The Advertising Age

Encyclopedia of Advertising

THE AdvertisingAge

Encyclopedia of Advertising

VOLUME 1

A–E

Editors
JOHN MCDONOUGH AND THE MUSEUM OF
BROADCAST COMMUNICATIONS

KAREN EGOLF, ADVERTISING AGE

Illustration Editor
JACQUELINE V. REID
HARTMAN CENTER FOR SALES, ADVERTISING, AND
MARKETING HISTORY OF DUKE UNIVERSITY

FITZROY DEARBORN
An Imprint of the Taylor & Francis Group
New York • London

Published in 2003 by
Fitzroy Dearborn
An imprint of the Taylor and Francis Group
29 West 35th Street
New York, NY 10001

Published in Great Britain by
Fitzroy Dearborn
An imprint of the Taylor and Francis Group
11 New Fetter Lane
London EC4P 4EE

10 9 8 7 6 5 4 3 2 1

British Library and Library of Congress Cataloguing-in-Publication Data are available.

ISBN 1-57958-172-2

First published in the USA and UK 2003

Typeset by Andrea Rosenberg
Printed by Edwards Brothers, Ann Arbor, Michigan
Cover design by Peter Aristedes, Chicago Advertising and Design, Chicago, Illinois

Front cover illustrations: *Duke Cigarettes* (American Tobacco Company). *J. Walter Thompson,* courtesy of the J. Walter Thompson Company. *Citroën,* courtesy of Citroën, © Citroën Communication. *Lux Toilet Soap,* courtesy of Unilever. *Leo Burnett,* courtesy of Leo Burnett Company, Inc. *Coca-Cola,* courtesy of The Coca-Cola Company, *Sears, Roebuck & Company,* reprinted by arrangement with Sears, Roebuck and Co. and protected under copyright; no duplication is permitted. *Green Giant Peas and Niblets Whole Kernel Corn,* courtesy of The Pillsbury Company. *Alka-Seltzer,* courtesy of Bayer Corporation.

Back cover illustrations: *Cadbury's Cocoa,* reprinted with permission of Cadbury Schweppes plc. *U.S. Army* ("I want YOU"). *G.D. Crain, Jr.,* courtesy of Crain Communications, Inc. *William Rembach,* courtesy of DDB. *Broadway and 47th Street, New York City.* ca. 1940. *Michelin,* courtesy of Michelin North America, Inc. *Clio Award,* courtesy of the Clio Awards. *Planters,* courtesy of Kraft Foods Holdings, Inc.

CONTENTS

INTRODUCTIONS

From John McDonough

An encyclopedia is typically an instrument of convenience, not scholarship. It offers an overview of otherwise widely available information assembled in a volume or two for handy and expedient access. This encyclopedia is, to a considerable degree, the exception. Unlike the well-documented histories of many other fields, much of advertising's past remains buried, reported only in rare contemporary press accounts and other primary sources. Even trained researchers have found this material difficult to locate.

The histories written about major corporations and marketers are typically silent on the specific role of advertising and ad agencies in their growth. There have been periodic general overviews of developments in advertising, most recently the excellent revised edition of *The Mirror Makers* by Stephen Fox. But not even that superb account could document the parade of important advertising agencies that were established, prospered, and then disappeared during the past 75 years or so. We hope these volumes will shed new light on their contributions to the profession.

There are several reasons why the agency side of the advertising business—as well as the advertising side of marketing—has been neglected. Anyone reading *Advertising Age*, the principal industry trade publication since 1930, will be struck by the extent to which the weekly coverage focuses on advertisers rather than ad agencies. Historically, the agencies, with a few exceptions, have preferred—or were obliged—to remain in the background. Like law firms, they regarded their customers as clients and were privy to much confidential information that required discretion. Also like law firms, they were agents, even alter egos, of their employers and resisted the scrutiny of outsiders and the media. While the actual advertising created by an agency in the name of an advertiser may have been aggressively public, the creative process itself was inclined to be intensely private.

Moreover, prior to 1962 agencies were, with one minor exception, privately held and under no obligation to reveal billings, income, or other financial data. Their role was to bring attention to their clients, not themselves. It was not until 1944 that *Advertising Age* undertook to publish annual rankings of agencies, first by billings and later by gross income and other measures. But the early rankings were in many cases based on estimates, not on hard data made available by agencies. All these practices contributed to the relatively low profile maintained by ad agencies, a barrier of secrecy breached only when a few individual agencies placed house ads in the trade press—and most prominently in *Fortune*, a magazine so expensive in the 1930s ($1 per issue) that agencies could be sure that no one below the level of senior management would ever see their advertising.

Yet another reason business historians have neglected agencies is their brittle, personality-driven nature. As corporate institutions go, ad agencies are uncommonly volatile entities, fundamentally different from the companies that hire them. During the formative decades of the advertising business, most advertisers had the advantage of manufacturing a product for the mass market that defined them as companies. They were capital-intensive organizations with factories, warehouses, and distribution systems. With such costly assets to protect, they necessarily operated as institutions and planned for continuity. The ad agencies that served them, on the other hand, were labor-intensive service providers. Their physical plants were rented office space. Their principal capital assets were their brains, which, as one agency observer noted, went down the elevator and out the door every night. They were also possessed of that most serious challenge to organizational discipline and persistence—dependence on a single individual. Thus, when the number-one brain died or retired, the agency that was its extension was often prone to failure. A business of personalities is a fragile thing, and many agencies, even today, are essentially mom-and-pop companies. Perhaps the most telling example was the decline and fall of Cecil & Presbrey, a New York City agency that prospered in the late 1940s and early 1950s. When founder James Cecil died suddenly in September 1954, the $21 million agency vanished within a month.

The uniquely different character of the agency compared to that of the marketer is demonstrated by their relative survival rates. Of the top 22 U.S. ad agencies billing more than $10 million in 1944 (then the threshold of top-tier status), 11 no longer existed 50 years later. Yet among the top 22 advertisers and/or brands during that same period, all still existed in some form in 1994. Even when mergers swallowed up huge advertisers such as General Foods Corporation, brands such as General Foods' Jell-O and Maxwell House coffee continued under the new parent organizations.

Why then are advertising agencies and their work important? Despite the impermanent nature of all but the most powerful agencies, not to mention the reputation for deception and wastefulness that has dogged them in popular film and literary portrayals, the modern advertising agency function is a crucial stabilizing gyroscope bringing supply and demand into balance. Manufacturing and sales are only two legs of the three-legged economic model of the modern consumer economy. The third, because it represents control of demand, is advertising. Demand became critical in the 20th century when, for the first time in history, production capacity of goods began to exceed the capacity of the market to absorb them. With the advent of mass production, the struggle to supply basic human needs was ending; the battle to stimulate demand was about to begin. If production and employment were to be free to grow, their only limits henceforth would be demand. So some means had to be found to radically increase and then control the size of the market. Without such regulation, capital and labor would face uncertainty and potentially destabilizing social chaos. Capital could not undertake the risks of financing a national economic infrastructure without predictable outcomes. And huge labor forces could not be assembled and organized without reasonable assurance of stable employment and living conditions. Advertising evolved as the most effective means of creating and amplifying demand, opening new markets to new products, and fighting for a share of mature markets. When as early as 1924 Procter & Gamble Company was able to guarantee its employees 48 weeks of continuous employment annually, it was largely advertising that had brought the company's sales to such predictable levels that it could make the commitment.

Does advertising sell people things they do not really need? You bet it does. The quality of a civilization is not judged by its capacity to meet basic needs but by its power to provide abundant choices, both material and intellectual. Advertising is a gauge of social development: the more advertising, the greater the development because the greater the choices available to individuals. It is not by coincidence that the world's largest advertising organizations are in the United States, England, France, and Japan. Advertising is the ultimate marketplace of choice. For many companies, the brand and what it stands for have become vastly more important than the manufacturing of the product behind it. Designers such as Calvin Klein, Ralph Lauren, and Tommy Hilfiger have gone so far as to abandon production altogether. They own no factories or workshops. Instead, they license the work of manufacturing to anonymous factories around the world, leaving themselves free for the more important work of expanding the power of their brands through advertising.

For these reasons and a good many more, the editors of the *Advertising Age Encyclopedia of Advertising* believed that this industry warranted a comprehensive reference source that provided as broad a perspective on the field as possible. The degree to which we were venturing into uncharted research territory soon became evident in the unexpected difficulties we encountered in enlisting contributors. A key problem was that many of the assigned topics had never before been researched, leaving would-be contributors with nowhere to turn for basic information. As a regular contributor to *Advertising Age* and being in Chicago, Illinois, I enjoyed the luxury of the remarkable resources of Crain Communications, Inc.: extensive clipping files and a library that, in addition to bound volumes of *Advertising Age,* also includes a rare collection of the *Standard Directory of Advertisers* and *Standard Directory of Agencies* (the so-called Red Books) going back to 1936, a resource that not even National Register Publishing, the current publisher of these directories, possesses. No single publication is more essential in tracking shifting agency-client relationships or in following the career progress of individuals. Contributors at colleges and universities around the country and the world were not so fortunate. Their efforts to assemble profiles on many agencies for which no formal histories had ever been written and no documents survived were often stymied for lack of resources. So late in 2000 *Advertising Age* and its parent Crain Communications joined our initial two partners in this venture, the Museum of Broadcast Communications in Chicago and the Hartman Center for Sales, Advertising, and Marketing History at Duke University.

Advertising Age brought to the task not only its library resources but also a staff of journalists and writers familiar with the advertising business. Among the results are profiles of more than 120 ad agencies around the world, not counting global holding companies and parent ad organizations. These include essays on some 80 leading contemporary agencies worldwide, plus, assembled for the first time, detailed articles covering more than 40 U.S. shops of historic interest that have either gone out of business or been absorbed by other entities. All, for different reasons, merit inclusion in this project. Many once ranked among the top 10 or 20 American ad companies. Their inclusion fills an important gap in the history of advertising. Tracking an agency's genealogy can be complex, and it is hoped that this work will help in that task. Unlike most major advertisers and large corporations, whose chief executive officer would never dream of imposing his or her name on the corporate identity, mergers and changes in agency management have been reflected in a dizzying succession of changing names on the masthead. It is ironic that companies that presumably are experts in building and sustaining the brand names of their clients are often startlingly indifferent to the brand concept when applied to themselves. In contrast to this volatility, it is also instructive to point out that of the six largest agencies as ranked by *Advertising Age* in 1944—the J. Walter Thompson Company; Young & Rubicam (Y&R); N.W. Ayer & Son; McCann-Erickson; Foote, Cone & Belding (FCB); and Batten Barton Durstine & Osborn—all continued to thrive in 2002 with their names substantially intact and unmolested by mergers or executive musical chairs. And five were still among the top ten.

We offer no general theories as to why these companies have survived and other former giants such as Ruthrauff & Ryan, Newell-Emmett, and the Biow Company have collapsed, only pertinent facts on which to speculate. As in any service business, the culture and success of an ad agency mirrors to a large degree the culture and success of its most powerful clients. Y&R grew up and prospered with General Foods, Campbell-Ewald with General Motors Corporation. But not even the most deeply rooted and conservative client can stabilize a company whose founders are unwilling or unable to turn themselves into an institution. For every David Ogilvy, there are dozens of Stirling Getchells; for every Leo Burnett, many more Milton Biows.

The initial list of topics to be covered in the encyclopedia was drafted by me, then submitted to the Board of Advisers, an international panel of authorities in the field, for additions and deletions. Also contributing invaluable suggestions were colleagues at the Museum of Broadcast Communications, the Hartman Center, and later *Advertising Age*. Our topic has frequently proved to be a rapidly moving target. Since the project was initiated in 1998, there have been major changes in the advertising field. Y&R became part of the WPP Group, Bozell & Jacobs was bought by True North (holding company of FCB), and True North itself was subsequently acquired by the Interpublic Group of Companies in 2001. As press time neared in 2002, Publicis Group of Paris, France, acquired Bcom3 Group, Inc., holding company of D'Arcy Masius Benton & Bowles and the Leo Burnett Company, one of the last holdouts among closely held major agencies.

Initially, the table of contents included far more biographical entries than remain now. As the list grew, however, it became clear to the editors that it would be redundant to discuss the lives of many men and women in individual biographies and then recapitulate much the same information within the context of the agencies or companies for which they worked. Consequently, much personal background has been consolidated into essays on more all-embracing topics. Nonetheless, the lives of 47 men and women, deemed by common if somewhat arbitrary consent to be of surpassing importance, are treated in individual biographies. In addition to the agencies, the encyclopedia profiles more than 160 corporate advertisers, brands, and/or campaigns that have had major lasting effects and in many cases have expanded the range and power of advertising in material ways. General histories of many of these companies can be found in other reference sources but none with the specific focus on advertising history that readers will find here. Another 20 or so essays focus on market research methods and theory and data-gathering institutions. And 52 essays explore the various systems, tools, and professional organizations that help make advertising work.

Advertising is not an insulated business. It speaks to the widest possible audiences. So to provide context and perspective for the discussions of agency and advertiser activities and how they interact with the marketplace, 68 thematic essays explore various social, cultural, and historic issues that influence advertising, among them ethical considerations, feminism, industry and government regulations, the shorthand of stereotyping, sex in advertising, and the impact of war on advertising. In addition, 25 essays profile the role and structure of the ad industry in as many countries and regions around the world.

What is not covered comprehensively by name is likely covered in part within related essays. From the beginning, many agencies grew through merger, resulting in a kind of musical chairs of agency names that often makes tracing an agency lineage a complex process. Doherty, Clifford, Steers & Shenfield, and the agency from which it was spun off in 1944, Pedlar & Ryan, for example, are both discussed as part of the history of the agency into which they ultimately merged in 1964, Needham, Harper & Steers, which itself was successor agency to Needham, Louis & Brorby. The pioneering radio advertising done by Blackett-Sample-Hummert is treated within the history of its successor, Dancer, Fitzgerald, Sample. The two are merely different generations of the same company, much the same way Newell-Emmett became Cunningham & Walsh in 1949 when management changed. Readers will find the story of Sullivan, Stauffer, Colwell & Bayles tucked into the larger stories of Ruthrauff & Ryan, from which it was first spun off, and

Lintas Worldwide, which subsequently acquired it. Rather than clutter the text with countless cross-references to other essays, the reader should regard the index as the principal guide to all such names not treated as separate essays.

By way of apportioning credit for these volumes, there is much to give and many deserving of mention. Initially, Robert M. Salkin of Fitzroy Dearborn undertook the task of commissioning editor, seeing the project through its basic structuring and the arrival of the first manuscripts. When the requirements of other projects forced his departure, the bulk of the assigning, editing, and organizational work fell for many months to his successor, Linda Tomchuck, a veteran of *Encyclopaedia Britannica* who entered the project a novice in advertising and leaves it an expert. In 2000 Fitzroy Dearborn approached David Klein, vice president and publishing/editorial director of *Advertising Age,* with a view toward making the project a joint venture. The arrival of *Advertising Age* and its parent company, Crain Communications, Inc., brought Karen Egolf, project development editor of *Advertising Age,* into the picture. Karen and her colleague, Richard Skews, provided further input on topics and brought forth many of the more than 240 writers whose contributions make up the heart of these pages, with invaluable help from researcher Steve Clover. The editors are also indebted to the two charter partners that helped to initiate and sustain the effort that has produced this work—the Hartman Center and the Museum of Broadcast Communications.

John McDonough
Coeditor
June 2002

From the Editors of *Advertising Age*

As an institution, *Advertising Age* is all about *now*: what happened this week, today, this minute. We publish all the news of the marketing business around the clock on our Web site and via e-mail, transmitted by fax and newsletter, and, of course, in ink laid down on paper in our print newspaper every Monday. We are journalists, not academics. So the idea of producing a full-blown encyclopedia, suitable for library archivists and agency historians, had to wait about 70 years before we got around to it.

But we are very glad we finally did. With our partner, Fitzroy Dearborn Publishers—which *is* an expert in the publishing of encyclopedias—we believe we have filled a long-standing void in our business. As John McDonough explains in his introduction, there is no easy central resource to turn to for historical information about advertising, marketing, and its various players over the past century and a half. As it happens, *Advertising Age* itself has one of the best archives of the business from its own coverage since its founding in 1930. But that archive is not really open to the public, it is in raw, news-clipping form, and it does not go back to the earliest days of advertising.

What we set out to do, then, was to pair Mr. McDonough with our own Karen Egolf, former editor of *Business Marketing* magazine and a longtime editor at the Ad Age Group, to assign, coordinate, edit, and organize the contents of the ground-breaking set of volumes you have in your hands now. In the months to come we will be working to bring out a searchable on-line version of this reference source for students and professionals, available via our Web site at adage.com.

Whether you are a veteran marketer, an agency information services specialist, an aspiring copywriter, or a college student embarking on the study of advertising, we hope you find the *Advertising Age Encyclopedia of Advertising* both informative and entertaining.

David Klein
Vice President-Publishing/
Editorial Director of the Ad Age Group
June 2002

From the Illustration Editor

To illustrate an encyclopedia of advertising is no small task. Most advertising is based on visual representation and would be difficult to describe accurately without illustration. The hundreds of illustrations in this work bring the words to life and enhance the volumes' usefulness to readers. Our team painstakingly selected each image and pursued permissions to use them. We actually found many more wonderful illustrations than have been included, but space considerations eliminated some.

Most of the images in the encyclopedia came from the extensive collections at the Hartman Center for Sales, Advertising, and Marketing History in Duke University's Rare Book, Manuscript, and Special Collections Library. The Hartman Center was selected to be the base camp for the Illustration Editor because of its rich resources relating to advertising history. It has easily proved itself a worthy resource. This project would not have been practical without the Hartman Center's vast and significant collections. Because most of the illustrations did come from the Hartman Center, we did not cite these images' sources individually. Illustrations with no source line come from the collections at Duke.

We spent almost two years pursuing copyright and trademark permissions with the copyright holders and companies mentioned in the courtesy lines. The process of obtaining permissions to use advertising as illustrations brings with it many pitfalls and obstacles not found in other types of illustrations. It may be necessary to get the permission not only of the company that owns the trademarks in the ad but also of the photographer and the models or the artists involved in creating the ad. We made repeated attempts to contact every existing company, or its successors, depicted in these ads. Most were cooperative and responded to our requests. Others were not and gave us no response after months of diligent efforts on our part. In these cases we made the decision to use the images and notified the companies of our intentions. Each company had the opportunity to deny permission to use its ads, and some did. We honored those injunctions. Our apologies go out to any company or copyright holder whose image appears in this book without proper credit. Please be assured that we have documented all our attempts to get the proper permissions and give the proper credit.

Many thanks must go out to the people involved in the process of illustrating this encyclopedia. I am very grateful to both Richard L. Collier, Jr., and Catherine R. Saleeby for their diligent and unwavering efforts as Assistant Illustration Editors. The illustration of these volumes would not have been possible without them. Thanks also to Amy Moulton, Farah Mehta, and Keturah Gray, Duke undergraduates who contributed significantly to the illustration process. Hartman Center Director Ellen Gartrell was responsible for bringing Duke University into this project, and she must be thanked for her support and advice from beginning to end. The Research Services staff of the Rare Book, Manuscript, and Special Collections Library at Duke University also deserves thanks for supporting our project. Thanks to Linda Tomchuck at Fitzroy Dearborn Publishers, who acted as our contact there and answered so many questions. It is impossible for me to thank each and every person who granted us permission to use the images in these volumes, although I wish that I could. Those of you who responded quickly and enthusiastically made our task so much easier. Finally, thanks to my husband, Michael Stenke, who put up with my late evenings and tolerated my rantings. I am very appreciative of his support.

For more information about the Hartman Center, please visit its Web site at http://scriptorium.lib.duke.edu/hartman/.

Jacqueline V. Reid
Illustration Editor
Hartman Center for Sales, Advertising, and
    Marketing History of Duke University
June 2002

Notes on the Encyclopedia's Contents and Organization

As John McDonough noted in his introduction, deciding what topics to cover in the *Encyclopedia of Advertising*—and, in the case of agencies with long and convoluted histories—determining the name under which to cover them, was not an easy task. And because we intended the encyclopedia to be international in scope, we required advice from experts around the world on which local agencies were the leaders in their respective countries. Also challenging was narrowing the list of individuals who would receive separate biographical entries, given that the lives of many agency founders would also be covered in the entries on their agencies. We hoped to provide as complete information as possible without being unnecessarily repetitive. The resulting list of topics is the product of a long collaboration between the editors, John McDonough and Karen Egolf, the international Board of Advisers representing both the profession of advertising and the advertising and marketing departments at countless academic institutions, and the editors and writers at *Advertising Age*.

The essays in these volumes can be divided into four very basic categories:

- agency histories (including entries on the major advertising holding companies);
- advertiser/brand/market histories;
- biographies;
- entries on theoretical, methodological, and practical aspects of advertising.

The last, extremely broad category includes advertising media (e.g., radio; television; newspapers), theoretical constructs (e.g., persuasion theory; archetype/stereotype), and myriad aspects of the practice of advertising (e.g., professional associations; package design; typography; targeting; the production of commercials; music and jingles). It also includes essays about how advertising influences and is reflected in the culture at large (e.g., cultural imperialism; impact of feminism; representation of minorities in advertising).

A word about the organization of the encyclopedia: entries are arranged alphabetically by the first letter of the most common designation. Thus, Carl Ally, Inc., will be found under *A*, the Leo Burnett Company under *B*, and S.C. Johnson & Son, Inc., under *J*.

At the beginning of each ad agency profile is a brief chronology of key dates in the agency's history, followed by a short, selective list of its major clients, past and present. The client lists are alphabetical. (Entries on holding companies have no client lists, as these are included in the essays on the individual agencies within the larger corporate entity.)

Essays on advertisers, markets, and brands are preceded by a selective list of the principal advertising agencies that worked on the account. Principal agencies are listed in rough chronological order, starting with the earliest.

Biographical entries include at the end of the essay a brief chronology and, where applicable, a list of selected publications by the subject.

To the extent possible, all entries are accompanied by a list of resources for readers seeking additional information.

ADVISERS

Marsha C. Appel
Beth E. Barnes
Joe Cappo
Larry Edwards
Stephen Fox
Gary R. Pfies
Ellen Gartrell
Robert Goldsborough
Sandra Gordon
Donald Gunn
Michele Hilmes

Tamotsu Kishii
Jaromir Loeffler
John C. Maloney
Atilla M. Ogud
Joel Raphaelson
Ralph W. Rydholm
Don E. Schultz
Juliann Sivulka
Wallace S. Snyder
Joseph Turow
William M. Weilbacher

CONTRIBUTORS

Debashis ("Deb") Aikat
Stuart Alan
Emmanuel C. Alozie
Eusebio Alvaro
Hussein Youssry Amin
Marsha C. Appel
Edd Applegate
Masaru Ariga
Jan Arrigo
Paul Ashdown
Christopher Bacey
Michael Baker
Siva K. Balasubramanian
Paul Barr
Thomas E. Barry
Joe Basso
Doug Battema
Cara Beardi
Kristen Beckman
Margo Berman
Joseph P. Bernt
Linda Bjone
Dana Blankenhorn
William H. Bolen
Nancy Bowman
Ian Brailsford

S. Adam Brasel
L. Clare Bratten
Pia Grahn Brikell
Edoardo T. Brioschi
Faye Brookman
Sheri J. Broyles
Michael R. Bullington
Christine Bunish
Michael Burgoon
Neal M. Burns
Rick Burton
Mercedes M. Cardona
Matthew Carmichael
Megan Cassada
Lynn Ann Catanese
Kara Chan
Roger Chapman
Hillary Chura
Claudia Clark
Eric Clark
Ken Clark
Philip B. Clark
Randall Clark
Steve Clover
Ann Cooper
Caryl A. Cooper

Kevin Cote

Anne-Marie Crawford

Anne Cunningham

Peggy Cunningham

Patricia A. Curtin

LeAnne Daniels

Sammy R. Danna

Amy I.S. Dattner

Derek Dattner

Bruce Davis

Judy Foster Davis

Wendy Davis

Destiny DeLinda

Nancy Dietz

Caitlin Dover

Bonnie Drewniany

Stephen Duncombe

Larry Edwards

Karen Egolf

Sandra L. Ellis

Craig Endicott

Nancy Engelhardt

Sunil Erevelles

Olan Farnall

Hanzada Fikri

James Fisher

Kate Fitzgerald

Vanessa Fonseca

Laurie Freeman

Jami A. Fullerton

David Goetzl

Robert Goldsborough

Elizabeth Goldsmith

Ian Gordon

Stephen J. Gould

Catherine Gudis

Charles S. Gulas

Louisa Ha

Jean Halliday

Carl Hamilton

Thomas L. Harris

Deborah Hawkins

Alexandra Hendriks

Cynthia Lee Henthorn

Wayne Hilinski

Julianne Hill

Michele Hilmes

Randall Hines

John H. Holmes

Andrew Hornery

Frederick B. Hoyt

Bruce A. Huhmann

Clark Hultquist

Kara Hunter

Randy Jacobs

Russell Johnston

Heather Jones

Richard Junger

Helen Katz

J.D. Keeler

Kevin L. Keenan

Sean Kelly

Marilyn Kern-Foxworth

Gayle Kerr

Lance Kinney

Sharon Kissane

Barbara Knoll

Tony Koenderman

Edmund Lawler

Elzbieta Lepkowska-White

Sheree R. Curry Levy

Hairong Li

Jerry B. Lincecum

Dan Lippe

Yuping Liu

Michael R. Luthy

Scott MacDonald

M. Carole Macklin

Normandy Madden

Rajesh V. Manchanda

Mark Mandle

Brett Martin

Ann Maxwell

William Mazzarella

Michael H. McBride

Allison McCracken

John McDonough

Norma A. Mendoza

Diane Mermigas

Debra Merskin

Tara Anne Michels

Sallie Middlebrook

Mimi Minnick

Yutaka Mizuno

Sara Teasdale Montgomery

Young Sook Moon

John Morello

Bourne Morris

Deborah K. Morrison

Margaret A. Morrison

Barbara Mueller

Dagmar Mussey

Jack Neff

Noel Mark Noel

William F. O'Connor

Gerard O'Dwyer

Patrick O'Neil

Denise T. Ogden

James R. Ogden

Ken Ohlemeyer, Jr.

Susan Ohmer

Kathleen K. Olson

Peter B. Orlik

Cele C. Otnes

Charles Pappas

Carol J. Pardun

Kartik Pashupati

Jennifer Pendleton

Francisco J. Pérez-Latre

Barbara J. Phillips

Mary Ellen Podmolik
James V. Pokrywczynski
Melvin Prince
Ali Qassim
Andrew Quicke
Joel Raphael
Karen Raugust
Bethel Ann Ravalo
Tom Reichert
Patricia Riedman
Daniel J. Robinson
Stuart C. Rogers
Patricia B. Rose
Billy I. Ross
Herbert Jack Rotfeld
Abhijit Roy
Paul Rutherford
Michael Ryan
Alan Salomon
Barry S. Sapolsky
Dave Saunders
Mark Schumann
Angela Schwarz
Mark Matthews Secrist
Trina Sego
Susan Seymour
Cliff Shaluta
Eric H. Shaw
Hanan Sher
Ron Shinkman
Jason Siegel
Juliann Sivulka
Allen E. Smith
Tommy V. Smith

Carrie Smoot
Lawrence J. Speer
Harlan E. Spotts
Marla Royne Stafford
Carolyn Stringer
J. Douglas Tarpley
Catharine Taylor
Brian D. Till
James B. Twitchell
Daryl Umberger
Anthony Vagnoni
Francisco Verdera
Vincent Vinikas
Wayne Walley
Jian Wang
Linda Wang
Brian Wansink
Hazel G. Warlaumont
Nancy Coltun Webster
Karen Weigert
William M. Weilbacher
Marc G. Weinberger
Laurel Wentz
J. Roberto Whitaker-Penteado
Jennifer Whitson
Kurt Wildermuth
Kristen Wilkerson
Thomas Wiloch
Joyce M. Wolburg
Wendy Siuyi Wong
James P. Woodard
Toshio Yamaki
Kenneth C.C. Yang

LIST OF ENTRIES

A

Abbott Mead Vickers/BBDO

Formed when David Abbott joined Peter Mead and Adrian Vickers at their newly established London, England, agency, Mead Davies and Vickers, and renamed it Abbott Mead Davies and Vickers, 1977; sold a minority share to BBDO Worldwide, Inc., 1991; acquired by BBDO and renamed Abbott Mead Vickers/BBDO, 1998.

Major Clients
British Telecom
The Economist
Guinness
Pepsi-Cola International
Pizza Hut
J. Sainsbury (retail grocery)

Abbott Mead Vickers (AMV) has consistently been both the largest advertising agency in London, England, and one of the most creative. Founded in 1977, the agency was independent until 1991, when it took over the tiny, floundering London shop of BBDO Worldwide, Inc., as part of the sale of a minority stake in Abbott Mead Vickers (AMV) to BBDO. The merged AMV/BBDO has been a major force in building BBDO's reputation as a highly creative international network.

David Abbott, creative director of French Gold Kenyon & Eckhardt, quit his job there in 1977 to buy a 22.5 percent stake in a fledgling London ad agency, Mead Davies and Vickers, which was immediately renamed Abbott Mead Davies and Vickers. Abbott eventually took over the creative department from the agency chairman, Peter Mayle, who soon departed for France (and who has become known for his books about living in southern France, starting with *A Year in Provence*). Abbott and Adrian Vickers had met at the University of Oxford, and both men had worked with Peter Mead at Doyle Dane Bernbach (DDB) in London. Within two years, the agency was renamed Abbott Mead Vickers and a minority stake sold to Scali McCabe Sloves, a U.S. agency then owned by Ogilvy & Mather Worldwide.

In November 1985 AMV obtained a listing on the London Stock Exchange. In its first deal as the publicly quoted Abbott

Mead Vickers Group, AMV bought London agency Leagas Delaney in July 1986; soon thereafter co-founder Ron Leagas departed. With AMV heading for full ownership by BBDO Worldwide in 1998, Leagas Delaney bought itself back in a $6 million management buyout in March 1998.

The AMV Group has bought or started a number of companies over the years. In 1996, for example, it acquired its own media specialist company, Pattison Horswell Durden, and renamed it New PHD, with Ken New, AMV's vice chairman, moving to its chairmanship. BHWG, a direct marketing company acquired in 1993, became the lead agency for Proximity BBDO. In 1994 the agency bought both public relations firm Freud Communications and custom publisher Redwood Publishing.

In 1991 AMV was eager to get out of its deal with Scali McCabe Sloves and gain access to an international agency network. After prolonged negotiations, the WPP Group sold Scali's share of AMV to the Omnicom Group, whose BBDO network ended up with a 22 percent stake in AMV. BBDO merged AMV with its own faltering London agency to form Abbott Mead Vickers BBDO. The agency quickly began winning pan-European business, including Wrangler jeans and ICI Dulux paints and became lead agency for Europe on international BBDO accounts such as Pizza Hut and Pepsi-Cola International. In 1994 the agency won the $80 million British Telecom business, believed to be the largest single U.K. account up to that time.

AMV/BBDO's ongoing creative success continued unabated during a period of transition following the retirement of Abbott, who stepped down as chairman on his 60th birthday in October 1998. A year earlier, he had handed over the creative reins to Deputy Creative Director Peter Souter. Soon after Abbott left, the creative department's heavy workload and the need for a senior creative figure led to the hiring of Tony Cox as creative director—and unofficial elder statesman. Cox had been executive creative director of BMP DDB, another of London's more creative agencies, for ten years. Abbott, meanwhile, was inducted into the One Club Hall of Fame in New York City in February 2001.

BBDO took full ownership of AMV at the beginning of 1999, and AMV executives began taking on broader roles in BBDO. In

"Surfer," created by Abbott Mead Vickers for Guinness, won more creative awards than any other commercial in 2000.
Courtesy of Abbott Mead Vickers.

March 1999 Peter Mead, group chairman of AMV, assumed the additional title of Omnicom vice chairman. To reinforce the three-partner management team, AMV hired Michael Baulk, an Ogilvy veteran, as managing director and chief executive. After BBDO took control of AMV/BBDO, Baulk in July 1999 added the job of chairman-chief executive officer (CEO) of BBDO Europe to that of chairman-CEO of the Abbott Mead Vickers BBDO Group in London. In 1995 the agency hired Andrew Robertson, CEO of London agency WCRS, to take over the managing director post. Robertson was subsequently named president and CEO of BBDO North America, a role that positioned him as a contender to succeed BBDO chairman-CEO Allen Rosenshine.

Over the years, much of the agency's best creative work was done by Abbott himself, working on accounts such as J. Sainsbury supermarkets, won in 1979, and Volvo cars. In the 1980s outstanding creative work came from the duo of Tom Carty and Walter Campbell.

The agency is best known for the Sainsbury ads that redefined supermarket advertising in the 1980s; the distinctive, witty post-ers for *The Economist* magazine throughout the 1990s; and the Volvo ads built around a safety strategy. Even after Volvo moved to Havas Advertising's Euro RSCG Worldwide as a global account in 1990, AMV/BBDO continued to do some local work on the car brand.

In 2000 AMV/BBDO won more creative awards than any other ad agency in the world. A series of print and TV ads for Guinness swept award shows, and one U.K. Guinness commercial called "Surfer" won more creative awards than any other in 2000. A series of commercials for Guinness was based on the theme that good things come to those who wait. In the $1.5 million "Surfer" spot, surfers wait to catch the perfect wave, a majestic cascade that is transformed into prancing white horses. In late 2000, when Guinness decided to consolidate its accounts, AMV/BBDO won the bulk of Guinness's global advertising, split with Saatchi & Saatchi.

The agency has always had a reputation as a hard-working but exceptionally civilized workplace, creative and humane but still profitable. Public holidays are often extended into longer breaks for the whole shop, and as of early 2001, the agency had adhered to a no-layoffs policy.

In 2000 Abbott Mead Vickers/BBDO was the third-largest ad agency in the United Kingdom, with gross income of $202 million, down 1.9% from 1999, on billings of $1.66 billion, according to *Advertising Age*.

LAUREL WENTZ

Further Reading
"AMV BBDO 20th Anniversary Advertising Supplement," *Campaign Magazine* (21 November 1997)
Ellison, Sarah, "Guinness Picks AMV BBDO and Saatchi to Handle All Ads," *Wall Street Journal Europe* (5 January 2001)
"Robertson to Control BBDO in U.S.," *Campaign Magazine* (9 January 2001)

Absolut Vodka

Principal Agencies
N.W. Ayer ABH International
Martin Landey, Arlow Advertising, Inc.
TBWA (later TBWA/Chiat/Day)

In 1977 Lars Lindmark, then chief executive officer (CEO) of Sweden's Wine & Spirits Corporation, decided that the state-owned liquor monopoly should make a bid for the export market. Sweden at that time was probably the least likely place in the world for the birth of what would become one of America's top-selling liquor brands. The Swedish liquor market was strictly regulated, and the country's parliament—as well as the company's board of directors—leaned toward abstinence and thus were opposed to all attempts to commercialize the operation.

Wine & Spirits lacked experience in marketing and advertising and did not have any products positioned for the international market. That deficiency turned out to be a blessing in disguise, however, as Lindmark found it necessary to hire several consultants, the most important being Gunnar Broman, a well-known advertising man in Stockholm, Sweden. While the product prides itself on a hundred-odd-year-old ancestry and 400 years of proud liquor tradition, Broman began with nothing—no brand name, no package, not even a vodka.

At a meeting in New York City with the top creative team from ad agency N.W. Ayer ABH International, Broman presented five different concepts for a Swedish vodka. In what was later to become a familiar pattern, the suggestion that met with the most vehement reaction—both positive and negative—was "Absolute Pure Vodka." Broman had borrowed this name from an inexpensive Swedish vodka favored by the less affluent classes and alcoholics. The provocatively simple bottle design, inspired by a 19th-century apothecary bottle, bore the brand name as well as a substantial block of copy, explaining the origins of the product, applied directly to the clear glass.

The basic ideas were there from the start: an uncompromising emphasis on purity in name as well as in packaging and a breakaway design that signaled a willingness to challenge the prevalent Russian vodka heritage in the quickly growing vodka market.

(Vodka at the time was typically packaged in tall bottles with large crimson labels, an abundance of crests, and Russian-sounding names.) It is ironic that a product that came to be highly praised for its design met with such strong initial opposition from art directors, liquor executives, and focus groups. It explains the huge difficulties Lindmark and Broman had to overcome before the product could find an importer.

An often repeated criticism at Ayer and elsewhere was that the highly unusual bottle, having no label and hardly any color, would be virtually impossible to see on liquor store shelves or in front of a bar mirror. Years later, well after the actual launch, Wine & Spirits and its U.S. agency were still working on various options that would solve this presumably unsolvable problem.

Probably the most ardent advocate of the original bottle design was Art Director Hans Brindfors, who created the first real glass bottle with the brand name and bottle copy applied to the exterior in silver. The first batch of bottles was made at the Saint Gobain glassworks outside Paris, France.

CEO Jerry Siano of Ayer received credit for being the first to recognize the full potential of the name *Absolut*. Mostly for legal reasons, but encouraged by Siano, the Swedes decided to change the name, dropping the "e" from "Absolute" as well as the "Pure," now felt to be redundant. The brand thus became "Absolut (Country of Sweden) Vodka." It is, of course, always and only known by the shorter name: Absolut Vodka.

Lindmark and the Wine & Spirits Corporation were unable to find an importer, despite courting major U.S. producers, importers, and agents. Finally, Broman found a small agent, Carillon Importers, mostly known for marketing the French liqueur Grand Marnier. The Absolut account was moved from Ayer to Carillon's agency, Martin Landey, Arlow Advertising, Inc., in New York City, which immediately demanded that major changes be made to the bottle design. After many creative clashes, Broman's partner, Creative Director Lars Börje Carlsson, finished the design: the name "Absolut Vodka" in large clear blue letters and the long copy on the bottle written by Broman, in elegant, black hand-drawn writing (the original type was actually borrowed from a Cadillac Seville ad).

Absolut launched its legendary campaign focusing on the distinctively shaped bottle with this 1981 advertisement.
Under permission by V&S Vin & Sprit AB. Absolut Country of Sweden Vodka & Logo, Absolut, Absolut Bottle Design and Absolut Calligraphy are trademarks owned by V&S Vin & Sprit AB. © 2001 V&S Vin & Sprit AB.

Thanks to Martin Landey's gentle prodding, Carillon CEO Al Singer finally decided to take on the Swedish vodka and entered into a 50-50 partnership deal with Wine & Spirits. Absolut Vodka was launched at the liquor trade convention in New Orleans, Louisiana, in the spring of 1979. By 1990 Carillon would be one of the most profitable corporations per employee in the United States.

Creative Director Arnold Arlow apparently remained uncomfortable with the bottle design. In the first ads Arlow did his best to hide the product; he also let his copywriter pen a new and different presentation than the one found on the bottle. Ironically, Arlow would later reappear at Absolut's next agency to manage the creative side of the campaign for more than ten years in collaboration with Peter Lubalin.

Shortly after the launch, Martin Landey, Arlow had to give up the Carillon account in connection with a merger. When pitching the account, the small but highly ambitious TBWA agency (formerly Barron Costello and Fine TBWA), led by Bill Tragos, suggested a whimsical two-word campaign: "Absolut [Something]," with the ads showing the strange bottle in a visual pun.

By most accounts, the first idea was "Absolut Perfection," in which the bottle was depicted with a halo. It was presented at the very first meeting between agency and client, and the same ad was still running in parts of the world 20 years later. The originators of the campaign were two young advertising men, Geoff Hayes (originally from South Africa) and Graham Turner (a native of the United Kingdom), recently hired by the agency's creative director, advertising legend Carole Anne Fine. The basic idea for the campaign could probably be characterized as every client's dream: the product is always the hero—and often the only thing shown in the ad—while the headline consists solely of two words, one being the brand name. Absolut Vodka sold well from the start, even before the TBWA ad campaign was up and running and long before the ads had been recognized in the advertising community as anything out of the ordinary.

A defining moment came when Michel Roux was unexpectedly promoted to the top position at Carillon, replacing Al Singer. Roux would quickly, through daring and hitherto unrivaled marketing panache, propel Absolut to the number-one spot among imported vodkas in 1985. Roux was a staunch believer in two tenets of marketing. First, never price-promote your brand (i.e., reduce price to stimulate sales). Second, funnel the quickly growing profits back into marketing—a strategy that suited the worried Swedes well, as they were anxious not to disclose anything of the huge and politically sensitive profits on their home turf. The advertising budget for Absolut in 1980 was $750,000; ten years later, it reached $25 million, and in 2000 it was $33 million, making it the most heavily advertised liquor brand in the world.

In 1985 the celebrated pop artist Andy Warhol offered to paint the bottle and display it as an ad in his *Interview* magazine. In spite of much hesitation at TBWA and Wine & Spirits, Roux decided to go ahead with "Absolut Warhol." The Warhol ad originally ran only once but got more free media coverage around the world than probably any other commercial product, anytime, anywhere.

This effort would mark the beginning of Absolut's long, spectacular, often entertaining, and occasionally pompous series of diversions into the realm of art, fashion, geography, design, furniture, cartoons, and Christmas greetings—the list is endless. Whether brilliant or contrived, the campaign masterminded by Roux always served to confirm the enormous strength in the word *Absolut*. The name could evidently be put in front of anything or anyone, ostensibly promoting cities, countries, artists, and celebrities—but always promoting the brand first and foremost.

The ads themselves have become collector's items, unparalleled since those created for Volkswagen in the 1960s by Doyle Dane Bernbach. Generally speaking, the campaign has been managed with consistency and continuity over the more than two decades since Hayes and Turner came up with the original idea. To the credit of TBWA and Wine & Spirits (today TBWA/Chiat/Day and V&S Vin & Sprit AB, respectively), they clung steadfastly to an original product design and a congenial ad campaign, seldom wavering from the basic idea.

Absolut soon become the signature account at TBWA, making it possible for Tragos and Dick Costello to build the agency into a success story in its own right. Fifteen years after winning the Absolut account, TBWA had billings of $7 billion and, under new owner Omnicom, was able to buy Chiat/Day.

In 1994 Wine & Spirits dropped Roux and Carillon in favor of Seagram, presumably to gain a worldwide distributor. The day after Roux left Absolut, he signed up with the competitor he had helped crush ten years earlier, Stolychnaya. Roux was unable to repeat his earlier success, however. And Absolut never again showed the growth figures of the 1980s and early 1990s.

Nevertheless, by the late 1990s Absolut was by far the best-selling import vodka in the United States and the second best-selling vodka after Smirnoff; by 2001 it was the third biggest international premium spirits brand. After a little more than 20 years in the market, Absolut was selling more than 65 million liters per year, primarily in the United States.

Over the years the Absolut Vodka campaign has won most of the advertising awards in the United States. It is considered by many in the industry to be among the best—if not the best—print campaign ever created. Absolut was voted into the Marketing Hall of Fame in 1995 at the same time as an older but equally famous beverage—Coca-Cola. In 2000 the Absolut brand alone, distribution rights excluded, was estimated to be worth more than $3 billion. Twenty years earlier Gunnar Broman received $150,000 for his work, all expenses included.

CARL HAMILTON

See also color plate in this volume

Account Planning

Account planning, a relatively recent development in the advertising industry, is an approach for generating consumer insights that aid in the development of strategy and tactics and in evaluating communications campaigns. Account planning was developed in the mid-1960s and can be traced to the British offices of two advertising agencies—the J. Walter Thompson Company and Boase Massimi Pollitt (BMP, which later became BMP DDB). The discipline gained in popularity and spread to the rest of Europe during the 1970s. In 1982 account planning was "discovered" by Jay Chiat of Chiat/Day and introduced into the United States, where it was widely embraced. By 1995 more than 250 people were employed in U.S. account planning, a figure that had grown to more than 1,000 in 1999. Account-planning departments are now fairly common in the U.S. advertising industry and are found in large full-service agencies as well as in medium-sized agencies and smaller creative boutiques.

Account planning originated from a need to concentrate client research, which in the 1960s was being somewhat diluted across marketing, advertising, and media-research departments. Society and the nature of consumerism were undergoing great changes. After World War II, more and more women entered the workplace, and the household dynamic—especially with regard to product purchasing—changed dramatically. Instead of cooking meals from scratch and keeping a spotless home, working women looked for foods that required little preparation and products that helped shorten the time it took to clean house. Entirely new product categories catered to the needs of women. Other cultural changes such as the Civil Rights movement, the growth of technology, and the rise of health and fitness concerns also influenced the advertising and purchasing of products. As a result of these changes, the number of companies conducting market research increased. These companies specialized in generating and selling information that analyzed and dissected the changing populace. Among the biggest purchasers of this information were advertising agencies.

However, while ad agencies were learning more about consumers, the surge in available data resulted in agencies being so deluged with information that the account-management team often was not able to put it to good use. In short, agencies continued to produce advertising without fully understanding the impact these societal changes were having on the consumer. Thus, account planning was born from the changing consumer environment and the need for a single department to assimilate and analyze relevant product data that could then be applied to the day-to-day decision making on an account. Furthermore, the presence of an account-planning department positioned an agency as having exceptional creative solutions and set it apart from competitors during the all-important stage of seeking to win new business. In employing account planners, an agency integrated functions formerly performed by other departments in the agency or by outside market-research consultants. This integration allowed the agency to act as a strategic partner with its clients and to retain control of business that might otherwise have been contracted out to independent research companies.

Role in Advertising

Account planners function as a liaison between the account executive and the creative department and between the creative department and the consumer. In this sense, account planners are both fully integrated members of the account team and advisors to the creative team. Account planning encompasses three key phases: strategy development, creative development, and evaluation of effectiveness. The primary responsibility of account planners is to understand the target audience and to "represent" it throughout the entire advertising-development process. This is accomplished through the use of market and research data on the product, the category, the market, the competition, and the client. The understanding that flows from this research leads to usable insights that help the creative and account-management teams produce advertising that is strategically and tactically relevant to the target market. Consumer insights—discoveries about the potential purchaser—enable advertisers to establish a connection between a brand and the consumer's life in a way that is innovative and meaningful. Effective consumer insights provide an understanding of what motivates consumers first to try a product and then to continue buying it.

Account planners rely heavily on a variety of qualitative research techniques that provide an unstructured environment and opportunities for intimate consumer contact aimed at revealing insights into the more "emotional" aspects of a brand. These techniques include traditional one-on-one approaches such as interviews and focus groups, as well as more innovative approaches such as accompanied shopping, word associations, use of visual prompts, video montages, projective techniques, and consumer diaries. Often, account planners employ experts (for example, semioticians, ethnographers, and cultural anthropologists) who do not work in advertising but may offer unique insight into a particular consumer situation. Account planners also depend on behavioral and attitudinal data from long-term studies to uncover social and cultural changes that may be relevant to advertising. In this capacity, they use primary and secondary research sources such as published market reports, usage and attitude surveys, and awareness-tracking studies.

While many of the techniques used by account planners are similar to those used by other research functions in an agency, account planning differs from more traditional research in that the research becomes part of the process instead of being used only in an advisory or evaluative capacity. For example, while more traditional research may uncover consumer insights, account planners take these consumer insights, interpret them, and advise the creative team how they can be used to develop creative strategy. In essence, the research used by account planners is more focused and integral to problem solving than is the case with traditional research.

Account planners are part of the account-management team and work as equal partners with account executives. While each has his or her own areas of expertise, there is substantial overlap between the two roles. The account executives and the account planner share responsibility for the development of plans, strategies, creative briefs, and most aspects of the agency's marketing input to the client, thus orchestrating the entire advertising-development process. However, while account planners complement the work of account executives by explaining through research findings how consumers respond to advertising, they do not sell the work of the agency. Account planners are useful to the account executive and client because of their close contact with the consumer and their knowledge of advertising and the entire marketing process. It is not unusual, for example, to find account planners working hand-in-hand with the account executive in obtaining the client's input on packaging, promotion, and product development. Account planning promotes a more integrated approach within the agency and better teamwork in satisfying the needs of the client, the demands of the market, and the expectations of the consumer. Clients recognize account planning as an enormous added value.

Account planning influences the entire creative development process except for production. It has a crucial role during strategy development in helping to incorporate the consumers' point of view. Research gathered by account planners is presented to the creative team in the form of a creative brief. The creative brief answers questions such as: why are we advertising; what is the goal of the advertising; what is the target market; what is the relevance of the product to the target market; what unique aspects of the target market will lead consumers to purchase the product; what is the main thought that needs to be expressed in the advertising; and what are some possible ways to achieve this? The creative brief serves as a blueprint for the creative team in the development of the advertising strategy. During creative development, account planners act as sounding boards for the creative team. They are responsible for researching the advertising before production to make sure it is as relevant as possible, and finally, once the ad appears runs, they monitor its effect in depth with a view toward improving subsequent executions and campaigns.

Use in Ad Campaigns

Account planning has been used successfully in a number of high profile campaigns. The following examples were taken from *Adweek*'s biannual coverage of campaigns that earned awards for their account planning insights in 1997 and 1999. The "Got Milk?" campaign, designed by the Goodby, Silverstein & Partners agency, was the first campaign to bring about an increase in milk consumption and sales during the 1990s. The original "Got milk?" campaign was regional in scope and had been initiated by the California Fluid Milk Processors Advisory Board. Per capita milk consumption had declined in California from 30 gallons in 1980 to 24 gallons in 1993. Further, the total volume of milk con-

The principles of account planning guided companies such as Stouffer's in marketing products directed toward the modern working woman. *Courtesy of Stouffer's Foods Corporation.*

sumed had been declining by an average of 2 percent to 3 percent each year since the late 1980s. The main reasons for the decline were concerns about milk's fat content, a feeling that "milk is for kids," and an overall boring image for milk in comparison with other beverages (mainly sodas). Past campaigns had attempted to stem declining milk consumption by giving milk a fun, trendy image and by running advertising that featured healthy-looking people. While this advertising had been successful in shifting attitudes toward milk (more than 50 percent of Californians agreed that "I should drink more milk than I do"), the new attitudes were not being translated into sales. Past campaigns had also targeted Californians who did not use milk or used very little of it. Instead, Goodby, Silverstein & Partners recommended targeting the 70 percent of the population that used milk frequently. Behind this recommendation was the basic belief that it is easier to get people to continue doing what they would normally do than it is to get people to start doing something that they have not done before.

Research by the account-planning department uncovered three "truths" about milk: it is largely consumed at home; it is rarely consumed alone but instead complements another food item (such as cereal or cookies); and, although these foods were "perfect" with milk, they were "ruined" without it. Planning played a key role in the development of the campaign and uncovered a basic truth about milk: the only time consumers think about milk is when they are out of it. This insight led to the "deprivation" strategy used in the campaign in which complementary food items were presented without milk in order to stimulate a desire for the product. All executions started with one of the food items—for example, a cookie or some cereal—for which milk is the perfect complement. The twist in the ads was that there was no milk available to accompany the food, so both the food and the moment were ruined. This insight was integrated into all levels of the campaign, including media and creative executions as well as promotional programs. As a result of the campaign, which later was expanded to the national level under the sponsorship of Dairy Management, Inc. (a national diary industry organization), overall milk consumption grew, frequency of use climbed, and sales increased.

When Yoo-hoo chocolate drink hired the Mad Dogs & Englishmen agency in the late 1990s, the company was suffering from declining sales. Research indicated that the brand was seen as old-fashioned, boring, and "not for me." Other soft drinks and beverages (such as Sprite or Minute Maid juice) were seen as more hip to drink. Additionally, in interviews with mothers (the obvious target market since they generally buy soft drinks for their children), it was found that they would buy the drink for their younger children but not their teenage children. Teenagers, especially boys, believed that Yoo-hoo was an old-fashioned drink and one for their little brothers and sisters, not something "adult." Since teenagers consume more soft drinks than any other demographic group, this was a serious obstacle and one that needed to be overcome in order to get the brand back on track. Hence, Mad Dogs & Englishmen recommended that Yoo-hoo aggressively target teenagers, not their moms.

Research by the account-planning team revealed that some teenage boys had created Web pages glorifying Yoo-hoo. The pages revealed that for these teens, Yoo-hoo represented goodness and a calming presence; in contrast, the advertising images of the more popular soft drinks portrayed people doing risky things such as jumping off cliffs or out of cars. While this Web group was small and not representative of how most teens viewed Yoo-hoo, it did give the account-planning team an idea of how to position the brand against larger competitors. The insight resulted in the facetious but charming strategy that "Unlike other drinks, Yoo-hoo makes a bad situation better." The sheer irony of the strategy and the joke behind it was a compelling message for teens. The ads showed teens in everyday situations in which the purchase of Yoo-hoo made things better, while its absence made things worse. Owing to the new advertising campaign, the decline in sales was reversed and distribution strengthened. Campaign evaluations concluded that the ads were functioning just as intended.

MARGARET A. MORRISON

See also color plate in this volume

Further Reading

Barry, Thomas E., Ron L. Peterson, and W. Bradford Todd, "The Role of Account Planning in the Future of Advertising Agency Research," *Journal of Advertising Research* 27, no. 1 (1987)

Bond, Jonathan, and Richard Kirshenbaum, *Under the Radar: Talking to Today's Cynical Consumer*, New York: Wiley, 1998

Dru, Jean-Marie, *Disruption: Overturning Conventions and Shaking up the Marketplace*, New York: Wiley, 1996

Fortini-Campbell, Lisa, *Hitting the Sweet Spot: How Consumer Insights Can Inspire Better Marketing and Advertising*, Chicago: Copy Workshop, 1992

Morgan, Adam, *Eating the Big Fish: How Challenger Brands Can Compete against Brand Leaders*, New York: Wiley, 1999

Steel, Jon, *Truth, Lies, and Advertising: The Art of Account Planning*, New York: Wiley, 1998

Sullivan, Luke, *Hey, Whipple, Squeeze This! A Guide to Creating Great Ads*, New York: Wiley, 1998

ACNielsen Corporation

ACNielsen Corporation is an international market research firm with 21,000 employees worldwide and operations in more than 100 countries. Although the Nielsen name has been associated primarily with television ratings measurement since the 1950s, about 80 percent of the company's revenue comes from measuring and tracking sales of consumer goods, while only 10 percent of revenue in any given year is attributable to media usage ratings. U.S. and Canadian television ratings are now measured by Nielsen Media Research, which was spun off from ACNielsen's operations during a corporate restructuring of the company's former parent, Dun & Bradstreet, Inc.

ACNielsen's founder, Arthur Charles Nielsen, was widely considered a marketing research visionary. He was the first to collect data on food and drug purchases, the first to use electronic sampling to track television viewership, and an early proponent of computers as a means of processing large amounts of data with speed and accuracy.

Emergence

Nielsen was born in Chicago, Illinois, in 1897. He graduated from the University of Wisconsin with a degree in engineering in

1918, then served in the U.S. Naval Reserve. After his stint in the service, Nielsen worked as an engineer at a number of companies but soon went out on his own. In 1923 he founded the A.C. Nielsen Company on $45,000 invested by a group of his fraternity brothers.

The company's mission initially was to monitor and measure the performance of production processes and equipment for industrial manufacturing companies. This business turned out to be a difficult one for the young A.C. Nielsen Company, which nearly went under twice but managed to hang on until the 1930s. The economy of the Great Depression, however, was almost the last straw because equipment manufacturers—Nielsen's main customers—suffered financially, in turn threatening Nielsen's business.

To prevent his company from going down with those of his customers, Nielsen developed a first-of-a-kind service in 1933 that tracked the retail sales of grocery and drugstore products. Called the Nielsen Food and Drug Index, the service was designed to enable manufacturers to measure their sales, on a brand-by-brand basis, against sales of competitors' products. Nielsen coined the term *share of market* to describe this yardstick and sold it on the basis that the information would help manufacturers make sound marketing decisions.

Nielsen believed that accurate information could be extrapolated from small samples and that, by taking sample measurements on an ongoing and regular basis, manufacturers could form a picture of how their sales and competitive positions stood at any moment and how they were changing over time. At first, manufacturers were skeptical because they lacked knowledge about statistics and statistical methods. They soon embraced the idea, however, and Nielsen became the leading U.S. market research company.

In 1936 Nielsen heard about a new measurement tool being developed by two professors at the Massachusetts Institute of Technology. It was this device, the Audimeter, that ultimately enabled him to launch a system for measuring television ratings, the service for which Nielsen would become best known. The Audimeter recorded the time radios were turned on and off and where the dial was set on a minute-by-minute basis. Nielsen acquired the Audimeter, modified it for his purposes, and patented it on behalf of A.C. Nielsen Company in 1938. After a pilot program, he began offering his radio measurement service, called the Nielsen Radio Index (NRI), in 1942. Like his earlier Food and Drug Index, this service drew some skepticism because it was new; many industry executives did not understand how radio signals worked and, consequently, did not believe they could be measured or captured mechanically.

Whereas Nielsen had been the first entrant in the food and drug measurement industry, his company had competition in radio listener measurement. In 1935 the C.E. Hooper Company introduced its Hooperating system. This was shortly joined by the Crossley rating system, which was devised by the network-supported Cooperative Analysis of Broadcasting (CAB) organization; by the late 1930s it surpassed the Hooperatings in use. Both used relatively simple sampling methods based on telephone calls

Arthur C. Nielsen.
Courtesy ACNielsen.

and personal interviews, providing a snapshot of listenership at the time of the contact. Though the Nielsen system could electronically track shifting listener patterns over the course of a day or evening period, it was more expensive than the Crossley and Hooper services, which remained the preferred methods into World War II.

Eventually, the networks, led by CBS, started to back Nielsen; when Nielsen began to offer national ratings in 1946, the networks abandoned CAB. In 1950 Nielsen bought Hooper's operation and went on to become the leader in the radio measurement industry. Nielsen at that time had 1,500 Audimeters installed in U.S. households, claiming coverage of 97 percent of the domestic market. All told, Nielsen spent more than $7 million to develop the NRI and the Audimeter, the most ever spent on a system to track marketing and advertising information up to that time.

NRI customers spent from $1,000 to $70,000 a year for the service, depending on their size and the amount of information they required (e.g., national or local). By contrast, customers of the company's food and drug industry tracking, which continued to be its mainstay business, paid Nielsen $15,000 to $100,000 for their marketing reports. (More than 30 years later, in 1980, the television networks were spending $1.5 million to $2 million a year on Nielsen rating information; they were the largest of several hundred companies using the service.)

Innovation

Nielsen was among the earliest proponents of computers as a means of improving efficiency. He found out about the evolution of an archetype of the first computer, called the ENIAC (Electronic Numerical Integrator and Computer), and, in 1946, signed a contract with the inventors to deliver a prototype of the machine to Nielsen within a year. Four years later, after cash flow problems and numerous delays, the inventors sold out to Remington Rand.

After this setback Nielsen contacted Thomas Watson, Jr., of the IBM Corporation. The two agreed that IBM would build on the progress made on the ENIAC. That resulted in Univac I, the first electronic computer in the world. IBM shipped one to A.C. Nielsen in 1955, allowing the company to produce its reports more efficiently and cost effectively than before.

In 1950 Nielsen moved into television audience measurement, using an adaptation of the Audimeter, and almost immediately took over 90 percent of the market. Families equipped with Audimeters supplemented that information by keeping viewership diaries and, for their trouble, were paid a small monthly stipend and reimbursed for repair costs on their TV sets.

When the networks and other Nielsen customers complained about the five-week delay in Nielsen's reporting of these results, Nielsen sought new technologies to shorten its reporting time. It was able to accomplish this goal within a year.

Among the statistics that Nielsen tracked in its television ratings reports were the number of television households tuned to a show (total and average) and the percentage, or share, of households watching TV that were tuned to a given program. Some of the company's services included the Nielsen Television Index (NTI), which measured national network ratings; the Nielsen Station Index (NSI), which tracked ratings in designated market areas; the Nielsen Syndicated Service (NSS), which monitored syndicated program ratings published in weekly "Pocketpiece" reports sent to subscribers; and the Nielsen Homevideo Index (NHI), which rated cable networks and superstations.

The Ratings Business

The quiz show scandals of 1958 and 1959 caused trouble for Nielsen's growing business. The U.S. Department of Commerce launched an investigation into whether Nielsen had tampered with the shows' ratings. The department took no action, but its probe led to another one by Congress, which began to look into the accuracy of ratings measurement in general and whether ratings measurement companies exerted undue influence over television programming decisions. Senator A.S. Monroney claimed that "the mumbo-jumbo cult of TV ratings" caused "the laws of the nation [to be] reversed and negated, because the network presidents supinely bow to this fictitious god that tells America what it may hear and see."

Congress's scrutiny was not limited to Nielsen's operations. Its competitors were also accused of creating poor-quality television by providing ratings that accounted only for the number of viewers watching (or households with sets on) and not for the characteristics of the show. Other companies in the ratings business in 1959 included Trendex, which gathered information through telephone interviews and used methodology based on Hooper's radio ratings methods; American Research Bureau (ARB, now Arbitron), which at that time used viewer diaries; and the Pulse, which went door-to-door for personal interviews. In addition, a company called Sindlinger and Company, Inc., used half-hour telephone interviews to garner information for specific clients on purchase patterns of viewers who watched particular shows. Nielsen had the largest market share of all of these, although its services were the most expensive, both to produce and for its customers to purchase.

All this investigative activity was one factor behind A.C. Nielsen's launch of the Nielsen Media Service in 1961. The new offering monitored the readership of magazines and magazine advertising, which Nielsen believed was a sector that would not be of much interest to Congress.

In 1963 Congress began to probe Nielsen again, along with seven of its competitors. This time it discovered inconsistencies in the way Nielsen measured ratings. As in 1959 the media got caught up in the story, blaming Nielsen and the other ratings companies not only for inaccuracy—a charge that had some validity—but also for creating a wasteland of poor-quality television programming. As he had four years earlier, Arthur Nielsen strongly disagreed with the latter accusation, noting that his service was not intended to assess quality and that he had never claimed to be a "tastemaker."

On the accuracy question, investigators found Nielsen's sample to be weighted toward lower-middle-income families who had enough money to buy a television set but valued the small monthly fee and therefore agreed to participate in the Nielsen program. The congressional report argued that Nielsen employees had not taken the time to compose a more demographically balanced sample but had simply chosen families who agreed to participate. Despite this flaw in its methods, and the unwelcome publicity that accompanied the accusations, Nielsen proceeded as before; the controversy did not seem to hurt its business.

In 1964 Nielsen stopped selling radio ratings, leaving the market to its competitor ARB. In large part, this move was due to Nielsen's belief that the Audimeter was incapable of adequately tracking the market, now that the proliferation of stations was crowding the radio dial.

In the 1970s Nielsen, at the forefront of technological advances that helped it improve its data measurement techniques, replaced its Audimeter with the Storage Instantaneous Audimeter. The improved device reduced to 15-minute periods the television set–usage information sent back to Nielsen.

Food and Drug Research

Despite all the attention devoted to its media measurement services, 80 percent of A.C. Nielsen's revenue during the 1960s and 1970s came from retail food and drug research. During these decades, Nielsen's consumer products tracking services were growing, with increases in both the number of clients served and the number of information management products offered.

In 1963 A.C. Nielsen began measuring sales at mass merchandiser chains, providing more data on consumer trends than had ever before been available. (From a technological standpoint, this amount of data would have been impossible to handle previously.) In 1966 Nielsen launched a service that tracked warehouse withdrawals and one that handled couponing operations for clients.

The development of Universal Product Code (UPC) scanners at retail stores in 1977 assisted Nielsen's business activities significantly, allowing the company to collect information on consumer purchases at the cash register as they occurred. In 1980 Nielsen introduced its national Scantrack service, which tracked specific market trends on a proprietary basis. As data processing software and scanners have improved, Nielsen has tried to keep abreast of technological advancements to offer the most up-to-date methods possible for retail measurement.

Arthur Nielsen retired from the A.C. Nielsen board in 1976, after a series of strokes—although he never really stopped working—and was succeeded by his son, Arthur C. Nielsen, Jr., who had assumed the position of president in 1957. By the time the elder Nielsen died in 1980, at the age of 83, the company he founded almost 60 years earlier had grown to $383 million in annual revenue. Television accounted for only 10 percent of the total. The company had subsidiaries in 23 countries, offering 80 different services.

The younger Nielsen sold the A.C. Nielsen Company to financial information company Dun & Bradstreet, Inc. (D&B), in 1984. D&B paid $1.3 billion in stock for the operation, which translated to 26 times earnings. Nielsen believed that as a member of the D&B family, the company would be able to benefit from the parent's technological know-how and its information databases.

After the acquisition, Dun & Bradstreet split its market research operations into three units. ACNielsen, as it was renamed, oversaw global packaged goods tracking and media measurement in 15 countries and was the largest of the three; Nielsen Media Research monitored television ratings in the United States and Canada; and IMS International became a leading provider of market research data to drug companies.

ACNielsen continued to grow under D&B. It entered into several marketing and technological partnerships—a strategy that is ongoing—and consistently introduced new products throughout the 1980s. In 1987 Nielsen created a joint venture, NPD/Nielsen, with market researcher NPD Group, to create an electronic consumer panel that tracked customer response to promotions in local markets, by brand, product category, and other variables. The panel comprised 40,000 homes by 1991. The following year, Nielsen purchased Logistics Data Systems, developer of Spaceman, a software package used by retailers to manage shelf space and other display areas in-store.

In the 1990s many of ACNielsen's product introductions were created to allow its customers to analyze results at workstations or personal computers in their own offices rather than in printed report form. Informational products launched in the early 1990s

included tracking services to measure purchases in national convenience store chains, food and drug combination chains, and discount drug chains; each of these included all the major U.S. chains in their respective sectors. ACNielsen also introduced other services, such as a modeling tool for financial firms targeting consumers, called WealthWise, and a service called ScorePlus, which tracked product-use data and demographics for specific geographic areas. ACNielsen's Spotlight system, launched in 1991, gave its customers the ability to account for volume and share changes in great detail on a brand-by-brand basis. In 1993 ACNielsen became the first company in the industry to provide scanning information from warehouse clubs.

Also in 1993 ACNielsen created an Efficient Consumer Response (ECR) division to help clients increase efficiencies in sales and distribution, allowing them, in turn, to sell products to their consumers at lower cost. Marketers, including Anheuser-Busch Companies, used the service to boost sales; Anheuser-Busch saw increases of more than $3 million in some individual retail chains due to the implementation of Nielsen's ECR service. Nielsen forged agreements with suppliers and distributors around the world in 1994 to form Nielsen Solution Partners, an entity that brought ECR to international markets.

Nielsen Solution Partners was just one of many efforts of the 1990s developed to increase Nielsen's global reach. The company had clients for its marketing information services in more than 34 countries by the mid-1990s, after having opened its first overseas subsidiary, in England, in 1939. By 1991 it had offices in 28 countries, and continued to open more, such as one in South Africa in 1994, in partnership with Integrated Business Information Services. Seventy percent of Nielsen's business came from overseas markets at this time. Meanwhile, Nielsen Media Research, the ACNielsen spin-off and sibling within D&B, remained the primary supplier of TV rating services in North America, a dominance that grew when its key competitor, Arbitron, got out of the local television ratings business in 1993.

Competition

ACNielsen's key competitor in the retail market research industry was (and continues to be) Information Resources, Inc. (IRI), a company founded in 1979. In 1987 D&B agreed to acquire IRI. The acquisition would have allowed the companies to place less emphasis on competition and more on developing new products. The deal did not go through, however, because of antitrust objections, and the two remained bitter rivals.

The year 1995 was a turbulent one for Nielsen, especially in its market research division. The company was in the midst of a competitive and legal battle with IRI; the latter had prompted a U.S. Justice Department probe into Nielsen's syndicated sales tracking services and whether its marketing tactics were anticompetitive. IRI argued that it was prohibited from entering markets where Nielsen was active.

Meanwhile, also in response to a request from IRI, the Canadian government prohibited Nielsen from forging deals with retailers for exclusive access to scanner data. This meant IRI would be able to enter the Canadian scanner information tracking market, valued at $70 million. Around the same time, ACNielsen's ECR division was integrated into its main business. Nielsen also outsourced some of its computer processing to another company to reduce costs, while increasing spending on trade advertising to attack IRI and other companies in the industry.

Throughout the early and mid-1990s, the two companies engaged in a price war. Many of Nielsen's clients had moved to IRI, which prompted the former to aggressively price its services in order to reacquire some of that business. Its price-cutting led to the government's interest in certain competitive practices of Nielsen's, including adding employees to a particular account without raising the price, cutting prices on scanner services, and adding international data at no cost to a domestic contract.

Both IRI and Nielsen suffered financially from the rivalry. Each had to make significant investments in technology to keep up with the pace of change and to continue to provide usable data. Because of price-cutting, they were not able to pass along most of these costs to their customers. In 1994 Nielsen invested more than $300 million in technology and acquisitions of companies that could help it remain technologically and globally competitive. It cut hundreds of jobs, particularly in its domestic operations.

IRI was hurt even more, since it did not have the strong financial backing of a parent company such as Dun & Bradstreet. Since 1992 IRI had been expanding globally, especially through deals with ACNielsen competitors such as GFK and Sofrès in Europe and Mitsui in Japan. In 1994 IRI suffered a loss of $15 million.

Meanwhile, ACNielsen had won back some of its clients earlier lost to IRI; each company was estimated to have about half the market for "continuous research" (the provision of scanner data on an ongoing basis). In 1994 Nielsen's worldwide revenue grew by just 3 percent, and the following year Nielsen's U.S. business lost $50 million, although its global operations had started to perform better. Within a year, however, Nielsen's U.S. operations had recovered.

At the height of this fevered activity between ACNielsen and IRI, Dun & Bradstreet was in the midst of a corporate restructuring, and in 1996 it spun off ACNielsen and another subsidiary, Cognizant Corporation, which focused on market research for the health care and television industries. Nielsen Media Research, as of 2000 a subsidiary of Dutch conglomerate VNU, went with Cognizant and retained the U.S. and Canada television ratings services with which the Nielsen name most often is associated. ACNielsen kept its consumer packaged goods tracking services, as well as many media tracking products outside U.S. and Canadian television, and went public.

The competitive battles with IRI continued, moving out of North America and into Europe, where the European Commission ordered Nielsen to cease offering discounts and exclusives to win contracts. The action was taken, as had happened in the United States, because of an IRI complaint. Nielsen agreed to stop, which satisfied the commission and also led the U.S. Justice Department to halt its inquiry into the company's European business. In 1997 Nielsen filed a countersuit to IRI's 1996 anticompetitive-conduct suit; the countersuit claimed that IRI had made false and misleading statements about Nielsen and its operations.

In 1997 Nielsen, now based in Stamford, Connecticut, went on a cost-cutting mission focused on streamlining its international operations. It cut jobs, especially in Japan, and consolidated services in several countries, including Australia, China, Hong Kong, and Japan. It also closed offices in some countries.

The late 1990s saw Nielsen boost its acquisition activity, especially to bolster its international business. In 1998 it purchased the Bases Group, a test marketing company that used simulation techniques to evaluate the performance of newly introduced products. The next year it acquired Media Monitoring Services, which tracked the British advertising industry. By this time, Nielsen was active in more than 40 countries. In February 2001 ACNielsen was acquired by VNU, putting it back in the same corporate family with Nielsen Media Research.

Internet Tracking

One of the company's highest-profile deals was a joint venture with NetRatings, a company that tracks Internet usage. In 1999 the two companies launched a global service—the first of its kind—to monitor Internet advertising and usage worldwide. The same year, Nielsen bought a 10 percent stake in NetRatings; it owns 80 percent of the joint venture. Nielsen and NetRatings had allied in 1998 to assess the audience size of U.S. Internet sites.

The global partnership, known as ACNielsen eRatings.com, measured Internet activity in 30 European, Asian-Pacific, Middle Eastern, and African countries by 2001. The sample size is between 2,000 and 7,000 users, compared to 33,000 for the U.S. sample. Research is performed using sampling software provided by NetRatings that tracks on-line activity in real time; this differentiates the venture's methodology from that of its main competitor, Media Metrix, which relies on PC users' periodically mailing in disks that have captured their on-line usage activity.

As of 2000 ACNielsen continued to invest in new technologies and forge partnerships to provide retail and media measurement on a global scale. It had more than 9,000 clients in 100-plus countries and was organized into four business segments. Retail Management consisted of consumer purchase tracking at the point of sale—through scanning, retail audits and in-store observation—and was available in 80 countries. Retail Management also included the Consumer Panel segment, which extrapolates from the purchases, demographics, and retail patterns of a panel consisting of 126,000 households in 18 countries. Customized Research comprises several different Nielsen offerings, including Customer eQ, which evaluates customer satisfaction, Winning B®ands, a brand equity measurement service, and Bases, the simulated test-marketing service acquired earlier.

The final segment, Media Measurement, included television ratings monitoring in 18 countries (Nielsen Media Research continued to provide that service in the United States and Canada) as well as radio ratings measurement in 12 countries and advertising expenditure monitoring in 31 countries. Some of the brands under the Media Measurement umbrella include Peoplemeter,

ACNielsen CABSAT Asia, AdEx International, Nielsen//NetRatings, NetWatch, WebAudit, and WebAdEx. It also includes ACNielsen EDI, formed through Nielsen's purchase of Entertainment Data, Inc., in 1997, which tallies box office figures for 45,000 movie screens in 11 countries.

Many of the services within the Media Measurement sector involve Web monitoring, a fast-growing segment for ACNielsen throughout the late 1990s and continuing as an important business in the early 2000s, despite the dotcom downturn. Nielsen// NetRatings, for example, is an ambitious service launched in September 1999 that is a joint venture between ACNielsen eRatings.com (itself a joint venture between Net Ratings and Nielsen), NetRatings, and Nielsen Media Research. It consists of a panel of 57,000 at-home and 8,000 at-work Internet users in the United States, as well as international users, for a total of 175,000 Internet users globally, the largest Internet measurement sample to date.

Nielsen also provides software to help retailers make merchandising decisions, as well as INF*ACT workstation software, which allows customers to work directly with Nielsen's data from their own computers.

In the retail management sector, Nielsen's primary competition remains IRI. For international television ratings, its rivals include several companies in Europe and Japan. The competitive landscape for Internet ratings is especially crowded, with companies such as Media Metrix, NetValue, PC Data, and IMR Worldwide all providing similar services to those of ACNielsen and its joint venture partners.

As ACNielsen entered the 21st century, it continued to expand its services, often through acquisitions or partnerships, with a focus on international territories and Internet measurement. In 2000, for example, it launched ACNielsen.online to measure Internet usage in the Asia-Pacific region. International territories account for nearly 70 percent of the company's $1.5 billion revenue worldwide, while 85 percent of the company's 21,000 global employees are based outside the United States.

While ACNielsen's flurry of activity in on-line measurement and international media measurement means its name continues to be associated primarily with television and other media ratings, media measurement accounted for just 7 percent of the company's total revenue as of 2000. The core of ACNielsen's business, generating 68 percent of worldwide revenue, continues to be retail measurement, the business sector that had its origin in Arthur C. Nielsen's first market research service.

KAREN RAUGUST

Further Reading

Basler, Barbara, "A.C. Nielsen, Who Devised System That Rates TV Programs, Dead," *New York Times* (4 June 1980)

Current Biography Yearbook (1951)

"Data Wars," *The Economist* (22 July 1995)

Elli, Caron Schwartz, "Nielsen, A.C.," in *American National Biography,* vol. 16, edited by John A. Garraty and Mark C. Carnes, New York: Oxford University Press, 1999

Fletcher, James E., "Nielsen, A.C.," in *Encyclopedia of Television,* edited by Horace Newcomb and Noelle Watson, vol. 2, Chicago and London: Fitzroy Dearborn, 1997

Goldberg, Michael, "Nielsen, Arthur Charles," in *Dictionary of American Biography,* supplement 10, New York: Scribner/ Simon & Schuster Macmillan, 1995

Meller, Paul, "Nielsen Agrees to Changes in Europe," *Advertising Age* (9 December 1996)

"The Only Wheel in Town," *Time* (14 January 1957)

Steinberg, Cobbett S., *TV Facts,* New York: Facts on File, 1985

Tedesco, Richard, "Nielsen and NetRatings," *Broadcasting and Cable* (27 September 1999)

"TV Ratings—The Men behind Them," *Newsweek* (18 May 1959)

Ad Council

Long considered the "conscience of the advertising industry" in the United States, the Ad Council was founded in 1942 by members of the Association of National Advertisers (ANA) and the American Association of Advertising Agencies (AAAA, or "Four A's"). It is an independent nonprofit organization dedicated to using the power of advertising to encourage individual action on important social issues.

In fulfilling its mission to "deliver the messages America needs to hear," the Ad Council, in concert with ad agencies working on a *pro bono* basis, has produced some of advertising's most memorable and compelling spokes-characters (Rosie the Riveter, Smokey the Bear, Larry the Crash Dummy, Crime Dog McGruff) and slogans ("Loose lips sink ships," "A mind is a terrible thing to waste," "Friends don't let friends drive drunk"). Its public-service work has won hundreds of ad industry and civic awards, and its success has inspired similar organizations in Canada, Japan, Eastern Europe, The Netherlands, India, and Russia.

Funded entirely by private donations, the council has produced as many as 35 complete advertising campaigns annually on a wide variety of topics related to health, education, safety, child welfare, the environment, and community involvement. Each campaign represents a five-part coalition consisting of: (1) the Ad Council; (2) a sponsoring not-for-profit public-service organization, foundation, or government agency; (3) a volunteer

THE ENVIRONMENT: AN AMERICAN TRAGEDY

But it's not too late to do something about it. Something as simple as acquainting yourself with local anti-pollution ordinances and abiding by them will help.
**People Start Pollution.
People Can Stop It.**

Keep America Beautiful

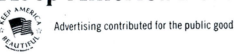

Advertising contributed for the public good

A 1971 public service announcement by Marsteller, Inc., for Keep America Beautiful alerted the American public to the need to protect the environment.
Courtesy of Keep America Beautiful.

executive coordinator from a major company; (4) volunteer writers, designers, and producers at a leading advertising agency; and (5) national and local media outlets that donate time and space to deliver the messages to the public.

To be considered for an Ad Council campaign, a project must be of national significance and have wide public appeal to warrant donations of time and space by the media. It must be noncommercial, nondenominational, nonpartisan, and not intended to influence legislation. Throughout its history, the Ad Council has produced campaigns for organizations such as the American Red Cross, 4-H Council, American Cancer Society, Crime Prevention Coalition, National Highway Traffic Safety Administration, National Institute on Drug Abuse, National Committee for Prevention of Child Abuse, National Urban League, American Mental Health Fund, Peace Corps, Social Security Administration, United Way of America, National Council on Alcoholism, Environmental Protection Agency, and hundreds of other groups. The campaigns do not promote the organizations themselves but rather disseminate a message calling for participation in a worthy activity—giving blood, donating an organ, preventing crime, voting, recycling, volunteering, wearing safety belts, and so forth.

Foundations in War

In November 1941 leaders of the ANA and AAAA met to discuss the anti-advertising sentiment prevailing in the United States after a decade of economic depression. Advertising icon James Webb Young of the J. Walter Thompson Company (JWT) suggested that "a greater use of advertising for social, political, and philanthropic purposes will help immeasurably to remove the distaste for advertising which now exists among many influential people." Other professionals agreed that advertising directed toward the public good might help advertising's own image problems and boost the long-term fortunes of the industry.

Less than one month later the United States entered World War II. In February 1942 the fledgling Advertising Council was officially renamed the War Advertising Council to support various nonmilitary war efforts. Advertisers and agencies, the latter including the Leo Burnett Company, JWT, Lord & Thomas, and Young & Rubicam Inc. (Y&R, whose chairman, Chester LaRoche, became the council's first head) joined together to create more than 150 advertising campaigns. They helped to raise more than $35 million in war bonds; promote the planting of 50 million victory gardens; recruit more than 2 million women into the workforce; salvage and recycle tons of necessary commodities such as fat, rubber, and metal; and guard national security. By the end of the war, more than $1 billion in labor hours and media time and space had been donated to the council's campaigns. Before the war ended President Franklin D. Roosevelt requested that the council continue its efforts as a peacetime public service organization to help solve pressing social issues.

Postwar Highlights

As the single-minded urgency of the war effort dissipated and political partisanship reemerged, the renamed Advertising Council needed to define the types of causes it would support in the postwar era. The president of the council, Theodore S. Repplier, developed a plan to promote nonpartisan programs serving the private sector as well as the government. He also established the basic operating structure of volunteers that still exists.

Three of the Ad Council's longest-running campaigns grew out of the war effort and continue today for the American Red Cross, the United Way, and the Forest Service. For the latter, the figure of Smokey Bear was created in 1947 as part of a campaign by Foote, Cone & Belding that urged individual responsibility with the slogan, "Only you can prevent forest fires."

One of the council's first major peacetime campaigns was created for the Cooperative for American Remittances to Europe (CARE) to address devastation and starvation in postwar Europe. The N.W. Ayer agency created the campaign featuring flying "CARE packages." The ads helped increase shipments of food and supplies by 300 percent in a single year, and the term became part of the American vernacular. The campaign ran for ten years.

In the early 1950s, during Sen. Joseph McCarthy's campaign to expose people suspected of Communist sympathies, Burnett's ad campaign "Our American Heritage" celebrated Americans' rights and responsibilities. In the late 1950s and early 1960s Ad Council campaigns began to take advantage of the visual power of television. One of the most effective was for the recruitment of Peace Corps volunteers. Ayer created "The toughest job you'll ever love" slogan while Y&R produced the corps' best-remembered television spot, "Beach," in which attractive, middle-class college students are shown lazily sunbathing on the beach, oblivious to a portable radio nearby on which an announcer is detailing problems and miseries being endured by the less fortunate around the world. During the height of the efforts, more than 50,000 responses a week were received.

The mid-1960s to mid-1970s were among the most turbulent years in U.S. history. During that time, the Ad Council was criticized by some for not taking harder-hitting, more partisan positions on issues. Robert Keim became president in 1966 and oversaw the creation of some of the organization's best work. Y&R's slogan, "A mind is a terrible thing to waste," created in the early 1970s for the United Negro College Fund, is still in use and has helped raise more than $1.4 billion. The "Crying Indian" TV spot (1971) created by Marsteller for Keep America Beautiful, Inc., is considered a classic. In this ad, Native American Iron Eyes Cody, wearing traditional garb, paddles a canoe down a river; as he banks the canoe, he sheds a single, eloquent tear over the land that is now ravaged by litter and pollution. Ketchum, McLeod and Grove's "Kitty" spot for the Urban Coalition/Crisis in the Cities Campaign was an effective shocker. In this darkly lit spot, the audience sees a close-up of a tenement including a large rat, while hearing the voice-over of a young child calling, "Here, kitty, kitty."

Child abuse, crime, drunk driving, and drug abuse became national concerns in the late 1970s and 1980s, and all were addressed by major Ad Council campaigns. In 1978 Dancer, Fitzgerald, Sample introduced the "Take a bite out of crime" campaign with canine detective Crime Dog McGruff, now almost universally recognized by American youngsters as a symbol of crime prevention. The simple but powerful "Crashing Glasses" (1984) television ad from Leber Katz Partners helped reduce drunk driving for the U.S. National Highway Traffic Safety Administration with the slogan, "Drinking and driving can kill a friendship."

Campbell-Ewald's "Word Pictures" (1989), with the message "Words can hit as hard as a fist," emphasized the insidious nature of child emotional abuse.

In the mid-1980s a powerful coalition that included the Ad Council, 200 agencies, and virtually all national media (including the ABC network, the *New York Times,* the *Wall Street Journal,* Hearst, Time Inc., and *Reader's Digest*) mounted a massive three-year battle against drug abuse through the Media-Advertising Partnership for a Drug-Free America. The effort sought donations of $500 million annually in media support, while the agencies produced more than 150 TV, radio, and print ads. (The volume of ads produced was similar in magnitude only to the war bonds effort.) The ads' imagery attempted to deglamorize drugs and dispel drug myths. Included was the celebrated anticocaine poster in which a teenager was shown snorting a gun.

In 1988 Ruth Wooden became the council's third president; and as the organization approached its 50th anniversary, there was much to celebrate. In its first half-century, more than $60 billion of media exposure and millions of dollars of creative talent had been donated to Ad Council campaigns—placing them among the most respected and durable in the advertising industry as well as making them permanent fixtures in American culture. The Ad Council logo had become a recognized symbol of quality and excellence, instantly communicating that a campaign was the work of top agency people supported by leading advertisers and media.

New Challenges

In the 1990s the Ad Council faced the same challenges confronting the advertising industry in general: intense competition, pressure for results and accountability, fragmented and waning media support, and the advent of new media. Thousands of local, national, private, and governmental organizations were competing for public and media attention with their public service messages. As the number of those messages grew, the Ad Council's share of the public service market decreased.

In 1995 the council made a strategic decision. While it would continue to support more than a dozen of its longest-running campaigns, it would concentrate new efforts around a single issue—the needs of children. This ten-year effort, called Commitment 2000, has produced campaigns related to topics such as early childhood development, education excellence, learning disabilities, mentoring, kids and the environment, child safety, talking with kids about tough issues, and recruiting new teachers—"Helping America's parents . . . reach America's kids." One of the largest efforts is "Connect for Kids" on behalf of the Coalition for America's Children and its 350 member organizations. The campaign's gritty images and theme ("Whose side are you on?") encourage people to get involved locally to support kids and parents.

Wooden placed a new emphasis on research and effectiveness. A major study released in 1991 demonstrated the impact of past public service advertising. Research work for new campaigns includes problem definition; pre- and posttesting of audience awareness, attitude, and action levels on issues; and media response. Data from these studies are especially important to the council's media partners.

The media have been essential partners of the Ad Council coalition since its inception and continue to donate nearly $1 billion annually in time and space. However, some critics see the deregulation of broadcasting, decline in ad sales, reduction of print pages, and creation of huge media conglomerates, with their inherent profit pressures, as deterrents to the use of public service announcements. Even prior to the advent of these trends, local stations traditionally placed public service announcements into some of the least desirable time slots, primarily slots they could not sell. Generally, however, stations identify a few key issues—chosen on the basis of their audience demographics—with which they wish to associate themselves for the purpose of demonstrating their commitment to public service. In 1990 the council formed an internal office to provide outreach to local and national media, thus giving media placement the same high priority as quality creative work. The group utilizes a marketing approach by providing information to the media on how the council's tailored messages can be useful to each media outlet's own public service efforts and audience segments. The council may even be able to make minor adjustments to the creative work to make it appear more customized for a specific station's market.

The council also recognizes its most generous media partners with an annual award.

In addition to its traditional work for TV, radio, newspapers, magazines, and outdoor advertising, the council has developed banners for web site placement. Working together, the Ad Council and the Internet Advertising Bureau are encouraging Internet publishers to donate 5 percent of their advertising space to banner public service announcements. More than 300 sites did so during the first year of the effort. The council also has developed its own comprehensive web site that allows the media to order materials online. Despite changing media, changing industry conditions, and changing social needs, the Ad Council entered the 21st century rededicated to its mission of "delivering the messages America needs to hear."

SUSAN SEYMOUR

Further Reading
Ad Council <www.adcouncil.org>
"Ad Council at 50: A Half-Century of Helping the Nation Face Change and Challenge in a Turbulent Era," *Advertising Age* (11 November 1991)
Advertising Age, various issues
Adweek, various issues

Advocacy Advertising

Advocacy advertising is advertising that is concerned with the propagation of ideas and the elucidation of controversial social issues deemed important in public policy terms. The first use of the term in its present context is attributed to John O'Toole, former president of the Foote, Cone & Belding advertising agency. Terms often used synonymously with advocacy advertising include *public affairs advertising, issue* (or *public issue*) *advertising, viewpoint advertising, opinion advertising, adversary advertising,* and *controversy advertising.*

Advocacy advertising is commonly regarded as a subset of corporate or institutional advertising. However, it differs from corporate image advertising in several respects. The primary objective of traditional corporate-image advertising is to build a favorable image and keep the advertiser's name in the public eye. By contrast, advocacy advertising attempts to tackle potentially controversial issues and to present arguments that project the advertiser in the most positive light. It may also attempt to influence public opinion on an issue directly affecting the advertiser's business.

As noted above, not all authorities use the term *advocacy advertising.* Albert Stridsberg, for example, titled his 1977 book on the subject *Controversy Advertising,* a term he finds preferable because it carries no litigative connotation. He notes that

controversy advertising is separated from other forms by its intention—namely, to exert influence in a matter of recognized public controversy.

History

Advocacy advertising in some form is as old as the practice of corporate institutional advertising. Shortly after the end of World War I, for example, the German textile industry initiated an advertising campaign to mobilize support for its efforts to regain property lost during the war.

Historically, advocacy advertising by some types of organizations (such as social welfare organizations and labor unions) has been accepted without much question in countries with strong advertising traditions. Similarly, political interest groups and organizations have long used paid advertisements as a means of expressing their viewpoints. In the business sector, corporations have traditionally articulated their views on controversial matters through collective bodies such as industry groups and professional associations.

The use of advocacy advertising by individual corporations is a relatively recent phenomenon, stimulated to some extent by business opposition to the reform policies of President Franklin D. Roosevelt's New Deal. In 1936 the Warner & Swasey Company, a Cleveland, Ohio-based manufacturer of machine tools, launched an ad campaign that was to run for more than four decades. Couched in language that was aggressive and often strident, the campaign's themes included a strong defense of the American free enterprise system, opposition to government regulation of business, opposition to U.S. foreign aid and loans, and various conservative policy proposals.

While advocacy campaigns were not uncommon in the 1940s, 1950s, and 1960s, scholars and practitioners generally agree that a sharp increase in the use of advocacy advertising occurred in the United States and Europe in the early 1970s— and particularly after 1973. This sudden surge of paid advertising to present corporate viewpoints is attributed to a combination of historical and cultural factors. The late 1960s and early 1970s were characterized by heightened public awareness of environmental and occupational health and safety issues. This concern was coupled with a heightened distrust of large corporations, which were seen as resisting pollution control and workplace safety measures in order to protect their profits and vested interests. The consumer movement spearheaded by Ralph Nader and others also served to mobilize public opinion against big business. Surveys conducted by Opinion Research Corporation in 1972 showed that the public's image of business and approval of its actions was then at its lowest point since the early 1960s. More than half the people surveyed thought that industry was doing "very little" about air and water pollution, and more than three-quarters felt that some form of consumer-protection legislation was necessary.

Distrust of large corporations increased even more during the 1973 energy crisis, when the oil industry was accused of creating sham fuel shortages and raking in windfall profits at the public's expense. Several oil companies, most notably Mobil and Chevron, felt the need to use advertising to counteract hostile public opinion. Mobil began a series of "op-ed" ads in 1971. In 1973, Mobil's public affairs department took full control of the creative work for the campaign. During the energy crisis, Mobil's ads aggressively defended the viewpoints of the company and the oil industry. Since then, the campaign has continued to express the company's position on a wider variety of subjects. Similarly, some of Chevron's advertising in the mid-1970s was intended to alter the popular impression that oil companies were making enormous profits at the expense of the American consumer. The ads provided information about the actual profits made by Chevron. The impetus for such information-oriented advocacy ads came from studies showing that the public held certain misconceptions about oil companies—believing, for example, that after-tax profits of these corporations averaged 28 cents on a sales dollar, whereas the actual figure was just over 4 cents. In the 1990s, Chevron's TV and print ads concentrated on projecting an image of the company as environmentally friendly—a clear effort to allay the concerns of environmentalists about the company's oil exploration activities and refining practices.

Objectives

In his book *Advocacy Advertising and Large Corporations* (1977), S. Prakash Sethi identified four major objectives of advocacy advertising: (1) to counteract public hostility to corporate activities based on ignorance or misinformation; (2) to counter the spread of misleading information by the critics of business and to fill the need for detailed explication of complex issues; (3) to foster the values of the free enterprise system; and (4) to counteract inadequate access to and bias in the news media.

These objectives have been fulfilled through a variety of strategies, ranging from public education (e.g., providing facts about the actual versus perceived profit levels) to pontification about the virtues of free enterprise and even to a strident defense of corporate viewpoints. The strategy of public education is based on the premise that negative public attitudes are the result of misinformation and can be changed by providing corrective information. In the 1970s in particular, many advocacy campaigns included expositions of the benefits of the free enterprise system; this theme grew out of the conviction held by large segments of the business community that the public did not really understand the role of business in a free market economy. As public awareness and acceptance of the part played by business in the economy increased in the 1980s and 1990s, this message strategy declined in relevance.

Stridsberg has classified the various strategies adopted in advocacy advertising into what he calls three main "postures": (1) defense of an economic or social point of view; (2) aggressive promotion of a point of view; and (3) establishment of a "platform of fact" that entitles the advertiser to have a voice in the controversy and to participate in its resolution. The third strategy is similar to corporate image advertising in that the ads are factual, do not present demands for action or justification of past events, and present information intended to put the advertiser in a good light. However, the intent of such advertising is not to create a favorable climate for financial activity and corporate development but rather to create a "platform of fact" in the public's mind to which reference can be made should the advertiser later find it necessary to advocate specific viewpoints or courses of action. The long-running television advertising campaign by the agribusiness giant Archer Daniels Midland (ADM) could be viewed as an example of this type of advocacy advertising. While the spots seldom focus directly upon points of controversy, they often include unmistakable advocacy content—the contribution of agribusiness to the value of U.S. exports, the company's responsible soil conservation practices, and the virtues of using ethanol additives in gasoline.

The advertising campaign of the Italian apparel maker Benetton can be seen as an example of an unusual form of advocacy advertising. Benetton's print and billboard ads have featured a series of controversial images: a nun kissing a priest, a man dying of AIDS, a black infant being nursed by a white mother, and the faces of prisoners on death row. Oliviero Toscano, the photographer and creative director behind many of these images, has said that these ads are intended not merely to sell clothing but also to

"Anticipate charity by preventing poverty."

Maimonides (1135-1204)

The American system of welfare has never really worked. But there is one solution to poverty that offers real hope. It is built on a partnership of business enterprise and the efforts of men and women who learn they can help themselves. It's called the Community Development Corporation. Thirty-six CDCs are now operating in large cities and in forgotten pockets of poorer rural areas.

The CDCs are not merely another anti-poverty project. They're a form of American capitalism. Residents of impoverished communities—black, Hispanic, Indian, white, urban or rural—form a corporation, usually nonprofit. The corporation shops for venture capital and seed funds from banks, businesses, and the federal government. Local businesses, big and small, are also tapped for technical assistance.

The pay-out? The community-formed corporations finance subsidiaries that often *do* make a profit—in dollars and cents and in benefits to the community. By providing training, ownership, employment opportunities for fellow residents. By bringing income into the community.

Only a seven-year-old concept, CDCs are now active in 30 states. They provide mortgage money for black homeowners and home-buyers in Brooklyn; health-care and job-training facilities for Mexican-Americans in East Los Angeles. One is manufacturing kitchen cabinets in the mountains of southwest Virginia. Another, run by Lummi Indians, "plants" salmon and oysters in the coastal and inland lake waters of remote Marietta, Wash., for harvest and sale to industrial markets.

Their product lines are as limitless as the economy itself. They manufacture toys, blue jeans, and electronic equipment. They develop shopping centers and farming cooperatives. They run motel franchises, industrial parks, pipe-bending plants, and restaurants. And many of the workers have never even held jobs before.

The granddaddy of the CDCs is the Bedford-Stuyvesant Restoration Corporation in Brooklyn. It serves the largest black community in New York City and is one of the most ambitious self-help programs in the United States. Since its birth in 1967, the corporation has invested more than $30 million in "Bed-Stuy." It is neither typical of the other 35 CDCs, nor a model for them. But it does prove what poverty-bred capitalism can achieve.

If you think you can help a CDC—with your expertise or with a market for good products—write the National Congress for Community Economic Development, 1126 16th Street, N.W., Washington, D.C. 20036. Its motto is the advice Maimonides handed down in the 12th Century: "Anticipate charity by preventing poverty; assist the reduced fellowman...by putting him in the way of business, so that he may earn an honest livelihood, and not be forced to the dreadful alternative of holding out his hand for charity." We believe that's still good advice.

In the 1970s Mobil Oil introduced a series of "op-ed" ads intended to help shape public opinion about the company and the industry.
Permission to reprint granted by Exxon Mobil Corporation.

provoke people into thinking about vital social issues. Unlike most other advocacy campaigns, Benetton's tend to be predominantly visual rather than verbal. The sole copy in many of these ads is the slogan, "United Colors of Benetton."

Media Choices

Advocacy advertising is seldom directed toward the general public. Rather, it is usually targeted toward narrowly defined segments. The major segments include: (1) individuals or groups opposing the advertiser's viewpoint; (2) individuals or groups supporting the advertiser's viewpoint; (3) uncommitted individuals who can be persuaded to support the advertiser's viewpoint; (4) key decision makers, such as legislators and government officials; and (5) key "influencers," such as journalists, educators, and intellectuals.

Both scholars and critics have noted that advocacy ads targeted at the first group—those who oppose the advertiser's viewpoint—are the rarest. This is true not only of advertising by large corporations but also of campaigns undertaken by interest groups such as environmentalists and labor unions. Underlying this strategy is the belief that it is extremely difficult for advertising alone—or any other form of persuasive communication—to induce a change of heart among individuals or groups already committed to a particular viewpoint. It is much easier to generate support among uncommitted members of the public and to strengthen the beliefs of those who are already supporters of the advertiser's point of view.

The target audience of a campaign is often reflected in the media choices made by advertisers. Advocacy advertisers have traditionally used print media—and especially newspapers—as the primary means of disseminating their messages. Following Mobil's campaign in the 1970s, advocacy advertising in the United States became virtually synonymous with ads on the "op-ed" page of newspapers. In Great Britain and Canada as well, advocacy advertising has been placed primarily in newspapers, with some going to the major newsweeklies such as *Time* magazine and others. In the 1990s, however, other media—most notably television—began to gain acceptance as a forum for advocacy ads.

The preference for newspaper advertising has traditionally been justified along the following grounds by both advertisers and agency personnel: (1) The controversial nature of an advocacy ad intrinsically requires many words. Print media are better suited than broadcast media to deliver lengthy messages with extensive amounts of copy. (2) Because advocacy ads often deal with topical issues, advertisers must respond rapidly to unfolding events. Newspapers have short lead times for advertising and are well suited for a quick response. Magazine ads require longer lead times, while television commercials have more elaborate production requirements and, therefore, call for even longer lead times. (3) Until recently broadcast media, even those in the United States, did not welcome controversial advertisements. Broadcast media in other countries often have even more stringent controls on ad content than their U.S. counterparts and may not permit advertising about controversial topics.

Critics have charged that the real reason for the preference for newspaper advertising is the perception of top management personnel that newspapers are a more "dignified" medium than radio or television, especially for offering detailed clarifications of their viewpoint. These critics also point out that not all advocacy ads deal with topical subjects and that, moreover, the sense of urgency about particular issues may be greatly exaggerated by those at the managerial level.

In the 1980s and 1990s, U.S. advertisers such as Chevron and ADM regularly used TV for advocacy ads, although the tone of such advertising was mild compared with the aggressive stance of other print advertisers. ADM has been a longtime sponsor of several political talk shows broadcast over U.S. television networks on Sunday mornings. While the audience share of such programs is not very high, the shows are keenly watched by influencers such as journalists and legislators, who constitute a crucial target audience segment for advocacy ads. Again, Benetton can be cited as an exception to the usual pattern. Because its advertising is visual rather than verbal, the company has used magazines and billboards rather than newspapers and TV as its chosen media for advocacy ads.

The newspapers that have probably benefited the most from advocacy advertising are those with a strong national reputation, such as the *New York Times, Washington Post, Wall Street Journal,* and *USA Today.* The editorially conservative *Washington Times* has been a beneficiary of advocacy advertising targeted toward influential Washington, D.C., residents. Both the *Washington Post* and its rival *Washington Times* experienced a lull in advocacy ads during the impeachment trial of President Bill Clinton in early 1999. Several advocacy ads were withdrawn from both newspapers because their sponsors were concerned that lawmakers—in their single-minded focus on impeachment—would not get around to discussing the issues raised in the ads. Both newspapers ran advocacy ads from sponsors on both sides of the impeachment issue, but any gain in revenue from these was more than offset by the losses on other advocacy ads.

Newspapers have long sought to consolidate their position as the medium of choice for advocacy ads. At the same time, they have also worked to expand the ranks of advocacy advertisers. Addressing the Philadelphia, Pennsylvania, chapter of the Public Relations Society of America in 1995, the advertising manager of the *Washington Post* exhorted public relations practitioners to abandon their disdain for paid advertising, urging them instead to view advocacy advertising as a valuable supplement to traditional public relations tools.

Concerns

By its very nature, advocacy advertising is controversial. During the 1970s, when this form of advertising was growing increasingly visible in the United States, law suits were filed challenging the right of business firms to engage in political speech. Courts in the U.S. have ruled decisively to uphold this right (as in the 1978 case of *First National Bank of Boston, et al. v. Bellotti, et al.*). Both practitioners and scholars of advertising have expressed concerns that corporations with vast wealth might be able to overwhelm or exclude the public expression of alternative viewpoints. Such critics are clearly skeptical of the motives of advertisers. However, large corporations and businesses are by no means the only sponsors of advocacy campaigns. Paid advertising is being used increasingly by other groups, including organized labor, voluntary private groups of all persuasions, government agencies, and even foreign governments.

Critics are also concerned about the increasing amounts of money spent on advocacy campaigns that attempt to influence elections. Expenditures on advocacy advertising remain outside the restrictions placed on regular campaign fund-raising and spending. Some people therefore fear that businesses and special interest groups with vast financial resources may be able to unfairly influence the electoral process. An article in a 1998 issue of *Broadcasting & Cable* estimated that the U.S. trade union AFL-CIO spent $35 million on advocacy advertising during the 1996 election campaign. Other highly visible advocacy advertisers that tried to influence elections in the U.S. during the late 1990s included pro- and anti-abortion activists, tobacco industry groups, and environmental groups such as the Sierra Club. Critics are concerned that the strong language and appeals to fear in TV commercials sponsored by these groups serve to increase the heat of the political process without shedding much light.

Because of its inherently political content—either tacit or overt—advocacy advertising cannot be judged simply in terms of whether it achieves the sponsor's objectives. Its impact needs to be analyzed in the larger context of the social responsibility of advertisers and its contribution to a balanced discussion of controversial issues.

KARTIK PASHUPATI

Further Reading

Hatfield, Stefano, "Should Brand Advertising Address Social Issues?" *Campaign* 6 (1995)

Nicholson, Joe, "Impeachment Obsession Is Hurting Advocacy Advertising," *Editor and Publisher* (19 December 1998)

Rosenberg, Marc, "The Power of Advocacy Advertising in Newspapers," *Editor and Publisher* (11 February 1995)

Sethi, S. Prakash, *Advocacy Advertising and Large Corporations: Social Conflict, Big Business Image, the News Media, and Public Policy,* Lexington, Massachusetts: Lexington Books, 1977

Sethi, S. Prakash, *Handbook of Advocacy Advertising: Concepts, Strategies, and Applications,* Cambridge, Massachusetts: Ballinger, 1987

Stridsberg, Albert, *Controversy Advertising: How Advertisers Present Points of View in Public Affairs: A Worldwide Study Sponsored by IAA Sustaining and Organizational Members,* New York: Hastings House, 1977

Tedesco, Richard, "Issue Ads to Boost Political Spending," *Broadcasting* (7 September 1998)

A. Eicoff & Company. *See under* Eicoff

Africa, Northern

The countries of Northern Africa, here considered to include Algeria, Egypt, Libya, Mauritania, Morocco, Tunisia, and Sudan, were all former colonies of England, France, Italy, or Spain. Each became independent during the mid-20th century, and in varying degrees their economies are still developing. As a consequence, advertising in the region is less advanced than in the developed world.

The political and cultural climates of Northern Africa have not been welcoming to the concepts of Western consumer marketing, and thus advertising has been limited. Democracy and open markets have been difficult to establish in the region. Socialist or Islamic rule in a number of the countries runs counter to many of the principles upon which advertising is based. There is little or no truly indigenous advertising industry, and several factors—including limited potential for profits, instability of governments and markets, and local concerns about cultural imperialism—have discouraged foreign agencies from establishing much of a presence.

Government ownership and control of the media is the common model in Northern Africa. Domestic media systems are limited in technology and distribution, and no audience research data are available in most Northern African nations. Low income levels and low literacy rates, along with the fact that in some Northern African countries no single language is fully accepted (although Arabic is by far the most widely used language in the region), are further barriers to advertising as it is practiced in the United States, Europe, and Asia. In many parts of the region there simply is not much private business to advertise, and in certain countries the government itself is the sole advertiser.

بسكويت مناسب لكل نوق ـ بسكويت حلو ـ سندويتش
بالكريمة ـ رقاقه ـ مكارو بز ـ نجدكل هذه الاصناف فن علبة
يك فرن العائلية المشكلة الاصنافـ كل صنف من هذه
الاصناف نحدها طازجة ـ لذيذ وذات طعم شهي
وانك لتفتخر عند تقديم هـنا البسكويت لضيوفك الممتاز ،
حيث انه مرتب ترتيب جاذب فن علب محكمة السدة ضامنا
حفظ الصنف فحالة جيدة كل الوقت ـ كل صنف من اصناف
البسكويت مصنوع من انفر العنا صـر فن معامل بيك فرن
وشركاه فنلندن ـ وصى اليوم بمقالك على علبة وناكد دائما
ان تكون الصنف بيك فرن لتنال هـنه المزايا ، الوكيل للقطر
المصرى بنيامين كوهين صندوق البوسته نمرة ٤٨٩ الاسكندرية

بيك فرين وشركاه ليمتد
معمل بسكويت ـ لندن

J. Walter Thompson Company's office in Cairo, Egypt, created this ad for
a brand of British cookies in the 1920s.

Despite these obstacles, certain advertising practices and
structures have emerged in Egypt and, to a lesser extent, in
Morocco and Tunisia. In these countries, which have more plu-
ralistic forms of government than their neighbors, the privatization of various industries has provided an environment that is
somewhat accepting of the consumer market system necessary
for modern advertising.

In Egypt, the largest country in Northern Africa, with a population of around 65 million people in 1999, official efforts to
encourage competition have stimulated the growth of advertising.
Government policies during the 1990s opened to private investors
business categories formerly controlled by the state. The advertising industry itself has benefited from this openness, and advertising has served as an important tool for new enterprises in other
industries. Over the course of the 1990s total spending on advertising in Egypt more than doubled, reaching approximately $260
million by 1999.

As practiced in Egypt, advertising is a mix of colloquial customs and international sophistication. A holdover from the
Nasser era, when all industry, including formerly private enter-

prises, was nationalized, the largest advertising agency in Egypt is
the state-run Al Ahram (The Pyramids). While Al Ahram is a full-
service agency, it also enjoys an advantageous affiliation with the
state newspaper *Al Ahram* and the state-run television system.

Private agencies in Egypt include Tarek Nour Communications, founded in 1979 as Americana Advertising and the largest
of about a dozen indigenous agencies. Multinational agencies
with Cairo offices include DDB Needham, Leo Burnett, McCann-
Erickson, and Saatchi & Saatchi. Some Western agencies, including Bozell and J. Walter Thompson, have formed relationships
with local agencies for handling projects in Egypt. A few Lebanese-
based agencies, such as Intermarkets Advertising, have locations
in Egypt as part of a Pan-Arab network of offices serving accounts
throughout the region. The Fortune Promoseven agency has
offices in Morocco and Tunisia as well as in Egypt.

The style of ads in Egypt, and throughout Northern Africa, is
for the most part an imitation of Western advertising with cultural
and religious sensitivities taken into account. The advertising of
alcohol is restricted. Appeals to the consumer based on sexual
imagery risk being censored or offending substantial segments of

Biscuiterie Industrielle du Moghreb (BIMO) is one of North Africa's
largest producers of snack foods. In a 1999 print ad BIMO's Caramel
Wafers provide the energy needed to "fly across the golf course."

the audience, although a common format in television ads involves unveiled dancing girls. Advertising themes that stress family relations are particularly effective, as are those that feature popular football or soccer stars.

During the Muslim holy month of Ramadan, television audiences in Egypt are substantially larger than during the rest of the year. Those advertisers that use television take advantage of this fact, spending as much as half or more of their annual budgets during Ramadan, and they often develop special campaigns that run only during the holiday month. Television stations increase their advertising rates at this time. Readership of newspapers and magazines actually declines during Ramadan, however.

Whereas television and print advertising have begun to be accepted in some parts of Northern Africa, radio advertising is still quite rare. There is outdoor advertising, especially in larger cities. Most stores are small shops or are found in bazaar settings, and there is very little point-of-purchase advertising. Direct mail advertising is limited by the poor reliability of postal service in the countries of Northern Africa. Internet penetration is quite low, making on-line advertising ineffective for all but the most elite target audiences.

The future of advertising in Northern Africa is likely to depend on the positions individual governments adopt toward the opening of markets and the media to competition. In 1998 the International Advertising Association held its biannual congress in Northern Africa for the first time when it met in Egypt, the country in the region with the most progressive system of advertising. In addition to Egypt, Morocco and Tunisia seem to be promising sites for future advertising industry growth. As for the rest of the region, unless there are significant changes in philosophies, laws, and habits, advertising will probably not develop much beyond the most simple and restricted practices that have prevailed for the past 100 years.

KEVIN L. KEENAN

Further Reading

Kamalipour, Yahya R., and Hamid Mowlana, editors, *Mass Media in the Middle East: A Comprehensive Handbook,* Westport, Connecticut: Greenwood, 1994

Mooij, Marieke de, *Advertising Worldwide: Concepts, Theories, and Practice of International, Multinational, and Global Advertising,* New York: Prentice Hall, 1991; 2nd edition, New York and London: Prentice Hall, 1994

Mueller, Barbara, *International Advertising: Communicating across Cultures,* Belmont, California: Wadsworth, 1996

Ochs, Martin, *The African Press,* Cairo: American University in Cairo, 1986

Africa, Sub-Saharan

Since the disintegration of the Soviet Union in 1991, democracy and market economics have been making inroads throughout Africa, turning the continent into a new frontier for marketing and advertising. Africa's 730 million people may be among the world's poorest, but they represent a virtually untapped market of considerable interest to suppliers of household products, detergents, food, soft drinks, and beer. While markets in many other regions of the world are saturated, African markets offer enormous growth potential.

Since gaining independence in the 1950s and 1960s, most African countries have had outdated economies ruled by authoritarian governments with strong socialist orientations. To a large extent, these nations were held back by cold war realpolitik, as both Western and communist powers propped up undemocratic regimes that drained wealth from their people for ideological and security reasons and for the sake of a few votes at the United Nations. After 1991, however, Russia and China were no longer able to pour aid into the continent, and the West became less interested in supporting its traditional African allies. Faced with the grim reality of declining levels of foreign assistance, many African nations have turned to market economics, and some have even held elections. This expansion of capitalism and democracy in Africa has had a marked impact on the growth of independent media, answerable to commercial imperatives rather than government fiat. In turn, at the end of the 20th century, the media were for the first time beginning to offer an appropriate platform for advertisers.

Despite the years of apartheid, South Africa has a long tradition of market-driven economic activity, and, as a result, the nation has a sophisticated advertising industry that has gained international recognition. In the 1990s, two South African advertising agencies (Ogilvy & Mather Rightford and TBWA Hunt Lascaris) were named "International Agency of the Year" by *Advertising Age.* In 1998 the British trade publication *Campaign* put South Africa's second-largest agency group, TBWA Hunt Lascaris, on its "dream team" of the world's best agencies. At the International Advertising Festival in Cannes, France, in 1999, jury chairman Keith Reinhard singled out South Africa as one of the emerging forces in advertising. South African media are well-developed, and the quality of research on both market trends and media consumption is high. Television and radio production facilities are excellent and have begun to attract growing numbers of international producers who hope to take advantage of the combination of high quality, low prices, and reliable weather. South

"We would have PERISHED from HUNGER..."

"ON October 6th, 1877 we were encamped in the Kaapse Mountains. Our food supply was nearly at an end. To add to our discomfort the chilly east wind rose. Terrifying clouds overcast the sky . . .

"Suddenly a loud thunderclap rent the heavens. The panic-stricken cattle stampeded. Cold and exhausted as my poor husband was, he had to mount his horse and follow them.

"For three anxious days I looked for his return. Tearful and heavy of heart, I remained on my feet to provide warm food for my small children and servants. The weather was so bad I never thought to see my husband again.

"In these dark days Royal proved a great friend to me. Our only food was rusks, bread and 'doughboys' made with Royal. My only oven was a hollowed out antheap, but the results of my cooking were delicious. Were it not for Royal, we would all have perished from hunger.

"On the third day I heard the whinny of a horse. How my heart leapt for joy.

My husband had returned to me from the dead. Half frozen and with an ugly wound on his leg—but safe."

This tale of hardship overcome by 'Trekker' courage is told by Mrs. A. M. Meyer of Standerton, Transvaal. This grand old lady of 74 has used Royal for nearly 55 years. "I regard Royal as the oldest and most faithful friend and ally in my home," she says.

* * * * *

Way back in the early 70's Royal was to be found in every trekker household. For Royal had already proved that it was the most reliable and economical baking powder obtainable. No matter if the oven was only a hollowed out antheap, Royal could always be depended upon to rise perfectly, quickly, unfailingly.

Now manufactured in South Africa, Royal is just as dependable and economical as it was when your mother was a girl. Made only from the most wholesome South African ingredients, Royal's purity and raising strength guarantee you success with your baking.

One of a series of incidents in the early days of South Africa, when Royal first proved itself to be the key ingredient which makes successful baking certain even under the most trying conditions

THE KEY INGREDIENT

ROYAL   *The Cream of Tartar* BAKING POWDER

Frontier life in the South African Transvaal is the theme of a 1932 ad for Royal Baking Powder, a U.S. brand also manufactured in South Africa.

Africa has good printers and reproduction houses and excellent communications systems, including telephones that work, daily international flights to and from Johannesburg, and a growing Internet-based sector. Advertisers working in Europe or the United States may take such facilities for granted, but South Africa is a lonely beacon of progress in sub-Saharan Africa.

Elsewhere on the continent, advertising is more primitive. Media research is rudimentary; production facilities are limited;

and budgets are small. The annual advertising expenditure of the continent was estimated in 1998 at nearly $2 billion. Expenditures in South Africa on advertising in television, radio, newspapers, magazines, cinema, and posters amounted to $1.2 billion, or approximately two-thirds of the continent's total. (If spending in South Africa on sponsorships, design, direct marketing, promotions, public relations, and all other "below-the-line" [marketing services] disciplines is considered, the total expenditure on advertising in that nation is estimated to be over $2 billion.)

During the apartheid era, South Africa's pariah status in the international community played a part in discouraging foreign advertisers' interest in the entire continent. With the election of the first majority government in South Africa in 1994, multinational corporations began to establish a presence in that country and to use that presence as a springboard into markets on the rest of the continent. Responding to client needs, advertising agency networks have also settled in Africa; at the end of the 1990s, there were 12 African networks. The biggest of these geographically (but not in billings) was McCann-Erickson, which had full agencies in 21 countries (as of 1999), with correspondent offices in another 8, giving the agency a claimed ability to meet the needs of advertisers in all 55 African nations from bases in 29 of them. McCann's pan-African billings were about $154 million, of which 25 percent were generated in South Africa. Ogilvy & Mather Africa covered 25 countries and had billings of about $187 million, of which 80 percent was South African. Other African networks are Saatchi & Saatchi Africa (22 countries),

Table 1.   Advertising Expenditures in Africa.*

Country	Amount (millions of U.S. dollars)	Population (millions)
South Africa	1,208.0	40
Egypt	288.5	66
Algeria	145.3	29
Kenya	45.8	29
Tunisia	44.5	9
Morocco	43.0	27
Nigeria	39.4	91
Zimbabwe	30.2	12
Ghana	21.0	18
Cote d'Ivoire	17.2	15
Uganda	15.6	22
Tanzania	11.9	31
Senegal	10.8	9
Namibia	10.5	2
Sudan	6.0	31
Total	1,937.7	431

Source: Optimum Media Direction, 1998

*top 15 countries in advertising spending

Table 2.   Advertising Networks in Africa.

Network	Number of countries	Number of employees	Total billing (millions of U.S. dollars)
McCann-Erickson Africa	29	850	154
Ogilvy & Mather Africa	25	373	187
Saatchi & Saatchi Africa	22	500	88
FCB Africa	13	750	125
Ammirati Puris Lintas	9	468	96
Grey Africa	9	310	80
TBWA Hunt Lascaris	9	668	171
Leo Burnett	8	330	
J. Walter Thompson	7	327	64
BBDO	5		
DDB International	5	81	16
Young & Rubicam	4	317	61

Source: Ad Focus (May 1999)

FCB Africa (13), Ammirati Puris Lintas (9), Grey Africa (9), TBWA Hunt Lascaris (9), Leo Burnett (8), J. Walter Thompson (7), BBDO (5), DDB International (5), and Young & Rubicam (4). Virtually all agencies have established centers that act as hubs servicing the needs of surrounding groups of countries through contact offices.

Together, these agencies serve approximately 80 Africa-based marketers, although few of those are active in more than a handful of countries. For example, 46 clients are serviced in five or fewer countries, according to a survey conducted by *Ad Focus*, an advertising annual published by the *Financial Mail* of Johannesburg. Among the multinational companies actively advertising in Africa are Unilever, Procter & Gamble, Nestlé, Coca-Cola, Reckitt & Colman, Mars, Colgate, British American Tobacco, Gillette, and Guinness. There is also a growing base of South African companies expanding into the African hinterland, including Multi-Choice (a satellite subscription TV service), MTN (a mobile phone network operator), South African Breweries, Standard Bank, Shoprite Checkers (a supermarket chain), and Nando's (a fast-food restaurant chain).

South Africa has also been an important catalyst for advertising in other respects. Media and marketing research companies based in South Africa have begun to expand northward, exporting their skills and systems to other African nations. In August 1999 at a conference held in Johannesburg, the Pan-African Media Research Organization was formed under the auspices of the South African Advertising Research Foundation (SAARF). SAARF produces the All-Media and Product Surveys, which, as the name suggests, are a comprehensive set of surveys measuring national levels of consumption of media (TV, radio, print, outdoor) and all product groups. These surveys are the envy of many Western nations, few of which have measurement tools that can match their comprehensiveness and methodological compatibility.

This cover for the design magazine *i-jusi #6* earned international recognition for the agency Orange Juice Design, based in Durban, South Africa.
Courtesy of Orange Juice Design, Durban, South Africa.

The surveys are funded by a levy on all advertising in member media.

The potential for economic gain that awaits bold marketers is evident in the rapid growth of consumption in Africa. In the 1990s, sales by some multinational companies in Africa (excluding South Africa, where market penetration was already high and competition was fierce) were expanding annually by 30 percent, supported by advertising budgets that were rendered particularly effective by low media rates and the fact that many African consumers responded with enthusiasm to simple marketing techniques.

TONY KOENDERMAN

Further Reading
Ad Focus (1993–)
Sinclair, Roger, *The South African Advertising Book,* 4th edition, Johannesburg: Thomson Publishing, 1997

African-Americans: Representations in Advertising

The depiction of African-Americans in advertising, always of interest to members of that group, became a matter of increasing concern to the advertising industry during the second half of the 20th century. Initially, many of the portrayals of blacks in advertising were highly denigrating, presenting them in the worst possible lifestyles, situations, and positions. Over the years, however, with changing social consciousness and new paradigms in the marketplace, the images of blacks in advertising have changed dramatically.

Historical Antecedents

Initially the images of African-Americans in advertising were derived from very early product packaging, much of it European. Chocolate, for example, was traditionally shown being served to Europeans by a diminutive black servant or page like the turbaned Moor trademark of the German confectioner Sarotti, his small stature and oversize eyes both suggesting a lapdog. A similar image was used in the marketing of coffee; typically, a little black servant was shown running to offer the drink to his masters.

The washing away of blackness was long a motif in the advertising of consumer goods, especially soap. Playing on the dualities implied by the opposition of black and white (dirty versus clean, dark versus light), the bathing image went to the foundation of the racial divide. The desire of whites to wash the color from black skin seemed to be an expression of the idea that blacks wished to be white. A recurring theme in a number of advertisements involved the black person who wanted to be white or the black child whose white peers would not play with him until he washed himself white. The black character was sometimes depicted as willing to do almost anything to change his color. A classic example of this was an advertisement for Pears' Soap that showed a black boy getting into a tub of water. In a second frame, after he had used Pears' Soap, the boy had a white body, although his head, which had not been immersed in the soapy water, remained black.

Pervasive Stereotypes

In the United States, African-Americans first appeared in advertising to sell products during the 1870s when color lithography was first used to print trade cards. Ranging from wallet- to postcard size and larger, trade cards were used to advertise virtually every type of product, including foods, tobacco products, medicines, shoes and boots, and a variety of household goods. They were given to those who purchased the products and became an especially popular form of advertising between 1870 and 1900.

The cards varied greatly in subject matter, although sports figures and ethnic humor were the two most popular motifs. Some of the images were positive representations of African-Americans, but others were blatantly racist. One of the most defamatory showed abolitionist leader Frederick Douglass with his second wife, a white woman, taking a product called Sulpher Bitters to lighten her skin.

From the beginning of the 20th century to the mid-1960s, advertising using stereotypical images of African-Americans was pervasive throughout the United States. Some of the images became American icons and are still used on products considered staples in many homes. It was difficult, for example, to prepare a meal without using products featuring the image of a stereotypical pickaninny, black mammy, or Little Black Sambo.

Thus, even in the 20th century, the use of pejorative and stereotypical images of blacks in advertising suggested that they remained emotionally bound to the idiosyncratic whims of their former masters. Blacks were made to appear to be subservient and ignorant, as well as ugly and grotesque. Advertising continued to portray blacks as wishing to be white. If domestic work or menial labor was involved, blacks were depicted as being best suited for the job.

Aunt Jemima was one of the best known of the stereotypical African-American advertising characters. Born of the aspirations of two businessmen in Joplin, Missouri, the trademark had its beginnings in 1889. It was a historical development for three reasons: Aunt Jemima, the first ready-made pancake mix, foreshadowed the era of convenience products; it was the first product to use a black person as a trademark; and the owners were the first to promote the idea of giving a product away to attract new customers.

During the 1920s criticism of the use of African-Americans in advertising focused on the Aunt Jemima logo. To ascertain the reactions of blacks, a study was conducted with two Aunt Jemima advertisements. The ads used the same fundamental selling appeal, the primary difference being that one had a prominent illustration of Aunt Jemima while the other focused on the pancakes The test was conducted in Nashville, Tennessee, and Richmond, Virginia, with 15 housewives and the heads of 15 families from four occupational classifications: unskilled and semiskilled labor, skilled labor, businessmen, and professionals. The advertisement in which Aunt Jemima dominated captured the attention of the respondents more quickly than the one in which her presence was downplayed. The researchers concluded that "just the presence of the Negro woman in the illustration was sufficient in many cases to gain attention quickly and thoroughly."

Thus, from the end of slavery in the 1860s to the period of the Civil Rights movement in the 1960s, advertising in the United States continued to show blacks as Aunt Jemimas, Uncle Bens, and Rastuses—individuals in subservient roles to whites. Trade cards, advertising stamps, blotters, tins, and bottles commonly portrayed blacks with thick lips, bulging eyes, and distorted grimaces. Many saw these images of servility as promoting a type of psychological bondage equally as detrimental as physical enslavement.

Even during World War II, advertisers continued to depict blacks in subservient and docile roles. As Robert Atwan, Donald

"Did you ring, sir?"

NEXT TIME you take a trip, chances are you can go in Pullman comfort.

That's because the way Pullman works with the railroads—through its centrally controlled "pool" of sleeping cars—makes it possible to take care of military needs and accommodate *more civilians*, too.

So, always *ask for Pullman space* when you plan to travel!

We'll welcome you aboard a sleeping car as we've welcomed every Pullman passenger for more than 80 years—with *service*, *comfort*, and *safety* that no other way of going places fast can match!

COMFORT! Pullman cars are clean and safe; Pullman beds are big and soft, with fresh linen every night. You get a wonderfully restful sleep!

SERVICE! Courteous Pullman employees are proud of their art in extending travel hospitality. They help make your Pullman trip a memorable event!

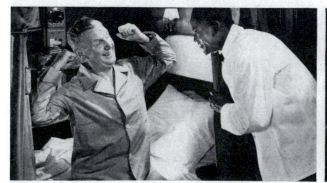 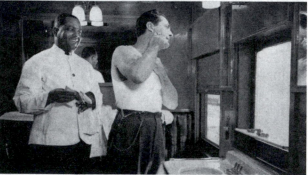

PULLMAN | *THE SAFEST, MOST COMFORTABLE WAY OF GOING PLACES FAST!*

Copyright 1945, The Pullman Company

In the 1940s ads continued to depict African-Americans in subservient roles, such as that of railroad porter.

McQuade, and John W. Wright wrote in *Edsels, Luckies, and Frigidaires* (1979), "Indeed, if one examines the vast amount of wartime propaganda issued by this nation's major advertisers, it is difficult to believe that blacks did anything in the war except serve as faithful porters on troop trains." During the war and after, the depiction of blacks as servants continued, even in advertisements in some of the best-known upscale liberal magazines, such as *The New Yorker*.

Africans-Americans as Consumers

African-American consumers were seen as a specific advertising market by whites as early as 1916, when a gas company in Rock Hill, South Carolina, worked with a church group and the local government to conduct a cooking school for "Negro" servants. Advertisements for their efforts led to the sale of 12 kitchen ranges by the gas company. In 1922 the Fuller Brush Company hired four teachers as salespersons for the black consumer market in Tulsa, Oklahoma. And the early recording industry discovered an important market among blacks when Columbia Records issued "Crazy Blues" by Mamie Smith in 1920. Other companies quickly began to cater to the market with blues and jazz performances made for and distributed to African-American population centers in the South and urban North. The companies grouped these records into separately numbered series that became known as "race records."

In the 1930s the National Negro Business League conducted a study of income and living habits of African-Americans. The investigation, one of the first national studies of black consumers, was commissioned by Montgomery Ward, Lever Brothers, and Anheuser-Busch. Based on the data they gathered, the researchers estimated the disposable income of black consumers at the time to be approximately $1.65 billion.

Breaking into the Industry

It was during the 1940s that African-Americans entered the advertising industry. The first black agency was Vomack Advertising of Inwood, New York. According to Stephen Fox, author of *The Mirror Makers,* in 1943 alone two new agencies were founded by blacks: David Sullivan in New York City and Fusche, Young and Powell in Detroit, Michigan. They were primarily involved in selling products made by blacks, targeted to blacks, and promoted through the black media. Because black agencies were not generally given business by mainstream advertisers, their financial stability was often threatened, which explains why Sullivan's agency closed in 1949. In the 1950s blacks began to be hired by mainstream agencies.

During the 1940s and 1950s other venues for the employment and portrayal of blacks in advertising opened up with the successful launch of several black-owned magazines, including *Jet* and *Ebony*. By 1967, 80 of the leading 100 national advertisers were among *Ebony*'s clients. The majority of the advertisements in such publications, however, were for skin lighteners and hair straighteners.

The 1960s: Era of "Firsts"

The Civil Rights movement enlightened the nation and led to more diversity throughout the advertising industry. In 1963 Lever Brothers, one of the largest TV advertisers at the time, proclaimed that it would show more blacks in its commercials. It was during this period that the first commercials for All detergent featured Art Linkletter talking with a black housewife about her laundry problems.

In 1963 a groundbreaking advertisement for the New York Telephone Company appeared featuring a nonstereotypical black male—a professionally dressed, distinguished-looking man shown anxiously entering a telephone booth. It was the first time such an ad had been run in general-circulation publications. Because the appearance of the ad was seen as a historic event, newspapers carried stories about it. The lead for an article in the *New York Herald Tribune* read: "What might well be the first use of a Negro model in a general circulation publication was published in this and other metropolitan area newspapers yesterday by the New York Telephone Company."

Despite progress, problems remained. Activists and national leaders of the Civil Rights movement denounced the atrocious images of African-Americans still being promulgated in some quarters. Organizations staging boycotts included the National Association for the Advancement of Colored People (NAACP), the Congress of Racial Equality (CORE), and People United to Save Humanity (PUSH). Despite the efforts of such groups, the depictions of blacks were slow to improve.

Following the 1968 riots in Chicago, Illinois, and Detroit, Michigan, the Kerner Commission's *Report on Civil Disorders* singled out the media as one catalyst for the unrest. The report placed particular emphasis on the advertising industry and recommended that "Negro reporters and performers should appear more frequently—and at prime time—in news broadcasts, on weather shows, in documentaries, and in advertisements." At the time blacks in advertising still had to be camouflaged as whites to be accepted (i.e., light-complexioned black models with European features were preferred over darker-skinned models with African features), and the title of Ralph Ellison's book *Invisible Man* might have been used to describe millions of black consumers. In 1969 Parke D. Gibson published *The $30 Billion Negro*, which revealed the value of the African-American consumer market. Gibson's observations were generally ignored, however, prompting him to write the 1978 update *$70 Billion in the Black*. In both books he tried to convince Madison Avenue that it was making a costly mistake by ignoring a lucrative market; the books also offered guidelines and tips on differences in targeting black and white consumers.

Integrated Advertising Arrives

Madison Avenue eventually began to respond to the changes occurring in society at large. By 1970 blacks, too, could finally be seen holding boxes of Wisk detergent and proclaiming, in an ad from Batten Barton Durstine & Osborn (BBDO), "No more ring around the collar." In 1972 Kodak and the J. Walter Thompson Company (JWT) took the groundbreaking step of using a black Santa Claus to advertise Kodak's pocket Instamatic camera in *Ebony* magazine. Another milestone was the debut on 2 March 1988 of the highly publicized four-part Pepsi commercial series, titled "Chase," starring pop singer Michael Jackson, who was paid $10 million, the single largest amount ever paid for an endorsement to that time.

Each year during February (designated Black History Month, which began as Black History Week in 1926) there is a proliferation of ads featuring African-Americans. One of the most highly regarded of these, which appeared in 1989, was a print ad produced internally by Polaroid Corporation to appear both in magazines for the general public and those targeted to blacks. The image in the ad was a 1948 snapshot of three small boys, one black and two white; the caption read, "Small wonders, big dreams."

During the 1990s the Benetton Group was catapulted into the spotlight by its use of black models. The company, which had some 5,000 retail outlets in 79 countries, created a stir in Europe and the United States with some of the advertisements in its $65 million campaign "United Colors." One controversial ad showed a black woman, a red sweater loosely draped about her shoulders, suckling a white baby. The ad won awards in France and Italy after failing miserably in the United States. For African-Americans the image was too reminiscent of a time in history when black slave women were forced to wet-nurse their owners' babies.

The 1992 signing of an African-American model by Cover Girl was a first for a marketer of mainstream cosmetics. Overall, the images of blacks proliferated in advertising in the closing years of the 20th century, and the portrayals became more positive, although stereotypes continued to appear from time to time.

Even while much progress was being made in and by the advertising industry, various organizations and legislators were working to enhance the process. In 1982 the Ad Watch Committee of the Black Media Association in North Carolina began to monitor the industry. It also developed guidelines, now under the jurisdiction of the Better Business Bureau, outlining ways to eliminate stereotyping in advertising.

In 1987 United Methodist Communications received a $57,000 grant from the General Council on Ministries of the United Methodist Church to create materials designed to combat racism in reporting and advertising. The group decided that the development of a training kit, including an advertising manual and a videotape that could be distributed worldwide, would be the most effective means of disseminating information. The videotape, *Racism in Advertising: From Frito Bandito to PowerMaster,* and the manual were made available in December 1991. They explored the impact of messages that relied on racial stereotypes and characterization.

Also in 1991, U.S. Rep. Cardiss Collins of Illinois reintroduced measures to curb discriminatory advertising. During the early 1980s, troubled by the absence of African-Americans in commercials, Collins had begun a process that led her to introduce a bill to eliminate tax deductions for advertisers discriminating against

multi-ethnic-owned advertising agencies. In 1986 she introduced a bill that would set aside at least 10 percent of Department of Defense advertising dollars for agencies owned by people of color.

At the same time employment in the industry for African-Americans remained low. *Advertising Age* focused attention on the problem in 1992 with the headline "The ad industry's dirty little secret." The article reported that African-Americans, who accounted for 10.1 percent of the total U.S. workforce, filled only 5.2 percent of all positions in the nation's advertising, marketing, and public relations agencies. A follow-up piece in June 2000 found that little had changed.

African-American agencies themselves seemed to be on a downward trajectory, and some agencies were not able to stay in business. A 1998 list in *Black Enterprise* indicated that the top three African-American agencies—Burrell, Uniworld, and Don Coleman—accounted for 54 percent of the billings of the 20 agencies listed. Through the mid-1990s the estimated 27 agencies owned by African-Americans were billing only approximately 1 percent of the industry total. In 1996, $865 million was spent advertising to African-American consumers, but of that amount only $337 million (39 percent) went to African-American agencies. In addition, African-American agencies found themselves competing with larger mainstream agencies such as JWT, Saatchi & Saatchi, BBDO, and the Leo Burnett Company, all of whom had created their own multi-ethnic groups.

African Images in Europe and Asia

As in the United States, blacks have generally not been presented positively in advertising in other countries. For example, the golliwog, the Beatles' mascot, has been England's most popular black figure since the beginning of the 20th century. Hailing originally from Canada, the doll was taken to England by a son of James Robertson, the founder of the Robertson's marmalade business. The figure, with its large black head and red lips, has always been offensive to black Britons, and in 1980 the National Committee on Racism in Children's Books initiated a campaign to ban golliwogs as a symbol. In 1980 alone the marmalade company distributed more than 20 million golliwog products. (In 2001 Robertson's announced that it was replacing the golliwog with figures from children's literature.)

In a 1988 article *Jet* magazine discussed the disdain blacks felt toward the Japanese advertising character Sambo. An ad for Sanrio beach clothes depicted the characters Sambo and Hanna, with the wide-eyed Sambo stating, "When I'm hungry there's no stoppin' me. I'll be up a palm pickin' coconuts before you can count to three." In addition to the Sambo line, the company marketed a black character named Bibinba, with fat, pink lips and rings in her ears.

Although blacks are not commonplace in Japanese advertising, when they do appear, they are usually shown as stereotypes. This was documented by the Japan-based Forum for Citizens' Television, which in 1991 conducted an analysis of the content of Japanese commercials in which *gaijin* (foreigners) appeared. The report indicated that both racist and sexist biases were evident in

TWICE AS NICE. LASTING LIPCOLOR THAT FEELS AS FABULOUS AS IT LOOKS.

COVER GIRL CONTINUOUS COLOR LIPSTICK. FASHION FRESH COLOR! THE STAY-TRUE FORMULA MAKES IT LAST AND LAST. THE CONDITIONING EMOLLIENTS MAKE IT SMOOTH AS SILK. FOR A LOOK AND FEEL THAT STAY FRESH AND FABULOUS. THAT'S CONTINUOUS COLOR. IN 36 ENHANCING SHADES.

COVER GIRL NIKI TAYLOR IN REALLY RED COVER GIRL TYRA IN RUM RAISIN

COVER GIRL®

CONTINUOUS COLOR LIPSTICK

© 1993 Noxell Corp.

REDEFINING BEAUTIFUL™

Tyra Banks—seen here in a 1993 Cover Girl ad, alongside white model Niki Taylor—was one of the first African-American models signed to represent a mainstream cosmetics marketer.

the depiction of *gaijin*. As an example, the report described a soft-drink commercial that focused on the waists and hips of two black females clad in tight leotards.

Darkie Toothpaste, a product manufactured by the Hawley & Hazel Group in Hong Kong for 62 years and long sold throughout Asia, was renamed Darlie in 1989. After much protest from black consumers, the logo was changed from an offensive image of a black man with a top hat and a menacing grin to a racially inoffensive silhouette.

In South Africa, where blacks account for 70 percent of the sales of consumer goods, only 30 percent of the advertising is targeted toward them. During the spring of 1994, when Nelson Mandela became the country's first black president, advertisers realized that the time had come for campaigns to reflect the majority population more accurately. One study found that 71 percent of whites living in Johannesburg-Pretoria viewed mixed-raced television commercials positively. In one beer ad a young black man sitting in a pub mused, "One thing you know about an Ohlsson's drinker. He's a man who is prepared to give change a chance."

MARILYN KERN-FOXWORTH

See also color plate in this volume

Further Reading

Atwan, Robert, Donald McQuade, and John W. Wright, *Edsels, Luckies, and Frigidaires: Advertising the American Way*, New York: Dell, 1979

Ayres-Williams, Roz, "A Battle for Billings: The Ethnic Market Has Never Been Hotter, but Black-Owned Ad Agencies Are Being Muscled Aside by Mainstream Firms," *Black Enterprise* 28, no. 11 (June 1998)

Dates, Jannette L., and William Barlow, editors, *Split Image: African Americans in the Mass Media*, Washington, D.C.: Howard University Press, 1990; 2nd edition, 1993

Kern-Foxworth, Marilyn, *Aunt Jemima, Uncle Ben, and Rastus: Blacks in Advertising, Yesterday, Today, and Tomorrow*, Westport, Connecticut: Greenwood, 1994

Kern-Foxworth, Marilyn, "Aunt Jemima, the Frito Bandito, and Crazy Horse: Selling Stereotypes American Style," in *Mass Politics: The Politics of Popular Culture*, edited by Daniel M. Shea, New York: St. Martin's/Worth, 1999

Pieterse, Jan Nederveen, *White on Black: Images of Africa and Blacks in Western Popular Culture*, New Haven, Connecticut: Yale University Press, 1992

Sivulka, Juliann, *Soap, Sex, and Cigarettes: A Cultural History of American Advertising*, Belmont, California: Wadsworth, 1998

Sturgis, Ingrid, "Black Images in Advertising," *Emerge* (September 1993)

Wilson, Clint, and Félix Gutiérrez, *Minorities and Media: Diversity and the End of Mass Communication*, Beverly Hills, California: Sage, 1985; revised edition, as *Race, Multiculturalism, and the Media: From Mass to Class Communication*, Thousand Oaks, California: Sage, 1995

Woods, Gail Baker, *Advertising and Marketing to the New Majority*, Belmont, California: Wadsworth, 1995

Age: Representations in Advertising

Advertising uses words and images intended to appeal directly to specific types of people. These words and images are carefully cultivated, based on information about how different types of consumers make purchases. The term *demographic* has been applied to the field of advertising to refer to particular audience categories. Over time, advertising experts have come to realize that age groups are invaluable demographics (or market segments) because sophisticated research methods, such as focus groups, allow advertisers to create messages designed to appeal to the wants and needs of specific age groups.

In the 1960s U.S. advertisers began to deliberately seek out the youth market. A large segment of the U.S. population was younger than 25, and this age group had a considerable level of discretionary income. Furthermore, in this era of hippies, rock music, experimental drug use, antiwar demonstrations, and feminism, youth culture and political activism were the focus of a great deal of media attention, and advertisers discovered that youthful images and the concept of "coolness" could be used to sell products to the general population as well. In other words,

youth itself became a commodity, and a variety of stereotypical images associated with particular segments of the youthful population were used by advertisers to appeal not just to those specific markets but to Americans in general.

Before they learned this lesson, companies typically advertised to the general public rather than targeting youth in particular. For example, during the first half of the 20th century, the Coca-Cola brand was sold to people from all walks of life in every part of the United States, and Coke was unrivaled in the marketplace. In the 1960s, however, Pepsi transformed soft drink advertising by appealing specifically to the youth market through the "Pepsi Generation" campaigns. Early "Pepsi Generation" ads featured young men and women in carefree situations with pop, folk, and rock-and-roll sound tracks, although later campaigns would expand the notion of the Pepsi Generation from a demographic to a state of mind.

The matrix for much youth imagery came from Hollywood in the mid-1950s, with the release of *The Wild One*, starring Marlon Brando; *Blackboard Jungle*; and—above all—*Rebel without a*

Cause, starring James Dean. Advertising adopted all these images and continues to appropriate the slang and fashions that differentiate various segments of the youth population. Ads today feature such stereotypes as rap artists, "Goth" groups, skateboarders, computer nerds, sexy adolescent divas, and prepubescent boys playing violent and sexually explicit video games. In part, these images are so popular among advertisers because U.S. teenagers have a great deal of purchasing power and because they buy more movie tickets and watch more TV than any other age group, a fact that makes them a relatively easy audience to reach through ads. Also, the lesson taught by the "Pepsi Generation" ads continues to resonate with advertisers: youth advertising sells to people of all ages because of the strong association between youth and carefree vitality.

In contrast to the positive images of youth, the elderly are usually depicted in advertising as either afflicted with specific medical ailments or, conversely, as robustly healthy and active. More than any other age group, the elderly are rigidly stereotyped, and the very old are seldom seen in ads. One reason these stereotypes prevail may be that research shows that this group usually makes purchases based on fixed perceptions and brand loyalty. These data have led advertisers to conclude that ads portraying and addressing the elderly in conventional terms are more effective than ads that try to be innovative.

Senior citizens are the segment of the U.S. population most likely to watch the network evening news, and therefore television commercials on these programs are often geared to that audience. These ads show consumer brands targeted to the infirm or impaired, featuring such products as adult diapers, arthritis medications, prescription drugs, or motorized wheelchairs. Other commercials aired during the news include spots for luxury cruises (one depicts a handsome middle-aged man with salt-and-pepper hair holding hands on deck with a slightly younger woman) and insurance ads that may feature a well-known senior citizen in a recliner extolling the benefits of the advertised product. Frequently, a spokesperson is chosen from former film and TV stars of a "certain age": June Allyson for Depend undergarments, Arthur Godfrey, Art Linkletter, and Ed McMahon for health insurance.

In a few instances, breakthrough advertising was achieved by daring strategies that defied common age-related stereotypes. In 1984, for example, the fast-food chain Wendy's sought to highlight the generous size of its hamburgers by calling attention to the meager portions of ground beef provided by competitors. The commercial created by Dancer, Fitzgerald, Sample showed three elderly women examining a hamburger from one of Wendy's competitors. The women appeared stereotypically polite and docile until the one on the right demanded in an unexpectedly assertive voice, "Where's the beef?" The phrase immediately entered the American idiom, and the woman who said it, Clara Peller, became an instant celebrity.

JAN ARRIGO

See also color plate in this volume

Further Reading

Frank, Thomas, *The Conquest of Cool: Business Culture, Counterculture, and the Rise of Hip Consumerism*, Chicago: University of Chicago Press, 1997

Agulla & Baccetti

Founded by Ramiro Agulla and Carlos Baccetti, 1994; won Topper footwear account, 1995; ranked by *Advertising Age International* as the fifth most awarded independent agency in the world, 1996; won Renault business, 1996; 20 percent of the agency acquired by Lowe Group Worldwide, 1997; won Telecom Argentina account and Levi Strauss & Company account, 1997; awarded HSBC Group business, March 2000; Lowe Group increased shares in agency to 40 percent, July 2000.

Major Clients

Direct TV
HSBC Group
Levi Strauss & Company
Loteria Nacional (National Lottery)
Renault Argentina
Telecom Argentina

If any one advertising agency in Argentina were to be singled out as the driving force behind the local industry's creative renaissance in the second half of the 1990s, garnering the country an international reputation for Latin creativity second only to that of Brazil, it would almost certainly be Agulla & Baccetti. Since its founding in Buenos Aires, Argentina's capital, in 1994, the agency established by the creative duo of Ramiro Agulla and Carlos Baccetti has consistently won a remarkable number of local, regional, and international creative awards. Servicing a growing list of prestigious clients—Renault, Telecom Argentina, HSBC Group—the agency has also seen a meteoric rise in billings, from $1.3 million in its first year to $70 million in 2000.

In July 1997, only a month after *Advertising Age International* had highlighted Agulla & Baccetti as one of the hottest creative shops in the world, the Lowe Group acquired a 20 percent stake in the agency. Lowe then doubled its holding in 2000.

The quality.   The price.

Jotter. Parker's new low price line.

✦ PARKER

A 1991 ad created for Parker Pen by FSB/Young & Rubicam features the work of one of the agency's premier creative teams, Carlos Baccetti and Ramiro Agulla. The two opened their own ad agency in 1994. *Courtesy Parker Pen Company.*

the company's advertising for free if the campaign proved to be a failure. If the ads were successful, however, Sanyo would agree to pay double the usual fee.

Agulla, the president of the agency, recalled courting Topper, an Argentine marketer of leather footwear, by challenging the potential client's marketing staff to a game of basketball. The move helped persuade Topper that the start-up possessed the freshness and audacity necessary to reposition its brand's tired image. The ensuing campaign was predictably controversial: two athletes facing off on a tennis court wearing literally nothing, except for their Topper shoes.

The bold tactics did not stop there. On one occasion, the executives of a leading Brazilian bank, Banco Itau, who were impressed with the agency's work, decided they wanted to drop by the shop. At the time, the shop was run out of cramped, rather unpolished premises, Agulla said. Fearing that the bankers would not be sufficiently impressed, the partners hired several men to appear on the day of the visit and pretend they were builders drafting plans to expand the office.

A growing number of established advertisers wanted to work with the agency but were hesitant at first. For instance, Renault approached Agulla & Baccetti in 1996 but initially gave the agency only half of its business (the rest was with Grey Advertising). Eventually, the agency acquired the whole account.

As the agency's billings continued to grow, reaching $20 million by the end of 1996, so did its creative reputation abroad. Several multinational agency networks, keen to get a foothold in the growing Latin American market, began to knock at Agulla & Baccetti's door, including Ammirati Puris Lintas and FCB Worldwide. The ideal partner came in the shape of Frank Lowe, chairman of the Lowe Group, who first flew to Buenos Aires for a meeting and then invited the duo to London, England, for further consideration. The three were almost immediately compatible. Agulla and Baccetti respected the fact that Lowe was not looking solely at profits but was also concerned with the creative product.

In June 1997 the Lowe Group bought a 20 percent stake in the Argentine shop as part of its regional expansion. To round out a momentous year for the agency, the Buenos Aires-based industry group Circulo de Creativos named Agulla & Baccetti the best agency of 1997.

In the next two years, the agency won more prestigious accounts, such as the newly privatized telecommunications company Telecom Argentina; the country's number-one beer brand, Quilmes; and, most significantly, Levi Strauss & Company, in what was the first time the jeans marketer awarded part of its business—in this case for its Think Dark brand—to a local agency.

Amid the awards, however, the agency suffered some disappointments. These included giving up the Quilmes beer account over "creative disagreements" and losing its hold on oil giant YPF, the country's biggest company, after it merged with Spain's mammoth Repsol. (Repsol insisted on keeping its lead agency, Young & Rubicam, for work in Argentina.) But offsetting those losses were major gains in the new century, including HSBC Group in March 2000 and in December 2000 a regional advertising

Even before opening their own agency, Agulla and Baccetti, who began their advertising careers in 1987 and 1980, respectively, were no strangers to creative acclaim. They first teamed up in 1988 at Young & Rubicam, Inc., working for clients such as Adidas, Colgate-Palmolive Company, and Visa International, and eventually being promoted to directors in 1992 after being named the most creative team in the company's international network. A year later, they moved together to the Verdino Bates agency as associate creative directors. By then, they were already impatient to open their own shop. "It wasn't just a dream of owning an agency," Baccetti has said, "we wanted to start a revolution, to transform the old-fashioned ways that agencies were run."

The shop was launched in September 1994 with a single client, JCA, a private postal service. The maverick pair wasted no time in shaking up the formal, rather stuffy relationship traditional between clients and agencies in Argentina. The unconventional and irreverent way they began to pursue new clients soon became the talk of advertising circles. The agency told Sanyo it would do

account for DirecTV Latin America-DTLA, a leading provider of satellite TV, previously with J. Walter Thompson Company. For the latter business, though, the agency was forced to resign its local business with DTLA's archrival Sky.

Now that it is firmly established as a top-ten agency in Argentina, Agulla & Baccetti's forthcoming challenges include expansion in international markets. Future projects include helping Lowe find a suitable candidate in Miami, Florida, to join the multinational network and establishing a partnership in the Spanish market.

Entering the new century the two partners remain as committed to developing creative standards in Argentina as they were in the early 1990s. This interest extends to ensuring that the local industry has an appropriate platform from which to nurture new talent. Toward that end they run part-time courses jointly with

the Universidad Di Tella aimed at developing the notion of creativity, Baccetti said, "in its widest sense of the word."

ALI QASSIM

Further Reading
"Focus: Creative Agencies: 'Renaissance' Men in Argentina: Agulla, Baccetti season talents with element of surprise," *Advertising Age International* (1 June 1997)
Gray, Kevin, "Jesus stars in Agulla & Baccetti spots that will not be seen at the Cannes fest," *Advertising Age International* (1 June 2000)
"The Hot Shop Everyone Wants to Buy," *Advertising Age International* (1 June 1997)
Mandel-Campbell, Andrea, "Faces of the Future," *Advertising Age International* (8 June 1998)

Air Canada

Principal Agencies
BCP (later Publicis-BCP)
Marketel (McCann-Erickson Ltd.)
FCB/Ronalds-Reynolds
Hamazaki-Wong

Air Canada is Canada's major national airline. At one time, however, the establishment of a Canadian airline was viewed as nothing more than an impractical dream. The nation was struggling through the Depression and was unable even to link its far-flung regions by rail. One government minister declared, " I do not think that Canada will ever have need of an air service."

Undaunted by such predictions, Trans-Canada Air Lines, the forerunner of Air Canada, was founded as a crown corporation (i.e., one owned by the Canadian government) by an act of parliament on 10 April 1937. Its first commercial route linked Vancouver, British Columbia, with Seattle, Washington. In one of its early months of operation the new carrier served a total of 144 passengers.

Flights across Canada were soon introduced, but because flying above bad weather was not technologically feasible, passengers often experienced harrowing, bumpy, uncomfortable—and long—rides; it took 15 hours to get from Vancouver to Montreal. The needs of the government and the armed forces were the airline's first priority during World War II, but in 1945 it introduced transatlantic passenger service. With the growth of international service came the need to adopt a name that required no translation. Trans-Canada Airlines thus became Air Canada in 1965 when it also unveiled its distinctive maple leaf logo. Throughout the 1960s and 1970s, Air Canada upgraded its fleet and ushered

in a host of new services and special prices for families, youth, and seniors. The airline survived the onslaught of government cuts, economic downturns, and increased competition in the 1980s to emerge as a privatized company in 1988–89. It launched its first loyalty program, Aeroplan, during the same period. The early 1990s were spent making the airline more efficient so that it could better meet its challenges as a private company in a competitive marketplace. These improvements enabled the company to exploit new opportunities when, in 1995, the "Open Skies" agreement was signed between Canada and the United States, enabling unrestricted access to carriers from both countries on transborder routes. Today, Air Canada's U.S. flight network accounts for 25 percent of its business.

In 1998 Air Canada celebrated its 60th anniversary. It has grown from its initial staff of 71 people to a company that now employs more than 24,000. In July 2000 Air Canada merged with Canadian, Canada's only other national airline. This merger helped Air Canada increase its revenues to CDN$ 9.3 billion. It operates 155 aircraft as part of its main operations and owns four commuter carriers that account for another 50 airplanes. It logs 1,200 flights a day and serves 120 destinations in Canada, the United States, the Caribbean, Europe, the Middle East, and Asia. To extend its services, Air Canada joined with five partners—United Airlines, Lufthansa, SAS, Varig, and Thai International—to form the Star Alliance, the world's first multi-airline coalition. The alliance enables Air Canada to provide passengers with seamless service around the globe.

Air Canada's goal has always been to communicate as clearly as possible with its customers. Its traditional advertising focus has been on its products and prices. This straightforward approach has been apparent in the company's advertising from its inception.

American business travelers have declared Air Canada "the Best Airline to Canada" for the fifth year in a row.

(Gosh, this is getting embarrassing.)

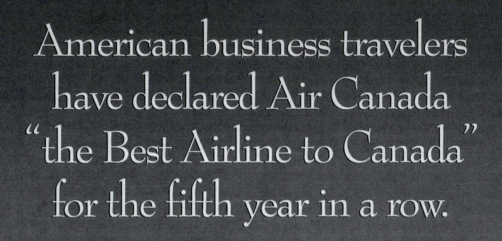

All of us at Air Canada would like to thank all of you in America (you know who you are) who so very kindly cast your vote for us in the Business Traveler International Magazine poll. We're all touched. We must admit, however, there have been times we were afraid we might appear a tad obsequious in our attempts at winning your business. We've done things like offer more nonstops between the USA and Canada than any other airline. Let's not forget all those extremely *convenient* connections within our *immense* global network. And we'll come clean, we even went and offered you your choice of Mileage Plus®[1], OnePass®[2] or our own Aeroplan®[3] miles. Our detractors may also be quick to point out how we really, really went over the top by introducing world-class, *dee*-licious Second Cup coffee on board every flight. There's more. But space prevents us from going on. Bottom line is, does America want to fly with a bunch of people who are so willing to show their appreciation for your patronage that they will stoop to *hospitality*? Evidently you do. Air Canada. We're like a regular airline, only we're not.

For more details, please call your travel agent or Air Canada at 1-800-776-3000.
Visit our Internet site at this address: http://www.aircanada.ca

[1]Mileage Plus is a registered trademark of United Airlines. [2]OnePass is a registered trademark of Continental Airlines. [3]Aeroplan is a registered trademark of Air Canada.

The **nicer** *way to fly.*™

Air Canada's strategy in the late 1990s, exemplified by this 1997 ad, focused on hospitality and service.
Ad courtesy of Air Canada.

In its early years, "marketing" at Air Canada consisted of selling tickets. The airline's main ad claim was simply that flying reduced travel time. Later, its ads took on a human face. A 1948 print ad showed a boy writing a love letter to a stewardess; the copy applauded the airline's shiny new planes and the employee's old-fashioned hospitality and helpfulness. In the 1950s, it moved more toward image advertising; ads featured glamorous people and hints of romance. As the company evolved, it learned to focus on customer needs and expectations. This focus helped Air Canada create advertising that became part of the Canadian culture. One radio and TV spot promised Canadians that all one needed to hop aboard an Air Canada flight for a southern destination was "My bikini and my toothbrush."

After it emerged from under the protective wing of government ownership, Air Canada's top advertising priority was letting Canadians know that it was no longer a conservative crown corporation but a vital company that was an integral thread in the fabric of the community. It had to stress its customer-driven strategy, and it did this with extensive television advertising that featured employees helping passengers. It also launched the memorable "Hello-Goodbye" campaign to reinforce the airline's "human dimension."

With the formation of the Star Alliance and Air Canada's move into the global marketplace, new communication challenges faced the company. It had to develop a global identity and project that identity onto a brand recognized worldwide. It also had to fine-tune and align its different media strategies. Air Canada's solution to these problems was unique. It brought together its 11 communication suppliers and put them in a room at a resort just north of its Montreal headquarters. There was no question about the ground rules: bring your expertise, but do not try to steal the other guy's business.

Using data from a comprehensive market survey, Air Canada management identified four strategic areas where improvement was needed to make the airline more competitive: its loyalty program; products and services; customer service; and brand positioning. The 11 agencies were asked to create a common vision to position the airline, taking into account Air Canada's history, its present challenges, and the research results. The agencies worked in teams and developed eight positioning options. These were tested in North America, Asia, and Europe. Instead of talking about better seats or more convenient schedules, the new integrated communication strategy focused on Air Canada's culture and its desire to make passengers feel like valued individuals. Its brand vision says it all: "I am not a seat number, I am a person." This statement promises customers that when they meet an Air Canada employee, whether a baggage handler or a ticket agent, they will have a different experience than they would with any other airline. The goal of every employee is to understand what customers want from an airline and to exceed their expectations.

PEGGY CUNNINGHAM

Further Reading

Air Canada <www.aircanada.ca/about-us>

De Wolf, Mark, "Air Canada Dream Team Scores," *Strategy: The Canadian Marketing Report* (16 February 1998)

Kotler, Philip, Gary Armstrong, and Peggy Cunningham, "Canadian vs. Air Canada: Surviving the Fare Wars," in *Principles of Marketing,* by Kotler, Armstrong, and Cunningham, 4th Canadian edition, Scarborough, Ontario: Prentice Hall Canada, 1998

Pratt, Laura, "Retrospective: Air Canada: Flying High for 60 Years," *Strategy: The Canadian Marketing Report* (16 February 1998)

Airlines, U.S.

The intrepid Wright brothers and the dashing aviator Charles Lindbergh did much to romanticize air travel in the early 20th century, but it took hard work by the airlines to sell the concept to the public. Since that time, numerous airlines have come and gone, but their ad campaigns have consistently focused on the same themes: routes, fares, safety, and convenience.

Interest in commercial aviation burgeoned after World War I. At first a skeptical public, while intrigued by the notion of flying, saw airplanes as noisy machines that performed at air shows—sometimes with disastrous results—and dropped bombs during wars. When U.S airmail routes were opened to private plane operators in 1925, 130 airlines started operations within a year, and they quickly worked to make their names known. Borrowing an idea from steamship companies, some fledgling airlines gave out free baggage stickers that detailed their routes and the makes and models of their aircraft. Hundreds of such stickers were issued until the practice ended at the close of the 1930s.

Charles Lindbergh, who became famous after his May 1927 flight across the Atlantic Ocean to France in the *Spirit of St. Louis,* was the "poster child" for passenger air service, and he went on to help start what would become Trans World Airlines (TWA). At the same time another U.S. aviation pioneer, Juan Trippe, was rapidly expanding international air routes. In 1927 he founded the Aviation Corporation of America and began building a route between Key West, Florida, and Havana, Cuba. Later that year Trippe bought up potential competitors and merged them to form Pan American Airways.

It took FIFTEEN YEARS to build our World Routes, now so vital to Victory

Every American knows the story of Lewis and Clark—the men who pioneered a trail across the North American continent to the Pacific.

But few Americans know the story of how Pan American Airways—our Merchant Marine of the Air—pioneered skyways across two oceans and down the length of South America in the short space of fifteen years.

In Central and South America, cloud-piercing mountains, hundred-mile swamps and deadly jungles blocked the path. For much of the territory, no accurate maps existed... None had been made since the 17th-century charts of the Spanish, Dutch and French explorers.

To equip some of our early airports on the route to the Panama Canal, gasoline had to be carried in by hand—long lines of natives, each with a five-gallon tin balanced on his head.

In the Pacific, at Midway and Wake Islands, there were no harbors... Construction mate-

rials had to be towed through heavy seas, floated over barrier reefs and landed on the beach despite the heavy breakers.

Across Africa also, airports had to be hacked out of jungles and built up on desert wastes. At some points the only available hauling power was furnished by camels... Native Africans who had never seen an airplane were employed as artisans.

In Alaska, summer is brief—roads did not exist. Airports had to be built on unfriendly swamp morass or, when it was available, on glacial gravel and sand.

* * *

Today all these routes are playing their part in hastening Victory for the United Nations.

Without exaggeration, it can be said that the existence of facilities pioneered by Pan American has saved the United Nations' aerial war transport many long months.

Wings over the WORLD PAN AMERICAN CLIPPERS

During World War II ads from airlines such as Pan American Airways focused on the role of commercial aviation in the war effort.

Pan American quickly won government routes into Latin America and was flying into Costa Rica and Panama by February 1929. The maiden flight was piloted by Lindbergh. The company also had significant equity in the RKO film company, founded in that same year, a relationship said to be the basis for RKO's 1933 hit film *Flying Down to Rio,* perhaps the most successful air travel promotion of its time. Advertising for Pan American was being handled by Batten Barton Durstine & Osborn. In 1935 Trippe launched transpacific service on the *China Clipper,* a huge flying boat that took off from and landed on the water, as no network of airfields was yet in place. Pan American began service to Europe on the *Atlantic Clipper* in June 1939, Egypt in 1941, and India in 1942.

"Safe. Swift. Clean. Comfortable."

Meanwhile the N.W. Ayer Company created a series of 17 ads that sought to illustrate the joy and necessity of flying; each ad focused on a particular aspect of passenger flight. Over the next 18 months the "Lift up your eyes" ads made their way into such widely read publications as the *Saturday Evening Post, National*

Geographic, American Boy, and *Vanity Fair.* Airline executives were crafting innovative marketing approaches, focusing on what they considered to be the basics of their industry. A 1929 ad from Delta Air Service read, "Safe. Swift. Clean. Comfortable."

In 1930 executives at Boeing Air Transport, an airline that would join with others to form United Air Lines a year later, came up with the idea of hiring stewardesses to take care of passengers on the airline's early, often turbulent flights. Instead of simply hiring pretty women, which was a good marketing tool because most of the passengers at the time were men, Boeing recruited nurses to boost its safety image. Almost 40 years later airlines continued to tout the comforts provided by their flight crews. A 1968 print ad from American Airlines, for example, featured a flight attendant curled up in a chair, with copy that read, "Think of her as your mother. She only wants what's best for you."

Taking the theme of safety and security one step further, American Airlines broke the advertising mold in 1937, running ads that openly talked about the fear of flying and discussed safety issues. One such ad featured an open letter from company President C.R. Smith with the banner headline, "Why dodge this question: afraid to fly?"

In addition to the speed advantage of air travel, other fringe benefits were promoted. During Prohibition, for instance, posters highlighted flights to the Caribbean, where alcohol was plentiful.

World War II and After

During World War II, with planes diverted to military use and airline employees dedicated to the war effort, passenger service was limited. But passenger carriers did not want to be forgotten. A 1940 United Air Lines ad in *Time* magazine focused on airline employees. Pan American Airways, in a wartime ad, stressed the important role that commercial aviation was playing in the war effort.

It was not until after World War II that advertising began to focus on fares. Americans' interest in air travel had grown, but flying remained prohibitively expensive for the middle class. To overcome this obstacle, Pam American introduced a marketing program called "Fly now, pay later," in which passengers could arrange an installment loan contract with Household Finance Corporation to pay for their flight. With the notion of vacation travel reappearing after World War II, airline ads reverted to their early ad themes, explaining why travelers would go to a particular destination on a particular company's planes.

Air travel slowly began to replace train travel, and as commercial aviation became more sophisticated, advertising slogans changed. In 1938 Continental Airlines' pitch was "Fly the old Santa Fe Trail." By the mid-1940s the slogan had become "The blue skyway." With the introduction of jet service in 1958, the J. Walter Thompson Company unveiled Continental's "First in the West with jet power flights." By the mid-1960s the agency and the slogan changed again as Continental chose to focus on its proud history, record profitability, and service levels. Needham, Harper & Steers emphasized these attributes with slogans such as "The airline that pride built" and "See the difference that pride makes."

Amenities, too, were emphasized. TWA in 1940 offered the first in-flight audio entertainment, providing individual receivers to passengers so they could listen to radio programs. In 1957 TWA was the first airline to serve freshly brewed coffee during a flight. And it was also the first airline, in 1970, to offer no-smoking sections aboard all flights. The introduction of business-class ambassador service prompted TWA's "whole new way to fly" slogan in 1970. A Braniff International campaign from the 1970s carried the slogan, "When you've got it, flaunt it." But at Eastern Airlines, Chairman Frank Borman scrapped the "Wings of man" slogan, on the grounds that it was pretentious. Reluctantly, he began acting as a spokesman for the airline in television ads.

Perhaps the most successful marketing jingle in airline advertising history debuted in 1965 when United and the Leo Burnett Company introduced the "The friendly skies." Two years later the airline launched a "Take me along" promotion to entice traveling businessmen to take their wives along on business trips. In 1969 "Come fly with me" made its first appearance as part of United's "Friendly skies" campaign. When employees took a 55 percent ownership stake in the company in the mid-1990s, that became the platform for all marketing efforts. The tag line was tweaked only slightly ("Come fly our friendly skies"), and employees sported buttons with sayings such as "Welcome to my airline" and "Ask me. I'm the owner."

In 1977 American Airlines' innovative marketing team introduced Super Saver fares, the industry's first restricted discount fares. The program offered dramatic savings for leisure customers willing to buy tickets far ahead of travel dates. Other airlines quickly followed suit.

Deregulation

Deregulation of the airline industry in 1978 changed not only the landscape for airlines but also the industry's advertising environment, which went from controlled to "anything goes." Before deregulation Eastern Airlines, during one cash-tight spell, had proposed paying for advertising by giving free tickets to agencies. United Air Lines tried to promote its winter flights to Denver, Colorado, by offering "snow guarantees," promises that a skier's fare would be refunded if there were no snow. Neither idea won regulatory approval.

Deregulation brought a flurry of upstarts, the ability for airlines to freely enter and exit markets, and an opportunity for carriers to spread their wings in advertising. Innovation was everywhere. Republic Airlines, a Minneapolis, Minnesota-based airline formed after deregulation by three regional carriers, offered prospective passengers a free ticket in 1982 in exchange for five box tops from Chex cereal.

Southwest Airlines, a brash upstart that began in 1971 as a regional airline in Texas, ratcheted up the competition for innovative marketing. Southwest recognized early on that its marketing would have to be special to attract attention. In its first year of operation, half of its $700,000 advertising budget was spent in the first month. Consequently, the airline quickly had to rely on word-of-mouth promotion of its outrageous personality. When it

The Natives are friendly

We know you don't fly just to be smiled at.
So we add efficiency.
We have schedules that are convenient for you.
We fly more jets to more U.S. cities (and carry more passengers)
than anybody else.
And United Air Lines is the only airline that connects with every other U.S. airline.
We add extra care for your creature comforts, too.
"Extra care" is doing things nobody tells us to do, or maybe even expects us to do.
We prepare your meals ourselves, coast to coast,
which is something no other airline does.
We pay top prices for steak, and we have European-trained chefs
with a proper respect for beef like that.
And we never forget that you like to be smiled at, too.

fly the friendly skies of United.

"We've got a great movie today, Mr. Bryant."

In 1965 United Air Lines launched its "Friendly Skies" campaign, introducing one of the most enduring airline slogans. *Courtesy of United Air Lines.*

did spend money, it had to get the biggest bang for its buck. Its first ad agency, the Bloom Agency, helped create Southwest's image; it came up with the idea of long-legged flight attendants in go-go boots and hot pants.

In 1973, just two years after getting its wings, Southwest showed its marketing tenacity in what it viewed as a David-versus-Goliath battle for passengers. The carrier had tried to woo passengers by cutting its fare from San Antonio, Texas, to Dallas, Texas, in half—to $13. Competitor Braniff quickly retaliated by reducing its fare from Dallas to Houston, Texas, Southwest's bread-and-butter market. Southwest's response: a spread ad in the Dallas and Houston newspapers from the Bloom Agency that was short and to the point. Accompanied by the picture and signature of company President Lamar Muse, copy on one page read, "Nobody's going to shoot Southwest Airlines out of the sky for a lousy $13." The ad explained Braniff's tactics and told passengers that Southwest would match the fare. Passengers were given the choice of opting for the $13 fare or paying the full $26 and getting a free fifth of liquor.

Airline deregulation provided maverick Southwest with the opportunity to fly outside Texas, and it continued marketing itself as "the low fare airline." With help from its two later agencies,

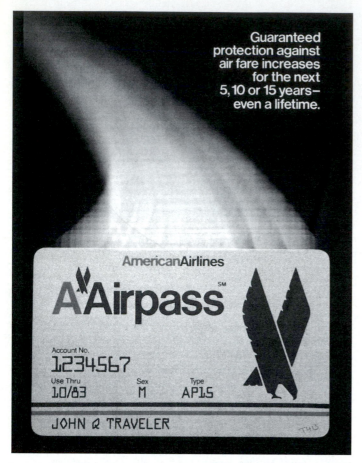

Guaranteed
protection against
air fare increases
for the next
5, 10 or 15 years—
even a lifetime.

AmericanAirlines

A'Airpass℠

Account No.
1234567

Use Thru   Sex   Type
10/83   M   AP15

JOHN Q TRAVELER

In 1981 American Airlines introduced its AAdvantage Travel Awards, the
first frequent-flier incentive, and AAirpass, a prepaid airfare program
aimed at frequent fliers.
Courtesy of American Airlines.

Austin, Texas-based GSD&M and Cramer-Krasselt of Chicago,
Illinois, Southwest tried to get the public to relate to its philosophy and its employees, reasoning that if they were accepted,
Southwest would also be accepted as a viable airline. Some campaigns were serious, such as Cramer-Krasselt's "Just plane smart"
appeal to business travelers. But others—such as a television spot
in which Southwest Chairman Herb Kelleher sat with a paper bag
on his head—were not.

The established airlines found themselves threatened by
upstarts such as Southwest, and the first expense they cut was
marketing. Troubled TWA, under the control of Carl Icahn in the
late 1980s, sought to reduce costs by trimming marketing. A
friend of Icahn's, an advertising man named Shelly Kravitz with a
reputation for getting the job done as cheaply as possible, was
brought in to negotiate better terms with TWA agency Young &
Rubicam, Inc. Kravitz convinced TWA to handle production of its
own commercials and to do them in black and white, changes that
did reduce production costs significantly. However, it also cost
TWA an agency; Young & Rubicam resigned the $45 million
account when Icahn demanded that the agency cut its fee from $6
million to $4 million.

Other airlines targeting Southwest's customer base toyed with
their own versions of campaigns touting themselves as low-fare
airlines. In the mid-1990s Continental Airlines crafted Continental Light. TWA, having gotten out from under the control of
Icahn, opted to move in the other direction, away from the low-
price image. New management initiated a $10 million, eight-week
campaign in early 1993 that focused on comfort. In one television
commercial from Backer Spielvogel Bates Worldwide, New York
City, the camera focused in on passengers' knees to demonstrate
improved legroom. Quick to react, American Airlines' domestic
agency, Temerlin McClain, of Irving, Texas, came back with a
series of ads that focused on its amenities. One ad showed an
Adirondack chair placed at the edge of a dock.

Seven years later TWA still was trying to upgrade its image
through ads detailing plans to replace its fleet. A $2 million TV,
print, and radio campaign from D'Arcy Masius Benton & Bowles,
St. Louis, Missouri, was aimed at business travelers. This group,
which flies more frequently than leisure travelers and pays more
for seats, became a key ad target.

In 1998 Continental launched a "Work hard. Fly right" campaign, which acknowledged the drudgery of flying but also highlighted industry problems of promising too much and delivering
too little. Sample copy in the primarily print and outdoor ads
from N.W. Ayer & Partners, New York City, read: We're only as
good as our last flight" and "Other airlines promise you the stars,
how about getting your luggage back?" The campaign was meant
to attract customers and to motivate the company's own employees, a common goal in airline advertising. "All the airlines fly
essentially the same kind of airplanes. Ultimately, the contact people have with us is the airline," Richard Metzner, Continental's
vice president of marketing programs, told *Advertising Age* in
1999.

The Frequent Flier

Years earlier American Airlines had understood the idea of solidi-
fying the relationship between passenger and airline. In 1981
American Airlines developed a marketing strategy aimed initially
at business fliers: the frequent-flier program. American had actually began rewarding loyal customers in 1936 with membership in
an "admiral's club" as part of its introduction of the DC-3 aircraft. That perk eventually went by the wayside when the regulatory authority for airlines decided that airport lounges must be
open to anyone willing to pay a fee. (The club lounge was later
reintroduced.)

The 1981 frequent-flier program was far more sophisticated,
thanks to computers and some insightful thinking by Doyle Dane
Bernbach, American's agency in the late 1970s. The agency suggested that American come up with a "loyalty fare" for its best
customers. This was the genesis of the AAdvantage program,
which made customers feel special and enabled American to track
individual members and their travel patterns. United Air Lines
came out with its own frequent-flier program 11 days later.

Frequent-flier programs are considered the most effective
industry-wide marketing program, and they are as popular with

leisure travelers as with business travelers. Earning miles has become a latter-day version of collecting Green Stamps, and corporations outside the travel industry now buy miles from the airlines to use as customer loyalty incentives. The programs have meant that airlines have to do less advertising and can more effectively market to select groups of customers.

In the 1990s American tried to break new ground by returning to its roots. In 1991 the carrier sought government approval to base ads on aircraft maintenance and safety issues. "We think it's time to put aside the notion that it's OK for airlines to compete on the thickness of their ham sandwiches and the breadth of their wine selections, but that it's not nice to talk about the quality of aircraft maintenance," American Chairman Robert Crandall told the Association of National Advertisers. Four years earlier American had benefited greatly from a campaign from Bozell/Southwest, of Dallas, Texas, that highlighted the carrier's on-time performance as measured by the U.S. Department of Transportation.

Quick responses to competitors' ads became critical, particularly as airlines placed growing emphasis on fares and conditioned the flying public to look for sales. In 1992, when American Airlines came out with its Value Plan, a major low-fare initiative, United was able to cut American's ad lead to less than 24 hours. In the end, though, the ability to respond quickly did not matter. Other airlines began advertising fares that were lower than American's, and the airline ultimately had to cut the price of its already discounted fares. While the entire episode was lucrative for anyone who had print or commercial time to sell, and leisure travelers took to the skies as never before, the fare war bloodied the airlines.

Ad slogans, particularly in the competitive and ever-changing airline environment, are continually changing. American Airlines' "Doing what we do best" became "Something special in the air." Delta's slogan, "We love to fly," was replaced in 1995 with "You'll love the way we fly." United Air Lines, not to be outdone, decided it needed a change—in both slogan and ad agency—and came away with the dubious distinction of dumping a tried-and-true winner for something that did not work. In 1996 United ended its relationship with Leo Burnett USA, in Chicago, Illinois, and abandoned its "Friendly skies" slogan. Instead, United said it had formed a "strategic partnership," giving its domestic advertising to Fallon-McElligott, of Minneapolis, Minnesota, and the international advertising and media buying duties to Young & Rubicam's Y&R Advertising, of New York City. The arrangement was similar to one at American Airlines, where Temerlin McClain handled domestic ads and DDB Needham Worldwide, New York, handled the international side.

United's domestic campaign from Fallon centered around a $1.5 million survey that the airline had commissioned to find out what passengers thought about traveling. From the survey responses, a "customer satisfaction philosophy" was developed. The resulting campaign, with the tag line "Rising," was intended to commiserate with business travelers about the pitfalls of traveling. United's longtime musical theme, George Gershwin's "Rhapsody in Blue," got an update. The same tag line was used

Delta's slogan, "We love to fly and it shows," emphasized comfort and service rather than fares.
Courtesy of Delta Air Lines, Inc.

internationally. "Rising" fell, however, and the campaign was dropped in the fall of 1999. Some thought the early work was promising but failed to connect with employees and passengers.

Fallon next created a campaign that focused on "uniting" people, using phrases such as "Be united" and "Feel united." After "Rising" was scrapped, Y&R produced its own campaign, which became United's first overseas branding campaign.

Consolidation and Change

By the end of 2000 United acknowledged that the team effort was not working and decided to consolidate the $80 million–$100 million global account with one of its two agencies. Its goal was to create a consistent voice and message worldwide and to reduce its annual spending by $6 million. Fallon Worldwide emerged as the winner.

United was not the only airline to opt for a big change as the end of the century neared. In 1998 Delta scrapped Saatchi & Saatchi's "On top of the world" campaign and put its $100 million global account up for review. Saatchi had only had the account for a year, winning it from BBDO South, Atlanta, Georgia, Delta's agency for 51 years. But it did not take long for the airline to grow dissatisfied with the result, which included commercials showing a woman sleeping on a bed of feathers, fanned by handmaidens. In 1999 the account was awarded to Burnett in Chicago.

International marketing also took on new importance in the mid-1990s. In 1997 American Airlines undertook its first multinational branding effort, aimed at overseas business travelers bound for the United States. This marketing effort came late in the game, given that 35 percent of the airline's revenue was generated by international fliers, and the international segment had been growing faster than domestic business.

When airlines were not trying to one-up their competitors, they were banding together and marketing alongside each other. Code-sharing agreements between U.S. and foreign carriers, such as Star Alliance and Oneworld, were marketed to tout the benefits of seamless worldwide air travel while still preserving each airline's own brand identity.

The Internet also grew in importance as a marketing and ticketing vehicle. Airlines began advertising Internet-only fares and revamped their Web sites to be more user-friendly. The benefits were obvious and immediate: ticketless travel cut down on backroom expense, and travelers booking their own trips online cut the commissions that airlines had to pay to travel agents. Following the lead of Northwest Airlines, Southwest Airlines launched a campaign in 2000 that focused solely on its Internet presence. The conventional tag line, "A symbol of freedom," became "A symbol of e-freedom."

Marketing programs that steer travelers first to the Internet and then to specific airlines are expected to continue to grow in importance. Orbitz, an airline ticketing service founded by the top five airlines, made a splashy spring 2001 debut. The consortium hired TBWA/Chiat/Day, New York City, to handle a $75 million advertising and marketing budget.

A subsequent industry wrinkle may not benefit the ad world. American's effort to rescue TWA from U.S. Bankruptcy Court may entail the consolidation of route structures, employees, and advertising.

Terrorist attacks on the World Trade Center and Pentagon on 11 September 2001, in which commercial aircraft from American and United Air Lines became in effect flying bombs, radically altered the creative direction of airline advertising. After a hiatus immediately following the attacks, airlines slowly returned to advertising; the message was no longer simply about fares and air-

craft features but now included patriotism and safety. Southwest, the first airline to run television spots after the incident, abandoned its trademark humor in favor of a serious commercial from GSD&M in which its president spoke of the tenacity of Southwest and the nation. In mid-October, United resumed its television efforts with a series of black-and-white commercials from Fallon in which employees discussed their feelings about the company, the country, and the American spirit. Low-fare ads again reappeared, with the theme of getting America moving again, but they, too, were more sober.

MARY ELLEN PODMOLIK

Further Reading

Allen, Oliver E., *The Airline Builders,* Alexandria, Virginia: Time-Life Books, 1981

Dagnoli, Judann, "American Wants to Air Safety Ads," *Advertising Age* (4 November 1991)

Freiberg, Kevin L., and Jacquelyn A. Freiberg, *Nuts! Southwest Airlines' Crazy Recipe for Business and Personal Success,* Austin, Texas: Bard Books, 1996; London: Orion Business Books, 1997

Gleason, Mark, "United Opts for 'Team' Approach with Fallon, Y&R," *Advertising Age* (21 October 1996)

Goetzl, David, "Rivalry Rising on United Account: Stakes Are High for Y&R As Shop Breaks New $50 Mil Int'l Campaign," *Advertising Age* (15 May 2000)

Goetzl, David, "United Shops to Duke It Out for Global Biz," *Advertising Age* (11 December 2000)

Goodrum, Charles A., and Helen Dalrymple, *Advertising in America: The First 200 Years,* New York: Abrams, 1990

Peterson, Barbara Sturken, and James Glab, *Rapid Descent,* New York: Simon and Schuster, 1994

Petzinger, Thomas, Jr., *Hard Landing: The Epic Contest for Power and Profits That Plunged the Airlines into Chaos,* New York: Times Business, and London: Aurum, 1995

Reed, Dan, *The American Eagle: The Ascent of Bob Crandall and American Airlines,* New York: St. Martin Press, 1993

Reiss, Bob, *Frequent Flier: One Plane, One Passenger, and the Spectacular Feat of Commercial Flight,* New York: Simon and Schuster, 1994

Serling, Robert J., *Maverick: The Story of Robert Six and Continental Airlines,* Garden City, New York: Doubleday, 1974

Alcoholic Beverages. *See* Beverages, Alcoholic

Alka-Seltzer

Principal Agencies
Wade Advertising Agency
Jack Tinker & Partners
Doyle Dane Bernbach
Wells, Rich, Greene, Inc.
McCann-Erickson Worldwide
BBDO

Developed for Miles Laboratories of Elkhart, Indiana, in 1928, Alka-Seltzer was known for "effervescent" tablets that emitted bubbles of gas while dissolving in water, creating a pleasing remedy consisting of buffered aspirin and antacid. Hub Beardsley, then company president, envisioned Alka-Seltzer as a medicine for various ailments, from headaches and stomach problems to colds and flu. The claim that Alka-Seltzer could treat concurrent symptoms helped to establish its success. However, the product would later be plagued by the legal implications of this very claim, as well as by product safety concerns. Throughout its period of popularity, Alka-Seltzer pitted itself against both headache and antacid competitors and succeeded in becoming a leader in both categories. Its greatest legacy, however, is some of the most memorable and humorous advertising of the 20th century.

Franklin Miles, a physician, founded Miles Laboratories in the late 1880s to promote his sleep remedy, Restorative Nervine, to other physicians both locally and by mail order. Just before his death in 1929, word reached him in retirement that the company was undertaking the initial testing of a promising new medication called Alka-Seltzer. It quickly became the leader in company sales and by the beginning of the 21st century had sold more than 2 billion tablets.

Alka-Seltzer was first introduced in 1931 in newspaper ads and radio spots run in cities near the marketer's Elkhart, Indiana, headquarters. Its agency at the time was Wade Advertising, a family-run shop that began with Miles in the early 1900s. The ads invited consumers to try a free sample in their neighborhood drugstores. Using a microphone held near two tablets dropping into a glass of water, the radio spot let listeners "Listen to it fizz!" One early tag line promoted Alka-Seltzer as a "new drink for health," treating a vast range of symptoms and conditions. Alka-Seltzer was presented to U.S. consumers nationally on the popular program *Saturday Night Barn Dance* on 200 stations on NBC's Blue Network, and despite the Great Depression, sales soared. In 1938 Alka-Seltzer's claims to remedy "systemic acidity" drew the attention of the Federal Trade Commission (FTC), which described Miles's advertising as "false, misleading, and deceptive" after research showed that the product assertions had little medical support. The company compromised with the FTC, agreeing to drop the claims and promising to submit all future copy to review by licensed physicians. Yet Alka-Seltzer's introduction to the country barely skipped a beat. Wade invested heavily in radio with long-term sponsorships of *Lum 'n' Abner*

(1941–47), *Hilltop House* (1948–55), *Queen for a Day* (1946–50), *One Man's Family* (1950–59), and most famous of all, *The Quiz Kids,* which was associated with the brand from 1940 into the mid-1950s on television.

Miles stayed with radio until the late 1940s, when the new medium of television came onto the horizon. Miles broke into the new platform slowly, but by the late 1950s Alka-Seltzer was the sponsor of a diverse group of well-liked American programs such as *Break the Bank* and *The Jack Paar Show.* Before World War II, Miles was spending between $1 million and $1.5 million a year on network radio, most of it on Alka-Seltzer, although Miles's Nervine received some support. In 1939 the company ranked 16th among radio advertisers, a tradition continued in television.

By the 1950s Alka-Seltzer was contributing the majority of Miles's earnings and received in turn the majority of its growing advertising budget. For years, Jeff Wade, grandson of the founder and by 1951 president of the agency, had wanted to create a character to represent Alka-Seltzer. In 1951 a Wade account representative implored a wartime flying buddy turned commercial artist, Robert Watkins, to produce a "Mr. Alka-Seltzer." The result was Speedy Alka-Seltzer, the very embodiment of fast relief. Speedy was a blue-eyed, redheaded sprite who sported an Alka-Seltzer tablet, caplike, on his head while another tablet formed his body. He appeared in magazine ads, point-of-purchase store displays, and stop-action animated television commercials in which he was given the voice of actor Dick Beals. Over the next ten years Speedy would appear in more than 100 commercials and garner Alka-Seltzer many awards, including selection by *Advertising Age* as one of the best commercials of the 1950s.

By 1958 Speedy's popularity and recognition level were at their height, both in the United States and abroad. Given Alka-Seltzer's increasing sales, Miles's decision to part ways with Wade after 40 years was a surprise. In April 1964 the company chose the Interpublic Group of Companies' think tank, Jack Tinker & Partners, a small group of Interpublic's best creative talents, who now had the challenge of becoming a full-service agency to administer Alka-Seltzer's estimated $12 million budget. Tinker took the brand in a new, more sophisticated direction. The agency's 1964 debut of the revolutionary "Stomachs montage," depicting series of images of midsections and featuring the tag line, "No matter what shape your stomach's in," was well received, after only 12 months with the new agency, Alka-Seltzer sales were up 64 percent compared with the last 12 months of Wade's tenure. Tinker's 1966 award-winning print campaign showing "Alka-Seltzer on the rocks"—a close-up of a glass of fizzing tablets on ice, the glass beaded with condensation—began a new advertising style that future ad designers would copy. The Tinker agency developed other popular and edgy commercials such as "Unfinished Lunch," which won a Clio Award in 1970. But Miles was concerned by the migration of top talent from Tinker to other agencies and moved the brand to Doyle Dane Bernbach (DDB) in the summer of 1969.

Alka-Seltzer
On The Rocks

You haven't tried it yet? / Oh boy. / Alka-Seltzer On The Rocks / works just like Alka-Seltzer / Off The Rocks . . . only / it's good enough to drink. / Maybe even delicious? / And even today, in 1966, / nothing relieves an upset / stomach and summer / headache faster . . . or better / than good old Alka-Seltzer. / Try it at a picnic. / Try it at the beach. / Plop two Alka-Seltzers in / water. Let it bubble away / a few seconds. Add ice. / A slice of lime. Cheers.

A 1966 Alka-Seltzer print campaign from Jack Tinker & Partners won awards for its creativity.
Courtesy of Bayer Corporation.

Miles gave DDB a generous $20 million advertising budget with which to confront a daunting challenge: although Alka-Seltzer's sales continued to rise with the help of its new cold remedy, Alka-Seltzer Plus, increasing costs were driving down earnings, and antacid tablet competitors were hurting market share. Television campaigns such as "Groom's First Meal" and "Mama Mia" also won Clio awards and scored extremely high with audiences for their comedic appeal. However, some observers criticized the agency's style as creativity for creativity's sake. In fact, later research on the popularity of "Mama mia," a humorous commercial within a commercial in which an actor ingests spicy meatballs take after take, showed that many viewers mistook the spot to be about tomato sauce, not a heartburn remedy. Alka-Seltzer continued to lose market share, and some in the industry blamed the decline on the introduction of Miles's new Alka-Seltzer Plus, which took loyal users away from the original product. After only 16 months at DDB, Miles moved its account again, this time to Wells, Rich, Greene, Inc., reuniting the brand with Mary Wells, agency founder and chief executive officer, and other former Tinker executives who had worked on the account in 1964. Miles had hopes for a more complete and serious campaign centered on the product.

Wells, Rich, Greene refocused Alka-Seltzer with a stronger message while still retaining a humorous appeal. Its first campaign, "Personalities," captivated the public with ads that made

light of Americans' vaunted tendency to overindulge. The famous tag lines, "Try it, you'll like it" and "I can't believe I ate the whole thing," became fixtures in American pop culture. But chewable and liquid antacids were gaining on Alka-Seltzer, even though the marketers of these products were spending millions less to promote their brands. Some observers believed Alka-Seltzer was becoming obsolete.

The brand was hurt in 1973 by the report of a U.S. Food and Drug Administration (FDA) panel that suggested that Alka-Seltzer was an overtreatment for many stomach ailments. Some medical professionals had raised concerns about possible stomach damage caused by aspirin. The result was a shift in marketing to a more straight-talking campaign. Its purpose was to ensure that consumers understood that the product was for conditions requiring both antacid and aspirin. In 1974 the company went further and introduced an aspirinless version of the original Alka-Seltzer, now called Alka-Seltzer Gold, which was designed to win back sales. It also agreed to clarify its message, specifying which ailments the remedy should be used to treat. In 1975 the brand was still positioned well in American homes through the memorable "Plop, Plop, Fizz, Fizz" jingle, and Miles even invited Beals, the voice of Speedy, to sing the catchy song in a new commercial in 1976. In 1978 Bayer AG of Leverkusen, Germany, acquired Miles Laboratories and retained the Miles name until 1995, when it became known as Bayer.

Wells, Rich, Greene kept the Alka-Seltzer account until 1983, when it was won by McCann-Erickson Worldwide. On an advertising budget that had reached nearly $50 million, McCann-Erickson marketed the product until all Bayer brands moved to BBDO, New York City, in 1995. In the 1980s and 1990s Alka-Seltzer and its marketers were faced with tough challenges to remain competitive within the drug market and relevant to both new and loyal consumers. Alka-Seltzer Plus, hosting an assortment of additional remedies such as nighttime cold, flu, and sinus medications, was outspent in advertising and outmaneuvered in technological developments by competitors such as the Procter & Gamble Company's Vicks Nyquil and Dayquil and Johnson & Johnson's Tylenol Cold products.

The late 1990s saw an explosion of direct-to-consumer advertising for prescription drugs after the FDA eased advertising restrictions in August 1997. The resultant boom in ad spending for the prescription drug market detracted from Alka-Seltzer's sales and diluted its marketing message (as well as those of other over-the-counter medications). In November 2000 the FDA announced that the drug phenylpropanolamine, an ingredient in many leading cold products including various Alka-Seltzer Plus cold medications, was unsafe. Bayer and other manufacturers immediately introduced reformulated versions without the banned drug, but the announcement had done its damage. Yet despite these setbacks, Alka-Seltzer entered the 21st century with a strong ad effort proclaiming that the brand was still a contender.

MEGAN CASSADA

See also color plate in this volume

Further Reading

Adams, Valerie, "Alka-Seltzer Opts for Straight Talk," *Advertising Age* (10 December 1973)

"Ad Sales Builds Talking Trademarks for Point of Sale," *Advertising Age* (3 April 1951)

Alka-Seltzer <www.alkaseltzer.com>

"The Alka-Seltzer Headache; or, Please Pass the Excedrin," *Advertising Age* (11 August 1969) (an editorial)

"Alka-Seltzer's Headache," *Advertising Age* (1 August 1977)

Bayer: History of Bayer Consumer Care <www.bayercare.com/bayerinfo/hist.html>

Cray, William C., *Miles, 1884–1984: A Centennial History,* Englewood Cliffs, New Jersey: Prentice-Hall, 1984

"Criticized Alka-Seltzer Ad to Go Back on Air," *Advertising Age* (8 September 1969)

Currie, Emmett, "Alka-Seltzer Names Interpublic's Tinker," *Advertising Age* (11 May 1964)

Danzig, Fred, "Despite Acclaim for Ads, Alka-Seltzer Is Becalmed in Share-of-Market Race," *Advertising Age* (21 August 1972)

Edwards, Larry, "Miles Tells New Alka-Seltzer Strategy," *Advertising Age* (10 November 1975)

Grant, Don, "Miles Seeks New Insights at DDB," *Advertising Age* (4 August 1969)

Grant, Don, "Alka-Seltzer Reported Eyeing Rivals of DDB," *Advertising Age* (7 December 1970)

Grant, Don, "Wells, Rich Gained Alka-Seltzer Account with Message That Hard Times Call for Hard Sell," *Advertising Age* (14 December 1970)

Grant, Don, "WRG's New Alka-Seltzer Strategy: Make 'Pylorus' a Household Name," *Advertising Age* (16 August 1971)

Grayson, David, "The TV Spot: If You Enjoy It, Maybe You Shouldn't Run It," *Advertising Age* (3 December 1973)

Hannon, Kerry, "Fast, Fast Relief for Sour Sales," *Forbes* (12 December 1988)

Howard, Niles A., "Alka-Seltzer Minus Aspirin Is Moving Out," *Advertising Age* (21 October 1974)

Howard, Niles A., "His Dream Comes True; Beals Rejoins Speedy," *Advertising Age* (11 October 1976)

"Miles Finds Rx for Flak: Alka-Seltzer sans Aspirin Bows," *Advertising Age* (4 March 1974)

Ornstein, Charles, "FDA Warns against Use of Dozens of Medications; Ingredient of Cough-Cold, Diet Drugs Linked to Stroke Risk," *Dallas Morning News* (7 November 2000)

Revett, John, "Headache Helps May Be Alka-Seltzer Target if Antacid Rules Pass," *Advertising Age* (9 April 1973)

"Tinker Views Alka-Seltzer As New Type Effort," *Advertising Age* (18 May 1964)

"What a Relief for Speedy—He's Revived by Miles," *Advertising Age* (12 July 1976)

Carl Ally, Inc.

Founded by Carl Ally, 1962; renamed Ally & Gargano, 1976; went public, 1983; purchased by Marketing Corporation of America, 1986; control sold to Wesray Capital Corporation, 1988; closed, 1995.

Major Clients

Dunkin' Donuts
Federal Express Corporation
Fiat
Hertz Corporation
MCI Communications
Polaroid Corporation
Saab
Volvo

In its glory days in the 1960s and 1970s, Carl Ally, Inc. (later Ally & Gargano [A&G]), earned a reputation with its "grab 'em by the throat" approach. The agency was the first to use comparative advertising and earned a reputation for representing fledgling companies—such as Federal Express Corporation (FedEx) and MCI Communications—that would go on to become industry leaders.

Carl Ally, Inc., was launched in 1962, after Carl Ally left Papert, Koenig, Lois, Inc. (PKL), to strike out on his own. Ally had been a copywriter at the fabled PKL, where he worked on the account of a little-known European automaker, Peugeot. A former Peugeot ad manager had gone to work for another obscure car manufacturer, Volvo, and offered Ally its $1 million account.

Ally's Aggressive Approach

Ally's affinity for cars began early on. He was born in Detroit, Michigan, in 1924, where his father, a Turkish immigrant, worked as a tool-and-die maker in the automotive industry. His interest in planes also began when he was fairly young. During World War II and the Korean War he served as a fighter pilot in the U.S. Air Force, winning both the Distinguished Flying Cross and a Presidential Citation. Between military stints, Ally became a copywriter at the General Electric Company through a training program he likened to a Harvard M.B.A. in marketing and advertising. He received an undergraduate degree from the

University of Michigan and later earned a master's from the same institution.

In 1955 Ally joined the Campbell-Ewald Company, a regional advertising agency in Detroit, Michigan. His supervisors there were so impressed with his work that they moved him from the Detroit main office to the New York City office, where he became manager. Ally was famously aggressive and headstrong; he often claimed he was the model for the Yossarian character in the novel *Catch-22* (a claim denied by the author, Joseph Heller). Ally's conviction that he was smarter than his bosses got him fired eight months after he arrived in New York. He then went to work for PKL shortly after it was formed. There he created subtle previews of what would become his signature technique: naming competitors in advertising. One memorable campaign for the *New York Herald Tribune,* aimed squarely at the *New York Times,* asked, "Who says a good newspaper has to be dull?"

Upon being offered the Volvo account, Ally convinced two former colleagues from Campbell-Ewald to join him: art director Amil Gargano and copywriter Jim Durfee. Carl Ally, Inc., with Ally as chairman and chief executive officer (CEO), was established in 1962 with $330,000 and one account, Volvo, along with billings of $1 million. Durfee later recalled that the agency was lucky to snag the account, considering it misspelled the client's name as "Valvo" on presentation materials.

With that first account, the agency showed off its "grab 'em by the throat" advertising philosophy, which shook up old-line agencies. Neither Ally nor Gargano fit the buttoned-down image of the advertising community's old guard, and Ally, in particular, saw the old school of advertising as dull and insipid. At the time Carl Ally, Inc., was formed, television rules barred an advertiser from mentioning its rivals by name. One Volvo spot got around that rule by using an aerial view that showed a Volvo, with the company's name visible on the roof, easily outracing five unnamed, but recognizable, competitors.

It was not long before the agency began naming names. One Volvo ad claimed the import was faster than a Ford. When a Ford lawyer called Ally to ask, in a rather threatening manner, "Well, what should we do about this?" Ally suggested, "Make your cars faster." Indeed, Carl Ally, Inc., is credited with helping lift the ban on comparative advertising, which the last of the major TV networks discarded in 1972, following suggestions from the Federal Trade Commission that the rules might be interpreted to represent restraint of trade.

Hertz had been losing market share to Avis, which, in a Doyle Dane Bernbach (DDB) campaign, had obliquely compared itself to Hertz by touting its "No. 2" status. The Ally agency's approach was more direct:

> For years, Avis has been telling you Hertz is No. 1. Now we're going to tell you why. If you were in the car rental business and you were No. 2 and you had only half as many cars to offer and about half as many locations at which to offer them, and fewer people to handle everything, what would you say in your advertising? Right. Your ashtrays are cleaner.

Hertz had seen its market share slide from 55 percent to 45 percent under the Avis assault. Six months after the agency's campaign was launched, Hertz rebounded to a 50 percent share. Avis was not the only DDB client that Ally met head on: in its campaign for Fiat, Volkswagen too was mentioned by name.

FedEx and Other Successes

It was not just cars that Ally identified with. He also had a weakness for planes and underdogs and perhaps that was no more apparent than with the agency's FedEx account. In October 1974 the one-year-old Nashville, Tennessee, company named Carl Ally, Inc., as its first consumer agency. With a $150,000 budget, the agency began test campaigns in New York City and Los Angeles, California. Business in New York increased 87 percent and in Los Angeles, 59 percent.

Not only did Ally's ads boost the shipper's business (the company had $400 million in annual sales in 1980), they helped launch an industry. The advertising strategy was accomplished in phases. The first goal was to build awareness, through the tag line, "America, you've got a new airline." The agency created many memorable ads, with slogans the company used for years, among them, "Why wait when you don't have to?" and 1979's famous tag line, "When it absolutely, positively has to be there overnight."

The agency's 1982 FedEx spot "Fast Talker," featuring "the world's fastest-talking man" garnered nationwide acclaim. It featured actor John Moschitta in a fast-paced telephone conversation on the importance of overnight delivery. It also showcased director Joe Sedelmaier's signature style of offbeat characters performing in minimalist settings. Although it was Moschitta's only role for the advertiser, Sedelmaier and Ally completed more than 80 commercials for FedEx in their six years of collaboration, relying on a comedic pitch to an audience that was once believed to shun advertising that pushed the bounds. In 1999 *Advertising Age* magazine ranked "Fast Talker" number 11 in a list of the 100 best ad campaigns of the century. FedEx became a cash cow for the agency, worth $25 million in annual billings by the time their relationship ended in 1987.

By some accounts, Ally was personally responsible for losing half the important clients the agency ever had, and Carl Ally, Inc., began a series of reorganizations. In 1976 the agency changed its name to Ally & Gargano, and in 1979 Ally sold his voting stock to Gargano. He also turned over day-to-day responsibilities to his longtime colleague, although he retained the title of chairman until his retirement several years later. Another major change in the executive suite occurred in 1979, when Edward M. Gallagher joined A&G as executive vice president and chief operating officer. Gallagher had previously worked for McCann-Erickson and Compton Advertising and had a strong background in packaged goods. He had also gone to college with William McGowan, who was then chairman of a small, upstart telephone company, MCI Communications, that became an A&G client.

By 1982 A&G's fortunes had turned, at least briefly, and *Advertising Age* named the company its "Agency of the Year," characterizing the agency's work as "some of the freshest, most arresting—and effective—advertising the industry has seen." The publication specifically noted A&G's work for FedEx, MCI, and the early-rising baker for Dunkin' Donuts. But the success was not to last; Ally, Gargano, and Gallagher clashed. Nonetheless, the agency went public in 1983, a decision that Gargano, at least, claimed to regret. A&G's finances took a nosedive; it reported a net loss of $160,000 for the third quarter, compared with year-earlier third-quarter net earnings of $312,000. Several major clients, including FedEx and MCI, cut back on their advertising budgets and several others, including Commodore computers and Franklin Computer, went bankrupt. At the same time the agency was rapidly increasing the ranks of its staff. In 1981 A&G had 75 employees; by 1984 it had almost 300.

Takeover by MCA

Six months after the company went public, Gallagher was out, after Gargano, acting for the board, fired him. Following Gallagher's termination, the company again reorganized. That reorganization created a greater daily role for Ally and an operating committee led by Senior Vice President and Media Director Larry Dexheimer.

By the time Ally retired in 1985 the agency had attracted several new, large clients, such as Ciba-Geigy Corporation's pharmaceutical division and Polaroid Corporation. Gargano added the title of chairman following Ally's departure. Several key clients left when Ally did, including Travelers Insurance Company, Polaroid, and MCI. In June 1986 Marketing Corporation of America (MCA) purchased A&G for $26.6 million. MCA merged A&G with its advertising agency, MCA Advertising, an effort that proved less than seamless. MCA Advertising focused on packaged goods, with clients including H.J. Heinz Company. Not all A&G employees were happy within the more conservative culture of MCA.

Gargano and Ally barely remained on speaking terms following Ally's departure. According to some executives, the rift centered partly on Gallagher's firing, a move that Gargano had not been comfortable with. The relationship between the two could not have improved when Saab, which had employed Ally as a consultant, moved its account from A&G to Lord, Einstein, O'Neill & Partners in 1988. (Ally insisted that he had no role in Saab's final decision to move its account, maintaining that consultants do not make those sorts of decisions.) For A&G the loss of the Saab account was particularly bitter, and not merely for financial reasons, although it certainly hurt the company's bottom line (the account had been with A&G for nine years and represented about $30 million a year in billings). The blow was also emotional; A&G had been closely identified with import cars, including Volvo, Fiat, and Saab, for most of its years in business.

Following the merger with MCA, the agency began losing key creative people. A&G employees who left after the merger formed Messner, Vetere, Berger, which went on to compete as one of the finalists for the Saab account. Noted alumni from Carl Ally, Inc., included David Altschiller, Bob Kuperman, Marty Puris, Ralph Ammirati, Bob Mayer, Bob Schmetterer, Ron Berger, Ed McCabe, Helayne Spivak, Ed Butler, Tom Messner, and Barry Vetere.

Carl Ally, Inc., created many memorable commercials for FedEx, its premier client, including this 1983 execution, a humorous look at the pitfalls of trusting deliveries to the "other" company.
©1983 *Federal Express Corporation. All Rights Reserved.*

The same year that Saab moved its account, A&G also lost the Ciba-Geigy and SmithKline Beecham accounts. In December 1988 MCA sold control and 50 percent of the agency for $30 million to Wesray Capital Corporation and Bill Luceno, who became chairman-CEO, in a leveraged buyout. A year earlier, Luceno had left Wells, Rich, Greene/Worldwide after 14 years as president. The debt from that reorganization, while not immediately crippling, meant that A&G could not afford further losses.

A&G brought several major accounts on board, including Shearson Lehman Hutton and Tambrands, Inc., but in 1991 Gargano left the agency as soon as his contract allowed. He opened Amil Gargano & Partners, taking with him three of the agency's top creative people and sparking a series of departures that represented an enormous drain on A&G's talent.

Turning Point

In 1992 A&G unsuccessfully competed for the Mercedes-Benz of North America account, which went instead to Scali, McCabe, Sloves. This failure marked a turning point in the agency's fortunes. A&G subsequently failed to make the finals for the $80 million BMW of North America account in 1993, although the shop was familiar with the product through its work for the New York City metropolitan BMW dealers association. While the agency won General Nutrition Centers' $30 million media account in September 1993, it also lost the $6 million Celestial Seasonings account and two brands marketed by Pfizer: Ben-Gay ointment and Plax mouth rinse.

In February 1994, after A&G President Warren Dechter left to return to MCA, Luceno took on a much larger role in client service, which left him stretched thin. As the end of 1994 approached, A&G was struggling but had managed to hold on to

about $250 million in billings (when accounts at its three main subsidiaries were included).

Nevertheless, in December longtime client Lorillard announced that it was pulling its $25 million account from A&G. That left A&G with two clients, Bank of New York and Dunkin' Donuts, and both were considering switching shops.

In January 1995 A&G was named a finalist in the $175 million Kmart Corporation review, an effort Luceno termed the agency's "last chance," but in March Kmart handed that account to Campbell Mithun Esty of Minneapolis, Minnesota. Soon after that loss, a parade of accounts began to leave A&G, including in April H.J. Heinz Company's $4 million Weight Watchers account and Bank of New York's $20 million account and, in June, Dunkin' Donuts' $40 million account.

Pressures continued to build until late in 1995, when the agency once described as "one of the great agencies of the 1970s and 1980s" finally succumbed. In 1991 agency founder Ally, the self-styled outsider, was inducted into the Advertising Hall of Fame. He died of a heart attack at age 74 in February 1999.

DEREK DATTNER AND AMY I.S. DATTNER

Further Reading

Davis, David E., Jr., "People: Some Fired, Some Drunk, One Dead," *Automobile Magazine* (May 1999)
Fox, Stephen, *The Mirror Makers: A History of American Advertising and Its Creators*, New York: Morrow, 1984
Petrecca, Laura, "Legendary Adman Ally Remembered," *Advertising Age* (22 February 1999)
Thomas, Robert McG., Jr., "Carl Ally, Hard-Hitting Adman, Is Dead at 74," *New York Times* (17 February 1999)

Almap/BBDO

Created by Caio de Alcantara Machado as Alcantara Machado Publicidade Ltda., or Almap, in São Paulo, Brazil, 1954; hired Alex Periscinoto, then advertising manager of Mappin Stores, São Paulo's leading department store, 1960; sold a share in the shop to Omnicom Group's BBDO, 1993; Periscinoto retired and was replaced by Marcello Serpa (creative) and Jose Luiz Madeira (management), 1997.

Major Clients
Banco Finasa S/A
Bayer S/A
Companhia Cervejaria Brahma/Miller Brewing
Éffem/MARS (candy)
Embratel-Empresa Brasileira de Telecomunicações S/A
Federal Express

Hellman's and Knorr Products–Refinações de Milho Brasil Ltda.
Iberia Airlines
Pepsico do Brasil Ltda.
Sarah Lee Coffees
Texaco Brasil S/A
UOL (Internet provider)
Visa do Brasil Ltda.
Volkswagen do Brasil Ltda.

Shortly after World War II, Caio de Alcantara Machado, a lawyer and businessman from São Paulo, Brazil, was working as a junior partner in a small advertising agency, ACAR Propaganda. Having had some early success in his real estate business, he decided to set up his own ad agency and invited his brother, Jose,

FourLink suspension.

In a 1997 Audi ad from Almap/BBDO, the automaker's logo is transformed into a graphic representation of the FourLink suspension's handling capabilities.

who also had some experience in advertising, to run it. Thus, in 1954 Alcantara Machado Publicidade Ltda.—or Almap, for short—was established.

In the 1950s Brazilian advertising agencies tended to be small businesses, geared more to the artistic than to the business side of the industry. The brothers had a new idea about what an ad agency should be: a prosperous business that sold creative advertising to other prosperous businesses. The concept was novel in Brazil at the time, and the plan worked faster than anticipated, even by its originators.

The first clients of the São Paulo-based agency were in real estate, but the success of its first campaigns attracted new clients: Lion, a Caterpillar dealer, Shaeffer Pens, Anderson-Clayton (food), and Sirva-se, the first supermarket chain to open in Brazil. Four years later year, in 1960, the agency was chosen by Volkswagen (VW) to advertise its first Beetles and Kombis imported from Germany, while the automaker built Brazil's first automobile factory.

In 1960, in what proved to be a fateful move, Jose de Alcantara Machado hired Alex Periscinoto, then advertising manager of Mappin Stores, São Paulo's leading department store. As retail ad manager of a major store, Periscinoto had visited Ohrbach's stores in New York City and had worked with the Doyle Dane Bernbach ad agency (DDB), under the direction of Bill Bernbach himself. With his move to Almap, Periscinoto had a new tie with DDB: the VW account. Brazilian advertising professionals tend to agree that DDB has been the one major outside influence in the country's style of ad creativity and that Periscinoto and Almap were the decisive force in introducing Brazil to the type of daring text and illustrations—and the humor—that were hallmarks of DDB in the 1960s.

Periscinoto established the system of creative "pairs" (one art director and one copywriter) at Almap, which was then adopted by all first-line agencies. Although the agency was not associated with any of the big international advertising groups at the time, it routinely brought to Brazil many of the great names in creative, design, research, and media, from Madison Avenue and Europe, to train Almap's employees. Almap was the first Brazilian agency to use computers in its media department.

By the early 1970s, Almap, then called Alcantara Machado/Periscinoto Comunicacoes, ranked among the top-three ad agencies in the country, with blue-chip clients such as Gillette, Xerox, Polaroid, General Foods, Groupe Danone, Rhone-Poulenc, R.J. Reynolds, and NEC Electronics, besides the faithful Volkswagen. In addition, it had important local clients, including Banco Real and Antarctica beverages. The agency ranked among the biggest prizewinners, both in local contests and in the international arena.

Jose de Alcantara Machado died in 1996; Periscinoto remained at the helm of the agency for 36 years. In 1993 the agency established its first official tie with an international group, selling a share in the shop to the Omnicom Group's BBDO.

In 1997 Periscinoto finally retired; he joined the staff of Brazil's President Fernando Henrique Cardoso as head of the government's Communications Secretariat. Alexandre Gama, Jose Luiz Madeira, and Marcello Serpa—all from rival agency DM9—were hired to form the new management team for the renamed Almap/BBDO. Gama soon left for Young & Rubicam and then opened his own agency, NeoGama. Serpa became chief creative officer and Madeira the management supervisor.

The year 1997 was a very successful one for Almap/BBDO. The agency had previously dropped from the ranks of the top-ten advertising agencies in Brazil, but in 1997 it moved into ninth place, with billings of more than $200 million, almost a 10 percent increase over the previous year. The agency managed to keep its existing clients and also acquired new accounts, including Samsung, CPC, Iberia, Texaco, Embratel (telecommunications), and UOL (Internet). The agency also set up a new company, NoMedia, specializing in design, merchandising, visual identity, and new media in general.

In 2000 Almap/BBDO, with 185 employees, ranked as Brazil's fourth-largest advertising agency. It was selected as "Agency of the Year" at the International Advertising Festival at Cannes, France. The agency won several silver Lion awards at Cannes: six in 1996, six in 1997, 12 in 1998, four in 1999, and ten in 2000.

In April 2000 Almap/BBDO was chosen as "International Agency of the Year" by *Advertising Age International* magazine. And it entered the Hall of Fame of the Ibero-American Advertising Festival (FIAP) for being the agency with the most prizes and for having been the first agency, in the 29 years of FIAP, to win two Grands Prix.

In 1998, 1999, and 2000, Almap/BBDO was the agency with the most prizes from the *Year Book* of the Creative Club of São Paulo, considered the benchmark of creative quality in advertising in Brazil. In 1999 Almap/BBDO was the Brazilian agency with the largest number of Clio awards; it also won a Golden Pencil and a Gold on Gold from the One Show.

In 2000 Almap/BBDO was elected—for the third consecutive time—"Agency of the Year" by the Advertising Columnists Association of Brazil. It also won, for the third time, the El Ojo de Iberoamerica prize, awarded by art directors from the Latin countries of Latin America and Europe.

J. ROBERTO WHITAKER-PENTEADO

Further Reading

"Cannes Presidency Lies in Hands of Quiet Brazilian," *Campaign* (23 June 2000)
"Cannes 2000: Interview with the President of the Jury, Marcello Serpa, Co-CEO and Creative Director of Almap/BBDO, Brazil," *Media Key Europe* (June 2000)
"The Lion's Share: Marcello Serpa the First Latin American Film and Press and Poster Jury President at Cannes," *Commercials Production Review* (June 2000)
Serpa, Marcello, "Un Brésilien sur la Croisette," *Strategies* (16 June 2000)
Wentz, Laurel, "Brazil Blitzes Festival with Flurry of Entries," *Advertising Age* (19 June 2000)

American Advertising Federation

The American Advertising Federation (AAF) is a nationwide association of advertising groups consisting of advertisers, agencies, media companies, and advertising clubs. The association sets standards for truthful and responsible advertising, works on advertising legislation, and actively influences agencies to abide by its code and principles. The AAF also brings together all parties involved in the field of advertising to educate policy makers, the news media, and the general public on the contribution of advertising to the well-being of society.

The principal mission of the AAF is to protect and promote the reputation of the advertising profession through a nationally coordinated grassroots network of advertisers, agencies, media companies, local advertising associations, and college chapters. The organization, formed in 1967 through the merger of the Advertising Federation of America and the Advertising Association of the West, adopted in 1984 "The Advertising Principles of American Business," defining standards for truthful and responsible advertising:

- Truth: Advertising shall tell the truth and shall reveal significant facts, the omission of which would mislead the public.

- Substantiation: Advertising claims shall be substantiated by evidence in possession of the advertiser and the advertising agency prior to making such claims.
- Comparisons: Advertising shall refrain from making false, misleading, or unsubstantiated statements or claims about a competitor or a competitor's products or services.
- Bait advertising: Advertising shall not offer products or services for sale unless such offer constitutes a bona fide effort to sell the advertised products or services and is not a device to switch consumers to other goods and services, usually higher priced.
- Guarantees and warranties: Advertising of guarantees and warranties shall be explicit, with sufficient information to apprise consumers of their principal terms and limitations or, when space or time restrictions preclude such disclosures, the advertisement should clearly reveal where the full text of the guarantee or warranty can be examined before purchase.
- Price claims: Advertising shall avoid price claims that are false or misleading, or savings claims that do not offer provable savings.
- Testimonials: Advertising containing testimonials shall be limited to those of competent witnesses who are witnessing a real and honest opinion and experience.
- Tastes and decency: Advertising shall be free of statements, illustrations, or implications that are offensive to good taste or public decency.

In 1971 the AAF joined with three other associations—the American Association of Advertising Agencies (AAAA), the Association of National Advertisers (ANA), and the Council of Better Business Bureaus—to establish the National Advertising Review Council (NARC). The mission of this self-regulating association is to sustain high standards of truth, accuracy, and social responsibility in advertising by relying on advertisers to police the accuracy of other advertisers. The council has two operating divisions, the National Advertising Division of the Council of Better Business Bureaus (NAD) and the National Advertising Review Board (NARB). The NAD/NARB has become the advertising industry's primary self-regulatory mechanism.

The AAF uses the talents of its members to help solve community problems. The association is also involved in the Alliance for Youth, a national nonprofit organization dedicated to improving the quality of life of more than 15 million at-risk youths. The alliance furthers AAF's goal of bringing more young people into the advertising industry. In a similar vein, in partnership with the Advertising Council, the AAF implemented Commitment 2000, a public service campaign designed to protect the health and welfare of young children. The AAF also worked with its local affiliate associations to produce and submit public service campaigns for distribution with the Ad Council logo. In 1997 the U.S. government's Office of National Drug Control Policy secured $195 million to fight teen drug abuse and worked with the AAF and its national network of clubs and federations to promote public service announcements in more than 100 target markets.

AMERICAN ADVERTISING FEDERATION
THE UNIFYING VOICE FOR ADVERTISING
Courtesy of AAF.

The AAF promotes diversity in advertising in many ways. It has encouraged the recruitment of people of diverse cultures. The association recognizes the importance of ethnic minority groups as customers and supports the use of media aimed at minority markets. The AAF Foundation awards the Crain Diversity Grants, sponsored by Crain Communications, Inc., publisher of *Advertising Age*, recognizing and funding exemplary cultural diversity initiatives undertaken by affiliated AAF local clubs. Entrants are required to document their diversity program initiatives in their respective local communities. In conjunction with Procter & Gamble, the AAF has also cosponsored a survey to measure ad industry diversity, and it has hosted a Congressional Summit on Diversity and offered scholarships and internships to promising minority students in the field of advertising.

The AAF supports a self-regulating system to protect consumer privacy on the Internet, and to that end the federation has joined the Online Privacy Alliance, which consists of more than 50 corporations and associations committed to protecting consumers' privacy online. The alliance has provided extensive guidelines for maintaining online privacy, particularly emphasizing ways to safeguard the privacy of children. In 1995 it implemented an enforcement policy that includes three elements: verification and monitoring, complaint resolution, and education and outreach.

In 1999 the organization surveyed 1,800 top managers and found that when it came to increasing sales, most executives placed a lower priority on advertising than on product development, strategic planning, or public relations. In light of these findings, the AAF selected Carmichael Lynch in Minneapolis, Minnesota, to create a two-year integrated campaign stressing the significance of advertising to the chief executive officers, presidents, and other leaders of 1,500 companies owning brands that have advertising budgets of $10 million or more. The AAF used direct mail, ads in major business publications and *Golf* magazine, banner ads on the Internet, and AAF-logo notepads at major airlines to spread awareness of both advertising and the federation among executives of the targeted companies. Hoping to persuade clients to increase their ad budgets, the group organized the campaign around the tag line, "Advertising: A new brand of business."

The AAF sponsors three major conferences. The American Advertising Conference is the premier annual conference; it attracts corporate members, local federation members, college students and professors in the field of advertising, corporate recruiters, exhibitors, and media representatives to discuss the latest marketplace trends and advertising strategies. The AAF Government Affairs Conference, held in Washington, D.C., each spring, gives the advertising industry an opportunity to voice concerns about legal issues directly to federal decision makers. Finally, AAF's annual Marketing Conference is held in the fall and provides an opportunity for participants to consider the latest industry trends and the future of advertising.

The federation publishes *American Advertising* magazine and *AAF Government Report,* as well as the *Communicator* for college students, the *Advisor* for college advertising professors, and the *Voice* for corporate members. The AAF has also joined the Career Community Network, an Internet-based job bank that assists individuals looking for career opportunities as well as companies looking for employees.

The AAF honors advertising excellence at various levels. The American Advertising Awards are the biggest creative advertising competition in the United States. Other awards include the Advertising Hall of Achievement, the National Student Advertising Competition, the Advertising Leader of the West award, the AAF Club Achievement Awards, and the Distinguished Advertising Educator award.

Perhaps the most prestigious award of all is election to the Advertising Hall of Fame, which was created in 1948 by the Advertising Federation of America to recognize lifetime achievement in the industry. The candidates for the Hall of Fame are judged on their advertising careers, their contributions to the betterment of advertising and its reputation, and their volunteer efforts outside the workplace. Upon induction, each member receives a "Golden Ladder" trophy. The trophy was designed by the legendary advertising executive Bill Bernbach and bears an inscription written by another great ad man, Tom Dillon: "If we can see further, it is because we stand on the rungs of a ladder built by those who came before us."

The first inductees were honored at the AAF's 45th annual convention on 31 May 1949, in Houston, Texas. By 1999 the AAF had honored 146 industry notables with induction into the Hall of Fame, including David Ogilvy, Bill Bernbach, Leo Burnett, and J. Walter Thompson, as well as notable personalities such as Benjamin Franklin, whose *General* magazine featured the first known advertisement in 1741.

The main office of the AAF is located in Washington, D.C.; the federation also maintains a western regional office in San Francisco, California. In 2000, there were 135 corporate members, 220 local advertising associations, 215 college chapters, and more than 50,000 individual members.

ABHIJIT ROY

Further Reading
American Advertising Federation <www.aaf.org>
Melillo, Wendy, "AAF to Probe Multicultural Marketing Practices," *Adweek* (26 April 1999)
Melillo, Wendy, and Aaron Baar, "AAF Launches Campaign for Ads," *Adweek* (21 June 1999)
Teinowitz, Ira, "AAF Survey: Ad Importance Flat," *Advertising Age* (21 June 1999)

American Association of Advertising Agencies

Founded in 1917, the American Association of Advertising Agencies (AAAA, known informally as the Four A's) is the national trade organization for advertising agencies. The AAAA has 545 member agencies with more than 1,200 offices in 303 cities in the United States and 1,800 offices and affiliates in 126 countries. The membership comprises agencies ranging from large multinationals to small and mid-sized agencies across the country. Its members handle approximately 75 percent of the total advertising volume place by agencies in the United States.

Election to the AAAA is the highest professional recognition an advertising agency or marketing communications company can achieve. In order to be elected to membership, a marketing communications firm must demonstrate professional ability, financial integrity, and a commitment to ethical business practices. Fewer than 6 percent of the nation's 13,000 agencies have qualified for membership in the AAAA.

The structure of the AAAA serves its three basic aims: to foster, strengthen, and improve the advertising agency business; to advance the cause of advertising as a whole; and to aid member agencies in operating more efficiently and profitably.

The association is based in New York City, with offices in Washington, D.C., and San Francisco, California, and an employee benefits subsidiary in Charlotte, North Carolina. The organization is run by a paid president–chief executive officer (CEO) and is governed by a national board of directors composed of chief executives from member agencies.

Each of the four AAAA regions (Eastern, Central, Southern, and Western) has a board of governors elected annually by member executives in its region. The AAAA regions are further divided into 26 local councils representing metropolitan areas. Councils sponsor activities of local interest such as seminars and training programs.

The AAAA has 47 committees that represent the major functions of agencies and marketing communications companies. The committees work with related industry groups and suppliers to solve industry problems.

In addition to its many local region and council meetings and workshops, the AAAA holds several large national conferences, including an agency management conference and annual meeting, creative conference, and a media conference and trade show.

The association provides extensive services to its members, including management surveys and advice, secondary research on U.S. and international topics from its Member Information Service, and media and production information and printed guides. The AAAA also represents the agency business in negotiations with talent unions. Its Washington, D.C., office, which opened in 1969, monitors federal and state government activity and works to protect agencies and the advertising industry against burdensome legislation and taxation.

Formation and Early Years

Between 1872 and 1912 the advertising agency business unsuccessfully attempted to form a national association five times. The attempts failed primarily because at the beginning of the 20th century advertising agents were viewed with distrust and suspicion.

The Association of New York Advertising Agents was formed in 1911, with William H. Johns of the George Batten Company as chairman. He, along with Frank Presbrey of the Frank Presbrey agency, was a leading proponent of a code of advertising ethics. By 1916 several other regional associations had been established. The regional groups had taken steps to improve agency practice and competition, but a larger and more influential body was needed. With a national association, agencies could accomplish collectively what they were unable to do individually.

In St. Louis, Missouri, on 4 June 1917, the New York; Chicago, Illinois; Philadelphia; and Boston, Massachusetts, associations and the new Southern Association of Advertising Agents formally announced the formation of the American Association of Advertising Agencies. The five regional groups became the original councils of the AAAA, which started with 111 charter members. Johns was named the first president (the role subsequently known as chairman). Later in 1917, James O'Shaughnessy sold his Chicago agency and moved to New York City to become the executive secretary (later called president) of the association, its first paid post and one he held until 1927. Subsequent presidents were: John Benson (1928–43), Frederic R. Gamble (1944–61), John Crichton (1962–77), William R. Hesse (1978), Leonard S. Matthews (1979–88), John E. O'Toole (1989–93), and O. Burtch Drake (1994–present).

The list of chairmen of the board reads like a "who's who" of advertising luminaries and included, in the first 50 years, A.W. Erickson, Stanley Resor, Roy Durstine, James Webb Young, H.K.

AMERICAN ASSOCIATION
of ADVERTISING AGENCIES
www.aaaa.org

Courtesy of AAAA.

McCann, Raymond Rubicam, Atherton Hobler, Sigurd Larmon, Fairfax Cone, and Marion Harper. Since 1967 the organization has benefited from the talents of such advertising leaders as Barton Cummings, John Elliott Jr., Richard Christian, Ed Ney, Stuart Upson, Eugene Kummel, Paul Harper, Louis Hagopian, Charlotte Beers, Keith Reinhard, Alex Kroll, and Shelly Lazarus.

The formation of the national association heralded and facilitated the coming of age of the industry. The AAAA brought together agencies that had formerly been hostile and suspicious, led them to respect and trust one another, and persuaded them to work together to further their common goals. According to O'Shaughnessy's memoirs, "The earliest concern of the AAAA was to efface the memories of the free-for-all days when knocking the other fellow was almost a social requirement."

According to *Printers' Ink* of 14 June 1917, the first association activities after establishing an office would be to

> work on such matters as information on which to base official recognition; uniform cost systems for agencies; uniform order blanks; the collection of data useful to agents; and in general to give a definite point of contact with [other industry associations]. In all the contemplated plans the underlying idea is to raise the standards of agency practice, and to make for better relations between agents, clients, and space sellers all round.

Traditionally agencies had acted as agents for the media, but that was gradually changing as more agencies began creating and placing ads on behalf of advertisers. In 1918 the association adopted a document called "Agency Service Standards." The statement defined agency service so that advertisers and publishers would know what to expect and agencies would know what should be required of them, thus discouraging the less professional and encouraging those equipped to provide effective services.

O. Burtch Drake was elected president of the American Association of
Advertising Agencies in 1994.
Courtesy of AAAA.

The advertising agency business found respectability in the 1920s, a decade when business reigned supreme. The crowning moment for the AAAA was when U.S. President Calvin Coolidge agreed to speak at the tenth annual meeting of the association in 1926. O'Shaughnessy proudly wrote to members, "The fact that our convention dinner was attended by the President of the United States and that he made it the occasion to deliver what is perhaps the most useful pronouncement for advertising that has ever been penned, may be taken as a national expression of the approval of the work of our association."

Media Relations

Pressure to form an association had come from the media, particularly newspapers, whose own growth was hindered by abuses and inconsistencies in procedures on the part of advertising agents. By the same token, agencies needed to strengthen their bargaining power with the media and protect themselves in the face of media consolidation. The need for standard practices in working with the media was a primary motivation for creating a national association and a major focus of its early years.

The association issued a media rate card in 1918 that standardized the reporting of media rates and allowed agencies to evaluate the media more effectively. In 1920 it published the first standard order blanks, copyrighted forms that facilitated relations with publishers and eventually covered all media. By 1921 the AAAA had obtained for agencies a uniform commission of 15 percent from most publishers. Another media relations success was the cash discount. After decades of persistent efforts to encourage a discount for cash payment, by 1956 nearly 90 percent of the major advertising media allowed the practice. The cash discount helped keep credit losses in national advertising to an infinitesimal amount and led to a more stable advertising agency business.

Over the years AAAA committees worked with each major medium to resolve issues of mutual concern. In the early 1980s the AAAA Newspaper Committee approached newspaper associations to fix a nagging problem, the huge variety of column sizes. Working together, they were able to reduce the number of standard advertising units accepted by newspapers from more than 390 to 57, thereby simplifying the agency production process and abetting the growth of newspaper advertising. The AAAA was also influential in the development of radio and television as advertising media. In the 1990s the AAAA and the Association of National Advertisers formed CASIE (Coalition for Advertising Supported Information and Entertainment), a joint task force to ensure and foster advertising's role in interactive media.

Ethics and Self-Regulation

The AAAA Standards of Practice was first adopted in 1924, and the Creative Code was incorporated into it in 1931. The statement of standards contains a professional code of ethics and covers topics such as fair competition among agencies. From the organization's inception a grievance process was established to address complaints against members for violation of AAAA codes of practice.

In 1945 the AAAA established a committee to deal with objectionable advertising. The AAAA Interchange of Opinion (1946) enabled members to register their comments whenever they considered an ad in bad taste or otherwise objectionable. If two or more complaints were received, they were passed to the offending agency, which could then take corrective steps. Shortly afterward, the AAAA put more bite into the procedure by authorizing the ejection of any member that refused to cooperate. In 1960 the association joined the Association of National Advertisers in a joint Committee for Improvement of Advertising Content. This was a major step in the development of self-regulatory efforts.

In 1971 the National Advertising Review Board (NARB) was formed with the support of the AAAA and other advertising organizations. Its members come from agencies, advertisers, and the general public. The National Advertising Division (NAD) of the Council of Better Business Bureaus is its investigative arm. NAD/NARB serves the public interest by policing advertising, with the goal of improving its credibility, and it minimizes the need for government regulation. Its value was recognized by Robert Pitofsky, chairman of the Federal Trade Commission, who said in the mid-1990s, "Advertising is nowhere near the problem it was 25 years ago . . . it has the best voluntary self-regulation device in American industry."

Public Service Advertising and the Advertising Council

Given that the formation of the AAAA coincided with the entry of the United States into World War I, it is not surprising that one of the earliest actions of the new association was to urge members to sound a patriotic note in ads to support the war effort. By December 1917 the Division of Advertising of the Committee of Public Information office opened under the auspices of the AAAA, with a government charter to coordinate all wartime campaigns, including advertising for the U.S. Army, U.S. Navy, liberty bonds, victory loans, and the Red Cross. After the war a 1919 navy request for a postwar recruitment campaign resulted in the formation of the Advertising Agencies Corporation, a composite agency that handled several government campaigns until its dissolution in 1928.

No sooner had the 7 December 1941 bombing of Pearl Harbor taken place than advertising leaders approached Donald M. Nelson, head of the Office of Production Management, offering once again to marshal advertising industry forces to assist in the war effort. The War Advertising Council, established in 1942, developed more than 90 different advertising campaigns for the home front, including campaigns for war bonds, victory gardens, the Women's Army Corps (Wacs), and mail for soldiers. Its anti-inflation task force developed the ubiquitous symbol of a hand pressing prices down and coined the slogan, "Use it up, wear it out, make it do, or do without." After the war, realizing its tremendous power to effect positive social change, the group evolved into the Advertising Council.

Under the philosophy that the "best public relations is public service," the AAAA has continued to sponsor the Ad Council in cooperation with advertisers and the media. It underwrites the agency share of the council's financing and provides the task force agencies that create the campaigns.

In 1985 Phil Joanou, chairman and CEO of Dailey & Associates, called upon the AAAA to marshal the forces of advertising once more, this time to wage a war of unprecedented scope on drugs. Enlisting the cooperation of several other advertising and media groups, the AAAA in 1986 led the creation of the Media-Advertising Partnership for a Drug-Free America. Twelve years and a President's Citation award later, the partnership could claim to be one of the most effective drug education groups in the United States and could take credit for launching the largest public service media campaign in history.

Education and Diversity

The AAAA Educational Foundation was established in 1967. Originally designed to act as a bridge between advertising and university research, it funded many academic research studies on marketing and advertising topics and jointly sponsored projects with the Marketing Science Institute and the National Bureau of Economic Research. In response to concerns of the government and critics that advertising was often misleading, the foundation underwrote a significant academic research project on the miscomprehension of advertising and other forms of communication. The result was a 1980 report by Jacob Jacoby, titled *Miscomprehension of Televised Communications,* that in essence proved that the public misunderstood about 30 percent of all communications, not just advertising, and, in fact, that it understood a larger percentage of advertising than programming content. A 1987 follow-up study on print communications supported the earlier conclusions. The AAAA Educational Foundation merged with the Educational Foundation of the American Advertising Foundation in 1983 to form the Advertising Educational Foundation.

The AAAA Multicultural Advertising Intern Program (MAIP) was born in 1973. In its first 25 years it placed more than 1,000 minority students in advertising agencies as summer interns, many of whom went on to careers in advertising. In 1997 the AAAA Foundation was established to provide scholarships to multicultural advertising students. Proceeds from the association's prestigious O'Toole Awards help to fund the foundation.

Other Industry Activities and the Future

The AAAA joined with the Association of National Advertisers in 1936 to establish the Advertising Research Foundation (ARF). It has continued to support the work of the foundation financially and through the volunteer contributions of time and effort by agency members of the ARF board and committees.

The AAAA has undertaken many projects over the decades to improve the image of advertising among consumers and to demonstrate the value of advertising and advertising agencies to clients. In 1961 it retained Hill & Knowlton to make recommendations for a public relations program for advertising. The result was a 1964 benchmark study of consumers' attitudes toward advertising, subsequently published by the Harvard Business School in a 1968 book, *Advertising in America: The Consumer View,* written by Raymond A. Bauer and Stephen A. Greyser. A follow-up study resulted in the 1976 book *Advertising and Consumers: New Perspectives,* by Rena Bartos and Theodore F. Dunn. In 1984 an advertising image campaign aimed at consumers was launched and then broadened to target business leaders as well. It was followed in 1991 by a "Top Guns" campaign, featuring CEO testimonials on advertising effectiveness. The MAX Project (Managing Advertising Expenditures for Financial Performance) started in 1997 to help marketers budget more efficiently for advertising.

The AAAA spent 80 years as the association for traditional full-service advertising agencies, but the 1990s brought sweeping changes to the industry. Advertising agencies no longer just created ads and bought media but also performed a host of marketing services, including public relations, direct marketing, sales promotion, interactive projects, and corporate identity programs.

In 1998, in recognition of the new realities of the advertising business, the AAAA changed its constitution to open membership to marketing communications firms in addition to advertising agencies.

MARSHA C. APPEL

Further Reading

"The AAAA Educational Foundation," *AAAA Newsletter* (November 1979)

"Agents Discuss Plan to Advertise Agency Service," *Printers' Ink* (14 June 1917)

Clapp, Roger H., "Prelude to the Four A's," unpublished paper, 1954

Forbes, Thomas, "The Early Years," *Agency* 3, no. 1 (Spring 1992)

"The 4A's Today," *Advertising Agency* (27 April 1956)

Hobler, Atherton W., "The First Fifty Years Are the Easiest," unpublished speech given at the 1967 AAAA Annual Meeting

Inside the AAAA, New York: American Association of Advertising Agencies, 1998

Turnbull, Richard, "Genesis of the American Association of Advertising Agencies," unpublished, 1969

Wharton, Don, "The Story Back of the War Ads," *Advertising and Selling* (June 1944)

American Home Products Corporation

(Wyeth)

Principal Agencies

John F. Murray Advertising Agency (in-house agency)
J. Walter Thompson Company
Ted Bates & Company, Inc.

Created as an umbrella company to buy up other companies, the American Home Products Corporation (AHP) has evolved through acquisitions into a large conglomerate of companies, divisions, and product categories. The company name itself never became a brand, but many of its products have become familiar to millions through years of advertising. These include Black Flag, Woolite, Chef Boyardee, and Easy-Off. AHP's Whitehall Division produced many personal hygiene brands and over-the-counter drugs, including Heet liniment, Guards cold tablets, Neet depilatory, Freezone corn remover, and, perhaps most famous of all, Anacin.

The company began in 1926 when a group of managers from Sterling Products, Inc., and Household Products, Inc., combined their resources to buy small companies as cheaply as possible. During the 1930s W.I. Kirn, the company chairman, led the early AHP expansion, which included the acquisition of Anacin in 1930. Growth became aggressive when Alvin Bush, a former Sterling executive, became chairman in 1935. More than 30 food and drug companies were absorbed, including Bisodol Company, marketer of Bisodol laxative; A.S. Boyle Company, marketer of Old English Floor Wax; Kolynos Company, marketer of Kolynos dentifrices; Wyeth Chemical Company, whose brands included Hills Nose Drops and Jads Salts; and Midway Chemical Company, marketer of Aerowax. It was a lineup of brands that made AHP a major packaged-goods advertiser under the leadership of Bush, which lasted into the middle 1960s.

The Move into Radio

Through the early 1930s AHP maintained a modest advertising budget, but its spending rose sharply in 1934 as it moved into radio sponsorships. By 1936 the company had become the eighth-largest advertiser in network radio, according to *Advertising Age* figures, a rank it held for the rest of the decade. Kolynos received the largest support, jumping from $231,000 in ad spending in 1933 to $356,000 in 1934. During that same period Bisodol spending jumped six-fold to $188,000. Then in 1936 Anacin ad expenditures more than doubled to about $422,000, surpassing Kolynos. Total AHP radio spending rose to more than $2.5 million in 1937 and remained at that level until World War II.

Blackett-Sample-Hummert, Inc., made AHP a major sponsor in daytime radio drama, starting with *Rich Man's Darling*, which helped account for the jump in Anacin spending in 1936; the program evolved into the long-running *Our Gal Sunday* the following year. AHP remained a sponsor of the show until 1955. Other pioneering soap operas sponsored by AHP included *The Romance of Helen Trent* and *Just Plain Bill*, both launched in 1933 for Kolynos, and *John's Other Wife* (1936) and *Front Page Farrell* (1942). The marketer was also active in evening programming, most famously with *Mr. Keen, Tracer of Lost Persons* (1937).

AHP bought a suntan lotion company in 1935 and reformulated the product, turning it into Preparation H, a hemorrhoid ointment. The following year it bought Three-in-1 Oil, followed by Black Flag insecticide in 1939. In the early 1940s AHP added Heet, Freezone, Mystic Hand Cream, Neet depilatory, and George Washington coffee to its roster. In 1943 it purchased the Canadian marketer Ayerst Laboratories, completing the foundation of its prescription drug business. Chef Boyardee Quality Foods, Inc., was acquired in 1946.

By the mid-1960s the company had five core businesses: prescription drugs, over-the-counter drugs, foods, housewares, and household products. At the time, it marketed the largest line of foods, drugs, and household brands of any U.S. company, and it has continued to be a leader in prescription and over-the-counter drugs. AHP's philosophy held that the best way to gain a strong new position in a particular market was to acquire a brand that was already competing in that market.

"American Home Profits"

By the early 1970s AHP had developed a reputation as a company that was run on an old-fashioned, hard-nosed, dollars-and-cents basis; and it demanded much from its employees and ad agencies. Its sales expenses remained virtually frozen at 3 percent for several years, and its profits held steady at 10 percent for about 15 years. Expenses were so minutely tracked that, according to a company history, employees had to buy tickets to attend the AHP Christmas party. Any expense of more than $500 had to be approved by the chairman. Wall Street loved it—some financial analysts dubbed the company "American Home Profits." It maintained its high levels of advertising spending; in the mid-1980s its ad budget was approximately $412 million. Yet, its tight-fisted ways sometimes became more than its ad agencies could tolerate. Both Ted Bates & Company, Inc., and the J. Walter Thompson Company (JWT) resigned AHP business at various times.

In 1982 AHP acquired Sherwood Medical Group, a medical supplies company. In 1987 it bought Bristol-Myers Company's animal health division and began to develop its new Fort Dodge unit (later called Fort Dodge Animal Health); in 1989 it acquired A.H. Robins Company, Inc., and its widely known consumer brands, including market-leading cough syrup brands Robitussin and Dimetapp. AHP's $9.7 billion acquisition of American Cyanamid Company in 1994 created one of the world's largest prescription drug companies.

AHP started to divest itself of businesses unrelated to health care in the 1980s, selling off Ecko Housewares Company and candy maker E.J. Brach & Sons, and in 1990, its Boyle-Midway household products subsidiary. It sold its American Home Food Products food business in September 1996.

AHP's strategy has been to focus on its pharmaceutical, biotechnology, consumer health care, and animal-care products businesses. Its most important products at the start of the 21st century were Advil and Dimetapp (handled by Y&R Advertising, the ad division of Young & Rubicam, Inc.), Robitussin (Grey Advertising Worldwide), and Anacin.

Throughout its history, AHP has been a low-profile advertiser, often using its own in-house shop, the John F. Murray Advertising Agency. In February 1943 it announced plans for a large institutional advertising campaign via JWT. As of April 1943 the company's advertising activities were coordinated by its Advertising Plans Board, and by the end of that year it had advertising expenditures of $13 million and 16 agencies on its roster, many of which came along when AHP acquired other companies.

Pardon me...
but your lips are showing.

Use 'Chap Stick' before you need it.

Look at your lips. Are they as smooth as they can be? Or aren't they kinda dry . . . kinda wrinkled? 'Chap Stick' lip balm helps you prevent all that. Keeps your lips comfortably moist and smooth. And keeps away chapping, cracking, roughness. Wherever you are, your lips are showing. So put on 'Chap Stick' protection, and smile like you mean it!

Use 'Chap-ans' for hands
BOTH ARE FAVORITES IN CANADA

'Chap Stick' and 'Chap-ans' are Reg. T.M.'s © 1966
Chap Stick Company, Lynchburg, Va., a subsidiary of A.H. ROBINS COMPANY

The Chap Stick brand was acquired by American Home Products Corporation in 1989. Early Chap Stick ads, such as this one from 1966, took a humorous approach to the problem of dry, cracked lips. *Copyright © Whitehall Robins/Wyeth and used with permission.*

Advil, a nonprescription form of the anti-inflammatory drug ibuprofen, was introduced in 1984.
Copyright © Whitehall Robins/Wyeth and used with permission.

Through the 1960s AHP took a tough approach in dealing with ad agencies that veered from its thrifty course. AHP was known as a client that kept its agencies on a tight rein. It also worked hard to hold down the cost of commercials; in some cases, agencies whose campaigns did not clear detailed preproduction meetings at AHP ended up footing the bill for those commercials.

Checkered History of Anacin's Ad Campaigns

With a few exceptions, agencies have not created particularly memorable advertising for AHP brands. Sometimes there have been conflicts. In the mid-1950s, under Rosser Reeves, Bates's legendary chairman, the agency created the widely known "hammer in the brain" commercials for Anacin. The agency resigned the then-$20 million account in 1967, however, citing interference from AHP executives in its staffing and creative work. AHP then reassigned Anacin to its house agency. The Bates ads, with the tag line, "Fast, fast, fast relief," were ranked 19th on the *Advertising Age* list of the top-100 advertising campaigns of the century.

AHP and the U.S. Federal Trade Commission (FTC) have disagreed more than once over advertising in the analgesics category.

In 1958 the FTC questioned claims from AHP, in ads from Bates, and four other analgesics marketers, charging that there was no truth to the claims that one brand relieved headaches faster than another. In 1961 the FTC again brought complaints against AHP's analgesics advertising, but the charges were dropped in 1965 after a long entanglement in procedural arguments at the federal agency.

Later run-ins over Anacin advertising lasted through the 1970s and 1980s. In early 1970 censors from the CBS and NBC networks, the National Association of Broadcasters, and the *Journal of the American Medical Association* (*JAMA*) all objected to AHP's using information from a *JAMA* article in an Anacin TV commercial created by Murray.

In 1973 the FTC opened yet another investigation into Anacin ads touting the remedy's use for the relief of tension. After six years, FTC administrative law judge Montgomery Hyun ruled that consumers still believed the advertising even though the company had stopped the claims in 1973. He ordered AHP to spend $24 million—an average one-year ad budget for Anacin at that time—on corrective ads disclosing that "Anacin is not a tension reliever." The FTC insisted that ads for all AHP products meet the tests applied by the U.S. Food and Drug Administration and the medical community to substantiate drug effectiveness.

In July 1983 *Advertising Age* reported that after ten years of legal maneuvering, the FTC had settled on a formula establishing the kinds of proof that three major analgesics marketers—AHP, Bristol-Myers Company, and Sterling Drug Company—must have before making performance and comparison claims. It required that studies and research proving superior performance be supported by two competent clinical tests. James C. Miller III, then chairman of the FTC, said that he supported the formula in part to resolve the long dispute.

AHP's Preparation H hemorrhoid treatment also has had a checkered history with the FTC. In 1967 the FTC ordered stringent limits on claims for Preparation H made in advertising created by Murray; three competing hemorrhoid remedies were also included in the order. The order prohibited the four advertisers from claiming that their products did anything more than provide some "temporary relief of pain and itching" associated with some types of hemorrhoids. AHP appealed, and in 1967 the Sixth Circuit Court of Appeals upheld most of the FTC order. In November 1968, in response to the court, the FTC noted there had been at least eight instances over the previous 30 years when the federal agency had challenged ads for Preparation H.

More Ups and Downs

AHP got involved in a controversy of another kind in 1973 when it pulled out of two episodes of the CBS TV sitcom *Maude* in which the middle-aged title character, played by actress Bea Arthur, decided to end an unwanted pregnancy with an abortion. The U.S. Catholic Conference attempted to keep CBS from repeating the first of the two episodes in the series. The National Organization for Women staged a demonstration in front of

AHP's offices in New York City, and a group called the Association for the Repeal of Abortion Laws accused AHP and four other advertisers of having "blacklisted" the episodes. AHP found itself caught in an advertiser's worst nightmare: a public controversy.

In the late 1970s and early 1980s, AHP was involved in several historic two-season buys on NBC, notable because they demonstrated the growing power of the television media market. In 1978 AHP signed a $100 million deal; in1982 it committed to a three-year buy valued at $250 million.

In 1984 AHP launched Advil, one in a new category of non-aspirin pain relievers. Ads for the new product were created by Young & Rubicam, Inc. By 1985 Advil had performed well enough to cause concern at Bayer Corporation, which marketed Bayer aspirin, as well as record promotional activity by Bristol-Myers for its own Nuprin brand. By 1989 Advil had overtaken Nuprin in sales.

In August 1992 AHP's Wyeth-Ayerst Laboratories lost a battle with the National Advertising Division, the self-regulatory arm of the Council of Better Business Bureaus, over claims for its SMA infant formula. It then appealed its case to the National Advertising Review Board. The board, however, enjoined AHP to modify claims for SMA made in brochures distributed to doctors' offices that said the brand was "closest to mother's milk" and would produce better health results than competitors' products. The review came after rival Mead Johnson challenged AHP's claims.

In August 1995 AHP launched the first of a new generation of pain relievers in the United States, ketoprofen, with agency Partners & Shevack. But the product further fragmented the already crowded $2.5 billion analgesics market, and by 1998 it was in trouble, with double-digit sales losses.

Meanwhile, American Home had been seeking a merger partner. After unsuccessful attempts to join with SmithKline Beecham PLC and then Monsanto Company, both in 1998, a deal was finally struck with the Warner-Lambert Company in November 1999. In a stock exchange estimated at about $72 billion, it was the largest drug company merger in history. The new company, to be called AmericanWarner, was expected to have revenue of $24 billion, based on 1998 numbers. The merger brought together a considerable roster of ad agencies. American Home, whose U.S. ad spending was about $322 million, used Young & Rubicam (Advil, Dimetapp), Grey Advertising (Anbesol, Preparation H), Lowe & Partners/SMS (Robitussin, Primatene Mist), and Carrafiello-Diehl & Associates (Centrum, Caltrate). Murray handled all media buying. Warner-Lambert, whose billings stood at $386.5 million, employed the J. Walter Thompson Company (Trident, Listerine, Schick) and Bates Worldwide (Neosporin, Quanterra, Lipitor).

In January 2000 AHP launched a $10 million ad campaign that sought to influence the up to 6 million users of the popular fen-phen diet-drug weight-loss combination, which had been withdrawn from the market in September 1997 after patients using the prescription drug combination of fenfluramine and phentermine developed heart and lung problems. The effort, from Tierney & Partners, urged those who had used AHP's Pon-

A 1986 ad for Robitussin is one of the first print ads from the acclaimed "Recommended by Dr. Mom" campaign.
Copyright © Whitehall Robins/Wyeth and used with permission.

dimin (fenfluramine) and Redux (dexfenfluramine) to call a toll-free number or go to a special Web site for further information about a class-action suit against the company. The effort encouraged those who had used the drug to participate in the class-action suit, for which the marketer had set aside $3.7 billion for a settlement, thereby limiting AHP's liability against further, individual suits.

A year later, in January 2001, AHP took a $7.5 billion charge against its fourth-quarter earnings, saying it had settled 80 percent of the lawsuits filed against it by dieters who had used the fen-phen combination. In April 2001 AHP, with revenue of $13.81 billion, was ranked 143rd among *Fortune* magazine's 500 largest corporations. It could no longer be called "American Home Profits," however, as the company lost $2.37 billion in 2000.

By the end of the 20th century, AHP was the 45th-largest U.S. advertiser, according to *Advertising Age*, with 2000 ad spending of $571 million. Its top-spending brands were: Advil, $82 million; Centrum, $57 million; and Premarin, $37.9 million. In 2002 the company changed its name to Wyeth.

MARK MANDLE

See also color plate in this volume

Further Reading

Hoover's Handbook of American Business (annual; 1992–)
O'Gara, Jim, "Inside Story of American Home Producers,"
    Advertising Age (20 November 1972)

"Variety Spices Up Ad Departments, AA Finds," *Advertising Age*
    (12 December 1960)
"Will Parity Products Slow AHP Money Machine?" *Advertising
    Age* (10 April 1972)

American Red Cross

Principal Agencies

J. Walter Thompson Company
D'Arcy Masius Benton & Bowles
Kaplan Thaler Group

In 1859 Henri Dunant, a Swiss businessman and philanthropist, visited Solferino, Italy, the site of a bloody battle between the Franco-Sardinians and the Austrians in the struggle for Italian unification. Dunant's publication in 1862 of a graphic book about the event, *A Memory of Solferino,* led to the formation of the Red Cross the following year.

Meanwhile, in the United States the Civil War was raging. Clara Barton, a former teacher turned nurse and government worker, helped soldiers wounded on the battlefield. Barton later traveled to other countries where nursing help was needed. Inspired by the European Red Cross movement, she founded the American Red Cross in 1881, with the goals of systemizing nationwide relief efforts, educating the public about safety and health issues, and helping people in need.

Today, the American Red Cross is one of the country's premier humanitarian organizations, with 1.2 million volunteers nationally, organized through more than 1,200 local chapters and 36 Blood Services regions. The organization provides relief during war, natural disasters, and other calamities. In addition to its disaster-relief program, the American Red Cross collects and distributes almost half the United States' blood supply. It also trains more than 15 million people each year in first aid, cardiopulmonary resuscitation (or CPR), swimming, and other health and safety skills. In the year 2000 more than 230,000 people volunteered to teach these courses. The American Red Cross Armed Forces Emergency Services keeps American families in touch with loved ones in the military around the world.

A nonprofit organization, the American Red Cross receives monies for its programs from fund-raising activities and contributions from individual and corporate donors. Its advertising efforts consist of broadcast and print public service announcements (PSAs), along with ads in new media (e.g., the Internet). The creative ideas behind the PSAs may change over time, but the overall message remains constant: the American Red Cross is always there to help save lives.

Before the advent of radio, television, and the Internet, the American Red Cross's advertising, promotions, and calls to action reached people via posters. From World War I through the mid-1950s, artists such as James Montgomery Flagg, N.C. Wyeth, Norman Rockwell, and James Chandler Christy created works for the Federal Committee on Public Information and the War Advertising Council, encouraging patriotism in wartime and publicizing Red Cross programs. These efforts increased citizen involvement.

"The Greatest Mother in the World," a poster from 1918, featured a woman in a Red Cross uniform holding a stretcher bearing a wounded soldier. "Knit Your Bit: Our Boys Need Sox," also from 1918, encouraged citizens to make clothing for soldiers overseas. "For Their Sake, Join Now," from 1936, reflected the needs of the Dust Bowl and Depression years. The boy and girl shown represent victims of fires, floods, and other disasters. "Blood Saves Lives" (1948) shows a man giving blood, attended by a nurse. "Mobilize for Defense" was popular in 1951, during the Korean War. Other posters carried general patriotic messages, such as "The Spirit of America: Join Now."

American Red Cross themes influenced other forms of popular culture during these years. They included the poem "Rhymes of a Red Cross Man" by Robert W. Service; "Rose of No Man's Land," an early popular song; Ernest Hemingway's novel *A Farewell to Arms;* and children's toys. Red Cross themes came to American television in the spring of 1988 when the ABC network aired the dramatic series *China Beach.* The show, which ran through the summer of 1991, starred Dana Delany as a nurse in Vietnam and Nan Woods as a Red Cross recreational worker. The American Red Cross continues to use posters as a form of advertising, and the organization has been depicted in films as well as in television programs such as *ER* and *Chicago Hope.*

The Advertising Council of America worked with the American Red Cross starting in 1946, assisted by the New York City–based agency Sullivan, Stauffer, Colwell & Bayles, Inc. In 1957 the American Red Cross chose the J. Walter Thompson Company (JWT) as its advertising agency. Through surveys, it was learned that younger people (18-to-34-year-olds) held some misconceptions about the American Red Cross—for example, that only snobbish nurses and wealthy elderly women worked in local chapters. Many in this age group also had the mistaken

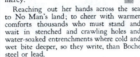

The GREATEST MOTHER in the WORLD

Stretching forth her hands to all in need; to Jew or Gentile, black or white; knowing no favorite, yet favoring all.

Ready and eager to comfort at a time when comfort is most needed. Helping the little home that's crushed beneath an iron hand by showing mercy in a healthy, human way; rebuilding it, in fact, with stone on stone; replenishing empty bins and empty cupboards; bringing warmth to hearts and hearths too long neglected.

Seeing all things with a mother's sixth sense that's blind to jealousy and meanness; seeing men in their true light, as naughty

children — snatching, biting, bitter—but with a hidden side that's quickest touched by mercy.

Reaching out her hands across the sea to No Man's land; to cheer with warmer comforts thousands who must stand and wait in stenched and crawling holes and water-soaked entrenchments where cold and wet bite deeper, so they write, than Boche steel or lead.

She's warming thousands, feeding thousands, healing thousands from her store; the Greatest Mother in the World—the RED CROSS.

Every Dollar of a Red Cross War Fund goes to War Relief

Courtland Smith's ad for the American Red Cross is widely cited as one of the organization's most memorable World War I efforts.
Provided courtesy of the American Red Cross.

erroneous belief that the act of donating blood placed one at risk for the disease) and PSAs about the blood-screening process helped bolster public faith in the safety of the blood supply. The education program continues under the guidance of the U.S. Centers for Disease Control and Prevention. The American Red Cross's HIV/AIDS education program has several facets, including a Workplace Program, an African-American Program, and an Hispanic Program—all of which address the topic from the perspective of, and with special relevance to, particular population groups.

In 1990 JWT created a hugely popular three-year PSA campaign called "Play Your Part," featuring the song "Gimme Shelter." The PSAs, targeted toward young professionals in the 18-to-34-year-old age group, featured a television spot with musicians Branford Marsalis, Carly Simon, Paul Shaffer, and Randy Travis. Each performer was shown helping out in a disaster relief

There's no such thing as a small disaster.

When Disasters Strike, Children are the Most Vulnerable

The American Red Cross will always be there, helping families and saving the lives of those devastated by hurricanes, floods and other disasters. You can help the families affected by disaster by contributing to your local Red Cross. Ninety-one cents of every dollar spent goes directly to programs and services that help those in need. We rely on your financial contributions when help can't wait.

To make a donation, call 1-800-HELP NOW or call your local Red Cross chapter.

☐ Yes, I want to support my local chapter
Name _____
Address _____
City _____
State _____
Zip _____
☐ $25   ☐ $50   ☐ $75   ☐ $100   ☐ Other _____
Please make your check payable to the American Red Cross and mail your contribution to: P.O. Box 37243, Washington DC 20013. Or call 1-800-HELP NOW.
For internet information: www.redcross.org   M06S+M7+ ++++ +MS+++

American Red Cross
We'll be there.

An ad from 1998 highlights the importance of continued public support for the Red Cross.
Provided courtesy of the American Red Cross.

impression that their money and time were unappreciated. To counteract this image, the slogan "Always there . . . with your help" was retired and replaced with the more upbeat "Join up . . . Join in." Seeking to emphasize the universality of the Red Cross, JWT launched a campaign that featured images of youthful volunteers in action. The campaign, which appeared in newspapers and magazines, on television and radio, and on posters, also encouraged young people to donate money to American Red Cross programs.

In 1970 JWT sought to spotlight unity, caring, and brotherhood in its "Roll Up Your Sleeves" campaign. The ads featured African-American boys in a city park and Native American youngsters in southwestern settings. The copy used language that reached out to everyone, regardless of ethnicity, background, or circumstances. In the mid-1970s singer Glenn Campbell performed a series of songs for PSAs emphasizing that the entire nation relied on this disaster relief agency in times of trouble.

The American Red Cross, after the advent of AIDS, invested in improved technology and screening procedures for its blood collection program beginning in the mid-1980s. An intensive AIDS education program (correcting, among other misconceptions, the

situation, and each activity had a musical tie-in. Musicians Michael Bolton, Tito Puente, and Richie Havens performed radio spots. Magazine and newspaper PSAs rounded out the campaign.

An increased effort to secure corporate sponsorship was also launched in the early 1990s. A total of $4 million, donated by FedEx Corporation, Anheuser-Busch Companies, MCI Corporation, and American Express Company, was used to develop and purchase spots for the "Help Can't Wait" campaign created by the Kaplan Thaler Group. Along with outdoor ads, PSAs were distributed to 1,000 daily and weekly English- and Spanish-language newspapers and magazines, 6,000 radio stations, and 1,200 television stations. In addition, local chapters used the campaign information to solicit local support. "We'll Be There," a campaign by the Kaplan Thaler Group launched in 1998, reinforced the organization's reputation for effective, caring relief efforts.

The American Red Cross develops its advertising in-house or with outside agencies on a project-by-project basis, devising a road map and setting the tone for the campaign. Then it tests the concepts with focus groups in several cities. Publicizing a huge disaster relief effort, such as those necessitated by Hurricanes Floyd and Mitch, requires a quick turnaround—often as little as 24 to 48 hours for broadcast and print PSAs. Such campaigns require merging of new images with ads prepared and donation information collected in advance.

The Red Cross avoids the use of guilt and scare tactics in its PSAs. For example, when D'Arcy Masius Benton & Bowles created the PSA called "The Gift" in 1995, the agency emphasized the confidentiality of the blood donation process as well as its lifesaving importance. The PSA showed strangers from all walks of life giving each other a wrapped box with a ribbon, symbolizing the 22,000 daily blood donations the Red Cross needs to service

hospitals nationwide. The same principle was employed in "Be a Source of Hope," an ad created in-house for the Somalian relief effort in the early 1990s. Instead of images of dead or starving children, the Red Cross chose to feature a photo of a youngster in obvious need but basically well cared for.

The American Red Cross does not advertise in other countries (out of respect for its sibling societies). Nonetheless, it is often asked to participate in international relief efforts, including, in the late 1990s, those in Mozambique, Kosovo, Turkey, and India.

CARRIE SMOOT

Further Reading
Berens, Robert J., *The Image of Mercy,* New York: Vantage Press, 1967
Goodrum, Charles A., and Helen Dalrymple, "Causes: Advertising in the Service of the Community," in *Advertising in America: The First 200 Years,* by Goodrum and Dalrymple, New York: Abrams, 1990
Hernandez, Debra Gersh, "Red Cross Begins Major Public Service Awareness Campaign," *Editor and Publisher* (18 March 1995)
Moorehead, Caroline, *Dunant's Dream: War, Switzerland, and the History of the Red Cross,* London: HarperCollins, 1998; New York: Carroll and Graf, 1999
Pryor, Elizabeth Brown, *Clara Barton: Professional Angel,* Philadelphia: University of Pennsylvania Press, 1987
"Red Cross Push Aims to Create a Younger Image," *Advertising Age* (5 February 1965)
Wojtas, Gary W., "Red Cross Unveils New Image," *Fund Raising Management* 21, no. 2 (April 1990)

American Telephone & Telegraph Company. *See* AT&T Corporation

American Tobacco Company

Principal Agencies
Williams & Cunnyngham
Caxton Advertising
Dorland Advertising Agency
Erwin, Wasey & Company
Wm. H. Rankin Company
Lord & Thomas
Foote, Cone & Belding
Batten Barton Durstine & Osborn

Sullivan, Stauffer, Colwell & Bayles, Inc.
Laurence, Charles, Free & Lawson, Inc.
Grey Advertising Agency, Inc.

The American Tobacco Company had its roots in a small family business, W. Duke Sons and Company, founded after the Civil War in Durham, North Carolina. By 1890 W. Duke Sons had captured 40 percent of the growing cigarette market in the United

States, and scion James Buchanan "Buck" Duke became president of the American Tobacco Company, which consisted of W. Duke Sons and Company and its leading competitors. Although the government forced the dissolution of the group, which came to be known as the "tobacco trust," in 1911, Duke's American Tobacco Company survived and thrived as an industry leader into the 1960s. It was a competitor of R.J. Reynolds Tobacco Company (RJR), Liggett & Myers Tobacco Company (L&M), and eventually the Philip Morris Company and Brown & Williamson Tobacco Company for dominance in the tobacco market. Innovative and influential in its first 50 years, American Tobacco began to lose ground in the 1960s and vanished as a market entity in 1994 when it was acquired by the British-American Tobacco Company, the parent of Brown & Williamson, which maintained the Lucky Strike and Pall Mall brands that had made American famous.

Early Years

W. Duke Sons and Company originally was devoted to the production and sale of smoking and chewing tobacco, a field in which it was a competent but undistinguished competitor. The Dukes were not able to compete with the neighboring Durham Company, the producer of Bull Durham smoking tobacco. James Green, creator of the Bull Durham mixture, merchandised his product widely and well, using premiums, gifts, billboards, posters, and what have been aptly described as the "unlikely endorsements" of the British authors Alfred, Lord Tennyson and Thomas Carlyle. In 1880 the Durham Company had the largest tobacco factory in the world. Buck Duke watched and learned, but he decided to compete in another field. In the early 1880s he turned his attention to the nascent cigarette industry and acquired the exclusive rights to the Bonsack cigarette-rolling machine.

Capable of producing billions of units annually by the end of the 1880s, Duke had a supply of Cameo, Duke of Durham, and other cigarette brands that actually exceeded the national demand. To correct this unprofitable situation, Buck Duke turned to international markets. More importantly, he applied and expanded on Green's aggressive merchandising techniques, working tirelessly to expand the domestic market for his product. From the 1880s onward, Duke offered the public a wide variety of incentives to purchase his cigarettes, everything from tags and coupons for rugs, clocks, and chromolithographic scenes and portraits that smokers' wives might covet to prurient picture cards that young boys and bachelors might dawdle over. He sponsored sports teams from baseball to roller-skating and held exhibitions in which crowds of potential customers received product information leaflets. Relying on the fame and allure of the French actress Madame Rhea and the American beauty Lillian Russell, he pioneered the use of celebrity images and endorsements to sell cigarettes, a practice that his successors learned to mimic.

By 1890 Duke had succeeded fantastically both at home and abroad. His products squeezed other brands off the nation's shelves, forcing several rival firms to unite with W. Duke Sons and Company in order to survive. Thus was formed the American

763   HELEN DAUVRAY,
DUKE CIGARETTES
ARE THE BEST.
W. DUKE, SONS & CO.

James Buchanan "Buck" Duke was a master of merchandising, popularizing the use of endorsements and picture cards in tobacco advertising.

Tobacco Company, which dominated the industry and acquired ever more properties. Competitors, including the Durham Company, found themselves forced to cave in to or to collude with American Tobacco. By 1898 American's holdings gave it an 85 percent share of the cigarette market.

The American Tobacco Company profited but also drew heavy fire from a growing antitobacco movement, from antitrust reformers, and from competitors. At the turn of the century, reformers objected particularly to cigarettes on grounds of morality and health, with special concern for the nation's youth. They directed most of their rhetoric toward the consumer but reserved criticism for the marketers and advertisers that offered what were called "indecent" pictures meant to titillate and attract young boys. (Even some within the industry criticized trade cards featuring scantily clad women in suggestive poses. While grown men might quickly discard such items, they suggested, "callow youths" would be tempted to buy cigarettes for the purpose of collecting the pictures.) The antismoking faction promoted a variety of products to aid in smoking cessation, but without much success. Morality was tough to package, and the images and endorsements used in advertising No-To-Bac and other cures were ineffective and even amateurish when compared to those used by the tobacco industry. The antitobacco lobby succeeded in getting laws restricting cigarettes on the books in 14 states, and such laws were considered by 21 other state legislatures. But the laws did little to slow the growth of cigarette smoking or to harm the trust.

Those who successfully assaulted the monopoly did not condemn the users, the products, or even the advertising. They attacked the business practices that worked to narrow the choices of both competitors and consumers. Muckraker Charles Edward Russell asserted that the "trust's pathway to success and profits has been over the ruins of the small tradesman's prosperity," and he decried the "enforced contributions of tobacco consumers and retailers" to the coffers of the American Tobacco Company.

In 1911 a federal court ordered the trust dissolved. A significant portion of Buck Duke's empire survived, however, as he personally had a hand in drawing up the plans for dissolution. A leaner American Tobacco Company, now headed by Percival Hill, was one of the four companies spun off from the old trust. (The other three were RJR, P. Lorillard Company, and L&M, all of which had existed prior to the formation of the trust and which had maintained varying levels of autonomy within it.) The new American Tobacco Company retained roughly a third of the cigarette and smoking tobacco market, a quarter of the plug (chewing tobacco) trade, and a very small fraction of the cigar market. Among the new company's leading brands were Bull Durham smoking tobacco and Sweet Caporal cigarettes, the latter an old Kinney brand and the only brand at the time that had anything approaching a national market.

The Era of the Hills

The efforts of Hill and especially those of his son George Washington (G.W.) Hill made the new American Tobacco Company every bit as much a force to be reckoned with as was the old company. The younger Hill was much like Buck Duke in his drive to put American Tobacco on top. He introduced packaging innovations—vacuum-packed tobacco tins, glassine-wrapped cigarette cartons, and product dating—that were meant to persuade retailers and consumers of the superiority and freshness of his company's products. He took American's pricey, all-Turkish Pall Mall brand to the top of the deluxe market with ads that stressed quality and distinction and that evoked images of London high society. This appeal to snobbish Anglophiles, which was a departure

from the exotic Oriental images used in advertising for other Turkish cigarettes, would be the approach used for Pall Malls for decades to come.

Hill's particular obsession, however, was the Lucky Strike brand, which debuted in 1916 in response to RJR's spectacularly successful Camel cigarettes. RJR was shut out of the cigarette market when the trust dissolved but was determined to profit from the growing popularity of cigarettes among the American public. Camel debuted in 1913 and broke every mold in the business. In an era that favored cigarettes of Turkish or domestic Bright tobacco, Camel blended a significant portion of Burley tobacco with Maryland, Bright, and Turkish. RJR did away with the premiums that had been a staple in the business and touted the departure as a boon to the consumer. "Quality, not premiums" was the guarantee. On top of this, RJR offered 20 Camels for a price of 10 cents, while its rivals L&M's Fatima, Lorillard's Zubelda, and American's Turkish Omar sold for 15 cents. Finally, RJR hired N.W. Ayer & Son to engineer a million-dollar national advertising campaign that preceded as well as accompanied the unveiling of the brand. The mysterious teaser "The camels are coming" whetted consumers' and retailers' curiosity and appetite long before the cigarettes themselves appeared on the shelves. By 1916 RJR had topped L&M in market share and sales and was closing in on industry leader American Tobacco. Within five years Camel took the lead, becoming the first truly national brand and transforming the way cigarettes were sold.

Under Hill's leadership in the 1920s and 1930s, American turned out virtually every tobacco product except snuff. The company sold nearly 500 brands, from Boot Jack, Gold Rope, and Old Honesty plugs to Roi Tan and Chancellor cigars. Incredible as it may seem, one of the company's best-selling smoking tobaccos was marketed under the brand name Nigger Hair, with some 425,000 pounds sold in the Milwaukee area alone in 1936. Other American cigarette brands included Egyptian Prettiest, Royal Nestor, and Svoboda, each with its own secret formula. All were profitable, but none gave American Tobacco a national brand identity.

Thus Hill quickly turned his hand to fashioning a challenger to the upstart Camel. Surveying American's old labels, he unearthed Lucky Strike, a brand of pipe tobacco, and updated the lettering and detail on the green label with the red bull's-eye. Considering a formula for the new cigarette, Hill decided on an all-domestic blend of tobaccos, even more heavily weighted toward Burley than was Camel. To suggest Lucky Strike's flavorful appeal, the early advertising relied on the simple slogan, "It's toasted" (1916). The new brand did well enough in its first year, capturing about 11 percent of the market, but its progress was stalled by the entry of the United States into World War I. Both Camel and Luckies went to war in Europe, but the U.S. government had contracted to buy cigarettes at prewar market shares, thus putting American in the shadow of RJR.

In 1924 American retained Lord & Thomas to work on the Lucky Strike account. Account executive Albert Lasker persuaded Percival Hill to focus the majority of the advertising budget on this single brand. By 1925 Lucky Strike had 16 percent of the cigarette market. This was progress to be sure, but Luckies were still

Good Sport and Good Smoke Go Together

There's more crisp, brisk, youthful vigor in an ounce of "Bull" Durham than in a pound of any other tobacco ever rolled up into a cigarette. It's the co-partner of the go-ahead spirit —the delight of the fresh, unjaded taste that goes with enthusiasm and energy. This grand old tobacco—the favorite of three generations—is today the liveliest smoke in the whole world.

GENUINE "BULL" DURHAM
SMOKING TOBACCO

Ask for FREE package of "papers" with each 5c sack

Within the last two years the "roll-your-own" idea has spread amazingly. Thousands of men have learned that their own hand-rolled "Bull" Durham cigarettes have a freshness and fragrance impossible to obtain in any other way. Made exclusively from mild, ripe Virginia-North Carolina "bright" tobacco leaf, "Bull" Durham is unique in its mellow-sweet flavor. Try it once and you'll smoke it always.

FREE An Illustrated Booklet, showing correct way to "Roll Your Own" Cigarettes, and a package of cigarette papers, will both be mailed, *free*, to any address in U. S. on request. Address "Bull" Durham, Durham, N. C. Room 1295.

THE AMERICAN TOBACCO COMPANY

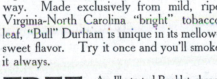

Although originally a competitor of "Buck" Duke's American Tobacco Company, the Durham Company and its popular Bull Durham brand were later acquired by Duke.

a distant third behind Camel (40 percent) and L&M's Chesterfield (25 percent).

Luckies attained market dominance after G.W. Hill ascended to the presidency of American in early 1926, after the death of his father. A company historian characterized the son as "a one-man ad agency." Others said that his "main interest in life" was to see that Lucky Strike gained and then retained first place in the race with Camel and Chesterfield. He reportedly devoted most of his time to thinking up ideas that might induce people to buy Luckies, and he spent millions of dollars annually to put his ideas into action. Immediately after World War I, he used skywriting to draw attention to his pet brand in cities across the nation. In the 1920s and 1930s he cajoled celebrities, respected businessmen, and even physicians into lending their names and images to his product. He made liberal use of page ads and ran them in every daily paper he could. When radio and television became viable mass media, Hill seized the opportunity, readjusted the advertising budget of American Tobacco, and sponsored a variety of popular shows that included the *Lucky Strike Dance Orchestra* (later the *Lucky Strike Hit Parade*, 1935–59), *The Lucky Strike Program with Jack Benny* (1944–1960), and *Information Please* (1940–43).

Hill was committed to understanding and exploiting the developing industries of advertising and public relations. To this end, he hired not only a bevy of advertising agencies but also top men in the new field of public relations, including Edward Bernays. With Bernays, Hill tackled the job of selling Lucky Strike to women, a little-exploited portion of the cigarette market. When Bernays was engaged by American Tobacco in 1928, women were already a recognized part of the smoking population, and their numbers were growing. Manufacturers, however, were timid about targeting them directly and were unsure how to do so effectively. (This even was true of Hill, who was timid about little.) For several years Philip Morris had had a small brand called Marlboro directed at women. The brand was packaged in white with a delicate script and was advertised to "discriminating smokers" as being "Mild as May." Earlier, small specialty brands such as Milo Violet cigarettes had been aimed at the female market. The lackluster performance of these brands, however, indicated that women were not interested in "feminine" brands; they were smoking the same cigarettes as men—industry leaders Lucky Strike, Camel, and Chesterfield. The question for American Tobacco and its competitors was how to make women loyal to their brands.

The Newell-Emmett Agency crafted the "Blow Some My Way" campaign for L&M's Chesterfield brand in 1926, suggesting that women as well as men enjoyed smoking. It was Hill's American Tobacco, however, that launched a sustained assault on the female market. Bernays orchestrated what was called the "Torches of Freedom March" down New York City's Fifth Avenue on Easter Sunday 1929. The sight of ten debutantes publicly puffing their cigarettes as they strolled down the avenue created a sensation on the nation's front pages, but there was no hint of a connection to American Tobacco in the press. Bernays had worked so effectively that the stunt seemed not a promotion but a validation of women's right to smoke and of any manufacturer's right to recruit female smokers. Hill already had made a strong bid in this direction in 1928 in the famous "Reach for a Lucky Instead of a Sweet" campaign, created by Lord & Thomas and named by *Advertising Age* among the top 100 ads of the 20th century. Asserting a connection between health, thinness, fashion, and Lucky Strike, Hill struck a chord with the American public, both male and female. Between 1925 and 1931 American's profits more than doubled, from $21 million to $46 million, and Lucky Strike moved ahead of Camel.

American Tobacco's triumph, however, was neither permanent nor without cost. In six years American's advertising budget nearly tripled—going from $8.7 million to $24.8 million—as it undertook a saturation campaign with print media, posters, theater programs, window displays, and radio. American scaled back its spending once it had achieved market dominance, but throughout the Great Depression, in an effort to maintain its position, it continued to spend at least $10 million annually on magazine and newspaper advertising, retail window displays, and, of course, radio broadcasting.

Luckies, Camel, and Chesterfield jockeyed for market position throughout the 1930s. The 1940s were a decade of change for Lucky Strike and American Tobacco. In 1942 Luckies' distinctive green package, on which Hill had lavished so much attention, gave way to white, and it was announced that "Lucky Strike green has gone to war." This patriotic declaration and the fact that cigarettes were regarded as essential to the soldier's kit, bolstered sales during and after World War II. Sales of Lucky Strike increased by 38 percent in the six weeks after the "Gone to War" campaign commenced. In 1946, as soldiers returned home, domestic sales increased by some 32 billion units. The year was also a turning point for Lucky Strike. Hill died in September 1946, and Lucky Strike ceased to be the focal point in the company's executive offices and advertising department.

Hill's son, G.W. Hill, Jr., had joined the company in 1936 and risen to become vice president of advertising. He was committed to continuing his father's aggressive, repetitive ads as well as the relationship with the agency that had crafted them for 22 years, Foote, Cone & Belding (FCB), which succeeded Lord & Thomas on the account in 1942. But within American Tobacco a power struggle quickly developed between Hill and Vincent Riggio, the president. On 19 March 1948 Hill quit, and three days later FCB president Emerson Foote startled the advertising industry by resigning the $10 million–$12 million account. It was the largest account any agency had ever resigned.

Lucky Strike was moved to Batten Barton Durstine & Osborn, which in turn resigned its Brown & Williamson Kool business (which went to Ted Bates Company). A smaller brand that had been in the American Tobacco line since the early 1930s, Herbert Tareyton, was assigned to the M.H. Hackett Company, a move that Hill had opposed on the grounds of nepotism, Monty Hackett being Riggio's son-in-law. Ayer continued as the agency for Lucky Strike's television advertising, which was still insignificant in 1948. Following Hill's resignation, Lucky Strike remained the company's principle brand, but American Tobacco would also begin to promote others more aggressively as well.

In 1907, before the breakup of the trust, Duke had bought Butler-Butler, Inc., a small company that made a high-priced Turkish cigarette called Pall Mall. Percival Hill, who was in charge of the cigarette division, decided that his son was ready to begin learning the marketing end of the trade and assigned him the brand. Within a few years G.W. Hill had built it into a leading name among Turkish cigarettes. It remained in production until 1936, when he decided to extend American Cigar, a division of American Tobacco, into the cigarette business by using Pall Mall as its flagship brand.

Pall Mall was re-created as a "modern" blend without flavoring and with a preponderance of domestic tobaccos, and just a hint of Turkish. In 1939 its shape was redesigned, with the cigarette made "more modern" by lengthening it to what was called "king size." And while the aristocratic red label was retained, the cigarettes were made available in a regular "cup" package rather than the more expensive box of the past. Using the tag line "Modern design makes the difference" in radio spots, print media, and billboard advertising, American Tobacco and agency Young & Rubicam doubled Pall Mall's sales in 1940. After 1946, as Lucky Strike went into a relative decline, Pall Mall's sales continued to expand.

With the ad shake-up of March 1948, Pall Mall was moved to Sullivan, Stauffer, Colwell & Bayles, a new agency formed in June 1946 by the group of former executives at Ruthrauff & Ryan, which had handled Lucky Strike and Pall Mall radio production. The account was estimated by trade sources at about $1 million. At the core of the original campaign for Pall Mall, in which the pronunciation of the brand was Americanized to "Pell Mell," was a single claim whose words and rhythms would persist essentially unchanged for decades and become one of the longest running copy blocks in advertising history: "Pall Mall's greater length of traditionally fine, mellow tobaccos filters the smoke and makes it mild. . . . Pall Mall, famous cigarettes, and they are mild."

A Changing World for Cigarettes

The decade after World War II was the high-water mark for the American cigarette industry. The public was in comfortable denial of any health risks posed by the cigarette habit, and more Americans smoked than ever before or since. Profits soared, and the industry met the government in court, congressional hearings, and Department of Justice investigations more than once concerning issues of trade collusion and fraudulent advertising and generally emerged triumphant. Certainly its public reputation remained unscathed. Early in the 1950s, however, health claims about cigarettes began to trouble the public's conscience and the industry's bottom line. In 1964 U.S. Surgeon General Luther Terry issued a report that specifically linked cigarettes to death and disease, and the tobacco wars began in earnest.

Well before Terry's report, the American Tobacco Company and its competitors tacitly recognized in their advertising possible health risks posed by smoking. They denied, however, that any cigarette posed a grave danger and certainly denied that their products posed even minor risks. Indeed, they protected themselves against the idea. Almost from the beginning, for example,

American claimed that the "toasting" of Luckies offered "Your throat protection–against irritation–against cough." In the 1940s ads claimed that the length of new, improved Pall Mall Kings "gentles the smoke," making it milder, cooler, and less irritable to the throat.

In the 1950s, however, numerous scientific studies began to assert clear, statistical links between cigarette smoking and lung cancer, not just scratchy throat and coughing. In the December 1953 issue of *Cancer Research,* Ernst Wynder and Evarts Graham of the Sloan Kettering Institute offered compelling evidence that cigarette smoking was probably linked to "bronchiogenic carcinoma," or lung cancer. In the wake of this article, industry leaders gathered to discuss their options. They formed a jointly funded research organization to examine issues of smoking and health, hoping to find perhaps either that cigarettes were not harmful or that they could be made safe without significant difficulty or loss of profit. In the meantime, however, they retained the services of John Hill, of the preeminent public relations firm Hill & Knowlton, determined to deny and refute all charges made in the scientific journals. They launched a public relations campaign that expressed concern for consumers' health, denied they would ever knowingly market a dangerous product, and called into question the validity of the charges leveled against them. The evidence, they said, was inconclusive, and to prove it the companies recruited their own scientists to study and disprove any link between smoking and cancer. The public, they said, should not worry. With little variation, this continued to be the industry line into the 1990s.

The public, however, clearly was worried. Per capita cigarette consumption declined 10 percent in the early 1950s. In response, the industry continued to deny that its products were at all dangerous, but simultaneously companies began to produce filtered cigarettes. They advertised the new cigarettes as healthier, thus calling into question the safety of their other brands. In 1952, for example, Lorillard promised low-nicotine delivery from its Kent cigarettes, while Brown and Williamson claimed, "The new Health-Guard filter makes Viceroy better for your health than any other leading cigarette!" By 1954 filtered cigarettes accounted for one of every ten sales.

American Tobacco, however, declined to enter the filter fray. President Paul Hahn believed that filters robbed cigarettes of their flavor, and he may have seen the dangerous inconsistency of the trend toward filters. In any case, his company alone failed to put any real effort into fielding a filtered brand in the 1950s. In 1954 he permitted the production of a filtered version of Herbert Tareyton Kings, but he did not budget extensively for advertising the new cigarette. The unfiltered version heavily outsold the filtered Tareyton, and American had nothing to compete with Viceroy, Kent, Winston, and the other filtered brands that were proliferating and gaining market share throughout the 1950s and 1960s.

Robert "Barney" Walker shifted the policy on filters when he assumed the company presidency in 1963, but the move failed to gain market share. He rolled out Carlton cigarettes in 1964 as being low in tar and nicotine, and between 1963 and 1966 he introduced a host of other filtered brands at the rate of seven a year. Waterford, Half & Half, Colony, a rejuvenated Sweet Cap, the old standard Lucky, and (specifically for the female market) Silva Thins were all filtered cigarettes that should have appealed to a newly health-conscious public, but none of them succeeded commercially. The "Unswitchables" campaign for Tareyton—featuring a smoker with a black eye proudly declaring "I'd rather fight than switch"—enjoyed brief success and made American a momentary contender in the filter field. Walker was making "safer" cigarettes available to the public but was unable to bring himself to market them as such, for he wanted to concede nothing to the industry's critics.

The debate over cigarette advertising in the 1960s, however, soon made Walker's reticence about health advertising irrelevant. In the months surrounding the surgeon general's report, the Federal Trade Commission (FTC) moved to restrict cigarette advertising and mandate strong health warnings on the packaging. The industry united behind the front of the Tobacco Institute, hired former Kentucky Senator Earle Clements to lobby Congress against FTC regulation. Clements's lobbying forces, which included the Advertising Federation of American and the National Association of Broadcasters, persuaded Congress to make an end run around the FTC. The Cigarette Labeling and Advertising Act of 1965 required mild health warnings on packaging but blocked state and local action against the industry while it prevented the FTC and other federal agencies from taking action to regulate tobacco advertising. Consequently, the industry was then free to pour advertising dollars into low-tar, filtered brands and to sell them to the American public as being safer. American's Carltons and Montclairs, though they failed to capture the market lead, began to receive more advertising attention.

When the FCC put a novel interpretation of the so-called Fairness Doctrine into effect in 1969 and gave significant airtime to antismoking forces, American Tobacco and the rest of the industry voluntarily withdrew from advertising on radio and television. Broadcast media had accounted for 80 percent of the industry's advertising in 1969, but the industry was able to effect a transition away from the broadcast media to print and outdoor advertising. In this manner it still managed to escape significant regulation of its advertising. Low-tar brands proliferated and by

1978 represented 28 percent of the domestic market, thanks in no small measure to the ability of companies to market the cigarettes as being safer.

The U.S. tobacco wars intensified in the 1980s and 1990s. In the 1990s industry advertising finally came under strict control. In an effort to curb the use of tobacco by teens, promotional giveaways were banned, and tobacco companies were forced to pay for a portion of the antismoking advertising seen on billboards and television. American Tobacco, however, was no longer a participant in the tobacco wars. In 1969 the company's vice president, Robert Heineman, engineered the takeover of Gallaher Limited in Great Britain and immediately increased American's overseas market. Also in 1969, Walker spearheaded the acquisition of nontobacco companies and the establishment of American Brands, of which American Tobacco became a subsidiary. By 1975 the majority of American's tobacco sales and earnings came from its Gallaher subsidiary, and by 1990 less than 10 percent of American Brands' revenue came from American Tobacco. Then, in 1994 the parent company sold American Tobacco to Brown & Williamson. There American's old marquee brands, Lucky Strike and Pall Mall, survived but with none of the luster of their heyday.

NANCY BOWMAN

See also Bull Durham

Further Reading

American Tobacco Company, *"Sold American!" The First Fifty Years (1904–1954),* New York: s.n., 1954

Hilts, Philip J., *Smokescreen: The Truth behind the Tobacco Industry Cover-Up,* Reading, Massachusetts: Addison-Wesley, 1996

Kluger, Richard, *Ashes to Ashes: America's Hundred-Year Cigarette War, the Public Health, and the Unabashed Triumph of Philip Morris,* New York: Knopf, 1996

Lewine, Harris, *Good-Bye to All That,* New York: McGraw-Hill, 1970

Petrone, Gerard, *Tobacco Advertising: The Great Seduction,* Atglen, Pennsylvania: Schiffer, 1996

America Online, Inc.

Principal Agencies

TBWA Chiat/Day
Carat Freeman
Gotham, Inc.

The company that was eventually to become America Online (AOL) emerged in 1985 from the ashes of a start-up gaming company called Control Video, Inc., whose GameLink service downloaded computer games to an Atari game console. Its failure left a young marketing executive, Steve Case, the brother of Control Video's largest backer, looking for work.

Case adapted some GameLink ideas into a bulletin board service, called Q-Link, for Commodore 64 users, founding Quantum Computer Services to market it. He also created a graphical user interface (GUI) for Q-Link, giving his bulletin board the point-

and-click attributes of Apple Computer's new Macintosh. A few years later, Apple asked him to rework Q-Link for its users, naming the service America Online.

AOL was a minnow in a sea of on-line services dominated by such big fish as H&R Block's CompuServe, IBM Corporation and Sears, Roebuck & Company's Prodigy service, and General Electric's GEnie service. But it had the GUI that Case had created, and a key ally in Apple. It also had Case, a native of Hawaii and a Williams College graduate who had made marketing his life. While his rivals went directly from school to the technology industry, Case sold hair-care products for Procter & Gamble Company and then conducted customer surveys and focus groups for PepsiCo's Pizza Hut chain.

Case's epiphany came while he was working for Pizza Hut in Wichita, Kansas. He bought an early personal computer (PC), called Kaypro, and a modem and then joined The Source, an early on-line service owned by the Reader's Digest Company. When an opportunity came to work for a graphic on-line service, Control Video, he jumped at it. His key insight was the need for alliances. Q-Link was an alliance with Commodore, then the largest marketer of PCs, which bundled the service with its machines. Tandy

In 2000 America Online's ads focused on the Internet service provider's accessibility, with tag lines such as, "So easy to use, no wonder it's #1." ©2000 *America Online, Inc. Used with permission.*

and IBM also became allied with Quantum, in addition to Apple. This meant that the PC makers did Quantum's marketing. Quantum became profitable within two years of its founding.

When AOL went public in 1992, it had only 150,000 subscribers, a fraction of the number claimed by rivals Prodigy and CompuServe. But the next year, Prodigy, with 2.5 million subscribers, dropped its flat-fee structure in favor of hourly rates. AOL cut prices and ran ads urging Prodigy members to switch to AOL. It also introduced new software whose interface looked more like that of Microsoft's Windows, which had exploded in popularity.

AOL then signed new alliances, this time with media companies such as Time-Warner, ABC, and the *New York Times*. For a small share of the revenue coming in from these companies' content, AOL offered direct marketing access to its customers. By the end of 1994, it had 1.5 million members. In 1995 it launched its first television commercials, 15-second spots from TBWA Chiat/Day, New York City.

AOL had offered its members access to Internet rivals for years. But with the rise of the World Wide Web, it also faced new competition from Microsoft Corporation, AT&T Corporation, MCI Communications Corporation, and thousands of small Internet service providers offering the same flat rates as AOL. While AOL kept growing rapidly, it suffered from technical bottlenecks (the service was once down for 19 hours because of a software problem), accounting controversies, and a growing number of lawsuits involving, among other things, its monitoring of on-line discussions and use of its network by children to access Internet pornography.

Yet, by 1997 AOL had 7 million subscribers and had become the first on-line server to reach $1 billion in revenue. It lengthened its lead over CompuServe and Prodigy, neither of which, under the umbrella of slow-moving parent companies, could compete with AOL. AOL thus became the first on-line company to make cyberspace a mass-market product. The company's advertising budgets increased rapidly during the mid-1990s, and by 1996 its total spending on marketing reached $333 million, $100 million of which went into television to build the AOL brand. TBWA Chiat/Day created a series of TV commercials set to the theme music of *The Jetsons,* a popular animated program of the 1960s. At the end of the year, the company introduced an unlimited-use pricing plan at $19.95 a month. AOL had emerged as the clear leader in what remained a highly competitive and challenging new market.

Case's answer to these challenges came in September 1997. He traded to Worldcom, Inc., his Internet-access business, ANS Communications, Inc., in exchange for CompuServe, his last major rival in the on-line services market, plus $175 million. At a stroke, Case shed his technical troubles and, with the addition of CompuServe's 2.6 million subscribers, emerged from the deal serving 54 percent of the on-line services market.

Exploiting these advantages required a new business model. Instead of sharing revenue with those who put content on its network, AOL could charge media companies for access to its members. AOL could also charge rent—including multimillion-dollar up-front fees—to merchants that wanted prime space in its on-line mall. In November 1998 AOL acquired Netscape Communications Corporation for $4.2 billion and entered into a related three-year alliance with Sun Microsystems, a move that undercut the notion that Microsoft would have the Internet to itself.

For fiscal year 2000, ended in June of that year, America Online had net income of $1.2 billion on sales of $6.8 billion. It had become the first company based on the Internet to join the *Fortune* 500, which ranks companies by sales, debuting at number 337. In January 2000 AOL announced that it would acquire Time-Warner for AOL stock worth $160 billion, creating the world's largest media company. Case, still in his early forties, would become chairman of the new company's board. AOL's shareholders would own 55 percent of the new company. Not only would AOL acquire some of the greatest content in the world—CNN news programs, Time-Life's magazines, Warner

Music, and the Warner Bros. movie studio—it also would pick up Time-Warner Cable, the nation's second-largest cable television network. The U.S. Federal Trade Commission approved the $111 billion merger in December 2000.

DANA BLANKENHORN

Further Reading

Stauffer, David, *It's a Wired, Wired World: Business the AOL Way,* Milford, Connecticut: Capstone, 2000

Swisher, Kara, *AOL.com: How Steve Case Beat Bill Gates, Nailed the Netheads, and Made Millions in the War for the Web,* New York: Times Books, 1998

Thornally, George, *AOL by George! The Inside Story of America Online,* Livingston, New Jersey: Urly, 1999

Ammirati Puris Lintas

Formed as Ammirati Puris AvRutick, Inc., in 1973 (a partnership within Young & Rubicam); became independent in 1977 after establishing a reputation for lush creative work on BMW; sold in 1987 to a British holding company, the Boase, Massimi, Pollitt Partnership (BMP), but subsequently bought by Omnicom; became independent again as Ammirati & Puris in a buyback from Omnicom, 1990; sold to the Interpublic Group of Companies, 1994; merged with Lintas Worldwide network to become Ammirati Puris Lintas.

Major Clients
BMW North America
Club Med, Inc.
MasterCard International
United Parcel Service
Waterford Crystal, Inc.

Ammirati Puris Lintas (APL) was born within Young & Rubicam (Y&R) in September 1973 as Ammirati Puris AvRutick, Inc. (APA), in an effort to avoid an anticipated client conflict within Y&R. Since the 1950s the agency had handled both the International Harvester (IH) heavy- and light-duty truck divisions as well as the business of Chrysler Corporation. Although IH's light-duty off-road vehicles approached an overlap with Chrysler's passenger cars, neither advertiser regarded the other as competition. Then in 1973 Chrysler announced it would introduce the Trailblazer, an off-road, four-wheel-drive wagon in direct competition with IH's Scout and Travelall models.

In an effort to eliminate the conflict, Y&R creative chief Alex Kroll initiated talks in March with Ralph Ammirati and Martin

Puris, who had met and worked together at the Carl Ally agency as art and copy group heads, respectively, since 1966 when they had joined within four weeks of each other. Ammirati had previously worked at N.W. Ayer, Campbell-Ewald, and Y&R; Puris had worked at J.M. Mathes on Canada Dry and at Batten Barton Durstine & Osborn (BBDO) on Pepsi-Cola. Both men were now eager to start their own agency. Kroll suggested a third partner in the new agency, Julian AvRutick, a 13-year Y&R veteran who then headed the company's Mexico City operations. Kroll then enlisted the support of Y&R president Ed Ney, who contributed a 50 percent financial stake of about $125,000. Ammirati Puris AvRutick opened in August 1973 in rooms at the Delmonico Hotel in New York City with a single small account, the Chrysler Trailblazer.

The new agency emphasized its independence from Y&R while at the same time promising would-be clients access to its resources. Early listings in the Standard Directory of Advertising Agencies ("Red Book") were under the Y&R banner. APA positioned itself as a midsize agency with large-agency depth. On that basis, it went after blue-chip accounts, declining to work with tiny companies in marginal product categories. It claimed that it rejected $3 million in potential business during its first year of operation. From Y&R's perspective, the formation of APA pointed to other specialized agencies it had recently acquired, such as the pharmaceutical ad specialist firm Sudler & Hennessey. In fact, the Y&R-APA partnership was in principle a small version of the larger holding company model as exemplified by the Interpublic Group of Companies, in which multiple agencies could join under a corporate umbrella to avoid conflicts.

The Chrysler business was so small, however, and the additional overflow from Y&R so slow in coming, that the agency soon recognized it would have to stand or fall on its own merits. In 1974 it was invited to pitch the BMW (Bavarian Motor Works) business in competition with Ted Bates and Benton & Bowles. Each finalist was given generous funding and three months to come up with a presentation. With only two weeks of operating income left, APA was awarded the business. Within the next six years it would go from billings of $900,000 to billings estimated at between $11 million and $15 million.

Meanwhile, Y&R sold its interest back to APA in December 1977 after a relatively brief but, according to Ney, "mutually profitable" relationship. Now fully independent, APA continued to add both small and midsize accounts over the next several years. In the spring of 1979 AvRutick resigned the presidency and was replaced by Puris. At the end of April, AvRutick's name was dropped, and the agency became Ammirati & Puris, Inc. (API). Billings by then had risen to about $17 million served by 32 employees; billings would double to about $34 million by the beginning of 1988. This put API in the position of paying competitive salaries and attracting talent from top agencies such as McCann-Erickson, Y&R, and Wells, Rich, Greene.

The agency made its reputation from several high profile campaigns. For BMW there was "The Ultimate Driving Machine." For Club Med in 1980 there was "The Club Med Vacation . . . the Antidote for Civilization." APA won Dataproducts, America's largest maker of computer printers, just as the personal computer revolution was about to take off in 1984. Overall, the look and sensibility of the agency's work became associated with "yuppie" values of acquisition and luxury brand names.

During the early years of API, its rather dry and witty creative reputation tended to overshadow its wish to be seen as a full-service agency. In 1983 the account management side of the shop was strengthened when Ed Vick came from Ogilvy & Mather to be chief operating officer. The agency sought and won the account of Schweppes ("The great British bubbly"), Pulsar Time, and United Parcel Service ("We run the tightest ship in the shipping business"), bringing its roster to eight clients and close to $120 million by the mid-1980s, even as it lost Club Med, whose French management could not imagine why anyone would want an antidote to civilization. Elegance and class became the agency's signature, along with a touch of arrogance in its client relationships.

API expanded into the direct marketing business in 1986 and in 1987 won the $15 million Reebok shoe account at a moment when the athletic shoe category was poised for explosive growth. But the API "arrogance" intervened, and the agency dropped the business almost as quickly as it won it, claiming that the client could not be satisfied and was demoralizing the shop. The account would later return on better terms.

In May 1987, after more than a decade of investment in money and time, Ammirati and Puris decided to join the rush of American agencies selling out to British buyers (a rush that included Ted Bates, DFS Dorland, Backer & Spielvogel, McCaffrey and McCall, Della Femina, Pace Advertising, and others). In a transaction that totaled $31.8 million, including $6.3 million in stock, plus future incentive payments dependent upon profit goals (which would not be achieved), API went to a British holding company, the Boase, Massimi, Pollitt Partnership (BMP), a publicly traded company. It was an ideal arrangement for the two founders, Ammirati and Puris, each of whom netted 37 percent of the sale, with 10 percent going to Vick and the balance to 17 other executives. Ammirati and Puris also retained their titles, their authority, and their autonomy.

Then in June 1989 BMP announced that in an effort to block a hostile takeover by Boulet, Dru DuPuy Petit, a French company, it would sell to the New York City–based organization Omnicom, which owned DDB Needham and BBDO. Not wishing to operate under the Omnicom banner and concerned about client conflicts, API, then billing $210 million, quickly entered into negotiations to buy itself back from its new parent. Talks went on for six months before a deal was worked out. In January 1990 the agency regained its independence for an estimated $30 million. Specifics were not disclosed, but the terms were reported to have dissatisfied Vick, who may have believed he deserved more. He left API a month later, in February 1990.

Growth continued, with the agency picking up $120 million in new business in 1992 alone, bringing API billings to the $400 million level. One of the biggest new accounts was MasterCard International, whose own growth had been stalled by Visa's appeals to upscale consumers and the emergence of the Discover Card. Another new account was Compaq Computer, which the agency sought to reposition as a blue-chip brand with lower-than-ever prices. But it was also the year that BMW announced a review of its agency affiliations. Puris considered whether it would be worth the possible humiliation of staging a fight and then losing what had been the agency's most profitable account. In what was widely regarded in the industry as a move of considerable wisdom, Ammirati and Puris quietly relinquished the BMW account.

In 1994, after four years of independence, API was approached by yet another potential buyer, the Interpublic Group of Companies and its chairman, Philip Geier, who saw a role for the agency within Interpublic's Lintas Worldwide network. Lintas had originally been founded in 1899 as the house agency for Lever Brothers, then a British soap company. A 49 percent stake was bought in 1969 by Sullivan, Stauffer, Colwell & Bayles, which itself was acquired by Interpublic in 1970. With Lintas and API there would be few likely conflicts, especially after IBM Corporation departed Lintas, thereby eliminating any problem with Compaq at API. After months of on-and-off talks—and four months after API won the Burger King business in March, bringing its billings to $500 million—Lintas and API reached an agreement on 18 July based on a swap of stock estimated at between $45 million and $55 million. About $17 million was used to retire the debt to Omnicom for the 1989 buyback. Puris received 45 percent of the balance; Ammirati, 15 percent; and the rest went to senior executives. The agreement called for the merger of API with Lintas Worldwide, whose New York City office billings had suffered recent declines after losing Diet Coke as well as the IBM business.

The combined agency became Ammirati & Puris/Lintas, with billings of $850 million, a figure that put it among the top ten New York shops and instantly made API an agency of international

This simple slogan developed by Ammirati Puris Lintas positioned Schweppes as a traditionally elegant beverage.
Schweppes® is a registered trademark of Dr Pepper/Seven Up, Inc. ©2001.

standing. Puris became president and Ammirati chairman. In characterizing the merger, *New York Times* columnist Stuart Elliott quoted actress Katherine Hepburn on what made the combination of Fred Astaire and Ginger Rogers successful: "Ginger gave Fred sex, and Fred gave Ginger class." Thus, API's "Fred" brought class to Lintas's "Ginger." Once consummated, the merger resulted in six client losses and staff layoffs of about 40. Seventeen months later Lintas Worldwide, one of Interpublic's three international networks, was formally renamed Ammirati Puris Lintas (APL), effective 1 February 1996.

But an unexpectedly high executive turnover along with significant client losses stalled progress. By 1999 Interpublic was the umbrella organization over four separate agency networks: McCann-Erickson Worldwide, the Lowe Group, Draft Worldwide, and APL. On 29 October 1999, in a move to achieve economies of scale, Interpublic folded APL into the Lowe Group, creating from the two networks a new agency name, Lowe Lintas & Partners Worldwide, billing nearly $6.5 billion with three U.S. offices and 94 others around the world, according to the 2000 *Advertising Age* Agency Report, which ranked the new company 13th among U.S. agencies.

Thus, in October 1999 the names Ammirati and Puris officially disappeared as an agency brand after 26 years as a force in U.S. advertising. Puris resigned as chief executive officer and also from the Interpublic board. Though in a press release he called the merger a "brilliant idea," he noted that he remained "an entrepreneur at heart" and said, "One merger in a lifetime is enough." Ammirati was in retirement at the time.

JOHN MCDONOUGH

Further Reading

Elliott, Stuart, "As Merger Partners, Ammirati Provided Style, while Interpublic Promises a Large Network," *New York Times* (19 July 1994)

Grant, Don, "New Y&R-Backed Shop Gets Chrysler Vehicle," *Advertising Age* (3 September 1973)

Kanner, Bernice, "The Other A&P," *New York Magazine* (25 November 1985)

Mandese, Joe, "Ammirati & Puris: Sense of Balance," *Adweek* (29 October 1994)

"Says IPG Chairman Philip Geier, 'The Building of the Two Organizations Was Obvious,'" *Adweek* (8 August 1994)

Anacin

Principal Agencies
Dancer, Fitzgerald, Sample
Biow-Biern-Toigo
Ted Bates & Company
Campbell Mithun Esty
Young & Rubicam, Inc.
Partners & Shevack
McCann-Erickson Worldwide
Grey Advertising Agency, Inc.

Anacin has had many advertising agencies over the years, but the campaign that put the pain reliever on the map was the "hammer-in-the-brain" effort created by Ted Bates & Company, New York City, under its legendary chairman Rosser Reeves. The TV commercial not only boosted Anacin's sales but also earned it a place in advertising history for the constant repetition that hammered home its message, "For fast, fast, fast relief."

Anacin's parent company, American Home Products, acquired Anacin in 1930 when it bought Van Ess Laboratories to get the company's hair tonic; the pain reliever came along as part of the deal. Early ad agencies for Anacin included Dancer, Fitzgerald, Sample and Biow-Biern-Toigo. Later agencies included John F. Murray Advertising, the house agency for American Home Products' Whitehall Laboratories Division; Campbell Mithun Esty;

Young & Rubicam; Partners & Shevack; McCann-Erickson; Lois/EJL; and Grey Advertising. But the shop that made the most difference to the product was Bates, which won the account in 1956.

Anacin was one of many over-the-counter pain relievers that had their origin in 1897, when a German chemist first produced aspirin. Aspirin was bottled by Bayer, which marketed its product to physicians rather than patients. When Bayer's patent ran out, Anacin emerged.

Anacin took what was essentially the same product as Bayer's and simply repositioned it. It was now marketed toward the consumer—the end user—as a powerful pain reliever. Anacin's first important campaign was a series of radio ads that ran in the 1940s and claimed that Anacin was ". . . like a doctor's prescription—not just one, but a combination of several medically active ingredients." Thus, consumers saw a new and different product, one that contained several ingredients and must, therefore, be superior to conventional aspirin—although aspirin remained the product's active pain reliever. Anacin was the radio sponsor of the popular daytime drama *Just Plain Bill* from 1936 to 1954.

Under Bates, the Anacin campaign concentrated on television. The advertising took advantage of the visual medium to show what a "tension headache" might look like. The spots were typical of the era, in that a simple theme was repeated along with a visual demonstration. One spot showed a mother, transformed from saint to devil by headache pain, snapping impatiently at her

Doctors Find a Big Advance Over Regular Aspirin With Buffering for Arthritis Minor Pain.

Regular aspirin with buffering. Note the large aspirin particles (magnified over 50 times). They dissolve more slowly and, therefore, are more apt to cause gastrointestinal heartburn.

Arthritis Pain Formula. Tiny pain-relieving particles (magnified over 50 times), soft as powdered sugar. Dissolve almost instantly, less apt to cause gastrointestinal heartburn.

Many arthritis sufferers who take large daily doses of aspirin suffer side effects of stomach irritation. So they take aspirin with buffering. This helps a little. But doctors have found a formula that solves the problem a lot more.

It's Arthritis Pain Formula, by the makers of Anacin®. First, it contains double buffering. But more than that, the pain reliever is micro-refined to be smaller than the human blood red cell. This allows Arthritis Pain Formula to reduce gastrointestinal heartburn—and at the same time give you 50% more pain reliever. Thus, you get both extra protection for your stomach plus extra medication for your pain. If you take aspirin with buffering to relieve arthritis minor pain and its stiffness—switch to Arthritis Pain Formula, by the makers of Anacin. You'll enjoy relief for hours—without so much stomach upset.

Special Offer: While Arthritis Pain Formula is more economical than regular aspirin with buffering, because you take fewer tablets per day, now you can save an extra 50¢ on a package of 180 tablets (or any combination of packages totaling 180). Get coupons with details of this offer at the store where you purchase Arthritis Pain Formula.

Arthritis Pain Formula
By The Makers Of Anacin®
Analgesic Tablets.

In 1969 Whitehall introduced Arthritis Pain Formula, perhaps the first instance of market segmentation in the analgesic category.
Copyright © Whitehall Robins/Wyeth and used with permission.

child. Then an angelic voice-over reminds her not to take her headache out on her loved one. Finally, a male voice-over says: "You need Anacin for fast relief. The big difference in Anacin makes a big difference in the way you feel." It continues, extolling the product's "combination of ingredients," which makes it "like a doctor's prescription." The demonstration segment depicted three boxes inside the skull of the headache sufferer: one contained a pounding hammer, one a coiling spring, and the third a jagged lightning bolt. Each of these was then shown to be relieved by tiny bubbles of Anacin making their way up from the stomach.

Reeves once commented that these hammer-in-the-brain ads "were the most hated commercial in the history of advertising." But during an 18-month period, they increased sales by $36 million, to $54 million. The secret of the campaign's success was that it made a clear and potent claim (Anacin is "like a doctor's prescription") and that it was repeated, in only slightly altered form, for years. Reeves attributed the ads' success to the fact that they were based on reasoning, going against the predominant trend at the time. This was an era when much attention was paid to moti-

vation research; ads were aimed at consumers' subconscious needs rather than at their ability to reason.

In taking an existing product and marketing it to a completely different market, Anacin showed the power of positioning as a means of gaining market share. The hammer-in-the-head campaign was also a strong example of Reeves's concept of the "unique selling proposition, or USP, in which a supposedly unique claim is made for a product, then repeated continuously so that it is always associated with that product. It did not matter that the pain reliever Anacin contained was simply aspirin; what mattered was that it was "like a doctor's prescription" and that it contained the pain reliever most recommended by doctors "plus an extra ingredient missing from leading aspirins. . . ."

Integral to the ads were the repeated triplets of claims and images: the three icons shown in the skull; the three dishes with the added ingredients; even the wording on the packaging, "Fast pain relief," "Headache, neuralgia, neuritis." Anacin's trademark slogan—"Fast, fast, fast relief!"—was ranked number 19 by *Advertising Age* in its list of the 100 best ad campaigns of the 20th century.

The dramatic typography and layout of this 1962 print ad for Anacin share design elements used in movie advertising of the period.
Copyright © Whitehall Robins/Wyeth and used with permission.

Ultimately, those in the ad industry concerned with the ethics of advertising focused on Anacin. The product's ads belittled plain aspirin ("Brand X"), despite the fact that "the pain reliever doctors recommend most"—the active pain-relieving ingredient in Anacin—was itself aspirin. "Doctors" who appeared in the spots were actually actors. And the USP claimed for Anacin was actually true of other brands as well, a fact acknowledged by Reeves: "The claims may be true for all brands, not just our own. But we tell people about them." The ads were discontinued in the late 1950s, to be replaced by slice-of-life ads that continued to position Anacin as a tension rather than headache reliever. In the 1970s, under pressure from the Federal Trade Commission, American Home Products eventually modified its advertising but not before being ordered to spend $24 million in corrective advertising that acknowledged the falsity of all claims that Anacin eased tension.

In 1969 Whitehall Labs created Anacin's Arthritis Pain Formula, becoming the first brand to fragment the analgesics market. The success of this product led to the creation of many other specialized analgesic products by other brands. This development, along with the introduction of Tylenol and various ibuprofen brands, significantly reduced the market share of each of the major aspirin brands.

BARBARA KNOLL

Further Reading

Fox, Stephen R., *The Mirror Makers: A History of American Advertising and Its Creators,* New York: Morrow, 1984
O'Gara, Jim, "Inside Story of American Home Products," *Advertising Age* (20 November 1972)
Twitchell, James B., *Twenty Ads That Shook the World,* New York: Crown, 2000

Anheuser-Busch, Inc.

Principal Agencies

D'Arcy Advertising
DDB Needham Worldwide

In a little less than 150 years, Anheuser-Busch, Inc., grew from a small local brewery to the largest in the world—commanding 47 percent of the U.S. market and selling more than 100 million barrels of its products worldwide. (Anheuser-Busch, Inc., is the brewing subsidiary of Anheuser-Busch Companies, which owns a number of businesses including Busch Entertainment Corporation, Manufacturers Railway Company, and the St. Louis Refrigerator Car Company.) Its dominance and leadership can be credited to the dynamism and determination of five generations of family management; technological innovation; efficient production expansions; a strong distribution system; and abundant advertising.

Two principles have guided the company's advertising practices: persistence and pervasiveness. The company has always believed strongly in continuity, advertising consistently in good times and bad. Even when products were unavailable or rationed or sales were in a slump, the company continued to place its name and those of its products before the public. Moreover, while advertising is the company's primary tool, it adroitly applies all the tools of savvy marketing communications—sales promotion, public relations, packaging, merchandising, sponsorships, product placement, special events, and specialty items. It believes that whenever, wherever, and however its customers relax, its products and messages should be part of the experience.

Throughout the company's history, its advertising messages have remained remarkably unchanged. They consistently center on five themes: the quality of the product itself achieved through its ingredients and brewing process; the traditions and heritage of the company and its leaders; beer as a beverage of moderation; beer as a reward; and beer as an essential element of hospitality and sociability (the company's internal motto for more than 100 years, "Making friends is our business"). Depending on political, social, economic, and marketing conditions at any given time, one or more of these themes may predominate.

Over the years, U.S. beer drinkers have come to believe that their brand choice is an "identification badge"—that not only do brands have their own personalities but they reveal the personality of the purchaser. From its start, Anheuser-Busch has tried to communicate a "leadership" personality.

Early Years

In 1860 Eberhard Anheuser, a creditor, acquired the small, failing Bavarian Brewery in St. Louis, Missouri. Four years later his son-in-law Adolphus Busch joined the company. Busch succeeded in doubling the company's capacity in just five years; introducing pasteurization to extend shelf life; and purchasing refrigerated rail cars and ice houses to establish a national distribution system. These innovations enabled him to introduce the country's first national beer, Budweiser, in 1876 and its "connoisseur" Michelob brand in 1896. They were among 19 beer brands sold by the company in the 1800s. Busch's contributions were recognized in 1879 when the company's name was changed to Anheuser-Busch Brewing Association.

In addition to his manufacturing and distribution achievements, Busch, a born marketer, left an indelible mark on the company's approach to marketing communications. In the late 1800s "corporate image" was largely a reflection of the personality of the head of the business, and Busch was a shrewd promoter. He developed a four-point plan to make Budweiser a national product. It consisted of: 1) massive distribution of saloon point-of-sale materials of a higher quality than those of his competitors; 2) a large cadre of traveling salesmen; 3) an extensive inventory of giveaway items; and 4) widespread use of print ads in national magazines, literary journals, playbills, sports cards, and on buildings, railroad cars, and billboards—including the first electric signs in New York City's Times Square, erected in the late 1800s. He wanted to be sure that there was no place a potential customer could turn without seeing some reference to Budweiser.

He lavishly entertained writers and editors in his private railroad car during his business trips around the country and was rewarded with positive press coverage for the expanding company. His promotional items included watch fobs, beer tokens, walking sticks, hat clips, and fine china (in anticipation of the transformation of beer from a tavern drink into a beverage for home consumption). He was famous for presenting a pocketknife in place of a business card. The knife was emblazoned with the company name and Busch's own portrait inside a peephole.

One of his most enduring point-of-sale items was an attention-getting print titled "Custer's Last Fight," which was distributed to retailers and prominently displayed in store windows. More than 1 million reprints were made to meet the demand for copies, and requests were still being received more than 50 years after its introduction. Other items included hundreds of lithographed metal signs, posters, and trays. At the time, these sales promotion items were as important as, or more important than, advertising.

Most brewery advertising sought to communicate proof of superiority. Anheuser-Busch ads compared the company's high-quality barley, hops, and malt ingredients with its competitors' cheaper corn, as well as emphasizing its brewing and aging processes. They also highlighted the many awards, medals, and accolades won at national and international brewing competitions and expositions, particularly in Europe. One series of ads listed the massive amounts of Budweiser already sold.

As the use of illustrations and color lithography became prevalent, Busch insisted on high-quality artwork and brilliant but "non-garish" color in the company's ads. At a time when narrow, condensed type was popular, he insisted that the Budweiser name be printed in broad, heavy letters. Ads and posters often featured lavish illustrations of ingredients, the Budweiser beer bottle with a label almost exactly the same as today's, the manufacturing plant, and mythological figures and heroic images of America's past. In general, creative "themes" and "campaigns" were not used in advertising then as they are today, but Busch pioneered the first use of a multiyear, single-element coordinated campaign with the introduction of the "Budweiser Girl" prints and tin signs. The series, which continued for 30 years, consisted of nine different

representations of attractive young women holding a bottle or glass of Budweiser. Their dignified presentation appealed to men without angering women.

Three of the company's most enduring symbols were born before 1900. The colorful red, gold, and brown "A-and-Eagle," trademarked in 1872, was gradually introduced into packaging, promotional items, and ads. With only minor changes, it is still in use today. Also from the 1800s were the bright-red beer wagons with shiny brass trim that Busch insisted be used to deliver his products; the wagons were also used to transport billboards around cities throughout the country. In 1898 the company produced its 500 millionth bottle of beer. Thereafter, all packages and ads carried the phrase "King of Bottled Beers."

War, Prohibition, and Depression

When Adolphus Busch died in 1913, he was an established beer baron who had placed his company and its flagship Budweiser brand among the leaders in an industry of nearly 2,000 brewers. However, his son, August A. Busch, Sr., would have to work tirelessly to ensure the survival of the company. For more than 25 years, some of the company's ads had identified Budweiser as a "beverage of moderation" and "strictly a family beverage . . . promoting the cause of true temperance." However, soon after World War I, another ominous battle was approaching for Anheuser-Busch and the industry—Prohibition.

In 1914 the company hired D'Arcy Advertising, which would remain its agency of record until 1994, one of the longest client-agency relationships in advertising history. Together they launched a year-long campaign in which all newspaper ad space was devoted to messages about the role of the struggle for personal liberty in U.S. history. Earlier, August A. Busch, Sr., had commissioned a series of oil paintings that depicted the growth and expansion of frontier America. They proved so popular that they were reproduced in book form. Both efforts were made in the hopes of preventing "the noble experiment," as Prohibition was dubbed by some, but in October 1918 wartime prohibition went into effect. In preparation for the worst, the company had developed Bevo, a nonalcoholic beverage that tasted like beer. For several years, the product was immensely popular and was sold in 20 countries. The first radio ad ever produced by D'Arcy Advertising was for Bevo in 1920.

During the 1920s the company was determined to stay in business and keep its employees on the job, so it manufactured and promoted a variety of nonbeer food products including nonalcoholic Budweiser, ice cream, soft drinks, root beer, malt syrup, ginger ale, corn syrup, and baker's yeast, in addition to truck and bus bodies, and refrigerated cabinets. Advertising for these products helped keep the company and product names before the public.

Throughout the decade D'Arcy resolutely promoted Budweiser malt syrup as a baking ingredient, insisting on its premium quality and ability to produce superior baked goods. Advertising expenditures for malt syrup increased more than 2,000 percent as ads moved from obscure baking trade magazines to consumer newspapers, magazines, outdoor advertising, and national network radio. Ironically, the public had discovered that good malt syrup also produced a superior home brew, a beverage that had not been outlawed by Prohibition.

When Prohibition was repealed in 1933, Anheuser-Busch had survived, while more than 50 percent of breweries had not. In celebration, August A. Busch, Jr., presented his father with a team of Clydesdale horses pulling a turn-of-the-century beer wagon. Wherever they went, the Clydesdales drew attention. Soon requests were being received from around the country for appearances. Thus was born one of the company's best public relations tools. Today, three teams crisscross the country, representing the company's quality and traditions.

On 7 April 1933 virtually every brewer in the country published a newspaper ad announcing that its beer was available again—except Anheuser-Busch. The company waited until the initial fervor was over; then it published a page ad in every major metropolitan newspaper and national magazine. The headline read, "Something more than beer is back," with the subhead, "Budweiser is back." The copy and illustrations were not product-oriented but instead focused on the traditions of industry, the work ethic, hospitality, sociability, quality, and bounty. Later that year, a page ad in color, "When gentlemen agree," ran nationally. It promoted sociability and "the good life." The two ads were among the most remembered in the company's history.

When Adolphus Busch III assumed the company's leadership in 1934, he was faced with a unique advertising challenge. He wanted to uphold the company's 70-year tradition of continuous advertising, but its supplies could not keep up with consumer demand. A hard-sell product-oriented campaign was not appropriate, so a campaign that today would be called a "lifestyle" effort was conceived. It continued the "When gentlemen agree" theme and associated Budweiser with the good things in life. But the country's mood began to darken as economic recession returned, and the decision was made to devote the entire 1938 advertising budget to a new campaign designed to "sell America to Americans" in 930 newspapers and magazines. The focus was on patriotic themes and symbols. Although sponsored by Budweiser, the bottle and the A-and-Eagle trademark were secondary graphic elements.

As the United States entered World War II, the company decided to create two advertising campaigns. The first was an institutional effort designed to reinforce the company's stature and highlight its participation in the war effort. Eight color print ads supported the theme, "All America knows Budweiser, but few know this." An accompanying subhead read, "Endless research in making the world's leading beer has led to other products." Although the ads carried the Budweiser signature, the copy described the company's other products essential to the war effort: vitamins, starch, corn syrup, yeast, and diesel engines. The second campaign was a public service effort that delivered the messages the U.S. government wanted people to see. Twelve print ads in the campaign featured large illustrations of average Americans and their daily lives in the 18th and 19th centuries. The copy drew comparisons between their contributions to building the country and the contributions needed for the war effort. Head-

lines included "You know the Minuteman . . . now meet the missus" (in support of women's efforts on the home front); "Thinking Americans today . . . are not too free with free speech" (to promote national security); and "Grandma knew just what to do . . . and what to do without" (in support of the effort to save food, fats, and fuel). A small ad-within-an-ad showed the Budweiser bottle and glass and promoted the product as a reward for hard work and wartime sacrifices.

Battle in the Marketplace

After the war, the company again found itself in the awkward position of being unable to meet the demand for its product but unwilling to cease advertising. D'Arcy again came through with a soft-sell image campaign. Carrying out the theme of "Great contributions to good taste," the ads highlighted personalities who had contributed to expanding Americans' culinary horizons. The secondary graphic element was the Budweiser bottle and glass accompanied by the slogan, "It lives with good taste everywhere."

By December 1950 production reached 5 million barrels per year. Mid-century ushered in a new era of growth and expansion for the company—and its advertising. Under the leadership of August A. Busch, Jr., a born marketer like his grandfather, the company became more determined than ever before to regain a leadership position and more assertive in its advertising. A new full-page, color magazine campaign was launched. It showed Budweiser as an essential part of social occasions, day and night, and emphasized that Budweiser was brewed and aged by the most expensive process. In 1952 an outdoor poster series with the headline, "The beer of your lifetime . . . too," celebrated the company's centennial with characters from the mid-19th century. But it also marked the use of outdoor advertising "spectaculars," animated electrical displays. The largest of these, 100 feet long and 80 feet high, featured a flying A-and-Eagle and Clydesdales atop New York City's Times Square. Similar displays appeared in major cities throughout the U.S., and outdoor advertising was a major component of the budget. Radio continued as a popular medium with the wholesalers, which bought time on regional stations that carried popular baseball broadcasts. Thus began a continuing practice of sports sponsorships.

It was a time of optimism and innovation. In 1950 the company tested the new medium of television and became the first brewery to sponsor a major network TV show, *The Ken Murray Show* on CBS. It was an hour-long variety show, and the commercials featured the show's star and guests, often seen drinking Budweiser on camera. The company noted that the sale of Budweiser increased twice as fast in areas that had television, so it quickly renewed its sponsorship at a cost of $65,000 per week. Television has been an important part of the advertising budget ever since.

Two additional graphic icons were introduced in the 1950s: the bow tie for the Budweiser brand and the mountains for Busch Bavarian, a popular-priced beer introduced in selected regions to offset low-priced competitive beers. Throughout the decade the company fiercely battled its competitors (Schlitz, Pabst, Ballantine's, Falstaff) to achieve the largest sales volume and become the

Given to August A. Busch, Sr., by his son to celebrate the end of Prohibition in 1933, the Budweiser Clydesdales became an enduring symbol of the company.
Copyright © Anheuser-Busch, Inc.-St. Louis, MO.

number-one brand in the country. At that time, there were still 200 brewers in the United States, most of them small with only local distribution. The industry was ripe for consolidation. Anheuser-Busch was ready with its national distribution, efficient new plants, and effective advertising creating a premium image that could command a premium price.

In 1957 Budweiser took the number-one spot and never let go. The achievement was due in large part to a breakthrough advertising campaign that marked the brewer's first use of photography. It showed real people in casual situations rather than illustrations of more formal occasions. Its "Where there's life there's Bud" slogan used the Bud nickname for the first time. It was cited in 1957 by *Printers' Ink* as one of the year's best integrated campaigns for its color magazine ads and 22 musical versions of the slogan arranged for various radio formats in styles from calypso to country. Credit also belonged to the "Pick-A-Pair" sales promotion that urged consumers to buy not one but two six-packs at a time. The summertime promotion was supported by radio, television, billboards, print, and point-of-purchase advertising. It endured for 30 years and was considered one of the most successful in industry history, accounting for the sale of more than 30 million six-packs in a 60-day period and helping the company become a major partner with supermarkets.

The company entered the 1960s still engaged in fierce competition, but its sales hit the 10 million barrel mark in 1964. In 1961 D'Arcy helped introduce the premium Michelob brand to the home market in a uniquely shaped bottle (it had previously been sold only in draft form) and positioned it as "the finest bottled beer in the world." Other ads continued the "sociable" people-and-parties creative approach with the "This calls for Budweiser" theme line. (In the early 1960s such themes were criticized by several in the profession as being too generic and too prevalent throughout the industry.)

Around that same time, the company commissioned consumer research and learned that the heaviest beer drinkers were middle-income working people who were highly conscious of quality and prestige. They wanted to buy and serve "the best" and could afford to do it. Thus, a matter of Busch family pride—the dogged insistence on quality—was reinforced as smart marketing. In 1964 the "That's Bud—That's Beer" campaign was introduced in television, radio, print, and outdoor ads. Although the images continued to depict sociable drinking situations, the copy explained why Bud was superior. An additional campaign called "Beer Talk" focused even more directly on the superiority theme but in a light-hearted way. It addressed issues related to serving and storing beer and positioned the company as the industry expert that could talk directly to the consumer in a personal way. The quality/superiority theme continued for the remainder of the decade. In 1965 the slogan "It's worth it, it's Budweiser" made the point. In 1967 "Budweiser is the best reason in the world to drink beer" took over and featured the Clydesdales in color print spreads offered as poster reprints.

Print campaigns ran in national magazines such as *Life, Look, Ebony, Playboy, Sports Illustrated, Outdoor Life,* and *TV Guide.* Network television began to supplant the practice of buying time on selected local stations, known as spot advertising. The company became a major sponsor of *The Tonight Show* in 1962 when Johnny Carson became the host, and Ed McMahon signed on as an important spokesperson for many years. Other sponsorships included Frank Sinatra television specials and broadcasts of professional baseball and basketball games. The ad budget was divided among Budweiser (70 percent), Busch Bavarian (20 percent), and Michelob (5 percent–10 percent).

Among the most popular and captivating print ads of the decade were spreads of the Budweiser label (meant to highlight the quality ingredients and aging processes), which customers framed as artwork. The company had always produced consumer sales promotion items on a limited basis, but it was inundated with requests for items bearing the product label. The first to be produced was a popular beach towel. It was followed by clothing, sporting goods, and recreational equipment.

This successful theme carried over into early 1970s advertising, in which the label was shown covering the bottom of a swimming pool, a rec room floor, and a hot-air balloon, accompanied by the slogan, "When you say Budweiser . . . you've said it all." A secondary theme, "Somebody still cares about quality . . . Budweiser," received its own ad push. A corporate campaign, "A pledge and a promise," promoted the company's environmental efforts.

The regional Busch Bavarian brand retained the mountain-and-natural-ingredient imagery as well as a musical tag line, "Busch after Busch after Busch." Michelob proclaimed, "Surprise people . . . serve Michelob." It gained its own song in broadcast ads and increased its association with golf sponsorships, as well as increasing its emphasis on women's print media.

Turning Point

The mid-1970s proved to be a turning point for the entire industry—and its advertising. Anheuser-Busch entered the decade with Schlitz as its largest rival but closed it out battling Miller in the number-two spot. It began with less than $20 million in annual media expenditures and finished with more than $100 million. Network television had taken over and accounted for more than any other medium, the emphasis being on sports and special-interest programming.

The company was rocked by the success of Miller's sports marketing techniques, the popularity of its Miller Lite brand (introduced in 1975), sales decreases among younger drinkers, and a damaging strike in 1976. All occurred just as August A. Busch III assumed leadership. He acted quickly and decisively to undertake a total analysis of every aspect of the company: management, operations, production, and marketing. The result was a makeover of the company and its advertising.

He attacked the light beer category with the successful introduction of Anheuser-Busch Natural Light, shortened to "Natural" in a humorous ad campaign with comedians Norm Crosby and Ray Johnson. Michelob Light quickly followed with "Good taste runs in the family," and together the two brands moved Anheuser-Busch into the number-two spot in the light category.

New or revised ad campaigns were initiated for the major brands. In 1979 Budweiser introduced one of its most popular and effective campaigns ever, the "salute to the worker" ads with the "This Bud's for you" slogan. The campaign, which ran for ten years, starred average working people in various jobs rewarding themselves with a Bud at the end of a hard day. Busch Bavarian's name was shortened to Busch and its brand personality solidified with crisp new packaging and the soaring imagery of the "Head for the mountains" campaign from Needham, Harper & Steers. Included was the popular "Buschsssssshhhhh" sound of the can popping, which was later translated into radio, print, and outdoor ads. The "Weekends Were Made for Michelob" campaign from D'Arcy-MacManus & Masius, with the smooth sound of Vic Damone's crooning and actor John Forsythe as a sophisticated spokesperson, combined the reward concept with class. Specialized campaigns began to be created for market segments. "It's my beer, too" for Natural Light ran in women's magazines. For younger adults, a pudgy, anti–super-hero Bud Man provided "beer facts" in print ads and promotions, and the "Taste Buds" provided the laughs on NBC's *Saturday Night Live*. Urban markets received customized versions of radio campaigns by popular artists and the "Great Kings of Africa" print series was a success with African-Americans.

Market Dominance

The new campaigns carried over into the 1980s, when the company started the decade with nearly a 30 percent market share and quickly hit the 50 million barrel milestone. Emphasis on segmentation, sales promotions, special events, and sports were the focus of all U.S. marketing communications efforts in the 1980s. The company worked closely with its distributors to tailor radio ads, sales promotions, point-of-sale materials, and special events to different audience segments, ethnic groups, and geographic preferences. Toward this end nearly 600 different package designs were introduced. New products were tested for different market segments, including L.A. (low alcohol) and King Cobra malt liquor.

The biggest product success story was the long-awaited national introduction of Budweiser Light in 1982. Its first campaign, "Bring out your best," was closely related creatively to the Budweiser campaign, showing the product as a reward for extra effort. In 1984, to counteract any confusion with Miller Lite in bars and restaurants, the name was shortened to Bud Light and a humorous campaign, "Gimme a Light" (1984), featuring bizarre light sources, reminded customers to ask for the product by name. Other efforts featured a bull terrier named Spuds McKenzie, the original "party animal," who later became a spokes-dog for moderation in alcohol consumption.

The biggest advertising story was the company's determined effort to wrest sports sponsorships from Miller. By 1985 it had succeeded, becoming the largest sports sponsor in the U.S. Each brand had its own sports affiliations based on brand consumer demographics.

The company also made two important corporate strategy decisions in the early 1980s. With increased pressure on the industry from anti–alcohol-advertising groups, the company increased its long-standing public service efforts in support of responsible consumption. It launched the major "Know When to Say When" media campaign, which has evolved into a multi-pronged effort including "Family Talk" to fight alcohol abuse and underage drinking. These efforts have received increased funding and media coverage ever since. The company also made the decision to venture into the overseas market, where the potential was three times that of the total U.S. market. It began with Japan, Britain, and Israel (1984). The move proved successful, owing to a growing worldwide preference for lighter beers, as well as a fascination with American imagery, particularly among younger adults. Advertising is tailored to each market, but quintessentially American images—the Grand Canyon, New York City, cowboys, rock-and-roll musicians—and themes of success and individual initiative have proven extremely popular and persuasive.

The company finished the decade with the introduction of the popular Bud Bowl sales promotion sweepstakes leading up to the 1989 Super Bowl. In the ads, animated Bud and Bud Light bottles played out their own game during each quarter.

In 1991 brand manager August A. Busch IV decided to emphasize humor and a return to tradition. Budweiser maintained its position as the "King of beers," the number-one brand, with campaign themes of "Nothing beats a Bud," "Proud to be your Bud," and then a return to "This Bud's for you." Memorable ads included the "Pool Hall/Classic TV" spot aimed at generation X, the football-playing Clydesdales, the guitar-playing granny, cut-out animated Bud Bowl players, "born on" freshness dating, the famous "Bud-weis-er" frogs, followed by the partying ants and the frustrated lizards.

The growth of other brands was even more rapid. In 1994 Bud Light achieved its goal of becoming the best-selling light beer, ahead of Miller Lite. Humorous campaigns helped—"Everything Else Is Just a Light" and "Make It a Bud Light." Ads included the "Beer Mooch" ("I love ya, man"), "Limo" ("Yes, I am"), and "Lawnmower" (maintenance slack-offs).

Anheuser-Busch developed a segmented marketing strategy in the 1990s and by the end of the decade was offering 38 brands. Many specialty products were introduced to compete with the increasingly popular microbrews, imports, dark beers, and draft products. O'Doul's became the best-selling nonalcoholic beer in 1997, positioned as a new-age drink with the ad theme, "When all you want is taste." Bud Ice, introduced in 1994, was the first ice beer introduced in the U.S. and became a hit with its "Just add ice" theme, musical penguins, and its association with professional hockey. DDB Needham Worldwide, Chicago, Illinois, was the agency for Bud Ice. In 1997 the Budweiser family of brands alone account for 30 percent of the domestic beer market.

Creative efforts were supported with record-breaking budgets: in 1990, for example, more than $200 million for traditional media for the Budweiser brands, in addition to millions for promotions, sports sponsorships, and new media. In 1992 the company formed its own in-house media group for all planning and buying. The company was among the first to make sizable media buys on U.S. cable television, as well as global cable sponsorship deals to support its international effort. In 1997 it signed a seven-year agreement (extending through the 2004 Olympics) to be the exclusive beer sponsor of the Olympic Games. The company also moved into cyberspace with its Bud Bowl promotion, other cyber promotions, sports sponsorships tied to space on team Web sites, and its first sponsored content area on the CBS SportLine Olympic site, as well as its own brand sites. Program-length infomericals were tested in the 1990s.

In December 1994 the company ended its long relationship with D'Arcy Masius Benton & Bowles and sent the $100 million Budweiser account to Bud Light's agency, DDB Needham Worldwide. The account moved without so much as a review, largely on the strength of Busch's satisfaction with DDB Needham's work for Bud Light. A company spokesperson said that no single agency would ever again manage all Anheuser-Busch advertising because the company, its number of brands, and its variety of marketing communications projects was simply too large. While DDB Needham continued as the principal agency of record, media planning remained an in-house function. Individual creative projects have been handled by a number of companies; sales promotion, special events, and ethnic, international, and new media projects have been handled by specialty agencies, including Goodby, Silverstein & Partners; Rodgers, Townsend; Open Mind;

and Waylon Company. In 1998 the "Lizard" ads were named the most popular ad campaign ever by USA Today, and the "Wassup?" campaign won a gold Lion at the Cannes (France) International Advertising Festival in 2000.

As Anheuser-Busch anticipated its 150th anniversary, it turned once again to a "heritage" campaign, in which Busch family members spoke directly to the American customer about the enduring themes of quality and tradition. While the company sought to maintain its dominance in the U.S. market, a new emphasis was placed on making Budweiser not only a national but an international brand, expanding beyond the 80 countries in which it was then sold. The strategy, too, remained similar: focus marketing and communications efforts on the Budweiser family of brands; uphold the quality image worldwide, through emphasis on refreshing taste, high quality ingredients, and first-rate brewing techniques; and use advertising and all other appropriate communications to make the brand an ever-present and congenial part of the customer's life.

SUSAN SEYMOUR

Further Reading
Krebs, Roland, *Making Friends Is Our Business: 100 Years of Anheuser-Busch*, St. Louis, Missouri: Anheuser-Busch, 1953
A Legacy of Quality, St. Louis, Missouri: Anheuser-Busch, 1998
Teinowitz, Ira, "This Bud's a Part of St. Louis History," *Advertising Age* (10 September 1990)

Animation

Since the 1940s animation has had a profound effect on how products are marketed. It allows advertisers amazing latitude for conveying their messages, transcending the boundaries of what is possible in photographic representation. It enables them to speak directly to children through cartoon characters and to target adults through eye-catching special effects. The costs of creating animated advertisements vary greatly depending on the type of animation and the amount of production time required to produce the advertisement. Often the cost is comparable to that of live-action spots, since animation usually does not entail rental of a site or location or the expense of hiring live actors and large film crews, but does require costly artistic talent.

In the early days of television advertising, animation was considered a costly technique. Most products were advertised either through live demonstrations or previously filmed "talking head"–style presentations. But the few animated television spots run in the early days of the medium attracted so much attention that advertisers soon looked past the cost and focused on the effectiveness of using animation.

The "Botany Lamb" series of commercials are often cited as the first animated television commercials. The 1941 commercial for Botany Mills, produced by Douglas Leigh and directed by Otto Messmer, promoted the company's wool ties. At the end of each spot an animated lamb would look into a telescope and predict the next day's weather.

Another early example of animated advertising was the character "Reddy Kilowatt," created in 1926 by Ashton Collins, Sr., then general commercial manager of the Alabama Power Company. The popular Reddy, who helped allay the public's fears about electricity in the home, was a friendly little character made out of five lightning bolts, with a round smiling face and a light bulb for a nose. Reddy evolved into a customer- and employee-education tool for the growing industry. In 1947 he was brought to life by means of cel animation by cartoonist Walter Lantz.

Cel animation was for many years the most popular form of animation. It involved filming a sequence of images drawn and colored on individual acetate or nitrate cels. The introduction of videotape in the early 1960s brought with it some new animation

One of the first animated spokes-characters in advocacy advertising, Reddy Kilowatt has appeared in ads for dozens of electrical utility companies since the 1920s. In this 1947 newspaper ad, Reddy rings in the new year.
Reddy Kilowatt is a trademark of Xcel Energy, Inc.

techniques, and advancements in computer technology made computer-generated imaging (CGI) an exciting animation tool in the late 20th century.

The Process

No matter which technique is chosen, all animation follows a basic development process. Animation starts with an idea. The idea is translated into a script and sound track before the drawings are created or the animation techniques chosen. The next step is the creation of storyboards. Sketches of main characters, backgrounds, and concepts are drawn out in a comic strip style. Usually models are made of the main characters, and the personality and psychology of the characters are decided.

Drawing the background where the action is to take place is the next step in creating cel animation. Sometimes the backgrounds are drawn as long panoramas; the camera can pan the landscape or be placed in specific sections of the panorama where the action is taking place. Having most of the action take place within a larger continuous setting is helpful in creating continuity. Sometimes backgrounds are drawn in layers to create the appearance of depth.

Next, the characters are added. In this step, the artists will often use live models or animals to study movements and anatomy as they draw the characters. Usually a head animator draws the most important phases of the movement using a "model chart" with "in-betweeners" creating the drawings that connect these phases. Special-effects animators fill in surrounding activities—everything that is not part of the actual character. These drawings are then tested to make sure that the movements are correct and that no detail has been left out before transferring them to the cels. Then the cels are colored with opaque paints or color washes for subtler shades. Once completed, the drawings are transferred to the final film or tape.

Often, before these drawings are colored, they are transferred to a computer. Instead of each scene being placed on separate cels, the production is completed digitally, including the special effects, and then output to film or videotape.

Origins

Persistence of vision is the fundamental principle of animation. If a series of images is presented in rapid succession, the human brain links them into continuous motion. A great deal of popular interest in this phenomenon was sparked by an article written in 1824 by Peter Mark Roget, who is best known for the *Thesaurus of English Words and Phrases,* published in 1852. Animation has its roots with the many toys and novelties that were invented based on this principle. The Thaumatrope of the 1820s, the Fantoscope (1832), the Zoetrope (1834), and the Kineograph (1868) all helped pave the way for the understanding and development of modern animation.

John Barnes Linnett invented the flipbook, or Kineograph, in 1868. Images were placed in a bound book in order of the sequence of movements. As the reader flipped through the pages, the drawings would seem to come to life. Inventor Thomas Edison took this idea and in 1895 developed the Mutoscope, a mechanical flipbook that used images on cards and was housed in a little box. In 1891 Edison invented the motion-picture camera and motion-picture viewer. The Lumière brothers invented the Cinematographe in 1895, the first portable cinema camera, film processing unit, and projector.

In 1895 Edison met vaudeville performer J. Stuart Blackton, known for doing high-speed drawings during his act, "The Komikal Kartoonist." Blackton was interested in putting his drawings on film. Blackton and Albert E. Smith founded the Vitagraph Company, one of the first film studios, under a license agreement with the Edison Company. Blackton's first creation, *The Enchanted Drawing,* released in 1900, used various tricks he developed to make one of his drawings come to life. Six years later he created *Humorous Phases of Funny Faces,* which features him creating drawings while tricks are used to animate the images.

Winsor McCay, an early pioneer in animation, began his career as a cartoon artist. He was known for his comic strip, "Little Nemo in Slumberland," first published in the *New York Herald* in 1905. McCay made 4,000 India ink drawings on rice paper to create the animated film *Little Nemo,* in 1911. He devised a wooden holder and put crosshairs on the corners of the paper to maintain continuity in the image as he filmed. Later animated films by McCay included *How a Mosquito Operates* (1912) and his most remembered work, *Gertie the Dinosaur* (1914). McCay began working with cels laid over a background in the film *The Sinking of the Lusitania* (1918). Working in this way, he eliminated the need to redraw the background for every drawing.

While McCay was creating his animated cartoons almost single-handedly, the animation studio came into being. The Raoul Barre Studio (1913), the John Randolph Bray Studio (1913), and William Randolph Hearst's International Film Service (1915) were among the early studios that created an assembly-line style of animation production.

The Raoul Barre Studio in New York City was the first professional animation studio; in 1916 it was renamed the Barre-Bowers Studio when Barre formed a partnership with Charles Bowers. Barre created the peg system of registering drawings to keep the paper in place. This system was still used into the 21st century.

The John Randolph Bray Studio is credited with standardizing the various studio staff positions of painters, checkers, layout people, background people, inkers, and camera operators, in its film *Colonel Heeza Liar in Africa* (1913). Before this, one person completed the entire series of drawings and backgrounds, and therefore these animated works were the creation of a single artist's vision. Bray's first animated film was *The Artist's Dream,* created in 1913. Bray patented many of his innovations in the animation process, such as the use of translucent paper that made it easier to position objects in successive movement. In 1914 Bray formed a partnership with Earl Hurd, who held the patent for using cels. The Bray-Hurd Processing Company had a monopoly on the animation process until 1932 when its patents expired and the process entered the public domain.

"I was all wound up and ready for stardom
...so Star-Kist made me a clock!"

Actual size
as shown.

A timely offer from Star-Kist
"CHARLIE TUNA" alarm clock
for only $3.50 and three labels from Star-Kist Tuna.

Your children will love it ... more than 5½ inches tall with a full-color picture
of Charlie, luminous hands and double brass alarm. Manufactured by Lux
Time Division, Robertshaw Controls Co. Great for nursery, children's room,
or a unique decoration for the family room.
    To get your "Charlie Tuna" alarm clock, just send your name, address,
3 Star-Kist Tuna labels, and $3.50 in check or money order (please, no cash
or stamps) to:

Charlie, the Star-Kist Tuna
P.O. Box 6133
Chicago, Illinois 60677

Look for specially-marked cans at
your grocer's.

Order now, while supply lasts.
Allow 3 to 4 weeks for delivery.
Offer void if taxed, restricted,
or prohibited by law.
© 1970 Star-Kist Foods, Inc.

Since debuting in 1961 Star-Kist's Charlie Tuna has appeared on
television, in print and packaging, and on a wide variety of promotional
products, as seen in this 1970 ad for a Charlie Tuna alarm clock.
Courtesy of Star-Kist Seafood, Pittsburgh, PA.

William Randolph Hearst's International Film Service (IFS)
was established in 1915. IFS took out a cel license from the Bray

Studio and began releasing animated films in 1916. These films
featured Krazy Kat, the Katzenjammer Kids, and Happy Hooligan, all comic strip characters from Hearst newspapers.

In 1919, while he was an employee of the Pat Sullivan Studio,
Otto Messmer created Felix the Cat. Since Felix was created as a
studio character, theater audiences could look forward to seeing
future releases featuring the mischievous feline. This also gave
Messmer the chance to develop Felix's character over time.
Because Felix was created within the Sullivan Studio, Pat Sullivan
took full credit and earned millions of dollars in royalties over the
years. It was not until long after Sullivan's death in 1932 that
Messmer was given credit for the creation of Felix.

In 1928 Disney Brothers Studio took the animation scene by
storm with its release of *Steamboat Willie,* featuring Mickey
Mouse in the first full-length animated feature film with synchronized sound. Disney was largely responsible for much of the
advancement in sound and color in animation. Walt Disney
encouraged his artists to create a more realistic style of movement
for the characters as well. Before the 1930s, many of the animated
characters moved as if they had rubber arms and legs.

The Disney Studio and its style of animation increasingly came
to dominate the field in the 1930s. In 1941 labor disputes spurred
the exodus of some Disney artists, who then formed United Productions of America (UPA). In a departure from the much-copied
Disney style, UPA's work featured a more simplified animation
style that appealed to the advertising community. Requiring far
less work, the UPA style of animation was much less expensive to
create than the more layered and complex Disney style; it also had
the advantage of allowing the main character or products to stand
out more clearly.

Animated Ads

As animation got a firmer foothold in advertising during the
1940s, many new studios opened to handle the work. The
Fletcher Smith Studios began animation work in the mid-1940s,
creating ads for New York's Roosevelt Raceway that featured a
talking horse. Smith also did work for Quality Bakers' Sunbeam
Bread featuring Miss Sunbeam. Tempo Productions did animated
work for Camel cigarettes, Standard Brands, Plymouth, the
National Dairy Association, Procter & Gamble Company's Tide,
and Clark Gum through the late 1940s.

The Ajax Pixies were created by Shamus Culhane Productions,
which also did spots for Muriel cigars and Halo shampoo. The
Ajax Elves displayed the high quality of the Disney work that Shamus Culhane had learned as a trainee at the Disney Studios. Grim
Natwick, Art Babbit, and Art Heineman animated the elves.

By the 1950s advertisers were beginning to see animation as a
way to stand out in a medium that was attracting more and more
commercials. It also offered companies a means for bringing certain brand icons to life. The Leo Burnett Company created Tony
the Tiger in 1951 for Kellogg's Sugar Frosted Flakes. Tony has
undergone many changes over the years. In his first appearances,
he walked on all fours and his head was shaped like an oversized
football. By the end of the 20th century, many cultural influences

had led to the development of a slim, well-muscled, 6-foot-tall cartoon tiger. In addition to Tony, Burnett was responsible for other major cel-animated icons of the 20th century, including Charlie the Tuna for Star-Kist Foods and the Jolly Green Giant for the Green Giant Company.

Other animated ad characters introduced in the 1950s included the Hamm's Beer bear from "the land of sky blue waters" created by Cleo Hovel of Campbell-Mithun in 1954, and Burt and Harry, animated spokesmen for Piel's beer, created in 1955 by UPA and Young & Rubicam (Y&R).

In 1957 the well-known Hanna-Barbera Studio opened when the animation division at Metro-Goldwyn-Mayer (MGM) was closed. William Hanna and Joseph Barbera had been working together at MGM, where they created Tom and Jerry, the famous cat and mouse duo. Hanna-Barbera created a "limited animation" technique with less detail in the characters and background, which was well suited for the small-screen format of television. This new style of animation was imitated by many of the studios active in television animation at that time and was attractive to advertisers as it was much less expensive to create.

By the 1960s animation had been widely adopted in TV advertising. Among the early adherents were the marketers of children's cereals, which created their own animated characters specifically to appeal to kids. In 1963 Quaker Oats chose Jay Ward Studios, creator of *Rocky and Friends,* to come up with a character for a new children's cereal, and Cap'n Crunch was born. Other popular cereal characters came from General Mills, which introduced the Trix rabbit, created by Stanley Baum at Dancer, Fitzgerald, Sample in 1960 for Trix cereal, and Lucky the Leprechaun, created by Saatchi & Saatchi in 1964 for Lucky Charms cereal.

But animation was not limited to the realm of children's advertising. For example, the early 1960s saw the rise of Mr. Clean, the Procter & Gamble Company's household cleansing icon created by Harry Barnhart and Ernie Allen of Tatham-Laird, New York City. Y&R created a commercial in 1960 for Bristol-Myers Company's Bufferin analgesic using cel animation to show how the remedy entered the digestive system, made its way into the bloodstream, and produced relief.

"Claymation" and Other Techniques

Cel animation is only one of many animation tools available. For example, Pillsbury's Doughboy, created by Rudy Perez at Burnett in 1965, was a sculpted figure filmed using a stop-motion technique that brought the character to life. This technique was developed decades before computer-generated imaging was possible. And S.C. Johnson & Sons used animated bugs designed by Don Pegler of Foote, Cone & Belding (FCB), Chicago, Illinois, to bring television life to its campaign for Raid insecticide ("Raid kills bugs dead").

Clay animation is a type of stop-motion animation in which clay (usually plasticine) figures are photographed frame by frame. Slight changes are made to the figures between each photographed frame. When these images are run in succession, the figures appear to move. An early, but shaky, example of clay animation is Gumby,

The television spots that supported this 2000 print execution, created by Wieden & Kennedy, Inc., for ESPN's Winter X Games, were done in the cut-out style of animation.
Courtesy Wieden & Kennedy, Inc., New York. Art director: Kim Schoen. Design/illustrator: Geoff McFetridge.

a popular children's television character from the 1950s and 1960s; a more recent—and much more sophisticated—example of the technique is the California Raisins. The California Raisin Advisory Board introduced the "dancing raisins" in 1986. FCB, San Francisco, California, and Wil Vinton brought these characters to life in commercials using the "Claymation" technique pioneered and trademarked by Wil Vinton Studios, in Portland, Oregon.

Eventually, instead of being built from clay, the figures were fabricated from metal armatures covered with latex skins, to better withstand the intense lights and constant repositioning required. Hundreds of heads or facial masks are often created to portray the subtle changes needed to convey speech and emotion for each character. In the mid-1990s, PepsiCo took advantage of these developments in a series of animated commercials for Lipton's Brisk iced tea that featured clay re-creations of Elvis Presley, Frank Sinatra, Babe Ruth, Bruce Lee, Bruce Willis, Sylvester Stallone, Coolio, Willie Nelson, and James Brown. The agency was J. Walter Thompson U.S.A., New York City; the production company was Loose Moose, Ltd., London, England.

With advancements in technology, computers began to play a larger part in animation, reducing the need for expensive artistic talent and speeding up the process. With computer-generated imaging the animator can use the computer to do much of the "in-betweening" that previously had to be done by hand; using CGI, artists need only draw every fourth picture in a series, and software can do the rest.

CGI software is also used in the 3-D modeling of objects that can then be animated. Software is continually being improved to render objects in greater detail through shading, color, and texture. Early uses of these techniques were incorporated in the 1982 movie *Tron*. But a more recent example was seen during Super Bowl XXXV in January 2001, in an ad for Hotjobs.com. Created by Weiss Stagliano Partners, New York City, the CGI commercial "Gravity Balls" brought to life a steel ball from a gravity ball set, complete with a personality and emotions. Pixel Envy, Los Angeles, California, was the animation studio that created the spot.

Often a combination of animation techniques is used to create TV commercials. In the mid-1990s Krech Productions created two 30-second spots for Ogilvy & Mather, Houston, Texas, and its client, Shell Conoco, using stop-motion and computer animation to bring to life marching armies of credit cards that could bend and wiggle on cue.

Other forms of animation include anime, pixilation, and cutout—styles that have made a few inroads into the world of advertising. Anime began gaining popularity in the United States in the early 21st century. Also called Japanimation, anime is a style of animation developed in Japan that is typified by characters that have a smooth and very realistic style. Portrayed through an economy of line to create the most expression with the least amount of drawing, these characters were also shaded more subtly than typical American animations. As used in Japan, the subject matter of anime is typically science fiction, action adventure, romance, and magical themes. American Honda Motor Corporation in its 1999 "The Coupe Mission" commercial from La Agencia de Orci & Asociados, Los Angeles, California, used the anime style to show that driving the Civic makes even a trip to the grocery store feel like an adventure.

In 1999 Sprite, through ad agency Burrell Communications, Chicago, Illinois, continued its "Obey Your Thirst" campaign (begun in 1992 by Lowe & Partners/SMS) by combining hip-hop and *Voltron: Defender of the Universe*, a popular anime-style cartoon. Wild Brain of San Francisco, California, handled the animation for the five-commercial series, while the live action was handled by A Band Apart Commercials, Minneapolis, Minnesota.

Pixilation involves animating living things by photographing them one frame at a time. Often this technique is used to place people in surroundings with inanimate objects that are brought to life. The Bolexbrothers production company of Bristol, England, created *The Secret Adventures of Tom Thumb* with this technique. It used a stop-frame manipulation of small-scale models and characters, along with live actors who posed as if they were also manipulated models.

The cutout style is seen in techniques used in the cartoon series *South Park* from Trey Parker and Matt Stone. Ortho, a pesticide and herbicide producer, featured cutout animation in a series of television spots created in 1996 through BBDO West, Los Angeles.

The use of animation in advertising continued to grow in the early 21st century, with rapid advances in computer technology having a significant impact on the field. The possibilities for creative advertising using animation appear to be limitless.

STEVE CLOVER

Further Reading

Barbera, Joseph, *My Life in 'Toons: From Flatbush to Bedrock in Under a Century,* Atlanta, Georgia: Turner, 1994

Crafton, Donald, *Before Mickey: The Animated Film, 1898–1928,* Cambridge, Massachusetts: MIT Press, 1982; with a new afterword, Chicago: University of Chicago Press, 1993

Hoffer, Thomas W., *Animation: A Reference Guide,* Westport, Connecticut: Greenwood Press, 1981

Kanfer, Stefan, *Serious Business: The Art and Commerce of Animation in America from Betty Boop to Toy Story,* New York: Scribner, 1997

Laybourne, Kit, *The Animation Book: A Complete Guide to Animated Filmmaking,* New York: Crown, 1979; new edition, New York: Three Rivers Press, 1998

Schneider, Steve, *That's All Folks! The Art of Warner Bros. Animation,* New York: Holt, 1988; London: Aurum, 1989

Solomon, Charles, *Enchanted Drawings: The History of Animation,* New York: Knopf, 1989; revised edition, New York: Wings Books, 1994

Taylor, Richard, *Encyclopedia of Animation Techniques,* Philadelphia, Pennsylvania: Running Press, and London: Focal Press, 1996

Thomas, Frank, and Ollie Johnston, *Disney Animation: The Illusion of Life,* New York: Abbeville Press, 1981; revised edition, as *The Illusion of Life: Disney Animation,* New York: Hyperion, 1995

AOL. *See* America Online, Inc.

Apparel. *See* Fashion and Apparel; Intimate Apparel

Apple Computer

Principal Agencies
Chiat/Day, Inc. (later TBWA Chiat/Day)
BBDO/West

Apple Computer was founded in 1976 by two friends, Steve Jobs and Steve Wozniac, who lived in Silicon Valley (south of San Francisco, California) and were part of a "homebrew" computer club, where members would meet and discuss their latest inventions. Wozniac created a computer that would later be called the Apple I. He intended to sell a few to his friends, but Jobs saw a brighter future for the new computer, and Apple Computer was born. During the early part of the 1980s, Apple grew on the strength of the Apple II line to become the number-two computer marketer in sales, second only to IBM Corporation.

In 1983 Jobs persuaded marketing maven John Sculley, then president of PepsiCo, to become Apple's chief executive officer (CEO). Between 1983 and 1985, a dynamic synergy formed between Jobs and Sculley as each pushed the other harder and embraced the revolutionary spirit that was to define not only Apple's internal culture but that of its customer base as well. One of Sculley's first goals was to improve Apple's visibility in the marketplace. During his first year, he raised the ad budget from $15 million to $100 million.

At the end of 1983 Apple was gearing up for a product launch that would become a milestone in both the computer industry and the advertising industry. Working with newly hired agency Chiat/Day, Inc., Marina del Rey, California, under the creative direction of Lee Clow, Apple moved to produce a commercial that would break all sorts of precedents. Both agency and marketer wanted a commercial that would generate tremendous buzz for the product. Chiat/Day created a 60-second spot, called "1984," which was inspired by George Orwell's novel of the same name. It was one of the first big-budget commercials ever made.

The spot, which cost between $400,000 and $600,000 to produce, ran only once—in the sixth slot during the second half of Super Bowl XVIII. Clow chose as the commercial's director the British film director Ridley Scott (*Bladerunner, Alien*), who created an effort that was typical of his work—dark, eerie, and stylistically severe. The commercial featured a female hammer-throwing champion, who used her hammer to destroy a big-brotheresque video monitor while row upon row of clonelike people looked on. The spot seemed to suggest that Apple rival IBM and the proverbial Big Brother were one and the same. More than 200 extras were brought in for the weeklong shoot, and many were paid $125 per day to shave their heads. The commercial mentioned Apple Computer only once, in a voice-over at the end of the spot announcing the launch of the Macintosh, a product that would ensure that the year 1984 was nothing like the one imagined in Orwell's dystopian vision.

On first viewing, Apple's board refused to run the commercial and demanded that the agency sell the $1 million time slot; but when Chiat/Day failed to find a buyer, the spot aired. It would later win more than 30 international advertising awards, including the Grand Prix at the International Advertising Festival in Cannes, France. *Advertising Age* magazine named Sculley its "Man of the Year" for 1984 and Chiat/Day the "Agency of the Decade" for the 1980s. In 1999 *Advertising Age* ranked "1984" 12th in its list of the century's 100 best campaigns.

Apple's role as a contender seemed assured. However, certain decisions—such as Sculley's insistence that the Mac be priced at more than $2,000 (against Jobs's wishes)—would eventually lead to a severely declining market share. Sculley's intent was to keep revenue high to help fuel the marketing budget. He positioned Apple as a leader in the education and home markets, a stark departure from other companies such as IBM, which were focused almost solely on business customers. Even more dire for the future of the company was the decision to keep the operating system and software proprietary, exclusively for the Apple and Mac product lines. By failing to license to other hardware makers, the company allowed IBM and Windows to become the standard around the world, thus isolating Apple and making its products incompatible with 90 percent of the world's computers.

In 1985 Apple was again taking aim at IBM during Super Bowl XIX with a spot called "Lemmings," which featured men clad in business suits walking off a cliff in unison. Many have suggested that this spot, which came at a critical juncture for Apple, had the effect of driving away the business market instead of embracing it. "Lemmings," some say, made the people wearing the suits feel as though they were not being invited to the revolution, and Apple's profit margin began to slip.

On 17 September 1985 the Apple board ousted Jobs from his role as president. The following year Chiat/Day also fell victim to Apple's declining sales, and BBDO/West, in Los Angeles, California, began its 11-year run with Apple, one of the longest in the computer industry. The next several years would see Apple and BBDO/West work through many different products and strategies in an effort to stabilize Apple, despite stiff competition.

In a major reversal of strategy, in 1990 Apple decided to refocus on building its share in the marketplace and slashed prices on the Macintosh line. In 1991 it launched the PowerBook, which quickly became one of the hottest-selling laptop computers. However, a sense that the product was underpowered and overpriced pervaded the marketplace.

Early 1993 saw the launch of the first major personal data assistant (PDA), the Apple Newton. Sculley put $5 million of the advertising budget behind its launch, but the product failed to meet consumer expectations.

Apple also shifted its strategy from decentralized advertising to global marketing, centralized at BBDO/West. Since its inception, Apple had wanted to seem like a local company, not a global one. But with international sales accounting for 45 percent of Apple's revenue, the board decided that there was too much at stake and that the brand was faltering across the globe. In June 1993 Sculley handed his CEO title to less advertising-focused President Michael Spindler. Sculley left Apple in October as the Newton floundered.

At this time, Apple was concentrating on selling product with its "Does more, costs less" ads rather than emphasizing its previous branding efforts. The company was also working with several other agencies for different projects. Wunderman Cato Johnson, San Francisco, California, was Apple's direct marketing agency of record, and CKS Partners, Campbell, California, was doing some work for the Newton on a project basis.

Apple's answer to the burgeoning on-line service market, eWorld, was launched in 1994. It created a friendlier user interface than its competitors, Prodigy, America Online, and CompuServe, but it was higher priced and failed to draw a large enough audience. eWorld fizzled in 1996. In 1994, more importantly, Apple launched the PowerPC chip, codeveloped with IBM and Motorola, which would fuel a whole generation of more powerful machines.

The end of 1996 marked the beginning of a number of shake-ups at Apple. Jobs sold his company Next to Apple and returned to the company as an "adviser." He began retaking control of the company. Jobs, still the CEO of animation powerhouse Pixar, became the "interim CEO" of Apple as well. An agency review was already under way for the U.S. business. Market share had dipped to a low of 3.3 percent compared to 13.8 percent when BBDO/West began work on the account in 1986. BBDO/West resigned entirely when the review was announced.

As Jobs took control of the review, all eyes turned to Clow and his shop, now named TBWA Chiat/Day, which had initially declined to take part in the review because of commitments to new client Taco Bell Corporation. But it was not long before the announcement came: Jobs, Clow, and Apple were reuniting. Ken Segall was hired as a creative director on the account, which Clow himself oversaw. He had worked on Apple at BBDO/West, and he worked with Jobs on the Next account at Ammirati & Puris, New York City.

Within six weeks the partnership was again producing award-winning work. In September 1997 Apple began running a 60-second spot titled "Manifesto," which featured voice-over by actor Richard Dreyfus and introduced Apple's long-running "Think Different" campaign. The ads, mostly print and outdoor, featured photos of individuals, such as the Dalai Lama, who had dared to "think different." TBWA Chiat/Day, riding on the success of this campaign and the immense popularity of another of its creations, the Taco Bell Chihuahua, was named *Advertising Age*'s "Agency of the Year" in 1997.

Apple's market share began to climb again in 1998, owing largely to the introduction of its iMac line of personal computers. The new machine, initially sold in blue but later produced in a variety of different colors, was backed by a large marketing push from TBWA Chiat/Day featuring images of the computer spinning across the screen. In later commercials actor Jeff Goldblum touted the simplicity of creating home movies and connecting to the Internet with the device.

Under Jobs's direction, Apple continued to create innovative products, releasing ever-faster and more stylish machines—including an eight-inch cube computer and a wide-screen, titanium-cased laptop. The company also began moving toward a stronger focus on software for the home user as computers increasingly became a part of everyday life in the new millennium.

MATTHEW CARMICHAEL

Further Reading

Braunstein, Marc, and Edward H. Levine, *Deep Branding on the Internet: Applying Heat and Pressure Online to Ensure a Lasting Brand,* Roseville, California: Prima Venture, 2000
Sculley, John, and John A. Byrne, *Odyssey: Pepsi to Apple—A Journey of Adventure, Ideas, and the Future,* New York: Harper and Row, 1987

Archetype/Stereotype

In advertising, an archetype is an artificial statistical construction in human form, an individual personification or representation drawn from research and observation of a group. The group can be defined by age, income, gender, race, education, ethnicity, nationality, profession, or any number of other characteristics. The resulting archetype is a distillation of shared characteristics, attitudes, and behaviors that correlate statistically to the given group.

The word *archetype* carries no particular connotation, positive or negative, and is a commonly used term among market researchers. The word *stereotype,* however, which carries substantially the same meaning, has come to have highly prejudicial and negative connotations, implying unfair social bias or bigotry against individuals based on the association and application of group profiles.

Market researchers and advertisers commonly use social stereotypes as a kind of shorthand to express what research has confirmed to be the values and general lifestyle patterns of a target market. A stereotype, therefore, is based on group data collected formally through research, though any given individual within that group may share few or none of its attributes. In other words, stereotypes are valid only for groups and not for individuals within those groups. To use an archetype or stereotype to characterize an individual is often called "profiling" and can be based on racial, ethnic, economic or other benchmark characteristics. Although it is a controversial practice when institutionalized in formal procedures, such "profiles" are a routine element of all first impressions. Archetypes and stereotypes are helpful to major advertisers because most advertisers seek to address mass markets. But their usefulness also depends on how valid and acceptable a given stereotype is in the wider social context. Thus, while scientific research may support a given stereotype with mathematically impartial evidence, it is useful to the advertiser only if it conforms to generally accepted perceptions based on nonscientific observation and judgments accrued informally through social contact.

Because advertisers typically have limited time and space to spell out their message, they cannot present fully formed characters in an ad or commercial the way a writer can in a play, novel, or film. Advertisers must rely on the shorthand of stereotypes, people who instantly define themselves to viewers in familiar ways that conform to social assumptions and relate to the product. For this reason, American advertisers for years resorted to the aproned housewife, the authoritative doctor, the powerful executive, the black maid, the Irish policeman—all stereotypical images, any one of which might properly frame a product without calling attention to itself. By the same token, similar stereotypical representations came to personify people from distant lands: the Frenchman, the Englishman, the Italian, the Japanese, the Chinese, the Mexican, the Russian. Based on limited data, ethnic stereotypes provide a representational way in which people may perceive others they will never likely meet.

From an advertising point of view, the making of an archetype is the result of a continuous interaction between individual viewers and the mass media. Thus, advertisers not only borrow from the vocabulary of the archetype, they also participate in the feedback loop that helps to create and enshrine it. In this process, advertisers have allies even more powerful than themselves. Through much of the 20th century, radio, motion pictures, and television have often been the most influential primary sources and distributors of social stereotypes. Compared to advertising, these communication channels have more time to create full-blown characterizations and more power and technology to drive

In this 1948 ad, the people who "make a good night's sleep" include African-Americans serving as porters, cleaners, and laundresses—stereotypes based on the social realities of American society in the 1940s.

them into wide circulation. Moreover, advertisers are averse to risk. With some exceptions, their primary mission—selling—makes them disinclined to introduce counterintuitive or untested archetypes. Instead, ad agencies typically feed off the most popular and accepted primary social models of movies and television, in particular, as a kind of secondary market, often distilling them into even more compact, abbreviated representations. When *The Godfather* came out in 1972, there was hardly an advertiser that did not immediately "make an offer you can't refuse" to customers using the Mafia imagery and Italian dialect of the hit film. The Frito Bandito of the Dallas, Texas-based Frito-Lay Company was first made widespread and socially acceptable through the Warner Bros. cartoon character Speedy Gonzales, introduced in 1953 and itself a variation on the character played by the Mexican actor Alfonso Bedoya in John Huston's *The Treasure of the Sierra Madre.* But then most archetypes have countless antecedents.

Although stereotypes often linger long into obsolescence in the popular culture, they also evolve in ways that make them surprisingly self-adjusting and correcting. This evolution occurs even more rapidly today, when so many channels of communication can bring so many points of view and images to bear so quickly. For example, in the 1940s African-American life was represented in only one program with weekly access to the nation through

How are <u>your</u> ethics today?

WE Americans are kind of squeamish about shooting down unarmed parachutists . . . abusing the daughters of conquered peoples . . . bombing schools and hospitals . . . executing men, women, and children by the thousands. But some people aren't squeamish about it. In fact, the Japanese are quite good at it, thank you. And how are your ethics today?

As men die without even a fighting chance, it makes you wild . . . crazy to get your hands on the enemy. You have only to reach into your pocket to do it. It's the old fire-fighting bucket-brigade system. You pass your War Bond dollars on to Uncle Sam. He turns them into cold, hard implements of war, and passes them on to men schooled in the art of modern warfare.

How many of your dollars so desperately needed to win this war have gone into things so inconsequential you don't even know where they went?

Ask yourself today . . . and every day . . . Am I doing enough? You'll find that you *can* do more . . . support the invasion . . . *buy more War Bonds!* One single hour's difference in the final Peace can mean saving thousands of lives.

How are *your* ethics today? Anything less than your complete and willing sacrifice is, in plain talk, sabotage.

FACTS ABOUT WAR BONDS

1. War Bonds cost $18.75, for which you receive $25 in 10 years—or $4 for every $3.

2. War Bonds are the world's *safest* investment—guaranteed by the United States Goverment.

3. War Bonds can be made out in 1 name—or in 2, as co-owners.

4. War Bonds *cannot* go down in value. If they are lost, the Government will issue new ones.

5. War Bonds can be redeemed in case of necessity, after 60 days.

6. War Bonds begin to build up interest after 12 months.

BACK THE ATTACK!   BUY BONDS...AND KEEP ON BUYING

A World War II–era ad features a sinister, laughing Japanese pilot.

network radio, *Amos 'n' Andy.* Most other Negro characterizations on radio and film were limited to maids and sleeping-car porters. This dominant archetype of the period represented an occupational reality of black Americans as a group at the time. A 1941 Shell Oil Company ad showing a black child happily enjoying a watermelon was not intentionally offensive, although it would be considered so in the context of later decades. In the 1940s, though, minstrel imagery was still regarded with nostalgic affection by the white target audience for which the Shell ad was intended.

In the 1960s the situation began to change as the Civil Rights movement opened new avenues to blacks, and the social realities on which their stereotypes were based began to shift. These new opportunities were first reflected in the evolving imagery of television programming. When it became safe for Robert Culp and Bill Cosby to function as equals on the TV show *I Spy,* it soon became safe for advertisers to routinely picture white and black people together in their commercials. By the 1990s the dominant black stereotype had evolved from the submissive, superstitious houseboy of Willie Best through the angry Black Power radical of the 1970s to the ultra cool "gangsta" rapper of the urban ghetto. But by the onset of the 21st century, there were a multiplicity of black archetypes with no one of them monopolizing perceptions. Also, the emergence of social diversity and "multiculturalism" created a heightened level of sensitivity to virtually all archetypal representations—of blacks, Hispanics, gays, American Indians, the elderly—causing advertisers to approach social imagery with caution, sometimes giving old stereotypes a satiric or ironic twist but more often working to keep new ones in tune with acceptable social models and free of potentially offensive content.

Not all groups sensitive to their advertising portrayals are minorities. The representation of women in advertising has expanded from the single pervasive model of wife and mother consumed with concern for dirty collars and scuffed floors to a range of representations spanning the professions. Like the evolution of other stereotypes, the images of women have evolved with the changing social and occupational realities. Advertising has picked up on these changes more quickly perhaps than it has on previous social shifts, because the profession itself saw the proliferation of women in top management positions in the last decade or so of the 20th century. With Rochelle ("Shelly") Lazarus as chief executive officer of Ogilvy & Mather and Charlotte Beers as chairman (1999–2001) of the J. Walter Thompson Company, advertising had two powerful women heading two of the most important agencies. More significant, however, was the increasing number of women moving into middle-management levels on the creative and account sides of the advertising business. Despite these changes, however, millions of women continue in their roles as mothers and housewives, buying Procter & Gamble and Lever Bros. brands, and will therefore continue as familiar and appropriate advertising archetypes.

Advertisers continue to rely on stereotypes because of the enduring truism that first impressions count. "No matter how far Americans think they have come in the ways they size up people," wrote *New York Times* columnist Janny Scott in December 2000, "they still judge a book by its cover . . . [and] automatically pigeonhole people by appearance." And as people are pigeonholed, so are brands.

JOHN MCDONOUGH

See also Minorities: Representations in Advertising; Women: Representations in Advertising

Further Reading
Lears, Jackson, *Fables of Abundance: A Cultural History of Advertising in America,* New York: Basic Books, 1994

Archives. *See* Museums and Archives

Argentina

The history of advertising in Argentina dates to the beginnings of journalism in that country and the appearance of advertisements in the early issues of the first Argentinean newspaper, *La Gaceta.* In 1898 an Austrian, Juan Ravenscroft, formed the first ad agency after negotiating a contract with English railroad companies and began selling advertising space in railroad stations and trains.

In 1929 J. Walter Thompson established the first U.S. advertising agency in Argentina, thus inaugurating a new era in Argentinean advertising history. The arrival of other foreign agencies, including Lintas and McCann-Erickson, further influenced the developing industry. The most influential of the country's talents, such as Manuel Marcelino Mortola and Ricardo Pueyrredon, were closely associated with some of these agencies.

LA JUNTA PROVISIONAL GUBERNATIVA

DE LA CAPITAL DEL RIO DE LA PLATA

A LOS HABITANTES DE ELLA,

Y DE LAS PROVINCIAS DE SU SUPERIOR MANDO.

PROCLAMA.

Teneis ya establecida la Autoridad que remueve la incertidumbre de las opiniones, y calma todos los recelos. Las aclamaciones generales manifiestan vuestra decidida voluntad; y sola ella ha podido resolver nuestra timidez á encargarnos del grave empeño á que nos sujeta el honor de la eleccion. Fixad pues vuestra confianza, y aseguraos de nuestras intenciones. Un deseo eficaz, un zelo activo, y una contraccion viva y asidua á proveer por todos los medios posibles la conservacion de nuestra Religion Santa, la observancia de las Leyes que nos rigen, la comun prosperidad, y el sosten de estas Posesiones en la mas constante fidelidad y adhesion á nuestro muy amado Rey y Señor Don Fernando VII y sus legitimos sucesores en la corona de España: ¿No son estos vuestros sentimientos? Esos mismo son los grandes objetos de nuestros conatos. Reposad en nuestro desvelo y fatigas; dexad á nuestro cuidado todo lo que en la causa pública dependa de nuestras facultades y arbitrios; y entregaos á la mas estrecha union y conformidad reciproca en la tierna efusion de estos afectos. Llevad á las Provincias todas de nuestra Dependencia, y aun mas allá, si puede ser, hasta los últimos terminos de la tierra, la persuasion del exemplo de vuestra cordialidad, y del verdadero interes con que todos debemos cooperar á la consolidacion de esta importante obra. Ella afianzará de un modo estable la tranquilidad y bien general á que aspiramos.= Real Fortaleza de Buenos-Ayres á 26 de Mayo de 1810. — *Cornelio de Saavedra.*— *Dr. Juan José Castelli.* — *Manuel Belgrano.*— *Miguel de Azcuenaga.*— *Dr. Manuel Alverti.*— *Domingo Mateú.*— *Juan Larrea.*— *Dr. Juan José Passo, Secretario.*— *Dr. Mariano Moreno, Secretario.*

CON SUPERIOR PERMISO:

Buenos-Ayres: en la Real Imprenta de Niños Expósitos.

A public notice from the provisional government of Rio de la Plata, ca. 1810, reassures the public that the new leaders will seek to restore calm through "the conservation of our Holy Religion and the observation of the laws that guide us."
Courtesy of the Rare Book, Manuscript, and Special Collections Library, Duke University.

The next phase in the evolution of the industry was marked by the appearance of national agencies such as Berg, Ricardo De Luca, Pueyrredon, Agens, Yuste, Lino Palacio, Nexo, Vincit, Gowland, Castignani y Burd, Cicero, and Solanas y Ortiz Scopesi. These national agencies provided excellent training for many influential ad executives in Argentina, including Pablo Gowland and David Ratto, who developed their talents at Pueyrredon and greatly influenced Argentinean advertising in the 1960s. Other important advertising masters of this time include Osvaldo Castagna, Carlos Mendez Mosquera, Juan Carlos Colonnese, and Ricardo De Luca, who with his colleagues Juan Carlos Martin, Julio Picco, and Hugo Casares perfected aesthetics in advertising. Casares, who first worked at De Luca and later founded his own agency, Casares Grey, was instrumental in modernizing Argentinean advertising practices. Finally, in the 1990s international companies such as Sony, Kodak, Coca-Cola, Philips, IBM, Xerox, General Electric, Toshiba, Microsoft, and Hewlett-Packard arrived in Argentina. Advertising in this era was also influenced by new developments in photography, radio, television, and, eventually, computers.

Industry Trends

In the early stages of advertising, much attention was given to the development of slogans, which, coupled with brand names, were the most important elements contributing to a product's success. Slogans were used as early as the 1930s when Untisal developed a slogan for its foot powder that read "Donde lo pongan, calma" ("Wherever you put it, it soothes"). Rhymes also became popular and were widely used. In 1942 Lamota, a clothing store, created the slogan "Casa Lamota, donde se viste Carlota" ("Lamota, where we dress Carlota"). Some other popular slogans included: "A usted lo beneficia . . ." ("You are our beneficiary . . ."), created by Banco Galicia in the 1950s and still popular today in ads promoting banks; "Cada día una copita" ("Every day a little zip"), developed by Jockey Club in 1956; and "Junto a las mejores cosas de la vida" ("Accompanying the best things in life"), created by Otard Dupuy in 1968. Over time, however, slogans became less important than images that conveyed messages by means of pictures, colors, and movement.

The use of celebrities has been popular in Argentinean advertising for many years. In 1900 Avelino Cabezas featured President Julio A. Roca and his cabinet as the first celebrities to promote clothing in an advertising campaign. In 1915 the image of Buitoni olive oil was enhanced by using Italian, Greek, Russian, and English monarchs in the ads. Later, pilots (Carlos Zatuszek in 1934 and Raul Riganti in 1945), soccer players (Rene Pontoni in 1949 and Angel Labruna and Jose M. Moreno in 1950), and movie stars (Olinda Bozan in 1931, Luisa Vehil in 1939, and Amanda Ledesma in 1940) appeared in advertising campaigns. Lever Brothers developed one of the most effective campaigns for Lux soap featuring celebrities such as Joan Crawford in 1930, Uruguayan actress Fanny Navarro in 1940, and Ava Gardner in 1951.

In the 1990s Argentinean advertising experienced a renaissance in creativity. According to the Asociación Argentina de Agencias de Publicidad (AAAP; Argentine Association of Advertising Agencies), total advertising expenditures in 1998 reached U.S.$3.37 billion, which represented a 2.9 percent increase over 1997. Nonetheless, annual spending for advertising per capita in Argentina remained low ($96 per capita) compared to that in the United States ($380 per capita).

Consumer Culture

Advertising in Argentina has had a tremendous impact on consumer culture. Even small towns have become popular targets for advertisements. Ads for beverages have been painted over the length of apartment buildings and on billboards, dominating the landscape. In northwestern Argentina, where water is scarce and rain falls only during the summer months, soft drinks have taken on the symbolic power once attributed to water. Today, the consumption of water is surpassed by the consumption of soft drinks such as Coke and Sprite.

Coca-Cola has been highly successful in Argentina. The company has used powerful advertising such as the "El sabor de ver-

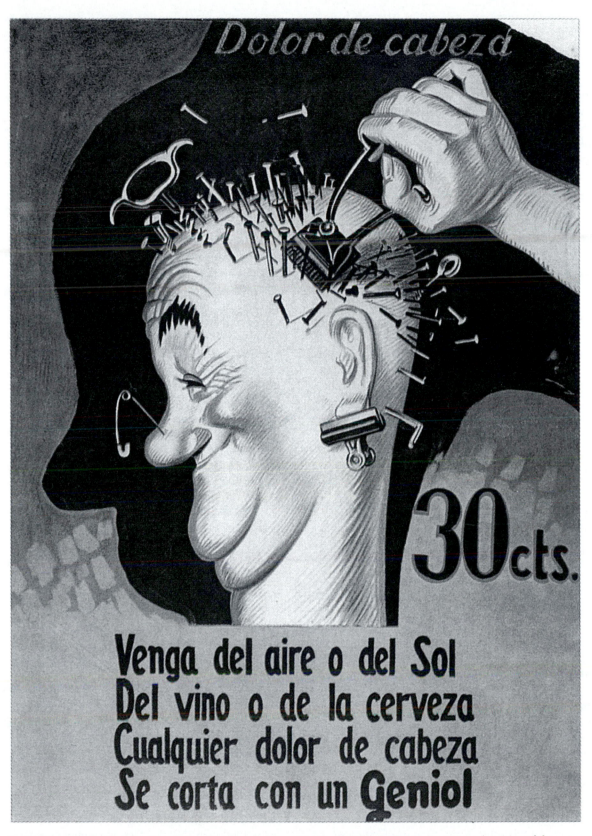

In the 1930s ads for Geniol, a brand of aspirin, featured one of the best-known slogans in Argentine advertising of the period. The quatrain reads, "Whether by wind or sun, by wine or beer, whatever kind of headache, a Geniol will take it away."
Courtesy of GlaxoSmithKline Argentina.

dad" ("Real Taste") campaign, which has attracted many customers. Even though its main competitor, Torasso, uses the slogan "El sabor argentino" ("Argentinean taste") as its theme, Argentineans tend to associate their country with Coca-Cola rather than with any other beverage. In some remote areas where people lack running water, Coca-Cola is distributed by mule.

Other companies that advertise heavily in Argentina include Unilever (U.S.$150.9 million in 1997), Presidencia de la Nación ($106.2 million in 1997), Procter & Gamble ($59.3 million in 1997), Editorial Agea ($51.0 million in 1997), Editorial Perfil ($47.1 million in 1997), Editorial Atlantida ($46.5 million in 1997), Cervecería Quilmes (a local brewery; $45.6 million in 1997), and Coca-Cola ($45.2 million in 1997).

These and other foreign companies have created a global consumer culture with local variations. A logo for a new Hipermercado Libertad, a huge "hypermarket" on the outskirts of the city of Tucumán, shows a stylized image of the Statue of Liberty. The logo probably symbolizes a new era of consumerism in Argentina in which the consumer is "free" to choose from a variety of domestic and foreign goods. Many products in Argentina are advertised with names and slogans in English because American goods are trendsetting and prestigious. One may find a brand of soft drink called Spill or a shoe and clothing store in downtown Tucumán called El Sportsman Drugstore. Some stores carry names that are a blend of Spanish and English words, an attempt to combine the local culture with an American image. Examples of such linguistic hybrids include names that end in *landia,* such as Radiolandia or Todolandia. The latter can be translated as "the place where you can do everything."

The Media

The most important advertising medium in Argentina has been television, which accounts for the highest advertising expenditures, followed by print and radio. In 1998, however, according to the AAAP, expenditures in television advertising dropped by 1.4 percent (total, U.S.$1.34 billion), whereas expenditures in print media increased by 10.6 percent (total, $1.2 billion). Prices for television advertising in Argentina are negotiable and vary from $540 per second to $2,400 for a 10- to 12-second spot aired at the beginning or the end of a program. Due to fierce competition among broadcasters, prices for television advertising in Buenos Aires are lower than in some provincial stations that have a local monopoly. In 1996 television advertising expenditures totaled $1.6 billion, with $1.5 billion in broadcast advertising and about $98 million in cable network advertising. In 1998 cable advertising represented 6 percent of total television ad spending.

Newspapers are a popular advertising medium, as they reach a wide audience. Approximately 60 percent of all copies of daily newspapers are distributed in Buenos Aires and about 40 percent in the provinces. In the mid-1990s there were about 160 daily newspapers in circulation; *Clarín, Cronista Comercial, La Nación, La Prensa, La Razón,* and *Ambito Financiero* were the most popular papers. Expenditures in newspaper advertising were U.S.$572 million in 1996. Magazines are a less sought-

after medium, as magazine ads are comparatively expensive. The cost per page in the largest-circulation publication may be as high as $17,200. In the second-tier magazines, costs may range from $8,000 to $10,000 per page. In terms of circulation, the leading magazines include *Viva, Nueva, Magazine Semanal,* and *Nuestra.* In 1996 expenditures in magazine advertising were $392 million.

Advertising in other media such as radio and movie theaters is less popular. However, radio advertising in Argentina is an effective way to reach groups who do not own televisions: there is approximately one radio for every 1.5 Argentineans. During the late 1990s consumers tended to switch from AM to FM stations. Although it is less expensive than television advertising, radio advertising is nonetheless often rather costly. In 1996 radio advertising expenditures totaled U.S.$190 million.

Other forms of advertising in Argentina include direct marketing and outdoor advertising. In the 1990s direct marketing was still in its early stages but seemed to be an increasingly attractive channel. With the technological advances in fiber optics, telemarketing and Internet marketing were growing in popularity. The major impediments to direct marketing in Argentina are payment methods and delivery systems. But these are continually improving, particularly with the growing penetration of credit cards (7 million credit card holders in 1998) and the privatization of postal services.

Billboard advertising has been rediscovered in Argentina with the help of costly technology introduced in 1998. An award-winning Argentinean advertising agency, Agulla & Baccetti, created a revolutionary billboard for Renault that pictured a man driving a Renault convertible. The man's head contained holes with turbines that made his hair move and created the impression that the hair was waving in the wind. Ramiro Agulla, the president and creative director of the agency, has said that billboard companies are now prepared to utilize new technologies and are open to receiving innovative creative proposals. Agulla & Baccetti's Renault billboard set new technological standards in Argentina. In the late 1990s Argentinean billboard advertising was employing the latest developments—front-lighting, back-lighting, the use of fabric, and moving parts.

Some companies—for example, Kellogg, the U.S. cereal producer—have crossed the border of good taste and have had to apologize to the Argentinean public for a billboard advertisement. Kellogg created an ad featured a naked boy walking toward a school bus with his back to the camera. The ad said: "If you don't send your child to school like this, why would you send him without breakfast?" The company apologized for violating advertising norms in Argentina in its efforts to creatively communicate the importance of a nutritious breakfast.

Self-adhesive ads on buses are being used with increasing frequency. Advertising agencies such as Stick! have utilized this type of promotion to advertise the Siembra Pension Fund and the Swiss food giant Nestlé. The two companies paid U.S.$4,000 a month to have 320 square feet of advertising affixed to buses that travel the most popular routes in Buenos Aires. According to Guillermo Salmeron, the president of Stick!, people like this type of advertising, and these ads directly influence consumers. In 1997 expenditures for billboards, buses, and outdoor structures such as lighted bus stops reached 8 percent of total advertising in Argentina, or $300 million.

Some citizens' groups and city officials are concerned with the spread of advertising in Argentina. In May 1998, after Gregorio Dalbon, president of Family Members of Victims of Traffic Accidents, successfully sued the city of Buenos Aires, Argentina's Supreme Court ruled that 380 billboards would have to be removed from the highway that connects the city to its most exclusive suburbs. Dalbon argued that ads featuring dinosaurs and three-dimensional clay figures were distracting drivers' attention and making the highway one of the most dangerous roads in Argentina. Advertising must now be placed at least 160 feet from a highway. City officials have also begun targeting illegal outdoor advertising. According to Ricardo Ostuni, general subsecretary of the city, Buenos Aires has been overwhelmed with this type of advertising. Moreover, outdoor advertising often does not adhere to the laws and creates "visual pollution" in the city.

Finally, there has been a growing trend toward the consolidation of media by large conglomerates in Argentina, which, some argue, will help provide multimedia advertising packages and lower rates. However, others contend that consolidation raises the potential threat of price fixing. In 1997 a merger was negotiated among U.S. Citibank, Telefónica Internacional SA (the international arm of Telefónica de Espana), and the U.S. cable programmer Telecommunications International (TCI). Together with Grupo Clarín and Grupo Uno these represented the major media giants at the end of the 1990s.

The Agency Landscape

A number of local agencies offer advertising services and provide market research information. These agencies are much more sophisticated than their counterparts in some other Latin American countries. The largest agency was created in October 1999 when Euro RSCG Worldwide acquired Lautrec, a major agency founded in 1974 by Gianni Gasparini and Raul Salles. Lautrec had long been successful because of its creativity and the quality of its services and has received 500 prestigious awards, including several Lions at the Cannes International Advertising Festival and medals at the Clio Awards and Foyer Internationale d'Art Photographique. In 1998 the agency's billings were U.S.$74 million, and its major clients included Budweiser and Banco Galicia. Euro RSCG is an international agency that began operations in Argentina in 1995 under the direction of Eduardo Plana. In 1999 it was one of the largest agency networks in the world, headquartered in New York City. Both Euro RSCG and Lautrec believed that by merging they would be able to share their competitive advantages and experience, Lautrec in advertising and Euro RSCG in marketing. The client portfolio of the merged entity included companies such as Peugeot, Citroën, Budweiser, Philips, Telefónica, Consolidar, Banco Galicia, and the dairy products marketer La Serenisima.

Lautrec NAZCA S&S's 1996 campaign for Sony, with its stark photography and memorable imagery, won numerous international awards.
Courtesy of Sony Electronics Inc.

In terms of creativity, the most honored agency at the end of the 20th century was Agulla & Baccetti, a Buenos Aires agency founded by Agulla and Carlos Baccetti in 1994. The agency's clients include Renault Argentina SA and Cervecería Quilmes SA. According to Baccetti, vice president and creative director, the agency's success is the result of taking risks and pushing the limits of conventional advertising while respecting consumers' suspicions about advertising. The agency believes that advertisements must also entertain and to that end creates commercials with a fast punch and bizarre humor that are easily remembered by the audience. In ads designed for Telecom SA, Agulla & Baccetti avoided a conventional message—guarantees of more reliable service and lower fees, which have little credibility among Argentinean consumers—and instead presented mischievous adolescents making prank phone calls. The campaign was a great success as it provided a human face for this previously anonymous utility company. In 1998 the agency won 156 awards, including a gold Lion for creativity at Cannes. Sales were expected to exceed U.S.$60 million in 1999, a growth of more than 40 percent over the previous year.

Among other important local and foreign advertising agencies in Argentina in the 1990s were ADV Vazquez SA de Publicidad, J. Walter Thompson, Young & Rubicam Argentina, Pragma FCB Publicidad, McCann-Erickson SA de Publicidad, Ratto/BBDO, Casares Grey, Lautrec NAZCA S&S, Leo Burnett Company, and Ogilvy and Mather. ADV Vazquez SA de Publicidad began operations in Argentina in 1987. Its sales grew steadily, reaching $20.1 million in 1992, $98.6 million in 1994, and $107.1 million in 1996. Major accounts include Air France, BASF, John Deere, Lloyds Bank, and Telecom SA. Thompson's sales have been growing steadily over time increasing from $48.8 million in 1992 to $96.8 million in 1996. The agency serves Kodak, Ford, Rolex, Unilever, Nestlé, Motorola, and Northern Telecom, among other companies. Both ADV Vazquez and Thompson develop ad campaigns mainly for television, newspapers, and magazines, with less emphasis on radio and other advertising channels. These and other leading advertising agencies are members of the AAAP.

ELZBIETA LEPKOWSKA-WHITE

Further Reading

Borrini, Alberto, *El siglo de la publicidad, 1898–1998,* Buenos Aires: Editorial Atlantida S.A., 1998

Corner, John, Philip Schlesinger, and Roger Silverstone, editors, *International Media Research: A Critical Survey,* London and New York: Routledge, 1997

Goodman, Joshua, "Entertaining the Argentines," *Multichannel News International Supplement* 5, no. 10 (1999)

Howes, David, editor, *Cross-Cultural Consumption: Global Markets, Local Realities,* London and New York: Routledge, 1996

Katz, Ian, and Elisabeth Malkin, "Battle for the Latin American Net," *Business Week* (1 November 1999)

Mandel-Campbell, Andrea, "Argentina's Massive Media Consolidation," *Advertising Age International Supplement* (October 1998)

Stewart, Beth, "Going Direct in Latin America," *Target Marketing* 21, no. 8 (1998)

Torreano, Rick, "Creativity in South America," *Communication Arts* 38, no. 2 (1996)

Arledge, Roone 1931–

U.S. Television Network Executive

Roone Arledge made his mark on broadcasting by bringing innovation and creativity to television news and sports. In the 1950s he forever changed the face of TV sports, transforming routine game broadcasts into "events" by using then-new technology to create the instant replay, slow motion, and multiple camera angles. Following his success in sports, he turned his showmanship skills to shaping the ABC News operation by spending money, pushing the industry envelope, and transforming sports commentators into big-name news stars.

Arledge was born in Forest Hills, New York, on 8 July 1931. He received a B.A. from Columbia College in 1952 and later was awarded honorary degrees from Boston University and Wake Forest University. As president of ABC Sports from 1968 to 1986, he matched bigger-than-life sports personalities such as Muhammad Ali with colorful commentators such as Howard Cosell to create a heightened sense of drama and confrontation. As executive producer of most major sports broadcasts for ABC, Arledge devised new ways of packaging live sporting events, interviews, commentary, and background reports in what soon became sports television staples such as *Wide World of Sports* (1960) and *Monday Night Football* (1970).

Arledge is credited with transforming televised sports, sports marketing, television sports economics, and competitive events such as the Olympic Games. He single-handedly raised the price broadcast networks would pay for on-air sports talent and events by bidding up their prices. One of his biggest gambles came in 1969 when ABC agreed to pay owners of the 26 National Football League (NFL) teams $25.5 million to televise Monday night games in prime time during the 1970, 1971, and 1972 seasons—after both CBS and NBC rejected a similar proposition. *Monday Night Football* became a launchpad, for both ABC and the NFL, for new talent and techniques.

Corporate executives often were frustrated when trying to rein in Arledge's free-spending ways and power, but his strong ties to the on-air personalities kept him secure, and he helped create a prestigious new image for advertisers willing to pay more for larger numbers of targeted viewers. He created a video haven for automobile manufacturers, beer companies, and high-tech firms seeking an otherwise-hard-to-find affluent and younger male audience. At the same time, he transformed ABC's also-ran news operations into the most watched and most admired of the three major broadcast networks, while making TV news a major, premium-priced venue for advertisers.

In what was considered by some a heretical move at the time, Arledge brought all his showman's sensibilities to the post of president of ABC News in 1977. He immediately set out to reshape

Roone Arledge.
Courtesy of Roone Arledge. © 1997 ABC, Inc. Photography: Enrico Ferorelli.

what had been the predictable, routine world of television news by developing the late-night, half-hour TV program *Nightline* out of the Iranian hostage crisis. Airing every weeknight, the program chronicled the daily events of the hostage crisis as well as other major news stories with a mix of fact and the medium's natural flair for drama. With a writing and commentary style that echoed that of TV news pioneers such as CBS's Edward R. Murrow, Eric Sevareid, Robert Trout, and Walter Cronkite, the newscast took an obscure TV newsman, Ted Koppel, and transformed him into a nighttime fixture in many U.S. homes.

In fact, Arledge is widely credited with reinventing ABC's news division with the creation of other program staples, such as *World News Tonight*, *This Week With David Brinkley*, *20/20*, *Prime Time Live*, and *Good Morning America*. He made stars out of on-camera newspeople, including Sam Donaldson, Diane Sawyer, Barbara Walters, Cokie Roberts, and Peter Jennings. Aloof but charming, Arledge enjoyed unwavering support from on-air talent who trusted his instincts as a producer and recruiter.

Arledge used snazzy graphics and packaged features on news programs, such as "Person of the Week," to attract non-news viewers. Among his more controversial moves was the use of hid-den cameras in a *Prime Time Live* investigation of Food Lion supermarkets, which led to an embarrassing and costly legal set-back for ABC News. He even had ABC's *World News Tonight* tracking major news stories such as the O.J. Simpson trial daily.

In 1986 Arledge was named group president of ABC News and Sports, making him the first TV executive ever to oversee both sports and news for a major broadcast network. (He had been responsible for day-to-day operations of both since 1977.) In that capacity, he relinquished daily operational control of sports, but remained ABC News president until long-time colleague and corporate attorney David Westin replaced him in 1997. By that time the dominant ratings position of ABC News was under assault, putting millions of television advertising dollars and Arledge's reputation on the line.

The move coincided with the acquisition by Capital Cities of ABC and with a move to make ABC Sports more fiscally prudent. Although it was one of ABC's most profitable operations, ABC Sports was under pressure to cut costs. Accounting for about $430 million, or 15 percent of ABC's overall annual broadcast revenue, ABC Sports had posted a loss in 1985 for the first time in recent memory. Arledge had just signed a new five-year, $2.1 billion contract for NFL broadcasts that was nearly triple that of the previous licensing deal, while maintaining costly licensing deals for Major League Baseball and the Olympic Games.

In the 1990s Arledge lost more battles than he won. He was unable to convince ABC's new owner, the Walt Disney Company, which acquired Capital Cities/ABC in 1995, to launch a 24-hour cable news effort. Nevertheless, Michael Eisner, chairman and chief executive officer of Disney, who worked with Arledge at ABC in the 1970s, is said to consider him a creative icon of the industry—"a legend."

In March 1997 ABC President Bob Iger named Arledge, age 66, chairman of ABC News, an emeritus role, and a senior vice president of ABC, Inc. He also began work on his life story in a book deal with HarperCollins, to be coauthored by *New York Times* sports columnist Robert Sam Anson.

DIANE MERMIGAS

Biography

Born in Forest Hills, New York, 8 July 1931; graduated with a B.A. from Columbia College, New York City, 1952; joined ABC as producer of *Wide World of Sports*, 1960; named vice president in charge of sports, 1964; promoted to president of ABC Sports, 1968; added position of president, ABC News, 1977; as group president of ABC News and Sports, became first TV executive ever to oversee both sports and news for a major broadcast network, 1986; named chairman of ABC News, an emeritus role, and a senior vice president of ABC, Inc., 1997.

Further Reading

Barnes, Peter, "Capital Cities/ABC's Arledge Gives Up Day-to-Day Sports Role for Group Post," *Wall Street Journal* (28 January 1986)

Burrows, Mike, "From Experiment to Monument: Monday Night Football Had Humble Beginnings," *Denver Post* (3 September 2000)

Gunther, Marc, *The House That Roone Built: The Inside Story of ABC News,* Boston: Little Brown, 1994

Gunther, Marc, "Is This Roone's Last Hurrah?" *Fortune 217* (February 1997)

Lafayette, John, "Westin Takes the Helm at ABC News Division," *Electronic Media* (1 June 1998)

Pope, Kyle, "Television: Roone Arledge Gives Up the Reins at ABC News," *Wall Street Journal* (7 March 1997)

"Roone Arledge on ABC's Wide World of News," *Broadcasting and Cable* (10 October 1994)

Zoglin, Richard, "ABC Ya, Roone," *Time* (17 March 1997)

Armando Testa. *See under* Testa

Asia, Southeast

In the last 15–20 years of the 20th century Asia experienced one of the most dynamic rates of economic growth of any part of the world. In the mid-1990s the World Bank estimated that by the end of the century this region would represent more than 50 percent of global gross national product growth.

The rapid economic development in Asia has had a tremendous impact on the advertising industry in that region. Billions of dollars have been spent on mass media advertising by multinational corporations striving to attract consumers newly arrived in the middle class. At the same time, advertising has affected the economic development of these countries. In the late 20th century the booming economy in Southeast Asia attracted many international advertising agencies to the region. For example, the Japanese agency Dentsu and the U.S.-based Young & Rubicam redefined their missions for their joint venture, Dentsu Young & Rubicam. Dai Ichi Kikaku, another Japanese agency, also targeted this region.

The economy of Southeast Asia has been fueled by several circumstances: the confluence of substantial human and natural resources; the region's fortuitous geographical location; and the enactment of government policies favoring economic growth. Traditional Asian values emphasizing the importance of frugality and hard work have also been instrumental in spurring economic growth.

Many countries in Southeast Asia, including Indonesia, Malaysia, the Philippines, Thailand, Singapore, and Brunei, are members of the Association of Southeast Asian Nations (ASEAN). By 2003 these six members plan to establish a common market. The Asia-Pacific Economic Council (APEC) intends to dismantle all trade barriers on goods manufactured in this region by the year 2020.

Colonial rule set the stage for the advertising industry in this region. In the Philippines, the development of the advertising industry was dominated by Americans from the 1890s until the 1940s. Under colonialism, the major advertisers and the most prominent advertising agencies in the Philippines belonged to the colonial powers. The first agency in the Philippines, Philippine Publicity Service, Inc., was established in 1921 and operated by an American, H. Edmund Bullis. All other operators of major advertising agencies at the time, including F. Theo Rogers, M.W. Jenkins, and Horace B. Pond, were also Americans.

Even in Thailand, which was never a colony, foreign powers affected the development of advertising. Advertising began in Thailand in 1845 when an American missionary, Dan Beach Bradley, published the first newspaper, *The Bangkok Recorder.* The newspaper carried the first advertisement in Thailand. The first modern advertising agency in Thailand was established in the early 1950s by an American, and in the early years of advertising in Thailand, very few native Thais were active in the executive or creative ranks of the industry, which were filled with U.S., European, and Japanese citizens.

As foreign products have dominated the advertising industry in Southeast Asia, there has been a trend toward using foreign (particularly American) modes of advertising. In Thailand—where some of the most prominently advertised brand names include Vidal Sasson, Toyota, Johnnie Walker, Nissan, and Fuji—advertisers commonly invoke the status of foreign products and cultures, insert foreign words and phrases into ads, and use endorsements by foreign celebrities to appeal to Thai consumers. Foreign advertisers in Southeast Asia also seek to influence consumers by sponsoring programs on the mass media. For example, Procter & Gamble Philippines introduced radio soap operas during the 1950s.

Although multinational corporations have dominated advertising in much of the region, those advertisers have often faced cultural challenges distinctive to Southeast Asia. Some Southeast

ขอโทษที่ที่ไม่ได้เปิดดี เพราะอยากให้ไปอยู่เฉย... ที่เซ็นทรัล เวิลด์เทรด, เดอะมอลล์ รามคำแหง, โรบินสัน รัชดาฯ, โอคิว มาบุญครอง

OP ให้อิสระในทุกรูปแบบ เพราะ OP คือ OCEAN PACIFIC.

Although this 1990 Ocean Pacific ad from Thailand is reminiscent of Western beachwear ad imagery, it uses a Thai play on words referring to a dish that bakes in the sun all day.

Asian nations have been receptive to advertising campaigns that have succeeded previously in other markets. Thailand has been characterized as culturally open and inclined to avoid confrontation, and many multinational corporations have found success in the Thai market simply by translating advertisements created elsewhere into Thai.

In the Philippines, centuries of Spanish and U.S. colonial rule deeply affected the political, cultural, and social structures of the country. Today, most Filipinos find it important to show concern and support for the well-being of the group as a whole, and they value conflict avoidance. These aspects of Filipino culture have deterred the practice of comparative advertising: Filipinos consider it offensive to name competitors or make comparisons in advertisements. Colonialism in the Philippines also taught that foreign products were superior to local ones, and a preference for imported goods remains prevalent among Filipinos today. Foreign brands and products are very popular, and Caucasian models and U.S. settings are often used in advertising.

Islamic governments in Southeast Asia have exercised considerable control over the content of advertisements in order to avoid the negative effects of advertising on existing religious, cultural, and political traditions. The Malaysian government set up regulations concerning the content of advertisements. Designed to safeguard Malaysian consumers against the danger of advertisements spreading foreign (particularly Western) cultures and values, the Advertising Code prohibits the "adaptation or projection of foreign culture that is not acceptable to a cross section of the major communities of Malaysian society either in the form of words, slogans, clothing, activity or behavior." The code promotes cultural sensitivity in advertisements aired or printed in Malaysia, and it is heavily influenced by the government's intention to promote Islamic principles and values. Similarly, the government of Indonesia formulated the Code of Ethics and Practices of Advertising in 1981 to create "correct, healthy and responsible" advertising.

In Southeast Asia the indigenous advertising industry developed much later than that set up by the region's colonial rulers. In many cases local advertising agencies were formed in reaction to the dominance of foreign-run agencies. In 1972 the Indonesian government helped local advertising agencies set up the Persatuan

Perusahaan Periklanan Indonesia, or the Indonesia Association of Advertising Agencies.

Despite the growth of indigenous advertising industries, foreign agencies remain very powerful in Southeast Asia. Most of the top ten agencies in the Philippines in the 1990s, for example, belonged to mega-agencies from abroad, including McCann-Erickson, J. Walter Thompson, Lintas, DDB Needham, Leo Burnett, and D'Arcy Masius Benton & Bowles. In Thailand, local agencies grew rapidly during the "Thai Era" (from 1977 to 1987) and the "Growth Era" (from 1988 to 1993), but the most prominent advertising agencies in that nation still belonged to foreign owners. In 1993 Lintas was the largest agency in Thailand, billing 3,148 million baht (U.S. $12,592 million), while Ogilvy & Mather ranked as the second largest firm. In Indonesia the top ten advertising agencies in 1994 included Lintas Indonesia and agencies affiliated with J. Walter Thompson, Dentsu, Young & Rubicam, Grey Advertising, Saatchi & Saatchi, and other foreign companies.

Advertising has fueled economic growth in Southeast Asia, and it has reduced the gap between the haves and the have-nots in that region. Such rapid development can also have detrimental effects on local cultures, however, and on the political independence of local communities.

KENNETH C.C. YANG

Further Reading

Anderson, Michael H., *Madison Avenue in Asia: Politics and Transnational Advertising,* Rutherford, New Jersey: Fairleigh Dickinson University Press, and London: Associated University Presses, 1984

"Asia, APEC, and the Pacific Community: A New World Dawns," *Business America* 115, no. 11 (November 1994)

Engardio, Pete, and Joyce Barnathan, "Asia: Breaking Down the Barriers," *Business Week* (14 November 1994)

Frith, Katherine T., editor, *Advertising in Asia: Communication, Culture, and Consumption,* Ames: Iowa State University Press, 1996

Gong, Gerrit W., and Keith W. Eirinberg, "Southeast Asia: Booming, but Not Everywhere," *Across the Board* 32 (January 1995)

Kilburn, David, "Japanese Giants See Potential in Southeast Asia," *Adweek* (Eastern edition) (28 November 1994)

Association of National Advertisers, Inc.

The Association of National Advertisers, Inc. (ANA), is the U.S. advertising industry's oldest trade association. It was founded in 1910 by 45 companies that banded together to bring cohesion to the then-nascent national and regional advertising industries.

The organization was originally known as the Association of National Advertising Managers. Its charter was established on 24 June 1910 at a meeting at the Hotel Pontchartrain in Detroit, Michigan. Among the founding corporate members were the Burroughs Adding Machine Company, N.K. Fairbank Company, Glidden Varnish Company, Macey Company, Sherwin Williams Company, National Lead Company, and Frederick Stearns & Company.

At the time of this first meeting, which was led by E. St. Elmo Lewis of Burroughs and O.C. Harn of National Lead, there were no standards or guidance for advertisers that wanted to reach a larger number of potential customers on a regional or national basis. The founding members had ambitious goals: they sought to foster cooperation between manufacturers and dealers; to substantiate magazine circulation claims; and to enhance advertiser-agency relationships. They also planned to establish national standards for measuring advertising results.

In a presentation titled "A Bridge From Problem to Solution," delivered to the ANA membership on 7 November 1982, Peter W. Allport, then president of the organization, gave this account of the founding:

> Once upon a time, back in the first decade of the century, the promising and still new concept of national advertising was in deep trouble. The trouble was that the pioneers, the 40 or so companies that were the first members of the ANA, could not know what they bought for their advertising dollars. Circulation figures were simply whatever a publisher wished or dared to claim, and rate cards were unreliable.
>
> It was then that the ANA was born. Your predecessors recognized that if national advertising was to work, it would be up to them, the buyers of advertising space and services, to build an orderly, honest advertising industry, tailored to the needs of advertisers, based on media they could trust. Their objective in forming ANA was to have an organization which would devote itself exclusively to their interests, and would serve as their trumpet to speak with a single voice.

According to the bylaws of the ANA, the organization's mission is to safeguard the essential values of advertising as a positive economic force; to enhance the science of advertising and marketing for the benefit of both industry and consumers; to improve efficiency in the marketing of goods and services through the use of responsible advertising; and to promote the common interests and welfare of its members as advertisers.

Within four years of its first meeting, the Association of National Advertising Managers had formed the Audit Bureau of Circulations to confirm the circulation figures of publications and monitor media rates. It was during this time that the organization formally changed its name to the Association of National Advertisers to better reflect its intentions.

The ANA played a key role in the development of the Crossley rating system, launched in 1930 as a joint effort between the ANA and the American Association of Advertising Agencies (AAAA, also often referred to as the "Four A's"), the major organization representing U.S. advertising agencies. The Crossley system was designed to establish standards for commercials airing on radio networks so that advertisers would have a rough measure of how many listeners they reached. The need for additional industry standards gave rise to the Traffic Audit Bureau, formed by the ANA and other industry groups in 1934, and the Advertising Research Foundation (ARF), which was spun off from an ANA committee in 1936.

In 1942 the ANA helped to establish the War Advertising Council to support the sale of war bonds. After World War II, the renamed Advertising Council began to address other public service issues—such as support for the Red Cross and antipollution measures—through pro bono advertising, with time and space donated by participating media companies.

In 1963 the ANA and AAAA established the Joint Policy Committee (JPC) for Broadcast Talent Union Relations, a committee that negotiates contracts with the Screen Actors Guild (SAG), the American Federation of Television and Radio Artists (AFTRA), and the American Federation of Musicians. In 2000 the JPC successfully negotiated a new contract with SAG and AFTRA after those unions staged a six-month strike demanding increased compensation for television and radio commercials. The new contract, agreed to by both sides in October 2000, provided on-air talent with a 7 percent to 9 percent raise over a three-year period.

The ANA plays an important role in industry self-regulation. In 1971 the ANA, the Four A's, and the American Advertising Federation, with funding from the Council of Better Business Bureaus (BBB), launched the National Advertising Review Board (NARB) to act as the appeals level of the National Advertising Division of the BBB. Complaints about the honesty of a particular ad go to the division, complaints regarding taste or social responsibility are heard by the NARB.

The ANA's current mission is to help its member companies build their businesses by building their brands. Representing more than 300 major companies (with 8,000 brands) that collectively spend more than $100 billion in marketing communications and advertising, the group's members market products and services to consumers and businesses. The ANA provides marketing and advertising industry leadership in traditional and Internet marketing, legislative lobbying, information resources, professional development, and industry-wide networking.

Membership dues are linked to a company's advertising expenditures. For most companies, ANA dues are in the range of one-tenth of 1 percent of expenditures for advertising and related services. ANA dues are tax deductible, with the exception of a percentage that is earmarked for lobbying expenses.

The organization maintains two offices, one in New York City and the other in Washington, D.C. The Washington office serves primarily as the organization's legal and regulatory "listening post," coordinating lobbying efforts on issues of concern to the advertising industry and serving as the industry's voice before federal, state, and local governments. This office lobbies against what it perceives to be anti-advertiser legislation and represents advertiser interests before regulatory agencies and within industry councils.

During the late 1980s and 1990s, the ANA's Washington office presented the advertising industry's position on issues such as tobacco advertising, food labeling, children's television, and privacy. The ANA helped defeat numerous proposals that would have imposed taxes on advertising, both locally and nationally. A law to enact an ad tax in Florida was overturned under pressure from the ANA.

The ANA is led by a board of directors; up to 32 directors may serve on the ANA board, with up to 16 new board members elected by the membership at the annual meeting and business conference every fall. The ANA also selects a new chairman each year; the staff is led by the group's president/chief executive officer. Members are invited to serve on the 15 committees that identify issues, trends, and opportunities in specific areas of advertising, marketing, and promotion.

The ANA sponsors regular conferences, forums, and training seminars for its members, as well as publishing a bimonthly newsletter, *The Marketer*, and its own magazine, *The Advertiser*, which appears six times a year and accepts outside advertising. The ANA maintains a Web site (www.ana.net) that includes member information and updates, and it also conducts periodic member surveys on important topics such as trends in Internet advertising and agency compensation. In addition, the ANA oversees the Family Friendly Programming Forum, a group of 48 member companies dedicated to encouraging the development of family-oriented prime-time TV programs.

LAURIE FREEMAN

Further Reading

"ANA to Allow Agencies to Join Trade Group," *Adweek* (Eastern Edition) (12 October 1998)

Association of National Advertisers Homepage <www.ana.net>

Association of National Advertisers, Inc., *Annual Report* (1990)

"A Bridge from Problem to Solution: Information about the Association of National Advertisers, Inc.," Association of National Advertisers, Inc. (1994)

Colford, Steve, "Putting ANA among the Big Boys: Helm Recalls a Decade of Making Group an Advocate for Advertisers," *Advertising Age* (19 October 1993)

Fox, Stephen R., *The Mirror Makers: A History of American Advertising and Its Creators,* New York: Morrow, 1984

Friedman, Wayne, and Richard Linnett, "Six-Month Strike Is Over, but No Victor Is Declared: Strike Scorecard: Unions Win Modest Fee Increases; New Long-Term Financial

Formulas Please Advertisers," *Advertising Age* (30 October 2000)

Sarsen, John J., Jr., "Why ANA Gates Are Opening to Agencies: ANA's Sarsen Cites Benefits of Broader Membership," *Advertising Age* (2 November 1998)

AT&T Corporation

(American Telephone and Telegraph)

Principal Agencies

N.W. Ayer & Son, Inc.
Newell-Emmett Company (later Cunningham & Walsh)
Young & Rubicam, Inc.
Foote, Cone & Belding
McCann-Erickson

AT&T Corporation is a long-distance, Internet, and wireless communications service provider in the telecommunications industry. Its history goes back more than 100 years. By the end of the 20th century the company was reporting yearly sales of more than $50 billion.

After the invention of the telephone in 1876, Alexander Graham Bell, along with several partners, formed the Bell Telephone Company in 1877. Two years later Theodore Vail became general manager of the new company and began the process of making Bell the one and only telephone company in America. He first made peace with Bell's major competitor, Western Union, which agreed to stay out of the telephone business in return for a share of Bell's licensing fees. In 1881 the company, now called American Bell Telephone Company, bought out Western Union's main supplier, Western Electric Company.

As Bell franchises grew, Vail envisioned an interconnected national communication system. In 1885 he set up American Telephone and Telegraph (AT&T), responsible for long-distance telephone business. At first a division of the Bell System, it became the hub of the corporation by 1900, providing long-distance connections to a network of wholly owned regional Bell subsidiaries plus many independent phone companies. By 1907, with financing from the industrialist J.P. Morgan, the company had consolidated virtually all its long-distance competitors under the AT&T banner, with Vail as president. In 1912 the government initiated antitrust action. Vail sought a compromise, and one soon was found. AT&T was declared a regulated "natural monopoly," a status it would hold for nearly 70 years, during which time it became the world's first company to have assets of more than $100 billion in 1978.

Advertising a Monopoly

The role of AT&T in the history of advertising is perhaps more central and fundamental than that of any other single corporation. It virtually invented the system of advertiser-supported commercial broadcasting that is common today in the United States and many other countries. The invention of radio was a dazzling technical accomplishment but one that presented no clear source of profit. In Great Britain and other countries, broadcasting became a noncommercial function of the government. But this was not a suitable model in the United States, where private ownership took the lead in taking it to the marketplace. In many cases early stations were owned by newspapers, stores, churches, unions, or other institutions, each of which hoped to use broadcasting to further its own commercial or social interests.

In 1922 AT&T owned a New York City radio station called WEAF. Having prospered for nearly 40 years in the telephone business by providing customers with the use of its facilities on a toll basis, it saw radio in fundamentally the same way. According to the WEAF model, anyone who wished to reach the public with a message was welcome to buy time on the station and go on the air. Thus, in the same way that AT&T provided line time on a toll basis to its telephone customers, WEAF offered airtime to its customers. On that simple premise, commercial radio was born as a common carrier in the business of selling time. It was a model that would not only make station ownership profitable, it would also largely free station owners from the responsibility of creating programming. That would become the sponsor's job, working through an ad agency.

It was also AT&T's long-distance lines that made live coast-to-coast broadcasting possible by carrying radio and early television network programs to local affiliates for local retransmission. And in 1926 AT&T was one of the original partners (along with General Electric, Westinghouse, and United Fruit) in the formation of the NBC network.

AT&T retained N.W. Ayer & Son as its principal advertising agency in 1908. Several years later it added Newell-Emmett Company, which became Cunningham & Walsh in 1949. Both agency

The more you hear the better we sound.

What would long distance service be
if it only served selected cities
at selected hours...
If there were no operator service...
no person-to-person or collect calling...
no immediate credit for wrong numbers...

We know one thing.
It wouldn't be AT&T.
Calling anywhere. Anytime.
Long distance operators.
And over a century of commitment.
That's AT&T.
The more you hear the better we sound.

AT&T
Reach out and touch someone

Actor Cliff Robertson served as AT&T Corporation's spokesperson in the 1980s.
Courtesy of AT&T.

---

relationships would continue uninterrupted through the 1970s. Although AT&T was a monopoly with no need to fight competitors for a share of the market, it still recognized the crucial value of advertising to help build a relationship of familiarity and trust with its customers, both business and residential. In many ways AT&T defined the special role of advertising for a natural monopoly. It used advertising to separate itself from the traditional bullying connotations of monopoly and portray itself as a benevolent servant working in the public interest and deserving of its special legal status. "We may be the only phone company in town," one ad said, "but we try not to act like it."

For AT&T, successful advertising was advertising that kept the political climate safe for its existence as a monopoly and protected it against latter-day trustbusters. Some have argued that the final challenge to its monopoly and the subsequent breakup of AT&T in 1982 can be blamed, in part at least, on the failure of the company's advertising to sustain that political climate.

The company maintained a high-profile corporate ad schedule in magazines and business publications such as *Fortune*. It also used radio consistently. Beginning on 29 April 1940 and continuing for the next 18 years, it sponsored *The Telephone Hour* on NBC (the *Bell Telephone Hour* after 1942). The program moved to television in January 1959, where it continued its format of presenting the finest classical, jazz, and popular artists (Van Cliburn, Pablo Casals, Rudolph Nureyev, Benny Goodman, Ella Fitzgerald, Louis Armstrong) without gimmick or sensation. Consistent with its position as a legal monopoly, the company used the program to project a meticulously distinguished corporate image of the highest quality, stability, and trustworthiness.

Music was not the only broadcast vehicle by which AT&T achieved that goal. In 1956 it sponsored the first of four science specials on CBS created by film director Frank Capra: "Our Mr. Sun," followed in 1957–58 by "Hemo the Magnificent," "The Strange Case of the Cosmic Rays," and "The Unchained

Goddess." The company also sponsored various news and dramatic anthology programs.

The company responded periodically to its marketplace with variations in the rigid uniformity of its service. For instance, in 1954 AT&T offered telephones in colors other than the traditional black, and in 1963 it introduced Touch-Tone service.

After the Breakup

During the 1970s the company was faced with various antitrust cases from Microwave Communications, Inc. (MCI), and the Department of Justice. The lawsuits culminated with AT&T's breakup on 1 January 1984. After this, AT&T had two primary businesses: as a manufacturer and seller of telecommunications equipment and as a long-distance telephone service provider.

In 1979 Ayer created the memorable tag line, "Reach out and touch someone," for AT&T. The accompanying visuals in print ads and TV commercials showed situations of warmth and affection. By 1985, however, AT&T was facing increased competition in the long-distance market. The company changed its advertising strategy and began to challenge its competitors. By 1989 the "Big Three" long-distance carriers—AT&T, U.S. Sprint, and MCI—had presented campaigns characterized by aggressive comparative price advertising. AT&T's "Put it in writing" campaign was described by Bob Garfield of *Advertising Age* as "the most powerful, poisonous, sinister, comparative assault of the decade." The campaign hinted that consumers would be wise to check competitors' savings claims. This campaign was followed by another series of commercials using the tag line, "The right choice," and featuring actor Cliff Robertson as spokesperson. After a $1.7 billion loss in 1988, AT&T rebounded with a $2.7 billion profit in 1989.

During the 1990s the company launched the Universal credit card with programs to promote card use. "True Rewards," for example, allowed cardholders to earn points (redeemable for frequent-flier miles or AT&T calling minutes) according to the dollar amounts charged. Because of the 1992 Federal Communications Commission rulings allowing increased competition in the 1-800 number market, AT&T was faced with another challenge. MCI had entered the arena with 1-800-COLLECT, although ads for the service did not mention MCI. AT&T responded with 1-800-OPERATOR.

In 1993 AT&T launched the "You Will" corporate teaser campaign for service innovations such as teleconferencing. That year also marked the introduction of the "i" plan, which consisted of providing "individualized" packages on services such as fax mailboxes and Universal credit cards. The "i" plan was an image campaign intended to portray the brand as personal and trustworthy, but the ads were discontinued because consumers apparently did not relate to them.

Meanwhile, competitive advertising among the "Big Three" continued with various calling plans as well as calling cards. AT&T introduced the PrePaid Card, while Sprint offered "Long-distance Greetings." At the same time, each company touted a calling plan: AT&T promoted "True USA," MCI introduced "Best Friends." In 1995 Sprint offered "Sprint Sense," in which long-distance calls during the evenings and weekends were billed at ten cents per minute. Advertising tactics ranged from emotionally driven ads to direct comparisons.

During the same year, AT&T acquired McCaw Cellular Communications, thus providing a foothold in wireless communications. With this acquisition AT&T created a new business unit, AT&T Wireless Services. In 1998 and 1999 AT&T Wireless Service bolstered its division with the Digital One rate plan, which included a Nokia phone.

Competing in the 1990s and Thereafter

The company reorganized in 1995, forming GIS, then AT&T's computer manufacturing division, and Lucent, a telecommunications equipment producer. AT&T continued in business, providing long-distance phone service, credit cards, and wireless service, and it introduced a brand extension, WorldNet, an Internet service provider. In 1999 the company's organizational structure once again changed. AT&T merged with the cable company TCI, entered into a joint venture with British Telecom, and sold its credit card business to Citibank.

From 1995 to 1997, the principal agencies handling the various AT&T divisions were McCann-Erickson Worldwide Advertising; Young & Rubicam, Inc. (Y&R); and Foote, Cone & Belding (FCB). In 1997 AT&T consolidated its advertising with Y&R and FCB. Advertising tactics in the late 1990s varied. Among these were commercials targeting cost-conscious consumers. The campaign introduced the Lucky Dog Phone Company, a wholly owned subsidiary of AT&T that competed against "dial-around" phone carriers. The company's product was the dial-around number 10-10-345; it countered MCI's 10-10-321. The name AT&T was not mentioned in the Lucky Dog ads.

AT&T's Villa Charla ("Chat Village") commercials promoted long-distance service to the Spanish-speaking public. The company also advertised in multicultural media such as Telemundo (Hispanic television channel) and the Ethnic American Broadcast Company's network (offering programming to U.S. audiences in Greek, Italian, Korean, Polish, Russian, and various Asian languages).

It was expected that the merger with TCI would enable AT&T to deliver data, video, and conventional telephone services over the same line. The initial advertising strategy included a phasing out of the TCI brand. The commercials—for example, "Teen Date," in which a teenage girl awaits an e-mail message from her boyfriend—focused on the impact of modern communications technology on daily life.

In October 2000 the company once again announced a corporate restructuring, this time splitting into four separate businesses: AT&T Wireless, AT&T Broadband, AT&T Business, and AT&T Consumer. The reorganization was scheduled to be completed by 2002.

BETHEL ANN RAVALO

Further Reading

Elkin, Tobi, "AT&T Augments Marketing Efforts against Students, Ethnic Consumers," *Brandweek* 39, no. 31 (10 August 1998)

Garfield, Bob, "AT&T Injects Emotion into Quiet Slices of Life," *Advertising Age* (30 November 1998)

Smith, George David, *The Anatomy of a Business Strategy: Bell,* *Western Electric, and the Origins of the American Telephone Industry,* Baltimore, Maryland: Johns Hopkins University Press, 1985

Snyder, Beth, "AT&T Joins Wave of Marketers Hiding IDs behind New Brands," *Advertising Age* (2 November 1998)

Vogelsang, Ingo, *Telecommunications Competition: The Last Ten Miles,* Cambridge, Massachusetts: MIT Press, 1997

Audit Bureau of Circulations

The convergence of a number of events led to the creation of the Audit Bureau of Circulations (ABC), an independent agency that measures and verifies newspaper and magazine circulations. Technological innovations in printing and transportation in the early 1800s allowed the mass production of publications and sped their delivery. Business practices, too, changed during the 1800s. Editors such as James Gordon Bennett and Benjamin Day ushered in the era of the so-called penny press. Rather than marketing newspapers through expensive annual subscriptions, they introduced daily newspapers that sold for pennies per copy. Editors competed for prominence by publishing sensational stories and vying to distribute the most newspapers. By 1860 most publishers agreed that for general-audience periodicals, a large circulation covering a wide geographical area made better sense than a small, limited circulation. Fueling this publishing strategy was advertising, which had become increasingly important to the newspaper and magazine business.

By the late 1800s, advertising agencies, advertisers, and publishers had come to consider circulation the primary factor in evaluating a publication's worth. Advertisers began to demand accurate audience measurement, but this information was not easy to obtain. Newspaper and magazine publishers considered circulation figures a business secret and did not always give advertisers or their agencies accurate figures. Newspapers, for example, frequently padded their circulation estimates by as much as 10 to 15 percent.

Inflated circulation estimates were not the only problem advertisers and their agencies faced. There was no consistent rate structure. As a result, a publication could give different rates to the same client.

Advertisers wanted to know what they were getting for their money, and they pushed their agencies to get the information. Some agencies arrived at probable circulation estimates by combining information from rival papers and by analyzing population data. The quality of the publication and the nature of the audience also became issues for advertisers. To address these issues, agencies established standards for analyzing such factors as the amount of advertising in a publication, newsprint quality, the number of issues printed, and the characteristics of subscribers.

In 1869 George Rowell, a broker of newspaper space, issued the first publication that brought together information on circulations. Rowell's *American Newspaper Directory* listed more than 5,000 titles and gave circulation estimates for each. The publication replaced the private lists compiled by individual agencies, which frequently contained contradictory information. Rowell's *Directory,* available to any advertiser at a cost of $5, represented the first blow to inflated circulation figures and the first step toward standardizing and establishing baseline values for the purchase of advertising space. Of course, even though Rowell's publication was available to everyone, agencies and newspapers questioned the circulation figures for the newspapers Rowell represented and the method he used to verify circulations.

By 1880 publishers actively supported the concept that advertising rates should be related to circulation. They also agreed that circulation could be measured and verified and that the advertiser had a right to know what he was buying. Yet it was advertisers, not publishers, that pushed for a method of auditing circulations.

In the late 1890s several advertising associations were formed to address the problem of verifying circulations. The first groups to be organized were the American Advertiser Association (AAA; later the American Advertisers Association), formed in 1899, and the American Society of National Advertisers, covering the western United States, which merged with the AAA in 1900. The first attempts to verify the circulations of newspapers and magazines were not successful. Because of privacy issues, publishers resented having outsiders examine their business records, and advertisers resented having to pay for information they thought should be provided without cost. In addition, not all publishers used the same record-keeping systems. As a consequence, it was almost impossible to establish standardized figures. The process was extremely expensive for the AAA, and the organization folded in 1913.

In 1914 two other organizations took up the task of measuring circulations: the Advertising Audit Association, which was made up of publishers, and the Bureau of Verified Circulations, an organization whose executive board was dominated by advertisers. The two groups met in May 1914 and merged to become the Audit Bureau of Circulations (ABC). The organization's board of directors included advertisers and representatives from advertising agencies as well as publishers of newspapers, magazines, and specialty periodicals.

At its initial meeting the ABC established as its mission the task of providing "facts without opinions" about the circulation of any newspaper, magazine, or trade, farm, business or other publication. "Each report issued to members shall embrace facts as the quantity, quality, and distribution of circulation, thereby enabling quality as well as quantity to be established." The organization had a measure of power: it could suspend member publications for fabricating or padding their circulation figures.

One of the first issues the ABC confronted was determining what constituted a publication's "paid circulation." In its simplest approach, a publication had a paid circulation if issues were paid for in cash. By 1916 the organization narrowed the definition to cover subscribers who received the publication by mail or carrier and who paid at least 50 percent of the regularly advertised subscription price.

Attempts to provide more meaningful information and equitable circulation standards have highlighted the bureau's subsequent history. For example, the ABC has grappled with the issue of measuring, and hence giving credibility to, publications distributed without charge to businesses and special consumer groups. In 1922 members voted to exclude from its audit those publications without paid circulations of 50 percent or more. In 1950, responding to pressure from magazine publishers, the ABC changed its audit requirement from 50 percent to 70 percent paid. In 1951 the ABC board voted to require the breakdown of unpaid circulations into "copies to advertisers and agencies, samples to prospective advertisers, samples to prospective subscribers, and all other unpaid," a move supported by media buyers. Others, however, primarily newspaper publishers, felt that the move would dilute the ABC's principal task of measuring paid circulations. Although opposed by daily newspapers, the board voted in the late 1950s to provide analyses of the unpaid circulation of business publications.

The ABC has remained the preeminent provider of information on circulations, although several other companies now provide

such data. BPA International, formerly Controlled Circulation Audit, began in 1931 in response to the ABC's reluctance to audit magazines with unpaid circulations. The company has come to specialize in auditing business publications and special-interest consumer magazines. For example, while ABC audits *Sports Illustrated*, BPA audits *Sports Illustrated for Kids*. Following a general trend in the business publication industry, the BPA has found itself auditing more business publications with paid circulations. The company currently audits approximately 1,800 business and 400 consumer publications. Like the ABC, the BPA also audits Web sites, E-mail newsletters, and attendance at trade shows.

The Verified Audit Circulation Corporation audits unpaid circulations. Formed in 1951, the organization verifies production claims and distribution and conducts readership studies for approximately 1,600 titles in the United States, Canada, and South America.

Although the ABC has continued to dominate the periodical auditing industry, the organization is not without its critics. Some advertising practitioners argue that circulation data alone do not help media buyers or planners assess a publication's worth. Rather, they suggest, factors such as the average price paid per issue, the average subscription term, and the renewal rate are better indicators of a publication's quality. The organization has withstood such criticism, however, and has modified its bylaws to address the needs of advertisers, advertising agencies, and publishers.

CARYL A. COOPER

Further Reading

Atkinson, Paul C., "How to Keep ABC Relevant," *Advertising Age* (26 October 1998)

Bennett, Charles O., *Facts Without Opinion: First Fifty Years of the Audit Bureau of Circulations,* Chicago: Audit Bureau of Circulations, 1965

Bennett, Charles O., *Integrity in a Changing World: Seventy-Five Years of Industry Self-Regulation through the Audit Bureau of Circulations,* Chicago: Audit Bureau of Circulations, 1989

Peterson, Theodore, *Magazines in the Twentieth Century,* Urbana: University of Illinois Press, 1956; 2nd edition, 1964

Presbrey, Frank, *The History and Development of Advertising,* Garden City, New York: Doubleday, 1929

Australia and New Zealand

The European cultural influence on Australia and New Zealand over the past two centuries is reflected in the development of each country's advertising industry. As former colonies of Great Britain, both countries were still considered far-flung outposts of the "Mother Country" during the first half of the 20th century.

Thanks to post–World War II European migration and the subsequent growth of Asian immigration, however, these countries today boast dynamic and diverse populations with their own identities, which are in turn reflected in sophisticated advertising industries. Existing in countries quite different in size—Australia with its 19 million citizens versus New Zealand with its 3.8 million—the Australian and New Zealand ad industries have faced different challenges to reach their current positions.

By 2001 Australia's ad industry was enjoying buoyant growth, while the New Zealand market had been stagnant for five years. In New Zealand globalization resulted in an increasing number of advertising accounts moving offshore, while the local agency scene was dominated by large multinationals working with locally owned agencies, usually one- or two-person "boutique" operations. In Australia there remained a large number of sizable Australian-owned ad agencies competing on an equal basis with the multinationals.

While catering to two mature markets that in many ways have more in common with the consumer patterns of North America and Western Europe than with closer neighbors such as Indonesia or Fiji, advertising in Australia and New Zealand remains distinct in style and tone from the work found in the United States and Europe. However, the Australian and New Zealand ad industries have developed historically along lines similar to those of the U.S. ad industry.

Australia

Among the earliest advertisements in Australia was a playbill for a performance of *The Recruiting Officer* at the Sydney Theatre on 8 March 1800. Advertising was also carried by the first Australian newspaper, the *Sydney Gazette and New South Wales Advertiser,* which began publishing in March 1803.

More than a century passed, however, before the first Australian advertising agency was established with the opening of the Weston Company in Sydney in 1906. Within a dozen years the Weston Company had many competitors, including Sydney ad agencies O'Brien; Willmot; Coudrey Arthur Smyth; Goldberg; and Catts-Patterson, along with Melbourne's Hugh Paton and Claude Mooney. Catts-Patterson, founded by George Patterson and Norman Catts, later grew to become the largest agency in Australia, George Patterson Bates, after George Patterson bought out a Depression-affected Melbourne ad agency and split from Catts in 2001. Media space brokers such as Gordon & Gotch and Besley & Pike, which dealt solely in newspaper advertising, were also operating early in the 19th century.

The advertising industry of the early 1900s reflected the rapid maturation of Australia, which was formed in 1901 by the joining of six previously separate British colonies. In the first decade of the 20th century the first foreign agencies began arriving on Australia's shores, starting with the establishment of the J. Walter Thompson Company to service the Unilever and General Motors Corporation accounts. Lintas, the Unilever house agency, soon followed its client to Australia.

While the contractors charged a fee for their work, it was not until 1911 that they began to claim commissions from the media for the space they sold. The move heralded the establishment of an advertising industry in Australia. Advertising agents began to form various "Institutes of Admen" in cities around the country, starting with a group organized by the five active advertising

agents in Melbourne in 1912. A national group representing advertising agents was not set up until 1946, when the Australian Association of Advertising Agencies (later renamed the Advertising Federation of Australia) was established.

The first Australian advertising convention was held in 1918 and another in 1920, which attracted representatives from five New Zealand–based advertising organizations. The 1918 convention, held in Brisbane, drew representatives from most of Australia's states. Participants discussed a "public declaration of the ethical character of and economic justification for advertising as a business force," reflecting issues that had been of social concern since the 1840s. For example, in 1854 a commentator wrote that Melbourne's daily press belonged "to the genus of gratis advertising sheets, with which is given generally a literary supplement to respite it awhile from base uses." However, advertising was already beginning to facilitate the strong sense of nationalism sweeping Australia.

Rise of Brands

The rise of the trademark in Australia was the result of the industrial revolution and the broad range of factory-produced products that were becoming available. In 1850 many Australian households made their own soap, candles, clothes, medicines, jams, bread, and butter. By 1900 factories were making these goods and selling them under distinctive brands and trademarks.

Between the 1860s and the 1880s the various Australian parliaments (pre-federation) passed the first laws to register trademarks, curbing "backyard" manufacturers that had found it profitable to copy the labels of well-known products. As late as 1874 a Melbourne maker of perfumes and soaps issued large advertisements warning the public that his labels were being copied by competitors. The registration and protection of trademarks was a simple answer to this commercial pirating.

A century ago the average Australian drank more tea than did his contemporaries in any other country, and many brands were widely advertised. The words of the Australian song "Waltzing Matilda," the country's unofficial national anthem, were first popularized in ads for a brand known as Billy Tea.

Boots were another commodity that encouraged the practice of trademarking. Boots and shoes were necessary but expensive. Boot polish was vital to maintain them and gave rise to some of the best-known trademarks in Australia. The brand name Nugget became the common word for shoe polish in many parts of the country. Gold rushes still fired the imagination of Australians and resulted in gold mining terms becoming popular in commercial trademarks.

Growth Spurt

The advertising industry grew quickly; by the 1920s there were many anecdotes about Australia's pioneers of advertising, such as Frank Goldbert, the Sydney advertising man who won the Johnnie Walker whisky account by catching the train from Sydney to Perth, a three-day trip, and boarding the distillery principal's Sydney-bound ship at Perth's Freemantle Port to show how keen

The 1984 campaign "Koalas Against Qantas" featured a koala that was unhappy because the airline was bringing travelers to Australia. *Qantas Airways, Ltd.*

he was for the business. George Patterson got the Palmolive account in 1921 by convincing the foreign sales manager of Palmolive that Australia would buy the soap when Asia would not because Australians already knew of it through American magazines. In 1925 Patterson ran the first free-sample-offer coupon ad; as a result, Palmolive became the biggest-selling toilet soap in Australia, beginning one of the longest client-agency relationships in advertising history.

The Australian advertising industry got another big boost with the introduction of commercial radio broadcasting in 1923, with two radio stations in Sydney, one in Melbourne, and one in Perth; in 2000 the country had more than 150 commercial radio stations. George Patterson Advertising sponsored so many radio programs in the 1940s and 1950s that the agency had a sizable department involved in the production of radio programming as well as the advertising that it carried.

Flourishing Postwar Industry

In April 1955 the federal government allocated two commercial television station licenses each to Melbourne and Sydney. The first commercial station in Australia, TCN, Channel 9, Sydney, began transmitting in July 1956 and opened with regular programming on 16 September 1956. Australia's first television commercial was a 20-second spot for Rothman's cigarettes through the now-defunct ad agency Jackson Wain. The Rothman's spot was followed by a 10-second "slide"—a still shot with voice-over—for Pepsi, through ad agency Fergus Canny Advertising. By 2001 there were more than 150 commercial TV stations in Australia as well as three pay TV networks.

In the 1960s advertisers, faced with the high cost of producing television commercials, often decided to run ads imported from their overseas affiliates. However, with pressure from domestic ad agencies, the Australian Broadcasting Control Board (later the Australian Broadcasting Authority, or ABA) began banning commercials not produced at home. The system was very difficult to administer because of conflicting definitions about what was "Australian content." In addition, advertisers lobbied to be allowed to bring ads created in other countries to Australia. In 1991 the ABA introduced new rules allowing that a maximum of 20 percent of a television licensee's total commercial time could be devoted to foreign commercials. The ABA's move was vigorously opposed by the TV commercial-production industry, which was concerned that foreign ads would flood Australian television, depriving the industry of income. Ironically, owing to favorable exchange rates and a highly skilled local talent pool, in 1999 and 2000 those same companies saw an unprecedented number of foreign ad agencies come to Australia to produce commercials.

Among the country's leading ad practitioners have been Bryce Courtenay, who is celebrated for his work for the Coca-Cola Company and Reckitt & Coleman's Mortein pest repellent; Leo Schofield, who is remembered for his Wool Board, Qantas, and British Paints campaigns during the 1970s and 1980s; John Singleton, who is known for popularizing "Ockerism"—stereotypical Australian character traits—and using Ocker spokespeople in Australian advertising; and the creative team of Allan Morris and Allan Johnson, founders of the ad agency Mojo, who are remembered for their use of folksy jingles such as "You Ought to Be Congratulated" to promote Meadow Lea polyunsaturated margarine (Morris has since said "congratulated" was the only word the pair could think of that rhymed with polyunsaturated).

The 21st Century

While advertising remains a major service industry in Australia with billings of $5 billion a year and more than 10,000 employees, the industry was changing as it headed into the 21st century. While the mainstream advertising industry enjoyed strong growth over the previous two decades, that growth was eclipsed by the rise of diversified marketing disciplines through the 1990s. Marketers began reacting to shifts in the demographic makeup of Australia and the fragmentation of mass media with the rise of the Internet, introduction of pay television, and proliferation of niche publications. Lifestyle and demographic changes—more females than males, couples living together rather than getting married, couples postponing parenthood, increased longevity, better health, and increased general literacy—all represent new advertising or media opportunities.

With these changes, Australian corporations have significantly increased their spending on establishing one-to-one relationships with their customers. In 1999 more than $7 billion was spent on direct marketing, outpacing other, traditional methods of marketing, including advertising. Telemarketing call centers and junk mail are winning out over glossy agency ads and 30-second television commercials in the battle for a bigger slice of corporate Australia's multibillion-dollar marketing budget.

Figures released by the Commercial Economic Advisory Service of Australia showed that spending on direct marketing initiatives, covering everything from catalogs to the Internet, surged 15.6 percent in 1999 to reach a record $13.8 billion. By comparison, spending on traditional mass media advertising on television, radio, and in newspapers and magazines increased just 3 percent.

New Zealand

As Australian advertising flourished, the ad industry in New Zealand had barely been established. The New Zealand Association of Advertisers, an industry body representing clients, was not set up until 1950, well after the creation of similar organizations in Australia and the United States. In fact, the New Zealand ad industry was not really established until the introduction of television in 1960.

However, a handful of advertising pioneers made their mark in New Zealand in the early part of the 20th century, including the Scotsman John Inglis Wright, who left the management of a printing business to open an ad agency in 1906 in Dunedin. New Zealand ad agencies' history started in 1911, the year newspaper publishers formed the Newspaper Proprietors Association. The association acknowledged the advertising agencies of the day—Haines, Illott; and Inglis Wright—with letters of commendation, a form of accreditation for agencies that the newspapers had found to be creditworthy.

By 1927 there were 11 accredited ad agencies operating throughout New Zealand, 5 with more than one office. During the 1930s New Zealand and Australia, like other industrialized countries, experienced the Great Depression; it was also the decade when commercial radio first emerged.

World War II provided a major catalyst for the development of New Zealand's advertising industry. The emergence of large-scale government advertising for war loans and patriotic appeals of all kinds provided much-needed work for ad agencies during lean times. These large-scale government advertising projects were handled by ad agencies on a panel basis, with three or four sharing the work and the responsibility. One important result was that politicians, not normally well-versed in selling or marketing, learned about the value and power of advertising for the first time. As a result, advertising became a key component in government communication.

The introduction of television in New Zealand in 1960 coincided with the influx of multinational advertising agencies, which bought out established agencies such as J. Ilott Advertising in Wellington. Sir John Ilott, considered a stalwart of the advertising industry in New Zealand, sold his business to Ted Bates & Company in the early 1960s. At the same time the center of New Zealand's ad industry began to move from its base in the capital city of Wellington to the country's center of population.

In the postwar years New Zealand agencies began to use market research seriously and some, partly through lack of outside facilities, developed their own research departments or spin-off companies. By the end of the 20th century New Zealand had established itself as a creative hotbed for global advertising agencies. The Auckland office of Saatchi & Saatchi alone won five gold Lions at the Cannes (France) International Advertising Festival in 2000.

New Zealand's advertising agencies employed 1,000 people at the turn of the century, with another 2,500 working in advertising-related services. Advertising revenue also contributed to the employment of another 10,000 people in New Zealand's publishing, radio, and television industries. At the end of March 1998 there were approximately 150 ad agencies in New Zealand, 30 of them multinationals. For the year ended March 1998, client spending on mainstream advertising was $572 million; another $220 million was spent on direct marketing. Approximately 45 percent of media ad spending was through advertising agencies, with agencies placing around 80 percent of advertising on television.

The Advertising Agencies Association of New Zealand is a group that represents the interests of its members on issues affecting the advertising industry and agencies. It has 40 member agencies representing about 85 percent of agency billings in New Zealand, with combined billings of about $360 million.

Both the New Zealand and Australian ad industries have systems of self-regulation. In New Zealand, the system is managed by the Advertising Standards Authority (ASA) and the Advertising Complaints Board. The authority's function is to promulgate a code of practice and develop policies on advertising standards. The board's function is to adjudicate complaints and advise the ASA on codes and public issues. In Australia the Advertising Standards Board is managed by the Australian Association of National Advertisers. The board is made up of a panel of individuals from different fields who meet monthly, discuss public complaints made about advertising, and decide whether to uphold or dismiss those complaints.

ANDREW HORNERY

Further Reading

Blainey, Geoffrey, "Behind the Label," in *Symbols of Australia*, edited by Mimmo Cozzolino and G. Fysh Rutherford, Ringwood, Victoria, and New York: Penguin, 1980

"Marketing and Media Milestones: Celebrating 50 Years of B and T Weekly," *B and T Weekly* (24 November 2000)

Wiggs, Grev, *New Zealand Advertising Agencies: The First 100 Years*, Auckland: Advertising Agencies Association of New Zealand, 1980

Automobiles

The histories of the automobile and advertising industries are inextricably intertwined. They grew up together, reflecting societal and cultural changes. Themes of high performance, luxury, safety, reliability, economy, and fun have been featured in auto ads through the decades, and the auto industry has produced some of the most memorable and award-winning ads of all time.

Matter-of-Fact Marketing

The brothers Charles and Frank Duryea, bicycle inventors and makers, are credited with starting the U.S. auto industry. In 1896 their Duryea Motor Wagon Company of Springfield, Massachusetts, built 13 gasoline-powered motor wagons. They are believed to have run the first illustrated auto ad in the inaugural issue of the trade journal *Horseless Age*. The ad, also significant in that it targeted female drivers, showed a woman dressed in a gown and hat driving the Duryea Motor Wagon with her similarly attired female

passenger. Copy was sparse, naming the marketer as "manufacturer of motor wagons, motors, and automobile vehicles of all kinds."

Many auto marketers of the day took the unromantic, unimaginative approach. Ads were short on art, generally using retouched photographs or an occasional drawing, and tended to be small—page ads were rare. Mechanical information was emphasized, and prices were usually included.

The headline in an 1897 Oldsmobile ad merely states: "Practically noiseless and impossible to explode." The ad depicts four adults in the open-topped carriage, none smiling or looking very relaxed. In 1901 founder Ransom Eli Olds advertised that to keep a horse cost $180 annually, versus $35 a year for his car's gasoline. His Olds Motor Vehicle Company targeted professionals and business owners after the first non–blue bloods started buying automobiles. An Oldsmobile ad from 1904, the year Olds resigned from his company in a tiff with investors, read, "Doctors, lawyers, merchants—You see them everywhere—in their

He drives a Duesenberg

This 1934 ad succeeded in associating social class and lifestyle with the Duesenberg—without the automobile itself appearing in the ad.

Oldsmobiles." "You see them wherever you go" was the brand's early tag line.

Olds, who went on to found the Reo Motor Car Company, created advertising and auto history in 1912, when, three years in advance, he publicized the 1915 "Reo the Fifth" model, which sold for $1,055. This type of advance advertising was unheard of at the time, although carmakers of the 1990s often promoted their upcoming new models as much as a year in advance at auto shows, on Web sites, or via direct mail to stir anticipation and build a database of prospective buyers.

Henry Ford, who wrote many of his own early ads, also took the practical approach. "Get behind the wheel and know the joy of driving this great new car," said an early Model A ad, which contained 500 words and took about two minutes to read. In 1904 Ford Motor Company showed the Model C, the Model F, and Model B and their prices with the headline, "Don't experiment. Buy a Ford." In 1907 E. Leroy Pelletier, Ford's first advertising man, penned the ad slogan, "Watch the Fords go by."

During the first eight years of the 1900s, more than 480 companies in the United States were making cars. Henry Ford emerged as one of the giants. In 1908 he made good on his promise of five years earlier to sell a car for the masses—the Model T. Ford sold 15 million Model Ts through 1927. During those years, Ford's ads hammered away at three selling points: the quality of the materials, his mass production techniques to lower prices, and mechanical benefits. Ford introduced the "buy now—pay later" installment plan after World War I, but by then the virtually unchanged Model T looked dowdy.

J.W. Packard personally wrote the first hit car slogan in the industry for his own Packard Motor Car Company in Detroit, Michigan. "Ask the man who owns one" premiered in a letter to prospects, and by 1902 the line was being used in all ads and promotional materials. The brand, the luxury leader into the late 1940s, used the timeless slogan until 1956.

Innovations

In the United States, the idea of applying artistic standards to car ads is generally credited to Ernest Elmo Calkins in 1903. Roughly five years later, his New York City ad agency Calkins & Holden was handling the account of the Pierce-Arrow Motor Company of Buffalo, New York, which had a steady waiting list of buyers. Calkins & Holden broke all the rules. The ads did not show the entire car, carried virtually no copy, and used splendid art. Experts rank Pierce-Arrow ads as among the top collectibles in auto art.

Pierce-Arrow took a laissez-faire approach with its agency. Adolph Treidler, an illustrator on the account at Calkins & Holden who started in about 1909, recalled that his client never knew what kind of scenes he would paint, nor did the client issue any rules before he created the ads. And, Treidler reminisced, "Pierce-Arrow never returned any of my paintings for change or correction."

The Cadillac Motor Car Company broke rules, too. Theodore F. MacManus, whose name was on the door of the ad agency that would later become D'Arcy Masius Benton & Bowles, penned a 1915 Cadillac ad on the back of an envelope during a train trip. Headlined "The penalty of leadership," the long copy discussed the difficulties that befall all who excel—emulation and envy, denial and detraction. It begins, "In every field of human endeavor, he that is first must perpetually live in the white light of publicity." No car is shown in the ad, only the Cadillac logo. It is considered one of the best car ads of all time and appeared on and off over a period of 50 years. D'Arcy still handled the Cadillac account at the beginning of 2001, as well as its General Motors Corporation sibling, Pontiac.

The real maverick of car advertising in the early 20th century was Edward "Ned" Jordan. He worked in advertising for the early Rambler and Jeffrey cars before starting his own Jordan Motor Car Company. Jordan introduced a dreamy style of copywriting into car ads—an innovation still studied today. He is remembered for having disdained "mechanical chatter" in auto ad copy. An ad for the Jordan Playboy model in the May 1919 edition of *Vanity Fair* dubbed the car "a spirited companion for a wonderful girl and a wonderful boy. It's a shame to call it a roadster. So full is this brawny, graceful thing of the vigor and boyhood of morning."

Jordan's legendary 1923 "Somewhere west of Laramie" ad, hailed as one of the greatest car ads ever, was ranked 30th among the 100 top ads of the 20th century by *Advertising Age* magazine in 1999. The ad shows a woman driving the convertible on a western road and says, "For it's always happy in the hills. The Playboy was built for her—the Playboy is an apt companion for Americans who dare never to grow old." The Jordan Motor Car Company was forced to close in 1931 during the Great Depression.

In the Roaring Twenties, the focus of auto ads shifted from mechanical reliability to freedom, comfort, and style. A 1925 ad for the American Mercedes Company shows an elegant woman in a long fur coat, with the car in the background. The "Mercedes" headline is the only copy. A 1923 ad for the Ford Runabout, with a price tag of $265, targets "the young businessman . . . who is making his mark in business and around school."

A 1925 ad for Chevrolet Motor Car Company, which had been acquired by General Motors Corporation (GM) in 1918, showed off the car's brightly colored finish, contrasting it with the industry's earlier all-black paint for mass-market models. A 1924 Chevrolet ad carries the headline, "Speed up success." It shows a suited man "watching others go by him" and points out that if one had a Chevy "to move your person twice as fast as some other chap, your chances for success are twice as good." The Campbell-Ewald agency of Detroit created the ad. Campbell-Ewald has handled Chevrolet since 1922, when the agency handled all GM nameplates.

The 1930s: Depression Themes

Even as the Great Depression cast a pall over the nation, Duesenberg targeted the wealthy with understated ads that showed off its sleek, classy cars. "He drives a Duesenberg" or "She drives a Duesenberg" were the simple ad messages under drawings of the pres-

Somewhere West of Laramie

SOMEWHERE west of Laramie there's a broncho-busting, steer-roping girl who knows what I'm talking about.

She can tell what a sassy pony, that's a cross between greased lightning and the place where it hits, can do with eleven hundred pounds of steel and action when he's going high, wide and handsome.

The truth is—the Playboy was built for her.

Built for the lass whose face is brown with the sun when the day is done of revel and romp and race.

She loves the cross of the wild and the tame.

There's a savor of links about that car—of laughter and lilt and light—a hint of old loves—and saddle and quirt. It's a brawny thing—yet a graceful thing for the sweep o' the Avenue.

Step into the Playboy when the hour grows dull with things gone dead and stale.

Then start for the land of real living with the spirit of the lass who rides, lean and rangy, into the red horizon of a Wyoming twilight.

JORDAN

JORDAN MOTOR CAR COMPANY, Inc., Cleveland, Ohio

"Somewhere West of Laramie," one of the most memorable car ads ever created, was used by Jordan Motors to market its performance coupe, the Playboy, to women.

tige automobiles driven by well-heeled men and women who showed no concern for the bleak economy.

Other brands targeted the little guy. Chevrolet's ad theme became, "Greater value in 1933." That same year, car chief Walter P. Chrysler appeared in the "Look at all three" ad next to the "New Plymouth with floating power." His lengthy statement in the copy below urged consumers to test-drive his model before making a deposit on another maker's car. J. Stirling Getchell created and produced the ad on speculation, and it saved the upstart brand and won the account for his J. Stirling Getchell ad agency. He pioneered the use of large, candid photographs in auto ads. Dodge picked up the style and added the tag line, "Dodge dependability." In two years, increases in the brand's annual sales boosted it from ninth to fourth place.

Celebrity advertising was in its heyday in the 1930s, as radio networks came into their own and talking movies matured. Dodge sponsored *Major Bowes Original Amateur Hour*. Comedian Jack Benny stumped for Chevrolet on his radio show in the early 1930s. Carmakers and moviemakers sometimes joined forces. A 1935 Buick ad carried the headline, "Hollywood—creator of style—chooses Buick for its own." The black-and-white photo showed Dick Powell and the Berkley Girls from Warner Bros.' upcoming film *Gold Diggers*. Actress Carole Lombard appeared in a 1938 Getchell ad for DeSoto that

informs readers of her appearance in David O. Selznick's *Made for Each Other*.

BMW of North America returned to this co-promotion practice in a 1995 deal with MGM/UA. BMW launched its Z3 roadster in the moviemaker's James Bond film *GoldenEye*. Fallon McElligott, Minneapolis, Minnesota, used scenes from the movie in its ads for the car. BMW repeated the move in two subsequent Bond movies. Other carmakers followed suit, including Mercedes-Benz USA for Steven Spielberg's *The Lost World: Jurassic Park* in 1997. Lowe & Partners, New York City, had the Mercedes account at the time. BMW's efforts, however, were the most effective and most acclaimed.

The streamlined shapes of Art Deco had a strong influence on automobile design in the 1930s. A 1934 Chrysler ad announced that "a new era of transportation brings functional design and Chrysler brings the floating ride." An Art Deco drawing of the car also contains a streamlined locomotive and a Zeppelin. As the Depression ended, car ads reflected the nation's optimism. A 1935 Studebaker ad for its Champion model showed the canary-yellow sedan and declared, "The biggest thrill in the world is to own a Champion."

Women were targeted in earnest during this period. A 1935 Cadillac headline reads: "For the first time it may truly be said—The perfect car for a woman." A 1937 ad for the 1938 Chrysler Royal Touring Sedan is written from a woman's point of view. She pokes fun at her husband's attempts to tell her about the brand's value, roominess, size, and quality—"As if I've never heard it." The ad also has a fashion connection, pointing out that her black pillbox hat is from the exclusive retailer Bergdorf Goodman.

The industry tried again to woo women in the 1950s. "Every woman needs a second love," reads the headline of a 1955 Chevrolet Belair convertible ad. It shows a young wife kissing her husband as he leaves for work in his Belair hardtop. Chevrolet's 1958 model was touted as "Chevy chic" because it came in colors such as Tropic Turquoise and Rio Red. A pink 1959 Cadillac appears in an ad with a fashionably dressed young mother and her young daughter, both wearing pink outfits. Dodge developed the La Femme model for women. It came with matching umbrella, purse, rain cap, and rain boots. (See Table 1.)

The "People's Car"

During the 1930s another important development in the history of the automobile and advertising was taking root overseas. In 1930 Adolph Hitler called for a car to be built for the masses, or, as the press soon started calling it, "Volkswagen" (VW), meaning the "people's car." The "Beetle" name first appeared in connection with the car in the *New York Times* on 3 July 1938. That year, Germans were informed in brochures that they could invest five Reichsmarks weekly to buy the upcoming "Dien KdF-Wagen" (Your KdF Car), from the car's name, *Kraft durch Freide* (Strength through joy). The money was used to build the car's plant. But the plant was instead used for making military

Table 1. Agency Affiliations in the 1930s.

Automobile Company	Advertising Agency
Auburn Automobile Company	P.P. Willis, Inc.
Buick	Arthur Kudner, Inc.
Cadillac	MacManus, John & Adams, Inc.
Chevrolet	Campbell-Ewald, Inc.
Chrysler Corporation	Ruthrauff & Ryan, Inc.
DeSoto	J. Stirling Getchell
Diamond T. Motor Car Company	Roche, Williams & Cunnyngham, Inc.
Dodge Brothers	Ruthrauff & Ryan, Inc.
Duesenberg	P.P. Adams, Inc.
Ford	N.W. Ayer & Son (later McCann-Erickson, then J. Walter Thompson)
Hudson	Brooke, Smith & French, Inc.
Hupp Motor Car	Stack-Goble Advertising
Lincoln-Mercury	N.W. Ayer (later Maxon, Inc., then Kenyon & Eckhardt)
Nash/Lafayette	J. Walter Thompson Company
Oldsmobile	D.P. Brother, Inc.
Packard	Young & Rubicam
Pierce-Arrow	Baldwin & Strachan
Plymouth	J. Stirling Getchell, Inc.
Pontiac	MacManus, John & Adams, Inc.
Reo Motor Car	Maxon, Inc.
Studebaker	Roche, Williams & Cunnyngham, Inc.
Stutz	(in-house staff)
Willys-Overland	United States Advertising

equipment for World War II, including an amphibious version of the car.

Production resumed slowly after the war. The first batch of Beetles was exported to the United States in 1949. VW's U.S. agency, Doyle Dane Bernbach, Inc. (later DDB Worldwide), which won the account in the late 1950s, dramatically affected the ad industry with its work for the Beetle. *Advertising Age* ranked the agency's "Think small" Beetle campaign as the best of the 20th century.

Led by the legendary William Bernbach, DDB's team included Helmut Krone, Julian Koenig, David Reider, Ed Russell, and Bob Levenson. Krone credited Russell, the account manager, with devising a series of "unique selling propositions" for "this dumb-looking car." Those selling points included the Beetle's promise that it would not change for change's sake; its rear, air-cooled engine; and the thoroughness of its assembly-line inspectors, which sparked the celebrated "Lemon" ad.

The VW team devised a stream of classic slogans, including "There are shapes you simply can't improve on" and "The VW runs—and runs—and runs." The car's advertising was simple, straightforward, and honest, capturing the Beetle's essence. The economy car developed into a "classless classic," driven by both housewives and multimillionaires. A 1969 ad showed the VW

logo on the moon-landing ship with the headline, "It's ugly but it gets you there." VW sold 15 million Beetles through 1979 in the United States. Richard Semenik, dean of the business school at the University of Montana and a board member of the American Advertising Museum in Phoenix, Arizona, has said that DDB's long-running Beetle campaign was influential for both its copy strategy and production with the use of massive white space.

DDB still had the account overseas in early 2001 but lost VW's U.S. account in the mid-1990s. The winning agency, Arnold Worldwide, Boston, Massachusetts, captured the essence of the earlier Beetle ads when, in 1998, VW launched an updated version of the car in the United States (the original Beetle had not been sold in the United States since 1979). The five TV launch commercials all used massive white space, as did the print ads. "If you lost your soul in the 1980s, here's your chance to buy it back," announced one TV spot aimed at baby boomers. "Less flower. More power," read another ad. Even before the New Beetle's introduction, Arnold was already getting industry attention for its VW brand and product ads, tagged "Drivers wanted." The agency shot tilted views of drivers in ads for the Jetta and Golf models and portrayed quirky, slice-of-life stories with catchy, non-popular music in the place of narration.

Wartime Themes and Advent of TV

During World War II U.S. carmakers used their plants for the military effort and touted the work in patriotic ads. The J. Walter Thompson Company (JWT), which won the Ford account in 1943, created an ad that featured the image of a crystal ball with the tag line, "There's a Ford in your future," indicating to soldiers that the carmaker would have vehicles waiting for them upon their return from service.

In May 1995 *Time* magazine published a special issue commemorating the 50th anniversary of V-E (Victory in Europe) Day. GM's Buick division was the sole sponsor of the reprinted 14 May 1945 issue. The special issue featured vintage Buick ads of the era. They carried the nameplate's wartime theme, "When better automobiles are built, Buick will build them," created by the Kudner Agency, Detroit. McCann-Erickson of Troy, Michigan, which won the Buick account in 1958, put the 1995 deal together and created an eight-page insert showing Buick's then-current lineup in front of a war-era B-24 bomber. The issue went to 750,000 *Time* subscribers matching Buick's over-50 target market and 250,000 consumers who had already bought Time Warner history books and videos.

Car production resumed after World War II. With the new medium of television catching on, carmakers sponsored and coproduced shows. Chevrolet sponsored Dinah Shore, who, from 1956 to 1963, opened and closed her TV show with the Chevy anthem, "See the USA in a Chevrolet." *Advertising Age,* in its 1999 special report, "The Advertising Century," ranked the jingle among the top ten of the 20th century, and the companion "See the USA" campaign ranked 41st. Campbell-Ewald revived the memorable jingle for a full Chevrolet car line commercial in 1999. Campbell-Ewald created other memorable Chevrolet tag lines over the years, including: "Baseball, hot dogs, apple pie" in 1975; "The heartbeat of America" in 1986; and "Like a Rock," using rock singer Bob Seger's song starting in 1992 for its truck line.

Selling Safety

In the 1950s a new ad theme emerged: safety. Ford was the first in the industry to focus on safety as a major theme in the fall of 1955. Ads from JWT focused on new, optional seat belts and padded dashboards. "At last! A car dedicated to safety first—the 1956 Ford," the headline read. For the first time Ford devoted more than twice as much advertising to new safety features as to any other feature.

Before long, however, Ford succumbed to complaints from a GM executive that the safety-focused ads took the romance out of the car business. At the time, GM was refusing to offer seat belts; GM executives made public statements that there was no conclusive evidence that seat belts helped prevent auto injuries. Ford ordered JWT to redo the campaign after two months to focus instead on styling and performance.

No other Ford option caught on as fast as seat belts did within a single year. In the 1964 model year, front-seat lap belts became standard in the United States. In 1959 Sweden's Volvo was the first to offer its three-point lap and shoulder belts as standard. Safety has been a cornerstone of Volvo's advertising, although in 1998, the brand began to emphasize emotional appeals and the fun of driving.

The 1950s were also the decade of one of the industry's most infamous missteps: Ford's launch of its Edsel division in 1957. The 1958 model Edsel was Ford's first new nameplate in 19 years. Foote, Cone & Belding handled the account. A launch ad touted the Edsel as unique. "This is the Edsel—never before a car like it—the one car that can look you in the eye and say you never had it like this before." Edsel, named after Henry Ford's son, offered a push-button transmission and dashboard compass. Another ad pronounced, "Dramatic Edsel styling is here to stay." The timing was bad—the nation's economy slumped in late 1957. The car's design was ridiculed by *Time* magazine, likened to "an Oldsmobile sucking a lemon." Dealers complained about sloppy workmanship, and critics noted that Ford already offered medium-priced cars. Production was halted in 1959.

This same year, GM's Pontiac division, still recovering from its worst sales year of some 242,000 units in 1958, had a new idea: the wide-track car. The trademarked "wide track" was used in Pontiac ads (by D'Arcy) from 1959 to 1972. The phrase stemmed from Pontiac's new wider, lower-slung bodies, which suggested a crouching animal. Ads for the cars used athletic analogies: one showed a baseball player moving his feet farther apart to achieve a better stance at the plate.

Throughout that period, Pontiac used artists Art Fitzpatrick and Van Kaufman, who airbrushed the print ads. By 1965 Pontiac was selling more than 800,000 cars annually, hitting a peak of 934,000 in 1969. However, Pontiac and other makers of high-performance, gas-eating "muscle cars" were hit hard by the gas crisis of the early 1970s. (See Table 2.)

Table 2. Agency Affiliations in the 1960s.

Automobile Company	Advertising Agency
American Motors	Geyer, Morey, Madden & Ballard
Buick	McCann-Erickson
Cadillac	MacManus, John & Adams, Inc.
Checker	Roche, Rickerd & Cleary, Inc.
Chevrolet	Campbell-Ewald, Inc.
Chrysler	Young & Rubicam
Citroën	Shevlo, Inc.
Dodge	Batten Barton Durstine & Osborn
Edsel	Foote, Cone & Belding
Fiat	Adams & Keyes, Inc.
Ford	J. Walter Thompson Company
Jaguar	Cunningham & Walsh, Inc.
Jeep (Willys)	Norman, Craig & Kummel, Inc.
Lincoln-Mercury	Kenyon & Eckhardt, Inc.
Mercedes-Benz	D'Arcy Advertising (later Ogilvy & Mather)
Nissan	Standard Advertising News Agency
Oldsmobile	D. P. Brother, Inc.
Peugeot	Needham, Louis & Brorby
Plymouth	N.W. Ayer & Son
Pontiac	MacManus, John & Adams, Inc.
Renault	Needham, Louis & Brorby
Rolls-Royce	Ogilvy, Benson & Mather, Inc.
Rover Motor Company	Sudler & Hennessey, Inc.
Saab	Gotham-Vladimir, Inc.
Studebaker/Packard	D'Arcy Advertising
Toyota	Clinton E. Frank, Inc.
Triumph	Doherty, Clifford, Steers & Shenfield, Inc.
Volkswagen	Doyle Dane Bernbach, Inc.
Volvo	Anderson & Cairns, Inc.

Japanese Brands

The gasoline crisis was not bad for all carmakers, however. It helped boost Japanese brands. Toyota Motor Sales USA started selling its small Toyopet Crown car in the United States in 1957. The marketer admitted in its own press materials that the car was underpowered. Industry experts at the time lauded the imports' quality and value. But it was Toyota's "Oh what a feeling" campaign, begun in 1978 during a second gasoline crisis, that "really put Toyota on the map," according to Joe Cronin, vice chairman of Saatchi & Saatchi Worldwide, New York City. Dancer, Fitzgerald, Sample, which was later acquired by Saatchi, created the ads. Cronin, who joined Dancer to head the account in 1985 as the campaign was ending, said the emotion-based campaign was unique to the category because it "was like non-car advertising" in its look, feel, and sound. Other agencies copied the style.

A standout TV commercial in the campaign showed a robed judge jumping and clicking his heels after a ride in his nephew's yellow Toyota pickup. It was the first of many spots to show ecstatic owners jumping with joy. Toyota's annual sales, just shy of 185,000 vehicles in 1970, jumped to 577,200 in 1985, according to *Automotive News*.

Japan's "Big Three"—Toyota, American Honda Motor Company, and Nissan North America—entered the luxury segment in the 1980s. Toyota has been the most successful. Toyota's Lexus Division premiered in ads in 1989 for the LS 400 and ES 250 sports sedan. Team One of Torrance, California, a Saatchi & Saatchi unit formed to handle the brand, developed the tag line, "The relentless pursuit of perfection." The campaign hammered home the cars' quiet ride, luxury, and performance. An eight-page magazine insert that complemented the launch TV spots discussed the Lexus vision and the positions of both models. In 2000 Lexus was the nation's best-selling luxury car brand for the first time.

Nissan flubbed its Infiniti luxury car launch in 1989. Hill, Holliday, Connors, Cosmopulos, Inc., of Boston created a series of nine Zen-like TV commercials that never showed a car. Instead, they showed rocks and trees. In a spot called "Summer storm," complete with lightning over a lovely bay, a voice-over intones, "You know, it's not just a car; it's an expression of the culture, an aesthetic that is connected somehow to nature, a way of saying, 'This is what we can do if we work hard at the highest level of our potential.' That's the level of the commitment behind a new line of luxury cars from Japan. Infiniti." Dealers demanded that Infiniti's Q45 sedan be shown in the ads. Hill, Holliday went back to the drawing board, and new TV commercials broke in February 1990. Although running footage of the Q45 appeared in the new ads, a "shaky camera" effect used in one execution and a special effect in another made it seem that the car was static as the scenery moved. The agency lost the account in 1992 to TBWA Chiat/Day, of Marina del Rey, California.

TBWA Chiat/Day was widely praised in the advertising community for its 1996 brand campaign for Nissan. One award-winning spot called "Toys" showed Barbie and G.I. Joe look-alike dolls tooling around in a red Nissan convertible. Another spot, dubbed "Pigeons," which broke during the Super Bowl in 1997, showed a squadron of the birds aiming to hit a clean, black Nissan car. Instead, the car foils them by zipping into a garage. Nissan's own dealers, however, criticized the spots as ineffectual. The agency switched to product-focused ads by early 1998 but kept the "Enjoy the ride" tag line.

1990s Tactics

Another campaign that made a big impact was the "New Dodge," which arrived in 1992. It coincided with the introduction of the limited-volume Viper sports car to change consumers' perceptions about the brand. The suburban Detroit office of BBDO developed an umbrella brand campaign that was carried into all product advertising. Dick Johnson, the executive creative director at BBDO, gave his team a few rules: use all red vehicles, shoot all ads on a stage, use title cards, and show no people but the spokesman, actor Edward Hermann. In 1999 Dodge changed its tag line to "Dodge. Different." The only other element that changed was

"Isuzu Trooper II. The 4x4 that conquered Everest."

What a snowjob.
The truth is, if you want to reach the top of Mt. Everest, you'd be better off driving a yak. On the other hand, you don't have to beat a Trooper II with a stick to get it moving. Simply shift into 4-wheel drive and its fuel-injected 2.6 liter engine will eagerly take you just about anywhere.
Shift back into 2-wheel drive, and it'll eagerly take you through long stretches of highway or cramped supermarket parking lots. Or fold up the rear seat and you've got over 71 cubic feet of storage space.
And unlike a yak, a Trooper II can be ordered with automatic transmission, captain's chairs, and 2-door or 4-door body styles. The result is something that handles like a station wagon. Hauls like a Sherpa. And looks like nothing else on or off the road.
All for thousands less than other comparable vehicles. Looks like our rivals have slipped.

ISUZU
Proud Sponsor of the 1988 Summer Olympics on NBC.

Isuzu's parody of car salesmanship, featuring the outrageous exaggerations of Joe Isuzu, proved to be the making of an extremely popular campaign.

Hermann, who was no longer seen on screen. Johnson retired from BBDO in June 2001, and new ad executives at the automaker dropped the longstanding Dodge executions. By this time, however, other carmakers had copied the strategy. Ford Division introduced its "Ford outfitters. No boundaries" in the summer of 1999 as an umbrella ad theme from JWT for its full line of sport-utility vehicles (SUVs) and individual models.

But perhaps the most memorable late-20th-century car campaign came from American Isuzu Motors in the late 1980s. Della Femina, Travisiano & Partners, of Los Angeles, California (later Della Femina McNamee), created the fictional Joe Isuzu as pitchman. In the commercials Joe, played by actor David Leisure, told whopping lies about the car; meanwhile, a printed disclaimer appeared on the screen below him. In a commercial for the Isuzu I-Mark sedan, for example, Joe Isuzu claimed that the car had a top speed of 300 miles per hour and that buyers would get a free house if they bought the car for $9. The gimmick, which elevated Isuzu ads to the ranks of the top-ten spots in consumer recall in April 1989, ran until 1990. Isuzu revived Joe for its 2001 model-year ads. Goodby, Silverstein & Partners, San Francisco, California, brought back Leisure for the role.

Jeep ads in the 1990s were among the most envied by competitors and the most honored internationally for the Detroit-area agency that created them. In 1994 Bozell, Southfield, Michigan (later bought by the parent company of Foote, Cone & Belding), became the first U.S. agency since 1986 to win a Grand Prix at the Cannes International Advertising Festival in France for its "Snow-covered" commercial. The spot did not show the SUV, nor did it utilize narrators. Instead, it showed something burrowing under the snow in a deserted Arctic-like region. At a stop sign, viewers could see the rear brake lights and blinker through the snow. Bozell was the first Detroit agency ever to win the coveted award.

Gary Topolewski, managing partner for creative work at the agency, told *Advertising Age* after the win that he had reviewed hundreds of concepts for Jeep ads. He credited Andy Ozark, senior vice president and art director, with developing the idea, inspired by a Bugs Bunny cartoon. Five years later, the agency won second place at Cannes for another Jeep commercial. It showed a zebra herd hiding from a lion by running in a straight line next to a Jeep Grand Cherokee. It was the only U.S. auto winner that year.

At the turn of the new century two venerable nameplates became history. Chrysler dropped Plymouth in 1998, and in 2000 General Motors announced that it would phase out Oldsmobile.

JEAN HALLIDAY

See also Chrysler Corporation; Fiat Panda; Ford Motor Company; General Motors Corporation; Honda Motor Company; Packard Motor Car Company; Studebaker; Toyota Motor Corporation; Volkswagen; Volvo

Further Reading

Curcio, Vincent, *Chrysler: The Life and Times of an Automotive Genius,* Oxford and New York: Oxford University Press, 2000

Fox, Stephen, *The Mirror Makers: A History of American Advertising and Its Creators,* New York: Morrow, 1984

Herndon, Booton, *Ford: An Unconventional Biography of the Men and Their Times,* New York: Weybright and Talley, 1969; London: Cassell, 1970

Levin, Doron P., *Behind the Wheel at Chrysler: The Iacocca Legacy,* New York: Harcourt Brace, 1995

Mair, Andrew, *Honda's Global Local Corporation,* London: Macmillan, and New York: St. Martin's Press, 1993

"100 Years of Auto Advertising," *Advertising Age* (8 January 1996)

Sloan, Alfred P., Jr., *My Years with General Motors,* edited by John McDonald, Garden City, New York: Doubleday, and London: Pan Books, 1963

Toyota Motor Corporation, *Toyota: A History of The First Fifty Years,* Toyota City, Aichi Prefecture, Japan: Toyota Motor Corporation, 1988

Volvo North America Corporation, *Forty Years of Selling Volvo,* Cobham, Surrey: Brooklands Books, 1995

Avis Rent A Car, Inc.

Principal Agencies

McCann-Erickson (later McCann-Erickson Worldwide)

Doyle Dane Bernbach, Inc.

Benton & Bowles

Batten Barton Durstine & Osborn

McCaffrey and McCall, Inc.

Bozell & Jacobs

Ted Bates & Company (later Backer, Spielvogel, Bates, then Bates USA)

The who's who list of major advertising agencies that have represented Avis Rent A Car is indicative of the turmoil that has swirled around the rental car giant over its roller-coaster history spanning slightly more than half a century. The brainchild of the flamboyant and entrepreneurial Warren Avis, a former Air Force captain who had flown combat missions in World War II, the company initially was called Avis Airlines Rent-A-Car Company. In his flying experience, both military and commercial, in the

1940s, Avis had been continually frustrated by his inability to rent automobiles at airfields. Hertz Corporation, the principal car rental company of the era, had no airport presence; its outlets were primarily in central business districts.

Putting up $10,000 of his own money and borrowing another $75,000, Avis moved quickly in 1946 to establish airport rental locations, first in Detroit, Michigan, and Miami, Florida, and soon after in other major cities. Within seven years, Avis had become the world's second-largest rental car operation after Hertz, which was slow in moving into the airport arena. Despite his company's rapid success, Avis soon grew restive; in 1954 he sold the company to Boston, Massachusetts, financier Richard Robie for an estimated $8 million and went on to other endeavors.

Over the next three-plus decades, Avis changed hands nine times, starting with Lazard Freres and going on to ITT Corporation, Norton Simon, Esmark, Beatrice Companies, Kohlberg Kravis Roberts & Company, and Wesray Capital Corporation. In 1987 an employee stock ownership plan bought the company for

Avis is only No.2 in rent a cars. So why go with us?

We try harder.
(When you're not the biggest, you have to.)
We just can't afford dirty ash-trays. Or half-empty gas tanks. Or worn wipers. Or unwashed cars. Or low tires. Or anything less than seat–adjusters that adjust. Heaters that heat. Defrost-ers that defrost.

Obviously, the thing we try hardest for is just to be nice. To start you out right with a new car, like a lively, super-torque Ford, and a pleasant smile. To know, say, where you get a good pastrami sandwich in Duluth. Why?

Because we can't afford to take you for granted.

Go with us next time.

The line at our counter is shorter.

© 1963 AVIS, INC.

This groundbreaking 1963 ad introduced the memorable Avis slogan, "We try harder."
Avis Rent-A-Car.

$1.75 billion, including debt assumption. In 1996 employees sold the company to HFS, Inc.

But for all the news Avis made on the financial page over the years, no story was as big as when it changed ad agencies in 1963, dumping McCann-Erickson and turning to hot creative shop Doyle Dane Bernbach (DDB). Avis wanted DDB so desperately that its new chairman, Robert Townsend, told DDB creative guru William Bernbach that if the agency would take the account, he would run the ads without any changes.

Initially, Townsend regretted this carte blanche when DDB came up with one of the most controversial—and revolutionary—campaigns in the history of American advertising. The first print ad, designed by DDB's legendary art director Helmut Krone with copy by Paula Green, appeared in March 1963. It was headlined, "Avis is only No. 2 in rent a cars. So why go with us?" The body copy began, "We try harder. (When you're not the biggest, you have to.)"

A storm of controversy followed, with virulent criticism heaped upon both Avis and DDB for their tacit admission that Hertz led the field. But the delayed reaction was markedly positive as a series of "We're No. 2" ads issued forth from the DDB idea factory. Avis's share of the market, depending on which survey was used, increased by as much as 28 percent. Whatever the figure, Avis came to be considered a co-leader with Hertz in the field, and "We try harder" became a pop culture mantra, as did "We're only No. 2." Hertz fought back. The headline of one ad (from agency Carl Ally, Inc.) read: "For years, Avis has been telling you Hertz is No. 1. Now we're going to tell you why."

The "We try harder" campaign continued until 1967, when DDB switched to a new line, "Avis is winning the battle of the bugs," a reference to the company's attention to maintenance. In 1969 the agency resigned the account, which went to rival New York City shop Benton & Bowles. Never again would an Avis campaign garner so much national attention.

That did not mean the excitement was over, however. In April 1973 Avis dropped Benton & Bowles and returned to Doyle Dane Bernbach, which hired movie actor Jack Palance as a spokesman in TV advertising. In 1976 DDB resurrected the "We try harder" campaign. But the magic was gone, and Batten Barton Durstine & Osborn (BBDO) soon won the Avis business.

By this time Norton Simon had bought the company, and its outspoken chairman, David Mahoney, wanted a celebrity spokesman for the advertising. He initially sought the highly respected newsman Walter Cronkite, although he knew Cronkite probably would not agree to appear in an ad. Finally, film actor Glenn Ford was chosen, but Mahoney felt that the resulting commercials were unsatisfactory. Ultimately, an agency review was held, and BBDO declined to participate.

The result was that in 1982 McCaffrey and McCall, Inc., became Avis's new agency. (One of its principals, David McCall, had been the creative director at the agency Mahoney once ran.) With this selection, Mahoney himself became the company spokesman in a series of TV commercials. The results were lack-luster; Mahoney appeared stiff and uncomfortable in the spots. Avis licensees, although giving half-hearted approval to these commercials, selected another agency, Bozell & Jacobs, for their own advertising.

In 1985 Avis switched agencies again, this time going to Ted Bates & Company. That fall, the new agency broke a "So easy" campaign, concentrating on younger business travelers and using music from Creedence Clearwater Revival. In 1988 Avis's agency, now Backer, Spielvogel, Bates, once again revived the "We try harder" approach, this time using actress Jamie Lee Curtis as the spokesperson in the TV spots. This campaign continued into 1990, although by then the focus had shifted to featuring actual customers in the commercials.

Another creative shift occurred in 1991, four years after Avis became employee-owned. In October the agency broke the "So why rent from anyone but an owner?" TV campaign, which featured company employees on-camera emphasizing service. But in 1997 the "We try harder" campaign tag was revived yet again, now with Bates USA as the agency.

In June 1999 Avis again threw its account into review. Bates resigned, citing creative and strategic differences. In September McCann-Erickson Worldwide won the business of the company, which by that time ranked only fifth in the car rental category.

Like Avis's advertising relationships, its ownership seems always to be in turmoil. In the fall of 1996 the employees sold out to HFS, a large franchiser of hotels and real estate brokerage offices. HFS oversaw an initial public offering of Avis stock in 1997. The same year, the company briefly became part of Cendant Corporation; soon after, Cendant, an international hotel franchiser, spun off all but 18 percent of Avis. In August 2000 Cendant was back, this time with a $742 million offer for the entire company. In March 2001 Cendant completed its acquisition of the portion of Avis Group Holdings it did not already own for $33 per share in cash, or approximately $937 million.

ROBERT GOLDSBOROUGH

Further Reading

Avis, Warren, *Take a Chance to Be First: The Secrets of Entrepreneurial Success*, New York: Macmillan, 1986

Fox, Stephen, *The Mirror Makers: A History of American Advertising and Its Creators*, New York: Morrow, 1984

Levenson, Bob, *Bill Bernbach's Book: A History of the Advertising that Changed Advertising*, New York: Villard, 1987

"Ownership Has Its Privileges," *Advertising Age* (21 October 1991)

Raissman, Robert, "David Mahoney: The Battling Maverick As Corporate Chieftain," *Advertising Age* (23 May 1983)

Ries, Al, and Jack Trout, *Bottom-Up Marketing*, New York: McGraw-Hill, 1988

Snyder, Beth, "McCann Wins Add Diversity to Roster," *Advertising Age* (13 September 1999)

Avon Products, Inc.

Principal Agencies
Luckey Bowman, Inc.
Monroe F. Dreher, Inc.
Ogilvy & Mather, Inc.
N.W. Ayer & Son, Inc. (later N.W. Ayer & Partners)

Avon Products, Inc., is one of the oldest direct-selling companies in America. It traces its origins to 1886, when David H. McConnell bought the Union Publishing Company of New York City and started manufacturing perfumes to give away with books. McConnell discovered that his customers were more interested in the fragrances than the books, and he decided to concentrate on selling perfumes. The business was renamed the California Perfume Company (CPC) in an effort to associate its products with the perceived beauty and novelty of the "Golden State." From the beginning, CPC sold directly to the consumer through a national network of sales agents, primarily women. During the late 19th and early 20th centuries, CPC grew rapidly and expanded its line of products to include cosmetics, household cleaners, food flavorings, and toiletries.

During the 1920s CPC sold several fragrance and cosmetic lines under various names, but the company lacked brand identification. In 1929 it established two separate product lines: "Perfection" (food flavorings and household cleaning products) and "Avon" (toiletries and cosmetics). According to promotional literature, the name Avon had been selected by the company's founder because he thought the area around the company's manufacturing site resembled the English countryside around Stratford-on-Avon. Later company publications admitted that the name Avon was chosen strictly for marketing purposes. CPC was officially renamed Avon Products, Inc., in 1939 to reflect the company's identification with its cosmetics and toiletries lines. McConnell had died two years earlier at age 81.

During its first 50 years, the company did little advertising; instead it relied on catalogs and product samples carried by sales representatives. During the Great Depression, in an attempt to boost sales of Avon cosmetics, CPC began to advertise nationally. It sponsored the radio program *Friends* in 1935 and launched its first continuous national advertising campaign with *Good Housekeeping* magazine in 1936. Within the next few years, Avon cosmetics were advertised in other national women's magazines and in the *Christian Science Monitor*.

Although CPC employed the Luckey Bowman agency during its early years of advertising, Monroe F. Dreher, Inc., created some of Avon's most memorable advertisements over a span of three decades. With the onset of World War II, the "Women of Achievement" campaign featured American heroines and depicted women's contributions to the war effort.

John A. Ewald became company president in 1944 and oversaw Avon's most successful and profitable period. He began his career with CPC in 1920, became the company's general manager, and was elected vice president in 1929 and put in charge of advertising. Because most of the company's top executives had been ad department managers with extensive marketing experience, there was a strong connection between advertising and career achievement at Avon.

Avon's advertisements during the immediate postwar years featured the company's sales representatives with the slogan, "Welcome her when she calls." The celebrity endorsement campaign (1949–52) linked Avon to the glamour of Hollywood and Broadway, professional sports, and high society, and featured such well-known figures as Jimmy Stewart, Celeste Holm, Loretta Young, and Joe DiMaggio.

Avon's spot television commercials first appeared on a limited basis in 1953 in the New York City and Chicago, Illinois, markets, where the company spent more than $100,000. The advertisements, featuring the "Avon calling" slogan and the quintessential doorbell-ringing "Avon lady," focused on Avon's personalized, at-home service. In 1959 its television commercials

An ad from 1975 features Avon's Sweet Honesty, a line of products for teenagers.
Courtesy of Avon Products, Inc.

Avon's arresting 1996 campaign, "Just another Avon Lady," featured extraordinary women such as 1920 Olympic diving medalist Aileen Riggin Soule.
Courtesy of Avon Products, Inc.

reached 99.5 percent of the 44.5 million television homes in the United States.

Avon expanded rapidly into the international market during the 1950s. Although the company had entered Canada in 1914, its operations were limited to North America. A Latin American division was established in 1953, and European offices opened in 1957. With the exception of language, the advertisements were nearly identical to those used in the United States. Advertising in international markets primarily consisted of print advertisements, supplemented in Latin America by the use of filmed commercials in movie theaters and limited television spots.

By the 1960s the advertising budget was approximately $700,000, or about 3 percent of sales. In the mid- to late-1960s, cosmetics and fragrances were highlighted, as well as popular product packaging, including decanters for men's colognes and Peanuts cartoon characters for children's toiletries. During the early 1970s, Avon's advertisements reflected the growing importance of the teen and African-American markets. The company

began advertising its teen products, such as Sweet Honesty, separately from its total line. Starting in 1974 print ads and TV commercials aimed at African-American consumers were produced by Uniworld Group.

Avon changed its primary advertising agency in 1972, retaining Ogilvy & Mather. Advertisements not only featured products but also recruited new sales representatives to its shrinking sales force with the "Someone you know sells Avon" campaign. In 1976 the company doubled the amount spent on print and television advertising for the campaign "You never looked so good." By the 1980s Avon began appealing to upscale, fashionable women, as reflected in the campaign "Avon now, Avon wow," which began airing in mid-1983.

In 1985 Avon retained N.W. Ayer & Son as its agency. During the 1990s much of Avon's advertising focused on the Anew line of anti-aging skin-care products. Ayer created new campaigns annually, including "Just another Avon lady" (1996), "Dare to change your mind about Avon" (1997), and "Claim your beauty" (1998).

Avon appointed N.W. Ayer & Partners (successor to N.W. Ayer & Son and a subsidiary of the MacManus Group) as its single global advertising agency in 1998; previously, the company had used local advertising agencies in international markets. In 1999, however, Avon dismissed Ayer. Instead, the company used its in-house advertising department to handle the creative portion of its advertising and launched its first global campaign with "Let's talk" in 2000. The company budgeted nearly $90 million globally for advertising (4 percent of sales), representing a 50 percent increase from 1999 spending. MediaVest, a unit of the MacManus Group/DMB&B, handled media buying for all markets. At the close of the 20th century, in an attempt to increase sales and develop international name recognition, Avon was promoting a unified brand image internationally and had relaunched established products such as Anew and Avon Color as global brands.

LYNN ANN CATANESE

Further Reading

Machan, Dyan, "The Makeover," *Forbes* (2 December 1996)

Manko, Katina L., "'Now You Are in Business for Yourself': The Independent Contractors of the California Perfume Company, 1886–1930," *Business and Economic History* 26 (1997)

Peiss, Kathy Lee, *Hope in a Jar: The Making of America's Beauty Culture*, New York: Metropolitan Books, 1998

Rudolph, Barbara, "Calling on Avon," *Equity: About Women and Money* (December 1998)

Awards

The contribution of advertising to the longevity, reputation, and economic success of businesses and other organizations undoubtedly accounts, at least in part, for the proliferation of awards programs honoring the creators of great advertising. Each year more than 40 well-known awards programs recognize outstanding work by individuals and groups in the advertising industry.

Some of the best-known and most widely publicized advertising awards programs are discussed in detail below. These include: the Clio Awards, considered by many in the field to be the industry's equivalent of the Oscars; awards sponsored by the American Advertising Federation (AAF), including the national ADDY and the National Student Advertising Competition (NSAC); the One Show award, sponsored by the One Club; the Pro-Comm Awards, sponsored by the Business Marketing Association; the Effie Awards, sponsored by the New York American Marketing Association; the ECHO Awards, sponsored by the Direct Marketing Association; the New York Festivals awards program, which sponsors eight categories of international advertising competitions; the Cresta Awards, sponsored by the International Advertising Association and Creative Standards International, Inc.; the London International Advertising Awards (LIAA); and the "Lions" awarded by the Cannes (France) International Advertising Festival, regarded, in international prestige and renown, as the ad industry's equivalent of the Cannes Film Festival. There are many specialty awards as well, including the Obie, given by the Outdoor Advertising Association of America, and the Radio Advertising Bureau award. All awards programs give prizes in various categories, and most have a single best-of-show award as well.

All of these awards programs are competitions. They have entry fees, guidelines, procedures, and deadlines that must be met for entries to be considered. Advertising agencies and other companies desiring to enter competitions usually set aside a small budget each year for entries, although smaller companies or agencies sometimes find the cost of entering prohibitive. Others believe the publicity generated from entering such competitions justifies the time, money, and effort. Many advertising agencies have found that their efforts are worthwhile because they put the agency's work on the same stage with that of larger, more successful shops while helping their agencies attract some of the brightest professional talent in the market. Conversely, several prominent agencies, including Leo Burnett and Ogilvy & Mather, have at times rejected award competitions as a matter of policy because they believe the awards reward only clever and amusing creative work without regard to strategic soundness or selling effectiveness. As an alternative, some companies have established in-house prizes based on specific standards established by the agency. But even these shops have found it difficult to resist the prestige and publicity of winning in a major competition.

The Clio Awards

The gold, silver, and bronze statuettes of the Clios have long been recognized as the ad industry's equivalent of the Oscars. The Clio Awards, founded in 1959 by Wallace A. Ross to recognize creative excellence in American advertising, remain the most widely known of advertising awards programs, with permanent representatives in 39 countries. The award is named for one of the nine muses in Greek mythology, Clio, who, like the award, was a proclaimer and celebrator of accomplishments as well as a historian.

In the early 1990s the Clio company went into bankruptcy, and ownership of the awards program changed hands. The new owner was Chicago, Illinois, magazine publisher Ruth L. Ratny, whose *Screen Magazine* publishes content about the production of commercials. After managing the awards program for a year,

Courtesy of the Clio Awards.

however, Ratny sold the company to Jim Smyth, a retired post-production executive. In 1997 Smyth sold the company to BPI Communications, its current owner.

Over the years the Clios have expanded to include not only television and radio commercials but also print and outdoor advertising, integrated media, advertising design, Web site and interactive advertising, and student advertising work. Every year in May, a week-long Clio Festival is held in New York City. The festival features conferences, seminars, and panels, a Digital Agency Open House, and a showing of commercials that have made the Clio TV advertising shortlist.

In 1999 the Clio Awards celebrated its 40th birthday with the release of a reel containing more than 100 classic television commercials from the "Clio Hall of Fame" collection. Among these were some of the most popular and memorable moments of four decades of advertising, including Alka-Seltzer's 1971 "Spicy Meatball," Coca-Cola's 1979 "Mean Joe Green" spot, and Apple Computer's "1984" commercial. Only one or two of a year's best television commercials make it to the Clio Hall of Fame. An executive jury selects new inductees, which, even to be nominated, must be at least five years old and the winner of at least one major international advertising award.

The Clio organization uses a democratic system to select annual award winners. A jury of internationally known industry executives votes on each entry. A first round of judging selects a shortlist of entries that advance to round two. After each category's entries are examined separately, members record an "impact" score. Votes for advertisements in each category are then tallied, and the total score is divided by the number of judges voting. Awards are bestowed upon entries scoring within a predetermined range. This scoring system makes it possible to award more than one gold, silver, or bronze award in a particular category. It is also possible that no entry will win an award in a particular category.

In 1965 the Clios expanded beyond U.S. borders to begin recognizing advertising creative excellence on a global scale. In the year 2000 the program attracted more than 18,000 entries from advertising agencies and production companies in 59 countries.

American Advertising Federation Awards Competitions

The American Advertising Federation (AAF), an organization with more than 50,000 members, strives to educate the public about the impact of advertising on the economy as well as on the culture. The organization sponsors a variety of awards and recognition programs. The AAF's most coveted professional award is the national ADDY. Competition begins at the "grassroots" level in local markets throughout the United States. Entries recognized as the best in their local markets can choose to compete against the best work in their districts. The 14 district winners then compete in the American Advertising Awards competition for the national ADDY trophy.

The largest and most representative competition for domestically produced advertising, the American Advertising Awards features categories for sales promotion, collateral material, direct marketing, out-of-home media, trade publications, consumer magazines, newspapers, Yellow Pages–type directory advertising, interactive media, radio, television, mixed media campaigns, industry self-promotions, visual and audio elements of advertising, advertising for the arts, and public service advertising.

Many college students in the United States compete in the AAF's collegiate version of its advertising awards competition, the National Student Advertising Competition (NSAC), begun in 1974. Competing in this event requires research, planning, and development of realistic and creative solutions, which are presented to representatives of nationally or internationally known corporate clients. The 1999 NSAC client was Toyota Motor Sales U.S.A. Fifteen student teams that had won top honors in their districts advanced to the national contest, where students from the University of California, Los Angeles, triumphed over students from the 14 other competing districts to secure the AAF's highest student honor. The NSAC is governed by the AAF's Education Services Committee, which is made up of advertising educators and practitioners from around the United States.

The AAF also recognizes advertising "legends"—individuals who have made outstanding contributions to the industry—with its Advertising Hall of Fame. Its Distinguished Advertising Educator Award honors those with records of distinction in teaching, scholarly research, writing, and student advisement.

In addition, the AAF pleads the cause of advertisers before policymakers, the news media, and the general public. It is the only ad industry association bridging the common interests of advertising agencies, media organizations, client companies and suppliers, and the academic advertising community.

The One Show

The One Show is an annual awards program sponsored by the One Club, an organization founded in 1975 to promote high standards among advertising artists and copywriters. Its top prize, a gold pencil, is one of the most coveted and sought-after symbols of creative success in the ad industry. The One Club also seeks to sharpen the creative talents of current and future generations of advertising artists and copywriters by sponsoring publications (including *One*, a magazine featuring content written by some of the top creative professionals in the United States), creative workshops and exhibitions, awards competitions, scholarships, portfolio reviews, and exhibitions of the work of college students.

Judging is by panels of the industry's most renowned creative directors. Categories of judging include television, radio, newspaper, magazine, billboard, and public service. In 1997 the club introduced the One Show Interactive, an event bringing together and honoring the most creative among interactive and new-media advertising professionals.

The One Club introduced a competition for young creative professionals in the year 2000. This competition hosts 30 teams of college students and junior creative professionals, who compete in the categories of print, interactive/new media, and television advertising. Award winners have their work published in the *One Show Annual*. In addition, the One Club College Competition

Courtesy of The One Club.

awards gold, silver, and bronze pencils to advertising campaigns produced by students. Besides the pencil trophies, winners of this competition receive cash awards and have their work published in the *One Show Annual*. In 1995 the club established an education department, which awards scholarships to students who demonstrate the highest standards of creative excellence in advertising programs at universities around the United States.

The Pro-Comm Awards

The Business Marketing Association (BMA) has sponsored the Pro-Comm Awards, an annual not-for-profit communications competition, since 1975. These awards recognize and reward excellence in business-to-business marketing communications. The competition is open to clients, agencies, and suppliers preparing or producing marketing communications directed to industry, business, or the legal and medical professions.

The BMA was established in 1922 to provide educational resources for its members. Its offerings include certification, conferences and seminars, career-enhancement programs, materials and services, and links to a global network of business-to-business marketing professionals. Since the category of business-to-business marketing communications is not included in many industry awards competitions, the BMA has taken the lead in encouraging and rewarding superior work in this category. Pro-Comm is the largest (and most prominent) awards competition of its kind.

Pro-Comm entries are judged by a panel of business-to-business marketing experts on the basis of visual impact, product identity, selling proposition, and effectiveness as related to stated objectives. Pro-Comm requires that all entries be accompanied by a brief statement of the communications objective, target audience, and, if known, results of efforts. Judging categories include space advertising campaigns, single advertisements, direct mail, total communications programs, promotional material, corporate identity, annual reports, newsletters/house organs, broadcast media, audiovisual presentations, electronic media, agency promotional materials, public relations, and exhibitions and trade shows. There are three levels of Pro-Comm awards: Professional Excellence awards, for excellence in business-to-business marketing communications; Best of Division awards, for the best single entry in each division or category; and Best of Show, for the single competition entry receiving the highest score.

The Effie Awards

The Effie Awards competition is sponsored by the New York chapter of the American Marketing Association (New York AMA), a group established in 1931. The first Effies were awarded in 1969, and the competition began accepting radio commercial entries in 1970. In 1976 the rules were changed to recognize campaigns rather than single advertisements. This highly respected award is primarily concerned with how well ads have performed in the marketplace: Effie is a shortened version of the word *effectiveness*. Since most well-known national advertising awards competitions do not include proven effectiveness as an entry criterion, this requirement alone sets the Effie apart. To win an Effie, an advertising campaign must prove that it has achieved its business objective. Winning entries must show evidence of effective planning, market research, media and creative strategy, and account management as well as evidence of successful brand management, which reflects a strong working relationship between the client company and the ad agency.

Top advertising and marketing executives serve as jurors for the Effie. Judging takes place in two phases. A "round one" panel examines the case brief, which contains a summary of the business results attributed to the campaign, accompanying each entry. Round one includes no creative materials, and no comparisons are made with other entries. Entries surviving to round two compete with others in their category on the basis of case briefs and creativity for the Gold (the Grand Effie), Silver, and Merit awards. Certificates of recognition are awarded to runners-up. Case briefs and creative materials are scored separately, and the final score is a weighted average of the two scores, with briefs counting more than the creative materials.

The year 2000 Effie competition offered awards in 46 campaign categories including agricultural/industrial/building products, Internet services, and travel/tourism/destination advertising campaigns. Since 1981, Effie Awards competitions have been established in numerous other countries, including Austria, Belgium, Chile, the Czech Republic, France, Germany, Greece, India, The Netherlands, Peru, Slovakia, and Switzerland. Each country or region establishes its own entry requirements and judges its own entries. Euro Effie, for example, requires that campaign entries have proven business success in at least three European countries. The New York AMA also sponsors local, national, and international conferences; publications; other awards; networking events; and career development services.

The ECHO Awards

The ECHO is an annual direct-marketing awards program sponsored by the Direct Marketing Association (DMA), the world's largest trade association for professionals involved in direct, interactive, and database marketing. Founded in 1917, the DMA provides its nearly 4,600 members in 54 countries with resources and services designed to help them achieve greater business effectiveness. Dubbed the "Oscar" of direct-marketing awards, the international ECHO award, established in 1929, honors direct-marketing strategy, creativity, and marketplace results. In 1999 the competition attracted nearly 1,000 entries, of which slightly more than half were from U.S. competitors.

The judges of the ECHO competition, some of the industry's top-performing marketing communications experts, examine 11 categories of entries each year, including nonprofit fund-raising, financial products and services, consumer services, business services, publishing, communications/utilities, automotive, manufacturing and distribution, packaged goods, retailing, and direct response sales. The ten media categories included are flat mail, dimensional mail, print, television/radio commercials, catalog, infomercial, internet/interactive media, telephone, alternative media, and multimedia/integrated media. Winning entries are awarded gold, silver, or bronze trophies. A Diamond ECHO is reserved for the "Best of Show," and the United States Postal Service Gold Mailbox is awarded for the most innovative and effective direct mail campaign.

The New York Festivals

The New York Festivals awards program began in 1957 to honor achievement in industrial and educational film and video. The program later expanded to include all types of media used by communications professionals. Television and cinema advertising were added in the 1970s; the category of international radio was added in 1982, including programming, production, and advertising. In 1984 print advertising, design, photography, and illustration were added to the roster. A category for new media, including competitions for interactive Internet communications and advertising, was added in 1992. The event attracted around 1,000 entries from around the world in 1979. By 1999 international entries totaled more than 1,600.

Judging of the New York Festivals is conducted by an international panel of communications professionals and business executives. Judges examine entries in eight categories: advertising and marketing effectiveness (AME), health-care, television and cinema, television programming and promotion, film and video, print and radio advertising, radio programming and promotion, and new media. The New York Festivals present three different categories of international awards. The "International" gold, silver, and bronze medals are awarded for the world's best work in advertising and marketing effectiveness. "Global" gold, silver, and bronze medals recognize the world's best work in health-care communications. "World" gold, silver, and bronze medals are awarded for the world's best work in educational, informational and industrial productions, home videos, short films, business theater, and multi-image.

The Cresta Awards

The International Advertising Association (IAA) and Creative Standards International, Inc., launched the Cresta Awards competition in 1993. Cresta, which stands for *creative standards*, reflects the goal of the awards program's two sponsoring organizations, which is to establish international standards of excellence for consumer and business communications. These organizations also assist advertising agencies, studios, and production houses in building international reputations.

The competition honors campaigns that have met an absolute standard for creative excellence in advertising and marketing communications. Cresta entries are judged by two criteria: originality of the creative idea and quality of execution. Even though entries are evaluated in categories, there can be more than one Cresta winner in a category if creative standards of excellence have been met by more than one entry. Similarly, it is possible for no Cresta to be awarded in a category if no entries meet Cresta's standards of excellence.

National and international advertising campaigns are eligible to compete for Cresta Awards. Advertising clubs, agencies, and IAA chapters from around the world organize the first phase of judging for the competition and submit a shortlist of finalists to an international grand jury comprising creative directors, film specialists, and graphic artists, which then votes to determine Cresta award winners. Award winners receive either trophies or diplomas. In the year 2000, 45 internationally known creative experts from 30 different countries served on the Cresta Awards grand jury.

London International Advertising Awards

The London International Advertising Awards program (LIAA), begun in 1985, attracts entries from international advertising agencies, production houses, and new-media development companies. The program has won praise from the advertising community for the degree of international diversity it brings to its competition. The organizers believe that the globalization of business and marketing has leveled the playing field for entrants in international advertising competitions such as the LIAA.

The LIAA includes five broad categories with many different subcategories, each of which may produce only one top prizewinner. The broad categories are television/cinema, print, radio, interactive advertising, and package design. In 1999 there were 17,200 entries from 84 countries, and the LIAA awarded 151 top prizes for creativity in advertising. Instead of convening a panel of judges during the awards program, the LIAA sends the entries to each judge separately to evaluate for a two-week period. The organizers believe that this system reduces peer and time pressures and removes politics from the judging process. Grand Prize–winners receive a bronze winged statuette.

Cannes International Advertising Festival

The Cannes (France) International Advertising Festival began in 1954, making it the longest running of the well-known international advertising competitions. The festival was started by the president of a cinema screen advertising sales company who had for many years attended the Cannes International Film Festival. He was so inspired by the annual celebration recognizing exceptional work in the motion picture industry that he and a small group of contractors working for his company decided to similarly acknowledge creators of advertising films. Thus the International Advertising Film Festival, as it was originally known, was born. For some years the festival was held in two cities, Cannes and Venice, Italy. The event became so popular, however, that after 23 years it outgrew its Venice facilities and was permanently established in Cannes.

The Cannes International Advertising Festival originally evaluated only cinema and television advertising according to categories based on technical attributes, such as length and whether they used animation or live action. After 13 years, with the maturation of television as an entertainment medium, festival organizers decided to begin classifying commercials based on product category. In the early 1990s festival planners added press (newspaper and magazine) and poster (billboard and other public site) advertising. Later categories for Web sites, on-line advertising, and, in 1999, media ideas were added. "Media ideas" is an innovative category that rewards outstanding ideas in media strategy, planning, and execution. This event attracted more than 421 of the world's best media planners from 30 different countries in its first year.

Judging is patterned after that of the Cannes International Film Festival. International advertising leaders gather during the weeklong program in June to judge the competition entries. The festival's highest honor is the Grand Prix. The program also includes a competition recognizing the on-site work of young creative professionals, seminars and workshops designed for client-side marketing departments, and events showcasing the latest in advertising production technology. The festival also stages creative seminars led by the world's top creative executives, hosts symposia examining case histories, and holds workshops on global selling and marketing.

SALLIE MIDDLEBROOK

Further Reading

Bishop, Todd, "Rival Club to Take Shot at the Addys," *Philadelphia Business Journal* (22 February 1999)

The Book: The American Advertising Awards, vol. 3, Washington, D.C.: American Advertising Federation, 1997

Bowen, Susan Brown, "Ad Awards Promote Agency Portfolio, Attract Talent," *The Business Journal of Jacksonville* (7 February 2000)

Caci, Fran, and Donna Howard, editors, *Winning with Promotion Power: 100 Best of the Best Promotions: The Reggie Award Winners,* Chicago: Dartnell, 1994

Eurobest 4: The Annual European Advertising and Design Awards, London: Booth-Clibborn Editions, 1996

Ficco, Jim, "Why You Should Care If Your Ad Agency Wins Creative Awards," *Pittsburgh Business Times* (17 February 1997)

Greco, Nick, editor, *3-Dimensional Illustrators Awards Annual II: The Best in 3-D Advertising and Publicity Worldwide,* Rockport, Massachusetts: Rockport, and Southampton, Pennsylvania: Dimensional Illustrators, 1992

Hatch, Denison, *Million Dollar Mailings,* Washington, D.C.: Libey, 1992

Matthews, David, "Small-Business Owners Practice the Art of Winning," *The Business Journal Phoenix* (28 June 1999)

Mull, Angela, "Anshell Scores at London International," *The Business Journal Phoenix* (8 December 1997)

Mullich, Joe, "Awards that Slam Commercials Are Anti-American" *Business First: The Weekly Business Newspaper of Greater Louisville* (10 August 1998)

New York Festivals: International Advertising Awards 7, New York: Hearst, 1999

Riordan, Steve, *Clio Awards: A Tribute to 30 Years of Advertising Excellence, 1960–1989,* Glen Cove, New York: PBC International, 1989

Silver, Linda, editor, *Print's Best Illustration and Photography,* New York: RC, 1993

Tascarella, Patty, "Upstart Shops Upstage Big Agencies at Addy Awards," *Pittsburgh Business Times* (17 February 1997)

Tascarella, Patty, "And the Winner Is . . . : Local Advertising Agencies Pursue Awards, but Does Victory Translate into Business?" *Pittsburgh Business Times* (5 July 1999)

Uyeno, Kristine, "Agencies Praise Clients Following Pele Awards," *Pacific Business News* (31 March 1997)

N.W. Ayer & Son, Inc.

(N.W. Ayer & Partners)

Founded as N.W. Ayer & Son by Francis Wayland Ayer in Philadelphia, Pennsylvania, 1869; purchased Hixson & Jorgenson, 1970, Frederick E. Baker, 1970; relocated to New York City, 1974; purchased by Cunningham & Walsh, 1986, Adcom Investors, 1993; merged with D'Arcy Masius Benton & Bowles and several smaller public relations and media services firms to form the MacManus Group, 1996; MacManus Group joined with the Leo Group and Tokyo-based Dentsu to form the global advertising and marketing services holding company Bcom3, 1999; merged into the Kaplan Thaler Group and closed, 2002.

Major Clients

American Telephone and Telegraph Company (later AT&T Corporation)

DeBeers Consolidated Mines, Inc.

Ford Motor Company

Philip Morris Companies

R.J. Reynolds Tobacco Company

Steinway & Sons

United Airlines

U.S. Army Recruiting Command

Western Union Telegraph Company

Founded in Philadelphia, Pennsylvania, in 1869, N.W. Ayer & Son was, for most of its history, a leader and innovator in the field of advertising. In 1876 Ayer pioneered the "open contract," a revolutionary change in the method of billing for advertising that became the industry standard for the next hundred years. It also pioneered the use of fine art in advertising and established the industry's first art department. It was the first agency to use a full-time copywriter and the first to institute a copy department. During the agency's long history, its clients included many blue-chip advertisers, among them AT&T Corporation, DeBeers Consolidated Mines, Ford Motor Company, Nabisco, and United Airlines. In later years, however, the inherent conservatism of Ayer left the agency vulnerable to the "creative revolution" of the 1960s and 1970s, the industry restructuring of the 1980s, and the economic recession of the early 1990s. The agency was bought by a Korean investor in 1993, and in 1996 Ayer merged with another struggling U.S. advertising agency, D'Arcy Masius Benton & Bowles, under the umbrella of the MacManus Group. Nonetheless, Ayer continued to operate as a separate, full-service agency until it was merged into the Kaplan Thaler Group in 2002.

Origins

However indirectly, N.W. Ayer traced its lineage to the first advertising agency founded in the United States, a Philadelphia agency begun by Volney Palmer in 1841. Palmer began his career in advertising as a newspaper agent, acting as a middleman between newspaper publishers and advertisers across the country. By 1849 Palmer had founded his own newspaper, *V.B. Palmer's Register and Spirit of the Press,* and had developed a complete system of advertising that included securing advertising space and placing ads in scores of commercial, political, religious, scientific, and agricultural journals. Palmer went one step further than the "space jobbers" of the day when he began offering "advertisements carefully drawn for those who have not the time to prepare an original copy." Always an enthusiastic promoter of advertising as an incentive to trade and economic growth, Palmer promised advertisers that "every dollar paid for advertising in country newspapers will pay back twenty-fold" and encouraged skeptical consumers that "he who wishes to buy cheap should buy of those who advertise." When Palmer died in 1863, the agency was bought by his bookkeeper, John Joy, who joined with another Philadelphia advertising agency to form Joy, Coe & Sharpe. That agency was bought out again in 1868 and renamed Coe, Wetherill & Company. In 1877 Coe, Wetherill was bought out by the newly formed N.W. Ayer & Son.

Francis Wayland Ayer was an ambitious young schoolteacher with an entrepreneurial streak. Having worked for a year soliciting advertisements on a commission basis for the publisher of the *National Baptist* weekly, he saw the potential to turn a profit as an advertising agent. In 1869 Ayer persuaded his father, Nathan Wheeler Ayer, to join him in business, and with an initial investment of only $250, N.W. Ayer & Son was born. Notwithstanding a smallpox epidemic in Philadelphia in 1871 and the general economic depression of the early 1870s, the agency flourished. The senior Ayer died in 1873, leaving his interest in the agency to his wife, but the son bought her out, consolidating his interest in the company's management. In 1877, with Coe, Wetherill & Company on the verge of bankruptcy and heavily indebted for advertising it had placed in publications for which Ayer acted as agent, Ayer assumed ownership of the agency.

Both Ayers had begun their careers as schoolteachers, and so their legacy included a commitment to the cause of education, with correspondence schools and institutions of higher learning historically well represented among Ayer clients. Just after World War I the agency was heralded as the "co-founder of more schools than any citizen of this country" for its conspicuous efforts to advertise private schools. Well into the 1960s, Ayer had an education department that prepared ads for more than 300 private schools, camps, and colleges, representing almost half of the regional and national advertising done for such institutions. In fact, to its clients Ayer presented advertising itself as being akin to a system of education. In 1886 the agency began promoting the virtues of the so-called Ayer way in advertising with the slogan, "Keeping everlastingly at it brings success."

Ayer's fortunes initially were tied to newspapers, and the agency began to make a name for itself as the compiler and publisher of the widely used *American Newspaper Annual*. During the first years Ayer's singular goal was "to get business, place it [in newspapers] and get money for it." After several years as an independent space broker, however, Francis Ayer resolved "not to be an order-taker any longer." This decision led the agency to a change in its mode of conducting business, a move that would revolutionize the advertising industry. In 1876 Ayer pioneered the open contract with Diggee & Conard, Philadelphia, a rose grower and agricultural supplier. Prior to this time, Ayer and most agencies had operated as independent wholesalers of advertising space; under this system, opportunities for graft and corrupt practices were virtually unlimited. In contrast, the open contract allowed the advertiser to pay a fixed commission based on the volume of advertising placed, aligned the advertising agent firmly on the side of the advertiser, and gave advertisers access to the actual rates charged by newspapers and journals.

Although adoption of the open contract by the industry did not come about overnight, by 1884 nearly three-quarters of Ayer's advertising billings were on an open-contract basis. Since Ayer was the largest agency in America by the 1890s, the switch to direct payment by advertisers had a significant impact on the industry, as other agencies were forced to respond to Ayer's higher standard. Just as important, the open contract helped to establish Ayer's longstanding reputation for "clean ethics and fair dealing." Its use of open contracts also helped establish Ayer as a full-service advertising agency. Ayer routinely offered advice and service beyond the placement of advertisements.

Ayer set another milestone for advertising in 1888 when Jarvis Wood was hired as the industry's first full-time copywriter. Wood was joined by a second full-time copywriter four years later, and the copy department was formally established in 1900. Ayer hired its first commercial artist to assist with copy preparation in 1898, and 12 years later Ayer became the first agency to offer the services of a full-time art director, whose sole responsibility was the design and illustration of ads. By 1918 the agency's billings had reached $6 million, and Francis Ayer predicted that they would soon hit $1 million a month. In 1924 they did.

In 1913 Ayer won the Camel cigarette account from R.J. Reynolds Tobacco Company, which was launching the brand to compete with the American Tobacco Company's Lucky Strike. Camel was a blend of tobaccos concocted by R.J. Reynolds himself, who boasted that "if you pay money for the best tobaccos, isn't that the best advertising you can get?" Ayer built Camel into one of the "Big Three" cigarette brands by the 1920s following Reynolds's lead with such simple slogans as, "No better cigarette can be made" and "The Camels are coming." Camel and Lucky Strike vied for the number-one position, and Ayer and Lord & Thomas (which handled the American Tobacco brand) became rivals. But Camel sales fell sharply in the late 1920s, and Ayer decided to respond with a massive $300,000 investment in newspaper space exposing "false and misleading statements in recent cigarette advertising." This "one sledge-hammer blow" did not stop Camel's decline, however. In 1930 Ayer lost the account to Erwin, Wasey & Company.

Creating Legends

Ayer's leadership in the use of fine art in advertising had its roots in this period but achieved its highest expression under the guidance of the legendary art director Charles Coiner. He joined the agency in 1924 after graduating from the Chicago Academy of Fine Arts. Despite early resistance from some clients, Coiner was adamant that "the use of outstanding palette and original art forms bring a greater return in readership, in impact and prestige for the advertiser." To this end, Coiner marshaled the talents of notable painters, illustrators, and photographers, including N.C. Wyeth and Rockwell Kent (Steinway), Georgia O'Keefe (Dole), Leo Lionni (DuPont), Edward Steichen (Steinway, Cannon Mills), Charles Sheeler (Ford), and Irving Penn (DeBeers). Coiner believed that there was a practical side to the use of fine art in advertising, and his and Ayer's success lay in the marriage of

An Interpretation of
MACDOWELL'S
Indian Suite

Painted for the
Steinway
Collection

by Ernest Blumenschein

STEINWAY

THE INSTRUMENT OF THE IMMORTALS

IT IS the way with art that once we know and love the best we cannot be satisfied with any other than the best. You who find your deepest satisfaction in the music of the immortals—men such as Wagner, Liszt and our own MacDowell—surely when you buy a piano, you can be satisfied only with the instrument which these men used themselves, the Instrument of the Immortals. Once your fingers touch the keyboard of the Steinway—once you know the eloquence of its response—once you drink the beauty of its tone, for you there can be no other piano. You would be just as unwilling to own another instrument as Paderewski would be, or Rachmaninoff, or Hofmann. Each time you hear the Steinway its voice means more to you. With each new year it grows into your life. Is it any wonder the Steinway is the piano chosen by the great composers, pianists and teachers? Is it any wonder so many people say: "It is the dream of my life to own a Steinway"?

Steinway & Sons and their dealers have made it conveniently possible for music lovers to own a Steinway.
Prices: $875 and up, plus freight at points distant from New York.

STEINWAY & SONS, Steinway Hall, 109 E. 14th St., New York

This long-running ad campaign and slogan by N.W. Ayer & Son, Inc., for Steinway is still cited for its elegant combination of image and copy.
N.W. Ayer Collection, Archives Center, NMAH, Smithsonian Institution. Courtesy of Steinway & Sons.

research and copywriting with fine art, an arrangement Coiner termed "art for business sake." Coiner's efforts won both awards and attention for a series completed in the 1950s for the Container Corporation of America. Titled "Great Ideas of Western Man," the campaign featured abstract and modern paintings and sculpture by leading U.S. and European artists. The artworks were linked with Western philosophical writings in what amounted to an early example of advertising designed primarily to bolster a corporate image. In 1994 Coiner was posthumously named to the American Advertising Federation's Hall of Fame, the first full-time art director ever chosen for the honor.

Coiner and fellow art director Paul Darrow also created the legendary "A diamond is forever" campaign for DeBeers, with ads featuring works by Pablo Picasso, Salvador Dali, and other modernist painters. The "A diamond is forever" tag line was written in 1949 by Frances Gerety, a copywriter at Ayer from 1943 to 1970. In 1999 Advertising Age cited the slogan as the most memorable of the 20th century.

Coiner also earned respect for his volunteer government service during World War II. He designed the armbands for civil defense volunteers and the logos for the National Recovery Administration and the Community Chest. As a founding member of the Advertising Council in 1945, N.W. Ayer associated itself with public service advertising. In the mid-1980s Ayer became a leading force in the "War on Drugs" campaign of the administration of President Ronald Reagan. Lou Hagopian, Ayer's sixth chief executive officer (CEO), brokered the establishment of the Partnership for a Drug-Free America, a media coalition that generated as much as a million dollars a day in donated time and advertising space aimed at preventing the use and abuse of illegal drugs.

By 1944 Ayer was the third-largest U.S. advertising agency, after the J. Walter Thompson Company (JWT) and Young & Rubicam, with billings estimated at $33 million. Among its major accounts were Chrysler Corporation's Plymouth division, whose growth after the war offset losses from Boeing Aircraft; the Birdseye division of American Home Products; and additional business from the Kellogg Company. Ayer also worked on the early television advertising for American Tobacco's Lucky Strike brand. The relationship was brief, however, ending when the account was consolidated at Batten Barton Durstine & Osborn in 1948. U.S. Army billings also expanded after the war, but the account went to Gardner Advertising and later Grant Advertising in 1949. Nevertheless, the agency celebrated its 80th birthday in that year with billings of about $65 million and a fourth-place ranking among the top agencies. After a healthy but static period in the early 1950s, growth took off again and carried Ayer over the $100 million mark in 1957.

Famous names appeared among Ayer's clientele from the very earliest days of the agency. They included retailer John Wanamaker, Jay Cooke and Company, and Montgomery Ward's mail-order business, all among the first Ayer clients. Over the years the agency represented at least 20 automobile manufacturers, including Cadillac, Chrysler, Ford, General Motors, Plymouth, DeSoto, and Rolls-Royce. Other major clients through the years included

Canada Dry, Cannon Mills, Hills Bros. Coffee Company, and Philip Morris. By the time of the agency's 100th anniversary in 1969, some of these companies had been Ayer clients for decades, and the longevity of these relationships was for many years a source of Ayer's strength.

Facing New Challenges

But the advertising industry began to change in the late 1960s and 1970s, due in part to what was called the "creative revolution." Small agencies won attention with provocative copywriting and art direction that more closely resembled art than advertising. Advances in market research allowed clients to tailor their ad messages to specific groups of consumers, which led to a rise in targeted marketing that could more readily be assigned to specialized "boutique" agencies than to larger, traditionally structured agencies. Thus it was that advertisers came to bypass the old, established firms such as Ayer, which maintained a tradition into the 1960s of originating all creative work in Philadelphia. Older, more conservative shops such as Ayer were hard pressed to compete, and by 1960 Ayer had dropped to tenth place among major agencies.

In 1969, in an effort to meet these challenges and to establish a foothold on the West Coast, N.W. Ayer bought out two smaller agencies—Hixson & Jorgenson (Los Angeles, California) and Frederick E. Baker (Seattle, Washington). The agency relocated from Philadelphia to New York City in 1974 in an attempt both to consolidate operations (Ayer had operated a New York office since the 1920s) and to be closer to the historic center of the advertising industry. Riding the wave of mergers that characterized the advertising industry from the 1970s on, Ayer continued to grow through the acquisition of Rink Wells & Associates, of Chicago, in March 1972 and Cunningham & Walsh, New York City, in 1986.

During this transitional period Ayer received widespread acclaim for its work for U.S. Army recruiting, which returned to the agency roster in 1967. "Be all that you can be," launched later in the decade, was widely credited with helping the army reach its recruitment goals, despite an unpopular war and plummeting enlistments after the elimination of the draft in 1973. The agency lost the account in 1986 amid government charges that an Ayer employee assigned to the account had accepted kickbacks from a New York film production company. In spite of Ayer's position as the 18th-largest U.S. agency (with billings of $880 million in 1985) and its selection by Advertising Age as the Agency of the Year in 1978, the loss of its second-largest account hit hard.

Ayer made up for the loss of the $100 million U.S. Army account and made headlines for being on the winning end of the largest account switch in advertising history to that date. This occurred when fast-food giant Burger King moved its $200 million account from archrival JWT in 1987. Ayer made headlines again, however, when it lost the account just 18 months later in another record-breaking switch.

A further devastating blow to the agency was the loss of its lead position on the AT&T account. N.W. Ayer had pioneered telecommunications advertising in 1908, when the agency was selected to craft advertising for the Bell System's universal telephone service. Despite valiant efforts to keep an account the agency had held for most of the 20th century, and for which it had written such memorable corporate slogans as "The voice with a smile" and "Reach out and touch someone," Ayer lost the business in 1996.

After a wave of mergers and acquisitions in the late 1980s, the economic recession triggered in 1987 hit Madison Avenue hard, and Ayer was particularly vulnerable. Despite the agency's long history and roster of blue-chip clients, it was not known for cutting-edge creative work. Moreover, although the agency had offices overseas, Ayer had never built a strong multinational presence. This left a serious void in the new climate of global marketplace consolidation. By 1990 earnings were declining (although Ayer was still among the top 20 U.S. agencies in billings), and the agency was suffering from client defections, a high rate of management turnover, expensive real estate commitments, and deferred executive compensation deals, all fallout from the high-flying 1980s. This was the atmosphere in 1993 when W.Y. Choi, a Korean investor who had already assembled a media and marketing empire in his homeland, began looking for an American partner to form an international advertising network. Jerry Siano, the former creative director who had recently been named Ayer's seventh CEO, was in no position to refuse Choi's offer of $35 million to buy the now-floundering agency. The infusion of cash was no magic bullet, however. Choi took a wait-and-see approach, allowing his partner Richard Humphreys to make key decisions about Ayer's future, including the purging of senior executives and the installation of two new CEOs in as many years.

Rebuilding

The agency's downward trend continued with the loss of another longtime client, the DeBeers diamond cartel, in 1995. *Adweek* reported that Ayer's billings had fallen from $892 million in 1990 to less than $850 million in 1995. Several top executives defected abruptly, and the agency failed to attract major new accounts. Ayer was facing the loss of revenue and personnel as well as much of the respect it had once commanded. Although Ayer remained among the 20 largest U.S. agencies, an aura of uncertainty hung over it. In 1995 Mary Lou Quinlan became the first woman to serve as the agency's CEO. A year later, Ayer and another struggling top-20 agency, D'Arcy Masius Benton & Bowles, were combined as part of the MacManus Group. In 1998 the MacManus Group had worldwide billings of more than $6.5 billion.

Under the MacManus Group, N.W. Ayer & Partners was able to expand its international operations and begin to rebuild a stronger global presence. Several important new clients were won in 1997 and 1998, including Avon, General Motors, KitchenAid, several Procter & Gamble brands, and, most notably, the worldwide account for Continental Airlines. In 1999 the MacManus Group joined with the Chicago-based Leo Group (parent company for Leo Burnett and other agencies) and Tokyo-based Dentsu to form Bcom3, a global advertising and marketing ser-

This campaign from N.W. Ayer & Son for the U.S. Army Recruiting Command was launched in 1981. The slogan remained in use for two decades.
Army materials courtesy of the U.S. Government.

vices holding company with more than 520 offices in more than 90 countries. Born in the 19th century, Ayer appeared to be one of a very few advertising agencies to successfully weather the economic and cultural transitions of both the 20th and 21st centuries. Then, in April 2002, Ayer was merged into the Kaplan Thaler Group and closed.

MIMI MINNICK

Further Reading

Ayer: 125 Years of Building Brands, New York: Ayer Worldwide, 1994

"Creativity at Ayer," *Back Stage* (special issue, 1981)

Cummings, Bart, editor, *The Benevolent Dictators: Interviews with Advertising Greats*, Chicago: Crain, 1984

Dunning, Deanne, and Blake Hunter, "The New Ayer," *Communications Arts* 12, no. 1 (1970)

Farrell, Greg, and Jennifer Comiteau, "Disappearing into Ayer," *Adweek* (Eastern Edition) (27 May 1996)

Fox, Stephen, *The Mirror Makers: A History of American Advertising and Its Creators*, New York: Morrow, 1984

Hower, Ralph M., *The History of an Advertising Agency: N.W. Ayer and Son at Work, 1869–1939*, Cambridge, Massachusetts: Harvard University Press, 1939; revised edition, as *The History of an Advertising Agency: N.W. Ayer and Son at Work, 1869–1949*, Cambridge, Massachusetts: Harvard University Press, 1949

"A Profile in Print: N.W. Ayer and Son," *Print* 13, no. 6 (November–December 1959)

B

Backer & Spielvogel, Inc.

Founded by William M. Backer and Carl Spielvogel, 1979; landed Miller Brewing Company's $85 million High Life, Lowenbrau, and Lite business less than two months after launch; acquired by Saatchi & Saatchi Company PLC, 1986; merged with Saatchi's Ted Bates Worldwide and the British firm Dorland Advertising, Ltd., to form Backer Spielvogel Bates Worldwide, 1987; Backer retired, 1993; Backer and Spielvogel names dropped from agency, 1994; Spielvogel resigned, 1994.

Major Clients
Campbell Soup Company
Cunard Line
Hyundai Motor America
Magnavox
Miller Brewing Company
Warner-Wellcome Consumer Products
Wendy's

Within a span of 15 years, Backer & Spielvogel burst onto the New York City advertising scene as a small, innovative, full-service agency, developed a reputation for creative risk-taking, became a unit of the Saatchi empire when its size seemed to limit expansion possibilities, and faced dissolution soon after the Backer and Spielvogel names were stripped from the agency's door and its two famous founders departed. Backer & Spielvogel's life cycle stretched over a period of feel-good economics followed by a general recession that was marked by agency mega-mergers and rampant consolidation. Its passing marked the end of an era for veterans of the golden years of 1950s and 1960s television advertising.

Backer & Spielvogel was launched in a Gotham Hotel suite in New York City in June 1979 by Carl Spielvogel and William M. Backer, two executives with big-agency experience, and five other partners. The fledgling company debuted without a single client.

A native of Charleston, South Carolina, Backer had begun his advertising career in 1953 as a copywriter at McCann-Erickson. He co-wrote the memorable "I'd like to teach the world to sing" and "It's the real thing" for Coca-Cola, created the mellow "Miller Time" campaign for Miller Brewing Company's Miller High Life beer, and the "Soup Is Good Food" campaign for the Campbell Soup Company.

The Brooklyn-born Spielvogel was a young reporter at the *New York Times* in 1958 when he was asked to pen the newspaper's first bylined column on advertising and marketing. Two years later, Marion Harper, chairman of McCann-Erickson Worldwide, invited him to join McCann as public relations director. Spielvogel assisted Harper in building the Interpublic Group of Companies and implementing Harper's idea of a worldwide network of agencies.

Spielvogel remained at Interpublic for two decades, leaving as vice chairman and chairman of the executive committee. Backer was executive vice chairman and creative director of McCann when he left that agency. Perceived by many as "the odd couple" among New York City ad agency heads, the patrician Backer and the street-smart Spielvogel did not seek "traditional, small-agency start-up accounts," Backer said at the agency's launch. "We're looking for the kind of client that knows the difference between good advertising and froth." "We've seen every mistake in the ad business. We'll just try not to repeat 'em," Spielvogel said.

Less than two months after opening, Backer & Spielvogel landed Miller Brewing Company's $85 million High Life, Lowenbrau, and Lite businesses, which had been at McCann-Erickson. It was the second-largest account switch in advertising history. Since Miller created the Miller Lite brand in 1973, Backer, Spielvogel, and another partner, Robert Lenz, had worked on the account at McCann; there, Backer and Lenz helped coin the memorable "Tastes great . . . less filling" tag line as well as "Everything you always wanted in a beer . . . and less."

Seven-Up, like Miller a unit of Philip Morris, Inc., awarded a new product assignment formerly at Leo Burnett Company to Backer & Spielvogel in February 1980. Two months later, the agency landed the $10 million Paddington Corporation liquor account and, soon after, a special assignment from Campbell Soup Company for its condensed soups.

It was not long before Backer & Spielvogel had made Dave Thomas, the founder of the Wendy's fast-food chain, into a household name and achieved success with irreverent commercials for

Magnavox television sets (starring John Cleese of the comedy troupe Monty Python) as well as cheeky ads for Hyundai that depicted a self-help group composed of Hyundai owners.

But the small agency with big ambitions began to feel the limitations of its size. In April 1986 Backer & Spielvogel agreed to be acquired by Saatchi & Saatchi Company PLC for more than $50 million. By that time the agency had total billings of about $450 million; clients included Arby's, Helene Curtis Industries, NCR Corporation, Philip Morris USA, and Quaker Oats Company. According to Spielvogel, joining the London, England-based Saatchi communications empire would provide worldwide facilities for the agency. He blamed the agency's lack of strong overseas connections for its loss of opportunities to service on a global basis brands it had developed in the United States.

In July 1987 Saatchi merged Backer & Spielvogel with its Ted Bates Worldwide and British Dorland Advertising units to form Backer Spielvogel Bates Worldwide (BSB), then the third-largest advertising agency in the world. Spielvogel emerged as its chairman/chief executive officer (CEO).

Despite Backer & Spielvogel's early claim that it harbored no desire to be the world's biggest agency—"big empires are just not as much fun," Spielvogel had once said—Spielvogel found himself presiding over one of the world's largest agencies. Known for building and nurturing close business relationships, Spielvogel attempted to maintain an attentive attitude toward clients. Some said, however, that his hands-on approach led him to spread himself too thin, and BSB entered the 1990s with a downturn. The agency lost the $25 million Xerox and $60 million Prudential Insurance accounts in 1990 and the $20 million Dole account in March 1991. The departure, also in March 1991, of the $110 million Miller Lite account—Backer & Spielvogel's original client—was perhaps its most stinging loss.

The flight of Miller Lite came after two years of attempts by the agency to devise a replacement for its long-running and once much-loved retired jocks campaign, which had gone flat. A leader in the light beer category, Miller Lite was losing market share to its rivals after several years of slow growth, while Anheuser-Busch's Bud Light and Adolph Coors Company's Coors Light had been growing steadily. The Miller Lite account went to Leo Burnett USA, in Chicago, Illinois, although BSB retained Miller Genuine Draft, Genuine Draft Light, and media buying for all Miller brands.

In a move to slow the exodus of clients, BSB hired Don Easdon as creative head in April 1991. A former creative director at Hill, Holliday, Connors, Cosmopulos, with a reputation as an original thinker, Easdon was perhaps best known for the Zen-like campaign that launched the Infiniti automobile.

In January 1993 Michael Bungey was appointed worldwide president/chief operating officer at BSB. He formerly had been chairman of BSB Europe and chairman/CEO of BSB Dorland, London. Under Bungey's leadership, the agency recorded substantial business gains, including Warner-Wellcome Consumer Products, with new products Benadryl, Certs, and Cinn-a-burst chewing gum from Young & Rubicam and Sinutab and Bubblicious gum from J. Walter Thompson USA. (BSB already had Burroughs Wellcome products Actifed, Sudafed, and Neosporin). Miller Lite Ice beer and Cunard Line also came on board.

The new business helped offset the summer 1993 loss of the lion's share of the Campbell Soup Company's $70 million red-and-white-label soup account and its $15 million print account, which went to the Omnicom Group's BBDO; BSB and Campbell had disagreed on a new marketing strategy to sell soup to a broader audience throughout the entire year. Philips Consumer Electronics also moved its account. Relations between Spielvogel and Bungey reportedly became strained, as Bungey assumed more control of the agency.

Backer retired as vice chairman and worldwide creative director of BSB in November 1993. Andrew Cracknell succeeded Backer as vice chairman (while retaining his position as executive creative director at BSB Dorland, the agency's London office), but he remained less than a year. Backer's and Spielvogel's names were dropped in June 1994, and the agency was rechristened Bates Worldwide. Four months later, Spielvogel resigned as chairman. He later became chairman/CEO of United Auto Group, the largest publicly owned group of auto dealers in the United States, and, in August 2000, was named U.S. ambassador to the Slovak Republic.

CHRISTINE BUNISH

See also color plate in this volume

Further Reading

"For Backer & Spielvogel, It's Miller Time," *Advertising Age* (13 August 1979)

Goldman, Kevin, "In BSB Strategy Shift, Saatchi to Drop Names Backer, Spielvogel" *Wall Street Journal* (14 April 1994)

Kanner, Bernice, "Await Backer & Spielvogel Trump," *Advertising Age* (25 June 1979)

Lipman, Joanne, "Ad Man Carl Spielvogel Now Thinks Big," *Wall Street Journal* (9 November 1987)

Lipman, Joanne, "Miller Lite Loss Prompts a Shift at Backer," *Wall Street Journal* (15 March 1991)

Wells, Melanie, "Top-Level Tumult at Bates Worldwide; Spielvogel, Cracknell Leave Disenchanted," *Advertising Age* (24 October 1994)

Ballyhoo Magazine

Ballyhoo magazine, published monthly by Dell Publishing Company, New York City, from August 1931 to February 1939, was a humorous publication that parodied advertising and publishing. Given that it was launched only two years after the stock market crash of 1929, its instant success surprised both its editor, Norman Anthony, and its publisher, George T. Delacorte, Jr. *Bally-hoo*'s quick rise to popularity also captured the attention of other publishers and worried an already nervous advertising industry. Stuffed with parodies of national advertisements and consumer magazines and sprinkled liberally with topical and risqué cartoons and gags, the 32-page debut issue in August 1931 sold 150,000 copies in three days. The 300,000 copies of the September issue disappeared in four days, and the 48-page October issue of 600,000 copies also sold out. In February 1932 *Ballyhoo* printed 2 million copies; some were peddled in the streets as if they were newspaper "extras." Anthony claimed that when *Bally-hoo* reached newsstands, he walked about New York City's Times Square and observed that nearly every pedestrian was carrying a copy of the colorful magazine.

The contents of this initially ad-free, fifteen-cent pulp publication were hardly so remarkable as to justify public embrace of all things *Ballyhoo,* including *Ballyhoo* scarves, neckties, rings, cuff links, greeting cards, toilet paper, a Manhattan nightclub, and a saloon in Havana, Cuba. In addition, the magazine—which resembled today's *Mad* magazine in size, editorial formula, and use of a mascot (*Ballyhoo*'s was named Elmer Zilch)—sold *Bally-hoo* games and puzzles. Anthony bankrolled a Broadway production called *Ballyhoo* that featured Bob Hope.

Even Anthony acknowledged that nothing in the magazine was so hilarious as to justify its enormous popularity, noting that much of the material was weak and should not have appeared. He attributed awareness of the magazine to its unusual cover. The front and back of *Ballyhoo* were a garish patchwork of multicolored squares with the magazine's nameplate in chunky capital letters. Initially, inside pages were printed only in black.

The contents of the inaugural issue typify most issues published during *Ballyhoo*'s first year. The inside front cover of the August 1931 issue featured an ad for *Ballyhoo* that promised "circulation of 5,000,000,000 by 1939," lampooning the outlandish readership claims made by other publications of the day. The first issue, sporting "Read a fresh magazine" and "Kept fresh by cellophane" as cover lines, parodied such national brands as Old Gold (Old Cold) and Lucky Strike (Ducky Wucky) cigarettes; Mobil (Nobil) Oil; Lifebuoy (Ohbuoy) and Lux (Lox) soaps; Simmons (Zimmons) beds; Absorbine Jr. (Shock Absorber Jr.); and du Pont's cellophane. Later issues revisited these brands repeatedly but also parodied most nationally advertised brands: Chesterfield and Marlboro cigarettes, Pond's cleansing cream, Ipana toothpaste, Barbasol shaving cream, Dentyne and Wrigley's chewing gums, Palmolive soap, Kodak cameras, Chrysler and General Motors, American Telephone & Telegraph, the Santa Fe and Pennsylvania railroads, Kellogg's, Tums, Vaseline, Campbell's soup, Parker pens, Elizabeth Arden, Arthur Murray, Sanka, Bon Ami, Texaco, Coca-Cola, General Electric, Hoover vacuum cleaners, Phillip's Milk of Magnesia, and Steinway pianos.

Advertising agencies and practices were satirized regularly. Batten Barton Durstine & Osborn was targeted in a yarn about Button, Button, Bitten, Betton & Button in which the partners shot each other one by one to accommodate the agency's shrinking revenues. Later *Ballyhoo* spoofed advertising puffery and offered lists of slogans, complete layouts on rubber stamps, and fill-in-the-blank advertising forms as a way to make expensive agencies unnecessary. An attack on magazines in the first issue recommended oblivion for *Vanity Fair, Life,* and *Arts Beautiful* magazines. *Liberty, Collier's, Time, Saturday Evening Post, Popular Mechanics, House and Garden,* and *Ladies' Home Journal* were parodied in later issues.

The 38 cartoons in the first issue addressed such topics as Prohibition, speakeasies, economic conditions, the homeless, tramps, and organized crime. Approximately 10 percent were mildly ris-

WHEN THE COUNTRY GOES RED

Lizzie Zilchski

prominent Street Cleaner of Leningrad endorses

BOOMSKI'S CREAM

(Pronounced "Boom-ski")

Comrade Lizzie Zilchski, prominent in street-cleaning circles, tells how she gives her face and hands that harsh-look.

"EVER since the revolution," says Lizzie Zilchski, "I have used Boomski's Cream and it's just too ducky. It gives my face and hands that rough, harsh look so necessary to a real worker . . . that look that makes Soviet officers think you're always on the job.

BOOMSKI'S CREAM

An ad in a 1932 issue of *Ballyhoo* magazine invokes Soviet communism to make fun of an American advertiser.

She thought:
"Migawd but that trollop has B. O.!"
But, to be polite,
She said:
"No, thanks, I never touch the damn stuff."

"B. O." cheated her out of popularity ...
(Bacardi Odor)

—but, my dear, she was invited everywhere!

PRETTY, gay, vivacious, with that insouciant *savoir faire* of the ultra cosmopolite —she should have been the life of every penthouse party.

But she wasn't! Why?

Everyone else knew—even the janitor. Luckily her sister-in-law was very frank.

SHE said, "Listen, Lizzie! you've got to get over the idea that you can drink the nation dry! You've got to stop falling on your nose!" Well, what happened?

Lizzie's still got "B.O."—Bacardi Odor—but she's learned how to hold her liquor, and now she's good company!

Ohbuoy Health Soap
—stops Bacardi Odor—

This mock ad from *Ballyhoo* magazine parodied Lifebuoy soap's "B.O." campaign.

qué, and such cartoons multiplied, as did nudity, when *Ballyhoo* faced competitors that emphasized bawdy humor. As sexual humor increased, the number of advertising parodies declined. The 32-page "Clean Number" issue (March 1934) featured two national brand parodies. The remaining advertisements were generic or paid, including one for Absorbine Jr., a liniment product *Ballyhoo* regularly lampooned. Of 19 cartoons, 11 involved nudity and risqué subjects.

Much of the success of *Ballyhoo* was attributable to Anthony and Delacorte's dislike of advertising and text-heavy magazines. Delacorte once caused a near riot in a movie theater because an advertisement accompanied the film. Most magazines Dell published did not depend on advertising. To Anthony's delight, Delacorte expected *Ballyhoo* to follow his company's formula. In the 1920s, as editor of *Judge* and later *Life* magazine, Anthony had produced burlesque issues that doubled circulation but troubled advertisers. The response of the advertisers angered him. "I felt a bitterness against rump-kissing advertising agents, rump-kissing advertising salesmen, and rump-kissing magazines," he wrote in 1946. This resentment emerged in advertising parodies, cartoons,

and short prose pieces—especially in critiques of *The New Yorker*'s mixture of advertising and editorial. Also important to *Ballyhoo*'s success was Anthony's experience working from 1920 through 1928 for *Judge,* the long-lived (1881–1949) American humor magazine that appealed to upper-class Republican readers, where Anthony tested concepts that were the foundation of *Ballyhoo*. He devoted the 17 November 1923 issue of *Judge* to advertising parodies; he considered it the "forerunner" of *Ballyhoo*. That issue earned Anthony the editorship of *Judge*, where he substituted illustrations for prose, as he did later in *Ballyhoo*.

No matter how independent Anthony and Delacorte were of advertisers, the timing of *Ballyhoo*'s arrival was fortuitous. In the Depression's second year, faith in business was crumbling. Advertising saw declining revenues, reductions in pay, and employee layoffs. Advertising expenditures in national magazines in 1931 were 18.2 percent lower than in 1929. Advertising practices had been attacked prior to *Ballyhoo*'s appearance. In 1926 Helen Woodward, a copywriter, published *Through Many Windows*, an insider critique of advertising. In 1927 consumer advocates Stuart Chase and F.J. Schlink published *Your Money's Worth*, which blamed waste on duplicitous advertising practices. Equally important was Silas Bent's *Ballyhoo: The Voice of the Press*, a 1927 critique of press and advertiser relations. The advertising industry even questioned its own future. Following the stock market crash, *Printers' Ink* and *Advertising & Selling* included articles by advertising executives about declining business, advertising's failure to spur economic growth, and public distrust of advertising. H.A. Batten, an executive at N.W. Ayer & Son, argued that rogue advertisers threatened the industry's survival; he advocated public ridicule of advertisers whose puffery offended good taste and public well-being—precisely the pillory *Ballyhoo* afforded Anthony and Delacorte, albeit more for profit than reform.

Ballyhoo magazine was profitable until its demise in 1939. While Anthony developed the magazine, Delacorte paid him $75 weekly and budgeted $500 to purchase art for the first issue. Ultimately Anthony, who received 17 percent of the profits, said he earned $250,000 and Delacorte more than $1 million during *Ballyhoo*'s nearly nine years. Although circulation quickly hit 2 million, it could not be maintained. By August 1933 circulation had fallen to 300,000. It continued to decline, finally dropping below 100,000 in 1938. Anthony blamed this on competition from *Vanity Fair* and use of cartoons in *Collier's* and *Saturday Evening Post*.

While competition contributed to *Ballyhoo*'s decline, the magazine managed to survive all but one of its 15 derivative competitors of the period. *Hooey*, published by Popular Magazines, closed in 1941. Other titles that mimicked *Ballyhoo*'s editorial formula and colorful cover design included *Aw Nerts, Boloney, Bunk, Bushwa, Haywire, Hokum, Jest, Kookoo, Merry-Go-Round, Slapstick, Smokehouse Monthly, Tickle-Me-Too,* and *Today's Humor. Hullabaloo,* a competing magazine Delacorte started in 1931, lasted six months; the others closed by summer 1933.

JOSEPH P. BERNT

Further Reading

Anthony, Norman, *How to Grow Old Disgracefully,* New York: Duell Sloan and Pearce, 1946

Marchand, Roland, *Advertising the American Dream: Making Way for Modernity: 1920–1940,* Berkeley: University of California Press, 1985

Peterson, Theodore, *Magazines in the Twentieth Century,* Urbana: University of Illinois Press, 1956

Pringle, Henry F., "The Anatomy of Ballyhoo: A New Type of Magazine—Smutty or Smart?" *Outlook* (6 January 1932)

Rorty, James, "The Logic of Ballyhoo," *The Commonweal* (23 March 1932)

Sloane, David E.E., "Ballyhoo," in *American Humor Magazines and Comic Periodicals,* edited by Sloane, New York: Greenwood Press, 1987

Turner, E.S., *The Shocking History of Advertising,* New York: Dutton, 1953

Barilla Pasta

Principal Agencies

Enneci
Venturini
Carboni
Colman Prentiss Varley
McCann-Erickson
Young & Rubicam
TBWA

In the late 1990s Barilla was the leader in Italy in the pasta and pasta sauce businesses and the world leader in the pasta business. In the bakery products segment, the group led in Italy and ranked third in Europe, with the Mulino Bianco, Panem, Pavesi, and Tre Marie brands.

Barilla operated 25 plants (20 in Italy and 5 elsewhere), as well as 6 mills that supplied 70 percent of the company's raw materials. Its employees numbered more than 7,000. Exports accounted for 14 percent of the output of its plants, with Barilla products being sold in more than 60 countries. Pasta was manufactured under joint ventures and alliances in Brazil, Japan, Greece, Mexico, Poland, Spain, South Africa, and Turkey.

By 2000 Barilla, which began in Parma, Italy, in 1877 as a pasta and bread shop, was the largest Italian food manufacturer. It has been managed for more than 120 years by the Barilla family, which has reached its fourth generation with the brothers Guido, Luca, and Paolo.

Pietro Barilla was the founder of the business. Under his son Riccardo, who focused on expansion and on innovation in the company's plants, the business assumed industrial dimensions. His grandson Pietro, father of the current owners, introduced modern commercial management oriented toward marketing, influenced largely by his first business trip to the United States in 1950. Later in the decade he also began emphasizing advertising. At the same time, he took an active interest in modern Italian culture and became one of Italy's foremost "enlightened entrepreneurs."

In 1952 the advertising campaign "With Barilla it is always Sunday," created by Erberto Carboni—one of the masters of Italian advertising—won the prestigious Palme d'Or at the International Advertising Festival in Cannes, France. Carboni's work for Barilla involved not only creating advertising campaigns but also forging an entirely new image for the business, including a trademark that called to mind an egg, distinctive blue packaging, displays for trade exhibitions, and catalogs. Barilla became the first Italian company to market its pasta—sold in bulk until 1955—in packages. In the second half of the 1950s, Barilla, recognizing the importance of the new medium of television, broadcast its first spots in the program *Carosello,* which featured well-known actors and the celebrated singer Mina. The collaboration with Mina continued for five years.

In 1960 Barilla became a joint stock company that was organized into seven operating units, a progressive management practice at the time. By then there were 1,500 employees and a sales force of 200. In 1968 Pietro Barilla began building a plant in Pedrignano; it was the largest pasta plant in the world in 2001. The high cost of operating the plant, together with social and economic difficulties, convinced Pietro and his brother Gianni to sell their holdings in 1971 to W.R. Grace & Company, an American multinational company that continued the expansion effort. By 1973 Barilla's share of the pasta market had reached 15 percent. It was at this time that Barilla acquired the pasta plant of its competitor Voiello in Naples, and, in the following year, the Altamura mill, the largest in Italy.

The 1970s were marked by advertising that focused on the product itself. In 1972 a television campaign on the cooking of pasta was created by Young & Rubicam. A 1974–75 TV campaign explained the difference between hard and tender wheat, the first being the fundamental raw material of pasta.

In 1975 Barilla introduced the Mulino Bianco (White Mill) line of bakery products. The use of a new brand name for the line was explained by the fact that although Barilla enjoyed a positive image, it was known primarily for its industrial and business

Italian singer Zucchero Fornaciari is featured in a television commercial
from Barilla's "Blue" campaign.
Courtesy of Barilla Historic Archives—Parma, Italy.

prowess. Packaging specifically for this new line was created by
the designer Giò Rossi. The product line's advertising campaign,
undertaken by the Troost agency, relied on nostalgia ("ancient
times . . . when the mills were white"), which was contrasted with
the cold impersonality of the industrial age. The Mulino Bianco
line was followed in 1977 by the introduction of other new products. In 1979 the Barilla family once again acquired a majority of
the company stock.

In the 1980s, through advertising created by TBWA, Barilla
emphasized good food and family values. In 1984 the renowned
film director Federico Fellini, a friend of Pietro Barilla, created the
celebrated spot "High Society." The public, however, simply
dubbed the ad "Rigatoni" after the type of Barilla pasta served in
the luxury restaurant shown in the ad.

From 1985 to 1990 the company relied on the television campaign, "Where Barilla Is, There Is Your Home," created by Young
& Rubicam under the direction of Gavino Sanna. The campaign,
which became very popular, was based on nine subjects and used
a well-known hymn by Vangelis, which came to be referred to as
the "Barilla hymn." The first of the ads—with the title "The
Train" and the theme of returning home—was unusual for its
length (two minutes). It was the first work from a new agency and
aroused the interest of the entire Italian advertising industry.

During the 1990s Barilla's advertising was tailored to its many
markets. For the French market, the film actor Gerard Dépardieu
agreed for the first time to appear in a testimonial ad. The celebrated tenor Placido Domingo appeared in an ad for the Spanish
market, and tennis player Steffi Graf for the German market.
Olympic ski medalist Alberto Toma, representing the athlete who
did not want to renounce the pleasures of food, appeared in Italian advertising. Barilla's advertising during the 1990s involved not
only television but also print and the use of recipe booklets.

In addition, Barilla undertook sponsorships. In 1981 the company began its sponsorship of the soccer team Roma that continued for more than a decade. In 1983 Barilla was among the first

businesses in Italy to support the participation of the Italian yacht
Azzurra in the America's Cup.

There were also a number of important developments in Barilla's business enterprises during the 1980s and 1990s. The company made several acquisitions, including pasta plants and, in
1992, the cookie maker Pavesi. Barilla also launched new products, including whole wheat pasta in 1985, a new line of sauces in
1989, fresh pasta in 1990, and Essere, a Mulino Bianco line, in
1994. In 1996 Selezione Oro, a high-quality product made from a
mixture of selected wheat, was launched. The company's objective
continued to be reinforcement of the image of quality.

During the 1990s the company benefited from the focus on the
health benefits of the Mediterranean diet. At the same time competition increased, and Barilla was forced to rely on discounts and
other forms of marketing. In 1994 the well-known singer Zucchero opened a new advertising campaign, sometimes dubbed the
"Blue" campaign. The objective of the campaign was to focus
consumer attention on Barilla's blue packages; every spot was
accompanied by a jingle devoted to the color.

When the younger Pietro Barilla died in 1993, he was honored
not only as one of the most celebrated industrial entrepreneurs in
Italy but also as an art collector. His collection of modern art is
now shown in the offices of the Pedrignano plant. Upon their
father's death, the sons conducted a search for a manager with an
international reputation. Edwin Lewis Artzt was hired as executive director. Under his management Barilla designed an ambitious strategy of expansion based on four principles.

In accordance with one of the principles—"To merchandise
products of higher quality at a good price"—Barilla abandoned
the sales promotion of its products to consumers in 1996. This
was a bold decision, especially given the promotion strategy for
which the business had long been known by the public and the
advertising community.

In accordance with another of its principles—"To introduce
our main brands in the most important world markets through
products meeting the local tastes and habits, but always presented
as authentic Italian ones"—the strategy of expansion was continued. Business in the United States in particular grew considerably,
and in 1997 a new plant was built in Ames, Iowa, the first for
Barilla in the United States.

Advertising was increased in 1997, with new emphasis placed
on the quality of the raw materials used in Barilla products and
the care with which they are processed. Since the 1980s Barilla
has been among the top ten Italian advertisers. In the late 1990s
its yearly advertising budget was approximately 220 billion liras
($100 million); the company ranks third (behind Fiat and Ferrero)
in ad spending in Italy. About 93 percent of Barilla's advertising
budget went to television and the remainder to print.

EDOARDO T. BRIOSCHI

Further Reading
Ganapini, Albino Ivardi, and Giancarlo Gonizzi, editors, *Barilla:
Cento anni di pubblicità e comunicazione*, Milan: Silvana,
1994; as *Barilla: A Hundred Years of Advertising and*

Corporate Communications, Parma, Italy: Archivio Storico
Barilla, 1994
Tassi, R., editor, *The Barilla Collection of Modern Art: The*

Barilla Family, Parma, Italy: Ugo Guanda Editore, 1993
Tedeschi, M.C., and A.I. Ganapini, *A Journey Inside a
Trademark*, Bologna: Barilla, 1990

Bartle Bogle Hegarty

Founded in 1982 by John Bartle, Nigel Bogle, and John Hegarty, who had worked together for nine years at Tragos, Bonnange, Wiesendanger, Ajroldi in London, England; opened an office in Singapore, 1996; opened New York City office, 1998.

Major Clients
Audi
Häagen-Dazs
Johnnie Walker
Levi Strauss & Company
Whitbread

Bartle Bogle Hegarty (BBH) first opened its doors in London, England, in 1982, a time characterized by conspicuous spending and increasing globalization. Owing to the impressive credentials of its three founders, it quickly established a reputation as a dynamic, ideas-based ad agency. BBH's work, especially that for Levi's and later for Boddingtons and Häagen-Dazs, has had dramatic impact on both consumer perceptions and product sales, while also giving the U.K. ad industry a huge shot of adrenaline.

In 1973 John Bartle, Nigel Bogle, and John Hegarty cofounded the London office of the advertising agency Tragos, Bonnange, Wiesendanger, Ajroldi (TBWA). Bartle, the son of a Leeds, England, bus inspector, moved from the post of marketing services manager at Cadbury Schweppes to planning director at TBWA. He became joint managing director of TBWA (along with Bogle) in 1979. In 1967, at the age of 19, Bogle started as a trainee with the Leo Burnett Company; he eventually became one of eight account group heads before becoming a founding partner of TBWA. Bogle was sharp, analytical, and one of the best account men in London. Hegarty began his advertising career as a junior art director at Benton and Bowles in 1965. He worked briefly for John Collins and Partners before joining CramerSaatchi consultancy (later Saatchi & Saatchi) in 1967. Within one year he became deputy creative director. At TBWA he was creative director.

Having helped build TBWA into a successful agency, winning *Campaign* magazine's "Agency of the Year" award in 1980, Bartle, Bogle, and Hegarty sought—but were denied—greater control of the company's equity. They finally decided to launch their own agency in Hegarty's front room, starting with plenty of enthusiasm and experience but no business. Within four months they had billings of more than £6 million ($8.4 million) and three major clients—Audi, Whitbread, and Levi Strauss—none of which came from TBWA (and all of which remained at BBH at the turn of the 21st century). The three men brought together three advertising disciplines—planning, account management, and creativity—and attribute their success, in part, to the equal importance they placed on each.

While many new agencies begin life by poaching their old company's clients, BBH started with a clean slate. The directors resisted the temptation to expand for the sake of expanding. And the agency refused to produce speculative creative work, although most advertisers select new agencies in this way. "Outstanding advertising is produced in partnership, not off the cuff," Bogle has said. By May 1989 billings had reached £100 million ($140 million).

Ever since its launch BBH has marched under the banner of "creativity." The aim has always been to create big advertising-led ideas that change consumers' perceptions and alter their behaviors. Hegarty's dictum, "Creativity is about breaking rules," constantly led to the creation of innovative campaigns.

In the 1980s the agency reenergized the sales of Levi's jeans by injecting liberal doses of sex, humor, and street savvy into its advertising. Hegarty's art department directed the 1985 commercial in which male model Nick Kamen stripped off his 501s in a laundromat. U.K. sales rose by 800 percent, and the commercial had to be taken off the air temporarily while Levi Strauss stepped up production to meet unprecedented demand. The sound track to this commercial—Marvin Gaye's "Heard It Through the Grapevine"—set the trend for a succession of rereleased hits. By 2000, seven singles linked to Levi's commercials had reached number one on the U.K. record charts. Levi's appears in the U.K. *Guinness Book of Records*, 2000 edition, under "Most chart hits produced by an ad campaign." Since the launch of the first pan-European campaign by BBH for Levi's jeans in 1985, the brand has continually achieved the market leader position in every European market, with TV and cinema campaigns running in 22 countries worldwide (not including the United States).

In an ongoing brand-building campaign for the motor manufacturer Audi, the company's existing slogan is presented in German, "Vorsprung durch Technik" (Advance through technology) and has entered the popular idiom in several European countries. The campaign has transformed the brand from a bland Euro-car to a member of the prestige car club and encouraged consumers to perceive Audi as forward thinking, daring in its design, and technologically innovative. The tone of voice used in the advertising is witty, confident, and understated.

In 1989 Whitbread, one of BBH's founding clients, bought a brewery in Manchester, England, that produced Boddingtons beer. Starting with crisp, clean print ads, the agency reversed declining sales by turning the established regional brand into a national brand with Mancunian roots. Canned Boddingtons became a market leader within 18 months of the advertising launch.

In the early 1990s BBH revolutionized the image (and fortunes) of the premium ice cream Häagen-Dazs. In a milestone U.K. print campaign, the agency eschewed the traditional television battleground for ice creams and repositioned the brand as an adult treat to be shared in a mood of sensual intimacy. The provocative ads fueled considerable controversy in the media, which decried the gratuitous use of sex. The agency defended its strategy by revealing research that described the experience of eating ice cream as "languorous" and "sensuous." In 1991 U.K. sales of Häagen-Dazs rose by nearly 400 percent over the previous year.

Acknowledging the agency's level of creative attainment, BBH was named "Agency of the Year" by *Campaign* magazine for 1986 and 1993. BBH became the first shop named "Agency of the Year" in 1993 at the International Advertising Festival in Cannes, France, winning more awards than any other agency in the world; it took the title again the following year.

By the end of 1996 billings had topped £200 million (US$280 million). As a measure of its success in "exporting" advertising abroad, BBH received the Queen's Award for Export Achievement in both 1996 and 1997, the only ad agency to hold this award. In 1997 BBH was also named "International Agency of the Year" by *Advertising Age* magazine. In 1999 it was voted number one for creativity for the 11th consecutive year by *Marketing Week* magazine, making it the leader every year since the awards began. The agency's founders have also received honors; Bartle was president of the Institute of Practitioners in Advertising (IPA) in London from 1997 to 1999. Hegarty was president of Design & Art Direction (D&AD) from 1988 to 1989 and won the D&AD President's award for outstanding achievement in the advertising industry in 1994.

BBH maintains that the traditional network agency, with offices around the world, works against the development of great international communication for global brands. The agency functions on the premise that, through influences such as travel, music, TV, and film, consumers have more similarities than differences, regardless of their cultural origins. BBH addresses those similarities in its advertising, thus creating international strategies that work well in most markets.

BBH operates as a single agency in three locations: London, Singapore, and New York City. The Singapore office opened in October 1996 and produces campaigns in several languages for such diverse markets as India, Japan, and Australia. Levi Strauss and Polaroid are among the agency's regional accounts. The New York City office opened in October 1998. From here the agency handles, among other accounts, Reebok's global advertising and

the U.S. accounts for Johnnie Walker, Lipton Foods, BBC America, and the Terence Conran Shop. In London the Identica Partnership was established in 1992 and merged with Tango Design in 1998 to offer strategic brand consultancy.

In December 1997 the U.S.-based advertising agency network Leo Burnett Company, Inc., purchased a minority stake in BBH. Both agencies were privately held companies owned by their employees, although Burnett later merged with the MacManus Group in November 1999 to form BDM with a view toward a future initial public offering (IPO); in March 2001, however, Bcom3—the new name for the holding company—postponed plans for an IPO owing to volatile market conditions. Both continued to operate as separate businesses in 2001, with only the media area overlapping. By providing, in particular, a global media delivery system, Leo Burnett helps BBH further develop the BBH brand internationally.

In January 2000 BBH and the Leo Group (parent of the Leo Burnett Company) confirmed the merger of their respective U.K. media operations, Motive and Starcom, to form a single operating entity called Starcom Motive Partnership. The merged company created the third largest media services company in the United Kingdom, with estimated annual billings of £440 million ($616 million), and it became the European, Middle Eastern, and African headquarters of Starcom global media network. Operating in 75 markets, Starcom worked for such clients as Coca-Cola (13 markets), Procter & Gamble (45 markets), McDonald's (15 markets), and Kellogg (32 markets). With 1998 international billings of £7.3 billion ($10.22 billion), Starcom ranked as one of the top ten media companies in the world.

In 1998 BBH employed a total of 429 staff and had total billings of £278 million ($389.2 million). With ads running in more than 60 countries, approximately half of BBH's clients were international. In 2000 Bartle Bogle Hegarty had worldwide gross income of £111.4 million ($77.8 million), up 24.1 percent over 1999, on billings of £871.5 million ($608.4 million), up 15.4 percent. It had 520 employees in three offices.

DAVE SAUNDERS

Further Reading

Butterfield, Leslie, *Excellence in Advertising: The IPA Guide to Best Practice,* Boston and London: Butterworth-Heinemann, 1997

Kanner, Bernice, *The 100 Best TV Commercials and Why They Worked,* New York: Times Business, 1999

McCarthy, John, and Jill Morrell, *Some Other Rainbow,* London: Corgi, 1994

Rossiter, John R, and Larry Percy, *Advertising and Promotion Management,* New York: McGraw-Hill, 1987; 2nd edition, as *Advertising Communications and Promotion Management,* New York: McGraw-Hill, 1997

Saunders, Dave, *The World's Best Advertising Photography,* London: Batsford, 1994

Saunders, Dave, *20th-Century Advertising,* London: Carlton Books, 1999

Steel, Jon, *Truth, Lies, and Advertising: The Art of Account Planning*, New York: Wiley, 1998

Temporal, Paul, *Branding in Asia: The Creation, Development, and Management of Asian Brands for the Global Market*, New York: Wiley, 2000

Wilmshurst, John, and Adrian Mackay, *The Fundamentals of Advertising*, London: Heinemann, 1985; 2nd edition, Boston: Butterworth-Heinemann, 1999

Wright, Ray, *Advertising*, New York: McGraw Hill, 1991

Bates Worldwide

(Ted Bates & Company; Ted Bates Worldwide)

Founded as Ted Bates, Inc., by Theodore Bates, 1940; achieved major growth as a television agency in 1950s; earned reputation for hard-selling ads based on "unique selling proposition"; bought Campbell Mithun, 1979, and William Esty Company, Inc., 1982; changed name to Bates Worldwide, 1983; acquired by Saatchi & Saatchi, 1986; merged by parent company with Backer & Spielvogel, Inc., to become Backer Spielvogel Bates, 1987; renamed Bates Worldwide, a unit of Cordiant Communications Group (successor to Saatchi & Saatchi PLC), 1994.

Major Clients

American Home Products (Anacin)
Bristol-Myers (Bufferin)
Carter Products, Inc. (Carter's Little Liver Pills)
Citizens for Eisenhower
Colgate-Palmolive-Peet, Inc.
Mars, Inc. (M&M's candy)
Mobil Oil
Standard Brands, Inc.
Warner-Lambert Company

Bates Worldwide ended the 20th century as the principal unit of the Cordiant Communications Group and the 17th-largest U.S. ad agency measured by both billings and gross income. It ranked as a major American agency from the day it was founded in 1940 and built its reputation on hard-selling advertising for inexpensive packaged goods.

Theodore Bates (no relation to pioneer copywriter Charles Austin Bates) was born in New Haven, Connecticut, on 11 September 1901, attended Andover Academy, and graduated from Yale University in 1924. He had no ambition for an ad career. Instead he went to work at Chase National Bank in New York City, looking forward to life in finance and banking. Shortly after joining Chase, however, he was assigned to take over the chores of the bank's ailing ad manager, a task he later claimed he was totally unprepared for. When a decision needed to be made, Bates told *Advertising Age* in a 1965 interview, he covered "the

mouthpiece of the phone . . . and [asked] a very efficient woman what to do."

Origins

In 1924 at the Yale Club, Bates met a senior employee of the George Batten agency named William H. Johnson. According to Bates, Johnson offered him a clerk's job at $25 a week. Bates, who was making $160 a week at Chase, did not explain why he took so deep a pay cut to change careers, but he insisted it was "the smartest decision of my life." Perhaps he saw more rapid advancement in the young field of advertising. He became a copywriter at Batten, working with Chester Bowles and mentored by J. Stirling Getchell. He continued through the 1928 merger that produced Batten Barton Durstine & Osborn (BBDO), becoming both chief copywriter and account executive on the Continental Baking (Wonder bread) account.

Meanwhile, Bowles had left the agency to form Benton & Bowles (B&B), and in 1935 he invited Bates to come over to B&B to play a major role in the huge Colgate-Palmolive-Peet account. Bates obliged and, after a reasonable period, brought the Continental Baking account with him.

By 1940, however, founders Benton and Bowles had both left the firm, leaving Colgate dissatisfied and in the market for a new agency. At this point, Bates was asked if he wished to launch a company that could take over the Colgate business. He did, and Ted Bates, Inc., was founded that year on initial billings of $2.9 million, which grew to $4.5 million within the first year. Although his name was never on the company logo, Rosser Reeves was the first copy director and chief creative theoretician at Bates. He became a partner in 1942. Nine years younger than Bates, Reeves had also started in banking. But his writing skills soon pointed him toward advertising, and he joined the Cecil, Warwick & Cecil agency (later Warwick & Legler) in 1934. When the job failed to work out, he joined Ruthrauff & Ryan, where he stayed for four years and then in 1938 moved to Blackett-Sample-Hummert, Inc., where he was schooled in the art of the hard-selling ad by bosses Duane Jones and Frank Hummert.

Here's why
ANACIN®
gives better TOTAL results in
PAIN RELIEF
better than aspirin...
even with buffering action

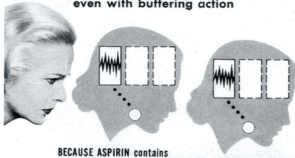

BECAUSE ASPIRIN contains
only one pain reliever.....   ADD BUFFERING ACTION
and you still have only one.

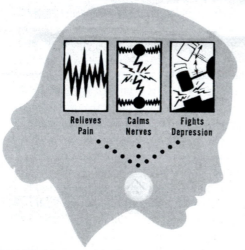

Relieves   Calms   Fights
Pain   Nerves   Depression

BUT ANACIN relieves pain, calms nerves, fights depression.

Anacin is like a doctor's prescription. That is, Anacin contains not just one but a *combination* of medically proven active ingredients. Anacin (1) gives fast relief from pain of headache, neuritis and neuralgia. (2) Calms jittery nerves—leaves you *comfortably relaxed*. (3) Fights depression. Thus, Anacin gives you better TOTAL results in pain relief than you get from aspirin, even plus buffering action. And Anacin does *not* upset the stomach. Buy Anacin Tablets today.

3 out of 4 doctors
recommend the ingredients
of ANACIN

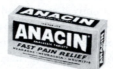

This 1957 print ad for Anacin is legendary for its graphic and dramatic portrayal of headache pain.
Copyright © Whitehall Robins/Wyeth and used with permission.

Many have pointed out the opposing temperaments of Bates and Reeves, who together would have such an influence on advertising over the next quarter century. Bates was a cultivated and soft-spoken New England aristocrat who avoided publicity with the same determination that he shunned fraternization with staff members. Reeves was a flamboyant extrovert with a philosophy of advertising structure that reduced the main creative function to discovering a product's "unique selling proposition," or USP, as it became known in the industry. This referred to a promised benefit that only the product in question could deliver. If none could be found, one would be invented. The Bates agency would take the old John E. Kennedy "reason-why" school of advertising, first articulated at the turn of the century at Lord & Thomas, to new heights in radio and television and become known for its repetitive, hard-selling campaigns that would continue for years without substantial change. Bates ruled his agency with a velvet glove, rarely issuing orders and delegating broadly to his senior management. Reeves was the chief author and enforcer of the company's methods.

Client Roster

When the Bates agency was launched, Colgate was the sixth-largest advertiser in network radio, spending nearly $2.8 million. Colgate, however, divided its brands among several agencies, including Sherman & Marquette; Ward Wheelock; William Esty & Company, Inc.; Lennen & Mitchell, Inc.; and Street & Finney, Inc. Bates had Colgate Dental Cream ("It cleans your breath while it cleans your teeth") and Palmolive shave products, which together raised the agency to rank 17th among U.S. agencies in 1945 with billings of $16 million. The other major account in Bates's early history was Standard Brands, Inc., whose Blue Bonnet margarine and Royal Desserts business made it the shop's second-largest client. The Brown & Williamson Tobacco Company (B&W) assigned Viceroy cigarettes to Bates during the war, and by 1945 the newspaper half of Raleigh cigarettes, which the agency shared with BBDO. In 1948, BBDO resigned B&W to take on American Tobacco Company's Lucky Strike, and Bates (now called Ted Bates & Company) inherited B&W's Kool. The agency also represented Carter Products (Carter's Little Liver Pills) and Minute Maid.

Bates was founded as a partnership and grew slowly but steadily after the war. At its height, there were 17 partners in the firm before sheer size required that it be reorganized as a corporation in April 1955. (Ted Bates & Company became the domestic division of parent company Ted Bates & Company, Inc.) The agency relied mostly on the internal growth of its short list of clients and prided itself on being above the new-business rat race. By the time it marked its tenth anniversary in 1950, it was a $25 million agency. That same year Bates won the account of the Anahist Company, Inc., which brought it and the marketer's Hist-O-Plus into the category of over-the-counter drugs, in which it would make a major impact.

In 1952 Bates became the agency for Citizens for Eisenhower. Four years before, Reeves had approached Republican presidential candidate Thomas Dewey and suggested that the Bates agency could handle his election campaign using the same principles it used to market products. Instead of concentrating on long speeches, short 60-second commercials could reach far more people with essentially the same messages. Dewey, who had close ties to BBDO, declined. But by 1952 television presented a media frontier, and Reeves approached Republican candidate Dwight D. Eisenhower with the same idea. This time Bates received approval to make 40 spots in which the candidate responded to specific questions from typical voters. The saturation campaign, personally produced by Reeves, became known as "Eisenhower Answers America." It was the first time spot advertising had ever been used on such a scale in a U.S. presidential campaign, and it set a pattern that would soon become the norm. BBDO was co-agency in the Republican effort that year.

In the 1950s ad agencies and television networks were engaged in a struggle for control of program production. Agencies had been the principal suppliers of programming in the heyday of radio, but this was not a practice the networks were eager to continue. Under Sylvester ("Pat") Weaver, NBC took the lead in developing an inventory of popular programs, mostly live variety shows, and selling segments to different advertisers on a participating basis. One of the most popular was the *Comedy Hour,* half of which Bates, acting on behalf of Colgate head Edward Little, bought for the company. According to Weaver, Bates and particularly Little, whom Weaver described as an ignorant "swamp fox," made it so difficult for the program's cosponsor (Fridgidaire) that it withdrew, leaving the entire show to Colgate. In 1954 Bates took over all production duties for the show, which, in a throwback to radio days, was renamed the *Colgate Comedy Hour.* The ad industry saw it as an attempt to reverse network incursion into programming and bring production costs directly under the control of the advertiser. It was applauded by *Advertising Age,* but in the long run Bates and the ad industry lost the war.

Top-Ten Status

Billings volume surged to $46 million in 1954, as Bates won M&M Ltd., the maker of M&M's candy that later merged with Mars. M&M's became a classic example of Reeves's USP system of creating advertising. For the soft chocolate candy sealed in a brightly colored hard sugar shell, Reeves came up with the famous line "melts in your mouth, not in your hands," a theme still associated with the brand.

Important new business (none more so than the Anacin account when it moved from Biow-Beirn-Toigo, Inc.) pulled Bates into the ranks of America's top ten agencies by 1956. Anacin was manufactured by Whitehall Pharmacal Company, a unit of American Home Products, and was said to bill $9 million, by far the largest single piece of Whitehall business. (Other Whitehall products included Bisodol, Infra-Rub, and Kolynos toothpaste.) Reeves devised a series of commercials in which three images appeared on the screen portraying the different kinds of headache pain that could be relieved by Anacin. One was a hammer banging inside a line drawing of a head. The ads promised "fast, fast,

fast relief" and were accompanied by one of the longest-lasting copy pitches in advertising: "Anacin is like a doctor's prescription. That is, Anacin contains not just one but a combination of medically proven active ingredients. . . ." In 1999 *Advertising Age* ranked it 19th among the century's 100 greatest campaigns.

By 1957 Bates had moved from $25 million to $103 million in seven years, a remarkable growth sprint. About 75 percent of Bates's work was in television, and the agency specialized in strong visual demonstrations. It was Bates that burned holes in handkerchiefs to demonstrate the power of stomach acid for Rolaids. By this time Ted Bates had moved to the position of honorary chairman, although he continued to work full time. Thomas Harrington became chairman in 1955 but died four months later. Reeves then moved into the chairmanship.

In the late 1950s Bates sought unsuccessfully to acquire Masius & Fergusson, an agency handling Colgate in London and the fifth largest shop in England (billing approximately $15 million). In 1959 Bates bought another Colgate agency, the London-based John Hobson & Partners, which became Hobson, Bates & Partners. It was Bates's first agency acquisition outside the United States, driven by a need to serve its increasingly global client interests. In 1960 and 1961 Bates bought additional agencies in Toronto, Canada, and Paris, France.

Setbacks

Although the agency would continue with impressive growth, the Bates juggernaut stumbled in the early 1960s. Since the shop's founding, it had boasted that it had never lost a client. That changed in 1961, when Minute Maid Corporation dismissed the agency. More important, some of its practices in the pursuit of the hard sell were exposed, to embarrassing effect. The Federal Trade Commission (FTC) targeted Bates for its claims that Colgate Dental Cream covered teeth with a "protective shield" called Gardol. It also forced the agency to admit that Carter's Little Liver Pills did nothing for the liver. But the best known Bates deception exposed by the FTC was the one for Colgate Rapid Shave in which a razor appeared to glide over a piece of sandpaper softened by the "super moistening" qualities of the shaving cream. In fact, the "sandpaper" was a piece of Plexiglas, substituted for "technical reasons" to compress the moisturizing time to fit into a commercial. The ruse prompted the chairman of the FTC to ask, "Is there something so special about television that we experts should amend the facts of life. . . ."

In January 1962 the FTC cracked down on Bates and Colgate with new rules against misrepresentation that had far-reaching implications for advertising generally. "They're going to take the fun out of commercials," one observer commented. Bates seemed to become a lightning rod for the suspicions of consumer protection groups. In 1963 the National Association of Broadcasters (NAB) code review board questioned the long-standing claim that Anacin was "like a doctor's prescription."

Reeves faced the FTC and NAB with neither doubt nor apology. Earlier, he had defended his methods down the line in his book *Reality in Advertising* (1961). Among other things, he

The classic slogan, "Melts in your mouth—not in your hand," coined by Rosser Reeves in 1954 (and seen here in a 1985 holiday ad), is still used for M&M's candies.

argued that a good campaign will wear out only when the product it supports becomes obsolete. Ad executive David Ogilvy declared he would buy 450 copies of the book to distribute to his staff and clients. One company that responded positively to the book was Mobil Oil, which promptly awarded Bates its $6 million account.

In December 1965 the agency celebrated it 25th anniversary. It ranked fifth globally with worldwide billings of $207.5 million, of which $180.4 million were domestic. Bates was building a far-flung empire in Belgium, The Netherlands, Sweden, Spain, and Japan. Ted Bates remained a hands-on presence, while Archie Foster, who joined the agency as a vice president in 1954, became president and chief executive officer (CEO) in 1965, launching a third generation of management.

Leadership Changes and Growth

More important, in February 1966 Reeves, pressured by a board that distrusted his financial intent with company stock, suddenly announced his retirement. He remained tied to Bates for the next ten years by an $80,000-a-year consultancy contract intended to encourage his withdrawal, after which he made a final unsuccessful try at launching a new agency. (In 1976 Reeves made it known to Bates management that he possessed the only copy of a secret history of the agency that had been originally commissioned by Ted Bates himself. The manuscript, which allegedly contained details of assorted misdeeds by the original partners, was offered to the agency by Reeves in exchange for undisclosed considerations, an offer Bates declined. The book has yet to become public, and Reeves's retirement effectively ended his active career in advertising. He died in January 1984 at the age of 73.) The following September Jerry Della Femina was brought over from Delehanty, Kurnit & Geller as Bates's creative director for $50,000, a move perhaps intended to bring the agency into closer register with the "creative revolution" of the 1960s. But Della Femina remained only a year before starting his own agency. Shortly after his departure, Bates surprised both its client and the industry by resigning its signature Anacin account (and American Home Products) to take on Bristol-Myers's Bufferin.

Even more far-reaching, however, was the arrival of Robert Jacoby as a vice president in 1965 from the recently merged Needham, Harper & Steers. Jacoby had been with the Doherty, Clifford, Steers & Shenfield, Inc., half of the 1964 merger and numbered among those he most admired Generals George Patton and Erwin Rommel. In December 1969 he became president of Bates's domestic division with the intent of asserting greater independence from the parent company. In March 1971 he became president of the corporation, succeeding Foster, who became chairman. Finally, in April 1973 Jacoby, at 45, became chief of the entire Bates organization, whose total billings were at $457.8 million, of which $205 million was outside the United States.

Ted Bates died on 30 May 1972, at which time the company was clearly on track to become one of the mega-agencies of the next decade. It finished the 1970s at $1.4 billion. Part of that growth was the result of the acquisition of the Stern Walters/Earle Ludgin, Inc., agency in Chicago, Illinois, and, more important,

Campbell Mithun, Inc., of Minneapolis, Minnesota (a major General Mills agency), for $130 million. Both acquisitions occurred in 1979, and the Bates–Campbell Mithun deal was the largest in ad history to that date. It was topped in February 1982 when Bates acquired the William Esty Company and its $450 million in volume. The move brought the Bates organization to the threshold of becoming a $2 billion company, although the two largest acquisitions retained a considerable measure of independence. Esty soon proved to be the weaker of the two properties, and on 5 July 1988, Bates announced it would merge it with Campbell Mithun to create Campbell Mithun Esty (CME), with combined billings of $800 million.

By 1984 Bates was second only to Young & Rubicam in world income. Reflecting its global coverage, the name of the agency was changed to Bates Worldwide in 1983. The agency expanded into the Hispanic market with the purchase of Conill Advertising in 1986, and into direct response with Kobbs & Brady that same year.

Mergers: Done and Undone

The management generation that had nurtured the enormous Bates growth (there were 108 offices in 48 countries) now faced a dilemma. As they faced retirement, they realized that their Bates stock had risen to a level where it was becoming too costly to buy back. This led Jacoby to seek a buyer for the agency. After a year of negotiations, in 1986 the agency was purchased by the London agency Saatchi & Saatchi, which had been acquiring American agencies at a startling rate. In the spring of that year, a furious race to consolidate was taking place, and no one wanted to be left out. On 27 April, Doyle Dane Bernbach, BBDO, and Needham Harper Worldwide merged to form Omnicom. Jacoby was in discussions with both Saatchi and the Interpublic Group of Companies but was interested only in a cash deal. When Saatchi agreed to pay more than $500 million for Bates's stock, more than twice its book value, the offer was accepted.

Jacoby personally made $100 million from the deal. But the larger consequences were significantly less beneficial. In June Bates lost about $300 million in billings from such disapproving clients as the Warner-Lambert Company and R.J. Reynolds Tobacco Company (RJR), which the Esty agency had served since 1933. The RJR loss, combined with the simultaneous loss of Nabisco, amounted to approximately $100 million. There was also a fierce power struggle within Bates, and in September Jacoby was stripped of his authority and replaced by his former lieutenant, Donald M. Zuckert. Jacoby left the agency later that month.

Within the Saatchi family, which also included Dancer, Fitzgerald, Sample; Compton Backer & Spielvogel; and CME, Bates was now just one more asset. On 16 July 1987, Saatchi merged Bates with Backer & Spielvogel, which had been founded in 1979, creating Backer Spielvogel Bates Worldwide (BSBW). It was an awkward name, as Bates was vastly larger and better known.

BSBW continued to expand its scientific approach to advertising, as symbolized by the old USP system. It invested in the development of an independent lifestyle tracking analysis called Global

Scan. Set up in 17 countries, it broke the psychographics of the consumer into five separate profiles: strivers, achievers, pressureds, adapters, and traditionals. Other agencies were using similar profiling systems in their research operations.

But the parent company, S&S PLC, had larger problems—including lawsuits, client losses, and the departure of Maurice Saatchi to form a new agency—which now directly affected the fortunes of Bates. When Maurice Saatchi's brother Charles left S&S in February 1994, S&S PLC became something of a fiction. The new name it adopted was Cordiant Communications Group, successor to the parent of the four agency networks that included Backer Spielvogel Bates, Saatchi & Saatchi Advertising, Campbell Mithun Esty, and Kobbs & Draft. Reportedly angry at not being consulted over Saatchi's departure and the name change to Cordiant, M&M/Mars pulled its $350 million in spending out of Bates after 40 years, forcing a 3 percent staff cut at the agency.

Later in 1994 the Bates-Backer merger was undone, and the agency once again became Bates Worldwide. Carl Spielvogel retired that year and chose Michael Bungey for the post of chairman and CEO. An offer from Richard Humphreys, a former president of Saatchi &Saatchi Advertising, to buy Bates was rejected that same year. Bates, which was now the major asset of Cordiant, continued to be the main bait in rumors of a takeover. But the parent company continued to steer its own course. With Bungey

as chairman-CEO, the agency celebrated its 60th anniversary in 2000 with total worldwide billings of nearly $7.9 billion.

JOHN McDONOUGH

Further Reading

"Ad Business Is Still Pretty Human, Says Bates," *Advertising Age* (20 December 1965)

"FTC Commissioners Flay Colgate, Bates for 'Sandpaper' TV Mockup," *Advertising Age* (16 October 1961)

Goldman, Kevin, *Conflicting Accounts: The Creation and Crash of the Saatchi & Saatchi Advertising Empire,* New York: Simon and Schuster, 1997

"Happy Clients Boosted Bates Billing 33% in '57," *Advertising Age* (13 January 1958)

Reeves, Rosser, *Reality in Advertising,* New York: Bates, 1960

"Reeves Departs Front-Line Post after 25 Years at Ted Bates Agency," *Advertising Age* (14 February 1966)

"Reeves' *Reality* and How It Works in Ted Bates Commercials," *Advertising Age* (17 April 1961)

"Ted Bates, a Quiet Adman, Is Dead at 70," *Advertising Age* (5 June 1972)

"Text of FTC Order Against Bates, Colgate," *Advertising Age* (8 January 1962)

Batey Ads

Established by Ian Batey in 1972 on the strength of winning the then-new Singapore Airlines account; various branches organized under the corporate holding of Batey Group; 30 percent stake acquired by WPP Group, 1997; WPP Group's share increased to 50.2 percent, 2000; Los Angeles, California, office closed, 2000; renamed Red Cell Asia, 2001.

Major Clients
Australian Broadcasting Corporation
Hewlett-Packard Asia Pacific
Mercedes-Benz
Raffles Hotel
Singapore Airlines
SmithKline Beecham
Swatch
Telstra
United Overseas Bank

Highly regarded in the Asia-Pacific region as an independent agency with a strong creative reputation, Batey Ads was launched in Singapore in 1972 by Ian Batey. The English-born Batey emi-

grated to Australia with his parents in 1948 when he was 13 years old. Leaving school at 15, he worked in Sydney as a runner for an advertising agency where he learned some basic copywriting skills. In the early 1960s he worked in Australia for the Jackson Wain Agency on the Qantas account, and later he handled the Malaysia-Singapore Airlines (MSA) account for the same agency. When the governments of Malaysia and Singapore terminated their joint operating agreement for MSA, and the Singapore government moved to establish Singapore Airlines (SIA), Batey pitched the account and won it. The agency and the airline commenced business on the same day, 1 October 1972. Batey's Singapore Airlines campaigns, featuring the Singapore Girl (represented by sarong-clad SIA flight attendants) and the slogan, "Singapore Girl, you're a great way to fly," helped establish the airline as the sixth-largest international carrier by 1987.

Batey had a reputation as a hard taskmaster but one supportive of creative talent. The agency claimed that it put art before profit because Batey believed that money would flow to the most creative work. His motto was, "Kill for the art; die for the client; and always be brief, direct, humble."

Rather than chasing new clients, Batey Ads concentrated primarily on developing relations with existing clients. At the end of

Award-winning 1995 work for Singapore Airlines, Batey Ads' signature client, advertised the carrier's Singapore-to-New York City flights. *Courtesy of Singapore Airlines.*

Michael de Krestser Consultants, John Hagely Communications, Tequila Asia Pacific, and Maximise Singapore as group partners. The Sydney branch, Batey Kazoo Communications, developed from a strong retail background to become a major-brand advertising agency handling such prestigious clients as the Australian Broadcasting Corporation, Telstra, and SmithKline Beecham. Batey Kazoo was Australia's fastest growing agency in 1995. Although the economic crisis in Asia cut the agency's billings in Thailand and halted its growth in Malaysia in 1997 and 1998, billings in Taiwan grew from NT$310 million in 1996 to NT$500 million in 1998. In 2000 the Taiwan office ranked 15th in the nation.

In 1997 the WPP Group, the largest communication services group in the world and owner of the J. Walter Thompson Company and Ogilvy & Mather Worldwide, Inc., took 30 percent equity in the Batey Group. Batey's management retained a majority on the board and controlled operations of Batey Ads. For the Batey Group, the association with WPP brought in some capital to facilitate its expansion. The WPP connection also enabled the Batey Group to win the global launch of Swatch's Skin line of watches in 1999 and the global campaign for Mercedes-Benz's C Class automobiles in 2000. In 1999 Ian Batey was awarded the inaugural Lifetime Achievement Award by the Singapore Advertising Hall of Fame.

In 2000 the WPP Group boosted its minority share to 50.2 percent; Batey Ads USA closed its Los Angeles, California, office that same year. For 2000 the agency had worldwide gross income of $21.4 million, up 11.6 percent from its 1999 figures, on billings of $143.8 million, up 8.5 percent from year-earlier numbers. In terms of 2000 gross income, Batey's Singapore office ranked fourth in the republic, after Dentsu, Ogilvy, and Saatchi & Saatchi. In 2001 the WPP Group gave the Batey Group a new name, Red Cell Asia.

IAN GORDON

the 20th century, the Singapore office had more than 20 clients. SIA had remained with the agency since the beginning. Other important Singapore accounts included the Singapore Tourist Promotion Board and Raffles Hotel.

In the 1990s the Batey Group sought to expand its reach in Asia, striving in particular to strengthen its three strongest branches: Singapore, Hong Kong, and Sydney. In Singapore Batey expanded into public relations and brand management, adding

Further Reading

Batey Ads: The First Twenty-Five Years, 1972–1997, Singapore: Batey Ads, 1998

Ling, Chan Siew, "Batey Ads Has the Right Mix to Be Singapore's Largest Agency," *Business Times* (8 April 1996)

Tan, Michael, "How SIA Created and Maintains a Successful Global Image," *SIA Perspectives* (April 1988)

Wee, Lea, "Advertising Guru: Flying High with Singapore Girl," *Straits Times* (13 October 1999)

Batten Barton Durstine & Osborn. *See* BBDO Worldwide, Inc.

Batteries

Although alkaline batteries have been available in the United States for just over 40 years, consumers—and their electronic devices—have developed a voracious appetite for them. This high demand has led to intense competition for sales and market share. Batteries are a highly profitable product, and ad campaigns over the years have sought to bring interest to a product category that does not stir much emotion in consumers.

The first alkaline batteries were made in the 1950s in response to the great demand for batteries after the invention of the transistor. Alkaline batteries replaced the shorter-lived zinc carbon batteries in most portable, battery-powered devices. In 1959 the Eveready Battery unit of Union Carbide introduced its alkaline product to consumers through its agency, the William Esty Company, Inc., and then rebranded the batteries under the Energizer name in 1980. The rival Duracell brand, made by the P.R. Mallory Company, was introduced in 1965 in a modest campaign by Needham, Harper & Steers. Energizer estimates that the alkaline batteries of the 21st century last 40 times longer than the first prototype. The attributes of power and longevity have been key to battery advertising.

Alkaline batteries made their television-advertising debut in 1974, after Peter G. Viele, president of the Duracell Products division of P.R. Mallory Company, decided to thrust them into the public consciousness. In an ad created by Needham, Harper & Steers, a roomful of stuffed, battery-operated pink bunnies beat drums until only one remained drumming—the one powered by a "copper-topped" Duracell. The tag line, "No regular battery looks like it or lasts like it," pointed to Duracell's longer life compared with its competitors. Not only did the battery have a long life, the pitch did too. The campaign lasted ten years and enabled Duracell to take the lead in the alkaline battery segment of the market.

In 1986 Ralston Purina Company acquired Eveready and sought to increase its market share through advertising. In ads from William Esty, actor Robert Conrad dared viewers to knock the battery off his shoulder and spunky Olympic gymnast Mary Lou Retton was featured to epitomize the battery's high energy. The ads did not resonate well with consumers, however, nor did a commercial featuring screaming Australian rugby player Jacko. The battery account was put up for review, and DDB Needham (successor to Needham, Harper & Steers) emerged the victor.

DDB Needham took a fresh approach with a familiar pink face—Duracell's old pink bunny. This time the bunny was less fluffy and sported Ray-Ban sunglasses. A commercial premiering in the fall of 1988 showed the drum-banging Energizer Bunny barging into ads for fictional products. While DDB considered this a one-shot effort, Eveready wanted to turn it into a full-blown campaign. Chiat/Day (later TBWA/Chiat/Day) replaced DDB after that first campaign in the fall of 1988, and in October 1989 Chiat/Day started a series of memorable parody commercials for fake products such as Chug-a-Cherry soda and a TV show about lady cops called "H.I.P.S." All the ads ended with a sudden inter-ruption by the bunny that "keeps going and going"—much like the campaign itself. (In the early years of the campaign, Eveready tried wrapping bunny ads around ads for other products from parent Ralston, including Purina Cat Chow, Hostess Twinkies, and Chex cereals, but the change in focus confused viewers.) Among the legendary villains who have appeared vainly seeking to block the bunny are *Star Wars'* Darth Vader and Looney Tunes cartoon character Wile E. Coyote.

Even the fall 2000 U.S. election season was used as a mock-serious background for one of these unstoppable-bunny ads. In this commercial, a fictional candidate named Bob Fremgen makes an appearance at a playground to demonstrate his interest in child welfare. While speaking, he is knocked down by a child on a swing just as the bunny marches past. Energizer went so far as to establish a fake political Web site for its faux candidate.

Duracell, meanwhile, came up with a new cast of characters. In the mid-1990s, a battery-operated, robotic-looking family, the

"Maximum power. Maximum value," an ad from 1997, was part of the campaign that reestablished Rayovac's place in the battery market. *Courtesy of Rayovac Corp.*

Puttermans, arrived on television screens in spots from Ogilvy & Mather Worldwide. In one commercial, the Puttermans—who all had Duracell copper-top batteries protruding from their backs—laughed during a family picnic when a relative without a Duracell ran out of power and fell over into a plate of spaghetti.

The nation's third-largest battery maker, Rayovac Corporation, was less active in advertising, but in the mid-1990s it emerged as a scrappy contender for its own market share. After Thomas Lee Company acquired the company in 1997 and installed a new management team, Rayovac set out to reinvigorate the value message of its lower-priced batteries. The pitch "Lasts as long as the other guys for less" was changed to "Maximum power. Maximum value," and Rayovac signed basketball superstar Michael Jordan for the ads, which were created by Young & Rubicam. In one spot, Jordan made disparaging comments about other batteries and offered consumers their money back if they noticed a performance difference between Rayovac and other brands.

The Gillette Company acquired Duracell in a $7 billion stock deal in late 1996 and in January 1998 fired Ogilvy, handing the estimated $75 million–$90 million advertising account over to BBDO Worldwide, which already worked with Gillette. That ended a 14-year relationship with Ogilvy.

Nearing the turn of the 21st century, the focus of the battery marketers became new product introductions and the expensive advertising that accompanied them. In 1998 Duracell launched its premium-priced Ultra battery, which promised to last 50 percent longer, for electronics that drain power quickly. The tab for the campaign from BBDO, New York City, was $60 million.

Energizer Holdings Corporation, spun out of Ralston Purina in the spring of 2000, introduced Energizer e2 with a $100 million marketing campaign—one that was not from TBWA/Chiat/Day and one that did not feature the bunny. DDB Worldwide won the account for the new titanium-based superpremium battery after an agency review that included the incumbent, TBWA/Chiat/Day. Shortly thereafter, Duracell launched the third generation of its Ultra battery, dubbed "M3" for "more fuel, more efficiency, more power." The ads were from BBDO Worldwide in New York City.

Meanwhile, Gillette had filed suit against Ralston over the Energizer Bunny ads. With a share of what had become a $2.6 million-plus market at stake, neither company was willing to turn the other cheek. In May 2000 a federal judge sided with Gillette and ruled that the Energizer Bunny could no longer continue to torch, crush, and pummel rival batteries in TV, Internet, and print ads. The ruling was not based on the attack bunny per se, but on the methodology of some battery performance tests.

MARY ELLEN PODMOLIK

Further Reading

Beardi, Cara, "Rayovac Will Spend $35 Million to Reinforce Value Position," *Advertising Age* (19 June 2000)

Beardi, Cara, "Energizer Powers Up e2 with $100 Mil Campaign," *Advertising Age* (24 July 2000)

Kanner, Bernice, *The 100 Best TV Commercials—and Why They Worked*, New York: Times Business, 1999

Savan, Leslie, *The Sponsored Life: Ads, TV, and American Culture*, Philadelphia, Pennsylvania: Temple University Press, 1994

Symonds, William C., "Can Gillette Regain Its Voltage?" *Business Week* (16 October 2000)

Bayer Bess Vanderwarker

Founded as Bayer, Bess, Vanderwarker & Flynn by Gary Bayer, Ronald Bess, William Flynn, and Anthony Vanderwarker through purchase of the Chicago, Illinois, office of Backer & Spielvogel, 1987; renamed Bayer Bess Vanderwarker with the departure of Flynn, 1988; purchased by True North Communications, 1996; merged into Foote, Cone & Belding, 1996.

Major Clients

Helene Curtis
Illinois State Lottery
Quaker Oats Company (Gatorade, Cap'n Crunch)

Bayer Bess Vanderwarker (BBV) was established in 1987 when Gary Bayer, Ronald Bess, Anthony Vanderwarker, and William Flynn purchased the Chicago, Illinois, office of Backer & Spielvogel. Rooted in Gatorade Thirst Quencher and Cap'n Crunch cereal, two Quaker Oats Company brands, BBV soon made a name for itself among mid-level advertising agencies in the Midwest. Within five years, it had nearly tripled its initial billings. Stalled in its efforts to continue this growth, in January 1996 BBV sold what had become the eighth largest full-service agency in Chicago to True North Communications. Despite initial statements that the agency would remain an independent entity within True North, by the end of 1996 it had been fully merged with Foote, Cone & Belding.

In 1969 Quaker formed an in-house agency, AdCom, which it sold in 1985 to Backer & Spielvogel, a unit of Saatchi & Saatchi. Because Saatchi & Saatchi was also the agency of record for a variety of Procter & Gamble products that competed with

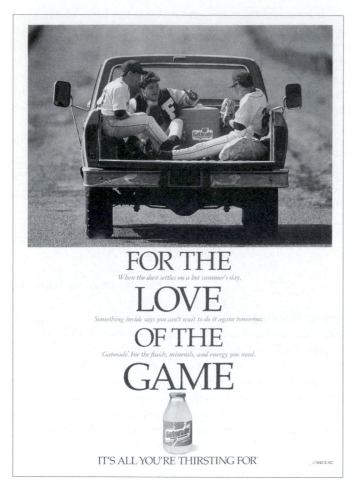

FOR THE
When the dust settles on a hot summer's day,
LOVE
Something inside says you can't wait to do it again tomorrow.
OF THE
Gatorade.' For the fluids, minerals, and energy you need.
GAME

IT'S ALL YOU'RE THIRSTING FOR

Bayer Bess Vanderwarker created this 1992 ad for Gatorade.
Courtesy of the Quaker Oats Company.

Jay Ward, whose cartoon characters included the popular Rocky and Bullwinkle squirrel-and-moose duo, the cereal gave BBV an inroad in the food and children's markets that it would later capitalize on when landing such accounts as Pro Set, the third-largest marketer of trading cards, featuring football, hockey, golf, and entertainment cards.

BBV began to build a reputation as a creative midsize agency and quickly acquired other accounts. One that would remain throughout the history of BBV was another Chicago-based account, Helene Curtis's Suave line, which BBV won in 1987. Another was the Illinois Lottery, with $19 million in billings, which became part of the agency's stable in 1991. BBV gradually added technology, services, and retailing clients and broadened its background of packaged-goods producers. For a time, it had the regional Domino's Pizza account, the Chicago Hilton and Towers, St. Paul Federal Bank for Savings, SpaghettiO's, and Ameritech corporate. By 1992 it had tripled its original billings, becoming the second largest independent agency in Chicago. It had also added staff to handle its newest account, Boston Chicken (which later became Boston Market). Despite the agency's growth, creative director Vanderwarker took what turned out to be a permanent leave in 1992.

BBV seemed to be at a crossroads. Efforts to expand were frustrated by clients such as Gatorade and Motorola, whose growth was increasingly international. In 1992 BBV affiliated with TBWA Advertising, which handled Gatorade overseas, but this was a short-term measure. The agency reorganized in December 1993; Brian Goodall was named general manager, allowing Bayer and Bess to focus on long-term growth and client development.

By late 1994, however, it was clear that this expected growth had failed to materialize, and reports in the media raised doubts about the agency's future. A merger with TBWA was proposed, but talks between the two broke down. Shortly thereafter, Boston Market put its account up for review; BBV lost the account—and 12 percent of its staff. Furthermore, Quaker acquired Snapple, and it did not appear that BBV had the resources to handle both Gatorade and Snapple. Complicating matters, Quaker was alarmed by BBV's talks with TBWA because that agency did work for competing General Mills brands.

Thwarted in its efforts to merge with TBWA, BBV turned to True North. In January 1996 BBV became part of True North Communications, a holding company. The merger provided a measure of symmetry: Bess, who had joined Foote, Cone & Belding (FCB) as an account executive when he graduated from the University of Illinois, was named president of FCB Chicago. Bayer continued as president of BBV, which was to operate independently under FCB Chicago.

The merger earned FCB honors as *Adweek*'s "Midwest Agency of the Year" in 1997. Praising the combination of the two companies as "straight out of Economics 101: merge two companies and watch the profits soar," *Adweek* noted the immediate rewards for the new FCB. Partly as a result of Quaker's positive experience with BBV, FCB won the Snapple account without a review. In August 1996 Bess's friendship with Herb Baum, a former DDB colleague who had become chairman of Quaker State (no affilia-

Quaker's, it decided to sell Backer & Spielvogel. Bayer, a DDB Needham veteran who headed Backer & Spielvogel's Chicago office, spearheaded a successful purchase to take the office independent, opening in 1987. His partners were Flynn, who was also in the Backer & Spielvogel office; Bess, a veteran of DDB Needham; and Vanderwarker, also from DDB Needham. Originally known as Bayer, Bess, Vanderwarker & Flynn, the agency became Bayer Bess Vanderwarker when Flynn left in 1988.

BBV had the accounts for several successful brands at its inception, including almost $50 million in billings from Quaker. Most prominent among them was Gatorade, which Backer & Spielvogel had won in 1985. The slogan, "Gatorade is thirst aid for that deep down body thirst," helped make Gatorade the best-selling drink in its category. By 1991 Gatorade was a $600 million brand, Quaker's largest. It helped that its spokesman was Michael Jordan, who in 1991 led the Chicago Bulls to the first of six National Basketball Association championships. Its ads featuring the extremely popular basketball superstar ran with the tag line, "Be like Mike. Drink Gatorade."

Cap'n Crunch was another of the initial products inherited by BBV. With its appealing "Cap'n Crunch" character designed by

tion with the Quaker Oats Company), earned FCB a $30 million Quaker State account, again without a review.

While FCB continued to avow that BBV had a place in the company, the jewels—Gatorade, Helene Curtis, and Campbell Soup Company—were shifted to FCB. Although BBV snared two new cereal accounts from Quaker during 1996, the last remnants of the agency were absorbed into FCB by the end of 1996. BBV ceased to exist; the 40 remaining staffers moved to FCB.

FREDERICK B. HOYT

BBDO Worldwide, Inc.

(Batten Barton Durstine & Osborn)

Formed in 1928 by merger of the George Batten Company (1891) and Barton Durstine & Osborn (1919); became major agency in radio and television; experienced major postwar growth under Bernard ("Ben") Duffy (1946–56), followed by international growth in 1960s and 1970s; combined in 1986 with Doyle Dane Bernbach and Needham Harper Worldwide to form Omnicom; continues as BBDO Worldwide, Inc., within Omnicom Group.

Major Clients

American Tobacco Company (Lucky Strike)
Apple Computer
Armstrong Cork Company
Brown & Williamson Tobacco Corporation
Campbell Soup Company
Chrysler Corporation (DeSoto)
E.I. du Pont de Nemours & Company
General Electric Company
General Motors Corporation
Hormel Foods Corporation
Lever Brothers
Pepsi-Cola Company
Polaroid Land Camera
Rexall Drugs
Time, Inc.
Toni

The roots of Batten Barton Durstine & Osborn (BBDO) go back to 15 March 1891, when George Batten opened the George Batten Company at 38 Park Row in New York City with one secretary and no clients. Batten had entered advertising as a space salesman for various religious papers but soon decided he preferred to run an agency of his own. After three months of precarious existence, the agency won its first account, the Macbeth Lamp Chimney Company, a business that was later acquired by the Corning Glass Works. The following year, 1892, Batten hired William Johns to work as his assistant—at $10 per week. Although Batten once fired Johns over a copy error, the two reconciled, and Johns later went on to head the agency and, in 1917, became the first president of the American Association of Advertising Agencies (AAAA, or Four A's). Among the most enduring contributions to American marketing attributed to Johns was the phrase "used car." After 17 years of steady growth, the agency opened offices in Boston, Massachusetts, and Chicago, Illinois, in 1908, and continued to prosper through World War I with such clients as Boyle waxes, Mallory hats, Regal shoes, Stevens-Duryea cars, Lehn & Fink Riveris brand talcum, and Armstrong Cork Company, which made linoleum ("For every room in your house"). When Batten died in 1918, Johns became president of the agency.

Meanwhile, during the war, three young advertising men had met while working on the United War Work fund-raising effort. They were Bruce Barton, Roy Durstine, and Alex Osborn. Barton recruited Durstine to assist with the war effort, and the two men subsequently brought Osborn into the effort from his agency in Buffalo, New York. Immediately after the war, Barton and Durstine talked of going into business, reportedly in the oyster bar of Grand Central Station. They opened their own agency on 1 January 1919, at 25 West 45th Street under the name Barton & Durstine Company. On July 1 the new agency announced the addition of Osborn to the partnership, thus adding the city of Buffalo to the coverage of Barton, Durstine & Osborn (BDO). Clients included *Scribner's* magazine, Wildroot Hair Tonic, McGraw-Hill, and the United States Chamber of Commerce.

In New York, Durstine managed the business while Barton took the lead writing the ads. Osborn ran the Buffalo operation and in 1949 authored a successful book on advertising called *Your Creative Power*. But it was Barton who would become the most celebrated of the partners. Born in 1886, he was the son of a successful preacher who traveled around the upper South before settling into prosperous church positions, first in Boston and then in Chicago. Barton went on to Amherst College and after graduation began a career in publishing with *Collier's Weekly*, where he began to dabble in advertising. Politically active and reform-minded, Barton wrote editorials for *Redbook*, *Everyweek*, and *American Magazine*, and then became involved in wartime fund-raising before starting BDO on a borrowed capital investment of $10,000.

The ads he wrote helped bring prominence to the agency. Among his most famous was one written for the Salvation Army—"A man may be down but he is never out"—which became an unofficial BBDO motto. In 1923, drawing on his background as a preacher's son, Barton began work on a book that was to make him one of the most popular spokesmen in America for the virtues of advertising and capitalism. Published the following year as *The Man Nobody Knows,* it argued that if Jesus Christ were alive in 1924 he would not be a pious recluse but an advertising man, eager to meet people, make friends, and above all sell his ideas—in the words of historian Stephen Fox, "Jesus Christ as George F. Babbitt." Barton's point was to erase the barrier between the secular and sectarian and to show that religion and business have much in common and much to learn from each other. It was a message in tune with its time, and the book was one of the decade's most interesting best-sellers. It was followed by a sequel dealing with the Bible, called *The Book Nobody Knows.* In 1932 Barton's career was tarnished by a sex-and-blackmail scandal in which a former mistress threatened to publish a fictionalized novel of their three-year affair.

A staunch Republican who worked for Calvin Coolidge and Herbert Hoover in the 1920s, Barton was appointed to Congress from New York City's wealthy "silk stocking" district. He was an enemy of the New Deal in 1937, and served two terms before being defeated in a 1940 run for the Senate. President Franklin D. Roosevelt immortalized him in a political speech during the 1940 campaign in which he referred to his three most prominent opponents: ". . . [Joseph] Martin, Barton, and [Hamilton] Fish." Following his career in politics, Barton returned to BBDO.

During the 1920s both the Batten agency and especially BDO ranked among the country's leading agencies. BDO attracted some of America's most prestigious companies, including General Electric (GE), General Motors, Consolidated Edison, and Du Pont ("Better things for better living through chemistry"). The agency developed a special reputation for so-called institutional advertising, which seeks to sell the company rather than its specific products. In need of larger offices, in 1927 BDO moved onto the seventh floor of 338 Madison Avenue, the same building occupied by the Batten Company. On 21 September 1928, a decade after the death of George Batten, it was announced that the two agencies would be merged into a single new agency to be called Batten Barton Durstine & Osborn.

The Batten Company had been the larger of the two agencies. Barton became chairman of the newly merged company; Johns became president and Durstine, vice president and general manager. Osborn oversaw the Buffalo office. The agency's philosophy was that an advertising person should be an all-around individual who could write copy as effectively as performing account executive functions. BBDO employed 600 people and was said to bill $27 million annually. It became a cliché to say that the name of the agency sounded like a trunk falling down stairs, a description ascribed to many but actually originated by a man named Stuart Peabody.

In 1929, according to figures provided by the agency to *Sales Management* magazine, billings for the agency's first year of operation reached $32.6 million. But the Depression would have an impact on even this powerful agency, which would see its billing drop by more than 50 percent to a low of $14.8 million. It would not be until 1944 that the agency would recover to its 1929 levels.

The 1930s were nevertheless a period of some accomplishment in the context of a constricted economy. BBDO acquired Bisell & Land for a position in Pittsburgh, Pennsylvania. It also bought the Harrison Guthrie Agency in Minneapolis, Minnesota, in 1931. Two years later, two key executives, Ralph Campbell and Raymond Mithun, left to form Campbell Mithun and took every account in the Minneapolis office with them except Hormel. Other famous advertising people to come out of BBDO included William Benton, Chester Bowles, Ted Bates, David Ogilvy, J. Stirling Getchell, Ed Ney, Jim Jordan, Hal Riney, Jock Elliott, and Ralph Ammirati.

One of the agency's most memorable radio successes involved the DuPont Corporation, which was suffering under the stigma of having engaged in profiteering during World War I. According to

In the 1930s ads from Batten Barton Durstine & Osborn introduced DuPont's "Cellophane," a revolutionary transparent cellulose film that provided protective packaging while allowing consumers to see what they were buying.
Courtesy of DuPont.

congressional investigations undertaken in the 1930s, the company had received more than a $1 billion in government contracts, nearly a quarter of which was profit. It was a major corporate scandal in a decade of corporate misbehavior. DuPont was also said to have motivated an isolationist Congress to pass the Neutrality Act of 1935 along with a general arms embargo. DuPont turned to BBDO to help repair a huge public relations problem that had shocked the nation, and the agency came up with a weekly radio series honoring the patriotic triumph of American history and biography called *The DuPont Cavalcade of America*. Among the young writers recruited from the Federal Theater Project to work for the show was the playwright Arthur Miller. Though the program never won a large audience, it was a favorite of opinion leaders and educators who saluted DuPont for its public-spirited efforts. This demonstrated precisely the purpose of institutional advertising.

BBDO became one of the first agencies to play an important role in radio, and in 1927 the first to set up a self-contained radio department able to write, cast, and produce programming for network broadcast. (The first radio network, the National Broadcasting Company, had been founded the year before.) BBDO's radio department was headed by Arthur Pryor, son of the famous bandleader. Pryor would create *The Atwater Kent Hour* and the *Soconyland Sketches*, said to be the first sponsored dramatic program.

He also created *March of Time* for *Time* magazine in 1931, a show that dramatized major news events of the week, into which the agency rotated various clients, including Remington-Rand (1933–36), Wrigley's gum (1936), Electrolux refrigerators (1937–38), and *Time* again until 1945. The agency created several music programs for GE, including *The Hour of Charm* with Phil Spitalny's all-girl orchestra (1936–46) and Fred Waring. It produced a Tommy Dorsey program for Brown & Williamson, Guy Lombardo for General Baking Company, and *The Burns and Allen Show* for Hormel, Swan soap (Lever Brothers), and B.F. Goodrich. In the 1940s it brought Rexall drugstores to radio on *The Phil Harris-Alice Faye Show*. To support its growing radio responsibilities, BBDO opened an office in Hollywood, California, in 1937.

In April 1939 Durstine left BBDO after several personal and financial reverses and soon formed his own agency, but it never became a major factor in the business. Johns became chairman of BBDO but was no longer involved in the day-to-day running of the agency. After his unsuccessful run for the U.S. Senate in 1940, Barton turned his full attention back to the agency. He and especially Osborn took measures to steer BBDO beyond its institutional typecasting and into a higher level of consumer package goods advertising, which was seen as the road to rapid growth and greater profitability. A copy department was set up in 1941 under Charles Brower and made up of specialists rather than the "all-around" people who had been doing both copy and contact work. In addition to winning Lever Brothers in 1939, the agency also took the Chrysler DeSoto division away from Ruthrauff & Ryan in 1944. It helped push billings to $33.7 million, the highest level since 1929, and made BBDO the sixth-ranking American agency, according to *Advertising Age*.

A large dinner gathering at the Waldorf-Astoria in 1942 celebrated BBDO's 50th anniversary as well as Johns's 50th year with the company. Johns died in 1944, the first of the founding partners to die. Durstine died in 1962 and Osborn in 1966. Barton continued as chairman until 1961 and maintained an office in the agency. His death in 1967 closed the book on the lives of the original BBDO founders. But it was Johns's death in 1944 that signaled the emergence of a second generation of leadership, led by Bernard ("Ben") Duffy.

Born in 1902, Duffy grew up in the Hell's Kitchen section of New York City's West Side and dropped out of high school to take a job as office boy at the Arbuckle Coffee Company in 1919. Not long after, his younger brother, who was working as an errand boy at BDO, told him he could make $1.75 a week more at the agency. He joined BDO that same year, went to night school, and was promoted to the media department in 1920. By the time of the merger with Batten, Duffy was ready to run the combined media operation. In 1938 he was elected vice president and in 1944 executive vice president. The following year he became general manager. Finally in 1946, after 27 years with the company, Duffy became president.

In 1948, upon hearing the stunning news that Foote, Cone & Belding had suddenly resigned the $12 million American Tobacco account, which included the flagship Lucky Strike brand, Duffy contacted American Tobacco and locked up the business within hours of the resignation announcement. (The agency resigned its Brown & Williamson business, which it had had since the early 1930s.) It was the largest account shift in ad history to that point and noted widely in the general press. BBDO took over production of the popular *Jack Benny Show* and the *Lucky Strike Hit Parade* and soon developed the long-running "Be Happy Go Lucky" campaign.

Later on, as the Lucky Strike name began to weaken in the 1960s, another American Tobacco brand, Herbert Tareyton, would begin to rise aggressively. With its name shortened simply to Tareyton, the brand became one of the big sellers of the decade as BBDO devised one of the most famous campaigns to emerge before the end of cigarette advertising on television in 1971: "Us Tareyton smokers would rather fight than switch."

Between 1947 and 1948 BBDO billings leapt from $59 million to $71 million. By 1950 the agency had 11 offices, more than 1,100 employees, and what many regarded as the largest billings in the new medium of television, $4 million. In 1951 the agency became the third advertising agency in history (after J. Walter Thompson and Young & Rubicam [Y&R]) to cross the $100 million barrier.

Duffy's involvement with Republican politics was almost as intense as Barton's had been. He was close friends with New York Governor Thomas Dewey and the agency had been involved in the Dewey presidential runs of 1944 and 1948, though as media advisor only. Commercials had yet to become a part of the election routine. Duffy's relationship with Dwight D. Eisenhower began when the general was president of Columbia University. When Eisenhower became the Republican nominee in 1952, BBDO played a major but not exclusive role. The Kudner Agency had been involved with Robert Taft's race for the nomination. But Dewey was an important Eisenhower strategist, and he pressed for BBDO's involvement after the convention. Thus, Kudner and BBDO became co-agencies. Y&R, which was the Eisenhower agency up through the nomination, was dropped. It was BBDO that departed from the normal practice of lining up broadcast clearances for campaign speeches and developed a series of 60-second spot announcements in which a "typical" voter would put a question to Eisenhower and the candidate would respond. These are generally considered to be the first presidential campaign TV "commercials." (The commercials were actually created and shot by Rosser Reeves of the Ted Bates Company, although the Bates agency was not otherwise involved.) BBDO returned for the 1956 campaign and Richard Nixon's run in 1960. The agency was also active in the Reagan campaigns.

BBDO was among the strongest agencies in the early days of television. It brought *Your Hit Parade, Jack Benny Show,* and *Cavalcade of America* from radio to TV, and developed *The General Electric Theater* around Ronald Reagan, *The U.S. Steel Hour, Armstrong Circle Theater, The Du Pont Show of the Month,* and *You Bet Your Life* with Groucho Marx for DeSoto and Plymouth. The agency acquired the Revlon account in January 1955 and had limited involvement in *The $64,000 Question,* which the company sponsored. But the agency was dropped in September 1957, nearly a year before the quiz show scandal would break and prove a matter of great controversy. An internal agency memo in June 1955 warned that "nothing will make Revlon look worse than if the public thinks there is some kind of trickery going on. . . ." BBDO was a major player in another controversy, that of "clearing" actors for work in TV during the blacklist of the Joseph McCarthy era.

By 1956 BBDO was billing $194.5 million, second to the J. Walter Thompson Company by only $500,000. In the same year Duffy suffered a serious stroke at age 54 during a meeting with General Foods executives, effectively ending his decade-long reign over the agency, although he retained the title of president. Charles Brower took over management of the company, becoming president in December 1959, while Duffy assumed the position of vice chairman. He died in September 1972. So dependent had the agency become on the cult of the Duffy personality that there was considerable uncertainty and several clients departures (including Revlon). In 1958, 150 employees were fired and growth was unimpressive. The agency won American Airlines and Chrysler's Valiant, both solid accounts, but there was no blockbuster win.

The year 1960 would be the turnaround year for the Brower regime. Although BBDO International was established with high hopes in 1954, the agency did not acquire its first major international position until the 1960 acquisition of Dolan Duckworth Whitcombe & Stewart in London, England. That same year, BBDO also won the Pepsi-Cola business, which pushed billings from $214 million to $243 million. Three weeks after John Kennedy proclaimed in his 1961 inauguration that a new generation had come to power, BBDO went after that generation on behalf of Pepsi. To the tune of "Makin' Whoopee," singer Joannie Sommers rolled out the campaign that would define the soft drink brand for the rest of the century—"For those who think young."

Four years later, in 1965, the youth positioning evolved into "Come alive, you're in the Pepsi generation," and the "Pepsi generation" became a common cultural reference point. (In 1999 *Advertising Age* ranked "The Pepsi generation" campaign 21st among the century's 100 most influential ad campaigns.

By the 1980s creative director Phil Dusenberry had become one of the stars of the industry through his work on Pepsi. He brought much attention to the brand and to BBDO when the agency signed the pop star Michael Jackson to do a Pepsi campaign to debut on a Grammy Award telecast. When a small fire broke out on the set during the filming, it brought still more publicity to the product. Less welcome was the attention the Pepsi-Jackson association drew in 1998 when the star was accused of alleged inappropriate behavior. The incident was a reminder of the risks a marketer assumes when it builds a high-profile partnership with a celebrity endorser. The creative output for Pepsi over the years to come would be a ladder that would carry many people to the top at BBDO, including future chairmen/chief executive officers (CEOs) Dusenberry and Allen Rosenshine.

Another long-lived campaign to come out of BBDO at about the same period was "Ring around the collar" for Lever Brothers' Wisk brand detergent. The 1960s were a period of renaissance under Brower's leadership. The company expanded domestically and internationally. In 1964 BBDO was the world's fourth-largest agency. That year it bought out Burke Dowling Adams in Atlanta, Georgia, the first agency merger activity since 1931. The following year it began discussions with Clyne Maxon, Inc., a major agency whose billings were 85 percent dominated by Gillette and GE. Clyne Maxon originated when Lou Maxon founded Maxon, Inc., in Detroit, Michigan, and built it into the city's second-largest agency after Campbell-Ewald by the mid-1940s. When Maxon suffered a heart attack in 1964, C. Terence Clyne, a former vice chairman of Interpublic who came to Maxon, Inc., in 1962, moved into the presidency and moved the agency to New York. This created a split. Clyne Maxon of New York opened in April 1965 and took the major share of the business, while Maxon, Inc., continued as an entirely separate agency in Detroit. On 1 January 1966, Clyne Maxon was acquired by BBDO. Two years later the merger was reversed at Clyne Maxon's request, and the agency became independent again. But BBDO came out of the brief partnership with the major part of the Gillette account.

An ethical scandal shook the agency late in the decade. For many years BBDO had been an agency for Campbell's Soup (along with the F. Wallis Armstrong/Ward Wheelock agency of Philadelphia, Pennsylvania). In the 1930s BBDO is said to have created the company's "Mmm mmm Good" campaign, ranked 25th on *Advertising Age*'s list of the top 100 campaigns of the century. In 1968 BBDO introduced Campbell's Chicken & Stars soup, a broth containing a mixture of pasta stars, small chicken chunks, and vegetables. In photographing the product for print ads, however, a problem developed when the solid ingredients sank to the bottom of the broth and could not be seen. Robert Ballantine, a BBDO art director, solved this by putting marbles in the bowl to push the chicken and pasta to the surface. The use of such artifice was not considered unethical in advertising, any

come alive!

You're in the Pepsi generation!

Take your choice: regular Pepsi-Cola or new Diet Pepsi-Cola. Pepsi cools a thirst fast, tastes clean and alive! Same goes for Diet Pepsi– honest-to-Pepsi taste with less than a calorie to a bottle. Either way, Pepsi is the official drink of today's generation!

A 1960s campaign for Pepsi from Batten Barton Durstine & Osborn firmly established the soft drink's identification with the youth market as "the official drink of today's generation."
Pepsi-Cola Company.

more than special lighting or photo retouching. Substitutes for ice cream, typically mashed potatoes coated with resin, were often used in photo shoots because the real thing melted too quickly under the lights. In apparel ads the models' clothes were often secured from behind with pins and clips to insure the desired fit.

The Campbell's campaign broke in April 1968 and promptly produced an inquiry from the Federal Trade Commission (FTC), acting on a complaint from an unknown source, later revealed to be the H.J. Heinz Company, a Campbell competitor. A representative of the Bureau of Deceptive Practices visited BBDO and was shown how the soup was "propped" for photography with the marbles. His report to the FTC stated that the advertising misrepresented the amount of chicken and pasta in the soup. In November 1968 Campbell and BBDO agreed they would not used such propping techniques in the future. The matter seemed closed with no one the wiser.

In February 1969 FTC Chairman Paul Dixon, who had been appointed by President John F. Kennedy in 1961, made the details public and instituted a formal proceeding against Campbell and invited public comment. The request had no precedent. The case was carried over into the administration of Richard M. Nixon. For the next two years, there were new petitions and appeals that would involve 14 federal judges. In December 1972 the FTC dismissed the complaint, and BBDO was not required to run corrective advertising.

BBDO ended the 1960s with billings of $336 million. BBDO International became a holding company in 1971, while Batten Barton Durstine & Osborn continued to be the name of the operating agency. Tom Dillon had succeeded Brower as president in 1964, pursued aggressive international expansion, and ultimately took the company public. Originally the plan was for a stock offering in October 1972, but depressed market prices at the time forced a postponement. Finally, in October 1973, 705,515 shares of BBDO common stock raised nearly $12.7 million with an opening price of $18.

Bruce Crawford succeeded Dillon as president in 1975, and by 1979 the company ranked seventh among U.S. agencies, with world billings just short of $1 billion, a threshold already crossed by the six top agencies. Also in 1979, BBDO acquired Arthur Meyerhoff Associates, an old Chicago agency long associated with Wrigley, and in 1980 Doremus & Company, a financial marketing specialist. The Meyerhoff name disappeared, while Doremus continued. The year ended with a spectacular gain of nearly 30 percent, putting world volume at $1.3 billion. Expansion through the 1970s, despite slow growth periods, proved as impressive as the fabled Duffy decade of 1946–56. By the time Crawford's presidency ended in 1984, BBDO had become a $2.3 billion giant.

But it was not big enough. Despite the prestige of being named "Agency of the Year" by both *Adweek* (1983) and *Advertising Age* (1985), BBDO found its relative position threatened in a decade that was seeing the merging of giants and the aggressive acquisition activity of two British agencies, the WPP Group and Saatchi & Saatchi. BBDO was not the only agency concerned with these developments. In 1985 Doyle Dane Bernbach (DDB) in New York City and Needham Harper Worldwide in Chicago were worried about the same things. On 25 April 1986, after seven months of talks, Keith Reinhard of Needham, Barry Loughrane of DDB, and Rosenshine, who had succeeded Crawford as chairman-CEO of BBDO the year before, agreed to form a new entity called Omnicom, a holding company that consisted of a merged DDB/Needham and BBDO. Rosenshine became chairman-CEO of Omnicom, while Norm Campbell became chairman of the new BBDO Worldwide, which was the largest of the agencies making up the merger. Reinhard headed DDB/Needham Worldwide.

Two years later Rosenshine moved back to head BBDO, while Campbell returned to run Omnicom. In 1987 the agency moved from the Madison Avenue offices it had occupied since 1928 to new quarters on New York's Avenue of the Americas. But the organizational structure put in place in 1986 remained substantially unchanged through the 1990s (although TBWA became a third major asset within the Omnicom family) and kept BBDO on a fast growth track. In 2000 BBDO Worldwide had gross income of $1.5 billion, an increase of 6.7 percent over the previous year, on billings of $13.6 billion, up 9.6 percent from 1999. It ranked eighth among U.S. agencies.

JOHN MCDONOUGH

See also Omnicom Group

Further Reading

Alter, Stewart, "Bates OKs Saatchi Talks, Fallout from BBDO Megadeal; $180 Million Departs," *Advertising Age* (5 May 1986)

Barnouw, Erik, *A History of Broadcasting in the United States*, 3 vols., New York: Oxford University Press, 1966–70; see especially vol. 1, *A Tower in Babel: To 1933*, and vol. 2, *The Golden Web, 1933 to 1953*

"Ben Duffy's Impact on Advertising Recalled," *Advertising Age* (11 September 1972)

"Bruce Barton, Agency Founder, Is Dead at 80," *Advertising Age* (9 July 1967)

Cogley, John, *Report on Blacklisting*, 2 vols., New York: Fund for the Republic, 1956; see especially vol. 2, *Radio-Television*

Crichton, John, "BBDO, Close to Top of Heap, Is Still Growing," *Advertising Age* (19 June 1950)

Duffy, Ben, "Ben Duffy Recalls How He Sold Ad Ideas to Alfred Sloan, GM, Crowell," *Advertising Age* (12 June 1961)

Fox, Stephen, *The Mirror Makers: A History of American Advertising and Its Creators*, New York : Morrow, 1984

Goodrum, Charles A., and Helen Dalrymple, *Advertising in America: The First 200 Years*, New York: Abrams, 1990

Hughes, Lawrence M., "BBDO Lay $104 Million on the Line," *Sales Management* (15 July 1952)

"Merger Unites Barton-Batten Ad Companies," *New York Herald Tribune* (22 September 1928)

Miller, Arthur, *Timebends: A Life*, New York: Grove Press, and London: Methuen, 1987

O'Gara, James V., "BBDO Will Miss Les Pearl's Copy Gems," *Advertising Age* (21 January 1957)

"TV Quiz Rigging Could Hurt Revlon, '55 BBDO Memo Said," *Advertising Age* (16 November 1959)

Bcom3 Group

(BDM)

The holding company Bcom3 is one of the largest advertising conglomerates in the world, with more than 500 units in 90 countries. It was formed in 1999 by the merger of the Leo Group, Chicago, Illinois, home of ad network Leo Burnett Worldwide, and the MacManus Group, New York City, whose flagship agency is D'Arcy Masius Benton & Bowles. The third partner was the Japanese advertising company Dentsu, which owned a 20 percent stake in Bcom3.

Other major agencies under Bcom3's umbrella include N.W. Ayer & Partners, New York City, and a 49 percent stake in Bartle Bogle Hegarty, London, England, of which 49 percent was owned by the Leo Group. In addition to including traditional agencies, Bcom3 also housed the media buying and planning powerhouse Starcom MediaVest Group.

Leadership was drawn from the ranks of longtime Burnett and D'Arcy executives. Bcom3 Chief Executive Officer (CEO) Roger Haupt rose through the ranks at Burnett, joining the agency in 1984 and rising to CEO of Leo Burnett Worldwide at the time of Bcom3's formation. Likewise, Bcom3 Chairman Roy Bostock first joined Benton & Bowles in 1964 and eventually became chairman-CEO of the MacManus Group. Bcom3 President-Chief Operating Officer Craig Brown was vice chairman-chief operating officer and chief financial officer of the MacManus Group. Bcom3 Vice Chairman and Chief Client Officer Arthur Selkowitz had previously been chairman-CEO of D'Arcy.

When first formed the new company was known simply as BDM; it was rechristened Bcom3 in March 2000. The "B" in the new moniker stood for "beacon," and the "3" represented the company's three major components: the Leo Group, the MacManus Group, and Dentsu.

The name *MacManus Group* was created in 1996 when D'Arcy was in the process of buying N. W. Ayer & Partners. The company wanted a name to distinguish its holding company function from its agency operation; it chose MacManus, after Theodore MacManus, whose agency MacManus, John & Adams merged with D'Arcy in 1972 to form what eventually became D'Arcy-MacManus & Masius, Inc. His name was dropped from the agency in 1985 when D'Arcy merged with Benton & Bowles and became D'Arcy Masius Benton & Bowles, or DMB&B.

Until 1999 D'Arcy and Burnett were fiercely independent rivals, often competing for the same business. Even so, by the time of the merger they shared several large clients, including the Coca-Cola Company, General Motors Corporation (GM), Philip Morris Companies, and Procter & Gamble Company. Each agency was a creative powerhouse in its own right, with ad campaigns that have long since passed into the realm of popular culture. The Marlboro Man, Tony the Tiger, and the Maytag Repairman were all inventions of Burnett. D'Arcy created Mr. Whipple, the grocer who implored customers, "Please don't squeeze the Charmin." D'Arcy also came up with the Budweiser beer tag line, "This Bud's for you," before Anheuser-Busch ended its 79-year relationship with the agency in 1994.

There had been a previous attempt at a merger between Burnett and MacManus, but talks collapsed in late 1998. Leaders of the two networks said at the time that they disagreed fundamentally on how to run a joint media operation. Ironically, when the merger was completed, Starcom MediaVest emerged as a particularly powerful entity. In August 2000 the agency won GM's $2.6 billion account for media buying and planning. That December Starcom won media duties for the $800 million Kraft Foods account.

Despite its strong media operations, Bcom3 relied heavily on traditional advertising. *Advertising Age* estimated that only one-third of Bcom3's revenue in 2000 came from nonadvertising billings, although many observers predicted this would become more important in the future. Since the merger, the traditional advertising agencies' fortunes have been mixed. Burnett was awarded the prestigious U.S. Army account, but its debut creative work, which sought to target the Gen X and younger crowd with the tag line "An army of one," was poorly received. In early 2001 Burnett laid off about 200 employees, or 9 percent of its work force.

N.W. Ayer suffered a devastating blow that triggered the closing of its Detroit, Michigan, office in October 2000, when GM moved its corporate image advertising and marketing account to McCann-Erickson, a subsidiary of the Interpublic Group of Companies. GM had been an Ayer client for 28 years.

When Bcom3 was formed its leadership announced plans to go public by the end of 2000, but with the stock market weak, the initial public offering was postponed. The company, however, did see some expansion during 2000. It formed an agency in Japan called Beacon and also became full owner of Pure D'Arcy in Australia; the agency had been called Pure Creative DMB&B and was 40 percent owned by Bcom3.

By the end of 2000 there was widespread industry speculation that one of the top-three holding companies—the Interpublic Group, Omnicom Group, or WPP Group—might make a play to acquire Bcom3. With the three largest holding companies seeking to expand and fewer small shops left to swallow up, industry watchers believed that holding companies that already owned global networks would be attractive merger partners. In 2002 Bcom3 Group merged with the Publicis Group, forming the fourth-largest communications group in the world.

WENDY DAVIS

Further Reading

"Ad Industry Review and Preview: As Big Ad Agencies Look to Buy, Few Smaller Companies Are Left," *Wall Street Journal* (22 December 2000)

Guy, Sandra, "Burnett's Expectation in Merger: Why Ad Giant Sought Outside Muscle," *Chicago Sun-Times* (4 November 1999)

Kranhold, Kathryn, and Steven Lipin, "Leo, MacManus to Form New Ad Giant," *Wall Street Journal* (3 November 1999)

MacArthur, Kate, and Laura Petrecca, "Burnett's New Leaders:

Wolf, Brennan Boosted: Hints of New Direction: Haupt Appoints Team to Oversee Bcom3's Top Shop," *Advertising Age* (2 October 2000)

BDDP Group

(TBWA/Paris)

Founded by Jean-Claude Boulet, Jean-Marie Dru, Marie-Catherine Dupuy, and Jean-Pierre Petit through purchase of Young & Rubicam's regional agency network, 1984; failed in hostile takeover of U.K.-based advertising network Boase Massimi Pollitt, 1989; bought 40 percent stake in U.S.-based agency Wells, Rich, Greene, Inc. (WRG), 1990; ownership in WRG increased to 70 percent, 1991; heavy debt load forced bank takeover, 1994; merged with U.K.-based Gold Greenlees Trott, 1996; loss of U.S. Procter & Gamble Company business led to friendly takeover by Omnicom Group and birth of BDDP/TBWA, 1998; renamed TBWA/Paris, 2001.

Major Clients
Absolut Vodka
Bic
FILA
France Telecom
McDonald's Corporation
Michelin
TAG Heuer

BDDP/TBWA traces its roots to 1984, when four executives launched Boulet Dru Dupuy Petit with the buyout of Young & Rubicam's regional agency network. BDDP quickly made a name for itself, winning high-profile accounts, turning out strong creative work, and becoming one of the five highest-billing ad agencies in France within three years of its founding. BDDP was born from the widely held idea in the 1980s that France was ripe for an independent agency network, outside the realm of the traditional leaders, Havas, Publicis, and RSCG, but not specifically linked to the U.S. giants. Such an agency would need to be provocatively creative, commercially minded, and international in focus. To put these ideas into effect, Jean-Claude Boulet and Jean-Marie Dru left top management positions at Young & Rubicam late in 1983, taking with them a regional network with 150 employees and about $10 million in gross income. The pair were joined by Marie-Catherine Dupuy, granddaughter of legendary French advertising man Jean-Pierre Dupuy and creative director at the

Dupuy & Compton agency, and Jean-Pierre Petit, whose local agency SNIP was merged into BDDP.

BDDP made a splash in 1984 with its first campaigns: a television spot for Hertz Corporation's rental cars by filmmaker Jean-Jacques Annaud (*The Lovers, Enemy at the Gates*) and an ironic print and outdoor campaign for women's ready-to-wear designer Rodier, featuring photographs by fashion guru Peter Lindbergh. At year-end, BDDP signed a partnership agreement with Chiat/Day, the U.S. lead agency for Apple Computer and Nike, and began adapting Chiat/Day's ads to the French market.

In 1985 BDDP bolstered its developing reputation by picking up a high-profile automobile account, Mazda Motor Corporation, as well as two other new clients that would make their mark on the agency's history: McDonald's Corporation, which chose BDDP to support its own rapid expansion across France, and Michelin, which tapped BDDP as the first outside agency to prepare pan-European ads using its classic marketing icon, Bibendum, also known as the Michelin Man. In 1986 new clients such as BMW and KLM offered additional international cachet, while creative work for Portuguese beverage marketer Porto Cruz set off what would be a decade-long string of award-winning print and outdoor campaigns.

In 1987 BDDP moved to a new, specially designed headquarters in the Paris suburb of Billancourt. The agency was selected by government officials to handle a series of privatization campaigns, winning rave reviews for its use of actress Catherine Deneuve in TV spots for the sell-off of industrial group Suez. But an avant-garde, photo-heavy campaign for retailer Printemps resulted in the loss of that account two years later.

BDDP began 1988 by laying the foundations for an international network. Recently arrived International Director Nick Baum targeted a Spanish agency, Solucion Diagonal, and a British shop, Waldron, Allen, Henry & Thompson, and then linked the pair to a Belgium-based creative shop, Booster BDDP, launched in 1987. Baum realized that global reach would be crucial if BDDP were to run international campaigns, such as the one it launched in 1988 for then-new client watchmaker TAG Heuer.

BDDP acquired a stake in Singapore-based Batey Ads in 1989, picking up the Singapore Airlines account and partner shops in

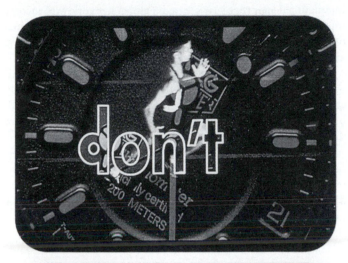

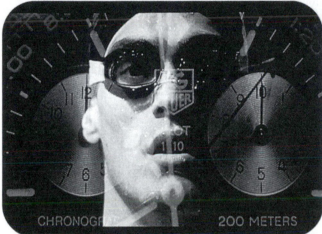

BDDP's award-winning campaign for Swiss watch manufacturer TAG Heuer featured arresting graphics of stressful moments superimposed on a watch face, along with the tag line, "Don't crack under pressure."

Hong Kong, Malaysia, the Philippines, and Taiwan. It waged a high-profile, but eventually unsuccessful, takeover bid for British ad agency Boase Massimi Pollitt. It scored a creative triumph at the annual International Advertising Festival in Cannes, France, coming home with three gold Lions.

However, 1990 marked the beginning of what turned out to be a dangerous liaison with Mary Wells Lawrence, a well-known advertising figure in the United States and chairman of Wells, Rich, Greene, Inc. (WRG). BDDP initially bought a 40 percent stake in the WRG network, then ranked 18th in the United States, and increased its holding to 70 percent in 1991. The WRG acquisition—valued at $140 million–$150 million—pushed BDDP's global billings beyond $2.1 billion and gave it a long-sought foothold in the American market, where its new division worked for blue-chip clients, including Continental Airlines, Chase Manhattan Bank, IBM Corporation, Philip Morris Companies, and Procter & Gamble Company (P&G).

In 1992 Dru introduced to the agency a then-revolutionary philosophy known as "Disruption." The new philosophy demanded that BDDP staffers worldwide adopt radical new approaches when designing new strategies for brand-name clients. Dru's book *Disruption: Overturning Conventions and Shaking Up the Marketplace* turned him into an international advertising guru, while the concept stoked global sales of previously unknown brands such as Absolut Vodka and British entrepreneur Richard Branson's Virgin brand.

But BDDP's inability to control its American subsidiary proved fatal. Faced with an estimated $250 million in debt, mounting annual losses, and the prospect of dismantlement, in 1994 BDDP's founders relinquished control of their agency to European Strategic Investments (ESI), a London-based investment group led by financier Walter Butler.

Petit was the first of the original partners to jump ship, in December 1994, accepting an offer from McDonald's to run its marketing in France as vice president of marketing. Baum followed suit, moving to Euro RSCG Worldwide, where as vice president-global account manager he handled Peugeot's advertising. ESI found a host of international suitors for the shop—including Grey International, Saatchi & Saatchi, and the WPP Group—but eventually sold the group in late 1996 to U.K.-based Gold Greenlees Trott (GGT).

The merged GGT-BDDP entity—led by a British advertising veteran, Michael Greenlees, as president—showed signs of promise as early as 1997, recording nearly $400 million in gross income and placing 15th on *Advertising Age*'s annual survey of international agency networks.

P&G dropped WRG in early 1998, pulling its Gain detergent, Oil of Olay face cream, and Pringles chips accounts, putting a halt to the experiment and slashing 12 percent off WRG's U.S. billings. Massive sell-offs at the London Stock Exchange halved GGT-BDDP's share price, making the agency a takeover target. With sharks circling, GGT-BDDP accepted a friendly merger offer from the Omnicom Group.

Although many BDDP loyalists had high hopes for the merger, Boulet shocked employees by tendering his resignation as co-chairman and chief executive officer (CEO) of BDDP Worldwide—created in 1996 when BDDP and GGT merged—in January 1998. The formal coupling between GGT-BDDP and TBWA

Jean-Claude Boulet, Jean-Marie Dru, Jean-Pierre Petit, and Marie-Catherine Dupuy.

International later that year created a global network with income topping $800 million, fulfilling Omnicom CEO John Wren's goal of launching a strong third agency network capable of standing alongside existing brands BBDO and DDB Worldwide.

Greenlees took over the presidency of TBWA International, with TBWA founder Bill Tragos as chairman. Dru, previously chairman-CEO of BDDP Worldwide, became CEO-international, based in Paris and charged with merging BDDP shops in more than 50 countries into TBWA.

BDDP/TBWA was France's fourth leading consolidated advertising group in 2000, with some 1,300 employees generating estimated gross income of $145 million. TBWA International dropped the BDDP brand in 2001, transforming BDDP/TBWA into TBWA/Paris, a division of TBWA/France.

LAWRENCE J. SPEER

Further Reading

BDDP (1984–1993), s.l.: s.n., 1994
"Merger: TBWA Formula Enriched with BDDP-GGT Enzymes," *CB News* (25 May 1998)
"GGT-BDDP Says Yes to the American Omnicom," *Strategies* (30 January 1998)

BDM. *See* Bcom3 Group

Beer. *See* Beverages, Alcoholic

Beers, Charlotte 1935–

U.S. Advertising Executive

In a career spanning four decades, Charlotte Beers has been the top executive of at least three advertising agencies, carving out a reputation as a sharp business executive as well as paving the way for women to become a competitive force in the advertising industry. Beers, the daughter of a Montana cowboy who later worked as an engineer for Standard Oil of Indiana, was born on 26 July 1935 in Beaumont, Texas. After her birth, the family moved to Houston, Texas, then Lafayette, Louisiana, following her father's

jobs in the oil fields. Beers often credited her father with helping her make career choices, saying he instilled in her the drive to "do something that would make a contribution and not just get married." Beers majored in mathematics and physics as an undergraduate at Baylor University.

After graduation in 1957, she moved to southeastern Texas to teach engineering algebra to petroleum managers in the oil fields. She soon realized she wanted to do something else and in the early

1960s accepted a job as a consumer market research supervisor with the Uncle Ben's division of food and candy marketer Mars, Inc., in Houston. She was promoted to brand manager for Uncle Ben's in 1966 and then group product manager.

In 1969, with her first marriage breaking up, Beers was offered a position as an account executive with the J. Walter Thompson Company (JWT), of Chicago, Illinois, which at the time was the ad agency for Uncle Ben's. At the agency, Beers discovered she enjoyed what she called "orchestrating service" for such clients as Alberto-Culver Company; Sears, Roebuck & Company; Gillette Company's personal care division; appliance marketer Sunbeam; and Quaker Oats Company. She became known for being able to forge close client bonds.

Within five years at JWT, Beers was elected the agency's first woman senior vice president. The agency did not promote her further, however, so in 1979 Beers accepted an offer from Jerry Birn, chief executive officer (CEO) at rival agency Tatham-Laird & Kudner, also in Chicago, to help put that agency back on a winning track. At the time, Tatham was struggling with low employee morale and tenuous client loyalty. Beers's hard work paid off, and in 1982 she was named CEO when Birn retired.

The 1980s were good years for the agency, which quadrupled its billings and developed a reputation for being a company that provided equal opportunities for women. Beers also prospered, becoming the first female chairman of the American Association of Advertising Agencies in 1988.

In 1991 Beers helped guide Tatham into its merger with Paris, France-based Euro RSCG and was named a vice chairman of the parent company. But she surprised the agency by quitting when she was required to move to France. She eventually accepted the chairmanship of Ogilvy & Mather Worldwide in 1992.

As chairman of Ogilvy, Beers helped the agency win the $500 million account of IBM Corporation in 1994 in what was the largest account consolidation to date. Ogilvy also signed other large accounts, including Kentucky Fried Chicken, with spending estimated at $80 million, and worked to woo blue-chip clients such as the American Express Company, Shell Oil Company, Ford Motor Company, Eastman Kodak Company, and Unilever. Beers helped develop the agency's strategy of "brand stewardship," or what she called the art of creating, building, and energizing profitable brands.

Beers is credited with bringing Ogilvy out of a slump and guiding it to become the sixth-largest U.S. agency. In 1996 Beers turned the company over to Shelly Lazarus, a longtime Ogilvy executive; the following year she retired to Florida, where she planned to write books.

But in 1999 Beers returned to the ad business as worldwide chairman of JWT, her first agency. Chris Jones, JWT's chairman, relinquished his duties in an unusual job-sharing arrangement, accepting instead the title of CEO. Beers's return to the agency was widely credited with helping JWT recover after a tough period. In an interview with the *New York Times* in 1999, Beers said she hoped to repeat her feats at Tatham and Ogilvy to help JWT regain ground lost to competitors. Within a year of her return to JWT, the agency won more than $700 million in new

Charlotte Beers.

billings, including Qwest Communications, Elizabeth Arden Company, Miller Brewing Company's Miller Genuine Draft, and Shell Oil Company. In March 2001 Beers's contracts with JWT and its parent WPP Group were not renewed, but she rebounded quickly with a nomination from President George W. Bush to become undersecretary of state for public diplomacy. The appointment was confirmed in September 2001.

LAURIE FREEMAN

Biography
Born in Beaumont, Texas, 26 July 1935; graduated from Baylor University, 1957; taught engineering algebra to petroleum engineers before accepting a market researcher position with Mars, Inc.'s Uncle Ben's rice, where she was promoted to brand manager, 1966; named account executive at J. Walter Thompson Company (JWT), Chicago, Illinois, 1969; joined Tatham-Laird & Kudner as chief operating officer, 1979; named chief executive officer (CEO) of Tatham, 1982; resigned after Tatham was acquired by Havas Advertising's Euro RSCG, Paris, France, 1991; named chairman-CEO of Ogilvy & Mather Worldwide, Inc., New York City, 1992; retired, 1996; named chairman of JWT, 1999; appointed U.S. undersecretary of state for public diplomacy, 2001.

Further Reading
Elliott, Stuart, "A Shift in Power for J. Walter Thompson As Madison Avenue's Steel Magnolia Climbs Aboard," *The New York Times* (9 March 1999)

"JWT Names Mrs. Beers First Woman Senior VP," *Advertising Age* (6 August 1973)

Kim, Hank, "Beers: I'm Better than Ever," *Adweek* (15 March 1999)

O'Leary, Noreen, "Charlotte's Web," *Adweek* (6 April 1992)

"She's Back: Charlotte Beers Says She's Excited about the Prospects for Cross Pollination of Talent at JWT," *Advertising Age* (15 March 1999)

Teinowitz, Ira, "Affairs of State: Looking for Love through Branding: Why State Dept. Tapped Beers for Image Overhaul," *Advertising Age* (9 April 2001)

Benetton

Principal Agencies
Chiat/Day (Benetton USA only)

Benetton was founded in 1965 in Treviso, Italy, a small town near Venice, by Luciano, Carlo, Gilberto, and Giuliana Benetton. Since that time the company has grown into a global fashion empire, producing more than 90 million garments per year for stores in 120 countries. Benetton, now based in Ponzano, Italy, is best known for its simple, colorful sweaters. The company is also known for its advertising, which often features unsettling images that depict social concerns such as racism, poverty, AIDS, and child labor. From the beginning, company President Luciano Benetton has sought out provocative issues that have kept his company in the spotlight. In addition to serving as head of the business, Benetton is a longtime political activist who was elected to the Italian senate in 1992.

As his business expanded, Luciano Benetton recognized the need for a coherent worldwide advertising campaign that could reach consumers in countries with different climates and cultures. In 1982 he turned to Italian photographer Oliviero Toscani, who was already known for creating the images of retailers Esprit and Fiorucci. Benetton named Toscani creative director of the company and handed him the company's entire advertising budget (which has consistently been 4 percent of total sales) and complete creative freedom. Although the company had stores around the world, until 1984 Benetton advertised only in Italy and France. That year, the company entered the international market with a campaign entitled "All the Colors of the World." The ads, featuring images of happy, Benetton-clad youth of varying ethnicities, carried undertones of racial harmony and peace, although the clothing remained the primary focus.

While catalogs and in-store posters continued to emphasize this multicultural theme, the company's advertising took an extraordinary turn in 1989: the merchandise disappeared from the ads altogether. The "United Colors of Benetton" campaign, a result of intense collaboration between Benetton and Toscani, featured symbolic photographs that many authorities in the field believe radically changed the face of advertising forever—among them, a black woman breast-feeding a white baby, a black hand and a white hand cuffed together, and an African-American child dozing on a pile of white teddy bears.

In 1991 Benetton's advertising took an even more controversial turn. Print ads launched at the beginning of the Persian Gulf War, depicting rows of crosses in a cemetery, were rejected in Italy, France, Britain, and Germany. Arab countries refused a photo of black, white, and Asian children sticking out their tongues, and a picture of a priest and a nun kissing on the lips incensed the Roman Catholic church. Nevertheless, the company consistently won awards in the advertising industry for these campaigns.

The next campaign featured actual news photos, including a duck covered in thick oil, a woman sobbing over the bloodied corpse of a Mafia victim, and a white youngster with a halo of blond ringlets posed beside an African-American child with two twists of hair shaped into devil-like horns. The most controversial ad of the group, "David Kirby," depicted a skeletal 32-year-old man who had just died of AIDS, surrounded by grieving family members. This photo in particular, originally shot for *Life* magazine and approved for Benetton's use by the Kirby family, fueled a debate that continues to this day. Proponents see the company's ads as brave, thoughtful, and groundbreaking. Those opposed to Benetton's ads feel that the company exploits powerful, emotional, painful issues for publicity and profit. While the ads have anticapitalist undertones—many convey messages of comradeship with the poor and exploited—there is no denying that they are intended to sell the Benetton product. Thus, many observers label the company's advertising hypocritical.

Moreover, Benetton has been accused of desensitizing the public to serious social issues by removing them from their familiar context in the news media and placing them in the advertising arena. Some critics argue that the company cheapens social problems by using these images as a means of advertising and attaching the Benetton name to them. Further, many are angry that while all of the ads display the Benetton name and phone number, none features a hot line number for the causes that they promote, nor do they urge people to take action.

Luciano Benetton has maintained that his ads appeal to his target market of 18-to-34-year-olds, who lack the historical framework of the previous generation and are accustomed to the somewhat random use of language and image. He has defended the

The "United Colors of Benetton" campaign promoted tolerance and celebrated diversity.
Concept: O. Toscani. Courtesy of United Colors of Benetton.

use of the photos, stating that Benetton's advertising is intended to do something much more meaningful than sell a product; the campaigns, he insists, are designed to spur people into activism. He also notes that the company does its share of charity work, spearheading clothing donation drives and contributing money to education, animal conservation, and AIDS organizations.

Despite the controversy, the company's global revenue has continued to grow, and Toscani has remained the creative force behind the company's campaigns in every country except the United States. Because of lagging sales and the belief that the ads had become so shocking that they were hurting business, Benetton USA replaced Toscani with the American advertising agency Chiat/Day in 1995. Chiat/Day's plain-vanilla ads, reminiscent of the earlier "All the Colors of the World" campaign, featured models of different ethnicities having fun while wriggling in and out of Benetton clothes. While this softer look prevailed in the company's limited U.S. market, the rest of the world continued to see the familiar Toscani ads. In the late 1990s one of the company's campaigns, entitled "Sunflowers," featured a group of German schoolchildren with disabilities. While the campaign stirred controversy in some circles, Benetton was actually praised by some Down syndrome groups for drawing attention to the cause and for portraying disabled people in a positive light.

Nevertheless, as Toscani's work became more edgy, resistance grew among consumers and, especially, retailers. In 1995 the company was sued by a group of German retailers that claimed the ads were undermining their own promotional efforts and affecting sales of all clothing. Toscani's most controversial series of ads came early in 2000 when the company entered the debate over capital punishment. One ad showed 25 convicted murderers on death row awaiting execution and gave each an opportunity to explain his case. Some claimed innocence, while others insisted they had found religion. The most extensive version of the "We on Death Row" campaign appeared in *Talk* magazine in a joint Benetton–Miramax Films venture of which Toscani was creative director. The ad was in the form of a 100-page insert that appeared in the February 2000 issue. It provoked immediate and widespread condemnation. "If the death sentence were handed out to those who are guilty of producing excruciatingly tasteless, ineffective advertising and inflicting it on the masses," ad executive Jerry Della Femina wrote in the *Wall Street Journal*, "Oliviero Toscani, the self-proclaimed 'genius' behind Benetton advertising, would be appearing in his own capital punishment ads." Toscani responded by dismissing Della Femina as "antiquated" and naïve.

In May 2000 Toscani left Benetton and the death row campaign was pulled; by then, however, the damage had been done.

Benetton's U.S. sales had been falling since the mid-1980s, and the company was counting on a marketing partnership with Sears, Roebuck & Company to increase its sales. In the summer of 1999 Sears launched a private-label line called Benetton U.S.A., but within weeks of the launching of the death row campaign, Sears withdrew from the deal. Moreover, Benetton was sued by the state of Missouri, which alleged that Toscani had lied to Department of Corrections officials to gain access to death-row prisoners.

While few would dispute that Benetton's ads have drawn attention to important social and political causes, many wonder to what effect on the causes and at what cost to the company. In February 2001 Benetton announced it would seek to rebuild its damaged U.S. presence with a fall campaign that would emphasize basic product attributes of color and style. Shot in New York City by James Mollison, the creative director who replaced Toscani, the ads continued to express the long-standing Benetton commitment to ethnic diversity but without the harsh elements of controversy. Nevertheless, Paolo Landi, the company's ad manager, insisted in an interview with *Brandweek* magazine that Benetton would continue to press social issues in future campaigns, and he alluded to the problems of refugees as a coming theme.

As of 2001 Benetton had only 150 U.S. outlets, down from a peak of more than 600 in the early 1980s. With only 15 percent of its $2.4 billion in world sales coming from the United States, the company announced plans to open several showcase "megastores" in key U.S. fashion markets.

KRISTEN WILKERSON

Further Reading

Ewen, Stuart, *All Consuming Images: The Politics of Style in Contemporary Culture*, New York: Basic Books, 1988; revised edition, 1999

Mantle, Jonathan, *Benetton: The Family, the Business, and the Brand*, London: Little Brown, 1999

Sivulka, Juliann, *Soap, Sex, and Cigarettes: A Cultural History of American Advertising*, Belmont, California: Wadsworth, 1998

Tinic, Serra A., "United Colors and United Meanings: Benetton and the Commodification of Social Issues," *Journal of Communication* 47, no. 3 (Summer 1997)

Williamson, Judith, *Decoding Advertisements: Ideology and Meaning in Advertising*, London: Boyars, 1978; New York: Boyars, 1979

Benton and Bowles, Inc.

Founded by William Benton and Chester Bowles, 1929; created *Maxwell House Showboat* radio variety program, 1932; three of the agency's sponsored shows were among the four leading network radio programs in the United States, mid-1930s; Benton sold his interest in the agency and joined academia, 1936; copywriter Ted Bates left the agency, taking the Colgate account with him, to open his own agency, 1940; Bowles resigned as chairman and began government career, 1941; agency merged with D'Arcy-MacManus & Masius to become D'Arcy Masius Benton & Bowles, 1985; merged with Leo Burnett Company, to form Bcom3 Group, 1999.

Major Clients

Anheuser-Busch (Budweiser beer)
Best Foods, Inc. (Hellmann's mayonnaise)
Colgate-Palmolive-Peet Company
General Foods Corporation (Maxwell House coffee)
E.F. Hutton & Company, Inc.
Procter & Gamble Company (Crest, Charmin)
Texaco, Inc.

Opening an advertising agency three months before the 1929 stock market crash and the start of the Great Depression in the United States might in retrospect seem inauspicious. But Benton and Bowles not only survived, it thrived as its founders, William Burnett Benton and Chester Bowles, pioneered the use of consumer market research, radio program sponsorship, and jingles.

Benton, born in 1900 and raised in Minnesota and Montana, was a graduate of Yale University who started his advertising career as a copywriter with New York City's Batten Company. "I don't set the world on fire writing copy," Benton admitted, but he did have a talent for market and consumer research. Researcher George Gallup dubbed Benton a "father" of advertising consumer research for Benton's development in 1928 of the first study of its kind measuring consumer preference.

Bowles, another Yale graduate who was one year younger than Benton, was hired by Benton as a junior copywriter at Batten. Bowles was a talented copywriter and skilled at assembling and managing a top creative team. Before long, Benton approached him about starting an agency of their own; Bowles was to become known as the key creative force behind the new agency.

When Benton and Bowles, Inc., opened in New York City, its first accounts were Hellmann's mayonnaise and Certo, a product used to make jam and jelly. Benton, Bowles, and their wives conducted door-to-door consumer surveys on the secrets of jam- and jelly-making; using the results, they created a magazine advertisement that helped boost product sales.

By the end of its first year, Benton and Bowles had billings of $40,000 and ten accounts, including additional General Foods

Pinch some pennies instead.

For Charmin bathroom tissue, Benton and Bowles, Inc., created Mr. Whipple, the grocery store manager who implored his customers not to squeeze the temptingly soft product.
Courtesy of The Procter & Gamble Company.

products, Bristol-Myers, and Colgate-Palmolive. In April 1933 Atherton W. Hobler joined the agency as a new partner, bringing with him $5 million more in General Foods brand accounts for Maxwell House coffee, Post bran flakes, Post Toasties, Log Cabin syrup, Walter Baker's cocoa and chocolate, and Diamond Crystal salt.

Once the country's best-selling coffee, Maxwell House had seen its sales decrease by 1932. Benton and Bowles conducted a survey to ascertain the cause of the decline and discovered that consumers perceived the brand as too expensive and not as high quality as competing products. The agency advised General Foods to improve the product, reduce the price, and increase brand awareness by sponsoring a one-hour radio variety show, which Bowles called *Maxwell House Showboat*.

Bowles also created radio shows and commercials to advertise Hellmann's mayonnaise and wrote and produced the radio soap opera *Young Doctor Malone* to promote General Foods products. He is credited with a number of radio firsts: using cue cards to generate laughter and applause from studio audiences, employing sound effects and jingles in spots, introducing dual sponsorship of shows, and crafting testimonial advertising. By the mid-1930s, Benton and Bowles's *Showboat, Palmolive Beauty Box,* and *Town Hall Tonight* (for Ipana toothpaste) were three of the nation's four leading network radio programs. In 1935 Benton and Bowles ranked sixth among U.S. agencies, with billings of about $10 million.

Although the savvy use of radio was central to the agency's rise, Benton advised educators and philanthropists to wake up to the medium's potential. "If the great universities do not develop radio broadcasting in the cause of education, it will, perhaps, be permanently left in the hands of the manufacturers of face powder, coffee, and soap, with occasional interruptions by the politicians," he said.

In 1936 Benton sold his interest in the agency, and Bowles became chairman. About this time, Bowles was credited with creating slice-of-life advertising. In addition, the agency's West Coast production office produced a number of high-rated radio shows, including the legendary *Burns and Allen*. By the end of the 1930s, Dr Pepper, Prudential Life Insurance, and Columbia Records had been added to the client roster. The agency was producing *Gang Busters* and *Hilltop House* for Palmolive, *Ripley's Believe It or Not* and Boake Carter, an anti–New Deal, anti-union isolationist news commentator for Post, *Myrt & Marge* for Super Suds, and *Stepmother* for Colgate.

By 1940 Bowles expressed a desire to leave the agency, but several major clients objected. Copywriter/account executive Ted Bates departed in December 1940 to launch his own agency, taking the multimillion-dollar Colgate account with him. Bowles, who had decided to stay on, landed Procter & Gamble's Ivory Snow in mid-1941.

Bowles finally resigned as chairman of Benton and Bowles later that year, handing the reins over to Hobler, who was to have a 60-year career in advertising. Hobler is credited with establishing the first agency copy-testing department and, with the advent of television, selling Procter & Gamble on sponsoring *The Loretta Young Show*.

For Texaco Benton and Bowles created the famous slogan "You can trust your car to the men who wear the star" in the 1940s. In the late 1950s, the agency boosted Procter & Gamble's Crest toothpaste with "Look, Ma! No cavities!" and, in the 1960s, Procter & Gamble's Charmin toilet tissue with "Please don't squeeze the Charmin" and brokerage house E.F. Hutton with "When E.F. Hutton talks . . . people listen." Budweiser's "This Bud's for you" slogan debuted in the 1970s; also during that decade, the agency revitalized General Foods' Post Grape Nuts brand by positioning it as a "100 percent natural cereal" and casting naturalist and wild foods expert Euell Gibbons in television spots for the product. With the financial power of General Foods and Procter & Gamble, Benton and Bowles remained among the last agencies to be active in TV program production. Lee Rich, head of the Benton and Bowles television department, played a major role in the development of *The Danny Thomas Show* and *The Andy Griffith Show,* both for General Foods, and *The Dick Van Dyke Show,* for Procter & Gamble.

Benton and Bowles's international billings climbed in the mid-1960s as domestic billings declined. The agency lost $21 million in U.S. billings from 1966 to 1967, while international billings more than doubled from $21.4 million to $47.5 million. Much of the gain came from newly acquired foreign agencies following a year of aggressive expansion. Benton and Bowles International was formalized as a separate corporate entity in February 1968. The $6 million Avis Rent A Car Systems account moved to Benton and Bowles in September 1969. In 1970 domestic billings were up slightly, and international billings continued their ascent, climbing more than 20 percent.

In 1985 Benton and Bowles joined with D'Arcy MacManus & Masius and became D'Arcy Masius Benton & Bowles (DMB&B), the eighth-ranked agency in the United States. By that time Benton and Bowles's accounts included Beatrice Foods' Tropicana orange juice, Hardee's Food Systems, long-distance phone company MCI, Nabisco Brands' Planters Nuts products, Texaco, and numerous Procter & Gamble and Richardson-Vicks brands. Today, the agency uses the short-form brand name D'Arcy and, like Leo Burnett Worldwide, is an operating unit of Bcom3 Group, Inc.

Benton and Bowles were young men when they retired from advertising and went on to illustrious careers in academia, publishing, and public service. Benton was to say, in retrospect, "I sold my interest in Benton and Bowles when I was 35, and I'd been taking three or four hundred thousand dollars a year out of it. Any business where a kid can make that kind of money is no business for old men."

In 1937 Benton accepted a position as a vice president of the University of Chicago at the urging of his Yale classmate and university President Robert M. Hutchins. In 1943 Sears, Roebuck & Company offered its Encyclopaedia Britannica unit to the university as a gift; when university trustees hesitated to accept the venerable publication, Benton put up the working capital and became responsible for running the publishing business. He continued as Encyclopaedia Britannica's owner and publisher until his death in 1973.

Benton was named U.S. assistant secretary of state for public affairs by President Harry S. Truman in 1945. Appointed to fill a vacant U.S. Senate seat late in 1949, he then won a special election to fill the remaining two years of that term. In the Senate, Benton was an early critic of Senator Joseph McCarthy's anti-Communist tactics. His other accomplishments include converting for peacetime the U.S. Information Service, cultural exchange programs, and radio's Voice of America, as well as serving as U.S. ambassador to the United Nations Educational, Scientific, and Cultural Organization (UNESCO) from 1963 to 1968. In 1948 he established the Benton Foundation, which is dedicated to demonstrating the value of communications for solving social problems.

Bowles served as Connecticut district director in the Office of Price Administration in 1942, UNESCO delegate in 1946, special assistant to the Secretary General of the United Nations from 1947 to 1948, and international chairman of the United Nations Children's Appeal from 1948 to 1950. He was elected governor of Connecticut in 1948 and twice served as U.S. ambassador to India, from 1951 to 1953 and from 1963 to 1969. He also was a member of the U.S. House of Representatives (1959–60) and a foreign policy adviser to Adlai Stevenson and John F. Kennedy. He was appointed undersecretary for political affairs and a special representative and adviser on African, Asian, and Latin American affairs in the Kennedy administration. Bowles died in 1986.

CHRISTINE BUNISH

Further Reading

Brower, Charlie, *Me, and Other Advertising Geniuses,* Garden City, New York: Doubleday, 1974

Hyman, Sidney, *The Lives of William Benton,* Chicago: University of Chicago Press, 1969

Leonard, Sheldon, *And the Show Goes On: Broadway and Hollywood Adventures,* New York: Limelight Editions, 1995

Webber, Gordon, *Our Kind of People: The Story of the First 50 Years at Benton & Bowles,* New York: Benton and Bowles, 1979

Bernbach, William (Bill) 1911–1982

U.S. Advertising Executive

Advertising's "brave new era" was born in the late 1940s, when advertising executives David Ogilvy and William Bernbach opened agencies destined to define a new style of conversation with the consumer. While Ogilvy made research the foundation of the work of his shop, Ogilvy & Mather, Bernbach anchored his philosophy in honest communication, ironic wit, and strong ideas. It was this new look and authentic voice, this "Bernbachian" affection for truth and delight, that led to advertising's much-touted "creative revolution" in the 1960s.

Though Bernbach did not necessarily set out to change the world of advertising, his vision for the industry and its creative product was firmly set before his famed agency opened its doors. His public school education in the Bronx, New York, and subsequent graduation from New York University formed the egalitarian nature of his creative style. A Jew who married an Italian (and suffered a lifelong split from his family because of it) and often quoted the Arab poet Kahlil Gibran's words of love and redemption, Bernbach early on found satisfaction in cultural risk-taking and flouting tradition.

Early career moves also betrayed Bernbach's maverick bent. After a stint at Schenley Distillers, he moved to the 1939 New York World's Fair as a promotional writer, reshaping the dreams of visionaries in terms the common American would embrace. Later, at the Weintraub Agency in New York City, where he worked beginning in 1941, he honed his simple and elegant writing style further. After a short time in the army, Bernbach returned to New York to be a writer for Grey Advertising, eventually rising to vice president for copy and art. There he met Ned Doyle and, along with Maxwell Dane, a friend who had worked at *Look* magazine, decided to open the agency (in June 1949) that would become the epicenter of change in the industry: Doyle Dane Bernbach (DDB).

Bernbach's new agency thrived on groundbreaking zeal. "I've got a great gimmick," he quipped in an early speech. "Let's tell the truth." And DDB advertising did just that. The funny and warm print ads for Volkswagen, Avis, Levy's, and Ohrbach's turned the traditional hard sell into strategic wit and honest communication. To many the Volkswagen "Think Small" campaign symbolized the creative approach of this new chapter in advertising history: it was honest, self-deprecating, radically inventive in layout and language (especially for this product category), and witty—all the while selling cars. In 1999 "Think Small" was named one of the best advertising campaigns of the 20th century by *Advertising Age.* Bernbach impressed upon his clients that in order to establish successful communication with the consumer, rules had to be broken. To begin with, the client had to be ready to sign on to something different in order to make the audience feel something different. "[A]ppeals to logic fail because the brain

William Bernbach.
Courtesy of DDB.

is not an instrument of logic at all," he noted. "It is an organ of survival, like fangs and claws." This philosophy is evident in the headline of a 1967 ad in favor of a nuclear test ban treaty: "We now have enough atom bombs to kill every Russian 360 times. The Russians only have enough to kill every American 150 times. We're ahead, aren't we?" These liberal creative ideals—fed by his love of literature and philosophy—were reflected in Bernbach's musings about hiring creative talent: "The real giants have always been poets, men who jumped from facts into the realm of imagination and ideas."

To create the powerful messages he vigorously advocated, Bernbach built a talent base like no other, eschewing Ivy League alumni (the traditional candidates for ad agency jobs) for graduates of art schools and English departments—and for middleclass, metropolitan types who had unusual perspectives. He hired Jews, Italians, Irish, women; the agency looked as different from others as it sounded. In the early 1960s, DDB became the creative shop where advertising writers and art directors, tired of the same old products from Madison Avenue shops entrenched in bulleted copy and predictable layout, wanted to work. Bernbach was their leader, their mentor, the father figure who passed harsh judgment on everything he saw but rewarded the work he approved with his careful attention. For the most part, the agency's work was attributed to Bernbach, causing some notable

resentment within his creative ranks. He was the conceptualizer and the headline writer; the "little words," he said, could be written by someone else.

Bernbach was responsible for at least four fundamental innovations in the industry. First, he changed the ethic of creativity. Before him, the work of producing an ad was a straightforward routine: sell the product through hard benefit. Bernbach, on the other hand, invented the concept of concept—that is, ideas with strategic force. He made writers and art directors into heroes of the business, engendering a respect evident today in the salaries of successful creatives. "Is creativity some obscure esoteric art form?" he once asked. "Not on your life. It's the most practical thing a businessman can employ." He regarded creativity as the professional advertising tool of choice. In a book of collected Bernbach wisdom published by Doyle Dane Bernbach, he wrote:

Merely to let your imagination run riot, to dream unrelated dreams, to indulge in graphic acrobatics and verbal gymnastics is NOT being creative. The creative person has harnessed his imagination. He has disciplined it so that every thought, every idea, every word he puts down, every line he draws, every light and shadow in every photograph he takes, makes more vivid, more believable, more persuasive the original theme or product advantage he has decided he must convey.

Second, Bernbach changed the advertising world by restructuring the creative side of agencies. His early work with Art Director Paul Rand at Weintraub proved his theory that writers and art directors created better concepts when they worked together. At the time writers customarily worked on copy while art directors made a layout; then they met and put the two together. Bernbach made teams of two—copywriter and art director—work together to form a strategy and then bring their idea to fruition. Rules were broken, and a passionate dedication to creative work was born. "I think Bill would be proud that his idea has not only changed how we work, it has changed where we work," noted Lee Clow, creative director of TBWA/Chiat/Day, in an essay on creativity in the 1990s.

Third, Bernbach profoundly changed the face and demeanor of advertising creativity. By hiring a new type of creative personnel—of diverse ethnicities and backgrounds and with new expertise—he moved the profession beyond the mystique of the "gray flannel suit." Bernbach and DDB nurtured the rebels and the new thinkers into a new breed of marketer: professional creative people who viewed their craft as art form. A number of industry luminaries worked with Bernbach during the heady 1960s and early 1970s: Ted Bell, Helmut Krone, Bob Gage, Bob Levenson, Carl Ally, George Lois, Phyllis Robinson, Julian Koenig, and Roy Grace, who likened the experience to being part of the 1927 New York Yankees. "[T]here was no other place to be at that point," Grace said. Interestingly, by enshrining the unconventional personalities and rebellious characters as the new gurus of advertising, Bernbach unwittingly inspired—but did not partake in—the late 20th-century phenomena of high creative salaries and the "hot shop" mentality as other agencies tried to lure away DDB creative personnel. Indeed, this cult of the creative individual is a point of departure in understanding the ongoing rivalry between proponents of the Ogilvy style and that of Bernbach. Ogilvy tried to systematize an agency style through long lists of dos and don'ts. Bernbach preferred to trust in the creative muse of individual talent. "Name one creative person ever to emerge from under Ogilvy," Bernbach once said.

Perhaps the most profound change to result from the "creative revolution" was wrought by Bernbach's work itself. Advertising Hall of Fame honoree Jerry Della Femina has remarked of the Volkswagen campaign, Bernbach's most celebrated: "That was the day when the new advertising agency was really born." Volkswagen is cited as the benchmark for changing not only a product category but the way to think about advertising. Bernbach's first creative coups were coupled with strong type and simple, often funny language. DDB television, too, was dramatic, entertaining as well as informing the audience. Again, it was a campaign for Volkswagen that showcased DDB's pathbreaking aesthetic for television advertising: the elegant simplicity of the visuals and the clarity of the idea "What does the snowplow driver use to get to work?" was superbly efficient in its use of the medium.

In an industry noted for its cynicism, Bernbach is still mentioned with reverence today. Those who worked for him continue to speak of that time with pride, and he is lauded in any advertising tome dedicated to great advertising campaigns, great talent, or great creative theory. In 1999 *Advertising Age* named him "Advertising Person of the Century." "We must develop our own philosophy and not have the advertising philosophy of others imposed upon us," Bernbach once wrote. Quite possibly the greatest tribute to Bernbach's memory is to reinvent what he invented: to continue his work of breaking rules and shaking up the status quo.

DEBORAH K. MORRISON

See also DDB Worldwide, Inc.; *and color plate in this volume*

Biography

Born in New York City, 13 August 1911; educated at public schools in New York City; received B.A. in English from New York University, 1932; married Evelyn Carbone, 5 June 1938 (sons John and Paul both became executives at Doyle Dane Bernbach); founded Doyle Dane Bernbach (DDB), 1 June 1949; named "The One Person Who Did the Most for the Progress of Advertising" by the AAAA, 1963, 1965–66; Man of the Year of Advertising Award, 1964–65; Who's Who in America, 1966–67; Top Advertising Agency Executive, 1969; Advertising Hall of Fame, 1977; retired from DDB, 1976; died of leukemia, 2 October 1982.

Selected Publications

Bill Bernbach Said . . . , 1989

Further Reading

Bowen, Croswell, "Ned Doyle, Maxwell Dane, William Bernbach," *Madison Avenue* 51 (August 1959)

Dobrow, Larry, *When Advertising Tried Harder: The Sixties, the Golden Age of American Advertising,* New York: Friendly Press, 1984

Fox, Stephen, *The Mirror Makers: A History of American Advertising and Its Creators,* New York: Morrow, 1984

Higgins, Denis, *The Art of Writing Advertising: Conversations with William Bernbach, Leo Burnett, George Gribbin, David Ogilvy, and Rosser Reeves,* Lincolnwood, Illinois: NTC/ Contemporary, 1965

Hixon, Carl, "The Bernbach Fantasies: Former DDB Chief's Poignant Legacy," *Advertising Age* (11 August 1986)

Levenson, Bob, *Bill Bernbach's Book: A History of the Advertising that Changed the History of Advertising,* New York: Villard, 1987

Sullivan, Luke, *Hey, Whipple, Squeeze This!: A Guide to Creating Great Ads,* New York: Wiley, 1998

Beverages, Alcoholic

Given that the production and sale of alcoholic beverages was one of civilization's earliest commercial activities, it should not be surprising that some of the earliest advertising—found on walls dating to ancient Greece—was for food and wine. Liquor has been a major sponsor of advertising ever since. Even after the 18th Amendment (1920) made the production, sale, and consumption of alcohol illegal in the United States, U.S. liquor manufacturers sponsored ad campaigns overseas. Anheuser-Busch marketed beer to Europeans during Prohibition, using storks as symbols of good fortune, social harmony, and family values. When the 21st Amendment ended Prohibition in 1933, alcohol advertisers were concerned with regaining lost markets and promoting the quality of their products. To avoid controversy, the U.S. distilled liquor industry agreed to refrain from advertising on radio, a policy it later extended to television. Distillers used mostly print media, and their ads appealed primarily to professionals and the upper class. Wine manufacturers portrayed their products as the drink of moderation to be consumed at mealtimes.

Beer

In the mid-1930s, as manufacturers began increasingly to package beer in cans, advertisements encouraged individuals to drink at home rather than in taverns. Marketed as a nourishing, healthy drink, beer became associated with physical activities. During the 1940s and 1950s, the beer industry began to sponsor all types of sporting events; for example, Anheuser-Busch purchased the St. Louis Cardinals, a Major League Baseball team, and began to advertise during all radio broadcasted games in the mid-1950s. In the Cold War years of the late 1940s and early 1950s, beer advertisements emphasized patriotism and freedom, depicting beer drinkers as independent, loyal, and dedicated individuals. In the late 1970s and 1980s, beer advertising tended to emphasize distinguishing brand characteristics (e.g., dry beer, ice beer, light beer) and, in response to growing public concerns about drunk driving, often reminded consumers to drink responsibly.

Through the 1980s beer advertisers targeted mass audiences through wide-circulation newspapers, billboards, and network television. In the 1990s, however, the growth of specialized media outlets (e.g., cable, satellite broadcasting, magazines, and the Internet) fostered a shift toward niche marketing. Marketers of premium beers and imported beers became prominent advertisers, promoting their products with the themes of independence and individuality (e.g., Molson's slogan: "We think it is a good beer, but you try it and decide for yourself"). Meanwhile, major brewers sought new advertising angles, as Anheuser-Busch did with its "Born On" campaign stressing product freshness.

In the last decades of the 20th century, beer became the most popular beverage in the United States and Canada, especially among young adult men, who consumed more beer than any other segment of the population. Not surprisingly, ads for beer tend to target men between the ages of 19 and 35. Ads aimed at this audience seek to associate beer with adventure, fun, excitement, escape, the good life, outdoor sports, and relaxation. They seek to convince young people that drinking beer will make them more successful, popular, and sexually appealing. Consequently, beer advertisements depict locations associated with good times— bars, beaches, and sporting events; they often feature water activities and images of cars and other motor vehicles that conjure up feelings of pleasure, power, and excitement.

A 1982 study of TV ads by Andrew Finn and Donald Strickland found that men outnumber women five to one in beer advertisements. However, they also found that at least one woman appears in half of all beer advertisements, usually as the object of male attention, often serving men. Furthermore, the study found that beer advertisements portray men in stereotypically "macho" roles: as ranchers, workers, athletes, adventurous sportsmen, and retired football players. Budweiser advertisements released in the 1970s and 1980s, for example, featured "the average working man." Busch advertisements, which once featured cowboys, adopted the slogan "Head for the mountains" by the 1990s. Anheuser-Busch's primary advertising agency during this period was D'Arcy Masius Benton & Bowles. A 1999 Coors campaign from Foote, Cone & Belding

(FCB) featured John Elway, former quarterback for the Denver Broncos.

Beer advertisers often use humor to appeal to young people. In a popular 1997 campaign developed by Young & Rubicam, New York, Molson Golden used Bob and Doug McKenzie, popular characters from a satirical skit on the television program *SCTV*, to promote its product and to poke fun at Canadians. Similarly, Rolling Rock made fun of its hometown of Latrobe, Pennsylvania, in its 1997 campaign developed by Ammirati Puris Lintas, which aired on ESPN. Other strategies included the use of animals and animated characters. For example, Budweiser campaigns developed by D'Arcy Masius Benton & Bowles and DDB Needham Worldwide in the early 1990s featuring frogs, dogs, and lizards generated substantial attention for their creativity and humor. In the late 1990s digital animation ushered in a new trend in advertising featuring quasi-human characters in a variety of bizarre settings. Some critics argued that such advertising appealed inappropriately to children and should be taken off the air.

Considering that young men are their most reliable customers, brewers naturally turn to sports events as a major forum for beer advertisements. A 1994 study found that beer was the most commonly advertised beverage during televised sports events (with wine and wine coolers ranking next). Sponsorship of sports teams and events enables beer brands to link themselves with the outdoors, fun, and sports in more subtle ways than are possible with direct advertising. Busch, for example, has sponsored NASCAR races since 1982. Beer advertisements show up in stadiums, at concession stands, on billboards, and as props (e.g., blow-up beer cans). Breweries also endorse sports teams; for example, Coors launched a professional female baseball team, the Silver Bullets, in 1994 and sponsors the Coors Light Classic, an annual beach volleyball tournament. Heineken sponsored the U.S. Open tennis tournament and launched its 1999 campaign during the National Football League playoffs.

Ethnic minority groups became an increasingly important consumer segment for beer advertising in the 1990s. In 1998 Corona Extra, a Mexican beer, became the top-selling imported beer in the United States, replacing Heineken, a beer from The Netherlands, in part by positioning itself in opposition to the macho image with ads by the Richards Group and Cramer-Krasselt featuring Corona in Mexican landscapes and promoting the idea of a vacation in a bottle. These trends have not gone unnoticed; more and more advertisements are focusing on ethnic diversity and the importance of heritage. In 1998 LaBatt USA aired radio advertisements for Tecate (from Ammirati Puris Lintas) that featured an elderly woman pleading with her sons not to forget their Mexican heritage. Even well-established European brands were advertised in the U.S. market with campaigns that made reference to ethnic authenticity. In 1999 Beck released a $20 million campaign that emphasized its origins as a German beer. Seagram promoted its Grolsch brand by highlighting its Dutch heritage in a $4 million print campaign created by Gearon Hoffman. One 1997 Grolsch ad showed a self-portrait of Dutch artist Vincent Van Gogh accompanied by the slogan, "The same bold taste since the days when body piercing meant cutting off an ear." This campaign ran in national magazines such as *Spin* and *Rolling Stone* and on local radio and in newspapers in New York, Miami, Los Angeles, Chicago, Atlanta, and Denver.

Wine

Although wine has been produced commercially in the United States since 1783, it only gained real popularity in that country at the end of the 20th century. By the 1990s, 90 percent of American wine came from California, and the United States ranked fifth worldwide in wine production. Wines produced in Canada gained popularity as well, but Canada still imported $350 million in wine, compared to exports of $1 million.

If beer is the drink of the young, then wine is the drink of the middle-aged, especially those between the ages of 35 and 54, according to the *Adams Wine Handbook* in 1997. Wine drinkers represent a small but loyal segment of the population. Wine marketers target a broader demographic audience than beer marketers, appealing to both men and women and focusing on consumers in their 30s and older. Marketers tend to perceive wine drinkers, who have above-average incomes, as more sophisticated than beer drinkers. Finn and Struckland's 1982 analysis of televised alcohol advertisements airing in the St. Louis market revealed that, compared to ads for beer, wine commercials tended to promote the quality of the product and to evoke wealth, affluence, and foreign settings.

A 1986 advertisement for the wines of Spain emphasized the quality of the product and its "remarkable value." A 1987 advertisement for Vina San Pedro touted its "pleasant, crisp and light, yet reasonably priced" wines noted for their "full-bodied taste." A 1997 radio campaign for Brown-Forman's Michel Picard line of French wines capitalized on the allure of foreign settings: "Every sip is like a stroll through the French countryside." These advertisements received attention through the underwriting of National Public Radio programs such as *All Things Considered* and *Car Talk,* which appealed to a more mature and sophisticated audience. A 1998 advertisement from Trone Advertising for Mystic Cliffs Premium Wines showed a hawk flying over vineyards and a couple enjoying wine by the fireplace, reflecting themes of freedom and affluence. In the same way, winemaker Domaine Chandon ran advertisements in travel and consumer magazines, targeted to upscale consumers, in a 1998 campaign for its California sparkling wine.

Other themes that appear frequently in wine commercials include love and romance, sex, camaraderie, tradition and heritage, humor, and physical activity. The advertisements tend to appeal equally to men and women. While people typically perceive wine as a dinner drink, reserved for special occasions, marketers have sought to expand audience perceptions of appropriate occasions for consuming wine.

The introduction of the wine cooler, a blend of wine and fruit juices, in the early 1980s was an attempt to reach a younger (aged 21–35) female audience. The wine cooler market soon represented the fastest growing segment of the alcoholic beverage market,

Paul Masson Vineyards' slogan, "We will sell no wine before its time," entered into general use as an adage for any endeavor requiring time and patience.
"Paul Masson" is a registered trademark of Constellation Brands, Inc.

exceeding all previous historical trends. Brown-Forman's California Cooler dominated this new niche, holding 60 percent of the market share in 1984. Other companies such as Heublein and Seagram soon offered their own wine coolers, and by the late 1980s more than 150 such brands were on the market. E.J. Gallo Winery's 1985 Bartles & Jaymes campaign, "Thank you for your support" (from Hal Riney & Partners), was the most recognized wine cooler campaign of its time. Despite the success of marketing efforts in the 1980s, wine cooler consumption decreased significantly during the 1990s. In 1986 wine coolers comprised 21.3 percent of the market for alcoholic beverages, but by 1997 they comprised only 2.6 percent. Advertising revenues for the product plummeted correspondingly over the same period.

Distilled Liquor

The rapid decline in popularity of the wine cooler may be due in part to the introduction of the liquor cooler in the 1990s. This type of cooler combines distilled liquors (instead of wine) and juices. Early popular brands included Brown-Forman's line of

Jack Daniel's Country Cocktails, Heublein's Jose Cuervo's margaritas, and Coors Brewing Company's Zima. Ads for these drinks followed the same format as those for the wine coolers, targeting young females with the message that the drinks are trendy and hip. For example, a 1999 print campaign from Hamon & Stern for Alizé liqueur, a mix of cognac and passion fruit, targeted young, dynamic women with the message, "Why bother with life's foibles when you can be having an Alizé drink instead?" The advertisements presented images of professional women trying to escape from life's mundane preoccupations.

While ads for distilled spirits are meant to appeal to the young, they tend to target an elite portion of the population. The heaviest consumers of distilled spirits are well-educated men and women, 25 to 35 years old, who make more than $60,000 a year. To appeal to this group, advertisements portray lifestyles characterized by wealth, success, class, intelligence, and prestige. They typically feature young adults, largely Caucasian, enjoying themselves while drinking.

An advertisement for Remy Martin's champagne cognac showed the bottle with two filled glasses, placed on a pedestal in the clouds. The tag line read, "Want to come up for a drink sometime?" One long-running campaign for Dewar's scotch presented the profiles of successful people who drink its whiskey. A 1999 ad told the story of former software developers who quit to develop a successful board game. "They're Dewars," the ad claimed—"doers," that is, intelligent and successful people. A 1997 advertisement for Campari, a bitter Italian liqueur, featuring the slogan "Escape from boredom," showed a woman complaining, "If someone offers me another glass of white wine I'll die." A 1998 advertisement for Southern Comfort, a bourbon whiskey, even suggested that the product was a way for married men to hang on to the swinging bachelor lifestyle. The advertisement, developed by Hill Holliday, showed a bride and groom walking down the aisle, with a noose drawn around the groom's head. The text read: "Life as you know it may change. Your drink doesn't have to."

Liquor advertisements show people in hip settings, often at upscale parties and celebrations, in order to portray the consumers of their products as trendsetters. A radio and print campaign by TBWA/Chiat/Day, New York City, for Seagram's gin targeted mainstream African-Americans with a hip-hop theme and slogans such as "the smooth groove" and "tonight's delight." An advertisement for Jim Beam bourbon whiskey featured a guitar player who appeared to be performing in a small club. The text in the advertisement described how Jim Beam supports up-and-coming musicians, giving the reader the impression that its customers are on the cutting edge. Other liquor advertisements use visual puns and humor to convey this same notion.

One of the time-honored advertising themes for distilled spirits is sexual desire. Often, the product is suggested as the catalyst of hedonistic pleasures to come. Typical of the genre was a 1999 TBWA/Chiat/Day print ad for Seagram's Lime Twisted Gin, which depicted the bumpy bottle in vibrant colors with a lime peel coming out of the top. The tag line read, "Your night is about to take an unexpected twist."

A 1934 print ad for White Horse Scotch Whisky treated the end of Prohibition in the U.S. as an occasion to reintroduce the brand to American consumers.

Some liquor advertisements focus on the virtues of the product, such as purity, quality, and other distinguishing characteristics. These ads often feature the bottle alone, sometimes placed in an inviting setting. As with beer, reference to tradition and authenticity is common. Jack Daniel's 1999 whiskey advertisements paired the "Old No. 7 Brand" logo with slogans such as "Tastes exactly like no other whiskey" and "Smooth Sippin' Tennessee Whiskey."

Occasionally, liquor advertisements also discuss alternative uses for the product, such as use in recipes. A French-Canadian advertisement for Bellini, an Italian liqueur made of peach nectar and sparkling wine, offered recipes for different types of margaritas. Promotional offers for items such as cookbooks, T-shirts, and shot glasses are not uncommon. Promotional items are often supplied to restaurants and bars to give away in raffles and contests.

Some advertisements have come under attack for promoting heavy alcohol consumption. An ad for Remy Martin showed a man pouring himself four times as much cognac as he poured for his guest, the tag line reading, "Looking after number one." Yet studies have found that most advertisements for alcohol neither encouraged nor discouraged heavy consumption. Nonetheless, Seagram, Anheuser-Busch, Miller Brewing Company, and Coors have each released campaigns encouraging moderate drinking (e.g., Anheuser-Busch's "Know when to say when" and Miller's "Think when you drink" campaigns). Critics argue, however, that these campaigns are not sufficient, as they fail to mention times when people should not drink even the smallest amount of alcohol.

Law and Policy: International Overview

Regulations governing the advertising of alcohol products vary substantially from country to country, and these restrictions, as well as cultural mores and attitudes toward alcohol, affect the content of advertisements produced internationally. In India, where Hindu scriptures refer to drinking alcohol as a sin, the advertising of alcohol is forbidden altogether (although only one state strictly enforces the prohibition of drinking it). Nonetheless, companies get around the advertising ban by sponsoring major sporting events and showing alcohol in advertisements for other brands. Saudi Arabia censors foreign media, removing alcohol ads from electronic and print media. Although advertisements for alcohol are widespread in China, appearing in broadcast and print media, their content is limited. For example, advertisements cannot associate drinking with personal, financial, or sexual success, nor can they show underage characters or claim that alcohol makes one stronger or relieves anxiety.

Regulation of alcohol advertising is also relatively strict in many European countries. A 1991 French law banned all types of alcohol advertising, causing, among other difficulties, French television to cancel broadcasts of foreign sports matches. Subsequently, the Ministry of Youth and Sport enacted the "good faith and moderation" principle, which discouraged alcohol distributors from buying stadium advertisement space in countries where they did not sell the products. The ministry also asked all networks to avoid shooting the advertisements during the events.

The Independent Broadcasting Authority, a regulatory body that was put in place following the Broadcasting Act of 1981 in the United Kingdom, adopted a complex advertising code (Rule 34) for alcohol in 1981. Unlike the codes adopted by U.S. advertisers, which are voluntary, the British code is imposed by law. It sets the following conditions for advertising: (1) advertisements may not appeal to children under 18 (anyone associated with drinking in an advertisement should appear to be 25 or older) or include children; (2) personalities with appeal for children may not appear in alcohol advertisements; (3) advertisements may not imply that drinking is essential to social success or that refusal is a sign of weakness; (4) advertisements may not encourage immoderate drinking; (5) advertisements may not claim that alcohol has therapeutic or stimulant qualities; (6) advertisements may not suggest that one drink is preferable to another due to its higher alcohol content; (7) advertisements may not show images of drinking and driving or machinery that could be associated with drinking and driving; (8) advertisements may not show alcohol being consumed during working time; (9) advertisements may not publicize a promotion that encourages multiple purchases of alcohol; (10)

advertisements may not suggest that drinking can contribute to sexual success; (11) advertisements may not suggest that solitary drinking is acceptable or that drinking is a way of solving problems; (12) advertisements may not imply that drinking is essential to masculinity; and (13) advertisements may not employ humor to circumvent the above requirements.

Before approving any ad for release in the United Kingdom, the Independent Television Companies' Association reviews it to ensure that it complies with the above rules. Similar regulations apply to cable, with the added stipulation that no ad may associate drinking with aggressive and antisocial behavior. Advertisements for alcohol are not aired during children's television, religious programs, or from 4 P.M. to 6 P.M. in Britain.

Other Western European countries also restrict alcohol advertising. Holland and Portugal restrict the airing of alcohol advertisements to certain times of the day; Denmark bans advertising for all drinks with high alcohol content; and France bans the advertising of alcoholic beverages altogether. In Canada provincial liquor boards control print advertising for alcoholic beverages, and a national commission has promulgated a code governing broadcast advertising.

Compared with the laws in other industrialized countries, regulation of the content of alcohol advertising in the United States is minimal, in some cases virtually nonexistent. Although early legislation (*Valentine v. Chrestensen*, 1942) denied First Amendment protection to commercial speech, a 1976 Supreme Court decision overturned this decision, and subsequent court decisions accorded liquor advertisements the same protection as other legalized commercial products. Furthermore, scientific evidence is lacking to establish a link between alcohol advertisements and increased consumption, and alcohol advertisers argue that their goal is merely to raise brand loyalty and share of market rather than encourage people to begin or increase consumption.

In the late 1990s politicians such as Senators Strom Thurmond and Edward Kennedy, along with lobby groups such as Mothers Against Drunk Driving (MADD), sought to ban alcohol advertisements during children's programming and to mandate warning labels on advertisements. They also advocated prohibiting all images of motor vehicles, cartoons, and athletes in advertisements for alcohol and banning any advertisements that encourage heavy consumption or link alcohol consumption with popularity, success, achievement, love, romance, and promiscuity. These legislative efforts failed, and the beer, wine, and spirits industries continued to maintain that self-regulation was a more reliable way to protect the public from harmful advertising.

Some U.S. beverage producers have adopted codes restricting alcohol advertisements. The Beer Institute, for example, published the *Advertising & Marketing Guide*, which clearly outlines unacceptable content in advertisements. The code urges ads to portray drinkers as responsible and to avoid depictions of drinking and driving, excessive drinking, intoxication, the sale of liquor to minors or drunk people, or other illegal activity. Advertisements should also exclude content that may appeal to children (e.g., Santa Claus, cartoon characters, and toys), and they should not be aired during children's programming or events.

According to the code, beer advertisements should neither encourage consumption during activities that require coordination and alertness nor convey the idea that beer has unique qualities or health benefits that have not been scientifically proved. While advertisers may associate favorable social and personal experiences with their products, the advertisements should not claim that social, personal, or professional success relies on beer consumption. The advertisements should not include indecent material, connect sexual passion with beer consumption, or employ religious themes. Finally, beer advertisements should not make untrue statements about competition, discuss intoxication, depict the act of drinking, show littering or other improper disposal of beer containers, or portray beer consumption on campuses as important to education. The Beer Institute distributes this code to all brewery employees, distributors, and agencies that advertise beer, and they investigate complaints when they arise. Similar codes exist for wine and distilled liquor advertisers.

Nonetheless, these codes of self-regulation are entirely optional, and the courts cannot prosecute violators. However, community watchdog groups can exert significant power through boycotts of companies that go too far in their advertisements. Heileman Brewing Company, for example, was forced to pull its 1991 ads for Colt 45 Powermaster malt liquor following numerous protests. These ads, targeting African-Americans, emphasized high alcohol content and alluded to the role of alcohol in sexual promiscuity.

In 1996 Seagram broke the 60-year voluntary ban on hard liquor advertisements on radio and television, airing advertisements (after 9 P.M.) for Crown Royal Canadian whiskey and Absolut Vodka on 21 stations operating in large markets across the United States. Seagram reasoned that advertisements for distilled spirits were not any more harmful than advertisements for other types of alcohol, because a standard serving of liquor contains the same amount of alcohol as a standard serving of beer or wine. The Distilled Spirits Council of the United States supported this decision. Despite the fact that other brands such as Bacardi, Jim Beam, and Chivas Regal followed suit, television advertisements for distilled liquor remain rare, with print media continuing to be the primary venues for this product category.

Role of New Media

As a consequence of the World Wide Web's ability to integrate sound, text, and video, many liquor marketers have begun to develop interactive advertising. Current Web sites for alcoholic beverages allow consumers 18 years of age and older to enter contests, buy products, discuss brands with other enthusiasts, play games, and download screen savers, animated e-cards, and icons related to the products. Heineken's Web site, for example, provides information on sporting events, corporate history, and national links. It also allows browsers to "hang out" in virtual bars and provides entertainment and merchandise in various forms. Kendall-Jackson's Web site lists events sponsored by the company, allows users to shop for wine, and provides education about the product. Bailey's Irish Cream sponsors play areas such as "PleasureDome" and the "Vault," which allow browsers to meet others, play games, discuss recipes, and buy collectibles.

These sites go a step further than regular advertising, as they permit viewers to get actively involved with the products, provide links to other loyal users, and suggest alternative uses for the products. Furthermore, Web sites allow advertisers to provide in-depth messages not permitted in one-page print advertisements or 30-second television spots. Web advertising is also appealing because advertisers can draw viewers to related product sites through banners and smaller advertisements that provide links to the corporate Web pages. Someone reading about wine tasting, for example, may be prompted with a banner that suggests visiting Kendall-Jackson's site. These advertisements target Web users with specific interests.

Many countries are concerned about the relative lack of control over Web content. Even though advertising of alcoholic beverages is restricted in countries such as France and India, citizens of these countries can access advertisements on U.S. Web sites. As policymakers struggle to find ways to regulate Internet alcohol advertising in light of the lack of boundaries, advertisers will work to continue to increase their market share by capitalizing on new technologies such as Web television and satellite broadcasting.

ALEXANDRA HENDRIKS

See also Absolut Vodka; Anheuser-Busch, Inc.; Heineken; John Smith's Bitter; Labatt Brewing Company; Miller Brewing Company; Molson, Inc.; Schlitz Brewing Company; Seagram Company, Ltd.; *and color plate in this volume*

Further Reading

Adams Wine Handbook (annual; 1997–)

Advertising and Marketing Code, Washington, D.C.: Beer Institute, 1997

Brown, Mary Louise, "The Stork and Anheuser-Busch Imagery, 1913–1933," *Gateway Heritage* 9, no. 2 (1988)

Circus, Philip, "Alcohol Advertising: The Rules," *International Journal of Advertising* 8 (1989)

Ellis-Simons, Pamela, "Hardly a Vintage Cru, California Cooler Creates a New Class of Sippers," *Marketing and Media Decisions* (Spring 1985)

Finn, T. Andrew, and Donald E. Strickland, "A Content Analysis of Beverage Alcohol Advertising: Television Advertising," *Journal of Studies on Alcohol* 43, no. 9 (1982)

Grant, Marcus, editor, *Alcohol and Emerging Markets: Patterns, Problems, and Responses,* Philadelphia, Pennsylvania: Brunner/Mazel, 1998

Madden, Patricia A., and Joel W. Grube, "The Frequency and Nature of Alcohol and Tobacco Advertising in Televised Sports, 1990 through 1992," *American Journal of Public Health* 84, no. 2 (February 1994)

McGowan, Richard, *Government Regulation of the Alcohol Industry: The Search for Revenue and the Common Good,* Westport, Connecticut: Quorum, 1997

Novak, Phil, "A Blend of Good and Bad," *Marketing Magazine* (8 March 1999)

Strickland, Donald E., T. Andrew Finn, and M. Dow Lambert, "A Content Analysis of Beverage Alcohol Advertising: Magazine Advertising," *Journal of Studies on Alcohol* 43, no. 7 (1982)

Tilles, Daniel, "French Government Revises Ad Law," *Adweek* (3 April 1995)

Turner, Ernest Sackville, *The Shocking History of Advertising!* London: Joseph, 1952; New York: Dutton, 1953; revised edition, London: Penguin, 1965

Beverages, Nonalcoholic

The Coca-Cola Company and the Pepsi-Cola Company have been responsible for some of the more memorable beverage advertising of the 20th century, but they are by no means the only soft-drink marketers to have come up with inventive—and constantly changing—sales pitches. Over the years many beverage companies have tinkered with their advertising—as well as their formulas—to make their products stand out.

Among the secondary cola brands, Royal Crown has endured the longest and with the most success. It came to the national U.S. market in the late 1930s, marketed by the Nehi Corporation, of Columbus, Georgia. At a time when Pepsi-Cola was just beginning to become competitive with Coca-Cola (Coke), Royal Crown was a distant third, despite the best efforts of Benton and Bowles, its first major advertising agency, and Batten Barton Durstine & Osborn, which had the account by mid-century. The business moved to Compton Advertising briefly in 1955 and then to D'Arcy Advertising in 1958, which had lost the Coca-Cola account three years before and was eager to have another soft drink client. It remained at D'Arcy for 11 years, during which time Nehi revolutionized the cola category with the introduction of the world's first zero-calorie diet soft drink, Diet-Rite cola.

Diet-Rite, sweetened with saccharine instead of sugar, was rapidly successful, but Nehi did not have the strength to hold its market leadership once Coca-Cola and Pepsi-Cola entered the field. Although it had invented the product category, its momentum weakened within a few years. By the end of the decade, Nehi opted for a creative approach keyed more to a youth-oriented lifestyle. In 1969 it moved the account to Wells, Rich, Greene, Inc., which shortened the Royal Crown brand to RC and developed some of the most aggressive advertising for both RC and Diet-Rite. Despite substantial spending ($8 million for RC in 1973–74), the brands failed to achieve hoped for market share. The RC account went to the Leo Burnett Company in 1974, then to Ogilvy & Mather, New York City, in 1978, and to other agencies after that. But neither brand would seriously challenge the market leaders. As of 2000, Royal Crown and Diet-Rite were a unit of Triarc Companies, Inc., a holding company whose beverage group also included Snapple. Deutsch, Inc., was the ad agency of record for these brands.

Life before Cola

Colas have not been the only beverages to build a mass market in the nonalcoholic drink field, which has a long and varied history. Housewives and pharmacists were at the center of the industry's beginnings. Charles E. Hires, a Pennsylvania native and drugstore owner, concocted a beverage he originally called an herb tea. He promptly changed the name to root beer, reasoning that Pennsylvania's coal miners would never drink something called herb tea. After giving away samples at the Philadelphia Exhibition in 1876—the same event that marked the introduction of Alexander Graham Bell's telephone, the Remington typewriter, and Heinz ketchup—Hires marketed the extract as a temperance drink. Ad copy read, "Drink it and the world drinks with you," while another ad touted use of the tonic to "purify the blood and make rosy cheeks."

Root beer advertising started in Hires's hometown newspaper, the *Philadelphia Ledger,* and expanded over the next decade into national magazines. Hires also borrowed an idea from Coca-Cola and began issuing advertising trade cards and promotional items such as mugs and metal serving trays. Some unusual tactics were adopted in the early Hires ads. For example, much of the text that accompanied the trade cards was religious in nature. Early print ads featured a drawing of a strange, dwarf-like child holding a mug of Hires root beer, and the drink's ingredients—including roots, barks, and herbs—were listed in the advertising. To cover all possible markets, the product, dubbed Hires, was sold in three forms—as a liquid concentrate, an extract, and in ready-to-drink bottles—during the 1930s, when its agency was O'Dea, Sheldon & Canaday, Inc. The company later used N.W. Ayer, Inc., of New York City, in the 1940s and 1950s and Maxon, Inc., in the 1990s.

Meanwhile, another soft-drink entrepreneur was quickly making a name for himself in Texas. The drink called Dr Pepper, concocted by Charles Alderton, a Waco, Texas, pharmacist, in 1885, made its initial splash with a wider audience in 1904 when it was introduced at the World's Fair Exposition in St. Louis, Missouri. It was not sold outside of Texas until the 1920s but then quickly grew in popularity, though a rural southwestern image lingered with the product for decades. A diet version came on the market in 1962 and was reformulated in 1991.

was crafted, and the company revived the "Be a Pepper" ads. The slogans subsequently changed a few more times, with "Dr Pepper makes the world taste better" appearing in 2001.

Arrival of the Uncola

The soft drink 7UP was a latecomer to the noncola category. Weeks before the 1929 stock market crash, and at a time when there were more than 600 lemon-lime beverages already on the market, a St. Louis businessman, C.L. Grigg, introduced Bib-Label Lithiated Lemon-Lime Soda. Regardless of the less-than-catchy name and the unusually strong amount of carbonation, the product sold well, helped by ads that promised a drink with a "real wallop." The name was soon changed to the more palatable 7UP, and the brand became the world's third-best-selling soft drink. Part of the attraction may have been its inventive marketing as a hangover remedy. One ad from the early 1930s by Philip Klein, Inc., touted its anti-acid qualities with the line, "Takes the ouch out of grouch." The company switched its advertising account to the J. Walter Thompson Company (JWT), of Chicago, Illinois, in the late 1940s and remained there for decades, during which time its greatest advertising was produced.

In 1967 JWT and the Seven-Up Company seized on the turbulent tenor of the 1960s and kicked off the "uncola" advertising campaign. It resonated loudly with younger consumers looking for anything that was considered anti-establishment. The imagery ranged from upside-down Coke glasses to brilliant mock–Busby Berkley visuals to the music of "We See the Light of 7UP." A few years later, JWT added the "uncola nut," an invented special ingredient that, as pitchman Geoffrey Holder explained in his deep voice, came from a tropical paradise and made the beverage so refreshing. Diet 7UP made its debut in 1970.

Cadbury Schweppes purchased Dr Pepper/Seven-Up, Inc., in 1995 and sought to reposition 7UP for a younger audience. The soft drink was rapidly losing market share to competitor Sprite, a Coca-Cola product. Leo Burnett USA, of Chicago, resigned the account, and the company moved 7UP to Young & Rubicam. In an effort to win consumers, the marketer experimented with the drink's recipe, and the agency brought back the "un" slogan with "Are you an Un?" This time, however, despite a $30 million campaign, the effort failed. Other ads used the line "It's an up thing." A 1999 campaign was built around the tag line, "Make 7UP yours," playing off the expression "up yours," and was targeted to 12- to 24-year-olds.

At the start of the new century, Dr Pepper/Seven Up, Inc., planned to more than double its ad budget in 2001 for its six flavored beverages—A&W, Canada Dry, Hawaiian Punch, Schweppes, Squirt, and Sunkist—because sales growth of the flavored soft drink segment was outpacing that of the rest of the industry.

Something "Kool"

Makers and marketers of fruity beverages knew that their ad campaigns could not be as sophisticated as those of soft drinks aimed

"Here's Your Hires, Ma'am"

BE sure you just say "HIRES" when ordering by the case from your dealer, or by the glass at the fountain. By saying "HIRES" you guard against an imitation drink which, being artificial, may be harmful.

Nothing goes into Hires but the pure healthful juices of roots, barks, herbs, berries and pure cane sugar. The quality

of Hires is maintained in spite of tremendously increased costs of ingredients. Yet you pay no more for Hires the genuine than you do for an artificial imitation.

Hires carbonated in bottles for the home is the same delightful drink, the same healthful, genuinely-invigorating drink as Hires the fountain favorite.

THE CHARLES E. HIRES COMPANY, PHILADELPHIA

Hires contains juices of 16 roots, barks, herbs and berries

Hires *in bottles*

Hires Root Beer, as seen in this advertisement from 1920, is one of the oldest beverage brands still marketed in the United States. *HIRES is a registered trademark used under license. ©2001 Dr Pepper/Seven Up, Inc.*

For its first 40 years, Dr Pepper used a lion as its symbol, accounting for one of its first slogans, "King of beverages," from 1910 to 1914. Later, other catchy phrases followed, devised by Tracy, Locke & Dawson, of Dallas, Texas (1930s), Benton and Bowles (1940s), and Ruthrauff & Ryan and Grant Advertising of Dallas, Texas. The slogans included "Drink a bit to eat at 10, 2 and 4" during the 1920s and 1930s, "The friendly Pepper Upper" in the 1950s, and "The most original soft drink ever" in the 1970s. But it was in 1977 that Dr Pepper hit advertising gold with its agency, Young & Rubicam, which that year coined the slogan, "Be a Pepper."

An investment group that owned Dr Pepper acquired the Seven-Up Company from Philip Morris Companies in 1986, and the combined company was bought by Cadbury Schweppes in 1995 for $1.7 billion. Between 1987 and 1992, the brand's household penetration grew 50 percent, an improvement the company attributed to the marketing of Dr Pepper not as the number-three soft drink overall (behind Coke and Pepsi) but as the number-one noncola. A new ad campaign, "Just what the doctor ordered,"

at adults, but they still found ways to whet youthful consumers' appetites for their products. In 1927 Nebraska-based Perkins Product Company decided to lower the production and shipping costs of its Fruit Smack soft drink syrup by making it into a powder and changing the name to Kool-Ade, which was later changed to Kool-Aid. The company's only ad agency during those years was Mason Warner Company, Inc., of Chicago. A year after General Foods acquired the product in 1953, the account moved to Foote, Cone & Belding (FCB), also of Chicago, which came up with the enduring symbol of the Kool-Aid pitcher. Marvin Potts, an art director at FCB, had been looking for a way to illustrate the copy message, "A five-cent package makes two quarts," and one day got his inspiration by watching his son doodling on a frosty window. The company tested three ads in the summer of 1954, one with the five-cent sign drawn on the pitcher's frost, another with a heart and arrow on the pitcher, and the third with a smiling face. By summer's end, it had become apparent that the smiling pitcher was the favorite.

It took more than 20 years, but in 1975 the perky pitcher grew legs and became the Kool-Aid man. In a series of television commercials from Grey Advertising Agency, Inc., New York City, the walking, talking pitcher happily crashes through obstacles to reach children who are yelling, "Hey, Kool-Aid!" More sophisticated ads followed, in which he played baseball and even tried break dancing. By the mid-1990s, computer technology enabled the Kool-Aid man to drive a car and ride a surfboard. In 1994 Ogilvy & Mather acquired the Kool-Aid account and decided to continue with the tried-and-true character but made him more athletic and showed him interacting more with children in the ads.

Adding to the lighthearted approach was Hawaiian Punch's "Punchy" character, who asked, "How about a nice Hawaiian Punch?" In 1992 Punchy declared himself a presidential candidate, running on the campaign slogan, "No one else has the punch." The campaign came two years after N.W. Ayer brought back Punchy as a spokesman, making him more "hip" and having him interact with children in the TV commercials. Procter & Gamble Company sold the Hawaiian Punch brand to Cadbury Schweppes in 1999.

Another beverage from General Foods was Tang, the orange-flavored powder drink introduced in 1965 after ten years in development. The National Aeronautics and Space Administration (NASA) space and Moon missions packed the mix, which initially contained no real juice, and the company, through its ad agency Young & Rubicam, quickly began marketing Tang as the beverage choice of astronauts. More than 30 years later, Kraft Foods (formerly General Foods) undertook a multiyear campaign to breathe new life into Tang by marketing it in convenient, ready-to-drink pouches and multiple flavors. Ads from Ogilvy & Mather, New York City, still featured the company "spokesman," an orangutan.

Sports Drinks and "New Age" Beverages

Isotonic beverages, electrolyte replacement drinks for athletes and aspiring athletes, became all the rage in the early 1990s, but it was the University of Florida's Gators football team that was responsible for giving the world Gatorade in the mid-1960s. Twenty years later, the Quaker Oats Company's purchase of Gatorade put the product segment on the map. By 1991 Quaker's ownership of the category seemed complete, as Gatorade signed basketball superstar Michael Jordan as its worldwide spokesman. Gatorade also became a sponsor of the first all-pro U.S. Olympic basketball team, led by Jordan. Bayer Bess Vanderwarker, of Chicago, Gatorade's ad agency, created the "Be like Mike" campaign, and Jordan signed a long-term contract with Quaker. Foote, Cone & Belding inherited the prized Gatorade account when True North Communications acquired Bayer Bess in 1996. The relationship between Gatorade and FCB ended in 2001. After PepsiCo's acquisition of Quaker Oats, PepsiCo shifted $350 million of work, including Gatorade, from the Interpublic Group of Companies' FCB to the Omnicom Group.

Other beverage makers wanted to get in on Quaker's success. Coca-Cola's PowerAde, Pepsi's lightly carbonated All Sport, and A&W Brands' Everlast helped double total ad spending in the "sports drinks" category to $70 million by 1993. All Sport's television commercials ran the gamut from those showing kids playing blacktop basketball to those aimed at women; PowerAde marketed itself directly against Gatorade, running spots from McCann-Erickson Worldwide, New York City, with the theme "More power to ya." Everlast, meanwhile, was positioned by Messner Vetere Berger McNamee Schmetterer/Euro RSCG as the drink for competitors in individual sports. Increased advertising fueled growth of the entire category, and many of those sales went to Gatorade. Nevertheless, the category leader took the competition seriously. Ad spending totaled $30 million annually, and new ads from Bayer Bess Vanderwarker refocused the brand on serious athletes rather than armchair quarterbacks.

Carbonated soda sales leveled off in the 1990s, and beverage marketers pinned their hopes on sports drinks. But sports drinks appealed to only one target audience, and companies needed another product for more sedentary consumers. Very quickly, store shelves became crowded with a new category—New Age beverages.

In 1972 the owners of a Long Island, New York, health food store started selling a fizzy apple juice later to be dubbed Snapple. In addition to fruit flavors, hot brewed iced teas were added to the product line of the company, which relied on delis and small stores for sales. Despite its mom-and-pop image, Snapple found itself at the center of negative publicity in 1992, when rumors began swirling in San Francisco, California, that the company had ties to the Ku Klux Klan, brewed some of its teas in then-apartheid South Africa, and supported Operation Rescue, a militant anti-abortion group. Snapple executives tried to deal quietly with the rumors, but in the fall of 1993 the company took out full-page ads in northern California newspapers. It also redesigned its labels, interpretations of which had fueled the rumors. "[The rumors] are so ridiculous we thought they would go away, but they didn't," Snapple President Leonard Marsh told the Associated Press at the time. "It reached the point [where] it was getting out of hand and we had to address it." Meanwhile,

The mid-1990s saw the creation of a new beverage segment, "New Age" drinks, introduced in ads that featured themes of expanded consciousness.
Courtesy of The Coca-Cola Company.

Wendy Kaufman, who worked in Snapple's order department responding to letters, quickly caught the attention of Snapple's ad agency, Kirshenbaum & Bond. The five-foot-two, 200-pound Kaufman, who was put in commercials reading letters and fulfilling fan fantasies, instantly became a hit.

When the Quaker Oats Company purchased Snapple in 1994, it sought to make the advertising more mainstream, and Kirshenbaum unsuccessfully tried to position Snapple against Coke and Pepsi. Foote, Cone & Belding subsequently won the account and undertook a huge $40 million sampling effort under the slogan, "Spread the good taste all over the place." Again, the effort failed.

Triarc Beverage Companies bought Snapple from Quaker for only $300 million in 1997 and parted ways with Foote, Cone & Belding. Deutsch, Inc., of New York City, created a new campaign that brought back Kaufman. By late 2000 Snapple had changed hands again, having been acquired by Cadbury Schweppes for $1.45 million.

Snapple was not the only line trying to take advantage of the New Age segment of the beverage market. Pepsi-Cola introduced a colorless drink that became one of the swiftest failures of the decade. Coca-Cola introduced its Fruitopia brand in early 1994 with a $30 million ad campaign and slogans such as "Fruitopia: for the mind, body, and planet." Marketing experts criticized the sales pitches as too trendy and noted that the product category was aimed at fickle younger consumers whose tastes were constantly changing. By the late 1990s the popularity pendulum had begun to swing back toward the cola drinks.

MARY ELLEN PODMOLIK

See also Coca-Cola Company; PepsiCo, Inc.; Seven Up

Further Reading

Dietz, Lawrence, *Soda Pop: The History, Advertising, Art, and Memorabilia of Soft Drinks in America,* New York: Simon and Schuster, 1973

Frank, Robert, "Beverages: Fruity Teas and Mystical Sodas Are Boring Consumers," *Wall Street Journal* (9 October 1995)

Goodrum, Charles A., and Helen Dalrymple, *Advertising in America: The First 200 Years,* New York: Abrams, 1990

Hammond, Dorothy M., and Robert Hammond, *Advertising Collectibles of Times Past,* Des Moines, Iowa: WH Books, 1974

Magiera, Marcy, "Gatorade Gains As Cola Giants Muscle In," *Advertising Age* (8 November 1993)

McKay, Betsy, "7Up Drops 'Un' for a New Ad Campaign," *Wall Street Journal* (15 September 1999)

Pollack, Judann, "Behind Wendy's Return to 'Her' Snapple Brand: 'Ambassador' Marketed Way Back to Role As Endorser of Triarc Drink," *Advertising Age* (23 June 1997)

Billboards. *See* Outdoor Advertising

Biow Company, Inc.

Founded by Milton Biow, 1918; became one of top ten U.S. agencies by mid-1940s; involved in tax scandal in 1953 that injured its reputation and sent billings into sharp decline, even though it was charged with nothing illegal; briefly became Biow-Beirn-Toigo in 1955; reverted to Biow Company and went out of business in 1956.

Major Clients
Benrus Watch Company
Bulova Watch Company, Inc.
Eversharp, Inc.
Lady Esther
Pepsi-Cola Company
Philip Morris & Company, Inc.
Procter & Gamble Company
RCA Victor
Schenley Distillers

The Biow Company, Inc., was created and functioned very much in the image of its founder, Milton Biow, a pioneering merchandising man who believed in the hard sell and thought that advertising should move goods as quickly and directly as possible. Biow was born in 1892. At the age of ten, he started his first job—sweeping floors in New York City for $4 a week. His first exposure to marketing after graduating from New York P.S. 171 (he never attended college) came when he joined Standard Mail Order doing statistical work. Biow's advertising career got under way in 1917 when he joined with Milton Weill to found Weill, Biow & Weill. He functioned as a salesman and account executive for the firm, but his strong sense of individualism made him a restless and impatient partner. In 1918 his partners left the company, which then became essentially a one-man shop, the Biow Company.

Though its billings would grow to $50 million before the end, the agency in many ways remained a one-man shop throughout its history. Biow was a loner who boasted that he never socialized with agency people and that his company was never a member of the American Association of Advertising Agencies, or "Four A's." He resisted delegation of authority and made few attempts to institutionalize his success. He considered himself a showman and merchandiser and prided himself on his ability to take a product from its inception to the top in its category. His company became a leader among major agencies by building a reputation for taking a client's poorest selling brand and making it a success.

Biow won the Bulova watch account in 1921 at a time when research showed that most men regarded wristwatches as feminine and preferred the traditional pocket watch. Biow launched the watchmaker into radio advertising in the 1930s and made "Bulova watch time" a regular part of network time cues. The campaign transformed Bulova from shoestring status to a company with estimated annual billings of $4 billion by the time it left the agency in 1954.

The Biow Company won the Philip Morris cigarette account in 1933 and created perhaps the most famous living human trademark in advertising history, Johnny Roventini, the diminutive bellboy whose cry, "Call for Philip Morris," would become familiar to several generations of radio and television audiences. Roventini was a real-life bellboy in 1933 working for $15 a week when Biow noticed him in the lobby of the Hotel New Yorker and, playing a sudden hunch, asked him to "page" Philip Morris. Soon Roventini was making $20,000 a year appearing in print ads, on billboards, and in radio commercials. He was given a contract for life that continued long after the company ended the campaign and was still in effect when Roventini died in 1999.

Almost immediately Biow launched Philip Morris and Johnny into radio with a program called *Johnny Presents*, a music-variety program with a dramatic segment. The *Philip Morris Playhouse* was spun off in 1939, continued intermittently until 1953, and then had a brief run on television. The program introduced "On the Trail," the opening theme from part three of Ferde Grofé's *The Grand Canyon Suite* (1931), as the Philip Morris musical signature. Other radio programs the company sponsored through Biow included *Crime Doctor, Casey Crime Photographer, My Little Margie,* bandleader Horace Heidt, *The Bickersons, It Pays to Be Ignorant,* and, in 1947–48, Milton Berle (just prior to his move into early television). It also created the original version of *This Is Your Life* on radio in November 1948. The agency handled other Philip Morris brands as well, including Marlboro, which was promoted with modest success as a woman's cigarette from the 1930s until it moved to the Leo Burnett Company in 1955.

Philip Morris was not Biow's only major radio advertiser. In 1940 the agency created a quiz show called *Take it or Leave It* for Eversharp razors. During the ten years Biow produced the program, it would launch the career of Jack Paar (later the host of the long-running late-night *Tonight Show* on NBC), contribute a new phrase to American culture ("the $64 question"), and provide the inspiration and format for the 1955 television hit, *The $64,000 Question* (though the agency had no role in the TV series).

Biow's greatest coup in television came in 1951, when he secured the *I Love Lucy* series for Philip Morris. When CBS President William Paley could not come to terms with Lucille Ball over bringing her radio series, *My Favorite Husband,* to television, Ball and her husband and co-star Desi Arnaz formed their own company and produced an audition program of *I Love Lucy*. Biow got an early look at the show, bought it immediately for Philip Morris, then bid it out as an independent production to both NBC and CBS. CBS offered the better time slot, Monday night at nine o'clock, and won the contract. The program went on the air on 15 October 1951 and quickly became the top show on television. Despite the huge ratings, however, Biow dropped the program in 1955 because he felt it was not increasing Philip Morris's sales.

Another account that would profoundly affect the agency's history was Schenley Industries, marketers of several leading wine and spirits brands, which the agency won in 1942. Though Schenley was mainly a print account (owing to the Distilled Spirits Institute code against advertising hard liquor on the air), Biow put the company's Roma Wines brand on radio in December 1943 as a sponsor of *Suspense,* one of broadcasting's most distinguished series, which CBS had been producing before selling it to Biow. The sponsorship continued into 1947.

In the key hard liquor category, however, Schenley sales were falling in the late 1940s. Once the largest among the distiller's 12 advertising agencies, with billings of $4 million, Biow was reduced to two brands by 1952, Roma Wines having moved to Foote, Cone & Belding in 1950. In 1952 Biow resigned the remaining Schenley business.

But in first winning and later trying to retain the Schenley business, Biow entered into relationship that would one day haunt the agency. Arthur Samish was a veteran California public relations man and lobbyist for the California Brewers Institute with direct business connections to Schenley Industries. In 1942 Alfred Lyon of Philip Morris introduced Biow to Samish with a view toward helping Biow secure the Schenley account, which he did in the spring of 1943. In consideration of his assistance, Biow retained Samish for a period of time as a consultant and also made substantial political contributions to causes favored by Samish. Morris Zimmerman, treasurer of the Biow Company, wrote checks totaling $110,000 to various payees designated by Samish. All the checks were cashed through Samish's office. In 1953 Samish was indicted and tried in federal court for income tax evasion on the basis of the Biow checks. Samish insisted the checks were deductible political contributions and gifts for business friends, but the government argued that they were disguised and taxable commissions to Samish for playing matchmaker in the Schenley-Biow relationship. Samish was convicted in November 1953.

Although neither Milton Biow nor his agency, which at the time was the eighth largest in the United States, with billings of $50 million, was ever accused of anything illegal, the affair severely tarnished the agency's reputation. Billings sank to $46

In its 1951 "More Bounce to the Ounce" campaign for Pepsi-Cola, the Biow Company, Inc., promoted Pepsi-sponsored television and radio shows on CBS.
Pepsi-Cola Company.

million in 1954, and the Biow Company's ranking dropped to 19th by 1955 as "ex-Biow accounts and account men became commonplace on Madison Avenue," according to *Advertising Age*. The company's decline was partially slowed by Biow's hiring in 1954 of Cecil & Presbrey executive J. D. Tarcher, who brought with him the Benrus watch business, and by increased spending by Pepsi, which the agency had won in 1949 and for which it created the slogan "more bounce to the ounce" for spokesperson Polly Bergen. In September 1955 Biow made the agency's President Kenneth Beirn and Vice President John Toigo, whose ties to Pepsi Chief Executive Officer Alfred Steel went back to the 1930s, full partners and changed the agency name to Biow-Beirn-Toigo. But the company's fortunes could not be reversed.

In December 1955 Pepsi shifted its $8 million account to Kenyon & Eckhardt, complaining that the advertising produced by Biow too closely resembled the work the agency was also doing for Philip Morris. American Home Products moved its $8 million Whitehall division business soon thereafter. The situation might have been saved by the $9 million windfall of new business the Joseph Schlitz Brewing Company awarded Biow the very same month. The agency resigned Ruppert Beer to take Schlitz, only to have Milton Biow turn around and resign Schlitz because of conditions that John Toigo had consented to without his approval. Toigo promptly moved to Schlitz as director of marketing, taking three key Biow executives with him. As a final blow, Philip Morris announced in February 1956 that it would leave Biow, taking with it another $8 million in billings. Only Procter & Gamble

remained among the major accounts committed to Biow, which handled the Downey and Top Job brands.

In April 1956 the Biow Company (once again back to its original name after the departures of Beirn and Toigo) announced it would close its doors on 30 June after experiencing losses of $25 million over the previous six months. In the end Biow sounded like a man whom time had passed by, clinging to the formative icons of his youth. "The agency business today is losing its drama," he told *Advertising Age* in December 1956. "Think of the days of Getchell and Albert Lasker and Kudner. They produced advertising with personality. Now we have run-of-the-mill advertising that obeys rules." Biow never returned to advertising. He died in 1976 at the age of 83.

JOHN MCDONOUGH

Further Reading

"Beleaguered Biow Folds His Agency," *Advertising Age* (9 April 1956)

"Biow (Sub-Consciously) Is Seeking New (and Big) Worlds to Conquer," *Advertising Age* (31 December 1956)

"Issues Are Cloudy as Pepsi and Biow Split," *Advertising Age* (12 December 1955)

"Samish Says Biow, Zimmerman Lied," *Advertising Age* (16 November 1953)

"Transcript of Lyon and Hesse Testimony in Samish Case," *Advertising Age* (16 November 1953)

Blacklisting

Blacklisting was a uniquely American political reaction to a perceived threat to internal security during the early years of the Cold War, when the United States regarded the Soviet Union as a major military threat and communist ideology as a primary intellectual one. In that political atmosphere there arose a growing public concern that individuals loyal to what was believed to be a Soviet-led "international communist conspiracy" might be secretly infiltrating American institutions, public and private.

Although there were a few highly publicized cases of actual Soviet espionage, blacklisting sought to confront the communist threat at the threshold of ideas rather than action. The assumption was that disloyalty was a kind of intellectual contagion to which Americans might be vulnerable if they were exposed to ideas sympathetic to the communist cause. Blacklisting sought to eliminate such ideas from mainstream communication channels. The means was simple: target individuals on the basis of their political beliefs. Thus, blacklisting addressed itself with particular

zeal to institutions dealing with ideas—higher education, motion pictures, and radio and television broadcasting.

The problems faced by universities and the film industry under blacklisting are outside the concerns of this essay. But the attempt by a few activists to control the hiring of creative talent in broadcasting drew advertisers and ad agencies directly into the deepest and darkest processes of blacklisting.

"Red Channels"

As early as 1934, long before the Cold War but during a long period of low-grade American suspicion of communism, a Chicago, Illinois, woman named Elizabeth Dilley published, at her own expense, a list of 1,300 names she called "The Red Network," but it had little impact in the media. Thirteen years later when J. Edgar Hoover, director of the Federal Bureau of Investigation (FBI), testified before the House Un-American Activities

Committee (HUAC), he claimed that the Communist Party had "taken to the air" as its "medium of propaganda." Hoover's statements were exploited by politicians and contributed to a growing atmosphere of suspicion toward radio.

HUAC, however, was not the principal trigger of the blacklist that would beset Madison Avenue. Some individuals believed HUAC was not doing an adequate job of policing the communist conspiracy. Three such men were ex-FBI agents in New York City: Ken Bierly, Ted Kirkpatrick, and John Keenan. In April 1947 they set up American Business Consultants, a private organization formed "to obtain, file, and index factual information on Communists, Communist fronts, and other subversive organizations." Its main instrument was a weekly four-page newsletter called *Counterattack: The Newsletter of Facts to Combat Communism*, whose content consisted largely of names and data collected from HUAC, the attorney general's office, and other lists, little of which concerned broadcasting during the first three years. Corporations that subscribed, however, included E.I. du Pont de Nemours & Company, Inc.; General Motors Corporation; Metropolitan Life Insurance Company; R.J. Reynolds Tobacco Company (RJR); and Bendix Aviation Corporation. The American Legion had its semi-monthly publication as well, *Summary Trends and Developments Exposing the Communist Conspiracy*, later renamed, more pointedly, *Firing Line*.

Prior to the blacklist itself, there were isolated incidents that foreshadowed the crucial role advertisers and ad agencies would play in enabling the coming process. In 1949 Phillips H. Lord, Inc., a radio production company, was packaging *Gangbusters* for General Foods Corporation through Young & Rubicam (Y&R) and *Counterspy* for the Pepsi-Cola Company through the Biow Company, Inc. Both programs were directed by William Sweets. One day the heads of General Foods and Pepsi received letters accusing Sweets of being a communist. The reaction was swift. After three weeks of quiet discussions, Y&R and Biow made it clear to Lord on behalf of their clients that Sweets would have to go.

In January 1950 a planned appearance by the dancer Paul Draper on the television show *Toast of the Town* with Ed Sullivan was criticized by several conservative newspaper columnists, who considered Draper's political sympathies pro-communist. The columnists encouraged readers to send protest letters to the offices of the program's sponsor, Ford Motor Company's Lincoln-Mercury division, and its ad agency, Kenyon & Eckhardt (K&E). The appearance of a dancer seemed so lacking in political content that K&E President William Lewis persuaded his client to support the booking. After the performance more letters arrived, persuading Sullivan that he wanted no further controversies on his show. He became both a subscriber to and supporter of *Counterattack* and its work.

Then on 22 June 1950 *Counterattack* published a special report that rocked the broadcasting and advertising industries, "Red Channels: The Report of Communist Influence in Radio and Television." The 215-page report virtually announced, albeit unofficially, the beginning of the blacklist. It named 151 individuals in the entertainment world suspected of having communist

The 1950 report "Red Channels" named 151 people in the entertainment industry—many closely associated with major advertisers—as having communist sympathies or associations.

sympathies or associations. Included were some of the most eminent figures in American arts and letters: Leonard Bernstein, Aaron Copland, Norman Corwin, Morton Gould, Langston Hughes, Arthur Miller, Artie Shaw, William L. Shirer, and Orson Welles. Many would continue working on the concert stage or in the theater, neither of which was subject to the public relations uncertainties of the mass media; they could afford to ignore blacklists. Also, loss of TV work was of little concern to people such as Bernstein, Miller, and Abe Burrows, a game show panelist on *The Name's the Same* when not polishing shows such as *Guys and Dolls* for Broadway.

At first glance the list seemed absurd; five years earlier Madison Avenue probably would have ignored it. But June 1950 was a flash point for the communist issue in America. The Soviet Union had recently acquired the atomic bomb; a communist revolution had swept China; a second trial had concluded that Alger Hiss was part of a Soviet espionage ring; Senator Joseph McCarthy had charged that there were communists in the State Department;

and it was widely believed (correctly, it is now agreed) that there were an unknown number of communists and communist caucuses active in trade unions, including those involved in the broadcasting industry. Above all, the very week "Red Channels" was published, the United States went to war with North Korea. Many American advertisers and ad agency executives suddenly gave up trying to distinguish between liberals and subversives in the face of a communist threat, both internal and external, that seemed to have a basis in fact.

With no clear strategy or expertise of its own, Madison Avenue first turned to *Counterattack*. Because the publication went into the hands of corporate subscribers, its circulation remained limited and surprisingly discreet. Executives in broadcasting and advertising found it easy to deny its influence while consulting its content.

In September 1950 Wildroot hair tonic dropped its sponsorship of the TV series *The Adventures of Sam Spade,* based on the Dashiell Hammett character and starring Howard Duff. Both men were mentioned in "Red Channels." The show was at the height of its popularity, but not even a quarter of a million letters could convince Wildroot to restore Duff. Wildroot replaced *Spade* with *Charlie Wild, Private Detective,* a play on its famous ad slogan, "Get Wildroot cream oil, Charlie." The show failed after one season. Another program based on a Hammett character, *The Fat Man,* was also a casualty of "Red Channels."

Dropping "Controversial" Performers

General Foods and its advertising agency, Y&R, once again found themselves at the center of highly publicized incidents in the wake of "Red Channels." In August 1950 Y&R cast actress Jean Muir in a TV version of *The Aldrich Family,* sponsored by Jell-O, even though Muir had been named two months before in the report. At first no one considered it important; she was only an actress. When Y&R, General Foods, and NBC began receiving letters and calls, however, concern mounted. The program's debut was postponed a week, during which time Muir was quietly replaced. With no evidence to support any wrongdoing by Muir and mindful of libel and slander laws, General Foods and Y&R made no accusations against her or offered any reason for her dismissal other than a desire to avoid "controversy."

The two companies faced a similar situation a few weeks later when Y&R was asked to drop Phillip Loeb, another name on the "Red Channels" list, from *The Goldbergs* TV series, which the agency produced. This time, however, the show's creator and star, Gertrude Berg, stood by Loeb. General Foods simply dropped the program at the end of the season "for economic reasons."

These incidents were highly embarrassing to General Foods and Y&R. To repair the public relations damage, General Foods announced in September a "temporary" suspension of the policy toward "controversial" performers. The suspension did not last, nor did it weaken the blacklist. It merely drove it behind closed doors and deeper into a shroud of discretion and denials by agencies, which, as producers of their clients' radio and television programs, were reluctantly obliged to become the blacklist's principal

enforcers. Neither proud of the task nor eager to defend their methods publicly, they mutually agreed that if it must be done, it had best be done in secret.

American Business Consultants was not the only group pressuring advertisers. In 1951 Lawrence Johnson, a Syracuse, New York, businessman, applied direct economic pressure on politically errant sponsors and agencies through his chain of four grocery stores. Because the grocery shelf was the primary outlet for the packaged-goods brands that accounted for 60 percent of radio and television revenue, he was in a position to wield an influence far out of proportion to the size of his businesses. Johnson's ultimate threat was to hang shelf signs alerting shoppers that particular brands were made by companies that employed communists or subversives. It was a threat that struck at every advertiser's most deep-seated fear—controversy at the point of purchase. When the local American Legion post became a Johnson ally and Johnson's daughter organized a mailing to Syracuse housewives, no Manhattan ad agency was eager to challenge him.

On the advertiser side, Paul Hahn, president of the American Tobacco Company, which invested millions annually to shape public opinion toward Lucky Strike cigarettes, saw no way in which his company could influence public opinion on the politics of blacklisting:

> The company which I represent . . . is owned by 85,000 shareholders. . . . When a company such as ours . . . sponsors a program, it does so . . . to reach the largest possible . . . audience, and to present its product in the most favorable light. . . . It follows that we would be wasting shareholders' funds were we to employ artists who . . . are likely to offend the public.

Another prominent figure of the period was Vincent Hartnett, a freelance talent consultant with his own files on various performers, who sold information to such Madison Avenue clients as Y&R and the Kudner Agency as well as to networks and advertisers. For information on a single individual he charged $20, but he also offered $5-a-head volume discounts. In December 1953 he formed a group called Aware, Inc., which published its own bulletins and worked in concert with *Counterattack* and the Syracuse group.

There were many gradations of blacklisting on Madison Avenue. Relatively few performers were actually considered totally "unemployable," according to John Cogley's "Report on Blacklisting" published in 1956 by the Fund for the Republic, Inc. It was on the "graylist" that many found themselves. They could work for certain sponsors, certain agencies, certain networks, but not for others. Some were suitable for radio but not television. When Johnson's Syracuse group tried to put pressure on Alcoa for sponsoring liberal newscaster Edward R. Murrow on CBS, it was unsuccessful because the aluminum foil wrap Alcoa sold in grocery stores represented only a small part of its business.

But the Block Drug Company, which made a chlorophyll-based toothpaste called Amm-i-dent, was not so well protected. It sponsored *Danger* on CBS, and when Johnson noted that the program featured such listed performers as Lee Grant, Morris Carnovsky, and Lou Polan, he told the company that his stores would display Amm-i-dent side by side with rival products from Lever Brothers Company, Colgate-Palmolive Company, and Procter & Gamble Company (P&G). A shelf sign would inform shoppers that Lever, Colgate, and P&G used pro-American artists and not "Stalin's little creatures." Block would be invited to write its own explanation of why it chose "communist fronters" for its programs.

Blacklisting was a business with which few executives wanted publicly to associate themselves, even if they had to do so privately. Advertisers tried to blame the practice on their agencies or the networks. "We buy *Studio One* as a package from CBS through our agency, McCann-Erickson," said Westinghouse Ad Manager L.W. Scott. "We expect CBS to screen as closely as possible to make sure we do not use anybody who has been proved to be a Communist." Texaco said that it "depends heavily on its advertising agency to determine the qualifications of . . . talent."

Robert Carney, speaking for Foote, Cone & Belding, laid out the common agency position: "As an advertising agency, it is our job to increase sales of our clients' products . . . and to enhance their public acceptance. It is our policy to refrain from employing anyone who may embroil our clients in controversies of any kind, for any reason."

Among the performers frequently cited as victims of the blacklist were Ireene Wicker, who told children's stories on the radio; Louis Untermeyer, a poet and charter panelist on *What's My Line?*; actress Judy Holliday; and actor Jack Gilford.

Agencies' Role

The blacklist became truly institutionalized when the major ad agencies and networks grew impatient dealing with meddling outsiders trying to dictate creative decisions. Rather than let others screen talent, they decided it could be done much more cleanly and discreetly in-house.

In 1954 four advertising agencies in the United States controlled $542 million—or 64 percent of the money spent in all media by the top 100 agencies. Because an estimated 42 percent of that figure, or about $229 million, went for broadcast time, those four agencies had enormous power over the networks and dominated the hiring of production and performing talent. The largest agency was Batten Barton Durstine & Osborn (BBDO) at $148 million, followed very closely by Y&R, J. Walter Thompson Company (JWT), and McCann-Erickson.

In taking talent screening in-house, these and other agencies established their own security departments. They typically appointed an employee at the vice presidential level with a legal or public relations background. As "security officer," his chief duties were to protect the agency and its clients from contact with suspect talent on the one hand and any complicity in the blacklist on the other. Many agencies publicly denied working with American Business Consultants or other freelance consultants and rarely admitted to any use of lists. "It will be our policy," wrote F. Strother Cary in 1955 speaking for the Leo Burnett Company,

"not to join with any other person, firm, or association in blacklisting any individual; and neither will we abrogate our right . . . to make our own decision as to the hiring . . . of any individual." If agencies took no responsibility for accusing, they took none for clearing, either. Controversy in the context of the blacklist was a problem of perception. It was not for the agency to publicly judge guilt or innocence, only to keep such questions as far from its clients' doorsteps as possible.

Privately, of course, agencies had to make judgments because they hired most of the talent, a responsibility that obliged them to produce winning programs as well as shield their clients from embarrassment. Although the Muir and Loeb affairs had given Y&R a high profile in blacklisting, the agency that built the toughest and, relatively speaking, fairest internal system of screening was BBDO, which controlled such programs as *Your Hit Parade* (Lucky Strike), *You Bet Your Life* (DeSoto, Plymouth), *Circle Theater* (Armstrong Floors), and *DuPont Cavalcade of America.*

In the early 1950s Jack Wren moved from public relations to become BBDO's security officer. By many accounts he exerted a quiet but significant influence among other agencies and at the networks. The CBS game show *I've Got a Secret,* for example, ran afoul of the blacklist in 1952 when the William Esty Company, America's 13th-largest ad agency, tried to oust panelist Henry Morgan on behalf of its client RJR and Winston cigarettes. During his fight to stay on the show, in which he was supported by producers Mark Goodson and Bill Todman, Morgan won additional support with a strong speech to a TV artists' union that was sympathetically covered in the *New York World-Telegram.* Wren not only arranged for the coverage but also wrote Morgan's speech. "BBDO has taken blacklisting for what it is," wrote John Cogley, editor of *Commonweal,* in 1955, ". . . a problem in public relations. For unlike most other agencies, [Wren] . . . takes part in clearance procedures. [He] will see listed performers and hear them out. Few other agencies will."

If the agencies were eager to take control of talent hiring from *Counterattack* and the vigilantes, the networks were just as eager to take control of it from the agencies. After 25 years of accepting programming produced by the Madison Avenue giants, NBC and CBS were determined to produce more of their own shows and sell them to advertisers. This meant that the networks, like the agencies, had to get into the business of security. CBS, which entered the 1950s with an unfashionably left-wing reputation, was more than willing to walk the extra mile in order to prove its anticommunist credentials. It became the only network to require a loyalty oath. From 1950 to 1955 CBS talent screening was run by Daniel O'Shea, a Harvard Law School graduate who, unlike many in similar positions, made no effort to conceal what he was there for. His openness made him accessible to any performer looking for clearance. His willingness to play the game so openly certainly helped make CBS synonymous with blacklisting among liberal opponents of the blacklist; but by the same token it also gave it credibility among anticommunists. This reputation tended to make a CBS clearance negotiable currency anywhere on Madison Avenue.

By 1955 security screening was functioning so smoothly and quietly in most of the larger agencies and the networks that it seemed to drop from public attention. The vigilantes continued to persevere, even though there were virtually no more names with a past they could offer up. This put them on dangerous ground. In 1956 Aware, Inc., the group founded by Vincent Hartnett in 1953, finally went too far. It attacked a CBS radio personality named John Henry Faulk, who had just been elected vice president of the New York chapter of the American Federation of Television and Radio Artists on a centrist ticket opposing the methods of *Counterattack* and Aware, Inc. In June 1956 Faulk launched a counterattack in a lawsuit against Aware, Inc., Hartnett, and his Syracuse-based collaborator, Lawrence Johnson. After five years in the courts, Faulk won a judgment of $3.5 million. More important, the trial revealed how a small group of right-wing extremists had brought America's largest advertisers, ad agencies, and broadcasting networks to heel. It was the verdict that finally broke the back of the independent blacklisters.

Although the 1960s saw no shortage of private right-wing organizations, including the John Birch Society, the Billy James Hargis Christian Crusade, and the Manion Forum, few targeted broadcasters or advertising agencies. Moreover, by the early 1960s rising costs and other factors forced advertisers to retreat from full sponsorships of programs to participating sponsorships. The old radio system in which ad agencies produced comedy and drama programs for single advertisers disintegrated. As control of production moved away from ad agencies and toward independent producers and the networks, Madison Avenue's once enormous influence over talent and creative decisions became limited to the production of commercials.

Lingering Remnants

Within the networks, remnants of old security mechanisms continued quietly in place. Perhaps the final act came on 10 September 1967, when Pete Seeger was booked to sing on the Smothers Brothers' CBS variety show. Because the singer and antiwar activist had recently been signed by talent executive John Hammond to the company's Columbia Records division (a move approved at the highest corporate level), the network felt it could lift the ban that had kept him off CBS since 1951. When the network then turned around and cut the song he had chosen to sing, "Waste Deep in the Big Muddy," a song about a misguided World War II training maneuver (written by Seeger earlier that year) in which network censors inferred an anti-Vietnam message, CBS found

itself waist deep in bad publicity. At a time when street protests against the war in Vietnam were rising to a fever pitch, the attempt to enforce a network policy held over from the blacklist days seemed almost comically absurd. Seeger returned on 25 February 1968, a month after the Tet offensive in Vietnam (a massive show of strength by the Viet Cong and North Vietnamese), and performed the song.

Blacklisting no longer exists among advertisers or ad agencies, although some performers may be denied employment opportunities owing to specific personal or professional controversies. Several motion pictures have been made that touch on the topic of blacklisting. Among them are: *Career* (Paramount, 1959), *The Way We Were* (Columbia, 1973), *The Front* (Columbia, 1976), *Guilty by Suspicion* (Warner Bros., 1991), *For the Boys* (20th Century Fox, 1992), and *Mr. Saturday Night* (Columbia Pictures/ New Line Cinema, 1992). A 1997 episode of the CBS television series *Touched by an Angel* also dealt with the issue.

JOHN MCDONOUGH AND JAMES FISHER

Further Reading

American Business Consultants, *Red Channels: The Report of Communist Influence in Radio and Television*, New York: Counterattack, 1950

Bernstein, Walter, *Inside Out: A Memoir of the Blacklist*, New York: Knopf, 1996

Cogley, John, *Report on Blacklisting*, 2 vols., New York: Fund for the Republic, 1956; see especially vol. 2, *Radio-Television*

Fariello, Griffin, *Red Scare: Memories of the American Inquisition: An Oral History*, New York: Norton, 1995

Foley, Karen Sue, *The Political Blacklist in the Broadcast Industry: The Decade of the 1950s*, New York: Arno, 1979

Goodson, Mark, "'If I'd Stood up Earlier . . . ,'" *New York Times Magazine* (13 January 1991)

McGilligan, Patrick, Paul Buhle, and Alison Morley, *Tender Comrades: A Backstory of the Hollywood Blacklist*, New York: St. Martin's Press, 1997

Navasky, Victor S., *Naming Names*, New York: Viking, 1980; London: Calder, 1982

Pope, John Marvin, "Trial without Jury: A Study of Blacklisting in Broadcasting," Master's thesis, University of Texas at Austin, 1972

Vaughn, Robert, *Only Victims: A Study of Show Business Blacklisting*, New York: Putnam, 1972

D.L. Blair, Inc.

Opened in New York City by Cy Draddy and Marty Landis, 1960; gained its first international client, Imperial Tobacco Company of Canada, 1969; acquired by global marketing agency Draft Worldwide to become part of the Interpublic Group of Companies, 1998.

Major Clients
American Greetings Corporation
Coca-Cola Company
Johnson & Johnson
Kraft Foods, Inc.
MCI WorldCom
Miller Brewing Company
New York Daily News
Oscar Mayer Foods Corporation
Philip Morris USA
Procter & Gamble Company
Reader's Digest Association

D. L. Blair, Inc., in the business of sales promotion since 1960, is best known as an innovator of many of the sweepstakes, contests, and games that promote products all over the world. It began the first preselected number sweepstakes ever for *Life* magazine in 1960 and followed that with the creation of the first scratch-off game for Tydol-Veedol in 1961. Throughout the agency's history it has created promotional marketing for blue-chip clients, establishing long-lasting relationships with many. One of its largest clients, the Procter & Gamble Company (P&G), has had an ongoing relationship with D.L. Blair since the agency opened its doors.

D.L. Blair was started by two college classmates, Cy Draddy and Marty Landis. One of their professors was moonlighting as a sweepstakes judge, and they were struck by the idea that there must be a more time- and cost-efficient way to handle the process. They entered into a partnership named for their last names and Blair House in Washington, D.C., which they happened to be walking past as they decided on a name. The agency began with fewer than 12 employees in a small loft on East 26th Street in New York City, and with two important clients: P&G's Mr. Clean brand and *Life* magazine.

D.L. Blair was one of the first promotion consulting agencies in advertising history, second only to a now-defunct company named Ralph Glendinning that opened just weeks before it. At the time, these agencies were involved mostly in store coupons and jingle contests, but as business grew more sophisticated and competition soared, sales promotion grew as well.

The agency's founders were more businessmen than they were marketers, but their methods for generating sales proved indispensable in the realm of sales promotion. In addition to the innovations for *Life* and Tydol-Veedol in the early 1960s, the company, namely Draddy, also introduced the first "matching-halves" game for Shell Oil in 1962 and the first "magic screen"

game for P&G in 1966. (A magic screen campaign requires that the consumer acquire a screen—usually a red plastic overlay—through an initial purchase; when the screen is placed over a picture or message on the packaging of a subsequent purchase, it reveals a message.) D.L. Blair's early work with P&G exemplified the way the agency addressed and executed its clients' promotional needs. Such big-client stakes taught Draddy and Landis to value strategy before tactics and results before creativity.

In January 1968, a few months after Landis left the company, Draddy hired Tom Conlon, a promotional marketing executive from Benton and Bowles, Inc. Conlon's approach to promotions fit the company's existing philosophy while giving it an additional push. Just as Draddy had been the innovator of many of the company's ideas for promotions, Conlon proved indispensable for his contributions in the area of creativity solidly grounded in results. For this, Conlon credited an old boss at Benton and Bowles who had impressed on him the saying, "It's not creative unless it sells." Two years after joining the company Conlon was named president. He became chief executive officer in 1975 following Draddy's death.

By 1969 D.L. Blair had crossed into international territory, working for Imperial Tobacco Company in Canada. Its campaign for the company drew the largest market share increase ever in the tight tobacco category, destroying assumptions about cigarette brand loyalty and giving new credibility to the power of sales promotion, even if used over a short time. The agency was asked to take Imperial's weakest brand, Sweet Caporal, and raise its market share from less than 1 percent. Devising a simple promotion involving scratch-off miniature playing cards, the company increased Sweet Caporal's market share 14 points in one month in the campaign's initial test market and raised the brand 22 points in just three more months after national expansion. Major competitors of Imperial enlisted the aid of the Canadian government to force the company to withdraw the promotion, but not before Sweet Caporal had gained 25 percent of the market in just seven months—more than any of Imperial's other brands combined.

The Canadian Parliament was not the only skeptic. In late 1969 and the early 1970s on the other side of the border, the Dingell Commission, led by John Dingell, a Democratic congressman from Michigan, urged the U.S. Federal Trade Commission (FTC) to recognize what he perceived as the damaging nature of sweepstakes practices in the United States. The FTC began naming top companies and advertising agencies in a legal suit to limit the use of sweepstakes as a promotional tool. Included in the suit along with D.L. Blair were such companies as McDonald's, P&G, and Reuben H. Donnelly, one of D.L. Blair's major competitors. As a compromise, those named in the suit were urged to sign a consent decree that would curb their use of sweepstakes. All signed but D.L. Blair, which refused because it was unwilling to say that it had deceived consumers. Taken to court, D.L. Blair triumphed over the FTC in January 1973. Meanwhile, those who did sign operated under the strict rules for more than 20 years, except for

D.L. Blair, Inc., created the sweepstakes featured on M&M's packages in 2001.

P&G, which successfully argued that its limitations be lifted several years earlier. For this victory D.L. Blair enjoyed a latitude of business practices that others did not. But the commission had stigmatized the sweepstakes business, and D.L. Blair often had to convince clients to try sales promotions.

By the 1980s D.L. Blair had an impressive client roster, including Kraft Foods, Inc. (which signed on in 1962) and Miller Brewing Company (1974). In the early 1970s Conlon had convinced Draddy that it made sense to open a fulfillment office for delivering premiums to winning consumers in a central location in the United States. Soon a large office in Blair, Nebraska, was opened. D.L. Blair had also expanded internationally, opening satellite offices to serve Shell Oil and the Kellogg Company in Sydney and Melbourne, Australia, in the late 1960s. In 1977 a small staff was

positioned in Windsor, England, to serve British American Tobacco.

In 1982 D.L. Blair was hired by American Greetings as its promotional agency of record. Through a successful campaign it revealed the usefulness of a promotions strategy that de-emphasized national advertising while targeting potential buyers at the point of sale. D.L. Blair convinced American Greetings to abandon its national television campaign and market to specific consumers within stores. Though the concept would not apply to all clients, the results for American Greetings were substantial. In 1985 Conlon created and trademarked a winning promotion sponsored by P&G as a way to involve a large audience. "Watch 'n' Win" was a new concept in which viewers wishing to enter into the sweepstakes needed information presented at the end of a prime-time television program, when TV viewership had usually declined dramatically.

Business for D.L. Blair was moving at a brisk rate as it entered the 1990s. It was executing one sweepstake, game, or contest a day—a rate that Conlon at one time believed would never be surpassed. In 1991 it was named the Coca-Cola Company's promotional agency of record, executing all promotions for all brands. Through its work for the soft-drink marketer, D.L. Blair learned that promotional ideas translate well from country to country. Successful promotions first executed in the United States could be duplicated internationally; thus, what worked in Des Moines, Iowa, could also work in St. Petersburg, Russia. In 1998 D.L. Blair ran an hour-long infomercial for Coca-Cola in Russia across six time zones combined with an "under the cap" contest already popular in the United States and gained the highest ratings to date for a TV program for that market.

In April 1997 D.L. Blair agreed to be acquired by the Interpublic Group of Companies under Draft Worldwide, a global direct-marketing agency, for an undisclosed sum of money. Since the mid-1970s D.L. Blair had been courted by various potential suitors, but Conlon could find "no comfortable philosophical fit." He worried that his employees might somehow be harmed by the acquisition or that D.L. Blair's business decisions would be inhibited. In the deal with Interpublic, the two parties agreed on a contract that allowed D.L. Blair to remain autonomous under its own name while establishing a mutually beneficial partnership that allowed for the sharing of capabilities and resources at a time when the line between sales promotion and direct marketing was becoming more and more obscured. For D.L. Blair the partnership meant significant growth in foreign markets at a rate that was no longer possible in the United States.

As the company entered the 21st century, it was the leader in its field, capable of executing eight sweepstakes, contests, or games a day—roughly 3,000 promotions per year. Anticipating further steady growth through the Internet, the agency, based in Garden City, New York, expanded its fulfillment facilities in Nebraska to house a large workforce to implement promotional work through the new medium.

MEGAN CASSADA

Further Reading

D.L. Blair <www.dlblair.com>
"FTC Examiner Declares Blair Sweepstakes Method Not Unfair," *Advertising Age* (15 May 1972)
"An Oldie but Goodie," *Promo Magazine* (October 1999)

Bleustein-Blanchet, Marcel 1906–1996

French Advertising Executive

If any one individual embodied 20th-century French advertising, it was Marcel Bleustein-Blanchet. Born Marcel Bleustein in the Montmartre section of Paris, France, to Jewish immigrant parents (he added the "Blanchet" to his name after World War II), he founded the French advertising agency Publicis, which would become one of France's—and the world's—leading agencies.

Bleustein-Blanchet had little formal schooling, dropping out at the age of 12. His final report card stated, "He knows how to read, write, and count." He went to work at his relatives' furniture store as a salesman at age 14. There he gained valuable experience in dealing with customers as well as advertising agents. After a few years of working for his relatives and performing his military service, Bleustein-Blanchet started his own advertising agency, Publicis, at the age of 20. Although he had little formal education, Bleustein-Blanchet had considerable charisma and organizational skills. His agency had modest beginnings; Publicis began as a two-room operation in a second-floor walkup, and its first clients were his family and friends in the Montmartre neighborhood. He had difficulty convincing merchants to advertise and later described a typical reaction to his sales pitch on the merits of advertising: "We have our own clientele. They know us. They know what we sell. Why do you want us to advertise?"

With persistence, Bleustein-Blanchet overcame such reluctance. By 1929, after three years of operation, Bleustein-Blanchet moved Publicis into a larger office and hired his first employees. At this time, Bleustein-Blanchet revolutionized French advertising by turning to radio. Agence Havas, France's largest agency and space broker, dominated the print media; Bleustein-Blanchet therefore explored radio as an ad medium. He traveled the French countryside approaching provincial stations and extending to them an exclusive contract to book advertising time in return for guaranteeing them yearly revenue. As a consequence, Publicis quickly became a powerful advertising force in France.

However, in 1934 the French government banned advertising for the state-run radio stations that comprised most of Publicis's clients. Undeterred, Bleustein-Blanchet bought his own Parisian radio station and christened it Radio-Cité. Radio-Cité transformed French radio by introducing a mix of news, game shows, commercial advertisements, and popular entertainers such as Edith Piaf, Maurice Chevalier, and Josephine Baker. Bleustein-

Marcel Bleustein-Blanchet.
Courtesy of Publicis Conseil.

Blanchet then explored cinema advertising in the mid-1930s and produced advertising shorts. He also established a subsidiary that managed the distribution of cinema advertising. By World War II, Bleustein-Blanchet had gained exclusive distribution rights to more than half of France's movie houses.

The war ended this first stage of his advertising career. With the advance of German forces on Paris, he and his family relocated to southern France. Radio-Cité was taken over, and the Vichy Government confiscated much of his personal property. After Germany occupied all of France in 1942, he made a daring escape to Spain, where he was imprisoned briefly. Finally, he made his way to Britain and served with the Free French flying reconnaissance missions. After the war he became a member of the French Legion of Honor.

At the war's end Bleustein-Blanchet had nothing. In his memoirs he wrote, "I was a millionaire at twenty-three, ruined at thirty-four, and obliged to begin all over again at the age of forty." He restarted Publicis but could not relaunch Radio-Cité because the French government had nationalized all radio stations. With his drive and personality, Bleustein-Blanchet regained many of Publicis's former clients, but more important, he gained his first U.S. client, Colgate-Palmolive Company, in 1947. (American clients were important because they gave Publicis advice concerning advertising and marketing techniques.) Other large clients followed, among them Shell, L'Oréal, Nestlé, and Renault.

With these important accounts Bleustein-Blanchet moved Publicis in 1957 to its present Champs-Élysées office, across the Place de l'Etoile from the Arc de Triomphe. On the ground floor he launched what was called "Le Drugstore," a swank café and retail outlet that sold magazines, electronic gadgets, and gifts. Such a combination was a marketing innovation for 1950s France. The French public responded enthusiastically.

Bleustein-Blanchet successfully guided Publicis to dynamic expansion through the 1960s and 1970s. In the 1960s this growth resulted mostly from acquiring new clients rather than acquiring new agencies; in the 1970s and 1980s, Publicis's growth came chiefly by acquistion of agencies. By the 1970s Publicis and Agence Havas were by far the two largest French advertising agencies. However, in world rankings they trailed American giants such as the J. Walter Thompson Company and Young & Rubicam. As a result, in the early 1970s Bleustein-Blanchet sold a minority stake of Publicis on the Paris Bourse and used the cash to acquire agencies in other European countries. Publicis cracked the world's top 20 advertising agencies with offices in all Western European countries by the 1970s and 1980s.

His last major act as director of Publicis was to promote the ill-fated merger with the U.S advertising agency Foote, Cone & Belding (FCB) in 1988. Bleustein-Blanchet and Publicis had longed to enter the lucrative U.S. market and saw an alliance with FCB as a mutually beneficial arrangement. Unfortunately, a clash of business cultures (American versus French) created mistrust and misunderstandings between the two. Bleustein-Blanchet retired from Publicis in 1990, after leading the agency for more than 60 years. He died in Paris in 1996, after which the merger officially ended.

CLARK HULTQUIST

See also Publicis Group

Biography
Born in Paris, France, 21 August 1906; left school at age 12, 1918; founded the agency Publicis, 1926; lost business in World War II; restarted Publicis after the war, 1946; gained first U.S. client, Colgate-Palmolive Company, 1947; engineered merger with U.S. advertising agency Foote, Cone & Belding, 1988; retired as director, 1990; died in Paris, France, 11 April 1996.

Selected Publications
Sur mon antenne, 1947; condensed and translated in *The Rage to Persuade: Memoirs of French Advertising Man,* translated by Jean Boddewyn, 1982

La rage de convaincre, 1970; condensed and translated in *The Rage to Persuade: Memoirs of a French Advertising Man,* translated by Jean Boddewyn, 1982

La nostalgie du futur, 1977; condensed and translated in *The Rage to Persuade: Memoirs of a French Advertising Man,* translated by Jean Boddewyn, 1982

Mémoires d'un lion, 1988

Les mots de ma vie, 1990

La traversée du siècle, 1994

Further Reading

Boutelier, Denis, and Dilip Subramanian, *Le grand bluff: Pouvoir et argent dans la publicité*, Paris: Denoël, 1990

Germon, Marcel, *Monsieur publicité*, Paris: Grancher, 1990

Martin, Marc, *Trois siècles de publicité en france*, Paris: Éditions Odile Jacob, 1992

BMP DDB. *See* Boase Massimi Pollit

Boase, Martin 1932–

British Advertising Executive

Advertising, revolution, and, perhaps briefly, religion are the three words that have played a significant part in the career of advertising luminary Martin Boase, a founder of Boase Massimi Pollitt (BMP). Boase was born in Sheffield, England, in 1932. As a youngster, Boase was a veteran of 14 different schools, including Bedales (from which, like many of the others, he was reportedly expelled), before a spell in the army (learning Russian in an interpreter's course) and at the University of Oxford (where he took a language degree).

It was face paint and film rather than advertising that beckoned after the army. But Boase apparently made little impression on the theater or with his directorial efforts at Elstree Studios near London, England. Nearly 50 letters, 22 interviews, and six job offers later, a then 26-year-old Boase found himself employed first by the London Press Exchange, then at the Robert Sharp & Partners agency for two years. In 1961 he took a job as account manager at London advertising agency Pritchard Wood and rapidly ascended to the position of managing director. But as Christmas 1967 loomed, the agency's future was threatened by the seeming lurch toward bankruptcy of its parent company, the Interpublic Group of Companies.

The board of Pritchard Wood offered up a management buy-out solution, but executives at Interpublic headquarters in New York City stalled until the following May, when the offer was accepted in person by Interpublic President Bob Healey. It was then, perhaps fortuitously for Boase, that negotiations, which should have started 48 hours later on a Saturday, stalled when Boase's Orthodox Jewish lawyer was unable to work on the Sabbath. By the following Monday, when Boase and his team were again ready to negotiate, the deal was off; Interpublic had found

the funding. No less than an advertising revolution followed on 9 May 1968 as Boase and nine other directors walked out to form Boase Massimi Pollitt.

In 1983 Boase, the only remaining of the three founding partners, took London-based BMP public. (Gabe Massimi left the company in October 1971, and Stanley Pollitt died in May 1979.) Since then the agency has forged relationships with many long-term clients, including Volkswagen and Anheuser-Busch Company. It also created one of the most memorable tag lines in British advertising history for Cadbury's Smash brand of instant potatoes: "For mash get Smash."

In 1989, two years after he had become chairman of Britain's leading trade organization, the Advertising Association, Boase was again creating advertising history. When BMP became a takeover target for French advertising giant BDDP, Boase suggested that the company's French suitors "frog off." It was a jingoistic line that caught the imagination of the media. He then negotiated a £125 million (approximately $187.5 million) white-knight offer from U.S. agency holding company Omnicom within a reported 36 hours.

As his career evolved, so did Boase's industry reputation for his democratic and encompassing profits-after-performance approach to the business. Once described by *Campaign* magazine as the "David Niven of the British advertising scene," he established a popular reputation for style, both personal and professional.

He served as chairman of Omnicom from 1989 to 1995 and has held various directorships with the British Television Advertising Awards (1993–2000) and as chairman of outdoor advertising company Maiden Group (1993–present). He maintains an office at London's BMP DDB, as the agency came to be known

Martin Boase.
Courtesy of Martin Boase/BMP DDB.

following the addition of Omnicom's U.K. agency network, which has its headquarters close to Paddington Station.

Boase, who sports a trademark beard, has been a longtime fan of horse racing. He is also known to be keen on Bentley automobiles, having owned eight in the same finish—dark green with beige leather interior. It made him a perfect advocate for a launch campaign for the automaker, which had never before advertised.

SEAN KELLY

Biography
Born in Sheffield, England, 14 July 1932; graduated from University of Oxford, 1956; became account manager at London, England, ad agency Pritchard Woods, 1961; left Pritchard Woods with nine other directors to form Boase Massimi Pollitt (BMP), 1968; took BMP public, 1983; sold agency to Omnicom and became chairman, 1989; resigned as chairman, 1995.

Further Reading
"BMP DDB 1968–1998—The BMP Launch" *Campaign* (23 October 1998)

Lindsay, Vincent, "The Failed Actor at BMP Who Stole the Show," *Observer Newspaper* (21 May 1989)

McEwan, Feona, "Empire Builders: Martin Boase," *Campaign Magazine* (22 April 1998)

Boase Massimi Pollitt

(BMP DDB)

Created in 1968 by Martin Boase and nine other former executives from the London, England, agency Pritchard Wood and Partners; went public, 1983; fought off a hostile takeover by French agency BDDP with a takeover by a U.S.-based holding company, the Omnicom Group, to become BMP DDB, 1989.

Major Clients
Barclaycard
Bentley
British Gas
Cadbury
Pepsi-Cola Company
Sony Corporation
Vodafone
Volkswagen

Created in 1968 through the failure of a proposed management buyout, Boase Massimi Pollitt began to make its mark from the moment it came into existence and continued to do so as it evolved into London, England-based BMP DDB. Led by Martin Boase and nine other directors, Boase Massimi Pollitt (BMP) was created when a religious matter held up management buyout negotiations for their agency, Pritchard Wood & Partners, from U.S. parent Interpublic, Inc. Interpublic, suffering financial problems, had agreed to sell the agency to its management team and scheduled the buyout meeting for a Saturday; the meeting was delayed until the following Monday because Martin Boase's lawyer, an Orthodox Jew, declined to break his Sabbath observance. By Monday Interpublic had secured the financing it needed and called off the deal.

Interpublic's withdrawal resulted in the largest-ever advertising agency executive walkout in the United Kingdom at that time, as Boase and his team left the agency to set up their own shop. If Boase and the other founding partners, American creative director Gabe Massimi and Briton Stanley Pollitt, thought it would be easy, they were quickly disabused of that idea. Only one client joined the upstart agency. But that one company, Cadbury, played a significant role in establishing the agency.

Key to the agency's success was its entrepreneurial, participatory, and ethics-led management style combined with innovations in account planning. Pollitt, usually credited with being the father of account planning, played a key role in the growth of the agency. The University of Cambridge graduate, who had boxed for the university between his law studies, started his pioneering work at Pritchard Wood & Partners, where he headed the agency's research efforts. In 1965 he introduced the role of account planner to the business, an act that would change the advertising industry. Increasingly his skills in identifying and analyzing relevant data, including consumer reaction, began to affect campaigns at Pritchard Wood and, later, at BMP. His ability to gather and use data to test campaigns soon caught on at other British agencies, though it was more than 15 years before the method started to find favor with U.S. agencies.

Pollitt's account planning skills attracted clients and served as a selling point for the agency, which has been noted for its democratic approach to client handling. During the 1970s as many as 5 percent of advertising graduates of British universities applied for planning jobs at the agency; by 2001 the agency was running a program designed to integrate graduates into the company. The program has seen at least seven of its former participants rise to the rank of executive director or higher within the agency.

Massimi left BMP in 1971, and the sudden death of Pollitt following a heart attack in 1979 dealt a major blow to the agency. His legacy of account planning remains at the core of the agency, which continues to reinforce its planning capabilities across the business. One example was the creation of the agency's Culture Lab, a unit that studies consumer behavior beyond information provided by electronic point-of-purchase data.

Creative efforts also played a major role in building the agency; its campaigns are the stuff of advertising legend. High up on the list is the 1973 "Lipsmackin'thirstquenchin'acetastin'motivatin'goodbuzzin'cool-talkin'highwalkin'fastlivin'evergivin'cool-fizzin'Pepsi" campaign on British television. A year later the agency created one of the most memorable lines in British advertising history for Cadbury's Smash brand of instant potatoes in an ad that featured robotic Martians poking fun at Earthlings, who mash their potatoes when they could have instant ones. If one asks British baby boomers to name their favorite advertising tag line, "For mash get Smash" still rolls off the tongues of this generation of British consumers. Other major campaigns over the years have included Volkswagen's "Affordability"; PG Tips's tea, with its famous chimps; and beverage marketer John Smith's, with the "Follow the bear" campaign for its Hoffmeister brand.

Boase Massimi Pollitt's 1974 "Martians" commercial for Cadbury's Smash instant potatoes brand was an instant hit in Britain.

In 1983 BMP went public as a $45 million business, with every employee receiving shares. At the same time the agency's client list and reputation for witty copywriting and creative messages grew. Work for the Greater London Council in 1984 resulted in the "Say no to no say" campaign against abolition of the council. The tag line was clever in its simplicity, but it was not enough to prevent the demise of the council.

The agency has trained and launched significant talents over the years, including Mike Greenlees, who formed Gold Greenlees Trott, (now part of TBWA Worldwide), Geoff Howard-Spink (at Lowe), and Jane Newman (now at U.S. shop Merkley Newman Harty). The agency's campaign work for the British newspaper The Guardian brought it in 1987 the Epica d'Or Award, given by the European advertising trade press in recognition of creative production in European advertising.

In 1989 BMP, with annual billings of $270 million, found itself under siege by French agency BDDP, which owned a 15 percent stake and was offering $178.5 million for the remainder of the agency. BMP, led by the somewhat jingoistic but highly effective "Frog off" rallying cry of Martin Boase, did more than fight back: it negotiated a $187.5 million white-knight agreement with the U.S.-based Omnicom Group. A deal was negotiated in 36 hours and resulted in a new and powerful advertising force with the merging of BMP and Omnicom's DDB office in London.

The 1990s provided continued growth and success, with award-winning campaigns for Volkswagen and Reuters, which became a client in 1997. BMP DDB's assignment to the Bentley account in 1999 was particularly sweet for Boase, who was a longtime fan of the car and had, as of 2001, eight of them. In 2000 BMP DDB had gross income of $88.3 million, a 14.3 percent increase over the previous year's income, on billings of $929.6 million.

SEAN KELLY

Further Reading

"Bentley Fanatic Boase Knows All You Need To about Yob's Best Drive," *Campaign* (29 January 1999)

"Campaign Supplement on BMP DDB 1968–1998: The BMP Launch," *Campaign* (23 October 1998)

McEwan, Feona, "Empire Builders: Martin Boase," *Campaign* (22 April 1998)

O'Leary, Noreen, "Martin Boase," *Adweek* (Eastern Edition) (30 October 2000)

Steel, Jon, *Truth, Lies, and Advertising: The Art of Account Planning*, New York and Chichester, Sussex: Wiley, 1998

Vincent, Lindsay, "Martin Boase: The Failed Actor at BMP Who Stole the Show," *The Observer* (21 May 1989)

Bonds, War. *See* War Bonds

Borden, Inc.

Principal Agencies

Young & Rubicam, Inc.

Benton and Bowles, Inc.

Ross Roy, Inc.

Tracy-Locke Company, Inc.

Grey Advertising, Inc.

BBDO Worldwide

One of the top dairy manufacturers in the United States, Borden, Inc., created the world's most famous cash cow in Elsie, named by *Advertising Age* as one of the top ten ad icons of the 20th century. Sixty years after her first appearance as the symbol of the wholesome goodness of Borden dairy foods, Elsie was still widely recognized by consumers, according to a 1996 American Dairy Brands Brand Equity Study.

Gail Borden, Jr., born in 1801, was a man with big ideas. He published the first permanent newspaper in Texas and is credited with having coined the phrase, "Remember the Alamo!" as a headline. Borden attempted to eradicate yellow fever in 1844 by refrigerating victims of the disease; however, there were no volunteers for his experiments. Borden next designed a "terraqueous machine," a combination wagon and sailboat, which capsized during a demonstration in the Gulf of Mexico. He created dehydrated meat biscuits that, while unpalatable, met with some success among the 1849 gold rush prospectors and pioneers.

Origins

Borden had long believed that all sorts of foods could be condensed and preserved. He turned his attention to fresh milk, which had a particularly short shelf life in the days when icehouses were the only means of refrigeration. Others tried—unsuc-

cessfully—to keep milk from spoiling by cooking it in the open air over a hot fire, but the milk burned, became discolored, or soured.

Borden decided to use a copper vacuum pan similar to one used by the Shakers for condensing fruit juice. Inside his vacuum pan, a heating coil warmed the milk slowly and evenly, allowing for evaporation without scalding. After the water had vaporized, what remained was condensed milk. Borden received a U.S. patent in 1856 for "producing concentrated milk in vacuo [in a vacuum]" and launched New York City–based Eagle Brand Sweetened Condensed Milk, which has been number-one in its category since its inception. He opened his first milk-condensing factory in Connecticut and insisted that farmers selling him milk follow strict sanitary guidelines.

In 1858 Borden's company became known as the New York Condensed Milk Company. That year Gail Borden wrote his first advertisement to convince housewives to try the new product, which, he said, "for purity, durability, and economy, is hitherto unequaled in the annals of the milk trade." It was published in the same issue of *Leslie's Illustrated Newspaper* as an expose of the unsanitary conditions of New York City dairies. Borden's sales began to rise.

Borden provisioned the Union Army with condensed milk field rations when the U.S. Civil War broke out in 1861. Demand far exceeded supply, however, so he licensed other manufacturers to use the Borden patent and trademark. By the war's end in 1865, so many competitors had appropriated his name—while often producing inferior products—that Borden devised the patriotic Eagle Brand trademark for his condensed milk.

Eagle Brand sweetened condensed milk, which used sugar as a preservative, was touted as a high-nutrition infant formula when diluted with water. The concoction was credited with significantly lowering the infant mortality rate in North America, but when medical studies began to show the effect of sugar on children's teeth, use of sweetened condensed milk as an infant formula began to wane. Borden then repositioned the product for use in desserts.

Gail Borden died in Texas in 1874, but his company continued to grow, adding fresh milk and evaporated milk to its product line. At the close of 1899, the Borden Condensed Milk Company, as it was then known, had annual sales of approximately $10 million.

Another name change, to the Borden Company, came in 1919 when the company tallied sales of $122 million. In 1928 Borden acquired the business and assets of the country's two leading ice-cream makers; a year later it added cheese to its product line. Borden selected five-year-old Young & Rubicam (Y&R), of New York City, as its advertising agency in 1928; Y&R was to remain the company's main agency for much of the next 40 years.

In 1931 Borden offered homemakers $25 for original recipes featuring Eagle Brand sweetened condensed milk and received more than 80,000 recipes. Booklets showcasing these recipes and others developed in the Borden test kitchen heralded the "Magic!" of cooking with Eagle Brand. The practice of offering recipes to consumers and food editors continued well into the 1980s.

Debut of Elsie

In the 1930s, "milk wars" between farmers and dairy processors led to the perception of big dairies as evil moneymakers. To counter this image, Borden adopted a friendly approach, promoting the cleanliness and high quality of its products.

Elsie the Cow was one of four bovines in a 1936 ad series in medical journals that proved so popular that doctors ordered reprints for their offices. In one of the ads, the cartoon cow was shown finishing a letter that read, "Dear Mama: I'm so excited I can hardly chew! We girls are sending our milk to Borden's now. Love, Elsie." The ads were created by Stuart Peabody, Borden's director of advertising, and illustrator Walter Early. Borden also tested the ad campaign in a few New York City–area newspapers.

In 1938 Borden sponsored radio newscasts with commentator Rush Hughes, who read the letters-from-Elsie commercials. They were a hit with listeners and became a regular feature of the program. Fan mail poured in. Borden recognized Elsie's tremendous appeal and launched a national campaign with a series of ads in consumer magazines.

In 1939 Borden opened an exhibit at the New York World's Fair featuring an automatic milking machine called a rotolactor. Visitors to the exhibit wanted to know not how the machine worked but which of the 150 cows milked by the rotolactor was Elsie. The most beautiful Jersey cow in the herd was selected to fill the public's need for a real, live Elsie. The next year at the fair, Elsie moved into a "Barn Colonial" boudoir dressed with whimsical bovine props such as milk-bottle lamps, butter-churn tables, and oil portraits of her ancestors. Elsie's popularity soared. Husband Elmer was introduced, appearing in a more masculine boudoir that looked like the site of nightly poker parties, while Elsie headed to Hollywood, California, to play the role of Buttercup in the movie *Little Men* and to await the birth of her calf. When

Elsie returned to the fair, the boudoir was redecorated as a nursery, and Elsie and her daughter, named Beulah, drew higher attendance figures than any other exhibit.

Magazines were still Borden's primary advertising medium. About 1941, the company abandoned any pretense that Elsie was just an ordinary four-legged Jersey cow. Elsie, Elmer, and Beulah went bipedal and took on the attributes of an average young housewife and her family in advertisements.

During World War II Elsie was a popular pin-up girl—flyers even named airplanes after her. She raised $10 million on a war bonds tour. After the war, Elsie began promoting an extended line of Borden-branded products. In 1947 she gave birth to a male calf behind temporary drapes in a Macy's department store window. A contest to name the baby brought in 1 million entries, an all-time record for an advertising contest at that time. The judges selected the name *Beauregard* in honor of the role of Confederate General P.G.T. Beauregard at the Battle of Bull Run in the U.S. Civil War.

In the postwar years, magazine advertising was being overtaken by television, but early attempts at animating Elsie proved unsuccessful. As a result, Elsie faded from TV ads, which shifted toward specific products. In 1951 the campaign introduced a trademark depicting Elsie with a garland of daisies around her neck and daisy petals encircling her face. While Elsie's advertising role was reduced to that of a trademark tag, her personal appearances continued with very little drop-off in attendance. At about the same time, Elmer assumed a similar role. Borden had introduced the first consumer white glue in 1947 under name Cascorez Glue. In November 1951 it was repositioned as Elmer's Glue-All, with packaging featuring Elsie's spouse and a magazine and direct mail campaign by agency James Thomas Chirurg Company.

Sponsorships and Contests

Network TV became an increasingly important component in Borden's ad budget, with Benton and Bowles handling Borden products for television. In 1956 Borden began sponsoring *Fury*, a children's series on NBC, and the sitcom *The People's Choice*, starring Jackie Cooper and a forlorn-looking talking basset hound named Cleo. Both enjoyed high ratings. In 1959 Borden added the co-sponsorship of *Ruff and Reddy*, a children's program that preceded *Fury*.

Borden celebrated its centennial in 1957 with a special ad campaign in *Reader's Digest*. It also kicked off a $100,000 contest to "Name the twins," the latest additions to Elsie's family, with ads in national magazines, food-business publications, and Sunday supplements as well as TV promotions. Y&R handled the contest advertising in cooperation with other Borden agencies. The contest drew nearly 3 million entries, and the winning names were Larabee and Lobelia—until Borden discovered that the lobelia flower was an antidote for poison in folk medicine. Thereafter Elsie's new calves were referred to as "the twins."

Elsie reappeared in 1959's successful "Borden's, very big on flavor" ad campaign, which placed a greater emphasis on appetite appeal. It featured an updated look for Elsie and her family. Commercials the following year for Starlac nonfat dry milk, from

"<u>Should</u> a child be named after a relative?"

ASKED ELSIE, THE BORDEN COW

"H<small>E SHOULD</small> NOT!" bellowed Elmer, the bull. "Why do you suppose I—I mean *you*—got Borden's to run a big $25,000 name contest to find him a name? So he *wouldn't* be named after a broken-down uncle!"

"But," protested Elsie, "maybe our son won't like the name the contest judges pick. Maybe we should wait till he's old enough to pick his own name."

"By that time," snapped Elmer, "you'll have him tagged *Fauntleroy* or *Percy!*"

"Don't worry about *that*," laughed Elsie. "I won't have a chance to name him anything! Right now, the judges are voting on the name my baby will answer to."

"Those judges," menaced Elmer, "better pick a good, he-man name — or Borden's will hear from me!"

"Oh," chirped Elsie, "Borden's hears from all sorts of folks. Nice things about wonderful *Lady Borden Ice Cream*. It's the world's smoothest ice-cream eating!"

"Woman," groaned Elmer, "how *can* you talk about ice cream when the wonderful-est son a guy ever had lies there without a first name?"

"Oh, Daddy," giggled young Beulah, "don't act so *icky*. Little Whosiz looks divinely happy."

"*Icky? Whosiz?*" frowned Elmer. "What in thunderation kind of talk is that?"

"It's just young folks' jargon, dear," explained Elsie. "Like my saying, as an exam-

ple — *Lady Borden Ice Cream sends me!*"

"Sends you?" exploded Elmer. "*Where?*"

"Into ecstasies over its creamy richness," tittered Elsie. "Lady Borden Ice Cream is made with golden cream, beautiful fruits, heavenly flavors — blended by master ice cream makers! It truly is *fit for a golden spoon!*"

"Get back on the line!" commanded Elmer. "Haven't the judges given you one *hint* as to what my son's name will be?"

"None," replied Elsie, "except to say the winning name will fit baby like a glove. As grand a fit, for instance, as the name None Such is for *Borden's None Such Mince Meat*. It makes the eatingest, spiciest, Thanksgivingest pie of them all! Old-fashioned mince pie — with luscious

fruit-rich filling made from a 62-year-old New England recipe!"

"Quit working yourself into a lather about None Such!" said Elmer.

"But, dear," objected Elsie, "there's no work to Borden's None Such Mince Meat. Those plump raisins—tart curls of citrus peel—pick-of-the-crop apples—are cleaned and chopped, then blended with savory spices from foreign lands!"

"Google, google, google—google, *google*, goo, goo, GOO!" crowed the baby.

"Elsie! Beulah!" cried Elmer. "My son's talk-ing—*talking!* Maybe he's telling us what to call him!"

"And maybe," teased Elsie, "he's just finishing off this ad for his mother. Maybe all those *Goo's* mean *if it's Borden's, it's GOT to be goo—goo—GOOD!*"

© The Borden Company

— if it's Borden's, it's <u>got</u> to be good!

In 1947 Borden sponsored a contest to name the new offspring of its bovine icons, Elsie and Elmer.
©1947 by Borden, Inc.

Dancer, Fitzgerald, Sample, had an animated Elsie opening and closing a live-action product demonstration.

In 1961 Borden net sales passed the billion-dollar mark for the first time. The President's Advertising Campaign for Expansion (PACE) was announced in the 1961 annual report with the goal of increasing the total impact of Borden advertising by providing specific product support where it would advance overall company interests, in addition to advertising normally conducted by the company's various divisions. TV and magazine advertising scheduled by PACE featured Elsie in real-life situations with real people. A 1963 Eagle Brand condensed milk spot featured an actress in a kitchen and a tiny, animated, fairylike Elsie perched on a shelf.

At the 1964–65 New York World's Fair, Borden staged a revue called "All About Elsie." In July 1964 the company signed the Fischer quintuplets, the most famous multiple-birth family of the era, to a three-year contract. In October of that year, Borden expanded its TV show coverage from eight to ten daytime programs on ABC and NBC. In January 1965, Borden promoted a host of products in 11 ads and a 24-page Eagle Brand cookbook insert in *Better Homes & Gardens* magazine, an effort coordinated by Y&R. Daytime TV advertising remained strong. But faced with the growing challenge of portraying Elsie in spots and the mounting costs of showcasing her on the road, the Borden icon again began to disappear from the consumer's daily life. An attempt was made to retire Elsie completely and develop a new Borden trademark, but a survey showed she was still one of the most recognized and beloved trademarks in the country.

In March 1966, the U.S. Supreme Court upheld a Federal Trade Commission decision that Borden must justify differences between Borden brand canned milk and private brand milk packed by Borden on the basis of cost, effectively ruling that advertising does not add to a product's value. Dissenting Justice Potter Stewart wrote, "The product purchased by the consumer includes not only the chemical components that any competent laboratory can itemize, but also a host of commercial intangibles that distinguish the product in the marketplace. The premium price paid for Borden brand milk reflects the consumer's awareness, promoted through advertising, that these commercial attributes are part and parcel of the premium product he is purchasing."

Fall 1966 found Borden recalling its Starlac product after traces of salmonella were discovered in samples. Soon after, the company became the first in the United States to use the U.S. Department of Agriculture inspection shield on its new product, Borden's Instant Nonfat dry milk, which premiered with heavy print and TV ad schedules plus point-of-purchase materials.

New Agencies, New Lines

In 1968 the company changed its name to Borden, Inc., and began running spots for milk, ice cream, and its food and chemical divisions during NBC's *Huntley-Brinkley Report*. This marked Borden's first connection with a major TV news program. In December 1968, Y&R resigned about $3 million in billings from Borden, Inc., effectively terminating its 40-year relationship with the company. Ross Roy, Inc., of New York City, won the cheese products business in March 1969. In 1970 Borden's total ad budget, in excess of $35 million, was divided among 18 agencies, including Tracy-Locke, of Dallas, Texas, which had the milk and ice cream accounts. In its biggest one-time ad venture to date, Borden cosponsored NBC's daylong coverage of the presidential inauguration in January 1969. The eight hours of coverage included 39 spots on TV and 17 minutes of radio commercials.

By 1970 Borden also marketed Wyler soups, ReaLemon concentrate, and Cracker Jack caramel popcorn. Lite Line ice milk and cottage cheese were introduced in limited markets in 1969 following the launch of Lite Line 99 percent fat-free milk the previous year. Despite these new products, Borden's dairy and services division closed some operations and consolidated others as the 1960s drew to a close. It withdrew from the milk business in the New York metropolitan area in 1970 because of unfavorable market conditions, terminated operations at some northern California dairy plants, and then stopped marketing milk and other dairy products in California.

In March 1970 Borden reentered outdoor advertising after almost a decade-long absence, with its dairy and services division promoting products primarily in the Midwest, South, and Southwest. In April 1970 a million-dollar magazine and Sunday supplement campaign broke with the theme, "Think cheese—think Borden."

Elsie Redux

Borden's sales exceeded $2 billion in 1971. With the help of technological advances, an animated Elsie returned to TV advertising that year in the first of several commercials geared to children. Elsie was also reborn on the travel circuit. About this time Grey Advertising, which had won the cheese account, created a costumed "spokesmouse" in TV spots introducing Lite Line cheese. A few years later, the agency signed tennis star Chris Evert to promote Skim American Slices. By 1988 Borden's sales had climbed to $7.2 billion. But the domestic dairy business was downsized in 1991 when the company withdrew from some highly competitive fluid milk and cultured product markets in the East, Southeast, and Midwest. An updated, fully animated Elsie returned to national TV in 1993 as the proprietor of Elsie's Market in a campaign from Grey.

An agreement for the affiliates of the investment firm Kohlberg Kravis Roberts & Company (KKR) to acquire all the shares of Borden was announced in September 1994. The affiliates completed the acquisition in March 1995. Through a 1997 licensing agreement with Borden and BDH Two, Inc., the Dairy Farmers of America (DFA), the largest dairy co-op in North America, obtained the rights to use the Borden and Elsie trademarks. DFA maintained Elsie's trademark on all packages of Borden Dairy branded products, gave her cameos in TV spots, and feted her 60th birthday at a Barnyard Bash in New York City's Bryant Park in 1999. American Dairy Brands, the marketing division of DFA for Borden branded products, is headquartered in Columbus, Ohio.

BBDO Worldwide, of Chicago, Illinois, which was awarded the Borden's Singles and Naturals cheese account in late 1998, introduced the tag line, "Borden brings the dairy home," in a pair of 1999 spots. They featured live-action cows enhanced by special effects and a cameo of an animated, winking Elsie. A national print campaign for Borden's Singles, also featuring Elsie, ran in the spring and summer of 2001.

CHRISTINE BUNISH

Further Reading

"Ads Don't Raise Value of Goods: High Court," *Advertising Age* (28 March 1966)

"Borden Co.'s Founder a Texas Firebrand," *Advertising Age* (16 October 1951)

Crowley, Carolyn Hughes, "The Man Who Invented Elsie, the Borden Cow," *Smithsonian Magazine* (September 1999)

"Ewen Tells How Borden Milked Elsie," *Advertising Age* (26 March 1962)

Bozell Group

(Bozell & Jacobs)

Founded as Bozell & Jacobs in Omaha, Nebraska, 1921, by Leo Bozell and Morris Jacobs; grew slowly but steadily on the basis of many public utility accounts; joined in 1958 by Charles Peebler, who became president, 1965; bought Emerson Foote, Inc., 1967, and moved headquarters to New York City; acquired by Lorimar, 1985, and merged with Kenyon & Eckhardt, 1986, to become Bozell Jacobs Kenyon & Eckhardt (BJK&E); bought back from Lorimar in 1988; BJK&E became holding company, 1992, and Bozell & Jacobs, as Bozell Worldwide, undertook the firm's advertising function; acquired by True North Communications, 1997; True North—and with it Bozell—acquired by Interpublic Group of Companies, 2001.

Major Clients

American Airlines
Boys Town
Merrill Lynch
Mutual of Omaha Insurance Company
National Fluid Milk Processor Education Program
National Pork Producers Council
Nebraska Power Company
Serta Mattress

Bozell & Jacobs (B&J) began in 1921 as an extracurricular activity of Morris Jacobs, a night police reporter for the *Bee-News* in Omaha, Nebraska, and Leo Bozell, a former editor of the *Omaha Daily News* then working for the local real estate board. The two men had met at the *Daily News* when Jacobs covered local business and Bozell was his editor. Their moonlighting venture was more public relations than advertising, a distinction neither considered important. Their work was good enough to attract the Nebraska Power Company, whose business enabled Bozell and Jacobs to put journalism behind them by 1923 and form a full-time agency. It was also an account that would typecast the new enterprise as a regional utilities shop.

Expansion

Five years later, the business of the Omaha & Council Bluffs Street Railway made it possible for B&J to open its first office outside of Omaha in Council Bluffs, Iowa. A third office opened in Chicago, Illinois, in 1934 under Morris's brother Nate Jacobs, and a fourth and fifth had been established in Houston, Texas, and Indianapolis, Indiana, by 1939.

It was a non-utility, pro bono account, however, that gained a national spotlight for the agency: Boys Town, the Nebraska orphanage started by Father Edward Flanagan. A B&J corporate history credits Morris Jacobs with coming up with the name and the PR push that eventually led to two motion pictures featuring Boys Town and starring Spencer Tracy and Mickey Rooney.

Amid the long list of utilities, a few consumer brands appeared by 1942, including Roper Ranges and the Amling Company, a florist chain. But overwhelmingly the pattern of B&J over its first four decades would be slow but steady growth within its utility and banking niche. In 1937 billings stood at less than $5 million, a level the agency would not exceed for another eight years. Meanwhile, the network of offices spread: Dallas, Texas (1939), Shreveport, Louisiana (1940), Seattle, Washington (1945), Minneapolis, Minnesota (1946, the year Leo Bozell died at 60), Los Angeles, California (1947), New York City and Washington, D.C. (1949), Baltimore, Maryland (1953), and on and on.

The agency's highest profile account was Mutual of Omaha, sponsor in the 1960s and 1970s of the weekly television show, *Wild Kingdom*. According to Chuck Peebler, who joined B&J in 1958, the agency grew steadily until the 1950s, then hit a plateau.

The B&J structure was far flung but extremely shallow and fragmented. Between 1951 and 1956 billings rose from $9.3 million to $20 million, healthy growth by any standard. But the total depended on a huge base of clients, each with only modest individual spending. By 1960, B&J's entry in the *Standard Directory of Advertising Agencies* filled six pages and listed more than 350 clients billing a static $20 million. By comparison, its future partner, Kenyon & Eckhardt, stood at nearly $90 million on a base of about 25 clients.

"B&J came from a different milieu," Peebler told *Advertising Age*. "We were not a club agency. We played the game differently. We did what people said couldn't be done. You couldn't move from here to there, you couldn't build simultaneously. The press never understood us because we didn't start in a center that was on their radar screen."

All that began to change in 1958 when Peebler came aboard. A native of Omaha, born in 1936, he had dropped out of Drake University with youthful dreams of a career in tennis. One of his regular tennis partners was department store owner J. L. Brandies, who induced Peebler to join his company and train for management. Peebler never returned for his junior year and after two and a half years ended up supervising a staff of 150, collecting a bonus equal to his starting salary, and fully expecting to become the youngest president of Brandies & Sons.

He might have, too, if he had not met and married another Brandies employee Susie Jacobs, whose father, Morris, at age 63, was eager to build a young management team of his own to take over B&J. Jacobs had a better offer for his new son-in-law. Thus, in 1958 Peebler joined the agency as the heir apparent. He became president in 1965. "I guess I would say I got where I am on talent," he once told *Advertising Age*, "but it certainly didn't hurt to have the boss's attention." (The marriage ended in divorce in 1977.)

In Peebler's first year as president, billings rose from $20 million to $23 million. He expanded the agency's profile outside of Omaha, and in 1967 he took on a living legend in advertising. Emerson Foote, 60, a founding partner of Foote, Cone & Belding and the man who ran the agency's Lucky Strike account for ten years, was coming out of a misbegotten partnership and needed money. Peebler needed connections and a stronger New York City office. In August of 1967 B&J bought Emerson Foote, Inc., for $500,000 and thus acquired a New York billing base of about $7 million. Added to the B&J New York billings, it gave the agency an eastern base of nearly $10 million. Foote remained with B&J as director and consultant for the next decade.

Entering the Big Time

Three months after the Foote acquisition, Morris Jacobs retired and sold controlling interest to Peebler, who became chief executive officer (CEO), and Alan Jacobs, a nephew. Peebler spun off B&J's offices in Minneapolis, Washington, D.C., and New York City to their executives and began to spend more time in New York, where Foote's offices at 575 Lexington became not only

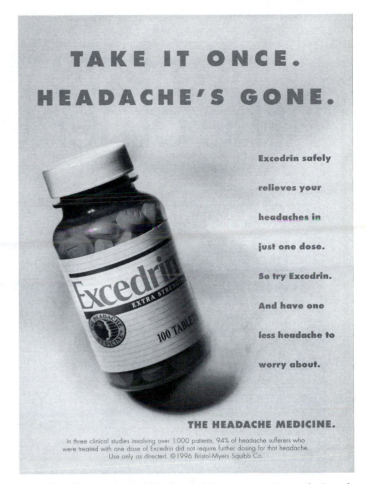

One of Bozell's most successful efforts of the 1990s was its marketing of Excedrin as "The Headache Medicine." Commercials from this campaign were memorable for the testimonial statement, "I had a headache THIS BIG, but I took Excedrin and it's gone."
Courtesy of Bristol-Myers Squibb Co.

B&J's eastern flagship but also the new corporate headquarters. The ties to Omaha were being cut. With a strong New York base not dependent on utilities, B&J began its move into the big time. Over the next five years the agency added more billings than it had in its previous 45 years, reaching $50 million on its 50th anniversary in 1971.

Though the account roster still lacked sparkle, Peebler pressed on with a strategy of agency acquisition that was generating momentum. The plan received a big boost in 1974 when B&J acquired Glenn Advertising of Dallas, a $29 million agency package that included pieces of American Airlines and Quaker Oats.

B&J acquired talent as well as billing and account muscle on its buying spree. Along with Glenn Advertising came its vice chairman, J. Liener Temerlin, whose agency, Temerlin McClain, would become a $550 million asset in the Bozell holding company. And in 1975 the purchase of Knox Reeves in Minneapolis brought B&J its first General Mills business along with its future chairman, David Bell, who assumed the title of CEO of Bozell

Have you tried the other white meat?

Pork Kiev

Pork Primavera

Pork à la King

Pork Divan

Pork Marsala

Pork Au Vin

If you think you have to serve fish or fowl to get the light, wholesome nutrition and easy convenience that today's life-styles demand, take a fresh look at pork — the *other* white meat.

Pork gives you the lighter meals and versatility you associate with white meat. Plus, it provides you and your family the great taste you want, and the nutrition and protein you need.

And of course the mouth-watering taste and savory flavor of pork blend deliciously with all kinds of sauces, spices, stuffings and side dishes.

Pork can easily be substituted for any other white meat in many recipes — in fact, in most meal preparation.

With a variety of new, leaner boneless cuts of pork to choose from, your menu plans have more flexibility than ever.

What's the best way to cook pork?

Often.

For a free recipe book containing light, easy, nutritious and creative ways to serve new meals with pork, just send a stamped self-addressed envelope to Pork Recipes, Box 10383-B, Des Moines, Iowa 50306.

The Other White Meat.

This message is brought to you by America's pork producers.

1987 National Pork Producers Council in cooperation with National Pork Board.

Bozell's "The Other White Meat" campaign successfully positioned pork as a healthy alternative to chicken.
Courtesy of Bozell Chicago.

Worldwide in 1996. Worldwide Creative Director Ron Anderson, creative mentor to Tom McElligott, Nancy Rice, and Jay Schulberg, Bozell's chief idea potentate at century's end, also joined the B&J talent pool.

B&J was now a $100 million company with certified membership in the top-20 club of American agencies. By 1979 it had nearly tripled to $287 million. One night in the Manhattan restaurant 21, Peebler walked over to congratulate Leo-Arthur Kelmenson of Kenyon & Eckhardt, a man he had never met, on his success in landing the huge Chrysler account. Neither man knew at the time that their biggest deal was still ahead of them.

They would meet again in 1985 when Lorimar Pictures, then the production company behind such popular TV shows as *The Waltons, Dallas, Knots Landing,* and later *Falcon Crest,* became interested in acquiring a major ad agency in order to vertically integrate sponsorship and production in one company. In a way, it was an effort to reconstitute the old network radio model, in which advertisers produced and controlled the content of the programs they sponsored. To this end Lorimar had bought Kenyon & Eckhardt in 1983.

Lorimar's stock went from 20 to 31 in six months, and by 1985 it had a reserve of $58 million in financing for more purchases. Chairman Merv Adelson talked about being a "communications company," and Adelson's partner, Lee Rich, a former Benton and Bowles executive who had worked with Sheldon Leonard to secure *The Dick Van Dyke Show* for Procter & Gamble, knew that the stability of a couple of big agencies could help smooth the boom-and-bust cycle of TV production.

In 1985 Lorimar put together the 14th largest agency in the country by acquiring B&J for $41 million and merging it with K&E. Peebler, who had been looking for a suitor with international links and a proper dowry, became CEO. At the time B&J was billing $808 million, compared with $412 million for K&E. "One of the reasons we got together with K&E," Bell told *Advertising Age,* "was that in order to jump start our growth, we really had to merge with somebody. When we decided K&E was a logical partner, we had to sell ourselves to Lorimar to do it." Peebler decided on a six-month trial before consummating the merger. In January 1986, B&J became BJK&E, with combined billings of more than $1 billion.

If the agency merger worked well, however, the combination with Lorimar did not. The failure to exert leadership at the holding company level left B&J and K&E to function largely autonomously while Lorimar went shopping for theme parks and other ventures. Meanwhile, K&E won Merrill Lynch, and B&J introduced "the other white meat" for the National Pork Producers Council.

But Lorimar started losing money. When BJK&E decided to buy itself back on 19 February 1988, the holding company did not fight the effort. It was glad to receive the cash windfall of $133 million. In 1987, shortly before the buy-back, Morris Jacobs died. He had lived to see his part-time agency of 1921 grow to nearly $1.4 billion—roughly the size of the entire federal budget the year he and Leo Bozell had begun the business.

Growth: the Only Option

K&E and B&J went into Lorimar as prominent midsize domestic agencies. They came out as BJK&E, on the threshold of the top tier of international agency holding companies, with 55 offices in 39 countries and positioned to nearly double its size in the next eight years. Among its accounts would be J.C. Penney, Excedrin, Scott Paper, Taco Bell, and Bell Atlantic. Growth became something of an obsession. "Because it avoids the opposite," said Bell, "in this business you must grow. There is no option."

In 1992 BJK&E reorganized; all agency functions were consolidated under the nameplate Bozell Worldwide, while BJK&E assumed the role of holding company for present and future agencies. The former made the ads, according to Peebler, the latter the deals. Growth continued in 1994 when Chrysler awarded all of its North American Jeep/Eagle business to Bozell, and the agency acquired the Detroit office of Campbell Mithun Esty. That same year the "milk mustache" campaign for the National Fluid Milk Processor Board was also launched.

In the fourth quarter of 1997, BJK&E was acquired in a friendly merger with True North Communications, Inc., the holding company of FCB Worldwide. The deal dissolved BJK&E as an entity and put Bozell Worldwide in the True North family along with former BJK&E holdings Poppe Tyson, Temerlin McClain, Bozell Sawyer Miller Group, McCracken Brooks, Bozell Wellness Worldwide, and the BJK&E Media Group. At the time of the merger, combined billings stood at $3.675 billion. David Bell subsequently became chairman of True North. In 2000 the agency, then known as Bozell Group, had U.S. gross income of $136.5 million, up 19 percent over 1999, on billings of $1.4 billion.

In March 2001 it was announced that True North Communications would be acquired by the Interpublic Group of Companies for $2.1 billion in stock, a move that would make Interpublic the world's largest advertising organization. At the time of the announcement the Bozell Group and Temerlin McClain were among the advertising agencies (along with FCB Worldwide) within the True North family. The merger created a company whose combined revenues would equal $7.2 billion, based on 2000 numbers.

JOHN MCDONOUGH

Further Reading

"BJK&E Buys Itself Back . . . ," *Wall Street Journal* (22 February 1988)

Dugas, Christine, and Paul B. Brown, "How Five Advertising Agencies Ran for the Bull," *Business Week* (14 April 1986)

Jacobs, Morris E., "You Ought to Know," *Advertising Age* (25 August 1958)

Kanner, Bernice, "Hollywood Squares," *New York Magazine* (16 May 1988)

McDonough, John, "Bozell at 75: A Commemorative," *Advertising Age* (8 April 1996)

Pauly, David, "J.R. Takes on Hollywood," *Newsweek* (9 September 1985)

Brand

The word *brand* has many meanings. It can mean the name by which a product, service, or organization is known. Coca-Cola, for example, is the name of a sweet carbonated beverage. FedEx is the name of an overnight delivery service. Merrill Lynch is the name of a company that supplies a variety of financial services.

But a brand is always more than its name. It is the unique combination of marketing characteristics that the brand name signifies. It is, first of all, a product, a service, or an organization with functional and performance characteristics that may, in turn, be extended into a number of brand variants. A brand typically has a price that reflects a pricing strategy. It is available in some retail outlets or venues but not others, and its sales are supported by networks of intermediaries such as sales organizations, dealer or franchise networks, and distributors. Finally, it is promoted in various ways: price promotions; promotions to build consumer loyalty; or promotions to link the brand to various activities (such as soccer or auto racing) and the star performers of those activities.

The brand name itself is given as broad exposure to customers and potential customers as possible. The name appears on billboards, in sports stadiums, as a sponsor of various activities and events, on race cars, on blimps, on apparel, and on anything else that can call attention to it. Above all, media advertising can send a consistent and positive message about the brand to a large potential audience.

A brand is a marketing entity with characteristics that distinguish it from competitive brands and from unbranded commodities. This collection of distinctive characteristics determines what the brand is and how it will perform for its customers. They provide the basis for consumer satisfaction, or the lack of it, in the use or consumption of the brand.

It is the task of the manufacturer to make sure that each of its brand entities, through its characteristics, promises and delivers distinctive benefits to customers and potential customers. If the maker does not ensure that its brand is distinctively attractive to this audience, most likely it will not survive.

Brand Managers and Branding

In most corporations the marketing responsibility for the brand resides at two levels. At the corporate level the responsibility for fundamental strategic development of the brand—basic decisions about product development and design, pricing, and distribution—are usually assumed by a core executive group, with the help of departments dedicated to specific functions. Such departments normally include research and development, product development, product design, distribution management, and consumer marketing.

The day-to-day tactical responsibility for making sure that the brand is attractive to consumers belongs to the brand manager, who typically functions within the marketing department. This person is responsible for managing all of the individual components of the brand and for combining them in a way that will attract buyers.

Designing and maintaining brands at both the strategic and the tactical levels is called "branding." Branding is what is done to create a unique and positive reputation for a given product. When a customer purchases a branded product or service or does business with a branded organization, he is buying what amounts to a group of perceptions that has been created by the branding process.

These consumer perceptions are formed by personal experience with the brand itself; by word-of-mouth impressions received from friends, relatives, and salespersons; brand name appearances; brand promotions; and brand advertising. The brand manager does his or her best to channel and control these consumer perceptions, but realistically, much of this perception formation by customers and potential customers is out of the brand manager's hands.

The process of branding involves a continuous interaction between the strategic and tactical brand programs and the final consumer perception of these programs, filtered through experience and the attitudes of others. Only the consumer can determine whether a particular brand at a particular time provides a promise of acceptable personal satisfaction.

Brand Image

A brand image is the collective impression people carry around in their heads about a given brand. It is the information—positive or negative—that a person has collected and distilled, consciously or unconsciously, about an individual brand. It is what remains after a person has been exposed to strategic branding activities, personal experience, word of mouth, promotion, and advertising.

Not all consumers have an image of every brand. Even those who do will not necessarily like or be attracted to all of the brands they know something about. But each successful brand generates consumer perceptions of distinctiveness that make it attractive to a mass market. It is typical for several competing brands in a product category to generate positive consumer images, and a consumer will frequently have positive images of competitive brands. Thus, branding is not a winner-take-all game.

Advertising is a controllable means of creating images about brands. But advertising is only a part of how information about a brand is communicated. Other elements of distinctiveness include the brand name itself, functional product characteristics, pricing characteristics, and distribution characteristics. There are relatively few brands that are distinctive solely because of the content of their advertising. In most cases advertising serves as a vehicle to communicate the other elements of brand distinctiveness. As these elements erode under competitive pressure, however, advertising may be called upon increasingly to bear the burden of maintaining successful branding. In some product categories brands exist without special distinctiveness. These are called parity products. For example, many major, nationally distributed brands of beer

The PENALTY OF LEADERSHIP

IN every field of human endeavor, he that is first must perpetually live in the white light of publicity. ¶Whether the leadership be vested in a man or in a manufactured product, emulation and envy are ever at work. ¶In art, in literature, in music, in industry, the reward and the punishment are always the same. ¶The reward is widespread recognition; the punishment, fierce denial and detraction. ¶When a man's work becomes a standard for the whole world, it also becomes a target for the shafts of the envious few. ¶If his work be merely mediocre, he will be left severely alone—if he achieve a masterpiece, it will set a million tongues a-wagging. ¶Jealousy does not protrude its forked tongue at the artist who produces a commonplace painting. ¶Whatsoever you write, or paint, or play, or sing, or build, no one will strive to surpass, or to slander you, unless your work be stamped with the seal of genius. ¶Long, long after a great work or a good work has been done, those who are disappointed or envious continue to cry out that it can not be done. ¶Spiteful little voices in the domain of art were raised against our own Whistler as a mountebank, long after the big world had acclaimed him its greatest artistic genius. ¶Multitudes flocked to Bayreuth to worship at the musical shrine of Wagner, while the little group of those whom he had dethroned and displaced argued angrily that he was no musician at all. ¶The little world continued to protest that Fulton could never build a steamboat, while the big world flocked to the river banks to see his boat steam by. ¶The leader is assailed because he is a leader, and the effort to equal him is merely added proof of that leadership. ¶Failing to equal or to excel, the follower seeks to depreciate and to destroy—but only confirms once more the superiority of that which he strives to supplant. ¶There is nothing new in this. ¶It is as old as the world and as old as the human passions—envy, fear, greed, ambition, and the desire to surpass. ¶And it all avails nothing. ¶If the leader truly leads, he remains—the leader. ¶Master-poet, master-painter, master-workman, each in his turn is assailed, and each holds his laurels through the ages. ¶That which is good or great makes itself known, no matter how loud the clamor of denial. ¶That which deserves to live—lives.

Cadillac Motor Car Co. Detroit, Mich.

This celebrated ad created a strong brand identity for Cadillac and has been lauded as one of the greatest automobile ads ever created. *Used with permission of General Motors Corporation media archives.*

Modess... *because*

For decades ads for Modess featured neither text nor images of the product, which sold on the strength of the brand name alone. *Courtesy of the Johnson & Johnson Company.*

fall into this category. But such brands gain distinctiveness through pervasive market presence. Budweiser is an example of a product that has overwhelming retail presence and allegiance because it has earned general customer acceptance simply because of the satisfaction it is known to give. Such brands also depend to an important degree on high brand exposure through tactical advertising and promotion to sustain their market share. This objective is accomplished in two ways.

First, the presence of large amounts of advertising for the brand reinforces and extends the inherent market presence of such brands. And second, advertising may also create a sense of value for the brand that reinforces the reality of its market presence.

The most compelling basis for brand distinctiveness is almost inevitably intrinsic brand characteristics rather than the extrinsic emotional attractions generated by advertising. It is usually the job of effective advertising only to provide a tactical basis of brand distinctiveness built into the product.

Focus on Advertising

In spite of the fact that advertising is only one component in a collection of ongoing marketing activities, advertising still seems to have a dominant role when marketers think about branding and brand management. There are three major reasons for this.

First, advertising reaches consumers and potential customers directly with a message designed to interest and influence them, independent of actual contact with the product. It provides a variety of ways and means to present a product's characteristics and virtues. And inherent in this flexibility is a license for the advertiser to control and manipulate what consumers come to believe about the product. Consumers may pay only limited attention to the brand's advertising. But advertising and the sales message it carries give the advertiser the opportunity to direct and enhance what consumers think about the brand.

Second, advertising has the potential to become a sales multiplier. Even if this does not happen either predictably or often, marketers usually believe that it is a possibility, and this is enough to keep marketers thinking enthusiastically about advertising as a continuing marketing tool.

Finally, and by far most important, is the fact that, of all the components that can contribute significantly to successful branding, advertising is the easiest, fastest, and least expensive to change. A new campaign can be conceptualized and produced in a matter of weeks. In addition, the cost of such new advertisements is, in the overall scheme of things, relatively modest. The largest cost in an advertising campaign is typically the media expense. Since media budgets are normally established on an ongoing basis, the only additional cost in changing advertising is in producing the new ads. It is much more difficult—and more expensive—to change the functional characteristics, pricing strategy, or distribution channels of a product. And before any of these can be changed, an alternative product, pricing approach, or distribution system must first exist.

Finding a new way to promote a product is not particularly difficult. The most easily available promotional option involves nothing more than lowering the price over the short term. Most marketers understand, however, that such price-cutting does little to enhance the brand's image and may lower the perceived value. At best, it can lead only to short-term sales responses. Thus, when the brand manager feels that something must be done with a brand, that some positive tactical step must be taken to improve its fortunes, it is always an easy, relatively painless decision to change the advertising.

For all of these reasons, advertising is likely to receive far more attention in the process of brand building than it may deserve on the basis of clear sales results. Whether the preoccupation with advertising is rational or not is beside the point; it is a reality. Only rarely does advertising actually expand the market in a mature product category such as bath soap, cigarettes, or beer. Its function typically is to allocate share of the market among competing brands, to attract new consumers at the expense of a competitor in the same product category.

This is not an insignificant goal, but it is a goal of considerably less consequence than most marketers routinely assume that advertising can accomplish. Advertising exists in a world in which consumers perceive brands in a variety of ways that are influenced by many branding and marketing actions in addition to advertising. Consumer brand choices are certainly affected by these collective marketing activities. Individual brand choices on particular shopping occasions are attributable to specific tactical brand marketing actions, including advertising. But the net effect of the day-to-day interplay of all marketing activities over time, including advertising, is the long-term maintenance of brand market share. Thus advertising, either alone or in concert with other activities, may exert a strong force in a particular purchase situation, but it may turn out to be only a weak force over time as the collective interplay of all marketing initiatives unfolds.

Brand Loyalty

The net effect of branding activity is to attract consumers to individual brands. In an ideal marketing world the collective force of branding would make individual consumers loyal to individual brands. This so-called brand loyalty would, then, cause individual consumers to purchase a particular brand consistently, constantly reinforcing the brand's market share. There is a good deal of continuing discussion among marketers about brand loyalty and a good deal of speculation about the best ways to create it. There is a growing body of evidence, particularly for package good brands, that consumers do not routinely become loyal to individual brands in particular product categories. Rather, consumers seem to identify a small number of acceptable brands. These form a "repertoire of brands," in the words of A.S.C. Ehrenberg, the Scottish statistician who has studied this phenomenon closely since the 1960s. For most consumers any brand within this repertoire is acceptable for purchase at any particular time, but over

time purchases will be spread almost randomly among all the brands in the person's repertoire.

This is why brands and branding are of such concern to marketers. Successful marketing depends upon creating a continuing excellence in all branding activities. Marketers that try to rest on their laurels are doomed to failure in the intense competition of brand marketing.

WILLIAM M. WEILBACHER

Further Reading

Aaker, David A., *Managing Brand Equity: Capitalizing on the Value of a Brand Name,* New York: Free Press, 1991

Aaker, David A., *Building Strong Brands,* New York: Free Press, 1996

Ehrenberg, A.S.C., *Repeat-Buying,* New York: American Elsevier, and London: North-Holland, 1972; new edition, New York: Oxford University Press, and London: Griffin, 1988

Jones, John P., *What's in a Name? Advertising and the Concept of Brands,* Lexington, Massachusetts: Lexington Books, and Aldershot, Hampshire: Gower, 1986

Kapferer, Jean-Noël, *Strategic Brand Management,* London: Kogan Page, 1992; New York: Free Press, 1994; 2nd edition, London and Dover, New Hampshire: Kogan Page, 1997

Steel, Jon, *Truth, Lies, and Advertising: The Art of Account Planning,* New York: Wiley, 1998

Weilbacher, William M., *Brand Marketing: Building Winning Brand Strategies That Deliver Value and Customer Satisfaction,* Lincolnwood, Illinois: NTC Business Books, 1993

Bravo Navalpotro, Julián 1936–

Spanish Advertising Executive

An advertising professional, entrepreneur, advertising researcher, scholar, and publisher, Julián Bravo Navalpotro has established a reputation as one of the foremost men in Spanish advertising. According to a 1994 survey of 50 leading Spanish advertising professionals, he ranks as one of the key figures of all time in Spanish advertising.

Bravo was born in Campisábalos, in the Spanish province of Guadalajara, on 14 February 1936. In 1958 he received a law degree, and he completed his university training in 1963 with a degree in business administration. He therefore belongs to the first generation of university graduates to enter the advertising profession in Spain.

In 1962 Bravo took a job with the advertising firm Publinsa, Kenyon & Eckhardt as an account executive. He worked at the

New York City office of Kenyon & Eckhardt from December 1963 to May 1964, and a year later he wrote his first study on advertising, which won second prize in the awards competition run by Alas, one of the most prominent Spanish advertising firms.

Spain was in the process of modernizing its economic and social systems in the 1960s, laying the groundwork for the economic transformation that came to be called the "Spanish miracle." It was during this period that the foundations of present-day advertising in Spain were established.

In the 1960s multinational advertising firms such as the J. Walter Thompson Company (JWT) expanded into Spain. Between 1964 and 1966 JWT was associated with the Spanish firm Alas, but in 1966 JWT established itself as an independent shop. On 1 May, Manuel Eléxpuru, one of the most highly regarded Spanish

Julián Bravo Navalpotro.
Courtesy of Julián Bravo Navalpotro.

advertising professionals, agreed to become general manager of JWT. Bravo left Publinsa, Kenyon & Eckhardt and was hired by JWT on 1 November. On 15 December, J. Walter Thompson, S.A., was officially established in Madrid.

Bravo would have a key role in the growth and expansion of the agency. In 1966 its clients included Camy ice cream, Ford Europa, Kodak, Nescafé, Pan Am, Rolex, and Liggett & Myers. In early 1967 the agency employed 22 people; by the end of the year, the staff had grown to 45. In 1969 the first governing board, made up of Bravo and three other members, was created. The agency was characterized by the constant growth of both its billings and staff as well as various innovations in business practices, including the improvement of the media department, the creation of the post of television program producer, and the application of the T Plan (which enacted JWT's philosophy that ads are not messages, but stimuli designed to produce a particular response from the consumer), as well as the production of the reports on advertising investment in Spain. With the founding in 1968 of the audience research organization Estudio General de Medios (EGM), Bravo, along with other agency members, advertisers, and media representatives, contributed to the professionalization of advertising in Spain. As a representative of JWT, Bravo was from the outset a member of the technical commission of EGM, a body that has proved to be a valuable instrument in the consolidation of audience research in Spain.

One of the characteristics of Bravo's professional life has been his close involvement with education, which he has combined with his career in advertising. In this way he has made an important contribution to the training of many Spanish advertising professionals. In 1971 the university degree in information sciences was created, with specialties available in journalism, audiovisual communication, and advertising and public relations. That same year Bravo, who had taught marketing to professionals in the Official School of Advertising of Madrid between 1965 and 1969, began to lecture on marketing in the School of Information Sciences of the Complutense University of Madrid, an activity he has since continued at other Spanish universities.

One of Bravo's principal concerns has been the professional excellence of future advertising professionals. He believes that advertisers must make an effort to train their staffs and create opportunities for young professionals and that universities must play a key role in preparing individuals to enter the field. According to Bravo, the profile of a good candidate for the field of advertising must include the desire to innovate, a broad cultural knowledge, and the willingness to work.

Bravo was appointed general manager of JWT in Spain during the presidency of Eléxpuru in 1974. Under Bravo's guidance the agency continued to increase its billings. In 1975 JWT Spain won the account of Ford Spain and launched the advertising campaign for the Fiesta car. Other new clients that year were Banco Pastor, Bacardi, Brummel, Monroe, Técnicas Reunidas, Seven-Up, Educa, and Williams Hispania. In 1983 JWT occupied the top place in a study conducted by McCann-Erickson on advertising agencies in Spain. According to its own sources, JWT had been number one in the ranking of agencies in Spain at least since 1975 and would continue in that position until 1987. In 1986 the Tom Sutton International Exchange Program was initiated, allowing young Spanish advertising professionals to spend a year in a JWT office in another country. JWT Spain already had considerable experience in the training of young people, one of Bravo's principal concerns, by means of a system of apprentice workshops.

One of Bravo's aims as general manager of JWT was excellence. He met his goals by establishing objectives and by assuring that his staff carried them through. Eléxpuru and Bravo were able to convert JWT Spain into an important Spanish firm while at the same time respecting its multinational nature. Indeed, by 1984 the agency was in charge of advertising for some 40 firms. All of its campaigns were created and produced in Spain, and only a few were exported. Only two campaigns were adaptations. JWT Spain won acclaim for its professional rigor and for the talent of its employees.

In 1980 Bravo began what would become an important contribution to modern advertising in Spain—the publication of a series of books on the subject. The bibliography of books on advertising in Spanish was rather thin in 1980, although there was a significant increase later in the decade and in the 1990s. Bravo believed that in order to understand the true function of advertising it was necessary to know the history of the field, including its origins, the changes it had undergone, and the leaders who had shaped the business. He therefore embarked on a project to make the classic works on advertising known in Spain. In 1980 he translated and published James Webb Young's *How to Become an Advertising Man* and published two books by Claude C. Hopkins, *Scientific Advertising* and *My Life in Advertising*. He also published Young's *A Technique for Producing Ideas*. Bravo's editorial work grew over time as additional books on advertising were published.

From 1981 to 1986 Bravo served as president of the Spanish Association of Advertising Agencies (AEAP), which was founded in 1977. Under his leadership the association was transformed into a highly professional body. The AEAP organized courses for

A 1976 ad, which announced both the arrival of the Ford Motor Company in Spain and the first Spanish-produced Ford automobile, captured the essence of Julián Bravo Navalpotro's design style. *Courtesy of Ford Motor Company.*

novices in the creative end of the business in Madrid and Barcelona, as well as courses for young account executives. Bravo created the Festival de Cine Publicitario, whose first meeting took place in Marbella and then moved to San Sebastián. In 1986 Bravo took an audiovisual exhibition on Spanish advertising in the 1980s to the Museo de Arte Contemporáneo of Madrid. At the same time, under his presidency the AEAP collaborated with music production houses to standardize the sound of television spots on Televisión Española. His term as head of the AEAP coincided with a period in which Spanish advertising experienced great growth in investment, number of brands advertised, and international recognition. In 1989 Spanish advertising agencies won the Grand Prize at the Cannes Festival as well as 24 Cannes Lions. According to one observer, this was the "definitive consecration" of Spanish advertising.

During the time he was president of the AEAP and up to 1987, Bravo was also involved as the director of and lecturer in seminars on "Advertising and New Technologies," "Advertising and the European Single Market," and "The Art of Advertising" at the International University Menéndez Pelayo (Santander). In 1984 he became a member of the board of the European Association of Advertising Agencies (EAAA) and in 1986 the treasurer of its executive committee.

In November 1987 Bravo was named executive president of the J. Walter Thompson Group in Spain and a member of the executive committee of JWT Europe. In 1988 he was elected to the board of directors of JWT Worldwide and appointed executive vice president. In the first year under Bravo's leadership a series of internal publications, *Cuadernos de Campaña*, was launched; Holos Media was created as a media planning and buying services company; a telephone marketing agency was founded;

and the agency incorporated two graphic design companies in Madrid and Barcelona. Between 1986 and 1991 the agency won more than 15 advertising awards. Under Bravo's presidency, agency billings continued to increase. By 1990 billings amounted to 18.704 million pesetas ($195 million), and there were 155 employees. The loyalty of JWT's clients was legendary, and in 1991 the agency had been working for Camy, Nescafé, Kodak, and Rolex for 26 years; Kraft and Sunsilk for 24 years; Lux for 23 years; Findus for 22 years; and DeBeers for 20 years. In October 1992 Bravo resigned from the presidency of the J. Walter Thompson Group in Spain as well as from his post on the executive committee of JWT Europe. In November he left the executive vice presidency and the board of directors of JWT Worldwide and the EAAA.

In 1993 Bravo worked as a consultant. That same year Jacques Delors, president of the Commission of the European Community, appointed him a consultant to that body. Along with three other external specialists he formed a working group, presided over by Willy De Clercq, which wrote the "Report on the Information and Communication Policy of the European Community."

In 2002 Bravo was executive president of the Association for Research of the Communications Media (AIMC), founded in 1988. The AIMC's membership includes advertisers, advertising agencies, media firms, television digital platforms, cable television operators, film businesses, press editors, radio stations, and television channels, as well as advertising consultants and researchers. Among other activities, the AIMC operates the EGM, audits the television audiometry system Television Audience Research System, and conducts research on Internet and cinema audiences as well as outdoor advertising.

Through his associations with JWT, the AEAP, the EGM, universities, and the field of publishing, Bravo has been a major figure in the development of modern Spanish advertising. His work as an educator of advertising professionals, his efforts in all areas within the agency, and his organizational activity in support of advertising have all elevated the quality of advertising in Spain.

FRANCISCO VERDERA

Biography
Born in Campisábalos, province of Guadalajara, Spain, 1936; received degrees in law and in business administration in 1958 and 1963, respectively; helped establish J. Walter Thompson Spain, 1966; appointed general manager of the agency, 1974; named president of the J. Walter Thompson Group in Spain and member of the executive committee of J. Walter Thompson Europe, 1987; elected executive vice president and member, board of directors, J. Walter Thompson Worldwide, 1988; resigned from JWT, 1992; became a full-time consultant, 1993; named as a consultant to the European Union, 1993.

Selected Publications
"El papel clave de las agencias en la historia de la publicidad," *Publicidad* 28 (1973)

J. Walter Thompson España de 1927–1936, 1978
"50 años de seducción: Historia subjetiva y desenfadada de la
    publicidad española" (with others), *Vogue GQ* (supplement to
    Vogue España) 70 (January 1994)

Further Reading
Esto no es un cuchillo de palo, Madrid: JWT, 1991
30 años de recuerdos, Estudio General de Medios, 1968–1998,
    Madrid: AIMC, 1998 Eguizábal Maza, Raúl, *Historia de la
    publicidad*, Madrid: Celeste, 1998

Brazil

Advertising in Brazil began to assume its contemporary shape and standards in the 1920s and 1930s when American business methods and organization were first introduced. This process began in 1926 when General Motors (GM) opened its Brazil advertising department in São Paulo. The department was instrumental in the early training of a group of Brazilian advertising professionals, forming what one Brazilian advertising man called the "initial nucleus" of the local offices of U.S. agencies, which began opening in the late 1920s and early 1930s. In 1929, however, GM's Brazil department was closed when the J. Walter Thompson Company (JWT) opened a São Paulo office to serve GM under a worldwide agreement between the automobile manufacturer and the advertising agency, making JWT the first U.S. advertising agency to establish full agency operations in Brazil.

JWT's Brazilian subsidiary, staffed by veterans of GM's advertising department, proved integral to the development of modern advertising in Brazil. The experience of working at JWT, or "Thompson," as the agency is known in Brazil, defined a generation of advertising professionals who learned their craft through JWT's celebrated trainee system. JWT's São Paulo office was largely responsible for the expanding use of photography in print advertising during this period, replacing the line drawings that had dominated the medium.

With JWT serving General Motors in Brazil, Ford was forced to import its own advertising agency, N.W. Ayer and Son, which opened an office in São Paulo in 1931 and one in Rio de Janeiro later in the decade (JWT had already opened an office in Rio by this time). Notably, Ayer carried out the most impressive market research of the period, an investigation for the National Department of Coffee that reached 12,000 consumers and 3,000 retailers in 19 states. It was the first study to gauge personal preference and consumer habits on the national level.

McCann-Erickson followed Ayer and JWT to Brazil, opening an office in 1935 to serve Standard Oil. McCann distinguished itself as the first U.S. subsidiary headed by a Brazilian, Armando de Moraes Sarmento.

With the growth of the U.S. agencies, advertising in Brazil increased in both volume and sophistication. Outdoor advertising was perhaps the most visible manifestation of this increase, as billboards—many of them featuring automobiles and automobile-related goods—proliferated throughout Brazil's larger cities.

Radio advertising also expanded dramatically, with U.S. advertisers sponsoring news reports, music broadcasts, and radio dramas.

The decade of the 1930s was also an important period for the development of Brazilian agencies. In 1933 Cícero Leuenroth founded Standard, which enjoyed notable success. It acquired a full roster of clients, including Colgate-Palmolive and Shell, and

This 1930s revolutionary poster exhorts comrades to "Keep up the
struggle until victory is ours."
*Courtesy of the Rare Book, Manuscript, and Special Collections Library,
Duke University.*

DM9 Publicidade's award-winning 1997 ad advised motorists who plan to drive to extremes that they had "better buy a Honda motorcycle."

established the country's first in-house recording studio for radio advertising. In 1938 Inter-Americana was founded by Brazilian advertising professionals, including Armando D'Almeida, who had previously led his own eponymous agency representing the Foreign Advertising and Service Bureau in Brazil. By the end of the decade, it was estimated that there were 56 agencies operating in São Paulo and Rio de Janeiro.

Other local institutions founded in the 1930s included the Brazilian Advertising Association and the São Paulo Advertising Association. In July 1938 the first Brazilian Advertising Conference was held in Rio de Janeiro. The period also witnessed the introduction of the first Brazilian trade magazine, *Propaganda*. In 1941 the magazine *Publicidade* was founded; it would later become *PN*, the most important Brazilian trade publication of the postwar era.

With the advent of World War II, advertising in Brazil assumed new dimensions. The Office of the Coordinator of Inter-American Affairs, headed by Nelson Rockefeller, hired JWT to study Brazilian attitudes toward the United States, Nazi Germany, and the war in Europe. JWT also produced advertising, both in print and radio, designed to foster hemispheric unity for the war effort. U.S. advertisers and Brazilian agencies (such as Inter-Americana) spon-

sored campaigns to encourage goodwill toward the United States and promote the pan-American ideal; meanwhile, *Publicidade* published caricatures of the Nazi leaders.

In the immediate postwar era, JWT and McCann-Erickson dueled for supremacy in the Brazilian market after Ayer shut down its Brazilian offices in 1942. McCann-Erickson won one early victory with the acquisition of the Coca-Cola account in Brazil in 1948. The account became especially important for the agency internationally because it prompted the Atlanta, Georgia–based soft-drink marketer to abandon its commitment to D'Arcy, a firm established at the turn of the century, and give its worldwide accounts to McCann. (This international coup was especially significant given that Brazil consumes more Coca-Cola than any other country in the world, with the exception of the United States.)

As the two U.S. giants—JWT and McCann—fought for leadership in Brazil's expanding market, advertising production grew steadily. The training of Brazilian advertising professionals was first formalized with the 1951 founding of the Museum of Art of São Paulo's School of Advertising. One example of the preeminent role played by the U.S. agencies in training Brazilians prior to the founding of any such institutions was the government's award of

In a 1990s campaign for Heublein, "The Choice for Pleasure," DPZ Propaganda used elegant photography overlaid with scientific images, making the consumer's choice of Heublein products seem a mathematical certainty.

the Order of the Southern Cross—the highest honor Brazil can bestow upon a foreigner—to JWT-Brazil President Robert F. Merrick for "his contribution to the development of the advertising business, technically and ethically; to the creation of a highly qualified group of Brazilian professionals; and, through this, to the economic development of the country."

The advertising industry was also important in the growth and professionalization of the Brazilian media. New magazines such as *Manchete* (founded in 1950) featured color advertising for a variety of products, thereby providing these publications with much-needed revenue. In radio, advertising revenue helped build on the successes of the 1930s and 1940s as the number of stations and owners of sets continued to expand. (Private ownership, public ownership, and official encouragement of investment coexisted in the expansion of Brazilian radio.)

In the new medium of television, introduced to mass audiences with the broadcasts of TV Tupi in São Paulo in the early 1950s, advertisers adopted a system of sponsorship under which they imported U.S. programs or commissioned local productions (this system persisted until the rise of Brazilian television giant TV

Globo in the late 1960s and early 1970s), while U.S.-based agencies imported the technology to produce television advertising locally. Although in 1960 television accounted for only 6 percent of advertising revenue, the stage had been set for tremendous growth. By the 1980s television consumed more than 60 percent of all advertising expenditures in Brazil.

While moving into television during the 1950s, Brazilian advertising also expanded outward from the central cities of São Paulo and Rio de Janeiro. Local offices and independent agencies were opened in provincial capitals such as Belo Horizonte, Recife, Pôrto Alegre, and Salvador. At the close of the decade, agency services were extended to Brasília, the new federal capital.

In the 1960s U.S. preeminence in Brazil's advertising industry received its first significant challenges. Mauro Salles Publicidade, founded in 1966, was perhaps the most important Brazilian challenger, particularly after its merger with Inter-Americana in 1967. DPZ, founded by Roberto Duailibi, Francesc Petit, Jose Zaragoza, and Ronald Persichetti the following year, was another important domestic agency. These and other Brazilian agencies proved to be tough competitors for private-sector advertising revenue; meanwhile, the growing advertising budgets of the state and national governments naturally went to local agencies. These challenges prompted U.S. subsidiaries to promote Brazilian executives to the highest possible positions (previously reserved for Americans), even in the U.S. parent companies, in order to "nationalize" themselves.

By the end of the decade, nationalist sentiment and the rise of Brazilian agencies had reached the point where even the largest U.S. agencies were feeling threatened. JWT was at one time seriously considering a merger in which it would hand over day-to-day control of its Brazilian operations to Mauro Salles. These concerns, however, did not stop other U.S. agencies from investing in Brazilian shops. Ogilvy & Mather and Leo Burnett Company, for example, acquired minority interests in the Brazilian agencies Standard and CIN, respectively, during the late 1960s.

During the 1970s—the decade Brazilian advertising agent Fernando Reis termed the country's "golden age of advertising"— Brazilian agencies grew more quickly than their U.S. competitors. In 1971 industry insiders cited expenditures of $430 million as evidence of this expansion. By 1975 advertising in Brazil constituted more than 1 percent of the country's GNP. At the institutional level, observers gained a hint of what was to come in the 1990s as Standard, Brazil's most successful and long-lived domestic agency, became a wholly owned subsidiary of Ogilvy and Mather, Inc., in 1972. The 1970s were also marked by the rapid expansion of television advertising, now in color. Campaigns for a variety of products—domestic and foreign—reached millions of Brazilians through this relatively new medium over the course of the decade.

By the 1980s Brazilian advertising professionals were widely recognized as some of the world's most creative and able. In 1980 *Advertising Age* referred to DPZ as "one of the most creative [agencies] in the world." Between 1981 and 1989, Brazilians received 16 awards at the International Advertising Festival, held at Cannes, France, including two gold Lions, two silver Lions, and one bronze Lion. In 1987 at the Ibero-American advertising festival (FIAP) in Punta del Este, Uruguay, Brazil had more than 300 entries and shared with Spain some 70 percent of the prizes.

Recognition of the talents and abilities of Brazil's domestic advertising agents did not go unnoticed by trade organizations and, most importantly, advertisers. In 1981 Mauro Salles was elected president of the International Advertising Association (IAA), representing 1,100 delegates from 50 countries, thereby becoming the first Latin American to hold this prestigious position. By the end of the decade, domestic advertising agencies finally reached preeminence in the country as four agencies in which Brazilian nationals held majority ownership led the market.

Since the 1980s Brazilian advertising has expanded into new media and formalized existing forms of marketing and merchandising. The Brazilian agency Norton distinguished itself in the early 1990s as the first Latin American agency to expand into cyberspace and secure Internet accounts. Product placement on Brazilian evening soap operas, a uniquely Brazilian form of mer-

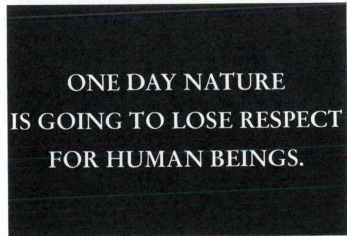

Standard O&M produced this critically acclaimed environmental advocacy ad for Brazilian media giant TV Gazeta in 1994.

chandising, continues to be integral to the marketing of consumer products. During the last 15 years of the 20th century, this form of merchandising benefited from the establishment of formal guidelines for the sale of product placement on television programs, replacing an older system somewhat prone to abuse, under which executives and producers or set designers negotiated such placement informally.

The move toward mergers and centralization that characterized much of the 1980s throughout the advertising world began to affect Brazil in a decisive manner in the 1990s, as multinational advertising concerns began to acquire substantial interests in Brazilian agencies. In June 1994 D'Arcy Masius Benton & Bowles (DMB&B) purchased a 40 percent interest in Salles/Inter-Americana de Publicidade. The resulting merger produced Salles/ D'Arcy Publicidade, then Brazil's second-largest agency. In 1996 Ogilvy & Mather acquired Denison Bates Advertising of São Paulo, making Standard O&M the largest agency in Brazil. That same year the French agency Publicis purchased a 60 percent share in Norton, which was renamed Publicis Norton. In 1997

DDB Needham Worldwide acquired a majority interest in São Paulo's DM9 Publicidade, creating the new DM9 DDB Publicidade agency.

Finally, Mercosur, the regional free-trade pact among Brazil, Argentina, Uruguay, and Paraguay, has opened an even larger potential market for Brazilian agencies and advertisers. The potential earnings for advertising agencies under Mercosur have been estimated at $4 billion per year, three-quarters of which are accounted for by Brazil.

McCann-Erickson Publicidade was the number-one agency in Brazil in 2000, with gross income for 2000 of $131.1 million on billings of $875.8 million, up 10.6 percent over 1999. J. Walter Thompson was second, with gross income of $78.5 million on billings of $345 million, up 32 percent. *Advertising Age* estimated that total gross income from advertising in Brazil in 2000 reached $929.3 million. Also in 2000 Brazil entered a total of 1,574 ads and campaigns in the Cannes festival, second only to the United States with 2,904 entries. Brazil's leading creative director, Marcello Serpa of Almap/BBDO in São Paulo, chaired the two main judging panels at Cannes that year.

JAMES P. WOODARD

Further Reading

"Brazilian Agencies Big on Creativity," *Advertising Age* (26 February 1973)

"Brazilian Agencies Growing Faster Than U.S. Shops," *Advertising Age* (19 February 1973)

"Brazil's Marketing Scene Reflects Nation's Growth," *Advertising Age* (12 February 1973)

Castelo Branco, Renato, Rodolfo Lima Martensen, and Fernando Reis, editors, *História da propaganda no Brasil*, São Paulo: Queiroz, 1990

Dougherty, Philip H., "Advertising; Brazilian Outlook: Expansionism," *New York Times* (15 March 1983)

Mattelart, Armand, *L'internationale publicitaire*, Paris: La Découverte, 1989; as *Advertising International: The Privatisation of Public Space,* translated by Michael Chanan, London and New York: Routledge, 1991

Riding, Alan, "On Brazilian TV, the Subtle Sell Pays Off Big, Too," *New York Times* (3 June 1988)

Tansey, Richard, Michael R. Hyman, and George M. Zinkhan, "Cultural Themes in Brazilian and U.S. Auto Ads: A Cross-Cultural Comparison," *Journal of Advertising* 19, no. 2 (1990)

Bristol-Myers Squibb Company

Principal Agencies

Geyer, Cornell & Newell, Inc. (later Cunningham & Walsh, Inc.)
Pedlar & Ryan, Inc.
Young & Rubicam, Inc.
Doherty, Clifford & Shenfield, Inc. (later DDB Needham)
Ogilvy, Benson & Mather, Inc. (later Ogilvy & Mather, Inc.)
Batten Barton Durstine & Osborn
Sullivan, Stauffer, Colwell & Bayles, Inc.
Ted Bates & Company, Inc.
Wells, Rich, Greene, Inc.
Foote, Cone & Belding Advertising, Inc.
Grey Advertising, Inc.
Corbett HealthConnect
Bozell Worldwide, Inc.

The Bristol-Myers Squibb Company traces its origins to 1887, when two former fraternity brothers, William McLaren Bristol, Sr., and John R. Myers invested $5,000 each in a failing Clinton, New York–based drug manufacturer, Clinton Pharmaceutical Company. After the usual early struggles, as well as the death of cofounder Myers in 1899, Bristol incorporated the company as the Bristol-Myers Company in 1900 in Brooklyn, New York. At first, the company made drugs for physicians, but after World War I it concentrated on the laxative Sal Hepatica and other over-the-counter proprietary drugs and entered the field of toiletries, notably with Ipana toothpaste. In 1929 Bristol-Myers was absorbed by a giant holding company, Drug, Inc., which dissolved during the Great Depression. In 1933 Bristol-Myers went public.

In 1943 the company returned to making drugs, and over the years it diversified by buying a number of other companies, including the hair-care and cosmetics firm, Clairol (acquired in 1959); Drackett, a household-products manufacturer (1965); and Mead Johnson, an infant-formula and nutrition company (1967). In 1989 the merger of Bristol-Myers and the Squibb Corporation (descendant of a company founded in 1858 by a U.S. chemist and Navy medical officer, Edward Robinson Squibb) created one of the world's largest pharmaceutical companies.

E.R. Squibb & Sons had been a manufacturer of various vitamin products, but the main focus of its consumer advertising was its toothpaste and tooth-powder products. Its principal agency for that purpose from the 1930s was Geyer, Cornell & Newell, Inc., which later became Newell-Emmett Company and finally Cunningham & Walsh, Inc., in 1949. Newell-Emmett brought Squibb into network radio briefly with the program *Academy Award,* which presented radio versions of award-winning motion pictures, often with their original stars. But the show, which ran during 1946 on CBS, was expensive, and the advertiser soon decided to return to print advertising. Squibb was acquired by the Olin Mathieson Chemical Corporation in the 1950s, prior to its merger with Bristol-Myers.

In the early 1900s, sales of Bristol-Myers's laxative mineral salt, Sal Hepatica, and of Ipana toothpaste, the first such product to contain a disinfectant, grew rapidly. In 1915 William Bristol's oldest son, Henry, became general manager, and he was joined in 1938 by his brothers, William, Jr., and Lee. Lee was responsible for advertising. Pedlar & Ryan (P&R) and Young & Rubicam (Y&R) became the company's principal agencies and made it a force in radio, first with the *Ipana Troubadours* (1926–34) and later with *Town Hall Tonight* (with Fred Allen), *Duffy's Tavern, Mr. District Attorney,* and other shows. During the Depression and the years following, the focus remained on those two best-sellers; the company's slogan was, "Ipana for the smile of beauty, Sal Hepatica for the smile of health." By 1939 the company was spending $1.4 million in network radio and was the 19th largest network advertiser.

Midcentury: Conflict with the FTC

In 1949, in what was to be the first of many scraps with the Federal Trade Commission (FTC), Bristol-Myers was ordered to cease advertising Ipana toothpaste using the "Pink Toothbrush" theme, which depicted the highly processed, "soft" American diet as harmful to gum health. Ruling that the claims were false and not backed by dentists, the FTC placed responsibility with Bristol-Myers and gave a clean bill of health to P&R and Doherty, Clifford & Shenfield, Inc. (DC&S), Ipana's advertising agencies of record associated with the campaign. (DC&S was a 1944 spin-off of P&R that later merged with Needham, Louis & Brorby to form Needham, Harper & Steers.) It said that both agencies "acted at all times under direction and control of Bristol-Myers, with whom rested the final authority and responsibility for such advertising." The "Smile of beauty" theme was not affected by the ruling.

In 1950 Bristol-Myers increased its advertising expenditures to give special emphasis to Resistab, an antihistamine touted as a cold preventative. Kenyon & Eckhardt handled the launch and account at that time. It was not long before the FTC again lashed out at Bristol-Myers—along with the Anahist Company, maker of Anahist—claiming that neither company had proof that its antihistamines prevented or cured colds.

In 1951 Bristol-Myers added another TV program to its schedule. It sponsored the first 15 minutes of *Foodini the Great,* highlighting Ipana. In 1952 Ipana was reformulated to include chlorophyll. The new ad copy read, "Now! In one great new toothpaste—science's great decay fighter plus nature's great deodorant!" Ipana also used radio spots to promote the toothpaste. Beginning early in 1953, Bristol-Myers was a featured sponsor of the *Jackie Gleason Show.* In 1954 it changed its approach to Ipana, adopting the celebrity testimonial format. The first of these ads ran in *Life* on 22 March 1954 and featured Garry Moore, whose CBS television show also advertised Ipana.

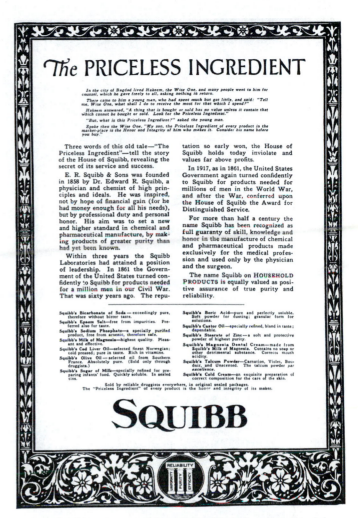

Raymond Rubicam's 1921 ad for E.R. Squibb & Sons introduced the slogan that became one of the most famous of its era: "The priceless ingredient of every product is the honor and integrity of its maker."

At this time DC&S, now called Doherty, Clifford, Steers, and Shenfield, Inc. (DCS&S) handled the Ipana account.

In 1954 Bristol-Myers introduced a lotion deodorant and antiperspirant called Ban in an applicator that worked much like a ballpoint pen. The advertising, handled by Batten Barton Durstine & Osborn, hailed Ban as "a completely new kind of deodorant" and prominently featured the fact that "it rolls on." This very successful campaign led Ban to the number-three spot in deodorant sales in only eight months.

The advertising of laxatives on TV presented a problem, especially for an all-family audience, and especially on Sunday night, when Bristol-Myers presented its Alfred Hitchcock-produced drama on CBS. But the Sal Hepatica commercials, with their lilting tunes and amusing animation, were widely agreed to be in good taste and to offend no one. Y&R's Jack Sidebotham was the art director for those commercials, which were written by Bernice Brilmayer and filmed by Academy Films.

Bristol-Myers's other deodorant product, Mum, handled by DCS&S, generated quite a stir in 1956 with a four-color poster

Does she...or doesn't she?

Hair color so natural only her hairdresser knows for sure!

You can see it dancing in his eyes . . . the fun and pride in having a mother whose happy spirit, whose radiant hair keeps her looking younger, so pretty *all* the time!

With Miss Clairol hair color, radiance is something which comes almost naturally! It's so quick and easy. And finished tone is always lively, young, yet soft and ladylike under brightest holiday lights. So even in this busiest of seasons, she wisely plans the little time it takes! And with Miss Clairol, it takes *only minutes* . . . to add clear, shining color to faded hair . . . to hide gray . . . to beauty-treat difficult texture to new softness. Miss Clairol is lasting color. *Never* muddies or darkens—*never* brittleizes your hair.

That's why America's hairdressers rely on Miss Clairol — recommend Miss Clairol, have given Miss Clairol treatments by the millions. With results so sure, why should you deny yourself the joy and confidence of knowing you're a younger-looking, happier-looking, completely attractive woman?

Try Miss Clairol yourself. Today. In the Creme Formula or Regular. There's sure to be a shade that's a "natural" for you . . . whether it's Topaz®, Moongold, Sable Brown or any of the many other lovely colors.

CREME FORMULA

miss **CLAIROL**®

HAIR COLOR BATH®

- Stays Put...Will Not Run
- Lightens as it Colors
- No Pre-bleaching
- Covers Gray Completely
- Natural-looking Color
- Simple Application
- Fast Development

©1956 Clairol Incorporated, Stamford, Conn.

miss CLAIROL® hair color bath®

MORE WOMEN USE MISS CLAIROL THAN ANY OTHER HAIR COLORING

Launched in 1956, Clairol's "Does She . . . or Doesn't She?" became one of the most widely recognized ad campaigns of all time, and the provocative query became part of the vernacular.

that received more fan mail than any other ad in the product's history. The copy read simply, "For security reasons . . . new Mum. The doctor's discovery that now safely stops odor 24 hours a day." "Mum's the word" became the ongoing slogan. Advertising expenditures in 1956 rose to the enormous sum of $21 million to promote a product line that included Bufferin, Ipana, Ban, Mum, Mum Mist, Sal Hepatica, Trushay, Ammens powder, Minit-Rub, and Vitalis.

In 1957 Robert F. Wilson, Inc., agency of record for Bristol-Myers's prescription drug products, resigned its inactive portion of the account to make room for a competitive account. Its work was reassigned to Paul Klemtner & Company. Noyes & Sproul and DCS&S were the other two prescription drug agencies working with Bristol-Myers at that time.

"In the Mature Male . . ."

By 1959 Ogilvy, Benson & Mather (OBM) had taken over as agency of record for Ban. Because no network wished to show real people applying deodorant, Reva Korda, a young copywriter who would later rise to head OBM creative operations, decided to represent the idea of the human anatomy with a flowing montage of nude statues over a discrete voice with a British accent: "In the mature male and the mature female. . . ." It was too classy to be erotic, but too detailed to set viewers at ease, thus provoking the attention of the Federal Communications Commission (FCC). The issue was not the credibility of advertising claims, which would have come under the jurisdiction of the FTC. Instead, the question was one of suitability under prevailing broadcast standards of taste. The FCC found nothing offensive in the campaign, which nevertheless was withdrawn after several months. More than $2 million was spent to advertise Vitalis. Grove Laboratories, a subsidiary, heavily promoted its products such as NoDoz (caffeine pills) and the 4-Way line of cold remedies. Bristol-Myers ranked number 16 in the nation in advertising expenditures that year.

In 1960 OBM assured potential Ban buyers that this deodorant would "take the worry out of being close." In June of that year, Bristol-Myers was cosponsor of the Johansson-Patterson heavyweight championship fight, paying half of a total tab of $250,000 and getting six minutes of commercial time. In July the company bought a one-sixth participation in the presidential conventions and election coverage. In March 1960 Bristol-Myers had been cited for alleged misleading advertising for Bufferin. The company responded that "clinical research over more than ten years . . . proves the reliability of our basic advertising claim, and the case we have taken to offer the public a product of the highest quality and effectiveness." Also in 1960, Bristol-Myers moved the advertising of its new antibiotic, Staphcillin, from Sproul & Associates to Sudler & Hennessey and then, along with several other new products, to Burdick & Becker. Sudler & Hennessey, a specialist in medical advertising, was later named to handle all advertising for Bristol Laboratories products.

In an effort to keep up with the competition, Bristol-Myers again altered its flagship product, Ipana, in 1961, adding sodium

Bristol-Myers used its sponsorship of the 1992 U.S. Olympic team to position Nuprin as "standard equipment" for treating the aches and pains that often result from athletic training.

fluoride in the wake of the success of Colgate-Palmolive's Crest. Ipana also contained chlorophyll in the form of hexachlorophene. The company advertised the product as effective in destroying decay-causing bacteria and strengthening tooth enamel. DCS&S continued to handle the Ipana account at that time. Also in that year, Bristol-Myers launched a new headache remedy, Excedrin, with a multimillion-dollar national campaign. Combining three analgesics and an antidepressant, Excedrin was touted as an "extra-strength pain reliever." Y&R handled the account. Television was the dominant advertising medium in 1961, with Bristol-Myers promoting its well-known proprietary brands on such shows as *Candid Camera, Naked City, Rawhide, Alfred Hitchcock Hour, Laramie, The Virginian,* and *Ben Casey,* as well as on newscasts and *CBS Reports.* That same year, Bristol-Myers named Grey Advertising to handle Trushay hand lotion and two new products.

Children's Bufferin was introduced in late 1962 and promoted in network and spot TV and magazines. Samples were distributed to pediatricians and to women's organizations. Y&R was the agency of record. In March of that year, Bristol-Myers switched its $1 million Mum and Mum Mist accounts from DCS&S to Grey Advertising. Bristol-Myers of Canada consolidated its advertising in that country with Ogilvy & Mather (Canada), switching approximately $500,000–$750,000 in billings from Vickers & Benson. Heavy airplay was given to Y&R's Bufferin commercial, which featured a woman suffering from a tension headache. As a loud ticking sound was heard in the background, the voice-over said, "If you had taken Bufferin when this message started, Bufferin's pain reliever could already be starting into your bloodstream, speeding relief straight to the pain."

In 1967 Bristol-Myers's subsidiary, Drackett Company, spent $3.6 million promoting Behold furniture polish. In the August 1967 issues of *Life* and *Look*, Excedrin, Ban, and Vitalis were promoted in connection with "pop art" posters, surfboards, record albums, radios, and other popular items. Ogilvy & Mather and Y&R were agencies for this promotion. Windex also made its debut in 1967, represented by Grey Advertising, as the "spray cleaner with guts."

In 1972 the FTC issued a cease-and-desist order with regard to "false and deceptive advertising" of Bufferin. In 1979 an FTC administrative law judge ordered Bufferin advertising to be pulled. In both cases the advertising claims or implications—that nervousness, tension, anxiety, or depression would be abated with the use of Bufferin and would enable a person to cope with the ordinary stresses of life—were ruled to be deceptive. The advertising agencies, Ted Bates & Company and Y&R, were cited for promoting the products even though they were alleged to have known that the claims were dubious. In 1983 the FTC, in a ruling that rejected the advertising claims of Bufferin, again cited ad agencies Bates and Y&R. Ads making the claim of "proven safety" were required to be supported by clinical testing. This particular chapter finally ended in 1985, when the Supreme Court refused to hear an appeal from Bristol-Myers against the 1983 FTC order.

"The closer you get, the better you look" was the 1964 slogan for Clairol's Nice 'n Easy Shampoo-In Hair Color. In the effort to persuade graying women to dye their hair, Foote, Cone & Belding's (FCB) award-winning copywriter Shirley Polykoff hit one of many home runs with this catchy phrase. At that time, only 7 percent of American women had ever dyed their hair. After Polykoff's first bold Clairol campaign ("Does she or doesn't she?"), that number rose to 50 percent. Because hairdressers were concerned over the competition from home-use products and could conceivably boycott other Clairol products, the phrase was added, "Hair coloring so natural, only her hairdresser knows for sure." Another FCB hair-color hit came in 1965 with the Clairol advertisement sporting the phrase, "Is it true blondes have more fun?"

Peter A. Georgescu, a 34-year veteran at Y&R, one of Bristol-Myers's long-standing advertising shops, was an early and strong influence at Bristol-Myers. A senior executive at Bristol-Myers had once objected when a youthful Georgescu, brimming with enthusiasm, kept referring to what "we" were going to do for the product they were discussing. "Young man," the executive said, "it is not 'we.' It is our money. It is Bristol-Myers." Georgescu's reply turned the executive into a firm ally: "Sir, I believe that you pay us to have the same kind of loyalty to your products and your objectives as you do. I don't see a difference between Bristol-Myers and Y&R, sir."

Rick Glosman, chief executive officer of creative media at the end of the 1990s, began his career in 1969 as a media research assistant at Ted Bates, where he worked on the Bristol-Myers spot TV account. After two years, Bristol-Myers hired him to work for it directly. He spent 11 years with the company, where he was responsible for all broadcast negotiations, ancillary support, programming, and control of the $150 million advertising budget. While there, he supervised the development of wholly owned Bristol-Myers broadcast vehicles such as *In Search of . . .*, *Young Dr. Kildare*, *Laugh Trax*, and *Alive and Well*.

Bristol-Myers launched a nonsteroidal anti-inflammatory drug called Nuprin in 1984 with a giant advertising budget and received disappointing sales for its efforts. Bristol-Myers's estimated $25 million investment brought sales of only around $35 million for Nuprin in 1985.

New Challenges

Direct-to-consumer (DTC) promotion of prescription drugs swept the U.S. pharmaceutical industry in 1997. New, more liberal guidelines from the Food and Drug Administration (FDA) for television advertising opened the floodgates, allowing the airing of commercials that made claims for specific brands along with abbreviated references to side effects. Commercials had to provide a toll-free number or cite a print advertisement where consumers could obtain more information. By the year's end, dozens of the new DTC commercials had premiered on U.S. television, and the industry had spent an estimated $1 billion on all forms of DTC promotion, up from $80 million in 1992. Bristol-Myers spent a total of $126 million advertising the cholesterol-lowering drug Pravachol in 1997 and 1998, only to lose market share to Merck's Zocor. Later Bristol-Myers discontinued its consumer advertising of Pravachol. In 1999 Bristol-Myers Squibb named GHBM Healthworld Corporation as agency of record for the global launch of a new antihypertensive agent in development at the time. (GHBM Healthworld was the U.S. medical advertising agency of Healthworld Corporation.)

In February 2000 Bristol-Myers Squibb Company, in partnership with Gillette Company, selected DDB Corbett as agency of record for the global launch of Vaniqa (eflornithine hydrochloride) Cream, a topical treatment for unwanted facial hair. DDB Corbett, a new agency with global influence, was chosen to handle all professional communications, direct-to-consumer advertising, and Web site development. The product launch was to reach five countries, beginning with the United States. DDB Corbett, a joint venture between Frank J. Corbett, Inc., one of the largest health-care advertising agencies in the United States, and DDB Chicago, a broad-based marketing communications and advertising agency, offered consumer and health-care communications expertise under one roof. Also in the year 2000, Bristol-Myers Squibb awarded Corbett HealthConnect the account for the antidepressant Serzone (nefazodone).

In keeping with the trend of marketing direct to the consumer via the Internet, Bristol-Myers Squibb boasted an extensive Web site (www.bms.com) with multiple linked sites categorized by product line, country, and business. Consumers who clicked on a heading such as "Look Good & Feel Great" were directed to the Web sites of Clairol, Matrix, Sea Breeze, and other beauty product lines. Web users could also find information about both prescription and over-the-counter drugs for conditions ranging from anxiety to insomnia to urinary-tract infections.

DESTINY DELINDA

See also Ipana Toothpaste/Sal Hepatica

Further Reading

Bristol-Myers Company Special Report: The Next Century, New York: Bristol-Myers, 1987

Blochman, Lawrence Goldtree, *Doctor Squibb: The Life and Times of a Rugged Idealist,* New York: Simon and Schuster, 1958

Dubrow, Larry, *When Advertising Tried Harder: The Sixties, the Golden Age of American Advertising,* New York: Friendly Press, 1984

Goodrum, Charles, and Dalrymple, Helen, *Advertising in America, the First 200 Years,* New York: Abrams, 1990

Hall, Jim, *Mighty Minutes: An Illustrated History of Television's Best Commercials,* New York: Harmony Books, 1984

British Airways

Principal Agencies
Foote, Cone & Belding, Ltd.
Tinker Campbell-Ewald, Inc.
Saatchi & Saatchi Advertising
M&C Saatchi

British Airways is recognized as a leader in international air travel, outlasting the once-monolithic Pan American Airways and a host of upstart airlines. Its instantly recognizable supersonic Concorde aircraft and its exultant tag line, "The world's favourite airline," have been advertising mainstays. But the path to the top has not been easy in the formerly highly regulated, ultracompetitive air travel industry.

British Air's roots reach back to 1919, with the formation of Aircraft Transport and Travel Limited (AT&T), the first airline in the world to offer daily international air service between London, England, and Paris, France. Two-and-a-half-hour flights from London's Hounslow Heath to Paris's Le Bourget carried a single passenger and cargo ranging from newspapers to fresh grouse. By 1999 British Air served more than 1,000 nonduplicated routes, and parent British Airways Group carried more than 45 million passengers annually.

After a spate of airline consolidations in the 1920s and 1930s, two dominant British carriers, Imperial Airways and British Airways, emerged. In 1939 each was nationalized, and the two were consolidated to form the British Overseas Airways Corporation (BOAC). BOAC introduced service to New York City in 1946, Japan in 1948, Chicago, Illinois, in 1954, and the U.S. West Coast in 1957, while British European Airways (BEA) handled Continental European and intercity British flights. In 1958 BOAC opened operation of the first transatlantic jet service between London and New York City.

In 1960 the British government formed the Air Transport Licensing Board to oversee the airline industry. BOAC and BEA were the dominant carriers. BEA eventually swallowed many smaller carriers, including Cambrian Airways and Northeast Airlines. Seven years later, the British government stepped in again, creating a holding board to oversee BOAC and BEA. In 1972, the boards of both airlines were combined; a full merger under the British Airways banner was completed two years later.

In 1974, with the merger of BOAC and BEA finalized, British Airways launched a $5 million ad campaign, the largest in the British travel industry to date. The campaign, developed by Foote, Cone & Belding, London, was comprised of 89 television spots, eight national newspaper color pages, and 100 "super site" poster and billboard locations.

By the mid-1970s British Air was ready to introduce its most famous aircraft, the supersonic Concorde. On 21 January 1976, a pair of Concordes, one from British Air and the other from Air France, took off to far-flung points amid a flurry of media coverage. To drum up support for eventual transatlantic service, British Air, through ads by Tinker Campbell-Ewald, ran spreads in national editions of the *Wall Street Journal,* the *Chicago Tribune,* the *Houston Chronicle,* the *Washington Post,* and the *New York Times.* The same newspapers also carried four identical teaser ads featuring actor and British Air spokesman Robert Morley pointing out the spreads to readers.

But plans for transatlantic Concorde flights encountered some turbulence with the U.S. Department of Transportation, which was responsible for granting the supersonic aircraft landing rights. Environmental groups decried the Concorde—which could complete a New York-to-London flight in less than four hours—as harmful to the Earth's ozone layer, noisy, and fuel inefficient. Concorde supporters responded that the aircraft's environmental impact was minimal and the outcry a product of competitors'

For more information on British Airways, call 1-800-AIRWAYS.

WE
RELUCTANTLY ADMIT
THERE IS
SOMEONE WHO
FLIES TO MORE
PLACES THAN
BRITISH AIRWAYS.

© 1988 British Airways

BRITISH AIRWAYS
The world's favourite airline.®

For years, British Airways' advertising proclaimed that the airline flew to more places than any other. In this 1988 tongue-in-cheek print ad, the company issued a "correction."

envy. The Concorde's proponents won that battle, and in May 1977, London-bound Concorde service took off, with high-speed and high-priced transatlantic flights between Heathrow Airport and New York City's John F. Kennedy International Airport.

In 1977 British Air also found itself embroiled in a battle over tourist class fares with competitors Air India, Pan-American World Airways, and Trans World Airlines. After an August announcement of a $256 round-trip fare (London–New York City), these and a handful of other airlines embarked on a fare war that brought such fares to a bargain-basement level. One ad from British Air's agency Tinker Campbell-Ewald touted a $156 one-way trip with a return fare of $10.

But some passengers who signed up for the budget fares never left the ground, as the U.S. Civil Aeronautics Board—the primary airline watchdog until deregulation in October 1978—did not approve the fee schedules previously advertised by the airline. The board's decision prompted last-minute changes to all air carriers' announcements and produced headaches for their ad agencies' creative departments.

After deregulation made cheap fares the rule rather than the exception, global air travel skyrocketed, only to be put into jeopardy in the 1980s by a new threat: global terrorism. A month after the U.S. raid on Libya in April 1986, British Air rolled out an ambitious $8 million newspaper campaign that featured a host of giveaways, ranging from free trips on its flagship Concorde to $153,000 worth of stocks and bonds. The campaign worked. Bookings came in at a rate of 64,000 per week, far from the low point of a net loss of 27,000 bookings per week immediately after the raid.

The promotions were indicative of the desperation all international air carriers were experiencing during the terrorism crisis. Sales promotion agency Howard Marlboro Group, of New York City, conducted a series of top-secret planning meetings to prepare for British Air's "Go for it, America!" program, which culminated in the giveaway of all its 5,200 seats for flights on 10 June 1986. As another part of that promotion, one passenger on each flight that June won a free round-trip ticket on the Concorde. The winner was determined via a contest distributed onboard each flight, consisting of seven multiple-choice questions plus a tiebreaker. British Air sustained the campaign through October 1986, giving away a prize to one passenger on each of its flights. A year later, the British government privatized the airline.

Concern over airline terrorism seemed to be subsiding by early 1988 (although it would return at peak levels in December of that year with the bombing of a U.S. airliner over Lockerbie, Scotland). But during those relatively carefree months when air travel began to increase, British Air commissioned Saatchi & Saatchi Advertising to create a campaign for the carrier's introduction of its Club World and Club Europe business-class sections. In one spot, aired in the United States and the United Kingdom, the camera cut back and forth between a cabal of corporate plotters and their intended victim, an executive traveling on short notice to an overseas meeting. Presumably, the jet-lagged businessman would be too exhausted to negotiate successfully. In the commercial, the "victim" settled comfortably in his British Air business class seat,

In one of British Airways' best-known commercials, several thousand students held up cards forming the image of a giant face that "winked" when viewed from the air. Later in the commercial, a flip of the cards created an image of the globe.

ate a lavish meal, slept, and worked on a report due at the meeting. The Machiavellian corporate plotters were shocked to see the traveler arrive refreshed and alert. The voice-over said, "British Airways' new business class delivers you ready to do business."

In 1990 Saatchi & Saatchi enlisted the director of the film *Chariots of Fire,* Hugh Hudson, to produce a 90-second extravaganza that included a collage comprised of more than 3,000 schoolchildren holding color-coded placards. The spot, aired during college football games and holiday programming, depicted a face in British Air's red, white, and blue motif. On cue, the face, viewed from a helicopter overhead, was transformed into a globe, alluding to the carrier's 38-country reach. The effort was supported by a $22.5 million ad budget.

In 1995, during an acrimonious legal battle between the holding company Cordiant and Saatchi & Saatchi founder Maurice Saatchi, British Air made waves throughout the advertising industry when it moved its $96 million global ad account to the Saatchi brothers' breakaway shop, M&C Saatchi. In August of that year British Air launched its first campaign by M&C Saatchi with four British television spots directed by Oscar-winning animation director Daniel Greaves. The commercials, touting British Air's World Offers campaign, featured a sheep, giraffe, peacock, and trapeze artist in four separate watercolor-like cartoons. Each asked the question, "Where is everybody?" The implied response: "everybody" had taken advantage of British Air's World Offers bargain fares program.

Along with a change in corporate identity, British Air in 1997 announced a three-year, $10 billion investment in new services, products, training, and aircraft, with the rollout of a TV campaign from M&C Saatchi. This branding campaign included the introduction of the "Speedmarque" logo, a red, white, and blue three-dimensional adaptation of British Air's former "Speedwing" logo. The "Speedmarque" logo was developed by Newell and Sorrell, London.

In October 1997 British Airways launched a three-month, $15 million campaign (from M&C Saatchi, New York) in 18 major U.S. cities highlighting the airline's international reach. Another TV spot introduced the carrier's business-class service and the Club World seat. The airline termed the overall campaign its "single largest wave of brand advertising" in the United States.

In 1999 British Air came under fire from a new rival, which challenged the carrier's "World's favourite airline" tag. Entrepreneur Richard Branson's Virgin Atlantic Airlines filed a complaint with the National Advertising Division (NAD) of the U.S. Council of Better Business Bureaus disputing the truthfulness of the "world's favourite" claim. The NAD said British Airways declined to participate on the grounds that the U.S. Department of Transportation, not the NAD, was the official U.S. regulator for airlines. At that time, the NAD said it would forward the complaint to the Department of Transportation for review.

In February 2000 British Airways named international Internet consultancy Agency.Com the exclusive global interactive services partner in its e-commerce division. In a multiyear agreement estimated at more than $30 million, British Airways and Agency.Com planned to develop and implement its interactive initiatives.

After the 25 July 2000 crash of an Air France Concorde—an aircraft identical to those flown by British Airways—killed 113 shortly after takeoff from Charles de Gaulle Airport in Paris, British Airways and Air France officials began working with government investigators and regulators to find ways to keep the planes in service. Shortly after the crash, regulators grounded the Anglo-French aircraft based on concerns that its fuel tanks could leak and catch fire if hit by ground debris.

In an attempt to win back customers and satisfy the concerns of regulators, British Airways announced in January 2001 that it would modify its Concordes. The seven revamped British Airways aircraft were to include armored fuel tanks, along with a cabin retrofit to include more modern seating. The armor material was designed to prevent a repeat of the massive fuel leak that contributed to the summer 2000 crash. The British government reinstated the Concorde's airworthiness certificate on 5 September 2001, and British Airways relaunched its service to New York City on 7 November 2001.

DEREK DATTNER AND AMY I.S. DATTNER

Further Reading

"British Airways Airlines Jump on $256 Bandwagon," *Advertising Age* (22 August 1977)

"Concorde Ads Cover Cities in U.S., Where It Cannot Land," *Advertising Age* (26 January 1976)

Haugh, Louis J., "Low Air Fares to London Turn into Tumult for Travelers and Carriers," *Advertising Age* (19 September 1977)

"Merger-Made British Airways Gets $5,000,000 U.K. Push," *Advertising Age* (1 October 1973)

Moran, Brian, "Airlines Try New Efforts to Lure Overseas Fliers," *Advertising Age* (26 May 1986)

"Saatchi & Saatchi's London Office," *Advertising Age* (8 January 1990)

Wentz, Laurel, "Business Jet-Set: British Air Scores in New Spot Aimed at Traveling Executives," *Advertising Age* (7 March 1988)

"World News Roundup," *Advertising Age* (11 January 1988)

British Telecom

Principal Agencies

KMP/Compton
J. Walter Thompson Company
Simons Palmer
Abbot Mead Vickers/BBDO (consumer market)
Saatchi & Saatchi (business-to-business advertising)
St. Luke's (youth campaign)

British Telecom (BT) has long been one of the largest advertisers in the United Kingdom. It has a storied past as England's dominant telephone company, providing local and long-distance phone service as well as Internet access, leased lines, data transmission, and other telecommunications services.

Key events that prefigure the origins of BT include the British government's adoption in 1795 of a semaphore, or apparatus for visual signaling, with three pairs of movable arms that could transmit a message 70 miles; the opening of the first public telegraph line, between London and Gosport, to transmit Queen Victoria's speech at the opening of Parliament in February 1845; the formation of the British Telegraph Company in 1852; and the takeover of British Telegraph by the Post Office in 1870. Finally, in 1879 the Telephone Company Ltd. opened Britain's first public telephone exchange, serving eight subscribers.

The company's advertising legacy goes back to 1 October 1934, when, as part of the Kingsley Wood plan for advertising and popularizing the telephone, the Post Office first introduced cheap night rates of five pence maximum for trunk telephone calls. In early 1965 Prime Minister Harold Wilson proposed that the Post Office be converted to a nationalized industry, and a government study led to a decision to split the agency into two divisions: post and telecommunications. Twelve years later, in 1977, the Carter Committee, commissioned by the government, recommended a further separation of postal and telecommunications services. Those findings led to the British Telecommunications Act in 1981 and the creation of British Telecom as a separate public corporation on 1 October 1981. That same year, the first steps were taken to introduce competition in the United Kingdom's telecommunications industry.

Before 1981 the Post Office and British Telecom alone had decided what could and could not be connected to Britain's telecommunications network. The 1981 Telecommunications Act established an independent procedure to set standards and approve equipment for connection to the network.

Faced with marketplace competition for the first time, British Telecom dropped its Busby spokes-character, an amiable fat yellow bird it used in advertising in the 1970s that had become known as "the friendly face of BT." Instead, British Telecom's advertising agency, KMP/Compton, launched the "It's for you" television advertising campaign featuring characters such as Neptune and the Hunchback of Notre Dame. A series of animal-themed advertisements followed, and the campaign ran until 1985.

In March 1989 British Telecom instituted a major change in its strategy, launching its "Customer Service Guarantee," a compensation program covering telephone line installations and repairs. Customers were able to claim compensation or a fixed reimbursement if they were without telephone service for more than two working days because of British Telecom's failure to install a line on the agreed-upon date or to repair a telephone line promptly. The Customer Service Guarantee was revised and reissued several times over the following years.

At the same time in 1989, BT's new advertising agency, the J. Walter Thompson Company (JWT), launched a campaign known as "Beattie," starring British comedienne, actress, and writer Maureen Lipman. The commercials were broadcast until 1991, and Lipman came to be identified as the matriarch on the Golders Green omnibus, a vehicle used by British Telecom to explain its services to the public until 1992.

On 5 March 1991 the British government issued a report entitled "Competition and Choice: Telecommunications Policy for the

In a commercial for British Telecom, actress Maureen Lipman plays a grandmother talking to her grandson about his exams.
Courtesy of Abbott Mead Vickers BBDO Ltd. and Maureen Lipman.

1990s." It ended the duopoly of BT and Mercury Communications, henceforth allowing customers to acquire telecommunications services from competing providers using a variety of technologies. (In 1983 the British government had established BT and Mercury as sole co-providers of services.)

About a month later, on 2 April 1991, British Telecom was relaunched, using the BT piper symbol. Then on 20 September 1991, BT unveiled its "BT Commitment," an outgrowth of the earlier Customer Service Guarantee designed to further the company's new corporate identity and focus on meeting customer needs. The BT Commitment specified target response times for orders, repairs, and connection rates and speed of connection. It guaranteed compensation for missed targets, particularly if a customer suffered financial loss as a result. The company also launched special discounts for business called "Customer Options."

"Putting customers first" was then launched in the northwest of England in January 1992, followed by a national rollout on 30 March 1992. The program aimed to transform customer perceptions of BT and was based on different initiatives to highlight quality, value, and responsiveness.

Simons Palmer, BT's ad agency in 1992, then created the "Get through to someone" television ad campaign that ran until 1994. The commercials featured a series of real-life situations, such as a college girl calling home.

In 1993 BT and MCI Communications Corporation announced a joint global alliance through a new international joint-venture company that eventually was named Concert. The two companies intended to merge, but a bidding war instead resulted in MCI's later merger with WorldCom. BT later partnered with AT&T Corporation, and the two opened another international joint venture—following the dissolution of the BT-MCI co-venture—which also used the Concert name. The 1993 alliance did lead to BT's adoption of one of MCI's more prominent promotional campaigns and discount plans, "Friends & Family," in February 1994.

It was also in 1994 that BT hired Abbot Mead Vickers/BBDO as its lead agency for the consumer market. The new agency then launched a series of TV and radio spots featuring actor Bob Hoskins and directed by Ridley Scott. The campaign, with its tag line "It's good to talk," sought to persuade people to spend more time on the phone.

The campaign was judged the most effective piece of British advertising between 1994 and 1996 by the Institute of Practitioners in Advertising, which said that the campaign had revolutionized telephone usage in the United Kingdom, encouraging men to chat on the telephone and tackling public misconceptions about the cost of calls. The campaign also helped increase the average amount of time residential customers spent on the telephone, from eight minutes to nearly ten minutes a day. Some analysts estimated the campaign brought in as much as $500 million in new revenue for BT.

In 1995 the work of agency Partners BDDH for BT's business customers featured a small company "soap opera," while Saatchi & Saatchi created the highly regarded corporate campaign that featured the renowned physicist Stephen Hawking. In the commercial, Hawking, speaking via the voice synthesizer that enables him to talk despite a disease that has robbed him of his speech, describes images of deserts turned into palaces of technology; he concludes, "Mankind's greatest achievements have come about by talking and its greatest failures by not talking."

In 1996 another campaign from Abbot Mead Vickers/BBDO featured comic Rory McGrath and a cast that included a dog, a pig, and a duck. After two years of "It's good to talk," the agency created a successor campaign made up of TV spots and consumer print ads that highlighted specific examples of BT's contributions to the community.

At the time, according to BT, its regular market research detected a small increase in negative public reaction to its higher profile as a result of its increased spending on mainstream advertising. BT was commonly thought to be spending at least $240 million a year. Later that year, however, "It's good to talk" was revived with a series of spots that featured the British TV and film actor Hugh Laurie. The company then shifted to a "BT friends & family" TV campaign in which actual BT customers and their friends and relatives are seen enjoying exotic vacations courtesy of BT.

In late 1997 soccer star Kenny Dalglish and his daughter, Kelly, were featured in another "It's good to talk" commercial, and in 1998 weatherman Ian McCaskill starred in a comic TV commercial for BT pay phones. BT's commercials moved away from celebrities after that, picking up the tag line "Tell someone" to portray ordinary people using the phone to tell friends and family about their day, an embarrassing situation, or a memorable occasion.

In April 1999 BT entered into an exclusive agreement with Universal Studios and director Steven Spielberg to use the E.T. character from the movie *E.T. the Extra-Terrestrial* in a new campaign from Abbot Mead Vickers/BBDO. In the commercials, E.T. used BT technology to "phone home" and introduced yet another slogan, "Stay in touch."

In April 2000 Sir Peter Bonfield, BT's chief executive, outlined another restructuring of the company, designed to support its position as a leader in the next wave of the communications revolution. The plan included separating the company into different businesses, including BT Ignite, a broadband Internet protocol business focused on the corporate and wholesale markets; BT Openworld, a mass-market Internet business; BT Wireless, a mobile business; and Yell, a new international directory and e-commerce business.

WAYNE WALLEY

Further Reading

Beesley, Michael E., *Liberalisation of the Use of British Telecommunications Network: Report to the Secretary of State,* London: HMSO, 1981

Beesley, Michael E., and Bruce Laidlaw, *The Future of Telecommunications—An Assessment of the Role of Competition in UK Policy,* London: Institute of Economic Affairs, 1989

Dru, Jean-Marie, *Disruption: Overturning Conventions and Shaking Up the Marketplace,* New York: Wiley, 1996

Great Britain Department of Trade and Industry, *Competition and Choice: Telecommunications Policy for the 1990s,* London: HMSO, 1990

Harper, John M., *Monopoly and Competition in British Telecommunications: The Past, the Present, and the Future,* London and Washington, D.C.: Pinter, 1997

Schultz, Don E., and Philip J. Kitchen, *Communicating Globally: An Integrated Marketing Approach,* Chicago: NTC Business Books, and London: Macmillan, 2000

Brown & Williamson Tobacco Corporation

Principal Agencies
Batten Barton Durstine & Osborn
Ted Bates, Inc. (later Bates USA)
Russel M. Seeds Company, Inc. (later Cunningham & Walsh)
Grey Advertising Agency, Inc.

Brown & Williamson Tobacco Corporation (B&W) has marketed tobacco products in the United States and internationally for more than 100 years. Well-known B&W brands through the years have included Viceroy, Raleigh, Nashville, Filtip, Kool, Capri, and Queen Bess (named for England's Queen Elizabeth I).

Brown & Williamson Tobacco Company was founded by George T. Brown and Robert F. Williamson in North Carolina in 1893. The partners had two things in common: they both came from families that owned tobacco factories, and they were brothers-in-law. The business was launched in the fall of 1893, selling Red Juice and Red Crown brands of chewing tobacco and a granulated smoking tobacco called Golden Grain.

The company moved from North Carolina to Louisville, Kentucky, in the early 1900s. In 1927 B&W was acquired by the British-American Tobacco Company (B.A.T.), which was based in London, England. The driving force behind the acquisition was Sir Hugo Cunliffe-Owen, chairman of the board of B.A.T. The purchase gave B.A.T. a foothold in the burgeoning U.S. cigarette business.

The year 1927 also saw the launch of a new B&W brand whose marketing reflected its parent company's British ownership. Raleigh, offered to U.S. consumers at 15 cents per pack of 20, soon became the fifth-largest-selling brand in the United States. But when the Great Depression hit in 1929, Raleigh was viewed as overpriced. In response, B&W cut the price and adopted a sales promotion strategy using on-pack coupons. In the U.S. cigarette industry, promotions such as coupons had nearly been abandoned as a result of a strategy adopted by R.J. Reynolds Tobacco Company. Reynolds's Camel cigarettes bore the following message on every pack: "Don't look for premiums or coupons, as the cost of the tobaccos blended in Camel cigarettes prohibits the use of them." Raleigh introduced a coupon redeemable for such premiums as playing cards or a card table. Later, the company offered other prizes such as electric toasters and irons. In a depressed economy, such items were available cheaply enough to be factored into the selling price while keeping the brand both competitive and profitable. Coupon redemption became an integral part of the B&W marketing plan. The coupons and the various prizes figured prominently in the brand's advertising.

B&W also believed that instead of trying to compete with industry leaders such as Reynolds, Philip Morris, and Liggett & Myers, it should not concentrate on a single, strong entry. Instead

B&W's strategy was based on developing a stable of distinctive specialty brands.

In February 1933 B&W introduced Kool, the first nationally sold menthol-flavored cigarette. Kool competed against a regional mentholated brand, Spud, marketed by Axton-Fisher, also of Louisville. Menthol, a chemical compound extracted from the peppermint plant and classified by medical science as a mild local anesthetic (sometimes used in veterinary medicine), served to mask the harsher taste of nicotine and other elements in cigarette smoke. In effect, it numbed the throat to the irritating effects of tobacco without diluting the pleasant sensations associated with smoking. The Kool specialty brand, which later in 1933 was first paired with what would become its longtime penguin mascot, went on to become one of B&W's best-selling brands and created the important menthol segment niche of the cigarette market.

Kool, priced at 15 cents per pack when introduced, was five cents cheaper than Spud. Kool ads featured the penguin and copy that narrowly skirted the sort of blatant message that big brands employed. "Give your throat a Kool vacation!" was a headline in a typical ad. The copy block from the same ad read: "Like a week by the sea, this mild menthol smoke is a tonic to hot, tired throats. The tiny bit of menthol cools and refreshes, yet never interferes with the full-bodied flavor."

In September 1936 B&W moved into network radio. Batten Barton Durstine & Osborn (BBDO), its longtime agency, produced the *Raleigh-Kool Program*, a variety program on NBC that began as a vehicle for comic Jack Pearl. But the focus soon shifted to popular music and the Tommy Dorsey swing band, which had the kind of young high school and college age following that all cigarette makers targeted. While Raleigh and Kool sponsored Dorsey, Camel had Benny Goodman and Bob Crosby; Old Gold had Goodman, Artie Shaw, and Glen Gray; Chesterfield had Glenn Miller and Harry James; and Lucky Strike had *Your Hit Parade*. B&W continued sponsoring Dorsey well into the 1940s.

B&W sought to capitalize on the demand for low-priced cigarettes during the Great Depression by decreasing the cost of its popular Wings brand in late 1932 from 15 cents per pack to ten cents. This reduction resulted in a huge surge in sales. While none of B&W's brands was overwhelmingly successful during this period, its entries held their own while selling half as many units as Liggett & Myers by 1940. B&W ranked fourth in the U.S. cigarette market.

In 1945 B&W hired Ted Bates, Inc., New York City, to create a campaign for Viceroy, a brand introduced in 1936. Viceroy featured a filter made from cellulose acetate, a highly malleable substance that was more effective in certain configurations than the crimped-paper and cotton-wadding filter offered by Parliament, a premium brand introduced a few years earlier by a small independent tobacco company, Benson & Hedges. Rosser Reeves of Bates, which already handled B&W's Kool account, noticed a pack of Viceroys on the desk of the president of B&W and asked him which agency handled the brand. The client replied that the brand was not promoted heavily and that other B&W brands were more popular. After Reeves discussed his hard-sell advertising philosophy, B&W's president authorized him to create a campaign for Viceroy but gave him a budget of only $41,000—revenue remaining from Kool's production budget. Reeves's copy and visuals for Viceroy, then a filter cigarette that cost marginally more than nonfilter products, were quite successful. Reeves's initial campaign for Viceroy, incorporating his famous "unique selling proposition" tactic, helped increase sales. Six years later he and his agency received approximately $18 million a year for advertising campaigns for Viceroy.

Meanwhile, in 1948 American Tobacco's Lucky Strike account became available when Foote, Cone & Belding suddenly resigned the business. BBDO moved quickly to pick up the $12 million account and resigned the Raleigh account. B&W then turned to the Russel M. Seeds Company, Inc., in Chicago, Illinois, where Freeman Keyes would run the account for years to come.

In the early 1950s the first studies appeared warning of the health hazards of smoking. Bates, whose largest client at the time was B&W, stood to lose a lot of money if the public took this research seriously and people decided to moderate their smoking habit or even to cease smoking altogether. Reeves, determined not to let this happen, countered the medical profession's bad news by developing a "reassurance campaign" for Viceroy cigarettes. His television commercials calmed smokers' fears by asserting that "the nicotine and tars trapped by the exclusive Viceroy filter cannot reach your nose, throat, or lungs." The copywriter's sales pitch sounded so authoritative that it convinced millions of consumers to continue puffing away. The success rocketed Viceroy into first place in sales in the United States. Over the next six years, B&W sold approximately 22 billion Viceroys; revenue from the brand reached $200 million.

In 1953 B&W retained the services of the public relations firm Hill & Knowlton (H&K), New York City. H&K said: "It is important that the industry do nothing to appear in the light of being callous to considerations of health or belittling medical research which goes against cigarettes. Moreover, the tobacco moguls ought to understand that their past advertising may have created a degree of skepticism in the public mind that could initially hamper a public relations effort to mitigate the health scare." In endorsing an industrywide research initiative, H&K called for the formation of a scientific advisory board consisting of individuals "whose integrity is beyond question."

Reeves's ads for Kool cigarettes were equally as effective as his Viceroy campaign. "Break the chain of the hot cigarette habit—with Kools," he penned. Customers misconstrued this message. It was not the cigarette's refreshing menthol taste that attracted them; it was the implicit suggestion that by switching to Kool they would eventually be able to quit smoking. The Kool campaign also targeted weary travelers and families seeking a hot-weather meal in an air-conditioned restaurant. Many a plate-glass restaurant door displayed a decal featuring the Kool penguin, the Kool pack, and the fact that the establishment was air-conditioned. The decal beckoned: "Come in, it's Kool inside."

To help make two B&W brands "safer" for consumers, a fiber-based filter was added to both Kool and Raleigh for the first time in 1957. The filters contributed to the success of both brands. In 1956 R. J. Reynolds sought to unseat entrenched segment leader Kool when it introduced Salem. Kool retained its lead even though Reynolds's onslaught against the brand in both advertising and promotion was effective and backed with millions of dollars. Clearly the 1950s were successful for B&W and its niche brand lineup. However, Reynolds was poised to increase its lead in the 1960s.

Growth for B&W brands in the 1960s and 1970s slowed from the heady days of the 1950s, and B&W moved its account to Post-Keyes-Gardner, Inc. (PKG), in Chicago. PKG was a successor to Russel M. Seeds, whose board chairman, Freeman Keyes, set up Keyes, Madden & Jones (KM&J) in September 1957 to handle the Raleigh business. Then in March 1963 KM&J merged with another Chicago agency, Post, Morr & Gardner, Inc., to form Post-Keyes-Gardner, which took over the whole B&W account. Kool remained the top-selling menthol brand, fueled by strong sales among blacks. This was one of the factors that led B&W to sponsor the New York Jazz Festival, which was renamed the Kool Jazz Festival through the 1970s and 1980s. More brand extensions were introduced to compete in new niches. For example, the new "light" category was used to extend Viceroy, Kool, and Raleigh brands.

In 1980 B&W introduced Barclay, an ultralow-tar entry. The brand won a one-milligram rating from the Federal Trade Commission (FTC). The headline in the Barclay ad stated: "The pleasure is back," implying that the brand offered more flavor than other brands in the category. B&W claimed that Barclay employed a different cigarette "technology" from that of its competitors, thereby producing a keener taste sensation.

B&W believed that Barclay could capture a quarter of the ultralow-tar market and budgeted $150 million in advertising and sales promotion costs for the launch. Within nine months, Barclay had a 1.2 percent market share; however, envious competitors were growing suspicious of Barclay's success. Reynolds and Philip Morris researchers tested Barclay and found that the air tunnels in its filter produced a slightly ridged effect to the touch. Competitors stated that consumers would be tempted to smooth the small bumps by crushing them down level with the rest of the paper filter overwrap, using their fingers or mouth. Critics said this action negated the diluting effects of the Barclay filter and raised the tar yields well above the rating recorded by the FTC's smoking machines. The reasoning was that the machines, being devoid of tactile sensation, had no tendency to exert pressure on the raised paper filter surface.

B&W was urged by Reynolds and Philip Morris to modify its claims. B&W refused. The FTC named a panel of independent experts who concluded that the Barclay air tunnels were "compromised with great regularity." The panel reported to the FTC that the design flaw gave a true tar yield in the three- to eight-milligram category. Eventually the FTC settled on a three-milligram rating for Barclay; however, the initial sales momentum of the brand faded after peaking at a 1.3 market share figure.

In 1994 B&W acquired American Tobacco, owner of the venerable and still-popular Lucky Strike, Pall Mall, and Tareyton brands. B&W's plant in Macon, Georgia, was expanded to help produce the new B&W brands. On 21 April 1995 the FTC gave final approval to a consent agreement with B.A.T. Industries and its subsidiary, Brown & Williamson Tobacco Corporation. The agreement settled antitrust charges over B.A.T.'s acquisition of the American Tobacco Company of Stamford, Connecticut, a subsidiary of American Brands, Inc., of Old Greenwich, Connecticut. The consent order ended litigation over FTC allegations that B.A.T.'s acquisition of American Tobacco would substantially reduce competition in the U. S. cigarette industry, potentially giving B A.T. and other companies in the market greater ability to collude. Upon acquisition, B&W divested the following American Tobacco brands: Montclair, Riviera, Malibu, Bull Durham, Crown, and Special Ten. B&W retained American's Tareyton, Silva Thins, and Tall brands, even though the FTC had originally ordered the company to divest the labels. B&W also retained American's Lucky Strike and Pall Mall brands.

Kool, now billed as the "classic menthol" cigarette, has continued as the mainstay and the largest-selling brand in the B&W lineup. Kool Natural Lights was introduced as a brand extension. The product was the first national mainstream cigarette brand to be positioned as a "natural" product. The ad campaign was estimated at $40 million. In advertising created by Grey Advertising, Inc., New York City, which took over the account in the mid-1990s, Kool Natural Lights were billed as: "A special blend of tobaccos and natural menthol with other natural flavors for a smooth, fresh taste. We add no artificial flavors to this blend." Also, in keeping with "health" statements about Kool from the 1950s, the copy on the pack in the 1990s said: "We're not saying these cigarettes are safer than other cigarettes, but we think you'll enjoy the perfectly balanced taste." In a bit of irony, the campaign for Kool Natural Lights was the last for the Kool brand under Grey. The brand returned to its former agency Bates USA (previously known as Ted Bates, Inc.) on 1 January 1999.

In 1999 B&W's lineup of domestic cigarette and specialty tobacco products (ranked by respective market segments) included: value-for-money—GPC, Misty, Viceroy, Raleigh Extra, Richland, and American Lights; full-revenue—Kool, Carlton, Capri, Lucky Strike, Barclay, Belair, Raleigh, Pall Mall, Tareyton, Silva Thins, and Tall; private label—Private Stock, Prime, and Summit; and specialty tobacco products—Kite, Bugler, Sir Walter Raleigh, Bloodhound, Brown & Williamson's Sun Cured, Red Juice, and Tube Rose. Its export brands of cigarettes included Lucky Strike, Kent, Barclay, Capri, Kool, Viceroy, and Pall Mall.

TOMMY V. SMITH

Further Reading

American Tobacco Company, *"Sold American!": The First Fifty Years (1904–1954)*, New York: s.n., 1954

Applegate, Edd, editor, *The Ad Men and Women: A Biographical Dictionary of Advertising*, Westport, Connecticut: Greenwood, 1994

Brooks, Jerome, *The Mighty Leaf: Tobacco through the Centuries*, Boston: Little, Brown, 1952; London: Redman, 1953

Brown and Williamson <www.bw.com>

Campbell, Tracy, *The Politics of Despair: Power and Resistance in the Tobacco Wars*, Lexington: University Press of Kentucky, 1993

Cox, Reavis, *Competition in the American Tobacco Industry, 1911–1932: A Study of the Effects of the Partition of the American Tobacco Company by the United States Supreme Court*, New York: Columbia University Press, and London: King, 1933

Fairholt, F.W., *Tobacco: Its History and Associations*, London: Chapman and Hall, 1859; reprint, Detroit, Michigan: Singing Tree, 1968

Finger, William, *The Tobacco Industry in Transition: Policies for the 1980s*, Lexington, Massachusetts: Lexington Books, 1981; Aldershot, Hampshire: Gower, 1982

Fox, Stephen, *The Mirror Makers: A History of American Advertising and Its Creators*, New York: Morrow, 1984

Heimann, Robert, *Tobacco and Americans*, New York: McGraw-Hill, 1960

Higgins, Denis, *The Art of Writing Advertising: Conversations with William Bernbach, Leo Burnett, George Gribbin, David Ogilvy, Rosser Reeves*, Lincolnwood, Illinois: NTC Business Books, 1986

Kluger, Richard, *Ashes to Ashes: America's Hundred-Year Cigarette War, the Public Health, and the Unabashed Triumph of Philip Morris*, New York: Knopf, 1996

McGowan, Richard, *Business, Politics, and Cigarettes: Multiple Levels, Multiple Agendas*, Westport, Connecticut: Quorum, 1995

Meyers, William, *The Image-Makers: Power and Persuasion on Madison Avenue*, New York: Times, 1984

Nicholls, William, *Price Policies in the Cigarette Industry: A Study of "Concerted Action" and Its Social Control, 1911–1950*, Nashville, Tennessee: Vanderbilt University Press, 1951

Rankin, Watson Smith, *James Buchanan Duke (1856–1925): A Great Pattern of Hard Work, Wisdom, and Benevolence*, New York: Newcomen Society in North America, 1952

Reeves, Rosser, *Reality in Advertising*, New York: Bates, 1960

Reynolds, Patrick, and Tom Shachtman, *The Gilded Leaf: Triumph, Tragedy, and Tobacco: Three Generations of the R.J. Reynolds Family and Fortune*, Boston: Little, Brown, 1989

Robert, Joseph, *The Tobacco Kingdom: Plantation, Market, and Factory in Virginia and North Carolina, 1800–1860*, Durham, North Carolina: Duke University Press, 1938

Robert, Joseph, *The Story of Tobacco in America*, Chapel Hill: University of North Carolina Press, 1949

Schudson, Michael, *Advertising, the Uneasy Persuasion: Its Dubious Impact on American Society*, New York: Basic Books, 1984; London: Routledge, 1993

Siegel, Frederick, *The Roots of Southern Distinctiveness: Tobacco and Society in Danville, Virginia, 1780–1865*, Chapel Hill: University of North Carolina Press, 1987

Sivulka, Juliann, *Soap, Sex, and Cigarettes: A Cultural History of American Advertising*, Belmont, California: Wadsworth, 1998

Sticht, J. Paul, *The RJR Story: The Evolution of a Global Enterprise*, New York: Newcomen Society of the United States, 1983

Tilley, Nannie, *The Bright-Tobacco Industry, 1860–1929*, Chapel

Hill: University of North Carolina Press, 1948

Whelan, Elizabeth, *A Smoking Gun: How the Tobacco Industry Gets Away with Murder*, Philadelphia, Pennsylvania: Stickley, 1984

Winkler, John, *Tobacco Tycoon: The Story of James Buchanan Duke*, New York: Random House, 1942

Bull Durham

Principal Agency
(in house staff)

A slight error in product research did not deter Bull Durham from becoming an early marketing success and from thriving for more than 50 years. During the U.S. Civil War, Union soldiers occupying Virginia, Georgia, and the Carolinas became accustomed to local tobacco products that were lighter than the Turkish blends popular at the time. During a cease-fire near the end of the conflict, Yankee and Confederate troops discovered a tobacco factory in Durham Station, North Carolina, a tiny town along the North Carolina Railroad with fewer than 100 residents. John Ruffin Green's Genuine Durham Smoking Tobacco company made shredded pipe tobacco and sold it in small cloth bags with a picture of a bull on the side. Enjoying the taste of the Bright leaf tobacco, the soldiers carried home their leftover treasure from Durham. Soon the discharged soldiers—especially the ones from the North—were sending letters back to the factory requesting orders for "that Durham tobacco." As word spread, the company with its celebrated bull trademark grew beyond anyone's imagination.

The famous Bull Durham logo actually owes its origin to some careless market research. Over a meal of fried oysters, Green's friend John Whitted pointed out the bull's head on a tin of imported Colman's Durham Mustard on the table. He suggested that Green call his tobacco Bull Durham Smoking Tobacco and incorporate a bull into the logo; the combination of the name and the symbol would, he proposed, suggest a link between Green's products and the popular English condiment. Whitted also urged Green to adopt the name and logo from the mustard because, Whitted believed, both the pipe tobacco and the mustard were made in towns called "Durham." Although Whitted's predictions concerning the success of Bull Durham were right on the mark, his presumption about the origin of Colman's mustard was incorrect. That mustard was actually produced in Norwich, in the eastern section of England; it was Ainsley Celebrated Durham Mustard that was manufactured in Durham. (However, both enterprises used the same recipe developed by a woman in Durham, England, in the 18th century. The head of the bull, surrounded by what appear to be mustard leaves, had become the decorative trademark for Colman's mustard in 1855.)

The name Bull Durham was initially considered impolite in some circles, which considered the term *cow-brute* more delicate than the word *bull*. Before long, however, the popular product was commonly known as Bull Durham.

Green died in 1869, and the company was bought by former storekeeper William T. Blackwell. The Bull Durham name became internationally renowned under the leadership and marketing expertise of Blackwell and his assistant, Julian Shakespeare Carr. The image of the bull appeared on billboards and murals throughout the world, thanks to several talented artists. At least one Egyptian pyramid—Giza's Great Pyramid—had the bull painted on it. Blackwell's factory had a steam whistle for shift changes that roared like a bull, and it could be heard for 13 miles. The baseball term *bullpen*, an area beyond the playing field where relief pitchers warm up before entering the game, was reportedly derived from the giant bull on the Bull Durham ad painted behind the New York Yankees dugout.

Advertising trading cards—forerunners to today's baseball cards—became a popular Blackwell and Carr marketing device in the 1870s. One particular card appealed to both political parties, depending on how it was folded. It featured New York Gov. Samuel Jones Tilden on one side and President Ulysses S. Grant on the other. Bull Durham also served as the first U.S. example of "image marketing," using the names of famous satisfied customers, including authors Thomas Carlyle, William Thackeray, and James Russell Lowell, to advertise its tobacco.

Along with success, Blackwell and Carr found themselves having to protect their trademark from infringements. A few of the advertising imitators during the late 1870s were Pride of Durham, Old Bull, Billy Boy Durham, and Sitting Bull Durham.

By the early 1880s Blackwell's Bull Durham factory was the largest tobacco processor in the world. Its plant employed more than 1,000 workers in a single building. The company was spending $100,000 per year on advertisements in small-town newspapers and $50,000 annually for ads in daily newspapers in larger cities. The company was also active in specialty advertising. The round tabs featuring a bull tied to the ends of the drawstrings for the small cloth sacks of tobacco could be exchanged for premi-

Roadside billboards were used to advertise Bull Durham in the 1920s.
Courtesy of The R.C. Maxwell Company.

ums: around $60,000 worth of clocks were offered as premiums during one year.

By 1890 Bull Durham was considered among the most famous trademarks in the world. In that same year, five of the largest cigarette producers—including Blackwell Tobacco Company, the maker of Bull Durham—joined forces to form the American Tobacco Company. Led by James Buchanan Duke, the consortium used the skills of advertising director Edward Featherston Small to increase the popularity of trading cards among the American public. On one set of cards, Small substituted portraits of Madame Rhea, a well-known French actress, for the Indian trademark normally used by Duke. The competition used similar gimmicks on their trading cards, numbering the cards to encourage customers to collect complete sets. Small then created a campaign in which customers could obtain "Sporting Girls" cards, but only

after redeeming 75 certificates from American Tobacco Company products.

Bull Durham, longtime advertising leader, made its last hurrah with the following page ad in the 4 May 1918 *Saturday Evening Post*:

ANNOUNCEMENT

Our Government has requested that we put at the disposal of the War Department our entire output of "BULL" DURHAM tobacco.

And we have complied—fully, gladly . . . .

We have been sending immense qualities of "Bull" to our men at the front, and at the same time trying to supply consumers at home. But now we are asked to give all our output: 36,000,000 sacks, 2,000,000 lbs., 100 carloads of "BULL" DURHAM every month.

This call means more than just huge figures to me and I know it will mean more than figures to the hundreds of thousands of men everywhere in the country who look upon that little muslin sack of good old "Bull" as a personal, everyday necessity . . . .

"Bull" will come back, with ribbons of honor. Have no fear.

The message was signed by Percival S. Hill, who had been president of American Tobacco since 1912.

Although it is no longer an advertising giant, Bull Durham's legacy continues: the "Bull City" nickname is still used for Durham, North Carolina, and a popular 1988 movie, *Bull Durham,* comically depicted the lives of players in a fictionalized version of the town's minor league baseball team, the Durham Bulls.

RANDALL HINES

Further Reading

Boyd, William K., *The Story of Durham, City of the New South,* Durham, North Carolina: Duke University Press, 1925

Glascock, Ned, et al., "Durham: The Town Tobacco Built," *The News and Observer* (Raleigh, North Carolina) (11 August 1996)

Goodrum, Charles, and Helen Dalrymple, *Advertising in America: The First 200 Years,* New York: Abrams, 1990

Burger King Corporation

Principal Agencies
Hume, Smith, and Mickelberry
Batten Barton Durstine & Osborn
J. Walter Thompson Company
UniWorld Group, Inc.
N.W. Ayer, Inc.
D'Arcy Masius Benton & Bowles
Saatchi & Saatchi Advertising
Ammirati Puris Lintas (later Lowe Lintas & Partners)
McCann-Erickson Worldwide Advertising

After nearly 50 years of advertising and marketing, Burger King Corporation found itself at the outset of the 21st century striving to remake its image. Yet the fast-food chain's enduring slogan, "Have it your way," developed by Batten Barton Durstine & Osborn (BBDO), has remained in the public consciousness.

Founded in 1954 in Miami, Florida, by James McLamore and David Edgerton, Burger King of Miami, renamed Burger King Corporation in 1972, began as a fast-food restaurant with indoor dining. The "Whopper" sandwich was introduced in 1957, and Hume, Smith, and Mickelberry advertised the future number-two hamburger chain with the theme "Home of the Whopper," running local television ads in 1958.

By 1961 the company was offering national and international franchising rights. Forty years later, Burger King Corporation owned nearly 10 percent of the company, while franchisees held the remaining 90 percent. The company had more than 2,500 international franchises, in Latin America, Europe, Asia, the Middle East, Africa, and Canada.

In 1967 Pillsbury Company acquired Burger King Corporation as a subsidiary for $18 million and hired BBDO, which developed its first major promotion, "The bigger the burger, the better the burger." Initial billings by the agency were estimated to exceed $4 million to represent 274 restaurants with sales of nearly $80 million.

By 1971 the chain had expanded to 800 restaurants, and it made a change in its marketing tactics, switching its focus from adults to children. With a $6 million budget, it promoted an animated spokesman, the Little King, coupled with the theme, "Where kids are king." The campaign advertised heavily on television on Saturday mornings and prime-time family and adult shows. Radio spots continued to provide quickly adapted advertisements for specific markets and captured an important audience, Americans in cars. Tossing discs called King Zingers were given away in 1972, the beginning of decades of toy and free promotions offered by Burger King and its chief rival, McDonald's Corporation.

Shaking McDonald's with the "Have it your way" campaign in 1973, Burger King put service in the spotlight with the jingle, "Hold the pickle, hold the lettuce. Special orders don't upset us." An advertising success, the campaign increased ad awareness by 50 percent, a feat never yet to be repeated despite attempts to revive the theme in subsequent years. The Little King was retired and "Have it your way" was adapted to target children with "All kids are different" and "Pickle-less Nicholas."

After four years of rapid growth, Burger King consolidated operations, but the reorganization strained its relationship with BBDO. In 1976 the J. Walter Thompson Company (JWT) won the $25 million Burger King account. JWT had just lost the Shakey's Pizza account, a loss accompanied by a failed pitch to Pizza Hut. Featuring customers on location, "America loves burgers, and we're America's Burger King" was JWT's first campaign for Burger King. The theme music was a variation of "Have it

In 1982 Burger King waged war on its competitors, claiming that taste tests showed its Whopper to be the choice of American consumers.
BURGER KING® print advertisments used with permission from Burger King Brands, Inc.

Lassen Sie sich nicht mit gewöhnlichen Hamburgern abspeisen.

Bei uns gibt's den Hamburger de Luxe.

Für sage und schreibe 35 Pfennig mehr als ein ganz gewöhnlicher Hamburger gibt's den Hamburger de Luxe bei Burger King: 100% Rindfleisch, auf dem Rost gegrillt, knackiger Eisbergsalat, Tomaten, Gurken, Mayo und Ketchup – wenn das nicht nach Ihrem Geschmack ist. **Vom Feuer schmeckt's besser**

Der neue Hamburger de Luxe für heiße DM 2,15.

BURGER KING RESTAURANT

The "Battle of the Burgers" went worldwide, reaching West Germany in 1984, in spots such as this one, with the tag line, "Don't let yourself settle for an ordinary hamburger."
BURGER KING® print advertisments used with permission from Burger King Brands, Inc.

your way," created by BBDO. In February 1978 "Best darn burger" ran on one evening of prime-time television programming during a four-hour period, targeting 140 million viewers.

Capitalizing on the differences between Burger King and its two major competitors, McDonald's Corporation and Wendy's International, Inc., JWT launched a burger war effort in 1982 with the slogan "Battle of the burgers." A hamburger taste-test comparison among the three fast-food giants proclaimed the Whopper to be the best-tasting, spawning lawsuits against Burger King from both McDonald's and Wendy's. McDonald's request for an injunction was denied, but Burger King agreed to phase out its ads. Four months later, Burger King ads emphasized that McDonald's hamburgers were fried, while Burger King's hamburgers were broiled and therefore superior. The company agreed to phase out those comparative ads after consultation with its rivals. Meanwhile, UniWorld Group, Inc., was added to the ad

agency list for U.S. markets in 1983 and remained the company's African-American agency of record into 2001.

The *Wall Street Journal* reported in October 1983 that sales had increased in the United States but that European operations were losing money. The following year, a version of the "Battle of the Burgers" campaign began in West Germany and other European as well as Asian countries. In 1985 a London, England, high court granted McDonald's Corporation injunctive relief to stop Burger King ads with the slogan "It's not just big, Mac" and fine print reading "Unlike some burgers, it's 100 percent pure beef." The judge in the case ruled that Burger King had misled the public into thinking the McDonald's Big Mac was a Burger King product. Meanwhile, in the United States, the $40 million "It's not too late, Herb" campaign was being planned by JWT. Herb was a nerdy character, introduced in two TV spots during the Super Bowl broadcast, who had never tried a Burger King hamburger. The four-month promotional campaign failed to increase sales, however. A promotion offering prizes to customers who spotted Herb in a Burger King restaurant also failed to stir interest. Critics of the offbeat campaign found it irritating and pointless.

Ringing in 1987 with a hostile takeover of parent company JWT Group by the U.K.-based WPP Group, JWT lost Chairman Joe O'Donnell as well as its 11-year Burger King account and Pepsi's Slice soft-drink account. N.W. Ayer, Inc., took over the Burger King account for two years, developing "We do it like you do it," a reintroduction of the broiling-versus-frying campaign. In 1988, however, Pillsbury, along with its Burger King unit, was acquired by Grand Metropolitan, which chose D'Arcy Masius Benton & Bowles to handle Burger King's advertising. That work, which lasted three years, echoed the famous "Have it your way" campaign.

Saatchi & Saatchi Advertising, New York City, later launched the Burger King Kids Club national program, before handing the account to Ammirati Puris Lintas in 1994. In 1997 Burger King again changed hands. Grand Metropolitan merged with Guinness, and a new company, Diageo PLC, was created. That year, Ammirati Puris Lintas introduced a new spokes-character, Mr. Potato Head, for Burger King's new $70 million french-fry campaign; the figure was created as a clay animation character, originally targeted at Hispanic and African-American audiences.

Lush food graphics, copy slides (slides of text or words), and popular music were featured in the three-year "Food and Music" campaign by Ammirati Puris Lintas. In 1999 the agency, by that time merged and operating under the new name Lowe Lintas & Partners, featured actress Kathleen Turner's sexy voice in its "Got the urge?" campaign, introducing the new "X-treme double cheeseburger." In early 2001 Burger King switched its $400 million account to McCann-Erickson Worldwide, New York City, as lead agency, with Campbell Mithun handling its children's work. Later that year, however, the fast-food company decided to phase out McCann.

LINDA BJONE

See also color plate in this volume

Further Reading
Burger King Company Information <www.burgerking.com/company.htm>
Iacobucci, Dawn, editor, *Kellogg on Marketing*, New York: Wiley, 2001
MacArthur, Kate, "BK Flame-broils McCann," *Advertising Age* (1 October 2001)

McCarthy, Michael, "Burger King Follows Urge to Jilt Turner," *USA Today* (25 September 2000)
McRoberts, Flynn, "A Tarnished Crown," *Newsweek* (13 November 2000)
Ries, Al, and Jack Trout, *Positioning: The Battle for Your Mind*, New York: McGraw Hill, 1981; 20th anniversary edition, 2001

Burma-Shave

Principal Agencies
Olmsted-Hewitt, Inc.
Meyer Associates
Leo Burnett Company
Abramson Ehrlich Manes

Perhaps no U.S. outdoor advertising campaign achieved more fame than the roadside signs of Burma-Shave, a shaving cream manufactured and marketed by the family-run, Minneapolis, Minnesota-based Burma-Vita Company. The roadside Burma-Shave campaign ran from 1926 through 1964. Each installation consisted of a series of six signs, the first five bearing a single line of a rhyming jingle and the last featuring the Burma-Shave logo; approximately 600 different Burma-Shave verses appeared in more than 7,000 locations in 45 states.

Starting with $200, a can of paint, and some wood salvaged from a wrecking yard, Allan G. Odell, one of two sons of Burma-Vita founder Clinton Odell, set out in 1925 to advertise a new product—a brushless shaving cream—and thus to save the family's failing business. Taking his inspiration from filling station signs that gave motorists advance notice of amenities available ahead, he planted six 10-by-36-inch red-painted wooden signs 100 feet apart along Minnesota highways 65 and 61. Verses such as "Does your husband / misbehave / grunt and grumble / rant and rave / shoot the brute some / Burma-Shave" offered motorists a humorous reprieve from what, at the going speed of 35 miles per hour (in the early years), could often be a tedious drive, especially along rural roads. The campaign's droll take on the mundane events of daily life posed a welcome contrast to the pastoral landscape. Families made a game of reciting the jingles, gleefully chanting their sightings both coming and going, frontward and backward.

The product, which contained a mixture of camphor and other essential oils, was originally concocted by Clinton's father, Minneapolis lawyer Robert Ransom Odell, from a recipe he claimed to have gotten from an old sea captain. It was Clinton, a retired insurance agent, who gave the mixture its name: Burma (for the country where the ingredients came from) and Vita (Latin for life). For years the Odell family struggled to sell Burma-Vita to local druggists. They soon realized that in order to build a market, they would have to find more daily uses for their aromatic salve.

With the help of a chemist, Carl Noren, whom the family had befriended years before, the Odells created a formula for a brushless shaving cream modeled after a British product called Lloyd's Euxesis. They set out to introduce it to the American public with their few available means: they traveled from town to town handing out free "Jars On Approval" to men on the street and small-town druggists. But even this mass giveaway was not enough to capture a market for the product.

In the mid-1920s Allan and his brother Leonard began posting the wooden signs bearing their handwritten, slightly irreverant advertising messages (later they used aluminum sheets, copper stencils, and spray paint). They did the work themselves, one at the wheel of the truck, while the other jumped out to ask permission from the landowner and to dig the post holes. The first signs—with unrhymed verses such as "Shave the modern way / no brush / no lather / no rub-in / big tube 35 cents drug stores / Burma-Shave"—were put up on the main highways leading into the towns of Albert Lea and Red Wing, outside Minneapolis. Within weeks local druggists were calling the Odells with orders, and the brothers began erecting signs throughout Minnesota, Wisconsin, and Iowa. By the end of the year sales had jumped from almost nothing to $68,000; the next year sales rose to $135,000. By 1945 the company was grossing $3 million annually.

Even in the midst of the Great Depression, Burma-Shave signs—and sales—increased in number. Allan Odell offered his own explanation for the campaign's success, remarking in 1930 that "the most remarkable aspect of the whole program is that the advertising does not ask the consumer to buy Burma-Shave, but creates a friendly feeling toward it by the whimsical humor of the treatment." This amiable atmosphere was enhanced by the company's jingle contests. Offering $100 and up for winning entries, the yearly competitions were received with enthusiasm; in one year there were more than 15,000 submissions. The Odells also

As travel by automobile gained popularity in the United States early in the 20th century, *Burma Shave's* signature roadside signs won over more and more consumers.
Courtesy of Bill Vossler.

won over the farmers and others from whom they leased roadside space by keeping in regular contact through mailings of the chatty house organ *Burma Shavings.*

Burma-Shave copy was clean and wholesome and had a folksy tone that appealed across regions, ages, and religions yet still had an edge: "He played / a sax / had no B-O / but his whiskers scratched / so she let him go / Burma-Shave" and "Are your whiskers / when you wake / tougher than / a two-bit steak! / use / Burma Shave." Though selling a new product to a modern motoring audience, the Burma-Shave signs retained an old-fashioned charm that was refreshing, especially to Depression-era Americans, who were quick to blame big corporations for the country's economic ills. It may also have helped that many of the verses were publicly minded: "Past a schoolhouse / take it slow / let the little / shavers / grow / Burma-Shave," "Many a forest / used to

stand / where a lighted match / got out of hand / Burma-Shave," and "From bar / to car / to / gates ajar / Burma-Shave." Perhaps this atmosphere of good will explains why, in the face of rising public opposition to outdoor advertising in the 1930s, Burma-Shave remained unscathed. Despite its 42,000 individual signs dotting the landscape by 1935, the company was not targeted by critics of billboard advertising.

In the 1940s, however, as a consequence of new legislation regulating the distance of outdoor advertising from the highway's edge, the Burma-Shave signs had to be placed farther away from the roadside—which also meant that they had to be made bigger if they were to remain visible. After the passage of the 1956 Federal Interstate Highway Act, which funded the construction of high-speed limited-access roads, visibility from a distance became more difficult for roadside advertisers. Although by 1960 the size of the signboards had increased by one-third, it had become easier for speeding motorists to bypass the Burma-Shave messages— just as they bypassed the country roads and small towns the interstate highways enabled them to avoid. The 1965 Highway Beautification Act, which regulated outdoor advertising on federally funded roadways, marked the final death knell for the Burma-Shave campaign.

For much of the history of the company, Burma-Vita advertised direct, using no agency at all. In the late 1930s it turned to Olmsted-Hewitt, Inc., a small Minneapolis shop, with a budget of $200,000. By 1950 it was using Meyer Associates for domestic advertising and Vance Pidgeon & Associates for all other assignments. A decade later the company was again without an agency, having returned to advertising direct.

The signs were retired after the Philip Morris Companies bought the Burma-Vita Company in 1963 and directed the $200,000 outdoor advertising budget into television and radio ads. Burma-Shave became part of Philip Morris's American Safety Razor unit, and all advertising was assigned to the Leo Burnett Company in Chicago, Illinois. In a eulogy for the roadside campaign one journalist wrote: "Super highways / super speed / people have / no time to read."

In 1989 American Safety Razor was taken over by the Jordan Company of New York City, which tried to resuscitate the brand name in 1996 by positioning it as a premier-priced niche product aimed at the 50-something man nostalgic for the roadside jingles of his youth. Abramson Ehrlich Manes of Washington, D.C., was the agency. Although Burma-Shave products are available today, the outdoor advertising campaign remains only as a fondly remembered icon of the American road.

CATHERINE GUDIS

Further Reading

Rowsome, Frank, *The Verse by the Side of the Road: The Story of the Burma-Shave Signs and Jingles,* Brattleboro, Vermont: Greene Press, 1965

Vossler, Bill, *Burma-Shave: The Rhymes, the Signs, the Times,* St. Cloud, Minnesota: North Star, 1997

Burnett, Leo 1891–1971

U.S. Agency Founder

In 1935 Leo Burnett opened an ad agency in Chicago, Illinois, that grew to be among the largest in the United States, largely on the strength of enduring campaigns that captured the essence of different brands in symbols that exhibited strong emotion and humor. In 1999 *Advertising Age* named Burnett the third most important advertising person of the century. And of the top ten advertising icons created over the century, four were associated with Burnett's agency: the Marlboro Man, the Jolly Green Giant, the Pillsbury Doughboy, and Tony the Tiger. No other agency had more than one.

Leo Noble Burnett was born 21 October 1891 in St. Johns, Michigan, the first of four children born to Rose Clark and Noble Burnett. After graduating from high school in 1909, he worked as a teacher for a year before entering the University of Michigan in 1910. Active in the campus newspaper and other literary activities, he became a member of Sigma Delta Chi, a journalism fraternity, before graduating in 1914. After a brief period as a reporter for the *Peoria* (Illinois) *Journal,* he went to work for the Cadillac Motor Car Company editing a company magazine and had frequent contact with Theodore MacManus, the legendary advertising man responsible for Cadillac's ads. After marrying in 1918 and serving in World War I, Burnett joined five other men and founded LaFayette Motors in Indianapolis, Indiana. Though the failure of the venture was swift, it brought Burnett to his first agency job with the Homer McKee agency, where he remained until 1930.

That year Arthur Kudner, copy director at Erwin, Wasey & Company in Chicago, Illinois, offered Burnett a position working on the account of the Minnesota Valley Canning Company, the marketer of the Niblets and Green Giant brands of canned vegetables. Burnett accepted the job and moved his family to Chicago. He also worked on the agency's Hoover Vacuum Cleaner business and Realsilk Hosiery. His five years at Erwin, Wasey gave him new experience in package-goods advertising as well as in network radio. But he became increasingly unhappy with the creative product of the agency. Equally dissatisfied was Kudner, who was running the agency's copy department in New York City. In the summer of 1935 Kudner left to form his own agency, a move that gave Burnett the final push he needed to do the same. He resigned on 1 August 1935 and on 5 August founded the Leo Burnett Company, Inc., at 360 N. Michigan Avenue in Chicago. The three charter accounts were Minnesota Canning, Hoover, and Realsilk. The new agency's motto became "reach for the stars."

The agency's growth in the 1930s was steady but unspectacular. Burnett became an influential member of the War Advertising Council in 1942 after the shock of the 7 December 1941 attack on Pearl Harbor, and helped mount a major campaign for the war effort to collect scrap metal. He also volunteered his agency's efforts on behalf of the meat rationing program of the Office of Price Administration.

After the war the agency grew swiftly with the rise of television. In 1946 it broke into the ranks of the top agencies, then defined as those billing $10 million a year or more. But growth took its toll. In 1947 Burnett, at 55, suffered a serious heart attack. Though it was a signal to him to slow down and delegate more responsibility to others, he remained fully engaged in the agency's creative work during the defining decade of the 1950s. In creative meetings, subordinates carefully watched the position of Burnett's lower lip as an index of his reaction to copy and layouts; the greater the protrusion, the more work for everybody else.

Although a short, somewhat stout man with little physical charisma or pretense, Burnett became a central figure in the Chicago advertising scene as his agency grew competitive with the major New York shops. In 1953 the Leo Burnett Company broke into the top ten of American agencies with billings of $46.4 million. The following year it won the Philip Morris, Inc.'s Marlboro account; Burnett took a personal role in repositioning the brand from a women's cigarette to a men's with the introduction of the Marlboro Man campaign. The Burnett style became increasingly associated with such characters, created to personify brand images. These included Morris the cat for Nine Lives, Charlie the Tuna for Star-Kist, the Maytag repairman for Maytag, and many more. Burnett gave frequent interviews in which he expressed a philosophy of simplicity that emphasized the primacy of the "big idea" and the carefully crafted word. He reportedly kept a file of "corny phrases" in his desk to use on such occasions. His tastes were conservative, some said quintessentially Midwestern. When an ad ran in *Life* magazine showing a partially naked woman in sheer panties, Burnett objected personally to publisher Henry Luce, saying he was "ashamed of *Life*" and pointing out his displeasure at having five Leo Burnett Company ads appearing in the same issue.

Although agency operations had passed to younger people by the 1960s, Burnett remained on the scene both as chairman and as the central cultural icon of the company, choosing to intervene with the full force of his personality where he deemed necessary. As long as he was part of the company, this proclivity undermined the efforts of would-be successors.

In the summer of 1967 senior management asked Burnett to step down from his seat on the agency's creative review committee because his sheer presence was having an inhibiting effect on the evolution of the agency's creative work. Burnett reluctantly complied, assuming the title of founder-chairman. That December at the annual employee breakfast, Burnett delivered an address that has become his most succinct personal credo. The speech was called "When to Take My Name Off the Door," and a film of the speech is still shown to every new Burnett employee.

Leo Burnett.
Courtesy of Leo Burnett Company, Inc.

On 7 June 1971 Burnett died of a heart attack at his home in suburban Lake Zurich, Illinois, after putting in a full day at the office. None of his three children followed him into advertising, and his stock was returned to the privately held company.

JOHN MCDONOUGH

Biography

Born in St. Johns, Michigan, 21 October 1891; graduated from the University of Michigan, 1914; became an editor for a company publication for the Cadillac Motor Car Company, 1915; served as seaman second class during World War I in Great Lakes, Illinois; co-founded LaFayette Motors, in Indianapolis, Indiana, 1919; began advertising career at Homer McKee agency, 1920; joined Erwin, Wasey & Company, in Chicago, Illinois, 1930; founded Leo Burnett Company, 1935; named founder-chairman at Burnett, 1968; died at home in Lake Zurich, Illinois, 7 June 1971.

Selected Publications

"Leo Burnett Tells 'What I Have Learned' about Writing Ads and the Advertising Business," *Advertising Age* (7 November 1955)

"Famed Copywriter and Agency Head Answers Some Questions about Copywriters and Copywriting," *Advertising Age* (8 July 1957)

"Leo Burnett Urges: Don't Be Dull, High Falutin' or Clever with Words—Be Simple, Believable, Different," *Advertising Age* (28 November 1960)

"Adman Burnett Gets a Gold Key, Cracks Heads Together, Talks Ad Philosophy, and Makes Bold Bid for Writers," *Advertising Age* (1 May 1961)

"The End of the Creative Line; or, An Ad Is Not an Ad until the Client Has Okayed It," *Advertising Age* (4 September 1961)

"Leo Burnett Talks about How He Writes Copy," *Advertising Age* (12 April 1965)

"How Do You Sell Advertising to Today's 'Critical' Youth?" *Advertising Age* (19 June 1967)

"Leo Burnett Discusses the Agency and the Ad Business, Parts 1 and 2," *Advertising Age* (23–30 October 1967)

Further Reading

Fox, Stephen, *The Mirror Makers: A History of American Advertising and Its Creators,* New York: Morrow, 1984

Hixon, Carl, "Leo: When You Toiled for a Legend, Your Life Overflowed with Exhilaration, Frustration, Pressure—And Fun," *Advertising Age* (8 February 1982)

Kufrin, Joan, *Leo Burnett: Star Reacher,* New York: Leo Burnett, 1995

"Special Report: Burnett—An Animated Celebration of Longevity," *Advertising Age* (1 August 1985)

"Leo Burnett: Still Reaching for the Stars after 60 Years," *Advertising Age* (31 July 1995)

Leo Burnett Company, Inc.

Founded in Chicago, Illinois, in 1935; grew steadily, breaking into the ranks of the top ten American agencies in 1953 with billings of just over $46 million; rose to become largest U.S. agency by the mid-1990s and tenth-largest worldwide; merged with D'Arcy Masius Benton & Bowles to form Bcom3 Group, 1999.

Major Clients

Atchison, Topeka & Sante Fe Railway System
General Motors Corporation (Oldsmobile)
Green Giant Company
Keebler Company
Kellogg Company
McDonald's Corporation
Miller Brewing Company
Philip Morris, Inc.
Pillsbury Company
Pure Oil Company
Joseph Schlitz Brewing Company
Star-Kist Foods
United Air Lines

When the Leo Burnett Company was born on 5 August 1935, a brief item appeared in the *Chicago Tribune* noting its founding. Its first address was in the London Guarantee Building at 360 North Michigan Avenue, first on the 18th floor and then on the 15th floor.

Early Years

When Leo Burnett left Erwin, Wasey & Jefferson to form his own company, he took five people and three accounts with him. DeWitt O'Kieffe (whom Burnett had met in Indianapolis, Indiana) and Margaret Stevens formed his copy department. John Olson was the agency's first art director; Strother Cary was its first account executive; and Mary Keating continued as Burnett's assistant. The business of the agency was originally centered on three clients, each with an unusual personal loyalty to Burnett: the Minnesota Valley Canning Company, marketer of Green Giant and Niblets; the Hoover Company, which made vacuum cleaners; and Realsilk Hosiery, which went back to Burnett's Indianapolis days. Together they made for billings of approximately $900,000. The Erwin, Wasey & Jefferson Agency went on to merge with Ruthrauff & Ryan, Inc., in the 1950s before disappearing into Interpublic in the 1960s.

Within a year Burnett would find a strong new business specialist in a fellow Michigan native named Richard Heath. He joined the Burnett agency in 1937 as a vice president with a background that included a stint as night city editor at the *Detroit Free Press* and as a salesman for Curtis Publishing. He was a handsome and gregarious man who led a modest push for new business that included Brown Shoes, A.B. Dick, Standard Milling

(marketer of Ceresota flour), and the American Meat Institute. The early years of the agency were spotty and unspectacular—a kind of "quiet fermentation," as one person called it. In 1938 billings inched over the million-dollar mark. Standard histories identify the $2 million American Meat Institute account in July 1940 as the breakthrough in Burnett's march to national stature. But it was the Pure Oil business ("Be sure with Pure"), also acquired in 1938, that not only made the Burnett agency a player in network radio but also permitted it to play a role in the history of wartime broadcast news.

Burnett was a lifelong Republican, and according to his biographer, Joan Kufrin, he never cast a vote for Franklin D. Roosevelt. This put him in harmony with most of his conservative clients. But he diverged from the party on one central article of heartland conservative dogma: isolationism. Burnett was an internationalist who had no illusions that two oceans could insulate the United States from Nazi and Japanese aggression. Among those who agreed with him was H.V. Kaltenborn, a veteran journalist who became the center of national focus when he reported the Munich crisis in September 1938 on CBS radio. Kaltenborn was also convinced that the proper role of the newsman was to explain and comment on the news as well as to report it; he often did so on his program, *Kaltenborn Edits the News*, sponsored by General Mills.

Kaltenborn's commentaries made him controversial and the owner of CBS, William Paley, nervous. The issue of commentary bothered Paley in principle. He feared the prospect of wealthy anti-Roosevelt sponsors plowing their ad budgets into their own personal notions of news and commentary, which were invariably anti-administration and occasionally fascist-friendly. So Paley decided that CBS must protect itself with an iron shield of objectivity. Burnett, account executive Paul Harper (whose son, Paul, later became chairman and chief executive officer of Needham, Harper & Steers Advertising, Inc.), and Pure Oil management shared Kaltenborn's fears of Nazism more than General Mills. General Mills canceled Kaltenborn's show in March 1939, saying, "It is not a proper function of a company [making] products for general consumption to involve itself in [politics]." Almost immediately Burnett bought Kaltenborn for Pure Oil.

With the outbreak of World War II in September 1939, Kaltenborn's opinions grew even more controversial in a country officially neutral by an act of Congress. But Burnett and Pure Oil were happy with his opinions and the sales they produced. In December, CBS told Burnett that it would no longer have a 15-minute time period in its evening schedule. It offered a daytime slot, knowing that Pure Oil would reject it. Burnett was cornered by its lack of influence in buying time. Thus it proposed an unexpected alternative: move Kaltenborn to NBC, where the limits on opinion were less severe. In March 1940 *Kaltenborn Edits the News* switched networks. Two months later, on May 10, Hitler invaded Holland, Belgium, and France, sealing the certainty of world war and propelling America into the status of an international power. During the war Burnett produced and promoted a series of Kaltenborn war maps for Pure Oil so that listeners could follow the geography of the battles.

The relationship between Burnett and Kaltenborn continued into television well into the 1950s. After the war, Burnett was the agency that brought television's first panel show, *Who Said That?*, to the air. In selecting the panelists, Burnett and Pure Oil insisted that Kaltenborn be a regular member. The Burnett-Pure Oil partnership continued under the Union Oil Company, Pure's corporate successor, for a total of 59 years, until the historic relationship ended in 1994.

Development of the Burnett Culture

In the 1940s Burnett slowly started to blossom. In 1944 it opened a small branch office in New York after having added a merchandising department in Chicago four years earlier. Perhaps as a result, the agency began to learn the tricks of merchandising itself. As Burnett picked up more local honors, he began assembling his thoughts and making speeches. In 1947 he gathered them in a booklet called *Good Citizen: The Rights and Duties of an American,* printed by the American Heritage Foundation. If an agency's job is to organize mythology, the Leo Burnett Company worked up a textbook case on itself.

Burnett knew that he was not a glamorous man, and in his public statements he wisely offered no illusions of glamour about advertising. Instead, he turned this seeming weakness into a strength by fashioning himself a personification of the redemptive power of the simple rural virtues of hard work, long hours, short vacations, and inconspicuous consumption. He became the personification of such values for several reasons. First, he consciously embraced Chicago's own mythology of broad shoulders and straight talk. In addition, in an industry associated with "snake oil" and slickness, he set his agency apart with a powerful profile of the work ethic. Above all, the image fit the man. From his simple beginnings, a company culture of work took root and began to gain critical mass. It centered on the founder and would have enormous influence on lifelong Burnett employees.

For other employees the ideology was a problem, and it sometimes drove them to escape. If advertising was as simple as Burnett claimed, some people asked, why was the process at the Burnett agency so long and full of frustration? One writer said that, after six months at Burnett, he had not been able to produce a single ad. To some the hard work and long hours seemed an end in themselves, a ritual of paying dues more important for exhibiting dedication to the ideology than for making an ad. There were stories of highly paid people sitting around deep into the night battling over how many peas to put on a plate or whether a product photo should be an eighth of an inch to the right or the left. At various times the phrase "creative sweatshop" was heard in connection with the agency.

Yet for those who stayed and thrived, it helped considerably that Burnett was driven by what he saw as the pure beauty of ads, not the desire for personal wealth. He was not a money-driven man. He disparaged "the gray suits and homburgs" and what he called the "wisenheimers." Dedicate yourself to making the ads, he said—"our kind of ads"—and the money would come. When it started coming, he made good on his word by lavishing it on his employees. In 1943 he set up a profit-sharing program that would become the envy of the industry. By the early 1950s he was paying a stunning 22 percent of base salary to employees as a profit-sharing bonus.

Not a share of Burnett stock ever left the company, however. Burnett made private ownership a core article of faith. He made many people rich with salaries that were prodigal by 1950s standards. Around 1957 a young Burnett account man traveled to Cincinnati by train with his boss, Ed Thiele, who was soon to become the agency's president. After a couple of drinks in the club car, Thiele asked the man, "Guess how much I'm making." "I couldn't do that," the young man said. "Come on, guess." The neophyte said nothing. Thiele grinned: "$33,000 a year!" Like all myths, Leo Burnett's was an amplification of fact. But more than anything, his lack of greed persuaded those who stayed with him that he meant what he said.

This also helped give credibility to Burnett's notion of himself as just a simple copywriter who knew nothing about money or big business and who had just stumbled onto his fortune. To make sure that he never showed too cosmopolitan a face to the world, he kept a file folder of "corny language" in his desk. Even at the height of his personal success and wealth in the 1950s and 1960s, he pretended not to know or care how big and rich his company had become. "I'm just an ink-stained wretch," he told people.

Many people suspected that Burnett knew more than he let on. He was smart enough to know that he needed businesspeople, even if he did keep their profiles low. Burnett was loyal but not especially sentimental where business was concerned. In 1964 one of his charter clients, Hoover, began selling washers and dryers in the United States, creating a conflict with the larger but more junior Maytag account, which had come to the agency in 1955. Nevertheless, Burnett had no hesitation in resigning the Hoover account.

Burnett constantly pressed to get new business. Santa Fe (". . . all the way") came in 1942, followed by Pillsbury Company three years later and Kellogg Company in 1949. In November 1957 he ran an ad he called "The Vanishing American" in the Detroit papers, telling workers and management that he wanted a car account. Three months later he got one in Chrysler. The agency would target and circle potential clients relentlessly for as long as it took. It spent nearly two years courting United Air Lines before winning most of its $12 million budget in June 1965.

The ways of new business were often mysterious. Burnett had a propensity for taking in young account and media trainees, building them up to executive potential, and then seeing them hired away by his clients, where they would have the background to constitute a vast fifth column for new business. But this cut both ways. One executive who started at Burnett in 1961 went on to fire the agency when he became chairman of Kentucky Fried Chicken and later rehired it when he became president of Kraft.

Leo Burnett Company, Inc., was responsible for the classic Green Giant ad icon, shown here in a 1945 advertisement.
Courtesy of The Pillsbury Company.

Jack Stafford, on the other hand, started at Burnett in 1960, working on Procter & Gamble Company (P&G) and Green Giant, and ended up 25 years later as CEO of Pillsbury, which had acquired Green Giant in 1979.

The Television Age

After World War II, Burnett's growth came to a large degree from within. (The Green Giant trademark, for example, grew to such proportions by 1950 that it replaced Minnesota Valley Canning as the corporate name.) Billings went from $7 million to $22 million between 1945 and 1950, when Burnett ranked as America's 20th-largest agency. Burnett was pleased that on the 15th anniversary of his agency, its growth was being driven almost entirely by his first love, print advertising. But his reputation for black pencils and notepads perpetuated the agency's image as a print shop at a time when television was growing rapidly. The image was not entirely accurate, however, for by 1950, 25 percent of its billings were in broadcast media, including *Howdy Doody* (Kellogg and Mars), *Arthur Godfrey Time* (Pillsbury), and *Art Linkletter's Houseparty* (Green Giant). By 1952 this figure rose to 40 percent.

The demands of television put new pressures on the agency. A growing list of package-good brands, culminating in the first P&G business ("L-A-V-A . . . L-A-V-A," for radio's *FBI in Peace and War*) in 1953, was pouring through the door and demanding TV campaigns. The agency had to find ways to adapt its print-prone approaches to the camera. A growing menagerie of simple animals and cartoon critters accumulated in Burnett's TV work, starting with Tony the Tiger for Kellogg's Frosted Flakes in 1951. The agency would soon discover that such icons could be powerful long-term instruments for building brand identification for its clients. In 1952 Burnett leased space at 360 North Michigan Avenue and set up its first broadcast department, with recording and film editing capacities and a screening room for 70 people.

In November 1954 the agency took over Philip Morris, Inc.'s Marlboro brand and, using the image of a cowboy on horseback, transformed it from the women's cigarette it had been for decades into a product for men. In 1999 *Advertising Age* named the campaign, which was still running 45 years later, the third most important of the century. (It was the only Burnett campaign to appear in the magazine's top 50 selections.) A decade later Burnett launched Virginia Slims as a cigarette for women ("You've come a long way, baby, to get where you got to today. . . ."). With P&G and now Marlboro, Leo Burnett was proud to be beating Madison Avenue at its own game. The next month an industry trade magazine named him third among America's top ten agency men. In December 1954 the agency paid a record $425,000 in profit sharing.

By the agency's 20th birthday in 1955, as a new generation of employees was beginning its climb, the founders and their early protégés were at the pinnacle of their careers, ruling an agency of 625 people, 28 clients, and some $71 million in billings. Of seven company officers, three had been present at the creation: Burnett,

O'Kieffe, and Cary. Heath and Ross Gamble came a year later. Only Andy Armstrong (the original model for the Marlboro Man) and William Young had joined after the war. Seventy-two employees held Burnett stock. Leo Burnett decreed himself chairman that year, and Heath became president.

In October 1955 everybody celebrated with a Pabst, which marked the agency's reentry into the beer business after an odd four-month encounter with Joseph Schlitz Brewing Company in 1952. The Schlitz experience was not wasted, however. Burnett merely shelved its campaign based on the slogan "What'll you have?" and sold it to Pabst three years later. Schlitz, the country's leading beer in the mid-1950s, would come back to Burnett in 1961, a poor second to Anheuser-Busch. But all the "Gusto" in the world could not save it from an aggressive move by Miller Brewing that pushed Schlitz to number three by the 1970s, and the brand would leave Burnett for good in 1978.

In November 1956 Burnett moved into five floors of the new Prudential Building, where the agency would remain for the next 33 years, after which it opened its own building. By the late 1950s the old guard began to yield, and a second generation began to emerge. Don Tennant joined as a copywriter in 1950, and Draper Daniels as creative director in 1954. Three years later Daniels replaced Armstrong and Bill Tyler as head of what was then called

In 1955 the Leo Burnett Company took on the Pabst Blue Ribbon beer account.
©2000 *Pabst Brewing Company, Milwaukee, WI.*

the "art, television and copy departments," just as the agency hit $100 million. Robert Noel, Don Keller, Gene Kolkey, and Rudy Perz were among the many who arrived during this period, all eager to work on television, which accounted for nearly 60 percent of the agency's billings.

The critter population was growing faster than the agency billings. Keller and Tom Rogers created the first Charlie the Tuna in 1958. But it was the self-effacing Noel who ended up heading the agency's unofficial "department of elves and gnomes," as he helped bring forth Hubert the Harris Lion for Harris Bank, the Little Green Sprout for Green Giant, Morris the Cat for Star-Kist Foods' 9 Lives cat food, the Keebler Elves, and a TV version of the Green Giant himself.

By the time Pillsbury ("Nothing says lovin'") introduced a line of fresh dough products in the mid-1960s, the agency was running low on lovable characters. "People thought the first thing we did when we got a new assignment," Perz told Advertising Age, "was hit the Golden Book of Animals to see which creature hadn't been taken yet." What Perz came up with for Pillsbury was an endomorphic lump of dough that blushed when poked in the tummy. At the Creative Review Committee (CRC), another manifestation of Burnett corporate culture that brought creative iconoclasm to heel and enforced a type of quality control, Burnett smiled and asked what his name was. "How about Poppin' Fresh?" Perz suggested. "That's it! That's it," Burnett said.

In 1999, when Advertising Age looked back on a century of advertising, the magazine chose the most identifiable brand icons of all time. Of the ten selected, four were created or mentored by the Burnett agency: the Marlboro Man, the Green Giant, the Pillsbury Doughboy, and Tony the Tiger. No other agency or company was associated with more than one.

Strains in the Culture

The Burnett company culture was enforced more loosely among the creative staff as time went on. Writers and art directors were often hired at senior levels, remained for a time, and then moved on. One frequently told story was about the day Burnett was waiting for an elevator in the Prudential Building. It was the late 1960s, and when the door opened, a hippie with a mane of wild hair, a bushy mustache, and threadbare jeans stepped out. Burnett turned to an associate. "Is he one of ours?" he asked in a mumble. "Yes," the man said. Burnett shook his head: "He'd better be good." The young man was Richard Fizdale, who would later preside over the company as CEO.

The story has its ironies. Burnett may have been a writer and have staked his company's reputation on its creative product, but his top management was to be developed almost entirely from the ranks of account service. The creative department enjoyed prestige and prosperity but not power. Burnett did not distrust creative people, but he saw them as nonconformists, indifferent to details. Above all, he recognized their reluctance to surrender identity to a larger culture. He preferred to keep them creating.

The latitude Burnett allowed the creative staff was severely tested in 1964 when John Matthews, one of the top members of the creative inner circle, published an impatient book called The Copywriter. Not since Frederic Wakeman (The Hucksters) had an insider debunked the business so severely. "The asininity that passes for top strategy thinking," Matthews wrote, "would be funny if it weren't so wasteful." When he compared the ritual of the creative meeting, meaning the Burnett CRC, to "burying a horse hair under the light of a full moon to [eliminate warts]," he struck at the heart of Burnett culture. Burnett personally disavowed the book, yet two years later he promoted Matthews to senior vice president. The creative meeting was central to the agency's method. "We have absolutely no pride of authorship here," Burnett told Advertising Age as far back as 1950. "Nobody knows for sure who produced which of our ads." In his speeches he questioned the notion that only the individual, never the group, could create. "Too many young writers are more concerned with keeping their identity," he warned. He had faith in creative teamwork. Individuality smacked of the prima donna.

But Burnett was not as high on teamwork when it came to collaborating with another agency. In early 1963 Burnett was awarded the account for the Republican National Committee at a time when the party was deeply divided over ultraconservative Senator Barry Goldwater. Burnett writer Otto Whitiker, a Great Society liberal to the core, wrote the campaign line "In your heart you know he's right." After Goldwater's nomination, however, the party chairman, Dean Birch, suddenly decided to assign the presidential campaign to another agency, keeping Burnett on the Republican National Committee account. Burnett objected. In a stroke of irony laced with reprisal, the business went to Erwin, Wasey, Ruthrauff & Ryan, the shop from which Burnett had taken the three accounts that launched his business in 1935.

In 1967 billings exceeded $260 million. That figure included nearly $38 million that came with the acquisition of the D.P. Brother agency, Detroit, which became an incorporated division of Burnett on 20 March 1967. Brother had been formed as a spin-off of Campbell-Ewald in 1934, when General Motors decentralized the advertising for its divisions among several agencies. Although Brother's ownership structure remained in place after the 1967 acquisition, it would ultimately be folded into Burnett, bringing with it its long-standing Oldsmobile business. Burnett would help the Olds Cutlass displace Chevrolet as the top-selling American car. In the later 1980s and into the 1990s, Burnett would proclaim to a younger generation that the brand "is not your father's Oldsmobile." The brand continued at Burnett until it was announced by GM that the division would be discontinued shortly after the turn of the century.

In February 1967 Burnett transferred all of his voting stock to a charitable foundation, and on July 1, at age 75, he stepped down as CEO. Philip Schaff became chairman, and Burnett assumed the title of founder-chairman. It was a period of transition, not all of it smooth. Burnett had effectively passed his company and its ideology into the hands of a committed management, but there would soon be restlessness in the creative departments. Tennant had been groomed for a top creative job since he came to the agency in 1950 from ABC. In 1962 Tennant replaced Daniels and in 1966 became CRC chairman, succeeding Burnett himself.

He organized the department into four groups under Matthews, Bob Evans, Cleo Hovel, and Bob Ross, all of whom left the agency by 1969 over differences in "total ad making philosophy." Finally, in October 1970, Schaff fired Tennant himself without notifying Burnett. Tennant offered no details. Burnett protested, unwilling to let go of his authority, at which point Schaff and other senior executives confronted the founder and told him that it was time to let the managers manage. Less than a year later, on 7 June 1971, Burnett died at age 79.

The Agency after Burnett

By the early 1970s the agency had acquired such size ($423 million in total billings), momentum, and overall power that only a total management disaster could have stopped its trajectory. Still, many felt that after Burnett's death there was creative drift. Norman Muse, who would later take over the creative functions, claimed to see a sterility and "a distance between the advertiser and the consumer." Yet billings soared, and by 1980 Burnett crossed the $1 billion mark. One reason was Schaff's decision to go global in the 1960s, a move Burnett had had little enthusiasm for. Various agencies were building international networks to keep clients with worldwide operations from going to other shops. Burnett knew what it needed to do, and Gordon Rothrock implemented what Schaff decreed. The changes began in London with the purchase in April 1962 of Legett, Nicholson & Partners, whose principal clients left for other shops when the name was changed to Burnett-Nicholson. Except for United Air Lines and Green Giant, none of Burnett's domestic clients seemed eager for a global agency. After several years, Schaff began looking for a more fruitful purchase opportunity, and he found it in the London Press Exchange (LPE), an old London agency with overseas offices that had once figured in an Agatha Christie mystery. The purchase was accomplished in May 1969, Burnett-Nicholson was merged with LPE, and Burnett found itself a global player. To keep control of the creative process, Rothrock said, the agency moved people to Chicago and assigned senior Chicago people to the branches, including Armstrong, who came out of retirement. Noel traveled the world giving seminars.

Using LPE as a base, Burnett began filling in the holes with acquisitions in Puerto Rico, Colombia, Brazil, and Argentina. When Burnett bought the Jackson-Wain agency in Sidney, Australia, in one sweep it became a presence in Hong Kong; Bangkok, Thailand; Singapore; and Tokyo, Japan. Other buys put the agency in what was then Rhodesia and in South Africa and Malawi. Currency fluctuations proved to be one of the problems of a global operation. Two sets of book were devised, one with blue sheets for the U.S. dollar, which told Chicago how the company was doing, and another with gray sheets for the local currency, which told management how the agency was doing competitively in the local market. In the 1970s and 1980s overseas divisions of Burnett's domestic clients began adding business.

In 1981, with 36 overseas branches in operation by the agency's 46th birthday, Chairman Jack Kopp split the international and domestic divisions into autonomous entities, each with its own chief executive. At the time, international was contributing only a fraction of worldwide billings. By 1995, with 64 offices, it would lead domestic billings by $200 million.

An international presence also played a role in landing the $75 million McDonald's Corporation business in October 1981, one of the largest account shifts in advertising history up to that time. Kopp talked about a plan of strategic encirclement: win McDonald's business in outposts such as Belgium, Holland, and France; show the client what the agency could do; and then strike directly at the company headquarters in Oak Brook, Illinois. The strategy worked, and Burnett soon crossed the billion-dollar line.

Ironically, however, the McDonald's victory also undermined one of the founder's most basic notions of the primacy of creative. It was widely agreed that Needham, Harper & Steers Advertising, Inc., the loser in the competition, had built a brilliant body of creative work over 11 years with McDonald's. To some the shift seemed a bitter and cynical reward for such work and a cruel reminder that, while creative might win accounts, it lacked the power to keep them.

Balance.

2% LOWFAT MILK VITAMIN A & D ADDED

Meat, potatoes and milk.
Balance comes from eating a variety of foods. Because nutritionists agree, no one food provides all the necessary nutrients.
At McDonald's, we offer 100% pure American beef. We offer fish and poultry. Lettuce and tomatoes. And more. Variety in our menu means you can balance what you order.
And make sure your McDonald's meal balances with other meals you eat. Because we want McDonald's food to fit comfortably into your well-balanced diet. Better for you. Better for us.
For more information about all our menu items, ask your McDonald's® Restaurant Manager.
IT'S A GOOD TIME FOR THE GREAT TASTE.

One of McDonald's most successful ad themes of the 1980s was Burnett's "It's a good time for the great taste of McDonald's."
Courtesy of McDonald's Corporation.

In the late 1990s there were increasing rumors of an initial public offering. With worldwide billings in the billions, the agency was moving farther away in time from its founder. CEO Fizdale would be the final senior officer whose career overlapped with Burnett's. The agency continued to take its culture and its traditions seriously, but business ideologies evolve in ways that are not always apparent.

It therefore came as a major surprise on 3 November 1999 when the parent companies of Leo Burnett and D'Arcy Masius Benton & Bowles (DMB&B), both closely held, announced the creation of BDM, a new company with a combined value in excess of $2 billion. Many in the industry assumed that a public offering would soon follow and that the announcement marked the end of the era of the larger privately held agency. But the new company was less eager to go public than many had first thought. Within a month of its formation, the name BDM was abandoned and replaced by the Bcom3 Group. Under whatever name, however, it immediately assumed its place among the world's top 10 advertising holding companies. In addition to the assets of DMB&B and Burnett, Bcom3 also included N.W. Ayer & Partners, Bartle Bogel Hegarty, Starcom Media, and other units.

Roy Bostock, chairman of the MacManus Group, parent of DMB&B, became chairman; and Roger Haupt, CEO of the Leo Group, parent of Burnett, assumed the title of CEO of Bcom3, which immediately became the world's fourth-largest ad company with combined revenue of $1.7 billion on billings of more than $13 billion. A 20 percent stake in Bcom3 was held by Dentsu, which had been in negotiations with Burnett for several months. The merger created a number of conflicts. In the airline category,

for example, Burnett had Delta Airlines; DMB&B had TWA; and N.W. Ayer, a unit of the MacManus Group, had Continental Airlines. The two agencies also shared many clients, including Coca-Cola Company, P&G, and General Motors Corporation. An IPO was expected later in 2000, but a slowing economy forced a postponement until the stock could be issued at its maximum price. A deepening economic slowdown in 2001 reached the level of a major advertising recession, further delaying a public offering. At the end of 2001, the Leo Burnett Company remained what its founder and a succession of top managers intended it to be, a privately held agency.

JOHN MCDONOUGH

Further Reading

Elsner, David M., "Burnett, an Ad Agency in Chicago, Eschews Flash . . . ," *Wall Street Journal* (12 January 1977)

Hixon, Carl, "Leo: When You Toiled for a Legend, Your Life Overflowed with Exhilaration, Frustration, Pressure—And Fun," *Advertising Age* (8 February 1982)

Kufrin, Joan, *Leo Burnett: Star Reacher*, New York: Burnett, 1995

Levin, Gary, et al., "Burnett: An Animated Celebration of Longevity," *Advertising Age* (1 August 1985)

McDonough, John, et al., "Commemorative Section: Leo Burnett," *Advertising Age* (31 July 1995)

O'Kieffe, DeWitt, "Leo Burnett's Favorite Ad Campaigns," *Advertising Age* (10 January 1972)

O'Kieffe, DeWitt, "Leo Burnett's All Time Favorite Ads from Other Agencies," *Advertising Age* (17 January 1972)

Burrell Communications Group, Inc.

Founded as Burrell McBain, Inc., in Chicago, Illinois, by Thomas J. Burrell and Emmett McBain in 1971; renamed Burrell Advertising upon McBain's departure in 1974; acquired DFA Communications, Inc., in 1996, naming the subsidiary DFA Advertising and renaming it Burrell Yagnik Relationship Marketing, 1999.

Major Clients
Bacardi-Martini USA
Bahamas Ministry of Tourism
Bell Atlantic Corporation (later Verizon Communications)
Brown-Forman Distillers Corporation (Martell brand)
Chicago Tribune
Coca-Cola USA
Ford Motor Company
Johnson Products Company, Inc.
Kellogg Corporation
Kraft General Foods (Stove Top and Maxwell House)

McDonald's Corporation
Procter & Gamble Company (Crest, Tide, and Pantene)
Quaker Oats Company
Sears, Roebuck & Company

Burrell Communications Group, founded in 1971 in Chicago, Illinois, is known primarily as a leading African-American–owned marketing communications agency. The company has a reputation for creating advertising that strikes a strong emotional chord by portraying African-Americans in a positive and realistic manner.

Tom Burrell began his career in 1961 in the mailroom of Wade Advertising in Chicago while a student at Chicago's Roosevelt University. Within six months he was promoted to copywriter on such accounts as Alka-Seltzer, Robin Hood flour, and Toni home permanents. By 1971 Burrell had been a copywriter at the Leo

Burnett Company and Foote, Cone & Belding and a copy supervisor at Needham, Harper & Steers. In the early 1970s there was scant research on African-American consumers. Advertisers, just starting to recognize the significance of the African-American market, had little experience in targeting African-American consumers. Using a market niche approach as a way to attract clients, Burrell founded his own agency with Emmett McBain, who had worked at the African-American–owned agency Vince Cullers Advertising.

Before the 1970s portrayals of blacks in advertising were either scarce or limited to stereotypical, dated, and sometimes offensive images. Burrell is credited with developing an advertising technique called "positive realism," which depicted African-Americans using consumer products in a manner that was authentic and relevant. This technique is believed to have influenced the depiction of African-Americans in advertising. The agency also used research and strategic planning to develop advertising campaigns. For example, in 1971 Burrell and McBain created an urban Marlboro Man for Philip Morris using research that revealed African-American men's concepts of masculinity. Finding that black men saw the traditional Marlboro Man as a lonely, rural outcast, Burrell's version was family oriented, urban, and social. Its successful ad campaign increased the brand's market share among African-American males.

As the agency's reputation grew, it attracted the attention of large corporate advertisers. In 1972 and 1973, McDonald's and Coca-Cola, respectively, selected Burrell to create their African-American–targeted advertising. (In 1983 Burrell opened an office in Atlanta, Georgia, to provide increased service to Atlanta-based Coca-Cola.) When McBain departed in 1974, the firm was renamed Burrell Advertising. The agency won its first Clio Award in 1977 for "Street Song," a 1976 TV commercial for Coca-Cola featuring African-American youths singing a cappella about the joys of drinking Coke. Television commercials such as "Street Song" and McDonald's touching "Daddy's Home" in 1977 significantly increased the recognition of Burrell's work. Research showed that these ads "crossed over"— that is, they appealed to general as well as African-American audiences. Between 1971 and 1979 volume grew from a $1,000 monthly retainer from a single client to about $10 million in total client billings.

The agency chalked up other significant successes during the 1980s. Burrell scored a major coup in late 1983 when Procter & Gamble (P&G) hired the agency to create a campaign for Crest toothpaste targeted at African-Americans, the first time P&G had gone outside its usual roster of agencies. Burrell's work for the consumer marketing behemoth raised the agency's profile considerably within the advertising community and is regarded as instrumental in the agency's subsequent success. In 1985 the agency was awarded its first general market account, Martell Cognac, when its slogan, "I assume you drink Martell"—originally developed in 1981 for the African-American market—was found to achieve greater recall among all consumers than themes developed by the brand's mainstream agency. Other general market assignments followed, including work for McDonald's ham-

burger with lettuce and tomato (the "McDLT") and Chicken McNuggets. By 1985 Burrell led all African-American–owned agencies in billings, climbing to a total of $50 million.

Recognizing that marketers needed a broader scope of communication services, Burrell established a public relations division in 1986. Like most advertising agencies, Burrell suffered cutbacks in the late 1980s when the advertising industry experienced business losses during a general recession. The agency, however, continued to win industry awards for its creative work and new assignments for several blue-chip clients, such as Ford Motor Company.

The 1990s brought economic recovery for Burrell; in 1990 it was awarded the African-American assignments for P&G's Tide detergent and Kraft Foods' Stove Top stuffing. Underscoring its expanded commitment to various types of marketing communications, the agency was renamed Burrell Communications Group in 1992. In 1994 Sarah Burroughs, a 20-year veteran of Burrell and former head of its Atlanta office, was named president and chief operating officer. That same year Burrell, along with Goodby, Silverstein & Partners and the Partnership for a Drug-Free America, took top honors at the American Marketing Association's Effie Awards, winning its Grand Effie for "Who Wants?"—a campaign aimed at changing the attitudes of inner-city youths toward drug use.

Early in 1996 Burrell further expanded its services with the acquisition of DFA Communications, a general market advertising and direct marketing firm based in New York City. This acquisition broadened Burrell's communications scope to include direct marketing, in addition to establishing a presence in the influential New York advertising community.

In February 1996 the American Advertising Federation recognized African-American contributions to the advertising industry and cited Burrell, along with other agencies, in a special awards program. In 1998 the American Association of Advertising Agencies honored Burrell with the O'Toole Award for Creative Excellence in Multicultural Advertising. Later that year the Chicago Advertising Federation presented Burrell with its Silver Medal Award for contributions to the advertising industry. In June 1998 *Black Enterprise* listed Burrell as the largest African-American-owned advertising agency, reporting billings of nearly $168 million.

Despite significant advertising industry recognition and financial success, Tom Burrell has expressed frustration with being limited to work that mainly targets African-American consumers and with the difficulty of attracting substantial general market assignments. As mainstream marketers court ethnic consumers more aggressively, Burrell and other African-American–owned advertising companies must also contend with encroachment upon their traditional market niche base. As a survival and growth strategy, Burrell Communications has expanded its services to include advertising, public relations, event marketing, and consumer promotions. Direct marketing efforts are handled by its New York City office, Burrell Yagnik Relationship Marketing.

In an effort to garner more general market assignments, in mid-1999 Burrell sold a 49 percent stake in the agency to the Publicis Group, a French communications conglomerate. Tom Burrell viewed this development as a means to pursue mainstream accounts where African-Americans make up a significant part of the customer base. In 2000 Burrell Communications Group ranked number 98 in terms of U.S. agency brands by gross income, with $23.9 million, up 4.5 percent over 1999, on billings of $174.4 million.

JUDY FOSTER DAVIS

See also color plate in this volume

Further Reading

Dates, Jannette L., "Advertising," in *Split Image: African Americans in the Mass Media,* edited by Dates and William Barlow, Washington, D.C.: Howard University Press, 1990; 2nd edition, 1993

Fawcett, Adrienne W., "Perseverance Pays Dividend at $128 Million Burrell Shop," *Advertising Age* (3 June 1996)

Kern-Foxworth, Marilyn, *Aunt Jemima, Uncle Ben, and Rastus: Blacks in Advertising, Yesterday, Today, and Tomorrow,* Westport, Connecticut: Greenwood, 1994

Business-to-Business Advertising

Long before the term business-to-business (B-to-B) advertising was coined, the practice known as "industrial marketing" was flourishing. Regardless of the name, the goal of the practice is the same—to prime the pump for the sale of a product or service not to a consumer but to another business or to a government entity.

While personal selling is the primary technique for generating B-to-B sales, advertising can help predispose a corporate or government buyer to the sale. Advertising can reach those who influence corporate buying in a way that a sales representative cannot, and an effective B-to-B ad campaign can help lower selling costs.

Crucial Distinctions

Advertising, the most conspicuous element in the marketing mix, has traditionally taken on a different look when the goal is to persuade a business customer rather than an individual consumer to buy a product or service. Compared with print ads directed at consumers, B-to-B print ads tend to include more information and often more visuals of the product or service. Sophisticated B-to-B audiences appreciate a wealth of information, because a misguided buying decision could jeopardize the company and hence the buyer's career. Fear-based appeals are common in B-to-B advertising because there is so much at stake.

B-to-B ads also tend to be more technically oriented and more narrowly targeted than consumer advertising, as the advertiser may be attempting to reach a purchasing manager, a design engineer, a chemical engineer, a chief information officer, a department head, or a distributor. Unlike a consumer, who can act individually and sometimes impulsively, a business decision-maker must carefully consider his or her purchase and often has to justify the buying decision to someone else in the company. In the corporate world, buying decisions often are made by committees, and advertising is often the best way to communicate the existence of a product to a diverse group of people, all of whom influence purchasing within the target company.

Industrial products, such as telecommunication systems, mid-range computers, office furniture, jet engines, and assembly line equipment, are vastly more expensive than most consumer products. The orders are larger, the products are more complex, and the risk to the purchaser is far greater. It is no wonder that the same marketing communications strategies cannot be used for these two very different categories.

Another key difference between consumer and B-to-B advertising is the level of respect each discipline commands. B-to-B advertising has long been dismissed as a creative backwater, while consumer advertising is considered glamorous and big budget. Television has been the favored medium for consumer advertisers since the 1950s, when that medium came into its own. B-to-B advertising put its roots down in print, primarily in highly targeted trade journals and direct mail.

Evolution

The perception that B-to-B advertising lacked cachet began to change in the 1990s as ads for new high-tech products and services narrowed the creative gap. Multinational advertising agencies such as Ogilvy & Mather, McCann-Erickson, Grey Advertising, and Leo Burnett, whose stock in trade was consumer advertising, began to take on computer, e-commerce, Internet, and telecommunication accounts. The work—which was presented in print ads, TV spots, direct mail, or online advertising—was impressive and equal to the work that big agencies did for their consumer clients. B-to-B advertising had traditionally been done in-house or by small- to medium-size ad agencies that specialized in B-to-B. Some of those agencies were later snapped up by multinational agencies to handle their growing rosters of B-to-B clients; other B-to-B agencies were content to remain independent.

In the 1980s, the early days of high-tech B-to-B advertising, marketers made heroes of their products, banking on the notion that superior technology would allow a product's gadgetry to

It's easy to jump to the H-200

Do you have more work than your out-dated business computer can handle?

Why not take a big leap forward — and order the new, low-cost, high-performance Honeywell 200.

We've made conversion easy. If you have a 1401, for example, your present magnetic tape files can go right on the H-200. And your programs, thanks to Honeywell's exclusive "Liberator" concept, can be converted automatically to fast-running Honeywell 200 programs. Your programmers won't have to be re-trained. Your new Honeywell 200 will be humming away in record time.

And you already know what the H-200 can do — it's a fact, not just a promise. For instance, it can read, write, print and punch simultaneously while computing at two-microsecond speeds. It's already hard at work for major companies coast to coast.

A Honeywell EDP salesman will be delighted to give you all the facts. Call him — he'll hop right over.

Honeywell
ELECTRONIC DATA PROCESSING

A 1964 Honeywell ad, featuring a grasshopper created from computer parts, challenged businesses to switch from IBM to Honeywell computers.
Reprinted courtesy Honeywell, Inc.

stand apart from the competition. The ads typically would boast of a stupefying laundry list of performance features accompanied by several visuals and daunting blocks of copy. It was dull stuff, but it usually worked. As the technology revolution accelerated, product life cycles became shorter, and technical product distinctions between one competitor and the next all but disappeared. It was no longer the horsepower that mattered, it was the message.

No longer merely a dry recitation of product features, the messages being delivered by high-tech B-to-B advertisers are increasingly focused on benefits to the business customer. The images and the language are more human. Single visual elements—which often are not even images of the product itself—tend to dominate the ads. The visuals in B-to-B advertising have become more metaphoric, as in consumer advertising. Emulating their consumer counterparts, high-tech B-to-B advertisers in the 1990s began selling on the strength of their brands, not their product features. It is now the brand that helps differentiate a technology product, which is no longer much different from the competition.

In the 1990s B-to-B marketers began supplementing the traditional channels—trade journals, direct mail, trade shows—with on-line advertising; commercials on cable TV, business programming, and broadcast network TV; airport transit boards; general business magazines; and drive-time radio. Trade magazines were not abandoned, however; a 2000 study by market research company Veronis, Suhler & Associates projected that B-to-B communications spending in those publications would reach $19.2 billion by 2004, compared with $10.9 billion in 1995. On-line B-to-B ad spending, which barely registered in 1999, was also projected to grow rapidly; Jupiter Media Metrix predicted that B-to-B advertisers would be spending $3 billion annually by 2005.

Brief History

B-to-B advertising has come a long way since the beginning of the 20th century. In the early 1900s, B-to-B—or industrial advertising, as it was then known—was fighting an uphill battle for respect. The revolutionary technology of the early 20th century virtually sold itself. Businesses did not need to be convinced that electricity, telephones, and internal combustion engines could help their productivity. Industrial marketers preferred to peddle their wares through their salesmen, who could zero in on the key people influencing purchasing at target companies.

Still, industrial advertising did appear in the trade journals of the day, primarily to help "warm the doorknob" for the salesmen. According to an article in the September 1999 Crain Communications' *Business Marketing* (later *B-to-B*):

Industrial advertising was primitive when compared with the advertising of such consumer products as Coca-Cola or Ivory Soap. With little incentive to dramatize their products with compelling stories or eye-grabbing visuals, industrial advertisers were content to have their perfunctory print ads prepared by the business publications themselves. Ad agencies wouldn't touch industrial accounts because the trade

press didn't offer agencies the 15 percent commissions for insertions that were standard on the consumer side.

In 1916 G.D. Crain, Jr., the founder of Crain Communications, Inc. (publisher of *Advertising Age*), started a trade journal called *Class,* whose mission was to help industrial ad managers do their jobs better. By the 1920s industrial advertising was gaining acceptance in the corporate suite, but its creativity was overshadowed by the increasingly stylish work being done on New York City's Madison Avenue by ad agencies on behalf of their consumer marketer clients. However, a handful of industrial advertisers began to imitate consumer-style design and the more conversational, storytelling tone of consumer advertising. A key example was a 1926 ad for Rome Wire Company that featured a four-color illustration of a lineman scaling a wooden utility pole. Under the headline "Out on the copper highways," the copy began: "In blazing sun and blinding blizzards, the bronzed guardians of service carry on."

Industrial advertising took a great leap forward in 1936 when *Class,* which had been renamed *Industrial Marketing* in 1935, launched a feature initially called "O.K. as Inserted," which, in a subhead, described itself succinctly as "a few nods in the direction of the unsung industrial copywriter." The feature was later renamed "Copy Chasers" and eventually came to be known simply as "Chasers" in *B-to-B* magazine. The column was written from its inception until 1982 by Howard G. ("Scotty") Sawyer, a legendary industrial advertising man. In his introductory column, Sawyer wrote of the advertising world:

It is a handful of Manhattan boys who get most of the plaudits—the Conrads of Consumer Copy who strum their fingers over the heartstrings of the masses, swaying millions from Chesterfields to Camels and back again. These are the fellows who get their names in the lights of advertising—and rightly so. But so far there has been no one to pass the bouquets to the industrial copywriter. Successful industrial campaigns and noteworthy industrial advertisements come and go—credit for them seldom gets further than the logo at the bottom of the page. So in order that the best not go unnoticed, the intention of this feature is to cull from the hundred-odd trade and technical magazines the best examples (in our opinion) of industrial selling in-print and bring them to your attention.

Here, industrial marketers were given a standard by which to measure their work. The "Copy Chasers Criteria," ten essential guidelines, became the golden rules of industrial advertising. According to the Copy Chasers Criteria, ads should be visually magnetic; they should promise and support a reward; they should speak person to person; they should sell the service before the source; and they should reflect the company's character. The craft evolved during World War II and the prosperous years of the postwar boom, although the creative handiwork was still not the match of the more visible, high-budget work being done for the masses by the consumer marketers.

This 1991 ad was among the first to encourage both businesses and home computer users to purchase computers with "Intel Inside."
Courtesy of Intel Corporation.

Inspired by Madison Avenue's "creative revolution" in the 1960s, business-to-business advertising, as it was then coming to be known, began to emphasize the more emotional soft sell instead of the traditional rational, hard-selling tone. Advertisers began to experiment with what the Copy Chasers called the "big picture" look. Visuals became more dominant as a way of stopping the reader in his or her scanning of the pages. The big picture was not necessarily the product itself but a borrowed-interest image designed to involve the reader in the advertiser's selling story.

A 1970 ad for Otis Elevator did not show a picture of the elevator but an image of skyscrapers at sheer angles, thus underscoring the danger of a faulty elevator. Warning the reader of a possible loss was certainly fair game in business-to-business advertising. The 1970s also saw the first use of television by B-to-B advertisers. The most notable efforts included Xerox Corporation's Brother Dominic, a fictional monk who secretly used a copier to impress his superiors at a monastery. Starting in 1982 Federal Express, the overnight delivery service, featured its famous "Fast Talker" in a series of TV spots designed to convince secretaries and clerks at corporations that the service could "absolutely, positively" get a package to its destination by the next busi-

ness day. The campaign by Ally & Gargano ranked 11th in the *Advertising Age* top 100 of the century.

Technology began to seize the day in the 1980s, but like the early 20th-century industrialists, computer industry entrepreneurs believed that their products needed to be sold on nothing more than the strength of their engineering. As a result, the creative work was unremarkable. By the 1990s, however, personal computers and microchips had become price-sensitive commodities that needed to be branded. No longer could technology alone sell the product.

Fresh Solutions

The switch from a product orientation to a customer-based brand orientation marked a significant trend in B-to-B technology advertising. In his 1995 book *TechnoBrands*, Chuck Pettis, then an executive with Floate Johnson (a high-tech advertising agency in Kirkland, Washington), argued that in the face of intense global competition, mature markets, and rapid change, marketers could no longer succeed simply by building a better mousetrap. It was a brand name that would assure success. "In our complex and confusing world, brand is needed as an 'editor,'" he wrote. "Brands symbolize the safe choice; they simplify decisions, eliminate surprises, and guarantee quality." Pettis encouraged B-to-B marketers to borrow liberally from their consumer counterparts:

> The brand marketing concepts created a hundred years ago to sell Ivory Soap provide a tremendous wealth of knowledge and experience that can be put to use selling high-tech products today. For starters, the definitions of branding terms such as brand equity and brand associations are the same. Techniques for identifying brand associations and brand extension strategies translate directly.

A shining example of the trend toward technology branding was the "Intel Inside" campaign launched in the early 1990s by Dahlin Smith White, Salt Lake City, Utah (the agency later became Euro RSCG DSW Partners). The print and TV campaign was designed to make both corporate and individual buyers of personal computers (PCs) conscious of an invisible microchip that drives the computer. It was a bit like suggesting that car buyers base their buying decision primarily on the type of engine under the hood. But the campaign worked, as buyers began to insist that their computers have an Intel chip inside. Intel became one of the giants of the technology industry.

B-to-B marketers not only have become more adept at developing and nurturing a brand, but they have also grown more conscious of the need to integrate their marketing communications messages across the ever-widening spectrum of media vehicles. Integrated marketing communications (IMC) is a strategic orchestration of all the elements in a company's marketing mix that allow it to speak in a clear, consistent, and continuous voice. IMC ties together every element—from public relations to packaging to sales promotion to direct marketing to Internet banners to broadcast and print messages. The net result is to leave no doubt in the prospect's mind as to what the brand stands for.

The best B-to-B advertisers present their brand or product messages in fresh, new, surprising, and relevant ways. Most important, the advertiser must offer a solution to a customer's problem. The solution-based messages must have impact, which comes from stating a message in a way people never before considered. A B-to-B advertiser's promotions need not be outrageous—but they should be impossible to ignore.

EDMUND LAWLER

Further Reading

Callahan, Sean, and Lawler, Edmund O., "Century's Legacy: B-to-B Marketing Comes of Age," *Advertising Age's Business Marketing* 84, no. 9 (September 1999)

Lawler, Edmund O., *Copy Chasers on Creating Business-to-Business Ads,* Lincolnwood, Illinois: NTC Business Books, 1994

Patti, Charles H., Steven W. Hartley, and Susan L. Kennedy, *Business-to-Business Advertising: A Marketing Management Approach,* Lincolnwood, Illinois: NTC Business Books, 1993

Pettis, Chuck, *TechnoBrands: How to Create and Use "Brand Identity" to Market, Advertise, and Sell Technology Products,* New York: AMACOM, 1995

Sawyer, Howard G., *Business-to-Business Advertising: How to Compete for a $1 Trillion-Plus Market,* Chicago: Crain Books, 1978

C

Cadbury

Principal Agencies
Euro RSCG Wnek Gosper
TBWA GGT Simons Palmer
Delaney Lund Know Warren
DDB Needham Clemenger/BBDO
Bartle Bogle Hegarty and Colman RSCG
Young & Rubicam, Inc.
Leo Burnett Company, Inc.
Gold Greenlees Trott

John Cadbury, a 22-year-old Quaker, opened his first shop in 1824 on Bull Street in Birmingham, England. Originally selling tea and coffee as his main business, he also offered cocoa and drinking chocolate that proved to be very popular. Cadbury's first advertisement appeared in the *Birmingham Gazette* on 1 March 1824 and read: "John Cadbury is desirous of introducing to particular notice 'Cocoa Nibs,' prepared by himself, an article affording a most nutritious beverage for breakfast."

His shop attracted considerable attention from passersby because it had a plate-glass window rather than the usual bottle glass more common at that time. Cadbury also employed a man dressed in a Chinese costume to preside over the counter.

The foundation of the Cadbury manufacturing business was laid in 1831 when John Cadbury rented a small factory on Crooked Lane in Birmingham and became a manufacturer of drinking chocolate and cocoa. Eleven years later he was selling 16 different drinking chocolates and 11 cocoas. Some of his earliest brands were Churchman's chocolate, Spanish chocolate, Fine Brown chocolate, Iceland Moss, Pearl, and Homeopathic cocoas.

Cadbury rented a larger factory on Bridge Street in Birmingham in 1847. After his brother Benjamin joined the business, they adopted the name Cadbury Brothers of Birmingham. At the same time, John's nephew, Richard Cadbury Barrow, took over the retail side of the business, which became Barrow Stores, trading in Birmingham until the 1960s.

Cadbury Brothers received its first Royal Warrant on 4 February 1854 as "manufacturers of cocoa and chocolate to Queen Victoria"; the company continued to hold these royal warrants into the 21st century. The mid-1850s also saw a reduction in taxes on cocoa beans, which brought cocoa and chocolate products within the budgets of a wider section of the population.

John Cadbury's sons, Richard and George, took over the company when their father retired due to failing health in 1861. Richard and George, both in their early 20s, had a difficult time keeping the company going and considered taking other professions. In 1866 they reached a turning point. Using a cocoa bean processing technique they learned on a visit to a Van Houten factory in Holland, the brothers began marketing a new cocoa essence as "Absolutely pure—therefore best." With the passage of the Adulteration of Foods Acts in England in 1872 and 1875, Cadbury received a measure of publicity for its new, purer cocoa. An earlier bill passed in 1860 had failed to prevent marketers from offering impure cocoas; so Cadbury cocoas, which followed a "rule of purity," became highly sought after.

In the late 1890s, Cadbury moved to a new factory in Bournville, about four miles south of the center of Birmingham. The company introduced "fancy chocolates," an assortment of fine chocolates sold in decorated boxes with small pictures children could cut out and glue in scrapbooks. Richard Cadbury often used his own original paintings to decorate these boxes. Elaborate chocolate boxes were popular as gifts in late Victorian culture, and remained so until the marketer phased out the boxes at the beginning of World War II.

With the dawn of the 20th century, Cadbury began to further expand its line, increasing its revenues through frequent new product introductions. A merger with J.S. Fry & Sons of Bristol in 1919 gave it other product successes. Many of the Fry brands, such as Fry's Chocolate Cream (launched in 1853) and Fry's Turkish Delight, were still popular in the United Kingdom at the end of the 20th century.

Several of Cadbury's best-selling—and most enduring—products were introduced in the early 1900s. Dairy Milk, launched in 1905, became Cadbury's best-selling line by 1913. Through the 1920s Dairy Milk had become a brand leader, a position it held into the 21st century. Beginning in 1928, advertising for Dairy Milk carried an image of milk pouring from a pitcher into a chocolate bar; the tag line read, "A glass and a half of full cream

"OUR GRAND FATHERS DRANK IT"

CADBURY'S COCOA

THE OLDEST AND STILL THE BEST
ABSOLUTELY PURE COCOA.

Cadbury's slogan in this 1900 print ad pointed to the brand's long history as a household favorite.
Reprinted with permission of Cadbury Schweppes plc.

milk in every half pound produced." In later years, singer and U.K. television personality Cilla Black and actor Arthur Lowe appeared in advertising for Dairy Milk. In 1988 the phrase "the chocolate, the taste" was used to update the product's image. The tag line was later updated, in 1998, to "the chocolate and a half."

The Bournville brand was introduced in 1908 as a classic British dark chocolate. Named after the town where Cadbury chocolates were produced, Bournville was advertised as having a "strong, dark taste." Advertising in the late 1980s emphasized the product's heritage with the tag line, "The original plain chocolate."

Flake, a crumbly milk chocolate, debuted in 1911. In the late 1950s, "The Flake Girl" became an advertising icon, appearing in television spots set in exotic locations around the world to promote the brand as a way to let consumers escape from it all. In September 2000 Cadbury introduced Snowflake, a white chocolate flake covered in milk chocolate. The launch was backed by a

$4.2 million campaign handled by TBWA GGT Simons Palmer, London, England.

Cadbury's Milk Tray, introduced in 1915, got its name from the way the original chocolate assortments were delivered to shops—in trays of fine chocolates that were sold loose to customers. A half-pound box with the traditional purple background and gold script was introduced in 1916 followed by a one-pound box in 1924. By the mid-1930s, Milk Tray assortments outsold all competitors and continued to hold its place as a brand leader into the 21st century. "The Man in Black" has enjoyed a long history as Milk Tray's advertising icon. This James Bond–like character was used from 1968 through the 1990s. Originally created by Leo Burnett Company, these commercials usually featured the anonymous "man in black" going through daredevil feats to deliver a box of Milk Tray to a mystery woman. The character was played by Australian model Gary Myers for nearly 20 years. The "man in black" image was used again in February 2000, when fans finally saw the woman getting her man. In December 2000, viewers were allowed to see the face of this mysterious man in black for the first time in a commercial by the London, England, agency Euro RSCG Wnek Gosper. Without the usual antics, he simply hands the chocolate box to his lady, played by English supermodel Jemma Kidd; her response: "Nice packet."

Fruit & Nut was launched in 1921. Until the 1970s Fruit & Nut and Wholenut were advertised together. The most popular Fruit & Nut commercial, from 1977, featured Frank Muir, singing "Everyone's a Fruit and Nut Case" to music from Tchaikovsky's *Nutcracker Suite*.

Crunchie was introduced in 1929. "Thank Crunchie it's Friday" and "Get the Friday feeling—you can't keep it in" were slogans Cadbury used to associate the candy bar with the pleasant connotations of the end of the work week. Cadbury also used animated commercials to give Chrunchie a fun personality, with the Pointer Sisters singing "I'm So Excited." A television campaign from Euro RSCG Wnek Gosper featured comedian Marcus Brigstocke in 2000.

Cadbury's Roses, a twist-wrapped confection, has been popular since its introduction in 1938. The first television campaign for the brand featured comedian Norman Vaughan and the theme "Roses grow on you." In the 1980s the advertising for Roses shifted to a "Thank you" theme that continued through the end of the 20th century as "Thank you very much." These commercials, also handled by Euro RSCG Wnek Gosper, showed people in the streets singing, "Thank You Very Much."

During World War II, chocolate products were seen as essential foods for both civilians and the armed forces. As a result, governments began to oversee production of chocolates and cocoas. However, as sugar and other raw materials were in short supply, rationing of chocolate continued until 1949.

With the introduction of new technologies and rebuilding of infrastructure in Britain, Cadbury again took off in the 1960s, adding new plants in Marlbrook, Herefordshire, for processing fresh milk, and Chirk, North Wales, for processing cocoa beans. In 1962 Cadbury's overall corporate structure was reorganized as

If we took away our creamy Cadbury's Dairy Milk Chocolate,

you'd think we were nuts.

And you'd be absolutely right. Cadbury's new 7-oz. and 3.5-oz. bars are packed with whole nuts, not stingy little slivers. And don't worry, you get Cadbury's Dairy Milk™ Chocolate in every bar—made smooth and creamy with luscious ladles of milk. So try Roast Almond, pure Dairy Milk Chocolate, Fruit & Nut, Whole Hazels, Brazil Nut, and Caramello. You'd be nuts to pass them by.

© Peter Paul Cadbury Inc. 1984   Now in three affordable sizes.   *Cadbury's*

In 1984 Cadbury made an all-out effort to gain a share of the U.S. candy bar market.
Reprinted with permission of Cadbury Schweppes plc.

the company went public. In 1969 Cadbury merged with Schweppes, a soft drink marketer. The combined operation became a major force in the confectionery and beverages market internationally.

By 2001 Cadbury's number-one selling product in the first three months of the year had become its famous Creme Eggs. In the United Kingdom there have been many memorable advertising campaigns for the Creme Eggs. For example, in one ad in the 1970s, a boy enters a local store and asks for 6,000 Creme Eggs; in 1985 Cadbury launched the "How do you eat yours?" campaign; and from 1990 through 1993 ads used the signs of the zodiac to show how different people ate their Creme Eggs. Variations on this theme were used through the end of the 20th century, including contests on the company Web site and special telephone numbers where fans could relate how they ate their Creme Eggs.

In addition to its traditional favorites, Cadbury continued to add new products through the end of the 20th century. In 1976 it launched Double Decker, using England's famous double-decker buses as an integral part of the candy bar's advertising. For example, a news feature about a bus falling into a hole prompted Cadbury to release a print ad with the line, "Nothing fills a hole like a Double Decker." The launch featured British comedian Willy Rushton and the tag line, "Crunchy in a chewy sort of way." In 2001 Cadbury backed the brand with its first ad campaign in ten years. Created by Euro RSCG Wnek Gosper, the campaign starred Charlie Chuck of the British comedy series *Reeves and Mortimer* telling tall tales about the Double Decker candy bar, prompting the tag line, "Are you missing something up on top?"

Other new products included the Wispa chocolate bar, launched in 1983 with a $10.5 million marketing campaign and commercials featuring personalities in pairs—Dennis Waterman and Rula Lenska; Mel Smith and Griff Rhys-Jones; Victoria Wood and Julie Walters; and Paul Nicholas and Jan Francis. Another new product, the Boost chocolate bar, was introduced in 1985 with the tag line, "Cadbury Boost—it's slightly rippled with a flat underside"; and Cadbury's Miniature Heroes, premiered in September 1999, backed with a campaign by TBWA GGT Simons Palmer, with the tag line, "The people magnet."

As part of its U.K. marketing efforts, Cadbury has been among British independent television's biggest sponsors. In 1996 it began sponsoring Granada Television's popular serial *Coronation Street* in a three-year contract for $16 million a year.

The company had tried on occasion to market in the United States on a modest level. In the late 1960s and 1970s it worked with a small Connecticut agency, Wilson, Haight & Welch, Inc., but to little effect. Its last attempt to market its products independently in the United States was an enormous $16 million advertising push through Young & Rubicam. The 1984 campaign focused on Roast Almond Cadbury with the tag line, "If you took away our Cadbury's smooth, creamy, dairy milk taste, you'd think we were nuts." Finally, in 1988 Cadbury decided to license its brands to the Hershey Foods Company.

John Sunderland became chief executive officer of Cadbury Schweppes in 1996. In spring 2000 Sir Dominic Cadbury retired and relinquished the chairmanship to Derek Bonham; it was the first time the Cadbury family had not been represented on the board.

STEVE CLOVER

See also color plate in this volume

Further Reading

Broekel, Ray, *The Chocolate Chronicles*, Lombard, Illinois: Wallace-Homestead, 1985
Cadbury <www.cadbury.co.uk>
Schlager, Neil, editor, *How Products Are Made: An Illustrated Guide to Product Manufacturing*, Detroit, Michigan, and Washington, D.C.: Gale Research, 1994

Calkins, Earnest Elmo 1868–1964

U.S. Agency Founder

Earnest Elmo Calkins was cofounder of the first modern advertising agency, Calkins and Holden. Calkins was an innovator who continually set new standards within the advertising industry. He was also the author of several books defining and defending the business he was so instrumental in forming.

Calkins was born in Genesco, Illinois, on 25 March 1868. A childhood bout of measles left him with progressively worsening deafness. As a result, Calkins's early fascination with letters, words, and print grew, and he became a voracious reader, which later gave him material for his career. When he was 12, he acquired a hand press and type. With these he began to publish broadsides and the occasional periodical. In high school he worked for the local weekly newspaper. Among other duties, he set patent-medicine ads into type, gaining his first taste of advertising. Calkins went on to graduate from Knox College, in Galesburg, Illinois, where he helped to edit a literary monthly.

An apprentice in a local print shop, Calkins launched his advertising career quietly with a few small local advertisements. In a move that was unheard of at the time, he began using artwork in his ads. He also changed his ads on a more frequent basis than once per month.

Calkins began to think seriously of moving his advertising career to New York City, rather than continuing to work in a small town, when he won an ad contest with a piece he created for a small Galesburg hardware dealer, the G.B. Churchill Company. One of the three judges of the contest was Charles Austin Bates, an agency founder/owner and one of the early important copywriters.

Calkins sent samples of his work to Bates in New York City, and Bates hired him as a copywriter. Calkins was successful at Bates's agency and was given increasingly important work. It was during his tenure there that he began to see more clearly the desirability of incorporating art into advertising. Art would bring form to the ads, he believed, strengthening their design and visual appeal. A visit to an art exhibit at the Pratt Institute in Brooklyn, New York, was a turning point, and he enrolled in design classes there.

It was at the Bates agency that Calkins met Ralph Holden, who was in charge of new accounts for the agency. At the time, Calkins was having creative differences with the artists at Bates. This disaffection probably made him more receptive to Holden's suggestion that they set up business for themselves. Holden, businesslike and meticulous, would take care of the sales that Calkins, who by now was totally deaf, believed to be beyond his sphere; Calkins, creative and imaginative, would produce the advertising copy.

Together, the two have been credited with founding the first modern advertising agency. Created in 1902, Calkins and Holden grew into a vital company, with clients including H.J. Heinz, E.R. Squibb, Beech-Nut, Pierce-Arrow, Thomas A. Edison Industries, and Ingersoll Watch. The company also handled promotions for the *Saturday Evening Post, Woman's Home Companion,*

McCall's, and *McClure's* magazines. The success of the agency stemmed largely from its emphasis on design.

When the agency first opened, Calkins had to sell the concept of advertising itself. He presented a series of ads to various manufacturers depicting advertising as the key to capitalizing on the changing climate of business. One such ad persuaded Cyrus Curtis to hire the fledgling company to prepare a campaign on the advantages of advertising in the *Ladies' Home Journal* and *Saturday Evening Post.*

At the time, advertisers commonly bought large blocks of advertising for the cheapest rates possible. A method of announcement, rather than promotion, was used. Calkins and Holden changed this by convincing advertisers that it was the quality of the ad rather than the size of the space that mattered.

Calkins was a visionary regarding the role of art in advertising. He believed that business held great opportunities for artists; in time, he predicted, the great artists of the day would create artwork for advertising, and ads would be a venue for defining and displaying great art. Advertising, in turn, would have an impact on the artistry of the products, as packaging had to be changed to meet the demands of this new type of ad.

In reality, most artists stayed away from commercial art entirely, viewing it with distrust. Eventually, Calkins and Holden hired Earl Horter, who drew in a broad, uncluttered style, and Walter Fawcett, who produced delicately etched silhouettes. As others were added to the staff, the agency's art department became the model and standard for the advertising industry.

Calkins also set the standards for copy. He firmly believed in the power of truth and integrity in advertising. He was outspoken in his criticism of paid testimonials as diminishing public confidence and thus diluting the effectiveness of all advertising.

Notable earlier campaigns by Calkins included the "Phoebe Snow" verses for the Lackawanna Railroad and the "Sunny Jim" jingles for Force breakfast cereal. Each of these appeared as serial stories, eagerly followed by their audiences. Sunny Jim took on a life of his own, as songs, musical comedies, and vaudeville skits were written about him. Both campaigns relied on trade characters; they did not actually present the products' specific merits, but did keep them before the public. Perhaps the most famous of the campaigns in this mode was "The Arrow Collar Man," in which the product was reflected by the accomplishments of the men who wore them. The ads were illustrated with elegant renderings by Joseph Leyendecker, whose work was already famous through his many covers for the *Saturday Evening Post.* The campaign continued when collars were replaced by shirts as the principal Arrow product. In later years, Calkins himself pointed out that this was not necessarily the best type of product advertising—for instance, people knew Sunny Jim but did not necessarily buy Force cereal. Yet these campaigns were considered to be cutting-edge work at the time.

In 1931, five years after the death of Holden, Calkins retired from the advertising business. His deafness had finally become too great a handicap as the advertising industry began turning to radio campaigns.

In 1925 Calkins became the first person to receive Harvard University's Bok medal for distinguished personal service in advertising. Calkins and Holden merged with Fletcher Richards in 1959 to become Fletcher Richards, Calkins and Holden. In 1964 it was merged into the Interpublic Group of Companies.

BARBARA KNOLL

Earnest Elmo Calkins.

Biography
Born in Genesco, Illinois, 25 March 1868; cofounded Calkins and Holden, 1902; first recipient of Harvard University's Bok medal, 1925; retired from Calkins and Holden, 1931; died on 4 October 1964.

Selected Publications
Modern Advertising (with Ralph Holden), 1905
The Advertising Man, 1922
Louder Please! The Autobiography of a Deaf Man, 1924
Business the Civilizer, 1928
The Business of Advertising, 1928
And Hearing Not—: Annals of an Adman, 1946
"The Transition—Magazines into Marketplace in 50 Years," *Advertising Age* (18 November 1974)

Further Reading
Fox, Stephen, *The Mirror Makers: A History of American Advertising and Its Creators,* New York: Morrow, 1984
Rowsome, Frank, Jr., *They Laughed When I Sat Down: An Informal History of Advertising in Words and Pictures,* New York: Bonanza Books, 1959

Calkins pioneered the concept of impressionistic advertising, or the "soft sell," wherein an ad establishes an atmosphere and makes sales pitches by association. This approach was used for products ranging from shirt collars to cars.

Campaign Palace

Founded in Melbourne, Australia, by Gordon Trembath and Lionel Hunt, 1972; opened Sydney, Australia, branch with founding partners Bob Isherwood, Reg Bryson, Chris Martin, and Jack Vaughan, 1982; George Patterson Bates, owned by the Cordiant Group, buys 25 percent interest in the Melbourne office, 1984; George Patterson Bates bought 25 percent interest in the Sydney office, 1985; George Patterson Bates completes buyout of Campaign Palace, 1992

Major Clients
Apple Computer
BHP (metals, mining)
Coles Myer
News Limited
Pacific Dunlop
Qantas
Sanyo
Taronga Zoo
Telstra
Westpac bank

The award-winning ad agency Campaign Palace has been responsible for much of the advertising that has become part of Australia's popular culture, such as the Aussie Rules football anthem "Up There Cazaly." The agency started in Melbourne when art director Gordon Trembath left the high-profile Masius agency to set up his own shop in 1972. Six months later, copywriter Lionel Hunt joined Trembath to establish the Campaign Palace, which at the time was doing work both for other ad agencies and directly for clients. By 1976 the number of direct clients had grown significantly, and the founders decided to become a fully accredited advertising agency.

Trembath was known within the industry as a "details" man, designing everything down to the swizel sticks for client Dunk Island, a resort on tropical Dunk Island in the Great Barrier Reef. Other major clients included packaged goods manufacturer Pacific Dunlop, a long-standing account.

The Melbourne agency built a reputation for breakthrough work, such as the "Blue denim" brochure for Qantas to target the youth market. The brochure is considered part of one of the most successful travel campaigns ever conducted by the airline.

Throughout the 1980s, the agency remained centered at the Melbourne office after the Campaign Palace suffered several false starts in setting up a Sydney office. The Campaign Palace finally opened its doors in Sydney in 1983, when Trembath left Melbourne to personally oversee the agency's northern expansion. Anchoring the Sydney office was the Sanyo account, which reportedly saved the shop from yet another failure when it signed on even as a moving van was en route to pack up the operation.

In the mid-1980s the Campaign Palace attracted a menagerie of clients ranging from zoos to Apple Computer, which the agency launched in Australia in 1984. The Sydney office's first television commercial, "You Belong in the Zoo," for Taronga Zoo, was part of one of the most successful campaigns the zoo ever conducted. However, the agency lacked a major consumer goods client and suffered a period of financial instability as it attempted to continue to grow. Rival agency George Patterson Advertising bought a 25 percent stake in the Melbourne office in 1984 and a 25 percent stake in the Sydney operation the following year.

George Patterson progressively increased its ownership in the Campaign Palace, and by 1987 it owned 100 percent of the Melbourne operation; by 1992 it had acquired the outstanding shares of the Sydney shop as well. The Sydney office hit full speed during the early 1990s, when the agency overtook the Melbourne office in billings. In 1995 the agency opened a separate media specialist agency, the Media Palace.

In 2000 the Campaign Palace employed 120 people in its Sydney and Melbourne operations. The agency had gross income of $9.4 million, down 33.2% over the year earlier, on billings of $82.6 million. Its clients included Australian marketers such as Westpac bank, telecommunications giant Telstra, Pacific Dunlop, News Limited, metals and mining company BHP, and retailer Coles Myer.

In 1997 the trade magazine *Campaign Brief* declared in its review of the Australian advertising industry, "Of all the creative factions of the last 10 years, none has shone so consistently

Elaborately dressed models are used to form words in this 1980s commercial for *Harper's Bazaar* from Campaign Palace.

brightly as the Campaign Palace Sydney. . . . If we had to choose just one agency of the decade, the Palace would be it."

The Campaign Palace has not always been as popular within the ad industry, however. The agency has long had a tradition of rocking the boat. In 1999 the agency's chief executive, Reg Bryson, published a giant foldout ad in Australia's major daily newspapers that challenged the country's business leaders:

> Thinking of advertising? Don't waste your money. . . . The advertising industry has been low on many of the vital signs over the past decade [and] too many of today's advertisers seem content to simply follow the crowd. Too many businesses are simply going from A to B following the well-trodden conventional path.

However pugnacious its attitude, the Campaign Palace has continued to dominate Australia's advertising awards. During the 1970s the agency won 11 Australian Writer's and Art Director's Awards (more than any other agency), Australia's most prestigious industry accolade. It was the top award-winner in the 1980s with 22 trophies and again in the 1990s with 17.

ANDREW HORNERY

Further Reading

Shoebridge, Neil, *Great Australian Advertising Campaigns*, Sydney and New York: McGraw-Hill, 1992

Campbell-Ewald

Founded by Henry T. Ewald and Frank Campbell in 1911; Campbell sold his interest and left, 1917; hired by General Motors Corporation, 1919; Ewald died, 1953; acquired by Interpublic Group of Companies, 1972; following a series of name changes starting in 1976, returned to Campbell-Ewald Company, 1996.

Major Clients

AC Delco (auto replacement parts)
Chevrolet
Delta Faucet
General Motors Acceptance Corporation

Campbell-Ewald (C-E) Advertising was created in 1911 by Henry T. Ewald and Frank J. Campbell; the newly formed agency opened its doors on 7 February 1911 with six employees (by 2000 it would employ 685). The early agency slogan was, "We care not who makes the nation's cars, if we may write and place the nation's ads." The agency's slogan immediately suggested the area of advertising the agency would focus on—the automobile business. Its first client was Hyatt Roller Bearing Company. Campbell sold his interest and left the company in 1917, and Ewald became president. In 1919 a fledgling auto company called General Motors (GM) asked C-E to help place newspaper ads for its Chevrolet line of cars. Three years later GM officially assigned the account to C-E, which included advertising work not only for Chevrolet but also for other lines at the time—Cadillac, Buick, Oldsmobile, Oakland (which later became Pontiac), and GMC Trucks. This focus has continued, with C-E still handling Chevrolet advertising as well as work for GM's parts (AC-Delco) and finance (General Motors Acceptance Corporation, or GMAC) divisions.

Campbell and Ewald were already deeply involved in the automobile business when they met at a gathering to organize an advertising club in Detroit. Both had worked for various car companies before Campbell started Campbell Advertising Service in 1907 to handle newspaper advertising for several auto manufacturers. After successfully launching the Adcraft Club of Detroit, a still thriving organization, Campbell convinced Ewald to join him to create Campbell-Ewald Company in 1911. Although the agency's success would come with GM, it also handled other advertising categories, including presidential politics. In 1924 Ewald, by then president of the agency, coined the famous political slogan, "Keep cool with Coolidge."

By 1929 billings were estimated at $26 million, but the Depression hit car sales hard, and spending on advertising was sharply reduced. Billings at Campbell-Ewald dropped to a reported $8 million by 1938. In 1942, when all civilian auto production ceased until the end of World War II, Campbell-Ewald saw its billings drop to $5 million.

In addition to reducing its spending, General Motors had long since split its various divisions among several agencies, with Mac-Manus, John & Adams handling Cadillac and Pontiac; Arthur Kudner, Inc., Buick; and D.P. Brother, Inc., Oldsmobile. But it was Campbell-Ewald that would handle Chevrolet, which was the GM division competing with Ford and Plymouth for the largest part of the automobile mass market. At the time a Chevy sold for between $400 and $700, and together these makes constituted the so-called low-priced three. In the early 1930s C-E made Chevy a sponsor of Jack Benny's radio program, although the association ended after 1934. Magazines carried the main weight of the advertising for Chevrolet, and wartime prosperity propelled growth as institutional advertising more than offset the cessation of car production. C-E also served other clients, including U.S. Rubber and Eastern Airlines, both handled out of the agency's strong New York office. By 1945 combined billings were estimated at $13 million.

Body by Fisher

$\mathscr{P}$ossession · · · **Makes the Heart Beat Faster**   ◆   ◆   ◆

BUICK this year is widening the tremendous favor it holds with people who live in the modern manner. Its beauty, its luxury, its air of quiet sophistication, are in their language and their mode, as its sturdy dependability and mighty performance are in the universal language of motoring.

In today's Buicks, engineering creates a different and finer kind of motoring—the Buick kind. It adapts Knee-Action wheels to Buick's own requirements for the gliding ride.

But it doesn't stop there. It goes all the way to the gliding ride as only Buick gives it. It builds in a new balance of weight and springing, and a new ride stabilizer; it equips with new air-cushion tires.

Then it provides center-point steering for your greater surety of control; vacuum-power brakes for your greater safety; automatic starting and other operations for your greater convenience and ease, and your car's increased efficiency.

In less than an hour you can learn why Buick is cresting the flood of popularity—and discover that just the thought of possessing it for your own makes your heart beat faster.

· B U I C K ·

WHEN · BETTER · AUTOMOBILES · ARE · BUILT — BUICK · WILL · BUILD · THEM

The slogan featured in this 1920s ad for Buick from Campbell-Ewald—"When better automobiles are built—Buick will build them"—continued to be used by the automaker for decades.
1988 GM Corp. Used with permission of GM Media Archives.

Then in 1946 cars began rolling off the lines again, and C-E soared to new prosperity, thanks in part to the arrival of television. Campbell-Ewald became a pioneer in television as it created commercials for Chevrolet and developed Chevy-sponsored programs. In 1946 Chevrolet became the first auto company to sponsor television programs, an effort that helped boost C-E billings to $25 million by 1950. By the late 1950s the agency was generating about 2,000 broadcast commercials per year, as well as producing variety programs such as *The Dinah Shore Chevy Show* and *Pat Boone's Chevy Showroom*. By 1960, thanks largely to Dinah Shore, "See the USA in your Chevrolet" was among the most famous ad slogans in the country.

In addition to the pioneering work done in television and radio for Chevy, C-E was innovative in other media, for example, creating the first 3-D billboard for Chevy in 1955 after an earlier failed experiment with talking billboards that gave passersby updates on new Chevy products. In 1959 C-E won the first of four gold Lions in five years at the International Advertising Festival in Cannes, France.

The 1950s were a period of major changes in management at C-E, as well as a time in which the agency overhauled its business. Agency cofounder Ewald died at age 67 in 1953. Henry Little, known as "Ted" to friends and "Big Daddy" to employees, became chairman after Ewald and put a renewed emphasis on developing additional accounts. Although his pursuit of new business was slow, Little was successful during this time in hiring many of the people who would succeed him in management, including Tom Adams, who would become chairman after Little's immediate successor, Lawrence R. Nelson (chairman 1966–68). He also gave opportunities to young creative people who later developed well-known agency names on their own, specifically Carl Ally and Amil Gargano. Increases in ad spending by Chevrolet lifted C-E billings to $58 million by 1955 and nearly $100 million by 1960.

Adams took over the leadership of the agency in 1968. After a rocky start (billings at C-E for 1970 were $20 million below those for 1960) he managed to propel Campbell-Ewald into the kind of growth that Little had sought. Rockwell Standard (later Rockwell International) added substantial new business billings, and there was further expansion of the agency's traditional Chevy business. By the end of 1972 billings had edged up to nearly $113 million, making Campbell-Ewald the 19th-largest U.S. agency. In November of that year C-E was acquired by the Interpublic Group of Companies, a holding company whose agency businesses also included second-ranked McCann-Erickson. It was at the time the largest merger of ad agencies. C-E would continue to operate autonomously but as a wholly owned operating company within Interpublic. Adams's plans for the future management of the company were upset when his president and heir apparent, Hugh Redhead, was killed in a plane crash in 1975. By the early 1980s, however, he had begun to groom Richard O'Connor, the ranking executive vice president on the Chevrolet account, for the chairmanship.

John DeLorean's arrival as head of the Chevrolet division in 1970 required adjustments at Campbell-Ewald in how the

Campbell-Ewald's "Heartbeat of America" campaign for Chevrolet ran through the 1980s and early 1990s.
Used with permission of GM Media Archives.

account was managed and financed. For example, DeLorean demanded that agency compensation be linked to product sales, a previously unheard-of philosophy. DeLorean's impassioned desire for new advertising emphasizing brand reliability drove C-E down a creative path that ultimately led to the highly successful "Baseball, hot dogs, apple pie and Chevrolet" campaign, which debuted in 1975.

Interpublic reshaped Campbell-Ewald in several different forms in the first dozen years after it acquired the shop. In 1975 Campbell-Ewald International, set up by Interpublic, linked C-E to the parent's overseas holdings. The next year, C-E was renamed Campbell-Ewald Worldwide, as the Detroit and London offices were merged with two smaller Interpublic properties—Tinker, Dodge & Delano and Clinton E. Frank Advertising. In 1978 the agency followed its chief client, Chevy, and moved its headquarters to Warren, Michigan, a suburb of Detroit, where it erected its own building 100 yards from the automaker's new offices. Then in 1980 Interpublic again rechristened the shop, now Marschalk Campbell-Ewald, which itself was again renamed Campbell-Ewald in December 1984, at which time Richard O'Connor was named chairman.

The synergy between C-E and Chevy extended the shop's run of creative successes, culminating in the 1986 "Heartbeat of America" effort for Chevy. By 1989 the campaign had won more than 400 awards. But at the same time it was being lauded for its work, C-E suffered financially when GM, the parent of its major client, began to renegotiate compensation with all its suppliers, including its agencies. Commissions in some cases fell to almost half of what the automotive giant had previously paid. This added financial pressure, combined with the announcement that Chevrolet was decreasing its advertising budget by $80 million, ushered in the 1990s with one of the largest layoffs in the agency's history.

In 1991 the agency, by now renamed Lintas: Campbell-Ewald in a move by Interpublic that made the shop a unit of Lintas, produced the first ads in the "Like a rock" campaign for Chevy truck. That year the company was named *Adweek* magazine's "Midwest Agency of the Year." In 1994 O'Connor was elected chairman of the largest trade association in advertising, the American Advertising Federation, providing evidence of national recognition for C-E and its advertising work.

History shows that C-E has gone the extra mile for Chevrolet—restructuring, moving, even going to jail over a paperwork mishap involving a commercial shoot in North Carolina. But it is also clear that C-E has grown to be far more than "the Chevy agency." At the outset of the 21st century the agency was ranked 15th in billings in the United States. Campbell-Ewald Company reported gross income of $209.4 million in 2000, up 12.6 percent over 1999, on billings of $1.9 billion, an increase of 16.7 percent over the previous year.

JAMES V. POKRYWCZYNSKI

Further Reading

Hampton, William, *The First 80 Years: An Informal History of the Campbell-Ewald Company*, Warren, Michigan: Lintas/Campbell-Ewald, 1991

Campbell Mithun

(Campbell Mithun Esty)

Started by Ralph Campbell and Ray Mithun, who left Batten Barton Durstine & Osborn to set up the new agency in Minneapolis, Minnesota, 1933; sold to Ted Bates & Company, New York City, 1979, which was subsumed by London, England's Saatchi & Saatchi in 1986; combined under Saatchi with William Esty Company to create Campbell Mithun Esty, 1988; bought itself back from Saatchi with help of Interpublic Group of Companies, 1995; renamed Campbell Mithun in 2000.

Major Clients

American Dairy Association
Andersen Corporation
G. Heileman Brewing Company
General Mills
Land O'Lakes, Inc.
Northwest Orient Airlines
Theo. Hamm Brewing Company

Ray Mithun used to recall that he and partner Ralph Campbell opened their ad agency on the 12th day of March 1933 when President Franklin Roosevelt closed the banks. Although the exact opening date is not firmly established, the two did set up shop in Minneapolis, Minnesota, in the depths of the Great Depression, with $3,000 in borrowed money. Both left the Twin Cities office of Batten Barton Durstine & Osborn (BBDO) to strike out on their own, apparently after Campbell, who was manager of the BBDO outpost, had a disagreement with Roy Durstine, who wanted Campbell to move to New York City. Campbell, for reasons Mithun later said were unknown to him, decided to leave BBDO and chose Mithun to join him as his partner.

Campbell was the agency president; he died of a heart attack in 1949. Mithun, named president in 1943, was to stay on until his retirement in 1983, when the agency was billing $250 million. But for him retirement meant entering another business, since he had earlier sold his own stock to the other agency employee stockholders; Mithun became a banker. He died in 1998, at the age of 89.

Following Campbell's death, Mithun recruited Albert Whitman to be agency vice president. Whitman became president in 1960, when Mithun moved to the post of chairman. The agency had grown steadily and had $43 million in billings at the time and additional offices in Chicago, Illinois, Los Angeles, California, and New York City. A key account in Chicago was the American Dairy Association, which the agency had taken over in 1943 from the Lord & Thomas agency. Whitman had overseen the Pillsbury Company and Theo. Hamm Brewing Company accounts since joining C-M in 1950.

In an unusual claim to fame, Campbell Mithun in 1962 acquired outdoor advertising businesses in St. Louis, Missouri. This was said to be the first time an ad agency had purchased an ad medium. Mithun vowed to keep this investment separate from

Hamm's!
From the land of sky blue waters

A 1956 billboard displayed the memorable slogan created by Campbell Mithun for Hamm's beer.
Courtesy of Miller Brewing Company.

his agency operations. The move did encounter problems, however, because of bylaws of the American Association of Advertising Agencies (AAAA, sometimes referred to as the "Four A's"), of which C-M was a member. Eventually, Mithun sold the outdoor operation to agency stockholders to get around the Four A's rules; it was later sold to Combined Communications. Around this time, C-M gained acclaim for handling the Hong Kong tourism account, which it had gained via its position as the agency for Northwest Orient Airlines. In 1961 it got its first automobile account, Mercedes-Benz, the German automaker whose sales in the United States were handled by Studebaker. It kept the account for only about three years but would get back into auto advertising later.

Cleo W. Hovel, who had joined the agency in 1949 and who is credited with creating the "Hamm's bear," left the agency in 1963 to develop animated TV characters at the Leo Burnett Company. He went back to C-M in 1966 as executive vice president-director of creative services and in 1969 was elected agency president, succeeding Whitman. In 1968 Pillsbury, a 16-year client, shifted its remaining business out of Minneapolis, and that same year C-M acquired business from the flour miller's cross-town rival, General Mills. It would retain that account into the next century. Hovel died suddenly, at age 48, in 1970. He was succeeded in 1971 by Richard Bowman, a New York City advertising man credited with the Ajax "White Knight" and the "Let Hertz put you in the driver's seat" campaigns. That year also saw George Gruenwald join C-M as an executive vice president; he specialized in new products and would become agency president in 1972, when President Stan Blunt moved to chairman. The agency billed $72 mil-

lion that year. Gruenwald later served as chief creative officer, after Bill Dunlap had followed Blunt into the agency's top management. Dunlap, who had joined the shop in 1981 as president, became chief executive officer and then chairman, holding that post through several agency ownership changes and into the new millennium. Early in 2001 Les Mouser was elected president-chief executive officer.

Campbell Mithun was sold in 1979 to Ted Bates & Company, New York City, the agency made famous by advertising pioneer Rosser Reeves and his "unique selling proposition" approach. But C-M continued as an autonomous unit within Bates. Then, in 1986, Bates was taken over by Saatchi & Saatchi, of London, England, for $450 million, a price that sent the advertising business into a frenzy. The deal eventually resulted in other mergers, as Saatchi & Saatchi acquired numerous U.S. agencies; it combined Campbell-Mithun with the William Esty Company in 1988, creating an agency—Campbell Mithun Esty (CME)—with $800 million in billings. The deal did get C-M back into the car business; Esty's Detroit, Michigan, office handled the Chrysler Corporation's Jeep account, after the Chicago-area Oldsmobile Dealer Association dismissed the Chicago office. CME won numerous creative advertising awards in the 1990s for its Jeep advertising. With much irony, Germany's Mercedes-Benz acquired Chrysler—and the Jeep, a vehicle made famous by its service to the Allies in World War II—in the late 1990s.

In 1990 CME linked up internationally with Saatchi & Saatchi's KHBB, London, England. But all the arrangements came apart when the Minneapolis-based agency bought itself back from Saatchi in 1995, with the help of New York City–based conglomerate the Interpublic Group of Companies. Interpublic supplied the initial funds, but CME management soon reacquired a majority share of its stock. In the summer of 2000 the agency dropped Esty from its name, calling itself Campbell Mithun. In 2000 Campbell Mithun had gross income of $103.2 million, up 7.5% over the previous year, on billings of $1.03 billion.

LARRY EDWARDS

Campbell Soup Company

Principal Agencies
F. Wallis Armstrong (later Ward Wheelock Company)
Foote, Cone & Belding
Batten Barton Durstine & Osborn (later BBDO Worldwide)
Leo Burnett Company
McCann-Erickson
Media Edge

As a manufacturer, the Campbell Soup Company has always associated itself with a single product. As an advertiser, the company has long taken an unusually active role in its campaigns and promoted itself in a variety of media. The strategy has worked: today, the name Campbell is virtually synonymous with soup.

The company began in 1869 as a partnership between Joseph Campbell, a fruit merchant, and Abraham Anderson, a manufacturer of iceboxes, in Camden, New Jersey, where the company's corporate offices remain. Soup was originally only one of its offerings; Campbell and Anderson also sold canned vegetables, tomatoes, minced meats, jellies, and condiments. Canned goods of any sort were a relatively recent market innovation at the time the company was founded, and Campbell and Anderson entered the market very slowly, packaging each can by hand and then selling them around the Camden area from the back of a horse-drawn wagon.

A major development in the company's promotional efforts came in 1876, when Campbell and Anderson entered some of their foods, including their soup, into competition at the Centennial Exposition in Philadelphia, Pennsylvania. The soup won a medal for quality. The prize was not a particularly prestigious one, but it proved to Campbell that winning awards could translate into good public relations. (He later incorporated a different medal into his company's logo.) The award also inspired Campbell to move beyond the confines of New Jersey and try selling his products nationwide. Months after the exposition, Campbell bought out Anderson's share in the company, took on a new partner, Arthur Dorrance, and founded Joseph Campbell and Company, later called the Joseph Campbell Preserve Company.

Campbell retired in 1894 and died in 1900, but by that time the Campbell name was so recognizable as a brand that Dorrance, who had become president and general manager of the company, retained it. He also established an advertising committee within the company in 1895 and began Campbell's first true advertising campaign that year. The campaign was quite simple, consisting only of signs and billboards in Philadelphia, New York City, and St. Louis, Missouri, but it was effective enough to demonstrate to Dorrance the value of both advertising and the committee itself. Campbell has subsequently remained highly involved in its campaigns.

The Campbell Preserve Company began moving toward the production of soup exclusively in 1897, when Dorrance hired his 24-year-old nephew, John T. Dorrance, an unemployed chemist. The company has perpetuated the story of John Dorrance's hiring as part of its promotions, creating a virtual myth around him. According to Campbell, John Dorrance had been very well-educated in Europe, but he was unable to find a suitable job after returning to the United States in the late 1890s. He became so determined to work at Campbell that he offered to establish a laboratory for the company at his own expense and to accept a salary of only $7.50 per week. While working as the company chemist, Dorrance discovered a means of preparing commercially condensed soup. Eliminating water from the contents made it possible to put more soup in a smaller package; the costs of packaging, shipping, and storage all dropped accordingly, and Campbell was soon able to market its soups at 10 cents for a 10-and-1/2-half-ounce can, compared with competitors that sold their soups in 32-ounce cans for 30 cents. The company furthered its exposure of the Campbell brand by placing five varieties of condensed soup into stores nationwide: vegetable, chicken, tomato, consommé, and oxtail. John Dorrance also oversaw a program to present free samples of Campbell's soup to housewives in major metropolitan areas. Campbell's profits increased dramatically, and, again according to company lore, Dorrance was given a raise to nine dollars per week.

The company's publicity department has also perpetuated a story about the development of the famous red-and-white Campbell's soup cans, which were introduced in 1898. During the first year that the new condensed soups were on the market, they were packaged in white cans with gold letters; that color combination was a standard of the time and did little to draw attention to Campbell's soups on grocery shelves. According to the legend, Herberton Williams, an executive at Campbell, attended a football game between the University of Pennsylvania and Cornell University in 1898, where he was so captivated by the Cornell team's new red-and-white uniforms that he persuaded the company to use those same colors for its soup cans.

As Campbell grew, John Dorrance took an increasingly active role in its advertising, personally overseeing most campaigns. In 1899 Dorrance placed advertising signs on the sides of street cars in New York City; the campaign doubled Campbell's sales in New York. Dorrance then authorized other street car advertisements, which he viewed as an effective means of reaching the working-class customers that Campbell desired. In 1900 Campbell's soup was entered in a competition at the Paris Exposition. The soup won a gold medal, which was immediately incorporated into the company logo. The red-and-white Campbell's can embossed with the gold medal has since become an advertising classic, one of the most easily recognized packages in the world and an American cultural icon brought to the level of art by Pop art painter Andy Warhol.

Dorrance's most significant advertising creation, however, came in 1904, when he introduced the Campbell's Kids characters. Designed by artist Grace Wiederseim, the Kids were first used in a series of advertisements placed on trolley cars across the United States, which specifically targeted working mothers who needed foods that could quickly and easily be prepared for evening meals. The chubby, red-cheeked Kids have become advertising icons; one of the earliest examples of using characters rather than objects, symbols, or logos to establish a company name, they were still being used in Campbell's advertising campaigns nearly a century after their first appearance (albeit in a slimmed-down version in the health conscious 1990s). The Kids also provided Campbell with another means of promoting the company when Campbell's Kids dolls were offered for sale in 1910. The sale of the dolls increased company profits and introduced Campbell to the concept of merchandising, but it had the even more important consequence of raising Campbell's profile around the United States. Today, merchandising accounts for a minor but steady part of Campbell's sales; customers can purchase products as diverse as toys, porcelain bric a brac, clothing, and greeting cards.

Campbell's first magazine advertisement appeared in *Good Housekeeping* in 1905. The ad emphasized variety, noting that there were "21 kinds of Campbell's soup—16 million cans sold in 1904." In keeping with the variety theme, the company introduced new varieties of soup throughout the decade, including chicken with rice and cream of celery. Dorrance, who had been made director and vice president of Campbell, phased out preserves, condiments, jellies, and minced meats but did approve one new product for the company, Campbell's pork and beans, which remains on the market.

In 1911 Campbell became one of the first companies to employ market research; specifically, Dorrance wanted to know if there was any relation between a consumer's income level and the likelihood that he or she would purchase Campbell's soups. The study proved to Dorrance that there was no class-related stigma to canned soups, which were eaten even in upper-income households.

John Dorrance became president of the company in 1914 and owner in 1915 after buying out his uncle, Arthur. The new owner greatly increased magazine advertising and made one firm demand of all periodicals: Campbell's advertisement in any magazine must be the first ad in the publication; it must appear on a right-hand page; and it must face a full page of text. Now highly coveted, such placement remains known today as "the Campbell's Soup position."

In 1916 Campbell publicized another use for its products when it published a pamphlet-sized cookbook, "Helps for the Hostess," the first cookbook to use condensed soups in its recipes. The patriotic fervor of World War I was also exploited when Campbell promoted its vegetable beef soup as a nutritious meal for soldiers.

During the 1920s Dorrance changed the business name to the Campbell Soup Company and authorized Campbell's first color magazine advertisements. It was the last campaign led by Dorrance; he died in 1930 and was succeeded as president by his brother, Arthur C. Dorrance.

Campbell also began to use agencies to create its advertising in the decade of the 1920s. The company's first agencies were based in Philadelphia, including the F. Wallis Armstrong agency, which worked with Campbell in the early part of the decade, and its successor shop, Ward Wheelock Company, with which Campbell worked into the 1940s.

The Campbell Soup Company first entered network radio in 1934 with a modest budget of just of $205,000. That sum increased by 500 percent in 1935, when the company bought the *Burns and Allen Show* and sponsored the first of five consecutive Christmas Eve presentations of *A Christmas Carol*, starring (except in 1938) Lionel Barrymore. By 1936 the company was spending more than $1.3 million in radio and had become the 11th ranking network advertiser. Three years later, it rose to the seventh position, with a budget of more than $2.7 million. Campell sponsored *Amos 'n' Andy* during the program's declining years as a 15-minute serial (1938–43). However, its most notable coup came in December 1938. Three weeks after Orson Welles's *Mercury Theater on the Air* startled the United States with its "War of the Worlds" dramatization, Campbell bought the show and sponsored it under the name *The Campbell Playhouse*, with Welles continuing as producer and star as well as product spokesman until the spring of 1940. Welles assumed the role, fellow actor John Houseman dryly observed in his memoir, "of a sophisticated world traveler, who, having savored all the greatest broths and potages of the civilized world, still returned with joy and appreciation to Campbell's delicious chicken-and-rice, tomato and pea." Del Sharbutt became the principal voice in Campbell's radio commercials. Foote, Cone & Belding (FCB) joined the Campbell agency roster during World War II. In 1946 Campbell, through the Wheelock agency, sponsored the CBS radio nightly news program, *The News 'Til Now,* first with Robert Trout, then Edward R. Murrow.

Radio would prove a major medium for the company. One advertisement on *Amos 'n' Andy* had lasting repercussions. During a live broadcast, the actor portraying Amos, Freeman F. Gosden, was supposed to refer to Campbell's chicken with noodles soup, but he misspoke and instead referred to "chicken noodle soup." Rather inexplicably, that unofficial name change made a huge difference to consumers; the sales of chicken with noodles

It's the soup that makes the whole meal sparkle!

That delightful glow of well-being and satisfaction! What else gives it so surely and delightfully as a plate of tonic, invigorating soup! Campbell's famous Tomato Soup or any of the 20 other delicious Campbell's blends! What enjoyment every day! 12 cents a can.

See the full list of 21 Campbell's Soups printed on the label.

Send me lots of Campbell's Soups
And don't you be too slow, sir.
I know you have all twenty-one—
That's why you are my grocer!

MEAL-PLANNING IS EASIER WITH DAILY CHOICES FROM CAMPBELL'S 21 SOUPS

An ad from 1930 features one of the Campbell's Kids, enduring advertising icons introduced in 1904 and still used today. *Provided courtesy of Campbell Soup Company.*

soup had been lackluster, but grocery stores nationwide reported a great demand for "chicken noodle soup" following the *Amos 'n' Andy* broadcast. Recognizing a sales success in the making, Campbell changed the name of the soup a few weeks later.

The most significant development in Campbell's advertisements of the 1930s—perhaps the most significant in the history of the company—came with its first radio ads, which introduced the "M'm! M'm! Good!" jingle. The jingle's lyrics are rather simple, even by the standards of a commercial, consisting entirely of "M'm! M'm! Good! M'm! M'm! Good! That's what Campbell's soups are! M'm! M'm! Good!" The jingle's very simplicity, however, has been one of its strongest attributes; virtually everyone in the United States, it seems, knows the Campbell jingle. It became a national catch phrase by the end of the decade, and while Campbell has used other slogans and campaigns, the "M'm! M'm! Good!" jingle has been used regularly since its inception. The Campbell corporation likes to point out that many of its slogans have entered American popular culture, including "Wow! I could have had a V-8!" and, every child's favorite, "Uh-oh, SpaghettiO's." All of these have undeniably caught the public's fancy, but none have been as enduring as "M'm! M'm! Good!"

During the 1930s Campbell strengthened the reputation of its soup as a food that could be used as an ingredient in many recipes, as well as a dish unto itself. In particular, cream of mushroom soup, which was introduced in 1937, was sold as a product that could also be served, undiluted, as a sauce. By the 1940s Campbell had in-house home economists who devised recipes that could be printed on its cans. The company published its first book-length cookbook, *Easy Ways to Good Meals*, in 1941, and sales of Campbell's soups topped $100 million that year.

In the 1950s the company moved heavily into television sponsorship. The television medium, combining both audio and video, allowed Campbell to merge its two most successful advertising creations, the "M'm! M'm! Good!" jingle and the Campbell's Kids, who were depicted in animated form, eating the soup and singing the jingle. Campbell ran the first such advertisement, its first-ever television ad, in 1950.

Like many corporations in the early days of television, Campbell took over the entire sponsorship of one program, with the provision that the company name be used in the series title. *The Campbell Playhouse*, a dramatic anthology series, premiered in 1952 and ran until 1954; the program's name was changed to *Campbell Soundstage* in 1953. The company also advertised on several family-oriented programs, including *Lassie*, *The Donna Reed Show* (the star also appeared in commercials for Campbell), and NBC's regular broadcasts of *Peter Pan* starring Mary Martin. One major change in Campbell's advertising came in 1958, when the company stopped having the Campbell Kids sing the "M'm! M'm! Good!" jingle. Both the Kids and the jingle were still used, usually separately, but the Kids' voices would not be heard again until 1990.

In 1954 Campbell undertook a major restructuring of its agency affiliations. As a result, the company ended its long association with Ward Wheelock Company, which went out of business later that year. Campbell then appointed a search committee, which included a retired Raymond Rubicam, to survey 15 agencies. The major winners were Batten Barton Durstine & Osborn and Leo Burnett in what became the largest account change of the year.

Campbell presented two new lines of soup through campaigns in the 1960s and 1970s. Manhandler soups, created in response to requests from homemakers for more substantial foods for their spouses, were introduced in 1968. The jingle "How do you handle a hungry man? The Manhandlers!" was used to foster the image of soup as a satisfying main course, no matter how large one's appetite. Chunky soups, which featured larger-than-usual pieces of meat and vegetables, were introduced in 1970 and promoted with the slogan "So chunky you could eat it with a fork."

In the 1970s McCann-Erickson introduced a new and effective jingle for Campbell (the company's first since "M'm! M'm! Good!"): "Bring on the Campbell's. Soup is good food." Created by Bill Backer, who also oversaw the Coca-Cola Company's "I'd like to teach the world to sing" campaign, the "Soup is good food" advertisements created a slightly more adult and modern image for Campbell. In the 1980s the company successfully launched its Home Cookin' line as part of the "Soup is good food" campaign and even approached rock star Bruce Springsteen, who reportedly consumes a bowl of Campbell's soup after each performance, about becoming part of the campaign (he declined). In 1990, to further modernize its image, Campbell ran a series of television ads in which the Campbell's Kids performed a rap song about the nutritional values of soup.

Always highly involved in its own campaigns, in 1995 Campbell created the Campbell Media Alliance (housed at True North's offices in New York City), which consolidated buying and planning with a client-dedicated team. Campbell was the first packaged-goods marketer to adopt such a strategy, which effectively moved media to an earlier point in the process of determining strategy. When the company's biggest new-product campaign to date came in 1996, a number of agencies were involved. Nineteen new soups were introduced to the market, including two new Chunky soups, one new Home Cookin' product, seven ramen noodle soups, and four soups in the Creative Chef line, which were primarily used in recipes. The Healthy Choice campaign was handled by Campbell Mithun Esty, while the Chunky soups were promoted by FCB/Leber Katz. All the others were handled by BBDO, which was by this time Campbell's primary agency. It was BBDO that oversaw Campbell's "Good for the body. Good for the soul" campaign in 1998. That campaign, which featured dramatizations centered on families at mealtime, was neither as effective nor as long-lived as "Soup is good food" had been. In 1999 Campbell shifted its account to Young & Rubicam's Media Edge, effectively shuttering the media alliance at True North. Campbell Vice President Tim Callahan explained that the move was made because Young & Rubicam had an independent media unit, while BBDO did not.

During its advertising history, Campbell has occasionally had problems with government regulators. In the 1960s Campbell's competitor, Heinz, tipped off the Federal Trade Commission (FTC) that Campbell and its agency, BBDO, had placed clear glass marbles in the soup used in its television commercials to make the broths look thicker. In 1989 the FTC charged that Campbell misrepresented many of its soups by claiming that they were linked to a reduced risk of heart disease, when, in fact, Campbell's soups are frequently high in sodium. In 1992 Campbell agreed to change its advertising.

Campbell has purchased many other corporations over the years, beginning with its acquisition of Franco-American in 1915; although it is best known today as a maker of Italian foods, Franco-American was at the time one of the other major soup companies in the United States. Other Campbell acquisitions have been intended to diversify the company. These include V-8 in 1948, Swanson in 1955, Pepperidge Farm in 1960, Godiva Chocolate in 1966, Vlasic Foods International in 1978, and Pace in 1995. Most of these brands were spun off into a separate corporate entity in 1997.

Although it has competitors, Campbell's recognizable logo and familiar advertising slogans and jingles have made it the best-selling soup maker in the world for over a century. The company estimates that 99 percent of U.S. homes have at least one can of Campbell's Soup in their kitchens.

RANDALL CLARK

See also color plate in this volume

Further Reading

Dotz, Warren, and Jim Morton, *What a Character! 20th-Century American Advertising Icons,* San Francisco: Chronicle, 1996
Kovel, Ralph, and Terry Kovel, *The Label Made Me Buy It: From Aunt Jemima to Zonkers: The Best-Dressed Boxes, Bottles, and Cans from the Past,* New York: Crown, 1998

Canada

Although the Toronto agency of Holtby, Meyers & Company was placing advertising in newspapers in the late 1870s, it is generally acknowledged that the first advertising agency in Canada was A. McKim & Company, established in Montreal in 1889 as a newspaper advertising agency. Anson McKim, who worked in the advertising department of *The Mail* newspaper in Toronto, was sent to Montreal in 1878 to open the first interprovincial branch advertising office of a Canadian newspaper. Soon afterward, in an effort to secure more business, McKim and other members of the staff began compiling rates and data on other newspapers and formed the Mail Advertising Agency. This effort culminated in the publication of the Canadian Newspaper Directory in 1892, the first complete listing of Canadian newspapers and periodicals. By then, however, McKim had left and opened his own agency, A. McKim & Company, in January 1889. McKim was one of a group of pioneering founders of Canadian agencies that bore their owners' names; others included Harry "Red" Foster, John Aiken "Jack" MacLaren, Warren Reynolds, Russell Kelley, James Lovick, and Palmer Hayhurst. Branch offices of U.S. agencies entered the market in the 1890s, the J. Walter Thompson Company being among the earliest.

Emergence of an Industry

The earliest advertisers in Canada were British firms whose products were already well known by the immigrant population from Great Britain. Among the first were soap makers such as Pears' Soap, which had been advertising in England since 1880 and in the U.S. since 1883. Lever Brothers began advertising Sunlight Soap in 1891. Following the bar and powdered soap advertisements, other products were advertised including baking powders, meat extracts (such as Oxo and Bovril), cocoa and chocolate candies (such as Laura Secord, a Canadian company), cereals, and ales.

Although McKim was the first agency in Canada, arguably the most influential modern Canadian agency was MacLaren. The agency began in Toronto as a branch office of U.S. agency Campbell-Ewald of Detroit, Michigan, which had been established to service the Canadian General Motors account in 1923. Six years later, branch manager Jack MacLaren bought the agency and began making Canadian advertising history. He has been called the "dean of Canadian advertising."

In 1922 Conn Smythe, owner of the Toronto Maple Leafs, granted sole rights to MacLaren for broadcasting of hockey games from the soon-to-be-built Maple Leaf Gardens. The deal, made over a handshake on a golf course, is regarded as the most significant event in Canadian radio advertising history. *Hockey Night in Canada,* sponsored by General Motors and later Imperial Oil and Molson breweries, began broadcasting in 1931 and soon became a Canadian institution.

MacLaren was the first agency in Canada to establish separate departments for radio, advertising research, direct mail, sales promotion, poster, and store display. By 1954 MacLaren was Toronto's largest advertising agency and one of the top 50 companies in North America. With its early success in radio broadcast production and advertising, MacLaren was prepared to be a major player in the early development of television in Canada. By the time the Canadian Broadcasting Corporation began in 1955, MacLaren dominated the medium; agency staff wrote and produced about 85 percent of network programming, including *Gen-*

eral Motors Presents, Cross Canada Hit Parade, CGE Showtime, and, of course, *Hockey Night in Canada.*

By 1960 MacLaren was Canada's largest agency. When the Interpublic Group of Companies bought MacLaren in 1988 and merged the agency with Lintas Worldwide, it acknowledged the importance of the Canadian agency by naming the new entity MacLaren: Lintas. In 1995 MacLaren absorbed McCann-Erickson operations in Canada, and the agency was renamed MacLaren McCann. Having already been recognized as "Canadian Agency of the Year" in 1988, MacLaren added to its reputation by regaining that title in 1995, 1996, and 1999.

MacLaren's original client, General Motors (with Jack MacLaren since 1923 and the agency since 1929), still remained with the agency at the beginning of the 21st century, making this agency-client relationship one of the most durable in advertising history. Other major clients include Nestlé, Royal Bank of Canada, and Lever Pond's.

Leading Agencies and Advertisers

In 1999 MacLaren McCann was the largest Canadian agency in both billings ($424 million Canadian dollars) and gross income ($63.6 million). The rest of the top ten included Cossette Communications, Young & Rubicam, Inc., BBDO Canada, Ogilvy & Mather, DDB Group Canada, FCB Canada Worldwide, Carlson Marketing Group, Publicis, and the Leo Burnett Company, Inc.

Canadian advertising agencies have always been concentrated in the population centers of Toronto and Montreal. Because many agencies are subsidiaries of U.S. ones, the U.S. influence on the Canadian advertising industry is a significant and continuing concern among Canadian advertising leaders. In the early 1960s only three agencies among Canada's top 15 were foreign owned. By 1984 seven of the top ten agencies were still Canadian owned and operated. As has been the case in the United States, however, many independent Canadian agencies—such as James Lovick, Ltd., F.H. Hayhurst Company, Baker Advertising, and Ronalds-Reynolds—have disappeared as a result of mergers and acquisitions, many involving U.S.-owned agencies and holding companies.

In the late 1980s, the trend toward more U.S. ownership of Canadian agencies was accelerated by the purchase of F.H. Hayhurst by Saatchi & Saatchi and Ronalds-Reynolds by Foote, Cone & Belding. In the early part of the next decade, Interpublic acquired two of the biggest Canadian agencies. Foster Advertising was absorbed by McCann-Erickson, and, as previously mentioned, MacLaren was merged into Lintas. By 1999 only one of the top ten agencies, Cossette Communications, founded in Quebec City in 1972, was Canadian owned.

The volume of advertising spending in Canada (in Canadian dollars) reached $9.5 billion in 1998. Broken down by media, the spending was $2.3 billion in television, $2.4 billion in daily newspapers, $765 million in community newspapers, $921 million in radio, $381 million in general magazines, $277 million in trade magazines, $49 million in other print media, $250 million in out-

FOR THOROUGH CLEANSING
—a special cream

Your skin pays for every dusty ride you take. Dust and fine particles of dirt bore into your pores and ordinary washing cannot remove them. Your skin becomes dull. It loses its clear, fresh look.

If you wish your skin to keep its youthful freshness you must give it a thorough cleansing after every dusty trip. For this you need a cleansing cream with just enough oil to remove every bit of dirt from the pores and never stay to overload them—Pond's *Cold* Cream.

This cream is soft and light and will not stretch the pores as stiff creams do.

Smooth it on with the finger tips. Let it stay a minute and it brings out all the dirt. Now gently wipe off both cream and dirt with a soft cloth. Notice how soft and refreshed your

skin feels after this. Regular use of this delicate cleansing cream will keep your skin soft and white.

Use this special cream after every dusty trip and regularly for the nightly cleansing. It contains nothing to promote the growth of hair. The Pond's Extract Co., 146 Brock Avenue, Toronto, Can.

To complete the care of your skin another cream is necessary. Pond's Vanishing Cream protects the skin against exposure and holds the powder on for hours. Always smooth it on before going out and before powdering.

POND'S
Cold Cream for cleansing
Vanishing Cream to hold the powder

MADE IN CANADA

The Canadian office of the J. Walter Thompson Company, one of the first branch agencies in Canada, created this 1922 advertisement for Lever Pond's, one of the country's first advertisers. *Courtesy of Lever Pond's Canada.*

door advertising, $1.3 billion in catalogs and other forms of direct marketing, and $935 million in Yellow Page advertising.

Major advertisers in Canada in 1998 included General Motors and Procter & Gamble. Unlike in the United States, government ranks among the biggest advertising spenders in Canada; the federal government has often been at or near the top and the government of Ontario usually among the top ten advertisers. In election years, campaign spending has contributed significant revenue and national prominence to Canadian agencies.

As a percent of gross domestic product, Canada has consistently spent less on advertising than many other countries. In 1998 it ranked ninth behind Mexico, Japan, Germany, and the United States, among others. Economists suggest several reasons for this. First, many products sold in Canada already have wide acceptance in the United States, and spillover advertising from the

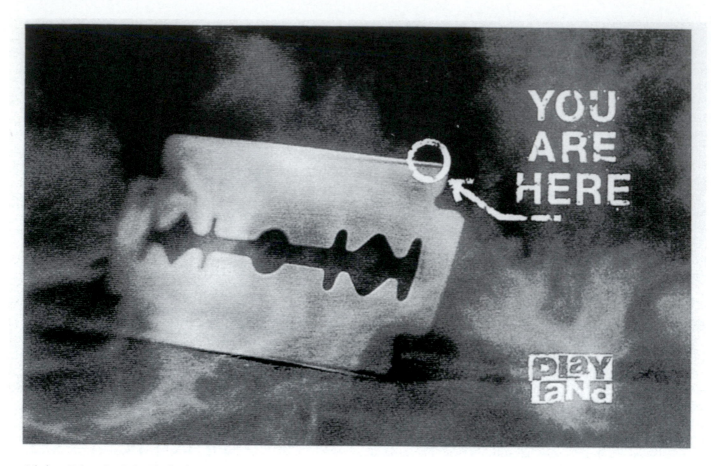

Ads from Palmer Jarvis for Playland, a Vancouver, British Columbia, amusement park, took home honors from Canada's prestigious Marketing Awards in 1997 and 1998.
Courtesy of PNE.

U.S. helps to sell those brands in Canada with less need for heavy Canadian media spending. Second, Canadians tend to be more conservative than Americans, who seem more influenced by advertising and more eager to try new products.

A Unique Culture

Because economic decisions frequently outweigh national or cultural considerations, Canadian advertisers often use ads and commercials conceived and produced in the United States. Yet some Canadian advertising executives contend that the apparent similarities between the two countries are misleading. A former president of Foster Advertising has said that "to be productive advertising must take into account the ethnic, cultural, linguistic, and regional diversities of Canada." An obvious difference between the countries is that Canada has two official languages, English and French, so advertising campaigns must be developed and communicated in both languages.

To fully understand the nature of Canadian advertising, one must appreciate the presence of U.S. advertising in Canada—both from media spillover and the use of U.S. commercials in the country—and its cultural impact. Both English- and French-speaking Canadians have strong feelings about the possible dilution of their unique cultures. A report by the Special Senate Committee on Mass Media in 1970 illustrates this concern:

> The degree to which the advertising industry borrows from foreign cultures and attempts to persuade listeners or viewers to alter attitudes and habits unique to Canada should be of concern in the preservation of our own way of life . . . To the greatest possible extent, such agencies should be controlled by citizens of this country. The decisions which will affect profoundly the buying habits of consumers and the marketing procedures of our industries should be taken by those who understand and wish to protect those attitudes which distinguish Canadians from other inhabitants of the North American continent.

Those sentiments were echoed in a 1991 article by the well-known Canadian author Pierre Burton:

> Our culture has already been badly eroded by the torrent of foreign material pouring over the border. We can't stop it nor should we. But why this reluctance to celebrate our

own talent? I thought we'd got rid of the old Canadian inferiority complex that held if it's American, it must be better, but I stand corrected.

Government regulation of advertising is generally more restrictive in Canada than in the United States, with the Canadian Radio Television Commission and the Department of Consumer and Corporate Affairs having major oversight for Canadian advertising. Provincial governments also have significant powers over advertising such as regulating alcohol advertising on a province-by-province basis. In 1980 the province of Quebec passed Bill 72, which virtually eliminated all broadcast advertising aimed at children under age 13. The resulting lack of advertising support has significantly reduced the amount of French-language children's programming in Quebec, leading some legislators to consider revising the bill.

Industry groups are organized along the same lines as in the United States. The Institute for Canadian Advertising (ICA) represents agencies, while the Association of Canadian Advertisers (ACA) represents advertisers. The ICA (originally called the Canadian Association of Advertising Agencies) was organized in 1905 and incorporated as a trade association in 1923. In 1957 the Canadian Advertising Advisory Board was incorporated by the ICA and the ACA to administer a Canadian Code of Advertising

Standards. That function has come to be performed by an organization called Advertising Standards Canada.

As in other countries where advertising is a significant industry, Canada honors its creative advertising with a host of awards shows sponsored by organizations including Magazines Canada, the Television Bureau of Canada, the Radio Advertising Bureau, and Mediacom, an outdoor advertising organization. By far the most prestigious and sought after annual prize is the Marketing Award given by *Marketing* magazine. The most honored Canadian agency in 1998 and 1999 was Palmer Jarvis DDB, of Vancouver, which won the most Marketing Awards in those years and also won the Gold Billi award from Mediacom for the best outdoor advertising in 1999.

WAYNE HILINSKI

Further Reading

Rotenberg, Ronald H., *Advertising: A Canadian Perspective,* Toronto, Ontario: Allyn and Bacon, 1986

Scotland, Randy, *The Creative Edge,* Toronto, Ontario: Penguin, 1995

Stephenson, Harry Edward, and Carlton McNaught, *The Story of Advertising in Canada,* Toronto, Ontario: Ryerson Press, 1940

The Uncertain Mirror: Report of the Special Senate Committee on Mass Media, Ottawa, Ontario: Information Canada, 1970

Canadian Tourism Commission

Principal Agencies

Publicis-BCP, Montreal
Vickers & Benson Advertising, Toronto
FCB Direct, Montreal

The Canadian Tourism Commission, established in 1995 by the Canadian federal government, replaced the earlier Federal Department of Tourism. The creation of the new body had three objectives. The first was to increase the amount of money available for promoting Canada as a tourist destination. When the commission was formed, the federal government increased funding from the $15 million a year it had provided to the department to $50 million (Canadian) a year for three years. At the end of the century, the federal government was contributing $65 million a year.

The second objective was to increase private-sector participation in tourism promotion. For years the tourism industry had been urging the federal government to allow it a greater role in determining how Canada was marketed as a travel destination. In return for greater participation the industry promised to match the government's contributions with cash from its mem-

bers. Since the commission's founding, and hence the formation of the partnership between government and the private sector, the tourism industry has been either matching or exceeding the support provided by the federal government. Still another objective of the government in establishing the commission was to provide timely information to industry members to help them make sound business decisions. The commission sees itself as industry led and market driven. The Canadian tourism industry wants visitors to see Canada as a premier four-season travel destination where people can connect with nature and experience diverse cultures and communities.

From its first day of operation, the organization faced a daunting task. For several years Canada had been experiencing a "travel deficit." In the early 1990s Canadians were spending $8.2 billion more on travel outside their country than foreign travelers were spending to visit Canada. Part of the commission's job was to reverse this trend. It has undertaken a number of efforts to solve the problem. First, 10 percent of its budget is spent within Canada. The commission has created ads encouraging Canadians to spend more of their vacation time traveling within their own country. One such effort involved a series of special sections, called "Great Canadian Escapes," in Canadian newspapers; they featured lavishly illustrated articles highlighting travel destinations throughout the country—locales for either weekend excursions or extended vacations.

The balance of the commission's budget is reserved for international marketing efforts. These have included a *Canadian Vacation Planning Guide* for worldwide distribution as well as a high-visibility television campaign designed specifically for the United States. A television infomercial was created to air in both France and the United Kingdom promoting Canadian winter vacations. Via Rail (Canada's passenger rail service) and Air Canada joined in the production of the TV campaigns. The commission also tries to support small tourism operators. For a nominal fee, it makes advertising space available in its guidebooks for businesses as small as independent bed-and-breakfasts.

Partnerships such as these have been key to increasing Canadian tourism. For example, the Canadian Tourism Commission and Air Canada teamed up with 12 organizations (Via Rail, Canadian Pacific Hotels, Thomas Cook Travel, All Canada Travel, and eight provincial tourism boards) to entice U.K. travelers to visit Canada during the off-season (late fall to early spring). Rather than using mass communication, the group used a direct marketing campaign. Mailing lists were compiled from databases belonging to Air Canada, Thomas Cook, and All Canada Travel, as well as from the commission's lists of people who had requested information about travel to Canada.

Research conducted prior to the campaign revealed that U.K. residents were intrigued by Canada's "vastness, beauty, and natural wonders." These images were translated into a campaign theme, "A vacation excursion that is larger than life." Colorful foldout brochures were created that combined photos of western Canada's natural and urban attractions alike, sending the message that tourists could enjoy Canada's natural wonders in an urban setting, if desired. The brochures also stressed the superior value that travelers would receive if they booked their vacation through partner agencies. To increase response, a contest called the "Western Canadian Getaway" encouraged consumers to call a toll-free phone number to receive more information on available packages.

The commission and its partners believe that although the program was effective, they should have built tracking devices into the program so that they could precisely measure its results.

In 1996 the commission developed a partnership with the Ford Motor Company of Canada, resulting in a campaign called "Rediscover Canada." It consisted of TV spots featuring tourist destinations across Canada and two Ford vehicles, the Escort and the Windstar, which were recommended as the means of seeing these destinations. Ford supplemented the TV ads with messages on the back of its product brochures urging customers to call a toll-free number to get more information about Canadian travel.

The commission's efforts have had considerable success; the travel deficit has begun to shrink, and tourism spending in Canada has grown steadily. From July to September 2000, tourism spending grew by 6 percent. During this period, domestic and foreign travelers spent $19.5 billion (Canadian). There has been a marked increase in the number of U.S. tourists visiting Canada. In 1995, 37.3 million U.S. citizens visited Canada; in 1997 their numbers reached 40.5 million, an 8.5 percent increase. In the last quarter of 2001, the number of U.S. visitors continued to grow (up 2.6 percent). There have also been marked increases in visitors from the United Kingdom (up 8.3 percent); however, visitors from other countries, such as Australia and South Korea, have declined as rising fuel prices have made the cost of travel more expensive. Greater access to Canada by air resulting from the "Open Skies" policy (deregulation of the Canadian air transportation market, which liberalized travel throughout North America) and the comparatively low level of the Canadian dollar in the late 1990s also helped improve Canada's tourism picture. In the wake of the terrorist attacks of 11 September 2001, however, all tourism entered a state of crisis.

PEGGY CUNNINGHAM

Further Reading

Bosworth, David, "Case Study: Tourism Suppliers Lure Brits West," *Strategy: The Canadian Marketing Report* (13 April 1998)

Caples, John 1900–1990

U.S. Advertising Copywriter

John Caples was a pioneer in the application of scientific methods to advertising. One of the great copywriters of his time, he devoted more than 50 years to testing advertising's effectiveness. He is credited with developing and standardizing the techniques necessary to evaluate an ad's ability to reach its audience and produce the desired results.

Caples was born on 1 May 1900 in New York City. His father was a physician, a general practitioner; his mother, a bright, edu-

cated woman who imparted her love of learning to her son. She taught him to read and write at an early age, instilling a love of language that would serve him well throughout his life.

Caples was admitted to Columbia University in New York City. With the outbreak of World War I, he became an apprentice seaman as well as a Columbia student, but he did not remain at the university. Ironically, his freshman English class stood in his way. His professor required each student to prepare and deliver a two-minute speech to the class. Caples, long a loner, was terror-stricken. Called upon the first day and unprepared, he began to skip class, worried that he would be called to speak as soon as he showed up. Eventually he dropped out of college, knowing he could not graduate without passing freshman English. At this point, he believed himself to be a failure for life.

Caples enlisted in the United States Navy as a regular seaman. Although the war had ended, he took the competitive exams for the United States Naval Academy at Annapolis, Maryland. He passed and was admitted to the class of 1924. While the curriculum was focused on engineering, Caples satisfied his desire to write by becoming the associate editor of the academy magazine.

After graduation from Annapolis in 1924, Caples worked for the New York Telephone Company as an engineer, then for Certain-Teed Products Company primarily performing clerical duties. At the same time, he began taking writing courses at Columbia. After conferring with several advisers, he set his sights on a career in copywriting. This would allow him to do what he wanted—write—and the necessary brevity inherent in ad copy would help him to hone his writing skills.

After trying unsuccessfully to find a job in the advertising field, Caples took a summer course in copywriting at Columbia. The professor, Bill Orchard, was a copy editor at the George Batten Advertising Agency. The copy Caples wrote for class formed the basis of his portfolio; he found that copy chiefs were interested in the samples he had written for class and in Orchard's comments.

In 1925 Caples began his advertising career working for Ruthrauff & Ryan (R&R), a leading mail-order company at the time. He quickly learned the secret behind mail-order copywriting: responses show which ads are successful and which are not, so the wise copywriter learns what characteristics place an ad in the former category.

During his first year as a copywriter, Caples wrote one of the best-known direct-mail ads of all time. Advertising a home-study course offered by the United States School of Music, the piece was headlined, "They laughed when I sat down at the piano, but when I started to play!" It was an overnight success, providing fodder for columnists, comedians, and other copywriters. Using one of his own principles, Caples reworked that success into a subsequent ad for Doubleday, Page & Company: "They grinned when the waiter spoke to me in French—but their laughter changed to amazement at my reply." It was another plum for the young advertising man.

Following his success with R&R, Caples sought a position that would allow him to learn more about the industry. In 1927 he joined Barton Durstine & Osborn—which would become Batten Barton Durstine & Osborn (BBDO)—as a copywriter and account executive. Here, he continued his quest for information, asking questions and pressing to separate fact from opinion. He clarified his own principles of advertising, continually trying to find out what made ads work.

Caples's third major ad success was written for the Phoenix Mutual Life Insurance Company in 1928. It showed an old man relaxing with a fishing rod in his hands. It was headlined: "To men who want to quit work some day." This ad, as well as "They

John Caples.
Photo courtesy of BBDO New York.

Laughed," appear in Julius Watkins's book *The 100 Greatest Advertisements*.

Caples would remain with BBDO for the remainder of his career. He became a vice president in 1941 and later was named creative director. His career was interrupted for a stint in the U.S. Navy during World War II; he served from 1942 through 1945.

Because he began his work in advertising in the mail-order business, Caples was involved with copy testing from the beginning of his career. In a sense, each ad written for the mail-order industry was a test; the ads were continually being judged according to the concrete results they provided.

Caples spent his more than 50-year career as an advocate of testing the effectiveness of advertising. Although he was not a trained researcher, he supervised continuing test campaigns for the *Wall Street Journal* and *Reader's Digest*. He oversaw advertising research for DuPont, U.S. Steel, General Electric Company, Johnson & Johnson, B.F. Goodrich, the United States Navy, Lever Brothers Company, and several other large organizations. Caples's research focused not only on the copy, but the medium, size, color, position, and seasonal attraction of ads as well. He believed that only tried-and-tested elements should be used to create new ads.

Caples began to experiment with split-run ads in the 1940s; by the 1970s, he was running 40-way split-run testing. In a simple split-run, if an advertiser has two different ads, it runs both on the same day in a single publication with each appearing in only half the circulated copies. Coupons in each ad to be sent back to the marketer are coded, so the advertiser knows which ad is eliciting more response from consumers. Caples believed this to be the most scientific means of testing copy. While his methods were at first ridiculed, the concept eventually became an accepted part of ad testing and development.

Caples advocated reworking old successes as a first step in creating new ones, and he recommended a direct approach to writing ad copy. He also maintained that the headline of an ad is all-important. He followed some basic guidelines for writing headlines: self-interest of the reader, news, curiosity, maintaining a positive viewpoint, and the suggestion of a quick and easy way to accomplish a task. "Keyed" advertising, which used the lure of samples or information to obtain a response, was one of Caples's mainstays. And he advocated the use of two campaigns at all times: one major national campaign and one local test campaign.

Caples went on to teach copywriting at Columbia Business School from 1952 to 1954. He authored dozens of articles for trade journals, as well as writing a column for *Direct Marketing* magazine. His five books each garnered international acclaim, with *Tested Advertising Methods* (1932) becoming an immediate success. This work codified many of his beliefs concerning advertising and the scientific approach to writing and testing ads; four chapters are devoted to headlines.

Caples was inducted into the Copywriters Hall of Fame in 1973 and into the Advertising Hall of Fame in 1977. The John Caples International Awards, established in 1978 to honor "creative solutions to direct marketing problems," are awarded annually by a volunteer board of members of the direct-marketing industry.

Caples was forced to retire in 1983, after 56 years with BBDO, when he fell off a ladder and broke his back. He died on 10 June 1990.

Throughout his long career, Caples was a powerful force. His call for a scientific look at the effectiveness of advertising resulted in new standards within the industry. He popularized the concept of testing and was a forerunner in developing experimental methods of testing; he conducted and recorded a great volume of research; he gleaned principles of advertising from his experience; and he left many writings to record his findings. His principles of copywriting and the testing of advertisements remain relevant, accepted, and useful.

BARBARA KNOLL

Biography
Born in New York City, 1 May 1900; attended Columbia University; served in the United States Navy during World War I; graduated from the U.S. Naval Academy at Annapolis, 1924; began his career in advertising at Ruthrauff & Ryan, 1925; moved to Barton Durstine & Osborn (later Batten Barton Durstine & Osborn) in 1927, where he would remain for the remainder of his career, with the exception of service once again with the U.S. Navy from 1942 to 1945, during World War II; died in New York City on 10 June 1990.

Selected Publications
Tested Advertising Methods, 1932; 5th edition, 1997
Advertising for Immediate Sales, 1936
Advertising Ideas: A Practical Guide to Methods That Make Advertisements Work, 1938
Making Ads Pay, 1957
How to Make Your Advertising Make Money, 1983

Further Reading
Fox, Stephen R., *The Mirror Makers: A History of American Advertising and Its Creators,* New York: Morrow, 1984
White, Gordon E., *John Caples: Adman,* Chicago: Crain Books, 1977

Carl Ally, Inc. *See under* Ally

Carter's Little Liver Pills

Principal Agencies
Street & Finney, Inc.
Small & Seiffer, Inc.
Ted Bates, Inc. (later Bates USA)

Carter's Little Liver Pills were first marketed in the late 1800s. The product was considered a patent medicine, a term that originally referred to quack remedies sold largely by itinerant peddlers.

Its manufacturer, Carter's Products of New York City (later Carter Medicine Company and Carter Products, Inc.) was a member of the Proprietary Association of America, a national organization of less-than-reputable physicians, patent medicine makers, and medical device manufacturers. Although the product had its greatest success in the United States, it soon became well known in other countries as well.

An ad in *The Illustrated London News* on 16 July 1887 carried the headline, "Torpid liver." The illustration showed a black bird holding in its beak a banner bearing the logo of Carter's Little Liver Pills. The subhead proclaimed: "Torpid liver positively cured by Carter's Little Liver Pills."

Patent medicines were big business in the United States in the late 1800s and early 1900s. The census of 1900 placed the annual wholesale value of all such products at $59,611,355. The retail value was more than $100 million. It was estimated that $40 million per year was spent on newspaper ads for these products.

In 1929 Henry Hamilton Hoyt, Sr., who had recently graduated from Princeton University, took over his father-in-law's business making Carter's Little Liver Pills. Hoyt bought control of the company anonymously, assigned advertising to the agency Street & Finney, Inc., and immediately cut dividends in order to begin accumulating capital. John Wallace, a chemist and soon-to-be partner, was enlisted by Hoyt to develop new products. Wallace was mainly responsible for the introduction of Arrid deodorant in 1935, Nair hair remover in 1940 (both assigned to Small & Seiffer, Inc., for advertising), and Rise shave cream in 1949. During World War II the company manufactured many health-related products, including foot powder, for the military. However, the company's contribution to the war effort did little to allay the charges that Carter's Little Liver Pills were not effective in treating liver ailments.

In 1943 the efficacy of Carter's Little Liver Pills was officially challenged by the Federal Trade Commission (FTC). The case was not resolved until 1959, when a U.S. Supreme Court decision called for removal of the word *liver* from the product name. The case against Carter contained some 11,000 pages of testimony and included 750 exhibits.

The complaint against Carter's had its basis in the 1938 Wheeler-Lea Act (itself an outgrowth of a 1914 federal statute), which was intended to strengthen the FTC's policing powers over advertising and promotion. The law was designed in part by members of the House of Representatives who wished to prevent the Food and Drug Administration from gaining control over drug advertising and promotion. The act expanded the scope of the FTC and increased the sanctions at the agency's disposal. The 1914 statute had declared that "unfair methods of competition" were illegal. The 1938 act also made illegal "unfair or deceptive acts or practices in commerce." The Wheeler-Lea Act thus explicitly guaranteed consumers that they would be protected, giving them greater power to question false claims. Consumers no longer had to rely completely on a product's competitors to challenge its claims.

It took 16 years for the FTC to get the word *liver* removed from Carter's Little Liver Pills. When an order was finally confirmed in court in 1959, no penalty—saving some bad publicity—was levied against the offender. By then, the company had adopted a new advertising and promotion approach.

In the late 1940s Ted Bates, Inc., of New York City, took over the Carter's Little Liver Pills account. In charge was pioneering advertising executive Rosser Reeves. When Carter's was forced to drop the word *liver* from the product name in 1959, Reeves and Bates were also forced by the FTC to drop any liver claims from ads. In response, "Carter's Little Pills" was born. The basic for-

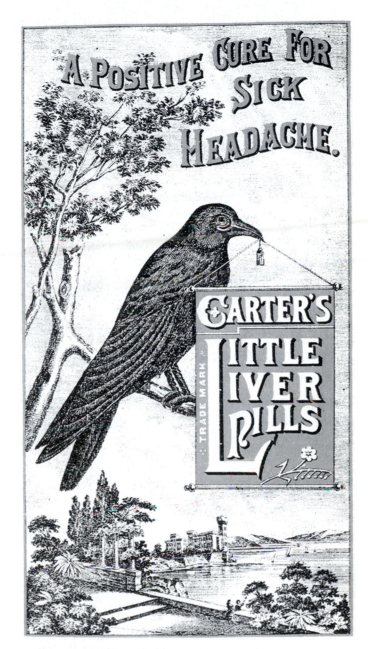

Early ads for Carter's Little Liver Pills featured highly detailed artwork, a simple slogan, and the Carter's brand logo—a black bird holding the trademark banner.
Reprinted with permission of Carter-Wallace, Inc.

mulation, unchanged since its inception, consisted of 16 mg of aloe and 4.0 mg of podophyllum resin. Direct competitors at the time included Feen-A-Mint and Ex-Lax. By 1961 the Carter's Pills advertising account was still at Bates despite a drop in sales from the heady days of the 1950s.

During the 1960s, Carter-Wallace expanded via acquisition. The company's lead product, Carter's Little Pills, began to show signs of aging. The company refused to let the remedy become extinct, however. But while Carter-Wallace continued to promote and advertise its other products in the 1970s and 1980s, it devoted no advertising and promotion dollars to Carter's Little Pills, and the venerable product had no advertising agency of record. The pills continued to be marketed in the familiar red-and-black-labeled cylinder (although plastic replaced metal as the material). The package label claimed Carter's Little Pills could relieve sluggishness, bloated feeling, headache, and nervousness—but only when these symptoms were due to constipation.

In 1985 the Carter-Wallace company acquired Trojan condoms. (At the start of the 21st century, the Trojan line represented more than 50 percent of the U.S. condom market.) Henry Hoyt, Sr., died in 1990 at age 95, and his son, Henry, Jr., took over the management of the company. It was estimated that the Hoyt family owned approximately $750 million in Carter-Wallace shares.

Church & Dwight Company, Inc., acquired Carter-Wallace in the fall of 2001 and continues to market the remedy, now called simply Carter's Laxative. The familiar logo with the big "L" still appears on the red package. The sole active ingredient is bisacodyl USP 5 mg, along with the inactive ingredients acacia, carnauba, gelatin, lac, magnesium stearate, polyvinyl acetate, phthalate, starch, stearic acid, sucrose, talc, titanium dioxide, and white wax. The product survives—but with no advertising or promotion budget.

TOMMY V. SMITH

Further Reading

Adams, Samuel Hopkins, *The Great American Fraud,* New York: Collier, 1905

Applegate, Edd, editor, *The Ad Men and Women: A Biographical Dictionary of Advertising,* Westport, Connecticut: Greenwood, 1994
Cramp, Arthur, editor, *Nostrums and Quackery: Articles on the Nostrum Evil, Quackery, and Allied Matters Affecting the Public Health,* 3 vols., Chicago: American Medical Association Press, 1911–36
Fox, Stephen, *The Mirror Makers: A History of American Advertising and Its Creators,* New York: Morrow, 1984
Handbook of Nonprescription Drugs, Washington, D.C.: American Pharmaceutical Association, 1967; 11th edition, 1996
Higgins, Denis, *The Art of Writing Advertising: Conversations with William Bernbach, Leo Burnett, George Gribbin, David Ogilvy, Rosser Reeves,* Lincolnwood, Illinois: NTC Business Books, 1986
Reeves, Rosser, *Reality in Advertising,* New York: Bates, 1960
Savan, Leslie, *The Sponsored Life: Ads, TV, and American Culture,* Philadelphia, Pennsylvania: Temple University Press, 1994
Sivulka, Juliann, *Soap, Sex, and Cigarettes: A Cultural History of American Advertising,* Belmont, California: Wadsworth, 1998
Strohbach, G., *Quacks and Grafters,* Cincinnati, Ohio: Cincinnati Medical Book Company, 1908
Young, James Harvey, *The Medical Messiahs: A Social History of Health Quackery in Twentieth-Century America,* Princeton, New Jersey: Princeton University Press, 1967; London: Princeton University Press, 1974

Casadevall Pedreño

Established in Barcelona, Spain, as Rilova, Casadevall, Pedreño, 1979; bought by Saatchi & Saatchi, 1986, becoming RCP/Saatchi & Saatchi Advertising; Casadevall and Pedreño resigned from RCP/Saatchi & Saatchi, 1989; Casadevall Pedreño & PRG (Piera, Roda, García) founded as new advertising agency, 1991; won Grand Prix at Cannes (France) International Advertising Festival, 1992; named *Advertising Age* "International Agency of the Year," 1993; majority share bought by French Publicis Group and name changed to Publicis Casadevall Pedreño & PRG, 1998.

Major Clients
Coca-Cola Company
El Corte Inglés
Group Danone
Iberia Airlines
Sara Lee/Cruz Verde-Legrain
Seat

The founders of Rilova, Casadevall, Pedreño (RCP) were Ernesto Rilova, Luis Casadevall, and Salvador Pedreño. Prior to starting the agency in 1979, Rilova and Casadevall, the future creative talents of RCP, who already knew Pedreño, a marketing executive, worked at Montfort, Moliné, Lorente, Borsten (MMLB), a "creative boutique" founded in 1971 and perhaps the most representative Spanish agency of the 1970s. MMLB's accounts included Osborne's Magno, Bitter Kas, Banco de Bilbao, and Trinaranjus.

Although each of the three partners made his own contribution to RCP, the agency itself had a distinctive style. A 1999 article in *Anuncios Revista,* the magazine supplement to *Anuncios* (a weekly trade paper of Spanish advertising and marketing), cited the following characteristics: simplicity of forms, categorical ideas, and a unique sense of aesthetics.

In its first five years RCP won clients and fame rapidly. The period started with two billboard campaigns, for Rives Gin and

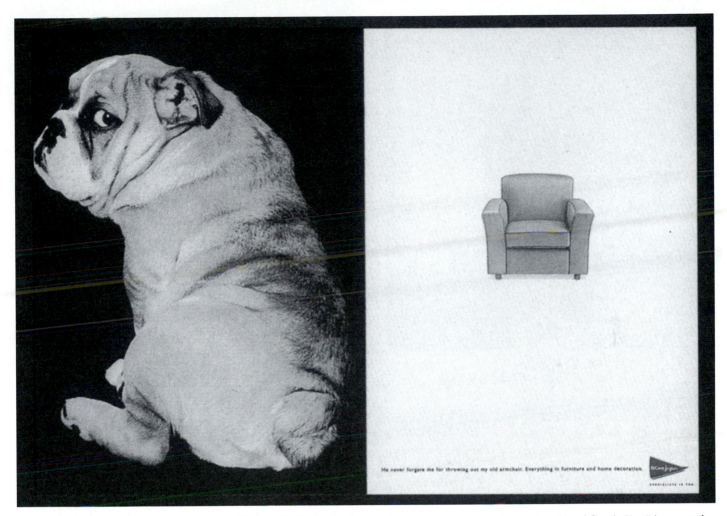

In 1992 Casadevall Pedreño won the account of El Corte Inglés, Spain's leading department store. A 1996 campaign, "Specialists in You," juxtaposed unexpected images that matched demand with supply.

for the sales department of Caixa de Barcelona (Savings Bank of Barcelona), the latter breaking established molds and marking the beginning of RCP's notoriety. The billboards for the Caixa were filled with images of cakes, capsules, lettuces, screws, and bottles; the messages (e.g., "Headaches cannot be given to a pharmacy") contained double meanings, plays on words, and irony.

One of the agency's main contributions to the Spanish ad industry was that it started modern television advertising in Spain. An important example was a spot called "Viva España," on behalf of the Association of Blood Donors of the Hospital Clínico of Barcelona. In 1981 the spot won RCP its first gold Lion at the Cannes (France) International Advertising Festival. Two years later the agency won the second gold Lion in its short history, for a campaign for Ambipur, an air freshener from Cruz Verde.

In the 1980s one of the major campaigns from RCP was "Learn from Your Children," for Danone, which won a silver Lion at Cannes. As part of a new marketing strategy by Danone, the campaign sought to encourage adults to eat yogurt through spots in which children introduced their parents the product. Another major campaign of the 1980s was for Vileda, a marketer

of household cleaning products; in a typical ad, a Vileda dishcloth managed to support a tower of wet glasses while another brand of dishcloth became saturated, causing the stack of glasses to tumble and break.

In the mid-1980s Rilova left the agency because of disagreements among the partners. In 1986 RCP won six of the seven Lions awarded to Spanish shops at Cannes. The agency was awarded a gold Lion for ads for Danone and a silver Lion for an antidrug campaign for the city of Barcelona.

In 1986 Saatchi & Saatchi bought RCP. The English multinational was attracted by the good work of the agency, and RCP thought that an entity combining the Saatchi and RCP names would be unbeatable. Two years later the new agency won another gold Lion for its ad "A Story of Love" for the Red Cross. But in 1989 a lack of mutual understanding prompted Casadevall and Pedreño to part company with the multinational company.

In spring 1991 Casadevall founded Casadevall Pedreño & PRG (the latter initials stood for the names of José María Piera, Ramón Roda, and Xavier García), a new creative agency. Some time earlier, Casadevall and Pedreño had created Casadevall

Luis Casadevall.
Courtesy of Publicis Casadevall Pedreño & PRG.

for industrial use and not known by the general public, controversy surrounded this award. In 1993 *Advertising Age* named the agency its "International Agency of the Year."

That same year the shop became the first Spanish agency to handle an international account for the Coca-Cola Company, specifically the European account of the soft drink Aquarius. By 1995 it was representing other multinational companies, including Swatch and Benckiser, a marketer of household products. The agency was exporting creativity to international advertisers, which bought its campaigns and then used them in various countries. For its campaigns for Spanish companies such as Iberia Air Lines and Seat, the agency worked with several multinational agencies: it provided the creativity and the others the international coverage. In July 1998 the French Publicis Group bought a majority share of Casadevall Pedreño & PRG, and the agency changed its name to Publicis Casadevall Pedreño & PRG. The possibility of establishing an agreement with a multinational agency—contacts were maintained with several companies—had been considered since the mid-1990s. In the words of Pedreño, "When an agency reaches our size, it either becomes a multinational or it falls behind." The main shareholders of the new agency were the Publicis Group, Casadevall, Pedreño, Roda, Xavier García, and Pepino García. In 1998 the agency's clients included Coca-Cola Spain (Aquarius), the Spanish Red Cross, Douwe Egberts, El Corte Inglés, Sociedad Nestlé A.E.P.A., and San Miguel Fábricas de Cervezas y Malta.

FRANCISCO VERDERA

Pedreño & SPR (Toni Segarra, Piera, and Roda). They started with the reputation gained in the 1980s, a good team of creative people and strategists, and a series of campaigns publicizing the new agency. New employees soon departed, among them Segarra, one of the founders, who left after six months. With the entrance of García as partner, the agency was renamed Casadevall Pedreño & PRG. Seven years later Piera, the P of PRG, left to found El Sindicato.

In 1991 the new agency won the account of Galerías, a Spanish department store chain. In the same year it won the account of Sara Lee/Cruz Verde-Legrain and became the lead agency worldwide for its Sanex brand of toiletries. In 1992 El Corte Inglés, the largest department store chain in Spain, moved its account to the agency. In addition, Casadevall Pedreño & PRG worked for Macy's, a U.S. department store chain.

In 1992 the agency won the Grand Prix at Cannes for "Nuns," an irreverent spot for Talens glue. Because Talens was a product

Further Reading

Bravo, Julián, et al., "50 años de seducción: Historia subjetiva y desenfadada de la publicidad española," *Vogue GQ* (supplement to *Vogue* España 70) (January 1994)

"La década prodigiosa, RCP: El paradigma de la creatividad publicitaria," *Control* 330 (1990)

Jordán, Antonio, *Publicitarios de frente y de perfil*, Madrid: Eresma and Celeste, 1995

"La mejor publicidad del fin de siglo: Los grandes anuncios de las últimas dos décadas del milenio," *Anuncios revista* 77 (December 1999)

Las mejores agencias de publicidad de España 1999, Madrid: Consultores de Publicidad, 1999

Catalogs

The word *catalog* is derived from the Greek *katalogos*, meaning "to list." Catalogs were first published in 15th-century Europe and included listings of books and gardening supplies. By the end of the 18th century, such catalogs had proliferated in England.

America's first mail order catalog, produced in 1744 by Benjamin Franklin, also offered books. Catalogs multiplied in the post–Civil War United States, where farmers, in particular, faced high prices and limited selections at local general stores. The

Absolut Vodka.
Twenty years after the launch of the "Absolut [Something]" campaign, Absolut's ads continued to feature its distinctively shaped bottle in new guises.
Under permission by V&S Vin & Sprit AB. Absolut Country of Sweden Vodka & Logo, Absolut, Absolut Bottle Design and Absolut Calligraphy are trademarks owned by V&S Vin & Sprit AB. © 2001 V&S Vin & Sprit AB.

Account Planning.
The "Got Milk?" ad campaign, created in the 1990s by Goodby, Silverstein & Partners, helped halt a 20-year decline in milk consumption. Its strategy was to target frequent milk drinkers—in this ad, for example, reminding them that milk is the perfect accompaniment to certain foods—rather than targeting consumers who drank milk only occasionally or not at all.
Photographer: Terry Heffernan.

African-Americans: Representations in Advertising.
Kodak became a pioneer in advertising to African-Americans when it featured a black Santa Claus in 1972.
Reprinted courtesy of Eastman Kodak Company.

Age: Representations in Advertising.
In an ad targeting newlyweds, Hoover used the image of happily married seniors to evoke the longevity and reliability of its vacuum cleaners.
Courtesy of The Hoover Company.

Alka-Seltzer.
With its humorous take on Americans' penchant for overeating, the "Plop Plop, Fizz Fizz" campaign, created by Wells, Rich, Greene, Inc., in the 1970s, was one of Alka-Seltzer's most successful efforts.
Courtesy of Bayer Corporation.

American Home Products Corporation.
A 1945 Wyeth ad from the "Pioneers of American Medicine" campaign celebrated the achievements of William Procter, Jr., who some called the "father of American pharmacy."
Copyright © Whitehall Robins/Wyeth and used with permission.

Backer & Spielvogel, Inc.
In the early 1990s commercials for Wendy's International from Backer & Spielvogel, Inc., featured the restaurant chain's founder, Dave Thomas.
Courtesy of Wendy's.

Benetton.
A controversial series of Benetton ads from the 1990s used provocative images to depict the peaceful coexistence of opposites.
Concept: O. Toscani. Courtesy of United Colors of Benetton.

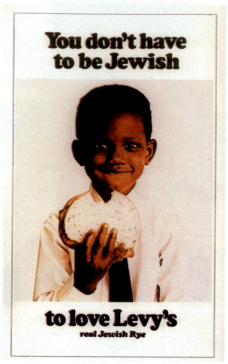

Bernbach, William ("Bill").
William Bernbach's fresh approach to advertising was exemplified in the Levy's rye bread campaign that agency Doyle Dane Bernbach launched in the New York City area in 1949. This print ad dates from 1963.
Courtesy of Bestfoods.

Beverages, Alcoholic.
This 1986 print ad exhibited a persistent theme in Beck's advertising in North America—the marketer's celebration of the beer's German origin and heritage.
© Beck's North America, Stamford, CT.

Burger King Corporation.
A 1978 print ad from Burger King's "Best Darn Burger" campaign emphasized the flame-broiled burger's appeal to all age groups.
BURGER KING® print advertisements used with permission from Burger King Brands, Inc.

Burrell Communications Group, Inc.
Featuring popular rap artists such as Kid 'n' Play, Burrell Communications Group, Inc., capitalized on the growing mainstream appeal of rap music in this 1991 campaign for Sprite.
Courtesy of The Coca-Cola Company.

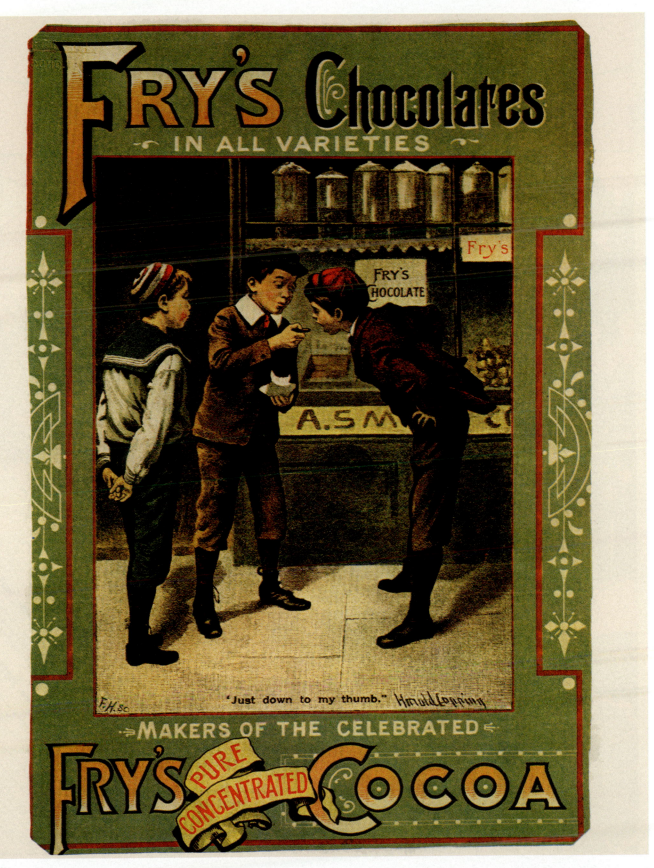

Cadbury.
In 1919 Cadbury merged with Bristol, England, chocolatier J.S. Fry & Sons. Fry's confections remained popular favorites in Britain into the 21st century.
Reprinted with permission of Cadbury Schweppes plc.

Campbell Soup Company.
In the 1960s the Campbell Kids became flower children, and Campbell Soup Company's enduring "M'm! M'm! Good!" slogan, introduced in the 1930s, was updated as "M'm! M'm! Groovy!"
Provided courtesy of Campbell Soup Company.

Catalogs.
Sears, Roebuck & Company's general-merchandise catalog, represented here by the cover of the spring 1920 issue, was launched in the late 1800s.
Reprinted by arrangement with Sears, Roebuck and Co. and protected under copyright. No duplication is permitted.

Children: Targets of Advertising.
Candy marketers have often used children's periodicals to target the young audience, as in this ad for Bubble Tape, which appeared in the June 2001 issue of *Nickelodeon* magazine.
Courtesy of Amurol Confections. Designer: Yvonne Demski. Illustrator: Gary Rose.

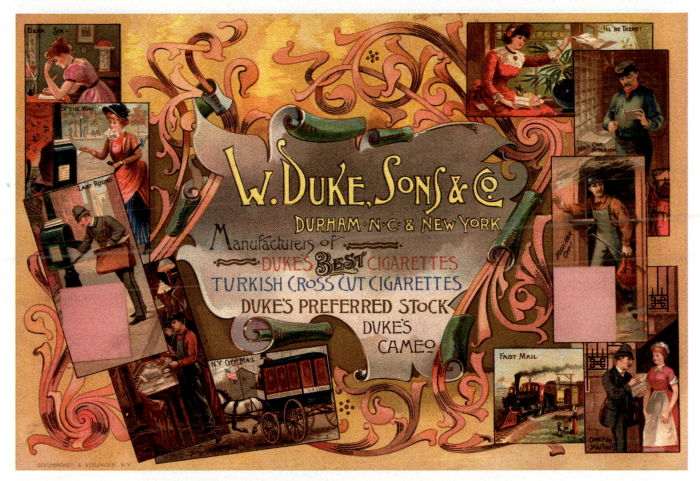

Cigarettes.
Trade cards were a common form of promotional material used by cigarette marketers in the early 20th century.

Cigarettes.
In this award-winning 1999 campaign, the California Department of Health Services turned the tables on one of the best-known advertising icons in the world.
Courtesy of the California Department of Health Services.

Coffee.
For 21 years the fictional housewife Mrs. Olson, seen here in a 1978 print ad, extolled the virtues of Folger's coffee.
Courtesy of The Procter & Gamble Company.

Intermission–

Drink Coca-Cola

Delicious and Refreshing

It's just a pause . . . you can make it *the pause that refreshes*

Scenes like the picture above are always before you around theatres and at dances. So will you welcome ice-cold Coca-Cola on the happiest occasions—to make intermissions *the pause that refreshes*. This great drink gives you a tingling, delicious taste. It quenches thirst. It leaves a wholesome, cool after-sense of refreshment.

And remember this about Coca-Cola: It contributes to the busy day in stores, offices and workshops the same life and sparkle. Only a minute is long enough to enjoy it to the full. The minute is never lost. It means a fresh start, and you do more work and better work. The Coca-Cola Company, Atlanta, Ga.

LISTEN IN
Grantland Rice—Famous Sports Champions—Coca-Cola Orchestra. Every Wed. 10:30 p. m. Eastern Standard Time Coast-to-Coast NBC Network.

OVER NINE MILLION A DAY . . . IT HAD TO BE GOOD TO GET WHERE IT IS

Coca-Cola Company.
Coca-Cola's celebrated tag line "The pause that refreshes," introduced in 1929, the year of the stock market crash, was credited with helping the soft-drink marketer maintain strong sales throughout the Great Depression.
Courtesy of The Coca-Cola Company.

Colgate-Palmolive Company.
Early advertisements for Palmolive soap advised modern women that legendary beauties such as Cleopatra owed their radiant complexions to the same natural oils used in Palmolive.
Courtesy of the Colgate Palmolive Company.

Computers.
With the slogan "The power is within your reach," the low-priced Timex computer entered the market in 1982.

Cosmetics.
Max Factor transformed the cosmetics industry when he began marketing his makeup—originally developed for motion pictures—for everyday use and featuring Hollywood stars such as Judy Garland, seen here in a 1947 ad, to promote the products.

Made as France makes her finest toilet soap!

FREE CAKE!

To introduce this luxurious new toilet soap the makers of LUX are giving you a full size cake absolutely FREE!

Just take the attached coupon to your grocer or druggist—buy one cake of LUX TOILET SOAP and he will give you another cake FREE!

TEAR OFF HERE AND TAKE TO YOUR DEALER   [OVER]

Valuable Coupon
Take this coupon to your dealer — Buy one cake of
LUX TOILET SOAP
And he will give you another cake
FREE!

No. 508727

3028TS

TO DEALERS — This coupon, when terms of the arrangement have been complied with, will be redeemed at the retail price. Lever Brothers Company, Cambridge, Mass.

Coupon.
A Lux toilet soap promotion from 1928 included this coupon for a free cake of soap.
Courtesy of Unilever.

Crest.
This 1950s ad campaign for Crest combined heartwarming sketches by artist Norman Rockwell with one of the era's most memorable ad slogans, "Look, Mom—no cavities!"
Courtesy of The Procter & Gamble Company.

Cultural Symbols.
James Montgomery Flagg's 1917 depiction of Uncle Sam, created for the World War I recruitment effort, remains the most enduring image of this cultural symbol.

Dancer, Fitzgerald, Sample.
Dancer, Fitzgerald, Sample created the "Our L'eggs fit your legs" slogan for the introduction of L'eggs pantyhose in the early 1970s.
Courtesy of L'eggs Products, a division of Sara Lee Corporation.

Seaside Romance . . . painted for the De Beers Collection by Raoul Dufy

Keeper of dreams   No flower ever was so gay, no sun so bright, as your engagement diamond. Token of love, guardian of dreams, it will lend its lovely light to all your years. Guiding your thoughts to one another through days of parting, it will dance for joy at your reunions. And all the happy moments, all the changes and responsibilities you share, will be recorded in its magic depths. Though it be modest in cost, choose your diamond with care, for nothing else on earth can take its place. And...may your happiness last as long as your diamond.

De Beers Consolidated Mines, Ltd.

DeBeers Consolidated Mines, Inc.
The French painter Raoul Dufy, known for his whimsical scenes of French life, was featured in DeBeers's 1951 "Great Artists" ad series.
DeBeers.

Direct Marketing/Direct Mail.
Lands' End, with its seasonal catalogs, represented here by the cover of the fall 2000 edition, was one of the largest U.S. direct-mail retailers at the turn of the century. Direct marketing accounted for more than half of all U.S. advertising dollars in 1999. © Lands' End, Inc. Used with permission.

For Bill Demby, the difference means getting another shot.

When Bill Demby was in Vietnam, he used to dream of coming home and playing a little basketball with the guys.

A dream that all but died when he lost both his legs to a Viet Cong rocket.

But then, a group of researchers discovered that a remarkable DuPont plastic could help make artificial limbs that were more resilient, more flexible, more like life itself.

Thanks to these efforts, Bill Demby is back. And some say, he hasn't lost a step.

At DuPont, we make the things that make a difference.

Better things for better living.

REG. U.S. PAT & TM OFF

E-Commerce.
Consumers accustomed to traditional bricks-and-mortar retailing had to be educated about shopping on the Internet. This 2000 BestBuy.com ad used humor to explain the options for returning merchandise.
BestBuy.com/Tribal DDB.

Your bones may be in jeopardy.

One in five osteoporosis victims is male. Luckily, fat free milk has the calcium bones need to help beat it. Beating your Harvard Ph.D. opponents? Well, that's another story.

got milk?®

Endorsement.
The familiar face of *Jeopardy!* game show host Alex Trebek is among many that have worn the "milk moustache." Courtesy of Bozell Worldwide, Inc.

Texaco took a break from drilling for oil to help others dig for gold.

Texaco is a proud sponsor of the U.S. Women's Soccer Team, because we know
what it's like to dig down deep and go for more.

A WORLD OF ENERGY.
texaco.com

Events.
Events marketing has the potential to reach a broader audience than other types of advertising and can boost a company's image. In association with the 2000 Olympic Games, Texaco also sponsored the U.S. Women's Soccer Team.
Courtesy of Texaco, Inc.

development of the railroads and the U.S. postal system served to bolster catalog businesses.

Rural America was largely responsible for the early success of the catalog giants Aaron Montgomery Ward and Richard Sears. In 1872 Ward published a discount general merchandise catalog as a price list on a single, unillustrated sheet of paper. By 1884 Ward's catalog, offering "satisfaction or your money back," had expanded to 240 pages and offered 12,000 items. Sears was a railroad agent in 1886 when he purchased an unclaimed shipment of watches. Using a mailing list, he resold the watches for a profit and started a catalog of watches and jewelry. By 1895 Sears and his business partner Alvah C. Roebuck were issuing a general merchandise catalog of more than 500 pages.

During the first half of the 20th century several apparel catalogs—including Spiegel (1904), L.L. Bean (1912), and Eddie Bauer (1920)—were launched; at the same time, general merchandise catalogs aimed at the rural population enjoyed strong growth. After World War II the catalog business began to diversify. Recognizing opportunities overlooked by "big-book" general merchandise catalogers, specialty catalogs such as Spencer Gifts and Sunset House emerged to supply the middle-class market with household items and gifts.

Between the 1960s and 1980s, a confluence of socioeconomic forces led to a momentous change in catalog advertising. The increased participation of women in the workforce created dual-income households with greater discretionary income but a correspondingly greater need for convenience. Catalogs provided this convenience, offering a range of merchandise, essential product information, guaranteed satisfaction, and prompt delivery. Toll-free telephone numbers and credit cards simplified the ordering process. Consumers became receptive to purchasing virtually any product by catalog, from prime beef (Omaha Steaks) to peignoirs (Victoria's Secret).

Advances in technology enabled catalogers to better target those consumers likely to respond favorably to their particular offerings. Computers compiled mailing lists of upscale consumers from zip code–level census data, which provide information about the economic characteristics of neighborhoods. Department stores such as Bloomingdale's and Saks Fifth Avenue began preparing multiple versions of their catalogs for selective mailing based on consumer buying habits. Even Sears, built on its general merchandise catalog, adopted these techniques in the early 1980s, producing up to 19 specialty catalogs ranging from western wear to toys.

Competition intensified, and by 1982 more than 5,000 catalogs were being published in the United States; the average household received 40 catalogs a year. Glossy specialty catalogs (e.g., The Sharper Image, Williams-Sonoma) that targeted niche markets were emerging as dominant and, by 1984, attracted approximately 66 percent of all catalog sales.

Although the industry experienced double-digit annual growth during the 1980s, it experienced a shakeout too. Many upstart catalogs failed due to undercapitalization, lack of marketplace knowledge, an insufficient customer base, or poor order fulfillment. Most noteworthy was the failure of old-line general merchandise catalogs. Alden's catalog folded in 1982, unable to sustain profits from its downscale customer base, and Montgomery Ward ceased catalog advertising in 1985 after several years of $50 million losses due to operational inefficiencies.

The mid- to late 1980s saw the catalog industry take some unexpected turns and encounter new challenges. With industry sales reaching $45 billion in 1985, The Sharper Image, Spiegel, Neiman-Marcus, and Marshall Field's began selling advertising space in their catalogs to defray operating costs. Many competitors reacted negatively to these "magalogs." Meanwhile, other catalogers embraced storefront retailing to attract customers from among the estimated 43 percent of catalog-resistant U.S. households. Talbot's accelerated its store openings, reducing catalog sales to about 40 percent of the company's total revenue. Brookstone and Banana Republic pursued this strategy as well.

Catalog advertisers were also confronted with competition from television home shopping, leading them to partner with shopping channels or shows or to produce their own "videologs." Sears had an interest in QVC Network, which sold Sears products for several years; Hanover House catalogs were pitched on *Value Television;* and Royal Silk ran 30-minute videologs on TWA's Travel Channel.

By the early 1990s aggressive U.S. catalogers were mailing more than 13 billion catalogs each year. In those difficult economic times a slowdown in consumer spending was compounded by rising production and mailing costs. Although general merchandise catalogers Sears and J.C. Penney Company entered the decade as the industry leaders, they found that they must either adapt or die. Catalogers responded to this intensely competitive environment with efforts to pinpoint, by name and address, targets for ever more specialized collections of merchandise. Lands' End issued *Coming Home*; Talbot's mailed books promoting dress-up clothes for children; and Sears published 50 specialty catalogs in addition to its semi-annual big book.

To distinguish themselves from the competition and build greater reader involvement, especially among women, catalogers implemented catalog makeovers in the image of magazines. Distinct editorial points of view were communicated in entertaining themes and informative copy. The J. Peterman catalog is perhaps the best exemplar of this practice; its copy is vivid, personal, and chatty, often telling a story about the merchandise. For example, the copy accompanying the "Hemingway's Cap" reads, "I had to go to some trouble to have this one made for you and me, but it had to be done. The longer bill, longer than I, at least, ever saw before, makes sense."

In 1992 J.C. Penney supplanted Sears as the nation's largest cataloger, thanks not to its 1,400-page big book but to its 100-plus specialty books. The venerable Sears catalog, losing more than $100 million annually, shuttered its operation in 1993. Apparel catalogers Spiegel, Lands' End, L.L. Bean, and The Limited held firm as industry leaders; however, they would soon be displaced by rapidly growing computer product catalogers such as Dell Computer, Gateway, and IBM.

By the mid-1990s catalogers faced further expansion of shopping alternatives such as TV infomercials and interactive technology. Cooperative CD-ROM catalogs were developed as "malls on disk," with multiple catalogers displaying their merchandise on a single disk. Williams-Sonoma, Lillian Vernon, L.L. Bean, and 1-800-Flowers joined music and video sellers in full-color, multimedia environments.

On-line catalog shopping was the next innovation. Speedy personal computers and modems allowed consumers to explore the World Wide Web. Businesses of all kinds rushed to establish Web sites, thus launching the era of electronic, or "e," commerce. From virtually zero in 1995, on-line sales jumped to more than $8 billion in 1998. And with about 84 percent of catalog companies on the Web, on-line selling, rather than replacing paper catalogs, appeared to be aiding them, as Web customers often requested print copies for leisurely review. Catalog sales reached about $110 billion in 2000, up from $96.8 billion in 1999. Forecasts indicate continued growth to $155 billion by 2005. Indeed, history suggests that by adapting to social, economic, and technological change, catalog advertising is likely to remain a viable form of merchandising for some time to come.

RANDY JACOBS

See also color plate in this volume

Further Reading

Horovitz, Bruce, "Catalogue Firms Are Narrowing Their Focus to Remain Afloat," *Los Angeles Times* (3 August 1993)

Muldoon, Katie, *Catalog Marketing: The Complete Guide to Profitability in the Catalog Business,* New York: Bowker, 1984; as *How to Profit through Catalog Marketing,* Lincolnwood, Illinois: NTC Business Books, 1996

Roberts, Mary Lou, and Paul D. Berger, *Direct Marketing Management,* Englewood Cliffs, New Jersey: Prentice Hall, 1989; 2nd edition, Upper Saddle River, New Jersey: Prentice Hall International, 1999

Schnorbus, Paula, "Home Shopping's Direct Challenge," *Marketing and Media Decisions* 22, no. 6 (June 1987)

Cecil & Presbrey

Successor to Frank Presbrey Company, founded in New York City, 1896; Presbrey succeeded by son Charles, 1931; became Cecil & Presbrey when James Cecil joined agency, 1939; dissolved after Cecil's death, 1954.

Major Clients

Block Drug Company (Ammi-dent, Poli-Grip)
IBM Corporation
Lamont, Corliss & Company (Nestlé)
Lever Brothers, Inc. (Rayve)
Philip Morris & Company, Ltd. (Marlboro cigarettes)
Sylvania Electric Products, Inc.

Founded as Frank Presbrey Company in 1896, Cecil & Presbrey enjoyed a steady, peaceful existence as a midsize New York City agency through the first half of the 20th century. After World War II, however, the agency quickly became a significant consumer advertising shop. But its place in the history of advertising perhaps owes more to the unusual swiftness and completeness of its decline, over nine days in 1954, than to any single ad campaign it devised.

James M. Cecil, born in 1891, launched his advertising career in Richmond, Virginia, after serving in the Naval Air Corps in World War I. With his brother John and another partner, he formed Cecil, Barreto & Cecil in 1917. While the agency was based in Richmond and had small branch offices in New York City and Baltimore, Maryland, James Cecil soon realized that the agency needed to be headquartered in New York City. About 1932 he partnered with H. Paul Warwick, who had been with the National Lithographic Printing Company, and his younger brother, J.R. Warwick, and formed Cecil, Warwick & Cecil, Inc. John Cecil remained in Richmond and continued to run the original office as a branch of the new company, and the agency soon became known simply as Cecil & Warwick, Inc.

In 1936 Henry Legler left a senior creative position at the J. Walter Thompson Company and became a vice president at the agency, which again changed its name, this time to Cecil, Warwick & Legler, Inc. (CW&L). In September 1938 Legler and Warwick both resigned amicably to form a new agency, Warwick & Legler, Inc., and in December 1938 James Cecil left to become president of Frank Presbrey & Company, taking with him several remaining clients (including the George Washington Coffee Refining Company; Elizabeth Arden; Lamont, Corliss & Company; and Selznick International Pictures, Inc.) to the renamed Cecil & Presbrey, Inc. (C&P). John Cecil and several other senior people also moved. The Richmond office of CW&L became an outpost of C&P, and CW&L was dissolved.

Frank Presbrey was born in 1855 and graduated from Princeton University in 1879 in the same class with Woodrow Wilson, Cyrus McCormick, and Mahlon Pitney, who would go on to become an associate justice on the U.S. Supreme Court. Presbrey worked in the railroad business and in publishing before forming Frank Presbrey & Company, an agency he built largely around travel advertising. About 1900 he started working with the Shredded Wheat Company and made its product among the first breakfast foods to be advertised on the basis of its health benefits. The Presbrey agency began working with the Computing-Tabulating-Recording Company (which in 1924 became IBM Corporation) in 1914. It also handled advertising for the American Tobacco Company until 1918, when the account was split along brand lines. Presbrey believed it was unethical to retain a portion of the account, so he stepped aside; Lord & Thomas became American Tobacco's principal agency in 1925. Presbrey also handled Lamont, Corliss & Company, which marketed Nestlé's EverReady Cocoa and Nestlé's chocolate bars, as well as several dental products, including Polident and Jiffy Toothache Drops. "No one creation of man," Presbrey wrote in *Outlook* magazine in 1922, "has done more [than the toothbrush] to lift the individual out of the sordid slough of mediaevalism [sic] and place him on a new aesthetic plane."

In 1931 Presbrey, then 76, relinquished the presidency to his son Charles, although he remained active until his death on 10 October 1936. But Charles Presbrey lacked his father's passion for the profession. When Cecil came in as president in January 1939, he quickly became the de facto head of the agency. In 1943 Charles Presbrey withdrew from active involvement within the agency, though he continued as nominal chairman until 1953.

It was not until after World War II, however, that the agency began to experience aggressive growth. In 1948 alone billings rose from $6 million to $8 million, based to some degree on campaigns for the Ronson Art Metal Works' Ronson brand lighters and Speidel Corporation, a marketer of watch bands. Even more dynamic was the growth of the Block Drug Company, which in 1940 had acquired the various dental brands earlier handled by the old Presbrey agency. Block Drug remained with Cecil & Presbrey and was a major factor in its growth thanks to its development and introduction of new products such as Poli-Grip in 1946 and Ammi-dent toothpaste in 1948. The hugely successful launch of Ammi-dent alone pushed billings to more than $10 million. Introduced by C&P with newspaper and magazine ads and later through "unrehearsed" commercials on Block Drug's radio show, *Quick as a Flash,* Ammi-dent's drugstore sales soared within 24 months to propel the brand to second place in the category in drugstore sales in 1950, behind Colgate. In the 1949–50 season, Ammi-dent sponsored *The Burns and Allen Show,* a popular radio program at that time.

C&P also won the Rayve Home Permanent account from Lever Brothers in 1946 and produced *Grand Marquee* on NBC for the marketer. More business arrived in 1949 when Thomas J. Maloney returned to the company as a senior vice president. Maloney had been a C&P production manager a decade earlier before leaving to become a partner at Newell-Emmett. When Newell-Emmett became Cunningham & Walsh, Inc., in 1949, Maloney decided to return to C&P and brought with him about $2 million in billings, including Bymart, Inc.'s Tintair home hair coloring brand. In 1953 Maloney became C&P president and Cecil, chairman.

In 1950 *Advertising Age* ranked C&P, with $15 million in billings, as the 25th-largest U.S. agency. Shortly after that, the agency acquired yet another client, Sylvania Electric Products, Inc., and another weekly TV production, *Beat the Clock.* The agency was already overseeing production of *Mystery Playhouse* for Block Drug and *Suspense* for Electric Auto-Lite Company.

In December 1952 the agency took another step forward, merging with J.D. Tarcher & Company, Inc., a $5 million agency that had been founded as Hommann, Tarcher & Cornell in 1924. As a result of the merger, C&P added the Benrus Watch Company account along with four other clients, plus about 20 account executives and creative people. Tarcher president Jack Tarcher came in as a vice president. But Cecil's growth strategy had one flaw. In bringing in a series of account executives, each with his own proprietary accounts, he was not building a cohesive agency but an amalgamation of little agencies.

The fragility of C&P's structure, despite agency billings of nearly $22 million in 1953, became evident when Block Drug and Sylvania departed in late summer 1954. At the same time Nestlé was reviewing its agency situation, and Tarcher was talking with Milton Biow about bringing Benrus to the Biow Company, Inc., which was on the verge of losing the Bulova watch business it had handled for 33 years. The fatal blow to C&P came on 21 September 1954 when James Cecil died unexpectedly after a short illness. His death set off a chain reaction that brought the agency to a quick end. Two days later, on 23 September, Tarcher announced his departure from C&P.

Remaining clients rushed for the exits. IBM, which had started with the Frank Presbrey Company 40 years before, left the agency; other accounts and brands also left, including Mennen Company, Inc.; Cunard Steam-Ship Company, Ltd.; New York City's Union Dime Savings Bank; and Block Drug's Poli-Grip, which had remained with C&P after the earlier departure of the marketer's Ammi-dent. The agency also lost Philip Morris & Company, Ltd., which had assigned some of its lesser brands, including Marlboro cigarettes, to C&P. What had been a prosperous business only a few days earlier, *Advertising Age* wrote, "was miraculously vanishing into thin air."

On 1 October, ten days after Cecil's death, Cecil & Presbrey announced its liquidation. McCann-Erickson, Inc., picked up the Nestlé and Mennen accounts; Benton & Bowles, Inc., got IBM; and the J. Walter Thompson Company picked up Sylvania. In summing up C&P's sudden collapse, *Advertising Age* commented:

> There may have been faster disintegrations in the advertising business . . . but surely no agency of comparable size has fallen apart so fast in recent years. . . . [It] was not surprising. . . . Cecil & Presbrey was not so much a single agency as it was a kind of convenient tent under which a half-dozen groups . . . chose to hang their hats rather than to construct their own individual tents. . . . Under such circumstances, it sometimes becomes painfully obvious that a crowd does not necessarily make a team.

Stockholders were paid off, and some older executives even walked away with modest capital gains. Final dissolution came on

31 December. "Cecil & Presbrey," Mahoney wrote in a letter to *Advertising Age* three weeks later, "relinquished its place in advertising's future, but not its past."

JOHN MCDONOUGH

Further Reading

"Building Rug Products into Leaders Is Specialty for Cecil & Presbrey," *Advertising Age* (6 November 1950)
"Cecil & Presbrey and Tarcher Join Forces," *Advertising Age* (1 December 1952)
"Fast Work on the Agency Front," *Advertising Age* (11 October 1954)
"Frank Presbrey, 'Agent's Agent,' Joins Majority," *Advertising Age* (19 October 1936)
"James M. Cecil, Agency Head, Died in New York," *Advertising Age* (27 September 1954)
Presbrey, Frank, *The History and Development of Advertising*, Garden City, New York: Doubleday, 1929; reprint, New York: Greenwood Press, 1968
"Tarcher Departs Cecil & Presbrey" *Advertising Age* (27 September 1954)

Censorship by Advertisers

Over the decades, advertisers have often been accused of using their economic influence to dictate media content. Because advertising pays the bills, managers of newspapers, magazines, and television and radio stations have a compelling reason to want their advertisers to be happy.

The balance of power in the relationship between advertisers and media companies has not been static, however. In the mid-19th century, U.S. magazine publishers placed ads in the back pages because advertising messages were considered an intrusion on the reader. But by the 1890s, when advertising revenue was becoming increasingly important to publishers, ad agencies were able to persuade publishers to position ads throughout magazines and weave them around the editorial matter. The mid-20th century brought another change—advertisers began to choose the editorial environment they wanted their ads to appear in not on the basis of expected reader interest but for its ability to create the proper "buying mood" for products. This strategy was based on the assumption that serious articles did not always create a positive environment for ads, particularly those that depended on fantasy or promoted a less serious product. The 1970s ushered in an era in which publishers created entire magazines that targeted an identifiable audience.

Advertisers usually exert pressure on the media in one of two ways: by threatening to withhold advertising (and the revenue it produces) as leverage against unfavorable coverage of the company or product or by withdrawing advertising support from media vehicles whose content they find too controversial. Examining the first strategy, researchers Lawrence Soley and Robert Craig found in 1992 that 90 percent of the editors of daily newspapers said that advertisers had attempted to influence the content of stories appearing in their papers; 37 percent acknowledged having capitulated to this pressure. Examples included a car dealership that withdrew its advertising from a newspaper for two months and tried to convince three other dealerships to follow suit after the paper ran a page-one story outlining a mechanical problem with a car sold by that dealership, even though the story was accompanied by another noting that no local customers had experienced problems.

Similarly, in 1986 the Los Angeles *Herald Examiner* documented widespread practices of short-weighting and overcharging by southern California grocery stores. One of the largest local chains, Ralph's, canceled a $250,000 contract with the newspaper, and other newspapers based in the area declined to cover the story, even though the Los Angeles country board of supervisors investigated the charges, a development that could have interested readers.

The conflict of interest between publishers and advertisers surrounds magazines as well and was identified by *Ms.* magazine founder Gloria Steinem as the cause for the demise of the original *Ms.* magazine in 1987. For example, Bristol-Myers-Squibb Company withdrew ads for its Clairol haircolor after *Ms.* ran a story about a congressional hearing into certain hair dyes thought to be carcinogenic. Ultimately *Ms.* returned in 1990 without advertiser support by raising subscription prices and reducing its frequency of publication.

The second tactic mentioned above, that of withdrawing advertising support from media vehicles that carry controversial content, gained attention when the Chrysler Corporation, in 1997 the nation's fourth-largest advertiser, notified 50 magazines that it would require summaries of upcoming articles and advance notice of any editorial content that encompassed sexual, political, or social issues or any editorial that might be construed as provocative or offensive. These summaries were to be forwarded to Chrysler's ad agency in ample time for rescheduling of ads. Milton Glaser, co-founder of *New York Magazine*, predicted that other advertisers would follow suit if editors and publishers did not resist, and he claimed that the practice would have a "devastating effect" on the idea of a free press and of free inquiry. In July 1997 the American Society of Magazine Editors met to discuss the issue of pressure by advertisers, and they issued a statement expressing "deep concern" over the trend to give "advertisers advance notice about upcoming stories." They stated their belief that some advertisers "may mistake an early warning as an open invitation to pressure the publisher to alter, or even kill, the article in question. We believe publishers should—and will—refuse to bow to such pressure." Despite this comment, Chrysler spokesman Mike Aberlich later claimed that all the magazines in question had signed the agreement to provide advance notice and summaries of upcoming articles.

There are many other examples of loss of advertiser support due to controversial content both in print and in broadcasting, including:

- In 1973 CBS repeated an episode of the TV series *Maude* in which the leading character obtained an abortion. No national sponsors purchased ad time, and 39 CBS affiliates refused to run the episode.
- In 1983 McDonald's Corporation sent a memo to franchise holders advising them not to advertise on the ABC miniseries *The Thorn Birds*, in which a Roman Catholic priest became involved in a love affair.
- The NBC series *Quantum Leap* faced advertiser withdrawals amounting to $500,000 in 1992 when an episode addressed homosexuality in a military school.
- In 1994 the TV show *NYPD Blue* won more Emmy nominations than any other series in history, but because of controversy surrounding the show's use of partial nudity and salty language, ABC was unable to sell sufficient advertising time and consequently lost money.

Most advertising agencies are motivated by a desire to serve their clients well and promote products and services. Helping clients become profitable is how ad agencies themselves remain profitable, and if the editorial content of a media vehicle is too controversial for certain products and companies, most agency executives believe it is their job to recommend a more suitable vehicle. While most advertisers may have a personal interest in supporting an uncensored media environment, they feel no obligation to support the media at the potential expense of their clients. A problem arises when advertisers, acting in their best interests, find those interests conflicting with those of the media or the public.

JOYCE M. WOLBURG

Further Reading

Bagdikian, Ben H., *The Media Monopoly,* Boston: Beacon, 1983; 5th edition, 1997

Baker, Russ, "The Squeeze," *Columbia Journalism Review* 36, no. 5 (September/October 1997)

Mencher, Melvin, *News Reporting and Writing,* Dubuque, Iowa: Brown, 1977; 7th edition, Boston: McGraw-Hill, 1997

Richards, Jef I., and John H. Murphy II, "Economic Censorship and Free Speech: The Circle of Communication between Advertisers, Media, and Consumers," *Journal of Current Issues and Research in Advertising* 18 (Spring 1996)

Soley, Lawrence C., and Robert L. Craig, "Advertising Pressures on Newspapers: A Survey," *Journal of Advertising* 21, no. 4 (December 1992)

Censorship of Advertisers

Many American consumers are under the mistaken impression that all print advertisements and broadcast commercials are screened by a government agency before they can be published or aired. In fact, no such local, state, or federal practice exists in the United States. Reviewing media messages in advance of their appearance in the media and forcing changes or blocking publication or broadcast is called prior restraint, or censorship, and is prohibited by the First Amendment to the Constitution, which protects free speech and a free press. Commonly referred to as the "preferred position amendment," the First Amendment contains guarantees that are considered by most Americans to be vital to the continuation of a free and open society.

Protection for advertising and other forms of "commercial speech" under the First Amendment dates back only to the mid-1970s. Historically, most U.S. court rulings regarding the protection of commercial speech have concerned attempts to block advertisements for information considered socially valuable—

positions on social issues such as health care, for example—or to purchase ads for political candidates. The Supreme Court has consistently shown little interest in protecting advertisers' right to sell soft drinks, cars, dog food, and the like.

At least theoretically, the ban against censorship of information in the United States extends to commercial speech and advertising. No governmental agency is empowered to review ad messages or to preemptively block advertisements that might be false, inaccurate, misleading, or deceptive. Instead, any person or group contending that a given advertisement is libelous, obscene, or otherwise harmful must seek legal restitution after the offending advertisement has been published or aired.

Individual newspapers, magazines, and radio and television stations, however, have the right to review advertisements, demand changes, or block commercial messages prior to publishing or broadcasting. The U.S. Supreme Court has generally held that the right to publish carries with it the right *not* to publish various messages, including potentially harmful advertising messages. Broadcast and print media may draft general policies concerning the forms of advertising that they will or will not accept, or they can make decisions on individual advertisements. Any newspaper, for example, can review an advertisement submitted to it for paid publication and refuse to print it. The now-defunct St. Louis, Missouri, *Globe-Democrat* had both an office and individual with the title of "advertising censor." Another newspaper, the *Columbia Missourian,* has a standing written policy that it will not accept advertising from palm readers, hypnotists, and nudist colonies. Other publishers and broadcasters have drafted policies forbidding ads for tobacco, alcoholic beverages, or "adult" products.

In the 1980s, faced with the AIDS epidemic, U.S. television networks drafted policies regarding ads for condoms. Broadcasting executives recognized that the product could help prevent sexually transmitted diseases, but they feared that the advertisements might contain tasteless or sexually explicit messages. It was decided, therefore, to bar condom commercials from the three major broadcast television networks, which go unrestricted into every American home, but to allow local affiliates to accept or reject condom commercials based on the local executives' sense of their own communities' standards. Many stations and publications then drafted their own policies for condom ads. These included barring advertisements that addressed the use of condoms as a form of birth control or contained "wild weekend" themes.

A medium may censor advertisements based on the content of an individual message or an individual execution. The broadcaster or publisher can review a single ad, can declare it inaccurate, tasteless, violent, or otherwise harmful, and can demand changes or refuse to air or publish it. One midwestern daily allowed advertisements from both sides of the abortion issue in the 1970s as a matter of policy—even including an ad featuring a photo of a fetus in a trash can—which prompted a great deal of outcry from readers. Any medium can demand changes in advertising art and copy. It can reject advertisements that feature inaccurate, unhealthy stereotypes; gratuitous sex and nudity; poor taste; questionable claims; or glorification of violence.

Often, however, potentially harmful ads are accepted for publication or broadcast because they provide needed sales revenue for the medium. In the United States newspapers, magazines, radio, and television provide a useful information service to the public and can serve as one check on government abuses, but they are also businesses that cannot be journalistically vigorous if they are not financially sound.

Legally, decisions to reject advertisements must be made on the basis of fairness. Declining one restaurant's advertisements because a local advertising manager's brother-in-law owns a competing restaurant is not protected under the First Amendment but under fair trade laws designed to prevent restraints on commerce.

Although the U.S. government does not have direct authority in the prior restraint of advertisement by individual media, it can have influence. A radio or television station that is broadcast over the public airwaves must periodically renew its license with the Federal Communication Commission, and stations that air irresponsible advertising may be refused renewal.

Government control of advertising and direct state intervention in publishing and broadcasting are much more common in countries other than the United States. Such restriction and limitation may be grounded in the governmental system, cultural norms, or state ownership of the media. In several countries, governments have the power to restrict or censor advertising. Typically, this power is used to limit advertisements aimed at children, to regulate comparative advertising, and to control advertising for products such as alcoholic beverages, tobacco, and pharmaceuticals. Many European governments restrict outdoor advertisements and telemarketing activities, and they place limitations on commercials, often following European Community guidelines concerning the acceptable length of individual commercials and the amount of daily airtime a station can use to broadcast commercials.

Cultural differences affect how various societies regard the censorship of advertising. Nudity and overt sexual themes are much more commonly allowed in Latin America and Europe than in the United States. In some Muslim countries, for example, advertisements that might offend the standards of Islam are prohibited.

In countries in which the media are state-owned, the government has full power to censor advertising. However, the economies of China and the former U.S.S.R., two of the most notable examples of nations that censored ads, were characterized by a shortage of goods, few luxury items, and a very narrow range of consumer choices basis; advertising was therefore not nearly as pervasive and powerful a force as in developed capitalist economies.

KURT WILDERMUTH

Further Reading

Fueroghne, Dean K., *Advertising and Law,* Chicago: Copy Workshop, 1995

Gordon, A. David, and John Michael Kittross, *Controversies in Media Ethics,* White Plains, New York: Longman, 1996; 2nd edition, New York: Longman, 1999

Moore, Roy L., Ronald T. Farrar, and Erik L. Collins, *Advertising and Public Relations Law,* Mahwah, New Jersey: Erlbaum, 1998

Overbeck, Wayne, and Rick D. Pullen, *Major Principles of Media Law,* New York: Holt, Rinehart, and Winston, 1982; 2nd edition, 1985

Zelezny, John D., *Communications Law: Liberties, Restraints, and the Modern Media,* Belmont, California: Wadsworth, 1993; 3rd edition, 2001

Census

A census is a periodic governmental enumeration of a population. It provides countries with the ability to use statistical methods to create population tables and calculate growth rates. Changes in the number and composition of the population of various regions can be calculated and future population trends projected. Demographic comparisons tend to promote national pride, as countries can compare themselves to each other or compare progress from census to census. Demographic data may also foster efforts at understanding among the different segments of a nation's population; if it is discovered that the demographic makeup of the nation is changing, administrators can attempt to better anticipate the needs of the various population segments.

Census data describe the state of the nation, area by area. These data have a variety of uses. Governments use the data for social and financial planning. Marketers use them to make product, distribution, promotion, and pricing decisions. In the United States and many other countries trained researchers help to ensure consistency in data collection procedures.

Countries throughout the world collect census information. Many, such as India, the United Kingdom, and the United States, conduct full population counts every ten years—known as a decennial census. The Indian census is the most extensive in the world. Enumerators collect a wide range of data on the billion people living in more than 4,000 towns and 600,000 villages. The registrar general and census commissioner, who is responsible for the count, sends enumerators to every household. Even the homeless are counted. According to Indian government estimates, the undercount at the last census was only 1.76 percent. The 2001 Indian census employed about 2 million enumerators and 400,000 supervisors. The United Kingdom, too, was scheduled to conduct a population count in the year 2001. Although the census is administered separately in England, Wales, Scotland, and Northern Ireland, most of the statistics published are common to all countries. This census covers a wide range of topics that describe the characteristics of the British population, including household and family composition, housing, ethnicity, birthplace, health status, economic status, occupation, workplace, transport mode to work, car ownership, and language spoken.

The U.S. Census

In the United States a census has been taken every ten years since 1790. The government agency responsible is the Bureau of the Census, an organization with 12 permanent regional offices. In the United States federal financial aid is distributed on the basis of census data; thus a given community may miss out on monies if too many residents fail to complete the census form.

Businesses and advertising agencies use this information in several ways; for example, census data help to predict, with some accuracy, the demand for certain types of businesses, the growth of various market segments, and the lifestyles of consumers. Census information is desirable commercially because it is an impartial and virtually free source of information. Retailers and retail advertisers base projections of market area growth on census data and use the data to determine which types of products and brands to stock. Site location specialists utilize the data to determine where to locate distribution centers and retail outlets. Often advertisers will cite population numbers when providing a rationale for pursuing a certain segment of the market. For example, in 1950 the U.S. Census Bureau reported that average life expectancy was 68 years. At the end of the 20th century, the bureau reported that life expectancy had risen to 82 years. These data could have far-reaching implications for the health care and leisure industries. By understanding and capitalizing on these trends, several companies have developed products that appeal specifically to older adults. Thus, the astute marketer can spot many opportunities by paying attention to changing demographics as reported by the Census Bureau.

Between 1880 and 1900 statisticians began to use the information collected by the census for more sophisticated interpretations of the numbers. It was at this time that private research organizations began to codify the census information. On 6 March 1902, legislation was passed to create a permanent federal agency, the Bureau of the Census. During the 1900s, the Census Bureau became more involved with data gathering and conducted more frequent surveys at all times of the year. Thus, information was available to advertising agencies on a more timely basis than in the past. Between 1903 and 1933, leadership of the Census Bureau came from the Division of Manufacturers because many people were interested in business and were requesting industry data on a continuous basis. It was during this time that the Census Bureau became involved in supplying businesses and advertising agencies with requested information.

Starting with the 1960 census, the government increasingly separated out data such as per capita income and population density because it recognized the differential wealth of various states. Commercially these two measures were important because they gave businesses and advertising agencies more information on different segments of consumers. They could now identify specific areas of the United States on the basis of per capita income. These measurements also made the targeting of advertisements much easier. The trend toward providing more detailed information had begun. In the 1960 census, information was provided for smaller and smaller geographic areas, data on educational attainment was broadened, and data about place of work and means of transportation to work were collected. This information provided advertising agencies with more specific lifestyle data than had been available previously, enabling agencies to be more accurate with projections and strategy planning. Census information about the racial makeup of the United States was used by advertising agencies and businesses to segment their marketing efforts by race as well as to determine the location of people from various racial backgrounds. The census detected the post–World War II birthrate increase, which prompted the coining of the term *baby*

"Plaza San José" por Manuel Hernández Acevedo—Museo de Arte de Puerto Rico

Cómo Puerto Rico Sabe lo que Puerto Rico Necesita

Censo 2000 Puerto Rico
Departamento de Comercio
Municipal de: 2000

No Dejes Tu Futuro en Blanco.

USCENSUSBUREAU

In 2000 the U.S. Census Bureau broadened its efforts to identify ethnic minorities through an intensive advertising campaign. A poster targeted to Puerto Rican residents featured "Plaza San José" by Puerto Rican painter Manuel Hernández Acevedo.

boomers to describe the individuals born in this era. Recognition of the rise in births allowed advertisers and businesses to focus their attention on the growing population of new mothers and to promote products for infants and children.

The 1970 census was the first to be distributed by mail. A decision was made to use a mail census for 60 percent of the country, primarily the large metropolitan areas. It was also decided that more detailed information was needed on the African-American and other minority populations. One of the major publications that used the 1970 census data was the *New York Times,* which used the census information to analyze its market segments that subscribed to the paper and to identify potential customers.

For the 1990 census, the bureau block-numbered the entire country and had counts for each of the 8 million–12 million blocks. Advertisers and businesses were in a position to analyze the information on a block level. They could identify the demo-

graphic characteristics of the people living within the blocks, which provided the accuracy that clients wanted.

The year 2000 census was played out against a political controversy over whether each person should be counted individually, in the time-honored way, or whether sampling techniques, widely used in advertising research, should be employed. Advocates for minority groups contended that their numbers would be undercounted using the traditional method because of the inability or reluctance of many people—immigrants and the homeless, for example—to complete census forms. They favored sampling as the way to ensure the most accurate count. Others held that the Constitution required a traditional count and that it was each citizen's responsibility to respond.

The debate was not solely over methodology, however; each alternative implied its own political consequences. Compared to a traditional count, sampling would be likely to show increases in the numbers of economically disadvantaged individuals and members of minority ethnic and racial groups. These increases would have an impact on the redrawing of congressional districts in a manner favorable to the election of Democrats. On the other hand, a traditional count could overlook many in these groups, which would diminish their impact in congressional redistricting and presumably favor Republicans. With a Republican majority in both houses of Congress, it was decided that the Census Bureau would conduct a traditional count. Most market research professionals had confidence that modern methods of sampling would have delivered an accurate count. But it was fundamentally a political decision not a scientific one.

Advertising the Census

From 1950 through 1990, U.S. censuses relied on pro bono advertisements to promote participation. Because these ads did not attract the attention that paid ads typically receive, they did little to increase the response rate. Thus, in the year 2000 census, paid advertising was used for the first time in U.S. history. The campaign promoted census awareness and participation, especially among those segments of the population that have historically had a low response rate.

The goal of the paid advertising program was to increase response rates by generating public awareness of the census. Advertising messages were developed to educate the public on the importance of census data in allocating funds for schools, health care, and other vital services. The ads urged people to complete the form, to mail it promptly, and to cooperate with census enumerators who called on them personally. The campaign's slogan was, "This is your future. Don't leave it blank." The advertising campaign was extended through several other marketing vehicles, including direct mail (advance letter, questionnaire, and reminder postcard), promotions, and special events.

After a competitive solicitation and evaluation process, the Census Bureau selected Young & Rubicam (Y&R) to design, develop, and implement a paid advertising campaign in support of Census 2000. Four Y&R divisions were chosen because of their expertise in advertising to specific markets or population groups:

In the 1990 census the U.S. Census Bureau began to encourage ethnic minorities to participate through a promotional campaign that celebrated ethnic heritage. This poster featured American Indian artist Jerry Ingram's painting "Calling the Eagles."
"Calling the Eagles" by Jerry Ingram. Water Color, 16x24.

the Bravo Group, specializing in the Hispanic audience; the Chisholm-Mingo Group, specializing in the African-American and emerging African and Caribbean audiences; Kang & Lee, specializing in Asian Americans and emerging audiences in Russia, Eastern Europe, and the Middle East; and g&g, which specializes in targeting messages to American Indians.

While Y&R developed the overall strategy for the campaign and developed ads for the "majority" portion of the campaign, the four partner agencies researched and developed creative and media plans for their specific target audiences. The Census Bureau

expected to pay more than $160 million for the entire ad campaign. The majority was earmarked for media purchases to deliver the messages as effectively as possible. If successful, the campaign may influence other countries to consider paid advertising to promote census participation.

Implications for the Future

According to a 1999 report from the U.S. Census Bureau, the world's population, which stood at a little more than 6 billion at the turn of the century, will reach 8 billion by 2026. The greatest population growth will take place in developing countries, particularly those in Africa, Asia, and Latin America. The agency projects that the world's total population will reach 9.3 billion by 2050, and the report confirms that the world's population is becoming progressively older. By 2050, it is estimated that there will be 370 million people over the age of 80, up from 66 million in 1998. The population of people age 100 and older will grow from 135,000 in 1998 to more than 2.2 million in 2050. The aging of the world's population and the growth of the Third World will have far-reaching implications for social and political policy and are certain to profoundly affect commerce. As it has in the past, the advertising industry, too, will change to suit the changing times.

DENISE T. OGDEN

Further Reading

Alonso, William, and Paul Starr, editors, *The Politics of Numbers*, New York: Russell Sage Foundation, 1987

Anderson, Margo J., *The American Census: A Social History*, New Haven, Connecticut: Yale University Press, 1988

Goyer, Doreen S., *The Handbook of National Population Censuses: Latin America and the Caribbean, North America, and Oceania*, Westport, Connecticut: Greenwood, 1983

Meyers, Janet, "Census to Give Marketers a Hand," *Advertising Age* (12 March 1990)

Stablein, Marilyn, *The Census Taker: Stories of a Traveler in India and Nepal*, Seattle, Washington: Black Heron, 1985

Van Matre, Joseph G., and Darell R. Hankins, "Census Data: A Primer for Business Applications," *Journal of Small Business Management* 18, no. 3 (July 1980)

C.F. Hathaway Shirt Company. *See under* Hathaway

Charren, Peggy 1928–

U.S. Consumer Activist

Before 1968 children's television received only cursory attention from the Federal Communications Commission (FCC). In the commission's 1960 programming statement, children's programming was not even defined. Advertising to children, while growing rapidly, was still in its infancy. The hosts of television's popular *Romper Room* and *Captain Kangaroo* endorsed products during broadcasts of each show, and the claims made in those endorsements went unchecked. But these practices changed following an informal meeting in the living room of a Massachusetts woman named Peggy Charren.

In January 1968, dismayed by Saturday morning animated programs that featured cartoon violence, hucksterism, and irresponsible messages, Charren and her associates formed Action for Children's Television (ACT). The group focused on the Communications Act of 1934, which stipulated that in return for their use of the public airwaves, broadcasters were obligated to serve the public interest. ACT contended that industry practices were placing the needs of advertisers and programmers above the needs of children.

ACT studied *Romper Room* broadcasts for four weeks in spring 1969, surveying advertising and program content. It documented the airing of violent cartoons, program hosts hawking products, and child participants selling products. ACT took its data to station executives at WHDH in Boston, Massachusetts. Armed with those data and the expert testimony of physicians and psychologists, Charren in 1970 drafted a one-page petition calling on the FCC to require programming for children and eliminate commercials on children's television. Charren and two ACT members met with FCC commissioners to discuss the issues, the first time the agency had met with members of the public. ACT began its rise to prominence that same year when it joined with the Kennedy Memorial Hospital for Children and the Boston University School of Public Communications to host the first National Symposium on Children and Television.

No "Little Housewife"

Charren had a witty, acerbic personal style that served her well in Washington, D.C. Her straightforward recitation of the wrongs in the network programming mentality tagged her with a Ralph Nader–style reputation—an activist turned interventionist who was not easily deterred. To her opponents, Charren was abrasive and demanding, traits her proponents interpreted instead as aggressive and unyielding. At a 1969 meeting with CBS network executives in New York City, Charren asked to speak to the network's director of programming. When he arrived, the discussion

Peggy Charren.
Couretsy of Peggy Charren. Reprinted with permission of the Gutman Library, Harvard University.

turned to the network's lack of a director of children's programming; within a week, executives at the network had appointed one.

Her typical approach was to charm her opponents with candor and sensible information, belying the dismissive "little housewife" label with which programmers initially tagged her and other ACT members. Eventually Charren would become the expert whom FCC members called upon for advice.

ACT quickly grew to a national organization with 10,000 members; after its first year, Charren was the only original member remaining. In 1970 a petition drive inspired thousands of letters supporting ACT's position, which was endorsed by such prestigious professional groups as the American Academy of Pediatrics, the American Public Library Association, the Consumers Union, and the National Association of Elementary School Principals. Those endorsements positioned ACT and Charren as formi-

dable defenders of children and, within a decade, major strides were made in the planning, approach, and production of children's TV programming. ACT managed to affect changes in children's programs in the 1970s that included: removal of commercials that presented children's vitamins as candylike products; reduction of commercial time to nine minutes and 30 seconds per hour on weekends and 12 minutes per hour on weekdays; prohibitions against program hosts endorsing or selling products; reduction of frequency of program interruptions; requirement of nutritional messages to balance product announcements; and insertion of five-second separator devices called bumpers before and after commercials to help children distinguish between program and non-program material.

In 1974 the FCC agreed with ACT's initiatives, turning the ACT requests into a set of guidelines known as the "Children's Television Policy Statement." The statement, viewed as a recommendation rather than a mandate, suggested stations provide a reasonable amount of children's programming, much of it informational and educational.

The FCC was against banning all advertising on children's programming, saying that to do so would ruin the economic foundations needed to create such viable programming. ACT's efforts in part led to the 1978 Federal Trade Commission (FTC) recommendation that TV advertising to children be sharply curtailed because it exploits their immaturity. The concept, first formally advocated by ACT, was hailed as visionary.

The Reagan Years

"The horrible nature of children's advertising is directly attributable to [President] Ronald Reagan," Charren said in the 1980s, charging the Reagan administration with "gutting" past promises of consumer protection. Early in the Reagan presidency, Charren, in a speech before the FTC, outlined the problems with children's television:

> As a psychological matter, children are cognitively incapable of understanding all television commercials directed to them, and no amount of consumer education can do much to improve this natural age-based limitation. As a factual matter, highly sugared foods and toys are the products most often advertised directly to children on television, and the average child spends an inordinate amount of time watching television programs and commercials targeted to him. As a practical matter, it is unrealistic to expect parents always to mediate between their children and television commercials, especially when the commercials are directed to the children.

The FTC—and later Congress—disagreed with Charren. In 1980, with new appointees in place, the FTC formally dropped its inquiry into children's programming. In 1981 Congress restricted the focus of its own inquiry into children's programming due to intense lobbying efforts by the networks and advertisers.

In 1981 Reagan appointed Mark Fowler as the chairman of the FCC; Fowler was an attorney who opposed regulation of either advertising or programming. In 1983 the FCC lifted its children's policy guidelines and allowed television stations to air as many commercials in a given time period as they thought necessary. That decision unraveled ACT's work in the 1970s, resulting in what came to be called "program-length commercials." At the same time, understanding that the milieu of programmers and networks had changed, the networks cancelled much of their educational children's programming (which was expensive to produce) and significantly reduced the number of after-school specials and other programming they aired. ACT turned its focus toward Congress and political action.

Children's Television Act of 1990

Aligning with Representative Edward Markey of Massachusetts, ACT formed strong coalitions with children's advocacy groups, children's health organizations, and other grassroots movements to push its agenda in Congress. Following congressional hearings that included testimony from Charren, the Democrat-controlled Congress in 1990 passed the Children's Television Act, which established the National Endowment for Children's Educational Television. The bill, sponsored by Markey, required stations renewing their licenses to demonstrate that they were fulfilling the educational and informational needs of children age 2 to16.

"This is like the first year of the clean air regulations," Charren said at the time. "Probably one-third of the new shows will be nifty, one-third will be terrible, and one-third will be the ones whose educational value is debated." The law, though later admitted to be ill-defined in scope and direction, made a philosophical difference at the time. Then in 1996 a new bill was passed that created core educational programming, with the premise of educating children under clearly stated, age-targeted objectives. Moreover, commercials were given no more than 10 1/2 minutes per 30 minutes for weekends and 12 minutes for weekdays. From 1990 to 1997 eight of nine Peabody Awards for children's programs were awarded to informational or educational programs, a result of the law's influence on programmers.

With the passage of the Children's Television Act—and a strong legacy of change in the children's programming industry—Charren shuttered ACT in 1992. She chose the Center for Media Education (CME) as the designated successor to ACT based on its mission, which she found closest to that of ACT's initial mandate, and remained involved in its foray into Internet regulatory matters. In 1996 President Bill Clinton named Charren to the Presidential Advisory Committee on Public Interest of Digital TV Broadcasters, which opened the Internet chapter of her advocacy story. She believed that on-line advertising posed two threats to children: tracking of children's on-line computer activity by advertisers and the solicitation of information from them. Through both her committee involvement and CME, Charren continued to work for regulation of children's on-line advertising and Web sites.

Controversies

Charren's role as an advocate thrust her into debate throughout her tenure as ACT president. She took aggressive stands in three separate areas: advertising, censorship, and parental responsibility.

First, Charren labeled advertising to children a "dastardly phenomenon" affecting their well being. She focused in particular on the inability of young children to discern what advertising is. Critics argued that her "no advertising is the right policy" philosophy worked against children developing a healthy consumer ethic in a culture that demands educated, informed consumers. One battle she won was that to remove commercials for multivitamins that resembled candy and were promoted by entertaining, kid-friendly cartoon characters. The National Association of Broadcasters in 1972 agreed to prohibit selling vitamins to children. In 1976 the FTC issued an order prohibiting such advertising, stating that "children are unqualified by age or experience to decide for themselves whether or not they need or should use multiple vitamins."

Charren also sparked controversy regarding her stance on First Amendment rights. Throughout her skirmishes with broadcasters and the FCC, she remained adamant that the best method for dealing with poor quality programming was not to censor specific shows. Instead she pushed for regulation that would "raise the bar" for programmers. At the same time, she advocated the removal of advertising as well as specific programs from the air. The two philosophies—advocating the banning of programs while opposing censorship—made for an inconsistent vision.

Charren's advice to parents dealing with these issues was simple: "when it comes to controlling what's on TV in American homes, I think the off button is pretty good." At the end of the 20th century V-chip technology—a programmed gatekeeper for television—suggested that further parental control options were at hand. Yet for Charren the V-chip was an imperfect solution, as it does not block advertisements during children's programming.

Because of Charren's liberal politics and outspoken views, her agenda aligned her with such other causes as civil and women's rights, and antiwar efforts. Though the causes never formally intersected, they became line items on the same agenda for politicians, activists, and the media, helping to paint social reform—such as ACT's mission—in liberal colors. Charren's work for children, especially during the Reagan years, sometimes took a backseat to the conservative-liberal struggles that marked the 1980s.

Some critics saw the efforts of ACT and Charren as overbearing. Entertainment options proliferated, and the brave new world that ACT and Charren envisioned (that of *Mr. Rogers' Neighborhood* and *Sesame Street*, with no advertising) evolved into *Mighty Morphin Power Rangers* and a new assault of product-sponsored programming such as the animated cartoons *Strawberry Shortcake* and *GI Joe*.

Charren's Legacy

This subtle evolution in governmental philosophy, pressed for by Charren for more than 30 years, reflects a change in American culture. Children in the United States increasingly have been more closely scrutinized, their interests protected through media discussion and government regulation, their needs becoming the object of intense research. Meanwhile, children's entertainment and purchasing power increased exponentially from the 1950s to the 1990s. Perhaps the powerful children's entertainment industry, with specific channels as well as cable and network programming mandated to educate and edify children, are unintended results of Charren's focus. This dedicated youth culture grew in part when the emphasis on children and their world became a prominent subject of public discussion. But whether or not children's programming is actually better than it was in the early 1970s is unclear.

During its two decades of existence, ACT was lauded as one of the most feared and respected public-interest groups in the nation. Charren's legacy, however, seems bound in personal optimism and tenacity. "I am ever convinced I can change the world all by myself," she said in 1996. In many ways, she has.

DEBORAH K. MORRISON

See also Children: Targets of Advertising

Biography
Born 9 March 1928; received bachelor of arts from Connecticut College, 1949; founded Action for Children's Television, 1968; named to Task Panel on Public Attitudes and Use of Media for Promotion of Health as part of the President's Commission on Mental Health, 1977; received honorary degrees from: Regis College, 1978, Emerson College, 1984, Bank Street College of Education, 1985, Tufts University, 1988, Wheelock College, 1990; named a visiting scholar at Harvard Graduate School of Education, 1987; awarded Emmy for children's advocacy, 1988; received Peabody Award, 1992; awarded Presidential Medal of Freedom, 1995; named to Presidential Advisory Committee on Public Interest of Digital TV Broadcasters, 1997; received Annenberg Public Policy Center Award for Distinguished Lifetime Contributions to Children and Television, 1998.

Selected Publications
Changing Channels: Living (Sensibly) with Television (with Martin Sandler), 1983
The TV-Smart Book for Kids: Puzzles, Games, and Other Good Stuff, 1986
editor, *Television, Children, and the Constitutional Bicentennial* (with Carol Hulsizer), 1986

Further Reading
Hendershot, Heather, *Saturday Morning Censors: Television Regulation before the V-Chip,* Durham, North Carolina: Duke University Press, 1998
Moody, Kate, *Growing Up on Television: The TV Effect, a Report to Parents,* New York: Times, 1980

Cheil Communications, Inc.

South Korea's first modern advertising agency, created by Samsung Group founder Lee Byung Chul as the in-house ad agency for Samsung, 1973; began conducting Korea's first nationwide lifestyle surveys, 1977; began publishing Korea's first *Advertising Yearbook,* 1979; set up a joint venture with Bozell, 1989; formed an alliance with Edelman Public Relations, 1991; set up Hakuhodo-Cheil, 1999; began working with True North Communications' FCB Worldwide, 2000.

Major Clients
Cheil Jedang
Daum Communications
Dong Suh Foods
Korea Exchange Bank
Korea Telecom Freetel
Samsung Electronics
Seoul Milk
Tongyang Confectionary

Cheil Communications was founded in 1973 by Lee Byung Chul, the pioneering Korean entrepreneur who founded Samsung Group. Cheil, established as Samsung's in-house advertising agency, was the first modern agency in South Korea. It introduced advertising and its related businesses of marketing and media research to Korea's booming economy.

Cheil gradually expanded its client base to include non-Samsung customers, established offices overseas, and built alliances with foreign companies. Major campaigns, such as those for Hite Beer and Pulmuone Foods, completely reversed the fortunes of what were once minor companies. Cheil remains Korea's industry leader, setting high standards for the competition.

Well before the 1950–53 war devastated the Korean peninsula, Lee Byung Chul was establishing businesses that would ultimately help propel South Korea into the club of rich nations in its half-century postwar growth spurt. In 1938, four years after dropping out of Japan's Waseda University, Lee started a company called Samsung Sang Hoe in Taegu, South Korea, to export Korean fish

Craving!

Cheil Communications.

Take a bite. You will never leave it.
We are ready to offer you a variety of services, say, traditional
advertising, SP, PR, sports marketing and even cyber-marketing on the
internet.
You want to go international? No problem. Because we are
aleady there to serve you in New York, London, Tokyo, Beijing
Singapore, etc.
Proud of our unique strategy and creativity praised in Clio,
New York and Cannes Festival, we are on the verge of growing to be one
of the leading global agencies in the world.
Our vision? To serve your taste better.
So, are you ready to take a bite?

CHEIL communications

Internet http://www.cheil.co.kr　Seoul Headquarters +82-2-724-0303 Cheil Communications America +1-201-229-6055 LA +1-213-388-4211 Miami +1-305-599-9367 Tokyo +81-3-5641-9573
Beijing +8610-6510-1522 Hong Kong +852-2862-6410 Singapore +65-420-8152 London +44-181-391-4550 Frankfurt +49-6196-666700 Moskow +7-502-213-9250 Dubai +971-4-218891

A house ad for Cheil Communications promoted the agency's creative services and global presence.

and produce to China. Soon after, Lee set up Cheil Sugar, and later a confectionary called Cheil Industries, Inc. In 1965 he founded what was to become one of Korea's largest daily newspapers, the *Joong-Ang Ilbo*. In 1969 he started Samsung Electronics.

By the time he founded Cheil Communications in 1973, Lee had already built a formidable business empire. He had long benchmarked South Korea's economic development with that of Japan, which historically has been several decades ahead of Korea. Lee was a close friend of the president of Japan's Dentsu ad agency, who in the late 1960s suggested that Korea would soon be ripe for mass advertising and marketing that would drive consumer demand. Lee recognized that an in-house agency could help sell Samsung products.

Lee recruited journalists from his *Joong-Ang Ilbo* newspaper to help set up the business and invited co-founders with a variety of backgrounds in pharmaceuticals, foods, industrial products, and financial services. Half of the co-founders came from Samsung companies and half were outsiders. They provided funding and the promise of advertising business. Therefore in the beginning, half of Cheil's clients were Samsung companies and half were outsiders; the latter included Lotte Confectionary, Jinro

Soju, and Dongwha Pharmaceutical. Along with Lee's companies, these were some of Korea's largest advertisers. Cheil had to learn fast. Soon after opening its doors, Cheil established an alliance with the Japanese agency Hakuhodo and began sending workers to Japan to learn about the ad business and a variety of related services.

Over the years Cheil expanded into promotions, public relations, brand consulting, research, marketing, and Web page design. In 1977 it began conducting Korea's first nationwide lifestyle surveys—part of its effort to provide clients with sound demographic information. In 1979 it began publishing Korea's first *Advertising Yearbook*, which would continue as the reference of record for the industry.

In the mid-1970s, as durable goods made by Samsung Electronics became popular and more widely affordable, Cheil campaigns carried them into the popular consciousness. A Samsung washing machine became a runaway seller after ads portrayed a young wife pleasing her husband with clean laundry. The message was that even in Korea's patriarchal society, a woman could control her man by using a Samsung product.

Another classic ad that tapped into Korean cultural values was a 1989 campaign for Tongyang Confectionery Corporation's "Choco Pie Chung." The sweet moon-pies were paired with the Korean concept of *chung,* a feeling of deep-seated affection that develops between people. Ads featured poignant story lines such as a young man giving a Choco pie to his teenage brother, who needed encouragement on a school test.

Some campaigns won international acclaim for Cheil. In 1987 it received a Clio award for a Samsung Electronics TV commercial called "Human Touch." In 1997 Cheil was awarded a gold Lion at the Cannes (France) International Advertising Festival for its "Baby Eyes" commercials about wide-screen TV sets.

As Samsung grew into an international marketer, Cheil grew as well. In the late 1980s it began setting up an overseas network of 15 offices on five continents. In 1989 it set up a joint venture with Bozell, called Cheil-Bozell, which expanded its skills and enabled it to add new clients that would otherwise conflict with existing Cheil clients. In 1991 Cheil formed an alliance with Edelman Public Relations to expand its public relations business and build its own marketing institute.

Cheil steadily built a reputation for top-notch service, closely following its customers' needs through basic research, planning, execution, and evaluation. As of 2000 approximately 64.5 percent of its clients had been with Cheil for more than 20 years.

Some Cheil campaigns were particularly effective. In 1981 Bukwang Pharmaceuticals' Brandax toothpaste expanded its market share from 3 percent to 19.9 percent after a campaign portrayed the toothpaste as a medical product that could significantly influence the health of its users. A campaign in the early 1990s for Hite Beer boosted its market share from 5 percent to 32.8 percent. The ads emphasized the deep-rock spring water used in making Hite at a time when the parent company of Hite's major competitor was in the news for spilling toxins into the Naktong River near Pusan, a port city at the southeast tip of the Korean peninsula. Similarly, Cheil emphasized the pure and natural qualities of

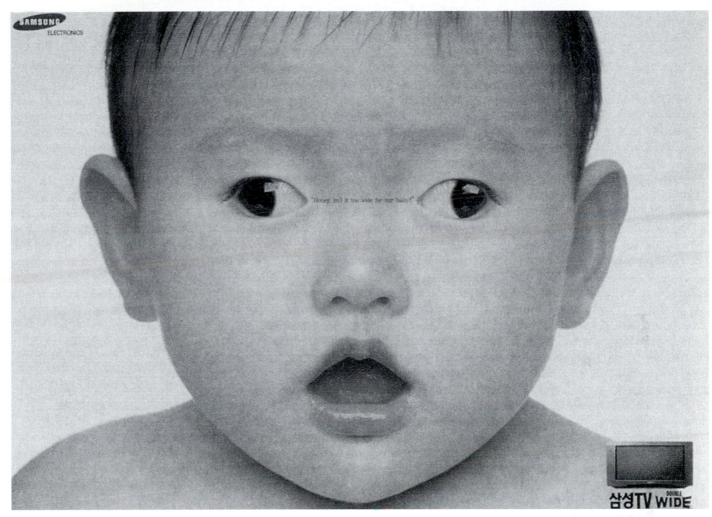

A 1996 ad—captioned "Honey, isn't it too wide for our baby?"—created by Cheil Communications for Samsung won a merit award in the 1997 Art Directors Annual.

Pulmuone foods at a time when the unpleasant aspects of industrialization were becoming apparent in South Korea. Pulmuone's success allowed it to expand abroad, and soon after the ad campaign, it built a factory in China.

Observers point to only one nonprofessional aspect of Cheil Communications—Lee always appointed his Samsung associates as its president rather than choosing advertising professionals. This practice did not necessarily harm Cheil. Its president since 1981, Pae Chong Yeul, is largely credited with the agency's many successes during his tenure. Even at the lowest point of South Korea's economic crisis in 1998, Cheil turned a $7.4 million profit. Pae accomplished this by listing Cheil on the Korea Stock Exchange and expanding into the Internet business. That year Cheil built Korea's number-one portal site in terms of customers for Daum Communications. A new economic boom helped Cheil rebound quickly, and in 2000 it reported profits of $40 million.

Cheil expanded into sports marketing with Samsung Electronics' Olympic sponsorship both at the 1998 Nagano, Japan, games and in 2000 in Sydney, Australia. The two campaigns were valued at $35 million and $79 million, respectively.

Cheil continues to strengthen old relationships and establish new ones. In 1999 it set up Hakuhodo-Cheil, and in 2000 it began working with True North Communications' FCB Worldwide, which won Samsung Electronics' $400 million global advertising account in December. Although it has expanded internationally and increased its non-Samsung client base to comprise 60 percent of its business, Cheil has yet to recruit many accounts from international marketers in Korea. As of 2001 it had only six international clients, including Pizza Hut, 3Com, and General Motors. As of 2000 Cheil had gross income of $150.4 million, up 15.1 percent over the previous year, on revenue of $949.3 million.

MICHAEL BAKER

Chesebrough-Pond's, Inc.

Principal Agencies
McCann-Erickson
J. Walter Thompson Company

Chesebrough-Pond's, which owns several well-known brands, including Pond's, Vaseline, and Dr. Scholl's, was formed in 1955 through the merger of Pond's Extract Company and Chesebrough Manufacturing Company. Prior to the merger Chesebrough, which produced Vaseline products, had an established relationship with McCann-Erickson, the agency that produced the long-running radio series *Dr. Christian* for the company. Pond's was represented for many years by the J. Walter Thompson Company, which remained after 1955 and was joined by Norman, Craig & Kummel, Inc.; Compton Advertising, Inc.; and William Esty & Company, Inc.

With the consolidation of the two companies, a diverse range of products, including Pertussin cough medicines, Prince Matchabelli fragrances, Ragú spaghetti sauce, Aziza cosmetics, and Q-Tips cotton swabs, were brought together under a single management. During the 1960s the company went international, acquiring subsidiaries in Argentina, Australia, Brazil, and India. Chesebrough-Pond's also acquired Health-tex, a children's clothing manufacturer, in 1973. During the 1970s Chesebrough-Pond's launched Vaseline Intensive Care lotion and Pond's Cream & Cocoa lotion. By 1980 it had captured one-fourth of the lotion market. During this same decade, however, the company was troubled by poor financial performance from some of its divisions. Unilever took over the company in 1986 and streamlined both its product line and operations.

Part of the Unilever strategy involved concentrating on the company's core products. In 1991, for example, it launched a campaign titled "Skin Science Updates" for the Vaseline Intensive Care products. That same year it expanded its cold-cream franchise with a body-care line of cleansers and creams. In 1993 the company invented a fictitious beauty treatment research center, the Pond's Institute, whose spokespeople are featured in Pond's ads dispensing skin-care advice. In 1998 the company introduced the Ultra Silk body-care collection, which included lotions, hand creams, foot lotion, and bath capsules. Clear Solutions, another product line promoted that year, was a skin-care line targeted to women ages 18 to 34. Dr. Scholl's extended its body-care product line with loofah sponges, brushes, body gels, and creams. These introductions seemed consonant with the enormous growth of the category: skin creams and lotions ranked as the second-fastest-growing category in Unilever's sales within the health and personal care segment from 1997 to 1999.

In addition to its body-care line of products, Chesebrough-Pond's entered the U.S. toothpaste market with its Mentadent brand in 1993. Among the brand's distinguishing characteristics were its baking soda and peroxide ingredients and a two-chamber package system. Mentadent advertisements featured a testimonial from a dentist's wife praising the product's taste and "tingle sensation" and stating that that her husband recommended the toothpaste's ingredient combination. By 1997 the brand ranked fourth after Crest, Colgate, and Aquafresh, with total sales of $164 million.

By the end of 1998 the company was preparing for the launch of Mentadent Crystal Ice. Positioned as a toothpaste to whiten teeth and freshen breath, the product was a response to the market trend toward toothpastes with multiple benefits. In 1999, however, Mentadent reported sales of $154 million, a 10.7 percent decrease. The decline was attributed partly to increased competition from other brands and partly to the maturity of the toothpaste market in the United States, Japan, and Western

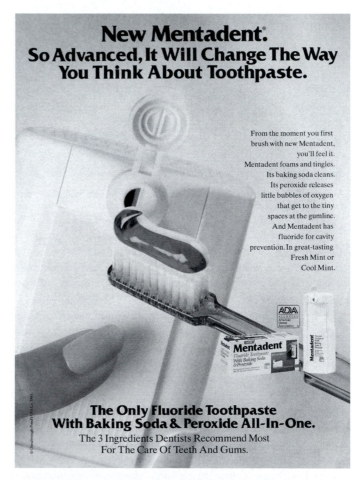

In 1993 Chesebrough-Pond's introduced Mentadent, a toothpaste whose unique packaging and ingredient combination helped it capture a significant share of the market.
The MENTADENT print ad was reproduced courtesy of Chesebrough-Pond's USA Co.

What one of Society's twelve most beautiful women says about the care of the skin

PORTRAIT BY NEYSA McMEIN

Mrs. Biddle Duke

"The woman who achieves loveliness must be exquisite at all times. Her skin should be so perfectly cared for that every situation finds it the same—smooth and transparently clear—unlined by fatigue, showing no trace of exposure. And this I believe any woman can accomplish with the careful use of Pond's Two Creams."

Cordelia Biddle Duke

OF COURSE if one did nothing but recline upon a chaise longue in a foam of Venise lace and chiffon, such terms as fatigue and exposure would be unknown.

But the woman who is active in society leads a very different sort of life.

The younger ones (to say nothing of their mothers and aunts) are almost invariably enthusiastic sportswomen. Indeed their strenuous daytime programme of skating, riding, or golf only serves to inspire their slim silver sandals right through until four o'clock the next morning.

But sports and late hours combine in an insidious attack upon woman's dearest possession — her complexion.

The icy wind that sweeps across the frozen pond is leaving tiny cracks and roughnesses. The merciless sun of seasides is bound to burn and coarsen. The laughing hours of post-midnight dancing will show next morning in faint lines of fatigue around eyes and mouth.

But—"exquisite at all times" is the society woman's code, as Mrs. Biddle Duke says. And exquisite at all times she is.

Long ago the women who led an active social life discovered a sure and simple method of skin care that actually frees the skin from the injuries their strenuous life would cause—keeps it at all times as clear and fresh and delicate as their position has always demanded.

This method is the famous one devised by Pond's. After years of study and research, the Pond's chemists pronounced the two skin essentials for every woman to be—Cleansing and Protection. And to this end they worked and experimented until Pond's Cold Cream and Pond's Vanishing Cream were produced.

Exquisite women use this Method

Pond's Cold Cream for cleansing is a deliciously soft pure cream that not only cleanses the skin thoroughly, but restores its natural satin suppleness. Dip your fingers into its fragrant softness and rub an ample amount on your face and neck. The fine oil in it sinks deep into the pores to dislodge all of the dirt, excess natural oil, and powder that invisibly clog those tiny cells. Now wipe it off with a soft cloth and don't be ashamed if the cloth is black. *Do this twice.* How clean your skin is, how soft and velvety and above all how fine! That is because the tiny pores now have a chance to breathe and function normally.

Pond's Vanishing Cream is now smoothed on. This light delicate cream is used after every skin cleansing, leaving a new fresh loveliness that prepares your skin perfectly for the necessary finish of powder.

As Miss Cordelia Biddle of Philadelphia, young Mrs. Duke began her social life against the brilliant background of one of America's most exclusive families. She is one of the most prominent and most admired of the younger women of society and is well-known on both sides of the Atlantic. Her captivating personality is coupled with a beauty that made Neysa McMein, well-known

artist and illustrator, whose charming portrait of Mrs. Duke is shown above, choose her as one of the twelve most beautiful women in America.

TODAY, ALL WOMEN WHO MUST BE EXQUISITE HAVE A NEW CONCEPTION OF SKIN CARE. ITS FOUNDATION IS POND'S TWO CREAMS—ONE FOR THE NEW REJUVENATING CLEANSING, ONE FOR THE DELICATE PROTECTIVE FINISH THAT FOLLOWS . . . . . .
EVERY SKIN NEEDS THESE TWO CREAMS

Smooth on only a little. There's a *pearly* glow to your whole face—and how extraordinarily young you're looking! The powder will go on more smoothly than ever and will last almost indefinitely.

Together these two creams provide the balanced treatment that every skin requires. Pond's Cold Cream effects a deep purifying of the skin that a mere surface cleansing can never accomplish. And immaculate Pond's cleanliness is the sure prevention and cure for such distressing blemishes as a lifeless muddy skin and over-active oil glands that result in the bane of all women —a shiny nose.

Pond's Vanishing Cream actually protects the skin from the constant attacks of every-day life that are so hard to realize. Fine lines and wrinkles that every woman dreads, chapping and rough places are the result of simply every-day exposure. Wind that dries and roughens, sun that burns and coarsens are to be met with whenever one goes out of the house. But the woman who cares about her skin can laugh at these ever-present foes, for she *knows* that her complexion, protected as it is by Pond's Two Creams, has nothing to fear from them.

When to use it

Every night give your face and neck a thorough cleansing with Pond's Cold Cream. If your skin is inclined to be dry, put a little more cream on for the night and let the skin absorb naturally the oils it lacks. And by all means rub a little into the point of your elbow if you want a soft rosy accent to your arm instead of the dreadful *turkey* look that so many elbows have.

In the morning freshen your face with water—Pond's Cold Cream, again, if your skin is dry—then apply Pond's Vanishing Cream for a delicious texture and perfect powder base. Powder and, if you wish, a trace of rouge. This cream should be used just as often as you cleanse your face.

After a long motor ride, a dusty journey by train, a windy afternoon of golf, be sure to use Pond's Cold Cream as soon as you come in, following it, of course, with Pond's Vanishing Cream before powdering.

If you are entertaining or going out in the evening use Pond's Cold Cream followed by Pond's Vanishing Cream for smooth clear loveliness.

Remember, that transparent clearness for which the fashionable woman is distinguished is the result of daily care. Begin this method at once and you will see the same loveliness reflected in your own mirror. Pond's Two Creams may be had at all drug and department stores. The Pond's Extract Company.

Free offer

Mail this coupon at once and we will send you, free, tubes of these two famous creams that usually sell for ten cents each.

THE POND'S EXTRACT COMPANY, 124 Hudson Street, New York

Please send me free one tube each of Pond's Cold Cream and Pond's Vanishing Cream — the size that usually sells for ten cents.

Name _____

Street _____

City _____ State _____

For much of its history Pond's has used testimonials, as in this 1924 advertisement from the J. Walter Thompson Company featuring socialite Cordelia Biddle Duke.
The POND'S print ad was reproduced courtesy of Chesebrough-Pond's USA Co.

Europe. Also in 1998, Unilever Health & Personal Care (HPC) USA was formed through the combination of the Chesebrough-Pond's, Lever Bros., and Helene Curtis business units.

BETHEL ANN RAVALO

Further Reading
Mehegan, Sean, "Vaseline Ups Ante via Anti-Bacterial," *Brandweek* (26 May 1997)
Popolillo, Melissa, "Health and Beauty Aids," *SuperBrands* (15 June 1998)

Chiat/Day, Inc.

(TBWA/Chiat/Day)

Chiat/Day formed by merger of Jay Chiat & Associates, Inc., and Faust/Day Advertising, 1968; merged with Hoefer, Dieterich & Brown to form Chiat/Day/Hoefer, 1980; named changed back to Chiat/Day, 1981; purchased Mojo MDA Group, Ltd., to form Chiat/Day/Mojo, Inc., Advertising, 1989; sold Mojo MDA Group, Ltd., 1992; merged with TBWA International to form TBWA Chiat/Day (later TBWA/Chiat/Day) and subsequently acquired by Omnicom Group, 1995.

Major Clients
ABC Television
Apple Computer
Everyready Battery Company
Nike
Nissan Motor Corporation
Samsonite Corporation
Taco Bell Corporation

Chiat/Day was renowned for its provocative, innovative, even disturbing work for such clients as Apple Computer, Nike, Reebok, and Eveready. Its creative reputation was matched by a reputation for an offbeat, determinedly bohemian work environment, where employees enjoyed television breaks and tricycle races, and a relaxed "virtual office" concept held sway. The creative, yet seemingly anarchic style had its detractors, who charged that the agency could be erratic, self-indulgent, and not responsive to its clients. As Jay Chiat acknowledged in a 1990 interview with *Adweek,* "We have a reputation that polarizes clients. We're perceived as being arrogant and pedantic." On the other hand, many of Chiat/Day's campaigns are widely recognized as brilliant, and other Madison Avenue agencies often mimic the agency's daring work.

Chiat/Day was founded by Jay Chiat and Guy Day. Chiat was born in the Bronx, New York, in 1931 and raised in New York and New Jersey. After serving in the U.S. Air Force, he was discharged in California in 1954 and decided to stay on the West Coast. After writing advertising for an Air Force contractor, he joined a small agency and then founded the Los Angeles, California-based Jay

Chiat & Associates in 1962. Inspired by the early ads of such "hot" agencies of the 1960s as Doyle Dane Bernbach—noted for its work for Avis and Volkswagen—Chiat began carefully studying and emulating this new approach, and he soon enjoyed a reputation for making moves that surprised everyone, from the consumer to the media to other advertising professionals.

Day was a partner in the California advertising agency Faust/Day in the 1960s. After merging that agency with Chiat's in 1968, Day served as president of the agency most of the next two decades, although he left the agency from 1976 to 1982, before departing permanently in 1988 because he opposed Chiat's decision to borrow $60 million to buy back control of the agency from employees.

A third major force in the history of Chiat/Day was the creative director and former president Lee Clow, who was already creative director at a rival ad agency in 1971 when he decided that he wanted to join Chiat/Day, which he saw as creatively unique. To get hired, he began a year-long self-promotional campaign. Using the slogan "Hire the Hairy" (a reference to his then-long mane), Clow sent stickers, posters, and even a jack-in-the-box with a miniature Lee Clow doll to Chiat. The effort finally paid off. Clow became creative director of Chiat/Day and is credited as the agency's leading creative visionary.

According to Chiat's own explanation published on the TBWA/Chiat/Day Web site, Chiat/Day was formed in 1968 after he received a phone call from rival Guy Day, who had just broken with his business partner. After an initial one-hour meeting, the two men went to a Los Angeles Dodgers baseball game, where they closed the deal. Both parent agencies were small and focused on technical advertising for the computer industry, and both men wanted to move into consumer-product accounts. The new agency of about 50 employees, with Day serving as president, won its first major account—the Equitable Savings Bank—within a month of the agency's founding. In 1969 Chiat/Day added Western Harness Racing to its list of clients, in part because Chiat bet the company president that his ads would raise track attendance by 15 percent; Chiat won the bet. In 1970 Chiat/Day's ads for the community youth organization Direction Sports, featuring the

The Energizer bunny, shown here in a 1992 advertisement, has proven to be one of Chiat/Day's most memorable creations.

In the late 1990s TBWA Chiat/Day's "TV Is Good" campaign for ABC, with its thought-provoking, tongue-in-cheek phrases, won accolades from both advertising professionals and viewers.
Courtesy of the ABC Television Network.

provocative slogan, "My hero, the pimp," won further acclaim and attention for the fledgling agency. In addition to the agency's innovative ads, Chiat has credited his agency's growth to the rise of new industries in the Southern California market and the increasing presence in the United States of such Japanese businesses as Yamaha, Pioneer, and Mitsubishi. Among Chiat/Day's most notable campaigns were the 20-page-long magazine ads for Yamaha motorcycles (an unprecedented length for print ads) and the agency's Honda ads from the early 1970s, which won a host of awards.

Whereas the agency's earlier efforts had been well-received by clients and the public, it was Chiat/Day's work for Apple Computer in the early 1980s that made advertising history. To introduce Apple's new computer model, the Lisa, in 1983, Chiat/Day shot a 60-second commercial starring then-unknown actor Kevin Costner. The spot begins with an unshaven Costner riding a bicycle through empty city streets at dawn, his faithful dog running at his side, headed for the office. When he arrives, he eagerly begins typing a new idea into his office computer, something he has been mulling over during the night. The phone rings and Costner answers, smiles, and says "Yeah, I'll be home for breakfast." The commercial's interweaving of work and home life, suggesting the possibility of happily merging the two by using an Apple computer, struck a chord with American consumers, who dreamed of such a utopian existence.

Also in 1983 Chiat/Day launched the first of its ads for the sportswear manufacturer Nike. Nike initially wanted an upbeat, humorous campaign, but Chiat/Day argued forcefully for a campaign featuring sweaty, hard-working athletes wearing Nike attire and bearing the tag line, "We haven't forgotten why they're called sweats." The campaign's message: Nike understands the struggles that serious athletes face as they strive to succeed. Nike was happy with the results, and the campaign garnered the agency a

number of awards, indicating the respect the agency had earned in the industry.

In 1984 the agency created a controversial—and now legendary—ad for Apple's new Macintosh computer. Called "1984," it was directed by British filmmaker Ridley Scott and aired during that year's Super Bowl. The commercial offers a stark Orwellian vision of a future dystopia ruled by Big Brother. Mindless, zombielike workers chant in awe before an authority figure preaching to them from a huge television screen. The entire scene is tinted blue, a reference to IBM's nickname, Big Blue. Then the spot shows a young woman running into the room and throwing a sledgehammer into the television-screen face of the dictator, a symbolic challenge by the upstart Apple to IBM's dominance in the computer market. Although nervous executives at Apple tried to pull the ad at the last minute, Chiat/Day fought hard for it, and the commercial aired once during the Super Bowl at a cost of some $800,000 and in 11 regional markets. Network news broadcasts also replayed the spot as an example of innovation in advertising. The ad won every major advertising award that year, including the Grand Effie; a gold Lion at the prestigious International Advertising Festival at Cannes, France; a Belding bowl; and a Clio award. *Advertising Age* named the spot "Commercial of the Decade." The ad's success is credited with making the Super Bowl the premiere showcase for new commercials. Chiat/Day also picked up major new accounts thanks to the Apple ad, including Bristol-Myers, 3M, and Pizza Hut.

For the 1985 Super Bowl, Chiat/Day launched an ad for Apple that did not work out well for either party. Dubbed "Lemmings," the spot features a line of business executives dressed in monotonously similar dark suits and wearing blindfolds. As they snake their way through a desolate countryside, the sound track plays a dirgelike rendition of the Seven Dwarves' song "Hi Ho, Hi Ho, It's Off to Work We Go" from the Walt Disney Company's animated film *Snow White*. Reaching a cliff, the blinded businessmen walk over it one by one. This spot, like the previous year's effort, tries to place Apple's rival IBM in a bad light—implying that those who purchase IBM computers are too blind to see the future in front of them—but the spot lacks the liberating feeling of the earlier commercial. The only moment of hope comes when one of the blindfolded businessmen, pausing at the cliff's edge and lifting his blindfold, stops and saves himself. Chiat defended the ad's allegorical impact, but the spot did not receive a positive reception.

In 1987 Chiat/Day acquired the Nissan Motor account, worth some $90 million in billings. The new account put the agency among the nation's top 25 advertising agencies, with annual billings of more than $500 million. Also in the late 1980s Chiat/Day launched one of its most successful campaigns, this one for the Eveready Battery Company. Starring an unstoppable, drum-banging pink toy bunny powered by Eveready's dependable Energizer batteries, the campaign was among the most popular of the 1990s. The bunny and the familiar slogan, "Energizer Batteries. They keep going and going and going . . . ," were still being used at the end of the 20th century, as the agency had created variations on the simple concept to keep it fresh. A series of spoofs of other television commercials, ending with the obnoxious bunny bursting in and spoiling the proceedings, were a big hit. That campaign was followed by a series in which famous Hollywood villains tried unsuccessfully to stop the bunny. By the late 1990s, the bunny was being pursued by a dedicated crew of "Bunny Chasers" who, much like those seekers after Big Foot or the Loch Ness Monster, attempt to glimpse the Energizer bunny.

In 1989 Chiat/Day merged with the Australian agency Mojo MDA Group Ltd.; the executives hoped that the merger would create an agency better able to serve large accounts in U.S., Australian, and New Zealand markets. By 1992, with these hopes not materializing and an economic downturn leading to such major accounts as American Express and Shearson Lehman leaving the agency, Chiat/Day sold Mojo to Foote, Cone & Belding Communications. Other hardships also hit Chiat/Day in the early 1990s. The San Francisco office was sold in 1990, and Thomas McElligott , a founder of Fallon McElligott Rice (later Fallon-McElligott), was hired and lost within a nine-month span.

The agency rebounded in the early 1990s with new and distinctive headquarters in Venice Beach, California. Designed by architect Frank O. Gehry, the building is comprised of two wings joined by a three-story-tall pair of binoculars designed by Pop artist Claus Oldenburg. Among the rooms are "the fish," a meeting room resembling a whale.

Along with the change in architectural design was a much-ballyhooed move to a "virtual office" concept in which staff members no longer had assigned desks but kept their supplies in lockers and carried their laptop computers to wherever they needed to be. Video conferencing, working at home, and the use of extensive e-mails were expected to change the face of how business at Chiat/Day was done. More than $8 million were spent on technology for the new office alone.

In 1995, after 27 years as an independent agency, Chiat/Day merged with TBWA, a traditional Madison Avenue agency best known for its Absolut Vodka ads, to form TBWA Chiat/Day. The merger created an ad agency with more than $2 billion in annual billings. TBWA was strong in foreign markets, having offices in more than 30 countries, but it had only a weak presence on the U.S. West Coast. Chiat/Day had been looking for foreign business since its earlier merger with Mojo. The merger led Chiat to leave the agency. In 1998 he became chief executive with Screaming Media, a broker of editorial content for Web companies. He died in 2002.

TBWA Chiat/Day became a unit of the Omnicom Group. In 1999 TBWA Chiat/Day opened an innovative office complex, designed by Clive Wilkinson Architects, in Playa del Rey, California. Among other unusual features, the new offices include a basketball court and pool tables where employees can unwind. The agency subsequently restyled its name as TBWA/Chiat/Day. In 2000 TBWA/Chiat/Day had gross income of $240.3 million, up 11.7 percent over 1999, on billings of $6.6 billion, up 12.5 percent.

THOMAS WILOCH

Further Reading

"Absolutely Fabulous: Advertising Mergers," *Economist* (4 February 1995)

Chiat, Jay, "This Is How It Happened," <www.chiatday.com>

"Chiat/Day's 1983 Ad for the Apple Lisa Sparked a New Ideal for What Work Could Be,", Inc. (18 May 1999)

Colvin, Geoffrey, "Long Hours + Bad Pay = Great Ads," *Fortune* (23 July 1984)

Gross, Len, "Chiat/Day and Hoefer Two Years Later," *Adweek* (10 May 1982)

Landler, Mark, "Chiat/Day Is Winning, After Losing, After Winning . . . ," *Business Week* (2 December 1991)

O'Leary, Noreen, "C/D Highers the Hairy: Clow Is President," *Adweek* (4 March 1985)

O'Leary, Noreen, "Chiat's Day of Reckoning," *Adweek* (20 March 1995)

Ouroussoff, Nicolai, "In Chiat/Day's New Playa del Rey Headquarters Complex, the Real World Is Represented but It Doesn't Actually Intrude," *Los Angeles Times* (31 January 1999)

Peischel, Bob, "Chiat/Day Breaks Free from Pack," *Adweek* (March 1984)

Rapaport, Richard, "Jay Chiat Tears Down the Walls," *Forbes* (25 October 1993)

Rosenbaum, Ron, "Chiat's Day," *Manhattan, Inc.* (April 1985)

Seo, Diane, "Things Are Clicking for Chiat as CEO at Screaming Media," *Los Angeles Times* (8 October 1999)

Shamoon, Sherrie, "Lunch with Jay Chiat," *Adweek* (7 May 1990)

Sharkey, Betsy, "Clow Riding High on Chiat/Day Creative Wave," *Adweek* (6 August 1984)

Children: Targets of Advertising

While children have always been the target of advertisements for products of special appeal to them—toys, dolls, games—advertising to children has been a topic of special interest and, indeed, controversy only since the early 1970s. At that time the argument was advanced, particularly by the U.S. consumer group Action for Children's Television (ACT), founded in 1968, that advertising to children is inherently "unfair." Consumer advocates contended that because young children are cognitively immature, they are unable, first, to understand ad messages and, second, to understand the commercial intent of advertising directed to them. Under the leadership of activist Peggy Charren, ACT went so far as to call for the elimination of advertising from children's TV programs. Although the debate has cooled somewhat in subsequent decades, it has not been resolved. Moreover, in the intervening years, the size of the children's market has grown worldwide, and marketers have become more attuned than ever before to the importance of youthful audiences.

Children in the United States spend an estimated $24 billion on direct purchases and influence family spending of another $188 billion. Television advertising directed to this market amounts to more than $1 billion in the United States alone. The 1996 *Roper Youth Report* estimated that American boys and girls aged 8 through 12 watch an average of almost 30 hours of television each week. Children are also targeted as a market through magazines (for example, *Sports Illustrated for Kids*, *Nickelodeon* magazine, and *Nintendo Power*), radio (*Radio AAHS*, *Disney*, *Fox*), newspaper inserts, and Internet sites (*legos.com*, *barbie.com*, *disney.com*, *hotwheels.com*). Not only have marketers recognized the importance of the children's market, but the economic influence of children is predicted to grow in areas where the birthrate remains high.

What Children Know—and When

Two major theories have been advanced to explain the effects of the communications process on children. One is the theory of cognitive development put forth by the 20th-century Swiss psychologist Jean Piaget. His age-related theory of cognitive development proposed four main stages: (1) sensorimotor (from birth to two years of age); (2) preoperational (two to seven years); (3) concrete operational (7 to 11 years); and (4) formal operational (11 years through adulthood). Youngsters at different stages exhibit vast differences in cognitive abilities. For example, children at the preoperational stage are "perceptually bound" and so tend to focus on a single dimension of information. Children at the concrete operational stage are able to consider several dimensions of a stimulus at the same time and to begin to think more abstractly. Children in the formal operational stage are considered to be more like adults in their thinking and are thus more capable of abstract and hypothetical thought. Cognitive orientation by age has been used as the basis for explaining children's understanding of advertising. For example, preschoolers are believed to be less able than older children to distinguish commercials from programming, to understand the selling intent of commercials, and to recognize deception and bias in advertising.

Researchers also use a second explanation, information processing theory, to understand the effects of advertising on children. This theory focuses on how children's skills and abilities develop in the acquisition, encoding, organization, and retrieval of information. Limited processors (children under seven years of age) are characterized as exhibiting "mediational deficiencies," which means that they often have trouble using storage and retrieval strategies even when they are prompted to do so. Cued processors (7 seven to 11 years) show "production deficiencies," meaning that they have the ability to use processing strategies but typically need to be aided by explicit prompts or cues to enhance information storage and retrieval. Strategic processors (12 years and older) are able to use a variety of strategies for storing and retrieving information. Information processing theory also provides an explanation of children's abilities at various ages to use the information they retrieve. For example, although cued processors know a great deal about advertising, their ability to use the knowledge they have is still developing.

Researchers have posed a number of questions. One is whether or not children understand the intent of advertising. The most accurate answer depends on the definition of the term *intent*. If it is defined as the advertiser's aim to provide information on items for purchase, the answer is that many preschoolers begin to show such understanding. Both verbal and nonverbal measures indicate that children as young as four or five begin to connect ads with items available for purchase in stores. If, however, intent is defined to include the persuasive nature of advertising, only older children demonstrate such understanding. By the age of seven or eight, children seem to understand that ads appear on television in order to "get people to buy something." Older children are thus able to distinguish the availability of items for purchase from the desire of marketers to sell the items.

Considerable research, much of it conducted during the early 1980s, has addressed the question of whether or not children distinguish commercials from programming. The bulk of the studies indicate that children begin to distinguish commercials from programming as they progress through the preschool years. Three- and four-year-olds, for example, have been shown to discriminate between the two. Research indicates, however, that many preschoolers appear to base the difference on audio or video cues or on affective (i.e., emotional) aspects, for example, the fact that commercials tend to be funnier than the programs. Children may have to be somewhat older before they clearly understand that a commercial is inviting or urging them to purchase something. Therefore, while young children may recognize a commercial as being distinct from the program they are watching, they may not grasp the fact that the ultimate purposes of the two are inherently different, that the commercial's purpose is to sell, whereas the program's purpose is to entertain.

Children differ in their ability to process product-related information and thus to comprehend the message of an ad. A report by the Federal Trade Commission (FTC) concluded that young children neither recall much of the content of commercials nor fully understand them. Studies have also indicated that there is a positive correlation between age and comprehension. For example, research has reported a high positive correlation between age and the awareness of brand names. It should be noted that such a relationship is consistent with Piaget's theory, especially in view of young children's perceptual boundedness.

Such studies, however, have generally used verbal measures to collect data from young children. Preschoolers are not usually very good at providing verbal responses, and thus it is difficult to assess their level of understanding. When pictures and other non-verbal measures are used, young children appear to exhibit greater understanding than when their comprehension is assessed verbally. In her 1983 article "Do Children Understand TV Ads?" (*Journal of Advertising Research*), M. Carole Macklin presented findings based on both traditional verbal and specially designed nonverbal measures. She found that very few preschoolers measured by the traditional technique of verbal recall would be classified as exhibiting moderate or high understanding of the content of commercials. More than half of those measured by methods not dependent on expository abilities, however, seem to understand the content.

Research conducted during the 1970s addressed the question of children's ability to discern deception in advertising by asking them if "commercials always tell the truth." What researchers found was that children become more skeptical with age. One study, for example, found that half of kindergartners believed that advertising never or only sometimes told the truth, whereas 88 percent of third graders and 97 percent of sixth graders believed this. Younger children have also been shown to be more trustful of commercials and to like them better; yet as they progress through the elementary school years they like commercials less. This may be explained by their increasing understanding of the persuasive intent of commercials, additional years of exposure to television advertising, and parental and peer influence.

A Special Audience

It is important to understand that advertising to children results from what is called "targeted marketing." During the 1950s most advertising and marketing were directed toward a general audience. In the 1960s, however, advertisers began to develop targeted marketing, exploiting the differences between people. As a result of targeted marketing (along with the increased cost of airtime), television commercials have become shorter. Moreover, many TV ads in the 1950s were live, with the host of a show often touting the product, a practice that was banned in the 1970s. In the 1950s many ads were woven into the content of the program, another practice that is no longer allowed. Whereas many products were targeted to both adults and children in the 1950s, today ads for such products as toys, cereals, candy and snacks, and fast foods are directed toward children. (Toys, cereals, candy, and snacks

account for more than three-quarters of all ads shown on the Saturday morning schedules of the major U.S. television networks.) The average amount of time given to commercials in the 1950s was less than that allowed by law in 2000. Thus, both the targeting of messages and an increase in commercial time occurred as marketers came to recognize that children represented a growing and lucrative market niche.

Some aspects of children's advertising have not changed much from the 1950s, however. The promotional content is much the same, particularly the use of "fun" appeal. In addition, commercials aimed at children today do not show any increase or decrease in the use of controversial selling techniques. Finally, a majority of commercials, as in the 1950s, are live (as opposed to taped), even though hosts are no longer involved.

The techniques and media used to reach children of different age groups vary. Dan S. Acuff, author of *What Kids Buy and Why: The Psychology of Marketing to Kids* (1997), has described five locations where children can be reached: at home, in stores, in the community, in schools, and in automobiles. The pathways for appealing to children include TV programming and advertising, packaging, promotions, magazines, newspapers, radio, computer programming, and the Internet. The age of the child must be considered when deciding which methods and media are most effective.

Acuff contends that the average three- through seven-year-old can be reached by all of the above pathways. There are other considerations, however. The packaging, for example, should include bright colors, bold graphic designs, and fun characters. In addition, the younger child—who does not yet have the logic and reasoning skills of the 8- to 12-year-old—accepts advertising. Thus, to be effective, ads for small children should show the product in concrete, highly visual ways. Slapstick works well, as do role models such as sports figures.

Somewhat older children, those between 8 and 12, are more discriminating. Children in this age group are more reality-oriented and therefore prefer more realistic ads. They may consider simple magic and more childish characters as being beneath them. Rather quick pacing, slapstick and more abstract humor, and both realistic and heroic role models are appropriate for children of this age. Acuff has said, "The marketing goal is 'like me' associations with kids of the target child's own age and upward 'emulation' associations." He also has pointed out that the packaging for the 8–12 group should be different than for younger children. The graphics should be more abstract, the colors more neon than primary, the characters more realistic and complex, and the messages more verbal and detailed-oriented.

As children enter their early teen years, between the ages of 13 and 15, they can be reached via the same media. Acuff argues, however, that a major difference emerges with this age group. The typical young teen does not perceive him- or herself as a "kid," and any advertising or promotion that directly identifies kids or children as the target or that communicates this through visual means is likely to be regarded as "for younger kids." Moreover, young teens read more newspapers and use the Internet more frequently than do their younger counterparts.

South of the Border, a Mexican-themed attraction in South Carolina, uses billboards to lure youngsters riding with their families on Interstate 95. *Courtesy of South of the Border and Ace-Hi, Inc. Photography: Cat Saleeby.*

Other researchers have made similar observations. Barrie Gunter and Adrian Furnham, authors of *Children as Consumers: A Psychological Analysis of the Young People's Market* (1998), have pointed out that reaching young consumers with advertising messages requires knowing how they respond to different types of products and promotions. According to them, four rules of thumb apply: (1) never talk down to youngsters, (2) be totally straightforward and sincere, (3) give young people credit for being motivated by rational values, and (4) be as personal as possible. A message stands out if the marketer observes the following precepts: know the niche; position the product; talk the talk; use pictures to sell; put it to music; move it along; do not preach; make it fun; remember that groups are dynamic; and use the new but familiar. Reaching children effectively requires a high level of skill and is often more difficult than communicating with parents. Furthermore, children are not a homogeneous market. They can be differentiated by age, stage of cognitive development, needs, desires, interests, and personality. Advertisers must establish what segments they are aiming for and must create promotional messages that position the product clearly to these segments.

Selina S. Guber and Jon Berry, authors of *Marketing to and through Kids* (1993), advise advertisers to put themselves into the mind of a child and to think like one. They suggest that ads should tell their stories in straightforward ways, with clear narratives, much as fairy tales do. Ads should be kept simple, with only a limited number of points being made. The ages for which the ad is intended should be clear, although the appearance in the ad of models older than the targeted children has proven effective. The communication should be fun, bright, and lively. It is important that ads reflect what children care about, and the advertiser must recognize that children pride themselves on being different from grown-ups. Advertisers also should remember that children tend to try to find the good aspects of things and people, and they enjoy whatever is new. Timing is important as well; while Saturday morning is an effective time for reaching younger children, older children are fans of after-school and prime-time television.

Success in the toy industry depends on good product positioning and clear advertising messages. The success of Mattel is a case in point. By 1958 Mattel had become the industry leader in musical toys and toy guns, but the company needed a product for girls to balance its action toys for boys. It was this deficiency that prompted Mattel in 1959 to introduce the Barbie doll, which subsequently became the most popular toy product in history. Cy Schneider, an authority on children's television, has written, "More than any other children's product before or since, the Barbie doll is testimony to the influence of television advertising on children. . . . [The doll's] essential appeal, how it is positioned, how it affects children, and why it has lasted so long, is a significant social commentary on the television age." Barbie was based on a German doll, Lili; Mattel purchased the rights to the doll and renamed it. The company engaged the services of Carson/Roberts, which saw the potential of the doll in helping growing girls make a fantasy leap to their teenage years. Carson/Roberts created television commercials that depicted Barbie not as a doll but as a real-life teenage fashion model. Each 60-second ad told a story about the life of Barbie, with the events allowing for a change of her costume. In this way Barbie became a fashion icon, and the Ken doll was created a few years later as an escort for Barbie in her best-selling wedding gown.

Guber and Berry have argued that Barbie's continued success is partially attributable to Mattel's ability to reinvent her to keep up with the changing times. Mattel has introduced many line extensions, a strategy that encourages girls to continue to collect Barbies. Guber and Berry also argue that it is important for a marketer to understand the differences between the sexes, and they point out that successful marketers such as Mattel often split their product lines into separate divisions, one for boys and one for girls. It is clear that children do adopt sexual roles and behavior, whether as a result of genetics or socialization or a combination of the two. This is a controversial area of research, but as Acuff has noted, many studies point out the importance of genetics, particularly hormonal differences, as the primary factor influencing behavior. "Given that the higher presence of testosterone in males has been shown to lead to their increased aggressive tendencies," he wrote, "it would only be natural that boys would prefer aggressive toys such as action figures over dolls."

Whatever the causes, the differences in the behavior of boys and girls are important in the marketing of toys. Considerable time and money have been invested in efforts to interest girls in traditionally male toys and games and, to a lesser extent, to get boys interested in traditionally female products and programs. As Acuff has observed, "Girls make up approximately 20 percent of the electronic-game-playing audience. . . . Given that there are as many girls out there in the marketplace as boys, manufacturers' profits would increase substantially if they could penetrate boy and girl markets."

Guber and Berry have concluded that research can serve as a road map for marketers in developing new products. They suggest that cars, trucks, action figures, and building sets will continue to be mainstays for boys and that dolls and arts and crafts will be continue to be popular with girls. Some products, such as stuffed animals, will continue to be popular with both, however, particularly at younger ages.

Impact of Ads on the Young

The potential of advertising to children to shape society is a central concern of social theorists and critics of advertising. A 1978 report by the FTC expressed alarm over the effects of advertising on children under the age of eight—that is, those who are unable to perceive that the purpose of television advertising is to sell. The report expressed particular concern for the youngest children, those who are incapable of comprehending the influence that television advertising exerts over them: "It appears that a large proportion of pre-schoolers think that the persons or animated figures on television are addressing them personally, and that the animated figures are real and in some sense appropriate for emulation." Although regulatory interest in the issue subsided during the 1980s, many people continued to voice concern over the effects on children who are too young to make informed decisions about buying or to understand the difference between real life and the world shown in commercials. While the influence of television is the primary concern, the persuasive effects of other media have been well recognized. Thus, some municipalities have restricted billboard advertising of alcohol and tobacco products in close proximity to schools.

Concern has also mounted over the widespread diffusion of Channel One advertising. Whittle Communications, a Tennessee-based marketing and communications firm, introduced the program in 1990. It consists of a 10-minute newscast, with 2 minutes of advertising, aimed at middle- and high-school students. More than 12,000 U.S. middle and high schools show the program, and some 8 million students are viewers. In exchange for delivering the program to the students, the schools receive telecommunications equipment—satellite dishes, TV sets, and so forth. Some critics charge that the exchange takes unfair advantage of children, making them a captive audience. Other initiatives targeted to children, including kids' clubs, product placement in child-oriented movies, and ads on schoolbook covers, have also come under fire from consumer groups. In fact, Consumers Union has accused major marketers of launching an unfair advertising assault on children.

Channel M was created during 1994 as an advertising and promotional network to target children and teens in video game arcades at shopping malls. Using from 4 to 16 monitors in each of the Aladdin Castle arcades (with its more than 100 locations throughout the United States) Channel M broadcasts two-hour programs that include top music videos, highlights from professional sports, movie trailers, and bloopers. Each commercial spot runs 330 times a month in each location and reaches more than 2 million children. Advertisers use the network's customized promotions for point-of-purchase displays, contests and sweepstakes, cross-promotions, product samples, and couponing. Although Channel M is located in malls rather than schools, critics have expressed their fear that, as with Channel One, children will be unduly influenced by the barrage of messages.

Marketers argue, however, that advertising to children is carefully monitored by self-regulation. In 1974 the National Advertising Division of the Council of Better Business Bureaus, Inc., established the Children's Advertising Review Unit (CARU) to help marketers deal with advertising in a manner that is sensitive to children's needs. CARU reviews and evaluates advertising directed at children under the age of 12. Using written guidelines that were revised in 1977 and 1983, CARU honors five basic principles regarding advertising directed to children: (1) advertisers should take into account the level of knowledge, sophistication, and maturity of the audience to which their messages are primarily directed; (2) realizing that children are imaginative and that make-believe play constitutes an important part of the growing-up process, advertisers should exercise care not to exploit the imaginative nature of children; (3) recognizing that advertising may play an important part in educating a child, advertisers should communicate their information in a truthful and accurate manner, with full recognition that a child may learn practices from advertising that can affect his or her health and well-being; (4) advertisers should capitalize on the potential of marketing to influence social behavior by developing advertising that, wherever possible, addresses social standards generally regarded as positive and beneficial, such as friendship, kindness, honesty, justice, generosity, and respect for others; and (5) although many influences affect a child's personal and social development, the prime responsibility for providing guidance to children remains with parents, and advertisers should contribute to this parent-child relationship in a constructive manner.

Setting Standards

Throughout the world there are established traditions for treating children as a special audience. Quotas on the number of spots in children's TV programming and other such restrictions are common. Most countries have laws intended to protect children from exploitation by advertisers. The European Union has enacted a "Television without Frontiers" directive. Australia has set standards for children's television, while in Great Britain the Independent Broadcasting Authority has a similar code, and a 1993 code adopted in Canada gives details for self-regulation by the advertising industry.

In the United States, Congress passed the Children's Television Act in 1990, and in 1996 the Federal Communications Commission (FCC) used the act to set standards for the broadcasting industry. The law restored the 10.5-minute-per-hour ceiling for commercials in children's weekend television programming and the 12-minute-per-hour limits for weekday programs. The act also restored rules requiring that commercial breaks be clearly distinguished from programming and rules barring selling by program hosts, tie-ins, and other practices that involve the use of program characters to promote products.

Some have suggested that children should be better educated as to how advertising works. Those in the field of media education advocate that youngsters be taught to view television critically and to question what they see. On the other hand, there are those who argue that advertising actually helps prepare children for the real world. The CARU guidelines, for example, encourage advertisers to capitalize on the potential of advertising to influence positive and beneficial social behavior. The debate over the ethical aspects of advertising to children has been going on for more than three decades, however, and the different viewpoints are unlikely to be reconciled any time soon.

M. CAROLE MACKLIN

See also Charren, Peggy; *and color plate in this volume*

Further Reading

Acuff, Dan S., *What Kids Buy and Why: The Psychology of Marketing to Kids,* New York: Free Press, 1997

Alexander, et al., "'We'll Be Back in a Moment': A Content Analysis of Advertisements in Children's Television in the 1950s," *Journal of Advertising* 27, no. 3 (Fall 1998)

Federal Trade Commission, *FTC Staff Report on Television Advertising to Children,* Washington, D.C.: Federal Trade Commission, 1978

Guber, Selina S., and Jon Berry, *Marketing to and through Kids,* New York: McGraw-Hill, 1993

Gunter, Barrie, and Adrian Furnham, *Children as Consumers: A Psychological Analysis of the Young People's Market,* London and New York: Routledge, 1998

Macklin, M. Carole, "Do Children Understand TV Ads?," *Journal of Advertising Research* 23, no. 1 (1983)

McNeal, James U., *Kids as Customers: A Handbook of Marketing to Children,* New York: Lexington, 1992

McNeal, James U., "Tapping the Three Kids' Markets," *American Demographics* 20, no. 4 (April 1998)

Schneider, Cy, *Children's Television: The Art, the Business, and How It Works,* Lincolnwood, Illinois: NTC Business Books, 1987; new edition, 1992

Wackman, Daniel B., et al., "Learning to Be Consumers: The Role of the Family," *Journal of Communication* 27, no. 1 (Winter 1977)

Ward, Scott, Daniel B. Wackman, and Ellen Wartella, *How Children Learn to Buy: The Development of Consumer Information-Processing Skills,* Beverly Hills, California: Sage, 1977

Young, Brian M., *Television Advertising and Children,* New York: Oxford University Press, and Oxford: Clarendon, 1990

China

Contrary to those arguments that trace the roots of advertising to ancient China, modern advertising as an organized industry and a form of mass communication was a Western invention introduced to China at the turn of the 20th century. Advertising first flourished in Shanghai, China's commercial center, during the 1920s and 1930s. Its development was interrupted when the Chinese Communist Party came to power and began to institute a central command economy in the 1950s. Commercial advertising became irrelevant in the transformed Chinese socioeconomic system, serving as a government instrument for political control, and eventually disappeared from the mass media. Its return in the late 1970s was the direct outcome of market-oriented reforms in post-Mao China. Advertising has since enjoyed tremendous growth. From 1987 to 1996 ad spending in China increased by almost 900 percent, establishing the nation as the world's fastest growing advertising market.

The advertising industry in China has been formed by economic forces both within and outside Chinese society and by the development of China's mass media system. China's trade with foreign colonial powers around the beginning of the 20th century had a crucial influence on this history. China began trading with the West at least as early as the 17th century, but trade relations only became full-fledged in the aftermath of the Sino-British Opium War in 1842. At this time the direction of trade between China and the West shifted—previously China had sold more than it bought from foreign countries, but now it bought more than it sold.

Under Foreign Influence

Westerners not only brought in goods and capital but also introduced China to modern mass media and advertising, which were employed to promote the increasing flow of goods and expand sales in the untapped Chinese market. Foreign companies were the first to advertise in newspapers and magazines and on billboards in China. Most of the early newspaper ads were for foreign products. Because of a high illiteracy rate among the Chinese population, pictorial billboards were one of the most effective advertising media. In 1915 an Italian named Bruno Perme established the first foreign ad agency in Shanghai, which primarily created outdoor advertising. During the 1920s and 1930s Carl Crow, Inc., Millington's Advertising Company, the Consolidated National Advertising Corporation, and the China Commercial Advertising Agency were the four largest agencies, known as the "Big Four," in Shanghai's burgeoning advertising industry. A few smaller agencies were based in other cities, such as Beijing, Tianjin, Chongqing, and Guangzhou. There were approximately 30 advertising agencies in Shanghai in 1937, of which five were foreign owned.

Two of the agencies in the Big Four—the China Commercial Advertising Agency and the Consolidated National Advertising Corporation—were Chinese-owned companies. Both C.P. Ling, founder of the former agency, and L. Lewis Mason, manager of the latter, had studied in the United States before becoming advertising executives. Ling received his bachelor of arts degree from the University of Rochester in New York state and went on to obtain a master of arts degree from Columbia University in New York City, where he studied advertising. He started his ad agency in Shanghai in 1926. When it celebrated its tenth anniversary in 1936, the China Commercial Advertising Agency had a roster of 97 clients, including Heinz, Parker Pen, Gillette Industries, Quaker Oats, and Welch's Grape Juice.

One of the pioneering agencies in China, Carl Crow, Inc., was owned and run by Carl Crow, a U.S. journalist-turned-businessman. Over a period of 20 years, he ran a successful advertising operation in Shanghai, and his company was credited with teaching the Chinese how to be consumers. His best-selling *Four Hundred Million Customers* (1937), a winner of an American Booksellers Association award, recounted tales of his advertising adventures in China.

Advertising in the early 20th century concentrated on—and appeared most effective in the marketing of—such consumer goods as cosmetics, clothing, food products, and pharmaceuticals. Initially, patent medicine marketers and cigarette manufacturers were the two major categories of advertisers. Among ads in the *Shun Pao* (one of the largest dailies in China) in 1925, those featuring medicines appeared most frequently. Consumer advertising predominantly targeted the affluent Chinese, a small segment of the population, and Western expatriates in foreign enclaves of Chinese cities.

Mass marketing and advertising were also pursued, however. With its introduction of the Mei Foo kerosene lamp, the Standard Oil Company became the first to succeed in mass merchandising a foreign product in China. Another early mass-marketed product was cigarettes. These were a novelty in China, where the water pipe was the traditional form of smoking. Foreign cigarette brands quickly attracted many Chinese consumers. The British-American Tobacco Company dominated the cigarette market.

Effects of Communism

Advertising's role and influence in China was altered dramatically when the Chinese Communist Party came into power in 1949. The People's Republic of China (PRC) embarked on a different road to development and modernization than that of capitalist nations in the West. The Chinese government under Mao Zedong implemented a highly centralized economic, political, and cultural system. Private ownership and production were abolished through consolidation with government-owned enterprises in the urban areas and through the commune system in the rural regions. The central government exercised firm control over economic planning and implementation; little local autonomy was allowed. The restructuring of the Chinese economy during the first decades of the PRC was also exemplified by the increased emphasis on developing heavy industry rather than the service sector. Consumption was discouraged, and many food staples and other daily necessities were rationed. China allied with and drew support from the U.S.S.R. in the 1950s, later adopting a policy of self-reliance. Between 1949 and the 1970s, China's economic contacts with Western industrialized economies were extremely limited.

These developments hindered the growth of the advertising industry. As the press came under government control, and as the socialist economy developed, commercial advertising was considered irrelevant and virtually disappeared from China.

At the dawn of the Communist victory in China's Civil War, Shanghai had about 90 advertising agencies. In 1950 the city's ad agency association had a registered membership of around 100. Then the Chinese government began to transform private ownership into state ownership, a process declared complete by 1956. All of the independent Shanghai ad agencies were consolidated into a single state entity, called the Shanghai Advertising Corporation.

With the transformation in China's economic structure and mass media, advertising was no longer viewed as a viable marketing

Calendar posters, which combined Western products and art techniques with the traditional Chinese New Year painting style, were a popular form of advertising in Shanghai in the early 20th century.
Courtesy of the Colgate-Palmolive Company.

tool. Nonetheless, the potential of advertising to convey messages was not ignored by the Chinese government. At a meeting on commercial advertising in Shanghai in 1959, the Chinese state outlined the concept of "socialist advertising," asserting that such advertising must serve the purposes of production, consumption, distribution, and the beautification of the urban environment; socialist advertising must not only be true and artistic but must also reflect communist China's policies, ideology, and cultural identity. Instead of serving commercial interests, advertising in China began to be seen as a communications tool to showcase the nation's economic achievement.

Outdoor advertising was the first commercial casualty of the Cultural Revolution. Commercial messages on billboards were replaced by political propaganda; neon signs advertising shops and products were destroyed. The main duty of the Shanghai Fine Arts Company (formerly the Shanghai Advertising Corporation) was to design political propaganda posters. Countless goods were labeled "problem products" by the state. Cosmetics, jewelry, Western-style dress, traditional Chinese dishes, chocolate, and whiskey were among the goods that the government condemned as embodying outmoded feudal and bourgeois lifestyles; brand names, logos, and advertisements that evoked traditional cultural motifs and themes were also regarded as problematic. Many brands and stores adopted new names, such as "Red Guard," "People," and "Workers and Peasants," which conveyed compatibility with goals of the proletarian class. Commercial advertising, deemed a wasteful capitalist business practice, was unable to survive in the drastically changed political economy.

The Open Door

China's new open-door policy in the late 1970s, which began to lift trade barriers and accept some levels of consumption, was welcomed by the world's developed capitalist economies. As economic reform policies have been implemented, there has been a phenomenal increase in the influx of foreign goods and capital into China. For three consecutive years—1993, 1994, and 1995—China was the largest recipient of foreign direct investment among the developing nations.

One concomitant development of the expansion of foreign business has been the return of foreign advertising to the Chinese market. The number of media outlets has grown remarkably, and the amount of airtime and ad space to be filled has increased. Commercial advertising has again become a legitimate—and, in most cases, indispensable—source of income for Chinese media.

Advertising reappeared in the Chinese mass media in January 1979, when Shanghai TV made history by airing the first television commercial in China (a 90-second ad for a Chinese medicinal wine). In 1979 the Shanghai-based *Liberation Daily* carried the first print ad (for a Minolta camera) after an almost ten-year absence of advertising from the Chinese press. The first foreign product reintroduced to Chinese consumers through television advertising was the Swiss Rado wristwatch. By 1981 at least five multinational ad agencies were actively engaged in discussing business opportunities with the Chinese government. The Japa-

China's first advertising trade publication, *International Advertising Press,* debuted in 1985. The May 2000 cover spotlighted articles on the 1999 Euro Effie awards and the bookselling Web site Amazon.com. *Courtesy of the* International Advertising Press, *with cooperation from Advertising Age.*

nese agency Dentsu was the first foreign ad agency to open offices in China in 1979. Despite the small presence of their products in the Chinese market, Japanese companies used advertising to create brand awareness for Sony, Mitsubishi, Sanyo, and their electronic products and appliances. The U.S. agency McCann-Erickson formed a joint venture with Jardine Matheson & Company, a Hong Kong trading firm, and became the first Western ad agency to establish a representative office in China. Other early arrivals included Young & Rubicam, Inc., Ogilvy & Mather, and the Leo Burnett Company.

The efforts to restore advertising in China were endorsed by the central government's propaganda ministry. But despite such official support, the reintroduction of advertising was not a smooth process, in part because the government faced the challenge of legitimizing both a business and an economic practice it had earlier vehemently denounced. Nonetheless, like the general economic reform policies, commercial advertising withstood criticism and challenges and continued to expand and prosper, especially in the 1990s.

In 1981 advertising revenue made up about 0.02 percent of China's gross national product (GNP). From this insignificant start, the Chinese advertising industry achieved an annual growth rate of about 48 percent between 1981 and 1995, rising to 0.47 percent of China's GNP in 1995. The number of advertising agencies increased from just over 1,000 in 1981 to slightly more than 57,000 by the end of 1997. Likewise, the number of people employed in advertising grew from fewer than 20,000 in the early 1980s to around 500,000 in the mid-1990s.

The Chinese Ad Industry

The sheer number of ad agencies may be large, but the agencies themselves are generally small in size, most having fewer than ten employees. (This latter number has remained steady over the years since commercial advertising was reintroduced.) Of the 48,082 advertising agencies registered in 1995, only about one-quarter were full-service agencies; most of the rest were engaged only in certain aspects of advertising (e.g., creative work or media buying). Some are simply "ghost agencies."

The Chinese advertising industry is also characterized by an unbalanced agency-media relationship, in which the still mostly centralized state-run media overpower weak agencies. Despite the proliferation of media outlets and the decentralization of media management, the government media still prevail, and only in rare cases is there genuine competition. Wielding their tremendous social and political influence, media organizations often expand their reach into advertising, setting up their own shops and quoting low rates to compete with ad agencies for clients.

Chinese companies tend to emphasize ad placement over ad production, being more concerned with the media-buying function, while ignoring ad execution and production quality. By and large, the economically more developed coastal region represents the top echelon of advertising development, with the inland region in the middle, and the outlying areas at the bottom. This regional disparity is a corollary of the different levels of economic and social development in China. Advertising is concentrated in three cities: Beijing, Shanghai, and Guangzhou. Advertising revenues generated in these three cities accounted for half of the national total at the start of the 21st century.

Foreign ad agencies have grown increasingly enthusiastic about working in China. Major players in global advertising, such as the J. Walter Thompson Company and Saatchi & Saatchi, have set up shops in mainland China, representing a wide array of global consumer product manufacturers. During the early 1990s Grey Advertising, BBDO Worldwide, and DDB Needham each formed joint ventures with local Chinese companies to conduct business inside the country. At first, these agencies primarily served multinational clients in China, but this situation was changing as more and more Chinese domestic advertisers sought multinational agencies.

Whereas China's first exposure to consumer products and advertising culture occurred in the 1920s and 1930s, the 1990s witnessed China's second major encounter with a global consumer culture. This time, the experience was more massive and far-reaching: the potential market of Chinese consumers, around 400 million in the 1930s, had grown to more than 1 billion by the turn of the 21st century.

JIAN WANG

Further Reading

Crow, Carl, *Four Hundred Million Customers*, New York: Harper and Brothers, and London: Hamilton, 1937

Lee, Winston, "China's Ad Industry," *Media* (16 December 1994)

Seligman, Scott D., "China's Fledgling Advertising Industry: The Start of Something Big?" *China Business Review* 11, no. 1 (January/February 1984)

Stross, Randall, "The Return of Advertising in China: A Survey of the Ideological Reversal," *The China Quarterly* 123 (1990)

Xu, Bai Yi, *Marketing to China: One Billion New Customers*, Lincolnwood, Illinois: NTC Business Books, 1990

Chrysler Corporation

(DaimlerChrysler)

Principal Agencies

J. Stirling Getchell Agency
Lee Anderson Advertising Company
Ruthrauff & Ryan
McCann-Erickson
N.W. Ayer & Son

Batten Barton Durstine & Osborn
Grant Advertising
Ross Roy, Inc.
Young & Rubicam, Inc.
Kenyon & Eckhardt
Campbell Mithun Esty
PentaMark Worldwide

Chrysler Corporation has made many significant contributions to the history of advertising and automotive marketing. Chrysler was the inventor of the factory rebate concept for automobiles. It pioneered the minivan. It used spokesmen such as actor Ricardo Montalban, sportscaster Joe Garagiola, and its own inimitable chairman, Lee Iacocca, in memorable campaigns. And perhaps most famously it successfully dealt with negative publicity generated by the nearly unprecedented large-scale national bailout of a U.S. corporation. Through it all, Chrysler soldiered on, creating both memorable vehicles and enduring advertising slogans.

The company was founded by Walter P. Chrysler, a former railroad engineer and manager who rose through the ranks at General Motors Corporation (GM), first as a production manager and then as president and general manager of Buick Motor Company. In 1919 he became vice president in charge of production at GM. In 1920, owing to differences with GM President William C. Durant, Chrysler resigned. He was soon retained by the creditors of Willys-Overland Company as an executive vice president on a two-year contract. He was given a mandate to turn the company around, which he did by restructuring it from top to bottom. At the same time, the creditors of Maxwell Motor Company, 90 percent of which was owned by Chalmers Motor Company, retained Chrysler for similar purposes, giving him the title of chairman of Maxwell-Chalmers Company in 1921. As the company began to recover it was renamed the Maxwell Motor Corporation, and ads touted "The good new Maxwell."

Birth of the Nameplate

While at Maxwell, Chrysler and a team of engineers were also working on the development of a totally new car. During the 1924 New York Auto Show the group unveiled the first car bearing the Chrysler nameplate. Denied access to the Auto Show itself since the car was not yet available for sale, Chrysler staged a showing of the new Chrysler Six in the lobby of New York City's Hotel Commodore. The showing was a success, and the car received significant press and industry attention. Production began later that year, and the Chrysler Six sold nearly 20,000 units by the end of 1924. Due to the success of the new vehicle, in June 1925 Maxwell Motor Corporation was renamed Chrysler Corporation. Chrysler Canada was established the same year, and in 1926 Chrysler climbed from 27th to fifth place in ranking by sales of American automakers. The 1926 Chrysler line included three models; the top model in price and luxury was the E-80 Imperial.

The year 1928 was pivotal for Chrysler. To compete with GM and cover all market segments, the company introduced two car brands for the 1929 model year. The Plymouth brand was launched in the lower-priced market segment; the De Soto was launched in the mid-priced field. Chrysler Corporation further expanded by acquiring Dodge Brothers, Inc., a company that had been in the auto and commercial truck business since 1914. Advertisers, Inc., by then handling advertising for Chrysler, took over the Dodge account as well as adding Plymouth and De Soto. With its three new brands, the company sold nearly 365,000 units

in 1928. The expansion made Chrysler Corporation one of the "Big Three" U.S. automakers for the first time. It was also a record year for the Chrysler brand, which sold 171,514 units. Although its new marques would continue to sell well, the Chrysler brand would not top this number again until 1965.

In 1931 the first Chrysler eight-cylinder engines appeared in the Chrysler Eight and Imperial; in 1932, with new engine mount and drive-train mount technology, Plymouth four-cylinder models were advertised with the slogan, "Smoothness of an eight, economy of a four." In early 1932 Chrysler awarded the De Soto account to the J. Stirling Getchell Agency. Getchell won the Plymouth account as well a few months later, while Ruthrauff & Ryan took over the Dodge account. The Chrysler brand and corporate accounts briefly remained with Advertisers, Inc., before going to Lee Anderson Advertising Company. In the most famous of the early Chrysler Corporation ads, in 1932 Getchell ran a Plymouth print ad featuring a photo of Walter P. Chrysler with his hand on the radiator of a Plymouth. The copy urged prospective car buyers to "Look at all three!" low-priced cars. By encouraging people to consider Plymouth along with Ford and Chevrolet, the ad is credited with making the Plymouth brand a credible competitor of the other two makes.

Chrysler Corporation introduced revolutionary streamlined styling in 1934 on models dubbed the Chrysler Airflow and the De Soto Airflow. Though other Chrysler vehicles sold well that year, the Airflow was not well received, and Chrysler soon returned to more conservative styling. In 1935 unit sales reached 682,168, up 44.1 percent over the prior year. In 1936 total Chrysler Corporation unit sales were up another 35.9 percent, with strong Plymouth sales alone reaching nearly half a million units. Walter Chrysler resigned as president of the company in 1935 but stayed on as chairman. He remained active in the company until he became ill in 1938; he died in 1940 at age 65.

Because of a brief downturn in the economic recovery, U.S. auto sales declined significantly in 1938; in that same year Chrysler de Mexico was established. In 1940 Chrysler built its first two "idea cars"—Chrysler Thunderbolt and Chrysler Newport—to showcase and test new engineering and styling concepts. The Chrysler Town & Country station wagon was launched in 1941 with a unique wood-and-steel body and visible wood ribbing. The ads for the 1941 models encouraged buyers to "Be modern—buy Chrysler!" After J. Stirling Getchell's death in 1940, the Getchell agency was closed in 1942, leaving Plymouth and De Soto without agencies. The Chrysler brand and corporate accounts went in house by 1942, but in 1943 Chrysler sought a corporate campaign that would publicize its wartime activities and keep its name before the public. In 1943 Chrysler made three new agency appointments: Plymouth went to N.W. Ayer & Son, and soon afterward the Chrysler brand and corporate accounts went to McCann-Erickson. De Soto was given to Batten Barton Durstine & Osborn (BBDO), while Dodge cars remained at Ruthrauff & Ryan, and Dodge trucks remained at Ross Roy, Inc.

From 1942 to 1945 civilian manufacturing ceased at U.S. automakers as factories were converted to wartime production for

In the 1930s Chrysler automobiles entered a period of aerodynamic styling and innovative engineering. A 1934 ad associated Chrysler's models with the most advanced technology.
The Chrysler and Plymouth advertisements are used with permission from DaimlerChrysler Corporation.

World War II. Chrysler's wartime efforts included the production of 25,000 tanks, 18,000 B-29 Superfortress airplane engines, 29,000 marine engines, and 438,000 Dodge trucks for military use. Chrysler would maintain a large defense division for years to come, including work on such high-profile projects as the Jupiter research rockets of the early 1950s.

When civilian automobile production resumed in 1946, automakers began turning out slightly modified versions of prewar models. Chrysler introduced new sedan, coupe, and convertible versions of the Chrysler Town & Country. Starting in 1947 ads for Chrysler brand cars touted "The beautiful Chrysler," a theme that continued for three years. Postwar ads for Dodge called it "The smoothest car afloat." The tag for Plymouth was "Plymouth builds great cars," while De Soto's tag was "The car designed with you in mind." The first all-new Chrysler models since the war were presented in 1949, a year in which Chrysler Corporation unit sales topped 1 million for the first time.

In 1950 the Italian design house Ghia created the first of many concept cars for Chrysler, and these made the rounds of the auto shows. In 1951 Chrysler engineers designed an engine with hemispherical combustion chambers. This legendary Hemi V8 engine successfully powered Chrysler race cars and enhanced the company's engineering reputation. It was Chrysler's first V8 and established American high-performance standards in the 1950s and 1960s; versions of the engine were eventually used in the so-called muscle cars of the late 1960s.

Expansion of Advertising

Chrysler had concentrated its advertising almost exclusively in print before the war, with relatively little being invested in radio. After the war that began to change as the company moved its accounts to experienced broadcast agencies such as BBDO and McCann-Erickson. Quiz shows were especially favored: *Hit the Jackpot* and *It Pays to Be Ignorant* for Chrysler and, starting in October 1950 on both radio and television, *You Bet Your Life* with Groucho Marx for De Soto. The latter program remained on the air through 1961 and gave the brands their strongest TV profiles during the years of Chrysler sponsorship (1950–58).

In the record-breaking U.S. car market of 1955, Chrysler unit sales rose 62.3 percent to 1,254,124 vehicles, a record for the company. Ad spending was $68.6 million, up 60.8 percent over the prior year; this more than doubled newspaper spending, and nearly doubled network TV spending. The Imperial nameplate was used as a stand-alone luxury brand that year, and 1956 ads for Chrysler products touted a new "Magic Touch" push-button automatic transmission.

With an eye toward improving Chrysler's traditionally weak presence in Europe and Latin America, McCann-Erickson was appointed to handle its export business, succeeding Ross Roy, which maintained Dodge truck and corporate sales and service accounts. Chrysler's efforts abroad were aimed primarily at Europe and Latin America. Ad spending in 1956 dropped to about $60 million, mainly due to a cutback in newspaper spending, as unit sales fell 23 percent. Ads of the era for all Chrysler brands touted the new "Forward look" of the finned cars. The introductory ads for the 1957 Chrysler products proclaimed "Suddenly—it's 1960!" and the Chrysler brand cars were advertised as "The most glamorous cars in a generation." Chrysler Corporation ad spending in 1957 grew by 20.3 percent, and unit sales were up 17.2 percent.

In 1958 Chrysler bought a stake in French automaker Simca and began selling Simca vehicles in the U.S.; Richard N. Meltzer Advertising was retained as the brand's agency. In February, McCann-Erickson caused a stir in the ad industry by resigning the Chrysler corporate and Chrysler and Imperial car accounts to take on the Buick business. McCann had held the Chrysler account since 1943. Chrysler named Young & Rubicam, Inc. (Y&R), which had resigned the Lincoln car account, to handle Chrysler and Imperial brand advertising; the Leo Burnett Company was tapped for corporate advertising. Ad spending was down 18.7 percent in 1958, and Chrysler Corporation's unit sales tumbled 40.4 percent in a falling auto market.

In addition to Chrysler's broadcast sponsorship of Groucho Marx's radio and television programs, Dodge sponsored national TV broadcasts of *The Lawrence Welk Show* from 1955 through 1960. A sponsorship conflict flared in 1958 when Chrysler offered singer Gordon MacRae a pair of 1958 De Sotos, as well as new 1959 and 1960 models when they came out, if he would appear in television commercials for the brand. But MacRae had already been scheduled to do a half-hour Oldsmobile-sponsored TV special later in the year. MacRae lost the special, as well as his fee. Oldsmobile then took him off Patti Page's *The Big Record,* and Lincoln-Mercury canceled a season's worth of MacRae's guest spots on Ed Sullivan's *Toast of the Town.* Such was the power of advertisers over program content in the 1950s.

To compete in the new small-car segment, which was dominated by Volkswagen, Chrysler introduced the Valiant compact car in 1959 for the 1960 model year. The Valiant account was given to De Soto agency BBDO. Valiant, a stand-alone nameplate at first, would eventually become a Plymouth model. In the Dodge line, a lower-priced Dart series was added for the 1960 model year. The Dart more than doubled Dodge's unit sales over the previous year and accounted for about 85 percent of the division's sales in 1960. The De Soto was not faring as well. The company dropped the brand after producing only about 3,000 1961 De Sotos (at its peak in 1953, the car sold 122,342 units) In 1960 Chrysler's agency alignment was overhauled. BBDO lost Valiant and De Soto but gained both Dodge cars (from Grant Advertising) and Dodge trucks (from Ross Roy). N.W. Ayer & Son, the Plymouth agency, took over Valiant and the soon-to-be-axed De Soto, mirroring the divisional alignment of the company. Chrysler also reorganized its Canadian accounts, loosening the grip that Ross Roy of Canada had over the entire account there. Ross Roy retained the Chrysler and Plymouth accounts, but Grant Advertising of Canada got the Dodge and De Soto accounts.

Reorganization

In 1961 Chrysler named Administrative Vice President Lynn A. Townsend to the post of president of Chrysler. Divisions were reorganized, with Plymouth-Valiant and Chrysler-Imperial merged into a single Chrysler-Plymouth division. Townsend remained president through 1967, when he was appointed chairman. The mid-1960s saw strong growth in the U.S. auto market, and Chrysler capitalized on this trend under Townsend. Unit sales for the decade peaked at 1.6 million in 1968, nearly a million more cars than the 663,000 the company had sold in 1962. Chrysler's earnings also skyrocketed, as did ad spending, reaching more than $82 million in 1966. During this period Chrysler spent heavily on TV sponsorship, including the weekly *Bob Hope Theatre* and Bob Hope specials on NBC.

Y&R, which had held the Chrysler and Imperial business since 1958 and had been given the corporate account in 1962, was awarded the $30 million Plymouth account in 1966. At the time, this was the largest single account switch in history. Y&R also picked up Chrysler International, based in Geneva, Switzerland, from BBDO that same year. Y&R's first campaign for Plymouth, for the 1967 models, used the tag line, "Plymouth is out to win you over," dropping Ayer's 1966 theme, "Let yourself go." For the 1968 Plymouths, the tag was changed to "The beat goes on," and the campaign featured English pop singer Petula Clark in the TV and radio spots. A controversy developed in early 1968 during the filming of a Petula Clark TV special sponsored by Plymouth on NBC. The Chrysler-Plymouth advertising manager strongly objected to minor physical contact during a duet between Clark, who was white, and singer Harry Belafonte, who was black. The incident was reported widely in the general press, and the ad manager was relieved of his duties soon after.

Also in 1968 Plymouth premiered its Road Runner muscle car, purchasing the rights to the animated Warner Brothers Seven Arts Road Runner cartoon character created by Chuck Jones. The cars featured a horn that echoed the "beep-beep" of the character, and the animated character was used in print and broadcast ads. On the Dodge account, BBDO used the tag line, "Join the Dodge rebellion," for 1966, and continued it with a military theme for the 1967 models. The theme was changed to "Dodge fever" for the 1968 and 1969 model years.

Association with Mitsubishi

As a recession hit in 1970, Chrysler Corporation's earnings fell sharply. Ford and Chevrolet were introducing U.S.-manufactured subcompact cars, the Pinto and the Vega, and American Motors Corporation (AMC) would soon have the Gremlin. Chrysler, lacking a comparable model, began to import subcompact cars for 1971 from Mitsubishi Motors Corporation of Japan and rebrand them as Dodge Colts. This was the start of a long, sporadic association with the Japanese manufacturer. For Plymouth, a version of a subcompact from Chrysler's British arm was rebadged as the Cricket. The Plymouth model was plagued with quality problems and withdrawn from the market after two years,

The sports car you can afford after you've put a small fortune in sports equipment.

Plymouth Barracuda. The under $2500* fastback that seats five and has a 7-foot cargo space.

The Plymouth Barracuda beat Ford's Mustang to showrooms by several weeks and set off a "muscle car" war that preoccupied manufacturers and enthusiasts alike for the next decade.
The Chrysler and Plymouth advertisements are used with permission from DaimlerChrysler Corporation.

but the Colt continued on as a "captive import" for Dodge and later Plymouth as well. Chrysler moved its corporate ad account out of Y&R in 1970; the TV portion went to Dodge agency BBDO, and print and radio advertising went to Ross Roy. In 1971 Chrysler Corporation bought an equity stake in Mitsubishi and stopped importing Simca models from France.

In 1972 Chrysler Corporation unit sales jumped 16.5 percent over the prior year to a record 1.7 million, and peaked for the decade in 1973 at 1.8 million. Ad spending for 1973 was nearly $96 million. Chrysler's compact cars, the Plymouth Valiant, Duster, and Dodge Dart, sold well in the early 1970s, and the company returned to profitability after suffering a loss in 1970. Dodge trucks, riding on the rising popularity of the recreational vehicle market, surged 72 percent in 1972, and another 23 percent in 1973 to a record 358,394 units sold. The advertising theme for 1972 Dodge cars and trucks was "Dodge. Depend on it." In the fall of 1973 the 1974 Plymouth Dusters and Valiants were introduced with a comical fictional spokeswoman named "Mean Mary Jean." The popular character, a tough captain of a women's football team, was used in radio, newspaper, and TV ads.

Energy Crisis and Recession

With an energy crisis and recession hitting hard, the bottom dropped out of the U.S. car market in 1974. Chrysler's unit sales fell sharply for two straight years, to approximately 1.3 million cars and trucks sold in 1975, as the company suffered operating losses. Facing a large inventory of unsold cars, Chrysler introduced the "Chrysler Car Clearance Carnival" on Super Bowl Sunday in January 1975, promising buyers of select Chrysler products a rebate check of $200 to $300. The ads, featuring former baseball player Joe Garagiola, introduced the concept of automotive incentive advertising, which has been heavily used by automakers ever since. Chrysler's incentive advertising used Garagiola through the 1980 model year. Decades later, automakers still bemoan factory rebates as a drain on profitability.

But Garagiola did not have the impact of another celebrity spokesman: Ricardo Montalban. When Chrysler Corporation introduced a new, intermediate-sized Chrysler coupe for the 1975 model year, Y&R, then the Chrysler-Plymouth agency, came up with an ad campaign showing the car in a Spanish-style courtyard. In the TV spots a guitar strummed as Montalban walked around the car, extolling its virtues. His elegant demeanor and rolling R's, most apparent as he described the "rich Corinthian leather" of the car's upholstery, apparently appealed to buyers. The new Cordoba was a success, responsible for more than doubling Chrysler brand sales in 1975, an otherwise poor year for the company and the industry. Though Chrysler featured many celebrity endorsers in the 1970s and 1980s, Montalban was the most enduring, becoming nearly synonymous with the Cordoba. Chrysler was so pleased with Montalban that they featured his son, Victor, in ads for the 1980 models to try to appeal to younger car buyers. When the Cordoba was discontinued after the 1983 model year, the company used Ricardo Montalban for the next several years in ads for the Chrysler LeBaron, as well as in umbrella ads for the corporation.

Montalban's popularity was not enough to stem the tide of losses for the carmaker, however. In 1975 Chrysler suffered a financial loss of more than a quarter-billion dollars; but by late that year the corporation had finally updated its aging compact car lines with the introduction of the Dodge Aspen and Plymouth Volaré. In addition to Montalban, other celebrities were used in the advertising campaigns for the new 1976 cars, a practice that continued through the 1980s. The 1976 campaign featured, among others, Rex Harrison for Aspen and Sergio Franchi for Volaré. Compact sales increased with the introduction of the new cars. Chrysler's U.S. ad spending for calendar year 1976 topped $100 million for the first time, as unit sales soared 32 percent over 1975 on the strength of a rebounding U.S. auto market. The company returned to profitability. Although its new compacts were a hit, Chrysler dropped the slow-selling Imperial nameplate, and the company still had no domestically produced subcompact car. Outside the U.S. and Canada, Chrysler unit sales neared 1 million vehicles. In nonautomotive business, the company sold its Chrysler Airtemp airconditioner division.

Chrysler's ad expenditures were up another 15.4 percent in 1977, largely due to boosts in magazine and direct-mail spending, although unit sales slipped due to late introductions of 1978 models. In January of 1978 the company finally introduced the Dodge Omni and Plymouth Horizon models, which were the only domestically produced front-wheel-drive subcompacts. They were backed by a major ad push of $15 million, with the Omni being billed as the car that "Does it all" and the Horizon tag being "Relax. Horizon can handle it." The cars sold well, but their reputation and that of the corporation were later damaged by an "unacceptable" rating given the cars by the Consumers Union due to handling peculiarities.

Difficult Times

The following year marked the start of a disastrous period for Chrysler Corporation in which the company nearly went bankrupt. Although in 1978 Chrysler Corporation had its popular new subcompacts, production was constrained by Chrysler's contracting of the four-cylinder engines for the cars from Volkswagen. It could not buy enough engines to satisfy consumer demand. At the same time, production glitches delayed its new line of large cars. When the company finally introduced them for 1979, a gas crunch hit, curtailing demand in that category. By the end of 1978 Chrysler Corporation had suffered a loss of more than $204 million. Ad spending had been increased a staggering 48 percent to nearly $189 million, but despite that effort, unit sales slumped. Lee A. Iacocca, who had been fired earlier in 1978 from his position as Ford Motor Company president, became president of a desperate Chrysler Corporation in November. Within a year he was given the title of chairman. Chrysler also curtailed its international operations, selling its European arm to PSA Peugeot-Citroen while obtaining a 15 percent stake in Peugeot. Chrysler sold its Brazilian operations to Volkswagen.

Iacocca was involved in Chrysler advertising from the start, going so far as to choose the colors of the cars pictured in the ads. He participated in a direct-mail campaign, comparing Chrysler's cars to Ford's, and exhorting buyers: "Find out for yourself. I did." One of Iacocca's early actions, in 1979, was to fire several long-time agencies. Y&R, which had been the Chrysler-Plymouth agency since 1958, was let go. BBDO, which had owned the Dodge account since 1960 and De Soto prior to that time, was also booted. The recipient of both accounts was Kenyon & Eckhardt (K&E), headed by Leo Arthur Kelmenson, who had developed a strong relationship with Iacocca when he was at Ford. K&E quickly resigned the Lincoln-Mercury account. At the time, the shake-up constituted the biggest account switch in history—approximately $125 million in billings. K&E's first campaign for Chrysler touted a new optional extended warranty plan.

In 1979 Chrysler slashed its advertising expenditures by nearly 40 percent as it became the first U.S. corporation to lose more than $1 billion. Its U.S. market share for cars and light trucks slipped to less than 10 percent. In the last half of the year, the company spent $200 million on sales incentives and cash rebates in a futile attempt to stem losses; it also launched a nearly

$10 million corporate-image campaign to improve public perception of the company. The corporate campaign featured astronaut Neil Armstrong touting Chrysler engineering expertise. By August, Joe Garagiola, Chrysler's perennial rebate spokesman, was again featured in ads telling potential buyers: "Get a car. Get a check."

Chrysler Turns to the Government

With the company's financial situation worsening in 1979, Chrysler Corporation took the drastic step of turning to the U.S. government for relief. While the politicians considered the matter, Chrysler introduced its 1980 models, and Dodge's long-running "Dodge trucks are ram tough" tag debuted. Iacocca appeared on camera in brief tags to existing commercials saying, "I'm not asking you to buy a car on faith. I'm asking you to compare." As October sales dropped 57 percent over the prior year, Iacocca touted a new round of rebates, the earliest ever in the model year, calling them a "special introductory offer." In late 1979, after much debate, Congress approved a $1.5 billion loan guarantee package to bail the company out. Chrysler ran newspaper ads on the last day of the year, saying that the company was "in business to stay," and referring to itself as "The new Chrysler Corporation," echoing "The new good Maxwell" of decades before. President Jimmy Carter signed the Chrysler Corporation Loan Guarantee Act into law in early 1980, setting the stage for Chrysler's recovery.

That year Chrysler continued "The New Chrysler Corporation" corporate advertising theme, and tried to lure customers back into showrooms by offering a money-back guarantee, free auto club membership, no-cost maintenance, and $50 for test-driving a Chrysler vehicle. Iacocca became the company's chief public spokesman, appearing in a series of TV spots and magazine ads. In the summer of 1980 Frank Sinatra offered his services to the company for $1 per year and appeared in corporate ads with Iacocca talking optimistically about the company. He was later featured, in the tradition of celebrity spokesmen for individual Chrysler models, in ads for a new 1981 luxury car with a revived Imperial nameplate, though the car never achieved sales success and was soon discontinued.

A new line of front-wheel-drive compact cars, dubbed K-cars, was slated to be launched in the fall for the 1981 model year, but 1980 was another year of huge losses for Chrysler Corporation, more than $1.7 billion worth. Ad spending was increased in an effort to stay in the game, though sales fell to barely more than 1 million units, and hovered at that level through 1982. With the introduction of the K-cars, the Dodge Aries and Plymouth Reliant, the company boosted ad spending again, to $193 million in 1981. Themes for the new cars' introduction were "The American way to beat the pump" and "America's not going to be pushed around any more"—the latter a reference to the cars' front-wheel drive and to the success Japanese automakers were having at the expense of the Big Three. Chrysler Corporation reportedly received breaks on advertising costs in 1980 and 1981 from media outlets sympathetic to its plight.

Recovery

The K-cars were instrumental to the company's recovery, quickly becoming the best-selling cars in the lineup. In the second quarter of 1981 the company turned a profit for the first time in two years, and K&E devised a newspaper ad with a drawing of a car bursting out of a grave marked "Chrysler R.I.P." The caption read, "The reports of the death of Chrysler were greatly exaggerated." This was still a year of losses—more than $475 million—but with corporate cost-cutting, the sale of Chrysler's defense division in early 1982, and the strong-selling K-cars helping profitability, the company seemed to have turned a corner.

In 1982 Chrysler finally had a profitable year again, at the same time increasing ad spending. Although the base K-cars saw a sales decline, this was more than compensated for by the strong sales of the new, more luxurious Chrysler LeBaron and Dodge 400 K-car derivatives. Lee Iacocca continued to appear in ads, challenging consumers, "If you can find a better car, buy it." Chrysler made an effort to better differentiate the three car brands. Ricardo Montalban became spokesman for the entire Chrysler brand lineup, while Plymouth's theme for 1981 and 1982 was "The American way to get your money's worth." Dodge used "America's driving machine" for cars and continued the "Ram tough" tag for trucks. In late 1982 Chrysler rehired BBDO as the Dodge agency, and its first new commercials for the brand broke in early 1983.

Strong profits returned in 1983, and the Chrysler Corporation repaid its bailout loans—seven years ahead of schedule. The company introduced a new type of family vehicle in the fall of 1983 for the 1984 model year. These were similar to compact station wagons but much taller and were an immediate hit. Soon, the Dodge Caravan and Plymouth Voyager came to be called minivans, and a new segment of the auto market was born. The minivans sold out production by spring of 1984, and some orders went unfilled, but Chrysler's minivans would come to dominate the segment for many years. In August BBDO began a new campaign for Dodge in an effort to create a stronger identity for the brand. The tag line was "We are Dodge. An American revolution."

Chrysler's recovery seemed complete in 1984, as it logged record profits of nearly $2.2 billion and unit sales surged 31.6 percent. Ad spending grew to $344 million, including large increases in network TV and magazine spending. The company took a minority stake in Italy's Maserati and announced plans to bring an Italian-built luxury sports car to the U.S. in 1987. The car finally arrived after many delays, but the venture was unsuccessful and was soon dissolved. In the spring of 1985 Chrysler Corporation announced plans to expand its holdings in Mitsubishi Motors to 24 percent and launch a joint venture, called Diamond-Star Motors, to build sporty subcompact cars for 1988 in a new Illinois plant.

By 1986 Chrysler Corporation's advertising spending topped half a billion dollars, and sales continued to climb as the company resumed exports to Europe and bought Lamborghini (later sold, in 1993). The following year Chrysler acquired American Motors Corporation (AMC) for $800 million. This gave Chrysler the Jeep

Boldly go.

PT CRUISER®

Presenting the new Chrysler PT Cruiser. Ingenious functionality. Stand-out styling. Surprising affordability. Guaranteed to recharge any road. Get details at 1.800.CHRYSLER or www.chrysler.com.

CHRYSLER

The Chrysler PT Cruiser was one of the most highly anticipated automobiles of the 1990s. Its distinctive styling still drew stares and stopped traffic long after its introduction.
The Chrysler and Plymouth advertisements are used with permission from DaimlerChrysler Corporation.

brand of sport-utility vehicles, including the Chinese joint venture Beijing Jeep. AMC had purchased the Kaiser-Jeep Corporation in 1970; this was formerly Willys-Overland Company—the same company Walter P. Chrysler had helped to rejuvenate decades earlier. The Eagle brand of cars was introduced beginning with the Eagle Premier, a car jointly designed by AMC and its former partner, Renault. With the AMC acquisition, Chrysler Corporation's unit sales topped 2 million for the first time in 1987. Chrysler retained AMC's former ad agency, William Esty Company, soon to be Campbell Mithun Esty, as the agency for the Eagle and Jeep brands. The agency continued its "Only in a Jeep" tag for the line of sport-utility vehicles. The Jeep brand would prove to be the major asset of the AMC deal, as the sport-utility market was poised for spectacular growth.

In 1989 Chrysler signed an agreement to produce minivans, and eventually Jeep Grand Cherokees, in Austria with Steyr-Daimler-Puch. Chrysler also set up its Pentastar Transportation Group, Inc., consisting of four rental car companies it had purchased, including Thrifty and Dollar. For 1989 Dodge advertising changed its tag line to "The new spirit of Dodge," while Chrysler brand vehicles used the tag "Driving to be the best," using perennial Chrysler spokesman Ricardo Montalban. Iacocca by this time had a reduced role in corporate advertising, appearing in a small number of ads touting "The car buyers' Bill of Rights."

In the early 1990s unit sales for Chrysler Corporation dropped sharply in a softening auto market, reaching just over 1.5 million units in 1991. Nonetheless, the company's ad spending was more than a half-billion dollars for 1990 and 1991. In 1991 the company introduced a luxury Chrysler brand minivan, dubbing it Town & Country, reviving a name from the past. That year the corporation also sold its stake in Mitsubishi Motors, as "Advantage: Chrysler" became the corporate theme. In November of 1990 Chrysler announced a $40 million deal with Time Warner that included special single-advertiser issues of *Fortune, People,* and *Life* magazines built around the theme "Rediscover America."

Early in 1992 Dodge introduced the Viper, a low-volume V-10-powered sports car intended to be the brand's image leader. Also introduced at the same time was the Jeep Grand Cherokee, which would become instrumental for the company as the sports-utility market began to experience explosive growth. The period also marked the end of an era: Iacocca announced plans to retire at the end of the year. In March of 1992 Chrysler appointed Robert J. Eaton, formerly president of General Motors Europe, to the position of vice chairman and chief operating officer, poised to succeed Iacocca. In his last ad campaign appearance for the company, Iacocca introduced the new family-sized LH cars, the Dodge Intrepid, Eagle Vision, and Chrysler Concord, which were launched at the end of the year as 1993 models.

These new models were supported with heavy advertising, and in 1993 the company's spending rose more than 38 percent to $756 million. Network and spot TV and magazines saw hefty increases. Advertising for the new LH cars focused on their "cab forward design." Sales of the new cars, as well as sales of Jeep vehicles, surged with these new products, and Chrysler Corporation's unit sales grew nearly 20 percent, topping 2 million units once again. In 1994 Chrysler Corporation's earnings reached an all-time high of $3.7 billion, and the new Dodge Ram full-sized pickup was introduced. BBDO used "The new Dodge" as the umbrella tag for the brand, as all Dodge cars and trucks were shown in bright red in ads focusing on the product. The 1993 Intrepid was introduced with the theme "We're changing everything." The campaign was an attempt to shift the perception of the brand as boxy and boring. The red cars, along with voice-over and appearances by actor Edward Hermann, continued for several years. For the 1998 models the theme was "We're changing everything again," as Dodge truck sales alone topped 1 million units, and for the 2000 models the tag became "Dodge. Different." Late in 1997 Bozell introduced a new corporate theme, "Great cars. Great trucks."

Formation of DaimlerChrysler

But perhaps nothing could have been so different for the auto industry as Chrysler's next stunning move. In 1998 Chrysler Corporation and Daimler-Benz, maker of Mercedes-Benz cars and trucks, agreed to combine their businesses in a so-called "merger of equals." The deal, in actuality a buyout of Chrysler Corporation, would give Daimler-Benz mass-market brands in North America to complement the luxury Mercedes-Benz brand. Daimler-Benz also owned the Smart brand of mini-cars marketed in Europe. The resulting company was called DaimlerChrysler. Daimler-Benz Chairman Juergen Schrempp and Chrysler Chairman and Chief Executive Officer Robert Eaton were "co-chairmen" of the new company until Eaton's retirement in 2000, when Schrempp became sole chairman.

By the end of the 1998 model year, the Eagle brand, which peaked at just 71,225 unit sales in 1993, was discontinued. In 1999 DaimlerChrysler announced the phase-out of the dwindling Plymouth brand as well, which had sold only 264,624 units in 1999. To improve access to Asian auto markets and facilitate development of small car platforms worldwide, in 2000 DaimlerChrysler bought a controlling 34 percent stake in Chrysler Corporation's old Japanese partner, Mitsubishi Motors, and a 10 percent stake in Hyundai Motor Company of South Korea.

The new company transferred North American advertising for Mercedes-Benz vehicles, which had been with Lowe & Partners/SMS, to Merkley Newman Harty, a boutique shop of the Omnicom Group, in 1999. This move turned out to be a harbinger of further agency consolidation. In late 2000 the company consolidated the estimated $2.4 billion global advertising account for the Chrysler group of brands with BBDO Worldwide. BBDO, which had previously handled the Dodge brand and all media buying for DaimlerChrysler through its PentaCom unit, assumed the Chrysler and Jeep brand accounts as well. The new combined account constituted the largest in the automotive industry. PentaMark Worldwide, formed in 1998 by BBDO to oversee all of the agency's Chrysler business, assumed the additional work in January 2001. The creation of DaimlerChrysler marked a new era in the U.S. auto industry, transforming the venerable American company that had been rescued from disaster into the U.S. arm of a new global corporation.

SCOTT MACDONALD

Further Reading

Brown, Arch, *Jeep: The Unstoppable Legend,* Lincolnwood, Illinois: Publications International, 1994

Curcio, Vincent, *Chrysler: The Life and Times of an Automotive Genius,* Oxford and New York: Oxford University Press, 2000

Levin, Doron P., *Behind the Wheel at Chrysler: The Iacocca Legacy,* New York: Harcourt Brace, 1995

Moritz, Michael, and Barrett Seaman, *Going for Broke: The Chrysler Story,* Garden City, New York: Doubleday, 1981

"100 Years of Auto Advertising," *Advertising Age* (special issue, 8 January 1996)

"The Sales Statistics in *The-100 Year Almanac and 1996 Market Data Book,*" *Automotive News* (special issue, 24 April 1996)

Vlasic, Bill, and Bradley A. Stertz, *Taken for a Ride: How Daimler-Benz Drove Off with Chrysler,* New York: Morrow, 2000

Cigarettes

Long popular with American Indians, tobacco was introduced to Europeans by Christopher Columbus in the 15th century. Tobacco originally took the form of plugs (for chewing), cigars, pipe tobacco, and dry snuff. During the mid–19th century, Europeans created an inexpensive smoke of loose tobacco rolled in paper; it was called *papirossi* in Spanish, which translated into "paper cigar" or "cigarette."

Compared with other tobacco products, cigarettes had a limited market in the middle of the 19th century and were fashionable mainly in Paris, Madrid, London, Moscow, and Istanbul. In the United States they were considered effeminate compared with the masculine cigar and were initially confined to eastern seaboard cities. Two distinct markets existed in the United States: the wealthy, who favored imported cigarettes, and the poor, the immigrants, and the young, who could afford little more than low-cost domestic brands or loose tobacco they rolled themselves.

Although the manufacture of cigarettes was introduced to the United States in 1860, it remained a cottage industry until 1884 when James Bonsack, financed by tobacco company owner James ("Buck") Duke, invented the first viable cigarette-rolling machine. Many inventions and innovations converged at the turn of the 20th century, providing the opportunity for the mass marketing of cigarettes. Modernization of tobacco farming, curing, blending, and manufacturing allowed tobacco companies to mass-produce cigarettes. Innovations in transportation and warehousing cigarettes allowed companies to mass distribute them. Improvements in standardizing, packaging, and labeling allowed companies to mass merchandise branded cigarettes. It was largely the power of advertising, however, that allowed tobacco companies to create an appetite for the mass consumption of cigarettes.

From the 1860s to the 1900s, cigarette prices varied widely. A bargain brand containing Bright and White Burley American tobaccos (e.g., Durhams, Sweet Caporal, Cyclone, Full Dress, Cameo, Straight Cut) cost a nickel; mid-priced cigarettes using an American-Oriental blend (e.g., Halves) were 15 cents; and premium brands using Latakia and Xanthi Turkish and Russian tobaccos (Sultana, Moscow, Turkish Elegantes) were priced at a quarter.

One of the earliest cigarette promotions was the premium, pioneered in the 1860s by the English manufacturer P. Lorillard, which randomly placed money in packs of Century brand cigarettes—and then heavily advertised this fact. Among the most successful premiums were cigarette cards, introduced in 1878. By the mid-1880s these cards, featuring the images of Indian chiefs, baseball players, political figures, and the like, were being numbered to encourage collection of the complete series and thus multiple purchases. In 1888, to promote the new Cross Cut brand, Duke introduced "Sporting Girl" cards featuring actresses and models in exotic poses. Cigarette cards advertised brands and created customer loyalty through repurchase, while the stiff cardboard prevented cigarettes from being crushed in their soft paper packages.

Although the Bonsack rolling machine could produce 250,000 cigarettes a day, not enough smokers existed to buy them. Duke's first step was to popularize cigarettes, an undertaking that required extensive advertising. In 1889 the Duke Tobacco Company spent $800,000 on billboard and newspaper advertising, an amount unheard of at the time.

Duke established the Tobacco Trust in 1890, the same year the U.S. Congress enacted the Sherman Antitrust Law. By slashing prices and vastly expanding advertising spending, Duke threatened to bankrupt his competitors, and one by one they succumbed to acquisition. When the cigarette-marketing war ended, Duke's trust owned the premier cigarette manufacturer (American Tobacco Company), the second largest cigarette manufacturer (Allen & Ginter), and the third largest (Kinney), as well as Liggett & Myers (L&M), Reynolds, Lorillard, and a host of smaller firms. After swallowing up most of America's tobacco companies, Duke's trust proceeded to raid British tobacco firms from 1900 to 1902. The British companies consolidated to fight the trust and eventually agreed to a merger as the British American Tobacco Company (BAT). Ignored by the trust because it was too small, a minor British company set up shop in 1902 in New York City to sell cigarettes: Philip Morris.

In 1907 antitrust charges were filed, and the following year the Tobacco Trust was found guilty of violating the Sherman Act. The Supreme Court rejected its appeal, and in 1911 the trust was dissolved into its principal components: American Tobacco Company, L&M, Lorillard, Reynolds (which had 20 percent of the pipe and plug trade but no cigarette brands), and several smaller cigar and cigarette companies.

Another dark cloud emerged on the tobacco industry's horizon when, in 1908, England and Canada passed legislation prohibiting cigarette sales to children under the age of 16. Though the ban was generally ignored, cries for legislation to restrict or outlaw cigarettes and their advertising continued through the decades, returning later to haunt the cigarette industry.

The trust's breakup resulted in a cigarette brand explosion during 1912 and 1913. Demand was segmented, with different groups of smokers wanting different products. Consequently, the leading firms began expanding their lines to appeal to specific market segments. American introduced Omar, advertising it as a premium Turkish brand. L&M brought out Chesterfield, positioning it as an Anglophile brand to compete with Pall Mall's English snob appeal. Lorillard launched Hassan and Mecca, promoting the former as a premium brand and the latter as a mid-priced smoke, both targeting customers with a Turkish preference. All of these brands were either local or regional.

A National Market

Conditions were ripe for the introduction of a national cigarette brand. The proliferation of brands represented improvements in tobacco leaf curing and chemists' ability to create cigarette flavors and tastes at will. During 1912 not only did the Moslin Machine Company patent an improved cigarette-rolling machine, but cellophane for packaging was invented by Edwin Bradenberger. The transcontinental railroad connected the United States from coast to coast. Paved roads crisscrossed the land linking railroads to small towns. Wholesalers distributed branded merchandise, including tobacco, to mom-and-pop stores in every locale. More than 10,000 department and chain stores were in business, capable of handling large-scale cigarette distribution as well as carrying point-of-purchase displays. There were a number of well-established advertising agencies, including N.W. Ayer and Lord & Thomas, and new agencies were springing up in major cities. The *Saturday Evening Post* was being distributed nationally, and more than 15,000 newspapers were being published across the country. Also in 1912, book matches were perfected by the Diamond Company, a development that facilitated the shift from chewing tobacco to cigarettes. The convenience of matches enabled smokers to dramatically increase their cigarette consumption, and matchbook covers were an obvious place for cigarette advertising. This confluence of conditions provided the ideal circumstances for the mass production, mass distribution, mass advertising, and mass consumption of cigarettes.

It was R.J. Reynolds who produced the first truly national brand, providing a model for the entire industry. Recognizing that he could not afford to advertise local and regional brands for every market segment, as his major competitors were doing, Reynolds opted for a single brand. After several unsuccessful attempts, he introduced Camel in 1913. It contained mostly American Burley with some Bright leaf and a little Turkish Latakia. Billed on the package as a "Turkish & domestic blend," it vastly exaggerated the amount of Oriental tobacco in the blend and was heavily flavored with additives to taste like expensive Turkish cigarettes. The package also stated the cigarette's quantity and price: "20 for 10¢" as well as an intimation of quality, "No premiums or coupons," implying that such marketing ploys were precluded because of the brand's expensive Turkish leaf and low selling price. In reality, though, Camel was really quite profitable.

Reynolds's advertising agency, N.W. Ayer, developed a $680,000 three-part nationwide ad campaign that simultaneously used billboards, newspapers, and magazines. The first ads showed a picture of "Old Joe" (the Barnum & Bailey Circus camel pictured on the package) with the caption, "Camel." The next proclaimed: "The Camels are coming." The third triumphed: "Camel cigarettes are here!" Sales skyrocketed. The ad budget almost tripled to $1.9 million in 1914. Billboards across the United States displayed Camel ads; Reynolds later constructed a landmark billboard in New York City's Times Square picturing a man holding a cigarette from which emerged three-foot smoke rings that grew to 15 feet in the air. Camel ads were painted on the sides of barns visible from roads. Ads appeared in newspapers ranging from the *Wall Street Journal* to New York's Yiddish-language *Daily Forward* as well as local papers. Camels were advertised in magazines, including the first double-page spread in the *Saturday Evening Post*. Camels were pictured on thousands of matchbook covers and on point-of-purchase displays in thousands of retail

stores. By 1915 Camel had become the top-selling U.S. cigarette as well as the first national brand, selling in all 48 states.

Camel's success story inspired competitors. George Hill of the American Tobacco Company responded with Lucky Strike in 1916, resurrecting an old pipe-tobacco brand name reminiscent of the California gold rush days. Informally called "Luckies," the brand was an all-American blend with even more Burley leaf than Camel. Lucky Strike was also priced at ten cents for 20 and, like Camel, refrained from offering cigarette cards, signaling the end of premium promotions. On the package Luckies offered a money-back guarantee, and the ads touted its flavor, proclaiming, "Its toasted!"

Another Camel competitor, L&M, reformulated its 1912 Chesterfield blend by increasing the Burley and the additives. Befitting its aristocratic English name, the brand was given the understated slogan, "They do satisfy." At 15 cents for 20, Chesterfield targeted the more affluent and better-educated smokers. Its advertising played down the domestic leaf and proclaimed its Oriental quality, although the blend was mostly Burley with some Bright leaf: "The Chesterfield blend contains the most famous Turkish tobaccos—Samsoun for richness, Cavella for aroma, Smyrna for sweetness, Xanthi for fragrance, combined with the best domestic leaf." By 1917 it had captured 10 percent of the market.

Reynolds's Camel, American's Lucky Strike, and L&M's Chesterfield—the "Big Three"—dominated the cigarette market during World War I. Prices stabilized at 20 cents for a pack of 20 cigarettes for the duration of the war and afterward dropped to 15 cents. Most older Bright leaf brands such as Sweet Caporals, Sunshine, and Home Run were declining in sales, and many higher priced Turkish brands were eliminated altogether.

Advertising during the war featured pictures of exhausted doughboys smoking cigarettes in the trenches, accompanied by messages such as: "After the battle, the most refreshing smoke is Murad." The war helped to further popularize smoking. Soldiers' rations included packs of cigarettes. U.S. General John J. Pershing was quoted as saying, "You ask me what is needed to win this war. I answer cigarettes as much as bullets." At war's end, soldiers around the world returned home as smokers.

Advertising continued to play a critical role in the cigarette industry. In a market with minimal product differentiation, advertising quickly emerged as the essential ingredient of the marketing mix. One example of successfully using advertising, rather than actual product differences, to differentiate brands in the minds of consumers was the 1921 $8 million ad campaign "I'd walk a mile for a Camel." Another example, the 1933 "Call for Philip Morris" ad campaign, was made famous by the distinctive voice and image of Johnny Roventini—the first living person to become a brand trademark—dressed in a bellhop's uniform complete with pill hat, to give the impression of Philip Morris as a refined, upper-crust "English blend." Each of these notable slogans suggested that the advertised brand was special—at least worth walking or calling for—but there was little mention of product, price, or distribution distinctions. This market strategy of using advertising to create a slogan or image to distinguish one brand from another set the pattern for the remainder of the century. Because of the obvious importance of advertising, the principals of the major cigarette companies—Reynolds himself, Duke's successor Percival Hill and his son George Hill, and Caleb Dula at L&M—were personally involved in ad planning and execution.

By 1930 the leading advertising trade journal, *Printers' Ink*, recognized that "the one feature which has contributed more than any other single factor to the enormous growth of the cigarette industry is advertising." Advertising not only expanded overall cigarette consumption, it also affected demand for individual brands. In 1938 *Consumer Reports* magazine concluded in blindfolded taste tests that cigarette brands were nearly indistinguishable, a finding that further demonstrated the power and importance of advertising.

Targeting Women

From the start, the cigarette industry had targeted men, historically the heavy users of tobacco products, but it soon became obvious that men represented only half of the potential market. Although smoking had been considered effeminate in the mid–19th century, the converse was true by around 1910. Smoking was generally considered "unladylike" in much of the United States as well as many other countries. It was illegal for women to smoke in public in many cities, although the laws were usually ignored and soon were repealed or declared unconstitutional. The cigarette industry ultimately overcame the social prohibition against women smoking by using the power of advertising.

Early attempts to target women had limited results. Lorillard's 1919 Murad newspaper and magazine ad campaign, which showed women with open cigarette packs, but not holding cigarettes or smoking them, proved unsuccessful. A similar ad campaign for Helman and Players, an English brand, also failed. A 1925 Chesterfield ad campaign showing a woman enviously watching a man smoking, with the headline, "Blow some my way," implied if he could smoke so could she. Yet none of the ads put so much as an unlit cigarette in a woman's hand, let alone showed her smoking.

A now-famous strategy soon emerged: associate smoking with the women's emancipation movement. The American Tobacco Company hired the advertising and public relations executive Edward Bernays to address women's reluctance to smoke in public. In a legendary promotional event, Bernays hired ten fashion models and debutantes to walk down New York City's Fifth Avenue during the 1929 Easter Parade. Dressed as "Statues of Liberty," the models held Lucky Strike cigarettes aloft like "torches of freedom." Photos of the women appeared in newspapers nationwide, and the event became a turning point in the public's tolerance of women smoking.

Another successful advertising strategy aimed at women involved the association of smoking with weight control. Albert D. Lasker, head of Lord & Thomas and one of the pioneers of modern advertising, developed the 1928 Lucky Strike ad campaign "Reach for a lucky instead of a sweet." Numerous celebrity endorsers were employed. One ad featured aviatrix Amelia Earhart with the slogan, "For a slender figure—reach for a Lucky instead of a sweet." Regarded as one of the most successful campaigns in advertising history, the ads caused the candy industry to react furiously, leading to a public relations war between cigarette and candy manufacturers. At the end of the 20th century, the link between smoking and weight control continued to be a major component of many cigarette ads aimed at women.

The *U.S. Tobacco Journal* estimated that in 1924 women consumed only 5 percent of all cigarettes. The advertising strategies of associating smoking with women's suffrage and linking cigarettes to weight reduction were so successful that women's consumption increased to 13 percent by 1929 and jumped to 40 percent by 1950. Smoking became so common among women that when Philip Morris introduced Virginia Slims in 1968, it capitalized on the progress of the women's liberation movement with the congratulatory "You've come a long way baby" ad campaign, The campaign was a resounding success, the phrase entered the popular lexicon, and sales soared.

Along with advertising's successes in targeting women came failures. Philip Morris attempted to redesign its Marlboro cigarette specifically for women, right down to its red filter tip designed to hide lipstick marks. Its 1927 ad campaign "Mild as May" featured women. Directed at the refined lady, the ad copy read, "Women quickly develop discerning taste. That is why Marlboro ride in so many limousines, attend so many bridge parties, and repose in so many handbags." Sales were disappointing.

In an ironic twist of fate, a quarter of a century later Philip Morris successfully repositioned Marlboro from a women's brand to the quintessential filter cigarette for men. The rugged outdoor Marlboro cowboy image was created in the 1950s by the Leo Burnett Company and became a cultural icon. The "Come to Marlboro country" campaign launched in the early 1960s propelled Marlboro to the number-one sales position worldwide by 1972. Many women also preferred the brand's masculine image, helping Marlboro, by 1998, to claim more than 33 percent of the U.S. market and 8 percent globally. The cowboy image became recognized internationally as a symbol of Marlboro cigarettes, making it one of the best-known brands in the world.

The Role of Media

Print continued as the cigarette industry's dominant advertising medium in the early decades of the 20th century, but a number of new media emerged. Radio in the 1920s, product placement in films from the 1940s, and television from the 1950s also became important advertising venues.

Cigarette advertising helped build radio as a viable medium, and radio, in turn, helped build cigarette sales. Cigarette companies sponsored many radio shows during the 1920s and 1930s, such as the *Philip Morris Playhouse* and *Camel Pleasure Air*, featuring some of the day's best-known performers, and Lucky Strike's *Hit Parade*, a pop music show from 1935 to 1958. Among the top 100 network radio advertisers in 1939, American Tobacco ranked ninth with $2.5 million in ad spending, Brown & Williamson 11th with $2 million, L&M 12th with $1.9 million,

Reynolds 13th with $1.7 mllion, and Lorillard a distant 26th with $800,000.

By sponsoring radio programs and hiring celebrities, cigarette advertisers created an association with success and glamour. Many campaigns also featured sports celebrities, thus linking cigarettes with health, vitality, and athletic performance. These associations and a large advertising budget in 1930 allowed Lucky Strike (with 43.2 billion cigarettes sold annually and a $19 million ad budget) to finally surpass arch rival Camel (35.3 billion in sales, $15 million for advertising). In third place was Chesterfield (26.4 billion), and moving into a distant fourth but rising fast was Lorrillard's Old Gold (sales of 8.5 billion). Old Gold's radio ads appealed to the desire for the good life: "Eat chocolate. Light an Old Gold. And enjoy both! Two fine and healthful treats." Another Old Gold ad campaign, foreshadowing future health concerns, proclaimed: "Not a cough in a carload." By 1930 these four brands, representing a 90 percent share of the cigarette market, were the starter brands for the overwhelming majority of new smokers.

Menthol cigarettes were an innovation introduced in the 1930s. Some people found cigarette smoke too harsh, so menthol was added for its "anesthetic" properties. The first successful brand was Brown & Williamson's mentholated Kools. The 1934 ad campaign featured a penguin cartoon character. The headline read, "No need for Nyquil," and the copy emphasized that "your throat and tongue stay cool and smooth, your mouth clean and fresh. Change to Kools." Coupons were included as further incentive to buy the brand. Sales growth was slow, however, and menthol cigarettes remained a niche market until the 1970s.

Even with substantial cigarette advertising budgets invested in radio, print media continued to dominate. The 1931 "I'd walk a mile for a Camel" print campaign was run in 1,700 daily papers, 2,300 weeklies, and 400 financial and college periodicals. In addition to radio and print, peripheral advertising appeared in a variety of other media. During the Great Depression, men with sandwich boards were an inexpensive walking form of display advertising. In a new advertising medium, airplanes were used to skywrite brand names using letters one mile high. Low flying airplanes also broadcast slogans to pedestrians in small towns and cities and to audiences at outdoor social and sporting events.

During World War II Luckies used the ad slogan "LS/MFT—Lucky Strike means fine tobacco." The initials evoked the military's use of Morse code. Later the slogan "So round, so firm, so fully packed" was added. The sexual allusion implied that the servicemen might substitute a cigarette if a woman was not available. Camel ads of the early 1940s targeted the armed forces, with different tag lines for the different branches of the service.

From the 1940s on, movies began evolving into a popular venue for cigarette advertising. Cigarettes had always been faddish among Hollywood stars, including James Cagney, Maureen O'Hara, Fred Astaire, Rita Hayworth, James Dean, Linda Darnell, and Cary Grant. It was Humphrey Bogart, however, who elevated smoking to a new level of artistic expression in the popular 1943 film Casablanca. This single film was credited with dramati-

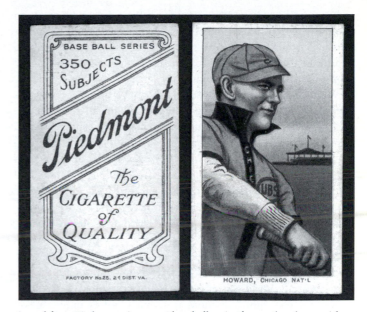

A card from Piedmont cigarettes' baseball series featured a player with Major League Baseball's Chicago Cubs.

cally increasing smoking initiation rates for men. In the Maltese Falcon, Bogart (who in 1957 died of lung cancer) played tough guy detective Sam Spade, who was shown chain-smoking Lucky Strikes throughout the movie. Subsequently, most major movie stars were pictured with a cigarette dangling languidly from their lips or held suavely between their fingertips.

Paid product placements became an effective and subtle advertising form that flourished in subsequent decades. In 1979, for example, Philip Morris reportedly paid $40,250 to have its Marlboro brand prominently featured in the movie Superman II—a film ostensibly for children. Although Lois Lane, a role model for girls, appeared in a series of comic books without ever smoking, she was portrayed chain-smoking Marlboro Lights in the movie. In one climactic scene, Superman was thrown into a van with an enormous Marlboro sign on its side. In another scene he fought through a maze of Marlboro billboards. Throughout the 1980s and 1990s, long after the ban on TV cigarette commercials, the movie Superman II was frequently shown in prime time.

By the 1970s, 29 percent of film characters were portrayed as smokers. Cigarettes developed into such a common feature that a study of the top-grossing films released between 1990 and 1996 found that 80 percent of male lead characters smoked on camera. More important, the characters who smoked were portrayed as successful and attractive, heroes rather than villains. Product placements in movies appealing to young people were an effective component of overall cigarette advertising strategy. Cigarettes even appeared regularly in animated films for children, such as 101 Dalmatians, All Dogs Go to Heaven, The Hunchback of Notre Dame, and Anastasia.

Cigarette placements in movies had several important advertising advantages. They allowed companies to show popular celebrities using their products, thus establishing role models for current and potential smokers. Moreover, they allowed the companies to effectively circumvent the mandated health warnings on advertisements. They also provided an instant visual demonstration of the wealth, health, and success that the cigarette companies wanted people to associate with smoking.

With the rapid growth of television in U.S. homes, the 1950s were the golden age of TV cigarette advertising. In 1950 the Big Three cigarette brands were still on top and were using television to stay that way. Camel, first in sales (98.2 billion cigarettes annually), sponsored the *Camel News Caravan*. Lucky Strike was in second place (82.5 billion) and sponsored *Your Hit Parade* and the *Jack Benny Program*. Chesterfield was third (66.1 billion) and sponsored Arthur Godfrey's show. Philip Morris, not even in the top-five best-selling brands, sponsored the number-one TV show, *I Love Lucy*.

Much of the advertising of this era claimed or implied that cigarettes were "healthy." In one ad, news commentator John Cameron Swaze assured the public, "When your nerves are shot, Camels set you right." In another, Arthur Godfrey publicized an alleged scientific study showing that "smoking Chesterfield would have no adverse effects on the throat." Later, as absolute health claims diminished, ads focused on the advantages of reduced tar levels; these competing claims introduced what became known as the "Tar Derby." Nicotine content was also a concern. After *Consumer Reports* rated cigarettes by nicotine level, Camel ad copy claimed "28% less nicotine than the average of the four other largest-selling cigarettes tested—according to independent scientific tests of the smoke itself!"

By 1960 Pall Mall took the lead in cigarette sales from Camel, now second. Reynolds's Winston, introduced in 1953 with a substantial ad budget and popular slogan, "Tastes good like a cigarette should," quickly became the leading king-sized filtered cigarette and third-leading seller overall. By 1965 Winston overtook Pall Mall as the overall sales leader. Lucky Strike dropped to fourth, and Reynolds's king-sized, filter-tipped mentholated Salem, introduced in 1956, was in fifth place. Menthol served a niche, but kings and filters were the wave of the future.

Robert "Brand-a-Month" Walker became American Tobacco's president in 1963 and, as his nickname implied, proceeded to develop a new brand for every conceivable market niche. He launched brands with heavy advertising, supporting those that caught on and immediately dumping brands that were unsuccessful. One of the newly launched brands was Carlton, a low-tar and low-nicotine cigarette that entered the market in January 1963, advertising its "air-vent" filter. Another was Montclair, introduced in May 1964, a mentholated, low-tar filter brand. Later that year Walker created a family of Lucky Strike brands with seven variants: regulars, filters in regular size, king-size, and a new 100-millimeter "luxury length" cigarette, as well as menthol filters in regular, king, and 100-millimeter sizes. In January 1965 several variations of Pall Mall were introduced. Sweet Caporal was also reformulated and reintroduced in October 1965 with the ad slogan, "Sweet news for you from 1870"; within a few months the brand was withdrawn. In 1967 Walker launched Silva Thins, which were actually slimmer than the industry standard cigarette,

in filtered 100-millimeter regular and menthol versions aimed at weight-conscious women.

By 1969 there was a massive proliferation of product variations by brand. The number-one brand in 1970, Winston (with sales of 81.9 billion cigarettes), came in four forms. Number two, Pall Mall (58.0 billion), came in three. And in third place, but rising fast, Marlboro (51.4 billion) came in five variations, including mentholated Marlboro Greens. Each variation of the family brand required a significant initial advertising budget to see if it would catch on. None of the original top-three (Camel, Luckies, and Chesterfield) from the 1920s to the 1950s made it into the top-five best-selling brands of the 1970s.

A small independent company of the 1920s and 1930s emerged with a trend-setting brand in the 1960s. The Benson & Hedges Company (B&H) spent little on advertising through most of its early history. In 1937 its budget with the Paris & Peart agency was little more than $10,000. Spending grew in the 1940s with Maxon, Inc., and later the Kudner Agency; most of the ad budget supported the flagship Benson & Hedges brand and secondary brand Virginia Rounds. Then in 1946 the company added Parliament to its roster and began building it through heavy spending before merging with Philip Morris in 1953. The new owners turned Virginia Rounds into a repositioned Virginia Slims, and Parliament became the leader within the old B&H line, with the Benton & Bowles agency employing newsman Mike Wallace as spokesman. The B&H brand was assigned first to Burnett and then to Doyle Dane Bernbach without great effect. It was not until it became an extra-long, 100-millimeter cigarette in the 1960s, and ad agency Wells, Rich, Green, Inc., touted its length as a "disadvantage," that Benson & Hedges broke through as a major brand. "Oh, the disadvantages of Benson & Hedges" became one of the most memorable campaigns of the 1960s. In 1999 *Advertising Age* named it 32nd among the century's 100 greatest campaigns.

Health Scare

Despite a growing body of research demonstrating the toxicity of cigarettes, most people remained uninformed about the health dangers of smoking. The absence of information was partially due to the ability of cigarette advertising to foster media self-censorship. Many magazines were financially dependent on cigarette advertising; they therefore avoided publicizing information about the health risks of smoking, fearful that large tobacco companies such as RJR Nabisco, parent company of R.J. Reynolds, and Philip Morris, which also had large stakes in food and other heavily advertised products, would withdraw their advertising.

A dramatic exception was *Reader's Digest,* which did not carry advertising in its U.S. edition until 1955; in December 1952 it published an article, "Cancer by the carton," marking the beginning of the "health scare" era. The tobacco industry responded to growing health concerns with several tactics, such as improving filters, stressing health benefits in ads, and increasing advertising budgets. Benson & Hedges touted Parliament's cotton "recessed filter," and in 1952 Lorillard's Kent introduced the "micronite filter." L&M's "pure white miracle tip of alpha-cellulose" was advertised as "Just what the doctored ordered" in 1953. American Brands' 1955 ad for its cork-tipped Tarryton emphasized the brand's new, improved charcoal filter. Filters were important: in 1950 only 2 percent of cigarettes were filtered; this number rose to 50 percent by 1960 and to 90 percent by 1980. Yet the most important strategy for dealing with the health scare was to substantially increase advertising budgets. Spending on cigarette ads rose 178 percent between 1950 and 1960.

In December 1953 six of the seven major tobacco companies (L&M would join later), in association with growers and warehousemen, funded the formation of the Tobacco Industry Research Committee (TIRC), which in turn promptly hired Hill & Knowlton, one of the largest public relations firms in the United States. In January 1954 TIRC, working with ad agency Fuller & Smith & Ross, which had no cigarette account, placed ads in newspapers around the country promising a joint industry research program run by scientists "disinterested in the cigarette industry." The headline was: "A frank statement to the public by makers of cigarettes." It was the industry's first open move to confront the cancer issue and was prompted by some of the most damaging publicity in the history of the industry, including articles in *Life, Time,* and a feature piece on *See It Now,* the prestigious CBS news program hosted by Edward R. Murrow. The same week the TIRC ads ran in January, a story in *Business Week* said that after years of growth, total industry sales for 1953 had fallen by 2 percent, the first drop since 1932. The magazine blamed the cancer scare for the decline.

In 1960, after growing industry criticism, cigarette manufacturers agreed to a voluntary ban on claims for reduced nicotine and tar. At the same time, consumer research revealed that switching from explicit to implicit health claims in advertisements would not only stop reminding smokers about health risks, it would help broaden the market to nonsmokers as well. Consequently, explicit ads were discontinued, and implicit ads were made an integral part of the advertising strategy. Many of these implicit messages, based on the presumed benefits of new filters, used euphemisms such as light, pure, clean, mild, natural, and fresh. Advertising's primary goal was to reassure both smokers and nonsmokers that cigarettes were not dangerous. Cigarette advertisements began stressing visual elements instead of verbal content. The visuals featured young, athletic-looking adults engaged in vigorous activities and surrounded by pristine environments. Even the smoke disappeared from the picture.

This shift in advertising strategy was quite successful. Smoking among teenagers rose to 40 percent in 1963. Because of these high rates the Federal Trade Commission (FTC) concluded, in 1964, that cigarette ads were aimed directly at young people. This coincided with the second wave of the "health scare" following the 1964 Surgeon General's Report linking smoking with cancer and lung and heart disease and led to the 1965 National Association of Broadcasters' Cigarette Advertising Code limiting ad claims on television and radio. More significantly, Congress passed the Cigarette Labeling and Advertising Act in 1965, requiring manufacturers to place warnings on cigarette packages but not in the ads, although this distinction was short-lived. In 1966 the FTC required the display of health warnings on all cigarette advertisements; banned advertising aimed at people younger than 25 years of age; and prohibited ad claims of the healthfulness of cigarette filters or products.

Restrictions and Response

The industry responded to health concerns and advertising restrictions by further increasing its substantial television advertising. In the middle of the 1960s, R.J. Reynolds alone sponsored 21 different television shows. By 1970 cigarette advertising represented 7 percent of total television advertising.

Antismoking ads began appearing on television after the Federal Communications Commission initiated the "equal time" Fairness Doctrine. Some ads featured well-known actors, such as Tony Curtis and Tony Randall, and overall were successful in reducing smoking. By 1970 the cigarette companies agreed to put an end to TV advertising in exchange for a halt in the antismoking ads. Beginning in 1971 the Public Health Smoking Act required a stronger warning on cigarette packages and advertisements than had been called for in the earlier 1966 FTC regulation. More important, the act also banned cigarette advertising on television and radio. Although appearing to be a major blow to the industry, this restriction was immediately circumvented by cigarette company sponsorship of popular televised sporting events. Philip Morris launched the Virginia Slims tennis tournament, and R. J. Reynolds initiated the Winston Cup auto race, prominently displaying billboards and cars bearing cigarette colors, logos, and brand names on television.

By the mid-1970s health authorities worldwide had issued warnings about cigarettes. Warnings appeared on packaging and advertising, and school educational programs were put in place. Growing public awareness and concern about the health consequences of cigarettes constituted a serious threat to the industry. Cigarette manufacturers turned to increasingly sophisticated consumer research to guide their advertising strategy. In 1976 Philip Morris introduced the Merit "low-tar" brand, backed by a $40 million advertising budget. Low tar implied lower health risk, and within a year, Merit captured a 1.5 percent share of the U.S. cigarette market.

To counter the extremely low-nicotine and low-tar brands, such as Philip Morris's Saratoga and Merit, American's Carlton, and Reynolds's Now, Winston took the reverse tactic and pointed out the obvious: the lower the nicotine and tar, the poorer the taste. In the mid-1970s Winston's ad campaign showed handsome, athletic-looking men; the slogans read: "If I'm going to smoke I'm going to do it right" and "Some people smoke a brand for image. . . . I smoke for taste." In 1980 Marlboro was in first place (with sales of 103.6 billion cigarettes); Winston fell back to second (81.0 billion); Kools, which had taken up sponsorship of major jazz festivals, moved up to third (56.7 billion); and Salem remained in fourth (53.2 billion). Annual consumption peaked in 1981 with sales of 640 billion cigarettes.

WE THOUGHT IT
WAS TIME TO
CLEAR THE AIR.

Giving you smoke-
free flights is
just one way
Northwest has seen
its way clear to
making your in-
flight experience
more pleasant.
Unlike other
airlines which only
prohibit smoking
on flights under
2 hours, every
Northwest flight
throughout North
America is smoke-
free.
Our position is
perfectly clear.

NORTHWEST

IN NORTH AMERICA
FLY SMOKE·FREE ◎ NORTHWEST AIRLINES
U.S. RESERVATIONS AT 1-800-225-2525 OR INTERNATIONAL RESERVATIONS AT 1-800-447-4747.   © 1988 Northwest Airlines, Inc.

**Northwest Airlines was the first U.S. carrier to institute smoke-free flights.
With this 1988 campaign advertising the policy, Northwest became a
pioneer in antismoking advertising.**
Courtesy of Northwest Airlines.

Throughout the 1980s members of the U.S. Congress proposed
limiting, reducing, or prohibiting the tax deductibility of cigarette
advertising. However, tobacco companies were traditionally
among the largest contributors to political parties and candidates.
The millions of dollars given to political campaigns and lobbying
efforts constituted a virtual stranglehold over Congress and
helped ensure that bills unfavorable to the tobacco industry were
not passed. Of the 174 pieces of federal health legislation introduced in the late 1980s and early 1990s, only two antitobacco
bills passed. At the state level, the influence of tobacco lobbying
and political campaign money was at least as effective.

The 1990s were characterized by the increasingly aggressive
promotion of cigarettes. In 1993 the tobacco companies spent
more than $6 billion on marketing in the United States alone, of
which $1.2 billion was spent on point-of-purchase displays, out-
door, newspaper, magazine, and direct mail advertising. Point-of-
purchase displays were particularly effective: a tobacco trade
journal reported that "cigarette purchases are 2.5 times as great
when an in-store display is present compared to when no advertising or display treatment is employed." Cigarette ads accounted

for 10 percent of outdoor billboard advertising in 1997; then in
the 1998 tobacco industry settlement with the state attorney's
general, outdoor billboard advertising was eliminated. To compensate, cigarette advertising shifted to magazines. At the beginning of 1999, cigarette ads in magazines were up 33 percent in
just two months to $60 million and rising. The remaining $4.8
billion was spent on a variety of other marketing vehicles and promotions, such as retail incentives, branded merchandise, and
sports and other sponsorships.

In 1996 the Food and Drug Administration imposed sweeping
restrictions on cigarette advertising in an attempt to protect children. Some U.S. municipalities set their own limits on cigarette
advertising, although many states had laws prohibiting stronger
local ordinances by municipalities and thus were preempted from
restricting cigarette ads. In many developing international markets, cigarette advertisements often linked U.S. brands with an
affluent and sophisticated lifestyle, an advertising strategy that
proved quite effective. In 1988, to offset global cigarette growth,
the World Health Organization had started an annual "World
No-Tobacco Day." International restrictions on cigarette advertising grew, and by 1995 more than 20 nations had enacted total
cigarette advertising bans. The European Union was planning to
ban tobacco advertising starting in 2006.

One example of a U.S. government victory was the termination
of the Joe Camel advertisements—a cartoon version of the "Old
Joe" character appearing on Camel cigarette packages since 1913.
On Camel's 75th anniversary, the McCann-Erickson ad agency
had reintroduced Old Joe in the "Smooth Character" campaign of
1988. The Old Joe ads were so successful that in 1991 Saatchi &
Saatchi tested a campaign for Kools revising the old 1930s cartoon penguin with a more modern version of a "hip penguin"
wearing sunglasses and Day-Glo sneakers. Old Joe raised more
public concern than previous cartoon characters in cigarette ads
because of the campaign's effectiveness with teens and children. In
the four years after Joe's reintroduction, Camel's share of the
underage market jumped to 61 percent. Mounting criticism from
government officials and antismoking advocates followed, and
RJR Nabisco withdrew the popular Joe Camel character from its
ads in 1997.

Antismoking Ads

The cigarette industry's most powerful marketing weapon—
advertising—also proved an effective antidote in the effort to
reduce underage cigarette use. In 1988 Saatchi & Saatchi designed
Northwest Airlines' very successful "Smoke-Free Skies" campaign. RJR Nabisco was so incensed it withdrew the Oreo cookie
account, which Saatchi had held for 18 years.

Antismoking ad campaigns in the late 20th century proved just
as successful as cigarette company ads when using the same
sophisticated consumer research techniques; in fact, sometimes,
they were too effective for their own good. For example, in 1992 a
California antismoking campaign used aggressive and sometimes
shocking ads that condemned the industry for deceitful and dis-
honest practices. Surveys showed that the campaign was working;

cigarette consumption declined significantly. Nevertheless, the governor forced the development of less confrontational antismoking ads, and the legislature reduced the advertising budget. Not surprisingly, smoking rates began to rise. Similar scenarios occurred in Massachusetts, New York, Arizona, and Florida, illustrating, some observers said, the power of political lobbying and campaign contributions. Nonetheless, the power of advertising, when guided by sophisticated consumer research, was underlined.

Creative Strategies for a Hostile Climate

In the 1990s, in part to counteract the growing threats of legislation and advertising restrictions, cigarette advertising focused on the introduction of a variety of new media and promotional opportunities. These included sporting and cultural sponsorships, music videos, branded merchandise, and the Internet, each becoming an important component of cigarette advertising worldwide.

Event sponsorship—the subsidizing of social or sporting events—became increasingly popular after the broadcast ban in 1971. Sponsorships had three main advantages for the cigarette industry. First, these promotions were technically not classified as advertising; they therefore allowed the industry to circumvent restrictions, including television broadcast bans. Second, sponsorships provided for the development of a thankful constituency of financially dependent recipients who tended to support and defend the cigarette industry. Finally, sponsorship psychologically linked cultural and athletic excellence with cigarettes, leaving a powerful mental association in the consumer's mind.

Since its introduction in the 1980s, the music video has been a popular medium appealing to young people. Like movies, music videos provided another opportunity for cigarette advertisements in the form of product placements. A survey in the late 1990s found that 25 percent of MTV videos portrayed musicians or actors smoking. Ascertaining how often cigarette manufacturers paid for these portrayals was difficult, and estimates varied considerably.

Increased attention was paid to another medium, namely the merchandising of items displaying cigarette names and logos, such as shirts and toys. These items were not required to bear health warnings and could be easily obtained by children and teens. Industry expenditures quadrupled from $184 million in 1991 to $756 million in 1993. Camel's advertising expenditures for merchandise alone were $40 million in 1991. Although U.S. federal laws prohibited the sale of these items to those under age 18, many children and teens still wore hats, T-shirts, sweaters, backpacks, and other gear emblazoned with cigarette brand names and trademarks. Some critics called these youth "walking cigarette billboards."

The Internet is the newest medium to host cigarette advertisements. Though cigarette ads were less common on U.S. Web sites than on those originating from other countries, they were widely criticized by antismoking groups because of the Internet's great popularity with youngsters. Many Web sites promoting cigarettes actively encouraged children's visits. For example, one German cigarette Web site offered a cute virtual pet that a child could care for and play with. Internet ads did not require health warnings and were not limited by restrictions placed on conventional advertising in many countries where Internet users live. Thus, like advertising in movies, videos, and branded merchandise, Internet ads avoided restrictions and yet were subtle and effective in reaching youthful targets.

Conclusion

The success of cigarette advertising is a potent example of advertising's enormous power and economic value. From the birth of the cigarette industry, advertising was instrumental in creating a mass market and apportioning shares among brands. At the end of the 20th century, guided by increasingly sophisticated consumer research, advertising continued to increase the size of the market, despite an expanding awareness of health risks and increasing advertising restrictions. Cigarette advertisers became adept at targeting every conceivable consumer niche and developing an impressive array of advertising and promotional tools to reach them.

Campaigns throughout the 20th century demonstrated that in addition to directly increasing primary demand for cigarettes, advertising could be highly effective in developing selective demand for individual brands, particularly during their introduction. Advertising also had other less quantifiable benefits for cigarette companies: it promoted the continued social acceptability of smoking and encouraged the incorrect belief that the majority of people smoke.

The start of the 21st century presented both unique opportunities and growing challenges for cigarette advertising. Although U.S. sales were declining, markets in Asia, Eastern Europe, South America, and Africa offered significant financial opportunities for the industry. International advertising restrictions forced companies to become increasingly sophisticated in their promotional strategies, as well as to rely on new, unregulated media, such as the Internet. If the history of cigarette advertising in the 20th century is any predictor of the future, it clearly suggests that in the 21st century the tobacco industry will adapt, persevere, and remain a vivid testament to the power of advertising.

ERIC H. SHAW AND STUART ALAN

See also American Tobacco Company; Brown & Williamson Tobacco Corporation; Hamlet Cigars; Philip Morris Companies; Product Placement; R.J. Reynolds Tobacco Company; *and color plate in this volume*

Further Reading
Calfee, John E., "The Ghost of Cigarette Advertising Past," *Regulation* 20, no. 3 (Summer 1997)
Glantz, Stanton, et al., *The Cigarette Papers,* Berkeley: University of California Press, 1996
Johnson, Paul R., *The Economics of the Tobacco Industry,* New York: Praeger, 1984
"Joint Tobacco Group Tackles Cancer Fear," *Advertising Age* (4 January 1954)

Kluger, Richard, *Ashes to Ashes: America's Hundred-Year Cigarette War, the Public Health, and the Unabashed Triumph of Philip Morris*, New York: Knopf, 1996

Meyers, William, *The Image-Makers: Power and Persuasion on Madison Avenue*, New York: Times, 1984

Miles, Robert H., *Coffin Nails and Corporate Strategies*, Englewood Cliffs, New Jersey: Prentice-Hall, 1982

Mullen, Chris, *Cigarette Pack Art*, New York: St. Martin's, and London: Hamlyn, 1979

Petrone, Gerard S., *Tobacco Advertising: The Great Seduction*, Atglen, Pennsylvania: Schiffer, 1996

Pollay, Richard W., "The Subsidizing Sizzle: Shifting Strategies in Print Advertising, 1900–1980," *Journal of Marketing* 49, no. 3 (Summer 1985)

Pollay, Richard W., "Filters, Flavors . . . Flim-Flam, Too! On 'Health Information' and Policy Implications in Cigarette Advertising," *Journal of Public Policy and Marketing* 8 (1989)

Pollay, Richard W., "Targeting Tactics in Selling Smoke: Youthful Aspects of 20th Century Cigarette Advertising," *Journal of Marketing Theory and Practices* 3 (Winter 1995)

Sobel, Robert, *They Satisfy: The Cigarette in American Life*, Garden City, New York: Anchor/Doubleday, 1978

Strasser, Susan, *Satisfaction Guaranteed: The Making of the American Mass Market*, New York: Pantheon, 1989

Sullum, Jacob, "Cowboys, Camels, and Kids," *Reason* 29, no.11 (1 April 1998)

Tate, Cassandra, *Cigarette Wars: The Triumph of "The Little White Slaver,"* New York: Oxford University Press, 1999

Citroën

Principal Agencies
Wallace and Draeger
Theo Brugiere
RSCG (later Euro RSCG Works)

The French automobile brand Citroën originated in 1919 when industrialist André-Gustave Citroën converted a World War I munitions factory into an auto plant. Citroën, an engineer trained at France's renowned École Polytechnique, launched the new venture with two core beliefs: first, that assembly-line manufacturing was the only way to produce automobiles that would be accessible to the masses, and second, that advertising and brand recognition would be key to selling these cars.

To meet his technological and industrial objectives, Citroën imported U.S. assembly-line manufacturing methods developed by industry legend Henry Ford, whom he had met during a visit to Detroit, Michigan, in 1912. To promote the new venture, Citroën developed a communication strategy that would set the standard for car companies for the next century.

Citroën placed his first advertisements in the French press early in 1919, before production of the Type A model had even begun at the company's factory on the banks of the river Seine. The half-page ad was product oriented, featuring a drawing of the three-seat Type A, details on optional configurations, and a base sticker price. It also promoted the brand, highlighting the Citroën name and double chevron logo and promising scarcity-plagued consumers "output of 100 cars per day from April 25."

When the company had trouble meeting consumer demand in the early days, Citroën pushed forward with his promotion strategy. He placed detailed, full-page ads throughout the French press, seducing existing and would-be car owners alike with a barrage of technical facts that heaped credibility onto cars that had yet to be produced. In hindsight, industry experts credit Citroën with helping invent "prelaunch" advertising.

Citroën quickly realized that his success would be linked to that of the industry as a whole. Thus, his early mass-circulation print ads from the Paris, France, agency Wallace and Draeger promoted the automobile as a practical and economical form of transport offering the freedom of the open road. The campaigns broke new ground in several respects, from putting a woman behind the wheel of a snazzy convertible to associating Citroën's cars with seemingly contrary adjectives: "Both breadwinner and joy-bringer," read one popular tag line.

While the agency's approach bore fruit, Citroën opted to move advertising in-house in 1920. Pierre Louys, a 24-year-old former medical student, was appointed art and photography director, marking the debut of a decade of revolutionary promotional activities for the company. Louys's arrival saw Citroën redirect advertising toward single-message print ads focusing on product attributes—fuel consumption, comfort—or the prestige of owning a Citroën. Text was pared down, and graphics, headlines, and eye-catching techniques such as the use of white space led the consumer's eye to a basic message and the Citroën logo. Finally, Louys ushered in the lifestyle ad, depicting Citroën models such as the new 10 HP against the backdrop of the countryside or the beach, over tag lines offering the explicit promise of a good time: "Flee the city and savor the pleasures of a trip to the country," read one popular ad used throughout the 1920s.

Having pioneered print advertising, Citroën quickly turned to other means of promotion. In 1922, as the company launched its first budget model, the 5 HP, Citroën paid a stunt pilot to write the company's name in smoke above the famed Champs-Élysées, just hours before the opening of the annual Paris Motor Show.

Citroën also inaugurated a traveling motor show that presented the company's entire range of vehicles in cities, towns, and even villages nationwide. A visit from "La Caravane Citroën," as the traveling show was known, was a major local event, attracting media from across the region as well as the majority of the local population. Most hoped to sit in, and perhaps even drive, one of the new models on display. Thus, the road show was the birth of the no-questions-asked test drive.

Citroën's publicity department closely coordinated the road show. Its executives created ready-to-publish advertising for local print media. Outdoor advertising, from posters to fliers and pamphlet handouts, was used. And in an early form of direct marketing, company officials in Paris sent letters and fliers to existing Citroën owners and prospective customers. Citroën also made use of hidden advertising, instructing local dealers to disguise paid print ads as articles written by journalists. When this practice was contested by some media owners, the company turned to "advertorials," or sponsored pages, to promote the road-show concept, which was later exported to Belgium, Denmark, Italy, Spain, and France's North African colonies.

The 1920s were also a time of massive event marketing. Citroën sponsored the first motorized trip across the Sahara Desert in late 1922, and then capitalized on the feat the following year with a film produced by French cinema leader Léon Gaumont. The company was to copy this promotion several times in the future, sponsoring expeditions across Africa and Asia that later gave birth to the famed Paris-Dakar rally.

Citroën launched its first line of miniature toy cars specifically for children in 1923. A line of pedal cars followed in 1924. Citroën once said he would "see to it that babies' first three words are Mummy, Daddy, Citroën," recognizing before his rivals that children play a role in their parents' decision making and eventually become car owners themselves. During 1924 Citroën also attacked its primary opponent, Renault, in the Paris taxi market, and by year's end it operated a fleet of more than 1,000 yellow cabs—not to make a profit, but rather to develop new word-of-mouth advertising for the brand.

In 1925 Citroën scored its biggest coup, illuminating the famed Eiffel Tower and turning the landmark into the world's largest brand advertisement. Covering the Eiffel Tower with the Citroën name and logo was a massive and costly endeavor, but the promotion, which lasted in various forms until 1934, kept the company's name squarely in the limelight.

Although the Eiffel Tower stunt was the company's most spectacular outdoor promotion, it paled in comparison with Citroën's national leadership in signposting, a public-service activity that saw all major tire and auto manufacturers assume the costs of branded road safety and direction signs. In 1926 the company planted its 100,000th branded road sign in France, a figure that would rise to 165,000 signs across France and its colonies by 1932.

Citroën ushered in the era of celebrity marketing in 1927, inviting aviator Charles Lindbergh to visit the Citroën factory the day after the pilot completed the first solo, nonstop, transatlantic flight. The visit was captured on film by the world's media, as was

This 1919 Citroën ad boasting "Production-100 autos per day beginning April 25" was remarkable in that the vehicles were being marketed even before they had been manufactured. Citroën was the first mass-produced automobile in France.
Courtesy of Citroën, © Citroën Communication.

Lindbergh's declaration—probably prompted—that he was guided to Paris's Le Bourget Airport by Citroën's lights on the Eiffel Tower.

Citroën was among the first to recognize the advertising value of celebrities, inviting singer-dancer Josephine Baker to perform at company galas, tying his promotions to films starring silent-movie legend Charlie Chaplin, and inviting top French politicians to participate in newspaper advertorials.

A new front opened during the 1928–29 period, when Citroën inaugurated glamorous showrooms and service garages in Paris and the provinces that were hailed as models of architecture by critics of the era. The showroom policy, which extended to distributors and service stations across Europe, was managed by house architect Maurice-Jacques Ravaze and was specifically designed to boost Citroën's brand prestige.

The 1930s were not nearly as vibrant an era for Citroën; the Great Depression brought the automaker dwindling sales, crippling strikes, and, finally, bankruptcy. The company was taken over by the tire manufacturer Michelin in 1934. André-Gustave Citroën immediately retired from the car business; he died the following year at the age of 57.

By the 1950s Citroën was focusing its advertising on its technological sophistication; this 1959 print ad highlighted Citroën's hydro-pneumatic suspension, which eventually replaced the springs used on virtually every other make of auto.
Courtesy of Citroën, © Citroën Communication.

Concerned with Citroën's unstable finances, Michelin vowed to do away with all nonessential expenses, starting with advertising. Sales of new models soared, however, pushed by André-Gustave Citroën's last design, the Citroën Traction. Ensuing political uncertainty and World War II put the company in limbo until the 1948 unveiling of the economy compact 2CV. Advertising for the car was minimal, limited to posters from the Theo Brugiere agency and technical brochures created in-house.

The 1955 launch of another Citroën classic, the elongated DS, brought in a fresh era of advertising, managed by a new marketing director, Claude Puech. Disgusted by Citroën's existing advertising, Puech looked abroad for inspiration, finding a model in the art-heavy approach of Italian tire manufacturer Olivetti as well as in a relatively new medium: television.

Puech ran the first Citroën television commercials in the late 1950s. He brought in celebrated photographers Robert Doisneau and Pierre Jahan for high-profile DS campaigns. And he approved poster campaigns from The Netherlands designed by graphic artist Karel Suyling, a 2CV fanatic. The success of Suyling's early work, marked by a pure, elegant, and modern style, launched him on a 20-year collaboration with Citroën that would see him create more than 200 ads.

The company entered an advertising renaissance in 1960, when Puech hired avant-garde publisher Robert Delpire to produce an in-house magazine, *Le Double Chevron*, intended for dealers. Delpire Publicité hired legendary photographers such as Henri Cartier-Bresson and Marc Riboud from the Magnum agency, ordering them to shoot Citroën's cars from new angles and in original contexts. This approach gave way over the ensuing decade to a series of exceptional brochures and catalogs for the 2CV and DS that were loaded with beautiful art and photography and remain collector's items to this day.

The advent of international competition in the 1970s led Citroën to greater reliance on sales-oriented press and television advertising. Advertising also suffered from a 1976 change in ownership, when Michelin sold the car company to its leading French rival, Peugeot. The changes saw Delpire sell his agency to RSCG, a young upstart that was the predecessor to the Havas Advertising–owned agency Euro RSCG Worldwide.

The Citroën account fell into the hands of Jacques Seguela, a Citroën devotee who had driven a 2CV around the world in 1958, written a best-selling book about the exploit, and worked with Delpire and Puech on the company's advertising. Seguela was well placed to take on the account but saw only mixed results until 1980, when a new marketing director, Georges Falconnet, gave him carte blanche to differentiate the brand from its competitors.

RSCG convinced Citroën to dedicate 15 percent of ad spending to brand promotion. This led to a highly acclaimed poster campaign from artist Raymond Savignac and one of the decade's most memorable TV spots: wild horses running across the desert in the formation of Citroën's double chevron logo.

Seguela next asked French President Francois Mitterand—for whom he handled political advertising—to "loan" RSCG an aircraft carrier and a nuclear submarine for an outlandish ad for the

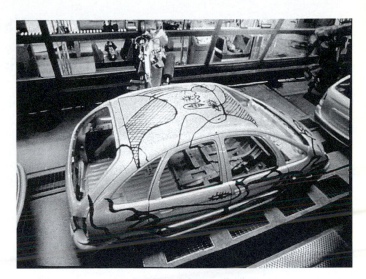

In a major celebrity endorsement coup, Citroën in the 1990s obtained the rights to name its new model the Picasso.
Courtesy of Citroën, © Citroën Communication.

Visa GTI. He rolled an AX across the Great Wall of China and into a revered Tibetan monastery. And he brought back celebrity advertising, placing pop singer Grace Jones in a series of spots for the CX2.

A sales slowdown in the early 1990s saw Seguela create a new division, Euro RSCG Scher Lenoir Lafarge, dedicated specifically to Citroën advertising. Campaigns in the mid-1990s for the AX and Xantia models, based around the now-classic "Nothing moves you like a Citroën" tag line, won rave reviews. So did new celebrity advertising, such as that featuring supermodel Claudia Schiffer in a filmed crash-test ad for the Xsara compact.

The departure of Gilbert Scher and Christophe Lafarge in 1999 saw Seguela form a new division, Euro RSCG Works, to launch Citroën's first model of the new millennium, a compact minivan named, at Seguela's prompting, after the artist Pablo Picasso. Citroën paid an undisclosed, but reportedly massive, fee for use of the name and the right to associate the car with his artwork. Prelaunch advertising depicted Picasso looking off into the distance, while a caption in a child's handwriting asked, "Mummy, why's that man got the same name as the car?" Although some critics deemed this commercial use of the Picasso legacy tasteless, consumers voted with their pocketbooks, pushing demand far beyond Citroën's production capacity. In the wake of this success, Citroën marketing executives justified the cost of acquiring the Picasso name as a relatively cost-effective means of achieving global brand recognition.

Rather than duplicate the Picasso affair, Citroën planned to base future product launches around the once-popular practice of using coded numerical names reminiscent of signature models such as the AX, the BX, the 2CV, or the classic DS. The back-to-the-future approach would allow Citroën to scale back its $200 million global ad spending of 2000 while advancing sales beyond the million-unit mark.

LAWRENCE J. SPEER

CKS Group

(USWeb/CKS; MarchFirst, Inc.)

Founded as CKS Partners by Bill Cleary, Mark Kvamme, and Tom Suiter in Campbell, California, 1991; incorporated as CKS Group, 1994; merged with two extensions of the CKS brand—CKS Pictures and CKS Interactive, January 1998; CKS Partners merged with USWeb Corporation to form USWeb/CKS, 1998; USWeb/CKS merged with Whittman-Hart, 1999; renamed MarchFirst, Inc., March 2000; declared bankruptcy and went out of business, 2001.

Major Clients
Apple Computer
Levi Strauss & Company
MCI WorldCom
Microsoft Corporation
United Air Lines

In 1991 three former executives of Apple Computer—Bill Cleary, Mark Kvamme, and Tom Suiter—formed CKS Partners in Campbell, California. In so doing they created a new breed of advertising and marketing agency that combined creative skills with new technology to take advantage of the emerging new-media environment. CKS Partners pioneered what became known as "interactive advertising," combining advertising and e-commerce with the capabilities of personal computers. By the end of the decade, that combination had become an almost required facet of any traditional ad agency. CKS was among the first shops to be named interactive agency of record for many of its clients.

CKS revolutionized traditional advertising by opening new channels of production, design, and delivery of its campaigns via technology. In December 1995, the agency, incorporated as CKS Group, went public with one of the first initial public offerings (IPOs) in its segment of the industry. In 1998 CKS Group merged with the Internet services company USWeb of Santa Clara, California, to form USWeb/CKS. In December 1999, business-to-business Internet services provider Whittman-Hart, Inc., of Chicago, Illinois, acquired USWeb/CKS, and the combined shop became the largest Internet professional services company of its kind, with 9,000 employees worldwide and, the following year, a new name: MarchFirst, Inc.

The three founders of CKS Partners first met as executives at Apple Computer in the mid-1980s. Kvamme was an internal hardware manager for the Apple IIc, Cleary a consumer marketing manager, and Suiter a creative director for the computer giant. Kvamme, CKS Partners' president-chief executive officer (CEO) and later chairman-CEO of CKS Group, was only 29 when he cofounded CKS Partners, but the successful ad agency was not his first major business endeavor. Kvamme, it has been said, was born with a "silicon spoon" in his mouth. His father's connections in the Silicon Valley, an area just south of San Fran-

cisco, California, that is considered the birthplace of U.S. high technology, helped Kvamme get a job with Apple in 1980 when he was a freshman at the University of California at Berkeley. Kvamme's task at Apple was to help iron out early problems with the new Apple II computer, which taught him programming skills he later applied to agency work. He subsequently went to Europe to study and helped to launch Apple France at age 21. He returned to work as a hardware manager for Apple in 1983 but later that year quit to begin his own company, International Solutions, which developed computer hardware for foreign consumers. At the same time he completed his studies at Berkeley in 1984. In late 1985, his growing company dissolved as the personal computer market crashed. For the next three years, Kvamme took on several endeavors to pay off his debts to investors in his failed company—the biggest to Apple cofounder Steve Wozniac—by creating and marketing the "Cellular Phoney," a popular fake cellular phone. He also held management positions at Pillar Corporation and Wyse Technology.

In 1989 Kvamme rejoined former Apple acquaintance Cleary, who had been employed at International Solutions and in 1987 had created an eponymous marketing company. Kvamme bought a 50 percent share of the company to create Cleary & Kvamme, in Campbell, the forerunner of CKS Partners, with the intention of adding advertising and product packaging to the company's existing capabilities. In 1991 the two were joined by Suitor, who came from a position as a creative director at San Francisco's Landor Associates, a corporate identity consultancy.

CKS Partners was set up to be a one-stop shop: an agency that combined traditional advertising and media placement with product design, corporate identity solutions, and multimedia content for technology and nontechnology-oriented clients. Kvamme had a vision to bring new efficiencies to marketing. Technology companies were cutting their normal product development cycles in half to rapidly roll out new products. They needed marketing strategies that would integrate with newly available advertising media such as CD-ROMs, the Internet, and the World Wide Web. To Kvamme, the way to accomplish these efficiencies was through a great investment in new technology, including personal computers for every employee and skilled programmers to create the software and applications to drive their enhanced design needs. The advertising industry was slow to accept these changes, but as CKS Partners began to capitalize on the new advances, the industry began to take notice.

CKS Partners was named the largest ad agency in Silicon Valley by a San Jose, California, newspaper in 1993. Executives from traditional agency backgrounds disputed that ranking, claiming that less than half of CKS's $44 million in billings came from traditional media-based advertising; the rest came from new media services and consulting fees. Kvamme, in response, said, "The agencies that just do advertising are dead. Evolve or face the music." Computers had begun to change the way agencies did business. They allowed for new ways to create and review campaigns as well as new methods to deliver ads to their intended media vehicle through complex computer networks and the ability to "push" data through phone lines.

CKS, however, did not work only for California-based software companies in its early years. In the second half of 1992, United Airlines chose the shop to handle an image overhaul that encompassed everything from its logo to its ticket counters. CKS utilized new technologies pushed to their limits, as it had only six months in which to design and implement the new blue and gray look for United. In early 1993, CKS partnered with BBDO Worldwide in what was referred to by an Apple spokeswoman as an "equally important" role in rolling out Apple Computer's Newton MessagePad hand-held digital assistant. As Kvamme described the agencies' interrelationship to *Advertising Age*, "BBDO's job is to create a shopper. Our goal is to turn a shopper into a buyer." CKS helped with Newton's packaging and created in-store displays and brochures. The shop also developed a 90-second digital in-store demonstration of a MessagePad written by CKS programmers.

In 1994 the partners incorporated under the name CKS Group, with headquarters in Cupertino, California, and offices in Campbell; San Francisco; Portland, Oregon; and London, England. The company began operating 24 hours a day, seven days a week to maintain a data center and their clients' Web sites. It designed and implemented Web sites and integrated marketing campaigns for Microsoft Corporation, McDonald's Corporation, General Motors Corporation, Clinique Laboratories, Inc., and Prudential Insurance Company of America.

In November 1994, the agency began the first of several large projects for MCI Telecommunications, Inc., to develop and maintain a new on-line service, internetMCI. Later, in May 1996, CKS began a campaign to introduce MCI One—an integrated communications service that provided customers with services ranging from long distance to the Internet for a flat fee—with packaging, a Web site, direct mail, and after-market services, as well as the company's corporate Web site.

At the beginning of 1995, CKS Group caught the eye of the Interpublic Group of Companies, an agency holding company. Interpublic invested heavily in CKS, then valued at approximately $20 million, and came away with a minority stake and a means to advance the integration of its own technological aspirations. CKS in turn gained access to Interpublic's considerable resources. The deal caught the attention of other investors, and CKS began an IPO in December 1995 at a valuation that had exploded to more than $200 million. Interpublic in 1996 sold back many of its shares, keeping a 20 percent stake. CKS's successful IPO inspired a revolution of similar considerations for some of its contemporaries such as Interpublic's Poppe Tyson and True North Communications' TN Technologies.

After CKS went public, it began pursuing a program of acquisitions beginning in August 1996 with New York City advertising agency Schell/Mullaney, Inc., and continuing with another New York City shop, Donovan & Green, Inc., and Raleigh, North Carolina's McKinney & Silver, both in January 1997. In March of that year, CKS purchased both Electronische Publikationen GmbH of Germany and Gormley & Partners, Inc., of Greenwich, Connecticut, followed by another interactive ad agency, SiteSpecific, Inc., in June 1997.

Acquisition of outside companies proved a popular trend for a while among integrated marketing companies, which could increase resources and revenue more quickly through acquisitions than by building from within. But in November 1997 CKS Group announced fourth-quarter earnings for that year would remain significantly below expectations; as a result, investors began to abandon the company, and its stock dropped to an all-time low. The company explained the disappointment as the result of accounting methods that relied heavily on expected future projects, making valuation hard to pinpoint. Investors, however, feared that the company had gotten too caught up in an industry not yet come of age.

At the beginning of 1998 CKS's creative reputation was still riding high, as the agency tallied more 1997 Web awards from the Web Marketing Association than any other interactive agency, including three Best of Industry Web Awards and five Outstanding Web Site awards for a number of clients. Later that year CKS won an assignment from Levi Strauss & Company to set up its first e-commerce endeavor that would allow customers to purchase products on-line. It was one of CKS's final endeavors as an independent company.

In September 1998 CKS Group reached an agreement with another Internet-consulting pioneer, USWeb, of Santa Clara, California. In a stock swap valued at $300 million, the two businesses merged, forming USWeb/CKS. While each company brought to the merger resources the other lacked, analysts warned that the differing corporate cultures would be hard to meld. USWeb, fresh from its own acquisition track, wanted to establish itself as a large Web architecture company but needed CKS's creative skills; CKS needed USWeb's technological resources to win and retain larger clients. The combined company had more than 1,800 employees in more than 50 offices in six countries. USWeb's chief executive officer, Joe Firmage, became CEO of the newly merged company, while Kvamme became chairman, and Toby Corey moved from president-chief operating officer of USWeb to those same titles at the merged company.

USWeb/CKS proved the viability of its merger when it landed the account of kitchenware marketer Williams-Sonoma, which began its search for an interactive agency while the two companies were in their merger process. The marketer needed a company large enough to meet its aggressive plans for expansion on the Web. USWeb/CKS created a wedding registry site for the company and, a year later, an entire on-line store.

In November 1998 the company recruited Robert Shaw, the executive vice president for Oracle Corporation's Worldwide Consulting Services. Shaw took over as CEO from Firmage, who moved to the new position of chief strategist until leaving the company with Corey in January 1999. Kvamme relinquished his post as chairman later that year to become a partner in the venture capitalist firm Sequoia Capital; he remained on USWeb/CKS's board. Shaw continued to try to meld the 47 different businesses

USWeb and CKS had made in the preceding four years. These acquisitions allowed USWeb/CKS to maintain its number-one position in Internet consulting.

In December 1999 Shaw found himself at the helm of a company—now with 4,000 employees in 13 countries—preparing to merge with business-to-business technology consultant Whittman-Hart, Inc., led by President-CEO Robert Bernard. The merged company claimed combined revenue of $991.8 billion in 1999, with 9,000 employees in 70-plus offices worldwide, making it the largest consultancy devoted entirely to the Internet. On 1 March 2000, the venture announced its new name, MarchFirst, Inc.

The idea behind the merger was to combine USWeb/CKS's creative, e-commerce, and emerging applications service provider (ASP) business with Whittman-Hart's sound back-end legacy systems expertise and mid-size business customers. A successful merger was dependent on a sound economy still fueled by growth of dot-com businesses as well as retaining staff.

One month after the merger's completion, Shaw abandoned the new entity, resigning his position to launch his own venture capital firm. Bernard was left at the helm of a company that was exploding with opportunity but that faced a major challenge: how to meet expectations that its massive size and talent could integrate its complex systems and marketing strategies in record time for several hundred clients all at once. In its first several months, MarchFirst took on more than 1,500 clients looking for Internet professional services. Clients included several dot-com companies seeking to catch the wave of the Internet, as well as established brands such as FAO Schwarz, which looked to MarchFirst to revamp its on-line store, fao.com.

Despite strong early projections, by November 2000 it seemed that the company was not reaching its intended goals. MarchFirst's stock had dropped nearly 100 percent since the day it began, to just over a dollar; the company cited too much dependency on dot-com clients. Bernard, who had become the chairman-CEO, was forced to lay off a considerable portion of MarchFirst's employees. Bernard declared a change in strategy that included building tighter and more strategic relationships with MarchFirst's key clients, and cutting contracts with more than 1,000 mostly dot-com companies to focus on top clients. In April 2001, MarchFirst filed for protection from creditors under Chapter 11 of the U.S. bankruptcy code. Subsequently, it was liquidated.

MEGAN CASSADA

Further Reading

Andrews, Whit, "USWeb-CKS Face Challenges in Merging Businesses," *Information Week* (7 Sept 1998)

Angwin, Julia, "CKS Acquires High-Tech Ad Company," *San Francisco Chronicle* (11 November 1997)

Cuneo, Alice Z., "High-Tech CKS Sees beyond Media Ads; Agency 'Evolves' into Other Forms of Communication," *Advertising Age* (13 September 1993)

Cuneo, Alice Z., "Mark Kvamme," *Advertising Age* (17 April 2000)

Donaton, Scott, "Peacock Net Taps CKS As Fledging Interactive Shop" *Advertising Age* 65, no. 40 (26 September 1994)

Elgin, Ben, "Merger Turns Bulls into Bears," *Sm@rt Reseller* 2, no. 33 (20 December 1999)

Evangelista, Benny, "Internet Pioneers Merging: USWeb, CKS Group in $300 Million Deal," *San Francisco Chronicle* (3 September 1998)

Gottesman, Alan, "CKS Group's Bonanza: The Interactive Ad Shop Has the Cash—and Imitators: Now What?" *Adweek* (1 April 1996)

Greenberg, Herb, "Why CKS Group Stock Was a Disaster Waiting to Happen: Analysts Saw Hints of Trouble in Accounting," *News and Observer* (Raleigh, North Carolina) (12 November 1997)

Hayes, Mary, "Mark Kvamme: Connections Helped, but Success Is Self-Earned," *Business Journal* 10, no. 15 (27 July 1992)

Johnson, Bradley, "New Links for Telecommunications," *Advertising Age* (13 September 1993)

Johnson, Bradley, "CKS Touts Technology over Creative," *Advertising Age* (25 April 1994)

Johnson, Bradley, and Alice Z. Cuneo, "Here's Newton, but No Ad Blitz; Low-Key Intro Paving the Road for Integrated Campaign," *Advertising Age* (30 August 1993)

Nee, Eric, "An E-Consultant Cleans Up Its Room: After 47 Acquisitions in Four Years, USWeb/CKS Is Growing Up; That's Good, Now That Its Clients Are Old-World Types Like Chevron and Sears," *New York Times* (29 November 2000)

Obermayer, Joel, "Ad Execs Claim CKS Doesn't Spell Panic" *Raleigh News & Observer* (12 November 1997)

Rogers, Amy, and Jerry Rosa, "A Marriage of Convenience—USWeb/CKS-Whittman-Hart Merger Creates Soup-to-Nuts, Web Integration Powerhouse," *Computer Reseller News* (17 April 2000)

Wilder, Clinton, "Deal Helps USWeb Reinvent Itself," *Computer Reseller News* (17 April 2000)

Williamson, Debra Aho, "Williams-Sonoma Spearheads Efforts for the Housewares Marketers," *Advertising Age* (26 July 1999)

Willis, Clint, "Try, Try Again (Young High-Technology Entrepreneurs' Transitions from Failure to Success)," *Forbes* 159, no. 11 (2 June 1997)

Classified Advertising

In a sense, classified, or "want," advertising has existed almost since humans learned to communicate and express needs that they could not fulfill themselves. Classified ads continue to provide an important source of revenue for daily newspapers even as these types of ads move increasingly into specialized newspapers and magazines and onto the Internet.

Ads and Print: Early Link

In the late 1430s Johannes Gutenberg's invention of movable type opened up a new world for those who wished to disseminate information to the general public. Prior to 1441 signs, small notices, and criers constituted all the media available. The first ad in English appeared in 1477. The first ad in an English newspaper was printed in 1625 in *Mercurius Britannicus* and concerned the publication of a book. The term *advertising* was introduced in 1655. By 1704 the first U.S. newspaper began carrying advertisements.

In the earliest days, the most prevalent forms of small ads—similar to those today termed *classified*—were of a personal nature. For instance, in May of 1658, England's *Mercurius Politicus* featured an ad for a runaway servant, listing the items she had allegedly stolen from her employer's home. A major difference between newspaper advertising at its beginning and today is that at first newspapers were, for the most part, the only advertising medium. In 1682 a London newspaper, the *City Mercury*, displayed a list of articles for sale: coal, masks, leather, painted sticks, and quills. The editor of this publication, John Houghton, was the first to advocate that a newspaper should include a variety of features and not merely print the news.

Much of colonial American advertising, by today's standards, would actually come under the heading of classified pieces. The third issue of the *Boston News Letter* (the first American newspaper, founded in 1704) carried the first known paid ads in the colonies—appearing on the back page under "Advertisements." These included offerings of real estate for sale. While a good many of the ads in colonial newspapers concerned commerce, competitions (contests), and public events, many looked very much like modern-day "classifieds." Often the phraseology was extremely clever; the majority of these ads were labeled "highly personal." There were ads seeking "lost" husbands and requesting the return of borrowed books. A man whose wife had left him submitted an ad notifying the general public that he was not accountable for her debts. A May 1704 ad in the *Boston News Letter*—offering real estate for sale or rent in Oyster Bay, Long Island, New York—was more like today's classifieds than any of its predecessors.

Richard Steele's English newspaper the *Tatler* distributed 3,000 copies of its first issue in April 1709. Its circulation rose to about 4,000 in a short time. This meant that advertisers had a potentially large audience, and the newspaper took advantage of it. The ads included personals, houses for sale or rent, dry goods for sale, book and play announcements, and notices of financial schemes seeking investors. In addition, long lists of articles both lost and stolen were always present—usually, offering rewards with "no questions asked."

In 1710 the *Tatler* devoted an entire issue to advertising, including a discussion that gave the word new meaning. Up until then, *advertisement* meant any kind of notice; henceforth, the Tatler would use the term to refer only to business announcements.

In 1729 Benjamin Franklin, often considered the "father of American advertising," began publishing his newspaper, the *Pennsylvania Gazette*. His journal soon boasted the largest circulation and the largest advertising volume of any newspaper in the American colonies. There were ads for ship sailings and for quills, books, wine, tea, chocolate, and many other commodities. It was Franklin who began the practice of using white space to separate each ad from its neighbors. He also initiated the use of a large heading for each ad. In addition, he is thought to be the first American to use illustrations to promote a product. Ads for real estate and notices of ship sailings were the two largest categories that used such illustrations.

Ships for sale and notices of those sailing were among the most numerous classified-like ads in colonial America. They were particularly common in newspapers in coastal cities and seaports. By midcentury these ads were using cuts depicting the type of vessel spoken of in the ad.

Wants ads were not uncommon, however. On page one of the *New York Gazette* for 13 January 1763, a middle-aged woman advertised for a job performing housework, indicating that she "can be well recommended as to her honesty." A few months later, there appeared in the same paper, on page three of the 3 March 1763 issue, a "Wants a Place" ad submitted by a wet nurse who was also "well recommended." The *Pennsylvania Evening Post* and the *Virginia Gazette* each printed the Declaration of Independence on 6 July 1776 and 20 July 1776, respectively. Want ads were included in the same editions.

Between 1775 and 1875 both men and women placed small matrimonial messages in American and English newspapers. While some discussed friendship, others mentioned marriage right up front. By 1776 London alone boasted 53 newspapers, many of which provided a medium for advertising. The *Times* of London, founded by John Walter, devoted the entire front page of its first (1 January 1788) issue to advertising. This practice continued until relatively recent times.

The evolution of classified ads can be followed in the *Times* of London. In the late 1780s advertisements of all sorts were on the first page of the paper. The messages included announcements of dramatic presentations in local theaters and advertisements for various products ranging from "medical" wares to haberdashery, drapery, and hosiery. In addition, there appeared requests for the return of lost goods and marriage and death notices. These followed one another in no particular order, leaving to interested parties the task of searching and reading almost

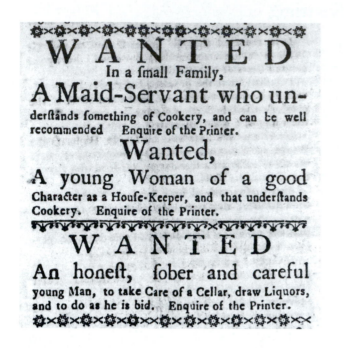

The *Boston (Weekly) News Letter* was among the first American papers to run paid ads. The classified advertisements shown appeared in the 9 June 1768 edition.
Courtesy: Rare Book, Manuscript, and Special Collections Library, Duke University.

everything, even if looking for only one thing in particular. Within 50 years, however, there appeared specific "Wants" columns, both for those looking for positions and for those looking for someone to fill positions. While there were still death notices and special announcements, as well as theater schedules and for-sale listings, these appeared gathered together under the appropriate heading. Thus, the reader could readily find an item of particular interest.

By the time the American colonies had become the United States, there were 30 newspapers throughout the country. The ads carried by these publications, like those appearing in their English counterparts, were mostly what one would describe as "classified"; newspapers represented the largest class of media in the early 20th century. In personals ads people did not hesitate to ask for exactly what they wanted, whether it be a job, a companion, or simply money. By 1789 New York City's *Independent Gazette* was running as many as 34 "classifieds"—that is, small ads similar to what would today be called classifieds.

Evolving Form

As the 18th century came to an end, London's *Morning Herald* was going so far as to classify its "Wants" columns by category— "Want Places," "Sales by Auction," "To Be Sold," and "To Be Lett"—while cooks, servants, housemaids, teachers, coachmen, and ladies' maids offered their services in shorter advertisements. Virtually all of London's newspapers were replete with advertising.

In America advertising became a part of newspaper publications almost from the beginning. By 1800 most English and American newspapers were not only supported by advertising but were the primary medium carrying it. As with the English newspapers, the front pages of the Boston, New York, and Philadelphia newspapers consisted of relatively small, classified-like ads. The back page was often filled with ads as well, and there were others on page three (these journals usually comprised only four pages total).

As of 1790 there were 106 newspapers in the colonies; by 1800 the number had increased to 260, serving a population of more than 5 million. By 1820 there were 532 newspapers, providing reading for a population of about 9.5 million—and more than 1,000 other journals had been started and shuttered. For the most part, these were weekly newspapers, with three to four columns devoted to news and some editorial comment while the rest of the publication consisted of advertising.

In 1833 the *Penny Press* came on the scene and began charging for the small classified-like ads. That same year Benjamin H. Day founded the *New York Sun*. He became the first publisher to hire people to contact advertising prospects.

Most advertisements looked more like today's display ads— before the modern classified-like system was developed in the early 1800s with illustrations placed above the copy. In 1835 James Gordon Bennett, founder of the New York *Morning Herald*, chose to classify each ad type in rows with an appropriate cut illustration, for example, a ship for all shipping notices.

The *Philadelphia Public Ledger* is said to have invented "modern" classified advertising shortly after the U.S. Civil War (circa 1865). Essentially, it was the first to promote this type of advertising as a special department. The first time the column heading "Wants" is known to have appeared is in the *New York Herald* on 8 January 1836. Thus, to some extent, this publication gained a foothold in classifieds.

In the early days of newspapers—just as at present—the want ad afforded the individual an opportunity to carry a message to the masses at a relatively small cost. "Auction Sales" and "Marine Intelligence" (sailing times, etc.) were the first classifications most editors adopted, although "Amusements" were also generally grouped. Then came categories such as "Commercial Advertisement" and "Houses."

By 1842 the idea of actually "classifying" ads into various categories had made considerable progress. The following are the categories mostly in use at the time: Perfumery; Hotels; Boarding; Oculists; Medical; Miscellaneous; China, Glass, and Earthenware; Dentistry; Regular Packets, Railroads, and Steamboats; Books; and Stationery. Medical classifieds were usually the biggest category, but they were often fraudulent, many of them offering nothing more than the products of quackery.

Between 1839 and 1844, a cut illustration, two type-lines high, was placed to the right of the ad. In 1848 the use of illustrations in classifieds disappeared. In the 1850s newspapers introduced white space around ads, allowing classified buyers to purchase blank space to make their message stand out among the crowd.

The 20th Century and Beyond

Nonpersonal classified ads of the 20th century generally fall into one of five major categories: employment, automobiles, real estate, rentals, and merchandise. Overall, the classified ad form accounts for as much as 40 percent of a newspaper's income. For years classifieds have cushioned newspapers from drops in revenue from other ad categories.

During World War II, "help-wanted" advertising increased dramatically as men left their employment to enter the armed forces. This left a tremendous number of jobs that needed to be filled. During July of 1943, for instance, the *Chicago Tribune* noted that such ads had swelled its classified section to the point where 51 percent of the newsprint consumed that month had been used to print the classified ads.

This increase in help-wanted ads presented the *Tribune* with a double-edged sword: because of the war, newsprint was at a premium; yet the Chicago newspaper wished to maintain its dominance as a classified medium. The solution combined switching to a nine-column format and using smaller type. Not only did this solution address the two aforementioned considerations, it actually increased the average number of revenue lines per column by 20 percent.

Although analysts are not sure why, from the later 1960s to the late 1980s, classifieds tended to maintain their strength when other advertising categories lagged. In 1989, however, classified ads suffered a severe decline, falling from a growth rate of 10.1 percent in 1988 to one of only 2.8 percent, a rate well below that of inflation.

By the early 1970s want ads had come under sharp attack for gender discrimination, mostly against women (Pittsburgh Press Company v. Pittsburgh Commission on Human Relations, U.S. Supreme Court, 1973). At this time newspapers began eliminating the gender-specific column labels "Jobs—Male Interest" and "Jobs—Female Interest" from the help-wanted ads. Today, the two major categories of advertising in newspapers are classified and display. Classifieds constitute a major part of a newspaper publisher's income—approximately 27 percent of all newspaper revenue.

In *Principles and Practices of Classified Advertising*, Ken Harrington refers to classifieds as "the people's marketplace." They are the only type of advertising the average person can buy on a line or word basis at reasonable cost. No particular knowledge or training in the art of printing is needed—although care should be taken in writing the text—so classifieds are the easiest type of advertising. One can go to the newspaper office or telephone, and an ad-taker writes and schedules the ad; the whole process takes just a few minutes.

Since newspapers derive a large portion of their revenues from classified ads, it is no surprise that publishers are wary of the competition provided by the new electronic information services. However, evidence shows that newspapers—because they can, on a daily basis, advertise in their own electronic services—are greatly helped by technology. This is but one of the newspaper's advantages over competing forms of classified media.

Besides the benefits of being able to keep their services in the forefront in their own journals, newspapers have additional advantages. A big operation has a classified staff to help process and generate orders on a daily basis—whereas, for instance, directories of Yellow Pages traditionally have sold their listings on a yearly basis. Want ads, covering all sorts of human "wants" and "needs" today, are basically similar to those of yesteryear.

The different categories of classifieds can appear in any order in a given newspaper. Some newspapers list them in the order of their strength; others place the less-used classifications, for example, announcements, up front; still others use the order their readers are most accustomed to.

Then, within each classification, ads are placed in a particular order. While the oldest method is by size, another approach is to put them in numerical order, which is extremely useful in the case of rental classifieds, where a reader is interested in the location of the property involved. Still another method is in alphabetical order, which has proved to be a good way to list jobs because it makes various occupations easy to find.

According to Vicki Liepelt, classified systems manager for the *Chicago Tribune* during the 1990s, most people still preferred print when looking for a job, car, apartment, or real estate. Over the last ten years of the 20th century, consumers became more savvy and looked for information before making a buying decision. While they still use the classified print products to help them in their search, there are a growing number who are using both print and the Internet, or just the Internet.

The Internet classified scene had changed a great deal by the year 2000; initially, it needed "content" to draw consumers. So some newspapers posted some or all of their classified newspaper ads on the World Wide Web at no additional cost to the advertiser. As Internet usage began to increase, many people became willing to pay to have their ad on the Internet. As of the year 2000, some newspapers were charging an additional fee to post these ads.

While the introduction of web ads has not decreased the number of print ads, it may have slowed the growth of the latter. Nevertheless, newspapers are still the stiffest competition for web ads because they have years of experience and expertise in their corner. Nevertheless, electronic classifieds continue to grow in popularity and in the number of advertisers served by this medium.

Help-wanted ads experienced ups and downs during the mid-1990s, but by the year 2000 things evened out. Real estate, auto, and job ads accounted for a great deal of the Internet's classified business. The *Chicago Tribune* had most of its classified content on the net, including cars, help wanted, real estate, rentals, and merchandise.

Millions of people peruse the classifieds regularly to find work, household help, shelter, or transportation. That audience makes the small ads a potent medium no matter the form in which they are presented.

SAMMY R. DANNA

Further Reading
Barrow, Robert Mangum, "Newspaper Advertising in Colonial America, 1704–1775," Ph.D. diss., University of Virginia, 1967
Dunn, Samuel Watson, *Advertising: Its Role in Modern Marketing*, New York: Holt Rinehart and Winston, 1961; 8th edition, by Dean M. Krugman et al., Fort Worth, Texas: Dryden Press, 1994
Grogan, Marge, editor, *Classified Telephone Selling*, Lafayette, Indiana: MacDonald, 1980
Kleppner, Otto, *Advertising Procedure*, New York: Prentice-Hall, 1925; 14th edition, as *Kleppner's Advertising Procedure*, by J.

Thomas Russell and W. Ronald Lane, Upper Saddle River, New Jersey: Prentice Hall, 1999
Presbrey, Frank, *The History and Development of Advertising*, Garden City, New York: Doubleday, 1929; reprint, New York: Greenwood Press, 1968
Sutphen, Richard, *The Mad Old Ads*, Minneapolis, Minnesota: Sutphen Studio, 1966
Towle, Felix S., editor, *Encyclopedia of Classified Advertising*, New York: Association of Newspaper Classified Advertising Managers, 1947
Wood, James Playsted, *The Story of Advertising*, New York: Ronald Press, 1958

Cliché

Some of the largest advertisers in the world—in particular such packaged-goods marketers as the Procter & Gamble Company and Unilever—produce some of the most formulaic advertising. This type of advertising, all too familiar to regular TV viewers and newspaper readers, includes such time-worn devices as split-screen comparisons of laundry detergents, scenes of women cheerfully immersed in household chores, and before-and-after demonstrations of hair-care products. Marketers of such products justify the clichéd quality of their advertising with voluminous research suggesting that a straightforward focus on the functional efficacy of their products results in increased sales.

Advertising clichés are not confined to the packaged-goods market. Indeed, narrative conventions that help to distinguish advertising as a genre of communication occur frequently across most product categories. A typical clichéd commercial establishes a problem at the outset, then resolves it with the timely appearance of the advertised product. Critics of advertising have charged the industry with encouraging and reproducing stereotypical, clichéd, and banal images. Others—in particular sociologist Michael Schudson—have argued that advertising, as a particular kind of language, is inherently clichéd; that is, advertising must use stereotypical images and hackneyed phrases not so much to reproduce a dominant ideology as to reduce it to a kind of social shorthand to communicate effectively. Schudson calls advertising "capitalist realism," drawing a parallel with the artistic style known as socialist realism, the official state-sponsored style of the former Soviet Union. He argues that advertising shares several programmatic characteristics with socialist realism, among them the objective of picturing "reality in simplified and typified ways so that it communicates effectively to the masses," and showing this reality "not in its individuality but only as it reveals larger social significance." The effect of such requirements is to eliminate contingency and eccentricity from advertising imagery.

Schudson offers the example of the "Reach out and touch someone" campaign created by N.W. Ayer & Son in 1979 for the AT&T Corporation. Searching for locations to shoot the ads, Ayer's staff sought not just actual homes, but homes that would look "real"—in other words, stereotypical.

These principles operate even in more narrowly targeted media, such as cable television and the Internet. Here, many argue, the increasingly pressing requirements of brevity and concision, together with the need to achieve emotional resonance with the target audience, are more likely to produce technical innovation than originality in content. This is because the content of an advertising message, regardless of its specific audience, must nonetheless function as a kind of cultural shorthand that can be assimilated speedily. The size of media budgets in markets such as the United States also tends to make advertisers risk averse when it comes to content, directing their attention to media-buying clout rather than the originality of their messages.

To break through the clutter and establish credibility, some advertising for style-led product categories—such as designer clothing and fragrances—has rebelled, particularly since the 1980s, against the conventions of advertising. Such efforts as Calvin Klein Cosmetic Company's TV campaign for its Obsession fragrance dispensed with even a mention of the product other than a voice-over of the word Obsession. The idea was to construct a resonant, atmospheric brand identity. Ironically, the very abstraction of these spots struck many observers as a sign of the insubstantiality of the commercials' claims, leading their ethereal tone to be parodied humorously in subsequent campaigns from other marketers. Visa tried a similar approach in its "Identity" campaign in which store clerks failed to recognize well-known celebrities who lacked proper identification. Through mocking the pretensions of "non-ad" ads, these parody spots reestablished a more conventional link to advertising as sincere.

market perceived to be "media savvy" and resistant to formulaic approaches. In the United Kingdom a spot for Peugeot automobiles self-consciously referenced a highly popular Heineken beer commercial, and U.S. television has seen the Energizer bunny humorously used in ads for fictional products that at first glance appear to be selling those products—but in reality are selling batteries.

Nostalgia is another mode in which advertising has knowingly played on the conventions of a genre, particularly through pastiche and the recycling of domestic images from the 1950s. From a present-day perspective, these images carry an almost delirious innocence and optimism that, when transplanted into 21st century advertising, evoke a peculiarly postmodern blend of irony and longing.

The increased self-consciousness with which some campaigns refer to advertising clichés is in part motivated by the need to encourage stronger consumer involvement with brands. An ironic approach to advertising's own clichés has become one way for marketers to provide instantaneous intelligibility to address the strategic need for building a higher consumer involvement with a brand.

WILLIAM MAZZARELLA

By associating raisins with memories of childhood, Sun-Maid capitalized on nostalgia, a clichéd, albeit successful, advertising approach.
Courtesy of Sun-Maid Growers of California.

Further Reading

Brierley, Sean, *The Advertising Handbook,* London and New York: Routledge, 1995

Goldman, Robert, *Reading Ads Socially,* London and New York: Routledge, 1992

Ogilvy, David, *Ogilvy on Advertising,* London: Pan, and New York: Crown, 1983

Rothenberg, Randall, *Where the Suckers Moon,* New York: Knopf, 1994

Schudson, Michael, *Advertising, the Uneasy Persuasion: Its Dubious Impact on American Society,* New York: Basic Books, 1984

Cross-referencing between ads has become increasingly common, particularly in commercials targeted at segments of the

---

CLM/BBDO

Founded in Paris, France, by Allen Chevalier, Jean-Loup Le Forestier, and Philippe Michel, 1972; won major accounts, including Nestlé's Vittel mineral water and Levi's; Christophe Lambert appointed chief executive officer, 1996; won non-U.S. Pepsi-Cola account, 1998.

Major Clients

France Telecom
Kookai (ready-to-wear)
Nestlé
Pepsi-Cola
TotalFinaElf
Walt Disney Company

CLM/BBDO traces its roots to the Dupuy Compton ad agency of Paris, France, which hired Allen Chevalier, Jean-Loup Le Forestier, and Philippe Michel in the late 1960s and gave them free reign over much of its account and creative activity. Using an "anything goes" style that fit the era, the trio produced audacious campaigns that shook up the Paris advertising scene and pushed Dupuy Compton into the upper echelon of French agencies.

On the strength of their success, Creative Director Michel and client directors Chevalier and Le Forestier demanded in 1972 that Dupuy Compton give them a share of the business. When the French and British owners of the agency balked at offering their top managers an ownership stake, the three looked elsewhere, eventually accepting an offer from U.S.-based BBDO to open a new French agency under its name. The deal struck between then-BBDO President Bruce Crawford and Chevalier, Le Forestier, and Michel gave the new French group a majority stake in Team France, the Paris office of BBDO's principal German subsidiary, BBDO-Team, Düsseldorf. It also offered Michel—a one-time Maoist and hippy—a pulpit for preaching a new vision of advertising; ultimately he rose to become the father of the French advertising family.

CLM/BBDO opened in October 1972 with little fanfare. By year-end the agency's future seemed secure, after executives convinced former clients of Team France, including Audi, E.I. du Pont de Nemours & Company, and appliance marketer Bosch, to give the new creative shop a try.

For CLM/BBDO, 1973 was a golden year. The agency won a number of major accounts, including former Dupuy Compton clients Levi Strauss & Company and footwear retailer Eram, and it turned out its first ads for what would become an anchor client, Nestlé's Vittel mineral water. The "Drink-eliminate" ads launched that year, as well as the "Drink-urinate" ads produced in 1974, created an uproar in traditional France, but the simultaneous jump in Vittel sales established CLM/BBDO as an effective agency.

The agency created a similar buzz around Levi's, turning the American jeans into an essential item of clothing for any self-respecting hippy. In one famous ad from his Dupuy Compton days, Michel had superimposed a photo of a 1960s love-in on a view of the somber Place de la Concorde. At CLM, he took the concept a step further, mixing imagery from the rock opera *Jesus Christ Superstar* with partially nude dancers reminiscent of the earlier musical *Hair* to help establish Levi's as a brand in tune with the era's young consumers, many of whom remained loyal into the 21st century.

The Vittel and Levi's campaigns were CLM/BBDO at its best: strong creative ideas aimed at shocking or irritating some sectors of the public with an intentionally provocative tone that won widespread recognition—and increased market share—for the brands. They also set the tone for things to come.

Over the next two decades CLM launched a number of advertising campaigns that became textbook examples of how to create lasting brand identity and customer relations. The Eram shoe effort, launched in 1973, was typical of the CLM approach. The signature slogan—"Eram: you'd have to be crazy to spend more"—played up the brand's long-standing tradition of offering bargain-basement prices, while a series of humorous films from then-unknown copywriter Etienne Chatiliez (who later became a well-known feature film director) won the company the loyalty of young customers, not necessarily justified by the quality of its shoes.

A cult of personality developing around Michel, who wielded control over the agency, saw founder Chevalier leave CLM/BBDO in 1981. Under Michel, the agency went on to develop some of France's first official political ads (for President Valery Giscard d'Estaing's failed reelection bid in 1981) and to engineer one of the agency's biggest coups to date, a nationwide teaser campaign for outdoor advertising company Avenir that held France spellbound for the better part of a week.

The first installment of the outdoor ad effort featured a beautiful bikini-clad model named Myriam who promised to take off her top in a coming ad. In the second installment, a now-topless Myriam promised to take off her bikini bottom in two days. When she did so in the final, eagerly awaited installment, CLM/BBDO launched the memorable tag line: "Avenir, an outdoor company that keeps its promises." The nationwide campaign using the outdoor company's own billboards showed that a marketer could reach all of France using a single medium.

CLM followed the Myriam effort in 1983 with an equally provocative series of ads for a little-known French ready-to-wear brand called Kookai. The campaign focused on a cheeky, Lolita-like adolescent who practiced "girl power," tempting and tormenting the boys and men who expressed interest in her. The "Kookaiette" would go on to star in the company's advertising over the coming decade, turning Kookai into an internationally known brand and winning creative accolades for CLM/BBDO at ad competitions worldwide.

The mid- to late1980s and early 1990s marked a notably creative period at CLM/BBDO, by now alternatively revered and detested by the rest of France's ad community for its flair for winning accounts and awards and for turning out fresh approaches to product advertising. Le Forestier left in 1984 to take a job as general manager of Grey Worldwide, just as CLM/BBDO launched its first ads for Apple Computer. The ads moved computer advertising away from the performance and technology-driven spots of the early 1980s and put people at the center of the high-tech revolution.

In one now-famous French ad for Apple, CLM/BBDO depicted a distinguished businessman in the backseat of a chauffeured car, explaining to his son, seated next to him, that creativity has nothing to do with productivity—a lesson that the heir should keep in mind when he takes over the company. The voice-over begins, "There are different ways to run a company. This is one. Happily, there are others," appearing to explain the quizzical look on the son's face. Viewers associated his unspoken disagreement with the philosophical debate at the time between Apple and its competitors. Characters and text in the ad never mention Apple by name, however, a tactical approach that Michel, in an interview with the French advertising magazine *Strategies,* said stemmed from his belief that "people will always remember something that was never said in the first place."

CLM/BBDO did not always take the understated approach, however. The agency launched a campaign for Mamie Nova yogurt starring a pair of "nasty" grandmothers that broke with tradition for dairy product advertising, which tended to show attractive actors or actual consumers enjoying the product.

The agency again found itself at the heart of a high-profile battle in favor of the then-controversial discount approach to selling everything from gasoline to books and groceries taken by leading

Non, Leclerc ne veut pas être présent partout.

Avec votre aide, mettons fin à la pollution par les sacs en plastique.

This award-winning 1996 poster campaign, created by CLM/BBDO for the French retailer Leclerc, drew public attention to the growing problem of plastic bag pollution and highlighted Leclerc's concern for the environment.

retailer E. Leclerc, which was vilified by rivals and politicians as unfairly undercutting competition. In 1988 Michel handled the advertising for the failed presidential campaign of center-right politician Raymond Barre, creating the slogan, "It's time to trust the French people." The ads, which suggested that President François Mitterand had been less than forthcoming with the truth, made Michel new enemies on the political left, but he stuck by what he said was a question of principle.

In recognition of his contributions to the group's international network, Michel was appointed to the board of BBDO Worldwide in 1990. CLM/BBDO won the account for French oil company Total that year, holding onto the account for the next decade as Total went through several rebrandings linked to a mergers-and-acquisition crusade that saw it swallow up Belgian oil company Fina and French rival Elf-Aquitaine.

By 1993 CLM/BBDO had become France's number-five agency, with more than $62 million in gross income and a roster of blue-chip clients. But when Michel, age 53, suddenly died on 24 July 1993, the agency was plunged into chaos just as it prepared to move to a new headquarters: a modern facility, shaped like a cruise liner, on the banks of the Seine River designed for CLM/BBDO by architect Jean Nouvel.

Michel left a lasting impression on France's advertising industry. Among the people he had mentored during his career were filmmaker Chatiliez; Gerard Jean, founder and president of the independent agency Jean & Montmarin; Pierre Berville, cofounder of Grey Worldwide's Paris shop, Callegari Berville Grey; Benoit Devarrieux, president of Havas Advertising–owned Devarrieuxvillaret, Paris; Marie-Catherine Dupuy, cofounder of BDDP Worldwide and later creative director at TBWA, Paris; Nicolas Bordas, president of BDDP & Fils; and Anne de Maupeou, who became creative director at CLM in 1996.

Alain Poiree, who had served since 1988 as managing director of CLM/BBDO as well as its La Compagnie marketing services division, initially replaced Michel. At one-time a creative staff member at CLM/BBDO, Benoit Devarrieux left the vice presidency of McCann-Erickson, Paris, to replace his former boss as creative guru. The new management team had several notable successes, including a 1994 pitch to handle the government's privatization of automaker Renault and a series of ads for the then-state-owned bank Credit Lyonnais.

Gross income continued to rise, topping $70 million by 1995, and CLM/BBDO maintained its fifth-place standing among French agencies. A malaise set in, however, with the departure of several longtime clients, including Eram, Kookai, and E. Leclerc. By 1996 Poiree's days seemed numbered.

That year, BBDO's U.S. executives hired Christophe Lambert, president of the local ad agency Operal-RLC, to replace Poiree. Lambert brought de Maupeou with him from Opera, appointing her CLM/BBDO's first creative director, a previously unofficial post that had always been held by Michel himself. The duo saw immediate results, winning back the Kookai ready-to-wear account and launching an award-winning "Save men" campaign in which a grown-up "Kookaiette" first tormented but later rescued a cast of miniaturized men from a series of impending disasters.

In 1998 Lambert convinced U.S. executives at BBDO and PepsiCo to let CLM/BBDO oversee the soft-drink marketer's account outside the United States. CLM/BBDO was put in charge of managing creative work in more than 100 countries, dramatically increasing its billings and revenue. The agency's success continued in 1999, when it won a European account for Federal Express Corporation and a national budget for top French mail-order retailer 3 Suissess.

In 2000 CLM/BBDO captured the high-profile $60 million account for utility Electricite de France and consolidated its hold on PepsiCo's remaining drink business outside the United States. Gross income rose to nearly $90 million, ranking CLM/BBDO sixth among French agencies. Also in 2000, the agency was voted the most creative among French agencies by the local professional press. In 2001 CLM/BBDO lost the mobile telephone business of France Telecom's Itineris brand but then won the estimated $40 million consolidated global advertising account for oil giant TotalFinaElf.

LAWRENCE J. SPEER

Further Reading
"CLM: Du mythe a la réalité," *Strategies* (28 May 1990)
"La pub lui dit merci," *Strategies* (17 August 1993)
"Philippe Michel: La mort d'un géant," *CB News* (August 1993)

Clothing. *See* Fashion and Apparel; Intimate Apparel

Clutter/Ad Ubiquity

Experts estimate that the last time the average American living in the 20th century might have gone an entire day without seeing or hearing a single advertisement would have been around 1915. By 1945 such an individual would have been exposed to 143 advertising messages a day, and by 1999 it was estimated that he or she would have seen or heard anywhere from 250 to 5,000 or possibly as many as 15,000 marketing messages per day—and the end was nowhere in sight. This gradual but relentless encroachment of advertising into every available venue—from stickers on fresh fruit touting Internet search engines to sports stadiums named for corporate monoliths to ads sculpted into the sand at public beaches—has become known to many by the pejorative term *ad creep*.

But the ubiquity of advertising in the late 20th century is different only in degree, not kind, from what went before. Once limited to reams of newspaper promotions, highway-long stretches of billboards, mailboxes bulging with junk mail, and more comically, roads dotted with Burma Shave signs, advertising has, with advances in communications technologies, taken root in places—over the airwaves, for example—undreamed of in earlier times. What was communicated by word of mouth in the preindustrial world could be spread farther and faster after the development of movable type. In the 17th century, weekly newspapers in London, England, began to carry advertisements; by 1900, ads might cover some 50 percent of a newspaper, and as much as 65 percent of it half a century later. In 1893, when *Munsey's* magazine, burdened by stagnant circulation and growing debt, slashed its cover price from 25 cents to 10 cents and made up for it with advertising, it set a precedent. In 1900, for example, *Harper's* magazine ran more ads than it had in the previous 22 years combined. The

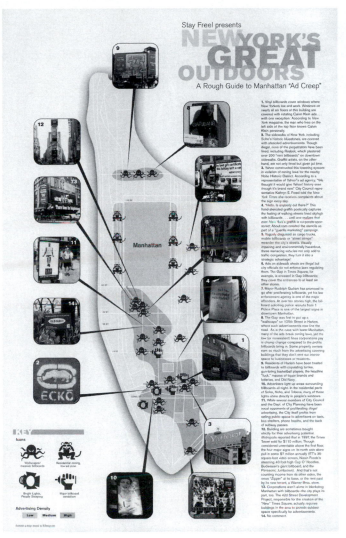

Volunteers associated with *Stay Free!*—a magazine devoted to the issue of commercialism and its impact on American culture—scoured Manhattan for billboards and created this map to make a statement against "ad creep" in New York City.
© *Carrie McLaren/Stay Free!*

more obvious and perhaps more disturbing in print. Radio content—largely popular music—was sponsored by merchandisers, resulting in such phenomena as the "Goodrich Silvertown Orchestra," the "A&P Gypsies," and the "Kodak Chorus." Thus, the gulf separating programming and advertising had been successfully—and irrevocably—closed. Scientific research supported the efficacy of broadcast advertising. It was shown, for example, that the brain understands a spoken word in 140 milliseconds, 40 milliseconds less than it takes to comprehend the printed word, and that a visual image disappears from the brain in about one second, while an aural image lasts four or five times as long. Not surprisingly, radio ad expenditure continued to grow, from $310 million in 1945 to almost $18 billion in 2000.

Television proved an even more fertile breeding ground for advertising than its predecessor media. Launched with great fanfare (albeit to a limited audience) at the 1939 New York World's Fair, television was never a medium with program content occasionally interrupted by commercials, but one of commercials occasionally interrupted by content. Watching television is largely a passive, even soporific experience. In 2000 U.S. viewers spent an average of four hours per day with the medium, a rate nearly eight times what they spent with newspapers and 14 times that for magazines. As a consequence, by the time American children graduate from high school, they have seen an estimated 360,000 TV commercials. The advent of the World Wide Web took advertising even further. Seen by 161 million North Americans, and 378 million people worldwide, Internet advertising can, like radio, cross editorial/advertising lines; like television and print, it bombards viewers with visual images; and, like direct mail, it is capable of targeting consumers with great precision. The electronic medium allows for niche marketing on an unprecedented scale. Nine out of ten Internet "surfers" receive so-called spam—unwanted commercials transmitted via e-mail—at least once a week, while 50 percent receive six or more. In the year 2000 unsolicited advertising accounted for approximately 10 percent of the 10 billion e-mails sent per day, and e-mail traffic was expected to increase to 35 billion by 2005.

Thus, while exposures to commercial solicitations in traditional media might be measured in the thousands, on the Internet they can be gauged in billions: banner ad impressions (essentially, the number of times a banner ad is rendered for viewing) appeared at a pace of about a quarter-trillion per year in 2000. Unhindered by physical borders or set blocks of time, pop-up ads and banners can be seen by computer users throughout the time they spend viewing a page. As customer-acquisition costs for Internet businesses decline, and as on-line advertising causes an increase in message association (the link the consumer makes between the company and the ad) and banner advertising raises brand awareness, the surfeit of ads is bound to continue over time.

At the same time, the popularity of marketing on the Web does not in any way detract from marketing in the traditional formats. With biblical simplicity, ad creep only begets more ad creep as companies fight to get their messages heard over those of others.

uneasy balance between editorial content and advertising in magazines tipped from a 54:46 editorial-to-ads ratio in 1970 to a near-standoff of 50.6:49.4 by the end of the century. Magazine ad revenues topped $12 billion in 2000 (almost double 1990's total), and newspaper ad revenues were nearly 800 percent higher in 2000 than in 1971.

When commercial radio debuted in the United States in November 1920 with KDKA in Pittsburgh, Pennsylvania, advertising had the potential to move from the (in some ways) more tangible print medium to the amorphous medium of sound. Probably the earliest radio advertisement—on New York City's WEAF in 1922—cajoled tasteful listeners to purchase housing at Hawthorne Court in the New York City borough of Queens. The genteel soft sell of the ad stealthily traversed the barrier between advertising and program content in a way that would have been

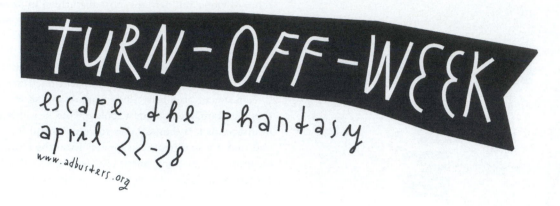

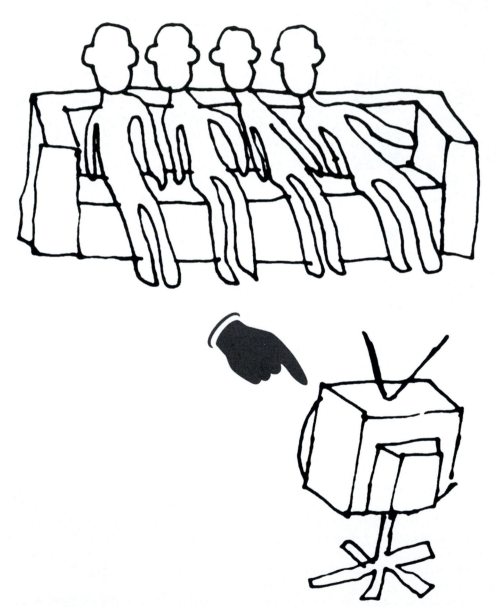

Each year Adbusters Media Foundation asks consumers to turn off their television sets for one week and consider who has been shaping the way they think.
Image courtesy of www.adbusters.org.

A photograph of the intersection of Broadway and 47th Street in New York City shows the ubiquity of advertising as early as the 1940s.

And the virtually infinite space offered by the Web may be helping to increase ad creep overall, as advertisers liberate themselves from the sense that any surface is taboo: a space either has information or it does not.

The result has been that advertising is not only abundant but inescapable and ubiquitous. A Mexican restaurant in San Francisco, California, went so far as to offer free lunches for a lifetime to customers who would have the eatery's logo tattooed on their bodies. Formerly information-free white paper take-out bags sport the messages of specialty cafes, delis, and marketplaces. In the United States, Channel One broadcasts a daily ten-minute television newscast—with commercials—to 12,000 schools. Stickers for the Internet search engine Ask Jeeves were placed on millions of bananas and apples, and future fruit campaigns were being planned by other businesses. Not limited to appearances on produce, the Ask Jeeves logo, a portly butler, also strode into popular culture as a balloon in the November 2000 Macy's Thanksgiving Day parade in New York City. Ad-displaying TV monitors have been installed atop self-serve fuel pumps, while motion-activated audio players have been positioned near urinals. Billboard-size signs are pulled behind boats along the Florida coastline. Private cars are wrapped in garish vinyl promotions, while "Adcaps"—ad-emblazoned hubcaps—spin on other moving vehicles.

Sports events have proved an irresistible venue for advertising. In Miami, Florida, Joe Robbie Stadium (named after the Miami Dolphins football team owner) was renamed Pro Player Stadium, for the sports apparel division of Fruit of the Loom. Similarly, in California the San Francisco 49ers stadium, Candlestick Park, was renamed 3Com Park. The Jacksonville (Florida) Jaguars and the Carolina Panthers score touchdowns in Alltel Stadium and Ericsson Stadium, respectively. NBC, ABC, Fox, MTV, and other television networks use virtual advertising, wherein paid ads that look like real scenery, such as a billboard for Dodge in the Cleveland Browns stadium or Canada's Global Television blimp floating over Pro Player Stadium, are blended into live broadcasts. Long-established college bowl games have been rechristened as, for example, the Nokia Sugar Bowl, the FedEx Orange Bowl, the Tostitos Fiesta Bowl, and the Chick-Fil-A Peach Bowl. Wearable computers woven into clothing promise a 21st-century version of the sandwich board, while by 2005 the mobile/wireless advertising market will be beaming $16.4 billion worth of ads, including commercials, to cell phones and personal digital assistants from interactive billboards aimed at the more than 125 million Americans who commute to work every day. And the sky is no longer the limit: Pizza Hut affixed its logo to a rocket sent to the international space station.

The public response to ad creep has been largely passive or amused, as evidenced by the high comfort level of most consumers with clothing that sports product logos or designer labels and the transformation of the Super Bowl from a sporting contest into a much-anticipated and much-analyzed debate over who runs the most ingenious ads. But ad creep can spark consumer resistance and suspicion, evidenced by the coinage of new words:

"advermation" (an ad offering specific information about a product or service), "advertecture" (ads covering the entire sides of buildings or walls), and "advertorials" (ads designed to look like traditional editorial content). As early as the 1960s, outrage over ad creep manifested itself in the U.S. Highway Beautification Act of 1965, which regulated outdoor advertising along the 306,000 miles of federally funded primary, interstate, and national highway. Since the passage of the act, nearly 750,000 "illegal" signs have been removed—yet outdoor advertising still reached $5.2 billion in 2000 and was growing at 9 percent annually.

Overall, legislation in response to ad ubiquity has taken a backseat to grassroots movements. "Subtervising"—advertisements carrying an antimarketing theme—is the weapon of choice among "culture jammers," who believe it is possible to parody cultural images (especially those in advertising) and thereby sabotage their message. The best known of culture jammers, Adbusters, organizes Buy Nothing Days and TV Turnoff Weeks, distributes spoof ads (e.g., Joe Chemo in place of Joe Camel), and promotes like-minded groups such as the Billboard Liberation Front, which modifies outdoor advertisements with jarring alterations (superimposing "Think doomed" over Apple Computer's "Think different" slogan).

Despite these insurgent acts and occasional grousing by the consumer in the street, ad creep is probably here to stay. Materialism, to paraphrase cultural critic James B. Twitchell (*Twenty Ads that Shook the World,* 2000), is the basis of all political systems, and advertising is its prophet.

CHARLES PAPPAS

Further Reading

Cross, Gary S., *An All-Consuming Century: Why Commercialism Won in Modern America,* New York: Columbia University Press, 2000

Klein, Naomi, *No Logo: Taking Aim at the Brand Bullies,* New York: Picador, 1999

Lasn, Kalle, *Culture Jam: The Uncooling of America,* New York: Eagle Brook, 1999

Savan, Leslie, *The Sponsored Life: Ads, TV, and American Culture,* Philadelphia, Pennsylvania: Temple University Press, 1994

Seabrook, John, *NoBrow: The Culture of Marketing the Marketing of Culture,* New York: Knopf, 2000

Twitchell, James B., *Adcult USA: The Triumph of Advertising in American Culture,* New York: Columbia University Press, 1995

Twitchell, James B., *Lead Us into Temptation: The Triumph of American Materialism,* New York: Columbia University Press, 1999

Twitchell, James B., *Twenty Ads that Shook the World,* New York: Crown, 2000

Coca-Cola Company

Principal Agencies
Massengale Agency
D'Arcy Advertising Company, Inc.
McCann-Erickson
Wieden & Kennedy, Inc.
Lowe & Partners
SSC&B: Lintas Worldwide

Coca-Cola, the world's leading soft drink, has been a leading advertiser since its inception in 1886. Over the years, the Coca-Cola Company has availed itself of almost every promotional and ad device accessible, and it has launched some of the best-known campaign themes, ranging from "Drink Coca-Cola" (1886) to the endearing "The pause that refreshes" (1929), and from the clever "Sign of good taste" (1957) to the ingenious "Always Coca-Cola" used in contemporary ads.

The sipping of soda fountain drinks, such as lemonade, root beer, and ginger ale, had already become an American tradition when Dr. John Pemberton introduced Coca-Cola in 1886 as a nonalcoholic patent medicine. Pemberton placed ads for the new drink in newspapers during the year of its debut. Also in that year, oil-cloth signs were hung from drugstore awnings, suggesting simply: "Drink Coca-Cola. Delicious. Refreshing." According to Pemberton, by the end of 1886, he had spent almost $74 on advertising, but he had sold only 50 gallons of cola syrup at $1 per gallon.

In poor health, Pemberton sold two thirds of his Coca-Cola interests in 1887 to Willis Venable, who in turn sold out in the same year to Atlanta, Georgia, druggist Asa Briggs Candler. Documents show that Pemberton also sold parts of the business to other smaller investors. But by 1891 Candler had bought up all Coca-Cola assets, including the formula, for a total of $2,300. Candler's first Atlanta newspaper ad for Coca-Cola appeared in 1888. On 1 May 1889 he published a page ad for Coca-Cola in the *Atlanta Journal.* In that ad, Candler promised Coca-Cola drinkers "Refreshment and relief" and called the soft drink a "wonderful nerve and brain tonic," good for treating "headache and exhaustion."

Candler touted his wholesale and retail cola syrup business as the "sole proprietors of 'Coca-Cola . . . Delicious. Refreshing. Exhilarating. Invigorating.'" On 31 January 1893 he registered

Coca-Cola as a trademark. Joseph Biedenharn in Vicksburg, Mississippi, first bottled and sold Coca-Cola in 1894. In 1899 Chattanooga, Tennessee, was the site of the first franchised bottling plant for Coca-Cola. By 1900 the familiar Coca-Cola script could be seen on plain, rounded bottles made of clear glass. The green hobble-skirt bottle that has become a symbol of the company was patented in 1915 and began regularly appearing on the market in 1916.

A firm believer in marketing, Candler hired the Massengale Agency in 1895 and distributed thousands of coupons for a complimentary glass of Coca-Cola, as well as a variety of novelties (such as fans, clocks, and calendars) displaying the Coca-Cola trademark. The Massengale Agency's first campaign for Coca-Cola featured upper-class ladies and gentlemen drinking Coca-Cola in elegant surroundings. In the early years, Coca-Cola also used sports heroes to promote the drink.

Around 1900 Coca-Cola shifted the focus of its advertisements from "health" to "refreshment." To convey the latter idea, the company linked the product with wholesome images of the pleasant things in life and depicted beautiful people drinking Coca-Cola. From 1886 to 1903 Coca-Cola's ad campaigns mainly exhorted, "Drink Coca-Cola." Later slogans included "Delicious and refreshing" (1904); "Coca-Cola revives and sustains" (1905); and "The great national temperance" (1906).

At the beginning of the 20th century Coca-Cola introduced the "Coca-Cola girls" ads, featuring celebrities such as actress Hilda Clark and opera star Lillian Nordica. Between 1903 and 1905 the latter's picture appeared on serving trays, sampling coupons, magazine advertisements, metal signs, menus, bookmarks, and the famous Coca-Cola calendars.

In point-of-purchase advertising, large stand-up displays decorated various store windows, reminding thirsty consumers that Coca-Cola was just a step away. Ornate leaded-glass chandeliers with Coca-Cola logos adorned many soda fountains during the first quarter of the 20th century.

Coca-Cola dropped Massengale in 1906 and chose the D'Arcy Advertising Company, Inc., as its next agency. In its first endeavors for Coca-Cola, D'Arcy (which would be Coca-Cola's ad agency for the next 50 years) maintained the continuity of the theme of pleasantness already established in earlier Coca-Cola ads: "Pleasant people in pleasant places doing pleasant things as a pleasant nation went pleasantly on its course." While the overall theme was maintained, by 1910 the images of people in the ads had shifted subtly to appeal more widely to Americans across classes, genders, and age groups. Another theme, used in 1909, was "Good to the last drop," a slogan later associated with Maxwell House Coffee. In 1917 the Coca-Cola advertising campaign theme became "Three million a day."

In 1919 Asa Candler sold Coca-Cola to a group led by Ernest Woodruff, who, in 1923, asked his son, Robert, to take the reins of the company. Many merchandising concepts accepted today as commonplace were considered revolutionary when Robert Woodruff introduced them. He pioneered the widespread use of colorful metal signs to advertise the soft drink, and hand-painted Coca-Cola signs, often with the merchant's name incorporated in the overall design, were placed in the windows of numerous restaurants and stores.

By the 1920s bottling had become a critically important packaging innovation for Coca-Cola, making the drink available to consumers anytime and anywhere—not just in the soda fountain. Coca-Cola Company first manufactured and field-tested one of the industry's most powerful merchandising tools, the innovative six-bottle cardboard carton, in 1923. By the end of 1928 Coca-Cola in bottles outsold the fountain drink. In 1929 the company introduced open-top metal coolers (later replaced by refrigerated units), making it possible for Coca-Cola to be served ice-cold in retail outlets, factories, offices, and other institutions. The now-famous bell-shaped fountain glass was adopted as standard by the company in 1929, and it greatly helped to popularize Coca-Cola. Coca-Cola began using billboards nationwide in 1925.

Coca-Cola's first practical coin-operated vending machines appeared by the early 1930s. The automatic fountain dispenser—introduced at the Chicago, Illinois, 1933 World's Fair—proved to be another great innovation for the company. Within only four years, Coca-Cola had become standard in soda fountains. The company also was one of the first beverage producers to sponsor radio programs.

Outside the 1928 Olympics in Amsterdam, The Netherlands, small shops called "winkles" served Coca-Cola in bottles and from soda fountains. D'Arcy's 1929 campaign for Coca-Cola, "The pause that refreshes," was ranked second by Advertising Age when it compiled its list of the top 100 ad campaigns of the 20th century.

From 1904 onward print ads for the soft drink, featuring quality illustrations by such noted artists as Norman Rockwell, appeared in the Saturday Evening Post. Works by these artists were seen as the hallmark of early campaigns in premier magazines. When Archie Lee, Coca-Cola's advertising guru in the 1930s, devised the brand's 1931 Christmas campaign, he enlisted Haddon Sundblom to create portraits of a realistically human Santa Claus, and these images indelibly shaped the 20th-century image of Santa Claus. Among other things, Sundblom helped popularize the already-established representation of Santa as wearing a red-and-white suit (Coca-Cola's official colors). Sundblom's association with Coca-Cola lasted more than three decades; his last Santa advertisement appeared in 1964, and his illustrations created a romanticized portrait of the United States that was as clear and compelling as that of Norman Rockwell.

When Woodruff took over the Coca-Cola Company, he aimed to move the product into the world market, and under his leadership the company invented a beet sugar–based syrup-concentrate (a thick, flavored extract that, when mixed with aerated water, becomes the soft drink) that was suitable for export. At the outbreak of World War II, Coca-Cola was bottled in 44 countries, including those on both sides of the conflict. When the United States entered the war in 1941, Woodruff ordered that every American in uniform should be able to get a bottle of Coca-Cola for five cents "wherever he is and whatever it costs."

The availability of Coca-Cola during the war did more than just lift the morale of the U.S. troops. In many areas, it gave the

Coca-Cola's depiction of Santa Claus—shown in a 1998 French advertisement but created by D'Arcy Advertising Company's Haddon Sundblom in 1931—shaped the 20th-century image of Santa.
Courtesy of The Coca-Cola Company.

local people their first taste of Coca-Cola—a taste they obviously enjoyed. From 1941 to 1946 the company sponsored the "Victory Parade of Spotlight Bands," which featured popular orchestras playing for military audiences. When peace returned in 1945, Coca-Cola was poised for unprecedented worldwide growth. In 1948 the company copyrighted the term *Coke* for the first time, in the slogan, "Where there's Coke, there's hospitality." From the mid-1940s until 1960 the number of countries with bottling operations nearly doubled.

Coca-Cola's advertising after the war essentially ignored the social realities of the war in Korea (and later, Vietnam) and the Civil Rights movement. The soft drink continued to be presented as a pleasant and rewarding part of life in an idealized, harmonious world. D'Arcy's philosophy for postwar Coca-Cola advertising was "keep it wholesome" and never make exaggerated claims in ad copy.

From the late 1940s to the 1970s the Coca-Cola Company experienced its most dramatic changes in marketing and merchandising since the advent of bottling in 1894. With better and bigger packaging in the 1950s and 1960s, Coca-Cola employed a retail-oriented strategy, focusing on price, size, and value. The company also moved into television advertising, airing its first commercial in 1950 during a live Thanksgiving Day special featuring Edgar Bergen and Charlie McCarthy. Prior to the 1950s the company had been only a minor presence on network radio. In 1940 it spent less than $100,000 on radio and was not even among the top 100 radio advertisers.

In 1955 Coca-Cola introduced 10-, 12-, and 26-ounce bottles. Also in 1955 William Robinson and H.B. Nicholson became president and chairman, respectively, and promptly ended the company's 50-year relationship with D'Arcy, installing McCann-Erickson, which took over in the spring of 1956. The account billed $15 million at the time.

The company began marketing Coke in 12-ounce metal cans, originally developed for use by the armed forces overseas, in 1960. In 1963 the "Things go better with Coke" jingle, sung by such groups as the Supremes, Jan and Dean, the Four Seasons, and the Moody Blues, was aired on the radio. Applying the principles of market segmentation, the company decided in the mid-1960s to use TV as an all-family medium.

In 1970 Coca-Cola changed its strategy, launching the "It's the real thing" campaign. The company wanted to present the brand as real, patriotic, and original—an escape from phoniness. "It's the real thing" was ranked 53rd on *Advertising Age*'s 1999 list of the century's 100 best ad campaigns, and the jingle for the campaign (written by McCann-Erickson Creative Director William Backer) placed ninth among the top ten jingles and became a hit record by the Seekers.

During the 1970s the company faced increasing competition from the Pepsi-Cola Company. Against Coke's "It's the real thing" campaign, Pepsi designed a campaign for the "Pepsi generation," associating its beverage with youth and free spiritedness, and offered the "Pepsi challenge," in which consumers were invited to compare Pepsi to Coke in blind taste tests. In 1979 Coca-Cola countered by hiring "Mean" Joe Greene, a member of the Pittsburgh Steelers football team, to star in a sentimental Coke commercial with a young boy. In the ad, Greene gives his jersey to the boy, and the boy shares his Coca-Cola with Greene. This campaign, with the tag line "Have a Coke and a smile," did not convince Pepsi-Cola drinkers to switch brands, however.

Later Coca-Cola campaigns, including "Coke is it" (1982) and the worldwide "Always Coca-Cola" (1993), have been more successful, increasing Coke's market share over that of Pepsi. In another effort to improve Coke's competitive edge over Pepsi, the Coca-Cola name was lent to other soft-drink products from the marketer in the 1980s, with Coke spending $50 million in 1982 alone on advertising for its newly extended line of soft drinks.

Coca-Cola introduced Tab, its first low-calorie soft drink, in May 1963. At that time, Coca-Cola executives decided not to name that beverage "Coke" because they thought that the trademark should not be used for more than one product. Two decades later, however, marketers for Coca-Cola changed their thinking, debuting "Diet Coke" in the United States in 1982 and internationally in 1983. At the onset, the Diet Coke ad campaign emphasized "Just for the taste of it." Nothing was said about the fact that the drink was low in calories. The campaign was created by SSC&B: Lintas Worldwide, which handled Diet Coke in all English-speaking countries. By the end of 1983 Diet Coke had become the best-selling diet drink in the United States, and by 1984, it was the third-most popular soft drink overall, replacing 7 UP in the ranking.

Following the introduction of Diet Coke, the Coca-Cola Company further expanded the number of products sold under the Coke trademark. Caffeine-Free Diet and Regular Coke debuted in 1983; Cherry Coke was introduced nationally in 1985; and Diet Cherry followed in 1986. Despite the success of Diet Coke, however, Coke's market-share against Pepsi crumbled to a margin of 4.9 percent by 1984, and Coke sales were trailing those of its arch-rival in grocery stores by 1.9 percent, even though Coke continued to lead Pepsi in institutional outlets such as McDonald's and Burger King.

In this competitive context, executives at the Coca-Cola Company concluded—erroneously—that marketing was not the problem. Rather, they believed, it was the product itself that was the problem. Americans simply seemed to prefer the taste of Pepsi. Working from this supposition, on 23 April 1985, Coke introduced its new formula for Coca-Cola, which was noticeably sweeter than the recipe it superceded. Moreover, the new product was intended to permanently replace the original formula, becoming the one and only Coca-Cola. Almost instantly, there was a national outcry against the new Coke and a resounding demand for return of the old Coke. Complaints to the Atlanta headquarters numbered as many as 1,500 a day. By July 1985 old Coke was back on the market under the name "Coca-Cola Classic." Coca-Cola President Donald Keough even appeared in Coke commercials, apologizing to consumers at large for underestimating their passion for the original formula.

In the months after the New Coke/Coca-Cola Classic debacle, Coca-Cola adopted a "megabrand" marketing/advertising strategy. Because the campaign counted all the products marketed under the Coke name (including Diet Coke, Cherry Coke, Caffeine-Free Coca-Cola, and Diet Caffeine-Free Coca-Cola), it provided a new way for Coca-Cola to position itself as the best-selling brand in the soft drink market.

In 1988 Coke debuted the first three-dimensional TV commercial, featuring the trendy cartoon character Max Headroom, during the season finale of the popular series *Moonlighting*. That same year, Coca-Cola also began an ad campaign pitting Diet Coke against Diet Pepsi in an attempt to boost sales of the Diet Coke brand.

In 1989 the company concluded a deal making Coca-Cola the official soft drink of the National Basketball Association. It also signed an agreement with Major League Baseball and became the official soft drink of the National Hockey League. Also in 1989, Coke unveiled the "Can't beat the real thing" campaign, which was intended to incorporate elements of traditional Coke ads in a fresh appeal to contemporary consumers. The following year Coke signed a 16-year agreement with the Walt Disney Company to tie Coca-Cola products into the studio's films and to sell Coke products at Disney theme parks.

In August 1989 Coca-Cola challenged the traditional agency-client relationship when it hired Mike Ovitz's Creative Artists Agency as a consultant, a move that New York City's Madison Avenue agencies regarded as a threat to their control over creative work. Three years later, in 1992, Coke launched its first global advertising campaign, which used similar commercials in each country. Another move that shook Madison Avenue was the October 1993 decision by Atlanta-based Coca-Cola to shift $95 million in Diet Coke billings from Lintas, which had launched the product in 1982, to Lowe & Partners. It was the first major change in the otherwise stable Coca-Cola agency structure since Coke switched from D'Arcy to McCann-Erickson in 1955–56. All the agencies involved were part of the Interpublic Group of Companies.

In 1993 Coke launched its "Always Coca-Cola" campaign created by the Hollywood talent shop Creative Artists Agency. The campaign included an unprecedented 26 different TV commercials, which were as diverse as the global audience for Coke itself. The campaign's theme was a reinterpretation of the "Real thing" concept for the 1990s and an extension of the "Coke is it" slogan. A spokesperson for Coke explained the strategy behind the ads by asserting that, "in this age of media clutter, it is imperative to make ads that are personally relevant and that are so visually stimulating as to make the audience want to watch them."

"Always Coca-Cola" is considered the epitome of the strategy of all-situations positioning, which attempts to nullify other brands' specific situational positioning. "Always" ranked 86th on *Advertising Age*'s 1999 list of the top 100 campaigns.

In 1993 Coca-Cola created a new campaign with nostalgic elements, including the return of old-style contoured Coke bottle and core brand icon graphics. That year sales of Coca-Cola Classic jumped nearly 8 percent.

The Coca-Cola Company's Sprite (lemon-lime soft drink) proved to have the fastest rising sales on the U.S. soft drink market during 1997 and 1998. Sprite's marketing strategy sought to

Table 1. Major Coca-Cola Campaigns.

Year	Campaign
1886	Drink Coca-Cola
1904	Delicious and refreshing
1905	Coca-Cola revives and sustains
1906	The great national temperance
1917	Three million a day
1922	Thirst knows no season
1925	Six million a day
1927	Around the corner from everywhere
1929	The pause that refreshes
1932	Ice cold sunshine
1938	The best friend thirst ever had
1939	Coca-Cola goes along
1942	Wherever you are, whatever you do, wherever you may be, when you think of refreshment, think of ice-cold Coca-Cola.
1942	The only thing like Coca-Cola is Coca-Cola itself. It's the real thing
1948	Where there's Coke, there's hospitality
1949	Coca-Cola . . . along the highway to anywhere
1952	What you want is a Coke
1956	Coca-Cola . . . making good things taste better
1957	Sign of good taste
1958	The cold, crisp taste of Coke
1963	Things go better with Coke
1970	It's the real thing
1971	I'd like to buy the world a Coke
1975	Look up America
1976	Coke adds life
1979	Have a Coke and a smile
1982	Coke is it
1985	We've got a taste for you [Coca-Cola and Coca-Cola Classic]
	America's real choice
1986	Catch the wave [Coca-Cola]
	Red white and you [Coca-Cola Classic]
1989	Can't beat the feeling
1990	Can't beat the real thing
1993	Always Coca-Cola

get consumers—especially the youth market—to ignore image and "Obey their thirst."

Whatever the medium, advertising for Coca-Cola has always reflected the mood and the look of the time. Today it is even more carefully targeted to reflect the various outlooks of different audiences within single markets, while always underscoring the universal appeal of the refreshment.

Coca-Cola was initially presented only as a thirst quencher, but its makers soon positioned the drink as a symbol of America itself, an integral part of the nation's happiest and most rewarding activities. Over the years, advertising and other promotions of Coca-Cola have been designed to make the product an inherent part of people's lives and habits, a means of contributing to their pleasure. To that end, the company has preferred advertising that shares the properties of the product itself.

Seeking to make Coca-Cola stand out clearly amid the clutter of other promotions, today's creators of advertising for Coca-Cola strive for one sound, one sight, and one sell. Thus, the Coke "look" is carefully applied to uniforms, emblems, point-of-purchase materials, delivery trucks, and other related objects. To communicate the uniqueness of the soft drink, Coke's marketers have concentrated on four specific elements (in addition to the distinctive flavor of the drink) that, according to marketing research, help consumers identify the brand: (1) the familiar script lettering of the Coca-Cola trademark; (2) the trademark "Coke"; (3) the bright red color of Coke packaging; and (4) the unique contour of the bottle.

With characteristic thoroughness Coca-Cola has recognized that the image of Coke is influenced by far more than the product itself and its promotional elements. The company's claim is that, since its inception in 1886, it has made only one promise concerning the brand: "an ice-cold Coke is delicious and refreshing."

SAMMY R. DANNA

See also color plate in this volume

Further Reading

"Advertising and Marketing," *Facts, Figures, and Features* 7–8 (1996) (published by The Coca-Cola Company)
Louis, J.C., and Harvey Yazijian, *The Cola Wars,* New York: Everest House, 1980
Oliver, Thomas, *The Real Coke, the Real Story,* New York: Random House, and London: Elm Tree, 1986
Sivulka, Juliann, *Soap, Sex, and Cigarettes: A Cultural History of American Advertising,* Belmont, California: Wadsworth, 1998
Watters, Pat, *Coca-Cola: An Illustrated History,* Garden City, New York: Doubleday, 1978

Cockfield, Brown & Company, Ltd.

Founded by Harry Cockfield and Warren Brown in Montreal, Canada, in 1928; became a pioneer in market research services; had strong ties to Canada's federal Liberal Party from the 1930s until the 1950s; suffered sudden bankruptcy, 1983.

Major Clients

Bell Telephone Company of Canada
Canada Packers, Ltd.
Imperial Oil, Ltd.
Molson

Cockfield, Brown & Company, Ltd. was established in Montreal, Canada, in December 1928 by Harry Cockfield and Warren Brown. Cockfield, an austere, cost-accounting businessman, had managed the Advertising Service Company since its founding in 1913. The ebullient, backslapping Brown had worked at National Publicity since 1920. It was thought that their complementary styles would make for a winning formula in the advertising business. Each brought with him a number of clients, and billings in the first year were a respectable $2 million. A second office in Toronto opened shortly afterward, in 1929.

Cockfield, Brown was Canada's first agency to develop an extensive market research capability. In 1930 it formed a commercial research and economic investigation department, which employed university economists, marketing specialists, and Harvard MBA graduates. Along with this in-house operation, it hired on a contractual basis some 80 research associates nationwide, often as survey interviewers.

The agency's marketing studies combined desk and field research. Business and governmental statistics were analyzed and incorporated into marketing reports, while original market research was conducted for dozens of clients, such as Campbell Soup Company, Molson's brewery, and Imperial Oil. A marketing study done for the Orange Crush Company in 1932 involved an assessment of suitable retail outlets based on local business and weather conditions and on a national poll of soft-drink consumers. In the words of a company official in 1930, Cockfield, Brown's research program sought to "transform advertising from a haphazard adjunct of high-pressure salesmanship into a scientific and essential function of modern business."

Cockfield, Brown also succeeded in securing many new clients, a none-too-easy feat during the Depression. Among the more prominent firms to sign on were Dominion Securities Corporation (1929), Dominion Textile Company (1930), Great-West Life Assurance Company (1930), Molson (1930), Bell Telephone Company of Canada (1931), Massey-Harris Company (1932), Royal Bank of Canada (1932), Welch's Grape Juice Company (1932), Canadian Goodrich Company (1933), and Gruen Watch Company of Canada (1936).

Capitalizing on its research expertise, the agency forged close ties with the governing Liberal Party. In 1944 Cockfield, Brown beat out Canadian rival MacLaren Advertising for control of the party's national English-language advertising. Cockfield, Brown executive H.E. Kidd (who would become Liberal Party secretary

A 1950s house ad for Cockfield, Brown & Company, Ltd., showed the agency's new headquarters building.

in 1949 while still working for Cockfield, Brown) coordinated the first-ever opinion survey in an electoral riding for Liberal M.P. Brooke Claxton in 1944. That year the agency also conducted a national opinion survey to test the appeal of party slogans. Most significantly, in the spring of 1944 it supervised a series of 43 opinion polls in Ontario ridings to assess Liberal support. The surveys constituted the first uses of polling by a Canadian political party and were pioneering examples of political marketing.

In the 1945 election Cockfield, Brown handled radio, newspaper, and poster advertising for the winning Liberal Party. Afterward the agency worked closely with Liberal officials, in the process securing millions of dollars in advertising contracts before the party lost office in 1957. Also in 1945, Cockfield, Brown became the only Canadian agency to be listed in the first annual agency rankings compiled by *Advertising Age*. The company ranked 29th out of 51 large and midsize agencies, which were otherwise all based in the United States. Cockfield, Brown continued to grow at a rapid pace after World War II, and in 1948 it became the first Canadian agency to surpass $10 million in billings.

By the late 1950s Cockfield, Brown had grown significantly, ranking consistently among the top five agencies in billings (its 1958 billings topped $26 million). Its clients included such prestigious companies as Canada Packers, Imperial Oil, Lever Bros., and Merrill Lynch. The agency employed a staff of nearly 500 in its Montreal, Toronto, Winnipeg, and Vancouver offices. In addition to advertising and market research expertise, the agency offered services in merchandising, media analysis, and public relations. Cockfield had died in 1942, but Brown continued to be active in the firm. In 1956 the Association of Canadian Advertisers awarded him its Gold Medal and he remained the agency's president until 1968.

At a time when other agencies were growing, Cockfield, Brown's fortunes began a downward slide; its billings remained unchanged between 1958 and 1964. Although it still secured, thanks to Liberal Party ties, the $6 million account for Montreal's World Fair Exposition in 1967, the agency faced greater competition from rivals Vickers & Benson and MacLaren, which in 1960 became Canada's largest agency. The "creative revolution" of the 1960s, which emphasized original, bold, and dynamic advertising, stood at odds with the general conservatism of Cockfield, Brown. Although the agency was respected for its sound management practices, its creative work garnered scant praise. Questions were raised about the executives' large bonuses, seemingly not justified by profit levels. A mounting rivalry between the Montreal and Toronto offices further sapped the agency of morale and vigor.

In 1969 Cockfield, Brown became the first Canadian agency to go public. It issued shares at $7 each, but the stock soon fell in value. Generally preferring companies with material assets rather than the human ones typical of ad agencies, investors balked at the opportunity. Moreover, the company's bottom line was not inviting. In 1970 Cockfield, Brown counted $34 million in billings, $5 million in revenue, but only $361,000 in net profits. By 1977 net earnings had dropped to $172,000. By the late 1970s approximately 70 percent of the company's shares were in outside hands, leaving it a ripe candidate for a hostile takeover.

A chain of events culminated in Cockfield, Brown's insolvency in 1983. In 1980 Peter Hunter, the owner of a smaller ad agency, offered to merge with Cockfield, Brown, but he was turned down by the board. A year later, John Francis, president of the Calgary-based Williams & Johnson advertising agency, bought 22 percent of Cockfield, Brown in a bid to merge the two companies, but he, too, was rejected by Cockfield, Brown officials.

Meanwhile, another group vied for Cockfield, Brown. This group was headed by Jacques Krasny, a senior vice president of health care conglomerate Extendicare, which had recently bought a controlling interest in the communications and marketing firm Caldonia Corporation. The other partner was Jerry Goodis, president of Jerry Goodis, Inc., and a flamboyant agency executive noted for his creative work and close links to the Liberal Party.

Hunter and Francis joined forces in October 1981 when together they controlled 44 percent of Cockfield, Brown shares. Cockfield, Brown officials in turn issued their remaining shares to Extendicare, granting it approximately 40 percent of the company's stock. At a bitter meeting of Cockfield, Brown shareholders in February 1982, the Hunter-Francis forces seized control of the company, which prompted the immediate resignation of the board, including company president Rick Gallop. Don McDougall, a beer marketing expert, became the new chief executive officer and chairman. Incredibly, Extendicare, which owned 43 percent of Cockfield, Brown shares, was not represented on the board. This tumultuous affair sparked the departure of many major and long-standing clients, including Gilbey Canada, Imperial Oil, Bell Canada, and Molson.

The agency's outlook continued to deteriorate. More accounts left, including Canada Packers, a 53-year client. McDougall resigned in February 1983, and in the following month the company released its 1982 annual report, showing a net loss of $474,300. Clients began withholding payments to Cockfield, Brown, fearing that it would go under before paying its media bills. Soon afterward the company's banker refused to honor its line of credit and payroll. Cockfield, Brown's directors resigned, and in May 1983 one of Canada's oldest and largest advertising agencies filed for bankruptcy protection.

DANIEL J. ROBINSON

Further Reading

Blankenship, Albert B., Chuck Chakrapani, and W. Harold Poole, *A History of Marketing Research in Canada,* Toronto, Ontario: Professional Marketing Research Society, 1985

Brown, Warren, "The Past, Present, and Future of Ad Agencies," *Marketing* (21 November 1958)

Hayes, David, "Who Killed Cockfield, Brown?" *Saturday Night* 99 (February 1984)

Robinson, Daniel J., *The Measure of Democracy: Polling, Market Research, and Public Life, 1930–1945,* Toronto: University of Toronto Press, 1999

Coffee

As it entered the 20th century, the United States was the world's largest consumer of coffee. At the time Americans were just becoming accustomed to the idea of buying prepackaged, branded coffee rather than blends purchased in bulk from the local grocer. And they were willing to spend more for branded coffee from regional companies than from national ones. The largest companies at this time were J.A. Folger & Company and Hills Brothers, which competed for the western market in San Francisco, California; Maxwell House coffee from the Cheek-Neal Coffee Company in the South; Arbuckle Brothers Coffee, a leader in New York City; and Chase & Sanborn Coffee, which held leading market positions in Boston, Massachusetts; Chicago, Illinois; and parts of the South, as well as in Montreal, Canada.

Early Rivalries

Coffee marketers learned their first lessons in effective advertising not through competition with each other but rather in the struggle to stave off popular coffee substitutes that had emerged in response to health claims against coffee. One in particular, Postum, a grain-based "healthful" coffee substitute created in 1895 by C.W. Post, of Battle Creek, Michigan, effectively propagandized against "coffee nerves." Postum, a national product backed by a $1.5 million advertising budget, was touted with sensationalized copy that targeted consumers' concerns that drinking coffee was an unhealthy weakness. "Is your yellow streak the coffee habit?" one ad read. When Post's Postum Cereal Company hired its first ad agency, Young & Rubicam, in 1924, it continued its unrelenting attack on coffee. In an ironic twist, Postum began buying a number of companies in the mid- to late 1920s, and one of them was coffee giant Maxwell House, in 1928. In 1929 Postum became General Foods Corporation.

The coffee industry faired well in the early 1900s, using premiums, direct mail, and in-store promotions to get consumers to commit to individual brands. When U.S. servicemen went off to war in 1917, coffee went, too. George Washington, a small coffee roaster in New York state, had recently developed an instant coffee brand, and the U.S. Army requisitioned his company's entire inventory for U.S. soldiers. The company advertised, "G. Washington's refined coffee has gone to war." The company's agency, Cecil, Warwick & Cecil, Inc., would later bring the brand to radio in the first network quiz program, *Professor Quiz* (1936). Soldiers returned from World War I with a taste for the drink. Coffee marketers also got a boost when Prohibition went into effect in 1919. During the 14 years that alcohol was banned in the United States, coffee sales rose steadily, and coffeehouses began replacing bars in the 1920s as social gathering places.

Meanwhile, the regional coffee marketers began looking to broader markets for their products. Of the brands battling for leadership in the West, Hills Brothers' "Red Can" brand began moving eastward in the 1920s. In 1921 Hills Brothers hired N.W. Ayer, Inc., to promote its brand on every streetcar west of the Rockies. In 1928 Hills Brothers coffee rolled out in Minneapolis, Minnesota, and Chicago, with ads proclaiming, "The robust West loves its vigorous drink."

In the mid-1920s, Maxwell House worked its way north and east with the help of the J. Walter Thompson Company (JWT). The agency's extensive surveys of women revealed that flavor was the biggest factor in determining their coffee brand. However, a JWT account manager concluded that housewives sought social status more than good taste, and he was right. The agency tried a new way to advertise coffee, playing up a romantic, prestigious image for the brand. Maxwell House was positioned as the aristocratic drink of the Old South that was "Good to the last drop"—praise the coffee company claimed was first awarded its product by U.S. President Theodore Roosevelt in 1904 after finishing a cup during a visit to Nashville, Tennessee's Maxwell House Hotel, from which the brand took its name. By 1927 the now leading national brand had moved to Chicago as well as New York.

Despite the Great Depression, coffee marketers continued running big advertising efforts through the 1930s. Maxwell House was facing strong competition from Chase & Sanborn coffee, now owned by Standard Brands, and its novel concept of dating coffee packaging to ensure freshness. With the brand war heating up, coffee companies turned the new medium of radio into their battlefield, sponsoring radio hours branded with their names. In 1932 the weekly variety show *The Maxwell House Show Boat* premiered, created for the brand by its new agency, Benton and Bowles, Inc., of New York City. Listeners were told, "Your ticket of admission is just your loyalty to Maxwell House Coffee," and the show was a hit. Sales for the brand rose 85 percent by December 1933, one year after a price cut for the coffee was announced on the show. Chase & Sanborn countered with the *Chase & Sanborn Hour,* from JWT, another popular variety show begun in 1929 and featuring a succession of hosts including Maurice Chevalier, Eddie Cantor, and, most famously, Edgar Bergen and Charlie McCarthy from 1937 to 1948.

Coffee marketers urged consumers to try their blends for their exceptional taste but often played on housewives' insecurities by suggesting that brewing an exceedingly good cup of coffee was difficult—especially when using the wrong brand. Trying for humor, print advertisements of the 1930s depicted housewives being nearly divorced or even abused for choosing the wrong brand of coffee. One cartoon for the Chase & Sanborn blend showed a woman getting bad coffee thrown at her by her husband as she cries, "I'm all black and blue!" She offers Chase & Sanborn coffee to him while wearing a catcher's mask. A Hills Brothers advertisement claimed, "There's nothing that soothes the savage masculine heart more quickly than steaming cups of this magnificent brew." (This line of marketing would not be left behind in these early decades. In 1965 one of Maxwell House's first color television spots urged women to "be a good little Maxwell House wife." If she was, her husband might "keep her around.")

During World War II, coffee was again part of soldiers' rations, and Maxwell House was quick to point it out with ad copy that declared, "Coffee's in the fight too!" Benton and Bowles handled Maxwell House at the time. The U.S. military again requisitioned America's entire supply of instant coffee for the war effort. In fact, coffee became so tied to the U.S. G.I. that it earned a new nickname, a cup of "Joe." After the war, high coffee prices, seemingly indiscriminant palates, and a long-awaited ease to coffee-making spurred a new popularity for this cheap instant drink, led in worldwide sales by Nescafé; that brand had been introduced in the United States by the Swiss company Nestlé in 1939 to compete with Maxwell House Instant. By 1952 instant coffee accounted for 17 percent of total coffee consumption in the United States; in Great Britain, instant coffee made up 90 percent of the total coffee market in the 1950s.

Meanwhile, regular coffee marketers were facing new challenges in the 1950s. Although surveys showed that nearly every U.S. home served some form of coffee, Americans were not drinking much coffee outside the home. Americans also were continuing the common wartime practice of "stretching" coffee, producing a diluted beverage that cut down on overall coffee consumption and satisfaction. At the same time, soft drinks, which had been in short supply during the war, were back full strength and significantly outpacing coffee in growth. Coffee industry organizations such as the National Coffee Association (NCA), a trade association for the U.S. coffee industry founded in 1911, and the Pan-American Coffee Bureau (PACB), a Latin American–funded organization established in 1936 to promote coffee consumption in the United States and Canada, launched campaigns to boost sales for the entire industry.

In 1952 the PACB and its ad agency invented America's "coffee break." This well-funded, multimedia campaign created the theme, "Give yourself a coffee-break—and get what coffee gives to you." The campaign was so well publicized that within months, 80 percent of U.S. companies surveyed had introduced a "coffee break" into their employees' work schedules. As the watchdogs for the coffee industry, these organizations also researched ways to use advertising to overcome coffee's problems—that coffee drinking was becoming routine, that consumers did not understand what coffee meant to them, and that housewives lacked the knowledge to brew good coffee—while the individual marketers focused on sales. One result was a joint campaign by the two organizations in 1958 promoting an acceptable formula for making a good cup of coffee; the recipe was printed on the packaging of 70 participating roasters and backed by an extensive print campaign.

That year a new association was formed, the International Coffee Organization (ICO), funded by 18 coffee-producing countries. The ICO was well organized and had more money than the PACB, which folded in 1963. The PACB's final campaign declared, "Good coffee is like friendship: rich and warm and strong."

In the early 1950s, General Foods, still with Benton and Bowles and coming off of a four-year radio association with George Burns and Gracie Allen, jumped into the new advertising medium of television, recognizing the unprecedented opportunity to demonstrate its products to new audiences. Other brands would not follow suit until later in the decade. Despite aggressive advertising, Maxwell House's share was eroding in an increasingly crowded market. Hills Brothers and Folgers were making gains, although Maxwell House was the overwhelming leader in instant-coffee sales.

Folgers brand coffee was especially aggressive, even before it was acquired by the Procter & Gamble Company (P&G) in the mid-1960s. In 1955 Folgers took over markets in the western states with its "doorbell promotion," helped in part by its agency, Fletcher Richards Calkins & Holden, of San Francisco. Backed heavily by local media, the campaign told housewives to be ready for the Folgers man who might come to their door; a housewife who used Folgers and could answer the question of the day would win a new Westinghouse appliance. In 1958 Folgers, based in Kansas City, Missouri, promised to ". . . bring a mountain to Chicago," a campaign that drew on its claim of blending "mountain grown" coffee. A year later, following an overwhelming media and couponing blitz, Folgers emerged with a 15 percent share of the U.S. market, while Hills Brothers dropped from a 25 percent to a 16 percent share, according to figures published that year in *Advertising Age*.

Classic TV Commercials

Maxwell House began the 1960s in a show of television leadership with what would become a classic ad created by Ogilvy, Benson & Mather, Inc. The commercial featured a musical beat that accompanied the spurtings of a percolator and grew into a catchy instrumental jingle that continued to be used in one form or another in the marketer's ads until 1975. The popular TV spot was brought back in near-original form in 1990 by Maxwell House's new agency, D'Arcy Masius Benton & Bowles, which replaced Ogilvy after more than 30 years on the account. The agency change was short-lived, however. General Foods returned to Ogilvy & Mather, the successor to Ogilvy, Benson & Mather, in 1991.

In 1960 America was also introduced to a new character, Juan Valdez, created by Doyle Dane Bernbach for the Colombian National Federation of Coffee Growers. The federation, founded in 1929, was promoting Colombian coffee in general; the coffee, the expensively and carefully grown main crop of Colombia, was blended into many U.S. brands. Juan Valdez was introduced first in newspaper ads to personify some 300,000 hardworking *cafeteros* of Colombia who, the ads said, produced a superior, hand-picked product. The copy in one ad explained that Juan Valdez "would sooner give up his *finca* (coffee grove) than pick a single coffee bean before it is ripe." Juan Valdez appeared in TV and radio spots in what the federation termed an "education" campaign that ran into the 1980s and won several Clio awards for its television commercials. In the late 1980s, the federation and its agency, then known as DDB Needham Worldwide, Inc., created an image campaign to meet America's cravings for quality products. All forms of transit, from planes to boats, turned around to get their Colombian coffee after it had been forgotten in humorous, popular commercials that also garnered a handful of Clios throughout their run. In a later television campaign, Juan Valdez and his trusty mule appeared unexpectedly in household cupboards or supermarket aisles. At its pinnacle, the federation produced a "100 percent Colombian coffee" logo that was used worldwide by different brands; the logo stood for quality and a rationalized added cost. The federation claims eventually to have reached an 83 percent brand recognition among U.S. consumers, up from 4 percent at the campaign's beginning.

In 1963 U.S. families were introduced to the character Mrs. Olson in commercials by Cunningham & Walsh for Folgers, which was not yet a national brand. Mrs. Olson, played by actress Virginia Christine, was a guiding light to housewives who could not seem to satisfy their husbands with their coffee. Mrs. Olson, who began as a cleaning lady but would come of age later in more glamorous circumstances, continued as the Folgers spokeswoman for 21 years, patching up marriages destroyed by bad coffee by telling couples to "just use Folgers." At the end of 1963, P&G bought J.A. Folger & Company and retained its ad agencies. P&G's reputation for market supremacy and deep pockets created fear not only among smaller roasters but industry leaders as well; the U.S. Federal Trade Commission, questioning the acquisition, issued a moratorium requiring P&G to refrain from expanding Folgers's marketing area for five years. During that time, General Foods went on the offensive with Ogilvy & Mather to create a Mrs. Olson imitation, Aunt Cora, played by actress Margaret Hamilton (best known for her role as the witch in the movie *The Wizard of Oz*). In the commercials, Aunt Cora was a shopkeeper who advised young couples about the best coffee, Maxwell House. General Foods used an ingenious strategy: although Mrs. Olson was the original, Aunt Cora beat her to the eastern states; when Folgers finally moved into eastern markets with Mrs. Olson, she appeared to be the imitation.

Brand Differentiation

Meanwhile, the coffee war was expanding worldwide. With their instant coffees already a success in Europe, General Foods and Nestlé were starting to fight for market share in Asian-Pacific regions, primarily Japan and Australia. General Foods began moving into these markets in the early 1960s, and by 1969 had garnered 30 percent of the Japanese instant coffee market. But its brand strategy faltered and by the mid-1970s, Nestlé was dominating the Japanese market, thanks to consistent brand imagery in its advertising from McCann-Erickson. Throughout the 1960s, Maxwell House had changed its brand name in different regions to attract consumers. The brand became Café Monky in Spain, and it dropped the "House" in countries such as France and Japan, fearing ties with royal imagery. By 1974 General Foods attempted to give its cans a "family look" to heighten brand recognition worldwide, but it was too late. In Japan, Nestlé's Nescafé and new Gold Blend, a freeze-dried Nescafé, accounted for 70 percent of instant coffee consumption compared with Maxwell House's 20 percent.

The 1970s saw a period of great innovation and brand differentiation as coffee marketers attempted to counter social changes that were hurting coffee consumption, including accusations that caffeine was unsafe. At the same time, Americans, enjoying more active lifestyles, were moving away from hot beverages, particularly in summer months, in favor of sweeter, more portable, and more refreshing soft drinks; younger consumers, in particular, were turning away from coffee. Coffee marketers turned their focus to decaffeinated brands, which had been around since the late 1920s, as the new growth area. In 1970 General Foods' Sanka decaffeinated freeze-dried instant held a 92 percent market share; that would be challenged the following year by Nestlé's introduction of a decaffeinated form of its new Taster's Choice instant coffee brand. An early and spirited Taster's Choice Decaffeinated sales promotion campaign offered one free jar of the

The perfect Sunday.

100% Colombian Coffee

The richest coffee in the world.™

The fictional character Juan Valdez, seen in a 1989 print ad, has appeared in numerous advertisements for the National Federation of Coffee Growers of Colombia.
Courtesy of the National Federation of Coffee Growers of Colombia.

new brand with a proof of purchase from an "old decaffeinated coffee."

Then, in 1972, an invention was introduced that took the focus away from instant coffee and returned it to regular blends: the automatic drip filtered coffeemaker. By the end of 1974, 35 percent of Americans had purchased an automatic coffeemaker, replacing the electric percolator and other traditional coffee-making devices. Mr. Coffee, made by North American Systems, was the clear leader in the category helped by its new spokesman, baseball legend Joe DiMaggio. Marketing Communications Associates, in Chicago, handled Mr. Coffee. Coffee marketers raced to roll out new blends ground strictly for the new machines—Maxwell House ADC was "specially developed for automatic coffeemakers," while in 1976 Hills Brothers and Mr. Coffee introduced a joint promotional campaign from Doyle Dane Bernbach with the theme, "The best thing one coffeemaker did for another."

But coffee marketers soon faced a new problem: failed Latin American coffee crops forced prices to spiral out of control from 1975 to 1977, and soft drinks finally moved ahead of coffee in per capita consumption. As coffee prices began returning to normal, the ICO pushed a $56 million campaign from 1977 to 1979 to try to fix the bad relations between coffee and its consumers, which included a boycott of the beverage.

"Lifestyle" Marketing

Advertising in the 1980s and 1990s turned largely to emotional "lifestyle" appeals. In such advertising, however, marketers risked instilling coffee drinking in general with a special feeling rather than increasing their own brand strengths. Maxwell House was the first to try emotional advertising in the early 1980s and finished strong in the year 2000. Efforts from agency Ogilvy & Mather linked the product's good qualities with consumers' special feelings; for example, one ad showed a mother playing with her daughter with the tag line, "Make every day good to the last drop."

P&G would prove to be the most effective at the lifestyle campaigns. In 1987 the company dropped Mrs. Olson and turned to the jingle, "The best part of waking up is Folgers in your cup," developed by N.W. Ayer, Inc. For 13 years, commercials showed "Peter," a young serviceman who came home for the holidays early in the morning—and announced his arrival by brewing a fresh pot of Folgers. Other ads showed doting parents and their dozing newborn with the same jingle, making the product a hero. In 2000 Folgers updated the tag line in an attempt to attract younger consumers, having a more "hip" group, Rockapella, sing the tag line as a group of young people decorate a Christmas tree outdoors, in an effort from D'Arcy Masius Benton & Bowles.

Perhaps the most publicized and popular commercials of this new romantic genre were Nestlé's soap opera–styled Taster's Choice commercials by McCann-Erickson Worldwide. The concept, first used in Great Britain from 1987 to 1993 for Nestlé's Gold Blend instant coffee, followed the romance of two apartment-building neighbors who first meet when one borrows some coffee from the other and is pleased—but not surprised—that the coffee is Taster's Choice. Each subsequent ad picked up the sto-

ryline and advanced the budding relationship a few steps. The same storyline, with minor modifications, was picked up in the United States in 1990 and ran until 1997, with new episodes of the tale released in a slow drip. The serial aspect of the campaign kept audiences eagerly awaiting the next installment. Although Taster's Choice remained in fourth place behind other leading instants, it enjoyed a level of brand recognition beyond expectations.

Upscale Marketing

Still, in a coffee industry that was struggling to recapture the market it enjoyed before its steady drop during the 1970s, brands sold to the home brewer did not see their biggest challenge coming until it was almost too late to act. In 1966 Alfred Peet introduced richer, darker, and more expensive coffee roasts through his Peet's Coffee & Tea shops in Berkeley, California. Three men from Seattle, Washington, learned the ropes of brewing great coffee from Peet and opened their first store, Starbucks, in 1971. Under new management, the chain exploded in the 1990s, with 3,300 stores globally by 2001. In addition, it set up co-marketing campaigns with Dreyer's Grand Ice Cream, United Airlines, and even Target Stores to serve Starbucks coffee exclusively. Its growth came largely through word of mouth; the chain barely advertised until 1997, when it launched a campaign tagged "Starbucks, purveyor of coffee, tea and sanity" from Goodby, Silverstein & Partners. Starbucks and rivals that started to spring up—such as Minneapolis, Minnesota–based Caribou Coffee—found a market that had not been tapped before in the United States, with young and old flocking to coffee houses at all hours to spend their money on expensive coffee drinks and darker roasts. The Starbucks brand succeeded by transforming coffee from a commodity into a lifestyle accessory.

Another development in coffee marketing that materialized in the prosperous 1980s was the emergence of the gourmet coffee line. General Foods International Coffees led with the largest effort, spearheaded by a campaign that showed singer Carol Lawrence serving a procession of specially flavored coffee blends to her friends. The strategy was that the mass market, which plainly could not afford luxury durable goods costing many thousands of dollars, would indulge itself in an affordable luxury from time to time as long as the extravagance was within financial reach. The advertising effort was supplemented by a public relations push in which beverage critics and gourmet journalists were retained to appear on such TV programs as Today and Good Morning America to discuss the subtleties of the blends and emphasize its affordability.

This shift away from traditional brews left the coffee industry reeling. In the late 1980s and early 1990s, the industry had seen mass consolidation and mergers, which resulted in more ad spending for the major brands. But by the end of the 1990s, the trend had shifted as companies such as Nestlé—which had purchased Hills Brothers coffee in 1984, in addition to Chase & Sanborn and others—sold the brands to Sara Lee Corporation in 2000. The market leaders scrambled to acquire and market their own specialty roasts, returning to their roots by selling whole beans at the grocery store, or to extend their existing brands with more upscale, flavored brands with nontraditional advertising that did little to boost market share. P&G, for example, bought Millstone, a specialty coffee retailer, in 1995 and offered its products via mail order and then in supermarkets. Through N.W. Ayer & Partners, the company attempted to take shots at Starbucks. Commercials in 1997 claimed that consumers preferred the taste of Millstone to the "leading specialty coffee chain," and a voice-over asked, "You have to wonder what business that leading specialty coffee chain is really in," while showing an "employee" hawking T-shirts and novelties.

In 1998 Starbucks joined Kraft Foods, under the Philip Morris Companies umbrella, to market and distribute Starbucks coffee beans in grocery stores. In early 2001 Folgers and Maxwell House both made a bid for market share through lifestyle appeals targeted at the Starbucks generation. Folgers, with 34 percent of at-home coffee sales, sponsored the Grammy Foundation through a music education program designed to reach the 25- to 35-year-old parents of elementary students. Maxwell House, with a 27 percent share of that market, did a movie promotion timed to coincide with the Academy Awards.

By the end of the 20th century, coffee was the number three beverage in average per capita consumption in the United States, according to the consulting company Beverage Marketing. Soft drinks ranked first, followed by beer. The overall U.S. coffee market was $18.5 billion in 1999, including $4.5 billion in at-home coffee sales, up from $13.5 billion in 1993, according to figures from the NCA. In 1998 there were an estimated 7,500 coffee houses nationwide, not including carts and kiosks, compared with fewer than 450 in 1991.

MEGAN CASSADA

See also General Foods; Gevalia Kaffee; *and color plate in this volume*

Further Reading

"Advertising Helps Folger's to Lead West Coffee Sales," *Advertising Age* (10 October 1955)

"Folger Enters Chicago Market in Teaser Drive," *Advertising Age* (30 March 1959)

"GF International Moves to Centralized Policies," *Advertising Age* (25 February 1974)

"Glamorize Java, Dicter Urges, Says Public Boredom Stalls Coffee Sales," *Advertising Age* (10 October 1955)

"If You Can't Make That Good Cup of Coffee Now, Mom, It's Not the Industry's Fault," *Advertising Age* (15 September 1958)

"Instants Make Hay, Roasters and Others Explain Prices in Rash of Ads," *Advertising Age* (15 February 1954)

MacArthur, Kate, "Iced Coffee Market Gains Ground," *Advertising Age,* 4 September 2000

"Market Percolates As No-Caf Taster's Choice Takes Aim at GF Brands," *Advertising Age* (29 January 1973)

Maxwell, John C., "Coffee Intake Rose in 1972 after Sliding for Five Years," *Advertising Age* (23 July 1973)

O'Connor, John J., "Coffee Marketers' Nerves Atwitch at Folger Market Expansion Rumor," *Advertising Age* (7 February 1972)

"P&G Sets Folger Unit to Handle Its Coffee Marketing," *Advertising Age* (9 December 1963)

Pendergrast, Mark, *Uncommon Grounds: The History of Coffee and How It Transformed Our World,* New York: Basic Books, 1999

Thompson, Stephanie, "Coffee Brands Tie in Music, Movie," *Advertising Age,* 12 February 2001

Woodward, Helen, "About Coffee," *The Nation,* (25 December 1937)

Woolf, James D., "This Campaign I Like," *Advertising Age* (23 May 1960)

Colenso

(Cleminger Colenso Communications)

Founded by Roger MacDonnell, Hilton Mackley, and Michael Wall in Wellington, New Zealand, 1969; ownership gradually acquired by Australian-based Clemenger in 1970s and 1980s; forged long-term relationships with clients such as Toyota and Bank of New Zealand.

Major Clients
Bank of New Zealand
Cadbury
Taubman Paints
Toyota Motor Corporation
Zip Industries

Colenso has built a reputation for being one of New Zealand's truly creative-driven advertising agencies. In July 1969 Roger MacDonnell teamed up with Hilton Mackley and Michael Wall to open a new advertising agency in Wellington, New Zealand. The

Colenso/BBDO's clever commercial for *The Invisible Man* television show won the agency a Gold Pencil at the 2001 One Show.
Creative Director: Mike O'Sullivan. Art Director: Quentin Plister. Writer: Warwick Delmonte. Rosie the dog.

three men, all in their mid-20s, had worked together at another Wellington ad agency, Charles Haines. But the advent of television was changing the face of advertising in New Zealand, and the three decided to go out on their own to capitalize on the changing times.

The result was Colenso, the first new ad agency in New Zealand in more than a decade. The agency was named for a Cornish preacher, William Colenso, who established the first printing press in New Zealand. The founders learned of him while searching for a name that had a communications context and a unique connection to New Zealand.

The new agency was owned equally by the three partners. It worked hard to be recognized within the market as a creative-driven ad agency—a revolutionary concept at the time. Its first client was Zip Industries, an Australian-based manufacturer of electrical appliances. Other clients followed, including Taubman Paints, which led to Colenso's collaboration with a fledgling Australian ad agency, Singleton Palmer Strauss McAllan (SPASM), founded by John Singleton. Colenso and SPASM formed a nonfinancial link, with each agency helping the other with various accounts in Australia and New Zealand throughout the early 1970s.

The relationship ended in 1973 when another Australian-based advertising agency, Clemenger, began to expand into New Zealand and bought a 20 percent stake in Colenso. As with many other New Zealand-based businesses, the three Colenso partners realized that the future of their business would depend on embracing an "Australasian" attitude toward the company's growth.

Initially MacDonnell, Mackley, and Wall thought the Clemenger organization was "too conservative," but Clemenger boss Peter Clemenger convinced them to sell the stake in their agency. The Clemenger link gave Colenso access to a much larger and more financially powerful advertising network; Clemenger was 53 percent owned by its Australian and New Zealand staff and 47 percent owned by the Omnicom Group's BBDO Worldwide. During the late 1970s through the mid-1980s, Clemenger gradually acquired 100 percent ownership of Colenso.

Colenso's big break came in 1975 when the agency was chosen to handle the New Zealand National Party's election campaign. The National Party, which represents the country's conservatives, won the election by a landslide. The party's campaign was based around the notion of problem solving and used a series of animated TV commercials depicting members of the incumbent Socialist government as dancing Cossacks. Not wanting to align itself with any particular political party, Colenso turned down the National Party's next campaign account and instead worked for the socialist Labor Party, which won the election.

During the mid-1970s Colenso had started working for blue-chip brands such as Toyota Motor Corporation; it had also acquired the country's "establishment" accounts, such as the Bank of New Zealand and Cadbury. By the early 1980s Colenso had become one of the biggest ad agencies in New Zealand; its Auckland office, opened in the late 1970s, grew to become larger than the original Wellington office. In 2000 it was named by trade magazine *Campaign Brief* as "New Zealand Agency of the Year" and was regularly honored at international award shows. A characteristic trait of Colenso over the years has been the agency's ability to forge long-term relationships with its clients, such as the Bank of New Zealand and Toyota, which have each worked with the agency for 15 to 30 years. In 2000 Clemenger Colenso Communications had gross income of $21.4 million, down 5.1 percent from the year earlier, on billings of $142.9 million.

ANDREW HORNERY

Further Reading

Smith, Paul, *Revolution in the Air!* Aukland: Longman, 1995
Spicer, Barry, Michael J. Powell, and David M. Emanuel, *The Remaking of Television: New Zealand, 1984–1992,* Aukland: Aukland University Press, 1996

Colgate-Palmolive Company

Principal Agencies
Lord & Thomas
Benton and Bowles, Inc.
Ted Bates & Company (later Ted Bates Advertising/New York)
William Esty Company, Inc.
D'Arcy-MacManus & Masius, Inc.
Norman, Craig & Kummel, Inc.
Young & Rubicam, Inc.
Foote, Cone & Belding Communications, Inc.

The company that became known as Colgate-Palmolive was founded by William Colgate, a candle, soap, and starch maker, on Dutch Street in New York City in 1806. Colgate-Palmolive is one of the oldest companies in the United States; its company headquarters remain in New York City. Its fiercest rival is the Procter & Gamble Company (P&G), the country's largest soap and detergent maker, which was founded in Cincinnati, Ohio, in 1837. In certain product categories, such as liquid soap, however, Colgate is the leader in the United States and worldwide. Colgate-Palmolive, a company worth over $9 billion at the end of the 20th century, has a long history of advertising and brand development.

"Inexpensive" Luxuries

The first Colgate advertisement appeared in a New York newspaper in 1817. Early advertisements emphasized the utilitarian benefits of using soap. After the Civil War, the public clamored for different kinds of soaps, and Colgate responded by manufacturing perfumes and essences and adding perfumed soap to its line. Cashmere Bouquet, the first milled, perfumed toilet soap, was registered as a trademark in 1872. Later, a spin-off product, Cashmere Bouquet perfume, debuted. A late-19th-century advertisement suggested that the perfume be dabbed on handkerchiefs. The copy read, "No luxury is so gratifying, harmless, or inexpensive as this perfectly prepared perfume. Colgate & Co.'s name and trademark on each bottle are a guaranty of excellence."

With increased public interest in soaps and perfumes came increased competition for Colgate. In addition to P&G, a soap company was formed by the Peet brothers (William, Robert, and James) in 1872 in Kansas City, Kansas.

Colgate expanded its product line to include toothpaste. In 1873 the company made aromatic toothpaste in a jar, and in 1896 it sold toothpaste that came in a collapsible tube. This tube was the forerunner of the toothpaste tube used today; it was portable and kept the product fresh. Since then Colgate has experimented with a variety of brands, formulas, and containers. Its earliest toothpaste in a tube was called Colgate Ribbon Dental Cream.

During the late 19th century and early 20th century, Americans showed a growing interest in indoor plumbing. Taking a bath became an art. Many of the Colgate advertisements extolled the pleasures of personal cleanliness. Women were typically portrayed as mothers helping their children or as attendants and maids in contemporary or ancient dress, helping their aristocratic mistresses.

As early as 1910 the company formulated an aggressive expansion program that included the establishment of Colgate operations worldwide. Given that most of its products are designed to enhance personal or household cleanliness, throughout its history the company has acted as if it were on a mission to improve living conditions around the globe. Colgate had an early advantage over other companies in terms of its international outreach: its products did not need refrigeration or delicate handling, so shipping abroad was easier than it was for companies selling perishables.

Colgate has had a long-standing company symbol—a large clock sometimes displayed as a logo in company publications or on product packaging. In 1906 the first Colgate clock, its face measuring 37.5 feet in diameter and covering an area of 1,104 square feet, was installed near the roof of one of its Jersey City, New Jersey, factory buildings. By 1910 the headquarters had moved from its original buildings on Dutch and John streets to Jersey City. The clock was moved in 1924 to Colgate's new factory at Jeffersonville, Indiana, and a new clock, the face measuring 50 feet in diameter, was placed on the Jersey City building, located on the banks of the Hudson River facing lower Manhattan.

Competition Leads to Advertising

In 1898 another major competitor, the B.J. Johnson Soap Company of Milwaukee, Wisconsin, emerged. Johnson marketed a line of soaps including Galvanic soap (a laundry soap) and Palmolive toilet soap, which, as the name implies, was made from palm and olive oils. Two men from Johnson approached Lord & Thomas about developing an advertising campaign. Ad executives Albert Lasker and Claude Hopkins persuaded the soap maker to invest $700 on a test campaign for Palmolive toilet soap in Benton Harbor, Michigan. The advertisement used the approach known as the "beauty appeal" and included a coupon for a cake of Palmolive that could be redeemed at any drugstore (thus developing a forced distribution—the retailer would stock the product so that he could get the redemption money from the manufacturer). The Benton Harbor trial was a success, similar trials were tried in other cities, and a national magazine campaign was mounted.

The agency created a series of ads based on the premise that Cleopatra and other legendary beauties of history used soaps similar to Palmolive. In the advertisements, an aristocratic beauty used the product with the assistance of attendants standing by her bathtub. The ad copy recommended that the bar soap be used for both skin and scalp. At this time few people used shampoo; instead they used the same bar of soap for washing both body and hair.

According to a Lord & Thomas magazine ad, if a grocer or druggist did not have Palmolive, readers could order a full-size cake directly from the company for 15 cents. In addition, if readers would send four cents in stamps to cover the cost of mailing and the names of the errant grocer or druggist, then they would receive a "beautiful oriental photogravure without advertising on it, suitable for framing." Owing to the immense popularity of Palmolive toilet soap, by 1916 the Johnson Company had changed its name to the Palmolive Company.

The 1920s advertisements for many toilet soap brands emphasized the themes of luxury and pleasure. The soap industry had come of age; behind the scenes, hard business deals were being made. The Palmolive Company and Peet Brothers merged to form the Palmolive-Peet Company. Then in 1928 Colgate merged with Palmolive-Peet, becoming Colgate-Palmolive-Peet.

Although the Great Depression ruined many businesses, the soap industry thrived; soap was both a necessity and an affordable luxury. For a few cents, users could be transported to a palm-fringed oasis or could pretend to be movie stars.

By 1939 Colgate sales reached $100 million. During the 1930s its biggest advertising accounts went to Lord & Thomas and Benton and Bowles. In 1936–37 total ad spending by Colgate-Palmolive-Peet included $1.3 million for magazines and $1.6 million for radio. Demonstrating the growing dominance of radio, by 1941–42 the marketer's radio budget had increased to $5.4 million, while its budget for magazines rose only slightly to $1.4 million. Colgate was among the top-five radio advertisers in the United States.

In 1947 Colgate introduced Fab detergent and Ajax cleaner. By 1953 the corporate name of Colgate-Palmolive was adopted. Its domestic and international headquarters were established in 1956 in the Colgate-Palmolive Building at 300 Park Avenue in New York City.

A switch to television was made during the 1940s in terms of dollars devoted to advertising revenue. There were only 200,000 television sets in the United States in 1947, making expensive productions infeasible; however, by 1948 there were enough television sets to make the debuts of the Ed Sullivan and Milton Berle shows successful and a harbinger of the future. By 1949 the number of TV sets in the United States had reached 2 million.

Colgate & Company's Cashmere Bouquet was the first milled, perfumed toilet soap. In the late 19th century, Colgate marketed a perfume of the same name.
Courtesy of the Colgate-Palmolive Company.

Sponsoring TV Programs

Because television shows were more expensive than radio shows to produce, Sylvester ("Pat") Weaver of NBC, formerly with Young & Rubicam, conceived the idea of finding multiple sponsors. He reasoned that having several sponsors would allow for increased creative freedom in developing the shows, as no single advertiser or agency executive would have a monopoly over a show's content and talent. Weaver's idea was slow to become popular. NBC personnel contacted large companies as potential sponsors, and Colgate was one of the companies it contacted.

After a succession of problems, Weaver launched the *Sunday-Night Comedy Hour* in 1950. The weeks with Bob Hope and Bobby Clark were sold to General Motors Corporation for sponsorship by its subsidiary Frigidaire. The Fred Allen, Eddie Cantor, and Dean Martin and Jerry Lewis weeks were sponsored by Colgate. Later Jackie Gleason and other comedians joined the show. Colgate Chief Executive Officer Edward Little wanted to gain

control by sponsoring the whole show. Little was a fan of Phil Silvers, Donald O'Connor, and Ray Bolger, but he did not like the overweight Gleason. Little's interaction with his cosponsor Frigidaire led to Frigidaire's canceling, and Little took over. Soon the show was renamed the *Colgate Comedy Hour,* much to Weaver's disappointment. In the long run, mostly because of the great expense involved in producing television shows, Weaver's idea of multiple sponsors became the standard in the industry. From the 1950s throughout the remainder of the century, Colgate, as well as other soap manufacturers, most notably P&G, became prominent advertisers on afternoon "soap operas," hence the popular name given to these shows.

Proliferation: Products and Agencies

In 1966 the company introduced Palmolive dishwashing liquid. Building on the reputation of Palmolive soap's gentleness, the advertisements for the dishwashing liquid emphasized how kind it was to hands—a departure from the hard-working, grease-cutting approach. Domestic servants began to disappear from many TV commercials and print ad in the 1950s and 1960s, mirroring the lessening of their numbers in the greater society. By the 1950s most middle-class women—and all but the highest echelons of the upper class—were doing their own housework; they valued soft, smooth hands that did not look like those regularly immersed in dishwater. The advertising emphasis on the gentle quality of the product appealed to these women. Sales of Palmolive dishwashing liquid passed the $1 billion mark in 1967.

In 1968 Colgate toothpaste was reformulated with monofluorophosphate fluoride (MFP), the best protection against tooth decay on the market at the time. That same year Ultra Brite, positioned as a cosmetic toothpaste, was introduced. By the 1990s Colgate, in its characteristic red-and-white tube, would become the number-one toothpaste brand worldwide.

Though the majority of Colgate products were pitched to women, some were aimed specifically at men. In 1972 Colgate introduced Irish Spring, a deodorant soap for "manly men," an account handled by the William Esty Company. Ted Bates & Company, another agency, promoted Palmolive Rapid Shave. D'Arcy-MacManus & Masius created the advertisements for Wilkinson Blades.

As Colgate's product lines increased so did its number of advertising agencies. In 1975–76 the agencies and products advertised included Bates for Colgate Dental Cream; D'Arcy for Palmolive soap; Norman Craig & Kummel for Ajax cleaner; and Esty for Ajax laundry detergent and Ultra Brite.

In 1976 Colgate-Palmolive acquired Hill's Pet Products, which was quite a departure from previous product lines. The advertising, produced by Young & Rubicam, Inc. (Y&R), New York, emphasized the brand's specialized diets, and by 1999 Hill's products were sold in 63 countries. Veterinarians served as spokespersons for more than 35 different prescription diet products recommended to manage such conditions as pet obesity, heart disease, and kidney disease. A May 1999 advertisement in *Southern Living* magazine featured a veterinarian and her pet cat with the tag line, "What vets feed their pets." Hill's products are sold primarily at pet specialty stores and veterinary clinics.

In 1981 the company celebrated its 175th anniversary and introduced another toothpaste, Colgate Winterfresh Gel. But three years later Colgate's advertising strategy marked a turning point. In May 1984 the *New York Times* reported that Esty had been dropped after 30 years of association with Colgate. Ted Bates; Y&R; and Foote, Cone & Belding were named as Colgate's global advertising agencies. According to the article, Esty, which operated exclusively in the United States, was unable to keep up with the growing global lines that had become increasingly important in Colgate's corporate development. Colgate reassigned Ajax Dishwashing Liquid to Y&R, which, over time, became Colgate's dominant international advertising agency.

Building again on the popular Palmolive name, Colgate introduced Palmolive Automatic Dishwashing Liquid in 1986; it was the first liquid soap for use in automatic dishwashers. The next

By 1914 Colgate had expanded its product line to include a range of shaving supplies.
Courtesy of the Colgate-Palmolive Company.

year Colgate acquired the liquid soap business from the Minnetonka Corporation and formed Softsoap Enterprises to market liquid hand soaps. The company also announced a major redevelopment project on the waterfront in New Jersey. Office space, a hotel, parks, and a marina were built on the site formerly occupied by its New Jersey plant.

The 1990s were marked by several mergers and increased international expansion. In 1990 the company acquired Javex Bleach from a Canadian company, making Colgate-Palmolive the number-one marketer of bleach outside the United States. In addition it acquired Murphy's Oil Soap, the leading wood cleaner in the United States; the international rights to Plax, an anti-plaque mouth rinse; and the Mennen Company, with its Speed Stick deodorants and antiperspirants and its Baby Magic product lines. By 1999 Mennen deodorant stick was the worldwide leader in that category. Advertisements in 2000 for Baby Magic's complete line of hypoallergenic, gentle bathing, and skincare products emphasized that its special moisturizers protect a baby's skin best.

According to Madge, the fictional manicurist featured in a campaign that ran for nearly two decades, using gentle Palmolive Dishwashing Liquid meant the end of "dishpan hands."
Courtesy of the Colgate-Palmolive Company.

Colgate's international growth included many new products and expansion to other countries, mainly in Europe, Asia, and South America. By 1997 Colgate's Softlan was the number-one fabric softener in Hong Kong with a 49 percent market share, and its position was strengthened by the introduction of Ultra Softlan. Sampling reached 40 percent of Hong Kong households, and a strong advertising campaign helped ensure the brand's success.

Also in the 1990s Colgate acquired the liquid soap brands of S.C. Johnson in Europe and the South Pacific, making Colgate-Palmolive the global leader in this category. The company built an oral care facility in Huangpu, China, and it acquired the Kolynous Oral Care Business in Latin America. Increasingly, manufacturing took place overseas. In the 1990s the company opened a factory and warehouse in Thailand.

Colgate is often cited as a leader in global markets. By 1999 it was valued at more than $9 billion, reaching people in more than 200 countries with its consumer products; only 26 percent of Colgate's sales came from the United States. Its five core businesses were oral care; personal care; household surface care; fabric care; and pet nutrition.

Because the company's products are associated with health and cleanliness, it makes an effort to maintain a quality image. For this reason it adheres to a strict advertising placement policy that precludes ads in contexts where there is gratuitous violence, offensive sexual behavior, or denigration of individuals because of their age, gender, sexual orientation, race, religion, or ethnic origins. Further, the policy states that "Colgate-Palmolive charges its advertising agencies and their media buying services with the responsibility of prescreening any questionable media content or context. If there is any doubt about media suitability for Colgate-Palmolive advertising, it is referred to Colgate-Palmolive media management for review and decision."

At the turn of the 21st century, the future held further growth for Colgate, especially in Asia and South America. In the United States Colgate Total brand toothpaste was a particularly successful 1990s product—the first toothpaste to receive the American Dental Association Seal of Acceptance for protection against plaque, gingivitis, and cavities. By 1998 combined sales of all varieties of Colgate toothpastes had recaptured U.S. leadership in that category—a lead the company had lost in 1962. P&G. remains Colgate-Palmolive's top competitor. The two companies have fought toothpaste, soap, fabric softener, and detergent wars. P&G took the lead in detergents after World War II when it introduced Tide. P&G has generally been a more aggressive user of advertising than Colgate, and it is one of the leading U.S. issuers of free samples and discount coupons. Colgate's strategy has been to build its international markets.

In the 1990s Colgate responded to the demand for so-called value-added products by offering, for example, added-value bleach products that have a variety of scents or all-purpose cleaners with bleach. Much of the long-term success of the Colgate-Palmolive Company can be attributed to its ability to respond to consumers' changing values and changing market trends.

ELIZABETH GOLDSMITH

See also color plate in this volume

Further Readings

Aaker, David, *Building Strong Brands,* New York: Free Press, 1996

Brooks, Tim, and Earle Marsh, *The Complete Directory to Prime-Time TV Shows,* New York: Ballantine, 1979

Rowsome, Frank, *They Laughed When I Sat Down: An Informal History of Advertising in Words and Pictures,* New York: Bonanza, 1959

Weaver, Pat, *The Best Seat in the House: The Golden Years of Radio and Television,* New York: Knopf, 1994

Collectibles

Limited-edition collectibles—plates, figurines, dolls, books, and the like that are issued for the purpose of collecting rather than for use—are most often targeted at adults. The market is divided into two parts: the "first-issue" segment, which consists of items produced as collectibles that may increase in value, and the secondary segment, items that are bought, sold, and traded among collectors rather than being purchased directly from the manufacturer. First-issue collectibles are normally released in limited-edition series.

Driven by direct-mail advertising, the collectibles market was valued at $10.4 billion in retail sales in 1999 in a study by Unity Marketing, a research and consulting company that tracks the market. Primary means of communication include Sunday newspaper magazines, women's magazines, and specialty magazines such as *TV Guide;* newspaper inserts; and database-driven collectors clubs established by the collectibles marketers to maintain customer loyalty. In the mid-1990s, Sunday magazines such as *Parade, USA Weekend,* the *Los Angeles Times Magazine,* and the *New York Times Magazine* attracted about half the industry's total ad spending and generated more than a quarter of industry sales. The Franklin Mint (a marketer of porcelain plates, coins, licensed memorabilia, and other collectibles) alone spent $31.5 million to advertise in national Sunday magazines in 1999. Two-thirds of industry sales were recorded in retail channels, while TV shopping generated 5 percent of purchases. (Fred Segel, founder of the Franklin Mint, also created QVC home-shopping network, which is an important marketer of limited-edition collectibles.)

Collector Clubs

Affinity marketing to collector clubs through direct mail is a key sales tool in the collectibles market. Collector clubs were booming in 1999, with revenue from memberships nearly doubling to $78.8 million that year versus $40.6 million two years earlier, according to Unity Marketing. Much of the growth was due to the launch of Ty, Inc.'s Beanie Babies collectors club, which boasted approximately 2 million active members in 1999. But other clubs saw growth in their membership rosters as well. In all, 4 million collectors in 1998 accounted for nearly 8 million memberships in collector clubs.

Some collector club offers are in the form of continuity programs, especially in the case of limited-edition series. Customers who buy the first in the series automatically receive subsequent series releases, with the option of returning the object without payment if they do not want it. These offers tend to be marketed through mail order, while direct-response newspaper ads and the like tend to feature individual items for purchase.

While revenue from club memberships represents just a small portion of the industry's total sales, clubs are important marketing tools because they generate increased loyalty and spending among members, who tend to be the best customers for collectibles marketers. A typical collector maintains four to five separate collections; collectors who belong to clubs spend about three times as much annually on their collections as nonclub members ($1,169 per year versus $572 in 1998, according to Unity Marketing).

The Enesco Group, with annual sales of $400 million to $500 million, is one collectible marketer that relies on collectors clubs to market its merchandise. It formed the Precious Moments Collectors Club in 1981—three years after introducing the first licensed Precious Moments figurines—and by 1994 the club had half a million members. The company created the Enesco Precious Moments Birthday Club in 1985 to encourage children to collect the figurines. Enesco uses collectors clubs for some of its other collectible lines as well, including Small World of Music, Memories of Yesterday, Cherished Teddies, Treasury of Christmas Ornaments, and Sports Impressions, in addition to several licensed and artist-identified collections. All told, the company's catalog features about 7,000 gift and collectible items, with about half of those new each year.

The collectibles business had been around for some time prior to the 1990s growth spurt in collectors clubs. Enesco was founded in 1958, the Franklin Mint in 1964, Danbury Mint in 1969, and Bradford Exchange in 1973. The Bradford Exchange was founded by Rod MacArthur, son of John D. MacArthur, founder of the John D. and Catherine T. MacArthur Foundation, one of the wealthiest U.S. foundations. The MacArthur business empire included a number of interests, including Marshall John Advertising, the predecessor to Draft Worldwide. Rod MacArthur worked for the agency and as a sideline operated his own private collec-

A 2001 print ad from the Danbury Mint shows die-cast vehicles and college memorabilia, two popular categories of collectibles.
© *MBI and the University of Illinois Urbana-Champaign.*

tors plate business in the early 1970s out of his father's Northbrook, Illinois, office. It was not a business the senior MacArthur saw much future in. But when it began to take off, he demanded a share of the profits in payment for his son's use of office and shipping facilities. Rod MacArthur refused and established his own business, the Bradford Exchange, in 1973.

Collectible Toys

A robust secondary collecting market for items such as dolls, trading cards, and comic books had also developed in the mid-20th century. However, these items were not marketed as collectibles until the late 1980s, when comic book and trading card marketers and toy companies started to issue limited editions made specifically for collecting (with artificial scarcity built into the design) in order to capitalize on the rise of the collecting hobby during that period. Prior to that, the products were intended for reading or playing with, not for collecting.

Several factors fueled the upward trend in toy collecting. First, baby boomers entered their prime collecting years—age 45 to 64—and began seeking collectibles that brought back memories of their childhood. Men began entering the market in greater numbers, particularly younger men, seeking anything from sports collectibles and die-cast vehicles to action figures and G.I. Joe dolls. Individual collector crazes, most notably Beanie Babies, brought new customers of all ages into the market. And new marketers entered the field, such as plush-toy, giftware, and, especially, toy companies.

Both Mattel and Hasbro increased their participation in the collectibles industry in the 1990s by issuing limited-edition, more expensive versions of the toys baby boomers remembered from their childhood. Ten thousand collectors attended Hasbro's first G.I. Joe International Collectors Convention in 1998, the toy's 30th anniversary year. The G.I. Joe Classic Collection consisted of foot-tall dolls, such as those issued by the company in the 1960s, selling for five to ten times more than the action figure–sized versions sold to children. Some of the collector releases included a Tuskegee Airman G.I. Joe and the first female G.I. Joe, both introduced in 1997.

Hasbro also marketed collectors' editions of the action figures in its "Star Wars," Starting Line-Up, and Beast Wars Transformers lines. By 1997 a Hasbro-sponsored study conducted by Unity Marketing found that 40 percent of the $2.1 million U.S. action figure market was products purchased as collectibles. The typical collector, a male age 18 to 40, spent between $1,000 and $2,000 on collectible action figures.

Meanwhile, Mattel was creating a large collector market for its Barbie dolls. It introduced its holiday limited-edition Barbies in 1988 and its Barbie Collectibles brand in 1993, starting a database-driven Barbie Collector Club to market the special limited editions, which retailed for as much as $900. In the program's first year, sales of Barbie Collectibles were $35 million; by 1997 the line accounted for $200 million of the Barbie brand's total $1 billion-plus sales. The line featured designer versions from top names such as Oscar de la Renta, Calvin Klein, Christian Dior, Bob Mackie, Dolce & Gabbana, Fendi, Louis Vuitton, and Vera Wang. Some were marketed exclusively through department stores such as Bloomingdale's, which sold $2.5 million worth of Donna Karan–designed Barbies and $1 million worth of Nicole Miller Barbies, both exclusives, in the mid-1990s. In 1995 Mattel estimated that 10,000 consumers collected Barbie dolls regularly.

Aside from designer versions, Barbie Collectibles included unique nostalgic pieces such as Rose Barbie, a pink-gowned doll packaged with a Barbie miniature rose bush; "Star Trek" Barbie and Ken, for $75, commemorating the 30th anniversary of the television show; Pink Splendor Barbie, which wore Swarovski crystal jewelry and a gown embellished with 24-karat gold threads; and Soda Fountain Sweetheart Barbie, created through a licensing arrangement with Coca-Cola Company and distributed only via Mattel's direct-mail list, Coca-Cola's collectibles catalog, and the Coca-Cola stores in New York City and Atlanta, Georgia.

In 1995 Mattel launched its first advertising effort directed at adults, a print campaign to support the Barbie Collectibles brand. The black-and-white ads, which ran in *People* magazine, women's magazines, and Sunday publications, were tagged "You're never too old for Barbie," with copy that read, "As a kid you loved her,

and shoe by hat by glove, you lost her. Reunite with an old friend." Ogilvy & Mather, which handled Barbie toy advertising along with Foote, Cone & Belding, handled the collectibles effort. Mattel also supported its collectible Barbies with sweepstakes and infomercials.

In the midst of the collecting boom in the mid-1990s, the five largest collectibles specialists—the Franklin Mint, the Bradford Exchange, the Danbury Mint, the Hamilton Collection (since 1997 part of the Bradford Group), and Lenox Collections—together spent $377.8 million in measured media, according to Competitive Media Reporting. The Franklin Mint accounted for $147.2 million, or 39 percent of that figure. (The company's advertising is handled in-house.) Additional spending came from other marketers of first-issue collectibles, including social expressions companies such as Hallmark Cards with its Keepsake Ornament line; die-cast vehicle marketers such as Ertl and Racing Champions; gift marketers such as Enesco and Hammacher Schlemmer; toy companies such as Mattel and Hasbro; and plush-toy marketers such as Applause and Steiff.

Plush-toy marketer Ty, Inc., was an exception; sales of its collectible Beanie Babies grew without benefit of advertising support. The company relied instead on word of mouth. Ty did, however, take advantage of promotional alliances, especially a series of tie-ins with fast-food giant McDonald's. The Beanie Babies partnership was McDonald's most successful promotional alliance to date.

First-issue collectibles marketers do business in an exceptionally competitive marketplace. In 1994 alone the Franklin Mint produced 1,000 new items. The key players tend to copy each other's successes, creating similar designs or themes, from realistic portraits of wolves to inspirational depictions of visions of the Virgin Mary (one of the best-selling collector plate series in the mid-1990s, initiated by the Bradford Exchange). Companies also try to differentiate themselves by signing licenses for brands such as Coca-Cola or Harley-Davidson, deceased celebrities such as Elvis Presley, fictional and cartoon characters, and sports figures.

Lenox Collections is typical of collectibles marketers in its use of a variety of direct-response media to reach its target audience, women age 45 to 60. As the direct marketing division of china manufacturer Lenox, Inc., Lenox Collections was founded in 1982 to sell collectibles, including sculptures, figurines, home décor, and jewelry. It mails more than 1,000 direct-mail packages a year and runs more than 900 print ads. Lenox's parent firm, Brown-Forman Corporation, handles its advertising in-house. Its six catalogs a year—the first went out in 1989—are sent to a total of 10 million names and account for 20 percent of the marketing mix, with the bulk of the remainder devoted to print coupon ads and noncatalog-related direct mail efforts. As with other collectible companies, TV and other media represent a small proportion of spending.

One controversial advertising technique undertaken by many leading collectibles marketers is "dry testing." In a coupon ad, the company offers a product that is not yet available and produces it only if there is enough response to warrant manufacturing. If the company decides not to produce the product, its sends customers who ordered the product a letter explaining that the item is unavailable.

After a decade-long run of substantial sales increases, the first-issue collectibles market started to decrease in 1999; sales were down 2 percent from the peak year of 1998. Reasons for the decline included the end of the Beanie Babies fad (Ty discontinued the original line in 1999), as well as competition from the secondary collectibles market—especially via the Internet—and softness in sales by some of the market leaders, such as Mattel and Hasbro in the collectible doll sector.

The market contraction was accompanied by several industry changes. First, the product mix changed. In 1994 figurines were the biggest segment, with 41 percent of total sales, followed by dolls with 23 percent, plates with 8 percent, and cottages (collectible ceramic buildings marketed by such companies as Department 56) with 6.5 percent, according to Unity Marketing. In 1999 figurines and dolls remained the top two, respectively, in market share, but sales were down 7 percent and 12 percent, respectively, from 1998. Meanwhile, such collectibles as ornaments, boxes, and musical items were becoming more popular. The industry also had begun to experiment with nontraditional collectibles, such as jackets.

As a result of soft industry-wide sales, some companies saw significant declines in their individual financial performance. Enesco's sales dropped 15 percent and profits 52 percent in 1999, causing the company to discontinue some of its collector clubs. The downturn also had an impact on ad spending; Franklin Mint's expenditures on Sunday magazines were down 37.4 percent in 1999 from 1998, for example.

As direct-response spending fell, marketers increased their focus on retail sales and on meeting retailers' needs. Lenox Collections set up a retail division in 1997 and changed its product mix to appeal to retail as well as direct-response customers. It continued to sell collectibles through Sunday supplements and major women's magazines but focused more on boosting its retail distribution and less on its direct-response activities.

New Outlets

At the same time, collector's items moved from primarily specialty distribution into new outlets such as department stores and, in particular, mass channels. Items ranging from collectible Barbies to die-cast vehicles to action figures were increasingly sold through mass merchants. These retailers embraced collectibles, which they had identified as a growing market and one that would bring new customers into their stores. Collectibles have 40 percent–50 percent profit margins, much higher than other similar products sold through mass merchants, and can be extremely profitable if properly merchandised.

Enesco and Hallmark both introduced collectible products into drugstores and large national mass retailers for the first time in the late 1990s. Some chains made Hallmark's Keepsake Ornament line the focal point of their advertising and promotions during the holidays. Longs Drug Stores Corporation ran a chainwide Keepsake event in 1997 marking the introduction of the new Keepsake designs for that year. It backed the promotion with TV ads and print teasers in July from Pickett Advertising and made sure its outlets were stocked with the new ornaments by the beginning of August. Its ad campaign used a "Don't miss out" theme to remind collectors of the limited quantities and spur them to purchase.

Another distribution-related change in the collectibles market in the late 1990s was the rise of the Internet, which occurred at roughly the same time as the downturn in industry sales. A portion of advertising spending moved to the Web. Lenox Collections, for example, which built an on-line site for its collectibles and figures in the late 1990s, advertised the site on other Web sites and portals, including using banner ads on About.com and Lycos.com.

Hasbro launched HasbroCollectors.com in November 1998 to offer information about its collectible products, such as details of manufacture, quantities, and dates of availability. Just a small slice of Hasbro's total sales of more than $3 billion came from the site, which offered a few exclusive collectible action figures in its G.I. Joe, Star Wars, Batman, Starting Line-Up, Beast Wars Transformers, and Action Man lines. To avoid competition with its retailer partners, the company limited the site primarily to information in the hope of driving retail sales.

Third-party collector sites have also generated interest from collectors. CollectibleTown.com was launched in 2000 and sold branded collectibles from Walt Disney Company, Warner Bros., Lenox, Ertl, Christopher Radko, Hummel, and about 70 other suppliers for a total of more than 10,000 dolls, figurines, plates, crystal pieces, and sports memorabilia items. Before it folded in January 2001, CollectibleTown.com's competition included Collectibles.com; Collectiblestoday.com, owned by the Bradford Exchange; and Gocollect.com, a network of 600 specialty collectibles retailers.

According to Unity Marketing, about 40 percent of collectors have used the Internet for collecting purposes. A total of 13.9 million Internet users purchased first-issue collectibles from an on-line store in 1999, while 10.2 million bought collectibles through an on-line auction site (such as eBay.com). Educated and affluent women younger than 40 were the most frequent users. More than a third of doll collectors have used the Internet to gather information on their hobby, while 21 percent have made a collectible purchase over the Internet. Memorabilia and die-cast collectors are two of the most active sectors; 16 percent of those who collect die-cast items shopped regularly on the Internet in 2000.

As distribution of collectibles expanded more toward nontraditional channels, specialty retailers of collectibles faced tough times at the end of the 1990s and in the early part of the new century. In 1999 retail sales through specialty stores were down 6 percent from the previous year. In the same year, there was a 19 percent decline in the number of stores, from 12,007 in 1998 to 9,778 in 1999. Young collectors were driving many of these changes in distribution as they sought collectible products from mass merchant chains, department stores, toy stores, and the Internet rather than from specialty collectibles stores.

Changes in distribution meant changes in the way marketers do business. For example, the Danbury Mint, a mail-order collectibles specialist, began to explore new distribution channels such as third-party catalogs (independent catalogs marketed by companies other than Danbury), inserts in products marketed by other companies that target customers in the same demographic group, and holiday brochures. Danbury also included information about its Web site in all of its print advertising. Meanwhile, it decreased its reliance on traditional channels such as free-standing newspaper inserts and women's weeklies.

With more than 200 companies in the business of marketing collectibles at the outset of the 21st century, no specialty retailer could stock all the products available. This meant that the trend toward alternative distribution, particularly on the Internet, was expected to continue. Yet it seems unlikely that collectibles marketers will move entirely away from the marketing tool that has driven the industry throughout its history: direct-response advertising through Sunday magazines, newspaper inserts, women's and specialty publications, and database-driven collectors clubs.

KAREN RAUGUST

Further Reading

Bryceland, Kristen, "Precious Moments Deal Nixed," *HFN* (3 July 2000)
"Collectible Market Growing; Nostalgia Is a Key Theme," *Research Alert* (4 April 1996)
Fitzgerald, Kate, "Hallmark Harnesses Disney 'Dalmatians' Tie-in for Holidays," *Advertising Age* (25 November 1996)
"Infighting Nasty for Collectibles," *Advertising Age 100 Leading National Advertisers* (7 September 1995)
Kehoe, Ann-Margaret, "Lenox Inc.'s New Chief Maps Out Growth Tack," *HFN* (13 July 1998)
Negus, Beth, "Big-Time Kid Stuff," *Direct* 11, no. 2 (February 1999)
Stephenson, Elizabeth, "Mattel Dolls Up Barbie for Adult Collectors," *Advertising Age* (9 October 1995)
Wallace, Andrew, "Bradford Group Purchases Hamilton from Stanhome," *Direct Marketing* (8 May 1997)

Collett Dickenson Pearce

Created from John Collett's Pictorial Publicity by Ronnie Dickenson and John Pearce in London, England, 1960; joined by Frank Lowe, who left to form his own shop in 1981; acquired by Dentsu, 1991.

Major Clients
Birds Eye
Cinzano
Fiat
Ford Motor Company
Gallaher
Hamlet cigars
Harvey's Bristol Cream
Heineken
Honda Motor Company
Parker Pens
Whitbread brewery

Collett Dickenson Pearce, later known simply as CDP, had much the same revolutionary effect on the British advertising scene that Doyle Dane Bernbach had in the United States. Founded in 1960, the London, England–based agency was responsible for some of the most creative, thought-provoking, and humorous advertising seen by the British public. The agency's roll call of classic campaigns includes evoking the "happiness" of a Hamlet cigar, the refreshment of a Heineken, and the attractions of Pretty Polly legs. Other memorable visions it created include the Cinzano-soaked blouse of actress Joan Collins and surreal images for Benson & Hedges cigarettes.

From the 1960s through the 1980s, CDP dominated creative awards and played a major role in advertising in the United Kingdom, gaining international recognition as a world leader in advertising creativity. Major clients during that period included Gallaher tobacco (Benson & Hedges), Ford Motor Company, and, later, Fiat, Birds Eye frozen foods, Whitbread brewery, Nestlé, Harvey's Bristol Cream sherry, and Parker Pens.

Over the years, the agency proved to be a veritable hotbed of talent and turned out a large number of British advertising's leading figures; CDP alumni include Colin Millward, Charles Saatchi, Alan Parker, David Puttnam, Frank Lowe, John Salmon, Alan Waldie, Paul Weiland, Gray Jolliffe, Neil Godfrey, Tony Brignull, Ron Collins, and Robin Wight. In turn, they brought in top photographers such as David Bailey, Don McCullin, and Patrick Lichfield, and film directors Ridley Scott and Hugh Hudson.

Unlike many agencies that were created by young upstarts eager to make their mark, CDP was founded by three executives approaching middle age. Ronnie Dickenson, a program controller for the television company ATV, and John Pearce, joint managing director of the stylish agency Colman Prentis and Varley (CPV), decided to set up their own agency and purchased John Collett's Pictorial Publicity to gain immediate recognition by the Institute of Practitioners in Advertising and thus entitlement to credit when buying media. They brought in Colin Millward from CPV as the agency's creative director.

Pearce, Millward, and Dickenson set the style and tone of the new agency, establishing an environment where unconventional creative people could flourish. The creative department was the hub of the agency, and the creative staff claimed a much larger share of the payroll than was the industry average. Even sample ads sent to clients were approved by the managing director—indicating that they had the backing of the agency management—still an unusual practice. CDP also became the first U.K. agency to put writers and art directors together in teams.

The creative concept extended to media. CDP was a pioneer in seeking more effective ways of using media to grab attention or deliver a particular audience. The agency even persuaded Britain's TV companies to be more flexible about the length of commercials they would accept. It also was instrumental in the success of newspaper color supplements, recognizing the launch of the *Sunday Times Magazine* as an opportunity to showcase print advertising for brands such as Benson & Hedges, Aer Lingus, and Whitbread Pale Ale.

In the late 1960s CDP linked with other agencies in Europe, and Millward passed the creative director's job to John Salmon who returned from Toronto, Canada, to concentrate on international creative work. The informal network, however, eventually fell apart owing to a lack of major international accounts.

In 1969 joint managing directors were appointed from within the agency: Bob Pethick, deputy creative director, and Geoffrey Pattie, account director. Meanwhile, Frank Lowe joined as an account executive and earned his corporate stripes on the Birds Eye frozen foods business. Lowe, recognized by agency management for his passion for advertising, presented only work he believed to be outstanding. So in 1972, when Pattie later moved on to politics and Pethick retired, Pearce appointed Lowe managing director and the agency entered another period of expansion that lasted through the rest of the decade, with Lowe working closely with Millward and Pearce.

CDP in the 1960s had made its reputation largely in print, but Lowe concentrated on raising the agency's TV and cinema work to the same standard. He signed Alan Parker, a former top CDP writer who had become an independent commercials director, to work exclusively for CDP.

In the 1970s Lowe caused a sensation when he resigned from the Ford account after a new marketing director at the automotive giant apparently demanded a selection of creative solutions for each ad. CDP's policy had been to submit what it thought was the best single creative solution. Luckily, Fiat moved its account to CDP soon after the loss of Ford, and CDP went on to create its famous "Hand-built by robots" spot for the Fiat Strada launch in 1978. The commercial, directed by Hugh Hudson (who directed *Chariots of Fire,* which won the 1981 Oscar for best motion picture), shows robots assembling the car to music from Gioacchino Rossini's *Barber of Seville.* Its climax shows the car hurtling round a racetrack.

Throughout the 1960s, 1970s, and 1980s, CDP's campaigns cemented the company's presence in the United Kingdom's

"Finishing School," a 1974 TV commercial from Collett Dickenson Pearce, emphasized the quality craftsmanship of Parker pens through a subtly humorous view of the pens' "snob appeal."
Courtesy Parker Pen Company.

national consciousness. "Happiness is a cigar called Hamlet" was the tag line for countless commercials depicting mishaps, such as a tennis spectator in a neck brace and a bald man in a photo booth trying—and failing—to arrange a few strands of hair across his pate before the four-photograph sequence was completed. The campaign's impact was enhanced by a musical theme, a Jacques Loussier version of Bach's "Air on a G String."

Music also played an important role in the shop's much-awarded Hovis bread campaign. The nostalgic TV spots featured a small boy in a turn-of-the-century northern mill town who enthused about the bread while a brass band play Dvorak's *New World* symphony.

The agency's best-known advertising was for Benson & Hedges cigarettes, in which it introduced surreal print and cinema ads with no headline or copy, only the Benson & Hedges pack replacing an object in the picture—or forming an additional object—to make a visual joke. Executions included one in which the agency added an extra pyramid to the famous trio in Giza, Egypt.

In 1979 Lowe handed the post of managing director to John Salmon but continued to manage clients he was closely associated with, such as Whitbread and Birds Eye. Two years later, he dealt the agency a major blow when he left along with Geoff Howard-Spink—the deputy managing director who had worked on Texaco and Clarks footwear—to set up his own agency, Lowe Howard-Spink, taking along key accounts including Whitbread and Birds Eye. The Gallaher tobacco account, however, remained at CDP, and the agency made up the billings loss within three years.

Pearce died following a heart attack in 1981. Salmon became chairman; John Spearman moved up from deputy managing director to managing director; and Dave Brown was promoted from deputy creative director to creative director. However, by the end of the 1980s the financial climate had changed, and the Euston

Road offices, formerly a key property asset, decreased in value. Some large clients moved, and the agency had to downsize.

In 1991 Japan's Dentsu came to the rescue, buying 40 percent of the agency and influencing the way it would be run. Ironically, it brought in David Jones from Lowe Howard-Spink as chief executive. However, he was lured back to take up the same role at Lowe in 1994. Ben Langdon of McCann-Erickson became CDP's next chief executive and moved the agency to Soho (London) in 1995. After securing new business such as the Honda Motor Company account and returning the agency to profitability, he, too, returned to his former agency in 1996. Langdon had appointed former Saatchi & Saatchi Director Chis Macleod as deputy managing director, and Macleod took over running the agency, becoming chief executive in 1998. Macleod, with Managing Director Simon Myers, operated CDP as a fully integrated agency, offering direct marketing, sales promotion, and public relations.

In 2001 Macleod succeeded Langdon as chief executive and, with managing director Simon Myers, brought the agency back to profitability, while reorganizing the shop as a fully integrated agency offering direct marketing, sales promotion, and public relations. Staff grew to 125 employees.

CDP once again began producing award-winning work. Hamlet's "Bummer" was voted the best U.K. radio commercial of 2000 at the Aerial Awards, the U.K.'s major radio awards. The integrated campaign for the recruitment company totaljobs.com won professional accolades for its creativity and its effectiveness. In 2000 CDP was the only agency to have four ads (for Hovis, Cinzano, Fiat Strada, and Hamlet) included in *Campaign* magazine's all-time top-ten ads.

Toward the end of 2001, as part of the trend toward agency consolidations, CDP merged with travissully, its sister Dentsu agency in London, to create cdp-travissully, an agency that aimed to combine on-line and off-line creativity. Chris Macleod became chairman of the merged operation; Peter Travis of travissully (formerly of CDP) became chief executive; and Gill Sully of travissully became managing director and creative director. The new agency had accounts such as Dell, NEC, and Six Continents hotels group in its portfolio.

SEAN KELLY

Further Reading

Garrett, Jade, "Media: Up in Smoke: The Government's Policy on Tobacco Ads Is in Disarray; Jade Garrett Says They Should Have Seen It Coming," *Guardian* (9 October 2000)
Inside Collett Dickenson Pearce, London: Batsford, 2000
McIntosh, Alastair, *From Eros to Thanatos: Cigarette Advertising's Imagery of Violation As an Icon into British Cultural Psychopathology*, Edinburgh: Centre for Human Ecology, University of Edinburgh, 1996

Commercials. *See* Director, Commercials; Production: Commercials

---

Commission System

Historically, when an ad agency places an ad for a client, the medium (i.e., newspaper, TV, radio) pays a commission to the agency. If, for example, the commission rate is 15 percent and an advertisement costs $1,000, the advertiser pays $1,000 to the advertising agency. The agency remits $850 to the medium and retains the remaining $150 as its commission. Thus, the commissions that an agency receives pay for the service provided to the advertiser by the agency.

In addition to media commissions, advertising agencies also usually mark up the cost of physically producing advertisements in a form that is acceptable to the media. If the media commission is 15 percent, for example, agencies will typically mark up production bills by a commission rate of 17.65 percent; that amount equals a return to the agency of 15 percent of the combined total of production expenses and agency commission. For example, if a production bill is $100 and the agency markup is 17.65 percent, the total paid by the advertiser is $117.65, and the agency commission ($17.65) is equal to 15 percent of $117.65.

In the jargon of the industry, media bills represent "gross" costs—that is, media rates including the agency commission. Production bills represent "net" costs, as they do not include commission and must be marked up (or "grossed up") to include the agency commission.

When advertising agencies emerged in the United States in the second half of the 19th century, they originally functioned as sales agents for newspapers and magazines. The agencies were compensated and encouraged by the media because they efficiently served the space-buying advertisers. Later, agencies evolved into media-space brokers. By the 1890s the agencies were taking on the additional responsibility of providing ideas for advertisements to fill the space they had sold to advertisers. Media proprietors welcomed this agency activity because they realized that the provision of such services was critical to increasing the sales of media space.

Around the turn of the century, the original advertising agency functions associated with the sale of advertising space gradually disappeared as agencies concentrated on providing the service that had, at first, been only incidental to their existence—the creation of ideas for advertisements.

Throughout this period, agencies were compensated by media commissions on the value of space used by the advertisers. These commissions varied from medium to medium and from time to time but were generally in the range of 10 percent to 25 percent of the gross cost of media space.

Around 1920 the rate for agency commissions granted by the media settled at 15 percent, even though advertising agencies no longer functioned as sales agents for the media. The establishment of the level of commission at 15 percent was not legislated nor was it formally derived from an industry-wide contract between agencies and media. Instead, the 15 percent rate reflected an accommodation between the media and the agencies for the creative service provided by the agencies to advertisers. The system was a subject of great controversy within the industry, pitting advertiser against agency. But ultimately it survived. The commission was allowed only to advertising agencies. If advertisers bought space (or later, time) directly from the media, they were charged at the gross, or undiscounted, rate. This accommodation between the media and the agencies had nothing to do with the intrinsic worth of the ideas for advertisements created by a particular agency. As the role of the advertising agency evolved, the 15 percent commission proved to be a compromise that satisfied not only its original architects but also the advertisers.

The 15 percent commission system served as a basis for agency compensation in the United States until 1956. In that year, the U.S. Department of Justice promulgated a consent decree that effectively abolished the 15 percent commission system. Under this decree, all media were henceforth required to sell space and time at the net price to all buyers, instead of charging advertisers that bought space or time directly from the media the gross rate.

Advertisers in the United States were now free to buy media at net rates and negotiate agency compensation on their own. The result was vigorous growth of alternative systems of advertising agency compensation.

Today, few, if any, agency compensation arrangements are exactly alike in detail, but three major alternatives to the traditional 15 percent media commission system have evolved:

(1) Flat-rate commissions at less than 15 percent.
(2) Downward-sliding scale commissions, in which an advertiser might, for example, pay the agency 14 percent on the first $10 million in media billings, 12.5 percent on the next $10 million of media billings, and 10 percent on all billings in excess of $20 million.
(3) Labor-based fees, calculated from the actual cost of the labor assigned to an advertising account, plus allocated agency overhead and agency profit at a stated percentage of revenues.

The greatest advantage of commission systems of agency compensation—even complex downward-sliding scales—is that they are simple to administer. The greatest weakness of commission systems is that the basis of agency compensation (media space/time) has no relation to either the quantity or the quality of the creative work and other services that are provided to the advertiser client by its advertising agency.

WILLIAM M. WEILBACHER

Further Reading

Beals, David, and Robert H. Lundin, *Trends in Agency Compensation,* New York: Association of National Advertisers, 2001

Jones, Charles B., *Agency Compensation: A Guidebook,* New York: Association of National Advertisers, 1989

Weilbacher, William M., *Choosing and Working with Your Advertising Agency,* Lincolnwood, Illinois: NTC Business Books, 1991

Commonwealth of Independent States. *See* Russia and the Commonwealth of Independent States

Comparative Advertising

Since the early 1970s U.S. consumers have been bombarded with comparative advertising—ads that openly name an advertiser's competition. Prior to 1972 advertisers and the media held to an unwritten "gentlemen's agreement" that vague and indirect wording—referring, for example, to "Brand X," the "leading brand," or the "best-selling brand"—was the preferred terminology when comparing brands in advertising.

In 1972 the Federal Trade Commission (FTC) issued a statement of support for comparative advertising, arguing that the format could benefit consumers by providing more and better information than had been available in the past, thus aiding consumers in choosing among brands or services. Through direct comparisons, the FTC said, consumers could learn which brands had the lowest price or the most relevant attributes or which tasted best. Comparative advertising, it was contended, would eliminate vague references to "Brand X" or the "leading brand," which were thought to be of little value to consumers.

While comparative advertising was never illegal per se in the United States, its basis of law lies in the Federal Trade Commission Act of 1914 and the Wheeler-Lea Amendment of 1938; the latter gave the commission the ability to stop companies from disparaging competitors even when those competitors lacked proof of injury. Early comparative advertising cases included *Rosenberg* v. *J.C. Penney Company, Hopkins Chemical* v. *Read Drug and Chemical,* and *Shevers Ice Cream* v. *Plar Products Company.* In 1974 what was to become the first landmark case involving comparative advertising went before the Council of Better Business Bureau's National Advertising Review Board (NARB), an industry self-regulatory group. The dispute involved a campaign by Schick and its ad agency for the Flexamatic electric shaver; the ad claimed that the Flexamatic shaved closer than products marketed by Norelco, Remington, and Sunbeam. A fourth competitor, Ronson, not named by Schick in the ads, asked the FTC to investigate, charging that Schick refrained from naming Ronson because Schick had copied Ronson's shaving screen. The NARB concluded that the Schick campaign was in part false and misleading. Although statistical data presented in the campaign were found to be valid, the board ruled that arguments based on those data had likely been misused.

Historically there has been little standardization among codes for comparative advertising. On 1 April 1975, the three major U.S. television broadcast networks presented standardized codes for comparison copy. Radio broadcasters and the American Association of Advertising Agencies also attempted to produce standardized codes in the mid-1970s. Yet at the end of the century, confusion still remained regarding comparative advertising standards, definitions, and effectiveness.

International Standards

Outside the United States, comparative advertising is legal in many countries, including France, the United Kingdom, Germany, The Netherlands, Denmark, Italy, India, Japan, Canada, Brazil, New Zealand, Australia, and Mexico. Hong Kong, South Korea, and Belgium, however, do not permit advertisers to engage in any comparative advertising. While consumers in the United States are frequently exposed to comparative advertising, consumers in other countries see and hear much less of it.

To deal with the diversity of standards in the European Community, the European Parliament on 6 October 1997 issued a directive to help integrate the highly diverse "laws, regulations, and administrative provisions of the individual member states." This directive permits the use of comparative advertising in member states where the following conditions are met: the comparative advertising does not mislead, create confusion, discredit or denigrate trade marks, or take unfair advantage of the reputation of a trade mark, trade name, or other distinguishing marks of a competitor.

Seeking a Taxonomy

Comparative advertising has been defined in many ways in the United States. Some researchers define it as advertising involving an explicit comparison, one that is obvious to the audience. Others suggest that the comparative format can be either direct or indirect, as well as being either substantiated or unsubstantiated. Still others define comparative advertising based on the intensity of the comparison and whether the comparison is one of parity or superiority. One proposed taxonomy of comparative advertising includes "inferiority comparatives," "parity comparatives," and "superiority comparatives." Another proposed taxonomy includes "no intended comparative," "inferiority comparatives," "parity comparatives," and "superiority comparatives"; in this taxonomy, the last three categories are further subdivided. "Inferiority comparatives" include implied category inferiority comparative, implied brand inferiority comparative, and direct brand inferiority comparative. "Parity comparatives" include implied category parity, implied brand parity, and direct brand parity. Finally, "superiority comparatives" include implied category superiority, implied brand superiority, direct brand superiority, implied combination comparatives, and direct brand partnership comparatives.

Comparisons based on inferiority are rarely used by advertisers because of the risk that comes with claiming, even in a humorous spirit, that one's own brand is inferior to others. On occasion, however, marketers do tell the world that their product is the smallest or the ugliest (Volkswagen's "Think small" campaign for the Beetle via Doyle Dane Bernbach, beginning in 1959) or "number two" (Avis Rent a Car's "We try harder" campaign from 1963, also from Doyle Dane Bernbach).

Marketers that want consumers to believe their product is as good as another marketer's brand use parity comparisons. A 1998 newspaper ad for BellSouth compared its Interactive Paging service with rival Skytel's Skywriter. After listing a number of features that

You guessed it! In a coast-to-coast test among consumers of both burgers, the Whopper beat the Big Mac for best taste overall. In a similar test, the Whopper beat Wendy's Single.* And that's just for openers.

Broiling beat frying almost two to one in another survey. Burger King broils. McDonald's and Wendy's fry. Takes the guesswork out of choosing a burger, doesn't it?

*Comparably garnished.

Burger King/Whopper — Reg. U.S. Pat. & TM Off. © 1982 Burger King Corporation

One of the most celebrated comparative campaigns in advertising history was developed by Burger King during the "burger wars" of the 1980s.
BURGER KING® print advertisements used with permission from Burger King Brands, Inc.

were offered by Skywriter as well as other competitors, the copy continued, "BellSouth Interactive Paging service lets you do all that and even more. . . ."

Superiority comparisons, the most commonly used type of comparative advertising, claim that one brand is superior in some way to its named rivals. Some examples include TV spots from Jack in the Box comparing itself to fast-food rivals Burger King and McDonald's and Tylenol PM's commercials comparing its effectiveness to that of Excedrin PM. In a 28 October 1998 *Wall Street Journal* ad, Canon USA, Inc., claimed that 70 percent of its digital copiers sold in 1997 were connected to a network, while only 15 percent of Xerox Corporation's digital copiers were net-worked. In one effort for Chevrolet's Malibu marque, advertising claimed that the Malibu had "More room for five than [Toyota] Camry or [Nissan] Altima." On-line marketers also were getting into the comparative advertising fray; a 1998 ad in *People* magazine for barnesandnoble.com read: "The online bookstore so big, it makes Amazon look tiny."

To Compare or Not to Compare

Whether to adopt the comparative format at all is a decision of some consequence for any advertiser. As with any advertising approach, be it humorous, logical, fear inducing, or otherwise, pros and cons exist.

One strong argument for using comparative advertising is that it provides useful information to consumers, helping them make better purchasing decisions. Comparative advertising also can help a start-up or low-share brand associate itself with an established brand, causing consumers to believe the two are similar. Comparative ads also garner high recall scores. Other reasons for using comparative ads include their ability to create confidence for the advertiser's brand, promote competition, stimulate comparison shopping, aid brand differentiation, lead to more rational consumption decisions, and make advertising more believable and less deceptive.

On the other hand, there are several reasons advertisers might choose to avoid the use of the comparative format in advertising campaigns. Comparative advertising occasionally can lead to marketers appearing to fight in the media, such as in the long-running comparative advertising battle between Coca-Cola Company and PepsiCo; the long-distance rate battle between AT&T Corporation and MCI Corporation from the 1990s; and the pizza superiority dispute between Papa John's Pizza and Pizza Hut that began in 1999. Another concern is that comparative advertising generates irrelevant information and can lead to confusion. Comparative campaigns, now common on television, sometimes leave viewers unclear as to which of several rivals showcased in a commercial is to be preferred—is it the sponsor's brand or the compared brand? Some studies have concluded that comparative advertising is less, or at least no more, effective than noncomparative advertising. Other concerns are that comparative advertising formats may decrease credibility, increase deception, unnecessarily promote competition, display bad manners, lead to misidentification, or create overly skeptical consumers.

A 1991 print ad for the Nissan Stanza highlighted its advantages over its chief competitor, the Toyota Camry.
Copyright, Nissan (1991). Stanza is a registered trademark of Nissan.

A survey conducted in 1991 by Thomas E. Barry (published in the *Journal of Advertising Research* in 1993) of creative executives from the top 35 advertising agencies in the United States found that respondents (25 of the 35 surveyed agencies) had mixed opinions regarding the use of comparative advertising. While some found it an effective and smart strategy, others questioned its use, citing a variety of concerns. Forty-eight percent of the respondents (12 agencies) estimated that between 16 percent and 50 percent of advertising was comparative in nature, while 44 percent (11 agencies) thought the range to be from 1 percent to 15 percent. Older studies from the 1970s and 1980s provided estimates of comparative advertising frequency ranging from about 4 percent to 15 percent, depending on the media used. Similar studies in the early 1990s provided higher estimates, suggesting comparative advertising frequency at 30 percent–40 percent of all advertising.

Assessing Effectiveness

Although comparative advertising has been studied extensively and is frequently used, its effectiveness remains unclear. Since the mid-1970s more than three dozen empirical studies have been conducted in the United States. Findings were analyzed along the "hierarchy of effects" advertising model, which contends that advertising is effective along a continuum ranging from cognition (attention, recognition, recall, information) to affect (attitudes toward brands, attitudes toward advertisements/commercials, credibility, loyalty attitudes) and culminating in conation (purchase intentions and purchase behavior, including consistent loyalty).

With respect to cognition, comparative advertising can be more effective in increasing attention, recall, brand awareness, and message processing. At the same time, however, it can also increase confusion among brands and services. Though this format can provide more information, noncomparative formats can be just as informative. Regarding affect, comparative advertising has the ability to diminish perceived differences between an advertiser's brand and the brand to which it is being compared. Still the comparative format can increase positive attitudes toward the advertising message itself as well as the sponsor brand. Conversely, comparative advertising can have a negative impact on the credibility of the message and so decrease the credibility of the advertiser. In addition, consumers who use the brand that is being used as a negative comparison react more negatively to the advertiser's brand when the comparative format is used. Perhaps of greatest importance to marketers, comparative advertising has been found to be more effective than noncomparative advertising in generating purchase intentions and actual purchase behavior, although market share levels, product involvement, and other variables often mediate these findings.

In 1998 Naveen Donthu of Georgia State University investigated the effectiveness of comparative advertising in Canada, Great Britain, and India using the United States as a control. His results, for the most part, supported previous findings; he concluded that comparative ads had higher recall than noncomparative ads. He also found, however, that respondents from all countries tended to react more negatively to comparative advertising than to noncomparative advertising, and this was especially the case in those countries where comparative advertising is seldom used.

THOMAS E. BARRY

Further Reading

Ash, Stephen B., and Chow-Hou Wee, "Comparative Advertising: A Review with Implications for Further Research," in *Advances in Consumer Research,* vol. 10, edited by R.P. Bagozzi and A.M. Tybout, Ann Arbor, Michigan: Association for Consumer Research, 1983

Barry, Thomas E., "Comparative Advertising: What Have We Learned in Two Decades?" *Journal of Advertising Research* 33, no. 2 (March/April 1993)

Barry, Thomas E., "Twenty Years of Comparative Advertising in the United States," *International Journal of Advertising* 12, no. 4 (1993)

Barry, Thomas E., and Daniel J. Howard, "A Review and Critique of the Hierarchy of Effects in Advertising," *International Journal of Advertising* 9, no. 2 (1990)

Barry, Thomas E., and Roger L. Tremblay, "Comparative Advertising: Perspectives and Issues," *Journal of Advertising* 4, no. 4 (Fall 1975)

Donthu, Naveen, "Comparative Advertising Intensity," *Journal of Advertising Research* 32, no. 6 (November/December 1992)

Donthu, Naveen, "A Cross-Country Investigation of Recall of and Attitude toward Comparative Advertising," *Journal of Advertising* 27, no. 2 (Summer 1998)

Grewal, Dhruv, et al., "Comparative Versus Noncomparative Advertising: A Meta-Analysis," *Journal of Marketing* 61, no. 4 (October 1997)

Miniard, Paul W., et al., "On the Need for Relative Measures When Assessing Comparative Advertising Effects," *Journal of Advertising* 22, no. 3 (September 1993)

Muehling, Darrel D., Donald E. Stem, Jr., and Peter Raven, "Comparative Advertising: Views from Advertisers, Agencies, Media, and Policy Makers," *Journal of Advertising Research* 29, no. 5 (October/November 1989)

Pechmann, Cornelia, and David W. Stewart, "The Effects of Comparative Advertising on Attention, Memory, and Purchase Intentions," *Journal of Consumer Research* 17, no. 2 (September 1990)

Robinson, Susanne, "One Message, Twelve Markets," *Journal of European Business* 5, no. 3 (1994)

Rogers, John C., and Terrell G. Williams, "Comparative Advertising Effectiveness: Practitioners' Perceptions versus Academic Research Findings," *Journal of Advertising Research* 29, no. 5 (October/November 1989)

Rose, Randall L., et al., "When Persuasion Goes Undetected: The Case of Comparative Advertising," *Journal of Marketing Research* 30, no. 3 (August 1993)

Compton Advertising, Inc.

Founded by Richard J. Compton, Leonard T. Bush, and Alfred Stanford from Blackman Advertising, Inc., 1937; acquired by Saatchi & Saatchi Company, 1982; name changed to Saatchi & Saatchi Advertising, 1988.

Major Clients

General Electric Company
Johnson & Johnson
Kaiser Jeep Corporation (later Jeep Corporation, American
    Motors Corporation)
Procter & Gamble Company
U.S. Steel Corporation (later USX Corporation)

Compton Advertising, Inc., was best known for its association with the Procter & Gamble Company (P&G), a relationship that began in 1922, when the agency was known as Blackman Advertising. Collaborating with P&G, Blackman, and later Compton, produced early daytime soap operas, such as *The Guiding Light*, for radio and television. Over decades of creating mundane "soaps-and-suds" advertising, Compton developed a reputation for its marketing skills rather than its creativity, emerging from the 1960s "creative revolution" without earning the label "creative agency." By following P&G around the world, Compton became a "big medium-sized" international agency with offices throughout Europe, South America, and the Far East.

Oscar H. Blackman and Frank Hermes founded Blackman Advertising in 1908. In 1922, with J.K. Fraser at the helm, Blackman became one of P&G's first full-service advertising agencies, handling the Ivory and Crisco brands. Fraser encouraged P&G's early desire to test radio advertising by recommending the *Crisco Cooking Talks* and other, similar morning programs in which recipes using Crisco were read.

Blackman also created a newspaper serial cartoon, *The Jollyco Family,* about a fictitious family of Ivory soap devotees and a Mrs. Percival Folderol who used another brand. P&G adapted this concept to a new daytime radio drama format that was dubbed "soap opera" because of the sponsorship by soap brands. Compton later extended the format to television, where Ivory was among the first products advertised.

During the radio advertising experiment, Richard J. Compton, who started with Blackman in 1917, was made a partner. He was appointed president in 1934, and Compton, Leonard Bush, and Alfred Stanford bought Blackman in 1935. The agency became Compton Advertising, Inc., in 1937. The first vice president was Marion Harper, who went on to found Interpublic.

A period of aggressive growth followed. Between 1939 and 1944, billings quadrupled to $22 million, making it the ninth largest agency in the United States according to *Advertising Age* rankings that year. Other clients in addition to P&G, which accounted for nearly half its billing volume, included Socony Vacuum, American Home Products, Allis-Chalmers, New York Life,

and United States Time. In 1948 Compton ushered P&G into television for the first time and made Neolite rubber soles from Goodyear Tire & Rubber Company a household name. It won Tender Leaf Tea and Chase & Sanborn Coffee from the J. Walter Thompson Company in 1949. Yet its billings were flat after 1944, and its rank dropped to 18 by 1950. Growth resumed in the 1950s largely on the basis of its television work. Though billings rose from $22 million in 1949 to $45 million in 1955, Compton's rank still stood at 18.

Compton's association with consumer packaged goods companies, known to be demanding clients, led it to build strengths in marketing and media. By 1955 Compton had established a merchandising department to help clients formulate sales promotion programs for their brands. Compton added a publicity subsidiary in 1956, developed a computer-based media planning program in 1964, and set up a direct-mail unit in 1969.

Fifty years after its founding as the Blackman Company, Compton employed 750 people, had 24 clients, and six offices. The agency's growth from the late 1950s through the 1960s occurred under the leadership of Barton A. Cummings. Cummings joined Compton in 1947, was made account executive on P&G's Duz soap business in 1949, and eventually supervised all P&G business. Cummings was named agency president in 1955 and chief executive officer (CEO) one year later, a post he held for 15 years.

Under Cummings, Compton's business and international presence expanded. Through the 1960s the agency won work from Seagram, Kaiser Jeep (later American Motors), U.S. Steel Corporation, General Electric, Johnson & Johnson, and the Quaker Oats Company. Still, P&G was Compton's largest client.

In December 1961 P&G moved its top brand, Tide, to Compton, which was already handling the company's Gleem, Crisco, Comet, and Ivory accounts. Although Compton's work for P&G lacked creative flair, some campaigns were enduring. Compton's television campaign for Comet featuring actress Jane Withers as "Josephine the Plumber" forged a strong brand identity. The campaign ran for 12 years.

Compton's international expansion began in 1960 with the acquisition of S.T. Garland Advertising Service Ltd., of London, England, a smaller, old-line British shop founded in 1928. The London agency was renamed Garland-Compton, Ltd., and its facilities expanded to service Compton's U.S. clients in Great Britain and Europe.

By the mid-1960s Compton had added offices in Paris, France; San Juan, Puerto Rico; Mexico City, Mexico; and Hong Kong, among others. As the 1960s ended, Compton had 39 offices in 22 countries outside the United States. Total billings rose from $86 million in 1960 to $175 million in 1968, making Compton the 14th largest U.S. agency.

Cummings was a staunch industry defender and a strong believer in public service. During his tenure Compton unveiled a campaign to combat anti-advertising attitudes among college stu-

Out of the kitchen by noon!

Recipes for a care-free afternoon and a delicious cold supper.

AN AFTERNOON on the veranda! A motor ride into the country! Visits with congenial friends! These and other alluring prospects beckon to you these warm July days.

"Yes," you say, "If I could only escape the kitchen occasionally."

You can.

A friend of ours did. In the cool of the morning she tried the menu given below. She found that with the help of Crisco its preparation became a sort of lark.

We believe you'll agree, too, when you learn what treats you can make with this pure *vegetable* shortening. See if your family doesn't compliment you on the delicious natural food flavors which Crisco leaves undisguised.

Yes, in bringing out the fine natural flavor of foods you will find Crisco a most helpful partner. And you will find the following facts very important if you wish your summer foods to digest easily.

What Fats do Children digest well?

Doctors unite in this warning: "Carefully select hot weather foods for your children." Speaking particularly of the digestibility of fats, a well-known professor of food chemistry says:

"If the melting point of the fat lies much above the body temperature, the fat will not become sufficiently fluid to be readily emulsified and digested."

Crisco (pure vegetable fat) melts at 97 degrees—which is below body temperature.

Think how easily your own little child will digest vegetable Crisco.

* * *

To assure delightfully uniform yet digestible cakes, pastry and fried foods order a can of Crisco from your grocer now. Today or tomorrow try the recipes given on this page. In welcoming Crisco for your own favorite recipes remember that you use ⅕ less of Crisco than you would of butter or animal fats.

Special Cook Book Offer

This unique book is entitled "The Whys of Cooking." It answers 164 puzzling questions about cooking and serving. Contains 143 delightful recipes. Gives 45 standards for cooking measurements. Illustrated in 4 colors. Written by the famous Janet McKenzie Hill. Simply mail 25c in stamps or coin to Section F-7 Dept. of Home Economics, The Procter & Gamble Co., Cincinnati, Ohio.

Small, medium and large sized cans Crisco is also made and sold in Canada

Try this **Cooling Summer Supper**

Fruit Cocktail
Cold Meat
Escalloped Potatoes
(Bake them in the morning. Re-heat just before serving. To brown, scatter bits of Crisco on top.)
Quick Nut Bread
(See Recipe at Right)
Asparagus Salad
French Dressing
Cherry or Berry Pie
(See Recipe at Right)
Iced Beverage

Quick Nut Bread

3 cupfuls flour
1 teaspoonful salt
3 scant teaspoonfuls baking powder
1½ tablespoonfuls sugar
1 cupful nut meats
1½ cupfuls milk
2 tablespoonfuls melted Crisco
1 egg beaten light

Sift well together first four ingredients. Add the well-beaten egg to the milk, then add the nut meats cut fine, then the two tablespoonfuls melted Crisco. Then mix all together and bake one hour in a moderate oven.

Cherry or Berry Pie

First make a plain pastry from this recipe:
1½ cupfuls flour
½ teaspoonful salt
½ cupful Crisco
4 to 6 tablespoonfuls cold water
(sufficient for one medium size pie)

With a knife cut Crisco into sifted flour and salt until mixture looks like coarse meal, then add slowly enough ice water to make a paste that clears the bowl. Take half of dough, roll out on lightly floured board until about ⅛ inch thick. Roll lightly from center outward. Use light motion in handling rolling pin. Line pie pan letting pastry emerge ¼ inch over edge. Mix one cup sugar with one teaspoonful flour and a pinch of salt. Mix this thoroughly with fruit. Fill pie pan, add bits of Crisco, moisten edges with cold water. Roll the remaining half of pastry to a thin sheet. Cover the pie. Press edges close together. Trim with knife and a few slits in center. Bake ½ hour in hot oven.

For delicious cakes which stay fresh longer.

For digestible and flaky pastry.

For crisp, digestible fried foods.

CRISCO
For Frying For Shortening
For Cake Making

Copyright 1922, by The Procter & Gamble Co., Cincinnati

Blackman Advertising, precursor to Compton Advertising, helped pioneer the use of recipes in advertising with client Procter & Gamble's Crisco brand shortening, as seen in this 1922 example.
Courtesy of The Procter & Gamble Company.

dents, created the ground-breaking "Why do you think they call it dope?" anti–drug abuse public service advertising (PSA) campaign, and developed a controversial PSA campaign that sought to improve the public's understanding of the U.S. economic system.

In October 1968 O. Milton Gossett was elected president of Compton after spending his entire career climbing the creative ranks at the agency. Gossett became Compton's CEO in 1975 and chairman in 1977. Gossett was intent on improving Compton's reputation as a creative shop. However, he would soon encounter the unorthodox business practices of Charles and Maurice Saatchi, and larger corporate challenges would take precedence over establishing a creative name for the agency.

In 1975 Ken Gill, a Garland-Compton partner, and the Saatchis entered into negotiations to merge the smaller Saatchi & Saatchi Company with Garland-Compton Ltd. Both sides saw value in the merger: Saatchi was known for its creativity but lacked marketing skills; Garland-Compton had the marketing expertise Saatchi sought but lacked a creative edge. Because Compton owned 49 percent of Garland-Compton, no deal could be made without its approval. Gill, Gossett, and the Saatchis reached an agreement: technically Compton bought the Saatchi shop, but in reality it was a "reverse" takeover by Saatchi. In September 1975 the agency became Saatchi & Saatchi Garland Compton. The merger was not considered important in the United States, where Compton billed $104 million and the Saatchi name was not widely known.

By 1977 the Saatchis were approaching New York City agencies in hopes of buying an established international network. Gossett became concerned that such a move would cause conflicts with P&G, which was the biggest account of both Compton and Saatchi & Saatchi Garland Compton. Gossett considered defensive options. When the Saatchis suggested that the Saatchi agency buy the non-U.K. offices of Compton (Compton's U.K. offices had already merged with Saatchi in 1975), Gossett was incredulous and planned an expansion of his own. Nevertheless, over five years the Saatchis slowly lured Gossett, and Compton, into their net.

Under Gossett's leadership Compton expanded internationally, entering Spain, Greece, Portugal, Denmark, Venezuela, Iran, and Kuwait. Major domestic acquisitions included Rumrill-Hoyt and Klemtner Advertising. Gossett recognized that Compton still had a sleepy image despite the firm's position as the 15th largest agency worldwide with 1979 billings of $525 million. To upgrade its creative product, Compton hired new talent with experience outside of packaged goods.

In 1981 Compton was growing fast; creating exciting advertising was a priority, and billings were expected to reach $1 billion in 1982. It unveiled a new logo to mark the agency's renewed vitality and revenue milestone. It also bought another agency in London, KMP Partnership. Just after closing the KMP deal, Saatchi made a formal offer for Compton. Furious, Gossett let six months pass before resuming talks.

By March 1982, however, the Saatchis had worn Gossett down and were able to buy the international advertising network they had sought. Saatchi & Saatchi purchased Compton Advertising for $29.2 million in cash plus performance-based incentive payments to Compton executives. It was the largest ad agency merger to date, with combined billings of $1.3 billion, and it rocketed S&S to seventh in worldwide billings from 25th.

Compton retained its name, but not for long. To erase its persistent image as a boring soap-and-suds shop, its name was subsumed under the parental moniker in 1984, becoming Saatchi & Saatchi Compton Worldwide. The history books closed completely on Compton Advertising in 1988, when the name became simply Saatchi & Saatchi Advertising.

RANDY JACOBS

Further Reading

"Compton Celebrates Its 50th; Cummings Heads Growing Agency," *Printers' Ink* (25 April 1958)

"Compton Returns to Acquisition Path," *Advertising Age* (15 May 1978)

Marshall, Christy, "Willinger Jazzes Up 'Largest Midget,'" *Advertising Age* (15 December 1980)

Schisgall, Oscar, *Eyes on Tomorrow: The Evolution of Procter and Gamble*, Chicago: Ferguson, 1981

Computers

Since the unveiling of the first commercial computer in 1946, the industry and its advertising have gone through several revolutions. Computer technology has evolved from mainframes to personal computers and the Internet, while the advertising of computers—along with its audience—has grown increasingly sophisticated. The ad media also have expanded, starting with specialty magazines and broadening to include TV and, finally, via the Internet, the computer itself.

Computers were first sold as "marvels of the future," arcane machines controlled by highly trained experts and housed in secure, climate-controlled rooms. In the 1950s they became tools for solving complex math problems. By the 1960s they were big boxes designed to manage money for big business. In the 1970s the first personal computers became the joy of hobbyists and the bane of small businesses trying to make them do something useful. By the end of the next decade they had become both a business necessity and a mass market. And in the 1990s computer networks became an advertising medium of their own, with the Internet drawing $8 billion in advertising by the year 2000.

In each decade the computer has been advertised differently, with ads targeted to different audiences, emphasizing different capabilities to different markets. As the pace of technological advances has accelerated, the industry, professions, and society as a whole have had to adapt to a situation of continuous change.

Early Advertising

In the beginning, computers were demonstrated rather than advertised. A Movietone newsreel from the mid-1940s marveled at the ability of a mechanical computer at the University of California-Los Angeles to solve complex math problems and plot the results on paper. The first computer was created under military contract to calculate mortar trajectories. It was called ENIAC—the Electronic Numerical Integrator and Computer—and caused a sensation when it was demonstrated by John Mauchley and J. Presper Eckert in 1946. At that time they announced plans to develop the machine commercially as the Universal Automatic Computer (Univac). Remington Rand delivered the first Univac to the U.S. Census Bureau in 1951, and 46 were eventually sold at $1 million each.

IBM Corporation, the dominant maker of office equipment such as typewriters and especially punch card machines, quickly saw a threat in the new machine, in part because Mauchley and Eckert wanted to replace punch cards with magnetic tape. IBM's first response was a calculating machine, the IBM 603 Electronic Multiplier, which processed numbers fed in by punch cards but did not store programs. IBM leased its machines through a dedicated sales force, and when it figured out how to make the device divide, it released the Model 604 and leased thousands of them. A 1951 color magazine ad for the Model 604 by Cecil & Presbrey, Inc., showed the calculator with its door open and its insides exposed, sitting next to an IBM punch card reader. An atom was drawn above the reader with its electronic pathways whirling around a central dot. "Getting your answers . . . at electronic speed," the copy promised, emphasizing its use in accounting calculations. Another picture of the setup is at the bottom of the ad, next to a woman wearing a businesslike red dress.

IBM staged its first effective demonstration of a computer, its Selective Sequence Electronic Calculator (SSEC), in 1948. This machine, 120 feet long with 12,500 tubes and 21,400 mechanical relays, was placed behind glass windows in the lobby of IBM's New York City headquarters, and a staff in white lab coats was put to work conducting calculations for corporate clients. The demonstration transformed IBM's image from that of an office products maker to that of an engineering outfit. Before being decommissioned in 1952, the SSEC produced the tables used for plotting the course of the 1969 Apollo Moon flight.

The IBM demonstration also set a tone for the industry that was maintained for decades: computers were complex machines that had to be carefully tended by experts in climate-controlled rooms, and they were leased, not sold.

In this 1960 corporate ad, "Who Won? You Did," IBM Corporation celebrated the first use of computers to tabulate U.S. presidential election results.

The IBM approach continued to dominate computing in the 1950s. As with the Univac, IBM's computing efforts began with a military contract, this one for a defense calculator during the Korean War. The commercial version of this computer was announced in 1952 as the IBM 701. First released in 1953, 19 were leased in the next three years to research labs, aircraft companies, and the U.S. government.

IBM was not a trendsetter, however. It did not invent the computer, it did not run the first computer advertising, and it did not even have the first computer on TV. That honor belongs to the Massachusetts Institute of Technology's Whirlwind, which appeared on Edward R. Murrow's *See It Now* program in 1951. The Whirlwind took six years to build, ran on tubes, and was said to be 90 percent reliable in 35 hours of weekly work.

Throughout the 1950s, computer development was chronicled in specialty magazines such as *Datamation*, targeted at engineers who yearned to own machines of their own. One of the more creative efforts of the period was the Bendix G-15, advertised in a print ad in 1958 from the Shaw Company, of Los

Angeles, California. A suited figure was drawn on the left holding a piece of paper, with the headline, "We learned to use the Bendix G-15 computer in just four hours." Copy explained how the G-15 could be used "by the men who know their own problems best, right in their offices and laboratories, and often at 1/10th the cost of 'computing center' installations."

The Bendix ad ran just two years after William Shockley, William Brattain, and John Bardeen won the Nobel Prize for their work on the transistor, a replacement for vacuum tubes announced by AT&T Corporation in 1948. Late in 1958, *Datamation* ran a news item from IBM, announcing its first "completely transistorized" computer, which would become the 7000 series. The computer age had been born.

Specialty-Magazine Ads

Computers based on transistors and later integrated circuits (for which Jack Kilby won the 2000 Nobel Prize) turned computing in the 1960s into a general-purpose office tool that could be sold through office automation channels. This was reflected in the pages of specialty magazines, which began taking page ads from computer makers rather than their traditional partial-page ads.

A January 1962 ad from Univac, working with Fuller & Smith & Ross, New York City, shows a woman holding a phone; the headline reads, "Quiet, please. Our computer is talking." The copy describes Unicall, a private computer network running at 20 characters per second that enabled data to flow from remote computers directly into offices.

Some advertisers used a mild form of sex appeal to humanize ads for computer-related devices. Computron, Inc., of Waltham, Massachusetts, which made magnetic computer tape drives, ran a series of ads in which a woman named Penelope made statements such as, "There's something magnetic about you, Computape."

Most ads of the period, however, focused on product features or office applications. NCR Corporation ran a series of "case study" ads in which customers such as American Greetings Corporation explained "Why we chose the NCR computer." In a decade when hardware and software were nearly always sold together, Packard Bell Electronics Corporation ran an ad in May 1962 promising "applications unlimited." A text-heavy ad from Control Data Corporation was headlined, "Why so many programmers prefer the Control Data 1604/1604-A," describing its Fortran and COBOL compilers in detail.

The decade's dominant computer was the IBM System/360. This was a family of machines in a variety of price ranges, all running the same operating system. Problems in software development and hardware manufacturing caused a major backlog and a crisis at the company, but its huge success made other machines obsolete. IBM's backlog for the 360 was so heavy it did not have to run many ads for the product. When it did advertise (via its agency at the time, Benton & Bowles), IBM's style was to break up text with subheads and add a huge headline on the top half of the page, a basic design it used into the 1980s. A 1966 ad for the 360 used the headline, "IBM's new Basic Operating System is not really basic," and the copy went on to explain what that meant.

Rivals sought either to outdo IBM with jargon or to position the computer as a business essential. A 1966 Raytheon Corporation ad showed a printout of sample test results. An NCR ad from the same period showed a lemonade stand with the headline, "Some businesses are too small to use electronic data processing."

The first serious challenges to IBM's dominance in computing came with the introduction of "minicomputers." These machines were sold, not rented; cost much less than IBM equipment; and mostly came from companies new to the field. While makers of minicomputers sold their machines through dedicated sales forces and support staffs, they used advertising to build consistent brand images.

The PDP-8 from Digital Equipment Corporation (DEC), introduced in 1965, was the first commercially successful minicomputer. It sold for $18,000, one-fifth the price of a small IBM mainframe. The company's ads emphasized value and availability, with an implication of honesty. One 1968 ad bragged, "We'll deliver a PDP-9 computer in 90 days. Seriously."

Hewlett-Packard Company (H-P) delivered its first minicomputer in 1966, the HP-2115. Its pitch was aimed at engineers familiar with its test equipment, emphasizing support for a variety of computer languages and quicker setup. By 1968 many of its ads also pictured a status box of blinking lights designed to reassure engineers the device was working.

Data General Corporation, launched by former engineers from DEC, tried to outdo DEC with the Nova, an $8,000 computer with 32 kilobytes of memory. Its ads, which often featured photos of company president Ed deCastro, also emphasized simplicity, an idea that would inspire many personal computer (PC) designs, including Steve Wozniak's Apple I board.

But by 1968 the dominance of the IBM 360 was secure, and order backlogs stretched for years. Rivals had to find niche markets. H-P pitched its machine to engineers, focusing on rapid setup or support for multiple languages and showing a box filled with blinking lights. Honeywell's ads from that period used photos of horses sculpted from wires and other electronic parts, billing the manufacturer as "The other computer company."

The 1960s also saw the emergence of the first independent software companies. Since hardware makers would not support competing software, a harder sell was called for. Thus, sex was introduced to computer advertising. National Computer Analysts, Inc., which wrote flow-charting programs, ran an ad in 1968 consisting mainly of a giant pink line-drawing of a woman swooning in the arms of a man wearing a loincloth. The headline reads, "You'll be amazed at the results you get . . . with QuickDraw."

By 1970 computers had become an accepted part of business practice. Advertising broke out of its base in technical journals and moved into the general business press. New computer niches were also developing. Small offices, for example, used low-cost minicomputers, consisting of a monitor with a green picture tube, a typewriter keyboard, and some simple electronics. Time-sharing services such as Automatic Data Processing Corporation gave small businesses access to mainframes with nothing more than a terminal connected by modem to the central machine and its software. Computer furniture and computer supplies came to be

George wanted to build a 3,000 mile wide computer

That may sound crazy, but Dr. George Feeney's crazy like a fox. Because he got his way - that computer exists.

I'll never forget that day I walked into his office and he said: "I want a central file you can access from anywhere in the country—or Europe, or the whole world."

(Sure, George, who's going to lay a new transatlantic cable for us?)

"And" he continued, "I only want the customer to have to pay for a local call."

(That had to be a put-on, but he's the boss. Did he have *any* ideas on how we pull this off?)

He did.

"Look," he said, "we've already developed the world's best communications system for our Mark II, using a GEPAC-4020 central concentrator hooked to the GE-635. Let's take the 8 remote concentrators that tie into that central concentrator and deploy them across the entire country.

Then, fan out a whole bunch of multiplexers from each one, so our customers can call a single system with a local telephone number from every major metropolitan area."

"You get it?", he said. As a matter of fact we didn't.

So he drew this diagram.

George's drawing

For more information, write Section 291-69, General Electric, 1 River Rd., Schenectady, N.Y. 12305.

Then he said, "Do it. And use a satellite to get to Europe. It'll be the Time-sharing system that only EDP people can love."

We did. And they do.

Oh, yes — we call it General Electric Network Service.

And EDP men across the country have really taken it to their hearts. They're using it for inventory control—all kinds— from auto parts to reservations.

They're using it for capital budgeting—with multi-location input.

They're using it for nationwide sales reports.

What else can it do?

Beats us. It's so versatile, new applications spring up everyday.

Somebody looks at our system and their requirements and off they go, making it do what they want.

And George says it's only the beginning.

In fact, he just called and said he wanted to talk about a new idea for hooking two systems together for super reliability.

Here we go again. . . .

GE Information Services
World Leader In Time-Sharing Service

291-69

GENERAL ELECTRIC

In the late 1960s and early 1970s, the first computer time-sharing and networking services were installed, a development highlighted in this 1970 General Electric corporate ad.

advertised in office supply magazines alongside typewriters and calculators.

Personal Computer Revolution

Outside the business world, however, a revolution was brewing. Hobbyist magazines such as *Scientific American* and *Radio Electronics* had been running articles and offering kits for "machines that think" since 1950, starting with Edmund Berkeley's Simon, a simple mechanical computer with blinking lights. Berkeley also designed a device called the Geniac in 1955 and sold it through his Berkeley Enterprises, influencing many people who would later fuel the personal computer revolution. The first computer kit, the Heathkit EC-1, sold for less than $200 in 1959, according to the Blinkenlights Archeological Institute of Irvine, California, established in 1977 to preserve early computing devices.

The fuel for the revolution was the integrated circuit, a complete "computer on a chip," requiring only input, output, and storage devices to be useful. In 1970 Intel introduced its first microprocessor, the 4004. It was quickly followed by competitors such as National Semiconductor and Texas Instruments. By 1972 and 1973 the first pocket calculators were reaching the mass market at prices starting at $100 for units that could merely add, subtract, multiply, and divide. Almost immediately hobbyists began trying to turn these "chips" into computer kits and even full-fledged computers.

A small but growing network of young hobbyists developed. Some, like teenagers Bill Gates and Paul Allen, traded programming knowledge for time on the then-popular PDP-series computers. Others, such as Steve Wozniak and Steve Jobs, tried to build and sell kits. By 1974 several new hobbyist magazines had been launched, such as *Creative Computing* and *Computer Hobbyist*. *Popular Electronics*, meanwhile, created a sensation with an article on a computer kit called the Altair, available for $439.

Like the mainframe ads of the 1950s, ads in these early magazines emphasized technical jargon, complete with part numbers and specifications. Both IBM and Digital Equipment commissioned work on simple computers but abandoned these projects in 1974.

Mass-Market Advertising

The launch of the Apple II in 1976 changed everything. Several companies—including Wozniak's employer, Hewlett-Packard—rejected his new computer design, so he and Jobs built a new company in Jobs's garage to make and market it themselves.

The Apple was the first all-in-one computer, with a keyboard for input and only the attachment of a monitor screen and printer required for output. But the real key to success was its advertising: color ads aimed at the mass-market. The ads starred accessible cultural figures such as Thomas Jefferson and featured the Apple logo, a multicolored apple with a bite taken out of it.

With the launch of the Apple II and dozens of competing PCs, computing became a battle of "suits" versus "geeks." A Data General ad in *Business Week* in October 1978 proclaimed, "When a businessman wants a computer system, he wants things kept simple." The Apple II ad's response, "Jefferson had one of the best minds of 1776, but today he could make better decisions with an Apple."

A host of new magazines emerged to serve the new market, including *Byte, A+,* and *The User's Guide to CP/M*. Each featured long articles on improving performance, new add-on products, and new software applications. Full-page display ads in these magazines branded the new machines and their makers. Commodore Business Machines, Inc., emphasized the low price of its VIC-20. Atari Corporation emphasized the quality of its graphics and usefulness for playing games. Radio Shack, in ads for its TRS-80, emphasized the support offered by its retail stores. Ads for smaller brands such as Cromemco tried to straddle the gulf between suits and geeks, showing both business applications and technical specifications.

Despite the growth of Apple and the other PC companies, however, the decade ended with the market divided. Hobbyists and small businesses bought PCs. Older, established business computer companies, such as IBM and Digital Equipment, sold mainframes, minicomputers, terminals, and networks.

Ads for these more powerful devices often ran in business magazines and emphasized their serious power for "real" applications, such as the on-line delivery of data to worker desktops. A March 1978 ad for the Data General Eclipse, via F.T. Brickman Advertising, Ltd., in *Management Today*, a British magazine, was typical. The ad featured a half-page picture of a trading room in a large commercial bank, prominently featuring Data General terminals. "Data General Eclipse minicomputers have arrived on the scene," the copy read. "Computers that give you up-to-date information where you need it. No waiting for batched processed information." Like the NCR "American Greetings" ad of 15 years ago, the copy continued in the form of a case study, identifying the office as that of Butler Till, a bank "handling deals ranging from hundreds of thousands to millions of pounds." This ad was the only computer advertisement in a 154-page issue of a magazine devoted to management problems. A few months later, the magazine featured a long story on adopting computers; it was surrounded by ads from competing suppliers.

Computer advertising really came into its own in the 1980s, as the mass market embraced computing and computer makers embraced mass-market media such as television. Apple had done some effective branding in the 1970s, and even some TV advertising, but when IBM entered the PC market in 1981 it set a new standard in every way. At the low end, Coleco, a toy company, introduced the first computer printer for word processing, the Adam, at less than $1,000.

The new IBM PC ran a new operating system, the PC-DOS (PC disk operating system), which it licensed from a start-up company called Microsoft Corporation. IBM prenegotiated the launch of an "official" magazine, called *PC*. IBM launched its machine with a huge TV ad campaign from Lord, Geller, Federico, Einstein, Inc., of New York City, starring actor Billy Scudder portraying Charlie Chaplin's "Little Tramp," complete with bowler hat, cane, and a rose in his buttonhole. The campaign's print ads used straightforward, carefully written copy that emphasized the simplicity of the machine and carried the headline, "A tool for modern times," an allusion to Chaplin's 1936 movie, *Modern Times.* The tramp character also made public appearances at trade shows.

As the IBM campaign evolved, the "Little Tramp" branding imagery evolved beyond use of the actor to the hat, the cane, and the rose, and finally just the rose, set in a vase next to the computer. The branding was applied to all product niches related to the PC, including software, service, and computer networks. IBM's PC introduction sparked a revolution in offices, which began replacing typewriters and calculators with the PC. Millions of PCs were linked to IBM mainframes as terminals, using programs called "terminal emulators." Millions more were connected to one another in PC networks, often running a network operating system called NetWare from Novell Corporation, a Utah start-up.

The PC was a massive success and spawned a host of "PC clone" start-ups, all of which licensed Microsoft's operating system under the name MS-DOS. The most successful of these companies was a Houston, Texas-based company, Compaq Computer Corporation, whose first machine was packaged in a 26-pound case and called a "portable." Compaq engineers carefully (and legally) copied the IBM PC design through a process called "reverse-engineering," producing a machine that ran nearly all the PC's software.

The PC revolution forced publishers to respond. Magazines devoted to the PC, such as *PC, PC Week,* and *PC Magazine,* became among the most profitable franchises in the magazine business. In an effort to compete, older titles devoted to office products, such as *Modern Office Procedures,* renamed themselves with titles such as *Modern Office Technology* in an effort to get ads from the PC makers.

Another success of the early 1980s was the first true portable, the TRS Model 80. Radio Shack took an operating system made obsolete by the PC, built its computer on a single circuit board, and packaged it with a tiny screen and full-sized keyboard with a plastic case weighing four pounds and with a price of $799. Print ads via Radio Shack's in-house Central Advertising Agency, Fort Worth, Texas, emphasized its strong product reviews from industry magazines, branding the Radio Shack stores as "the biggest name in little computers."

While the IBM PC and competing machines using its operating system, quickly dubbed "PC clones," would continue to hold their market leadership, the market still held its breath throughout the early 1980s, waiting for Apple's response.

That response was launched with perhaps the most famous TV ad in history. Director Ridley Scott, working with agency Chiat/Day, Inc., produced the spot for $1.5 million, and it ran only once, on the telecast of Super Bowl XVIII on 23 January 1984. The ad, dubbed "1984" after the futuristic George Orwell novel of the same name, featured a huge, one-color screen from which a man harangued a huge audience of people, apparently prisoners. This scene was intercut with a view of a young woman—wearing a white tank top and red shorts and carrying a huge hammer—running. As the figure on the screen reached the climax of his speech, "We shall prevail," the woman hurled the hammer at the screen, which exploded, showering the stunned audience in a white light. The voice-over intoned, "On January 24 Apple Computer will introduce Macintosh. And you'll see why 1984 won't be like *1984.*" The spot was ranked number 12 on *Advertising Age*'s list of the top 100 ad campaigns of the 20th century.

The Macintosh was revolutionary in many ways. For input it used a "mouse," a pointing device that controlled a cursor, and the screen held a visual interface, with pull-down menus and pictures, first developed at Xerox's Palo Alto Research Center in the 1970s. The Mac created entirely new computer applications, such as "desktop publishing," because pages designed on the screen would look the same when printed. Video applications were also promised.

Despite the success of the Macintosh, however, its high price and the huge installed base of PC clones in the business world restricted it to niche markets. Both IBM and Microsoft began work on a "windowing" interface for the PC that would match the Macintosh features. After a multiyear drama in which Microsoft's Bill Gates outmaneuvered a host of IBM executives, in 1990 Version 3.0 of Microsoft Windows was introduced, which finally brought the capabilities of the Mac into the computing mainstream.

Once Microsoft wrested the development of PC standards from IBM it became the industry's dominant company, although its revenue remained a fraction of IBM's. Microsoft ads have seldom been as creative as Apple's, nor are they as standardized as IBM's. The company did not begin advertising on TV until the 1990s, beginning with image ads that focused heavily on Microsoft programmers and the work they were doing. The company's growth and rising public profile, however, eventually did push it into becoming a heavy buyer of TV ads in the mid-1990s.

By 1990 the means and media for the advertising of computers seemed set. TV was used for brand awareness, print (mostly magazines) was used to advertise features, while radio was used by retailers to bring people into the stores. A Dell Computer Corporation ad from September 1990 was typical of the era's print ads. It shows a picture of the computer, a price on the monitor, a box with the specifications of the computer, the logos of trusted magazines, and a few paragraphs of copy focused on the computer's reviews.

But under the surface things were changing. Gateway 2000 ran an eight-page magazine ad that combined models and their features under the headline "PC saloon." A Toshiba laptop ad from the same month used a full-page picture of the computer, with the copy again describing the features.

The early 1990s represented the golden age for computer magazines. Publications such as *PC Magazine, Computer Shopper,* and *PC Week* were comprised of hundreds of pages, most of them advertisements for computers and related equipment. These ranged from multipage image ads for major makers to simple columns with one-line descriptions of products being offered by stores. Consumers and businesses relied on these publications. TV shows about computing were few and far between.

Dell Computer Corporation pioneered direct sales of personal and business computers. It also led the way in direct, on-line sales practices, as shown by this 1997 print ad.
Permission to reprint provided by Dell.

The dominant marketer in the computer category in the period was Microsoft Corporation. The Redmond, Washington-based software giant did not buy TV spots but concentrated on making its Windows operating system an "ingredient" brand inside boxes from Dell, Compaq, H-P, and other computer marketers. Windows allowed the PC to do most of what the Apple Macintosh did, but it cost less and was available everywhere. In addition, hardware companies provided a significant portion of the marketing muscle behind Windows, promoting their boxes as running the operating system. That allowed Microsoft to tag along on the marketing-budget coattails of multiple big-spending companies. By the mid-1990s Microsoft's Gates was being hailed as the richest man in the world.

Mail-Order Computers

The big change in how computers were advertised and sold in the early 1990s was mail-order, with Dell Computer leading the charge. Its computers were not produced until the company received an order, but the built-from-scratch machines were delivered within days, and often cost less than PCs bought from stores. Early Dell ads emphasized features and price, but as the decade wore on, the company's ads began focusing instead on the convenience of having a computer "made your way"—the Burger King message reinterpreted for the PC. Chiat/Day, Inc., of San Francisco, California, was Dell's agency at the beginning of the decade.

As Dell's direct sales channel grew (helped by Gateway, which copied many of its methods), the resellers that had dominated in PC magazines faded away. As computers steadily became more powerful, Dell began dominating business as well as consumer markets—the company grew 129 percent in 1993 alone.

At the same time, the creation of the Internet supercharged Dell's growth. Dell could reach its buyers directly through Internet advertising rather than buying expensive TV time. It also could take orders directly through the Internet instead of via the telephone. By 1998 Dell was bringing in billions of dollars of sales per year through the new channel, and direct PC sales seemed ready to overtake those made through all resellers.

By 1995 computers and software were such mass markets that even Microsoft was lured onto TV. It began with simple image ads but exploded in that year with the launch of Windows 95. TV ads for the new operating system featured quick cuts of people in homes, offices, and schools shown with the sound of the Rolling Stones singing "Start Me Up." Reportedly the Stones were paid $12 million for the song's license. Wieden & Kennedy, of Portland, Oregon, created the consumer campaign; Anderson & Lembke, of San Francisco, produced the trade ads as well as ads for applications software such as Office 95.

Apple and IBM, the dominant names of the 1980s, seemed tired by contrast. Apple had trouble following up on its huge success with the Macintosh. The company refused to license its operating system and thus lost most of the market to computers running Microsoft software. By the 1990s the cult built around its TV spots was dwindling. Apple launched its comeback with the return of Jobs as chief executive officer in 1997. The ad campaign he endorsed for the Apple's iMac broke new ground in that both the print and broadcast components carried the same story: puns on the various case colors available for the system. One print ad showed all the cases with the headline, "Collect all five." Broadcast ads focused on individual case colors backed by musical hits from the 1960s. TBWA Chiat/Day, then in Venice, California, was Apple's agency.

IBM, meanwhile, had lost control of the mass-market PC to "clone-makers," both foreign (Toshiba) and domestic (Compaq), which licensed their operating systems directly from Microsoft. IBM still dominated the market for mainframe computers and other powerful machines, but these markets were declining. Advertisements for these machines were mainly found in business magazines and a dwindling number of mainframe-specific titles such as *Datamation*. It was not until 1993 that IBM decisively changed course, hiring Louis Gerstner as its chief executive officer.

While IBM was still spending $150 million per year in 1994 on advertising, most of that was product specific; the company ranked last in "brand value" in a survey by *Financial World* magazine. Under Gerstner, IBM spent almost $1 billion in the mid-to-late 1990s on a branding campaign built around the "e-business" theme, via Ogilvy & Mather Worldwide. Rather than selling specific computers, the ads sold IBM's Internet expertise. At its heart were a series of ads using a movie-like "letterbox" format with blue bars across the top and bottom. The ads focused on the difficulty of making Internet hardware, software, and services work together. The subliminal message was that no company other than IBM was big enough to handle it. By the end of the decade, Gerstner was being hailed in both magazines and books for the "business turnaround of the decade."

Soon rival computer companies such as H-P were using TV in a similar way to advertise their corporate visions. When Carly Fiorina became H-P's new chairman in 2000, she launched an image campaign that showed a garage and the word "Invent." The nostalgic ad hearkened back not just to H-P's own beginnings in a Silicon Valley garage, but to IBM's ads from that earlier period, based on the single word "Think." By mid-2001 the company was under attack from Wall Street after it announced a proposed $25 billion acquisition of Compaq.

Under the headline, "Where do you want to go today?" Microsoft launched a $500 million, integrated marketing push from Wieden & Kennedy for its software in 1999. The ads focused on applications for business, home, and school. In 2001, however, Microsoft changed course, with a series of TV ads focused on the flexibility of its "enterprise" (big business) software from McCann-Erickson Worldwide.

As the new millennium dawned, advertising about the Internet reached its apogee. The giant Interpublic Group of Companies estimated at the time that the advertising industry's value was $215 billion, but advertising of computers—mostly Internet-related computer applications—was growing exponentially. The computer and related telecommunications categories were up 36 percent and 45 percent, respectively, and many of the ads on the Super Bowl XXXIV telecast in January 2000 were for new, Internet-related "dot-com" companies.

The collapse of the Internet stock bubble in 2000 had an impact on some of that advertising, but computer advertising remained strong. Television remained the focus of computer image advertising, while the Internet itself became the medium for detailed promotions and much of the order taking.

DANA BLANKENHORN

See also Apple Computer; IBM Corporation; Microsoft Corporation; *and color plate in this volume*

Further Reading

Forbes.com, "Forbes Faces: Steve Jobs," <www.forbes.com/2001/01/12/0112faces.html>

Freiberger, Paul, and Michael Swaine, *Fire in the Valley: The Making of the Personal Computer*, Berkeley, California: Osborne/McGraw Hill, 1984; collectors' edition, New York and London: McGraw Hill, 2000

Garr, Doug, *IBM Redux: Lou Gerstner and the Business Turnaround of the Decade*, New York: HarperBusiness, 1999; Chichester, West Sussex: Wiley, 2000

Gillies, James, and Robert Cailliau, *How the Web Was Born: The Story of the World Wide Web*, Oxford and New York: Oxford University Press, 2000

Godin, Seth, *eMarketing*, New York: Berkley, 1995

Greenia, Mark W., *Computers and Computing: History of Computing: A Chronology of the People and Machines That Made Computer History*, Sacramento, California: Lexikon Services, 1993

Hanson, Ward A., *Principles of Internet Marketing*, Cincinnati, Ohio: South-Western College, 2000

The Interpublic Group of Companies, Inc., "Advertising Industry Outlook," <www.interpublic.com/companynews/insider12_99.html>

Maddox, Kate, and Dana Blankenhorn, *Web Commerce: Building a Digital Business*, New York and Chichester, West Sussex: Wiley, 1998

Sterne, Jim, *What Makes People Click: Advertising on the Web*, Indianapolis, Indiana: Que, 1997

USA Today Tech Report, "H-P, IBM Compete for e-Customers," <www.usatoday.com/life/cyber/tech/ctf979.htm>

Watson, Thomas J., Jr., and Peter Petre, *Father, Son, and Co.: My Life at IBM and Beyond*, New York and London: Bantam Books, 1990

Zeff, Robbin Lee, and Brad Aronson, *Advertising on the Internet*, New York and Chichester, West Sussex: Wiley, 1997; 2nd edition, 1999

Michael Conrad & Leo Burnett

(Lürzer, Conrad)

Founded by Walter Lürzer and Michael Conrad under the name Lürzer, Conrad, 1975; merged with Leo Burnett Deutschland, 1980; name changed to Michael Conrad & Leo Burnett to reflect earlier departure of Walter Lürzer, 1986; became member of the BCom3 network through the merger of the Leo Group, the Mac-Manus Group, and Dentsu, 2000.

Major Clients

Coca-Cola Company
Condor Airlines
Fiat
Focus magazine
Heinz Company
Kellogg Company
Philip Morris Companies
Pillsbury Company
Procter & Gamble Company

Founded in Frankfurt, West Germany, in the mid-1970s by the creative team of Walter Lürzer and Michael Conrad, Michael Conrad & Leo Burnett (MC&LB) is known for producing standard-setting advertising in a variety of categories. The agency's work often opened new consumer markets through innovative creative treatments based on intense scrutiny of clients' products and the way consumers related to them. The agency also produced senior managers who were promoted to key positions at the highest levels of its U.S. parent, which was unusual for a German agency.

Conrad and Lürzer had already worked together in Frankfurt for Young & Rubicam and Heumann Ogilvy & Mather when they bolted to set up their first shop in Conrad's family apartment in 1972. When David Ogilvy suggested to Lürzer that he could make as much money working for an agency as he could owning one, Lürzer replied, "Well, I don't know a single copywriter with his own chateau in France." Conrad was 30, Lürzer, 28.

At the same time the Paris, France-based hot shop TBWA was looking for partners in Germany. Conrad and Lürzer shelved their plans and went into business with the Parisians instead, opening the Frankfurt office of TBWA. In 1974 the mercurial Lürzer resigned from TBWA, and not long after Conrad joined him to have another shot at running their own agency. This time they were hugely successful.

They picked up a half-dozen accounts within their first four months. By cleverly timing the release of the new business notices to the trade press, and by running a series of four self-promotion ads as pages in a business weekly, the new agency, called Lürzer, Conrad, created an immediate buzz within the industry.

In working on an early campaign for client Cointreau liqueur, Conrad and Lürzer discovered that most Germans knew the product but were not drinking it because it was too sweet. In 1978 Conrad traveled to Paris to convince company owner Max Cointreau that Cointreau tasted great on ice, which reduced the sweetness. The young agency then created a campaign based on the liqueur's twin lives as a pure or an on-the-rocks beverage. Cointreau's sales decline in Germany stopped instantly, and the idea of serving on ice for a more contemporary taste became standard for liquor marketers worldwide.

In the late 1970s some of the agency's clients, including Bosch, Braun, and Margaret Astor cosmetics, were increasingly concerned about pan-European advertising. Frankfurt was awash in international agency networks looking for talented partners. Conrad and Lürzer concluded that Leo Burnett Deutschland offered the best stable of fast-moving packaged-goods clients to complement the agency's roster of banks, appliances, and cosmetics. Leo Burnett Company Chief Executive Officer (CEO) John Kinsella invited them to a board meeting in Chicago, Illinois, and they emerged with a deal. In 1980 the merged agency was renamed Lürzer, Conrad & Leo Burnett.

The agency got off to a rough start as a Burnett shop. A downturn in the German economy and a client loss resulting from the merger was responsible for a 13 percent loss in billings in 1981. Then in 1982 the agency chairman, Dieter Karp, died in an accident. And although the agency would continue to bear his name for four years, Lürzer embarked on a solo career, eventually opening the Lowe, Lürzer office in Frankfurt.

That tumultuous period was critical to the future of both the Frankfurt agency and, eventually, Burnett offices worldwide. First, Reiner Erfert, who founded the Lintas agency's Frankfurt office, was hired to replace Karp as chairman. Also in this period, Lürzer, Conrad & Leo Burnett was charged with introducing a new economy car, the Panda, from Fiat; the iconoclastic advertising campaign swept up major awards in 1982 and 1983, raising the bar for creativity and effectiveness in auto advertising.

At a time when auto advertising in Germany was confined to dry technical specifications, the agency recognized that a large minority of potential auto buyers were enlightened, critical consumers looking for economical transport. They also would respond to emotional pitches poking fun at the Panda's awkward shape and small motor. Dubbing the Panda *die tolle Kiste* (the "mad box") and running witty headlines—including one that ran above a picture of a man speaking to his psychiatrist: "I'm in favor of pollution control. Against animal testing. For hand-knitted sweaters . . . and wholewheat bread. Against pre-fab housing. But for the Fiat Panda. Am I schizophrenic?"—the agency created a sensation around the Panda that propelled it to become the hottest-selling import in its class. Panda market share jumped from 5.9 percent in 1981 to 7.6 percent in 1982, helping make Fiat the largest exporter of cars to Germany. The Panda campaign continues to this day as one of the longest running in German ad history.

Mombasa in Kenia ist nur eines von 72 Condor Urlaubszielen.

Die Höhensonne ist zu klein, die Sauna zu voll und das Solarium immer ausgebucht. Das läßt Sie kalt? Dann haben Sie wohl längst einen Condor Flug in der Tasche.

Condor
Die Ferienflieger der Lufthansa

"The sun lamp is too small, the sauna too crowded and the solarium is always occupied. You don't care? Then you've probably already booked a Condor flight." This humorous advertisement won an Epica award for Michael Conrad & Leo Burnett in 1990.

In 1996 both Conrad and Lürzer were made honorary members of Germany's Art Directors Club, in part for their work for Fiat.

In 1986 Conrad remained a partner but left the Frankfurt agency to join Burnett's Chicago office as president of Leo Burnett

International. The move was controversial, but with the agency's creative legacy maintained by co-creative directors Klaus Küster and Heinrich Hoffmann, and with the strong supervision of Erfert, the agency prospered under the new name of Michael Conrad & Leo Burnett (MC&LB).

In the 1990s the agency lost some of the gloss of its initial years but produced solid, brand-building advertising for blue-chip clients that included the Philip Morris Companies, Kellogg Company, and Procter & Gamble Company. Among the throng of German offices of international agency networks, MC&LB enjoyed the reputation of remaining closest to its original guiding principles. The agency became a central creative force on Philip Morris Companies' Marlboro cigarettes, producing work that was executed throughout Europe and Africa, and it was the lead agency for Procter & Gamble's Secret deodorant in Europe.

In the mid-1990s MC&LB created the launch campaign for *Focus*, a newsweekly that quickly rivaled the entrenched *Der Spiegel* in both circulation and ad revenue. In what is generally regarded as the most successful magazine introduction in Germany, the agency promoted the weekly's pared-down editorial content and splashy graphics as the preferred read for Germany's "info elite" (Conrad's term) through the tag line, "Facts, facts, facts." The agency filmed actual editorial meetings on a Friday night, edited them into short TV spots, and broadcast them the next day to promote the Monday edition. Circulation soared.

As Conrad rose up the ranks in Chicago—in 1993 to the post of group vice president and deputy CEO—Erfert organized the expansion of Leo Burnett into Eastern Europe from Frankfurt. Erfert was appointed vice chairman of Leo Burnett for Europe, the Near East, and Africa in 1992. In 1995 he was appointed to the board of Burnett, Chicago.

After recruiting Heimar Schröter as CEO of MC&LB in 1997, Erfert officially withdrew from the Frankfurt agency in 1998. Today he is a vice chairman of BCom3 Group, the holding company for Burnett, MacManus, and Dentsu. In 1997 Conrad was named vice chairman and chief creative officer for Burnett, becoming the first German to hold the top creative job at a major international agency network.

KEVIN COTE

Consumer Electronics

Consumer electronics advertising has generally succeeded or failed on the merits of the gadgetry it promoted. The Radio Corporation of America (RCA) dominated the industry for years, reaching its advertising peak in the 1950s. RCA, Zenith Radio Corporation, and others created ads that reflected their time, producing wholesome images with the help of agencies such as the J.

Walter Thompson Company and the Leo Burnett Company, respectively.

Like many of its U.S. competitors, however, RCA found itself losing market share in the 1960s and 1970s to Japanese companies. It was a fertile time in the advertising world, with a loosening of moral standards and intense competition for the consumer

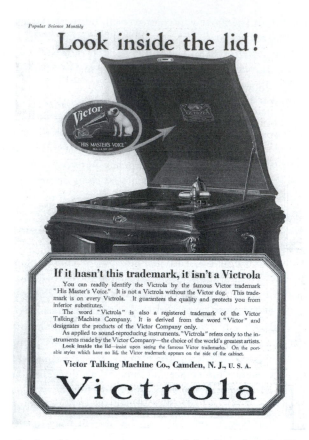

Popular Science Monthly

Look inside the lid!

If it hasn't this trademark, it isn't a Victrola

You can readily identify the Victrola by the famous Victor trademark "His Master's Voice." It is not a Victrola without the Victor dog. This trademark is on every Victrola. It guarantees the quality and protects you from inferior substitutes.

The word "Victrola" is also a registered trademark of the Victor Talking Machine Company. It is derived from the word "Victor" and designates the products of the Victor Company only.

As applied to sound-reproducing instruments, "Victrola" refers only to the instruments made by the Victor Company—the choice of the world's greatest artists. Look inside the lid—insist upon seeing the famous Victor trademarks. On the portable styles which have no lid, the Victor trademark appears on the side of the cabinet.

Victor Talking Machine Co., Camden, N. J., U. S. A.

Victrola

A 1918 print ad instructs consumers to look for the trademark "Nipper" the dog as a way of verifying that the product was made by the Victor Talking Machine Company.

dollar. The end result was increasingly racy ads featuring shocking images that would never have seen the light of day a few years earlier.

Early Days

RCA will forever be associated with its ad mascot, Nipper the dog, sitting attentively while he listened to an RCA Victrola phonograph. The image came from a painting titled *His Master's Voice*. RCA was established in 1919 to build radio receivers but did not acquire Nipper until 1929, when it purchased the Victor Talking Machine Company. By the 1940s and early 1950s, RCA was far ahead of its competitors in selling radios, but the radio was losing ground to the increasingly popular television set. Lord & Thomas was an early ad agency for RCA, but the agency lost the account in 1944 over a lingering disagreement between RCA Chairman David Sarnoff and Lord & Thomas Chairman Albert Lasker, even though Lasker had retired from advertising in 1943 and sold the agency to its three top managers—Emerson Foote, Fairfax Cone, and Don Belding, who renamed the shop Foote, Cone & Belding (FCB).

The J. Walter Thompson Company (JWT) took over most of the RCA account for the next 11 years (sharing it with Kenyon & Eckhardt (K&E) and Ruthrauff & Ryan), beginning an on-again,

off-again relationship that would last for decades. The first split came near the end of 1953 when RCA put its account up for review, prompting an unusual attempt by William H. Weintraub & Company to capture the $10 million business. Weintraub advertised for the business, purchasing a $5,000 back-page ad in the *New York Times*. The ad, which featured Morse code for RCA in outsized type, created a stir among *Times* readers. The ad did not persuade RCA, however, which awarded the account to K&E. RCA remained a major force in radio and television manufacture and radio broadcasting.

In 1959 JWT once again won over RCA. By this time, RCA was losing market share in the television segment to companies such as Zenith, and JWT was brought back to help the company fend off the competition. Despite its advertising efforts, RCA's hold on the industry continued to dwindle; a successful antitrust suit against the company further damaged its attempts to grow. RCA's total advertising budget—including nonconsumer electronics—was cut to $28.6 million in 1961 (from $31.7 million the year before), but the company raised it to $33.6 million in 1962 in an effort to hold onto its leading position in TV sales.

Zenith was another pioneer in the radio business, getting its start in 1918 in Chicago, Illinois, when two radio enthusiasts began assembling radios for other amateurs in the nascent industry. Zenith's slogan, "The quality goes in before the name goes on," was first used in 1929.

Zenith's own advertising account, though much smaller than RCA's at the time, was at H.W. Kastor & Sons in the 1930s, then E.H. Brown Advertising and MacFarland Aveyard in the 1940s, all Chicago agencies. It continued to be passed from shop to shop during the 1950s. Earle Ludgin & Company, Zenith's fourth agency in five years, was let go in 1957, having replaced Batten Barton Durstine & Osborn (BBDO), which had resigned the account in favor of Philco. But Zenith's tremendous growth was too much for the small Ludgin agency to handle. The much bigger FCB nabbed the account in 1958 and held onto it for many years. Zenith's primary products were TV sets and radios.

The Motorola Company, a diversified company, was another big spender. Motorola planned to spend $12 million on ads in 1953, using Ruthrauff & Ryan as its agency. The agency won the account using the then-innovative technique of finalist agencies making speculative presentations. Working with Ruthrauff, the company was one of the first to hire athletes to hawk electronic gadgetry; baseball's pitching great Bob Feller endorsed Motorola's All-transistor Pocket Radio in a 1957 ad appearing in *Sports Illustrated*.

The 1960s were an exciting time for consumer electronics, with portable transistor radios and color television growing rapidly in popularity, as Japanese companies such as Matsushita Electric Industrial Company and a small newcomer, Sony Corporation—with a $500,000 ad budget and a small agency, Ellis Advertising—tried to gain a foothold in the U.S. market. They were going up against such established giants as RCA, Zenith, and Motorola. One of the biggest battles among television set marketers was over quality of color, leading to the coining of such terms as Chromacolor (Zenith) and Total Automatic Color

(Magnavox), by which the various manufacturers sought to distinguish their products.

RCA and JWT scored a coup in 1964 with the publication of actual photos of the Moon taken from the Ranger 7 spacecraft in major newspapers. The pictures were used in ads that touted the National Aeronautics and Space Administration's use of RCA television technology. The ads were laid out in hours, the photos appearing only days after they were taken, a difficult feat for the time.

The Magnavox Company became an advertising force, too, hiring K&E for its $2 million account in June 1962 to replace McCann-Erickson. Toward the end of the decade, the Magnavox account became the target of an unusual approach to garnering business. Waterman Advertising, a relatively small agency, ran an ad in the *New York Times* chiding the Fort Wayne, Indiana-based Magnavox for spending so much money on its ads. Waterman suggested that it was "a place where big agency people aren't gagged by the smallness of big agency thinking." Waterman President Norman Waterman told *Advertising Age* at the time that the ads led to three or four appointments with advertisers but declined to name them.

Arrival of the Japanese

Given that World War II was still fresh in many consumers' minds, Matsushita wisely recognized that some Americans still resented Japan and would not buy products from a company with a Japanese name. Hence, in 1966, Matsushita phased out its name in the United States and became "Panasonic." Panasonic was just getting its feet wet in North American advertising, spending $1.2 million in 1966, according to *Advertising Age*. Its agency, Ted Bates & Company, created bold campaigns with proclamations such as: "Are you scared stiff your first color television set will turn out to be a $500 dog?" and "When you fall asleep while Wallace Beery is making love to Marie Dressler, will your next television set have the decency to shut itself off?"

Magnavox made headlines with its brash decision to dump K&E as its agency of record in 1970 in favor of the à la carte approach to buying advertising, seeking to save as much as 15 percent on commissions. The experiment lasted just two years, with the William Esty Company getting the $5 million account in November 1972 in a review with four other agencies.

Even if ads and their targets were getting more sophisticated, as the 1970s progressed, there were still indications that technology had a way to go in capturing the public trust. For example, Panasonic agreed to run a corrective ad in 1972 after the Federal Trade Commission investigated previous ads that implied Panasonic's television sets had passed a fire hazard test with flying colors. Today, most consumers assume that electronics are not going to burst into flames under normal use.

Sony and its agency, Doyle Dane Bernbach (DDB), created a stir with an ad that showed in profile 13 nude people and a dog sitting and standing in a field watching a Sony portable television set. "The Sony for sun-lovers," the ad stated. More comical than

Ted Bates & Company created this 1966 print ad for Panasonic's entry into the U.S. consumer electronics market. *Matsushita Electric Corporation of America.*

sexual, the ad nonetheless was refused by the *New York Times* ad department, although it was accepted by *Life* magazine.

Industry in Flux

The Motorola Corporation was one of the first U.S. companies to abandon the home consumer electronics market, citing excessive advertising costs as the primary reason. Motorola executives said that its 1973 advertising costs of $4 million–$5 million could not justify its sales of $244 million; it sold its television business to Matsushita, which renamed the company Quasar.

Through this period, Zenith remained the TV sales leader, eclipsing $1 billion in sales for the first time in 1973; *Advertising Age* estimated its ad budget at $25 million. Even then, Zenith was looking over its shoulder, because its products were considered to be of a lesser quality than those of many of its rivals. Zenith aggressively defended its turf, even asking U.S. Sen. Frank Moss of Utah to force Sony to stop using the results of a federal study in its ads. The "Sony. No baloney" ads, created by DDB, were based on a government study that found that Sony used rigorous standards in touting its technical achievements.

Meanwhile, the newly popular minicalculators, while growing fast in sales, were starting to get some advertising support. Sharp Electronics Corporation, the industry leader and first to market a calculator in the United States, spent about $1 million a year in TV and print via ad agency Wisser & Sanchez in 1973. Sharp held about 30 percent of the U.S. market at that time.

By the mid-1970s, much of the focus of consumer electronics marketers' advertising was on the emerging technology of videocassette recording. In early 1976 Sony became the first to offer consumers a home recorder, which used its own Betamax format. Sony planned to spend $2 million on advertising for the Betamax in autumn of that year when the product first reached national distribution. Sony did not use an outside agency for its video products, having brought its advertising in-house in July 1976.

Michel-Cather, the agency that had held the Sony videocassette recorder (VCR) account for five years, was hired by the number-two VCR company, JVC Industries, a deliberate act as it went head-to-head against Sony with a competing—and noncompatible—VCR format. JVC ultimately won the battle, with the marginally superior Betamax falling by the wayside in favor of JVC's VHS format, which could record up to six hours.

Sharp, another Japanese company, first advertised its TV sets in the United States in 1975, using the tag line, "One sharp picture is worth a thousands words." The ads were created by Wisser & Sanchez.

Another electronic toy, citizens band (CB) radio, caught on like wildfire in 1975 and 1976. CB radio advertisers first targeted consumers with their promotions in 1975 after initially focusing on niche publications such as *Electronics Hobbyist* magazine and *Popular Electronics* magazine. The craze was fueled further in 1976 by the hit song "Convoy," recorded by C.W. McCall, a pseudonym for ad executive Bill Fries. But CB radio never met early expectations for long-term growth. Predictions that sales would hit 10 million units a year by 1980 were way off, and by mid-1977, forecasts were scaled back severely, with CB manufacturers pulling back their promotions.

Meanwhile, RCA finally ended its relationship with JWT in January 1976, looking for a fresh start after 18 years of working together. The Leo Burnett Company won the estimated $100 million account.

Panasonic was still able to ruffle feathers with ads that would be considered tame by end-of-the-century standards. Ad industry professionals complained that Panasonic was promoting violence with 1977 ads for its TVs and radios. The offending TV copy headline stated: "Why horror movies are more horrible on the Quantrix II color picture tube." A Panasonic radio ad said: "The 6-inch speaker that makes fire, crime, and disaster sound beautiful."

Toward the end of the 1980s, experts were beginning to question the long-term viability of U.S. electronics companies. U.S. Trust, a major investment manager, favored Sony over U.S. companies such as Zenith as an investment. Recognizing their plight, U.S. manufacturers boosted their ad budgets. Zenith promoted its Chromacolor TV sets via FCB, RCA advertised its Colortrak sets using Burnett campaigns, while Quasar used DDB Needham

Compact Disc (CD) technology, co-developed by Sony Corporation and Philips Electronics in the early 1980s, was among the most significant innovations of the decade in consumer electronics. This 1983 print ad introduced Sony's first CD player.
Courtesy of Sony Electronic Inc.

Worldwide, Inc. While all of these companies were still in business as marketers of consumer electronics at the start of the 21st century, only RCA continued as a sizable presence.

Sony Supremacy

By the end of the 1970s Sony continued to take over U.S. consumer markets. If its Betamax was an abject failure, the company's portable Walkman was an unqualified success. Originally slated to be called the Sound-About in the United States, the Walkman took off immediately when introduced in 1979, despite a limited advertising budget.

The Walkman put new life into the audiocassette format. Home tape recording first hit the consumer market in the late 1940s using a reel-to-reel system that was a scaled-back version of the professional systems recording studios were starting to use. But the reel-to-reel recorders were relatively expensive and achieved only limited market penetration. Neither prerecorded reel-to-reel music tapes nor the introduction of stereo in 1958 did much to move the format forward. In 1960 most people still

TOSHIBA TECHNOLOGY SETS THE STANDARD.

Innovation. At Toshiba, it's the word we live by. It's also how we've approached multimedia technology from the beginning. This view has enabled us to create a range of exciting products that once existed only in the imagination. We're proud to have started a revolution that will help bring Hollywood and Silicon Valley together. But it's only just begun. Get ready for the ride of your life.

Dolby® is a registered trademark of Dolby Laboratories Licensing Corporation.

Since the first silent celluloid hero rode a flickering beam of light through a darkened theater, the medium has been evolving to this. At about 7 times the capacity of a CD, DVD's 4.7 gigabytes deliver feature-length films in unbelievable digital clarity. Dolby® Digital (5.1) surround sound. A choice of 8 language options and 32 subtitles. Three aspect ratios. Parental lockout. Random search. And no rewinding. Fasten your seat belt. The show's about to start. Call 1.800.631.3811.

In Touch with Tomorrow
TOSHIBA

http://www.toshiba.com

In 1996 Toshiba, co-developer of Superdisc technology, announced the arrival of the digital videodisc (DVD) format. A joint agreement with Warner, Sony, and Philips defined the standard for DVD, and a year later the first DVD products reached consumers.
Toshiba America, Inc.

regarded it as a novelty to hear their own voices. Then in the mid-1960s, Philips Electronics introduced the audiocassette, a miniaturized reel-to-reel tape format housed in a small plastic casing thinner than a cigarette pack. It not only simplified recording for the uninitiated, it made it portable enough to be installed as part of an automobile radio. Another portable tape format also came out in the 1960s that targeted the automobile market. But while the eight-track tape cartridge was simple and easy for prerecorded music, it lacked the flexibility needed for home recording and was prone to jam, working on the principle of a tape loop. By the late 1970s, the cartridge was as obsolete as the 78-rpm record.

The introduction of the Sony Walkman and similar products from other companies extended the market for the cassette by extending its portability. The Sony 110 recorder had reduced the size of the cassette machine to the size of a large novel, which could be carried about but not inconspicuously. The Walkman brought the size down to the dimensions of a small paperback book that one could put in a pocket or purse or clip to a belt while jogging. The ability to record was unimportant to most people, who wanted nothing more than a small and simple playback device. The audiocassette went into the 21st century still a healthy and thriving format, notwithstanding competition from the compact disc (CD).

Sony also had a hand in popularizing the compact disc format for music, introducing it in 1983 in Europe and North America. Though Philips N.V., the Dutch parent to Philips Consumer Electronics, invented the technology, Sony's marketing clout was able to help CDs become the primary format for listening to music. By 1986 Sony commanded 40 percent of a growing market, according to *Advertising Age*. With its finger in many pies, Sony's U.S. ad budget climbed to $53 million by 1984, with McCann-Erickson handling the account.

Sony also led the way in a new form of promotion that targeted component entertainment. The company advertised its products as a way for consumers to create a TV-based experience using a combination of inputs—such as cable, broadcast, and CDs—and customized outputs using a combination of television and external speakers.

New Technology

By 1982 others, including Zenith and Magnavox, jumped on the bandwagon. As part of that, rear projection TV sets were offered by a variety of manufacturers, including Sony, Mitsubishi, and Hitachi Ltd. By 1985 stereo TV sets were starting to hit the scene. Zenith, for example, advertised its sets' stereo capabilities via FCB with TV spots featuring the Preservation Hall Jazz Band, taped and broadcast in stereo, of course.

Toward the end of the decade, electronics companies scaled back on their advertising, though Philips's Magnavox brand was an exception. The Dutch company hiked its targeted ad spending in 1988 to $30 million, a 50 percent increase from the previous year and double RCA's budget, in an attempt to grab market share

from U.S. companies. Also, Philips began to put its Philips brand name on high-end electronics products in the United States, keeping it separate from its Magnavox nameplate.

Through the 1990s consumers were reaching new levels of sophistication in what they wanted from marketers. CDs were already old hat, and companies such as RCA, Philips, and Sony were happy to provide them with new products.

RCA, which had been acquired by Thomson Consumer Electronics in 1988, returned to its national broadcasting roots, so to speak, by offering a home-satellite system under the name DirecTV, which competed directly with cable television. In 1993 RCA opened a $120 million-plus marketing campaign for the $1 billion joint project with Hughes Communications and Hubbard Broadcasting. Agencies for the account were Ammirati & Puris for RCA, Bozell Worldwide for Hubbard, and Lintas Campbell-Ewald for Hughes.

Philips tried to turn the tide on its poor financial performance in the early 1990s with its first global image advertising campaign. The $40 million campaign from Euro RSCG, of London, England, was supposed to be a first step in overcoming its image of creating good products but not selling them. D'Arcy Masius Benton & Bowles, of New York City, was Philips's U.S. agency. Philips did make inroads in establishing itself in the U.S. consumer's mind, though it still stood in the shadow of Sony.

By the middle of the decade, companies had set their sites on the digital videodisc (DVD) format as the next big thing. Thomson; Sony; Philips; Toshiba America, Inc.; Panasonic; and others were expected to spend $150 million marketing DVD players, which quickly surpassed the LaserDisc format. The DVD first hit the scene in 1996, and immediately caught the fancy of electronics marketers and consumers. DVD had strong support from studios, an element missing from the LaserDisc.

Toshiba and Warner Home Video united to spend $30 million for ads promoting players and movies in late 1997. The next year, Philips even attempted an infomercial for DVDs in conjunction with print, TV, and cinema ads produced by Messner Vetere Berger McNamee Schmetterer/Euro RSCG. But advertisers did not abandon their roots. Sony reintroduced the Walkman in 2000 with a $30 million campaign created by Y&R Advertising, its largest yet for that unit.

By the beginning of the 21st century, electronics advertisers had begun to consolidate their global media buying—but not their creative work—under one umbrella agency. Both Sony and Philips took steps to do that in early 2001.

PAUL BARR

See also Motorola, Inc.

Further Reading

Fox, Stephen R., *The Mirror Makers: A History of American Advertising and Its Creators,* New York: Morrow, 1984

Nathan, John, *Sony: The Private Life,* Boston: Houghton Mifflin, and London: HarperCollinsBusiness, 1999

Sobel, Robert, *RCA,* New York: Stein and Day, 1986

Consumer Movement

In January 1940 *Advertising Age* wrote that the consumer movement had, over the previous decade, "developed from a slightly annoying but very tiny blot on the horizon to full stature as the symbol of *the* major problem facing business—and particularly advertising—as they enter the fifth decade of the 20th century." The trade paper listed 23 groups it regarded as most active in the consumer movement, adding that despite increased levels of protest, the effort still lacked the necessary focus and critical mass in public opinion to qualify as a legitimate movement.

According to a survey of the Association of National Advertisers at the time, consumer advocates had nine key objectives: (1) creation of a federal department of the consumer; (2) initiation of stronger lobbying efforts to influence legislation; (3) promotion of labeling containing real, usable information; (4) use of quality grading on labels; (5) establishment of minimum manufacturing standards; (6) general standardization of sizes; (7) adoption of wider use of product rating services; (8) commitment to greater honesty in advertising; and (9) use of consumer cooperatives. While manufacturers and advertisers tended to resist what they saw as efforts to interfere with the conduct of their business, such objectives had broad support among the majority of consumers. The economic reforms of the New Deal in the 1930s revived and redefined American capitalism on so many different fronts, however, that consumer issues failed to move to the top of the political agenda prior to World War II. It would be another 20 to 25 years before these objectives would begin to be codified into law, and when they were, it was largely due to the efforts of one man: Ralph Nader.

In the 1960s Nader almost single-handedly energized a consumer groundswell that resulted in a host of new government regulations and countless changes in how companies disseminated their advertising messages to consumers. But despite his many achievements in battling corporate excess and protecting consumer rights, Nader merely breathed new life into a tradition that had deep historical roots. As social science researcher Mark Green wrote in *Social Policy* (1998):

> When Nader jump-started the consumer movement in 1965 with *Unsafe at Any Speed,* the consumer's world was seemingly a much simpler place. There was only one kind of mortgage (fixed), one telephone company (AT&T) and just three TV networks (CBS, ABC and NBC). And you didn't pay a dime to keep your money in the bank—or take it out. But then again, the Corvair was killing people; you practically had to be an intelligence officer to break the date code on a carton of milk; and nobody had ever heard of a Freedom of Information request.

As a result of Nader's work consumers had more choices, and government took action to prohibit corporate excesses and abuses. The advertising industry, too, took note of the rising power of consumer advocates and began to produce messages that addressed consumers' concerns. Advertisers used the powerful ideas of the consumer advocates to help craft persuasive messages that would appeal to informed consumers.

The Muckraker and the Industrialist

In the 19th century, as the pace of industrialization in the United States accelerated, people increasingly began to rely on mass media for information. The migration from farm to factory was underscored by the importance of the dissemination of information and the social value placed on those people who were adept at formulating and distributing information.

Technological innovations such as the steam engine and the linotype reshaped the economic culture of the country. Technology also created a demand for better communication tools. However, this demand for information brought with it an expansion of social stratification. The gap between the social classes widened because of the different abilities of various groups to glean and to disseminate information via the mass media. Although industrialization enabled people to develop so-called economic capital— essentially, an individual's personal wealth—it also produced a greater disproportion in "cultural capital"—the opportunities for people to learn.

The era of the robber baron, led by figures such as railroad tycoon William Henry Vanderbilt, banker J. P. Morgan, oil magnate J. D. Rockefeller, and steel mogul Henry Clay Frick, ushered in an era of sweatshop labor and low pay. Business owners set the standard for the changing work environment. Unfortunately, they also set the standard for corporate abuses.

The modern consumer movement owes a great debt to a group of writers dubbed the muckrakers, who produced stinging exposés of corruption and exploitation. The term was coined by those who accused these investigative journalists of a desire to comb through society's "filth." One of the earliest of the muckrakers was Joseph Pulitzer, whose editorials supported labor in the Homestead, Pennsylvania, steelworkers strike of 1892. The slogan he coined for an early campaign, "the public be informed," presented a striking contrast to the attitude of Vanderbilt, summed up in his much-quoted statement, "The public be damned."

In the early 1900s *McClure's* magazine published a series of articles that aroused the public and alerted political leaders to the abuses of industry. Upton Sinclair's 1906 novel *The Jungle* exposed abuses in the meatpacking industry. In fact, Sinclair's novel provided the foundation for the enactment of federal standards for certifying the safety of food and drugs. Other prominent muckrakers of the time were Ray Stannard Baker, who wrote about child labor conditions; Ida Tarbell, who exposed the unfair labor practices of Standard Oil; and Frank Norris, whose novels *The Octopus* (1901) and *The Pit* (1903) attacked the railroads and wheat traders, respectively.

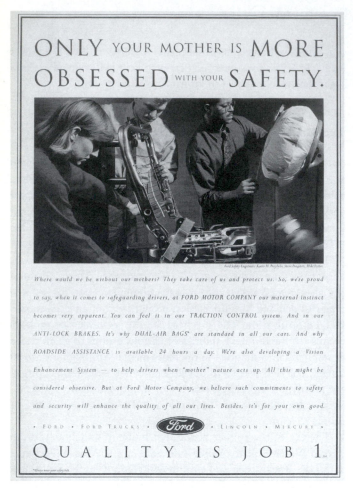

ONLY YOUR MOTHER IS MORE OBSESSED WITH YOUR SAFETY.

Where would we be without our mothers? They take care of us and protect us. So, we're proud to say, when it comes to safeguarding drivers, at FORD MOTOR COMPANY our maternal instinct becomes very apparent. You can feel it in our TRACTION CONTROL system. And in our ANTI-LOCK BRAKES. It's why DUAL-AIR BAGS* are standard in all our cars. And why ROADSIDE ASSISTANCE is available 24 hours a day. We're also developing a Vision Enhancement System — to help drivers when "mother" nature acts up. All this might be considered obsessive. But at Ford Motor Company, we believe such commitments to safety and security will enhance the quality of all our lives. Besides, it's for your own good.

· FORD · FORD TRUCKS · *Ford* · LINCOLN · MERCURY ·

QUALITY IS JOB 1.

Nearly 30 years after activist Ralph Nader energized the consumer movement with the publication of *Unsafe at Any Speed*, automakers continued to advertise their commitment to car safety. *Courtesy Ford Motor Company.*

Government Gets into the Act

President Theodore Roosevelt recognized the need for government action to uphold the public interest in battles involving management, labor, and consumers. Roosevelt used the leverage gained from the Sherman Antitrust Act of 1890, which protected consumers from the abuses of monopolies, to challenge business to address consumer concerns.

In 1899 the first national consumer group, the National Consumers League (NCL), was formed. The NCL provided leverage for cultivating the ideas of Harvey W. Wiley, a U.S. Department of Agriculture chemist, who for 20 years had pushed for passage of federal food and drug laws. Wiley's dream of governmental intervention was realized in 1906 with the passage of the first Pure Food and Drug Act. That same year, Congress passed the Meat Inspection Act, which enforced sanitary regulations in the meat-packing industry.

As the industrial era moved forward, technological advances helped narrow the intellectual gap in society. Acceptance of the

mass media as an information source bridged the information gap between socioeconomic classes. This resulted in more informed consumers who could now gather significant information about products, services, and ideas in order to protect themselves against corporate abuses.

The widespread use of media as a source of information paved the way for *Good Housekeeping* magazine to introduce its seal of approval in 1909; the seal is still in use today. *Good Housekeeping* forged a reputation for safeguarding its readers' welfare by carefully evaluating potential advertisers. In order to have the *Good Housekeeping* seal affixed to its product, an advertiser must first meet the strict standards imposed by the Good Housekeeping Institute and must successfully complete product testing by the magazine's test lab. Advertised products that meet the stringent testing requirements of *Good Housekeeping*'s test labs can use the seal for a 12-month renewable term in advertisements in the company publication. Advertisers are required to purchase at least one page of black-and-white advertising in the company publication.

The seal of approval entitles consumers who purchase defective merchandise to receive a replacement or refund if an advertised product fails to meet the promises of the advertised message. Writing in *Fortune* magazine in 1997, Paul Lucas, journalist, noted, "The review process is hardly a rubber stamp—in fact, [the magazine] stopped accepting cigarette ads long before the Surgeon General's landmark report." *Good Housekeeping* makes good on its promise to consumers several hundred times per year. Moreover, the magazine rejects several hundreds of thousands of dollars worth of advertising annually from products that fail to meet the quality standards of the test lab. According to research conducted by *Good Housekeeping*, 92 percent of women surveyed claim they are familiar with the seal and feel positive about it. Since the seal's inception, a number of products have had long records of acceptance, the longest held by Jolly Time Popcorn, which for 72 years has received the seal of approval.

The growing power of American consumers in the early decades of the 20th century prompted Congress to enact legislation designed to protect the public from unsafe products and services and to regulate business activities. In 1914 Congress passed the Federal Trade Commission (FTC) Act establishing an agency with the power to issue cease-and-desist orders against businesses that used unfair methods of competition. Later the same year Congress passed the Clayton Act, a law that supplemented the Sherman Antitrust Act and held that corporate officials who violate the act can be held individually responsible for damages created by monopolies.

The early part of the 20th century also saw a shift in the attitudes of American businesses. One reason for this shift was a growing recognition that women were making most of the family-related spending decisions. Businesses thus faced the challenge of determining if the long-standing economic view of consumers, based largely on the buying habits of men, applied equally to women. The prevailing view became that men were instinctive and rational consumers, while women were impulsive and irrational consumers. This view held throughout most of the 1910s and 1920s. In the late 1920s a different perspective began to take root, introduced by the noted industrial psychologist Lillian Moller Gilbreth, who devised methods for engaging women in the process of improving their own economic behavior and influencing the businesses that catered to them. The 1920s saw a parallel change in advertising messages directed at this redefined group of women consumers. Advertisers quickly adjusted their messages to meet the changing image of the female consumer and her demands.

Also during the 1920s, Stuart Chase and Frederick Schlink wrote *Your Money's Worth,* the first of the anti-advertising books. Schlink then followed by forming the Consumers' Club in White Plains, New York, in 1929, the organization that later gave rise to Consumers' Research. In the early 1930s numerous women's clubs took up the cause of consumerism. Organizations such as the Association of University Women, National Federation of Business and Professional Women's Clubs, Parent-Teachers' Congress, and League of Women Voters became active in the consumer movement.

The 1930s also gave rise to the notion of the consumer as a vital component of economic policy, alongside capital and labor. This idea was manifest in the creation of the Consumers' Advisory Board under the National Recovery Administration (NRA). Despite its presence, the Consumers' Advisory Board was deemed largely ineffective in promoting change. It served primarily as the protest arm of the NRA when its codes involved price increases and production controls. Despite its perceived failure, the Consumers' Advisory Board served as a catalyst for local consumer activity throughout the country.

The Consumers' Council of the Department of Agriculture came into being in 1933. The group served its constituents in two ways. First, it represented the public as consumers of farm products at all Department of Agriculture hearings, and second, it disseminated to the public consumer information of all kinds. The *Consumers' Guide,* the official publication of the council, advised consumers on how to make wise and informed purchases and upheld the rights of consumers to full and correct information on prices, quality of commodities, and costs and efficiency of distribution.

Congress amended the Clayton Act in 1936 with the passage of the Robinson-Patman Act and added to the existing legislation the phrase "to injure, destroy, or prevent competition." The amendment defined price discrimination as unlawful and empowered the FTC to establish limits on quantity discounts, forbid brokerage allowances except to independent brokers, and prohibit promotional allowances or the furnishing of services or facilities except where made available to all on proportionately equal terms. In 1938 Congress passed the Wheeler-Lea Act, prohibiting unfair and deceptive acts and practices regardless of the impact on competition. It also gave the FTC jurisdiction over food and drug advertising. The Lanham Trademark Act (1946) required that trademarks be distinctive and made it illegal to make any false representation of goods or services entering interstate commerce.

In the late 1950s, Congress passed new legislation designed to safeguard consumers from automobile industry abuses. The 1958 Automobile Information Disclosure Act prohibited car dealers from inflating the factory price of new cars. Also in 1958, the National Traffic and Safety Act provided for the creation of compulsory safety standards for automobile and tires.

Legacy of "Nader's Raiders"

Muckraking journalism had a revival in the 1960s, starting with Rachel Carson's *Silent Spring* (1962), which is often credited with initiating the U.S. environmental movement. In 1965 Nader published *Unsafe at Any Speed,* an exposé of the automobile industry; the target of this book was General Motors Corporation's Corvair, a vehicle deemed a road hazard by many. His well-documented attack resulted in a tremendous victory for the consumer movement. Although General Motors attempted to discredit Nader and his claim that the popular Corvair was dangerous, its efforts merely added impetus to the growing trend toward consumer activism. It took nearly 19 years after the publication of *Unsafe at Any Speed* for Nader and his followers to again claim victory against the auto industry, but they did so when the industry agreed to make air bags standard equipment in passenger cars.

Nader has been directly and indirectly responsible for influencing more government regulation of consumer products than any other person. His call to arms in the late 1960s spawned a sophisticated group of consumer activists who were prepared to roll up their sleeves and battle perceived corporate abuses. His work energized consumers and spawned an army of corporate whistleblowers who uncovered dubious business practices. He created consumer advocacy groups called Public Interest Research Groups (PIRGs), located on college campuses throughout the country, which investigated numerous consumer products, among them baby food and insecticides. This army of consumer advocates also amassed data on unfair insurance rates and coal mine and natural gas pipeline safety. Nicknamed "Nader's Raiders," these energetic and idealistic consumer advocates contributed greatly to a proliferation of consumer protection regulations, including the National Gas Pipeline Act of 1968, the Radiation Control for Health and Safety Act of 1968, and the Coal Mine Health and Safety Act of 1969.

In 1966 Congress again acted on the consumer's behalf by passing the Fair Packaging and Labeling Act. This law required manufacturers to list package contents and the proportions of ingredients. Also in 1966 Congress passed the Child Protection Act, which banned the sale of hazardous toys and articles. It was amended in 1969 to include items that pose electrical, mechanical, or thermal hazards. Congress enacted landmark consumer legislation in 1967 with passage of the Federal Cigarette Labeling and Advertising Act. This act requires cigarette packages to display the phrase, "Warning: The Surgeon General has determined that cigarette smoking is dangerous to your health."

The Truth-in-Lending Act of 1968 protected consumers by requiring lenders to state the true costs of a credit transaction. It also continues to outlaw the use of actual or threatened violence in collection of loans and restricts the amount of garnishments. In order to enforce this act, Congress established the National Commission on Consumer Finance.

The demand for child car seats, such as the Safe Embrace from Fisher-Price, was fueled by the consumer movement.
Advertisement used courtesy of Fisher-Price, Inc.

The issue of the environment became the focus of regulation in 1969 with passage of the National Environmental Policy Act. This act provided for the establishment of the Council on Environmental Quality. In 1970 Congress passed the Fair Credit Reporting Act, which ensures that consumers' credit reports will contain only accurate, relevant, and recent information and that the reports are confidential unless requested for an appropriate reason by a proper party.

The early 1970s also gave rise to the Consumer Product Safety Act (1972). This act established the Consumer Product Safety Commission and authorized it to set safety standards for consumer products and to exact penalties for failure to uphold the standards. In 1975 the Consumer Goods Pricing Act safeguarded consumers by prohibiting the use of price maintenance agreements among manufacturers and resellers engaged in interstate commerce.

Consumers were further empowered with passage of the Magnuson-Moss Warranty/FTC Improvement Act in 1975, which authorized the FTC to set rules concerning consumer warranties. It also expanded the regulatory powers of the FTC and gave consumers further means for redress with the enactment of "class action" suits against manufacturers.

Also in 1975, the Equal Credit Opportunity Act expressly prohibited discrimination in a credit transaction on the grounds of sex, marital status, race, national origin, religion, age, or receipt of public assistance. In 1978 the Fair Debt Collection Practice Act made it illegal to abuse any person and make false statements or use unfair methods when collecting a debt.

Congress further strengthened the consumer movement in the 1980s with the passing of the FTC Improvement Act (1980) and the Toy Safety Act (1984). The FTC Improvement Act provides the House of Representatives and the Senate jointly with veto power over FTC trade regulation rules. The Toy Safety Act gives the government expanded power to quickly recall toys when they are found to be unsafe. In 1990 the Nutrition Labeling and Education Act required that food manufacturers clearly label detailed nutritional information on food packaging.

The consumer movement of recent decades faced a more complicated situation than did that of the turn of the 20th century. As Green has observed, "Using President John F. Kennedy's 1962 proclamation of four consumer rights—the right to be heard, the right to be informed, the right to safety, and the right to choose—as a yardstick to measure consumer progress shows that the consumer movement's work is not done—and perhaps never will be." Consumers today have more choices and more opportunities than their predecessors, but they also have more information than ever before and are continually deluged with advertising messages designed to effect immediate behavioral changes. Moreover, much of this information is confusing and conflicting and leads to consumers' feeling overwhelmed and manipulated.

Response of Business

Business responded to the upsurge of consumer activism and the push for accountability by redirecting its marketing focus and placing significant emphasis on the approach known as "relationship marketing." Simply, business owners learned that consumer discontent as manifested in the form of unified activist groups could signal the death of market share. Most business owners learned that building relationships between socially conscious organizations that deliver good products and services and an informed consumer market builds lifetime associations.

One of the classic ways companies forge ties with consumers is by capitalizing on consumers' preference for patronizing businesses that offer both personal rewards and rewards for society as a whole. For example, children's clothing manufacturer Hanna Andersson developed a program called Hannadowns. Consumers trade in used Hanna Andersson clothing and receive a 20 percent discount toward the purchase of new clothing. The company, in turn, donates the returned clothing to various charities. In addition, the company donates 5 percent of its pretax profits to charities and shelters that benefit women and children. Social activism on the part of business serves to reinforce a positive public perception of the company and provides the company with much needed brand equity.

Beginning in the late 1960s businesses became increasingly aware of the need for ethical behavior in addressing the demands of consumers. The American Marketing Association, responding to the demand of consumers to regulate and guide business, developed its code of ethics. The code attempts to provide guidelines for conduct in dealing with consumers and includes the following key elements:

- Disclosure of all substantial risks associated with a product or service.
- Identification of added features that will increase the cost.
- Avoidance of false or misleading advertising.
- Rejection of high-pressure or misleading sales tactics.
- Prohibition of selling or fund-raising under the guise of conducting market research.

Ethical business practice, however, requires a business to measure itself on the basis of its response to consumer demands. The way a company responds to a customer's problem or complaint is often more influential in creating a negative perception of the

In 1990, responding to the concerns of environmentalists, Star-Kist demanded that all its suppliers adopt dolphin-safe fishing practices. Star-Kist began labeling its tuna products with this "dolphin safe" logo, and its competitors soon followed suit.
Courtesy of Star-Kist Seafood, Pittsburgh, PA.

company than is the occurrence of the problem itself. Likewise, an immediate and constructive response to problems goes a long way toward creating a positive corporate image. Procter & Gamble's voluntary withdrawal of its Rely tampons in 1980, within five months of the product's introduction, is an excellent example of an effective response in the face of a perceived threat to consumer safety. Although scientists found no causal link between Rely tampons and toxic shock syndrome (TSS), Procter & Gamble acted on the advice of the Food and Drug Administration and undertook an extensive advertising campaign to educate women about the symptoms of TSS and directed them to return boxes of Rely for a full refund. The company took a $75 million loss and withdrew a product that had already garnered 25 percent of the billion-dollar sanitary-product market.

Partly as a result of consumers' efforts, many federal agencies have been established to oversee consumer-related activities. These include the Department of Agriculture, FTC, FDA, Securities and Exchange Commission, and Environmental Protection Agency. However, government regulation of business practices is only one outcome of a sustained consumer movement. The push from consumer activists to fight fraudulent and deceptive advertising resulted in greater self-governance by the industry as a whole.

Consumerism and Advertising

Beginning in the 1960s, practitioners of advertising became increasingly aware of the connection between sales and consumer approval of products. Consequently, advertisers today pay more attention to product claims and concerns of consumers in preliminary research in order to cement a bond between consumers and the companies that they patronize.

An intricate network of consumer information groups—including organizations such as the Consumer Federation of America (CFA), the National Council of Senior Citizens, the National Consumer League, and the National Stigma Clearinghouse—continually investigates advertising complaints and conducts campaigns to halt objectionable advertising. If a company rejects the complaints made about its advertising and fails to act on the criticism, this politically active network goes on the offensive. Through the power of government intervention, strong support from the media, and an occasional lawsuit to obtain a cease-and-desist order, these consumer information networks possess the power to derail any consumer-targeted advertising campaign. Advertisers pay careful attention to these groups and attempt to cultivate good relationships through self-regulation and open communication.

With a competitive consumer market and an active and mobile consumer movement, advertisers must police themselves in order to gain consumer confidence in the advertising industry as a whole as well as in the products and services they market. In addition to self-regulation among advertising agencies, the industry has established a network of professional affiliations to monitor itself. This network includes advertising publications that seek to educate advertisers about current issues and legislation and professional trade associations that monitor the ad industry for abuses. Three of the most active and prominent member agencies are the Association of National Advertisers (ANA), founded in 1910; the American Association of Advertising Agencies (AAAA), founded in 1917; and the American Advertising Federation (AAF), founded in 1967.

The ANA comprises more than 300 major manufacturing and service companies that are clients of member agencies of the AAAA. These companies, pledged to uphold the ANA code of advertising ethics, work with the ANA to improve the content of advertising. The AAAA is an association of U.S. advertising agencies. It monitors agency practices and oversees the ethical standards agreed upon by the industry. The organization readily denies membership to agencies deemed unethical.

The AAF's Advertising Principles of American Business define the standard for truthful and responsible advertising. Its founding members helped establish the Federal Trade Commission, and its early vigilance committees were the forerunners of the Better Business Bureau. Together, the Council of Better Business Bureaus, AAAA, AAF, and ANA established the National Advertising Review Council (NARC) in 1971 to promote and enforce standards of truth, accuracy, taste, morality, and social responsibility in advertising.

In 1997 the Better Business Bureau Online and Internet Marketing Council began separate campaigns to protect consumers against suspect commercial Web sites. The efforts are designed to alert consumers about fraudulent Web sites and direct them to legitimate Internet commerce sites.

The NARC continues to look for ways to increase the industry's self-regulatory arm and protect the industry against outright government control of advertising. Beginning in early 2000, the NARC began exploring the possibility of asking for fees from participants. The organization's governing board—comprised of leaders of the ANA, AAAA, and AAF—would use the money to hire a new organization president as well as to seed other activities.

The strength of the consumer movement, the increased use of the media as a source of information, and the importance of legislation to protect the buying public established a relationship between business and consumers that continues to grow. Fostered by a sustained commitment from the business community to provide good products at fair prices, disseminated with truth and accuracy, consumers have entered the information age with the realization that their voice truly matters. The consumer movement—which took root prior to the 20th century and grew to become a driving force behind improved products, services, and legislation—was key in establishing the standards for the truthful and ethical behavior of business and protected the individual by earning respect for the power of activist groups. In turn, advertisers have developed higher standards of responsibility toward the dissemination of information and a better appreciation for their own social responsibilities.

JOE BASSO

See also American Advertising Federation; American Association of Advertising Agencies; Association of National Advertisers, Inc.; Consumers' Research; Consumers Union; Government Regulation

Further Reading

American Advertising Federation, "Advertising Principles of American Business" (adopted, San Antonio, Texas, 2 March 1984)

American Marketing Association, "Code of Ethics," revised edition, Chicago: American Marketing Association, 1985

Bourdieu, Pierre, *La distinction: Critique sociale du jugement,* Paris: Éditions de Minuit, 1979; as *Distinction: A Social Critique of the Judgment of Taste,* translated by Richard Nice, Cambridge, Massachusetts: Harvard University Press, and London: Routledge and Kegan Paul, 1984

Bovée, Courtland L., and William F. Arens, *Contemporary Advertising,* Homewood, Illinois: Irwin, 1982; 7th edition, by Arens, Boston: Irwin/McGraw-Hill, 1999

Edwards, Larry, "The Decision Was Easy," *Advertising Age* (20 August 1987)

Graham, Laurel, "Beyond Manipulation: Lillian Gilbreth's Industrial Psychology and the Governmentality of Women Consumers," *The Sociological Quarterly* 38, no. 4 (Fall 1997)

Green, Mark, "Consumers (General Consumer Movement)," *Social Policy* 28, no. 3 (1998)

Kotler, Philip, and Gary Armstrong, *Marketing: An Introduction,* Upper Saddle River, New Jersey: Prentice Hall, 1997

Lukas, Paul, "In Which We Bash a Baby Seal," *Fortune* (8 September 1997)

Newsom, Doug, and Alan Scott, *This Is PR: The Realities of Public Relations,* Belmont, California: Wadsworth, 1976; 7th edition, by Newsom, Judy Van Slyke, and Dean Kruckeberg, Belmont, California: Wadsworth, 2000

Newsom, Doug, and James Wollert, *Media Writing: News for the Mass Media,* Belmont, California: Wadsworth, 1985; revised edition, as *Media Writing: Preparing Information for the Mass Media,* 1988

"Online Seals of Approval," *Home Office Computing* 15, no. 11 (November 1997)

Seitel, Fraser, *The Practice of Public Relations,* Columbus, Ohio: Merrill, 1980; 7th edition, Upper Saddle River, New Jersey: Prentice Hall, 1998

Solomon, Michael R., *Consumer Behavior: Buying, Having, and Being,* Boston: Allyn and Bacon, 1992; 4th edition, Upper Saddle River, New Jersey: Prentice Hall, and London: Prentice-Hall International, 1999

Stewart, Thomas, "The Resurrection of Ralph Nader," *Fortune* (22 May 1989)

"What about the Consumer Movement?" *Advertising Age* (8 January 1940)

Teinowitz, Ira, "Ad Review Council Weighs Option of Changing Members; Top Priorities: Fill Presidential Vacancy, Seed New Programs," *Advertising Age* (31 January 2000)

Consumers' Research

Consumers' Research, an early linchpin of the consumer movement, was established in 1929 by Frederick Schlink and Stuart Chase. Schlink had worked at the National Bureau of Standards in Washington, D.C., and at the American Standards Association in New York City. Chase was a researcher and writer. In 1927 the two published *Your Money's Worth,* a book that sounded the alarm about the unscrupulous, often manipulative selling tactics used in advertisements. Schlink and Chase felt that the time had come to establish standards for manufacturers and advertisers and to conduct scientific tests of products for the benefit of consumers.

Your Money's Worth became a best-seller, and Schlink and Chase, with financial and editorial assistance from patrons and friends, transformed the Consumer Club of White Plains, New York—a group they had founded in 1927—into Consumers' Research, Inc. The headquarters of the new organization was in New York City.

Between 1930 and 1935 Consumers' Research published three separate periodicals. The *Handbook of Buying* (1930–35), which appeared either annually or semiannually, was an expansion of the *Consumers' Club Commodity List* (launched in October 1927). The bimonthly *Confidential Bulletin Service* (1930–32) featured the results of product tests conducted by or for Consumers' Research on products ranging from alarm clocks and automobiles to men's underwear and vacuum cleaners; it also published general articles on such topics of interest to consumers as food, fur coats, gardening, and heating. Another bimonthly, the *General Bulletin* (1931–35), contained information on consumer and political issues. Even in the midst of the Great Depression, the publications were successful. Indeed, the number of subscribers increased substantially during the first few years, reaching 33,000 by 1932.

In 1933 Consumers' Research moved from New York City to Washington, New Jersey, a small town near the Pennsylvania state line. The organization soon needed more office space, and the following year it moved to Bowerstown, outside of Washington. The board of directors included a number of prominent political liber-als. When Franklin D. Roosevelt was elected president, the organization increased its political activities, which included lobbying in Washington, D.C., on behalf of consumers.

Schlink and Arthur Kallet, who served as executive secretary of the board of directors, published *100,000,000 Guinea Pigs: Dangers in Everyday Foods, Drugs and Cosmetics* in 1933. The book examined the ingredients of certain popular products and called for legislation that would require companies to disclose ingredients and additives in food products. It became a best-seller and inspired other similar exposés. In 1937 the book also influenced Congress to revise the Food and Drug Act of 1906.

The organization suffered a major setback in September 1935 as the result of a dispute between employees and the board of directors. The employees had formed a union, primarily because of low wages and the lack of job security (several had been dismissed), and had requested a meeting with the board. The board considered the request, but certain members were dismissed when they agreed to meet with the employees.

More than 40 employees went on strike on 4 September 1935. The union had a number of demands, but Schlink and other board members refused to compromise. Eventually a riot erupted, and physical violence ensued. Members of the union later met with the National Labor Relations Board (NLRB), which heard arguments from representatives of both the employees and the board. The NLRB ruled in support of the union. When Consumers' Research appealed and lost, it chose to ignore the NLRB ruling.

The strike finally ended in January 1936. Kallet and Dewey Palmer, members of the board of directors who had gained the trust of the union, left Consumers' Research. Later that same year they helped form a rival organization, Consumers Union.

After the strike Consumers' Research maintained a smaller staff. The organization concentrated more on testing and rating products and less on political activities. Over the years the organization designed various machines to test products and also established a laboratory for the testing of ingredients in food.

Although *Consumers' Research* magazine contains no ads, this 1998 issue highlighted the power of advertising.
Courtesy of Consumers' Research.

Consumers' Research published the *Consumers' Research Bulletin* from 1935 to 1957, the *Consumers Bulletin Annual* from 1936 to 1973, *Consumers Digest* (1937–42), and *Consumers Bulletin* (1957–73). In 1973 the organization changed the name of its primary periodical to *Consumers' Research Magazine*.

In 1981, partly because of Schlink's advancing age, Consumers' Research was sold to conservative radio commentator M. Stanton Evans, who moved the enterprise to Washington, D.C. The testing laboratories in New Jersey were closed two years later. By this time membership was declining. *Consumers' Research Magazine* continued to be published, but because the parent organization no longer conducted product tests, the format was changed. The magazine, which now consists of articles based on government reports, has far fewer subscribers than Consumers Union's popular *Consumer Reports*.

EDD APPLEGATE

See also Consumers Union

Further Reading

"Chronology of Important Events Relating to Consumers' Research," Consumers' Research Archive, Rutgers University Library on the Web, http://www.libraries.rutgers.edu/rulib/spcol/cro3.htm

"Consumers' Research History," Consumers' Research Archive, Rutgers University Library on the Web, http://www.libraries.rutgers.edu/rulib/spcol/cro3.htm

Silber, Norman Isaac, *Test and Protest: The Influence of Consumers Union,* New York: Holmes and Meier, 1983

Consumers Union

Consumers Union was formed in New York City in 1936 following a dispute between the employees and the board of directors of Consumers' Research, a consumer advocacy organization established five years earlier. The employees had formed a union to protest low wages and lack of job security; several employees had been dismissed from their positions because they had disagreed with others. Union representatives requested a meeting with the board of directors, and when some board members agreed to the meeting, they were dismissed.

A strike began on 4 September 1935. The union made a number of demands, but Frederick Schlink, a co-founder of Consumers' Research, and other board members refused to compromise. Eventually, a riot erupted. Members of the union later met with the National Labor Relations Board (NLRB), which, after hearing

from both sides, ruled in favor of the union. Consumers' Research appealed but lost and then ignored the NLRB ruling.

The strike ended in January 1936. Later that year Dewey Palmer and Arthur Kallet, former members of the board of directors of Consumers' Research, helped form Consumers Union. Other board members of the new organization, including its president, Colston Warne, had worked at Consumers' Research or had supported it.

Schlink and others associated with Consumers' Research subsequently charged that members of the new organization were supporters of the Communist Party. They provided information about various Consumers Union members, including Kallet, to certain writers, who then produced disparaging articles about the new organization. One result of these attacks was that the primary publication of Consumers Union, *Consumer Reports,* was sometimes banned from newsstands and public schools. In 1940 the House Un-American Activities Committee, under U.S. Representative Martin Dies, issued a report that branded Consumers Union as a subversive organization. The stigma remained until 1954, when the organization was removed from the blacklist.

Schlink and his colleagues may have had several motives for depicting Consumers Union members as Communist sympathizers. They were defectors from Consumers' Research, for one. In addition, Consumers Union had become the major competitor of Consumers' Research. Further, the directors of Consumers Union had decided to run the organization on socialist principles, a practice opposed by Schlink and other members of Consumers' Research. Indeed, everyone at Consumers Union earned the same salary until 1937, when members of the board of directors realized that pay should vary to reflect people's differing responsibilities. In order to fill certain positions, the board then began offering different salary scales for different jobs.

Early issues of *Consumer Reports* contained articles about health issues, labor problems (e.g., long hours and low salaries), utilities' uneven quality of service, and cooperative buying plans, among other topics, as well as the results of tests of products as disparate as food, pencils, shirts, soap, shoes, silk stockings, and tissue paper. In general, these articles focused on the need for legislation to protect consumers from unethical business practices. When the organization shifted its focus to political issues in the late 1930s, however, several members of the board of directors resigned. They charged that testing was assuming a secondary role, as articles in *Consumer Reports* began increasingly to examine the working conditions under which goods were made. Product quality ratings were supplemented with evaluations of manufacturers' labor practices. In order to reinstate product evaluation as the first priority, in 1940 the organization designed its own testing laboratory. As a consequence, the tests became more scientific and the product information and ratings more reliable.

By this time *Consumer Reports* had 85,000 subscribers, most of them members of the middle class. Issues sold for 25 cents each; a year's subscription cost $3.00. A rival newsstand publication called *Consumers' Digest* continued to be published by Consumers' Research and sold for 15 cents per issue—or $1.50 a year. *Consumer Reports* was not always popular with other media. In fact, a number of major newspaper and magazine publishers refused to sell advertising space to the organization because they regarded product testing as an attack upon manufacturers.

During World War II Consumers Union also published *Bread and Butter,* a newsletter dealing with wartime problems such as price controls and housing shortages. The staff of the organization shrank when employees were drafted, and for a time, tests once again were conducted by outside firms.

When the war ended and the military was demobilized, men and women who had served in the armed forces returned home, and the demand for goods increased. There was also an increased demand for accurate information about products, and the number of subscribers to *Consumer Reports* more than quadrupled in five years, from about 90,000 in 1945 to more than 400,000 by 1950.

The testing program was expanded in the late 1940s under the direction of Morris Kaplan, a chemist by profession. Kaplan created separate departments for the testing of appliances, electronics, and foods, among other products. The organization also changed its political orientation. Kallet realized that the allegations made against Consumers Union had harmed both the group and its magazine. Members of the board of directors became more conservative politically, and the bylaws were revised. In addition, the magazine came to focus more on products and less on labor and political issues.

In the early 1950s the organization moved to a refurbished optical equipment factory in Mount Vernon, New York. Later, it relocated to Yonkers, New York. During this time Consumers Union suffered from internal disputes, especially among certain members of the board of directors. Warne, for example, favored increasing the consumer-oriented activities, while Kallet desired a much larger testing program. In 1957 Kallet lost his position and left the organization.

Consumers Union survived, however. By the late 1950s manufacturers began to realize that more and more consumers were reading reports about their products in *Consumer Reports*. If the ratings were good, it helped sell their products. If the ratings were poor, sales could suffer. Manufacturers sometimes responded to poor reviews by improving the product.

The circulation of *Consumer Reports* had increased to 800,000 by 1960. Twenty years later the magazine's circulation was more than 2 million, and by the late 1990s it was more than 4 million. Today Consumers Union informs people about products through its magazine, newsletters, and books. It even publishes a magazine for children. Reports also appear in newspapers and on radio and television. The organization has advocacy offices in Washington, D.C., San Francisco, California, and Austin, Texas. Advocates testify before legislative and regulatory bodies on behalf of consumers, and the organization has established the Consumer Policy Institute to promote consumer interests.

EDD APPLEGATE

See also Consumers' Research

Further Reading

"Chronology of Important Events Relating to Consumers' Research," Consumers' Research Archive, Rutgers University Library on the web, http://www.libraries.rutgers.edu/rulib/spcol/cr03.htm

"Consumers' Research History," Consumers' Research Archive, Rutgers University Library on the web, http://www.libraries.rutgers.edu/rulib/spcol/cr03.htm

Silber, Norman Isaac, *Test and Protest: The Influence of Consumers Union,* New York: Holmes and Meier, 1983

Consumption, Culture of

Culture of consumption is a phrase used to describe any society in which the acquisition of material goods is viewed a major defining feature of daily life. It is also a theoretical framework for analyzing the impact of such acquisition—and related activities such as advertising—on human social, political, and spiritual life. The phrase originated with the publication in 1983 of *The Culture of Consumption,* a collection of essays edited by Richard Wightman Fox and T.J. Jackson Lears, and marked a shift away from the narrower concept of *consumer culture,* a term with largely economic implications. The book appeared just as scholars were beginning to publish studies on the role of brands and commodities in shaping cultures, and the words came both to name and to provide a focus for an area of inquiry. In their essays, the various contributors analyzed different aspects of the culture of consumption and the "commodification" of society—that is, the transformation of virtually everything, from objects to experiences to feelings, into a commodity or brand that can be bought or sold. The sweep of their study across history, literary criticism, sociology, politics, and science inspired others to look to the role of commodification in shaping society.

Two important works that appeared in the years immediately before *The Culture of Consumption* were Stuart Ewen's *Captains of Consciousness* (1976) and Lears's *No Place of Grace* (1981). In his book Ewen described advertising as a means employed by the early industrialists to create new values that were compatible with consumerism and that would deflect dissatisfaction with the processes of modernization. Lears, on the other hand, argued that American consumerism was rooted in a therapeutic effort to overcome a social and spiritual ennui caused by modernization. In *Captains of Consciousness* and later books, Ewen presented the citizen as a consumer overwhelmed by mass culture. For Lears, Americans seeking refuge from the emptiness of modern life adopted practices (e.g., spiritualism) that merely reproduced the very problem they were meant to solve. These two books marked one area of disagreement among scholars undertaking work on the commodification of culture: Ewen implied that commodification was something imposed on society by capitalists, whereas Lears regarded the middle class as actively participating in its development.

The contributors to Fox and Lears's volume described how the ambivalence inherent in a modernist sensibility undermined attempts to critique such effects of modernization as the commodification of society. Specifically, they regarded the modern condition as a psychological rootlessness brought on by the erosion of a moral creed and the destructive effect of the market on traditional values. Into this void, according to these writers, stepped the entrepreneurs of mass-market amusements and the advertisers, who offered visceral, if illusory, sensations under the banner of "real life." One of the contributors, Jean-Christophe Agnew, held that in this ethereal, rootless world in which advertising had become an all-pervasive language, consumers adopted a strategy of "acquisitive cognition"—branded commodities were acquired

not simply through the act of purchasing them but also by gaining a deep-seated knowledge of their real and imagined qualities. Those who sought therapeutic release from the vacuousness of life in the industrial age found that this approach failed, however. The strategy of acquistive cognition could not provide a solid foundation for living; it simply reproduced the dynamic of change and uncertainty because the attributes of the objects acquired were not fixed—advertisers continually reinvented their products.

Much of the scholarship that developed in the late 1970s and the 1980s focused on the emergence of a culture of consumption in the last two decades of the 19th century and in the first decade of the 20th century. This scholarship did not, in contrast to Ewen, see the culture of consumption as something imposed on society. Rather, various scholars (among them, Lewis A. Erenberg on New York nightlife, William Leach on department stores and retailing, Kathy Peiss on women's leisure, Robert Snyder on vaudeville, and Susan Strasser on the shaping of a mass market) traced shifts in the American economy and society during these decades. These scholars pointed to the development of new technologies and new modes of transportation and communication that resulted in the large-scale industrial production of goods and an accompanying loss of craft skills; they noted the emergence of national markets and advertising and the growth of urban centers whose populations had sufficient income to participate in a new leisure culture—a culture of consumption. Thomas Richards, a British academic and author of *The Commodity Culture of Victorian England* (1990), made a similar study of England but used a slightly different chronology. Behind much of this work stood a critical tradition that was wide enough to include such diverse social and political theorists as Thorstein Veblen (*The Theory of the Leisure Class*), Walter Benjamin ("The Work of Art in the Age of Mechanical Reproduction"), Max Horkheimer and Theodor Adorno ("The Culture Industry: Enlightenment and Mass Deception"), Karl Marx, Herbert Marcuse, Daniel Bell, Clifford Geertz, David Riesman, Guy Debord, Warren Susman, and Christopher Lasch. Thus, the field and its intellectual debts are so broad that some of these authors would find themselves in unusual, perhaps even undesirable, company.

Another category of studies focused on how consumers use the goods they purchased. In these works there was a deliberate attempt to see the buying public as an "audience" engaged in something other than mindless consumption. Whereas Lears in 1983 suggested that the public was as least partly responsible for creating the culture of consumption, scholars such as Michael Denning, Janice Radway, George Lipsitz, and Lynn Spigel found that the audiences for such forms of entertainment as romance novels and television engaged in negotiated—and even oppositional (i.e., unintended)—readings of these forms. Like Lears, these scholars saw Americans as engaged with a commodified culture; nonetheless, they viewed the public as actively resisting the pervasive emptiness of consumption by grounding themselves in "user practices"—that is, using the objects of the culture to give meaning to life. In a sense these studies sought to investigate the "culture" of the culture of consumption rather than consumption per se as a social system. Such studies thus focused more on the psychological and symbolic use of goods than on the processes and ideologies involved in their production and distribution.

The Culture of Consumption suggested that the commodification of American culture began earlier than the 1920s, the period generally accepted as the decade of modernity. The authors argued that beginning around 1880 the market entered into areas of life that had previously been untouched and that, from this time on, existing modes of using goods and services began to be redefined. While not necessarily refuting the notion of a fin de siècle change, works by Susan Douglas, Roland Marchand, Martha Olney, Jeffrey L. Meikle, Susan Smulyan, and Joan Shelley Rubin restated the importance of the 1920s in shaping a fully realized culture of consumption. At the same time Lizabeth Cohen's work on Chicago's industrial workers during the 1920s and 1930s described their rich encounters with a mass culture of consumer goods, in which consumption and leisure were but part of an array of factors that could be used to define the self. The implication of Cohen's study was that these workers suffered less from spiritual emptiness than did Lears's subjects and that their use of material goods was, at least in part, different.

Other efforts to analyze the concept of consumption traced the origins of a consumer ethos to the early 17th century and earlier. Colin Campbell, professor of sociology at the University of York, England, argued that the same forces that gave capitalism life also provided the basis for a culture of consumption. Campbell centered modern consumerism on a notion of self-illusory hedonism that covertly consumed sensations. Chandra Mukerji, professor of communication and sociology at the University of California San Diego, argued that a modern materialism complete with consumer desire took shape in Europe during the 15th and 16th centuries. British historian Neil McKendrick found the marketing of Wedgwood pottery to be indicative of consumerism during England's industrial revolution. Harvard University academic Simon Schama delineated the rich pleasure the Dutch middle class in the 17th century derived from the commodities in their lives. Taking the analysis in another direction, anthropologists such as Mary Douglas and Grant McCracken argued that goods communicate meanings and serve as repositories of deep-seated ideals.

In 1994 Lears published *Fables of Abundance*, a work that set American advertising in the broader context of efforts to respond to the nation's material plenitude. He presented advertising as walking a line between its sideshow-like origins and the professionalization of the industry, part of the movement toward managerial efficiency in the early 20th century. He even suggested that advertising offered transformative experiences akin to earlier notions of religious redemption. Lears also pointed to advertising's role in ending, among modernists at least, a faith in language as anything more than arbitrary. At this point consumer goods became artifacts to be used, or not used, in a playful performance of life.

Stretched in these many directions, the notion of a culture of consumption might seem to have lost some of its interpretative power. Nonetheless, the body of scholarship that argues for significant transformations in American culture and society between the 1880s and the 1930s, along with studies that focus on consumption and consumer practices, demonstrates the ongoing significance of this concept for scholars of American life.

IAN GORDON

Further Reading

Brewer, John, and Roy Porter, editors, *Consumption and the World of Goods*, London and New York: Routledge, 1993

Denning, Michael, "The End of Mass Culture," *International Labor and Working Class History* 37 (Spring 1980)

Ewen, Stuart, *Captains of Consciousness: Advertising and the Social Roots of the Consumer Culture*, New York: McGraw-Hill, 1976

Fox, Richard Wightman, and T.J. Jackson Lears, editors, *The Culture of Consumption: Critical Essays in American History, 1880–1980*, New York: Pantheon, 1983

Fox, Richard Wightman, and T.J. Jackson Lears, editors, *The Power of Culture: Critical Essays in American History*, Chicago: University of Chicago Press, 1993

Lears, T.J. Jackson, *No Place of Grace: Antimodernism and the Transformation of American Culture, 1880–1920*, New York: Pantheon, 1981

Lears, T.J. Jackson, *Fables of Abundance: A Cultural History of Advertising in America*, New York: Basic Books, 1994

McKendrick, Neil, John Brewer, and J.H. Plumb, *The Birth of a Consumer Society: The Commercialization of Eighteenth-Century England*, Bloomington: Indiana University Press, and London: Europa, 1982

Strasser, Susan, Charles McGovern, and Matthias Judt, editors, *Getting and Spending: European and American Consumer Societies in the Twentieth Century*, Cambridge and New York: Cambridge University Press, 1998

Contrapunto

Founded in Madrid, Spain, by Teófilo Marcos, Rafael Sarró, José García, and José Luis Zamorano, 1974; sold a 30 percent share in agency to BBDO Worldwide, 1988; won Grand Prix at the Cannes (France) International Advertising Festival and was named "International Agency of the Year" by *Advertising Age* magazine, 1989; ownership stake of BBDO increased to 75 percent, 1993.

Major Clients
Canal +
La Cruz del Campo, S.A.
Organización Nacional de Ciegos Españoles
Osborne Group
Red Nacional de Ferrocarriles Españoles (Spanish state railway)

Contrapunto was founded in Madrid by Teófilo Marcos, Rafael Sarró, José García, and José Luis Zamorano, all of whom left another agency, Tándem, to open the new shop in 1974. The agency grew to become one of the major forces in Spanish advertising creativity in the 1980s. It also was the first Spanish agency to win the Grand Prix at the Cannes International Advertising Festival in France—in 1989, the same year it was named International Agency of the Year by *Advertising Age*.

Marcos, Sarró, and García worked together at Danis Advertising Agency but left in the early 1970s to establish Tándem, where they were joined by Zamorano. When the four subsequently left Tándem and opened Contrapunto, their first employee was Ana Botana, who was put in charge of research.

Among Contrapunto's notable efforts in the 1970s were campaigns for Riazor's lobsters, Apis's foie gras, and Trinaranjus beverages. In 1976 the agency won a part of the Osborne Group alcoholic beverages account, which it continued to handle until 2000. In 1978 Contrapunto won the Banco Urquijo account and launched a campaign to promote the bank's bonds. In 1979 Contrapunto began handling an account of the Spanish Public Administration and launched a campaign concerning government debt. This effort inaugurated a long period during which Contrapunto created both institutional and informational advertising for the Spanish Public Administration.

In 1983 the publication *Anuncios* ranked Contrapunto among the top 15 agencies in Spain in terms of billings. In 1980 Juan Mariano Mancebo joined the agency, and José María Lapeña joined the following year. In 1983 the two were appointed creative directors when Zamorano, who had been the agency's creative director, left. Mancebo and Lapeña, working as a team, created campaigns that many observers believe to be among the finest in the history of Spanish advertising.

From 1986 to 1995 Contrapunto handled the account of Red Nacional de Ferrocarriles Españoles (RENFE), the Spanish state railway, producing both institutional and consumer advertising. In 1987 Contrapunto won the account of Organización Nacional de Ciegos Españoles (ONCE), the Spanish national organization for the blind. ONCE had decided to launch a new commercial lottery. Previously, the group's lottery tickets had been marketed on a provincial basis, but Contrapunto's task was to develop a program to market a product at the national level. "The Great Ticket" (*El Cuponazo*), the new national product, offered the possibility of winning a prize of 100 million pesetas each Friday, an enormous amount of money for the time. Mancebo and Lapeña's campaign ran with the slogan "For 100 pesetas, 100 million" (*Por 100 pts. 100 millones*). In 1988 the campaign won a silver Lion at the Cannes festival.

In 1987 Contrapunto also won the account of Televisión Española (TVE), the Spanish public television corporation. In 1989 Contrapunto's "Learn to use television" campaign, created by Lapeña and Mancebo, won more than 30 awards, including the Grand Prix at the Cannes festival. It was the first time a Spanish agency won the award.

In 1988 Contrapunto sold a 30 percent share of the agency to New York City-based BBDO Worldwide, gaining access to overseas markets through its alliance with the international agency network. Two years later, *Advertising Age* noted the agency's financial health: "Gross income hit $11.8 million in 1989 while billings reached $78.8 million, each up 15 percent over 1988."

Marcos resigned as president of Contrapunto in 1991 and was succeeded by Sarró. By that time the Contrapunto Group, formed in 1988, consisted of six companies: Contrapunto, S.A., an advertising agency in Madrid; Contrapunto Sellarés, S.A., an advertising agency in Barcelona; Núcleo de Investigación, S.A., a consumer research corporation; M.B.O. Difusión, S.A., a public

Teófilo Marcos, one of the founders of Contrapunto, served as president of the agency until 1991.

José María Lapeña and Juan Mariano Mancebo were appointed creative directors at Contrapunto in the early 1980s.

relations company; C.P. Servicios de Comunicación, S.A., a direct-marketing company; and Media Services, S.A., a media buying service. In the early 1990s Contrapunto developed campaigns for the Exposición Universal 92, held in Seville, Spain, and for Quinto Centenario, the organization in charge of planning activities for the celebration of the 500th anniversary of the discovery of the New World.

Economic prosperity in the 1980s was followed by financial crisis in the early 1990s in Spain. A recession affected the advertising industry and resulted in salary freezes, personnel reductions, and the closing of agencies. Contrapunto also suffered as a result of the crisis, losing significant accounts such as those of the Exposición Universal 92 and Quinto Centenario. In 1993 BBDO increased its stake in the shop to 75 percent, providing additional financial backing to Contrapunto. In the reorganization that followed, two founders, Sarró and García, left the shop, and Contrapunto entered a period of transition. Tomás Corominas, a mining engineer and sociologist who had joined the agency in 1984, succeeded Sarró as president.

Contrapunto continued to produce award-winning campaigns for its clients, such as an effort for television company Canal+ that was honored with a gold Sun at the Festival Publicitario de Cine y Televisión of San Sebastián. Between 1996 and 1997 the Contrapunto Group consolidated its holdings into four companies: Contrapunto, direct-marketing shop CP Comunicación, CP Interactive, and CP Data. In 1999 Contrapunto began expanding internationally, opening offices in Lisbon, Portugal; Santiago, Chile; and Buenos Aires, Argentina. Some of Contrapunto's chief accounts in 2000 included Agencia Tributaria, Airtel-Vodafone, Canal+, Canal Satélite, Chrysler/Jeep, Mercedes Benz, and Wanadoo.

In October 1999 Pablo Alzugaray succeeded Corominas as president of Contrapunto Group. Carlos Martínez-Cabrera was

Contrapunto's 1988 campaign for Televisión Española won the agency the Grand Prix at the Cannes (France) International Advertising Festival, the first ever for a Spanish agency. The campaign featured a series of commercials in which a dog, "Pippin," packed his bags, while a voice-over said, "If your best friend leaves home, it may be because you're watching too much television."

named Contrapunto's general manager. Contrapunto Group expanded significantly internationally in 2000 and 2001. Although BBDO held the majority of shares of Contrapunto, the two remained distinct in Spain—they worked independently and competed in the Spanish market.

FRANCISCO VERDERA

Further Reading
Bravo, Julián, et al., "50 años de seducción: Historia subjetiva y desenfadada de la publicidad española," *Vogue GQ* (supplement to *Vogue* España) 70 (January 1994)
Contrapunto, S.A., "Contrapunto: Agencia internacional del año," *Cuadernos Contrapunto* 1991 (special issue)
Jordán, Antonio, *Publicitarios de frente y de perfil*, Madrid: Eresma, and Celeste, 1995

"La mejor publicidad del fin de siglo: Los grandes anuncios de las últimas dos décadas del milenio," *Anuncios Revista 77* (December 1999)
Las mejores agencias de publicidad de España 1999, Madrid: Consultores de Publicidad, 1999
Specht, Marina, "International Agency of the Year: Contrapunto Engineers Locomotion to Top Spot," *Advertising Age* (26 March 1990)

Cordiant Communications Group

Cordiant Communications Group is a modest-size holding company that came to be known primarily as the parent company of the New York City–based advertising agency Bates Worldwide and half-owner of the media agency Zenith Media Worldwide. In December 1997 Cordiant split from Saatchi & Saatchi of London, England. This "demerger" went starkly against the then-accelerating trend toward consolidation and left Cordiant a shadow of its former self. Before the split, Cordiant had been the sixth-largest advertising organization in the world; after the breakup, it ended 1997 as number 14.

The name *Cordiant* was created in 1995 by Siegel & Gale, of New York City, one of the ad agencies under the holding company's umbrella. The moniker was designed to represent the company's vision, which hinged on "accord" and a common purpose. Before the 1995 rechristening, the holding company was simply known as Saatchi & Saatchi—the same as its flagship agency, founded in 1970 by brothers Maurice and Charles Saatchi. By the time of the renaming, the Saatchi brothers had acrimoniously left the agency, and the new name was meant to separate the company from its founders in the public eye.

The falling out between the Saatchis and the agency's board of directors was one of the most talked-about advertising-world stories of its day. The drama began in December 1994, when the board forced out Maurice, the company's chairman. His brother Charles, whose role was more creative than managerial, left soon after. The brothers formed a new agency, M&C Saatchi, and took with them some of Saatchi & Saatchi's cornerstone clients, including British Airways.

Industry observers traced the feud between the Saatchis and the board to the brothers' ambitious growth plans, formulated in the 1970s and carried out through the 1980s. In 1976 Saatchi & Saatchi began acquiring other companies, first purchasing Compton Partners, London. A decade of rapid expansion followed, earning the company the nickname "Snatch-it & Snatch-it." In 1984 the Saatchi brothers hoped to diversify into management and consulting and purchased some financial companies. The agency was also at a creative high point during this period. High-profile work included the ad campaign that helped propel Marga-

ret Thatcher and the Conservative Party to victory in the United Kingdom in 1979.

In 1986, at the height of the agency's quest to merge, Saatchi & Saatchi bought New York City–based ad agency Ted Bates Worldwide for $450 million in cash. The size and scope of the deal was astronomical for its day, and in the end it proved unworkable.

In 1989 company profits plummeted, and the Saatchi brothers announced that they would no longer act as co-chief executives. Maurice became chairman, while Charles stayed on in a creative role. Any semblance of peaceful co-existence between the agency's board and the Saatchis ended in December 1994, and Maurice was forced out. The board then changed the holding company's name to Cordiant, although the advertising agency kept the name Saatchi & Saatchi.

The split between the Saatchi brothers and the board had severe repercussions for Bates. Outraged by the board's ouster of Maurice, the candy and pet food marketer Mars, Inc., immediately pulled $400 million of its business from Bates, which had handled Mars's work for 40 years. The agency, which created the slogan "Melts in your mouth, not in your hands" for Mars's M&M's, was left without a prestigious international client. In the fallout, Bates also lost Miller Brewing Company's $50 million Genuine Draft account. Faced with these client defections, Bates laid off 150 employees. In all, Cordiant (and its Bates unit) lost $53.5 million in 1995, although it did regain profitability the following year.

In April 1997 Cordiant announced the demerger plan, splitting the business into two publicly traded entities: Bates, which would keep Cordiant Communications Group as its parent company, and Saatchi & Saatchi. Cordiant and Saatchi each walked away with half of Zenith Media in the deal. At the time, Zenith was the number-one media agency in the United Kingdom and controlled $1.6 billion in media spending, according to *Advertising Age*. The move gave Bates the opportunity to emerge from Saatchi's shadow and rebuild an identity of its own. Cordiant's new-business billings more than doubled in 1998, to $580 million from 1997's $250 million, according to *Advertising Age*. New-business growth continued in 1999 and 2000, but not at the same pace. Bates gained approximately $180 million in new billings in 1999 and $190 million in new billings in 2000.

WENDY DAVIS

Further Reading

"Advertising Giant Stumbles: Saatchi & Saatchi Grew Too Fast, Diversified Too Far; Now, the Founders Are Stepping Back; Sliding Profits, Takeover Talk Roil Company," *USA Today* (13 October 1989)

"Cordiant, Saatchi Profits Soar: Former Siblings Like the Single Life; Both See Big New-Business Gains," *Advertising Age* (15 March 1999)

"Cordiant Unveils Plan to Revamp Empire Built by Saatchi Brothers," *Wall Street Journal* (22 April 1997)

"Mars Deals Saatchi a Mighty Blow by Pulling $400 Million Account," *Wall Street Journal* (22 February 1995)

"Who Will Woo Solo Agency Cordiant?" *Wall Street Journal* (18 December 2000)

Corporate Advertising

Corporate advertising, also known as institutional advertising, is advertising by a company or organization that attempts to create an image, address an issue, or communicate with specific audiences, including a company's own employees, about matters important to the company. Unlike consumer advertising—which promotes specific brands, products, or services—corporate advertising helps an organization operate more effectively in the context of its external environment.

The primary objectives of corporate advertising are to strategically position the company or its brand in key markets, increase awareness of the company, enhance the company's image, and educate the public on the nature of the company's business interests. Corporate advertising can redefine an organization after a name change or after the company has weathered rough times. Corporate campaigns can also serve highly specific short-term purposes, such as boosting a company's stock price in anticipation of an initial public offering or a merger. Corporate advocacy ads try to influence public opinion on a political or social issue. Magazines and the business press are the most widely used media for corporate advertising, followed by television, newspapers, radio, the Internet, special events, and direct mail.

As a part of its official launch in 1996, Lucent Technologies used corporate advertising to strategically position itself and increase awareness of the company. Created by a corporate restructuring of AT&T Corporation, Lucent was challenged to create awareness for itself even though it had 125 years of history and more than 100,000 employees. The new organization aspired to a scrappy, entrepreneurial, and customer-focused image. The result was a global corporate advertising campaign unveiling the new corporate name, Lucent Technologies, and its distinctive logo. The ads defined the company with the slogan, "We make the things that make communications work." The successful campaign ran globally in 14 languages.

Corporate advertising also provides marketing support for brands, products, and services. Nestlé, for example, uses its corporate name in advertising and on products to provide marketing support. The company has added the Nestlé name to some products, entirely renamed others as Nestlé, and put a smaller Nestlé "seal of guarantee" on additional brands. The purpose is to achieve a "halo effect"—that is, a product acquires the goodwill of consumers from its association with a familiar corporate name. When Nestlé advertises products that carry the corporate name, the advertising can reinforce or alter the target audience's perceptions of the product by reflecting the attributes associated with the company name.

Corporate advertising can also inform and influence shareholders and the financial community, especially for companies preparing for an initial stock offering or engaged in a proxy fight. In 1999 the utilities industry underwent government deregulation, spurring merger activity among utility companies. Columbia Energy Group, a Virginia-based energy concern, used corporate advertising as it tried to avoid a hostile takeover from NiSource, an Indiana-based energy company. Columbia rejected NiSource's unwanted advance and began to run a series of full-page print ads in Indiana smearing the company's environmentally friendly reputation. The ads attempted to shift public attention to NiSource's alleged environmental and financial problems as Columbia tried to avoid a takeover. Despite the ads, the two eventually agreed to merge.

Corporate advertising can also be used to communicate with the general public and a company's own employees during a company crisis as well as to attract potential employees or to retain existing ones. Drexel Burnham Lambert, for instance, was a brokerage firm under siege in the late 1980s for promoting high-yield bonds, also known as junk bonds, for financing purposes. To improve the public's perception of junk bonds, the company ran a television ad campaign to demonstrate how the bonds helped the economy. The ads featured day-care centers that were financed by junk bonds, told stories of entrepreneurial opportunities missed due to lack of financing, and showed playgrounds that would have closed if the bonds had not been issued. Other ads showed how junk bonds contributed to employment and the quality of life

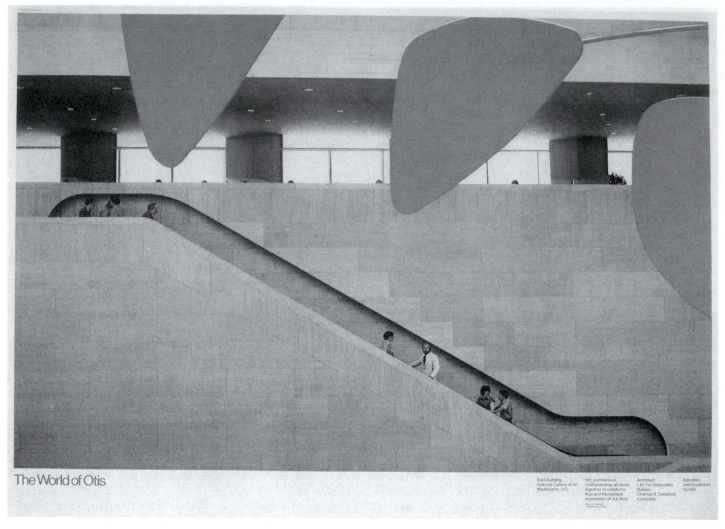

The World of Otis

A 1981 corporate ad for the Otis Elevator Company showing people on an Otis escalator in the East Wing of the National Gallery of Art in Washington, D.C., sought to draw prestige from the company's association with the noted architect I.M. Pei.
Courtesy Otis Elevator Company.

in the United States. Drexel Burnham Lambert also ran ads targeted directly at its employees. A separate campaign was created to celebrate the founding of the firm. The print ads, created by Chiat/Day, Inc., included the names of all 10,000 of the company's employees. The campaign was considered a significant morale booster and helped to reduce employee defections during the crisis.

Historical Background

Corporate advertising has a long history; the Dutch East India Company in the latter half of the 18th century was one of the earliest corporate advertisers. However, corporate advertising did not enter into more common practice until the beginning of the 20th century. The Industrial Revolution in the 19th century led to the formation of new companies in many industries, including transportation, utilities, oil, and steel. These large companies faced

heavy scrutiny from government regulators and muckraking journalists. The government regulators, or trustbusters, as they came to be known, sought to prevent the companies from exercising undue power in the marketplace. The muckrakers wrote sensational stories exposing unacceptable business practices and poor working conditions. Corporate advertising emerged in this environment as a tool to help companies rehabilitate their images by pleading their cases directly to the public.

In 1906 muckraking journalist Thomas Lawson exposed the fraudulent dealings of several major life insurance companies, including Mutual Life, Equitable Life, and New York Life. The negative revelations were reinforced by extensive coverage of the scandal in newspapers, along with investigations launched by the New York state legislature and the state attorney general. As the companies began to reform, Mutual Life hired N.W. Ayer & Son, one of the largest and most reputable advertising agencies of the day, to help improve the firm's image. The agency produced a series of ads to run in the national media as well as half-page ads to be featured in metropolitan newspapers. The ads featured dramatic headlines declaring, "The truth about Mutual Life" and "There is no good reason against good insurance." The campaign contributed to the rehabilitation of the company's reputation and caught the attention of future advertisers.

In 1908 American Telephone and Telegraph (AT&T) pioneered the field of corporate advertising. Faced with an unfavorable reputation, intense competition, and threats of public ownership, AT&T had an ambitious goal: to win the public's acceptance as a desirable monopoly. With that in mind, the company turned to N.W. Ayer, the agency that had produced the Mutual Life ads just two years earlier, to launch the first long-term effort to improve a company's public image. The first ads explained that AT&T was working for the public and gave instructions on how to communicate with the telephone operator. The monthly ads ran in many magazines and featured a prominent headline, a large body of text, and an illustration with the company logo. The advertising campaign was highly successful. There was no public backlash from the ads, and the company benefited from improved efficiency as its business rationale was better understood by employees and business partners.

By the 1920s more than half of AT&T's advertising budget went toward corporate advertising. A report prepared for the company in 1929 stated that the primary goal of company advertising was to create goodwill. Accordingly, the company's ads were directed toward the attitudes and emotions of the public. On 29 April 1940, AT&T began broadcasting the *Bell Telephone Hour* on the NBC network; over the next 28 years (1959–68 on television) the program presented a mixture of popular and classical music to U.S. audiences, always under the baton of conductor Donald Voorhees. AT&T's coordinated campaign of advertising and public relations over 30 years has been credited with protecting the company's monopoly status when large corporations were again under scrutiny by antitrust regulators in the 1930s.

Other companies took notice of AT&T's efforts and employed similar strategies. In 1916, during World War I, Bethlehem Steel undertook a last-minute advertising campaign to prevent the U.S. Senate from passing a bill that would authorize funds for a competing armor plant. The company's effort failed, providing advertising proponents with new ammunition for a long-term approach to changing public opinion. The meatpacking industry also turned to advertising, as companies such as Armour and Swift ran ads that defended their business practices against charges by muckrakers. The Pennsylvania Railroad ran ads featuring its employees, touting good service for customers while also providing employees with a model for ideal customer-service behavior. General Motors and General Electric began to use advertising to promote the idea of the company as one big family in hopes of thereby reducing the coldness of the corporate persona.

Radio—and TV—Days

Radio entered millions of homes in the 1930s, and corporate advertising quickly followed. In one instance, DuPont, a large manufacturer of chemicals and military explosives, had been accused of profiteering during World War I. The U.S. Senate held hearings to investigate alleged profiteers, DuPont among them, and the hearings generated much unfavorable publicity for the company. While the company had indeed sold explosives during the war, this business had been reduced dramatically to less than 1 percent of total sales by 1935. To combat the public's negative perceptions, DuPont undertook the sponsorship of a network radio program. The show, *Cavalcade of America*, was produced by ad agency Batten Barton Durstine & Osborn and presented historical vignettes dramatizing people and events in U.S. history. Along with the program the company introduced a new slogan: "Better things for better living . . . through chemistry."

Originally conceived to explain what DuPont produced, the campaign ran for 18 years and turned negative perceptions into favorable impressions of the company. In 1953 the *Cavalcade of America* left radio for the new medium of television and the opportunity to add faces and pictures to its corporate image. Although the TV program aired for only four years, the slogan remained in use until 1999. DuPont's radio and television success provided a template for other companies looking to communicate with the public. By the early 1950s Colgate, Texaco, and General Electric each sponsored television programs with eponymous titles: *Texaco Star Theatre, Colgate Comedy Hour,* and *GE Theatre* (the latter featured actor Ronald Reagan).

During World War II, the War Advertising Council was formed; members included representatives of leading advertisers, advertising agencies, and the advertising media. Its purpose was to work with the government's Office of War Information to produce public information in support of the war effort. After the war, the renamed Ad Council continued to work closely with business and the government to promote the virtues of the free enterprise system and to educate citizens against public policies that could undermine the system itself. One popular ad featured Uncle Sam rolling up his sleeves above the caption, "The better we produce, the better we live." Ads proclaiming themes of confidence were also produced to help combat gloomy economic predictions. Corporate advertising themes echoed the messages from the Ad Council spots. Sinclair Oil's advertising campaign told Americans that "your future is great in a growing America—remember to drive with care and buy Sinclair." American Can, U.S. Steel, and Prudential Insurance all filmed TV spots with similar messages.

While companies such as AT&T, DuPont, and General Electric advertised regularly in print and broadcast media, corporate advertising remained the exception rather than the rule until the 1970s, when the economic environment forced companies into a defensive position. Faced with the impending energy crisis and increased pressure from government regulators and consumer advocates, companies were forced to define and defend themselves before a demanding public. In 1970 the Mobil Corporation recognized that there were significant issues confronting the oil industry: foreign governments controlled much of the oil supply; the environmental lobby had ascended to the national stage;

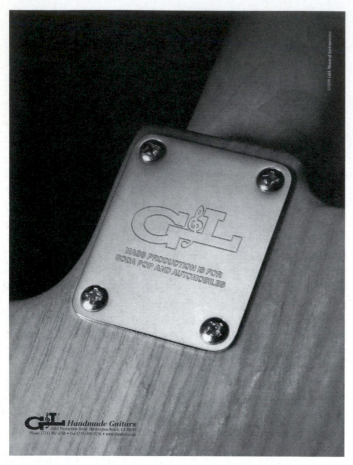

Even for relatively small and specialized companies such as G&L Handmade Guitars, corporate advertising helps build and maintain positive brand identity.
Courtesy of BRE Sound, Inc./G&L Musical Instruments. Copyright 2000. Photography by Randy Logan, Graphic Design by Troy W. Finamore.

and business institutions were generally held in low regard. Mobil could have remained silent, but the company believed that the severity of these issues warranted a response.

Mobil entered the arena by launching an advertising campaign aimed at the nation's opinion-makers and activists. Beginning with the debut of the *New York Times* op-ed page, Mobil ran a series of ads stating its position in view of a possible energy crisis. The first, a two-column text-only ad, called for improved mass transit, a position seemingly at odds with its corporate and industry objectives. Despite criticism from some of Mobil's traditional business allies, the ads were considered to be a major success, and Mobil's adversaries hailed the company for offering an opposing view. The success of the advertising effort convinced the company to run ads every week speaking out on issues important to the public. The tradition has been carried on for nearly 30 years. Although working with ad agency Doyle Dane Bernbach, Mobil itself directly generated the content of the corporate campaign.

New Challenges

The rise in consumer advocacy and increased pressure from government regulators questioning advertising claims led to other important challenges for corporations. In 1971 the Federal Trade Commission (FTC) enacted product-related regulations requiring advertisers to provide proof of accuracy of ad statements and to substantiate the claims made in their ad copy. The new climate also influenced corporate advertising. As the practice of corporate image advertising grew, critics charged that companies were telling only half-truths and that their ads were misleading. In 1974 six U.S. senators and representatives, through the Media Access Project, petitioned the FTC to extend its substantiation rules to all commercial advertising, including image and advocacy ads. However, the commission decided against making any policy decision on the grounds that regulation of corporate image advertising raised substantial First Amendment questions.

In response to demands for regulation, companies sought to create more responsible images for themselves. Instead of products, they advertised public interest programs, social responsibility, equal employment opportunity, and minority assistance. Some companies spoke out on political issues and referenda. In 1978 the Supreme Court increased First Amendment protection for corporate speech with its decision in *First National Bank of Boston* v. *Bellotti*. The court's ruling asserted that citizens have a right to receive political speech by corporations. After the decision in *Bellotti*, corporations began to recognize that silence was counterproductive, and they became more aggressive in response to criticism.

One such company was International Harvester. In the early 1980s the media reported rumors that the company was on the verge of bankruptcy. Indeed times were tough for International Harvester. The economy was in a slump, interest rates were high, and the company's major markets were depressed—but the company was not going out of business. International Harvester responded to the rumors with a full-page ad in the *Wall Street Journal* proclaiming, "We're not giving in. We're going on." The ad went on to explain the changes that had occurred within the company and asserted that it was "getting ready for tomorrow."

Ford Motor Company used corporate advertising as a cornerstone of its financial turnaround. From its inception Ford was known as a manufacturer of inexpensive, basic transportation. By the late 1970s large auto manufacturers in the United States faced industry challenges as Japanese imports were outperforming U.S. cars in quality, affordability, and efficiency. Negative stories circulated about product quality and Ford's perceived disregard for the public. In 1981 the company sought to refurbish its image by improving product quality and promoting the new slogan, "Quality is job one." The company developed in-plant quality programs reinforced by the ad campaign. Auto quality and sales surged as the company enjoyed a strong return to prominence. The campaign ran for 17 years until it was replaced in 1998.

Corporate advertising campaigns have not always been successful. The international conglomerate Beatrice Foods took a difficult route in trying to establish itself as the premier marketer of

A 1982 house ad for Ogilvy & Mather's London office detailed the history and successes of its corporate advertising campaign for the Shell Oil Company.

consumer products. Beatrice launched its first ad campaign in 1984, stamping its name on every product within the company. The ads, created by Marsteller, of Chicago, Illinois, showed Beatrice's products and then introduced the company with the tag line, "Beatrice. You've known us all along." The intention was for the lesser-known Beatrice name to borrow the prestige and good will associated with its established consumer brands such as Tropicana, Samsonite, and Playtex. The strengthened Beatrice name would then be used to add value to its food division products. However, the approach confused consumers, who questioned how a company that made orange juice could also make quality luggage and women's underwear. Ultimately, the company was bought out and its business units were sold.

Controversy

Some corporate advertising campaigns have ignited controversy. In 1989 Philip Morris, a company with significant tobacco interests, launched a campaign promoting its sponsorship of the upcoming 200th anniversary of the U.S. Bill of Rights. The television and newspaper ads depicted acts of free speech and exercise of religious freedom, ending with a mention of the company and a toll-free number for viewers to call to receive a copy of the Bill of Rights. The campaign sparked a reaction from antismoking activists and health organizations, which claimed the ads violated a 1971 law banning cigarette commercials from television.

For much of its existence the Italian clothing retailer Benetton has employed social and political messages in its advertising campaigns, which are designed to communicate values espoused by the company. The company has attracted both positive and negative attention for social message ads that have featured, among others, images of a person dying of AIDS, a nun kissing a priest, a black horse mating with a white one, and Palestinians and Israelis coexisting peacefully. In 1999, to foster debate on capital punishment, Benetton launched a series of ads featuring death-row inmates in U.S. prisons. The campaign drew heavy criticism from families of the prisoners' victims. There were also claims that the images were acquired under suspicious circumstances. Distributors of Benetton products were forced to cancel their contracts with the company after receiving threatening protests from offended consumers.

Sears, Roebuck & Company declined to stock the Benetton line, and ad executive Jerry Della Femina bitterly attacked the campaign in the *Wall Street Journal*. "If the death sentence were handed out to those who are guilty of producing excruciatingly tasteless, ineffective advertising . . ." he wrote, "Oliviero Toscani, the self-proclaimed 'genius' behind Benetton advertising, would be appearing in his own anti-capital punishment ads."

The Web and Beyond

The advent of the personal computer in the 1980s and the development of the Internet browser in the 1990s led a technological revolution around the world. Computer and software companies such as Dell, Apple, Microsoft, and Netscape grew quickly into corporate giants competing for the attention of consumers and investors. Gateway, a direct marketer and manufacturer of personal computers, used Holstein cows in its advertising to break through the highly competitive computer market. The cows were intended to symbolize the company's midwestern roots and to project a warm and friendly company image. The company's ads also featured employees in quirky scenarios to communicate its offbeat personality. Focusing on the company's humble origins, one ad asked, "Born in a barn?" and replied, "Actually, yes."

Companies have taken their corporate advertising to the Internet in the form of banner ads that allow viewers to click on the banner, which then takes them to more detailed information about a company. IBM used banner ads as part of its college recruitment efforts. The banners featured the names of colleges where the company had scheduled campus visits. Viewers could "click through" and receive more information about career opportunities at IBM.

Corporate Web sites also provide an advertising function. As corporate advertising increases company awareness, stakeholders (customers, employees, suppliers, stockholders, and distributors) are likely to visit corporate Web sites in search of information about the company. Many company Web sites include corporate mission statements, the company's guiding principles, recent press releases, financial data, and product information to help the viewer better understand the company and its business. Some companies have used the Internet to post their television and print ads to communicate more effectively with their stakeholders.

Since 1906, when Mutual Life spent $100,000 on the first modern corporate advertising effort, total corporate advertising expenditures have grown to more than $9 billion annually. As long as corporations and institutions need to communicate with their audiences, corporate advertising will continue to be a viable method for reaching them.

PATRICK O'NEIL

Further Reading

Biehal, Gabriel, and Daniel Sheinin, "Managing the Brand in a Corporate Advertising Environment: A Decision-Making Framework for Brand Managers," *Journal of Advertising* 27 (1998)

Flanagan, George, *Modern Institutional Advertising,* New York: McGraw-Hill, 1967

Gregory, James, *Marketing Corporate Image: The Company as Your Number One Product*, Lincolnwood, Illinois: NTC Business Books, 1991

Gregory, James, *Trends In Corporate Advertising,* New York: Association of National Advertisers, 1998

Liff, David, Mary O'Connor, and Clarke Bruno, *Corporate Advertising: The Business Response to Changing Public Attitudes,* Washington, D.C.: Investor Responsibility Research Center, 1980

Marchand, Roland, *Creating the Corporate Soul: The Rise of Public Relations and Corporate Imagery in American Big Business,* Berkeley: University of California Press, 1998

Marconi, Joe, *Image Marketing: Using Public Perceptions to Attain Business Objectives,* Chicago: NTC Business Books, 1996

Schmertz, Herbert, *Good-bye to the Low Profile: The Art of Creative Confrontation,* Boston: Little Brown, 1986

Sethi, S. Prakash, *Advocacy Advertising and Large Corporations,* Lexington, Massachusetts: Lexington Books, 1977

The Telephone Hour: A Retrospective, April 27–October 27, 1990, New York: Museum of Broadcasting, 1990

Corrective Advertising

Corrective advertising is one of the most severe penalties that can be imposed on an advertiser that knowingly fabricates false or misleading selling points to misrepresent a product's qualities to the public. It requires that the company invest a specified amount of its advertising budget to publish ads or air commercials that admit to potentially misleading messages and provide accurate "corrective" information.

Corrective ads are intended to correct two possible injuries resulting from false or misleading claims. First, corrective statements are supposed to counteract long-term negative effects of inaccurate information that appeared in prior ads. The injured parties in such cases are presumed to be consumers, who may continue to hold false beliefs about a brand well after dissemination of the offending ads has stopped. It is therefore not enough to simply cease making disputed or false claims because a future ad campaign, similar in other ways, may serve to reinforce the false claims, even though they are no longer a part of the new campaign. The advertiser must take affirmative steps to tell consumers they were misled.

The second possible type of injury corrective advertising is intended to redress is injury to a competitive brand, especially in cases of direct comparative ads. In a comparative campaign the advertiser not only makes specific claims about its own brand but also makes claims, typically negative, about a targeted competitor. In some cases the competitor's identity may be masked by a "brand X" pseudonym; in others, it may be named directly. In such cases, corrective measures are intended to restore the injured brand to the level of sales and market share that existed before the false claims were published. A shift in market share resulting from false advertising claims are likely to persist unless the offending advertiser aggressively informs the public that its ads were misleading.

Regulation of Advertising

At the federal level, the Federal Trade Commission (FTC) regulates advertising as part of its mission to protect consumers from unfair, deceptive, or fraudulent practices. Under Section 43 (a) of the Lanham Trademark Act of 1946, advertisers who are damaged or are likely to be damaged by false representations made by a competitor can bring suit.

The FTC, through the Bureau of Consumer Protection, regulates advertising. The Deception Policy Statement specifically defines deceptive acts or practices prohibited by Section 5 of the FTC Act. The commission usually takes action against advertisers when prompted by complaints from consumers, other advertisers, or other regulatory agencies. When the FTC believes a violation has occurred, it first attempts to obtain voluntary compliance from the advertiser through a consent order. If a consent agreement cannot be reached, the commission issues an administrative complaint, and a formal proceeding before an administrative law judge usually follows.

Once the FTC determines that an ad is deceptive, it may require that the advertiser disseminate information to correct consumers' impressions of a product. The commission often specifies and evaluates the content of corrective statements and makes recommendations regarding the format in which the statements must appear in all future ads. The main goal of the FTC is to protect consumers from any detrimental effects arising from a purchase based on false or misleading information. In the process, however, the commission is also ensuring a fair competitive environment. Punishing the advertiser is never the intent of corrective remedies.

The phrase "corrective advertising" entered the vocabulary of advertising in 1969 as the result of a campaign created by Batten Barton Durstine & Osborn (BBDO) for the Campbell Soup Company. The previous year the company introduced its Chicken & Stars soup, a broth containing a mixture of pasta stars, small chicken chunks, and other solid foods. In photographing it for print ads, however, a problem developed when the solid ingredients sank to the bottom of the broth and could not be seen. Robert Ballantine, a BBDO art director, solved this by putting glass shards and, later, marbles in the bowl to push the chicken and pasta to the surface where it could be photographed. The use of such artifice was not considered unethical in advertising, any more than was lighting or photo retouching. Substitutes for ice cream, typically mashed potatoes coated with resin, were often used in photo shoots because the real thing melted too quickly under lights. Additionally, clothing apparel on models was often secured by pins and clips from behind to ensure the desired fit.

The Campbell campaign broke in April 1968, prompting an inquiry by the FTC, which was acting on a complaint from an unknown source, later revealed to be the H.J. Heinz Company, a Campbell competitor. An investigator visited BBDO and was shown how the soup was "propped" for photography with the marbles. His report to the FTC stated that the advertising misrepresented the amount of pasta and chicken in the soup. In November 1968 Campbell and BBDO agreed that they would not use such techniques in the future. The matter seemed closed.

In February 1969 FTC Chairman Paul Dixon, who had been appointed by President John F. Kennedy in 1961, made the details public, instituted a formal proceeding against Campbell, and invited public comment. That October a group of law students at George Washington University calling themselves SOUP (Students Opposing Unfair Practices) petitioned that the company be required to include the following copy in every ad it ran: "In the past we used a certain photographic method . . . that gave viewers the impression there was more solid food than the can actually contains. What you see now is the way the soup will look on your dinner table." The request had no precedent. The case proceeded under President Richard Nixon, who appointed Caspar Weinberger as FTC chairman. For the next two years there were new petitions and appeals that would involve 14 federal judges. In December 1972 the FTC dismissed the complaint, and Campbell was not obliged to run corrective advertising. But the concept of corrective advertising had been born, and later the FTC would come to require it in serious cases of deceptive advertising.

FTC Targets: Listerine and Doan's Pills

The FTC's 1977 challenge of Warner-Lambert Company's Listerine advertising set the precedent as the first litigated case of enforced corrective advertising. Until that time, corrective orders were issued as consent agreements. For 40 years the Listerine brand of mouthwash had been advertised as having germ-killing properties that would prevent and cure colds and sore throats. The FTC found such claims to be false. Furthermore, it was determined that consumers' false perceptions of Listerine as a cure for colds were the result of such advertising. The FTC ordered Warner-Lambert to cease and desist from making such claims in all future advertising and to spend $10 million on a corrective campaign over a period of 18 months. The FTC even specified the language of the corrective disclosure to be included in the Listerine advertisements, which stated, "Listerine will not help prevent colds or sore throats or lessen their severity."

Carnation instant breakfast makes milk this kind of nutritious meal

**That's right.
You can turn a quick
glass of milk
into this bacon and egg
kind of breakfast
in an instant
– the instant it takes
to add the important nutrition
of Carnation instant breakfast.**

How can a glass of milk and a packet of Carnation instant breakfast give you so much nourishment?

Milk contributes substantial nutrition. (Read our package label for details). And then, to make milk a meal… Carnation instant breakfast contributes the rest of the protein, vitamins, minerals and food energy. It all adds up to a poached egg on toast, two strips of bacon and a glass of orange juice.

Now, that's the kind of balanced breakfast you want for yourself and your family when they don't have time for a regular breakfast.

Pick up a package of Carnation instant breakfast today. No family should be without it. Because no family should ever go without good nourishment in the morning.

Carnation® instant breakfast, Carnation Company, Los Angeles, California

In a 1971 print ad, "Turning Milk into a Meal," Carnation addressed concerns over nutritional claims for its Instant Breakfast drink by emphasizing the nutritional content of the milk with which it was intended to be mixed.

In its ruling against Warner-Lambert, the commission eluci-
dated the elements necessary to trigger corrective advertising as a
remedy. First, an advertisement must be deceptive; second, the
advertisement must have played a substantial role in creating or
reinforcing a false and material belief in the mind of consumers.
Finally, corrective remedies, the ruling stated, are justified if, even
after the false advertising has ceased, the false belief lingers in the
mind of consumers, affecting competition by its influence on consumer purchasing decisions.

Since 1977 the FTC has required corrective advertising in only
one other case. In 1999 the agency required Novartis, manufacturer of Doan's pills, to mount an $8 million corrective advertis-
ing campaign. The campaign was intended to correct consumers'
misbeliefs that Doan's is superior to all other analgesics in reliev-
ing back pain; according to the FTC, Novartis had no scientific
evidence to make such a claim. Doan's had been advertised as a
remedy for back pain since its introduction to the market, more
than 90 years earlier. Some of the claims used in Doan's advertisements included:

- "Doan's is made for back pain relief with an ingredient [other]
  pain relievers don't have. Doan's makes pain go away. . . . the
  back specialist."
- "If nothing seems to help, try Doan's. It relieves back pain no
  matter where it hurts. Doan's has an ingredient these pain
  relievers don't have."
- "Back pain is different. Why use these pain relievers? Doan's is
  just for back pain."

The FTC order specifically required that the packaging and the
advertising for Doan's include clearly and conspicuously the
phrase "Although Doan's is an effective pain reliever, there is no
evidence that Doan's is more effective than other pain relievers for
back pain." The FTC ordered that the statement be disseminated
for one year.

The Lanham Trademark Act

Advertisers who are damaged or are likely to be damaged by false
representations made by a competitor can bring suit under Section
43 (a) of the Lanham Trademark Act. Before 1989 the wording of
Section 43 (a) stated that potential damage to a plaintiff could be
claimed only when a false representation was made about the
defendant's goods or services. The revised wording allowed action
to be taken against an advertiser who makes false claims about its
own product and/or the plaintiff's products:

> False or misleading representations of fact, which . . . in
> commercial advertising or promotion, misrepresents the
> nature, characteristics, qualities or geographic origin of *his
> or her or another person's goods, services, or commercial
> activities*, shall be liable in a civil action by any person who
> believes that he or she is or is likely to be damaged by such
> act. (Act of 16 November 1988, codified as amendment at
> 15 U.S.C. @ 1125, emphasis added).

Corrective advertising can be used to dispel misconceptions about a
product as well as to provide further information, as seen in this early
1970s print ad for sugar.

Thus, to prevail in a case of false advertising under Section 43
(a), the plaintiff must first prove that the defendant made a false
or misleading statement regarding its own products. Specifically,
the plaintiff must demonstrate that the advertisement is either literally false, or if literally true is likely to mislead or confuse a substantial portion of the intended audience. The plaintiff must also
demonstrate damages or their likelihood. This can be accomplished by showing that sales have been diverted from the plaintiff
to the defendant or by showing a corresponding loss of market
share. A loss of goodwill toward the plaintiff or the plaintiffs'
product also constitutes damages.

Corrective advertising may be requested by the plaintiff to
counter consumers' false perceptions when these can be attributed
to the competitors' advertising. In fact, most litigants seek corrective remedies under Section 43 (a). The courts may grant corrective
advertising as part of the damages awarded to the plaintiff, who
then receives the necessary funds to disseminate corrective messages to counteract the false beliefs or confusion created by the
offending ad. On the other hand, the courts may order the defen-
dants to design and implement the corrective campaigns, for which
they assume all costs. In some instances both parties may be

required to disseminate corrective messages. In a case involving *Alpo Petfoods Inc.* v. *Ralston Purina Co.* (1989), the court ordered both the plaintiff and the defendant to distribute corrective materials to veterinarians, dog breeders, and dog owners to correct the lingering false impression left by the companies' advertisements.

The National Advertising Division of the Better Business Bureau

The National Advertising Division (NAD) of the Council of Better Business Bureaus is charged with independent responsibility for monitoring and reviewing national advertising for truthfulness and accuracy. The NAD reviews complaints regarding national advertising made by any person or legal entity, regardless of whether the advertisements were intended for consumers, professionals, or business entities.

A decision by the NAD that an advertisement has been substantiated does not constitute an endorsement of a company, product, or service by the NAD. Similarly, an advertiser's voluntary modification of advertising in cooperation with the NAD does not constitute an admission of impropriety. When an advertiser does not agree to comply with the decision of the NAD, the advertiser is entitled to a panel review of the National Advertising Review Board (NARB). When advertisers elect not to participate in the self-regulatory process, the NAD and NARB may prepare a review of the facts, which may be then forwarded to the appropriate federal or state law enforcement agencies.

In approximately half of all advertisements reviewed, the NAD will require the challenged claims to be "modified or discontinued." The wording of the claims may need to be changed to prevent consumers from forming false representations, or corrective disclosures may be included along with the claims. Once such a recommendation is published, the NAD may request that the advertiser report on the status of the advertisement at issue and explain the steps taken to comply with the decision. When compliance is at issue the NAD may refer the matter to the appropriate government agencies and report these actions to the public and the press.

Because participation is voluntary there is little more the agency can do in terms of enforcement. Corrective advertising is therefore less likely to be recommended in this setting. Still, given the acceptance by the advertising industry, a recommendation by the NAD involving corrective measures is likely to influence judicial opinions and regulatory actions.

Impact and Costs

Research suggests that corrective advertisements have little negative impact on the image of the company issuing the correction. In fact, in some cases consumers perceive companies as more trustworthy, presumably because they appear to have the consumer's best interest in mind.

Do corrective remedies have any impact on the beliefs they are intended to alter? Studies of the effects of corrective campaigns suggest that they are moderately effective in changing consumers' beliefs, but that at times the corrective messages are misunderstood. This finding is discouraging given the expense of corrective advertising, which includes both the costs of litigation and costs associated with changes in and delays to a company's promotion strategy.

Whether the high costs of corrective campaigns are viewed as a negative or a positive, however, depends on one's viewpoint. Regulators and consumer advocates argue that the financial burden of corrective orders serves as a deterrent, signaling to advertisers the potential consequences of disseminating deceptive messages. On the other hand, advertisers and others in the industry contend that corrective orders are extreme and represent serious restrictions on their ability to craft persuasive messages. Nonetheless, both sides acknowledge the role of corrective advertising in maintaining a competitive environment where consumers can rely on the information and credibility of promotional messages.

NORMA A. MENDOZA

Further Reading

Armstrong, Gary M., Metin N. Gurol, and Frederick A. Russ, "Corrective Advertising: A Review and Evaluation," *Current Issues and Research in Advertising* 2 (1983)

Belch, George E., et al., "An Examination of Consumers' Perceptions of Purpose and Content of Corrective Advertising," in *Advances in Consumer Research,* edited by Andrew Mitchell, St. Louis, Missouri: Association for Consumer Research, 1981

Ingersoll, Bruce, "FTC Orders Novartis Ads to Correct Claim," *Wall Street Journal* (28 May 1999)

Preston, Ivan L., "A Review of the Literature on Advertising Regulation," *Current Issues and Research in Advertising* 2 (1983)

Preston, Ivan L., *The Tangled Web They Weave: Truth, Falsity, and Advertisers,* Madison: University of Wisconsin Press, 1994

Richards, Jef I., *Deceptive Advertising: Behavioral Study of a Legal Concept,* Hillsdale, New Jersey: Erlbaum, 1990

Wilkie, William L., Dennis L. McNeill, and Michael B. Mazis, "Marketing's 'Scarlet Letter:' The Theory and Practice of Corrective Advertising," *Journal of Public Policy and Marketing* 48 (Spring 1984)

Cosmetics

The practice of adorning the face and body is believed to date back some 40,000 years. The ancient Greeks practiced beauty rites for both men and women, and the Roman poet Ovid wrote of cosmetics, "each maiden knows that art's allowed her."

The first "cold cream," a softener for the skin, was developed by the Greek physician Galen in the second century CE. Although the use of cosmetics declined in the early Christian era, the European Crusaders brought appearance-enhancing substances with them when they returned from the Holy Land. The English monarch Elizabeth I's fondness for perfumes and cosmetics helped spread the use of beauty aids throughout Europe, where they became common by the 18th century. Many other cultures around the globe, from African to American Indian, have made extensive use of cosmetics.

Days of Rice Powder and Roses

The first crude advertisements for cosmetics appeared in European newspapers during the 17th and 18th centuries. Powder made of white lead and ground rice was sold by the pound for whitening the skin and hair. Another product advertised was beauty patches, which were used primarily to cover the pockmarks left by smallpox and other diseases, as were rouge and lipstick. Early American newspapers featured similar ads, enticing colonists to imitate the latest fashions of London, England, and Paris, France.

The American and French revolutions, with their opposition to aristocracy and their republican ideals of homespun clothing and simple hairstyles, made cosmetics politically unfashionable and—with the exception of pomades used to control the hair—even dangerous, as wearers might be with Tories, Girondins, or even monarchists. Nineteenth-century Romanticism, with its emphasis on a demure and natural look, dictated that proper British and American women use only homemade cosmetics, such as rice powder, cucumber cream, lemon juice, and rose water, and then only in the privacy of the bedroom. That was not the case in France, which became the center of the invention, production, and advertising of cosmetics during the 19th century.

With the exception of hairdressings, however, there were at first no women's cosmetics to advertise in the United States. In 1846 Theron T. Pond, a chemist in upper New York state, invented witch hazel extract; a few years later Pond rediscovered an early formula for cold cream. In 1859 kerosene dealer Robert Chesebrough learned of a fatty substance collecting on oil drilling rods, which reputedly helped cure cuts and burns. Chesebrough's Vaseline Petroleum Jelly ("vasel" from the German *wasser* for "water," and "ine" from the Greek *elaion* for "olive oil") along with Pond's Cleansing Cream and Pond's Extract, became the first commercial American cosmetic products. (The two companies merged in 1955.) They were advertised primarily by means of colorful cards, product booklets, and testimonials placed in apothecary shops. Pond's became one of the J. Walter Thompson Company's first clients in 1886, and the Pond's Girl ad campaign won first place at a national advertising convention in 1904 with the slogan "Avoid sunburn, freckles and chaps. The out-of-doors girl can easily avoid the unpleasant effects of sun and wind on her delicate skin by always using Pond's Extract Company's Vanishing Cream."

The majority of cosmetics advertised in the 19th century, however, were purchased by men in barbershops. An 1851 ad for a Boston, Massachusetts, barbershop listed, among other products for sale, bear and buffalo oil, freckle wash, perfumed hair powder, two types of hair dye, lavender water, Macassar oil, and toilet powder. Talcum powder, made of crushed magnesium silicate, was marketed after the American Civil War primarily to men. Hair dye for men was advertised extensively, and some was presumably used by women. Rather than advertise cosmetics for women, *Godey's Lady's Book* and other 19th-century women's magazines advocated that readers keep their skin as white as possible with hats, veils, and parasols, redden their lips by biting them, and pinch their cheeks to produce a becoming blush. *Godey's* upper-class editor, Sarah Josepha Hale, even published recipes for homemade cosmetics such as hand lotion (lard, rose water, and coconut milk).

Gaining Respectability

The early 20th century saw an increase in the advertising of cosmetic preparations, although their use was still not commonplace. The discreet use of certain cosmetics—including hair tint, cheek rouge, and body powder on the arms and neckline—to cover the signs of aging was permissible. Lip rouge and eyebrow liner, on the other hand, were used only by actresses and prostitutes. Younger women could avail themselves of less obvious assistance. Cosmetic soaps, for example, had become an important business by the late 19th century when Pears' made the rather risky decision to use full-page magazine advertisements for its soap, "a speciality for improving the complexion." The ads made use of "high culture," employing paintings by popular artists and illustrators such as Frederic Remington, Maxfield Parrish, Will Bradley, and John Everett Millais, accompanied by eye-catching copy: "Good morning, have you used Pears' soap?" Pears' was also among the first products to use celebrity endorsements, including those of actress Lily Langtry and soprano Adelina Patti.

In 1891 John H. Woodbury introduced a beauty soap that was identified on package labels and in ads by a picture of his head. The image became so well known that it was lampooned by burlesque comedians as "The neckless head." The first advertisement for Woodbury's Facial Soap, with the slogan, "A skin you love to touch," appeared in 1911, the work of Helen Lansdowne Resor of the J. Walter Thompson Company (JWT). Palmolive soap, introduced in 1898, experienced a substantial increase in sales when Stanley and Helen Resor of JWT employed a subtle appeal to vanity with the slogan "Still—that schoolgirl complexion."

Like many cosmetics ads from the 1920s and 1930s, this 1925 ad advises women who use Pompeian Bloom that they can expect marriage as a "reward of beauty."

Some of the most memorable early 20th-century cosmetics advertising, however, was directed at men. In 1905 King C. Gillette introduced safety razor blades with his mustached face and signature on each package, and the distinctive Gillette diamond and arrow trademark was added to other products beginning in 1908. Clinton Odell began producing brushless Burma-Shave shaving cream in 1925, and his son came up with the idea of highway advertising signs four years later. The first ads for Shulton's Old Spice aftershave appeared in 1937 from Wesley Associates.

Meanwhile, homemade cosmetics remained the norm for most middle-class American women until 1917. A 1916 advertisement for Sunkist, a trademark of the Southern California Fruit Exchange, proclaimed the virtues of "a teaspoonful of lemon juice in a cup of warm water to soften the cuticle before manicuring." (Fruit growers continued to advocate homemade beauty preparations, hiring Lord & Thomas to produce a series of elegant high-fashion ads for Sunkist—"the real secret of beautiful hair is simplicity itself"—in the early 1930s.)

Cosmetic and beauty products, such as hair tonics, had always skirted laws designed to protect against unsafe drugs. The Pure Food and Drug Act of 1906 was supposed to include cosmetics, but they were eliminated from the act because they were not considered a serious public health problem. However, a death and a blinding owing to use of an eyeliner product forced Congress to enact the Food, Drug, and Cosmetic Act of 1938, dividing responsibility for the safety of cosmetics between the Food and Drug Administration and the Federal Trade Commission. In particular, advertising that made "therapeutic claims" equating cosmetics to drugs came under government scrutiny.

Arrival of Mass Marketing

With the advent of World War I, a combination of factors emerged that helped to make mass-market cosmetics not only acceptable, but also popular. The revolution was touched off in part when women, accustomed to long hair in the style of the pompadoured turn-of-the-century Gibson Girl and the actress Lillian Russell, began cutting their hair. Short hair was more practical for women working in factories, and for advocates of women's rights, "bobbed" hair asserted women's new freedom. By the early 1920s the hourglass figure of the 1910s had been replaced by the flat-chested boyish silhouette of the "flapper."

The flapper look required the use of cosmetics previously restricted solely to actresses and other not entirely respectable women. Mascara had been introduced by the former Empress Eugénie (widow of Napoleon III) around the turn of the century, but it did not become a standard cosmetics item in the United States until the plucked-and-penciled eyebrow of the flapper came into vogue. Before 1917 lip rouge was sold in pots and spread by the fingertips. During World War I, however, the first lipsticks were developed by the Scovil Manufacturing Company of Waterbury, Connecticut, and the company began selling solid, extendible lip "bullets" in the early 1920s, making possible the flapper's bright, puckered Cupid's bow mouth. As the marketing of cosmetics proliferated, beauty shops sprang up offering facials, hairdressing, and other services to help make women feel more youthful and appealing. By 1929 a pound of face powder for every woman in the United States was being sold annually, and there were 1,500 face creams on the market. At the same time the concept of color harmony in makeup was introduced, and major cosmetics companies began producing integrated lines of lipsticks, fingernail lacquers, and foundations.

Advertisers struggled to introduce consumers to the plethora of new cosmetic products and innovative makeup colors and styles. Although a 1928 ad for a skin lubricant still used the old-fashioned educational approach, advising women that "a youthful face loses half its charm when the throat below it looks middle-aged," such traditional messages, with their rational appeal, did not work well for "irrational" products such as cosmetics. Instead, manufacturers reasoned that just as stage actresses had introduced women to the rudimentary use of cosmetics a generation earlier, movie stars could now be used to demonstrate their proper use.

The success of tabloid papers such as the *London Daily Mirror* and periodicals such as *True Stories,* the first confessional magazine, demonstrated the potential of the emerging Hollywood movie culture as a mass-marketing tool. The movies offered people an escape from their mundane, everyday lives. And cosmetics were about escapism. Ad images evolved from the 1920s flapper as personified by Clara Bow, known as the "It girl," to the glitzy appeal of Jean Harlow and the elegance of Claudette Colbert or to the more sophisticated pale-lipped and flaming-fingernailed images of Norma Shearer and Madeleine Carroll in the 1930s. The enigmatic and seductive Rita Hayworth became the model for female workers during World War II, and the 1950s capitalized on the elfin appeal of Audrey Hepburn. In 1939 Lucille Ball starred in the RKO film *Beauty for the Asking,* the first movie to portray the marketing and advertising practices of the cosmetics industry.

Some early cosmetics advertising, especially for the highly competitive beauty soaps, appealed to women's feelings of insecurity. Just as magazine and newspaper advertising in the 1920s warned men that cultivating a good appearance in the workplace was critical to success, it also sought to remind women that beauty was directly linked to keeping a job—and a husband. A 1922 *Ladies' Home Journal* ad for Palmolive soap advised that "the charm of a perfect natural complexion attracts far more than elaborate dress and ornaments." A Woodbury ad of the same year promised that "the possession of a beautiful skin" would help women to face and overcome a hostile world "proudly—confidently—without fear." Another Woodbury ad in *Ladies' Home Journal* confided that "a man expects to find daintiness, charm, refinement in the woman he knows" and that "when some unpleasant little detail mars this conception of what a woman should be—nothing quite effaces his involuntary disappointment." A 1928 ad for Palmolive soap warned that "youth is a charm, and youth lost is charm lost." A 1930 *True Story* ad for Procter & Gamble's Camay soap, created by Pedler and Ryan, asserted that "someone's eyes are forever searching your face, comparing you with other women." And a *Ladies' Home Journal* ad for Pompeian Night Cream promised that lifelong marriage and security were "beauty's reward" for use of the product.

Early cosmetics advertisers also pioneered the use of sexual references and nudity to remind women of the power of their sexuality. A popular 1928 Palmolive ad by Benton and Bowles, Inc., depicted a lovely young mother adjusting her son's bow tie; it bore the caption, "His first love." A perfume advertisement of the era advised that "the first duty of woman is to attract. . . . It does not matter how clever or independent you may be, if you fail to influence the men you meet, consciously or unconsciously, you are not fulfilling your fundamental duty as a woman." A late 1920s beauty aids booklet featured a female nude on the front cover below the title "Your masterpiece—yourself." In 1936 Woodbury's soap became the first product to use the image of a nude woman in national advertising; the accompanying copy read, "Science enriches Woodbury Formula with benefits of "filtered sunshine," nature's source of beauty for the skin!" The implicit message in such ads was that the continued use of cosmetics products was necessary for women to preserve their psychological and sexual identity.

Products for People of Color

At the same time that cosmetics advertisers were promoting their products to the general population, advertising of cosmetics for people of color was helping to foster and support African-American newspapers and magazines. Before the 1890s black barbershops and beauty shops served both white and black clientele, but blacks were forced to adopt European beauty standards. Commercial hair straighteners and skin-whitening preparations, with names such as No Kink, Imperial Whitener, Mme. Turner's Mystic Face Bleach, and Black Skin Remover, were well advertised in the press in the late 19th and early 20th centuries, and some remained in use into the 1950s. In 1885 the *Nation* referred to these products as "the solution" to the race problem, and the advertising claims of at least one of them, Black-No-More, reinforced this view. "Colored people," one ad asserted, "your salvation is at hand. The Negro need no longer be different in color from the white man." The "greatest discovery of the age" was guaranteed to transform "the blackest skin into the purest white without pain, inconvenience or danger." Based on numerous complaints, the U.S. Post Office disagreed and in 1905 barred Black-No-More from the mail. It perished, but similar products were sold retail through newspaper and magazine advertising. Dr. Fred Palmer's Skin Whitener was still being advertised in the United States as late as 1960.

Anthony Overton's Overton Hygienic Manufacturing Company, established in Kansas City, Kansas, in 1898, was the first company to produce cosmetics created to accentuate black beauty. Advertisements for his High Brown Face Powder and other toiletry products became a staple in black newspapers, including the *Chicago Defender,* the first mass-circulation African-American publication, and the *Chicago Bee,* which Overton started in 1922. Annie M. Turnbo-Malone's Poro Company was another manufacturer of hair and skin care products and a major advertiser in African-American media. In 1905 C.J. Breedlove Walker, a onetime Poro agent who had learned advertising techniques from her newspaperman husband, revolutionized the hair and beauty culture industry by creating a treatment for hair loss, a common ailment among black and white women alike, which resulted from poor diet and harsh hair care treatments. Her Madame Walker Products Company had 5,000 agents and was the leading advertiser in black newspapers at the time of her death in 1919.

In the 1920s black activist Marcus Garvey attracted attention for pledging to refuse advertisements for hair straighteners and skin whiteners in his mass-circulation *Negro World,* but ads for Dr. Fred Palmer's Skin Whitener and for his Golden Brown Beauty Preparation, which claimed that light brown was better than white, occasionally found their way into his publication. Johnson Products, founded in Chicago, Illinois, in 1954 by George and Joan B. Johnson, marketed the first safe hair relaxant for men. Advertisements for the company's popular Ultra Sheen product line, using black advertising firms and models, aided the growth of *Essence* magazine and became a fixture on the *Soul Train* television program.

The unrelated Johnson Publishing Company, publisher of *Ebony* and *Jet,* produced Fashion Fair Cosmetics and Supreme Beauty Products. As a result of the efforts of black cosmetics manufacturers, *Ebony* was able to observe in 1957 that "the old definition of "the true Negro," one with black skin, woolly hair, a flat nose and thick lips, no longer stands." To defend such claims, in the late 1960s cosmetics ads in publications owned by African-Americans began using darker-skinned models. Meanwhile, black Chicago entrepreneur S.B. Fuller secretly purchased a white-owned cosmetics factory in 1947. His Fuller Products line, which advertised but relied primarily on the same door-to-door sales strategy as competitor Avon, was earning more than $10 million a year in sales until his ownership was revealed in the early 1960s. A boycott by southern whites, along with changing tastes, forced Fuller into bankruptcy in 1964. Beginning in the 1970s, the major cosmetics manufacturers began adding product lines that catered to customers of color, buying African-American-owned competitors such as Johnson Products and Soft Sheen Products and using black models in their advertising.

Marketing Beauty

The majority of cosmetics preparations have changed little in composition since the days of Pond and Chesebrough. For example, Pond's cold cream formula served more or less as the base for foundation cream, cleansing cream, vanishing cream, nourishing cream, moisturizing cream, and a variety of other products. Early cosmetics advertising overlooked such similarities, stressing reliability and convenience with slogans such as "Never hardens" and "The delicate fragrance lasts" or emphasizing safety and health benefits and anti-aging properties with promises such as "Never irritates," "Good for your skin," and "Keeps the schoolgirl complexion."

A growing body of market research after World War II indicated that the consumer's response to cosmetics was dictated more by the expectations and preferences of other women—what was called "other-directed" pitches—than by her own "inner-directed" goals such as age reduction or the promotion of health. One 1967 study of advertisements in three American women's magazines between 1913 and 1964 revealed that cosmetics were the only product among 13 categories surveyed that continued to stress an emotional, other-directed appeal.

As consumers continued to pay increasing amounts of money for essentially the same products, with only minor differences such as brand name and color, it was hardly a surprise that cosmetics manufacturers turned to psychological advertising. Perhaps the most famous cosmetics campaign, labeled "the most effective ads in cosmetics history" by *Business Week* and named best ad of the year by *Advertising Age,* appeared in 1952. Revlon kicked off a promotion for a new lip and nail color called Fire and Ice with two-page magazine spreads that featured redheaded model Dorian Leigh in a sparkling silver sequined dress with a crimson cape and the tag line, "Are you ready for 'Fire and Ice'?" Nine thousand window displays were devoted to the vivid red color, and it was also advertised in newspapers and on the radio.

"Fire and Ice" beauty contests were held across the country, and 22 hotels, from the Plaza in New York City to the Cornhusker in Lincoln, Nebraska, staged "Fire and Ice" preview parties. The color continued as a Revlon staple into the 21st century.

Revlon had been founded by New York cosmetics salesman Charles Revson in 1932. The company gained a virtual monopoly on beauty salon sales by 1940 through aggressive sales tactics such as salesmen "accidentally" destroying competitors' displays. "In the factory we make cosmetics," Revson said, "in the store we sell hope." Revlon borrowed the concept of "planned obsolescence" from General Motors Corporation about the same time it cornered its market. Until World War II, women had tended to use an entire lipstick or bottle of nail polish before purchasing a new one. While Revlon had already begun semiannual promotions based on seasonal colors, before Fire and Ice no shade had ever been introduced with such a splash and impact.

Leigh was already a leading model when she did her first Revlon promotion ("Fatal Apple—the most tempting color since Eve winked at Adam") in 1945, but the "Fire and Ice" campaign made her the first so-called Revlon Girl. She was joined by her sister Suzy Parker, actresses Barbara Feldon (Agent 99 of television's *Get Smart*) and Barbara Britton (Mrs. North on *Mr. and Mrs. North*), and model Lauren Hutton. Parker became so well known that she appeared on a *Life* magazine cover in 1957. Building on the "Fire and Ice" campaign, Revlon produced and sponsored the television quiz show *The $64,000 Question* in 1955. This popular program was such an effective advertising vehicle that one shade of Revlon lipstick, modeled by Britton on black-and-white television, sold out in ten days. *The $64,000 Question* disappeared from television in the quiz show scandal of 1958, but not before the show and the Revlon Girls had increased the company's sales by more than 100 percent. In fact, by this time Revlon was producing the number one brand of lipstick, hair spray, nail products, and foundation makeup.

Other cosmetics companies exploited the tried-and-true formula of actresses as role models. Maybelline, which began as a homemade petroleum jelly–based coloring for eyelids and lashes, has never missed a month of advertising since its first national magazine ads in the 1920s. It was the first cosmetic brand to use radio and television, and early on it made extensive use of celebrity tie-ins and endorsements. Hollywood star Hedy Lamarr promoted Maybelline in movie and confessional magazines of the 1940s, and Joan Crawford's ads maintained that she "would never be without" Maybelline. In spite of highly successful advertising by Revlon's and Cover Girl's glamorous models, in 1980 Maybelline hired television actress Lynda Carter, best known for the lead role in *Wonder Woman.* Carter appeared in ads for Moisture Whip skin care and cosmetics; Maybelline's sales increased by 200 percent during her first three years. She remained a spokesperson until 1991, when the brand was sold.

Max Factor, the brand sold by Sales Builders, Inc., traditionally spent less on advertising than the other major cosmetics companies because it capitalized on its historical ties with the motion picture industry. Founder Max Factor started his business in 1909 selling theatrical cosmetics and hair products but helped develop innovative makeup for filmmakers. A new type of film introduced around this time was more light sensitive than its predecessors and required makeup with more subtle variations in shading and light. A few years later, in 1927, Factor introduced his Color Harmony Make-up and Complexion Analysis Charts to the public. These products guided a woman to the best shades of makeup for her particular coloring. The company's principal agency during the 1930s and 1940s was a small Los Angeles, California, shop, Smith & Drum. Subsequently, advertising was handled by a house agency, the Ted H. Factor Agency, until Kenyon & Eckhardt became the agency of record in the 1950s.

While Factor continued to manufacture cosmetics for the entertainment industry, his mass-market products came to account for the major part of the company's sales during the late 1920s. His greatest advertising achievement came during the 1930s when the introduction of color photographic film made it necessary for cosmetics companies to create makeup that could provide natural-looking skin tones. Max Factor's Pan-Cake makeup, named for the round, flat container it came in, had a matte finish and more closely matched natural skin tones than had any previous makeup. The public learned of the product as it gained popularity in the motion picture industry, and Factor advertised it in a campaign of expensive, full-color magazine ads featuring movie stars Norma Shearer, Madeline Carroll, and Rita Hayworth. Factor died in 1938, but his company continued its ties with the entertainment industry by developing special makeup for television during the 1950s, including Erase, the first concealer product. Pan-Cake and the derivative Pan-Stik makeups have remained among the largest selling items in the cosmetics industry. Toward the end of the 20th century, Max Factor featured television actresses Jaclyn Smith and Jane Seymour in its ads, and although the ads did not reverse the decline in the line's market share, they evoked a nostalgic sense of Factor's earlier successes, with Smith remarking, "The glamour goes on" and "Thanks Max" at the end of the TV spots. Ultimately, Max Factor was bought by Procter & Gamble and renamed Procter & Gamble Cosmetics Company. Its agencies included Grey Advertising and the Leo Burnett Company.

Cover Girl built its product line on the age-old friction between the generations. Its cosmetics were based on Noxzema, which was Pond's 19th-century cold cream formula augmented with a mixture of clove, eucalyptus, menthol, and camphor. From its invention in 1914, Noxzema was marketed as a cure for eczema (its name means "no eczema"), sunburn, acne, chapped skin, facial blemishes, and tired feet, and it was sold briefly as a shaving cream. But in 1950 a company employee mentioned that she washed regularly with the product because it did not dry or irritate her face as soap did, and the company then began a long-running campaign advocating Noxzema as a replacement for soap. In 1961 Cover Girl cosmetics were introduced in an advertising campaign developed by Sullivan, Stauffer, Colwell & Bayles. Eschewing Max Factor's and Maybelline's tactic of featuring established movie stars, Cover Girl used beautiful, young, relatively unknown models (even the Revlon Girls were better recognized) and photographed them on

Hiring actress Lynda Carter, best known for her role as Wonder Woman, as its spokesperson in 1980 proved a profitable move for Maybelline.

fake magazine covers and taking breaks between photo shoots. In television ads an announcer intoned, "It's lovely Cover Girl Jane Rylander using Cover Girl Clean Make-Up." The maidenly Rylander, and the other models, then proclaimed, "Noxzema makes it, so I trust it," and offered the hope that even the viewer could be a cover girl.

The use of unknown models to advertise a major cosmetic brand was considered risky in the early 1960s, but the fresh, squeaky clean faces struck a response with Cover Girl's target audience of baby boomer teens and young women. Running until the 1980s, the campaign helped Cover Girl achieve an annual rate of growth in the double digits, putting it ahead of Revlon and Maybelline as the leader of the $2.6 million mass-market cosmetics segment. The brand and campaign also helped invent the so-called supermodel. Jennifer O'Neill, Carol Alt, Christie Brinkley, Cybill Shepherd, and Rachel Hunter all started as models for Cover Girl, and Cheryl Tiegs reigned as a Cover Girl model for a record 19 years. The first African-American and Latino Cover Girl models appeared during the 1990s, as did the first model under the age of 18. The declining market for cosmetics among teens and young women in the 1990s hurt Cover Girl's sales, however, even as the firm continued to outspend its rivals for advertising and to diversify with new products.

Smaller cosmetics companies have used less emotional, nontraditional, or even old-fashioned strategies to promote their products. Estée Lauder began as a product line sold exclusively in New York City department stores such as Saks Fifth Avenue. The company's founder, Josephine Esther Mentzer ("Estée Lauder" was a frenchified version of "Esther" and Mentzer's married name), did not have enough of an advertising budget in the late 1940s to attract even a small advertising agency. Instead, she spent the ad money on gift items that were included with the purchase of her products. The unheard-of practice puzzled retailers at first, but when it was discovered that the "free" samples actually served to demonstrate new products to consumers, other cosmetic companies also began giving gifts with purchases. Estée Lauder later employed snob appeal in its advertising, even though the company's ad budget paled in comparison to those of its competitors. Most of its magazine ads used stylish black-and-white photographs, which were cheaper than color. The company avoided television, preferring less expensive print advertising. It introduced a European-style skin care lotion called Re-Nutriv in 1960 with a full-page *Harper's Bazaar* ad that bluntly asked, "What makes a cream worth $115.00?" Other Estée Lauder products emphasized their uniqueness, a tactic used by many early cosmetics advertisers. The company also used in-house promotions, press releases, and even tree-planting ceremonies to publicize new products.

Pond's Cold Cream, still made according to the original formula, did not become highly profitable until other cosmetics became popular in the 1920s. For years it used the same testimonial advertising that it had in the 19th century, with endorsements from the likes of Princess Matchabelli (wife of the perfume maker) and Mrs. Nicholas R. du Pont, the wife of the chemical company magnate. A 1955 merger with the Chesebrough Manufacturing Company, makers of Vaseline Petroleum Jelly reinvigorated the century-old firm, but well into the 1980s the company's advertising continued to stress the medicinal benefits of Chesebrough-Pond's products. A repackaging of the entire line in 1988 and a $30 million network television, print, and promotional campaign developed by McCann-Erickson Worldwide in 1992 helped distance Pond's from its old-fashioned cold cream past.

Among other cosmetics lines, Oil of Olay, invented by a South African chemist to treat the burn wounds of British Royal Air Force pilots during World War II, was introduced to the rest of the world in the 1950s and 1960s through an advertising campaign that refused to define the purpose of the product. Instead, the ads emphasized the "mysterious" nature of Oil of Olay, a practice that persisted into the 1980s. Toward the end of the 20th century, the product and its derivatives received extensive advertising for their moisturizing abilities. Neutrogena soaps and hair and skin care products depended primarily on print advertising, although the company ran a successful television campaign in the 1980s with the slogan "For pure, beautiful skin, Neutrogena is pure necessity." And Avon became one of the leading cosmetics companies in the world through door-to-door sales, although over the years the company depended upon extensive radio, television, and

print advertising. Its most successful campaign, created by Monroe F. Dreher, Inc., began on American television in 1954 with the unforgettable dingdong chime and "Avon calling" slogan. The popularity of direct sales in the late 20th century, as epitomized by Amway and other network marketers, and the availability of Avon products on the Internet opened new vistas for cosmetics advertising.

Fashion innovations and cultural trends have occasionally transcended individual advertising campaigns. The 1920s flapper look originated with new products such as Scovil's lipsticks, which were duplicated by other manufacturers. Max Factor's movie star products and ads were immediately copied by competitors. The introduction of suntan products such as Bain de Soleil during the 1940s and Coppertone, which introduced its Little Miss Coppertone billboard ads in 1953, influenced cosmetics manufacturers to emphasize a "healthy" outdoor look in their ads. In the 1970s, in turn, concerns about skin cancer forced cosmetics advertising back indoors, leaving the manufacturers of suntan lotion scrambling for new formulations. A return to the pre-1920s natural look, sans makeup, was fostered by the women's movement of the 1960s and encouraged advertisers to abandon the heavy cosmetics look. At the same time, the images of women in cosmetics advertising became less sexually passive. Advertising in general had long subordinated women by distorting their appearance through artwork or camera angles or by showing them in horizontal rather than vertical poses. From 1973 to 1988, ads for Revlon's Charlie perfume, featuring tall, confident, working women dominating men, exemplified the new advertising image of women in positions of power and authority. They still wore cosmetics, but they did so to compete with other women on an economic rather than a sexual basis.

By the end of the 20th century the emotional image of many cosmetics overshadowed their other characteristics. Advertising and packaging had become the consumer's sole definition of a product, and each customer provided her own justification for a purchase based on confidence in a product and the attractiveness or "image" of the models using it. Cosmetics advertisers employed the so-called Modess Method in their ads, displaying the product name in large, distinctive lettering with copy following after the word "because." Viewers were encouraged to supply the rest of the ad, avoiding copy restrictions. Skeptics held that the copywriters did not know what to say.

A growing fear of synthetic chemicals, along with burgeoning consumer interest in the healthful qualities of products, encouraged advertisers to stress the simple and "natural" ingredients of cosmetics. Hypoallergenic cosmetics evolved from a specialty with only narrow appeal into a mass-market product, and advertising that emphasized a product's nonallergenic properties was directed at all women, including those who had no cosmetic allergies. As women became more active in sports, advertisers stressed the lasting qualities and convenience of makeup. The aging of the baby boomer generation by the end of the 1990s encouraged manufacturers to create new anti-aging products or to promote the anti-aging properties of existing cosmetics as much as the law would allow. Parallel with this tendency toward a utilitarian approach to cosmetics advertising was a trend toward surrealism, evident in ads with dreamlike or fantastic imagery. These ads proved the enduring appeal of glamour, first recognized by cosmetics advertisers more than half a century earlier.

RICHARD JUNGER

See also Avon Products, Inc.; Chesebrough-Pond's, Inc.; Procter & Gamble Company; *and color plate in this volume*

Further Reading

Ewen, Stuart, *Captains of Consciousness: Advertising and the Social Roots of the Consumer Culture,* New York: McGraw-Hill, 1976

Fox, Stephen, *The Mirror Makers: A History of American Advertising and Its Creators,* New York: Morrow, 1984

Goodrum, Charles, and Helen Dalrymple, *Advertising in America: The First 200 Years,* New York: Abrams, 1990

Gunn, Fenja, *The Artificial Face: A History of Cosmetics,* Newton Abbot, Devon: David and Charles, 1973; New York: Hippocrene, 1975

Jorgensen, Janice, editor, *Encyclopedia of Consumer Brands,* Detroit, Michigan, and London: St. James, 1994

Marchand, Roland, *Advertising the American Dream: Making Way for Modernity, 1920–1940,* Berkeley: University of California Press, 1985

Morton, Patricia Roe, "Riesman's Theory of Social Character Applied to Consumer-Goods Advertising," *Journalism Quarterly* 44 (Summer 1967)

Schudson, Michael, *Advertising, the Uneasy Persuasion: Its Dubious Impact on American Society,* New York: Basic Books, 1984

Stabile, Toni, *Everything You Want to Know about Cosmetics; or, What Your Friendly Clerk Didn't Tell You,* New York: Dodd, Mead, 1984

Twitchell, James B., *Adcult USA: The Triumph of Advertising in American Culture,* New York: Columbia University Press, 1995; Chichester, West Sussex: Columbia University Press, 1996

Vinikas, Vincent, *Soft Soap, Hard Sell: American Hygiene in an Age of Advertisement,* Ames: Iowa State University Press, 1992

Cossette Communication-Marketing

Founded by Jean-Claude Cossette, Claude Lessard, Louis Larivière, Paul Lefebre, Bernard Paquet, and Fernand Simard, from the reorganization of Cossette Associés, 1972; went public, 1999.

Major Clients

Bell Canada
Coca-Cola of Canada
General Motors of Canada
McDonald's Restaurants of Canada
Molson Breweries
Seagate Software

Cossette Communication-Marketing (CCM) was one of Canada's premier agencies of the 1990s. It was Canada's largest agency in billings and a perennial award winner for its creative work. It also bucked economic trends by remaining wholly Canadian-owned, an anomaly during a period when most of the leading domestic agencies were absorbed by global organizations. Creatively, it rose to prominence with a series of outdoor campaigns for McDonald's restaurants developed for the province of Quebec, a predominantly Francophone market with an Anglophone minority. In one campaign announcing the launch of a new menu item, CCM turned the trademark golden arches on their side and used them in place of the letters "z" in the word "Pizza!" The result, rendered in McDonald's signature red and yellow, was a one-word logo that linked the product with the brand in both languages. For the first time, the restaurant chain had allowed its trademark to be used in a playful manner; thereafter, it carried the "Pizza!" graphic into other countries and relaxed its rules governing use of the arches logo. For CCM the campaign established its ability to work across cultural barriers. Its McDonald's billboards have collected several Canadian and international prizes, including an Obie Award in New York City (1988) and a gold Lion at the Cannes International Advertising Festival (1992).

The agency had its roots in a Quebec City graphic design studio founded by Jean-Claude Cossette in 1962. Cossette offered his creative services to a regionally based Francophone market, and the business remained modest. Growth and agency status were contemplated with the adoption of advertising counsel in 1969, and Jacques Genest was recruited from MacLaren Advertising in Montreal, Quebec, to manage its transformation. Three years later the core of the present business took shape when five employees led by Claude Lessard bought out Genest and reorganized the still struggling firm as Cossette Communication-Marketing.

Since 1972 CCM has diversified its client services and branched out across Canada. To do so, it established seven affiliated companies to house its specialty services: Blitz, promotions and direct marketing (founded 1979); Optimum Public Relations (1980); Graphème, graphic design (1981); Impact Research, consumer research (1987); Geyser Création, branding (1989); Optimum

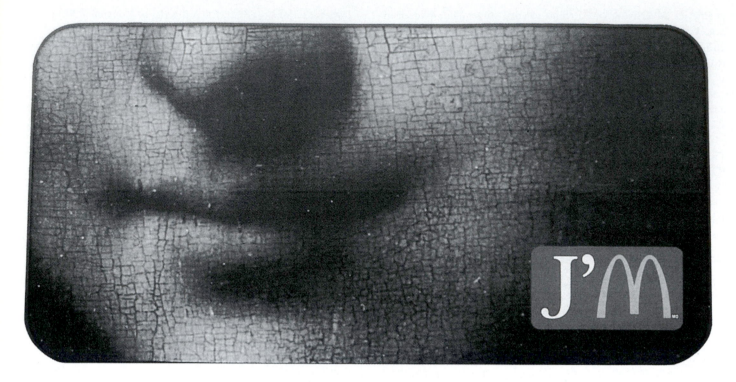

Cosette's "I Love (McDonald's)," an outdoor ad from 1988, was the first Canadian ad to win "Best of Show" at the Obie Awards. *Courtesy of McDonald's Corporation.*

Fusion, sponsorship (1993); and Cossette Interactive, new media (1995). Each was expected to operate and compete as an expert shop in its own field.

In 1999 about 40 percent of CCM's revenues came from these divisions; the remainder came from traditional advertising. In step with this expanding repertoire of services, CCM also expanded geographically. Quebec City was a provincial capital but distant from the country's major commercial centers. To better compete for national accounts, CCM opened branches in Montreal (1974); Toronto, Ontario (1981); Vancouver, British Columbia (1985); and Halifax, Nova Scotia (1999). It also expanded into the United States with the opening of Optimum Washington, in Washington, D.C., in 1997. To protect its corporate culture, CCM has usually developed its new ventures from scratch. There have been two exceptions: Kenmuir Brickendon Jones, Vancouver, formed the basis of Cossette Vancouver, and Pulse Marketing in Halifax became Cossette Atlantic.

The CCM brand was controlled by a limited partnership group, organized as a holding company named Groupe Cossette Communication, Inc. Although it began with the original six founders, the group included ten partners by 1999. By that time, the agency was the largest in Canada and stood among the top 40 in North America. Courted by global ad groups, the partnership chose to remain independent and expand internationally itself. It went public in June 1999 to raise capital to finance these goals. The partnership group maintained control through the issuance of multiple voting shares in conjunction with its initial public offering.

Jean-Claude Cossette opened his graphic design studio immediately after college, armed with a diploma in advertising art from L'École des beaux arts de Québec and in marketing from l'Université Laval in Quebec. However, he never left academia. He continued to pursue higher degrees in Canada and France, culminating in a Ph.D. in administration from Laval in 1975. By that time, he was teaching at Laval full-time and had ceased active participation in the business. When it was reorganized in 1972, he was asked to remain as "founding president" to provide it with some needed credibility; the five partners led by Lessard had an average age of 26. Cossette's association with CCM ended in 1982. As an academic, he published research on advertising and communication, including *La Publicité en action* (1987) and *L'Évolution des styles en communication visuelle* (1997).

Claude Lessard became chief executive officer in 1972. He was 23 years old, a graduate of Laval's business administration program with only one year of work experience—at Cossette's studio. The agency blossomed under his direction. Two important aspects of his administration stood out: his attention to organizational culture and to organizational structure. First, the firm's development into an agency was shaped by his desire that it retain the design studio's creative spark and informal culture. He also pushed his staff to think in terms of communication strategies rather than advertising campaigns per se. In practice, this meant that CCM constantly looked beyond traditional advertising to consider promotions and new media opportunities for all of its clients. Second, Lessard insisted that each new branch office nurture a regional flavor to ensure that it was sensitive to variations in local cultures. Each of the branch offices was relatively autonomous and competed for clients on its own merits.

CCM's origins were rooted in a period of dramatic social change in Canada. In 1960 the country's advertising trade was based in Anglophone Toronto. Francophone employees in agencies held few executive positions and wielded little influence, despite the fact that 28 percent of the Canadian market and 81 percent of Quebec spoke French. National campaigns were developed in the English language, then translated into French with little revision. Cultural differences were rarely addressed, and the persuasive power of this French-language advertising was severely compromised. The situation changed during the 1960s as French speakers won greater cultural and political authority within Quebec through a broad-based social movement known as the "Quiet Revolution." The movement's intensity prompted Anglophone businesses to develop original campaigns in French.

Cossette did not benefit directly from this new investment in the trade, but Lessard did. The design studio remained modest while Cossette pursued an academic career. When Lessard took control in 1972, it was facing bankruptcy. Only then did it draw upon its cultural capital to compete against English-language agencies. Its early clients were mainly concerns in Quebec appealing to the Francophone market, which included Assurances-vie Desjardins; the grocery chain Provigo, Inc.; and the provincial government. However, it also did French-language creative work for English-language agencies (notably Scali McCabe Sloves in Toronto), and an early creative success came with its own campaign for Automobiles Renault Canada in 1976. CCM drafted the slogan, *"J'ai attrapé le schnac"* (literally translated, "I caught the schnac")—a nonsense expression that managed to evoke the sensation of driving a Renault. The ads struck a deep chord with Francophone consumers, and Renault quickly became the top-selling car in the Quebec market.

The McDonald's account provided a model for CCM's handling of other accounts. In 1977 McDonald's gave CCM its work for one Francophone region of Quebec. Following a series of successful campaigns, the agency's responsibilities were widened to include all of French Quebec, and then English Quebec, until finally it won the entire national account in 1991. (Its first national campaign centered around a premium, a set of 31 hockey cards that could be collected in packs of four. As with the "Pizza!" campaign, the agency found a way to bridge the two language groups.) Lessard's strategy was to win a small portion of a client's total business—either through a CCM branch or a division—and then win the rest of the national account with a hands-on demonstration of its expertise. The pattern was repeated with clients such as Bell Canada, General Motors, and Coca-Cola, although it has had less success with Molson Breweries and Air Canada. Its future challenge will be to expand successfully beyond these accounts and beyond Canada's borders.

RUSSELL JOHNSTON

Further Reading

Bailey, Geoffrey, "The Little Agency," *Financial Post Magazine* (1 March 1983)

Daw, Lesley, "Canada's Agency," *Marketing Magazine* (30 November 1998)

Elkin, Frederick, *Rebels and Colleagues: Advertising and Social Change in French Canada,* Montreal: McGill-Queen's University Press, 1973

Foster, Cecil, "Once Ignored Agency," *Globe and Mail* (17 February 1984)

McLaughlin, Gord, "Arrogant But Good," *Financial Post Magazine* (December 1991)

Coupon

A coupon is a form contained in a printed advertisement, typically bordered by a dotted line indicating where the form is to be cut by the consumer. Once redeemed by the consumer, the coupon is eventually returned to the advertiser. Advertisers use two types of coupons. One type is a printed inquiry or order form to be completed by the customer with name, address, and other information; the customer then returns it to the advertiser either to request more product information or to order the product directly. The other, more common type is a certificate promising a discount, refund, free sample, or a combination offer, such as "buy-one-get-one free." Commonly called "cents-off" coupons, these entice retail customers to go to the store to make a purchase.

Cents-off coupons are a widely used and effective form of sales promotion for all types of advertisers. Marketers use coupons to achieve many promotional objectives, for example, to introduce consumers to new products or to encourage shoppers to try existing products or switch from one to another. Coupons can provide a price discount to customers who are price sensitive while not cutting the price for all customers. Unlike permanent price cuts, coupons offer customers temporary price reductions while allowing the brand to return to full price after the expiration date on the coupon.

Coupons may originate with either manufacturers or retailers. Manufacturer's coupons may be redeemed at face value by customers at any retail store carrying the brand. The retailer then returns the coupon to the manufacturer for reimbursement plus a small handling fee. Retailer-originated coupons are good for discounts on products carried by that retailer and redeemable only at that retailer's store. Supermarket grocery items account for the majority of redeemed coupons. Fast-food restaurants also use coupons as part of their promotional efforts, as do such service retailers as dry cleaners and beauty salons.

Cents-off coupons have several basic components: the offer, redemption instructions, the product's description, any restrictions, and an expiration date. The most important feature—the offer—is the part of the coupon that communicates the discount. The better the offer, the more likely that consumers will use the coupon. Although they are called cents-off coupons, the face value may be as much as one dollar or more, depending on the total price of the product. A coupon offer is not limited to a dollar amount; it may also be for a percentage off the total price of the product. Research has shown, however, that dollar-amount savings tend to be more attractive to coupon users than percentage discounts. The simplest offers with the least number of restrictions seem to work best. The expiration date is an important part of the coupon. A long expiration date may allow more customers to take advantage of the offer. A short expiration date, however, will create a sense of urgency, possibly enticing customers to take advantage of the coupon offer quickly, thus reducing the chance of the coupon being lost or forgotten.

Coupons are distributed through a variety of media. The most common distribution method for manufacturer-originated coupons for grocery store brands is freestanding newspaper inserts (FSIs). FSIs are color advertising supplements that often appear inserted inside newspapers. Fast-food restaurants and retailers frequently use direct mail to distribute their coupons to customers living near their stores. Other distribution channels include run-of-press newspapers (as opposed to preprinted flyers and inserts), magazines, product packages, and in-store distribution. In the late 1990s distribution of coupons electronically at store kiosks and over the Internet was proving an innovative and effective means of reaching customers.

Although coupons did not become widely used until the second half of the 20th century, the first coupons are thought to have been distributed by the C.W. Post Company for Grape Nuts cereal more than 100 years ago. Along with the expansion of mass discount retailing, the number of coupons being issued in the United States quadrupled during the 1970s. Coupon distribution continued to grow through the 1980s, though at a slower rate, peaking in 1992 at 310 billion and then dropping to 268 billion in the mid-1990s. In the year 2000, according to industry estimates,

some 300 billion manufacturer-originated grocery product coupons were distributed in the United States. This number does not include the millions of coupons distributed by restaurants and retailers. While only 27 percent of U.S. consumers say they use coupons each time they go shopping, in the late 1990s more than 80 percent reported using them at some time, compared to only 58 percent in the early 1970s.

While the number of coupons distributed and the number of U.S. residents using them have increased, redemption rates—that is, the number of coupons that consumers actually redeem as a percentage of the total distributed—have fallen. In 1978 the rate was about 5 percent; by 1995 only about 2 percent of coupons distributed were redeemed by customers. The 2 percent level is now considered a "good" redemption rate for most coupon programs, though redemption rates will vary, depending on the distribution method used, the coupon offer, and the time allowed for redemption.

The decline in redemption rates has persuaded some that coupons are losing their effectiveness as promotional tools. Many marketers have reduced the number of coupons they distribute each year, and others are looking for new ways to distribute them. Procter & Gamble chose to eliminate couponing in some test markets in 1996, though it later resumed coupon activities due to consumer demand.

Despite the declines in coupon redemption and distribution, there is little doubt that couponing will continue to be a widely used sales promotion tool for many advertisers. As long as consumers continue to clip the little slips of paper and redeem them for discounts on their favorite products, advertisers will continue distributing coupons.

JAMI J. ARMSTRONG FULLERTON

See also color plate in this volume

Further Reading

Blattberg, Robert C., and Scott A. Neslin, *Sales Promotion: Concepts, Methods, and Strategies,* Englewood Cliffs, New Jersey: Prentice Hall, 1990

Connor, John M., "Couponing as a Horizontal and Vertical Strategy: Theory and Effects," St. Paul: Retail Food Industry Center, University of Minnesota, 1997

Schultz, Don E., and William A. Robinson, *Sales Promotion Essentials,* Lincolnwood, Illinois: NTC Business Books, 1982; 3rd edition, by Schultz, Robinson, and Lisa A. Petrison, 1998

"Targeted Couponing Slows Redemption Slide," *Marketing News* (12 February 1996)

Crain, G.D., Jr. 1885–1973

U.S. Trade Publishing Executive

G.D. (Gustavus Dedman) Crain, Jr., was a major force in the world of business publishing for more than 50 years. He is best remembered for founding *Advertising Age* and developing Advertising Publications, Inc.—now called Crain Communications, Inc.—which published about 30 business and consumer titles in 2001.

Crain, who was born in Lawrenceburg, Kentucky, in 1885, had his first brush with journalism as a schoolboy, when he sold copies of the *Louisville Times.* "Money was a very scarce commodity in our family in those days," Crain recalled in *I Always Wanted to Be a Publisher,* a memoir of his career. He continued:

> Knowing copies of the afternoon papers could be purchased by newsboys for one cent and resold for two cents, I started my business career with a capital of five cents supplied by my mother. I purchased five copies [of the *Times*] at their offices and returned home a couple of hours later with a 100 percent increase in capital. I continued this for several weeks and finally found myself with about 25 regular purchasers . . . plus a number of others who were buying copies occasionally.

This entrepreneurial bent was a preview of things to come for Crain. After graduating from Centre College in Danville, Kentucky (he received both bachelor's and master's degrees in just three years), he became a reporter for the *Louisville Herald.* To supplement his income, he was also a correspondent for several trade publications. This led to his leaving the *Herald* and setting up an editorial service that supplied news and features to about 100 business publications in a variety of fields, including banking, insurance, and lumber.

But he had a desire to run his own publications, and in 1916 he founded not one but two trade magazines. Capitalizing on the boom in hospital construction, he introduced his first magazine, *Hospital Management,* in February of that year. In a publisher's letter, Crain wrote that the publication "will be devoted principally to the administration and executive departments of hospital work and will endeavor to be of practical value to the men and women in charge of the hospitals of the country."

Although the issue got good response from readers, advertisers were slow to respond. In part to help spur advertising in *Hospital Management,* the young publisher started another magazine, *Class,* in March. Also a monthly, this digest-sized publication targeted manufacturers and advertising agencies that were large users of the specialized business press. *Class* was so named because in that era, business publications fell into three general categories: retail; industrial—publications covering specific industries, such as railroads, steel, and construction; and "class" publications—periodicals aimed at classes of people who had the same general professional functions, regardless of the type of business or industry in which they were employed.

Advertisers, Crain said, "needed to be informed as to how to create effective advertising. We stressed the importance of market research. We encouraged publishers to feature market information in their advertisements and to offer information that would give advertisers a better knowledge of fields they were serving." In 1922 Crain was one of the founders of the National Industrial Advertisers Association, which is now called the Business Marketing Association.

Both of Crain's titles thrived during the Roaring Twenties—so much so that in 1929 Crain decided to launch a weekly publication covering the world of advertising and marketing. Despite the stock market crash in October, he launched the new venture, *Advertising Age,* in January 1930. "There was no indication at the time that a business depression of long duration was in prospect," Crain later wrote. But the bad times had indeed arrived, and he went from owning two profitable publications to overseeing three that soon were hemorrhaging money. However, Crain had a bookkeeper who negotiated payments with his suppliers, and he was getting good reviews from readers and advertisers, who said they would advertise in *Advertising Age* when times got better—and they did.

G.D. Crain, Jr.
Courtesy of Crain Communications, Inc.

The 1930s were tough, but so was Crain. With a still-small staff, he managed to keep all three publications afloat, although *Class,* by then renamed *Industrial Marketing,* was folded into *Advertising Age* for two years before reemerging as a free-standing title in 1935. However, better days were ahead for Crain, both professionally and personally. In the waning days of the Depression, his publications regained their health.

In 1936 the widowed publisher married Gertrude Ramsay, who would herself eventually become a powerful force in the business publishing world, as would their two sons, Rance and Keith, who later ran the company.

Advertising Age grew and strengthened throughout the late 1930s, the 1940s, and the postwar years, eventually supplanting longtime category leader *Printers' Ink,* which ceased publication in 1972 as the renamed *Marketing/Communications.* And although the company eventually shed *Hospital Management,* it was definitely in a growth mode, adding to its stable during Crain's watch *Business Insurance* in 1967, *Automotive News* (purchased from the Slocum family) in 1971, and *Pensions & Investments* in 1973. (*Business Insurance* was an idea he had 50 years earlier, when he ran his news service in Louisville.)

Crain died on 15 December 1973 at the age of 88, and his wife, Gertrude, succeeded him as chairman of Crain the following January. He was posthumously inducted into the American Advertising Federation's Advertising Hall of Fame in 1975. Ger-trude Crain was accorded the same honor in 1997, one year after her death. They were only the second husband and wife team to be inducted; the first were Stanley and Helen Resor of J. Walter Thompson Company.

At the outset of the 21st century, the company G.D. Crain founded had publications in the advertising, automotive, health care, insurance, pension, and wireless and electronic media fields and also published weekly business journals in New York City; Chicago, Illinois; Detroit, Michigan; and Cleveland, Ohio.

ROBERT GOLDSBOROUGH

Biography
Born in Lawrenceburg, Kentucky, on 18 November 1885; founded two trade publications to launch Crain Communications, Inc., 1916; introduced *Advertising Age,* 1930; died at age 88 on 15 December 1973; posthumously inducted into the American Advertising Federation's Advertising Hall of Fame, 1975.

Selected Publications
I Always Wanted to Be a Publisher, 1970

Further Reading
Goldsborough, Robert, *The Crain Adventure: The Making and Building of a Family Publishing Company,* Lincolnwood, Illinois: NTC Business Books, 1992

Cramer-Krasselt

Founded by Frederick Cramer and William Krasselt in Milwaukee, Wisconsin, 1898; purchased Hackenberg, Normann, Krivkovich and Alex T. Fritz, Inc., building strong base in Chicago, Illinois, 1980; became fifth-largest independent U.S. agency by 2000.

Major Clients
AirTran Airlines
Corona
Hyatt Hotels
Master Lock
Miller Brewing (High Life)
Mirro Aluminum
Wausau Insurance
Zenith Electronics Corporation

Cramer-Krasselt (C-K) has the distinction of being among the oldest continually operating advertising agencies in the United States, surpassed in longevity only by such enduring firms as the J. Walter Thompson Company and N.W. Ayer. That it continues to operate independently makes it unique among agencies of comparably modest size.

Frederick Cramer, born in 1878, was a typesetter by profession. William Krasselt, born in 1872, made his living selling cutlery to butcher shops. Both lived in the Milwaukee, Wisconsin, area and were members of the Badger Wheelman, a Wisconsin bicycling club. When the club decided to publish a house magazine, *The Wheelman,* the two men were asked to take on the job. They set up a company called the Pneumatic Press, and to finance the venture, the company decided to accept advertising. Soon both Cramer and Krasselt discovered that there was more profit in handling the magazine's advertising than they could earn in their regular jobs. With capital of $3,000, the Pneumatic Press became the Cramer-Krasselt Company, and in 1898 it opened its office on Grand Avenue in Milwaukee.

The company's printing origins served it well. In an early example of vertical integration, the company not only created its clients' ads but also printed them. Its printing activities included everything from simple fliers and newsletters to billboards and catalogs. Its printing operations would continue for 70 years. Early clients included local businesses that were heavily weighted toward the dairy and beer industries, as well as the emerging automobile business, which was still very much a cottage industry. C-K represented the Kessel Motor Company ("The car that stands up"), Miller High Life and Pabst beers, and Maytag washers. As early as 1909 C-K ads for Miller contained the celebrated tag line, "The champagne of bottle beer." Office hours at the agency were from 8 A.M. to 6 P.M. six days a week, which was typical for office workers in those days. The agency regarded itself as "progressive" when it closed at noon on Saturday during the summer. By 1910 C-K had 50 employees. Ten years later it claimed annual "sales" of $500,000, though its formulas for compensation were vague, making it difficult to translate such numbers into gross revenues. Growth was substantial enough, however, for the agency to open new offices in Detroit, Michigan; Los Angeles, California; and New York City. When C-K required larger quarters in downtown Milwaukee in 1927, it moved into two floors of the Graphic Arts Building at 733 North Van Buren.

During the Great Depression, the company's printing business helped compensate for lost ad revenues and was a major element of its survival. However, financial pressures still forced the agency's retreat from Detroit, Los Angeles, and New York City, and in 1937 it reported the first unprofitable year in its history. When Cramer died in 1934 and Krasselt in 1940, A. Walter Seiler, who had joined C-K in 1907 as a stenographer, took over the company. After World War II, C-K grew to be the largest agency in Milwaukee, though it was still a regional shop by national standards, with such clients as Milwaukee Gas Light, Wisconsin Telephone, and First Wisconsin National Bank. Mirro Aluminum and Evenrude were among the national brands C-K handled. By the mid-1950s reliable estimates put the agency's billing at $6 million. By the end of the decade, billings had grown to just over $10 million—only 10 percent of which was in the booming medium of television, however.

Growth continued at an unimpressive but steady pace through the 1960s, during which time C-K veterans William Faude, and later Robert Christiansen and Ted Wing, managed the agency. Its creative prestige began to grow through various awards. But by 1970 billings still were only about $15 million, limited by the huge competition for major accounts 90 miles south in Chicago, Illinois.

To break this barrier, C-K established a presence in Chicago in 1980 with the purchase of two agencies, Hackenberg, Normann, Krivkovich, founded in 1973 by two former account executives (Richard Hackenberg and Rolf Normann) from the Chicago office of Young & Rubicam, and Alex T. Franz, Inc. Another C-K office was opened in Phoenix, Arizona, and soon grew to become among the largest agencies in the southwestern United States. Wausau Insurance and Master Lock became platforms for some of the agency's best creative work, which further enhanced its reputation.

Moving against an industry trend toward consolidation and merger in the 1980s, the agency sought to position itself as a strong midsize agency able to serve mid-level advertisers. It built up its capacities in direct marketing (1981), research (1986), public relations (1987), and strategic planning (1996). By the late 1980s C-K claimed it was "master of the $2 million account"— the middle market. On that basis it successfully expanded into

A 1983 ad from Cramer-Krasselt emphasized the durability of handmade Allen-Edmonds shoes.
Courtesy of Allen-Edmonds Shoe Corp.

Orlando, Florida, in 1990. By 2000 C-K's midsize strategy had made it the 38th-largest agency and the fifth-largest independent U.S. shop. Billings for the first eight months of 2000, according to *Advertising Age,* were $470 million. Much of that volume came from its largest clients, Corona, AirTran Airlines, Hyatt Hotels, Kemper Insurance, and Zenith Electronics. The agency planned to extend its growth strategy to international markets between 2000 and 2005, seeking accounts in the $10 million–$20 million range. C-K continued to operate jointly out of offices in Milwaukee and Chicago, although Chicago accounted for about half the agency's billings in 2000.

JAMES V. POKRYWCZYNSKI AND JOHN MCDONOUGH

Further Reading

Bosch, Barbara, and Joseph Cahill, "Cramer-Krasselt Takes Middle Path," *Advertising Age* (1 January 1996)

Chura, Hillary, and Kate MacArthur, "Cramer-Krasselt Thinks Small," *Advertising Age* (11 September 2000)

The Cramer-Krasselt Story, Milwaukee, Wisconsin: Cramer-Krasselt, 1998

Hajewski, Doris, "A Century of Ads," *Milwaukee Journal Sentinel* (20 September 1998)

Crest

Principal Agency
Benton & Bowles, Inc. (later D'Arcy Masius Benton & Bowles)

Crest toothpaste debuted in test markets across the United States in 1955, boasting the active ingredient Fluoristan, a Procter & Gamble Company (P&G) trade name for a combination of stannous fluoride and a fluoride-compatible polishing agent. Fluoride was the latest hope in a series of unrealized experiments and panaceas in the dentifrice market of the 1950s, joining chlorophyll, ammoniation, and anti-enzymes. Three researchers at Indiana University patented a stannous fluoride compound, and P&G became the exclusive licensee of the resulting product. P&G underwrote the major share of the studies conducted on the product.

In January 1956 P&G introduced Crest nationally. Benton and Bowles, Crest's first and only agency, opened the campaign with spreads in *Life* and the *Saturday Evening Post* proclaiming "a new era in preventive dental care" and outlining "milestones in modern medicine," the latest being Crest's "triumph over tooth decay." The ad also described how the fluoride toothpaste "strengthens tooth enamel to knock out decay from within." The American Dental Association (ADA) greeted Crest's bold claims with scientific skepticism, stating that it was "not aware of evidence adequate to demonstrate the claimed dental caries prophylactic value of Crest" and that further clinical tests needed to be evaluated.

Crest was launched in the shadow of another P&G toothpaste, Gleem, which was introduced to challenge Colgate Dental Cream. Both Crest and Gleem attempted to knock Colgate out of its position as market share leader.

In 1958 Benton and Bowles broke what would become Crest's most memorable ad campaign: Norman Rockwell artwork depicted gleeful, smiling children showing off their flawless teeth and holding check-up cards from the dentist. The copy beneath them read, "Look, Mom—no cavities!" P&G spent more than $1.6 million advertising Crest that year, helping the toothpaste

succeed where other fluoride products had failed; however, it remained a distant No. 3 in market share, trailing Colgate and Gleem.

ADA Council on Dental Therapeutics continued to balk at toothpaste advertising in general and fluorides in particular. At a congressional hearing in July 1958 the assistant secretary of the ADA council on dental therapeutics said the Crest headline "Look, Mom—no cavities!" was "at best both a gross exaggeration and a misleading distortion."

That changed in 1960, a watershed year for Crest. In the 1 August 1960 issue of the *Journal of the American Dental Association,* the ADA recognized Crest as "an effective decay preventive agent." It was the first and only toothpaste at that time to receive any therapeutic acclaim from the ADA. The change of heart was not without its outspoken critics among dentists, who felt the ADA had no business endorsing a particular brand. In effect this announcement gave legitimacy to a product in a field with a history of unsubstantiated claims. Advertising could now simply cite the ADA's statement that Crest prevents cavities.

Furthermore, the ADA's endorsement extended only to the stannous fluoride used in Crest. The magnitude of this endorsement was certainly felt by competitors, and some viewed it as the biggest thing to happen in toothpaste marketing since the chlorophylls of the early 1950s. It would turn out to be much larger than that. Crest had only a 12 percent market share at the time, compared with Colgate's 35 percent share and Gleem's 20 percent. Propelled by the news, P&G's stock jumped sharply, and Crest unit sales jumped 3 percent in September 1960. By August 1961 Crest held an estimated 25 percent of the market, twice that of a year earlier, while Colgate had slipped to 28 percent.

Crest's advertising strategy nonetheless showed remarkable restraint. Clearly the company decided that this was a perfect opportunity to separate Crest from the irresponsible claims that marked the history of dentifrice marketing up to that point and position the brand as a modest but proven ally in the struggle for better teeth. Print ads stressed that Crest should be used as part of an overall dental program. One ad read, "Crest made news because it's effective against cavities—not because it's a cure-all." In the aftermath of the ADA announcement, when many stores reported increased Crest sales, ads claimed, "Your dealer may be temporarily out of stock in your favorite size. Because the benefits of Crest are so important, we hope you'll take another size until we catch up." A television commercial titled "Family Classics" showed an announcer interviewing children and young adults who had taken part in test groups using Crest. The ad concluded by claiming that those who used Crest had "25 percent to 49 percent fewer cavities" and restated the ADA's endorsement. P&G also placed ads in the *Journal of the American Dental Association* encouraging dentists to recommend Crest to their patients. It seems likely that Crest benefited in the long run by not overtly exploiting the ADA's endorsement.

In addition to traditional advertising methods and media, in 1963 P&G began sponsoring Crest Dental Health Month in first-grade classrooms across the United States. Teachers instructed students on the basics of brushing and flossing and introduced them to cartoon characters that illustrated dental health lessons. Many children remembered the program because they were given tiny discs to chew that turned their mouths red, highlighting plaque. Through the years the program continued, introducing Crest and dental care to children; in 1999 it was augmented with a Web site featuring an interactive environment called Sparkle City, after Sparkle Crest bubble gum–flavored toothpaste for children.

By 1964 Crest held a sizable lead in market share, at more than 30 percent, compared with Colgate's 25 percent. P&G made Crest an advertising priority. *Advertising Age* estimated ad spending at $12 million through Benton & Bowles that year, compared to $1.5 million in 1960. Crest received the most ad spending of any P&G product, a distinction it would retain until 1980.

After holding almost 40 percent of the market throughout the 1970s, Crest's position began to erode in the early 1980s because of the introduction of new brands such as Beecham Group's Aquafresh. In 1981 a "toothpaste war" erupted among Crest, Colgate, and Aquafresh. P&G increased spending almost 60 percent that year, putting about $45 million behind a campaign attacking those "fancy stripes and gels." P&G launched Advanced Formula Crest, which was based on sodium fluoride instead of the stannous fluoride of regular Crest. Crest advertising claimed the new formula was better tasting and twice as effective as the original. It again received the ADA's seal of approval.

After shoring up Crest's share of the market in the early 1980s, P&G still felt it necessary to develop and market new formulas. By 1985 Crest's market share dipped below 30 percent and became almost deadlocked with that of rival Colgate. The launch of Crest Tartar Control formula, backed with an estimated $50 million in ad spending through D'Arcy Masius Benton & Bowles (Benton & Bowles merged with D'Arcy-MacManus, Masius in 1985) returned Crest to a dominant market share of 40 percent. The advertising effort stayed true to Crest's strategy of professional endorsement and positioned Tartar Control Crest as the "dentist's choice."

In 1997 Colgate's Total bumped Crest out of the lead by less than one percentage point in the $1.7 billion toothpaste market. Crest had been the market leader for more than three decades. Advertising that year shifted away from the clinical "dentist approved" positioning to a more emotional approach with ads featuring the tag line, "Behind that healthy smile, there's a Crest kid."

The focus on the benefits of toothpaste continued in the late 1990s. Whitening formulas, mixtures of baking soda and peroxide, and breath-freshening ingredients were incorporated into new products that outsold the older formulas. The Crest ad campaign in 2000 featured the tag line "Open up and smile" and positioned the product as being for "real people with genuine smiles." Crest spent most heavily on its baking soda-and-peroxide whitening formula in 1999, with media expenditures of more than $20 million. P&G spent more than $90 million advertising all Crest toothpastes and toothbrushes that year.

MARK SCHUMANN

See also color plate in this volume

Further Reading

Procter & Gamble: The House that Ivory Built, by the editors of *Advertising Age,* Lincolnwood, Illinois: NTC Business Books, 1988
Swasy, Alecia, *Soap Opera: The Inside Story of Procter & Gamble,* New York: Times Books, 1993

Critics of Advertising

A comprehensive study of the social character of consumer goods advertising in the United States concluded, "It is difficult to think of another contemporary institution that has come under attack from so many different angles." The forms of most of these criticisms admit of no straightforward resolution. Nevertheless, the very miscellany of critical perspectives begs the question of why advertising as an institution has borne the brunt of so much antagonistic commentary.

Criticism of advertising has tended to focus on either its economic or its social functions and effects. Social critics of advertising have generally tended to focus not on price advertising or promotions but on national advertising for consumer goods and corporate brand-building efforts. Conversely, economists and critics of the economic efficacy of advertising have tended to be biased in the other direction. In *Images Incorporated: Advertising as Industry and Ideology* (1987), John Sinclair remarked, "Advertising which is economically significant may hold little ideological significance, and vice versa."

By and large, economically minded observers have been more favorably inclined toward the industry. Advertising, so the argument goes, provides consumers with information about goods in a market where reliable knowledge would otherwise be difficult to obtain. By communicating the virtues of products beyond the immediate context of their production, advertising helps to expand markets, theoretically lowering prices and creating more jobs in an ever-expanding economy. Critics of this position have argued that advertising—particularly advertising that is not overtly informative or price-oriented—cannot consistently be shown to be an effective way of increasing sales. Insofar as it may be a wasteful and inefficient business expenditure, advertising also adds to the purchase price of consumer goods. Whereas defenders of advertising argue that it allows up-and-coming entrepreneurs to make consumers aware of new products, critics point to the steep escalation in advertising costs as a significant barrier for smaller companies.

Although debates about the economic effects of advertising generally have been confined to relatively restricted concerns, critics of the social implications of the industry have blamed advertising for just about every conceivable evil of modern life. Nevertheless, certain key patterns have emerged across the political spectrum of complaint. Social critics have usually concurred with economic analysts of the industry in connecting the rise of advertising with the arrival of the "monopoly" stage of capitalism, which in the United States may be placed at about the turn of the 20th century.

The increased dominance of a handful of large corporate consumer-goods producers, together with the expansion of national markets made possible by innovations in distribution and communications, resulted in new economies of scale, which in turn led to the persistent threat of overproduction and market saturation. In this context, advertising was one of the central tools through which manufacturers attempted to keep consumer demand in step with production. The manner in which this persuasion was undertaken—indeed, the very fact that it needed to be undertaken at all—forms a key complaint in the social criticism of the industry.

Consumption of mass-produced goods came to be viewed as one of the crucial drivers of economic growth. Conversely, the social upheavals that accompanied industrialization and urbanization made reliance on manufactured goods—and, by extension, the advertising images that were created for them—a basic fact of life for an increasing proportion of the population. Finally, social criticism of advertising cannot be detached from the intimate relationship (particularly in the United States) between advertising revenues and the growth of the new mass media. If, as many theorists have argued, the mass media provide the basis of a sense of national community in modern societies, then their reliance on advertising places that industry at the core of how contemporary social life is imagined. On the one hand, it is argued, the advertising industry is systemically crucial to the reproduction of contemporary consumer societies. On the other, the messages that it produces carry specific—often undesirable—ideological overtones. In his 1994 book *Culture and the Ad* William O'Barr wrote: "In encouraging all manner of consumption, advertising helps support an economy of mass production. . . . Were we to minimize consumption, the fundamental nature of our social order would be challenged. Thus, advertising conveys ideas that are political and system maintaining."

One may—at a minimum—distinguish between "liberal" and "radical" strains in the social criticism of advertising. The former have generally focused on the cultural and psychological effects of the rise of consumerism and the prominence of advertising images that accompany it. Many deplore what they see as an increasing shift in advertising from an "informational" function to a "persuasive" function, arguing that much contemporary advertising propagates a hypocritical double message about modern life. On the one hand, we are told that the consumption of mass-produced consumer goods can assuage basic human problems and insecurities—for example, wear Tommy Hilfiger jeans and be admired. On the other, we are constantly reminded that no amount of consumption is enough; the emotional or psychological gratification to be had in consumption is at best fleeting and evanescent.

As Richard Pollay noted in a 1986 article in the *Journal of Marketing*, thinkers as diverse as Daniel Boorstin, Daniel Bell, Marshall McLuhan, Margaret Mead, and Erich Fromm have raised serious questions about the social consequences of advertising, particularly insofar as it may reinforce "materialism, cynicism, irrationality, selfishness, anxiety, social competitiveness, sexual preoccupation, powerlessness, and/or a loss of self-respect." Others suggest that advertising helps perpetuate sexist and racist attitudes. As O'Barr pointed out, a striking proportion of advertising images revolve around themes of domination and/or subordination and, by extension, the empowerment promised through the possession of the advertised product. Erving Goffman's classic study *Gender Advertisements* (1979) meticulously demonstrates the manner in which advertising imagery "hyper-ritualizes" stereotypical and hierarchical gender relations, a theme that O'Barr extended to the depiction of ethnic groups.

Literary voices such as those of British literary critics F.R. and Q.D. Leavis have mourned what they perceive as the rise of a banal and alienated popular culture, propagated through advertising as well as its effect on mass media content, whereas religious groups and social conservatives have attacked advertising for contributing to the decline of collective morality through its sexually exploitative imagery, thereby sometimes finding themselves in an unlikely ad hoc alliance with feminist voices from the left. Others, such as those inspired by "Frankfurt School" social theorists Theodor Adorno and Max Horkheimer (1973), have combined a broadly Marxist critical framework with a discussion of the close relationship between totalitarian politics and the homogenizing tendencies of mass markets. From this perspective, product differentiation merely hides a more fundamental standardizing mechanism. According to Adorno and Horkheimer, "Something is provided for all so that none may escape; the distinctions are emphasized and extended.

Adbusters Media Foundation's spoof ads seek to foster a critical perspective on advertising among consumers. *Image courtesy of www.adbusters.org.*

The public is catered for with a hierarchical range of mass-produced products of varying quality, thus advancing the rule of complete quantification." A "liberal" vision of this cultural dystopia, specifically concerned with the use of "motivational" psychological research techniques in advertising and marketing, was popularized by the success of Vance Packard's *The Hidden Persuaders* (1958), a title suggestive of a national capitalist conspiracy in a decade dominated by fears of a communist conspiracy.

Many liberal critics of advertising suggest that its evils may be tempered by regulations such as guidelines for the acceptable ratio of informational to persuasive content, controls on advertising to children, bans on the use of certain kinds of stereotypical images—particularly those relating to women and ethnic minorities—and restrictions on advertising for certain controversial or addictive product groups such as tobacco and alcohol. Conversely, radical critics of advertising, particularly Marxist commentators, have rejected such initiatives as superficial, calling instead for a critical reevaluation of the political economy, particularly the concentration of ownership underlying consumer goods production and advertising. In addition, Marxist theorists attack the centrality in modern consumer societies of what Karl Marx termed the "commodity fetish"—how the appearance and distribution of goods in industrial societies serves to concentrate people's attention on the relations among inert objects rather than on the living relations among human beings. This fraudulent prioritization of objects, leading to what Marx termed "reification," has a double ideological effect. First, it serves to obscure the manner in which exploitative social relations of power are maintained, and, second, it encourages individuals to think of themselves and others as little more than commodities.

Although the modern advertising industry was only beginning to evolve at the time of Marx's death, Marxist analysts have viewed advertising as one of the main devices through which energies that might otherwise be used for social transformation are diverted into narcissistic self-absorption. Whereas cruder versions of this thesis characterize advertising as a weapon in the hands of a conspiring elite, more sophisticated readings see its operation as far more diffuse and subtle, although no less corrupting.

Although the questionable ethics of encouraging conspicuous consumption in a social context in which millions struggle to subsist has been a standard feature of leftist attacks on advertising, both Marxist and liberal commentators have struggled with the question of whether advertising imposes false wants or desires on consumers. Countercultural as well as popular critiques of advertising in the 1960s and 1970s drew heavily on the kinds of consumer-manipulation models that writers such as Packard had helped to establish, a trend that found its most extreme expression in the largely unsubstantiated claims about subliminal advertising made in the works of Wilson Bryan Key.

In a more sober vein, John Kenneth Galbraith's highly influential *The Affluent Society* (1958) came to the conclusion that the very existence of such a large industry dedicated to consumer persuasion was incompatible with the stated marketing ideology of "consumer sovereignty," finding that the "central function" of the industry was to "create desires—to bring into being wants that previously did not exist." Advertising professionals have responded that such objections are mistaken on two counts. First, they counter, it is wrong to assume that goods have a single "natural" or "objective" value or meaning, and therefore that any one "true" want should necessarily correspond to a given object. For example, the legitimate significance of a coat is not simply to keep its wearer warm; it also forms part of a complex social language of fashion and style. Indeed, comparative anthropological evidence shows that objects and transacted goods in all kinds of societies take on any number of culturally specific meanings. Second, members of the industry argue, the very act of deeming the wants or needs of others as "false" or "excessive" is both arrogantly elitist and incompatible with the ethos of a democratic society. Indeed, the advertising industry often defends itself as a quasi-democratic populist mechanism, on the principles that "the consumer knows best" and that consumers "vote with their pocketbooks." With use of that analogy, advertising is—according to a much-used metaphor—only a "mirror of society."

While acknowledging the general validity of the first of these defenses, many critics have pointed to the disproportionate degree of public access that the meanings offered by advertising have in contemporary society, as well as to the consideration that these meanings have not evolved with regard to social interests, but instead to the interests of commerce. Most contemporary critics have abandoned the "brainwashing" model rejected in the second defense, but continue to emphasize the idea that if advertising is a mirror of consumers' preexisting needs, then it is a highly selective one. The populist claims of the industry must be weighed against the fact that the only needs relevant to the marketing and advertising complex are those that can viably be addressed in the form of consumer goods. Among this already restricted set of needs, moreover, those that are backed by higher levels of disposable income are granted a disproportionate amount of attention. Michael Schudson, a moderate critic of the industry, in 1984 questioned "the justice of focusing commercial development on the needs of consumers with the majority of dollars rather than on the needs of the majority of consumers."

In *Decoding Advertisements* (1978) Judith Williamson argued that advertising is not merely a selective mirror, it is a formative one. In an analysis that combined a generally Marxist perspective with structuralist semiotics and psychoanalytic theory, she suggested that the power of advertising rests in part precisely on the fact that it speaks to real human needs—loneliness, alienation, insecurity. Rather than imposing false or alien needs, advertising invites us to recognize the resolution of our preexisting needs (and therefore our own possible identities) in terms constrained by the imagery surrounding the lifestyles and product meanings in the ad: "Advertisements work by a process in which we are completely enmeshed . . . they invite us 'freely' to create ourselves in accordance with the way in which they have already created us."

A similar transformation in criticism has taken place in regard to the role of advertising for Western multi- or transnational corporations in the non-Western world. Much of the popular resistance to advertising in these contexts still revolves around two poles. First, critics point to the questionable ethics of advertising products to populations with a low level of media experience and not enough information to make properly informed decisions. An example of the tragedies that can result is the infamous mid-1970s case of Nestlé's marketing of baby formula to mothers in Africa, in which the company's ignorance of local conditions resulted in the deaths of a number of infants. To many observers at the time, the careless way in which the multinational company deployed its advertising seemed an example of the cultural indifference that often accompanied the expansion of Western companies across world markets. The combination of this type of multinational behavior with the seeming helplessness of many non-Western consumers formed the second pole of the critique: the specter of global cultural homogenization, also known as "cultural imperialism" or "coca-colonization."

The cultural imperialism thesis is in essence a politicized and globalized extension of the *Hidden Persuaders* thesis, and suffers from some of the same shortcomings. Particularly since the mid-1980s, as corporate structures have globalized to an unprecedented extent, it has become clear that marketing and advertising efforts for global brands employ a wide range of tactics, from total standardization to multi-local adaptation. Additionally, the experiences of "liberalized" consumer-goods markets, such as those of urban India, have demonstrated (to the detriment of several carefully crafted multinational marketing plans) that non-Western consumers are far from being mere pawns of Western commercial interests.

Again, many advertising professionals have pointed to such adaptations as proof that advertising performs its more-or-less passive mirroring function abroad just as it does at home. Critics such as John Sinclair, however, insist that although campaigns manifestly adapt their contents in deference to local cultural symbols, these adaptations must still be coordinated with nonlocal interests. Hence, a global system of "localities" is being produced in ways that are all the more restricted by their need to conform to global brand concepts. As Sinclair put it, "The transnationalization of the world proceeds not by making each nation conform to a universal, homogenized model, but by a very particular process of redefining each nation and its culture in commercial terms which are compatible with transnational interests."

The debate over advertising's manipulation of—or responsiveness to—consumers' needs has become so central to critical analysis that another theme that is perhaps more fundamental has often been obscured. This is the potentially alarming discrepancy between the enormous public prominence of advertising messages on the one hand and their lack of any coherently intelligible constructive social purpose on the other, beyond rather vague references to "improving the standard of living."

WILLIAM MAZZARELLA

See also Cultural Imperialism

Further Reading

Adorno, Theodor, and Max Horkheimer, "The Culture Industry: Enlightenment As Mass Deception," in *The Dialectic of Enlightenment*, by Adorno and Horkheimer, translated by John Cumming, New York: Seabury, 1972; London: Lane, 1973

Harris, Ralph, and Arthur Seldon, *Advertising and the Public*, London: Deutsch, 1962

Jhally, Sut, *The Codes of Advertising: Fetishism and the Political Economy of Meaning in the Consumer Society*, New York: St. Martin's Press, and London: Pinter, 1987

Nicosia, Francesco, editor, *Advertising, Management, and Society: A Business Point of View*, New York: McGraw-Hill, 1974

O'Barr, William, *Culture and the Ad: Exploring Otherness in the World of Advertising*, Boulder, Colorado: Westview, 1994

Pollay, Richard, "The Distorted Mirror: Reflections on the Unintended Consequences of Advertising," *Journal of Marketing* 50, no. 2 (April 1986)

Schudson, Michael, *Advertising, the Uneasy Persuasion: Its Dubious Impact on American Society*, New York: Basic Books, 1984; London: Routledge, 1993

Sinclair, John, *Images Incorporated: Advertising As Industry and Ideology*, New York and London: Croom Helm, 1987

Williamson, Judith, *Decoding Advertisements: Ideology and Meaning in Advertising*, London: Boyars, 1978; New York: Scribner, 1979

Vince Cullers Advertising, Inc.

First African-American-owned full-service ad agency in the United States, founded in Chicago, Illinois, by Vince Cullers, 1956; Jeffery Cullers promoted to president, while his father, Vince, remained chairman-CEO, 1997.

Major Clients

Amoco Oil Company (later BP Amoco)
Bristol-Myers
Chicago White Sox
Coors Brewing Company
Discover Card
Illinois Bell/Ameritech
Johnson Products Company, Inc.
Kellogg Company
Pizza Hut, Inc.
Sears, Roebuck & Company
United Negro College Fund
U.S. Department of the Treasury

Vince Cullers, born in 1929, founded the first African-American-owned full-service advertising agency in the United States with the help of his wife, Marian, in 1956. His interest in the business of advertising was sparked when he attended the Art Institute of Chicago and studied business at the University of Chicago. His career received its greatest boost when he became promotional art director for *Ebony* magazine. It was not an easy task in an era when the number of African-Americans working in advertising was extremely small. Thus, although his endeavor to found a black-owned agency was not immediately financially solvent, he had an idea of how to get mainstream businesses to adopt his concepts.

Cullers was dedicated to the proposition that "selling Black" required "thinking Black." Although black consumers were estimated to have $28 billion in annual disposable income in the late 1950s and early 1960s, mainstream advertisers did not readily embrace the idea of retaining a black advertising agency. As Cullers recalled:

> The general condition for blacks in the [advertising] business was bad. . . . When we began, white clients were reluctant to spend money on the black market. They didn't understand it. Some didn't believe it existed. We spent a lot of frustrating years knowing we had the knowledge to get a job done that others didn't even realize needed to be done.

Cullers did not let this state of affairs dampen his determination, and he used his knowledge and experience serving as a consultant to mainstream agencies interested in targeting black consumers. According to Terry Cullers, the agency's special projects director, most of the accounts acquired by the agency in the 1950s were very small and stayed with Cullers until the early to mid-1960s. By the late 1960s, corporate America had begun to appreciate the potential of multiracial markets, and Cullers had created the networks, clients, and financial stability needed to move ahead. The agency's first big break occurred in the mid-1960s, when it landed its first national account, Lorillard's Viceroy and Kent cigarette brands. Around the same time, the agency won Bristol Myers's Bufferin account. All of the efforts bore fruit when Lorillard became the first client to sign an advertising agreement, setting an example that encouraged other clients to follow suit. Before long, the agency had an enviable roster of accounts.

The late 1960s and early 1970s saw the advent of one of the agency's most memorable campaigns, for Johnson Products Company's Afro Sheen. It was this campaign that really put Vince Cullers Advertising, Inc., on the map. It also helped launch the long-running television show *Soul Train*, hosted by Don Cornelius, which served as a springboard for the multi-ethnic advertisements produced by the Cullers agency. It was a case of being in the right place at the right time. The show—still airing more than 30 years later—needed black-oriented commercials, and Cullers needed a national venue for his efforts. The effort that showcased the talents of Cullers, the "Watu-Wasuri" (Swahili for "Beautiful People") campaign for Afro Sheen, remains a classic. In the ads blacks showed their pride in their families and their heritage at a time when black people were just beginning to have a sense of their own identity. Johnson Products used another advertising firm from the 1980s to the early 1990s but made a brief return to the Cullers agency during the 1990s.

Cullers used his pioneering agency to educate, employ, and interest other African-Americans in the field of advertising. By the late 1990s, the agency had grown to a staff of 25 employees and reported annual billings totaling $18 million. In May 1997 the agency announced the promotion of Jeffery B. Cullers, Vince Cullers's son, from vice president and group account director to president of the firm. (Vince Cullers remained as chairman and chief executive officer.) Jeffery Cullers began working for the agency after earning a degree in marketing from the University of Illinois at Champaign-Urbana in 1980. As president, the younger Cullers intended to position the firm to tackle new challenges as it entered the new millennium. He also held the position of executive vice president and executive producer for SRELLUC Productions, Inc., a division of Vince Cullers Advertising. One of its major projects was the production of in-flight videos for United Airlines that promoted San Diego, California, as the site for the Republican National Convention of 2000 and Chicago as the site for the Democratic National Convention.

Over the years the elder Cullers has volunteered his time, money, and resources for Operation Breadbasket (now called Operation PUSH [People United to Save Humanity]), the National Association for the Advancement of Colored People (NAACP), the Cosmopolitan Chamber of Commerce, the Urban League, and the Assault on Literacy Program, working with these organizations to get mainstream companies to understand the importance of supporting black businesses. It was through these volunteer ventures, in fact, that he acquired his first account, Lorillard. In an interview with Gail Baker Woods, Cullers reflected on the evolution of advertising to African-Americans from the early days of his agency to the present:

> We were inventing the wheel. The market potential was enormous. The black consumer was not very difficult to target. Today, black people have gone through a dramatic metamorphosis. The emerging market is still black, but many of us are still trying to assimilate. This makes it more difficult to penetrate and reach the black audience.

At the start of the 21st century, the agency's largest client was BP (British Petroluem) Amoco, a company that had been with Cullers since 1985. Although it had won several Communications Excellence to Black Audiences (CEBA) Awards for television, radio, and magazine advertising, the agency showed no sign of slowing its pace. Promotions were being implemented for the Chicago White Sox and the United States Treasury Department. The agency had successfully resisted the trend, popularized during the latter decades of the 20th century, of achieving growth by being acquired by a larger, usually mainstream, agency. Its pioneering efforts, which paved the way for other African-American agencies, continued to be recognized, documented, and showcased within the annals of advertising history.

MARILYN KERN-FOXWORTH

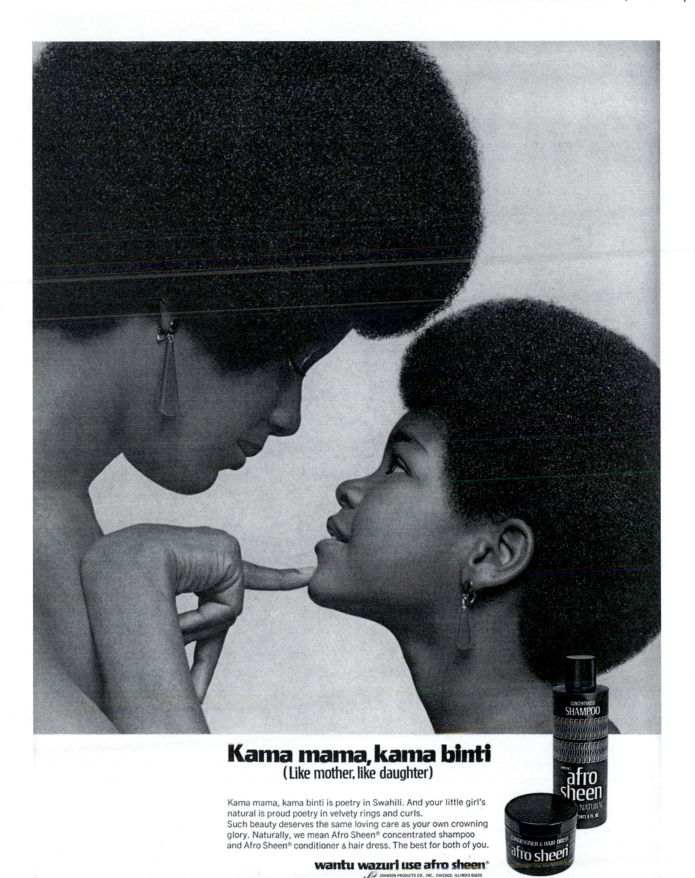

Vince Cullers's landmark campaign for Afro Sheen—"Wantu Wazuri Use Afro Sheen"—celebrated the African-American heritage.

Further Reading

"American Advertising Salutes Returning Congresswoman Cardiss Collins and Black Business Leader," *Jet* (15 April 1996)

"Chicago," *Advertising Age* (8 September 1997)

"*Jet* Editor Robert E. Johnson and Celebs Cited with Trumpet Awards," *Jet* (20 March 1995)

"Weathering Change: A Foundation for Success," *The Black Advocate* (May/June 1995)

Woods, Gail Baker, *Advertising and Marketing to the New Majority*, Belmont, California: Wadsworth, 1995

Cultural Imperialism

Cultural imperialism is a view of advertising as seen from the Marxist left that addresses the impact of a more powerful capitalist culture on a less powerful peasant one. It gained momentum in academe in the 1960s, most likely as part of the larger protest movement against growing U.S. intervention in Vietnam. But its roots lie in the traditional critique of capitalism set forth by both communist and noncommunist intellectuals of the left since the 1920s.

One of the better-known writers about cultural imperialism was Herbert Schiller, a respected U.S. media and social critic, who defined it in 1976 as "the sum of processes by which a society is attracted, pressured, forced, and sometimes even bribed into shaping social institutions to correspond to, or even promote, the values and structures of the dominating center of the system." While Schiller's definition identifies a power struggle between cultures, other definitions have an even more ominous tone and place the blame squarely on the West. In 1977 Jeremy Tunstall, author of *The Media Are American: Anglo-American Media in the World,* asserted that "authentic, traditional and local culture in many parts of the world is being battered out of existence by the indiscriminate dumping of large quantities of slick commercial and media products, mainly from the United States."

Four assumptions are common in most writings about cultural imperialism, each an updated version of the classic leftist view of transnational class conflict, but with the term *indigenous peoples* substituted for the more traditional phrase *workers of the world.* The first assumption is that the media—television, film, radio, print journalism, and advertising—are at the center of cultural imperialism. The second is that the process is carried out by the "invasion" of an indigenous culture by an outside one. Third, capitalism itself rather than any particular nation-state is the "imperialist power" because it spreads a culture of consumerism. And fourth, cultural imperialism presses a "modern" vision of society that includes urbanism, mass communication, and a technical-scientific-rational ideology.

The fear that long-established cultural values may be eroded by commerce and advertising is not limited to the poor and underdeveloped regions of the world. France, one of the cultural centers of Western civilization, is just as concerned for its own cultural future as are Third World countries. This view was clearly expressed by Jack Lang, former French minister of culture, who asked rhetorically, "Will technology enrich us by creating a diversity of channels for artistic expression, or might the truth be more ominous: the higher the satellite, the lower the culture."

Among the media products seen to promote cultural imperialism, global advertising plays an essential role. Opportunities for international advertising exist because population growth and potential for product consumption is often greater in less developed markets than in more developed ones. For example, the 300 million consumers in the European Union, the 253 million consumers in the United States, and the 125 million consumers in Japan are regarded as living in economically stable markets. However, the economy of the developing world is expanding at about 6 percent annually, according to Barbara Mueller in her book *International Advertising: Communicating Across Cultures.* As a result, manufacturers and distributors in developed countries have begun to selectively target consumers in developing markets. Some argue that this is done without proper regard for the values of the target culture.

Underdeveloped countries typically produce only those goods that meet the basic needs of their consumers, and whatever is produced will usually find a buyer. There is little need to stimulate demand through advertising in such a "sellers' market"— unlike in developed countries, where advertising expenditures per person can be 40 to 50 times greater than in most less developed countries.

Advocates of global advertising believe that allowing consumers in developing nations the opportunity to receive greater education about the availability of goods and services, along with more information to enable comparisons, helps prepare them for a higher standard of living. Messages promote social good through increased savings, reduced illiteracy, lower birth rates, and improved nutrition. Critics say that international advertisers attempt to re-create Western-style consumer cultures among populations that are vulnerable because of poverty, illiteracy, lack of experience with consumer goods, and lack of exposure to media messages. Further, less developed countries seldom have legal systems that protect consumers. Mueller accuses global advertisers with a long bill of particulars:

- International advertising unduly influences competition. Multinational corporations outspend local firms in advertising to such a degree that indigenous products cannot compete. For example, Kellogg has such great exposure in many developing markets that the name is virtually synonymous with "breakfast cereal." Foreign brands' higher level of advertising spending also provides them with significantly higher status.

- International advertising unduly influences domestic media by promoting commercialism and introducing Western media content. Many countries have shifted their media structures away from public- or state-financing models to Western models in which the media are supported by advertising. As a result, the advertising content of newspapers, magazines, and television has increased to such an extent that it is often much greater in developing markets than in the West. Multinational corporations have also been accused of attempting to influence media content by threatening withdrawal of advertising.

- International advertising agencies unduly influence local advertising institutions. This was particularly true in the 1960s, when local agencies were often staffed with Westerners who not only brought along marketing skills but personal values as well. While many developing nations have passed regulations limiting outside ownership and investment in domestic agencies, many upper-level, decision-making positions in agencies are still held by expatriates, leaving the locals to carry out decisions made by others and to handle routine tasks.

- International advertising has undue influence on consumerism. Advertising messages are thought to stimulate artificial wants and needs and encourage a demand of goods that exceeds the level of development for a given country. For example, a concern in Malaysia is that the advertising industry has created a consumer culture in which people measure their worth by "the size of their house, the make of their car and the possession of the latest household equipment, clothes, and gadgets," according to Katherine Toland Frith and Michael Frith in their 1989 paper, "The Stranger at the Gate: Western Advertising and Eastern Cultural Communications Values." The counterargument is that some consumerist messages create higher standards of living. Through its advertising of cereals, Kellogg introduced a nutritional concept previously absent in Brazil: the importance of eating breakfast.

- International advertising improperly allocates precious resources. International advertising strategies allegedly shift consumer behavior from rational consumption of locally produced goods to conspicuous consumption of foreign goods. To compete with foreign advertisers, local advertisers allocate large amounts of money to the promotion of goods—money that could otherwise be spent for health and welfare programs. For example, expenditures for soap advertising in Kenya are higher than those for rural health care

- International advertising creates a demand for goods that consumers cannot afford. When an unrealistic demand exists, the resulting dissatisfaction and frustration can potentially create social unrest or political destabilization. While affluent consumers exist in less developed countries, they cannot be targeted exclusively. Therefore, consumers in the most rural areas whose lifestyles are provincial and whose incomes are meager are exposed to the same messages as urban-center dwellers with sophisticated tastes.

- International advertising has undue influence on indigenous culture. In order to develop more efficient campaigns, many international marketers use a single message strategy across cultures. Despite their inappropriateness for certain target cultures, television messages that originate from the West provide 30-second lessons on what it means to be successful or attractive; what roles men, women, and children should play on the basis of gender, age, race, and ethnic group; and what freedoms an individual can expect to enjoy. As an example, according to Tony Koenderman in a 1994 *Adweek* article, while 85 percent of the South African population is black, and even though blacks account for about 60 percent of household expenditures, most models used in ads are white. This overrepresentation of whites sends a strong racial message to members of black cultures.

- International advertising has the potential to exaggerate product claims and deceive consumers. In developed countries, regulatory bodies were created in tandem with the advertising industry; however, more than half of developing countries have no regulatory agencies to protect consumers against misleading or deceptive advertising. This leaves such countries vulnerable to the promotion of defective products, such as unsafe chemical and pharmaceutical products banned in developed markets, packaged goods with overdue expiration dates, condoms that do not meet Western quality standards, and alcohol and tobacco products that are more heavily regulated in the West.

Alarmed by these prospects, some countries have raised barriers comparable to protectionist trade tariffs, except that the measures are designed to protect local culture more than local industry. Latin American countries limit foreign investment in ad agencies to 19 percent; India set the limit at 40 percent. In Peru 100 percent of advertising content must be locally produced in order to ensure that local values are projected. In Malaysia all TV and radio commercials are screened by a government censor board that provides guidelines for protecting the Malaysian national language, religion, culture, and tradition.

While these restrictions can be helpful in protecting indigenous cultures, most critics believe that more countries need to take action and make a much stronger effort. Such countries could follow the example set by France, perhaps the country most committed to preserving indigenous culture. When advertising is recognized as only one form of media product capable of imperialism, the sum total of cultural imperialism becomes even more significant.

Resistance to other cultural products exists, and J. Richard Munro, then co-chairman and co-chief executive officer of Time Warner, Inc., listed a number of examples of such resistance across various countries in a 1990 speech:

- Several countries limit the percentage of foreign films shown in theaters, including Argentina, Brazil, India, South Korea, Portugal, Greece, and Italy.
- Several countries have broadcast quotas, including Colombia and Ecuador.
- Many countries, among them India and South Korea, restrict the import of commercial home videos; others, such as Australia and Spain, levy high taxes on videocassette distribution and royalty.
- Canada restricts foreign investment in publishing, broadcasting, and cable television, in addition to restricting film distribution and investment.
- French law requires that 60 percent of all television programming be produced by companies within the European Community, and 30 percent must be produced by French companies.
- British government regulators advise independent networks that no more than 14 percent of broadcasts should be of non-European origination, outside of sports and cultural programming.

The defenders of the free flow of media products among cultures note that some countries have higher production qualities and that their products are naturally in high demand. In the same 1990 speech, Munro defended the popularity of U.S. products:

All over the globe people associate the American style with a way of existence that to one degree or another they wish to share in. The freedom they want is the freedom they see embodied in the images and idiom of America—an idiom that is optimistic and democratic, with an abiding faith in the ability to think as we wish, believe as we wish, worship as we wish but, equally, in the everyday freedoms of choosing what we wear or how we entertain ourselves.

Clearly, cultural imperialism is an emotionally charged concept, and its effects will continue to be hotly debated.

JOYCE M. WOLBURG

Further Reading

Frith, Katherine Toland, and Michael Frith, "The Stranger at the Gate: Western Advertising and Eastern Cultural Communications Values," paper presented at the International Communication Association Conference, San Francisco, 1989

Frith, Katherine Toland, and Michael Frith, "Western Advertising and Eastern Culture: The Confrontation in Southeast Asia," *Current Issues and Research in Advertising* 12, no. 1 (1990)

Golding, Peter, and Phil Harris, *Beyond Cultural Imperialism: Globalization, Communication, and the New International Order,* London and Thousand Oaks, California: Sage, 1997

Koenderman, Tony, "S. African Marketers Take New Direction," *Adweek* (3 January 1994)

Lang, Jack, "The Higher the Satellite, the Lower the Culture," *New Perspectives Quarterly* 12, no. 4 (Fall 1995)

Mueller, Barbara, "Social Responsibility and Ethics in the Global Marketplace," in *International Advertising: Communicating across Cultures,* by Mueller, Belmont, California: Wadsworth, 1996

Munro, J. Richard, "Good-Bye to Hollywood," *Vital Speeches of the Day* (14 February 1990)

Schiller, Herbert I., *Communication and Cultural Domination,* White Plains, New York: International Arts and Sciences Press, 1976

Tomlinson, John, *Cultural Imperialism: A Critical Introduction,* Baltimore, Maryland: Johns Hopkins University Press, and London: Pinter, 1991

Tunstall, Jeremy, *The Media Are American: Anglo-American Media in the World,* New York: Columbia University Press, and London: Constable, 1977; 2nd edition, London: Constable, 1994

Cultural Symbols

Advertising creates and uses cultural symbols as representations of essentially familiar ideas in order to fulfill its fundamental purpose: the selling of goods and services. Cultural symbols in advertising can take a number of forms, including corporate logos, real or fictitious celebrity figures, slogans, and all manner of social stereotypes (e.g., the American Indian as a symbol for the state of nature as deployed in the famous "Keep America Beautiful" commercial against littering). According to anthropologists such as Mary Douglas and Grant McCracken, the cultural symbolism of advertising and advertising figures is connected to the deep-seated ideals that people invest in goods. The trademark, brand name, or celebrity figure then serves as a sort of shorthand for the values consumers associate with particular goods and services.

The use of such symbols in advertising has been the subject of much academic inquiry. Some scholars have explored how advertising creates these symbols, while others have studied the symbols' effects. Within this latter category there are two streams of thought: one argues that advertising manipulates people through such symbols; the other suggests that consumers "read" advertising through their own experiences and often resist the sales message.

Some of the early uses of cultural symbols in advertising can be traced back to the 19th century when the first celebrity endorsements began to appear. For instance, when Henry Ward Beecher, the foremost preacher in America, endorsed Pears' soap in the 1880s, the purpose was to endow the product with some of Beecher's renowned godliness through a symbolic association.

Writers such as Judith Williamson and Matthew McAllister have referred to this kind of association as a system of referents through which advertisers hope consumers will link the character of the celebrity with that of the product. The drawback of this use of well-known figures is that aspects of their character that may be perceived in a less-than-favorable light by consumers may also be associated with a product. Williamson believes that advertisers can overcome such negative connotations by highlighting positive aspects and removing negative factors through "decontextualising" the cultural symbol. In his book, *All Consuming Images*, Stuart Ewen suggests that IBM successfully accomplished this goal when it used Charlie Chaplin's "Little Tramp" in its ads, despite the fact that in the film *Modern Times*, this hapless character's experiences with mechanization served to condemn technology. Indeed, when choosing to feature Beecher, the makers of Pears' soap may have hoped that association with its product would wash away some of the stain remaining on Beecher's character from the suit brought against him in 1875 by Theodore Tilton for alienating the affections of his wife, Elizabeth.

Sometimes the negative aspect of a cultural symbol, such as notoriety, is purposely employed in advertising, a memorable example being the mid-1980s Notorious Jeans campaign that capitalized on a political scandal by featuring Donna Rice, the girlfriend of married presidential hopeful Senator Gary Hart. For many years American Express ran an ad campaign based on the vagaries of fame. Under the slogan "Do you know me?" American Express ads featured individuals such as Mel Blanc, the voice of Bugs Bunny and Daffy Duck, and others whose names and faces might not be instantly recognizable, but who nonetheless are celebrities. Variations on this theme ran in markets such as Australia and Singapore, where well-known local personalities might not garner the attention due them when traveling without the support of the American Express card.

Historically the use of celebrity symbols in advertisements and the use of brand names and trademarks were closely linked. It was not until 1905 that trademarks received firm protection under U.S. law. Trademark law allowed companies to protect the sign or symbol that represented the company. Prior to the enactment of this legislation, companies seeking to distinguish their products often used copyrighted illustrations in their advertising—for example, Palmer Cox's drawings of Brownies (appropriated by Kodak and Ivory Soap), Rose O'Neill's Kewpies (Jell-O), and Richard Outcault's Buster Brown (the Brown Shoe Company and Buster Brown Apparel). The Brown Shoe Company of St. Louis, Missouri, adopted the comic strip figure of Buster Brown as a brand name for one line of its shoes, and Buster Brown Apparel came about through a series of mergers of companies in the clothing industry that also used the comic strip character in their marketing. These instantly recognizable figures were similar to celebrities in that advertisers chose them precisely because they carried established cultural connotations that could be transferred

to the products in question. Other companies developed their own fictional "celebrity" figures, most notably Aunt Jemima, who debuted as a symbol for a pancake mix at the 1898 World's Fair and who in different form continues to this day as the trademark symbol for a range of pancake-related products. Aunt Jemima was effective because she met the basic requirement of a cultural symbol in that she distilled a common American perception, rooted in slavery, of the turbaned black plantation-house servant. It would be hard to imagine such a trademark symbol originating in England or Japan, where no such tradition of slavery existed.

The Trademark Act of 1905 required that a company name be rendered in a distinctive style in order to be registered as a trademark. This requirement fit the needs of companies such as Coca-Cola, which had registered their names under earlier, less secure trademark acts. The distinctive ribbon-style letters of the Coca-Cola trademark allowed the company to register the name and vigorously defend any encroachment on its brand. This action, in combination with its dynamic advertising campaigns—which from 1900 onward featured healthy and lively young women and almost always incorporated the company's name and trademark—helped establish Coca-Cola as something more than a mere brand name. The symbolic association of Coca-Cola with a perceived American way of life was perhaps best epitomized by the U.S. soldier who supposedly said that he viewed his role in World War II, at least in part, as fighting for the right to drink Coke. Whether he meant Coca-Cola to stand symbolically for the way of life he was defending or simply meant that he fought for Coca-Cola, it is clear that the drink had acquired powerful meanings that motivated strong attachments.

Cultural symbols can also be created by government advertising campaigns. During World War I the U.S. government mounted a propaganda campaign through the Committee on Public Information in which the figure of Uncle Sam, as portrayed in a now famous recruitment poster by James Montgomery Flagg, emerged as a symbol of the nation rather than simply of the nation's imperial drive. World War II, on the other hand, witnessed an affirmation of "American-ness"—often presented as an association of democracy and consumerism—in various media and specifically in advertising for general goods and services. Thus, Republic Steel, Dixie Cups, McDonnell Aircraft Corporation, Birds Eye Foods, May Department Stores, General Motors Corporation, and Norman Rockwell's *Saturday Evening Post* magazine covers could not only symbolically represent the United States and American values but also could lay claim to embodying those values.

In the postwar years it was not unusual for a company's advertising slogan or image to be taken up by the public and adapted for other uses in metaphorical, metonymical, or synecdochical form. A prime example is the phrase "Where's the beef?" first introduced in 1984 by the fast-food chain Wendy's, which quickly became a metaphor for anything lacking in substance or detail. Likewise a range of Coca-Cola slogans proclaiming the product's authenticity—"The real thing" and "Coke is it"—lent themselves to such borrowings. In the hands of writer Tom Wolfe the "Pepsi Generation" of the early 1960s ad campaigns was transformed into the literary conceit of the "Me Generation." In the 1970s the

National Park Service's symbol Smokey Bear, shortened simply to "Smokey," became a synonym for a state highway officer. By the 1990s the designation 5-0, borrowed from the television series *Hawaii 5-0*, had replaced "Smokey." Internationally, Coca-Cola, Disney's Mickey Mouse, and McDonald's have been symbolically associated with the spread of U.S. culture and values.

Since the late 1980s there has been an increase in the identification of celebrity's names with brands. Sports figures such as basketball player Michael Jordan and golfer Greg Norman have endorsed entire product lines that carry their names. When Jordan endorses Nike shoes, Hanes underwear, and Gatorade, a synergy occurs in which Jordan himself and each of the brand names enhance the symbolic weight of the other. Not only are the brands united through the figure of Jordan, but he also becomes a brand himself. In a sense Jordan ceases to be real and becomes a mere symbol. As the memory of Michael Jordan the basketball player fades, he may be in danger of being remembered not as a symbol of sporting excellence but simply as a brand name. Such was the fate of Buster Brown, who began life as a comic strip character in 1902 but became known as the symbol of a range of products from shoes to pianos to bread. A century later "he" is remembered, if at all, only as the symbol for a brand of shoe.

Many other characters—and real people, as well—have suffered a similar fate, having been transformed through advertising into symbols more real than they ever were in other incarnations. One example of the process was nicely caught in the 1977 movie *Saturday Night Fever*. The British actor Lawrence Olivier had appeared earlier in the decade in a campaign to introduce a new line of Polaroid cameras. In the movie, one of the lower-middle-class characters does not know who Olivier is until he is told that he was the man in the Polaroid commercials. Polaroid had chosen Olivier because it wanted a great actor to lend his enormous prestige to a new product. But for those unfamiliar with Olivier, his name meant nothing. He became "the Polaroid man," and the prestige of the brand flowed to rather than from him. Thus, because of extensive media exposure through magazines and television, Olivier's symbolic significance was altered by the process of its own exploitation.

IAN GORDON

See also Archetype/Stereotype; *and color plate in this volume*

Further Reading

Douglas, Mary, and Baron Isherwood, *The World of Goods,* New York: Basic Books, and London: Lane, 1979; revised edition, New York and London: Routledge, 1996

Ewen, Stuart, *All Consuming Images: The Politics of Style in Contemporary Culture,* New York: Basic Books, 1988; revised edition, 1999

Gordon, Ian, *Comic Strips and Consumer Culture, 1890–1945,* Washington, D.C.: Smithsonian Institution Press, 1998

Kahn, E.J., *The Big Drink: The Story of Coca-Cola,* New York: Random House, and London: Reinhardt, 1960

McAllister, Matthew P., *The Commercialization of American Culture: New Advertising, Control, and Democracy,* Thousand Oaks, California: Sage, 1996

McCracken, Grant, *Culture and Consumption: New Approaches to the Symbolic Character of Consumer Goods and Activities,* Bloomington: Indiana University Press, 1988

Marchand, Roland, *Creating the Corporate Soul: The Rise of Public Relations and Corporate Imagery in American Big Business,* Berkeley: University of California Press, 1998

Strasser, Susan, *Satisfaction Guaranteed: The Making of the American Mass Market,* New York: Pantheon, 1989; London: Smithsonian Institution Press, 1995

Westbrook, Robert B., "Fighting for the American Family," in *The Power of Culture: Critical Essays in American History,* edited by Richard Wightman Fox and T.J. Jackson Lears, Chicago: University of Chicago Press, 1993

Williamson, Judith, *Decoding Advertisements: Ideology and Meaning in Advertising,* London: Boyars, 1978; New York: Boyars, 1979

Cunningham & Walsh

Formed by John P. Cunningham and Frederick H. Walsh in a reorganization of Newell-Emmett Company, New York City, 1950; advocated back-to-back 30-second TV commercials, 1960s; sold its Chicago, Illinois, office to management, July 1961; bought Post-Keyes-Gardner, 1978; named *Advertising Age* "Agency of the Year," 1974; acquired by Mickelberry Corporation and put under the new C&W Group umbrella, 1982; closed Fountain Valley, California, and Dallas, Texas, offices, and sold San Francisco, California, office, 1985; bought by N.W. Ayer & Partners and closed, 1987.

Major Clients

American Motors Corporation
Anderson Clayton Foods (Chiffon margarine)
Andrew Jergens Company
AT&T Corporation Yellow Pages
J.A. Folgers Company
Jos. Schlitz Brewing Company (Old Milwaukee beer)
Liggett & Myers Tobacco Company
Texaco, Inc.

Cunningham & Walsh, from its inception on 1 January 1950 to its absorption into N.W. Ayer & Partners in 1987, eschewed flamboyant advertising for good, sound selling. The attendant disciplines of selling—marketing and merchandising—were infused into the agency culture by John P. Cunningham, who, with Frederick H. Walsh, formed the agency in a reorganization of Newell-Emmett Company, a New York City ad shop founded in 1919 by Walsh, Clarence D. Newell, and others. Walsh served as the first president of Cunningham & Walsh, and Cunningham as its first executive vice president. The agency started with billings of $26.4 million and a rank of 15th among U.S. agencies.

Cunningham believed that "the key selling argument of any ad must be carried through to the point of sale and to three audiences—the salesmen, the dealer, and the consumer." That dimensional approach pushed billings from $26.4 million to $370 million over Cunningham & Walsh's 37 years and gave substance to some of the most memorable creative work on Madison Avenue: "It's not nice to fool Mother Nature" for Anderson Clayton Foods' Chiffon margarine; "Let your fingers do the walking" for AT&T Corporation Yellow Pages; "Tastes as good as its name" for Old Milwaukee beer from Jos. Schlitz Brewing Company; the cuddly but piqued koala muttering, "I hate Qantas," for Qantas Airways; the omniscient nature-mom, Mrs. Olson, offering up her steaming cup of mountain-grown coffee for Folgers.

By example, Cunningham showed others that copy had to be sound and practical. In 1952, when he was copy chief on the Texaco, Inc., account, he donned coveralls to pump gas for customers to test copy with reality. He found that few asked him to "fill 'er up" (as his copy had readily chirped) and that clean restrooms were of utmost importance. Out of this came the "Your friendly Texaco dealer" ad campaign and Cunningham & Walsh's internal Creative Merchants Plan, whereby the agency's research, account services, copy, art, and broadcast personnel took stints as gas station attendants and retail clerks. This program was memorialized in the self-promoting "The Man From Cunningham & Walsh" ads showing advertising people on the job.

Cunningham & Walsh put considerable stock in market research, to add an edge to its creativity and to tout itself in the marketplace. In the late 1940s and 1950s it conducted an annual Videotown USA survey in New Brunswick, New Jersey, to determine usage of the emerging TV set (or, rather, sets: the survey found 52 TV brands in New Brunswick in 1950, compared with 30 in 1949). The agency received quite a bit of press coverage from an annual survey in the 1980s on women in the workforce, which evolved into how the lives of all husbands and especially so-called "bachelor" husbands were changing.

Cunningham & Walsh, under the guidance of John P. Cunningham, was a lead agency in the mid-1960s in advocating that TV networks should allow back-to-back 30-second commercials from different clients. The networks at the time ran expensive 60-second commercials and would only allow back-to-back 30-second spots for different products from the same client, a policy that put TV out of reach of clients with unequal brand budgets or only one brand. Cunningham was given the moniker "industry guardian," and for good reason. In addition to advocating the

change in 30-second TV spots, he chaired the American Association of Advertising Agencies in 1952 and the American Advertising Federation (AAF) in 1961–62 and was a director of the American Research Foundation.

A key to Cunningham & Walsh's success was leadership continuity and mentoring. For the most part, upper management had been with the agency since its inception. Newell mentored Cunningham, who in turn mentored Carl W. Nichols and Anthony C. Chevins, the top two executives for the last 26 years of the agency.

Cunningham & Walsh was perhaps saved from an early death in 1961—called the "Year of the Locust" by Nichols—when management was forced to reinvent the company. For completely unrelated reasons, within weeks the agency lost Texaco, Smith-Corona Marchant, Italian Line, and Crown Zellerbach Corporation. Billings plunged from $54.5 million in 1960 to $39.1 million in 1962, creating serious cash-flow problems.

Nimble, energetic management was needed. Cunningham, 63, tiring from the demands of leadership, moved himself to honorary chairman (he retired the next year). Nichols, 37, took over as president and chief executive officer, and Chevins, 40, as executive vice president. The company was refinanced and a plan was developed to buy Cunningham's stock incrementally to incentivize management by spreading the ownership. The Chicago, Illinois, Cunningham & Walsh office (the former Ivan Hill, Inc.) was sold to its management when it balked at being part of the new structure; it became Hill, Rogers, Mason & Scott. Each remaining client was visited for its vote of confidence (none of them left). A decision was made to let 100 people go, and management set in motion a plan to develop a client base that would make the agency more marketing oriented and creative, with heavy emphasis on packaged goods and consumer products and services.

Sterling Drug Company became the first client of the rejuvenated Cunningham & Walsh. Fortunately, billings grew from existing accounts as well—American Home Products, Andrew Jergens Company, AT&T, and J.A. Folgers Company. It took five years for billings to surpass 1960 levels. As luck would have it, Folgers, an independent regional company in the early 1960s, soon came under the Procter &Gamble (P&G) umbrella. By the end of its agency run in 1987, Cunningham & Walsh drew about half its billings from P&G.

The push to become more consumer oriented was abetted in the 1970s when the agency won the Old Milwaukee beer, American Motors Corporation, and Liggett & Myers Tobacco Company accounts, Liggett & Myers having left the agency in the 1950s under Walsh's purview. Advertising Age named Cunningham & Walsh "Agency of the Year" in 1974 based on its creative output and the market-share growth of key clients. Its billings had surged to $108.2 million.

Growth by acquisition became the industry mantra in the late 1970s and 1980s. Cunningham & Walsh got into the act, purchasing Post-Keyes-Gardner (P-K-G), Chicago, in the fall of 1978. Much of P-K-G's nearly $80 million in billings came from Brown & Williamson Tobacco Company. The addition of this account led to the departure of Liggett & Myers because of the conflict. Cunningham & Walsh established a Dallas, Texas, office in 1982.

A koala presents his grievances about Business Class to Qantas management.

New leg rests and other comforts are discussed. Sometimes, heatedly.

KOALA: You've really done it this time, Qantas. Leg rests in Business Class. Not mere footrests like other airlines.
QANTAS: We're rather proud of that. They're the only Business Class leg rests in the world.
KOALA: It wasn't bad enough that Qantas invented Business Class. Now you go and make it better.
QANTAS: We do want our passengers to be comfortable.
KOALA: Comfortable? This is ridiculous. They can actually put their feet up and sleep.
QANTAS: The thought had occurred to us.
KOALA: Now more business travelers than ever will be coming to Australia. To disturb

my peace and quiet.
QANTAS: We're terribly sorry about that...
KOALA: And I suppose you're sorry about the Frequent Flight Bonus Program* with TWA, too.

QANTAS: Getting together with TWA was a stroke of genius, actually. Our passengers earn bonus points on both airlines. Good for travel on either.
KOALA: I hope they do their bonus traveling with TWA.
QANTAS: They could, of course. But we'd be delighted if they chose to fly to the South Pacific with us.
KOALA: And I assume that you're delighted about your schedules, too. More flights to Australia from North America than anyone else, including three non-stops a week from Los Angeles. And more destinations in Australia than any of the other international airlines.
QANTAS: Obviously, those things do provide us with a certain advantage.
KOALA: And scheduling your flights out of Sydney so they arrive in L.A.

in the morning. Does that give you an advantage, too?
QANTAS: It gives our passengers more connecting flights to choose from. So they'll be home in Chicago, or New York, or wherever, in time to have dinner.
KOALA: Speaking of dinner, I assume you're still offering a choice of delicious entrees, with complimentary wines and cocktails?

QANTAS: Yes. Served on real china and crystal. And you forgot the complimentary in-flight entertainment.
KOALA: This is getting unbearable. Do you have anything else up your sleeve?
QANTAS: Hmmm. No, I don't believe we do.
KOALA: That's good.
QANTAS: Wait a moment. Did I mention the increased baggage allowance for our Business Class passengers?
KOALA: I hate Qantas.

*Available to U.S. residents only.

QANTAS

For a humorous 1984 campaign for the Australian airline Qantas, Cunningham & Walsh created the traveler-shunning koala.
Qantas Airways, Ltd.

Having determined that clean restrooms were an important selling point for gas stations, Cunningham & Walsh capitalized on this knowledge in a 1952 advertisement for Texaco.
Courtesy of Texaco, Inc.

In 1982 the publicly traded Mickelberry Corporation, having bought Nadler & Larimer and Laurence, Charles & Free, hit the big time by acquiring Cunningham & Walsh. Saatchi & Saatchi Advertising, in London, England, and Univas, of Paris, France, had coveted Cunningham & Walsh as a U.S. building block, both having broken off merger discussions with the agency in the late 1970s. The Mickelberry deal allowed Cunningham & Walsh to become a public company without going through the process of going public, gave it access to greater financial resources, and allowed it to remain autonomous, Nichols said.

Mickelberry created C&W Group, placing the Cunningham & Walsh agency under it. Nichols moved up to group chairman and took on the self-imposed task of building the company through acquisition. Reiser Williams DeYong, of Irvine, California, and Direct Marketing Agency, in Stamford, Connecticut, were purchased in 1984, and BBDM, Chicago, in 1985. Billings for C&W Group peaked at $370 million in 1984, but those heady returns masked approaching troubles.

By the end of 1984, P-K-G/Cunningham & Walsh had lost $150 million in billings, largely from the defection of Brown & Williamson. Then, in late 1985 Mitsubishi Motors Corporation withdrew its $37 million account. The Cunningham & Walsh office set up to service Mitsubishi in Fountain Valley, California, was shuttered. The Dallas office was closed. Chicago operations had to let 124 employees go in a massive restructuring. Billings also were drying up in the Cunningham & Walsh San Francisco, California, office where management attempted a buyback. C&W Group opted to sell it instead to Allen & Dorward, then that city's largest agency.

N.W. Ayer & Partners bought C&W Group in the first quarter of 1987, just months after Nichols was named to the AAF's Advertising Hall of Fame, joining Cunningham, a 1973 inductee. The group's billings had dropped to $274.3 million by then, no doubt influencing the $25 million sale price, considered low at the time. Neither Cunningham nor Walsh was living when their names were removed from the agency shingle that year. Cunningham died in 1985 at the age of 87, Walsh in 1964 at the age of 79.

CRAIG ENDICOTT

Further Reading

"Adman in the News . . . John Cunningham," *Advertising Age* (5 June 1961)

"'Be Dedicated Admen' Is Motif of C&W Seminar," *Advertising Age* (29 February 1960)

Cummings, Bart, "The Benevolent Dictators: Carl Nichols Plays Key Role in Reviving C&W," *Advertising Age* (18 February 1985)

"Cunningham Elected President of C&W; Walsh Board Head," *Advertising Age* (22 March 1954)

"Cunningham Sums up Effects of TV on Videotown Family Living Habits," *Advertising Age* (14 May 1951)

"$11,500,000 Texaco Account Moves to B&B," *Advertising Age* (10 July 1961)

"Frederick Walsh, C&W Co-Founder, Is Dead at 79," *Advertising Age* (24 February 1964)

Marshall, Christy, "Mickelberry Buys C&W," *Advertising Age* (15 March 1982)

O'Connor, John J., "Industry Guardian Cunningham Dies at 87," *Advertising Age* (4 March 1985)

Quinn, Hugh, "C&W's Job for AMC Will Be to Promote Corporate Identity," *Advertising Age* (17 April 1972)

"TV Networks, Stations Reject C&W Proposal for 30-30 Joint Piggybacks," *Advertising Age* (22 August 1966)

Winters, Patricia, "Few Conflicts in Ayer-C&W Merger," *Advertising Age* (29 December 1986)

"You Ought to Know . . . John P. Cunningham," *Advertising Age* 7 (April 1952)

D

DaimlerChrysler. *See* Chrysler Corporation

Dancer, Fitzgerald, Sample

Opened as Blackett-Sample-Hummert, Inc., in Chicago, Illinois, 1924; became a major force in radio during 1930s, specializing in daytime dramas developed for clients General Mills and Procter & Gamble Company; largest buyer of network radio time for more than 20 consecutive years; new partnership formed creating successor agency, Dancer, Fitzgerald, Sample (DFS), 1943; moved to New York City, 1948; joined with Dorland Ltd., London, England, to become DFS-Dorland International, 1970; acquired by Saatchi & Saatchi, 1986; merged with Compton to become Saatchi & Saatchi DFS Compton, 1987; became Saatchi & Saatchi Advertising, 1991, ending Dancer, Fitzgerald, Sample as an active agency brand.

Major Clients
American Chicle Company
Best Foods, Inc.
Falstaff Brewing Corporation
General Mills, Inc.
Liggett & Myers Tobacco Company
Procter & Gamble Company
R.J. Reynolds Tobacco Company
Sara Lee Corporation
Sterling Remedy Company
Swift & Company
Toyota Motor Sales USA, Inc.
Wendy's International, Inc.

John Glen Sample, the one founding partner whose name remained in the agency name of Dancer, Fitzgerald, Sample through its entire history, was born 3 July 1891, in Lutsville, Missouri. After graduation from Will Mayfield College in Marble Hill, Missouri, he entered advertising by taking a job with the Finney Agency in Kansas City, Missouri, where he wrote ads for farm-product lines such as feed and tools. He moved to Chicago, Illinois, to take a position as a sales representative with Curtis Publishing's *Saturday Evening Post,* a career move that brought him into contact with Hill Blackett, an account executive at Lord & Thomas (L&T). Blackett, born in 1892, graduated from the University of Chicago in 1914 and began his career the following year at L&T, where he became a protégé of Claude Hopkins and rose to the position of copy chief. He worked on the agency's Sterling Remedy Company and American Home Products business.

In 1923 Blackett and Sample joined with a third partner, Hays MacFarland, to open a new agency in Chicago, which began operation in 1924 as Blackett-Sample-Hummert (B-S-H). MacFarland's name never appeared in the title, but Frank Hummert's did. Hummert was a writer who had been an associate of Blackett's at L&T and was among the first to be recruited into the new shop. He had been a key figure in the early advertising success of the Kotex account at L&T. In the 1930s he would become the creative force of the agency's growing radio department and a pioneer in the development of daytime network radio serials, that is, soap operas. Although Hummert's name was part of the agency's name and his salary rose to $150,000 by the late 1930s (he was rumored to be the highest paid writer of the period), he declined repeated offers from Blackett and Sample to become a partner. Not only did he prefer to avoid the responsibilities of management, he actually became less and less involved with advertising as his success as a creator of daytime serial programs grew.

Daytime Drama

The agency's innovations in daytime drama, according to Sample, began in the late 1920s with a popular daily serial story syndicated in newspapers. It was called "The Married Life of Helen & Warren." Hummert believed that the format had possibilities in radio for General Mills, and on 10 October 1932, it emerged as *Betty and Bob* on the National Broadcasting Company (NBC) Blue Network, one of two RCA-owned networks. The show centered around the continuing story of Bob Drake, the son of a wealthy family, and his lower-middle-class wife, Betty. The class differences were complicated by the fact that Bob lost part of his inheritance when he married Betty and had to go to work. Written by Hummert, it was the first daytime drama to explore the serious issues of love, money, jealousy, faithfulness, and life philosophy that would soon drive many other soap operas. By the time the program ended in 1940, it had given birth to an entire genre of daytime radio and had made B-S-H the most important producer of network soaps in advertising.

In the early 1930s, Sample suggested hiring Anne Ashenhurst, who had just returned to the United States after working in the Paris, France, office of the *Herald Tribune*. The agency's roster of clients marketed heavily to women, and both men recognized the value a woman's point of view could bring to the company's work. Ashenhurst was bright and intelligent, and she was hired despite her lack of background in advertising. She became involved in the agency's radio production from the start. In 1935 Ashenhurst and Hummert married, and the names Frank and Anne Hummert became synonymous with such radio soap operas as *The Romance of Helen Trent, Just Plain Bill, Lorenzo Jones, Stella Dallas, Mary Noble,* and *Backstage Wife.* To turn out the daily dialog, the Hummerts came to employ a huge stable of writers, one of whom was Ned Calmer, who wrote for *Mary Noble* and went on to become one of the legendary Murrow Boys of Columbia Broadcasting System (CBS) News.

Among the clients that laid the basis for B-S-H's success in radio was General Mills, Inc. In 1925 the company paid the agency $25,000 to study its advertising, which was then heavily invested in Gold Medal Flour. The product's long-standing slogan, "Eventually, why not now," was intended to suggest quality and had been devised by Benjamin Bull, advertising manager of Washburn Crosby Company, one of the companies that had merged to form General Mills in 1928. B-S-H found that the brand was widely known but little used. So the agency looked for a more forceful selling message. Although all flour millers sampled and tested their products, it was a process taken so much for granted that none talked about it. The agency suggested that General Mills seize that claim. When "kitchen tested" became the cornerstone of Gold Medal Flour advertising, market share reportedly rose from 11 percent to 20 percent.

The agency also introduced General Mills to the one-cent sale promotion to build market share for its cereals, which were competing with market leaders from Kellogg and Post. (In a one-cent sale promotion, the consumer buys one unit of the product at the regular price and can buy a second for one cent.) The radio serials

devised by the Hummerts also proved effective in selling to children. In 1933 the character Jack Armstrong of the fictional Hudson High School was developed by B-S-H for Wheaties cereal, which had been a client since 1925, before the formation of General Mills. The show aired for 18 years, although Wheaties moved to Knox Reeves Advertising, Inc., in 1937. (Wheaties returned to the agency, which had become Dancer, Fitzgerald, Sample, in 1970, where it remained for another 11 years.) Other famous children's serials created and produced by the agency (though not by the Hummerts) included *Little Orphan Annie* and *Captain Midnight,* both for Ovaltine, a product of the Wander Company.

The agency's package-goods success with General Mills led to a long association with Procter & Gamble Company (P&G) beginning with Oxydol, which in 1933 was running well behind Lever Brothers' Rinso among leading laundry soaps. The agency used a one-cent sale (i.e., the consumer buys one box of soap powder at the regular price and receives a second box for one cent) to encourage consumers to try Oxydol. Then it put the product into daytime radio when the Hummerts created *Ma Perkins,* the story of a down-to-earth widow who ran a lumber yard in the town of Rushville Center. The show was tested on WLW in Cincinnati, Ohio, in the summer and fall of 1933 and went national on NBC in December for a run that would carry it through 1960.

By 1934, according to the *Variety Radio Directory,* more than half of all sponsored network time was controlled by ten ad agencies. B-S-H was the leader, trailed by L&T; J. Walter Thompson Company; Benton and Bowles, Inc., Young & Rubicam, Inc.; and Batten Barton Durstine & Osborn (BBDO). At its peak in the early 1940s, B-S-H wrote and produced 45 different radio shows and spent $12 million on airtime. It was said to be billing nearly $50 million. The volume of work turned out by the agency was truly remarkable. One former scriptwriter told *Advertising Age* that the writers who worked for the Hummerts were valued far more for their typing speed than for their literary talents. Although the center of the agency's creative activity remained in Chicago, the agency opened a major office in New York City in the 1930s and later branched out to Toronto, Canada.

Reconstitution: Dancer, Fitzgerald, Sample

But from the beginning, the relationship between Blackett and Sample was one of convenience and opportunity, not necessarily friendship. Each recognized that the other brought his own essential skills to the operation: Sample, the creative flair and the ability to sell the agency to clients; Blackett, long experience in the general advertising business and his relationship with the Sterling drug company. The personality differences finally led to a breakup in 1943, when, shortly before entering the Navy (where he would become a decorated commander), Sample bought out Blackett's interests. Before his departure, however, he asked two senior officers of B-S-H, Howard "Mix" Dancer and Clifford L. Fitzgerald, to join him as partners and turned the agency into Dancer, Fitzgerald, Sample (DFS). Dancer had joined the company in 1937 from Henri, Hurst & McDonald, Inc., and had been president since 1940, running the General Mills and American Chicle

Company accounts. Clifford L. Fitzgerald was a B-S-H president with strong ties to the P&G account. In late 1943 the Hummerts, who had not been involved in advertising development for years, departed to set up their own production company, Air Features, and Blackett left to start his own agency, Hill Blackett & Company, which never achieved major status in terms of billings even though he took the Ovaltine account with him. Blackett later merged with Grant Advertising, Inc. He retired to a cattle farm in Newton, Georgia, in 1955 and died in December 1967.

DSF was a new agency in name only. It began life on 31 December 1943, 20 years after the founding of the original company, as the eighth largest U.S. agency, billing an estimated $23 million and carrying forward most of the key accounts on which B-S-H had built its reputation and size. Sample returned to the agency after the war, but preferred to take a less active role. In 1948 at the age of 51, he cashed out and retired to Florida, where he used his DFS money to start a new career as a land tycoon. He was never active in advertising again and died in December 1971 in Naples, Florida. The year he retired the new management decided to move the agency headquarters from Chicago, to New York City. The coolness that marked the partnership of Sample and Hummert continued in the relationship of Dancer and Fitzgerald. According to one senior executive, they would sit at opposite ends of the room in board meetings and would rarely converse on matters other than business.

The agency remained a leading presence in radio. In 1951, for the 17th consecutive year, DFS led all other agencies in radio billings by a huge margin, with billings of more than $19 million against $11.6 million for second-ranked BBDO. The agency's strength in radio was largely the result of the ongoing power of its position in the soap opera field. Research became another strength of the agency after the war. Lyndon O. Brown arrived at DFS in the late 1940s as senior vice president of merchandising and research. He came to advertising from an academic background at Carlton College, Northfield, Minnesota, where he had written an influential book called *Marketing and Distribution Research*. His impact on the agency was said to be considerable. By 1953 about one-fifth of the agency's 250 employees in New York City were involved in research. This was largely a reflection of the agency's deep involvement with P&G and General Mills, both of which were heavily committed to a strategic approach to advertising based on scientific and quantitative research.

Other major new business included Liggett & Myers Tobacco Company, which assigned the agency its three-year-old L&M Filters brand in 1956. The L&M Filters account would grow to $17 million before the company left DFS in 1961. In October 1952 DFS became the fourth agency to win the U.S. Army advertising business since World War II. The $1 million account was a politically sensitive one that had moved from N.W. Ayer & Partners to Gardner Advertising to Grant Advertising before coming to DFS, where it would remain until 1963. In 1958 the General Motors Corporation's Frigidaire Division gave the agency its first General Motors business, which amounted to $6 million and pushed the agency's total volume to about $80 million. On 21 November of that year, Howard Dancer died at the age of 60 of a heart attack.

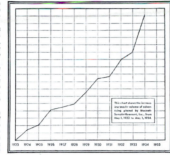

By 1934 Blackett-Sample-Hummert, Inc., predecessor to Dancer, Fitzgerald, Sample, was the leading U.S. agency in terms of sponsored network time and seemed unaffected by the Great Depression.

In February 1962 DFS announced it would close its office in Chicago, the city where the agency had been founded nearly 40 years before. The office, which had once been the agency's nerve center for much of the nation's radio soap-opera production, had fallen to a billings level of around $6 million, against $95 million for the New York City office. Sewall Gardner, Chicago senior vice president and general manager, led 25 DFS staffers to Post & Morr, which became Post, Morr & Gardner. Late in 1963 Post, Morr & Gardner merged with Keyes, Madden and Jones to form Post-Keyes-Gardner Inc., which became a major Chicago agency in the 1970s on the basis of its Brown & Williamson Tobacco Corporation business.

In 1965 DFS ranked seventh among U.S. agencies with billings of $139 million. This sum did not include the $16 million billed by Guild, Bascom & Bonfigli, Inc., with which the agency merged in September 1965 to strengthen its West Coast presence. The following year it won the Camel cigarette account of R.J. Reynolds Tobacco Company (RJR) after the brand's 33-year relationship with William Esty & Company, Inc. Nine years later the agency lost Camel, which went back to Esty, but added RJR's Winston brand.

In 1970 DFS turned its attention to building a more international scope for itself by partnering with Dorland Advertising Holdings Ltd. of London, England, and Dorland Werbeagentur of

Munich, Germany. (Although Dorland was a major company within the British advertising community, billing about $325 million, it was actually an American shop, founded by John Dorland in Atlantic City, New Jersey, in 1886. Dorland did not open a London office until 1905.) Through an exchange of stock, DFS created DFS-Dorland International (DDI) with combined billings of $237 million. DDI later affiliated with agencies in Paris, France, and Switzerland to expand its European coverage. In 1974 the agency's international partnership (by then known as DFS Dorland and Fortune) merged with Advico-Delpire, adding another $30 million in European billings. DFS had a 20 percent stake in the conglomerate. As the agency expanded in Europe, however, it retreated in Canada, selling out to McConnell Advertising in April 1973, which became McConnell/DFS.

Management changes in the mid-1970s included Stuart Upson as chairman and Peter McSpadden as president, with William Weilbacher as vice chairman. Billings then stood at $250 million. Within five years the agency's volume more than doubled to $558 million, including volume from 70 new European accounts acquired in 1980 alone. Among world agencies that year, DFS ranked 20th.

DFS added an enduring phrase to the American lexicon in 1984 through its work for Wendy's International, Inc., fast-food chain. Seeking to promote the larger size of the Wendy's hamburger compared to competitors' burgers, the agency hired the quirky director Joe Sedelmaier to shoot a commercial written by copywriter Cliff Freeman in which three elderly ladies examined an unnamed rival's product. "Where's the beef?" demanded one of the ladies, played with gruff determination by Clara Peller, who became a national celebrity through her exposure in the commercial. The campaign not only added a phrase to the language (presidential candidate Walter Mondale used it in his primary fight against Gary Hart). It sent Wendy's sales up 23 percent from a year earlier. But the campaign was an anomaly within the larger context of DFS. Although *Advertising Age* ranked the commercial number 47 among the top 100 ads of the 20th century, DFS had never achieved a strong creative reputation during or after the years of the "creative revolution." This was attributed to the fact that its major clients, P&G and General Mills, placed a high value on strategic depth and client service and did not encourage innovative creative work from its agencies.

By 1986 DFS continued to be a much-admired older agency that had maintained a leading position among major shops since its days as Blackett-Sample-Hummert in the 1930s. That made it a desirable acquisition target in a decade of intense merger and buyout activity. By far the most aggressive of the suitors was Saatchi & Saatchi Company, Inc. (S&S), which had acquired the Dorland agency in London in 1981 for $8 million. Dorland in turn bought out the DFS London office in 1984. Then early in 1986, Dorland "loaned" DFS $75 million in exchange for an option to buy 100 percent of the agency's common stock at any time. The "loan" was funded by Dorland's parent, Saatchi & Saatchi, and was in effect the agency's purchase price. On 24 February 1986, S&S announced the acquisition of DFS through a merger with Dorland. The new company was called DFS Dorland Worldwide (DFS/D) and became the world's 16th largest agency network.

DFS/D carried forward the old DFS relationship with General Mills. But a conflict developed when another supposedly independent S&S unit within its Compton group, Backer & Spielvogel, Inc., purchased AdCom, the house agency of the Quaker Oats Company. According to Kevin Goldman in his history of S&S, *Conflicting Accounts,* six months after the AdCom purchase, Maurice Saatchi told Carl Spielvogel that the S&S commitment to General Mills (by way of DFS) outweighed its interest in Quaker, thus forcing Spielvogel to resign the account and fire most of the AdCom people. This he refused to do. To resolve the problem, Spielvogel sold AdCom to itself for a nominal price, permitting it to retain its Quaker business.

On 21 July 1987, DFS was split off from Dorland and merged with Saatchi & Saatchi Compton to create a $2.3 billion giant with an equally gigantic name, Saatchi & Saatchi DFS Compton. The merger promptly cost the new shop about $84 million in billings from RJR (a DFS client since 1966), which objected when the newly combined agency created an antismoking campaign for another client, Northwest Airlines.

The new company was less an agency than an alliance of executive fiefdoms derived from other agencies, each seeking to defend some measure of turf. In 1991 the parent company simplified the name game by dropping DFS and Compton and rechristening the New York City flagship Saatchi & Saatchi Advertising. All reference to the names Dancer, Fitzgerald, and Sample thus disappeared as an agency name in American advertising.

JOHN McDONOUGH

See also Soap Opera; *and color plate in this volume*

Further Reading

Doherty, Lawrence, "Adman Sample? He's Florida Land Tycoon," *Advertising Age* (7 and 14 May 1962)

Goldman, Kevin, *Conflicting Accounts: The Creation and Crash of the Saatchi and Saatchi Advertising Empire*, New York: Simon and Schuster, 1997

D'Arcy Advertising Company, Inc.

Founded by William C. D'Arcy, 1906; merged with MacManus, John & Adams and Intermarco, N.V., to form D'Arcy-Mac-Manus-Intermarco, Inc., 1972; partnership established with Masius, Wynne-Williams, 1972; merger finalized to form D'Arcy-MacManus & Masius, Inc., 1976; merged with Benton and Bowles to form D'Arcy Masius Benton & Bowles, Inc., 1985; became principal subsidiary of the MacManus Group, 1996.

Major Clients

Anheuser-Busch, Inc. (Budweiser, Michelob, Busch beers)
Coca-Cola Company
General Tire & Rubber Company
Gerber Products Company
Glenmore Distilleries
International Shoe Company
Krey Packing Company
Milnot Company
Missouri Pacific Lines
Ozark Air Lines
Ralston Purina Company
Southwestern Bell Telephone Company
Standard Oil Company of Indiana

For nearly 65 years D'Arcy Advertising worked quietly but effectively for its local, regional, and national clients. It helped to build two of its clients' brands, Budweiser and Coca-Cola, into world leaders by creating some of the advertising industry's most memorable and effective ads. In so doing, it became one of the 20 largest advertising agencies in the United States and laid the groundwork for the international communications company it later would become.

William C. D'Arcy began his professional life as a paint salesman. After ten years, he moved to Western Advertising Company in 1901, one of only two advertising agencies in St. Louis, Missouri, as an account representative. His sales background is reflected in his writings on the role of advertising:

> A successful advertising man is a business doctor. He must diagnose the needs of business and prescribe the treatment or course of action that will lead to success. . . . Selling is the only reason for the existence of advertising. And to sell successfully through advertising, you must be a salesman in heart and mind.

His philosophy of advertising helped bring unprecedented global success to both his agency and its first client. According to agency legend D'Arcy struck up a conversation with a Coca-Cola salesman at the local train station while selling media for Western Advertising Company. He later sold streetcar advertising to the Coca-Cola Company but felt the company had much more potential as an advertiser. So he put his philosophy to work and made a

sales pitch. He won half the Coca-Cola account as the first client for his new agency, D'Arcy Advertising Company, Inc., which opened its doors in St. Louis on 23 August 1906.

Other clients that signed on in the first year, helping the agency eke out a $1,500 profit, included Plover Hams and Bacon, Three-Minute Oats cereal, Airline Honey, Seemore Soap, Nature's Remedy elixir, and Cascade Whiskey. Cascade brought the agency its first revenues, for three newspaper ads. Coca-Cola's initial ad budget was only $3,000, but D'Arcy's belief in the potential of Coca-Cola was borne out when its budget was raised to $25,000 for the second year, firmly establishing the agency's financial health.

Its work for Coca-Cola soon attracted the attention of another beverage manufacturer whose products eventually would achieve the same worldwide market dominance as Coke—Anheuser-Busch, Inc. That company awarded its nonalcoholic beverages Malt Nutrine and Bevo to the agency in 1914 and Budweiser beer a year later.

There were similarities between the two major clients and their advertising. Both companies had dynamic leaders who envisioned their products as national leaders and supported the technological developments necessary for nationwide manufacturing and distribution. They both insisted on quality ingredients and precise manufacturing processes. They both supported sizable sales forces and wide use of point-of-sale materials before extensive national media were available. Both believed in heavy use of advertising and all forms of marketing communications. They both saw their products as images of the good life in America and as a refreshing reward. These themes were reflected in the advertising produced by D'Arcy for both companies.

The agency's third major national account, General Tire, signed on in 1915 and another beverage product, Cook's Imperial Extra Dry Champagne, soon thereafter. With the addition of new clients, the agency successfully weathered the cutbacks of World War I.

In 1917 D'Arcy was elected president of the Advertising Federation of America, the forerunner of the American Association of Advertising Agencies, the industry's premier professional organization for agencies. He later served as board chairman of the organization.

In general, the 1920s were a period of growth, expansion, and innovation for the agency. It won the entire Coca-Cola account and opened its first branch office in Atlanta, Georgia, in 1923 to better service its rapidly growing client headquartered there. Two transportation clients, Missouri Pacific Lines (railroad) and the White Motor Company (truck manufacturing), joined the agency during this decade. And the General Tire business grew enough to justify opening a branch office in its headquarters city of Cleveland, Ohio, in 1929.

From the beginning D'Arcy's national clients were heavy users of available print media: magazines (e.g., *Saturday Evening Post, Literary Digest, Collier's, American Magazine, Life, Forbes,*

D'Arcy Advertising Company, Inc., helped make Coca-Cola, its first client, both a year-round favorite and an industry leader with this 1922 campaign.
Courtesy of The Coca-Cola Company.

Nation's Business), newspapers, and outdoor advertising. In the 1920s the agency became a leader in technological innovations in each area. George Eberts, head of the print production department, developed the technique of stripping in color separation negatives and combining that innovation with "wet-proofing" to change the entire industry's production process for color magazine ads. He and others in his department collaborated to invent ad "electrotypes" for newspaper illustrations. They improved newspaper matrices in smaller papers and offered more uniformity to print ads regardless of publication size, an important criterion for national clients advertising in hundreds of local papers. The agency and its clients were among the first to integrate electric lights into outdoor ads early in the century.

The agency produced its first radio ad for Bud Malt Syrup in 1920. During the following decade Coca-Cola became a sponsor of the Leonard Joy and Gus Haenschen orchestras on the CBS network, and General Tire sponsored a little-known comedian named Jack Benny during the spring and summer of 1934.

In the creative area, Archie Lee spearheaded a new campaign for Coca-Cola that changed the entire industry. The "Thirst knows no season" campaign helped reposition the beverage from a summer-only drink to a year-round one.

However, one of the biggest challenges in the agency's history occurred in 1920 with the dawn of Prohibition. Anheuser-Busch's flagship brand, Budweiser beer, was forced out of production, but the company was determined to stay in business and keep its name before the public. Percy J. Orthwein led the agency in developing ads for myriad new products, including soft drinks, truck bodies, refrigerated cabinets, and pharmaceutical ingredients. With the agency's help, the company achieved remarkable sales of baker's yeast, promoted for its high quality. The success was due in large part to the public's discovery that the yeast produced not only superior baked goods but better home brew, too.

When the 18th Amendment was repealed in 1933, Anheuser-Busch had survived, but more than half the other brewers in the country had not. The agency waited for the initial excitement to die down and for Budweiser's competitors to run their product-specific announcement ads. Then it ran a classic image ad in the *Wall Street Journal*, proclaiming: "Something more than beer is back . . . Budweiser is back." It firmly established a leadership image for Budweiser as the brand that could speak for an entire industry, promoting beer as an integral part of the American lifestyle.

Despite the harsh economic times of the Great Depression, D'Arcy's success continued. Although the agency had begun conducting consumer marketing research in 1917, it undertook its first major business-to-business market survey in 1930 for Shell Oil Company. At the time, Shell ranked 13th in the sale of fuel products for commercial aviation and wanted to know if the market justified continued attention. After visiting 733 airports, D'Arcy presented the findings that convinced Shell to aggressively pursue the market, where it ranked number two just five years later.

At about the same time, the agency began its own research project of collecting ads in more than 100 product categories dating back to 1890. The project continued for more than 40 years and grew to include almost 2 million print ads created by many agencies, primarily for consumer products. The purpose of the project was to provide a source of information and inspiration for agency staffers. (The "D'Arcy Collection" was donated to the Communications Library of the University of Illinois at Champaign-Urbana in 1983.)

In addition to that long-term research project, the agency also initiated one of the longest-running campaigns in advertising history—the Coca-Cola Christmas campaign featuring the now-classic image of Santa Claus, as created by illustrator Haddon Sundblom in 1931. Sundblom (who also created the Quaker Oats and Aunt Jemima trademark characters) started with an 1880s version of Santa by cartoonist Thomas Nast but made him taller and more robust. He added twinkling eyes, an ermine-trimmed red waistcoat and trousers, black leather belt and boots, and always a bottle of Coca-Cola. After his original model died, Sundblom used his own face as the model for Santa's. The Santa illustration was accompanied by the new slogan, "The pause that refreshes." The campaign was an extension of the "Thirst knows no season" campaign to increase winter sales and the decades-old slogan, "Drink Coca-Cola, delicious and refreshing."

Expansion continued with the opening of a New York City office in 1934 and the first international office in Toronto, Canada, in 1938. That same year, the agency gained Glenmore Distilleries' Kentucky Tavern, Glenmore, and Old Thompson brands. During the World War II years of the early 1940s, virtually every client cut its advertising budget. Some, like General Tire, devoted virtually all of their production facilities directly to the war effort. Many others were unable to obtain raw ingredients because they were needed for military purposes. Most consumer products were rationed, if they were available at all. Therefore, strong sales-oriented advertising was considered inappropriate. Most clients produced limited product-oriented advertising and undertook image campaigns to keep their names before the public. Major national advertisers such as Coca-Cola and Budweiser strongly supported the War Advertising Council's efforts and created campaigns to address war issues and efforts such as planting victory gardens, conserving and recycling raw materials, and buying war bonds.

Despite the hard times D'Arcy continued to add new clients, including Gerber baby foods, Laclede Gas, Bigelow and Lee Carpets, Philco appliances, Brown & Williamson cigarettes, and Listerine. A wholly owned subsidiary, Publicidad D'Arcy, was opened in Mexico City.

By the end of the war, billings had grown to $21 million. D'Arcy announced his retirement and was succeeded by J. Ferd Oberwinder, who had brought the General Tire account to the agency. D'Arcy spent his remaining years working on a project dear to his heart: a plan to build a 630-foot stainless-steel arch on the St. Louis riverfront to commemorate the city as the "Gateway to the West." He had been elected chairman of the Jefferson National Expansion Memorial Committee in 1936 and worked tirelessly for the rest of his life to see the dream realized. (When the last section of the Gateway Arch was lowered in place in 1965, many in the agency considered it a legacy to the personal efforts of D'Arcy.) After he died in 1948, D'Arcy posthumously became one of the first ten professionals to be inducted into the American Advertising Federation Hall of Fame.

During the late 1930s and 1940s, the D'Arcy agency had become the largest buyer of outdoor advertising space in America. Although most D'Arcy clients used outdoor advertising to some extent, Anheuser-Busch, Coca-Cola, General Tire, and Glenmore used it heavily. The agency's Charlie Horn helped found the National Outdoor Advertising Bureau and led the agency's innovative use of movable posters, rotating cutouts, and lighted "outdoor spectaculars" that drew attention in the 1950s. Two of the largest were created for Budweiser, one looming over Times Square in New York City and another along the Miracle Mile in Los Angeles, California. By 1959 the agency had placed $160 million in outdoor advertising over two decades.

The 1950s also saw pivotal changes at D'Arcy. The agency began experimenting with the upstart medium of television for its national accounts. Its first TV advertising was for Anheuser-Busch, with its sponsorship of the *Ken Murray Show* on Saturday nights on CBS. Guests performers on this live variety show also took part in the commercials. They were often seen drinking Budweiser on camera. Coca-Cola sponsored *Kit Carson,* a Saturday afternoon cartoon show for children. General Tire was an occasional sponsor of other shows.

As network radio and television took on greater importance in the Coca-Cola media plan, the account moved to the New York City office in 1951. But just four years later the agency suffered a devastating blow when Coca-Cola announced that it was moving the account to McCann-Erickson. The reasons were not clear. Some said the move was prompted by changes in top management; other cited the lack of a large international agency network. At the time of the transition, D'Arcy ran a large ad in the *Wall Street Journal* headlined "We hand it on with pride." The copy read, "And so Coca-Cola grew. Its advertising made its name better known than any other trade name in history. It won the respect and friendship of people everywhere . . . and its sales grew until it became by far the most popular soft drink in the world."

As the agency celebrated its 50th anniversary in 1956, it had billings of almost $60 million. Despite the loss of Coca-Cola, the agency saw its billings nearly triple from $28 million in 1950 to $80 million in 1960.

In the 1960s D'Arcy used comedian George Carlin to proclaim that "Go-getters go Ozark" for Ozark Air Lines; on the *Tonight Show* Ed McMahon insisted that "Where there's life there's Bud"; cows mooed, "If cows could, they'd give Milnot"; the animated Red Goose sang, "Half the fun of having feet is Red Goose Shoes"; every boy put the "spittin' image" Daisy air rifle on his gift list; and Michelob in bottles was introduced with "This is it." One of the most memorable campaigns of the decade began with one of the simplest print ads. To support a campaign theme of quality, the agency ran a large spread in *Life* magazine consisting solely of the Budweiser label, which details the product's ingredients and brewing process. The ad was a huge hit; readers pulled it out, framed it, and wrote the company demanding more items carrying the label. It created a mini-industry for the brewery, which eventually produced hundreds of items sporting Bud-

weiser's label and logo. It also provided the basis for a new ad campaign that showed the huge label covering the bottom of a swimming pool, a rec room floor, and a hot-air balloon. A similar approach was used successfully for Coleman outdoor products. The label covered expanses of grounds and woods with the tag line, "The greatest name in the great outdoors."

During the 1950s photography had replaced illustrations in most print ads, which still remained an important part of clients' campaigns. But the 1960s and 1970s saw the demise of national general-interest publications such as *Life, Look,* and *Saturday Evening Post* and the rise of more narrowly targeted publications. The 1960s also saw rapidly escalating use of television by marketers; radio and television together accounted for 55 percent of the agency's total billings during the decade. D'Arcy's outdoor department once again scored high in technological innovation, helping to create printed bulletins to replace painted ones. The former took less time to produce and post and guaranteed accurate reproduction of creative art. The first nationwide use of the new bulletins was for the outdoor portion of Budweiser's "Pick a Pair" sales promotion that grew into a multimedia ad campaign. The campaign ran for many years, and the promotion was perhaps the most successful in the brewer's history.

The 1960s also saw D'Arcy take the steps that would lead to its growth as an international agency and, ultimately, change it forever. In 1957 it had established an international department in the New York City office to serve clients overseas. In 1961 it opened its first European office. It formed a separate company, Synergie-D'Arcy, with French agency Synergie Publicité, one of the largest in France, to provide advertising and marketing support for Gerber products and its French canning partner. In 1966 D'Arcy formed Multi-National Partners, a group of cooperating international agencies. Membership in the group grew quickly and included agencies in The Netherlands, West Germany, Italy, Spain, France, Belgium, England, Sweden, Denmark, Norway, and Finland.

When the decade ended, billings had topped $100 million, and talks had begun with MacManus, John & Adams that would change the structure of William D'Arcy's company but not his vision of the essential role of advertising: to provide sales-oriented results for his clients. In November 1970 the two agencies merged and formed a partnership with Intermarco, an agency in Amsterdam, to become D'Arcy-MacManus-Intermarco, Inc., creating a company with total billing of $262 million. The merger became effective 1 January 1972. The following October D'Arcy-MacManus partnered with Masius, Wynne-Williams, a large London agency billing approximately $160 million, to become D'Arcy-MacManus & Masius, thus bringing to an end the history of D'Arcy Advertising as an independent agency.

SUSAN SEYMOUR

Further Reading

D'Arcy Masius Benton & Bowles <www.dmbb.com>
Peterson, Eldridge, "Advertising Centers of America: St. Louis," *Printers' Ink* (3 February 1956)

D'Arcy Masius Benton & Bowles

Established as D'Arcy-MacManus-Intermarco, Inc., in 1971 by merger of two longtime U.S. agencies, D'Arcy Advertising and MacManus, John & Adams, Inc., with European agency Intermarco; partnership established with Masius, Wynne-Williams, Ltd., in 1972 and merger finalized in 1976 to form D'Arcy-Mac-Manus & Masius, Inc.; merged with Benton & Bowles in 1985 to form D'Arcy Masius Benton & Bowles; became principal subsidiary of the MacManus Group (formed, 1996); joined with Leo Burnett Company to form holding company Bcom3 Group, 1999.

Major Clients

Amoco
Anheuser-Busch, Inc.
Avon Products (media)
Burger King Corporation (media)
Coca-Cola Company
Colgate-Palmolive Company
Corning Glass Works
Ernst & Young
Fiat
General Foods Corporation
General Motors Corporation
Hyatt International
Maybelline
M&M/Mars
Procter & Gamble Company
TWA (TransWorld Airlines)
Whirlpool

In November 1970, after three years of talks, D'Arcy Advertising Company, Inc. (ranked number 19 in the United States), and Mac-Manus, John & Adams, Inc. (MJ&A; ranked number 22), announced a merger of the two agencies and the establishment of a tie-in with Intermarco, N.V. (ranked fourth in Europe). The new entity, to be known as D'Arcy-MacManus-Intermarco (DMI), would be the eighth-largest agency in the world with billings of more than $250 million. (The two American agencies each brought billings of approximately $100 million and Intermarco brought $57 million.)

The principal agencies applauded the merger because of limited account conflicts, a common vision and management philosophy, and client approval. Each was highly respected and had a good account mix. Their growth and creative work had run a parallel course; they already had offices in several of the same U.S. cities and strong affiliations in Europe. The merger provided an increased presence overseas, with 25 offices in 15 countries, and an expanded list of blue-chip clients. D'Arcy brought American Oil Company, Anheuser-Busch, Bank of America, General Tire & Rubber, Gerber's, Ralston Purina, Royal Crown, the U.S. Air Force, and Bigelow Sanford. MJ&A's list included Colgate-Palmolive, General Mills, General Motors corporate as well as Cadillac

and Pontiac, Celanese Corporation, Bendix, Dow Chemical, and 3M Company.

After the D'Arcy-MacManus merger was finalized in January 1971, talks began almost immediately with Masius, Wynne-Williams (billings of $160 million), an agency founded by an American, Michael Masius, in London, England, after World War II. That agency was a leader in Europe, Australia, New Zealand, and South Africa. A partnership was established in 1972 (after Intermarco left the organization), and the company became known as D'Arcy-MacManus & Masius (DM&M). A merger was finalized in 1977. An aggressive expansion program in the early 1970s pushed the company into additional international markets. This effort added the DM&M logo to new offices in Australia, Hong Kong, Kenya, Germany, Spain, and Rhodesia (after 1980, Zimbabwe) in addition to 18 other countries. By the mid-1970s, more than half of the agency's 2,300 employees worked outside the United States.

The agency made impressive account gains throughout the decade. New business included accounts for Whirlpool Corporation; Rawlings Sporting Goods Company; the American Dairy Association; General Motors Corporation Parts Division; the *Chicago Sun-Times* newspaper; Burger Chef Systems; Heublein, Inc.; the *Detroit Free Press* newspaper; Knight-Ridder Newspapers; Red Lobster Inns of America; Mars, Inc.'s Milky Way candy bars; General Mills, Inc.'s Saluto Foods Corporation; Westinghouse Electric Corporation; International Telephone & Telegraph Corporation (ITT); Kal Kan Foods, Inc.; the American Soybean Association; Swensen's Ice Cream Company; Purex Corporation; American Telephone & Telegraph Company's national Phone Center Stores; Gallery of Homes; and Florists' Transworld Delivery Association, as well as increased business from the U.S. Air Force, Colgate-Palmolive Company, Anheuser-Busch, and Mars, Inc.'s Summit and Twix bars.

Success in the Seventies

Overseas gains included the accounts of Whirlpool International, ITT International, Colgate toothpaste, Rust-Oleum, Bank of America, Castrol, Corning Glass tableware, Uncle Ben's rice, Players cigarettes, the *London Sunday Express*, Haig whiskey, Marley Tiles, Golden Wonder Crisps, Dunlop motorcycle tires, Snugglers diapers, sherry maker Harveys of Bristol, Greyhound Coaches, Cinzano, Sherwin-Williams, General Foods, Barclays Bank, Norsk Citroen, Iberia Airlines, Lipton, Bayer, and the Colombian Coffee Federation. In 1979 alone, the company gained 119 accounts in 19 countries.

Notable television campaigns from the 1970s included those featuring "Mr. Goodwrench" for GM parts; Suzanne Somers singing, "Ace Is the Place with the Helpful Hardware Man"; Ed McMahon and, briefly, Frank Sinatra for Anheuser-Busch's Budweiser; John Forsythe and Robert Urich for Anheuser-Busch's Michelob and Michelob Light; a toothy, animated alligator for

Baggies; Ray Stevens for Flav-O-Rich; Ed Andrews for Southwestern Bell business long distance; the Handiwipes magician; Merlin Olson for FTD; and Jack Nicklaus for Pontiac station wagons.

Other memorable creative work included the "Pitch In" public service effort, Saluto's "Atsa lotsa mozzarella," "Red Lobster, where America goes for seafood," Pontiac's "Driving excitement," Michelob's "Weekends were made for Michelob," followed by "Put a little weekend in your week," "Downright upright" (for Harveys Bristol Cream Sherry), "You can call me Ray or you can call me Jay" (for Anheuser-Busch's Natural Light), "The little blue jug" (Dynamo), "Sooner or later, you'll own Generals" (General tires), "savagallonagasaweek" (Amoco), "Five kings of Africa" (Budweiser), the "mark of excellence" (GM), and "Milk's the one" (Dairy Promotion Federation). One of the best known and most enduring campaigns was Budweiser's "For all you do. This Bud's for you," which was revived in the 1990s.

Print, especially magazines, was important for business, industrial, and agricultural clients, including Amoco chemicals and plastics, Keene Corporation (marketers of fluid-handling and air-processing equipment), Avery labels, Dow chemicals, Bendix (auto parts), Budd (auto frame components), Fruehauf (trucking trailers), Detroit Diesel Allison (engines, generators, and transmissions), ITT, Hexcel (composite materials), and many divisions of 3M. These business and industrial marketers relied heavily on print advertising, but by the end of the 1970s newspaper and magazine billings accounted for only about 20 percent of the total agency billings, down from more than one-third at the beginning of the decade.

New business acquisitions and creative development benefited from the agency's consumer research. In the 1970s agency staff in St. Louis, Missouri, began expanding information gathered in research efforts looking for the "average" consumer who would be most likely to use a client's product. A systematic approach developed, called "The Man Who, the Belief That," which grew into "Belief Dynamics," a method for identifying factors that motivate consumers to make a purchase. The approach was adopted both nationally and overseas.

Tumultuous Eighties

The 1980s, a tumultuous decade for the agency, were marked by ambitious goals, modest gains, painful losses, a historic merger, restructure, and revitalization. By 1980 the agency had topped $1 billion in worldwide billings. Worldwide gross income of $156 million placed it tenth among U.S. agencies according to *Advertising Age,* but more than half of its income came from outside the United States, placing it seventh in overseas income. That year the agency gained approximately 170 new accounts overseas, including Datsun in Belgium, Citroen in Denmark, Munsingwear in Hong Kong, ITT Electronics in Italy, Akai video division in Norway, Waverly blankets in South Africa, Kimberly-Clark in West Germany, Ricoh copiers in the United Kingdom, Bluebird Music in Finland, and Banco Credito Industrial in Spain.

DM&M saw modest gains in billings and income in the early 1980s but began to look for another partner to strengthen both its New York City office and its overseas capabilities. Towards that end, the renamed D'Arcy MacManus Masius Worldwide (DMM) merged the de Garmo agency into its New York office in 1980, doubling the size of that office. De Garmo, Inc., brought in billings of almost $60 million from clients such as Drexel Heritage Furnishings, CPC International, Finnair, Pitney Bowes, Lorillard's True cigarettes, and Burlington Domestics. It also brought two subsidiaries: Poppe Tyson, a business-to-business agency, and Spanish Advertising Marketing Services, the largest U.S. Hispanic consumer agency with clients including Lorillard, Colgate-Palmolive, Libby, Bulova, and Standard Brands. (DMM lost the $20 million True account and others when John de Garmo, president and chief executive officer of de Garmo, Inc., resigned in 1982.)

In January 1984 the agency lost $40 million in overseas business from its longtime Colgate-Palmolive account when the client decided to consolidate business at a few worldwide agencies. That loss forced DMM to redouble efforts to improve its international network. Although it had a significant number of international clients, the agency was not among the top tier of multinational shops.

It formed a seven-member management team to concentrate on its then-current international clients and to search for new worldwide business. Until that time, each office had held responsibility for its own new-business efforts. At the end of 1984 DMM owned majority or maximum allowable stock in 51 overseas agencies, minority interest in 8, and had affiliations with 13.

DMM offset the Colgate-Palmolive loss with a $50 million gain: the Dairy Promotion Federation's fluid milk, cheese, and calcium campaign. But the same month of July 1984 brought the stunning loss of the longtime Michelob and Michelob Light business, totalling $60 million in the St. Louis office, which earlier had lost the $30 million Red Lobster restaurant business. Separately, the New York office lost $21 million in Mars business.

Industry's Largest Merger

DMM announced a merger with Benton & Bowles in June 1985. The $2.45 billion merger was the largest to date in advertising history and created the eighth-largest advertising agency in the world (based on 1985 billings). The Benton & Bowles agency had been founded in 1929 by William Benton and Chester Bowles. Its major clients included packaged-goods giants Procter & Gamble Company (P&G) and General Foods. Over the years its client brands included Tide, Maxwell House, Hellman's, Crest, and Ivory. It gave the advertising world Mr. Whipple and the slogan, "Please don't squeeze the Charmin."

The new agency, D'Arcy Masius Benton & Bowles (DMB&B), was led by D'Arcy's Hal Bay as president and chief operating officer, and B&B's John Bowen as chairman and chief executive officer. It had offices in nine U.S. cities and 24 countries. Combined media-buying strength made DMB&B second in radio, fifth in network television, third in spot television, sixth in outdoor advertising, and eighth in magazine placements. The new agency also would contain a number of subsidiaries: Direct, Inc., which specialized in direct marketing; Intergroup Marketing & Promo-

DMB&B created the popular Budweiser frogs, which made their television debut during the 1994 Super Bowl.
Anheuser-Busch, Inc. St Louis, MO.

tion (IMP), marketing and sales promotion; Manning, Selvage & Lee, Inc., public relations; Medicus Intercon International, health-care marketing and advertising; Poppe Tyson Advertising, business-to-business advertising; Ted Colangelo Associates, Inc., corporate communications; and Telecom Entertainment, which handled television production.

B&B's strong New York City office would complement the midwestern strength of DMM's St. Louis, Detroit, Michigan, and Chicago locations. Most important, B&B was P&G's largest U.S. agency, capable of filling the consumer packaged goods void left at DMM by Colgate-Palmolive. B&B benefited from the prestige of major auto and beer accounts, as well as access to DMM's stronger international network for P&G and its other multinational clients, including General Foods, Johnson & Johnson, Richardson-Vicks, and Texaco.

The transition was not entirely smooth, however. At the time of the merger B&B also had suffered major account losses, including Hardee's ($35 million), Nabisco ($17 million), Emery Air ($15 million), Tropicana ($15 million), and Zest ($10 million). B&B management attributed the losses to the normal cyclical nature of the business and to client personalities. Critics, however, attributed some of the losses to the lack of innovative creative work from an agency that had long been known for its marketing, media, and account management. During its first year the new agency faced other challenges as well. Corporate histories and cultures were different. DMM's independent offices had grown out of mergers and were not accustomed to more involved corporate oversight. B&B was primarily a New York agency with managers and a management style related directly to its largest client, P&G.

Worldwide billings dropped 5.8 percent in 1985 and rose only 1.3 percent in 1986, due largely to a 7 percent increase in overseas billings. The agency acquired offices in Japan, Mexico, Saudi Arabia, and Thailand, but sold Poppe Tyson to Bozell & Jacobs. The outlook improved with worldwide billings increases of 11.5 percent in 1987 and 23 percent in 1988, when billings topped $3 billion. Additional business from existing clients such as P&G,

Mars, Anheuser-Busch, and General Foods increased $305 million in 1988, including the consolidation of General Foods' entire $250 million network television budget.

After three years of work, the new agency scored big in 1989 with gains of $50 million from Maxwell House, $130 million from Burger King, and another $390 million in new accounts. Existing clients increased spending by $138 million, bringing a one-year increase of 13 percent over 1988. The agency also increased its acquisitions, including a 49 percent stake in Sosa & Associates, San Antonio, Texas, which won the Spanish-language portion of the Burger King account.

Gains continued into the early 1990s and included the accounts of Knudsen Dairy, the International Olympic Committee, Hyatt International hotels, Montgomery Ward & Company, Mexicana Airlines, and the American Plastics Council. The agency doubled its billings, from $3 billion in 1988 to $6 billion in 1998.

In 1991 DMB&B became the largest television buyer in the United States, with billings topping $1.4 billion. An important factor was Procter & Gamble's consolidation of $700 million at DMB&B. It gained another $450 million in buying assignments from Southwestern Bell, Pearle Vision, Kraft General Foods, Pillsbury, Pet, Inc., M&M Mars, and North American Philips. In 1992 *Mediaweek* estimated that the agency bought 25 percent of all daytime television. The agency credited its successes to early moves into syndication and cable for its clients, as well as a huge computer-driven strategic market analysis database begun in the mid-1970s. It was the first agency to use satellite transmission for spot buys to save money and increase accuracy. It scored other major wins in consolidated global media planning for Coca-Cola in 1995 and Avon in 1997. In 1996 DMB&B dominated U.S. agency television buying, accounting for one dollar of every seven dollars spent in network television.

By 1994 the agency exceeded $5 billion in worldwide billings. For the U.S. offices, however, it was the beginning of a two-year string of losses, including Burger King creative ($160 million),

FTD ($45 million), Blockbuster Music ($35 million), Whirlpool ($35 million), Kraft ($60 million), Amoco ($40 million), and Anheuser-Busch's Budweiser ($100 million), shortly after the famous "Frogs" commercial made its debut.

The Budweiser case was unique. Agency and client had been together for 79 years, one of the longest associations in advertising. For most of these years, there was a close personal and professional relationship between top management at the two companies. When DMB&B was dismissed by August Busch III, it was over a failure of internal communications. DMB&B's TeleVest media unit in New York City had accepted a small assignment from arch-rival Miller Brewing and had neglected to inform its St. Louis office or the client.

Reform and Revitalization

To revive its North American business, the agency restructured procedures for internal communications and built a management tier to provide consistency among offices and enable local directors to work more closely with clients. The reorganization also sought to turn the loose federation of agencies and offices into a cohesive network and to position the New York office as the U.S. network leader. In 1996 DMB&B acquired N.W. Ayer & Partners, whose New York City office claimed more than $500 million in billings, and the agency reorganized under a holding company structure. The MacManus Group, with DMB&B as its largest unit, was named for Ted MacManus, the founder of MacManus, Johns & Adams. He is best known for his 1915 ad "The Penalty of Leadership," which ran only once in the *Saturday Evening Post* but had such an impact that it was credited with positioning Cadillac as the world standard for luxury autos.

In 1996 DMB&B was the fastest growing international agency, based on the increase in number of countries served—from 30 in 1991 to 98 in 1996. It also increased from 5 to 15 the number of clients served in 10 or more countries. Its truly global clients remained Mars, Royal Philips Electronics, General Motors, and Procter & Gamble, but it also conducted extensive business for Maybelline, Hyatt, Bristol-Myers Squibb, and Australian Tourism in its Asia/Pacific offices; Western Union, Freudenberg, and Texaco in Europe; and CPC in Latin America.

By 1997 the agency had topped $1 billion in billings in both its New York and London offices and more than $500 million in Detroit. In 1999 the agency participated in the formation of Bcom3, a holding company for DMB&B, Leo Burnett, and other assets, including media operations Starcom Worldwide and MediaVest Worldwide. D'Arcy had worldwide gross income in 2000 of $724.8 million, up 9.1 percent over 1999, on billings of $6.7 billion, up 8.2 percent over the previous year. D'Arcy ranked 11th among U.S. agency brands in terms of gross income for 2000, with $278.3 million, up 7 percent over the previous year.

SUSAN SEYMOUR

Further Reading

Alter, Stewart, "Merger Finale for D'Arcy, B&B," *Advertising Age* (24 June 1985)

Alter, Stewart, "Wed in Woe: DMB&B Merger Bound Together 2 Stumbling Shops," *Advertising Age* (27 January 1986)

Alter, Stewart, "DMB&B Challenge: New Creative Profile," *Advertising Age* (10 February 1986)

Chase, Dennis, and Howard Sharman, "DMM Mulls All Options for '88 Goal," *Advertising Age* (27 February 1984)

D'Arcy Masius Benton & Bowles <www.dmbb.com>

Emmrich, Stuart, "D'Arcy Revamps Agency Image," *Advertising Age* (16 January 1984)

Farrell, Greg, and Jennifer Comiteau, "Wake Up Call," *Adweek* (4 March 1996)

Grant, Don, "D'Arcy MacManus Merger Complete, with Intermarco As Added Factor," *Advertising Age* (30 November 1970)

Grover, Stephen, "Benton and Bowles and D'Arcy Agree to Merge," *Wall Street Journal* (24 June 1985)

Konrad, Walecia, "The 'Bridesmaid' Ad Agency Finally Catches the Bouquet," *Business Week* (12 June 1989)

Mandese, Joe, and Jon Lafayette, "$700M Win Makes D'Arcy Top TV Buyer," *Advertising Age* (23 December 1991)

Schmuckler, Eric, "How D'Arcy Does It," *Mediaweek* (23 March 1992)

Wentz, Laurel, and Sasha Emmons, "AAI Charts Show Yearly Growth, Consolidation," *Advertising Age* (9 September 1996)

DDB Needham Worldwide. *See* Needham, Harper & Steers Advertising, Inc.

DDB Worldwide, Inc.

(Doyle Dane Bernbach, Inc.)

Founded in New York City as Doyle Dane Bernbach (DDB), 1949; went public, 1964; became part of DDB Needham World-wide in merger of DDB, Batten Barton Durstine & Osborn (BBDO), and Needham Harper Worldwide into the Omnicom Group, 1986; renamed DDB Worldwide, Inc., 1999.

Major Clients
Anheuser-Busch Companies
Avis Rent A Car System
Compaq Computer Corporation
Digital Equipment Corporation
Hertz Corporation
Michelin Group
Ohrbach's
Henry S. Levy & Sons (Levy's rye bread)
Polaroid Corporation
McDonald's Corporation
Volkswagen

The relationships that would eventually form Doyle Dane Bernbach (DDB) began in 1939—a decade before the agency was established—with the meeting of Ned Doyle, head of advertising for *Look* magazine, and Maxwell Dane, whom Doyle hired to be the magazine's advertising and promotion manager. During World War II Doyle joined the Marines, while Dane went to work as sales promotion manager at WMCA, a New York City radio station. In November 1944, after leaving WMCA, Dane started his own firm, Maxwell Dane, Inc. Meanwhile Doyle returned from the war and moved to Grey Advertising, where he met William Bernbach, the soft-spoken vice president of the Grey art and copy departments. Bernbach had begun his ad career as a writer with William Weintraub & Company in 1942 (which became Norman, Craig & Kummel in 1955) and came to Grey in 1945. Both he and Doyle were dissatisfied with Grey's penchant for rapid expansion, and they decided to strike out on their own if they could find someone who could actually run an agency. Doyle contacted his old friend Dane, who agreed to take on two new partners.

On 1 June 1949 Doyle Dane Bernbach opened its modest offices one story above the last elevator stop at 350 Madison Avenue. The agency began with 13 employees, all from the ranks of Grey. The Grey exodus also included DDB's first client, Ohrbach's department store.

Although he had scorned the speed with which Grey expanded, Bernbach soon found the same process occurring at DDB, as the agency's billings rose from $500,000 in 1949 to $5.1 million by 1953. The following year the upstart shop astonished the industry by winning seven out of the 50 awards given by the American Institute for Graphic Designers for the year's best ads. Among the DDB winners that year was early work for Ohrbach's

(two diapered infants were shown wearing adult accessories: "Smart people go to Ohrbach's for Mother's Day gifts"); Max Factor ("To bring the wolves out. . . ."); and Acrilan fabric ("Look mom, these suits made with Acrilan go right into the wash"). DDB won these early accolades simply because its ads were superior to those produced by other agencies—not because they were especially distinguished or innovative. It took the agency nearly a decade to develop the distinctive voice that would become the envy of the industry.

The early campaign that came closest to achieving the classic design purity later associated with DDB was written by Bernbach for one of the agency's smallest clients, Henry S. Levy & Sons. Capitalizing on the fact that Levy's rye bread was unusually firm—a contrast to the soft consistency most consumers associated with fresh bread—the first campaign asked: "Are you buying a bed or a bread?" When the fortunes of the bakery were reversed within a year, another ad proclaimed "New York is eating it up." But the tag line best remembered from this campaign was "You don't have to be Jewish to love Levy's."

Early Growth

Within five years of its founding DDB billed $8 million, employed 67 people, and had moved twice. By the time the agency moved again in the mid-1970s, its offices had grown to 250,000 square feet, housing about 1,800 employees. At that time DDB also had 18 other offices, more than half of them outside the United States. The largest of the branches remained the one in Los Angeles, California, DDB's first office outside of New York City. It was established in June 1954 to provide the agency with a West Coast staff capable of handling two major accounts: Ohrbach's was about to open in Los Angeles, and Max Factor was already headquartered there. The Los Angeles agency brought to DDB $1 million in new billings.

DDB suddenly lost the $3 million Max Factor account in March 1958, but by then the agency had a notable record both for selling and for winning awards. It had taken Levy's from a small Brooklyn bakery to the biggest selling brand of rye bread in New York City. In four years the agency had also created ads that nearly tripled Polaroid Land Camera sales to $65 million, and it had made El Al Airlines (which means "up to the skies" in Hebrew) a competitor among trans-Atlantic airlines with a single ad that ran once in the *New York Times*.

On 13 April 1959, a brief piece in *Advertising Age* noted that Bill Bernbach and Ned Doyle were in Germany to confer with executives at Volkswagen (VW) about taking on the company's advertising account. The other contender was Fuller & Smith & Ross. Volkswagen, a small company, made a small car that seemed destined for a small market in the United States. It was also less than headline news when DDB officially won the

Volkswagen account shortly afterward, although no one was more keenly conscious of the unlikely nature of the match between this "Jewish" agency and its German client than Bernbach and his colleagues.

In the late 1950s the upper tier of U.S. ad agencies remained conspicuously white and Protestant. Before the war the only important agency widely perceived as a "Jewish agency" was Grey Advertising, the shop from which most of DDB's charter employees, including Doyle and Bernbach, had come. After the war anti-Semitism was unfashionable on Madison Avenue, but the established, predominantly Gentile agencies and their clients remained hesitant about how to deal with products that might suggest anything Jewish. At DDB, however, the key people were Jewish, and they adopted an attitude of forthrightness that the old-line WASP agencies and clients were not yet ready to embrace. Only DDB could reassure reticent Gentiles that "you don't have to be Jewish" to enjoy Levy's rye or promote El Al with the slogan "The miracle of the lox that flies."

The essence of the style that DDB had been creating for a decade crystallized in its ads for Volkswagen. The campaign was so clear and timeless that it continued virtually unaltered when the redesigned VW Beetle was introduced in the late 1990s. The campaign was as striking in the pages of *Vanity Fair* as it originally had been in *Life* and *Look*. The classic ads offered a procession of small but penetrating insights, each of which mocked the pomposity of traditional car advertising.

The work for Volkswagen greatly enhanced DDB's creative reputation and drew the agency onto the world stage. Whereas other agencies were following their U.S. clients overseas, DDB was in the unique position of serving a blue-chip German client in the United States. In October 1961 the agency opened its first overseas office in Germany, a 50-50 partnership with Holzschuher & Bauer, a $5 million agency founded in Dusseldorf in 1949. A year later the German branch was named DDB, Dusseldorf, and handled VW business in Germany.

The agency celebrated its 12th birthday in 1961 by winning $6 million in business from American Airlines, which had considered DDB only two years before but passed because the agency, at $22 million, was too small. Twenty-four months later, it had become a $60-million agency.

In July 1964 as it opened an office in London, England, and exceeded $100 million in billings, DDB, the 18th-largest agency in the United States, announced a 25 percent initial public offering (IPO.). At that time only two other agencies had gone public: Foote, Cone & Belding (FCB) and Papert, Koenig, Lois.

The Glory Days

These were the glory days of DDB. It seemed to pull business away from other agencies with the force of a black hole; Mobil, Gillette, Ocean Spray, U.S. Rubber, General Foods, and Lever Brothers all became DDB clients. The agency was both envied and feared by its competitors, many of which were working overtime to copy "the Doyle Dane look." President John F. Kennedy was among the many who delighted in the Volkswagen work, and he

decided that DDB should handle his 1964 reelection campaign, in which he expected to run against conservative Arizona Sen. Barry Goldwater. After Kennedy's assassination in 1963, Lyndon B. Johnson chose DDB. Among the 40 or so DDB people assigned to the campaign were the art-copy team of Sid Myers and Stan Lee, and they were the ones who came up with the devastating "Daisy" spot, in which a little girl plucked the petals from a daisy, as if playing "He loves me, he loves me not" to a voice-over countdown to a nuclear detonation, implicitly asking voters who they trusted to lead the United States through the perils of the Cold War. Neither Goldwater nor the Republican Party was mentioned in the ad, but they immediately protested, and the spot was withdrawn. The Republicans may have protested too loudly, however. By rising to the bait, they created a level of interest that gave the commercial considerable exposure on countless news programs and election documentaries for years to come.

A commercial called "Ice Cream Cone" followed. In that spot yet another little girl, a personification of innocence, licked an ice cream cone while a maternal voice explained the physics of strontium 90, component of nuclear fallout, and the politics of Goldwater's recent vote against the nuclear test ban treaty. Finally, DDB produced a Johnson ad appealing to older voters—the spot showed a Social Security card being torn in two.

By 1968, however, President Johnson, DDB's "man of peace" in 1964, had to account for 500,000 U.S. soldiers in Vietnam and was not even welcome at his party's convention. The agency took on Democrat Hubert Humphrey's presidential campaign with far less relish than it had the Johnson one. Relations between DDB and the Democratic National Committee (DNC) quickly deteriorated, and the account passed to a Lennen & Newell election subsidiary.

The worst aspect of the story of DDB and the DNC came to light when the so-called Pentagon Papers were leaked in 1971 and it was revealed that in 1964 DDB had been fed misleading and sometimes inaccurate information by the DNC concerning the administration's future war policy. Bernbach confessed to being "disappointed to find out what had been going on behind the scenes." He was in the uncomfortable position of having to apologize for trusting his government, a new feeling to a man who had grown up in the age of Franklin D. Roosevelt, Harry Truman, and Dwight D. Eisenhower. Some younger members of DDB apparently were less shocked to find out that they had been deceived. Myers and Lee said they were not at all surprised. In July 1971 the agency announced a formal policy against handling any further election campaign advertising.

The political scandal did not diminish DDB's reputation. The agency had started a revolution in advertising, and other shops jockeyed to hire key members of its creative staff. As creative executives from DDB moved up and down Madison Avenue, the phrase "creative revolution" moved from the trade press to national weekly magazines such as *Time, Life,* and *Look.* People outside the industry learned to talk with expertise about ad campaigns, debating their merits and strategies as if they were sports teams.

In January 1963 Avis Rent A Car System left McCann-Erickson for DDB, which noted with interest that Avis was second

Lemon.

This Volkswagen missed the boat.

The chrome strip on the glove compartment is blemished and must be replaced. Chances are you wouldn't have noticed it; Inspector Kurt Kroner did.

There are 3,389 men at our Wolfsburg factory with only one job: to inspect Volkswagens at each stage of production. (3000 Volkswagens are produced daily; there are more inspectors than cars.)

Every shock absorber is tested (spot checking won't do), every windshield is scanned. VWs have been rejected for surface scratches barely visible to the eye.

Final inspection is really something! VW inspectors run each car off the line onto the Funktionsprüfstand (car test stand), tote up 189 check points, gun ahead to the automatic brake stand, and say "no" to one VW out of fifty.

This preoccupation with detail means the VW lasts longer and requires less maintenance, by and large, than other cars. (It also means a used VW depreciates less than any other car.)

We pluck the lemons; you get the plums.

Doyle Dane Bernbach's 1960 "Lemon" ad for Volkswagen is one of the most widely cited automotive ads in advertising history.
Volkswagen of America, Inc.

behind Hertz Corporation in the car rental field. With disarming forthrightness, DDB pounced on this fact, reasoning that a company that is number two is obliged to "try harder." Avis Chief Executive Officer (CEO) Robert Townsend hated this concept, but he stuck to his agreement with Bernbach "not to change a bloody comma." The Avis work became one of the agency's signature campaigns of the 1960s—second only to that for Volkswagen—and it increased Avis revenues from $16 million to $110 million in three years.

Troubled Times

One of the agency's most frustrating chapters began in 1969 in a flurry of celebration as Miles Laboratories moved Alka-Seltzer from Jack Tinker to DDB. DDB's only experience with analgesics had been its 1966 launch of Resolve, where the parody line "In your stomach you know it's right" proved no more successful than the original ("In your heart you know he's right") had been for Barry Goldwater's 1964 presidential campaign.

The agency produced two precedent-shattering masterpieces for Alka-Seltzer—"Spicy meatball" and "Wedding night"—only to lose the account in December 1970 to one of the many DDB clones that had sprung up in the 1960s: Wells, Rich, Greene (WRG). Joe Daly had succeeded to the DDB presidency in 1968. Although Bernbach continued as CEO, spiritual creative director, and teacher, management of the agency was changing hands. Doyle retired in 1969, and Dane left in November 1971. However, both men continued to influence affairs from the board. The agency went into the 1970s with a string of losses of high-profile accounts. In addition to Avis and Alka-Seltzer, Whirlpool, Sara Lee, Quaker, and Lever Brothers left the agency, taking $30 million with them. Morale slipped as ambitious young talents began feeling burdened, and idle senior members of the creative staff began foraging the floors for work. Some veterans of the agency, including Bernbach, were enjoying induction into one advertising hall of fame after another, suggesting that their careers were reaching the end.

The agency made some solid acquisitions in Europe, but it also had several misbegotten adventures into diversification that temporarily put DDB into the sailboat business (Snark Products) and the retail trade (Trade Mart, Inc.). To try to avoid future mistakes Bernbach began looking to strengthen his management team. Through 1974 DDB announced a procession of staff changes in the wake of losing the $10 million Uniroyal account. James Heekin, a former president of Ogilvy & Mather, became president, only to quit six months later just before he would have been ousted.

Bernbach was increasingly willing to listen to offers from companies hoping to merge with DDB. One interested party was a former DDB protege, Mary Wells Lawrence, who was eager to expand WRG into more global opportunities. With offices in Canada, Britain, Germany, and five other countries, DDB had a quarter of its billings outside the United States. Talks between Lawrence and Bernbach were necessarily brief to avoid making

clients of the two agencies nervous about potential conflicts of interest that might arise. Negotiations broke off in June 1974. Two years later DDB made a major move into direct marketing with the purchase of Rapp, Collins, Stone & Adler.

In August 1976 Bernbach turned 65 and handed his CEO title over to Daly. Much of the news the agency generated at that time concerned its expanding European network and further merger rumors. After acquiring agencies in Austria and Spain in 1980, DDB moved onto Sweden in 1982 and formed a European coordination unit in London called DDB Europa, which also included a Middle East operation set up in June 1979. DDB Europe was headed by Bernbach's son, John, who boasted that the agency now represented 31 U.S. clients abroad.

On the merger front, Ally & Gargano seemed willing to bring its $33 million together with DDB in 1978. Another suitor was the Wyse Agency. However, these agencies were small shops by DDB standards. Still another potential partner was the Chicago, Illinois, agency Needham, Harper & Steers, which ranked 20th in world billings (DDB was 11th). Around 1979 and 1980 Needham CEO Paul Harper, had several serious meetings with Bernbach with a view toward a package in which each would gain strength in the other's city. But nothing materialized.

A highly tempting and compelling combination was a merger considered between closely ranked DDB and Foote, Cone & Belding. The resulting $2.3 billion colossus would have been second only to Young & Rubicam in billings. In April 1982 the two parties agreed to merge, despite a number of client conflicts. It would have been the biggest agency merger in history—if the principals could have agreed on a name for the new firm. When they could not, the deal collapsed. That merger also might have been the ultimate victory in the legendary career of Bernbach. Instead, the failed deal was his final disappointment. Diagnosed a few years earlier with leukemia, he died on 2 October 1982.

Among the first things to change after Bernbach's death was DDB's policy on cigarette advertising. The agency had won Benson & Hedges in April 1958 and later took on Alpine, both from Philip Morris, but DDB left both accounts in 1961 because of a "mutual disagreement on policy." After that time DDB did not take on cigarette companies, by order of Bernbach. Within eight weeks of his death, the agency readmitted Philip Morris for the first time in 21 years and took on Parliament.

Other more profound changes signaled a slow atrophy of the Bernbach spirit, still openly honored but quietly ignored in the face of short-term growth pressures. The person most alarmed by this trend, however, had never worked at DDB: Keith Reinhard, at Needham, Harper & Steers, felt he was watching the agency that had inspired him turn into just another big ad factory. "My idea," he told *Advertising Age,* "was to get together with DDB for reasons of creative passion and bring Bernbach's ideas to life again." Reinhard also had the interests of his own agency in mind as he contemplated the merger. Needham CEO Paul Harper had put together a global network for that agency on relatively little money, leading Reinhard in 1984 to drop Steers and rename the company Needham Harper Worldwide, but the agency ranked only 16th in world income. Reinhard envisioned that DDB

Needham Worldwide would combine the geographic muscle of both firms.

After sorting out all the strengths and weaknesses of the two agencies, Reinhard approached Niel Austrian and Barry Loughran at Batten Barton Durstine & Osborn (BBDO) and John Bernbach, Bill Bernbach's son, in New York in the summer of 1985 to discuss a merger and other options, including the possibility of Reinhard's coming to DDB. Reinhard was at a disadvantage as a would-be partner, however, because at that moment DDB lacked a strong incentive to merge. By September talks were considered dead.

Merger Talks

In 1986 the situation changed. Saatchi & Saatchi had targeted DDB for a takeover and made a bid on 24 April. DDB, which had been talking to Needham and BBDO since 1 March, rejected Saatchi and at the same meeting approved the now legendary deal that joined Needham, DDB, and BBDO. BBDO became the third leg of the combination, with Omnicom serving as the holding company.

Together the three agencies accounted for almost $4 billion in billings, even though almost $200 million in business was lost because of conflicts among clients. For example, Needham's Los Angeles, California, office, which handled the $100 million Honda account, was sold so that DDB Needham could retain the $110 million Volkswagen business.

Reinhard, who had earned a reputation as an inspiring leader, was named chairman and CEO of DDB Needham Worldwide. He had joined Needham, Louis, and Brorby (as it was then called) in 1964. In 1969 he was a member of the team that helped Needham pitch and win the McDonald's account. He became the creative executive in charge of overseeing the McDonald's business, creating many slogans and jingles, including the famous "You deserve a break today."

Second in command at the new agency was John Bernbach, who was named president and chief operating officer of DDB Needham Worldwide. Although he once declared that the last thing he ever wanted to do was follow in his famous father's footsteps, John Bernbach joined DDB in 1972 and later became the first American chosen to be president of the European Association of Advertising Agencies. He was named president and CEO of DDB's new operating division in 1984 and elected to the executive committee and the board later that year.

In 1987 DDB Needham Worldwide had $2.6 billion in billings; by 1990 it had reached $4.6 billion. Under Reinhard's leadership, DDB Needham began a steady turnaround. To further the commitment to creative excellence, many of the executive slots at Needham's agencies around the world were filled with former creative directors. These new executives also had a mandate from Reinhard to break down the barriers between former Needham and DDB staff members and to create an entirely new corporate culture. When Susan Gillette was named president of DDB Needham Chicago, she removed the boundaries between research,

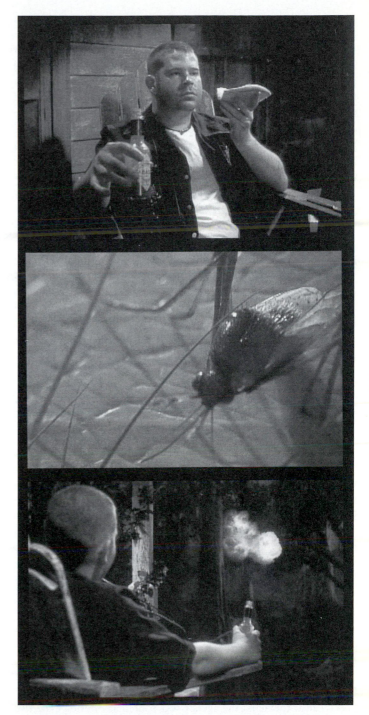

This 1997 commercial for Tabasco brand pepper sauce garnered many awards for DDB.
Courtesy of McIlhenny Company.

media, creative, and account departments, forming brand clusters where all personnel on an account were placed in proximity to each other.

In 1990 Reinhard instigated a new system of agency compensation for some of the clients at DDB Needham. Under this system, dubbed "guaranteed results," the agency's payment was no longer based on the amount of media commissions it earned from a client; instead, financial remuneration was tied to the effectiveness of its advertising. By the late 1990s about 20 of DDB Needham's accounts were participating in the guaranteed results program, and the move from media-based compensation to a more accountable fee structure was becoming more widespread throughout the advertising industry.

In 1995 DDB Needham Worldwide was named "Agency of the Year" by *Advertising Age,* which applauded the agency's memorable commercials for Anheuser-Busch's Bud Light beer and Frito Lay's Rold Gold pretzels. Bud Light overtook Miller Light, and Rold Gold's market share grew from 11 percent in 1992 to 25 percent. DDB Needham's promotional efforts for Anheuser-Busch have not been without controversy, however. Its "Bud Rewards" program, which enabled consumers to save points for Budweiser-related merchandise, was temporarily banned in California, when state alcohol regulators argued that it could lead to increased alcohol consumption. After a state court allowed the program to be reinstated, film director Spike Lee and DDB Needham Chicago produced a commercial that helped explain the new promotion to consumers in other regions of the country.

The late 1990s saw more gains for DDB Needham. The Chicago office was one of the most successful in the global network. *Adweek* chose DDB Needham Chicago as its "Midwest Agency of the Year" for 1997 after the agency secured more than $400 million in new business, including Montgomery Ward, Heinz, Sargento Cheese, General Mills' Golden Grahams, and Hefty. The greatest triumph for DDB Chicago was its acquisition of the $385 million McDonald's account from Leo Burnett. Reinhard in particular had been eager to recapture that business ever since Needham Harper Worldwide had lost the account 16 years earlier.

Confident in his ability to help spearhead a new creative record for McDonald's, Reinhard brought only one positioning line to the pitch: "Did somebody say McDonald's?" He argued that the line would resonate with consumers' emotional connections to McDonald's and that its "talk value" would be high among the general public. As Reinhard had predicted, the slogan became fodder for talk show comedians, and it helped to contribute to a turnaround for McDonald's. By 1998 DDB Needham was handling work for McDonald's in 47 countries.

In early 1997 another division of DDB Needham—Spike DDB—opened in New York City. With acclaimed film director Spike Lee at the helm, the agency was touted as offering expertise in "urban marketing," a euphemism for the African-American consumer segment. However, both black-owned agencies and the other large shops criticized Lee's lack of advertising expertise and the agency's lack of urban marketing experience. By 1998 Spike DDB had hired new principals to help position it as a more mainstream agency. Although Spike DDB garnered media attention, its creative output was small, and many of its assignments (for Fox Sports network, the Miami Heat basketball team, and ice hockey's Stanley Cup playoffs) put the agency in danger of becoming known as a sports marketing specialist. In June 1998 billings were estimated at $22 million.

International Expansion

That same year DDB Needham Worldwide became majority investor in two other agencies, DM9 in Sao Paulo, Brazil, and the internationally acclaimed Palmer Jarvis in Vancouver, Canada. Although remote from the business centers in eastern Canada, Palmer Jarvis had become known for its creativity. All of the activity in 1997 contributed to the selection of DDB Needham Worldwide as the Global Network of the Year by *Advertising Age.*

Although DDB Needham's account gains in the United States were impressive, much of the agency's growth following the merger occurred overseas. In 1988 DDB Needham had worldwide billings of $3 billion, 35 percent of which was in markets outside the United States; in 1998 DDB Needham had revenues of $11.7 billion, with 44 percent in international business. During the mid-1990s, DDB Needham agencies in Argentina, Australia, Brazil, Canada, Chile, India, Italy, France, The Netherlands, Poland, Russia, Slovenia, Sweden, and the United Kingdom were named *Advertising Age* "Agency of the Year" in their markets; eight of these agencies received this accolade in 1997. By 1999 DDB Needham was handling multinational advertising efforts for such clients as American Airlines, Johnson & Johnson, Michelin North America, PepsiCo, Sony, and Volkswagen. In 1999 the agency officially dropped Needham from its name, continuing as DDB Worldwide.

Like the work it created in the U.S. market, the agency's creative efforts overseas sometimes generated controversy. In February 1998 DDB France was forced to pull ads for Volkswagen. A spot featuring St. Francis carrying two trash bags and discussing his "conversion" after he saw the new Volkswagen Golf and an ad satirizing the Last Supper so angered French Catholics that they threatened to sue the agency if the advertising was not cancelled. The agency not only apologized for the campaign but also made a donation to the Catholic Emergency Fund in France.

CELE C. OTNES AND JOHN MCDONOUGH

See also Bernbach, William (Bill)

Further Reading

Arndorfer, James B., "Apple to Join Lizards in '98 Budweiser Creative," *Advertising Age* (16 March 1998)
Berger, Warren, "Palmer Jarvis DDB," *Communication Arts* 40, no. 8 (1999)
Dobrow, Larry, *When Advertising Tried Harder: The Sixties, the Golden Age of American Advertising,* New York: Friendly Press, 1984
"Execs Who Will Guide New Mega-Agency," *Advertising Age* (5 May 1986)
Fox, Stephen, *The Mirror Makers: A History of American Advertising and Its Creators,* New York: Morrow, 1984
Krajewski, Steve, "Southwest Agency of the Year: DDB Dallas," *Adweek* (Eastern edition) (9 February 1998)
Petrecca, Laura, "Pay-for-Results Plans Can Boost Agencies: Execs," *Advertising Age* (8 September 1997)

Petrecca, Laura, "Global Network of the Year," *Advertising Age* (30 March 1998)

Schmuckler, Eric, "Media Director of the Year: Page Thompson," *Mediaweek* 7, no. 46 (8 December 1997)

Selinger, Iris Cohen, "DDB Needham Turns a Clever Phrase," *Advertising Age* (10 April 1995)

Tilles, Daniel, "DDB France Pulls Religious VW Ads," *Adweek* (16 February 1998)

Vagnoni, Anthony, "Spike DDB Pursues Path to Mainstream," *Advertising Age* (1 June 1998)

Willens, Doris, "The Day DDB Went Up in Cigarette Smoke," *Advertising Age* (10 February 1992)

DeBeers Consolidated Mines, Inc.

Principal Agencies

N.W. Ayer, Inc.

J. Walter Thompson Company

Since its inception, the DeBeers cartel has controlled the availability and distribution of approximately 80 percent of the world's supply of uncut diamonds. Moreover, through its "central selling organization," DeBeers has orchestrated marketing efforts that have fueled the desire for diamond gemstones among consumers around the globe.

The history of the company dates to 1871, when the DeBeers brothers, Boer farmers who had settled in South Africa, paid a shepherd a 25 percent royalty for each diamond he found on their land. The next year the brothers sold their farm for $30,000; it would yield half a billion dollars worth of gems over the next 75 years. In 1881 the English-born entrepreneur (and, later, South African statesman) Cecil Rhodes bought the material rights on the farm. In 1888 Rhodes merged his DeBeers Mining Company with a nearby Kimberley mine to form DeBeers Consolidated Mines and control virtually all of the world's diamond production.

Under Rhodes and his successor, Sir Henry Oppenheimer, DeBeers controlled the flow of diamonds to world markets, often gearing levels of production to the projected number of engagements expected in the United States and Great Britain. While diamond engagement rings had begun to increase in popularity in the Roaring Twenties, fewer than 20 percent of American brides owned them by the end of the 1930s. Because antitrust laws prohibited DeBeers from directly conducting business in the United States, the company hired N.W. Ayer in 1938 to promote sales of diamonds in America, which had been languishing as a consequence of the Great Depression. The agency first used trade advertising to inform jewelers—who were concerned that advertising might "cheapen" diamonds—of their intent to launch a national magazine campaign to make diamonds desirable. From 1939 to 1948 the agency ran five separate campaigns, featuring romantic paintings of churches and couples in love; during World War II the ads informed consumers that diamonds used for jewelry were not the kind needed for the war effort. DeBeers supplemented these ads with integrated marketing efforts that employed public relations, product placement, and speeches on the desirability of diamonds.

In addition to issuing press releases about all aspects of diamonds, Ayer arranged for movie stars and celebrities to wear diamond jewelry from the DeBeers collection in movies and at gala events. Ayer also created a series of "seminars" on diamonds that were offered to women's clubs and high school assemblies. These efforts complemented those undertaken by DeBeers in Great Britain, where the marriage (in 1947) and coronation (in 1953) of Elizabeth II fueled the public's interest in diamond jewelry. To publicize the fact that Queen Elizabeth had loaned some of her diamond jewelry to the DeBeers exhibit at the British Industries Fair in London, England, the company purchased page magazine ads in Great Britain and the United States.

In 1948, before a major agency presentation to DeBeers, Ayer copywriter Frances Gerety scribbled the line, "A diamond is forever." Capturing both the durability of the stone and the romantic aspirations of couples entering into marriage, this slogan became the mainstay of the DeBeers campaign in the United States. It was incorporated into all advertising for the corporation, including the "Great Artist" series, which featured works by, among others, Pablo Picasso, Salvador Dali, and Raoul Dufy.

At the same time, Ayer developed the "Four Cs" of diamond buying—cut, color, clarity, and carat weight—and included this information in its advertising for DeBeers. These efforts, as well as events such as diamond fashion shows, allowed Ayer and DeBeers to establish diamonds as *the* gemstones for American and British women to envy.

By the end of the 1940s, the number of married women in the United States who owned diamond engagement rings had increased to 60 percent. By the 1980s, that figure was over 70 percent. Encouraged by its success in the United States, DeBeers decided to export the tradition of the diamond engagement ring to areas of the world where it had not yet been established. In Europe, for instance, diamonds had traditionally been viewed as portable "nest eggs" and insurance policies against the loss of wealth during political upheaval but, except for royalty, few women actually wore diamond jewelry. DeBeers launched an advertising campaign in 1963 to encourage the tradition of

Immer wieder blickt sie auf ihren Verlobungsdiamanten. Er leuchtet und strahlt. Ein Unterpfand des Glücks von dem Mann, den sie liebt. Und sie weiß, daß ihre Liebe so unvergänglich sein wird wie das Feuer ihres Diamanten.

Ein Diamant ist unvergänglich

Der Verlobungs-Diamantring ist das schönste Verlobungsgeschenk für die Braut. Sie trägt ihn neben dem Goldring, dem Zeichen der Bindung. Es ist ein ganz besonderes Erlebnis, wenn Sie Ihren Verlobungs-Diamantring auswählen. Sie sollten sich vorher über alles Wissenswerte informieren. Lesen Sie die Broschüre „Wenn Sie einen Diamanten kaufen…", die Sie kostenlos bei Ihrem Juwelier bekommen oder vom Diamant Informations-Dienst, Abt. 2J, 6 Frankfurt/Main, Bockenheimer Landstraß 104.

Fotografiert von Günter Kaufmann für De Beers Consolidated Mines, Ltd.

DeBeers's slogan, "A diamond is forever," translated for a 1968 ad in a German publication, crossed borders with ease. *DeBeers.*

diamond engagement rings, simply importing the "diamond is forever" slogan and translating it into several European languages.

Even more interesting was DeBeers's success in Japan. In 1968 the company commissioned the J. Walter Thompson Company (JWT) to create an advertising campaign that would help integrate the diamond engagement ring into Japanese wedding customs. When these efforts began, fewer than 5 percent of Japanese women received diamond engagement rings; by 1981, the figure was 60 percent. DeBeers's success in Japan can be attributed to JWT's inspiration that the ring should be positioned not as a gift from the groom to the bride, but as part of the array of gifts offered by the groom's family to the bride's household. DeBeers found Japan to be an especially lucrative market because the Japanese spend three or four months' salary on an engagement ring, as opposed to the "two months' salary" guide established by Ayer for American consumers.

In the 1980s and 1990s DeBeers and its advertising agencies continued to develop innovative marketing strategies. One of its most aggressive promotional efforts was the creation of the diamond "anniversary ring." In 1981 DeBeers began positioning diamond-studded wedding bands as gifts for special anniversaries. Ads by Ayer with headlines such as "The band that says you'd marry her all over again" began to appear in men's magazines. Just three years after the start of the campaign, 30 percent of all women could identify a diamond anniversary ring. By the late 1990s, one in ten women in the United States (which still accounts for more than one-third of all diamond jewelry sales) owned a diamond anniversary band.

In 1995 DeBeers ended its 57-year relationship with Ayer, awarding the U.S. account to JWT, which already managed the DeBeers account in the rest of the world. In response, Ayer unsuccessfully filed trademark applications for the "Forever" slogan, for jewelry names such as a "diamond anniversary band" and "diamond anniversary ring," and for the "Four C's."

DeBeers owed its remarkable success to its ability to control both the quantity of diamonds available and their price, which increased 50 percent from 1985 to 1996. However, it was the shaping of consumer aspirations—at a cost of some $200 million a year in ad spending in 34 countries—that made DeBeers especially noteworthy.

By 2000 DeBeers was facing increased competition from other diamond marketers, as particular areas of the globe—especially Canada and Russia—wrested diamond production away from DeBeers. Moreover, jewelers such as Tiffany and Bailey, Banks and Biddle were leading the way in diamond-cutting innovations, creating stones with more facets and branding these stones with special names. These initiatives undercut DeBeers's marketing efforts.

CELE C. OTNES

See also color plate in this volume

Further Reading

Dickinson, Joan Younger, *The Book of Diamonds: Their History and Romance from Ancient India to Modern Times,* New York: Crown, and London: Muller, 1965

Epstein, Edward Jay, *The Rise and Fall of Diamonds: The Shattering of a Brilliant Illusion,* New York: Simon and Schuster, 1982

"Glass with Attitude," *The Economist* (20 December 1997)

Koskoff, David E., *The Diamond World,* New York: Harper and Row, 1981

McGough, Jeanne L., "Brand Management: Glitter, Glitter Everywhere," *Madison Avenue* 26, no. 10 (October 1984)

Proddow, Penny, and Marion Fasel, *Diamonds: A Century of Spectacular Jewels,* New York: Abrams, 1996

Della Femina, Jerry 1936–

U.S. Copywriter

Jerry Della Femina has been quoted as describing the business of advertising as "the most fun you can have with your clothes on." Born 22 July 1936 in Brooklyn, New York, to Italian immigrant parents, Della Femina claimed that he learned to write by reading the newspaper. Before getting his first copywriting job with the Daniel & Charles Agency in 1961, Della Femina had spent seven years doing odd jobs as a messenger, shipping clerk, waiter, and salesclerk. But it was not long before he made a name for himself in the advertising world. The irreverent humor in his ad campaign for Talon zippers, in which a baseball catcher approaches the mound to tell the pitcher, "Your fly is open," was a signal of more daring things to come.

After years of butting heads with agency superiors at Ted Bates & Company and other shops, Della Femina and three associates, including Ron Travisano, opened their own New York City agency, Della Femina, Travisano & Partners, in 1967. By the 1970s it had become one of the industry's biggest revenue makers by stressing creativity.

In 1970 Della Femina wrote the book *From Those Wonderful Folks Who Gave You Pearl Harbor: Frontline Dispatches from the Advertising War,* taking the title from a slogan he proposed in jest for Panasonic. Through his own flair for publicity, he soon turned this insider's look at advertising into a best-seller. Throughout the 1970s Della Femina was at the forefront of a movement to transform advertising from an industry favoring reverence and hierarchy to one promoting humor and casual openness, just as U.S. society was changing in much the same way. This meant breaking some rules and creating controversy.

In 1986 a Della Femina campaign for Ansell-America's Life-Styles condoms was rejected by the *New York Times, Time* magazine, and three TV networks. The campaign highlighted safety but did not ignore sex; it featured a young woman saying, "I'll do a lot for love, but I'm not ready to die for it." Della Femina took to the airwaves, describing the campaign as a public service in the fight against AIDS, and soon the ads were being aired. But when John Silverman, president of Ansell, was quoted in *Time* as calling the AIDS epidemic a "condom marketer's dream," Della Femina quit the account, drawing support from his advertising colleagues, often labeled as people with no principles.

He created another controversy the same year by being the first to use the word *fuck* in advertising, in a print campaign for Perry Ellis cologne. A bit tamer was the agency's "Liar" campaign, featuring the Joe Isuzu character, for American Isuzu Motor Company, which played off the notion that car salespeople are prone to exaggeration. The agency also did notable creative work for Ralston Purina Company's Meow Mix cat food, Beck's beer, Schieffelin & Company's Blue Nun wine, and Pan American World Airways.

In 1986 the agency, then billing nearly $200 million, was acquired for $29 million by London, England-based Wight Collins Rutherford & Scott PLC; Della Femina himself received $23 million. He continued as chairman-chief executive officer of the agency (renamed Della Femina, McNamee, Inc., in 1988) and was offered $15 million in incentives over the next five years.

In June 1992 the holding company bought out his contract for $3 million, and he agreed not to use his last name on another ad agency nameplate; instead, he put his name on a restaurant in East Hampton, New York. By December of that year, however, he had opened a new agency, Jerry, Inc., promising to put the fun back in the business. In May 1994 Jerry, Inc., merged with the New York City office of Ketchum Advertising, forming Jerry & Ketchum. In 1998 the agency name changed to Della Femina/ Jeary & Partners. Della Femina was chairman-chief executive officer of the agency. In June 2000 Della Femina/Jeary & Partners merged with Grace & Rothschild to form Della Femina, Rothschild, Jeary & Partners.

Della Femina maintained his high profile, even being arrested in East Hampton for displaying pumpkins and flowers—considered "outdoor advertising" and thus illegal in East Hampton—outside his Red Horse Market. And he continued to share his principles, including characterizing a Benetton ad series on capital punishment as "excruciatingly tasteless, ineffective advertising." In 1999 *Advertising Age* recognized Della Femina as one of the top 100 advertising people, for his determination, sense of humor, dedication, and love of advertising.

NANCY DIETZ

Biography

Born in Brooklyn, New York, 22 July 1936; joined Daniel & Charles Agency, New York City, as a copywriter, 1961; founded Della Femina, Travisano & Partners, New York City, 1967; wrote *From Those Wonderful Folks Who Gave You Pearl Harbor,* 1970; sold his agency to London, England-based Wight Collins Rutherford & Scott PLC for $29 million, 1986; opened new agency, Jerry, Inc., 1992; merged with the New York City office of Ketchum Advertising, May 1994; changed agency name to Della Femina/Jeary & Partners, 1998; merged with Grace & Rothschild to form Della Femina, Rothschild, Jeary & Partners, New York, 2000.

Selected Publication

From Those Wonderful Folks Who Gave You Pearl Harbor, edited by Charles Sopkin, 1970

Further Reading

Gross, Michael, "Jerry Della Femina: (M)adman," *New York Magazine* (6 April 1998)
Nulty, Peter, "An Aging Boy Wonder Shakes Up the Ad Business," *Fortune* (13 April 1987)
Walls, Jeanette, "Advertising for Himself," *Esquire* (September 1996)
Wells, Melanie, "A Smaller, Happier World for Jerry Della Femina," *Advertising Age* (17 May 1993)

Demographics

In advertising the term *demographics* refers to information describing the characteristics of consumers or target audiences. (In the larger sense *demographics* is the social science that studies human populations, their size, geographic and age distribution, birth and death rates, and related factors.) Marketers, advertisers, and their ad agencies use demographic data to better understand the consumers of their products and the targets of their ad campaigns. Early advertisers were quick to realize the need for information about consumers. Frank Alvah Parsons, an advertising practitioner in New York City in 1913, was describing advertising when he said, "I understand it to involve a knowledge of men and what they want or need."

Such information is crucial to the success of advertising. In what is now considered a classic work—*Defining Advertising Goals for Measured Advertising Results* (now simply referred to as DAGMAR)—Russell Colley stated that for advertising to be effective, the advertiser needs to know the following:

- the number of people who constitute the present and potential markets, and
- complete information about these people, which is needed to communicate with them in terms of their particular needs, desires, and interests, including: their characteristics (age, sex, geographic location, socioeconomic group, and so on), their consumption habits (frequency and quantity of use of goods and services), and the relative buying influence of various people (e.g., adults vs. children, women vs. men, purchasing agents vs. engineers)

This information is used to make advertising more effective in both the media-planning and the ad-creation processes. In media planning, the demographics of the consumer can be matched with the demographics of the media user, allowing the media planner to match radio and television programs, magazines, and newspapers with the target audience. In creating the ad, the copywriter and artist will achieve a more effective creative strategy if they have a thorough understanding of their target consumer.

Marketers and advertisers generally describe the consumers of their products or services by using three broad types of analysis: psychographic, geographic, and demographic. Psychographic research concerns consumer lifestyles, attitudes, and behavior tendencies. One well-known model is the values and lifestyles system (VALS 2 Segmentation System) developed by the research company SRI International, in which consumers are segmented into eight different lifestyle groups: actualizers, fulfilleds, achievers, experiencers, believers, strivers, makers, and strugglers. Members of each group have different values and live distinct lifestyles. Geographic data describe where consumers of a particular product or service are located—nationally, regionally, or locally; in urban or rural areas; and so forth.

Of the three types of consumer information, demographic data are the most easily quantifiable and most readily available, which allows for computer analysis of the data and makes demographics the first and most commonly used of all consumer information. Demographic data usually include: age, gender, income, marital status and family size, race, education, and occupation.

Demographic Data

Age

Because age determines generation—and each generation shares a body of common life experience and cultural influences distinct from those of other generations—age is considered to be the most fundamental of all demographic criteria. Age distinctions became unusually sharp in the late 1960s and 1970s when marketers faced the challenge of selling to middle-aged buyers who had grown up during the Great Depression and World War II as well as to young adults who had been raised in a period of rising prosperity and comparative peace. Seldom had advertisers faced such a generational disjunction in the marketplace.

To better sort and classify generational subcategories, while at the same time developing data whose elements were mathematically compatible, the advertising industry created specific age groupings within which to analyze information: 5–11 (children), 12–17 (teenagers), 18–24 (college students), 25–34, 35–44, 45–54, 55–64, and 65–74. Other broader groupings included: 18–34, 18–44, 18–54, and so on; and 25–44, 25–54, and upwards. Adults are sometimes targeted as 18+ and older consumers as 55+ or 65+. In the 1980s a popular although unusual target breakdown was adults aged 18–49, unusual because it was so inclusive and potentially inefficient.

The designation of the correct ages of the target audience is extremely important to the success of the media plan and the creative strategy. Generally, advertisers believe that the target audience should be defined as narrowly as possible to minimize media costs and make the message more specific and, therefore, more effective.

Gender

Men and women have different media consumption habits and different buying behaviors. They also tend to purchase different types of products. For example, 64 percent of the purchasers of children's toys in the United States in 1990 were women, while men bought 62 percent of the powerboats sold that year. Traditionally, women have been the target of more advertising than men, because they are more often the purchasers of products, especially consumer goods. In the 1980s marketers started to compile demographic data for homosexual consumers, a relatively small group (2 to 3 percent of the population, according to the Guttmacher Institute for Reproductive Research) but one considered to exert a cultural influence larger than its numbers.

In this ad for *Time* magazine, a single demographic detail linked advertisers to thousands of potential customers.
Courtesy of TIME Magazine.

Income

Consumer income is a strong determinant of buying behavior, affecting what type of goods may interest particular consumers, how much they can afford, and which media they use. For years, advertisers such as Mercedes-Benz and Rolex have sought the "upscale" consumer—one with lavish tastes and the money necessary to purchase higher-priced products and services. Other marketers such as Walmart target consumers of average income with a message emphasizing low prices.

Marital Status and Family Size

Single individuals have different needs and interests than do married couples. Information on marital status and family size is relatively easy to obtain and may be quite meaningful in the target market analysis. Automakers target couples with children to sell them minivans and other child-safe vehicles that satisfy their needs.

Race

Many advertisers regard demographic data on racial differences to be prejudicial by its very nature. Others consider it to be useful in better understanding their target audiences. Certainly, cultural differences are strong determinants of consumer behavior and attitudes. As societies become more diverse over time, this type of analysis will perhaps become less important.

Education

Information on consumers' level of education is readily available in most nations. In highly developed societies, such as the United States, Western Europe, and Japan, educational data are available by consumer segments and even individually, so that direct marketers can mail their ads only to people with education above or below a certain level.

Occupation

For some widely used products and services occupation may be unimportant information. For other market situations—selling aircraft to pilots, for example, or accounting software to accountants—it may be crucial information.

After all this information is compiled for the consumers of a specific product or service, it may be developed into a "demographic profile" of the target audience. These profiles often become the basis for how advertisers present particular individuals in print ads and television commercials, thus helping to generate a base of social stereotypes through which people come to see themselves and others. In the 1950s and early 1960s the power of advertising helped to crystallize the images of "typical" homemakers, farmers, blue-collar workers, white-collar workers, teenagers, and other groups into a handful of idealized stereotypes.

Uses and Limitations

In the 1980s and 1990s, advertisers acquired the technology to look more deeply into their data and came—or were forced—to recognize subtle distinctions within group stereotypes. This growing consciousness of diversity has greatly expanded the range of acceptable social representations in advertising while at the same time exposing the limited insights available through data based purely on demographics. Although still widely used, many categories of demographic information are too general to be very meaningful to marketers when used alone. How does one know what demographic information is most important to the purchasing

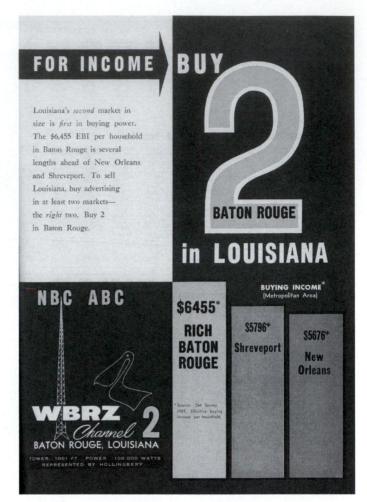

In this 1959 ad aimed at advertisers, WBRZ-TV of Baton Rouge, Louisiana, made bold use of demographic data to demonstrate the buying power of its audience.
Courtesy of WBRZ-TV.

decision? Without psychographic and geographic data, a demographic analysis alone may be misleading. Advertisers are best advised to consider all three types of information.

Demographic data are available from many sources: governments, private research firms, marketers, the media, and scholars. Broadcast media are particularly useful as sources of demographic information on their audiences. Private research companies in the United States such as Arbitron and ACNielsen Corporation are paid by television and radio stations to supply very specific and current demographic data about their audiences.

Magazines supply detailed demographic studies of their readership to potential buyers of advertising, as do large newspapers. Most local newspapers rely upon circulation and household data, with little demographic information available.

For other media, such as outdoor advertising, demographic information is very difficult to obtain and usually not available. For the Internet consumer information is readily available if individuals are willing to share it as they log onto specific Internet sites.

Standard Rate and Data Service (SRDS) is a private company that supplies advertising rates and data for all media in the United States, Canada, and Mexico, including demographic data broken down by states, counties, cities, and so forth. SRDS also publishes *The Lifestyle Market Analyst,* an especially useful annual study that integrates demographic and psychographic information, including a detailed list of consumer interests and hobbies, for all 211 designated market areas in the United States.

Other companies such as Simmons Market Research Bureau and MediaMark Research, Inc., provide comprehensive demographic information on the users of specific products and services, including users' media usage patterns, which helps to identify the target audience and to choose the proper media to maximize advertising effectiveness.

As social trends change, advertisers will become interested in the demographics of expanding market segments, such as working mothers or single parents. Along with psychographic information and geographic information, demographic information will continue to be important in understanding that all-important consumer of goods and services.

MARK MATTHEWS SECRIST

See also Psychographics

Further Reading

Bowers, Thomas A., and Alan D. Fletcher, *Fundamentals of Advertising Research,* Columbus, Ohio: Grid, 1979; 4th edition, Belmont, California: Wadsworth, 1991

Colley, Russell H., *Defining Advertising Goals for Measured Advertising Results,* New York: Association of National Advertisers, 1961; 2nd edition, by Solomon Dutka, 1993

Donnelly, William J., *Planning Media: Strategy and Imagination,* Upper Saddle River, New Jersey: Prentice Hall, 1996

Jugenheimer, Donald W., Arnold M. Barban, and Peter B. Turk, *Advertising Media: Strategy and Tactics,* Dubuque, Iowa: Brown and Benchmark, 1992

Parsons, Frank Alvah, *The Principles of Advertising Arrangement,* New York: Prang, 1912; 3rd edition, 1917

Sissors, Jack Zanville, and E. Reynold Petray, *Advertising Media Planning,* Chicago: Crain, 1976; 5th edition, by Sissors and Lincoln Bumba, Lincolnwood, Illinois: NTC Business Books, 1996

Surmanek, Jim, *Introduction to Advertising Media: Research, Planning, and Buying,* Lincolnwood, Illinois: NTC Business Books, 1993

Demonstration

In seeking to inform or persuade potential customers, advertisers often use a format known as demonstration. Demonstrations perform many functions: educating and informing audiences, establishing brand and store preference, generating immediate sales, and instilling long-term customer commitment. Demonstrations are instrumental in producing those results because they effectively convey the benefits of a product and/or how customers can best use it. Research confirms that the demonstration technique has consistently been associated with effective commercials.

In the context of advertising, a demonstration serves to substantiate an advertising claim through reasoning or a show of evidence. Depending on the nature of the product, the reasoning and evidence behind a claim may be conveyed in a demonstration in several ways: through illustration by examples or specimens; through testing; and/or by detailing the functionality, qualities, and/or benefits of an offering. Typically, the demonstration focuses on the rewards provided by an object's specific features, specifications, standards, and applicability. It is most useful when this explanation is unknown to the audience. The idea is to make the new and/or foreign familiar by showing off its properties and advantages.

Types and Characteristics

Demonstrations may be divided into many categories: the straightforward demonstration, the product test, the torture test, the comparative demonstration (such as the taste test), the before-after demonstration, and the whimsical demonstration. Straightforward demonstrations typically show how to use something, convey situational or lifestyle usage, or tout the simple benefits derived from using the brand, firm, person, or object. The product test demonstrates that a product meets a standard or set of standards established by experts or discerning users. The audience finds it believable because it involves state-of-the-art measurement equipment and experts who are more knowledge than they themselves are about the brand. The torture test shows how the product performs under adverse conditions rather than in ordinary circumstances. The before-after test compares the undesirable situation before use of the product to the desired state after use. Whimsical demonstrations incorporate humor and enjoyment into the message, for example, by employing an unexpected person as demonstrator or conducting the demonstration under unusual circumstances. Comparative demonstrations are used to achieve "head-on" positioning strategy: they explain the superiority of one brand over others on the basis of either subjective or objective judgments.

Demonstrations are product centered rather than audience centered. In other words, the focus of demonstrations is the product itself. The main argument in a demonstration concerns the product's applicability to a certain problem or situation and how to use the product. The crux of the demonstration generally entails the deterministic benefits of an offering's features, functions, standards, specifications, craftsmanship, design/form, or augmentation strategies (e.g., warranty, the functionality of the package, customer service programs). For example, to demonstrate the vehicle's superior traction, Ford ran its Explorer across the ice of a hockey rink. Demonstrations in conjunction with sound and sight deliver powerful arguments that can convey several benefits in a short time.

As a product-centered advertising format, demonstrations are most frequently used in supporting direct benefit-based claims—for instance, the braking power or trunk space of a car, the speedy drying time of a glue, the timely response of a consultant to a client's need, the comfort of an airplane seat—as opposed to promising higher-order gratification. Some of these benefits can be objectively measured using physical measurement (i.e., the braking power of a car, the drying time of glue). Other attributes noted can only be assessed subjectively. Subjective judgments cannot be measured using the instruments of physical measurement. Rather, mere preferences and liking expressed by a sample of people are used to support certain direct benefit-based claims, such as the comfort of an airplane seat or the taste of a bowl of chili. Demonstrations, therefore, are used successfully to establish favorable subjective and objective judgments. Thus, taste tests are frequently used to support subjective claims for foods and beverages. Objective demonstrations of gas mileage continue to be used to establish the superiority of economy cars.

Demonstrations are used less frequently than other ad techniques to establish the "higher-order gratification" often promised in advertising. Higher-order gratification is said to stem from perceptions of a brand's direct benefits along with other relevant observations, associations, and opinions held by individuals. Examples of higher-order gratification are power, prestige, learning and achievement, exclusivity, self-actualization, social acceptance, and the enjoyment of social rewards. FedEx Corporation successfully used a demonstration campaign which showed workers who scored points with their boss by using FedEx's fast, reliable delivery service and contrasted them with other employees who used a different delivery service, did not know the whereabouts of the packages, and lost favor with the boss. As the quality differential between many competing brands continues to decrease, demonstrations based on higher-order gratification rather than those touting direct benefit–based brand claims should prove of greater benefit to marketers.

Effectiveness

Credible demonstrations produce immediate sales because they persuade the audience that one brand actually works, provides

A 1999 ad used a comparative demonstration to highlight the advantages of the Swiffer Sweeper over the traditional dust mop. *Courtesy of The Procter & Gamble Company.*

key benefits, performs more functions than its rivals, or is safer and/or easier to use. Many advertisers have enjoyed immediate results from the use of demonstrations in advertising and other promotional programs. For example, Callaway Golf Company used demonstrations successfully to launch its Big Bertha driver. Callaway's advertisements and promotions showed a significant increase in the distance traveled by a golf ball after being driven by Big Bertha both in laboratory and on the course. Many golfers bought the Big Bertha soon after seeing the demonstrations in advertisements and in audio/video demonstrations at the point of purchase in golfing supply outlets. Having produced similar speedy results for many other companies, demonstrations are credited by experts as being able to produce immediate sales.

Demonstrations, moreover, yield important long-term results. Advertisers count on demonstrations to produce lasting loyalties among consumers to brands and firms. Demonstrations, for example, were used effectively by Foote, Cone & Belding in convincing consumers to associate Sears, Roebuck & Company's line of DieHard batteries with longevity, power, and reliability, especially under the harshest of winter conditions. In one famous commercial six cars were started simultaneously off of a single DieHard battery. In a similar vein, audiences associated Charmin bath tissues with softness as a result of whimsical demonstrations featuring a distracted grocery clerk unable to prevent shoppers from squeezing the Charmin (a creation of Benton & Bowles). For many years, Timex watches were subjected to "torture test" demonstrations to build a reputation for toughness and reliability in a campaign created by W.B. Doner & Company. Over the years, the continual use of demonstrations across advertising campaigns did much to establish customer-based brand equity for these and many other brands.

In some instances, advertisers may rely on the demonstration only for short-term periods. Periodically, advertisers may decide to influence newcomers to the market—consumers who typically know little about the product category, differences among competing brands, or product usage. They find demonstrations informative and helpful. Demonstrations may be used as a temporary strategy to launch new products and services. For example, Procter & Gamble Company's Dryel, a product that "dry cleans" clothes in consumers' home dryers, was launched using a "three-step, how-to-use" demonstration. After Dryel passed successfully through its introductory stage, P&G's agency, the Leo Burnett Company, abandoned the demonstration format. In finding that people had indeed learned how to use Dryel, its account planners drove Dryel into its growth stage by tying its use to sex appeal and a related promise of social rewards.

A problem faced by the Nestlé Beverage Company's launch of Taster's Choice freeze-dried coffee provides a different reason for using demonstrations in the short term. The manufacturer launched the instant coffee by claiming better taste. Initial sales were disappointing. Executives soon learned that people were not trying Taster's Choice because they simply did not know how to prepare freeze-dried coffee. Its advertising team turned to the demonstration format to show how simple the product is to make: just add a teaspoonful to a cup of hot water. Thus, demonstrations have both long- and short-term utility for advertisers.

Demonstrations are effective in handling ticklish promotional situations and thorny advertising challenges, as well. In the late 1990s Cover Girl selected playful demonstrations for a campaign designed to introduce young girls to make-up and cosmetics without antagonizing mothers, who fear that cosmetic ads encourage girls to grow up too fast. Recognizing that concern, Cover Girl marketers elected to set up kiosks in major malls across the United States. Advertisements invited girls and mothers to visit the booths, where, using computer demonstrations, girls from eight to ten years of age and their mothers had a fun and playful experience of make-up. Early indications were that the girls and mothers alike enjoyed the experience. Moreover, the smart approach to developing the Cover Girl demonstrations met the approval of mothers. That success story underscores the importance of knowing how the audience relates to an offering before designing the demonstration.

Demonstrations are best suited to specific audiences, including novices in the use of a product; risk-avoiders, who need assurance that a brand delivers on its claims and promises; dissatisfied customers or hostile audiences, who have had experience of one or more ineffective brands in the product category; experts desiring

to secure and extend their knowledge advantage; individuals who are attracted by novelty; people who are highly interested and engaged in the product category and actively seek information; business-to-business buyers and purchasing agents, who seek to select a brand that matches certain standards and specifications; and people who associate high levels of personal gratification and pleasure with a specific product/service category.

Demonstrations fit well with products that have so-called credence properties, features whose benefits cannot be judged at the time of purchase but only over the long haul. Demonstrations can show today the long-term benefits of a brand that users will eventually enjoy in the future. Likewise, the intangible qualities of a service can be explained and conveyed through demonstrations. Demonstrations tend to be effective in persuading audiences concerned with the ease, ergonomics, and/or efficiency of product usage.

Demonstrations are particularly useful in informing people about new products or showing how to use an existing brand in a new way. The latter is likely to become increasingly important to marketers seeking to increase incremental sales of established products at a time when annual sales growth has become increasingly difficult to achieve. One reason for slowed sales growth is product proliferation. Another is slowed population growth in the most economically advanced countries. In this challenging environment, demonstrations of new uses for a product may be one way companies can increase sales and grow. This is especially true when the demonstrator is someone who might normally use the product under the circumstances depicted.

Conversely, demonstrations may be less effective than other advertising formats in some situations. When a brand is mature and the audience already knows its benefits and how to use it, demonstrations make less sense. In that case, advertisers may find that whimsical, humorous, or absurd formats are more effective in increasing attention to and liking of the advertisements and in achieving other campaign goals. Similarly, price promotions may be more effective than product demonstrations in attracting deal-prone buyers. Deal-prone buyers, according to research, tend to find more utility in dollar savings than in product attributes or performance. A demonstration will not be effective if the audience senses that it is out of place or lacks a legitimate reason underlying its use. Also, a demonstration is less likely to be effective when its arguments are too difficult for the audience to comprehend or are perceived as being "too good to be true." Thus, it is important to match the demonstration to the audience's level of product acumen and persuasive tolerances.

Regulation

The Federal Trade Commission (FTC), the agency charged with regulating interstate advertising in the United States, recognizes the persuasive power of demonstrations. Although truthful and accurate demonstrations are encouraged, the FTC recognizes two potential problems caused by demonstrations. First, the FTC is concerned with protecting citizens from misleading and deceptive advertisements, and because demonstrations offer the promise of

This 1925 print ad features the legendary Fuller Brush Man, an advertising icon virtually synonymous with product demonstration. His real-life counterparts have traveled throughout North America since 1906, conducting in-home demonstrations of Fuller products such as the "Wonder Mop."
Reprinted courtesy of The Fuller Brush Company, Inc., a CPAC company.

reliable performance and/or tangible benefit, this is particularly relevant in the case of demonstrations. Moreover, audiences tend to believe demonstrations. Even though today's consumers are relatively savvy and experienced in coping with advertising, they can be misled by the power of a crafty or shady demonstration. And recent advances in computer and communications technology have made deception easier than ever before. Thus, demonstrations can be particularly detrimental to those who tend to fall prey to false claims or deceit.

Second, false and deceptive demonstrations can unfairly disparage competitive brands in the eyes of customers. Free and fair competition can be damaged by unscrupulous demonstrations. Therefore, the FTC carefully examines product demonstrations for accuracy and relevance.

Advertisers that use demonstrations must be prepared to prove that their testing procedures are valid and to provide support for the claims made in a demonstration. Demonstrations must not cause buyers to conclude more than is explicitly communicated in the advertisement. In addition, advertisers may be asked to prove that the test is relevant to the customary use of the product.

Finally, comparative ads must meet a set of criteria in order to be lawful. For example, nonusers of the advertised product cannot be used in preference tests, a marketer's superiority in distribution cannot be used to imply customer preference for its product, and the "triple association" method should be used in taste tests. (In a triple association test, subjects blindly judge—without brand names—three samples. Two of the samples contain the same brand; the third sample contains another brand. To subjectively judge one brand as being superior to the other, participants must successfully distinguish the two brands from one another and state a preference for one brand over the other.)

The sequence of steps in a particular act or process can be seen and/or heard. For example, General Motors Acceptance Corporation (GMAC) mailed audiocassettes to recent female college graduates with pointers on how to buy a car and arrange for an automobile loan. Some demonstrations permit people to learn by touching. An advertising director may learn which type of paper is best suited for a print ad or newspaper insert by touching the different types of paper on display at a trade exhibition. Learning through sight can be enhanced by a demonstration. How a product works, even in ways that are invisible to the audience, can be seen through graphic demonstrations. For example, the way a pain remedy travels through the bloodstream or the way an oil additive lubricates and protects a car engine can be dramatized by a graphic demonstration, even though the actual process is invisible to the naked eye.

The demonstration is a mainstay product-centered promotional tool. Demonstrations are generally persuasive because people are usually interested in what products will do for them. In addition to being heavily used in advertising, demonstrations can be a key ingredient in an integrated communications program. Demonstrations are frequently incorporated into sales plans and presentations, sales promotions programs, event marketing, trade and consumer shows, direct-marketing efforts, Internet communications, and public relations programs. E-commerce and the advances in virtual reality technology are opening newer and more effective ways to demonstrate products and services. At arm's length, customers sitting in front of their home computers can assess a hotel's rooms, activities, and amenities, no matter where in the world the hotel is located. Virtual reality, for example, allows high school students to tour universities before committing to one. As technology creates more sophisticated products and services, as competition continues to heat up, as buyers become more educated and demanding, and as new lifestyles emerge, demonstrations will continue to play a vital role in both advertising strategies and integrated communications programs.

ALLEN E. SMITH

Further Reading

Buchanan, Bruce, "Can You Pass the Comparative Advertising Challenge?" *Harvard Business Review* 85 (July/August 1985)
Dunn, Samuel Watson, *Advertising: Its Role in Modern Marketing,* New York: Holt Rinehart and Winston, 1961; 8th

edition, by Dean M. Krugman et al., Fort Worth, Texas: Dryden Press, 1994

Felton, George, *Advertising: Concept and Copy,* Englewood Cliffs, New Jersey: Prentice Hall, 1994

Moriarty, Sandra Ernst, *Creative Advertising: Theory and Practice,* Englewood Cliffs, New Jersey: Prentice-Hall, 1986; 2nd edition, 1991

O'Guinn, Thomas C., Chris T. Allen, and Richard J. Semenik, *Advertising,* Cincinnati, Ohio: South-Western College, 1998; 2nd edition, 2000

Schultz, Don E., and Dennis G. Martin, *Strategic Advertising Campaigns,* Chicago: Crain Books, 1979; 4th edition, by Schultz and Beth E. Barnes, Lincolnwood, Illinois: NTC Books, 1995

Tipper, Harry, and Harry Levi Hollingworth, *Advertising: Its Principles and Practice,* New York: Ronald Press, 1915; 5th edition, as *Advertising: Principles and Practice,* by William Wells, John Burnett, and Sandra Ernst Moriarty, Upper Saddle River, New Jersey: Prentice Hall, 1999

White, Hooper, *How to Produce an Effective TV Commercial,* Chicago: Crain Books, 1981; 3rd edition, as *How to Produce Effective TV Commercials,* Lincolnwood, Illinois: NTC Business Books, 1994

Dentsu, Inc.

Founded by Hoshiro Mitsunaga in Tokyo, Japan, 1901; served the dual functions of advertising and news service initially but became a specialized advertising firm, 1936; became the world's largest advertising company in terms of billings as a single agency brand, 1973; remains the world's largest ad company according to *Advertising Age.*

Major Clients
Coca-Cola Company
Japan Tobacco
Kao Corporation (beauty and cleaning products)
Nestlé S.A.
NTT Communications
Panasonic
Procter & Gamble Company
Suntory (beverages and pharmaceuticals)
Toyota Motor Corporation

Hoshiro Mitsunaga, a news reporter, established the company that would become Dentsu in 1901 in Tokyo, Japan. From the inception of the new company, Mitsunaga aspired to turn it into a modern news agency. At the time, Japanese news service companies lagged considerably behind their Western counterparts in equipment and quality. Mitsunaga's experience as a war correspondent during the Sino-Japanese War left him with a great desire to improve these services. He believed for a news service to be successful, newspaper publishers, from whom news service agencies received a fee in exchange for providing news, had to first be on firm financial ground. His idea was to found a company that would function as both a news service and an advertising agency; such a firm would be able to cover wire service fees with revenues.

Entrance into Advertising

Having founded a news organization called Dempo Tsushin Sha (Telegraphic Communication Company), Mitsunaga then established an advertising agency, Nippon Koukoku KK (Japan Advertising, Ltd.). In 1907 these two companies merged to become Nippon Dempo Tsushin Sha (Japan Telegraphic Communication Company, Ltd.) and subsequently began serving the twin functions of news reporting and advertising. The company name, Dentsu, is an abbreviation of the original name, combining the "Den" and "Tsu."

At the time of the merger five major advertising companies dominated the Japanese advertising industry. However, Dentsu was able to break this oligopoly by practicing fair trade based on reasonable commission. It then began to lay the groundwork for becoming the number-one agency in the Japanese advertising market. The news service side led the way, introducing, among other initiatives, a picture transmission system and establishing a relationship with the newly-founded United Press (UP; later to became UPI when merged with the International News Service). The agency grew to become one of the premiere wire service companies in Japan.

In 1931 a "national news agency" scheme entertained by the government called for a plan to merge all news service companies into a single government-owned news organization, Domei Tsushinsha (Domei News Agency). Its wire service operation was absorbed into Domei Tsushinsha in 1936. In exchange, the advertising arm of Domei Tsushinsha was incorporated into Dentsu, thereby allowing the company to relaunch itself as a specialized advertising agency.

The newly refocused Dentsu soon set up new departments devoted to marketing research and creative functions, thus consolidating its place as the market leader. Dentsu established what

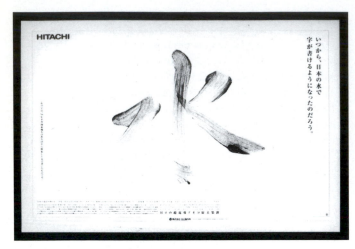

In this 1998 ad posing the question, "Since when have we been able to write with water?" the Japanese ideogram for *water* was drawn using polluted water from a Tokyo swamp. As Hitachi, Ltd., was the developer of equipment used to purify swamp water, Dentsu created this ad to demonstrate the company's commitment to the environment. *Courtesy of Dentsu Inc. and Hitachi Ltd.*

was the first advertising award in 1930, hosted an advertising lecture series for business executives in 1934, and subsidized various advertising studies. These initiatives, among others, helped spur the development of the advertising industry in Japan. Through talks with the government and newspaper publishers, Dentsu also worked toward standardizing newspaper advertising fees and the agency tariff in 1944. Business was scaled back considerably during World War II, however.

The Yoshida Years

In 1947, two years after the war ended, Hideo Yoshida became Dentsu's fourth president. Dubbed the "demon of advertising," Yoshida laid the foundation for postwar Japanese advertising, helping it grow into a modern industry. He was an integral part of this development as well as of the phenomenal growth Dentsu experienced during his 16-year tenure.

The Oni Jussoku, or Dentsu's 10 Work Guidelines, which set forth standards of behavior for Dentsu employees, epitomize Yoshida's philosophy toward work:

1. Initiate projects on your own instead of waiting for work to be assigned.
2. Take an active role in all your endeavors, not a passive one.
3. Search for large and complex challenges.
4. Welcome difficult assignments. Progress lies in accomplishing difficult work.
5. Once you begin a task, complete it. Never give up.
6. Lead, and set an example for your fellow workers.
7. Set goals for yourself to ensure a constant sense of purpose.
8. Move with confidence; it gives your work force and substance.
9. At all times, challenge yourself to think creatively and find new solutions.
10. When confrontation is necessary, do not shy away from it. Confrontation is often necessary to achieve progress.

This canon of behavior, which is otherwise known as the "Spirit of Dentsu," was unveiled by Yoshida in 1951 for internal use by the company, but it has since been adopted by many other companies.

During his tenure Yoshida called for an advertising strategy backed by modern theories; he also placed special emphasis on public relations and market research. The concept of public relations was introduced to Japan in 1947 when the General Headquarters, which was eager to see Japan democratize, recommended that local governments establish public relations offices. Dentsu brought the concept to the advertising world and promoted it through various publications. Yoshida also pioneered the field of market research, introducing random sampling through the polling of movie theater audiences (1948) and conducting surveys on supply and demand for pharmaceutical products. Dentsu proved a trailblazer in advertising market research.

When commercial radio was launched in 1951, Yoshida argued that the growth of private-sector broadcasting was vital not only for Dentsu but for the advertising industry as a whole. He made a concerted effort to help the broadcasting industry grow, providing capital to establish private broadcasting companies and dispatching personnel to these companies upon request.

Dentsu also played a pivotal role in the launch of commercial television in 1953. Yoshida worked to promote a system that involved both the government and the related industries, so that the new medium would take firm root. Dentsu created the first Japanese television commercial, which featured a Seiko time announcement. The company also conducted the country's first audience rating research.

Yoshida worked to modernize the ad industry in Japan. In 1950 he led a movement to establish disclosure of publication circulation figures and to promote fixed pricing for advertising. The inaugural meeting of the Japan Audit Bureau of Circulation Association was held at the Dentsu headquarters building in 1952. Dentsu also took steps to nurture advertising- and marketing-related industries and was actively involved in the establishment of the Japan Newspaper Advertising Agency Association (1950), predecessor of the Japan Advertising Agency Association, and the Japan Marketing Association (1957).

Among Yoshida's biggest contributions was his creation of the Dentsu Advertising Awards in 1947. These awards had their origin in the earlier Dentsu awards established in 1930, and although they bear Dentsu's name, the judging is carried out by some 500 independent judges. The contest is open to all advertisers and agencies. The first prize in 1948 went to the advertising for Matsushita's National brand radio. The contest, originally designed to reward excellence in newspaper advertising, later expanded to embrace ad prizes for magazine ads (1950); radio, posters, and outdoor advertisements (1952); television commer-

Denstu's "Kiss" campaign for NTT Communications, exemplified by this 2000 ad, hinted at the power of communication to break down barriers between those on opposite sides of an issue—in this case, Little Red Riding Hood and the wolf.
Courtesy of Dentsu, Inc., and Nippon Telegraph and Telelphone Corporation.

cials (1954); point-of-purchase and direct mail (1955); and movie theater advertising (1965).

Emphasis on Service

In 1958 Dentsu adopted a modified version of the American account executive system. Until then, employees in charge of media booking had doubled as client service representatives, but the new system had the account executive handle agency activities, communicate with appropriate internal departments in accordance with clients' marketing needs, and mobilize external resources as necessary. This system remains the essence of Dentsu's advertising operation. Each client works with an account director, marketing director, creative director, and sales promotion director. The account director acts as a coordinator, ensuring that the broad needs of the client are met. The company also consults with clients on marketing and business strategies. In 1978 the company name was changed from Dentsu Advertising, Ltd., to Dentsu, Inc., reflecting the shift in focus from the four major mass media to a broader range of communications objectives.

Dentsu handles advertising for most of Japan's major corporations and counts nearly 3,000 firms among its clients. (Unlike ad agencies in Western countries, Japanese agencies routinely handle the business of more than one company in a given industry.) Its large in-house planning organization includes strategic, research, promotion, and corporate communications planning. Ten percent of the approximately 4,000 employees based at Dentsu's headquarters in Tokyo work in these planning departments. While in-house planning also executes the plans, it is increasingly dedicated to strategy development as well. Implementation is often handled by affiliated specialty firms or outside organizations. Dentsu's affiliates include: Dentsu TEC, which produces advertising and promotional materials and executes events; Dentsu Public Relations; Dentsu Research, a marketing research organization; Dentsu Impiric, a direct marketing joint venture with the U.S. firm Wunderman Cato Johnson; and Dentsu Sudler & Hennessy, a

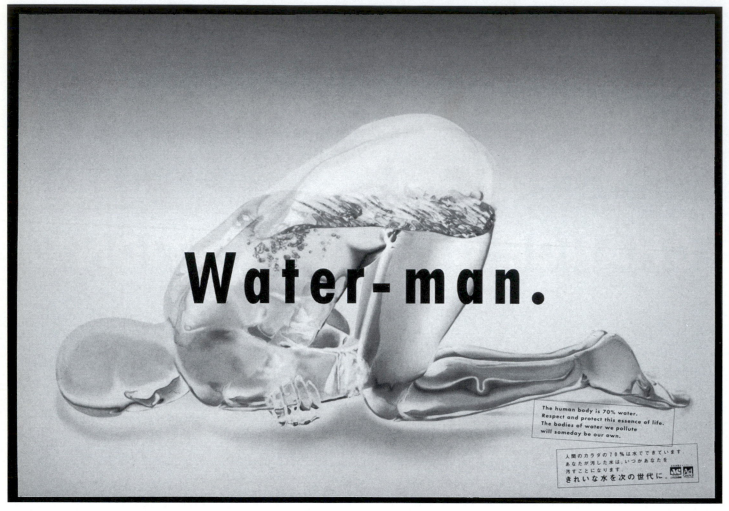

An ad from Dentsu for the Japan Advertising Council supports protection of environmental resources.
Courtesy of Dentsu, Inc., and Japan Ad Council.

health care marketing joint venture. All told, there were about 70 affiliated companies at the turn of the 21st century, and the total number of employees working for the Dentsu Group of companies was approximately 12,000.

In January 1999 the company implemented an organizational makeover with the aim of establishing a comprehensive and integrated planning capability. The hitherto independent departments of marketing, promotion planning, and corporate communications were integrated into a single division called Integrated Communications Planning. Each client works with an account service group, a creative group, and an integrated communications planning group, all housed under one roof, where all communication-related matters are proposed and implemented in an organic fashion. Advertising for the four major mass media—newspapers, magazines, television, and radio—accounted for 65 percent of the total group sales for 1999, but business outside of the four media was on the rise.

One such business is sports and event marketing, an area in which Dentsu's work is unusual. The Tokyo Olympics of 1964,

the first Olympic Games in Japan, provided the company with the opportunity to break new ground. Dentsu played an important role in the success of the event, dispatching employees to provide assistance to the press corps and to serve as officers to the games.

Building on this experience, Dentsu helped promote and support sports such as soccer, track and field, volleyball, and golf. Dentsu served as the marketing agency for the International Olympic Committee (IOC) in Japan and was responsible for courting Japanese sponsors for the summer Olympics, held in Los Angeles, California, in 1984; Seoul, Korea, in 1988; Barcelona, Spain, in 1992; and Atlanta, Georgia, in 1996.

As for event-related advertising, the 1970 World Exposition held in Osaka, Japan, provided the first opportunity. When the Commemorative Association for the Japan World Exposition 1970 was launched in 1965, Dentsu's role was limited to public relations and advertising. However, its activities expanded to include planning and administration of pavilions, nationwide publicity events and campaigns, compilation of official guidebooks, and radio- and TV-based live broadcasting of various programs and shows during the exposition. The event attracted more than 60 million visitors, far in excess of initial forecasts.

Dentsu's expertise in large event administration led the company to take on the role of producer of ceremonies associated with the Okinawa International Oceans Exposition (1975–76). During the 1985 World Science Exposition in Tsukuba, Japan, Dentsu was responsible for the administration of government exhibitions, staged two-thirds of the private-sector exhibitions, and executed the opening and closing ceremonies. For the 1990 International Garden and Greenery Exposition in Osaka, Dentsu was involved in the basic planning of the event, designed the event's symbol and mascot, and administered the press center. These experiences won the company kudos for its expertise in event marketing and led to its involvement in most of Japan's major nationwide events.

Such activities led Dentsu to city development-related enterprises, movies and content development, and other entertainment-related businesses. Dentsu has participated in the production of numerous films and has also begun to develop digital content. In the late 1990s it established a division dedicated to the merchandising of commercial characters.

Roughly 15 percent of Dentsu employees are involved in creative efforts. Since its establishment in 1989, the "Creator of the Year" award, sponsored by the Japan Advertising Agency Association, has gone to a Dentsu creative staff member almost every year. In addition to a number of other domestic prizes, Dentsu has also been the recipient of a handful of international awards, including Clios and prizes at the Cannes (France) International Advertising Festival.

The organizational structure of the creative department at Dentsu is different from those of U.S. and European agencies. Approximately 120 creative directors are in place to satisfy the needs of several thousand clients. Each director oversees all creative work for each client.

Going Global

Dentsu's overseas activities date to 1959, when the company set up an office in New York City. Dentsu and Young & Rubicam (Y&R) began informal contacts in the 1960s with the understanding that if Dentsu ever sought a more formal U.S. affiliation, it would be with Y&R. Ed Ney, chief executive officer of Y&R, worked hard to build the relationship through the 1970s. In 1981 Dentsu Young & Rubicam (DYR) was formed and became a force throughout Asia. To enhance the quality of its services in overseas markets, in March 2000 Dentsu formed its alliance with and made investment in Bcom3, a holding company that includes Leo Group, Chicago, Illinois (home of ad network Leo Burnett Worldwide); MacManus Group, New York City (whose flagship agency is D'Arcy Masius Benton & Bowles); and Starcom MediaVest Group.

Dentsu still has a way to go before it can describe itself as a "global agency." Its overseas revenue as a percentage of total sales were around 5 percent in 2000 on a consolidated basis. The company's overseas presence outside of Asia remains small, and the majority of its overseas clients are Japanese. Landing accounts with multinational and local corporations was therefore high on the agenda at the start of the 21st century. To adequately respond to this era of increasing competition, Dentsu has been intensifying its efforts to globalize its business since the mid-1990s.

The Asian market stands as an area of strategic focus for Dentsu and is one where the company's influence is strong. Dentsu's wholly owned subsidiary, Dentsu (Taiwan), Inc., for example, boasted the largest share in advertising in Taiwan. With the aim of increasing its planning capability in Asia, Dentsu is building marketing databases that incorporate findings from consumer research the company routinely conducts in more than 27 Asian cities outside of Japan. In 1996, as part of Dentsu's 95th anniversary observance, the company launched a Japan-China educational exchange program in advertising. Under this program Chinese teachers of advertising were invited to Tokyo, and Dentsu employees were dispatched to six Chinese universities.

Dentsu had been a privately owned company since its creation. It listed its stock on the Tokyo Stock Exchange in November 2001, when the company celebrated its 100th anniversary.

MASARU ARIGA

Further Reading

Japan Marketing and Advertising Yearbook (annual; 1991–) (published by Dentsu)

Design and Designers

From the Arts and Crafts movement in the 1880s through Art Deco in the 1920s and pop art in the 1960s to today, advertising design has reflected worldwide trends in fine art. At the same time, the look and feel of both print and television advertising have mirrored societal trends and have evolved as technologies have advanced.

The advent of photography in 1839 and lithography in 1860, as well as continuous innovations in printing capabilities throughout the mid-1880s, allowed advertisers to picture their products in ever more detailed and realistic ways. They also took advantage of the increasing variety of ad media—posters, handbills, trade cards, billboards, sandwich boards—especially because newspapers in the 1880s often had restrictive rules governing advertising design.

The showman P.T. Barnum is sometimes considered the first great advertising personality, and advertising in the mid-1800s reflected his sensibility. Patent medicines were one of the leading advertising categories at the time, and the design of these ads—mostly consisting of text, set in multiple fonts at the discretion of the newspaper—was typical of the period. Advertising design remained text-dependent throughout the 1800s, although the messages became more understated toward the end of the century, occasionally—as in the case of Royal baking powder and Ivory Soap—becoming subtle and even charming.

Trademarks, Brand Names, and Packaging

In the 1880s packaging became an important part of the brand image for the first time, and the appearance of the package became one component of the product's overall advertising effort. Trademarks started to be associated with specific products and were prominently displayed on standardized packaging that was consistent with the advertising message. One of the early, high-profile trademark designs of the time was the Quaker Oats man, whose head appeared on packaging and full figure in advertising. Procter & Gamble Company, Borden, Campbell's Soup, and H.J. Heinz Company were among the other companies that created corporate characters and brand names. They discovered that a well-known brand name, along with consistent packaging and advertising, allowed them to charge more for their products.

A notable innovation in package design occurred in 1887 when Patrick J. Towle, a St. Paul, Minnesota-based grocer, registered the trademark Log Cabin for a product that blended cane and maple syrups. He packaged his creation in a miniature log cabin–shaped tin box, which remained on the market for decades. In the years that followed, distinctive packaging became one of the most important components of a product's brand image.

Arts and Crafts, Art Nouveau, and Other Design Movements

One of the first art and design movements to have an effect on advertising was Arts and Crafts, which was founded by William Morris in Britain and began to take hold in the 1880s. In a reaction against the uniformity of mass production, Morris advocated a return to high-quality craftsmanship. He emphasized plain, solid, handcrafted work in all areas of design, including furniture, typography, graphic design, and printing. The main effect on advertising was to promote the use of simple designs featuring bold typefaces and to discourage the cluttered, type-heavy style typical of the Victorian period.

Another design movement, Art Nouveau, was developing alongside Arts and Crafts. Started in France, Art Nouveau left its mark on architecture, furniture, crafts, fashion, product design, graphics, and the arts. It was a romantic movement that protested against realism and industrialization, featuring an ornamental style characterized by natural forms, dark, graceful, organic lines, silhouetted figures, fanciful backgrounds, and flattened, repeated elements. It was influenced by Japanese prints, Arts and Crafts ideals, and 18th-century French rococo, as well as the paintings of French postimpressionists such as Vincent van Gogh and Paul Gauguin.

The rise of Art Nouveau occurred at the same time as the first illustrated ads, woodblock prints that appeared in *Harper's Weekly* and *Leslie's Illustrated* in the 1890s. Americans were becoming interested in advertising posters, a central component of the Art Nouveau movement. Consumers began to collect the posters, removing them from walls as soon as they had been posted. Both the colorful illustrated ads and the posters were made possible by advances in lithography.

Among the key Art Nouveau poster designers were Jules Cheret, Henri de Toulouse-Lautrec, Theophile-Alexandre Steinlen, Aubrey Beardsley, and Alphonse Mucha. Cheret is credited as the creator of the modern art poster and designed more than 1,000 posters for products ranging from cough drops to cigarettes. Mucha is known for his creations of sensuous women with flowing hair, which became a typical Art Nouveau image. Beardsley gained a reputation for shocking the viewer with his designs.

The 1880s and 1890s became known as the golden age of illustration. Some of the artists who created early magazine ad images were Edward Penfield, Jessie Willcox Smith, Maxfield Parrish, J.C. Leyendecker, Will Bradley, Ethel Read, Louis Rhead, and Frederic Remington. Rhead and Bradley became two of the best-known American Art Nouveau artists.

Artists' name recognition and growing appeal drove advertisers to seek well-known illustrators to create ads for them. By creating whole series of ads for the same brand and signing their work, the artists became indelibly linked with that product. The invention of photoengraving allowed these designs to be reproduced in a more painterly and less sketchy style. One advertiser that became linked with Art Nouveau was the Columbia Cycle Company. Its successful ads led other transportation companies to embrace the style.

Many of the advertising illustrators in the late 1800s portrayed women who were instantly recognizable as having been created by a particular artist. An example was illustrator Charles Dana Gibson's series of Gibson Girls, which influenced several other artists to create similar character groups through the first half of the 1900s, among them the Christy Girl, the Flagg Girl, and the Petty Girl.

The Birth of Graphic Design

Advances in printing technologies and the simultaneous increase in advertising during the second half of the 19th century led to the birth of graphic design as a profession. N.W. Ayer & Son, Inc., was one of the first advertising agencies to hire art directors. Several typefaces were created specifically for use in advertising, especially sans serif, slab serif, and decorative fonts. William Morris himself designed many advertising typefaces and inspired others.

The relationship between advertising art and text became strong and more equal at the turn of the 20th century, led by the efforts of Earnest Elmo Calkins, a partner at New York City–based Calkins & Holden. His agency was one of the first to have an art department. Calkins, who helped found the Art Directors Club of New York in 1920, believed advertising was more appealing when the graphics related to the copy, and he gave his staff detailed instructions on how the ads he wrote should be designed. Most of these ads followed a simple, stylized Arts and Crafts format. Some of Calkins's notable campaigns included the Arrow Collar Man (illustrated by Joseph Leyendecker), Force cereal, Wesson oil, Sherwin-Williams paint, Kelly Springfield tires, and Pierce-Arrow automobiles. Other agencies emulated the Calkins style, as well as his penchant for hiring well-known illustrators. Calkins also set up a department of "industrial styling" within his agency.

In 1907 the German *Werkbund* was formed in Europe as a movement that intended to link art and industry. It encouraged better design in manufacturing and led to an industrial look in advertising, with a particular focus on posters. Several separate but interrelated art movements followed in the 1910s and 1920s, especially in Europe and Russia, including futurism, suprematism, constructivism, dadaism, de Stijl, and Bauhaus. In the United States most of these movements did not affect advertising design, except in advertising posters. The look of advertising continued to be influenced by Art Nouveau and the evolving Arts and Crafts movement, which included American designers such as Daniel Berkeley Updike, type designer Frederic W. Goudy, and Bruce Rogers.

World War I brought war-related imagery into advertising, both as part of government recruitment efforts and as a way for companies to display their patriotism. The U.S. government's Division of Pictorial Publicity, part of the Committee on Public Information, produced more than 700 poster designs in support of the war and was led by Charles Dana Gibson. Many of the advertising images centered on sensual female images, often posed as icons such as Columbia or the Statue of Liberty. One of the most famous advertising posters of this era was James Montgomery Flagg's "I want you" recruiting poster for the U.S. Army. Many popular illustrators also continued to create advertising images for consumer products during the war, including N.C. Wyeth, who worked with Cream of Wheat and Coca-Cola, and Norman Rockwell, who contributed advertising images for Coca-Cola, Black Cat hosiery, Mennen shaving cream, and Perfection oil filters.

At about the same time, the U.S. art world was being introduced to the European avant-garde, the first exhibition of which occurred in 1913 and featured artists such as Pablo Picasso, Georges Braque, Vassily Kandinsky, Henri Matisse, and Marcel Duchamp. While the exhibition caused a sensation in the art world, it did not greatly influence wartime advertising design. In fact, the artists who created advertising posters to support the war effort disparaged the work of the avant-garde as "art for art's sake."

By the early 1920s a typical ad featured an illustration, usually showcasing ambitious or detailed photography or paintings. The art usually was placed on the top half of the page, under which

American artist James Montgomery Flagg posed in 1917 with some of the World War I posters for which he provided illustrations.

were a large headline and a half page of copy. Nearly every product category generated advertisements with this layout.

Just as style and design were important elements in advertising, they were also vital to the products themselves. The increased importance of product design was made possible by a fundamental shift in mass marketing that came to a head after World War I. For centuries people had struggled to produce sufficient goods to meet natural demand. But as the machine age permitted society to master the burdens of manufacturing, the ability to produce began to exceed natural demand. Advertising slowly turned to the task of stimulating new demand to keep pace with production levels. Reasons had to be provided to justify greater demand, and design became a major force. It was not enough for goods to be marketed on the basis of simple mechanical performance, where improvements were often subtle and usually invisible to the buyer. The sense of progress was, therefore, made manifest to the consumer in the form of style and design. The introduction of new models of durable goods—from refrigerators to cars—became an annual event in which the "improvements" offered were of an aesthetic nature, dramatic and instantly apparent. Shopping became a form of self-expression.

Not only did ad agencies focus on designing attractive products and brands for their clients, they also strived to design a stylized image for themselves. The J. Walter Thompson Company commissioned designer Norman Bel Geddes to create bold, modernistic interior designs for its conference rooms, auditorium, and lobby. The design of the interior reception floor of NBC Studios in New York City created in the early 1930s is clearly intended to make a powerful statement about NBC and its parent, RCA. A similar kind of advanced styling inspired by high art was filtered through the requirements of mass commerce and found its way in a modified form into many ads. McCann-Erickson pictured the 1928 Chrysler Imperial 80 in a cubist montage of modernistic illustrations in the April 1928 issue of *House and Garden*.

Art Deco

The Art Deco movement arose in the mid-1920s, profoundly changing the way advertisements were designed. Named after a 1925 exhibition in Paris, France—the Exposition des Arts Decoratifs—Art Deco attempted to create standards for architecture and decorative arts. The style encompassed a wide variety of classical imagery, including Oriental, Egyptian, African, and Aztec art, as well as new design ideals such as that of cubism.

Art Deco ads were known for their heavy ornamentation and for featuring images from antiquity. They employed naturalistic imagery and forms and normally did not focus on—or even mention—the product. The designs of Art Deco were highly stylized and geometric, featuring repeated patterns, smooth, parallel lines, sans serif typefaces, and an asymmetrical layout. Art Deco incorporated aspects of many of the fine art movements that had preceded it, including futurism, expressionism, cubism, and constructivism. One classic example of Art Deco is a 1926 advertisement by Franklin Booth for Willys-Overland automobiles. Its focal point was a detailed pen and ink drawing of a medieval castle. Other Art Deco artists and designers lending their talents to advertising included Thomas M. McClelland and Walter D. Teague.

Many observers consider ads created during the Art Deco period to be some of the most beautiful in history. Yet they received much criticism at the time, and the public seemed to find them too abstract, preferring the realistic, heartwarming style of illustrators such as Norman Rockwell. Still, many advertisers continued to promote their products with Art Deco; examples range from Perrin gloves to Ruxton Hansom automobiles.

While the Art Deco style prevailed during much of the period between World Wars I and II, both in Europe and in the United States, the stock market crash of 1929 and the subsequent Great Depression made it seem less attractive. The opulence that characterized Art Deco was antithetical to the concerns of the American public during the economic downturn of the 1930s. In fact, advertisers began to avoid using art, illustration, and color, and they refrained from following any particular design style.

Art Deco's influence could still be felt during the 1920s and 1930s through its successor, art moderne. The latter's smooth lines and simplified, streamlined forms were reminiscent of Art Deco, but the movement's focus was on mass production rather than the high end. Art moderne designers created affordable yet stylish furniture, posters, clothing, and silverware. Advertising design reflected the more simplified art moderne style, which remained prevalent through the New York World's Fair in 1939 but declined in popularity afterward.

Depression Trends in Advertising

An influential designer during the 1930s was Helen Resor of the J. Walter Thompson Company. She avoided the scientific approach taken by many of her colleagues and opted to intuitively follow the styles of publications she admired, such as the *Ladies' Home Journal* and *The Saturday Evening Post*. Resor created advertising that emulated the editorial look of these magazines and drew readers in because they seemed to be part of the publication's editorial content. Copy was subtle and was paired with paintings that appealed to the magazines' readership. One of her most famous campaigns was for Woodbury's Facial Soap.

Meanwhile, the Depression resulted in more hard-sell advertising, featuring large, exclamatory headlines and scantily clothed women. These types of ads pushed not only lingerie, but also products for the home and even industrial goods. Woodbury's, the same advertiser that embraced Resor's editorial style, also used nudes photographed by Edward Steichen to hard-sell its soap.

The 1930s witnessed the rise of polling as a factor behind the creation of advertising campaigns. Not only were the message and the copy style based on results of reader surveys, but so were the design and layout. Polls by organizations such as Gallup—which gained power during the 1930s—showed that comic strips, for example, were popular with the public, so they were incorporated into ads. Grape Nuts developed its own comic strip–style character, Little Albie, to discuss the merits of its cereal. Gallup's polls found readers preferred white space in their ads, so text-heavy layouts were replaced with airier versions. Readers, according to Gallup, also liked italic and boldface type, subheads to help them follow the copy, rectangular pictures, and photographs that were uncropped. All of these findings were incorporated into ad design in the 1930s.

Another design trend in this decade was the resurgence of photographs in ads. One leading supporter of this movement was the Getchell agency, headed by J. Stirling Getchell, which assembled a library of photos it made available to its clients. The photos formed the centerpiece of the agency's ad layouts, with typefaces and headlines—usually sensational ones—built around the photo. It hired well-known and highly regarded photographers such as Margaret Bourke-White, whose work promoted DeSoto automobiles.

Getchell also was behind one of the first comparative ads, published in 1932 for Plymouth automobiles. The pitch showed photos of the Plymouth and two competing models above the headline, "Plymouth Sets the Pace for All Three." Getchell created ads for everything from cars to Ritz crackers, all with his trademark attention-grabbing and—according to the critics of the time—somewhat ugly style. Although Getchell spent significant sums to create his photo archive, photographs in general were considered less expensive than illustrations and so became popular industrywide. Most showed eye-catching action and realistic scenes, influenced by Getchell's tabloid-style layouts.

While photographs were in favor for magazine and newspaper advertising, the popularity of paintings was on the rise when it came to advertising posters. In 1933 the government's Public Works of Art Project commissioned painters to design posters, many of which had an industrial, streamlined look. These designs helped support the perception that the economy, by 1936, had returned to strength after the long Depression.

Before World War II, several German artists and thinkers were forced to emigrate to the United States, Switzerland, and England. German modernist designers had a large impact on the commercial art in their new countries. The aesthetics of modernism evolved from previous movements, including de Stijl, constructivism, and the original Bauhaus.

One of the companies that significantly influenced advertising design in the 1930s and beyond was the Container Corporation of America (CCA), which commissioned one of the first comprehensive corporate identity programs encompassing all internal and external communications. Not only did it pioneer the idea of corporate identity, but it also embraced all manner of fine artists in its advertising, leading other advertisers to do the same. One of the key designers behind CCA's effort was Charles Coiner, who joined N.W. Ayer in 1924. Ayer was a leader among agencies in commissioning modern art for advertising campaigns; others included Erwin, Wasey & Company, Calkins & Holden, and the J. Walter Thompson Company. Coiner designed ads for DeBeers and Lincoln and Ford automobiles, as well as the Blue Eagle symbol for the National Recovery Administration during the Depression.

Ayer's work with CCA began in 1936, around the time advertisers began to look to artists, especially from the European avant-garde, to make their advertising and package design appear "modern." One of the innovations of CCA's ad campaign was that it concentrated on image rather than on the product. The campaign, known as the Great Ideas series, linked the CCA name with ideas and institutions of Western culture by commissioning well-known modern artists to abstractly illustrate phrases and quotes. Many critics still consider the campaign, which ran through 1960, as unique in the history of advertising design.

CCA, which made boxes, saw its sales increase from 22 million units in 1936 to 131 million in 1948. Coiner hired more than 100 freelance artists over the duration of the campaign, including Sasha Maurer, Alexey Brodovitch, Otto Kuhler, Josef Binder, and Otis Shepard. For CCA and his other clients, Coiner supported both European avant-garde artists and American designers. Some of the collaborations he arranged included Georgia O'Keefe and Isamu Noguchi for Dole Pineapple and Pablo Picasso, André Derain, and Raoul Dufy for DeBeers diamonds. Coiner also designed several government campaigns in the 1930s and 1940s, becoming one of the first American graphic designers to work on government projects. One of his most significant contributions to advertising design was narrowing the divide between fine and commercial artists, making graphic or applied art a respected profession. His work also resulted in a higher profile and more respect for the position of art director, which became a key role in the problem-solving process.

Another influential art director in the 1930s was Alexey Brodovitch, also associated with Ayer. In his commercial work, Brodovitch was known for a variety of styles. But his greatest influence was as a teacher and mentor of other art directors and advertising designers, including Sam Antiput, Raymond Ballinger, William Bernbach, Bob Cato, Herschel Levitt, Priscilla Peck, Otto Storch, Victor Trasoff, Henry Worl, Steve Frankfurt, Bob Gage, and Helmut Krone. Shortly after coming to the United States in 1930, Brodovitch established an advertising design program at the Philadelphia (Pennsylvania) Museum School of Industrial Design (now the Philadelphia College of Art), which he ran until 1938. He subsequently developed a series of design laboratories throughout his career, which were attended by many influential designers and art directors.

Modern art continued to influence advertising throughout the 1930s and 1940s, with Piet Mondrian, Max Ernst, Erté, A.M. Cassandre, Paul Rand, and Andy Warhol among the artists and art directors who brought modern art to advertising. At the same time, however, the kind of illustration that had been popular with the American public during the 1920s continued to appear in ads. These included George Petty's Petty Girls, which were a 1930s and 1940s incarnation of the Gibson Girls created by Charles Dana Gibson in previous decades.

Surrealism, a movement that started in 1923, was another branch of fine art that influenced advertising in the 1930s and 1940s. One of its key contributions was to infuse traditionally forbidden sexual imagery into advertising through the use of symbols and dreamlike icons, especially in categories such as women's fashions, perfumes, and cosmetics.

Other influential designers in the 1930s included Herbert Bayer, a Bauhaus student who made his mark in typography, including for CCA; Lester Beall, designer of posters for the Rural Electrification Administration and of packaging, advertising, and corporate identities for such companies as International Paper and Martin Marietta; and Paul Rand, who designed campaigns for Coronet brandy, Dubonnet aperitif, El Producto cigars, and Ohrbach's department store. Rand's ads integrated art and copy, foreshadowing a trend that would develop after World War II.

The New Bauhaus movement was founded in 1937 in Chicago, Illinois, and headed by Hungarian artist László Moholy-Nagy. It overlapped the end of Art Deco and art moderne and influenced advertising design throughout the 1940s, which became known as the "streamlined decade." Streamlined products from trains to teapots and from apparel to architecture appeared on the scene, and the same themes and design elements were included in advertising as well. Some of the designers who contributed to the evolution of the streamlined ideal were Bel Geddes, Raymond Loewy, Henry Dreyfuss, Harold Van Doren, and Walter Dorwin Teague.

The end of World War II launched a period of creativity in graphic arts, in which designers looked toward new ideas rather than staying with traditional, accepted methods of solving design problems. It also marked the rise of American-born graphic designers, who started to achieve recognition at home and abroad. They included Saul Bass, who created corporate identity programs and advertising for AT&T, Exxon, Quaker Oats, and Warner Communications; Lou Dorfsman, the art and creative director at CBS Television who specialized in on-air graphics; Gene Federico of Grey Advertising, who did work for advertisers and publications such as *Woman's Day* and the *Saturday Evening Post*; and Bob Gage, who worked with copywriter William Bernbach on campaigns for clients such as Ohrbach's department store.

Television and Postwar Consumerism

The 1950s marked the birth of television as a major communications tool. TV created a new style of advertising design simply because of its technical requirements and unique problems. The visual look was considered as important as—if not more than—the text. Television messages in the medium's early days tended to be understated, in contrast to the boisterous and hard-sell ads typical of radio. The advent of television also allowed a new type of advertising, the demonstration ad.

But there were deeper issues driving the changes in design that marked the 1950s. The history of marketing is in many ways the history of democratizing the playthings and status symbols of the wealthy in the form of knockoffs for the wider middle class. As the miracle of wartime production turned its capacities to the postwar consumer marketplace, this became possible to a greater degree than ever before. The aspirations of the Depression generation to own the finer things in life were about to be fulfilled, even if they were not really all that fine. It was sufficient that they simply appeared fine. A role of Con-Tact paper could turn a simple white surface into a richly grained wood-paneled wall or counter. Affordable antique reproductions could fill a home with illusions of tradition. But to most people style meant expressions of contemporary life, if not the future itself. It was a future of leisure time, push-button convenience, and freedom from drudgery. As confidence in the future generated economic expansion and new wealth, waste became permissible. Paper towels, TV dinners, and diapers became disposables. Designs in kitchens concealed reminders of work beneath smooth, almost-streamlined cabinetry, often built-in. Automobiles became aerodynamic abstractions of motion, with exaggerated tail fins suggesting the sweep of speeding through the wind. Money descended on whole new classes of consumers faster then they could cultivate the good taste to deal with the styling choices before them. Design sought to express a range of consumer emotions through lean abstractions. The boomerang became a varied and all too familiar design cliché, used in the Chrysler and Delta Airlines logos, the McDonald's arches, and even the design of the popular "butterfly" chair, with its canvas sling draped over four wrought iron boomerangs.

Such shapes and abstract forms were naturally reflected in the advertising of the postwar period, especially during the 1950s. Cartoon images became minimalist, sometimes almost sticklike.

Elements of the paintings and mobiles of Joan Miró and Alexander Calder were absorbed into countless advertisements in the form of abstract graphic shapes and blobs intended to suggest modernity and sophistication. The painter Paul Klee's meandering black lines were a common pictorial device among art directors. Older European art styles, such as Coca-Cola's impressionistic ads by McCann-Erickson, were appropriated to suggest urbanity and good taste in much the same way an advertiser might fall back on Luigi Boccherini's E Major Quintet to connote a gilded elegance. When they were not in aprons and frocks, women were dressed in long, thin sheaths to conform to the clean, uncluttered graphic landscapes in print ads. "Be sociable, look smart," Pepsi-Cola suggested in a 1950s campaign devised by the Biow Company. If nothing else, the 1950s were smart and adult. It was as characteristic of period style as psychedelic graphics would be in the 1960s, proving the wisdom of artist Austin Briggs, who said that "last year's fresh idea is today's cliché."

One of the key designers of the 1950s was William Golden, among the first graphic designers to be recognized for his work in television. He joined CBS Television in 1937 and is best known for creating the CBS eye logo, which he designed in 1951 and which was still in use 50 years later. Golden, who also created CBS's advertising, helped make the network a leader in graphic design during the early 1950s before his premature death in 1959. He was succeeded by his protégé, Lou Dorfsman, who would go on in the 1960s to create a total design scheme for CBS that would be built around its new corporate headquarters designed by Eero Saarinen and extend to everything from advertising to office artwork to the last ashtray in the building.

Some observers consider the 1950s a golden age of advertising. The decade saw the rise of advertising targeted at specific demographic groups, rather than toward a general audience. Teenagers became defined as a target group during this decade; previously they had been lumped in with either children or adults, depending on their age.

The 1960s were characterized by a wide variety of advertising styles with no one style dominant. More women, blacks, and ethnic minorities came into the advertising industry and into ad images. The decade was also characterized by a return to hard-sell messages, with short, simple copy and vivid visual images, typified by the work of Rosser Reeves of the Ted Bates Agency.

Photography played a central role in the 1960s. Bold photographs—such as Irving Penn's close-ups of Jell-O—with little copy were central to many of the most high-profile campaigns. Meanwhile, the illustrators who had gained popularity during the 1950s, such as Norman Rockwell, faded from prominence.

The "Creative Revolution"

Three agencies are credited with launching what was termed the "creative revolution" in the 1960s. They were the Leo Burnett Company, Ogilvy & Mather, and Doyle Dane Bernbach (DDB). Burnett was one of the first ad agencies to market itself primarily as a "creative agency," after what many had considered a creative lull in the 1950s, when advertisers and agencies had focused on realistic, representational art. Leo Burnett zeroed in on the product itself rather than relying on image or trendy creative devices. He introduced the modern Jolly Green Giant for the Minnesota Canning Company (later Green Giant), one of the agency's original clients, and went on to develop the Pillsbury Doughboy, Tony the Tiger, the Rice Krispies gnomes, the Marlboro Man, and other icons of print and television advertising. Burnett focused on what he called the "inherent drama" of the product and supported the message with quality artwork, information such as recipes, and often humor.

Doyle Dane Bernbach, and particularly William Bernbach himself, influenced the industry by advocating an integrated, symbiotic relationship between art and copy. Bernbach was a copywriter, but he believed that art and copy worked best as a team and that superior advertising was created when artists and copywriters acted as equal partners. The ads from DDB—its Ohrbach's and El Al campaigns being primary examples—were created through a back and forth process between art and copy. Bernbach's ads were clean and simple, usually incorporating humor. He was influenced by the theories of Paul Rand, with whom he had worked early in his career. Some of Rand's techniques included in Bernbach-influenced ads were the use of collages, symbols, and modern-looking typography, all of which combined for a dramatic, dynamic composition.

David Ogilvy was a proponent of image advertising but with a strong selling message. He specialized in high-priced status-symbol products such as Rolls Royce and developed a consistent formula of using an attractive picture, a long headline, and straight-talking copy. Ogilvy avoided humor until later in his career, believing that it distracted from the importance of the selling message. The Hathaway Man, the debonair eye-patch-wearing symbol of Hathaway shirts, was his best-known campaign. Each ad in the series, which ran exclusively in *The New Yorker* for four years, portrayed the Hathaway Man engaged in a different activity. Readers looked forward eagerly to his next adventure.

The social activism and upheaval of the 1960s, especially after 1965, affected trends in advertising design. Music, art, and fashion during the decade were often designed to shock viewers of conventional tastes. Television became an increasing force in American life. And the youth culture influenced all kinds of trends, with mod and hippie street styles becoming an artistic force both in fashion and in advertising. British music, fashion, and art, in particular, also began to have an effect on youth culture in the United States.

One subset of the youth culture was the drug culture, which gave rise to the neo–Art Nouveau style of Peter Max, as well as the intertwined styles of pop art, op art, camp art, psychedelic art, and funky art. While these movements did not necessarily appeal to mainstream consumers, they made some appearances in mainstream advertising, especially for products geared toward young people, such as posters, magazines, and records. These art styles were particularly evident in the poster craze of the late 1960s and early 1970s.

Although there were few rules or consistent trends in the 1960s, the eclectic design that emerged was characterized by wit and humor, flat outlines, bright colors, controlled yet personal images, and often-humorous juxtapositions. This style was pioneered by organizations such as Push Pin Studios, founded by Milton Glaser, Seymour Chwast, Reynold Ruffins, and Edward Sorel in 1954. The studio gained its reputation in the 1960s, creating both advertising and posters, as well as other graphic design.

In the 1970s the design of a product, whether a fashion item or a piece of furniture or electronic equipment, was of paramount importance, and marketing campaigns reflected this by focusing on design as a positive reason to purchase. Much of the advertising and graphic design during the decade evolved from an analytic approach to design problems. One of the leading advertising art directors of the 1970s was George Lois, who founded several agencies and was known for his irreverent, humorous, even outrageous style.

One of the design movements that made an impact on graphic design in the United States in the 1970s was Swiss design, which had first made an appearance in the late 1960s. But there was no consistent or overriding style. Advertising design in the 1970s was influenced by a myriad of movements, from American folk art and neo–Art Nouveau/psychedelic art to 1950s commercial art and Swiss New Wave.

In the 1980s the image advertising promoted by David Ogilvy in the 1960s underwent a resurgence, particularly in television. Cartoonish characters embodied a product's brand image. Some well-known examples included Spuds MacKenzie for Budweiser, Joe Isuzu for Isuzu automobiles, the fast-talking Federal Express spokesman, and the feisty senior citizen Clara Peller for Wendy's.

The 1980s avant-garde art movement, led by designers from The Netherlands, affected advertising design. Designers of ads tried to emulate the movement's focus on personal statements, its placement of photography, including photo-collage, in a central role, the incorporation of layers of imagery, and the use of a broad mix of media. Seemingly contradictory forces were often placed side by side, such as pairing provocative images with a refined overall look. Some of the American proponents of this postmodern design style, sometimes referred to as the New Wave, were April Greiman, Dan Friedman, and Willi Kunz.

Although it is difficult to look back on the 1990s and determine the lasting design trends, it is evident that technology drove many of the innovations in ad layout and themes, especially late in the decade. Most important, the advent of the Internet as an advertising medium added the potential for interactivity—both real and thematic—to advertising messages. In addition, the fast pace of technological change affected product design and, in turn, advertising design by driving a techno look, influenced by such highly designed products as the iMac and the reintroduced/redesigned Volkswagen Beetle. A combination of high-tech utility and colorful fun made its way into products and the advertising that supported them. Technological innovation continued to drive advertising design in the early years of the second millennium, affecting not only the way messages were delivered but also the ads' imagery and design.

KAREN RAUGUST

See also Package Design; Typography

Further Reading

Ainsley, Jeremy, "Graphic Design," in *Design History: A Student's Handbook,* edited by Hazel Conway, London and Boston: Allen and Unwin, 1987

Craig, James, and Bruce Barton, *Thirty Centuries of Graphic Design: An Illustrated Survey,* New York: Watson-Guptill, 1987

Fox, Stephen, *The Mirror Makers: A History of American Advertising and Its Creators,* New York: Morrow, 1984

Fraser, James Howard, *The American Billboard: 100 Years,* New York: Abrams, 1991

Goodrum, Charles A., and Helen Dalrymple, *Advertising in America: The First 200 Years,* New York: Abrams, 1990

Graphic Design in America: A Visual Language History (exhib. cat.), Minneapolis, Minnesota: Walker Art Center, and New York: Abrams, 1989

McQuiston, Liz, and Barry Kitts, *Graphic Design Source Book,* Secaucus, New Jersey: Chartwell Books, and London: Macdonald Orbis, 1987

Meggs, Philip B., *A History of Graphic Design,* New York: Van Nostrand Reinhold, and London: Allen Lane, 1983; 2nd edition, New York: Van Nostrand Reinhold, 1992

Remington, R. Roger, and Barbara J. Hodik, *Nine Pioneers in American Graphic Design,* Cambridge, Massachusetts: MIT Press, 1989

Sivulka, Juliann, *Soap, Sex, and Cigarettes: A Cultural History of American Advertising,* Belmont, California: Wadsworth, 1998

Thomson, Ellen Mazur, "Alms for Oblivion: The History of Women in Early American Graphic Design," in *Design History: An Anthology,* edited by Dennis P. Doordan, Cambridge, Massachusetts: MIT Press, 1995

Thomson, Ellen Mazur, *The Origins of Graphic Design in America, 1870–1920,* New Haven, Connecticut: Yale University Press, 1997

Deutsch, Inc.

Founded by David Deutsch, 1969; leadership assumed by his son Donny Deutsch, 1989; opened office in Los Angeles, California, 1996; expanded into Chicago, Illinois, and Boston, Massachusetts, 1998; named "Agency of the Year" by *Advertising Age,* 1998; acquired by Interpublic Group of Companies, 2000.

Major Clients

Ashford.com
Bank One Corporation
Baskin-Robbins USA
Domino's Pizza
Ikea
Revlon
Tommy Hilfiger
Triarc (Snapple)

Through a reputation for sometimes outrageous but always fresh campaigns, the boutique advertising agency Deutsch, Inc., grew to be the largest independent agency in the United States within the space of ten years. The roots of Deutsch, Inc., date back to an ad agency specializing in print ads, founded in New York City in 1969 by David Deutsch. He ran the shop for 14 years before his son Donny joined him as an account executive. Donny's only previous agency experience had been less than a year spent at Ogilvy & Mather Worldwide as an assistant account executive on the Maxwell House account.

The elder Deutsch in 1989 handed the business over to his 32-year-old son, who oversaw the expansion of Deutsch, Inc., into the nation's largest independent agency, with billings reaching $1.2 billion in 1999. Admirers dubbed Donny Deutsch a genius; detractors dismissed him as boisterous and cocky.

Deutsch's first work included controversial ads for the Swedish home furnishings marketer Ikea, which broke ground because they featured interracial and gay couples. At that time Ikea—a retail powerhouse in Europe—was still unknown to U.S. shoppers and needed to make a big impression. The campaign was so productive that Deutsch won Ikea's entire $40 million-plus account in 1997, succeeding Roche Macaulay & Partners Advertising and Ammirati Puris Lintas, both of Toronto, Canada.

Through the years, Deutsch kept Ikea's advertising fresh by replacing the ads that featured nontraditional families with spots showing that furniture from Ikea could make even a bowling alley, a hospital, or the New York City subway look better. Those spots began to air in 1998. Ikea, however, pulled the plug on Deutsch in 2000 to seek a new image, putting its advertising into review. Deutsch did not participate in the review.

The agency had struggled to break out of its image as a New York City–centric company. In 1996 Deutsch headed west and opened an outpost in Los Angeles, California. It was so successful that it was expanded and started exchanging its smaller clients, such as chef Wolfgang Puck, for bigger accounts. The next year, the Los Angeles office won the $60 million Bank of America account and the $25 million Baskin-Robbins USA business. Donny Deutsch added seven equity-holding partners to help silence comments that he was the agency's sole decision-maker. The partners were singled out to expand agency leadership and prepare for the future.

Things were going well at the New York City office, too. When Triarc Companies acquired Snapple in 1997, it hired Deutsch to handle the $30 million account. Of particular note was the agency's reintroduction of the brand's popular spokeswoman Wendy Kaufman, the renowned Snapple Lady from earlier ads created by Kirshenbaum & Bond. Although no longer the star of the ads, Kaufman traveled to 33 markets as part of a promotional tour. Deutsch also helped Snapple with the successful launch of its herb-spiked Elements fruit drink. In 1998 Deutsch added offices in Chicago, Illinois, and Boston, Massachusetts. It bolstered its integrated offerings by adding direct marketing and interactive capabilities.

One of the agency's biggest coups was its 1998 win of the Mitsubishi Motor Sales of America account, worth $250 million. The victory was especially significant because Deutsch had wrested the Mitsubishi account from McCann-Erickson Worldwide, a much more established agency. It also gave Deutsch the car company business the agency had coveted after losing out in competitions for Volkswagen, Mazda, and Acura.

That same year, Deutsch launched a $30 million effort that transformed Baskin-Robbins USA's pink spoon into a wry, animated icon for the ice cream retailer. Deutsch was lauded for the efforts and was named *Advertising Age*'s "Agency of the Year" for 1998.

The next year was one of continued success—the agency's biggest up to that time. Deutsch added premium clients such as Pfizer (Zyrtec allergy medication), Bank One Corporation, and Brink's/Citizen Watch Company of America, garnering a total of about $510 million in new billings. Deutsch seemed unstoppable, winning 11 of the 12 accounts it competed for (it lost Toys "R" Us). Tommy Hilfiger USA awarded Deutsch an estimate $60 million in spending without a review.

Deutsch then acquired the advertising account of Reflect.com, a Procter & Gamble Company (P&G) Web site marketing customized cosmetics on-line. The agency had resigned the Andrew Jergens Company's Biore skin care line account in order to take on Reflect.com. Hiring Deutsch was a departure from P&G's longstanding practice of awarding new business to its roster shops. At the time, Donny Deutsch said that his agency had been actively seeking the right dot-com partner. Deutsch also took on

creative responsibilities for the $100 million Ann Arbor, Michigan-based Domino's Pizza account. Borrowing a tactic from the Baskin-Robbins campaign, Deutsch created a character called Andy to help boost consumer awareness of Domino's.

Deutsch took on additional Internet clients, including Britannica.com, Ashford.com, and Myfamily.com, as well as opening dRush, a youth-marketing joint venture with rap musician and fashion magnate Russell Simmons's Rush Media. While the dot-com shakeout in 2000 affected Deutsch's client list, the agency retained Ashford.com and Reflect.com.

During 2000—with a client portfolio that included DirecTV, Domino's Pizza, General Nutrition Centers, Microsoft Corporation's Expedia, Mitsubishi Motor Sales of America, Pfizer's Zoloft antidepressant and Zyrtec, P&G's Reflect.com, Snapple, Sun America, and Timmy Hilfiger—Deutsch was ripe for acquisition. Donny Deutsch wanted to expand, especially internationally, as well, and he knew he needed to partner to do so.

The Interpublic Group of Companies acquired the agency in November 2000 for an estimated $250 million, thereby picking up one of the last major independent ad agencies in the United States. The deal was put in motion at a dinner at an American Association of Advertising Agencies meeting in 1999, when the wife of Interpublic Chairman Phil Geier tried to play matchmaker for the then-unattached Deutsch. A courtship of a different kind was ignited.

Interpublic also owns McCann-Erickson Worldwide and Lowe Lintas & Partners Worldwide and, as of March 2001, True North Communications. At the time of the Interpublic deal, Deutsch had offices in New York City, Los Angeles, and Boston. A London, England, office was in the works and was expected to use Interpublic's resources to make a global push for more international business.

FAYE BROOKMAN

Further Reading

Brandweek Online <www.adweek.com/adweek/issue_highlights/bwcover.jsp> (5 April 1999)

Competitive Media Reporting, *Description of Methodology: Competitive Media Reporting,* New York: Competitive Media Reporting, 1999

The Interpublic Group of Companies <www.interpublic.com>

Dichter, Ernest 1907–1991

Austrian-U.S. Psychologist and Motivational Researcher

Few men in the history of advertising have attracted such a following, excited so much controversy, and provoked as many detractors as Ernest Dichter, the "father of motivational research." Dichter was born in 1907 in Vienna, Austria. He studied psychology at the University of Vienna, where he

received his doctorate in 1934. He left his native Austria in 1938 via France after persuading the U.S. consul in Paris to give him a visa. He argued that he could help the United States solve its problems by getting to the root of why people behave in certain ways.

Ernest Dichter (with his wife, Hedy).
Courtesy of Hedy Dichter.

Determining why people do—or do not do—certain things was to occupy the rest of his life. He worked on behalf of worthy causes and organizations such as the United Nations, the Red Cross, and the American Cancer Society, but his most notable (and profitable) efforts were for the advertising industry. For years advertisers and agencies embraced him as a guru, the man they believed could tell them what truly motivated people to buy certain products or services.

Dichter made his reputation in advertising in the 1950s, as the ad industry turned more and more toward persuasion to sell the increasing number of products and brands that were pouring onto the market. Dichter offered aspects of Freudian psychology, with heavy emphasis on the symbolism of products. Thus, according to Dichter, what was important in selling cigarette lighters was the idea that the flame represented a desire for mastery and power. Or he might posit that indigestion-sufferers saw their affliction almost as a status symbol—it embodied their hard-working lifestyle.

His detractors laughed, but believers hung on Dichter's every word—and acted on them as well. It reached a stage, one advertising man recalled years later, when some advertisers would not listen to advice unless it came from a man with a thick Viennese accent and professorial mien; dozens of Dichter soundalike practitioners suddenly emerged.

But none had what Dichter had: a total conviction coupled with an ability to get his message across in Freudian-sounding terms that seemed to make sense. Whether or not the message was sensible increasingly became a subject for debate. But often enough marketing or advertising campaigns based on Dichter's theories had noticeable impact. Some observers, with justification, thought that the key element in the success was not so much his methods as his own personal genius at seeing a problem and formulating a solution.

Dichter's first attempt to establish his philosophy in the United States was not a success. Hired to research why consumers did or did not choose to drink milk, he argued that direct questioning was crude and unreliable. His superiors felt the same about the method Dichter proposed—namely, to interview consumers about their preferences but make no direct reference to milk.

Quitting this job, Dichter began a letter-writing campaign, presenting himself as a man who could increase sales by discovering the underlying reasons people chose certain products. The Compton Agency was one of the first to call him. Its Procter & Gamble Company product, Ivory soap, was not selling as well as the agency thought it should. Dichter interviewed 100 people at YMCAs and came to the conclusion that bathing was not just a matter of washing away dirt, but a psychological cleansing, too.

Procter & Gamble backed his insight and paid Dichter $400 for his work. The result was the slogan, "Be smart and get a fresh start with Ivory Soap . . . and wash all your troubles away." It was the first time, Dichter believed, that motivational research was actually used to sell a product. Years later, he recalled, "I knew bathing was a ritual. You cleanse yourself not only of dirt but of guilt."

Dichter was on his way—and so was motivational research. Hired by the Chrysler Corporation to help sell Plymouth cars, he uncovered the key role women play in men's buying decisions and recommended ads in women's magazines. The success that followed brought *Time* magazine's accolade, "Viennese psychologist discovers gold mine for Chrysler." Dichter was also responsible for the internationally famous Esso/Exxon advertisement, "Put a tiger in your tank." First emerging in 1956, the ad was a consequence of Dichter's insight that people associate cars with power.

That same year Dichter was featured in the best-selling book *The Hidden Persuaders* by Vance Packard, which depicted an advertising industry maneuvering consumers into buying goods they neither wanted nor needed. A number-one nonfiction bestseller in the United States for six weeks, *The Hidden Persuaders* still haunts many advertisers today because of its negative portrayal of the industry. It continues to sell thousands of copies each year, and for countless people it represents the "real truth" about advertising—that it is a black art that induces people to do what the advertiser wants, often against their will.

Dichter, a practical man, later admitted he saw Packard's book less as an attack than as a big break. "I got invitations of work from all over the world." He opened a dozen offices. He did not fail his new international audience. In London, England, for example, he explained that the British consumed vast amounts of candy and chocolates to channel their suppressed emotions. Even

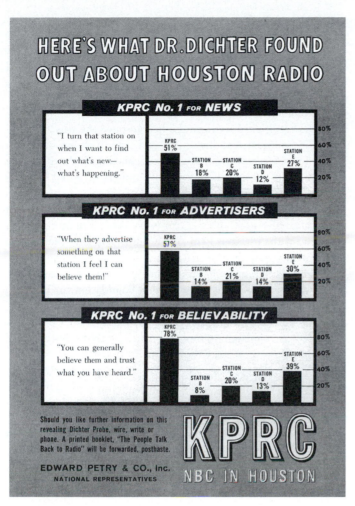

In 1959 KPRC-AM radio in Houston, Texas, used Dichter's research findings in its advertising.
Courtesy of KPRC 950 AM.

in his late 70s his client list still ran to hundreds. Companies that employed him included CBS, General Mills, Alberto-Culver Company, AT&T Corporation, Coca-Cola Company, and Sears, Roebuck & Company.

His reputation fluctuated wildly. Over the years he found himself attacked, ridiculed, consigned to history, and rehabilitated. His motivational research lives on in qualitative research, and his message that advertisers sell images is now considered a truism.

Focus groups (he claimed to be the first to coin the term) have become commonplace. No one today doubts that what people do—including what they buy—is often irrational and their motivations unclear. As Dichter himself put it, "Human behavior is still as strange to us as life on the moon would be if we settled up there."

ERIC CLARK

Biography

Born in Vienna, Austria, on 14 August 1907; received doctorate in psychology from the University of Vienna, 1934; emigrated to United States, 1938; founded the Institute of Motivational Research, New York City, 1946; elected fellow of the American Psychological Association; named "Man of the Year" by Market Research Council, 1983; died in Peaksville, New York, 22 November 1991.

Selected Publications

The Psychology of Everyday Living, 1947
The Strategy of Desire, 1960
Handbook of Consumer Motivations: The Psychology of the World of Objects, 1964
Motivating Human Behavior, 1971
The Naked Manager, 1974
Packaging, the Sixth Sense? A Guide to Identifying Consumer Motivation, 1975
Total Self-Knowledge, 1976
Getting Motivated by Ernest Dichter: The Secret behind Individual Motivations, by the Man Who Was Not Afraid to Ask "Why?" 1979
How Hot a Manager Are You? 1987

Further Reading

Barrett, Katherine, and Richard Greene, "Work Motivates Psychoanalyst," *Advertising Age* (1 November 1984)
Clark, Eric, *The Want Makers*, London: Hodder and Stoughton, 1988; New York: Viking, 1989
Fox, Stephen, *The Mirror Makers: A History of American Advertising and Its Creators*, New York: Morrow, 1984
Packard, Vance, *The Hidden Persuaders*, New York: McKay, and London: Longmans, 1957; revised edition, New York: Pocket Books, 1980; London: Penguin, 1981

Direct Marketing/Direct Mail

Direct marketing is an interactive system of marketing that uses one or more advertising media to effect a measurable response and/or a transaction at any location. Unlike traditional advertising and promotional activities, it attempts to develop an ongoing dialogue with an individual, household, or business. Direct-marketing materials are presented in a variety of formats including a merchandise or service order form, a card or other form for use in requesting further information (i.e., the process known as lead generation), a solicitation for a contribution or donation, or an invitation to visit a specific store or site. The direct-marketing piece normally provides the recipient with extensive information about the product, service, or organization being advertised, along with a means to execute the sale. This could be a coupon, a phone number, or other device.

Direct marketing's early history began with catalog publishers and, later, lettershop users (lettershops are mailing facilities where letters, flyers, brochures, and inserts are collated into a mailing package, labels and postage affixed, and the packages delivered to the post office). The first known catalog, Aldus Manutius's catalog of 15 books in Greek and Latin, was produced in 1498. Much later, in 1667, William Lucas, an Englishman, published a gardening catalog. In the United States, Benjamin Franklin published *Poor Richard: An Almanac,* which was distributed from 1732 to 1758. In 1744 Franklin published a book catalog listing some 600 volumes.

The Business Address Company of New York City, established in 1880, is credited as the first mailing house in the United States. However, the New York Life Insurance Company was using direct-mail promotions as early as 1872, possibly designing and collating them in-house. Buckley-Dement, the first direct-mail agency, was founded in Chicago, Illinois, in 1905. The Direct Mail Advertising Association (DMAA) was founded in 1917, helping to further organize the industry; 538 people attended the DMAA's 1918 convention. Though other direct-mail agencies were established in the 1920s, the majority did not appear until the 1950s.

Direct mail traditionally appeared in the form of post cards, letters, folders, circulars, catalogs, invitations, product samples, or research materials. In the mid–19th century the increased availability of goods and the drive for sales fueled the direct-mail industry's development. Though some companies used regularly scheduled mailings, with the distribution in 1844 of Orvis's catalog featuring fishing and camping gear, catalogs began to comprise the majority of direct mail. When penny postage debuted in 1863, boosting widespread mailing of merchandise, the catalog business was officially launched. By 1865 mail-order activity had expanded throughout the United States. As technology evolved, and the typewriter was invented (1867), direct marketing flourished. For example, Montgomery Ward and Company's first catalog, produced as a single page in 1872, had expanded to 240 pages by 1884. The growth of the railroad during this period greatly enhanced the distribution of printed materials. Richard

Sears entered the mail-order business in 1886; in 1887 he joined forces with Alvah Roebuck, and by 1893 the two were producing a 322-page catalog. Their catalog's distribution soared to more than 1 million copies by the spring of 1904. When Sears launched the Sears credit card in 1910, he helped pave the way for mail order's permanent establishment as a way of doing business. Retail stores and industrial advertisers refined the industry during the early 20th century. Predominant retailers included Neiman Marcus and L.L. Bean. The launch of the Book-of-the-Month Club in 1926 spearheaded so-called continuity programs, in which successive items are shipped to a customer upon receipt of payment for the previous item. While customers have the right to return items, they do not order each item seperately. Though political notices requesting donations were mailed occasionally during this period, it was the National Foundation for Infantile Paralysis (later to become the March of Dimes), founded in 1938, that established the use of direct mail for fund-raising purposes. Its successful campaign financed the research that eventually led to the development of the polio vaccine.

The postwar years continued to give rise to a host of specialty direct-mail companies. By the 1950s credit cards became commonplace. Diners Club introduced the first travel and entertainment card; American Express and Bank of America soon followed with their own versions. Supported by the flexibility of payment offered by credit cards, direct marketing expanded to both the magazine publishing business (Publishers Clearinghouse) and the music world (Columbia Record Club).

The mail-order business surged during the 1970s as working women, their numbers burgeoning, took advantage of the convenience of catalog shopping. Companies such as Lands' End, Lillian Vernon, and Spiegel became household names. And, with more women in the workforce and subsequently more disposable income, the acquisition of goods and services increased. In 1971 Roger Horchow founded the Horchow Collection, launching a groundswell for catalogs featuring upscale merchandise. Stores such as Neiman Marcus, Gump's, and Tiffany & Company, known for their luxury goods, also introduced catalogs, furthering the trend toward the use of direct marketing to cater to specialized, or niche, markets. (Neiman Marcus purchased the Horchow Collection in 1988.) With changing demographics—especially the decline in rural population—however, and increased postal costs, many general merchandise catalogs geared to lower- and middle-class families disappeared. Montgomery Ward, for example, withdrew its catalog in 1985.

Direct marketing has benefited greatly from advances in technology. By the beginning of the 21st century, the field had become entirely dependent on computers. Although the first general purpose computer was built in 1945, it was not until 1972 that the mainframe computer came into widespread marketing use, allowing for "merge/purge" programs and, hence, the elimination of duplicate mailings. These computers also facilitated the development of enormous databases and the collection of zip code and census tract data, enabling advertisers to target audiences more effectively and track responses to direct mail with precision. Advances in computer programming and the declining cost of computer equipment and, especially, the advent of the personal computer in the early 1980s, made it possible for advertisers to create promotions geared to varying target audiences with specific interests and unique buying patterns. Niches became even more narrowly defined, and relationship marketing (also known as one-to-one marketing)—whereby the company or service is willing and able to modify its behavior toward the individual customer based on the customer's needs—was established.

There was a negative side to this success, however. As direct-mail and direct-marketing appeals proliferated to the point where the average person received more advertising circulars per day than correspondence, the pejorative phrase "junk mail" came to commonly characterize direct advertising in the public's mind. Many direct-mail agencies employed ingenious ways to disguise the nature of their mailings. Affixed stamps replaced machine stamping and technology enabled machines to simulate handwritten addresses. Direct-mail pieces were designed to look like telegrams, checks, and even government documents, in the hope of fooling the recipient into opening the envelope rather than disposing of it, unopened and unread.

During the 1980s the entry of many low-budget advertisers into the field further impugned direct marketing's overall reputation. In the United States hundreds of local television stations had made available fringe time periods (after midnight and before 6 a.m.) for direct advertising. Payment for airtime was based on recorded sales, thus freeing advertisers from having to make costly media commitments. As a consequence of this practice direct marketing, long associated with novelty kitchen gadgets and cheap exercise equipment, became further tainted by the entry into the market of phone sex services, psychic hot lines, and fortune tellers, whose ads often appeared as inexpensively produced infomercials. Though several high-end advertisers, such as AT&T Corporation, used direct marketing during this period, the general public's negative opinion of it continued.

Direct marketing's expansion paralleled the growth of radio during the 1930s and of television during the 1950s, employing various calls to action. This trend, facilitated by AT&T's introduction of their toll-free 800-number service in 1967, paved the way for telemarketing and facsimile (fax) marketing in the late 1970s. The expansion of cable television and its niche stations enabled further targeting of audiences with specialized interests. At the turn of the century, direct marketing continued as an integral part of both radio and television, pervading the airwaves in the early morning hours. During this time, the Internet, with its rapid technological advances, became a powerful direct-marketing tool for the television and advertising industries.

Internet connectivity increased rapidly during the 1990s. Simultaneously, direct marketing and promotional disciplines became more intertwined. The Internet, originally thought of as peripheral to direct marketing, revolutionized the industry. Mailing lists, traditionally taken from sources such as driver's license rolls, subscription lists, and product purchase lists, had a new

This 2000 ad for Experian, a global information solutions company, promoted its INSOURCE database services, a resource for lifestyle-based target marketing.
Experian.

source of potential consumers, so-called e-lists, generated by Internet users. These lists grew rapidly, building a new frontier in direct electronic mail. The rapid expansion of on-line catalogs, promotions, and e-lists was responsible for U.S. e-commerce sales reaching $11 billion in 1999. During the year 2000, 35 percent of all U.S. Internet users made on-line purchases. It is projected that e-commerce sales will grow to $84.4 billion by 2004.

Changing technology transformed not only techniques of direct marketing but also the nature of the industry. In 1973 the DMAA modified its mission and changed its name to the Direct Mail/Direct Marketing Association. In 1983, with computers becoming more commonplace, the group changed its name again, this time to the Direct Marketing Association (DMA). Next, the DMA acquired two e-commerce trade associations, the Association for Interactive Media (in 1998) and the Internet Alliance (in 1999), acknowledging the Internet's impact and importance.

The year 2000 saw the majority of global and local companies phasing into computer-based direct campaigns with great success, whether delivered via diskette, CD-ROM, DVD-ROM, or the Internet. Revenues from direct-response advertising continued to increase—both from advertisements and infomercials—generating $1.5 trillion in U.S. sales during 1999 according to the DMA. Additionally, in 1999 direct marketing accounted for more than half of all U.S. advertising dollars. Corporations and marketers were coming to recognize the role of computer-based technology in enabling real two-way communication, increasing consumers' retention of key ad messages and thereby motivating them, and encouraging greater acceptance of direct marketing as a responsible form of advertising.

PATRICIA B. ROSE

See also color plate in this volume

Further Reading

Batra, Rajeev, *The New Direct Marketing: How to Implement a Profit-Driven Database Marketing Strategy,* Homewood, Illinois: Dow Jones-Irwin, 1990; 3rd edition, New York: McGraw-Hill, 1999

Bell, David E., and Dinny Star Gordon, *Note on the Mail Order Industry,* Boston: Harvard Business School, 1995

Gilmore, James H., and W. Joseph Pine, *Markets of One: Creating Customer-Unique Value through Mass Customization,* Boston: Harvard Business School Press, 2000

McDonald, William J., *Direct Marketing: An Integrated Approach,* Boston and London: McGraw-Hill, 1998

Sackheim, Maxwell, *My First 65 Years in Advertising,* Summit, Pennsylvania: G/L Tab Books, 1975

Stone, Bob, *Successful Direct Marketing Methods,* Chicago: Crain Books, 1975; 5th edition, Lincolnwood, Illinois: NTC Business Books, 1994

Wunderman, Lester, *Being Direct: How I Learned to Make Advertising Pay, New York:* Random House, 1997

Director, Commercials

A blend of marketing and artistry, the television commercial has elevated the sales pitch to a culturally significant, sophisticated medium, one involving some of the highest paid and most influential image makers in the world. The best work brings together inspired concepts, casting, and imagery, along with the perfect tag line, yielding an expression or image that can become an integral part of the culture. Among these enduring words and pictures are Bartles & Jaymes's "Thank you for your support" for E&J Gallo Winery; Apple Computer's "1984"; Alka-Seltzer's "Spicy Meatballs"; Wendy's International's "Where's the beef?"; Nike's "Just do it"; and the Coca-Cola hillside with its choir of fresh-faced youth teaching the world to sing.

At the center of every commercial is a director, who conducts the cast and crew and brings the creative team's vision to life in a collaborative effort. Over the years, the director's role—to manage the shoot and control everything going on around him or her—has remained the same, even though everything else has changed: the technology, the processes involved, and the structure and nature of the business.

In the early days of TV commercials, advertising agencies produced live black-and-white spots during the network programs their clients sponsored. The process was overseen by agency producers, who came from the radio departments and were assigned to networks rather than accounts. The advent of videotape in the 1950s made live commercials, with all of their associated risks, obsolete. Tape and film allowed commercials, for the first time, to be produced and prerecorded, thus offering a guarantee of content and quality.

Initially, industrial film producers dominated the field, being the only people qualified to assume the commercials mantle. But after the Korean War, when the ban on the start-up of new TV stations was lifted and stations began to proliferate, the business of making TV commercials changed radically. Within a short time a new job category arose within ad agencies: the television commercials producer.

At the same time, art directors were turning to still photographers, with whom they had developed relationships, to replicate their print look in motion picture film. While the early directors had been cameramen, new talent now came from the print medium. Early pioneers included photographers Norman Griner and Steve Horn of Horn/Griner Productions, Elbert Budin, Howard Zieff, Mike Cuesta, Richard Avedon, Melvin Sokolsky, Georges Gomes, Irving Penn, and Henry Sandbank. Horn and Griner, in particular, made important contributions to studio lighting.

Another print photographer who became an influential freelance director was Howard Zieff. Zieff's classic sample reel for Doyle Dane Bernbach (DDB) included Alka-Seltzer's "Spicy Meatballs" and "Stomach" commercials and Volkswagen of America's spot called "Funeral." The first to borrow from feature film techniques, Zieff combined subtle, sophisticated comedy with a virtuoso narrative performance.

Initially, advertising agencies purchased the services of the production company, not individual directors. As a result, there was a corresponding explosion in the number of commercial production houses supporting agencies, including MPO, Elliot, Unger, Elliot

(EUE), Screen Gems, Horn/Griner, Filmfair, Cascade, N. Lee Lacy/ Associates, Motion Associates, Habush, Filmways, and Pelican. The agency producer would select a small group of companies with established track records in the required specialty, then invite each to review the storyboards and submit a bid. During the shoot, formal protocol required that the agency communicate with the director through the producer, though that depended on the agency relationship with the production company or director.

During the 1970s an increasing number of agency art directors and producers began directing. Young & Rubicam (Y&R) and DDB became known as training grounds for such talents as Bob Giraldi, Stan Dragoti, Bert Steinhauser, Sid Myers, and Dick Lowe. Bob Giraldi started out as a comedy director who went on to develop a specialty in the flashy music video genre. He filmed singer Michael Jackson's "Beat It" video, followed by several blockbuster Jackson ads for the Pepsi-Cola Company. After innovative work for such musical performers as Stevie Wonder and Barry Manilow, he moved into the first ranks of the world's video directors.

In the 1970s agencies began requesting directors who specialized in such genres as slice-of-life, dialogue, "tabletop" (i.e., still life objects such as food and package displays), comedy, fashion, beauty, and cars. Joe Sedelmaier was a former art director for Young & Rubicam, Chicago, Illinois, who revolutionized the use of comedy, gaining professional and popular notoriety. The inspired dementia of his early work—the earliest being regional, such as a campaign for Chicago-area Pontiac dealers and Southern Airways—along with his celebrated "Fast Talker" commercials for Federal Express Corporation propelled the lunatic fringe into the commercial spotlight. "Fast Talker" was named number 11 on *Advertising Age*'s list of the top 100 ad campaigns. Sedelmaier was among the first commercial directors to cast real people rather than actors. His cast consisted of the dazed, disoriented, and disturbed: harassed office workers, sad-eyed salesman, and bewildered consumers, all filmed in the distorting perspective of wide-angle lenses. So popular was Sedelmaier's work that when "Where's the beef?" was uttered by octogenarian Clara Peller on behalf of Wendy's International, it entered the popular vocabulary as a metaphor for anything lacking in substance and even surfaced in the 1984 U.S. presidential race.

Another such specialist was Henry Sandbank, a former photographer who started out as a tabletop expert and then acquired a reputation for being able to come up with virtually anything the creative team wanted. He was known for his striking imagery and was one of the first to embrace special effects. His most celebrated spot, for American Honda Motor Company, featured an actor trying to drive the car off an art gallery wall.

During the late 1970s and early 1980s, fears of a recession pushed the U.S. ad industry into the creative doldrums. On the other side of the Atlantic, however, European agencies were enjoying a creative renaissance, and the first of the "new wave" directors, mainly British and French, invaded the U.S. market. Howard Guard was followed by Ridley and Tony Scott, Alan Parker, Hugh Hudson, and Adrian Lyne. Arriving with a fresh look, new ideas, and a more "crafted" approach, they quickly

Joe Sedelmaier.
Courtesy of Joe Sedelmaier, Filmmaker.

became known as "auteurs," involved with all stages of the pre- and post-production processes. Ridley Scott drew on French New Wave films of the early 1960s such as Alain Resnais's *Last Year at Marienbad* to create the carefully sculpted ambiguity of Chanel's "Share the Fantasy" campaign from DDB in 1979. He went on to direct one of the most talked about commercials of all time, Apple's "1984," and epitomized the British look, with his highly stylized compositions and dark vision. Another eccentric director was Tony Kaye, famed for his maverick behavior and impressive sample reel, which included work for Prodigy, Volvo, and a spot for Dunlop Tire reckoned by many observers to be the most surreal piece of abstract impressionism ever produced by a major agency, Abbott Mead Vickers/BBDO.

Following the British were the South Africans, led by Leslie Dektor, who was known for his versatility; he also became well known in the 1980s for his use of the "shaky cam," a hand-held, jagged technique for shooting, first used for Levi Strauss & Company's 501 jeans. Designed to simulate the nostalgic look of old home movies and to contrast with the slick production values displayed by most TV commercials, the technique remains influential. The 1984 campaign was ranked number 72 on *Advertising Age*'s list of the top 100 advertising campaigns.

New techniques meant increasing dependence on sophisticated visual effects. From a special effects standpoint, commercials were advancing by leaps and bounds. In the 1980s, West Coast companies such as Robert Abel & Associates, a groundbreaking effects house, made lasting contributions to the technology. Later, Abel's mantle was taken up by companies such as Lucasfilm's Industrial Light & Magic and Digital Domain.

Tarsem Singh Dhandwar.
Courtesy of Tarsem Dhandwar.

With the growth of technology and subsequent increase in the cost of production, both agencies and clients became more involved in the process of making commercials. Directors were brought in earlier than before for consultations and were expected to have presentation and sales skills in addition to directing talent. Clients, anxious about budgets, employed cost consultants, who soon became fixtures of every shoot.

A number of successful British commercials directors turned their hand to making feature films. Adrian Lyne directed 1983's *Flashdance* and 1987's *Fatal Attraction;* Ridley Scott's movies included 1982's *Blade Runner,* 1991's *Thelma & Louise,* and 2000's *Gladiator;* Tony Scott made 1986's *Top Gun* and 1995's *Crimson Tide,* among others; and Hugh Hudson directed 1981's *Chariots of Fire.* Each moved back and forth between films and commercials, contributing to the development of a new breed: the crossover director. While there were a few examples in the United States—Howard Zieff, who had hits with *House Calls* and *Private Benjamin,* and Stan Dragoti, with *Mr. Mom*—numerous other U.S. commercials directors who tried their hand at the feature film world were less successful.

Also in the 1980s, feature film directors, who had previously considered commercials beneath them, began noticing their slick production values. At the same time, agencies, in an effort to have their work stand out, believed they could enhance a commercial by using a star feature director. Previously, the two types of directors had remained largely separated—movie directors were centered on the West Coast, while the ad business was centered on the East Coast.

But the stigma attached to the making of commercials was fading fast. Big-name movie directors realized that making commercials was not only lucrative but also allowed them to hone their craft by telling a story in 30 seconds. Feature-film directors such

as Penny Marshall, Robert Altman, John Schlesinger, John Frankenheimer, Spike Lee, Tony Bill, John Badham, Martin Scorsese, and David Lynch began making themselves available for commercials work. Effects perfected in the world of advertising, such as quick cuts and extreme musicality, began showing up in movies.

In 1981 the launch of cable television's MTV, with its pulsing beats, high-energy rhythms, quick cuts, and tracking cameras that never stayed put, forever changed the look of TV commercials. Music video directors, with their in-your-face attitude and hip spontaneity, began to dominate commercials. The production house Propaganda (based both in New York City and Los Angeles, California), which specialized in the new in-demand talent, was at the forefront of the trend.

By the late 1980s, the fact that making commercials had become respectable and paid well was not lost on aspiring directors. New people swarmed into the industry from music video, editing houses, ad agencies, art schools, and computer graphics firms, as well as from feature films and still photography. Ray Lofaro, an impresario who started the first independent sales representation company, Lofaro & Associates, had a knack for finding unique talent and fanning new trends.

The MTV generation spawned many stars. One such standout was the India-born Tarsem Singh Dhandwar, better known as Tarsem, who in the 1990s became one of the most feted of commercials directors, known for his bizarre tableaus, mythological imagery, and offbeat humor. Tarsem, who directed R.E.M.'s "Losing My Religion" music video (which received six awards in the 1991 MTV Awards), went on to direct Nike's 1994 "Good Versus Evil" spot, which won a gold Lion at the Cannes (France) International Advertising Festival and a One Show award, as well as numerous Levi's spots for London-based agency Bartle Bogle Hegarty. Another standout director of the MTV generation was David Fincher, who brought a new look in cinematography and a different style of pacing to commercials for companies such as Nike. Fincher also became one of the first U.S.-born commercials directors to have success in features, with films such as *Alien³,* *Fight Club,* and *Seven.* Other MTV directors followed suit: Michael Bay made *The Rock* and *Armageddon,* and Spike Jonze made *Being John Malkovich.*

By the new millennium, more commercial directors than ever were bidding for the same amount of business, calling for extraordinary commitment on the part of aspiring directors. The increasingly global nature of the business also extended the competition to a range of international talents. Saatchi & Saatchi's Annual New Director's Showcase, launched in 1990, as well as the more general expansion of cable TV, satellite TV, and the Internet fostered a new openness to directors from all parts of the globe and from all divisions of the business—be it photography, production, music videos, or agencies themselves.

Although directors have come and gone over the decades, one perennial has been megastar Joe Pytka. Known as the consummate professional who always gets it right, he specializes in deft, subtle performances. His work is high profile, high budget, and high gloss. He got Michael Jordan and Larry Bird to tout McDonald's Corporation; Ray Charles to say, "Uh, huh," for

Pepsi; and fictional spokesmen Bartles and Jaymes to "Thank you for your support" of the Gallo wine cooler. And he got to know Bo Jackson, for Nike. With a reputation as a perfectionist and a tantrum thrower, Pytka is known for breaking the tension on the set with an instantaneous game of pickup basketball with the likes of Michael Jordan or Spike Lee. Pytka works with only a few agencies, such as BBDO Worldwide, the Leo Burnett Company, and Wieden & Kennedy.

By the 21st century, the business of producing commercials had changed dramatically from its early days. Gone were many once-thriving New York City production houses, as the industry shifted to the West Coast and became technology driven and increasingly global in scope. More directors were competing for fewer jobs. And more time was spent on presentation and selling and in postproduction. Specialization was the rule. Nonetheless, as in the early days, the director—and the director's vision—remained at the center of the process.

ANN COOPER

Further Reading

Davis, Brian, "The Yanks Aren't Coming" *Creativity* (6 July 1987)

Hume, Scott, "Joe's Beef: The Hard Sell," *Advertising Age* (9 November 1988)

Olds, Andrew, "Expatriate Gains," *Creativity* (4 June 1990)

Pendleton, Jennifer, "Hollywood Buys the Concept," *Advertising Age* (9 November 1988)

Shoot (November 2000) (40th anniversary supplement)

Vagnoni, Anthony, "Across the Great Divide," *Creativity* (4 June 1990)

Vagnoni, Anthony, "Lights, Camera, Action: Early Giants Were Print Guys, But TV Required Talent from Areas That Could Follow a 'Moving Target,'" *Advertising Age* (28 February 1995)

Vagnoni, Anthony, "Imagemakers Impart Advertising with Style, Special Effects, and 'Shaky Cam': Lights, Camera, Direction!" *Advertising Age* (29 March 1999)

D.L. Blair, Inc. *See under* Blair

DM9/DDB

Founded by Duda Mendonca in Salvador, Bahia, Brazil, in 1975; bought by Nizan Guanaes, a Brazilian advertising luminary, 1989; shares bought by DDB, 1997; Guanaes departed, 2000.

Major Clients

American Airlines/Brazil
AOL Brasil
Banco Itau
Batavia (milk products)
Blockbuster Video
Clorox do Brasil
Energizer do Brasil
Esso Brasileira de Petróleo (Exxon Mobil Corporation subsidiary)
Honda Automoveis do Brasil
Johnson & Johnson
Parmalat bakery
Philips Corporate
Shopping Center Iguatemi
Souza Cruz (tobacco products)
TAM Airlines

While the other major Brazilian advertising agencies originated either in Rio de Janeiro or São Paulo, DM9 was established in the state of Bahia, an area better known for its engaging musical rhythms and spicy food than for business enterprises. The agency opened in Salvador, Bahia, in 1975, under the initials of its founder, Duda Mendonca, a successful real estate salesman who liked to create his own ads, plus the number nine, "just for kicks," as he explained. But the agency was to become the brainchild of Nizan Guanaes, perhaps the most prominent advertising man of his generation in Brazil and in all of Latin America, as well.

Guanaes was born in Bahia in 1958, the son of a medical doctor father and an engineer mother. He studied business administration at the University of Bahia, but his real passion was advertising, and he joined DM9 as a teenage trainee after the other agencies in Bahia turned him down. Guanaes quickly outgrew DM9, which was still a small regional agency in the late 1970s, and moved to Rio, where he drew attention for his work for the agency Artplan Comunicaoes. In Rio he helped create an offbeat, humorous campaign for Brazil's Caixa Economica Federal. The

In this point-of-purchase display sign created for Honda in 1999 by DM9/DDB, a section of pavement showed the Honda logo, communicating the message that Honda automobiles are one with the road.

campaign proved so successful in drawing public sympathy that it had to be stopped because the bank could not cope with the onslaught of new clients.

In 1985 Guanaes was invited by Washington Olivetto, then creative head of agency DPZ in São Paulo, to join his team, considered the best in the country. Olivetto left DPZ in 1986 to set up a new shop that would eventually be known as W/Brasil, and Guanaes went with him as deputy creative director of the new venture. In 1989 Guanaes startled the industry by quitting his job at W/Brasil and returning to Bahia and his former agency, DM9, where he set up a partnership with Mendonca. Soon after, however, Guanaes bought the agency, with the help of the Icatu financial group; Mendonca went on to become one of Brazil's chief experts in political campaign advertising.

Between 1989 and 2000, Guanaes was the recipient of numerous advertising awards. In 1992 he became the first Brazilian to be president of a jury at the Cannes (France) International Advertising Festival. He is among the few Brazilians ever to be designated a "Marketing Superstar" by *Advertising Age* (in 1993). He also won the important Brazilian market award Cabore, as Best Entrepreneur/Communications Leader in 1997.

Under his leadership, DM9 became the fastest growing agency in the country, reaching billings of $300 million in 1998, and the first agency not headquartered in the United States or England to be chosen "Agency of the Year" in Cannes. As of 2001 DM9 and England's Bartle Bogle Hegarty were the only agencies that had won the title twice. DM9 is also one of only two Brazilian agencies that has won a Cannes Grand Prix (Almap/BBDO is the other).

As head of DM9, Guanaes coordinated two successful electoral campaigns (1994 and 1998) for Brazilian President Fernando Henrique Cardoso. He was chosen "Most Efficient Advertising Professional" and "Entrepreneur Leader of the Communication Industry" four times by the subscribers of *Gazeta Mercantil*, Brazil's equivalent to *The Financial Times*. With Mendonca, he also appeared on the cover of the Brazilian news magazine *Veja*. In 1997, in what has been billed as the biggest deal in Brazilian advertising, DM9 joined with DDB Worldwide, and Guanaes gained a seat on the DDB Needham board. However, he again surprised the market by quitting DM9/DDB in May 2000 to become chief executive officer of IG, an Internet service provider.

In the nine years under Guanaes, DM9/DDB garnered 43 Lions (in addition to the Grand Prix) at the Cannes Festival, including two Cyber Lions. It also won two Grand Prix at the New York Festivals and FIAP (Iberian-American Advertising Festival) and a Clio award. It was elected best Iberian-American Agency of 1994–98, receiving the El Ojo de Iberoamerica (The Eye of Iberian America), and won a Gold Pencil at the One Show Interactive. It also received the Marketing Best Award of the Century from the Getulio Vargas Foundation (a business school) and was elected the sixth most creative new media agency in the world by the International Digital Excellence Association.

After only one year without Guanaes, DM9/DDB managed to retain most of its clients and billings, which had reached $400 million in 1999, making it the country's number-two agency. Its new president, Affonso Serra, was elected "Adman of the Year" at Columnists Brazil in 2000 and was elected to the DDB Worldwide international board. In 2002 Guanaes returned to DM9/DDB, purchasing a 40 percent stake in the agency.

J. ROBERTO WHITAKER-PENTEADO

Further Reading

Berger, W., "DM9-DDB, Transformations," *Graphis* 327 (May–June 2000)

"International Advertisement Archives," *Archive* (November 2000)

"Scaling the Heights," *Wallpaper* (January 2001)

Donahue & Coe, Inc.

Established in New York City, 1920s; bought out by Edward Churchill, 1932; merged with Walter Weir agency, 1951; merged with Arthur Grossman, Chicago, Illinois, 1956; merged with Ellington & Company to become West, Weir & Bartel, 1964; name retired when agency was bought by MacManus, John & Adams, 1968.

Major Clients
Alpha Beta stores
Borg Warner Norge
Grove Laboratories
Metro-Goldwyn-Mayer
National Association of Ice Industries
New York *Herald Tribune*
Republic Pictures

Founded in New York City in the 1920s by M.J. Donahue and Sayers Coe, Donahue & Coe, Inc. (D&C), grew slowly until 1932, when it was bought by Edward Churchill, who became the agency's president. From then on D&C posted an average growth rate of $1 million a year until leveling off briefly around 1945 at $15 million in billings. Following a drop in revenue, it was slowly rebuilt through the 1950s.

Among the agency's 30 accounts in 1945, Grove Laboratories was a major client, but the largest part of D&C's growth was driven by the motion picture business. Metro-Goldwyn-Mayer (MGM); Lowe's, Inc.; Columbia Pictures; and Republic Pictures made up the largest share of D&C business for many years, accounting for as much as 50 percent in the late 1940s. Although movies were made in Los Angeles, California, the financial and marketing decisions of the film business were concentrated in New York City. Following World War II, the rapid growth of television hurt the movie industry, and D&C felt the blow; agency volume slipped about 15 percent as a result.

At the same time, Churchill decided to drop several small accounts he regarded as unprofitable. By 1950 the agency had recovered to near its 1945 levels and continued to grow steadily—reaching more than $33 million in billings by 1960—without significant reversals.

The Walter Weir agency merged with D&C in October 1951, bringing the combined shop's staff to 175. The Weir agency was established in 1945 by Walter Weir, who had served as copy director at several other agencies. He joined D&C as a senior vice president and later became its chairman. In 1955, when Cowan & Dengler folded, the agency's two principals, Stuart Cowan, Jr., and Horace Dengler, came to D&C, bringing with them several accounts, including Bankers Trust, Seamless Rubber, and Raytheon. In December 1956 D&C added a Chicago, Illinois, branch to its network—with offices in New York City; Montreal, Canada; and Atlanta, Georgia—when it merged with Arthur Grossman Advertising, bringing the Borg Warner Norge division

account. As a result of the diversification of its client base, billings rose to $27 million, and the agency's share of motion-picture volume dropped to around 18 percent.

In 1958 the agency finally opened a Los Angeles office. But the new branch served regional Pepsi-Cola Company bottlers and Alpha Beta grocery stores rather than the movie industry. Alpha Beta's system for compensation was both unique and pioneering in that it replaced the standard commission with a fee-based scale tied to sales on a cost-plus basis. Also in 1958 D&C's Chicago and New York City offices undertook an informal affiliation, but not a merger, with Keyes, Madden & Jones (which in 1963 would merge with Post, Morr & Gardner to form Post-Keyes-Gardner).

Donald West became president in 1959, and Churchill became chairman. The agency was expanding and attracting senior people from such agencies as Doyle Dane Bernbach, Ogilvy & Mather, and Dancer, Fitzgerald, Sample. Their experience in consumer advertising helped produce a swing toward increased packaged goods business, which by 1960 accounted for 30 percent of the agency's billings, with drugs making up 15 percent. D&C was no longer just a movie agency.

In 1961 the agency posted the most successful year in its history, billing nearly $35 million across four offices. It added the Squirt Company, maker of the Squirt soft drink, and several United States Tobacco Company brands; it even acquired another agency, Cohen, Dowd & Aleshire, which brought in Amstel beer, Grove's 4-Way Cold Tablets, the Lady Esther division of Chemway Corporation, Kiwi Shoe Polish, and the enduring home remedy, Lydia Pinkham's vegetable compound. Although it improved that volume slightly the next year, D&C lost Grove, Fitch dandruff shampoo, and Columbia Pictures.

D&C was hit hard by several account losses as well as the 1963 New York newspaper strike, which contributed to a reduction in volume of approximately $10 million from a 1962 high of $35 million. Following Churchill's retirement in 1962, West became chairman-chief executive officer (CEO). In 1963 Churchill sold his interest in the agency to a management group that included West; Weir; Bertram S. Nayfack, agency vice president; O.S. Kinsbury, administrative vice president and general manager; and A.B. Churchill, a vice president and Edward Churchill's brother.

Later that year the new management team merged the agency with Ellington & Company. Ellington had been founded in Philadelphia, Pennsylvania, in 1939 as Ivey & Ellington by Neil Ivey and Jesse Ellington. It became Ellington & Company in 1943, with Ellington remaining until 1954. In 1963 it was billing $18.3 million. In January 1964 the combined agency was officially renamed West, Weir & Bartel, Inc. (WW&B), with West as president and CEO and Walter Weir as chairman of the executive committee. William Bartel, who had been president of Ellington & Company, became chairman of the board. With approximately $40 million in billings, it was the 33rd-largest shop in U.S. advertising according to *Advertising Age*.

Donahue & Coe created this 1961 ad for the New York *Herald Tribune*.

But WW&B did not last long. In 1966 it lost the $3 million MGM account that had once been the financial backbone of its predecessor. Finally, in 1968 WW&B, by then billing about $20 million, disappeared in a merger with MacManus, John & Adams, taking with it the last remnants of Donahue & Coe.

JOHN MCDONOUGH

Further Reading

"Churchill Named Chairman of Donahue & Coe," *Advertising Age* (25 January 1960)

"D&C Merger with Ellington Just About Buttoned Up: Weir," *Advertising Age* (18 November 1963)

"E. Churchill Dies, Led Donahue & Coe," *Advertising Age* (1 April 1974)

"End of Agency Fee Revolt Is Seen as Cowan, Dengler Join D&C," *Advertising Age* (18 April 1955)

"Keyes, Madden & Jones, D&C Affiliate," *Advertising Age* (1 December 1958)

"Walter Weir Closing Shop," *Advertising Age* (1 October 1951)

Doner

(W.B. Doner & Company)

Opened in Detroit, Michigan, 1937; became the target of a Federal Trade Commission probe that resulted in the agency's reorganization, 1962; remains one of the few solid, independent, midsized U.S. agencies, 2001.

Major Clients

Atlantic Brewing Company (Tavern Pale Beer)
BP Oil International Ltd.
Chiquita Brands
Feigenson Bros. (Faygo soft drinks)
Hygrade Food Products Company
Iams Pet Food
La-Z-Boy Chair Company
National Brewing Company
Prudential Insurance Company of America
Speedway Petroleum Corporation
Timex Watches
Turtle Wax

Wilfred Broderick Doner was born in Detroit, Michigan, in 1914, the same year Henry Ford completed his first production line at the huge River Rouge Ford plant and Ted MacManus wrote his famous "Penalty of Leadership" ad for Cadillac (the ad would appear 2 January 1915). Doner graduated from the University of Wisconsin in 1936. After working briefly for a local Detroit area agency, only to get fired, he started his own company.

Doner went into business in March 1937 as Fink & Doner, a tiny "letter agency" that prepared handbills and radio announcements for Gross Pointe (Michigan) Quality Food Stores. Lionel Fink, the senior partner, took the titles of president and radio director, while Doner became secretary and treasurer. The client list remained small over the first three years. Only the La-Z-Boy Chair Company had come in by 1941 (and remained a client at the turn of the 21st century). In 1942 the company hired an art director, and its client roster grew to more than a dozen local merchants and manufacturers, including the Michigan Chandelier Company, which was owned by Doner's father.

That year also brought the first of the agency's growth clients: Speedway Petroleum and Speedway 79 gasoline. When Fink retired in 1943, Doner became president and began looking for new people who could bring their own business with them. Julian Grace had been working without pay for a small Detroit agency until 1935, when the Feigenson Brothers handed him a $2,000 budget to advertise their regional soft drink, Faygo. For the next five years, Grace worked as a one-man agency for Faygo. When he joined Doner in 1943, Faygo followed him. Three years later he became a partner.

Growth was slow and unspectacular during World War II. Automobile production stopped during the war as Detroit concentrated on Flying Fortresses and Liberators. Doner served in the army from 1944 to 1945 but never left the United States. While he was away, Grace and another new associate, Charles Rosen, kept the business going, despite a drop in billings.

"It's become a cliché that life begins at 40," Doner said on his 65th birthday in 1979. "Certainly this agency didn't really start to move until then. In fact, I wasn't sure it would make it." He "made it" by making his company less a traditional, "top-down" ad agency and more a federation of independent account executives sharing a common layout department but no creative department in the modern sense. After the war, it seemed like a convenient, if unusual, strategy for growth. Principals would come into the agency as "partners," each with their own accounts, and would contribute investment capital and receive a share in the agency. Each man was master of his own accounts, however, and under no corporate obligation to consult the other partners or even Doner himself. The early listings for the agency in the *Standard Directory of Advertising Agencies* (better known as the "Red Book") were unique: each account was listed with the name of its custodian.

It was a loose amalgamation that lent itself nicely to quick growth. After the war, the agency expanded into Chicago, Illinois, where Marvin Frank decided to leave his father's furniture business and open an office under the Doner name. In January 1947 he became a 50 percent partner, and Doner had its first branch office. A year later, Frank and Doner won the account for Tavern Pale, a local brewery that led the agency into television.

By the time Doner celebrated its tenth anniversary in 1947, Speedway 76 and Faygo were about to become the agency's springboard into the new medium of television in Detroit. In 1952 Doner won Hygrade Frankfurters, another account with a strong future in television. In Chicago, the agency landed the Plastone Company, which would soon launch an early and now legendary TV jingle composed by Frank: "Turtle Wax gives that hard shell finish—Turtle Wax."

Expansion remained on Doner's agenda, and by 1960 he had established his most dynamic office, in Baltimore, Maryland. There his strategy was a larger version of that followed in Detroit: entrepreneurship. Since Doner's clients were not national marketers, any Doner office in a distant city needed its own client base. Frank's Chicago operation would be the model. It was so independent it had a separate Red Book listing.

Doner's first probe into New York City in the late 1940s was short-lived. A brief association with Charles Higgins gave Doner 25 small clients and a Manhattan address, but it ended in 1951. In October 1958, with billings at $10.8 million, the agency returned to New York in a merger with Peck Advertising. The new agency, Doner & Peck, rounded off the numbers and claimed billings of $20 million.

Among the biggest clients it brought to Doner was the $3.5 million account of U.S. Time Corporation, maker of Timex watches and sponsor of many television network variety specials, including shows by Red Skelton, Steve Allen, and Frank Sinatra, NBC News' *White Papers,* and a famous series of Timex jazz shows. The live torture tests of Timex watches staged by John Cameron Swayze were often more entertaining than the programs they underwrote. When Swayze strapped a Timex to the propeller of an outboard motor and turned it on, it produced one of the most famous commercials in television history. When the motor was shut off a moment later, Swayze found the Timex had vanished. "But still ticking," he said, "wherever it is."

"One out of every three watches sold in the U.S. today is a Timex," Doner said later. "The advertising that propelled its revolution in the watch business consisted of only 109 network commercials on 46 shows over a period of six years." The Peck relationship fell apart when Timex moved to Warwick & Legler in February 1961, and a Peck executive left in May, taking five clients with him. In an attempt to stay in New York, Doner was absorbed by Lester Harrison Advertising, a retail and promotion agency, but the Doner-Harrison merger did not take root and was dissolved in January 1966. It was Doner's last attempt to breach New York.

The story of Baltimore would be different. It began in 1953, when the Detroit office won Altes Brewery, producer of a prominent but modestly budgeted regional beer. In 1955 National Brewing in Baltimore purchased Altes, and Doner prepared himself for the worst. To his surprise, National's chief, Jerry Hoffberger, not only liked Doner's work for Altes but invited him to handle the entire National account, which was many times the size of the Altes business. There was only one proviso: the agency had to have a Baltimore office. Frank recommended his nephew, Herbert Fried, who accepted with a promise of autonomy and a vice presidency.

Fried started with a handful of clients and within ten years built Baltimore into the agency's most aggressive office outside Detroit. In February 1968 Fried became an agency president and in 1973 succeeded Doner as chairman of the board.

The 1960s would see a shift away from the agency's early account structure that made each of its six senior account executives sovereign over his clients. On 21 June 1963 the Federal Trade Commission (FTC) charged that W.B. Doner & Company had created a phony research organization called the "Consumer Protective Institute" and put its seal on ads for its client Revco Discount Drug Centers. The Consumer Protective Institute was actually owned and run by Charles Rosen, who had been with Doner since 1944 and had brought in the Revco business in 1959. Doner claimed he knew nothing of Rosen's connection to the Consumer Protective Institute and severed his agency's relationship with Revco.

The Consumer Protective Institute was indeed a gimmick Rosen had invented in October 1961. Its only "employees" were his wife and brother-in-law. It claimed to test products but never

This Chiquita advertisement promoting bananas with the line, "Quite possibly, the world's perfect food," was created by the W. B. Doner agency in 1991.
© *Carol Kaplan Photography; Creative Director: Gary Wolfso, Art Director: Mike Ward, Copywriter: Lou Chiavone, Print Producer: Andrea Bates.*

did; moreover, its seal of approval was used only on Revco brands. By the time the case went to the FTC hearing board on 28 February 1964, Rosen had resigned from Doner. Still on the hook, though, was Doner himself, who argued that because of the "unique setup in which agency principals have complete and autonomous charge of their clients," he should not be liable for Rosen's mischief.

The FTC disagreed. "Doner cannot escape responsibility for its exec vp and half owner [Rosen actually owned 13 percent]," said Commissioner Maurice Bush on 10 July 1964, "in the performance of his function as account executive for Revco." An appeal in April 1965 was to no avail. No fines or penalties were assessed, but the decision sent both Doner and the industry a strong message about agencies' responsibility for their officers. The age of the all-powerful account potentate at Doner was over.

Other changes were also under way. The old copy-contact system had become a relic unsuited to the widely heralded "creative revolution" going on in advertising in the 1960s. So in 1963 Doner brought in Stanley Burkoff as creative director and told him to build a modern department of copywriter/art director teams. The results were soon apparent in the agency's work for STP motor oil, Vlasic pickles, I.J. Grass Soup, Dow Bathroom Cleaner ("Scrubbing bubbles"), and Tootsie Roll ("How many licks does it take?"). Among the people who would pass through Burkoff's department in the 1960s and 1970s were Lawrence Kasdan (who went on to write the scripts for the movies *The Empire Strikes Back* and *Raiders of the Lost Ark* and to direct such films as *The Big Chill*) and Cathy Guisewhite (who created the nationally syndicated cartoon strip *Cathy*).

In May 1964 the agency landed its first automobile account—the legendary Studebaker, which designer Raymond Lowey had made into a work of art in the 1930s but which was now too small to effectively compete with the power of the postwar "Big Three" automakers. Doner opened a five-person office in South Bend, Indiana, to service the business, but the billings were too small to sustain it for more than two years.

Back in Doner's "vest pocket" days, the partners had found it easy to accommodate client conflicts privately. Now growth and centralization brought new rules. When the Detroit office won the account of the Commercial Credit Corporation in 1966, it meant that Frank could no longer handle his biggest account, Commercial rival Dial Finance, in Chicago, so he left the fold to form his own shop.

W.B. Doner & Company now embarked on a race for growth between the Detroit and Baltimore offices; the latter had grown eightfold since 1955, largely on the strength of the Colt 45 Malt Liquor business. By 1972 they were in a dead heat, each billing $16.5 million. In 1976 the agency's appetite for international business was whetted as Max Fisher, chairman of United Brands and brother-in-law of Stanley Burkoff, now Doner president, moved Chiquita from Young & Rubicam to Doner. Within 20 years, the agency would be handling Chiquita's business in 58 countries and 48 languages.

The biggest leap into global marketing started in 1982, though, when Sohio gave Doner $168,000 to advertise the opening of five Procare auto service shops in Toledo, Ohio. The gasoline business followed, and soon after, the attentions of British Petroleum Oil International, Ltd. (BP), which had a majority interest in Sohio. Doner executives began flying regularly to London, England, and in 1987 they brought back the BP account itself, which, according to John Considine, a strategic planner at Doner, then covered Southeast Asia, Africa, Australia, Europe, and the United States. The agency did not disclose billings but claimed that BP was the biggest account on the Doner roster, which totaled $550 million.

Doner lived to see most of this growth and was still fully active in the agency as executive committee chairman. At the start of 1990 the company employed 550 people and had billings of approximately $350 million. On 4 January of that year Doner died of a cerebral hemorrhage at the age of 75. He had succeeded in institutionalizing his creation, then finding a generation of successors to run it.

During the 1990s the agency continued to seek healthy growth without yielding to the temptations of going public and being taken over by a major ad network. The agency's television work for the Iams Eukanuba premium dog food brand not only won wide praise but also a place in the Museum of Modern Art as an example of excellence in commercial filmmaking. Doner enhanced its position as a major beer agency when it won the Stroh Brewery account and took over work on such former G. Heileman brands as Colt 45, Old Style, and Special Export. It also continued its cautious international growth with the acquisition in 1995 of GKK in London.

Observers noted the continuing rivalry between the Detroit and Baltimore offices, based to some extent on Detroit's reputation as a retail shop and Baltimore's as a brand shop. In a 1997 interview in *Advertising Age* Herbert Fried, chairman of the agency, acknowledged that there had been a "competitive" relationship between the two offices in the 1980s but denied that it continued to exist in any sense of being a rivalry. His main concern was transition to a new generation of management headed by his hand-picked successor, Alan Kalter, who had joined Doner in 1967 and rose to the position of chief executive officer of the Detroit office in 1998 with Fried's retirement. *Adweek* magazine named Doner "Midwest Agency of the Year" in 1999. As of 2001 the agency continued as one of the largest and most successful independent shops in the United States and insisted it had no intention of selling or merging.

JOHN MCDONOUGH

Further Reading

"Agency Responsible for Execs' Activities, FTC Examiner Says," *Advertising Age* (3 May 1965)

"Frank Eschews Jingles; TV Ads Are Paris Goal," *Advertising Age* (14 September 1959)

"FTC Hit Doner, Revco on Use of 'Institute Seal,'" *Advertising Age* (19 July 1965)

McDonough, John, "W.B. Doner: 60th Anniversary," *Advertising Age* (3 March 1997)

"Rosen, Doner Hit in Examiner's Hearing," *Advertising Age* (13 July 1964)

Doremus & Company

Begun by Charles W. Barron in New York City, 1903; absorbed the Philadelphia and Boston News Bureau advertising agencies, 1920s; Philadelphia, Pennsylvania, branch of the company combined with the newly acquired Benjamin Eshleman Company of Philadelphia and operated as a wholly owned subsidiary, Doremus-Eshleman Company, 1952; Doremus & Company purchased by BBDO International, Inc., 1974, and placed within newly formed Omnicom Group, 1986.

Major Clients
Corning, Inc.
Credit Suisse First Boston
Dow Jones & Company
Goldman Sachs & Company
Hitachi
ITT Industries
Lehman Bros.
Morgan Stanley & Company
Salomon Smith Barney

Doremus & Company has been monitoring the pulse of America's financial transactions since the turn of the 20th century. From its inception, the company specialized in financial notice advertising, or "tombstones"—black-and-white newspaper advertisements of uniform design that announce business deals such as public stock offerings and mergers and acquisitions to the interested public. The company began as a part of Dow Jones & Company, supplying ad linage for Dow Jones publications such as the *Wall Street Journal* and, later, *Barron's*, as well as assisting other clients. The agency was in a unique position as the public's link to the nation's fast-paced financial dealings through advertising, and it was also instrumental in beginning the first business recruitment classifieds section after World War I. As the company approached its centennial, it underwent a restructuring. Moving away from its position as strictly a financial communications company to that of a more mainstream agency with corporate advertising accounts, Doremus remained firmly grounded in its finance-oriented heritage.

The company was started by Clarence W. Barron, a financial editor and publisher who had purchased Dow Jones & Company in 1902 along with the company's leading national financial publication, the *Wall Street Journal*. In the first few years he owned Dow Jones, Barron acknowledged a conflict of interest between the promotion of his advertisers and the integrity of the news. On 14 May 1903 he began a financial notice advertising agency in a corner of Dow Jones's office at 44 Broad Street in New York City with an assistant named Harry W. Doremus from the *Journal's* advertising department. For Barron, it appeared that "Doremus" was a name as good as any other, and Doremus & Company became the new name of the Dow Jones subsidiary—even though Harry Doremus had no equity in the company and left after barely more than two years after being blamed for authorizing editorial staff to sell advertising (most likely Barron's own decision).

Daily management of the *Wall Street Journal* was overseen by Barron's wife, Jessie, freeing Barron to manage Doremus, as well as other editorial ventures. At its inception, Doremus & Company placed primarily classifieds and tombstones as financial notices of business deals for just nine accounts that grew to be quite profitable under the part-time management of Barron, who was an excellent salesman. In 1914, at the beginning of World War I in Europe, Barron took official control of Doremus, assuming the title of president, and aided the company in taking on its first major campaign, the U.S. government's massive advertising effort to sell Liberty Bonds to raise money for the war effort. Shortly after the war, Doremus & Company assisted in beginning a special classifieds section of display advertisements in the *Wall Street Journal* that recruited personnel for executive and highly skilled positions; the purpose of this venture was to help returning soldiers find work. The innovation proved to be a top revenue-earner for the paper, and the practice was adopted by other major national newspapers.

Doremus expanded greatly in the 1920s and began to offer broader advertising services, such as stockholder and public relations, to a wider group of clients. New offices were established in Chicago, Illinois, and San Francisco, California; in Boston, Massachusetts, Doremus & Company absorbed the advertising agency business of the Boston News Bureau, which Barron had started before he bought Dow Jones. The company also took over the business of another Barron news service, the Philadelphia News Bureau Advertising Agency, in 1929.

Barron died in 1928, yielding the presidency and a final transformation of leadership to a younger team that included William H. Long, a vice president who had joined the company in 1919 as an account executive and would become chairman of the board in 1933. Long's Princeton University ties (he was an alumnus) proved beneficial in winning the company such major accounts as Dillon, Read & Company in 1919 and Morgan Stanley in 1935; Long earned a reputation as the company's best salesman.

In the early part of the 20th century, Wall Street banks and brokerage firms had been publishing entire prospectuses in national newspapers, making for grueling typesetting and proofreading tasks. However, in the 1930s the U.S. Securities & Exchange Commission (SEC) enacted restrictions on tombstones to prevent companies from making unfounded claims. The SEC allowed only the salient points of the cover prospectus and limited necessary information to be published, along with a notation to the effect that the placement was not a solicitation for business. This financial notice advertising, still Doremus's primary specialty, required a great deal of knowledge of the SEC, the stock exchange, and brokerage laws. Doremus was dominant in this particular advertising niche, handling the needs of the majority of the leading U.S. investment banking companies. Only one other

New York shop, Albert Frank-Guenther Law, Inc., was a direct competitor.

Doremus & Company underwent many changes in the mid-1930s. Under the direction of Long, the company had become independent of Dow Jones in the early 1930s and moved its headquarters to 120 Broadway. Long continued to oversee the company through the next three decades. In 1968 Doremus & Company announced its own initial public offering, having grown to 236 employees, with billings of $28 million and a roster of more than 500 clients in six offices. Long stepped down from his position as honorary chairman in 1968 to cede direction of the company to George Erickson as chairman and, nearly a decade later, Frank Schafer, both of whom served as chief executive officer (CEO). In 1974 BBDO International, of New York City, bought Doremus & Company, and in 1986 combined it with agency networks Doyle Dane Bernbach and Needham, Harper & Steers to form the Omnicom Group, an advertising agency holding company. At Omnicom, Doremus & Company is the financial services specialist of the diversified agency services arm.

Although Doremus & Company was long considered the premier business and financial advertising agency in the United States, its niche specialty of financial communications did not allow it to compete with the large agencies on Madison Avenue, nor did it beg the attention of a wider audience. In the churning economy of the 1980s and early 1990s, companies were not advertising their every financial move. Corporate and municipal bond advertising had dropped dramatically, and Doremus saw a corresponding drop in the use of tombstones. It also saw its long client list shrink dramatically as banks and investment houses began to consolidate. Doremus needed to alter its focus to match a changing economy and the changing needs of its clients, but its reputation for staid black-and-white notice advertising required a creative transformation.

That transformation came in the person of BBDO International executive Carl Anderson. Anderson joined Doremus in 1986 and was promoted to president by 1992; he was eventually elevated to the position of CEO in 2000. Anderson is credited with recognizing the opportunity to capitalize on Doremus's reputation for expertise in the financial world. Anderson expanded Doremus's work to begin corporate and consumer advertising, as well as launching corporate advertising campaigns for its existing clients. Since then Doremus has executed bold corporate branding strategies for ITT Industries; Corning, Inc.; and long-time client Morgan Stanley Dean Witter & Company (formed by the 1997 merger of Morgan Stanley Group and Dean Witter Discover Company) to communicate to potential business partners and consumers what these companies can do. Anderson hired new talent, recruiting top creative executives straight from large New York City shops to bolster new creativity.

One example of this new style of campaign was for Corning. Using its skills in corporate branding strategy, Doremus helped Corning explain that it was no longer a designer of cookware, having divested its cooking container business in 1998. In its first advertising campaign in more than 30 years, Corning highlighted its role as an innovator in the use of the thin glass strands that connect the world's telecommunications networks. The $22 million television and print campaign sought to illustrate the power of light through imagery and included copy that read, "The super-fast, super-broad boulevard called the global optical network. And there at the heart of it, you'll find Corning."

Edgier campaigns portrayed Doremus's use of humor to gain attention, such as a print campaign for Bloomberg, a financial publishing company. One ad showed a subway rider in New York City holding a copy of *Playboy* wrapped around a Bloomberg magazine. The copy read, "Satisfy your second most basic instinct."

Doremus also invested in newly available technologies. This investment, coupled with many client headquarters shifts to New York through consolidation, allowed for the streamlining of the agency. A single New York City office, located on Varick Street, handles much of the business; a San Francisco, California, office was opened in mid-1999. Anderson also drove an overseas expansion, aided by Omnicom resources, and established Doremus offices in Italy, Germany, Japan, Hong Kong, and Brazil; these joined a London, England, office that opened in 1981.

Although tombstone advertising still accounted for 40 percent of business as of January 2000, Doremus's specialty, according to its Web site, has become "what makes major corporate honchos and investors tick"—namely, e-commerce and technology-oriented business-to-business campaigns that target executive decision-makers. But despite moving away from the services that first established its success, Doremus reached $360 million in billings in 2000.

MEGAN CASSADA

Further Reading

Doremus <www.doremus.com>

Dumiak, Michael, "Bring On the Top 10 Agencies," *Financial Services Marketing* (September/October 2000)

McMains, Andrew, "Anderson Adds CEO Title at Doremus," *Adweek* (17 March 2000)

Norton, Justin M., "Doremus Finds Fast Track in San Francisco," *Adweek* (17 April 2000)

Norton, Justin M., "Hear Me Speaks Out via Doremus," *Adweek* (1 May 2000)

Rygor, Stanley, "Recollections of Doremus and the Street: An Overview," *Hotwire: A Doremus Newsletter* (2 February 1999)

Vranica, Suzanne, "Doremus Expands Its Client Base and Transforms Itself," *Wall Street Journal* (20 January 2000)

Wendt, Lloyd, *The Wall Street Journal: The Story of Dow Jones and the Nation's Business Newspaper,* Chicago: Rand McNally, 1982

Young, Shawn, "Corning's New Campaign Touts Shift to Glass Fiber," *Wall Street Journal* (5 December 2000)

Dorfsman, Louis 1918–

U.S. Graphic Designer

Beyond the presence of a logo, a marketer's design graphics and its advertising rarely coincide. A singular exception involved the work of Louis Dorfsman for CBS, which in the 1960s achieved a unity of design that embraced everything from cardboard coffee cups to architecture to advertising. Dorfsman's work for CBS made a vital contribution to the advertising movement of the 1960s known as the "creative revolution." As the man principally responsible for the design, comprehensiveness, and impact of CBS graphics, Dorfsman brought an imaginative use of typography and illustration to the business. His approach significantly influenced the work of Doyle Dane Bernbach, Ogilvy & Mather, Carl Ally, Inc., and other leading ad agencies that developed strong reputations in print and design layout.

Dorfsman, whose father was a sign painter, was born in New York City on 24 April 1918; he graduated from Roosevelt High School in 1935. His plans to attend New York University were derailed by the $300 annual tuition, which, during the Depression years, was a considerable sum. Dorfsman turned instead to the Cooper Union for the Advancement of Science and Art, whose degree program was both respected and free to those selected for admission. There he studied design, typography, and architecture and took his first courses in advertising. He graduated in 1939 with a Bachelor of Fine Arts degree. While at Cooper Union he held part-time jobs designing posters for the Trans-Lux movie theater and working on exhibits for the New York World's Fair of 1939.

Dorfsman served in the U.S. Army from 1943 to 1945. Medically exempt from combat because of a punctured eardrum, he was sent to the army design center in Dallas, Texas, where he worked on posters and public-relations exhibits. Two of his posters won first and second prizes in the national army arts contest in 1944. After the war he worked briefly as an art director at Reiss Advertising in New York City before joining the art department of CBS as assistant to William Golden, head of advertising and design, who had run the network's design department since 1937. In 1951 Golden created the famous CBS eye for a one-time television promotion, but CBS President Frank Stanton soon made it into the icon for the company.

In 1951 Stanton separated the television and radio divisions, and Dorfsman became art director for CBS Radio, where he created a series of provocative ads intended to remind the industry that CBS was still active in radio. Though NBC had largely abandoned radio except for news, CBS continued into the 1960s with *Art Linkletter's Houseparty, Suspense, Gunsmoke, Johnny Dollar,* and *Have Gun, Will Travel.* Arthur Godfrey remained on the network into the 1970s. The elegant balance and clean black-and-white graphics of Dorfsman's ads attracted industry attention, especially at cutting-edge shops such as Doyle Dane Bernbach and Jack Tinker & Associates. In 1959 Golden died at the age of 48, and Dorfsman took his place as the company's reigning design

guru, becoming creative director of the CBS Television Network the following year. In 1969 he was promoted to vice president–creative director of CBS Broadcast Group.

But it was the construction of the new CBS headquarters building at 51 West 52nd Street, in New York City, in the early and mid-1960s that provided Dorfsman with the occasion to focus and unify company graphics. The building, designed by the architect Eero Saarinen, was a matter of great pride to Stanton, who believed that a uniform physical sense of CBS should pervade every aspect of its space, uncorrupted by the tastes of the individuals who occupied it. Dorfsman began by taking the CBS initials, which had appeared for years in any number of typefaces, and fashioning them in Didot, a classic 17th-century face whose lines flowed gracefully from thick to thin with prominent serif trim. Dorfsman also designed a secondary sans serif face that later became known as CBS Sans. Every aspect of the building's lettering and signage conformed to Dorfsman's specifications. He even fought off the demands of New York City fire department inspectors, whose regulations for "exit" signs demanded letters of uniform thickness and no serifs.

Dorfsman's design edicts were all encompassing and covered all printed materials, from advertising to memo pads to stationery, all dominated by the Didot typeface. Even letters typed by CBS secretaries conformed to Dorfsman's design specifications. Every box of stationery contained a sample letter specifying format, line length, and content depth, as well as a tiny dot indicating precisely where the salutation should begin.

By the early 1960s the promotion of the fall television season had advanced to the point where the networks were buying heavy print schedules in local newspapers. In 1962 Dorfsman went a step further. He produced a magazine supplement with a spread that displayed the programming schedule for each day of the week and distributed the publication via Sunday papers in major markets. In 1963 he produced another supplement, this time replacing black-and-white photography with specially commissioned illustrations by cartoonist Al Hirschfeld, who depicted such celebrities as Judy Garland, Jackie Gleason, Jack Benny, Red Skelton, and Walter Cronkite. As the economic stakes mounted, networks began to pour increased budgets into promoting their fall lineups. By the mid-1960s Dorfsman was overseeing the first major fall television ad campaign to run on television itself.

As the pressure increased for profit growth each year, the amount of network prime time devoted to news and documentaries began to shrink, provoking criticism from Newton Minow, then chairman of the Federal Communications Commission, as well as from TV critics. CBS's advertising had to sell the network's entertainment schedule while at the same time maintaining its image as a provider of high-quality public service and news programming.

Although CBS used McCann-Erickson as its principal advertising agency in the 1950s and Sudler & Hennessey in the 1960s and 1970s, much of the day-to-day creative work in the early 1950s was done in-house under Golden's direction; by the time Dorfsman took over, virtually all of it was being done in-house, with the assistance of the art department at Sudler & Hennessey. The role created by Dorfsman for Sudler & Hennessey (primarily a medical ad agency acquired by Young & Rubicam in 1973) was an outgrowth of his lifelong friendship with Herbert F. Lubalin, a fellow member of the Cooper Union class of 1939 and head of Sudler & Hennessey Design. "In the CBS Broadcast Group," Dorfsman was quoted as saying in the 1987 book *Dorfsman and CBS*, "we operated our own self-contained advertising agency and design studio. Measured by our billings, in 1977 for instance, the Broadcast Group's Advertising and Design Department would have ranked as the 11th-largest agency in the United States."

Although the Didot typeface was the unchanging basis of the company's corporate graphics, Dorfsman varied its use in advertising, often using startling typographic devices as the central visual motif. But his bold black-and-white signature remained at the core of his print work, as did its clarity and legibility. When he resorted to color, he used it in fresh ways. A 1961 trade ad blanketed two pages of *Variety* with dense columns of real estate classifieds that framed a single one-third column classified ad in red type boasting of the number of homes reached by the CBS network. On television Dorfsman used color to create many lively variations on the CBS eye, rendering such effects as neon, fireworks, and marquee light patterns. His impact on advertising writing was equally direct and pervasive, resulting in clever headlines and sophisticated copy, according to those who worked with him.

Dorfsman officially retired from CBS in 1987 but continued to be active with the company and other clients through his own company, Lou Dorfsman Design, which he had begun operating out of his Great Neck, New York, home in the 1970s as a way of taking on freelance assignments that interested him. Among his most famous work was that done for Dansk International Designs, the European tableware designer that he took on as a client while still at CBS. The catalog Dorfsman created for the company became such an object of art in itself that orders became too overwhelming to fulfill. He subsequently designed a scaled-down version that the company could more easily supply.

Both during Dorfsman's CBS days and after his retirement, CBS Chairman William Paley often called upon him to take on special projects such as design work for the Museum of Modern Art in New York City, for which Paley was a trustee and board member. But few projects were closer to both Paley and Dorfsman than the Museum of Broadcasting, which to a large extent was a repository of CBS history. In exchange for his ongoing consultancy work for the Museum of Broadcasting, Dorfsman received the permanent use of office space in the museum building at 25 East 52nd Street.

Dorfsman also served as board member and chairman of the International Design Conference, Aspen, Colorado, and was trustee of the New York Institute of Technology and the Cooper Union. Over the course of his career he received 13 Gold Medals from the New York Art Directors Club, 50 Ad-of-the-Year Awards from various groups, and numerous Clio and Emmy awards; in 1978 he was inducted into the Art Directors Hall of Fame.

JOHN MCDONOUGH

Biography

Born in New York City, 24 April 1918; graduated from Cooper Union for the Advancement of Science and Art, 1939; named art director, CBS Radio, 1951; promoted to creative director, CBS Television Network, 1960; promoted to vice president–creative director of CBS Broadcast Group, 1969; retired from CBS, 1987, but remained active through his own company, Lou Dorfsman Design.

Further Reading

Hess, Dick, and Marion Muller, *Dorfsman and CBS*, New York: American Showcase, 1987

Doyle Dane Bernbach, Inc. *See* DDB Worldwide, Inc.

DPZ

Established in São Paulo, Brazil, by Roberto Duailibi, Francesc Petit, Jose Zaragoza, and Ronald Persichetti, 1968; won numerous awards for innovative creative work.

Major Clients
Ajinomoto of Brazil
Avon Products
Banco Itaú
B.A.T (British American Tobacco; for Souza Cruz)
Champion of Brazil
Citroën (retail sales)
Coca-Cola Company
Johnson & Johnson
Petrobras Distribuidora
Philco of Brazil
Sadia Food

DPZ is, by many standards, the largest and most important Brazilian advertising agency. It was founded 1 July 1968 by four advertising professionals: Roberto Duailibi, then manager of the São Paulo office of Standard Propaganda, Brazil's oldest agency, which later became the local branch of Ogilvy & Mather; Francesc Petit and Jose Zaragoza, two art directors from Catalonia, Spain, who ran a successful art studio called Metro 3; and Ronald Persichetti, a graphic producer.

DPZ is generally considered the first Brazilian agency established by a group of individuals from the creative side of advertising. It was a successful formula at the time, and the new agency soon became known for its daring copy approaches and stylish and colorful layouts. One year after its inception, it won São Paulo's ad of the year award for a print ad for Fotoptica, a retail optical store. The agency's approach translated well to color television, which was introduced in Brazil two years after the founding of DPZ.

The following decade was one of growth for DPZ, which added such clients as Rhodia (Rhone-Poulenc), Souza Cruz (cigarettes), Banco Itaú (Brazil's third-largest private bank), and Johnson & Johnson. In 1971 DPZ created a campaign for Sadia, a meat-processing company from southern Brazil; the effort was designed around a cartoon character, the fastest chicken in the world. The campaign helped Sadia take over the number-one spot in its market.

In 1972 DPZ received its first international awards, two bronze awards in the Venice Screen Advertising World Association festival. In 1975 the agency won its first gold Lion at the Cannes (France) International Advertising Festival for a film opposing workplace discrimination against people over 40.

In 1978 the agency introduced a media innovation, a four-and-a-half-minute commercial (for Louis XV cigarettes). Also in the 1970s the agency created the Bombril Boy character for BomBril

scouring pads (marketed by BomBril S/A), launching a campaign still running at the beginning of the 21st century.

In 1979 DPZ ranked number seven among Brazilian agencies and was described in *Advertising Age* as "one of the most creative agencies in the world." The following year, in an election by advertising columnists, DPZ was voted the "Agency of the Decade." In the early 1980s the agency began branching out to other areas of Brazil, opening offices in Brasilia (1980) and Rio de Janeiro (1981).

By creating a persona for the Brazilian Internal Revenue Service—a not-so-tame lion—DPZ contributed to a change in the public's image of the federal government and influenced government officials to make extensive use of modern communication techniques. Later, the Brazilian government—federal, state, and city—became the country's largest advertiser.

For Nestlé's Chambourcy line of yogurt and dairy products, DPZ created another first: a billboard that went beyond the standard size to accommodate the twice-life-size silhouette of a child. An ad for Artex towels showed, albeit discreetly, the first male nude in Brazilian advertising. In 1986 the agency's creative director, Washington Olivetto, who some considered responsible for the bulk of DPZ's large collection of awards, left to set up his own shop, with Swiss company GGK, now W/Brasil. DPZ's success continued, however, and by the end of the decade the agency ranked third in Brazil and had added the McDonald's Brazil account, the hamburger chain's fastest-growing national operation, to its list of clients.

During its more than 30 years in business, DPZ has been among the country's biggest and best agencies. It has appeared in *Advertising Age*'s ranking of the 50 largest agencies in the world more years than any other Brazilian agency. Its owners (now without Persichetti, who retired) estimate that the agency has helped some 1,540 clients sell $30 billion worth of goods and services. In 2001 DPZ had 40 clients and 270 employees in three offices: São Paulo and Rio de Janeiro and a branch in Buenos Aires, Argentina.

In the 1990s the agency was often the subject of reports that it was either about to merge with or was selling a controlling interest to one of several large multinational groups (DDB almost closed such a deal in 2000), but no such deal materialized. DPZ also functioned as a sort of school and "business multiplier"; many of the newer, mainly creative shops in Brazil were run by professionals who once worked there.

The agency planned to continue expanding in Latin America, following its successful experience in Buenos Aires. It formed a partnership with Mexico's Zeta Publicidad and was developing operations in Venezuela, Colombia, Peru, and Chile. In the area of direct marketing, DPZ was associated with Rapp Collins Worldwide in the United States.

J. ROBERTO WHITAKER-PENTEADO

Throughout the 1990s, DPZ produced a series of humorous, award-winning advertisements for Banco Itaú. The headline of this ad reads, "Driven by me. Protected by Itaucar."

Further Reading
Penteado, Claudia, and Laurel Wentz, "DDB on Verge of Long-

Sought Acquisition of Brazil's DPZ," *Advertising Age International* (June 2000)

Draft Worldwide

Kobs & Brady (K&B), direct predecessor of Draft Worldwide, founded in Chicago, Illinois, in 1978 by James F. Kobs and Thomas B. Brady; acquired by Ted Bates in 1986 but shortly thereafter became part of Saatchi & Saatchi Company; under leadership of Howard Draft, name changed to Kobs & Draft Advertising in 1988; repurchased from Saatchi & Saatchi parent Cordiant, 1995, and renamed DraftDirect Worldwide; sold to the Interpublic Group of Companies in 1996; became Draft Worldwide, 1997.

Major Clients
American Express Company
Bankers Life & Casualty Company
Bell Atlantic Corporation
British Airways
Home Box Office
Philip Morris Companies, Inc.
Sprint Corporation

Draft Worldwide is the most recent banner of an agency whose history goes back through five names. It began in May 1963 with Bankers Life & Casualty Company and its owner, John T. MacArthur, whose name is now attached to a foundation known for its so-called genius grants. The insurance company's agency, Phillips & Cherbo, had been one of the largest among a small niche of Chicago, Illinois, agencies specializing in direct mail work. When the agency fell on hard times, Bankers Life & Casualty invited its staff to form an in-house ad department and to take on any outside clients it could land. Marshall Edinger and John Egan became chairman and president, respectively, and, in an unusual gesture, they put their first names on the agency's nameplate—Marshall John & Associates. Also unusual was the agency's location, a Chicago neighborhood of working-class apartments and small businesses. According to Tom Brady, who had been among the Phillips & Cherbo employees absorbed by Bankers Life & Casualty and who would become a partner in the future agency, it was a part of the MacArthur empire. Things changed in February 1969 when MacArthur moved the agency to the Chicago suburb of Northbrook, where he put together a vertically integrated direct mail operation with a printing company, letter shop, list company, and agency under one roof. It achieved success, billing $12 million–$15 million at its height in the early 1970s. But Marshall John remained captive to the internecine squabbles of the MacArthurs.

By the late 1970s Edinger, who had taken time off to help launch the Capitol Record Club, and Egan were looking toward retirement. Tom Corcoran, who headed MacArthur Enterprises, began looking for a successor. The search led to Jim Kobs, an executive vice president of Stone & Adler, then Chicago's leading direct mail house. Kobs said that he was willing to take over Marshall John, but only if it could function as an outside business under a new name and have the appearance of a new agency.

Corcoran agreed, although MacArthur Enterprises would continue to control the agency, with minority shares going to Kobs, his partner Brady, and other senior management. But before the negotiations were completed, MacArthur died, making his assets, including stock in the agency, hostage to his estate. Corcoran asked Kobs if he would agree to a deal with the understanding that at some point he could acquire the whole agency. On 1 April 1978, Kobs & Brady (K&B) Advertising opened its offices on Michigan Avenue in Chicago. About two years later, a formal agreement was made for Kobs to buy the agency back on an earnout basis within three years. The real management authority belonged to Kobs, who took the title of president.

Kobs & Brady began with about a dozen people, mostly holdovers from Marshall John. Sandy Moltz, who has remained with Draft Worldwide as creative director, was hired from the Maxwell Scroge Agency, and Kobs took three people with him from Stone & Adler, one of whom was Howard Draft. "Howard was one of the best and brightest persons I ever worked with," Kobs told *Advertising Age* in 1998. "He understood the direct marketing business and was a quick learner. He also had good client skills and understood the numbers end of the business, how to control costs and how to make money."

Draft would become Kobs's protégé and receive a basic education in traditional direct marketing as it stood in the late 1970s. The agency grew swiftly. By 1982 Kobs, who had written *Profitable Direct Marketing,* one of the basic textbooks on the subject, had doubled K&B's revenue to nearly $26 million.

Major general agencies were eagerly buying direct shops. By 1984 Kobs & Brady was the only one of the top ten direct agencies still resisting acquisition. It was not for lack of suitors. According to Kobs, during the time the agency was moving through its earn-out with MacArthur, it was approached by each of the 15 top general agencies. But Kobs said that he did not want to sell something he did not yet own. While this was technically correct, the relationship to MacArthur seemed to serve more as a convenient cover for stalling potential buyers than as a real obstacle. The fact was that the earn-out was complete by the fall of 1982, K&B was private, and Kobs was the majority stockholder with the freedom to do anything he wished. He liked being his own boss and was in no rush to give up the privilege.

But Kobs also recognized that, as big agencies bought up direct shops, the playing field was no longer level for those who stayed independent. This became clear in the spring of 1982 when K&B lost a piece of potential business to a general agency with a strong direct mail division because the client expected to shift its spending between direct work and media advertising as needed. Kobs wanted the resources of a big agency without having to submit to its control.

The answer seemed to come in the person of Don Zuckert, who was heading the acquisitions committee at Ted Bates Worldwide in New York City. Bates had tried to set up its own direct division, had watched it sputter, and was now eager to buy a direct shop that could do the job right. With Bates clients such as the U.S. Navy and Prudential clamoring for direct services, the need was urgent, and Bates was in a hurry. But Zuckert was up against a man who was not.

Though Kobs was in no hurry for a merger, he would agree to a trial relationship. After four months of planning, K&B New York City opened its doors 4 October 1982 in a section of Bates office space at 1515 Broadway. It was the day after the earn-out with MacArthur was complete. To run the New York office, Kobs turned to Draft.

The move changed the history of K&B in ways Kobs could not have anticipated. Draft emerged as an aggressive force in building the agency. The Bates agency environment and Zuckert, who became Draft's new mentor, fundamentally changed the perspective on direct marketing Draft brought with him from Chicago. Within a year the New York office was bigger than the office in Chicago. Much of the volume was spillover from the Bates roster (Home Box Office, Chesebrough-Ponds), but Draft won Avis on his own, and when HBO moved to Batten, Barton, Durstine & Osborn (BBD&O), it kept its direct business at K&B.

Bates gave Draft a feel for general advertising. "It opened my eyes to what advertising was really all about," he told *Advertising Age.* What advertising was about was growth. And under its young manager, K&B New York became an engine of growth. When Draft returned to Chicago in February 1985, it was as president and chief operating officer. It was much the same K&B he had left two and a half years earlier, but it was not the same Howard Draft. He was no longer interested in small clients. He was ready to tell Kobs that times were changing, that Fortune 500 companies were recognizing the value of direct marketing, and that the agency must more closely align its work with the culture of general advertising. According to Zuckert, Kobs, who saw direct marketing as a distinct specialty, did not share Draft's view that the agency could no longer operate on a project basis but needed to move to contractual relationships along the lines he had seen at Bates.

"We all understood we could not continue independently forever," Kobs told *Advertising Age*. "We had always had a strategic plan that in order to compete we would have to sell to a general agency. . . . But we wanted to build ourselves up first to command respect." Respect meant money, and it came fast. The partners' differences were temporarily outweighed by a 35 percent growth spurt in 1985 that made K&B the envy of the big general agencies. Even during the relationship with Bates, other agencies came calling, including the Leo Burnett Company, McCann-Erickson, and the J. Walter Thompson Company. But negotiations with Bates were too far along. Although Kobs told the media not to expect a sale before June 1986, on March 6 he, Zuckert, and Bates chairman Bob Jacoby worked out a sale for a price said to be more than $10 million.

Six weeks later, however, Bates, to finance the retirement of a generation of senior management, sold itself to Saatchi & Saatchi. Kobs was faced with a new parent company and new people he had not chosen to work with. For the next year the fortunes of K&B appeared to be stable. In the emerging Saatchi hierarchy the agency continued to report to Zuckert, who saw a key role for Draft. Meanwhile, Saatchi sorted through its acquisitions, merging Bates with Backer & Spielvogel in July 1987 to form Backer Spielvogel Bates Worldwide, Inc. (BSB). In Chicago K&B moved its 140 employees to new quarters and on 1 April 1988 marked its 10th anniversary by changing its name to Kobs & Draft (K&D).

Meanwhile, the parent company wanted to move Kobs to Europe to help build an international network of Kobs & Draft direct marketing agencies. But Kobs was wealthy and without an appetite for further empire building. He suggested a number of alternatives, even proposing to buy back the Chicago office himself and letting Saatchi & Saatchi have the New York and international operations. According to Kobs, the proposal seemed to make sense and was approved by everyone at BSB.

Saatchi & Saatchi, however, was selling nothing. Negotiations went on for months, and in April 1988 Kobs took a six-month leave of absence. He never returned. For a short time he set up I.B.J. Consulting, which, if anyone had asked him, he would have explained stood for "In Between Jobs." The following March he established Kobs Gregory Passavant as a unit of Bayer Bess Vanderwarker and for the next six years enjoyed the singular distinction of seeing his name on two agency letterheads in the same city.

To be free of Saatchi & Saatchi, Draft would have to do what Kobs had tried and failed to do—buy back the agency. By 1994,

however, Cordiant, the Saatchi holding company, was out of cash. When Maurice Saatchi was fired by the board in December, Draft took advantage of the panic and offered $22 million in a buyback offer. The board rejected the deal, unwilling to concede yet that it needed to sell anything. Eight months of negotiations followed, during which Saatchi lost 6 percent of its business and fired 470 employees. Finally brought to heel, Cordiant agreed, and on 1 August 1995 Draft announced a deal valued at $27.2 million. Once again DraftDirect (DD), as it was renamed six weeks later, was its own boss, and Yvonne Furth, who had joined K&B out of college in 1981 became president of DraftDirect U.S.

Although Draft insisted that he would never again sell, within five months, in February 1996, he and Dan Ginsburg, president of DraftDirect, were in New York City talking to Philip Geier and Gene Beard, chairman and chief financial officer of the Interpublic Group of Companies. Each company had a weakness the other could fix. DD had a big debt, while Interpublic had a significant hole in its international direct services. Within about four weeks DD had agreed to become part of Interpublic. After buying itself back from Cordiant for $27.2 million, it now sold itself again, this time for a sum said to exceed $100 million, a 300 percent profit in six months.

It was a good deal for Interpublic, which saw its purchase double to revenues of $1.3 billion in 18 months while building specialties in the medical field, minority marketing, business-to-business selling, and other segments. Draft called Interpublic "a real savior" that permitted DraftWorldwide, as it was soon renamed, to resume its growth and acquisitions. In 1997 Draft Worldwide (as the company was renamed yet again that fall) bought D.L. Blair, MCA Marketing, Adler Boschetto Peebles & Partners, and Lee Hill, Inc. Draft acquired AG Worldwide, New York, in March 2000. Howard Draft remained chairman and chief executive officer. Worldwide gross income in 2000 was $430.9 million, up 26.6 percent over 1999, on billings of $3.6 billion, up 25.3 percent over 1999. Draft had U.S. gross income of $258.1 million, up 27.6 percent over 1999, on billings of $2.2 billion, up 32.5 percent over 1999.

JOHN MCDONOUGH

Further Reading

Draft, Howard, "TV: The Dominant Force in Direct Marketing," *DM News* (19 August 1991)

Goldman, Kevin, *Conflicting Accounts: The Creation and Crash of the Saatchi and Saatchi Advertising Empire,* New York: Simon and Schuster, 1997

Kobs, Jim, "Stop the Plane, I Want to Get Off!" *Advertising Age* (5 April 1982)

Kobs, Jim, "A Frog Becomes a Prince," *Advertising Age* (16 April 1984)

Levin, Gary, "The Infomercial as Steppingstone: Prepping for the Interactive Age . . . ," *Advertising Age* (12 July 1993)

Norris, Eileen, "An Insider's Look at the Battle for Independence," *Advertising Age* (11 October 1984)

Teinowitz, Ira, "Draft Maps Out Global Ambition," *Advertising Age* (18 April 1988)

Dr Pepper/Seven Up, Inc. *See* Seven Up

Drugs. *See* Pharmaceuticals

Duane Jones Company, Inc. *See under* Jones

E.I. Du Pont de Nemours & Company

Principal Agencies
Batten Barton Durstine & Osborn
McCann-Erickson Worldwide

Since its founding near Wilmington, Delaware, in the early 19th century, E.I. Du Pont de Nemours & Company (DuPont) has survived and prospered through three major corporate transformations, largely through the aid of advertising and public relations. Beginning as a gunpowder producer, DuPont evolved into a diversified chemical manufacturer in the 20th century and a life sciences company at the start of the 21st century. At every turn, advertising—whether by word of mouth, primitive signs, "educational" books and movies, or sophisticated campaigns—helped the company to remain a significant influence in the marketplace. Over time, DuPont orchestrated one of the most successful product introductions in advertising history, nylon, and one of the worst, Corfam.

Explosive Success

For the first 100 years of DuPont's existence, the company depended on "word of mouth" and primitive forms of advertising to sell its product, black blasting powder. The founder of the company was Eleuthère Irénée du Pont de Nemours, a French chemist who had emigrated to the United States. He began building a powder plant on the Brandywine River near Wilmington on 19 July 1802 and on 1 May 1804 began manufacturing and selling gunpowder. DuPont's black powder worked reliably, and that fact made the product popular with Americans who were dependent on guns for sustenance and defense and on blasting powder to clear agricultural land of stumps and rocks. Du Pont found his first "spokesman" when former President Thomas Jefferson sent

him a letter in 1811 praising the DuPont powder, which Jefferson had used on his estate, Monticello, and du Pont made ample use of the unsolicited endorsement.

Du Pont died in 1834, but his descendants carried on the family business through the 19th century. Powder flasks and broadsides were used not just to advertise the DuPont company but also to indicate the importance of gunpowder to the nation. DuPont's Eagle brand powder used the slogan, "Matchless for its power. Strong, swift and fatal, as the bird it bore." The company entered the smokeless powder and dynamite markets after the Civil War, but the railroads, quarries, mining companies, and other major consumers of high explosives controlled prices to such an extent that DuPont found itself limited to just 36 percent of the U.S. powder market at the turn of the 20th century. Upon the death of a senior partner, Eugene du Pont, in 1902, DuPont was in such poor financial condition that it was sold to Alfred I. du Pont, a great-grandson of the founder, and two of Alfred's cousins in a leveraged buyout that required only $8,500 cash. The new DuPont used sound management, luck, and hidden wealth to diversify, acquiring 54 companies within three years and increasing its market share to 75 percent. It quickly became one of the largest corporations in the United States, manufacturing 56 percent of the national output of explosives, with $60 million in estimated assets. The cousins also used a new organizational system based on family tree charts composed of levels of managers to run their rapidly growing company. The new structure revolutionized American business and worked so well that one of the partners applied it to the then-struggling General Motors Corporation. DuPont further diversified when the federal government used an antitrust suit to force the company to sell some of its black powder and dynamite holdings in 1913, on the eve of World War I.

As it sought to acquire and overcome rivals, DuPont turned to more sophisticated forms of advertising. Farmers needing to clear land were targeted as potential new consumers of dynamite. In addition to removing stumps and rocks, farmers used explosives to drain flooded fields, plow, dig ditches, plant trees, and even exterminate rodents and other animal pests. The company claimed in a 1916 sales report that "in almost every section of the country there is use for explosives on the farm as well as farmers who are in a position to pay for what they buy." Salesmen distributed free cloth hanger signs along with broadsides, felt counter mats, blotters, and calendars. The latter, which first featured the red DuPont oval insignia in 1907, were hugely popular items in farm households.

Salesmen were instructed to find the most effective locations for DuPont advertising and promotional literature. Signs lauding the uses of agricultural dynamite were placed in stores, hotels, railroad stations, and other public places. The company leased plots of uncleared land along well-traveled railroad routes, clearing half of each piece of land and planting crops on the other part to call attention to the "before and after" effects of dynamite. DuPont published a magazine called *The Agricultural Blaster* urging blasters to take on partners who would solicit work and leave them free to do the actual blasting. One early issue struck a blow for women's rights with "She Was not Afraid," the story of a woman in Alabama who, unable to find any men willing to help her use dynamite to plant trees, primed the cartridges, fired the shots, and planted the trees herself. The most important dynamite advertising appeared in "educational" blasting handbooks and booklets, which promoted DuPont products as they explained the proper use of explosives. The books were handed out at well-publicized demonstrations and shows and by traveling DuPont salesmen.

DuPont was one of the first U.S. companies to use the fledgling technology of moving pictures to advertise the proper ways to use its products. It paid for 37 copies of a silent film, *Farming with Dynamite,* in 1912, circulating and showing the movie around the country. In an era when moving pictures were still somewhat of a novelty, *Farming with Dynamite* and other DuPont productions were often all or part of the program in rural theaters, and DuPont films were also shown in noncommercial venues such as farmers' institutes and agricultural colleges. Prints of *Farming with Dynamite* no longer exist, but a *Scientific American* review stated that the film demonstrated "the real value of high explosives to the farmer." The motion picture and advertising campaigns were apparently successful: building a market where virtually none had existed before, DuPont sold American farmers around 17 million pounds of dynamite a year by 1920. The company continued to produce similar films, eventually with sound, into the age of television.

Diversification

In the early 20th century, corporate diversification led DuPont into a variety of markets that had nothing to do with explosives. The company established one of the first coal-tar dye factories in the United States, allowing DuPont to produce paints, varnishes, and cellulose, one of the earliest plastics. During the 1920s magazine ads for DuPont paints proclaimed that "tinted walls are now

DuPont's synthetic fibers helped revolutionize the apparel industry and dramatically altered household lifestyles when wrinkle-free, wash-and-wear clothing was introduced.
Courtesy of DuPont.

the vogue," as consumers were lured from traditional white to colors by many manufacturers. Fabrikoid, an early synthetic upholstery fabric that looked like leather, was advertised to affluent automobile purchasers. *Barron's* reported that Fabrikoid had proven indispensable because "all the cows on earth could not supply the demand" for upholstery leather by 1927. Pontoklene, a product used to remove tar from motor cars, was advertised in magazines as a "100% seller for DuPont dealers." Tubes of DuPont cement were advertised in newspapers and magazines with the slogan, "First aid for breaks and tears."

To sell these new products, DuPont needed to do more than increase consumer awareness. As was the case with dynamite, the consumer had to be instructed in their use, and DuPont responded with "educational advertising," in which exhibits played a pivotal role. One of the company's most successful educational efforts was the establishment of a permanent company exhibit on the boardwalk in Atlantic City, New Jersey, in 1916. Before the exhibit closed in 1955, more than 26 million visitors had learned of the wonders of DuPont chemistry. Traveling exhibits for schools, colleges, and even department stores were developed. The company considered such promotion valuable even if it did not directly sell products. "This company believes that all products of merit warrant publicity through instruction," *DuPont Magazine* stated in 1918. DuPont's emphasis on educating consumers did not mean the company was beyond hyperbole, however. A booklet produced by DuPont in 1928, *DuPont Pyraline: Its Manufacture and Use,* failed to note that its trademarked plastic Pyraline was exactly the same in composition and manufacture as cellulose, invented in 1869.

World War I and its aftermath proved to be a trying time for DuPont. The company, which remained a leading producer of explosives despite efforts by the government to curb the "powder trust," produced 1.4 million pounds of smokeless gunpowder between 1914 and 1918. Production of nitrocellulose, a key ingredient in the powder, increased from less than 1 million pounds per month to 1.5 million pounds per day. Overall, the company produced 40 percent of all explosives shot from Allied cannons during the war. It also manufactured chlorine and phosgene, poisonous gases, at a secret plant in southern New Jersey. Profits grew accordingly. Gross receipts jumped from $25 million in 1914 to $329 million in 1918. The company had so much extra money that it purchased more than 25 percent of existing General Motors stock in 1917 in order to establish a place to put managers it did not want to keep at DuPont. (DuPont remained GM's largest shareholder until 1961, when it was forced to divest its holdings after the U.S. Supreme Court ruled that its ownership of 23 percent of GM's stock violated the Clayton Antitrust Act.)

Along with other war industries, DuPont was singled out for criticism and special taxation during the war, but it did nothing to improve or clarify its public image. A special U.S. Senate committee on the munitions industry alleged in 1934 that DuPont had defrauded the government during the war by overcharging for munitions. The company was also accused of selling munitions to both sides. It survived most of the allegations, labeling the investigation a "trial without jury" but was labeled as a "merchant of death" in a famous editorial cartoon published in *Forum* magazine in 1934. The affair contributed to passage of the Neutrality Act of 1935, which for a time prohibited U.S. companies from selling munitions to belligerent nations. The law was justified in part by the belief that DuPont's arms dealings had encouraged World War I.

To survive the debacle and mark its second corporate transformation, this time away from gunpowder and explosives, DuPont hired Bruce Barton of Batten Barton Durstine & Osborn (BBDO) to personally handle its advertising. The agency began producing a comprehensive $650,000 program of advertisements, radio programs, films, and popular exhibits built on a new corporate theme. Launched in October 1935, "Better things for better living . . . through chemistry" became one of the longest lasting slogans in 20th-century American advertising history, ending in 1999. DuPont debuted its new slogan in the *Saturday Evening Post* and through a new network radio program, *The Cavalcade of America* (1935–53). The audience for *The Cavalcade of America* was not large, but it included many teachers, who encouraged their students to listen. Considering the public

relations function of the program, the stories emphasized humanitarian ideals. More importantly, they avoided any violence that might involve gunpowder. Writers, including future playwright Arthur Miller and historian Erik Barnouw, were prohibited as a matter of policy from dramatizing any battles. "The sound of a shot was taboo," Barnouw later wrote. "Even explosions were for many years forbidden."

DuPont also built a 1,600 square-foot display for the Texas Centennial Exposition in 1936. The display moved to New York's Museum of Science and Industry and was exhibited at the Franklin Institute Science Museum, Philadelphia, Pennsylvania, and the Museum of Science and Industry, Chicago, Illinois, in 1937. The dominant theme of the exhibit was the superiority of synthetics over natural products. A "chemical age" had dawned in which synthesized materials surpassed even nature's best handiwork. By associating compounds such as Lucite—which could take on any desired color and be molded, blown, sawed, cut, hammered, drilled, polished, or carved—with the cultural status of art objects, DuPont hoped to legitimate synthetics as products of "better living." The museums even allowed DuPont to stage opening night fashion shows, featuring clothing and accessories made with products of the chemical laboratory. Once again, DuPont used educational advertising to gain acceptance in the marketplace for its new products.

Nylon Arrives

DuPont's biggest, most spectacular exhibit was "The Wonder World of Chemistry," at the 1939–40 New York World's Fair, which cost $887,000 and was seen by nearly 10 million visitors. The exhibit showcased all DuPont's chemical products, but one in particular caught the public's eye. BBDO turned to a proven marketing approach to debut nylon, first patented by DuPont on 21 September 1938. Leo Baekeland, the inventor of Bakelite, had announced the introduction of his new plastic in the *New York Herald* in 1909. DuPont followed this precedent, purchasing a page ad in a special pre–World's Fair section of the *New York Herald Tribune* on 30 October 1938 that read, "DuPont announces for the World of Tomorrow [the fair's theme] a new word and a new material, Nylon." The ad and an accompanying speech by DuPont Vice President Charles M.A. Stine, which was reported as a news story in the paper, presented a number of prospective uses for the synthetic fiber, including toothbrushes, but the publicity materials dwelled more on "jobs for the men who make the raw material—jobs for the men who convert it into numerous articles for everyday service."

Curiously, the ad and speech failed to mention what would be the most popular use for the new product. For centuries, people had sought to create a synthetic fiber that imitated silk. That dream was realized the following year when DuPont introduced nylon hosiery for the first time, worn by live models at the Worlds Fair. BBDO's promotion of nylon stockings for DuPont was extraordinary. News stories claimed they were "as strong as steel," a contention DuPont was finally forced to deny. Journalists were told that a lit cigarette, a nail file, a razor, nor even a blowtorch could run nylon stockings, in contrast to the cheaper, more fragile silk. A boilerplate photograph sent free to newspapers showed an aerial view of DuPont's new nylon factory with the caption "$27,000,000 was invested by DuPont in nylon over 13 years." On a following page, the same newspapers published a cheesecake photograph of a lingerie-clad model wearing the new nylons with the caption, "10 cents is what DuPont receives for the nylon yarn in a pair of ladies' hose." Rumors that nylon was made from the "acids of corpses" had to be denied. DuPont sponsored a well publicized "Nylon Day" on 15 May 1940, in which stores offered nylon hosiery to women for the first time, at the extravagant price of $1.15 a pair. By the end of "N-Day," as the event came to be called, the entire initial production of 5 million pairs was sold.

The demand for nylon stockings was so huge that DuPont never met it before World War II forced the company to divert all nylon production to parachutes and other war uses. However, the stockings were so popular that their return to stores became an incentive for millions of female wartime workers and their military-bound mates to contribute to the war effort. Movie star Betty Grable auctioned off a pair of her nylons to help sell war bonds, and the wearing of a pair of nylons for the first time quickly became a right of passage for teenage girls. A hit song in 1943, "When the Nylons Bloom Again," created nostalgia for a product that many consumers had only heard about. At the end of the war, a second N-Day, on 14 February 1946, created "nylon beachheads," or "nylon riots," as women battled inside and outside stores to buy nylons as a reward for their wartime sacrifices. Never failing to miss an opportunity, DuPont chronicled its invention of nylon and part of the resulting craze in a 1940 educational film, *A New World through Chemistry,* which maintained that "nothing is impossible in plastics."

In contrast with other companies, DuPont scaled back its advertising during World War II, partly because the company returned to gunpowder and explosives production. Public service ads encouraged women to recycle old hosiery, sending "their nylons off to war" to make more parachute yarn, and other companies capitalized on the fame of nylon by advertising its use in their products, such as tires. According to one advertising trade journal, the end of the war and the resulting nylon craze created more free advertising for DuPont than had been received by any other company "in the history of [the] newspaper business," thereby decreasing DuPont's need to promote itself.

Wartime synthetics such as nylon and neoprene, an artificial rubber developed by DuPont in 1933, also created a level of consumer acceptance for chemicals that did not exist before the war. Even as DuPont saw its "merchant of death" label disappearing in the public mind, the nylon shortage led critics to charge that the company was greedy or even unpatriotic. One newspaper denounced DuPont as "the only company which knows the magic nylon secret" and proclaimed that nylon shortages "should cause women's pages from coast to coast to be bordered in black." To avoid antitrust litigation, the company eventually licensed the technology to other producers, and DuPont's favorable rating in opinion polls rose from 47 percent in 1937 to 84 percent by 1954.

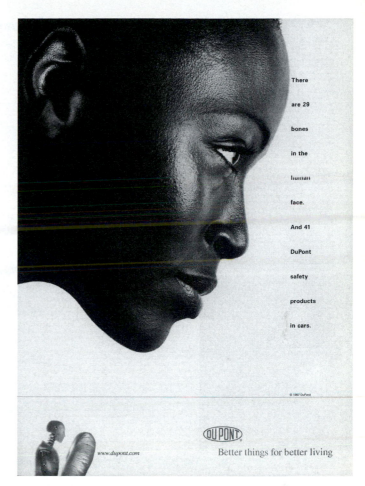

There are 29 bones in the human face. And 41 DuPont safety products in cars.

www.dupont.com   DUPONT   Better things for better living

This 1997 ad uses a stark, simple image and minimal copy to promote DuPont's safety products, an effort to show the company's ongoing commitment to improving the quality of life. *Courtesy of DuPont.*

Plastics and Polyester

The postwar years were the era of plastics. Tupperware, plastic Foster Grant sunglasses, and hula hoops were only three of the many well-advertised consumer products that made the United States the leader in plastics production. DuPont continued to make raw material plastics, a practice that had led it to avoid advertising before the war, although its habit of trademarking and publicizing innovations kept its name before the public in a variety of ways, not always positive. Delrin, a substitute for zinc and brass, was used in automobiles, as was a molded nylon called Zytel. The latter found its way into roller-skate and skateboard wheels and helped make the skateboard craze of the 1960s possible.

DuPont tried to imitate the success of nylon with polyester, a synthetic substitute for wool and other fibers in men's suits first marketed in the 1950s. By the 1960s, polyester derivatives had become commonplace, as had permanent-press clothing. A DuPont polyester film named Mylar changed audio and video tape recording and made boil-in-the-bag and microwave cooking

DuPont's corporate campaign, "The miracles of science," stressed the interaction between human life and technology in a series of enduring images from the company's "To Do List for the Planet."
Courtesy of DuPont.

possible. The same Mylar film was also used in the first satellites, making DuPont an early contributor to the space age.

Teflon, discovered the same year as nylon and used to help produce nuclear weapons-grade plutonium during the war, was promoted by DuPont to journalists as a nonstick cooking surface in the early 1950s. However, it was not introduced to consumers until 1961, owing to concerns that its fumes caused mild flu symptoms. Those fears were based on a persistent rumor that in the 1950s an unknown machinist had died within five minutes of smoking a cigarette contaminated with Teflon. The company responded in 1962 with a 20-page booklet, *The Anatomy of a Rumor,* that effectively debunked the health concerns, but the pamphlet appeared at the same time President John F. Kennedy was trying to convince the public that milk contaminated with strontium-90 was safe to drink. The observation that Teflon had been used to produce the same nuclear material that had filled the atmosphere with radioactive isotopes could not be avoided, and Teflon and its various DuPont-developed successors never became the best-sellers the company hoped they would be.

DuPont made its most serious advertising mistake in 1963, when it introduced Corfam, a synthetic shoe material that prom-

ised a scuff-proof leather substitute but never duplicated leather's flexibility. DuPont and BBDO created a sophisticated advertising campaign to market Corfam as a high-class product, much as they had once done with the leather-upholstery substitute Fabrikoid, but consumers disliked Corfam's inability to imitate the capacity of leather to shape to a wearer's foot and quickly equated Corfam with cheap vinyl plastic shoes. DuPont lost $70 million that it had invested in Corfam before abandoning the synthetic product and selling it to Poland in 1971. The product is considered one of the most serious flops in the history of American consumer culture, along with the Edsel and New Coke.

The public's appetite for synthetics began to wane long before the Corfam fiasco. In April 1959 the American Medical Association charged that polyethylene film bags used by dry cleaners had caused four children to die from suffocation in Phoenix, Arizona. A physician speculated that the static-electricity charged bags literally grabbed an infant "through electrical attraction to his face." By summer, the media reported that more than 80 children had died through mishaps with the bags, and ten adults were said to have used the bags to commit suicide. What DuPont had once called "those handy plastic bags" became a public relations nightmare for the company. Instead of effectively defending the company, a DuPont spokesman blamed "parental carelessness" in the deaths and maintained that the bags were "made to be disposable"—even though DuPont had previously extolled their reusability. Newspapers and magazines responded by printing photographs of breathless human faces wrapped in transparent plastic film. *Life* published a full-page picture of New York City Board of Health Director Leona Baumgartner sealed in what the magazine called a "thin bag of death." "After 20 seconds inside clinging plastic bag, Dr. Baumgartner gasps for breath, is near suffocation," the magazine observed. Better public relations by the Society of Plastics Industry and the introduction of warning labels helped soothe consumer concerns in what was called the "plastic bag war."

However, public distrust of plastics was further fanned in 1963 when author Norman Mailer began blaming plastics for everything from cancer to blotchy skin. Mailer was joined by writers such as Jack Kerouac and Gary Snyder and psychologist Robert Jay Lifton in criticizing a postmodern world made of synthetic rather than "real" natural materials.

DuPont continued to be plagued by rampant "chemophobia," which intensified during the 1960s and 1970s. Its "Better things for better living . . . through chemistry" slogan was adopted by users of the drug LSD and other synthetically produced hallucinogens. The deployment of napalm and other chemical defoliants in the Vietnam War was a public relations nightmare for the entire chemical industry. Earth Day on 22 April 1970 focused additional critical attention on plastics and other nonbiodegradable substances. DuPont temporarily abandoned its advertising slogan in 1972, although it later reinstated the tag line without the "through chemistry" phrase.

In 1974 the reputation of the company suffered further because of its alleged involvement in the suppression of Gerald C. Zilg's *DuPont: Behind the Nylon Curtain*, a 623-page history of the company and the du Pont family, which revealed, among other things, that the du Pont family "employs more servants than Britain's royal family, owns more yachts, cars, swimming pools, planes, and estates than any other family in recorded history." The book received a positive review in the *New York Times* and was scheduled to be a Book-of-the-Month Club selection. Then the selection was withdrawn by the club, and the publisher, Prentice-Hall, reduced the size of the first printing. Zilg charged that DuPont had launched a corporate plot to scuttle the publication. A federal judge awarded Zilg almost $25,000 from the publisher for reneging on a contract to promote sales, but the court threw out charges that DuPont had illegally interfered with sales. The damages were overturned by an appeals court, and the U.S. Supreme Court declined to review the verdict in 1984. The book became difficult to find, even in libraries.

The company responded to its increasingly negative public image by diversifying. It acquired the oil, natural gas, and coal company Conoco in 1981; started a pharmaceutical operation the following year (that company became DuPont-Merck Pharmaceutical Company in 1990); and made acquisitions in the agricultural industry. It also bought Shell Oil's herbicide and pesticide lines,

making DuPont the second largest U.S. agricultural chemicals producer. In 1986 Canadian liquor company Seagram bought a large share of DuPont stock, reducing family control. The following year, DuPont stopped making explosives, its original product.

"The Miracles of Science"

Foreign competition and a reduction in sales to traditional customers of its wholesale products forced DuPont to reinvent itself a third time in 1998; this time the company focused on life sciences rather than chemicals. DuPont divested itself of Conoco in a public stock offering, bought out Merck's share of their pharmaceutical company, bought its shares back from Seagram, and formed a partnership with competitor Dow Chemical to continue the innovative research that had been the basis of DuPont's success for much of the 20th century.

DuPont also began to market some of its products more aggressively, in particular Stainmaster carpet fiber. BBDO helped plan the campaign introducing the fiber in 1986. Most of the Stainmaster ads stressed the product's quality, durability, and stylishness in DuPont's typical "educational" format, but it was a 30-second television commercial first shown during the late innings of the 1986 baseball playoffs that captured consumer attention. The "Landing" spot showed an young child sitting in a high chair, with an airplane-shaped dish in front of him. As an air-traffic controller voice-over cleared a plane for takeoff, the boy sent his dish airborne, flinging its contents onto a Stainmaster carpet. Another spot showed a woman trying valiantly to stop a table full of food from falling on her carpet. DuPont's first humorous advertisements helped make Stainmaster a consumer success and DuPont the largest maker of carpet fiber in the country. Combined with nylon, which continued to account for one-quarter of DuPont's profits in the 1990s, and Lycra, used in Spandex athletic wear and Gortex products, fibers such as Stainmaster became the top brand names and profit makers for the company.

In 1998 DuPont was named the "most admired" company in the U.S. and global chemical industry by *Fortune*; it made *Working Mother* magazine's list of top 100 companies, was identified as one of the top 50 companies for minority employment by *Fortune,* and was listed as one of the 50 best companies for Hispanics by *Latina Style*. Also in 1998 DuPont changed advertising agencies, making McCann-Erickson Worldwide its corporate agency of record, although individual products continued to use other agencies. The most dramatic advertising change made by the reorganized company was the elimination of its 64-year-old "Better things for better living" slogan. To establish DuPont's new corporate image as a science rather than chemical company, "The miracles of science" tag line was created to emphasize products such as heat- and flame-resistant Nomex, Thermolite insulation, Kevlar (a bullet-resistant material with aerospace applications), and the Teflon replacement Silverstone. In newspapers (the same medium where it had once launched nylon), DuPont in 1999 revealed its new branding focus.

RICHARD JUNGER

Further Reading

Chandler, Alfred D., *Strategy and Structure: Chapters in the History of the Industrial Enterprise*, Cambridge, Massachusetts: MIT Press, 1962

Colby, Gerard, *Du Pont: Behind the Nylon Curtain*, Englewood Cliffs, New Jersey: Prentice-Hall, 1974

Corn, Joseph, "Selling Technology: Advertising Films and the American Corporation, 1900–1920," *Film and History* 3 (1981)

Cuff, Robert, "Private Success, Public Problems: The Du Pont Corporation and World War I," *Canadian Review of American Studies* 20 (Fall 1989)

DuBois, J. Harry, *Plastics History U.S.A.*, Boston: Cahners, 1972

E.I. Du Pont de Nemours and Company, *Du Pont: The Autobiography of an American Enterprise*, Wilmington, Delaware: Du Pont, 1952

Hensley, John, "Selling the Blast: DuPont's Agricultural Explosives Advertising, 1902–1920," *Delaware History* 22 (Fall/Winter 1986)

Meikle, Jeffrey L., *American Plastic: A Cultural History*, New Brunswick, New Jersey: Rutgers University Press, 1995

Rhees, David J., "Corporate Advertising, Public Relations and Popular Exhibits: The Case of Du Pont," *History and Technology* 10, nos. 1–2 (1993)

Sherrid, Pamela, "Please Pass the Bioengineered Butter," *U.S. News and World Report* (2 March 1998)

E

Eastman Kodak Company

Principal Agencies
J. Walter Thompson Company
Ogilvy & Mather Worldwide
Saatchi & Saatchi
Young & Rubicam, Inc.

George Eastman was born on 12 July 1854 in Waterville, a small town in upstate New York. He dropped out of school at the age of 14 to help support his family, working at an insurance company and a local bank. But even at that young age he was interested in photography and through his own practice realized that the dry-plate cameras and extensive equipment necessary to take pictures were both expensive and cumbersome. He began dabbling with chemical experiments in the evenings in his mother's kitchen and in three years found a dry-plate formula that was more practical.

Introduction of Film

In April 1880, at the age of 25, Eastman leased the third floor of a building in Rochester, New York, and began to manufacture the dry plates he had invented and patented. A year later Eastman and family friend Henry A. Strong partnered to form the Eastman Dry Plate Company, and Eastman resigned from his other job to devote his full attention to the business. His aim was to make the camera as easy to use as the pencil. Because the heavy glass plates were so cumbersome, in 1883 he invented what would become the foundation of the amateur photography revolution that he would pioneer: film. Within three years, the company was selling roll film and roll holders. The company's name changed a number of times through the late 1800s, until 1892, when it was christened the Eastman Kodak Company, the name it retained for more than a century.

In 1888 the name Kodak was trademarked and the company's first camera was launched, a $25 camera with 100 exposures that had to be sent to the headquarters in Rochester for processing. Less than one year after its introduction, more than 13,000 cameras had been sold, and the company was processing 60 to 70 rolls of film a day.

Easy-to-Use Cameras

The name Kodak came solely from Eastman's imagination; he chose it because it was short, easy to pronounce, and would not be associated with anything but the company's products. The next challenge was to get the camera into the hands of a new class of photographer, the mainstream consumer. The camera was introduced to the market with the slogan that embodied Eastman's desire to make picture-taking easy and affordable for the masses: "You press the button—we do the rest." The phrase, coined by Eastman himself, soon became familiar to the American audience.

In addition to the company's first slogan, Eastman penned many of the company's early advertisements, brochures, and magazines. Advertising was one of Eastman's four core business principles, which also included mass production at low cost, international distribution, and a customer-centered approach. He had the insight and foresight to recognize that successful advertising was the key to creating an amateur photography market. Until 1892 Eastman relied solely on himself as the company's creative ad mind, using two New York City agencies, Frank Seaman and the J. Walter Thompson Company (JWT), which would remain on the Kodak agency roster until 1997, as media buyers and advisers. Eastman soon learned that he could not handle all the marketing responsibilities on his own and in March 1892 hired Lewis Burnell Jones, a Syracuse, New York, newspaperman, to head up marketing.

Branding

By 1893 Jones—who was later identified as one of the five most influential people in assisting Eastman to shape the company—helped Eastman create and refine the company's first central ad image, the Kodak Girl.

The Kodak Girl stemmed from Eastman's belief that a picture of a pretty girl would sell more cameras than a picture of an

The Kodak Girl and the slogan, "If it isn't an Eastman, it isn't a Kodak," both seen in this 1902 ad, have earned a place in American advertising history.
Courtesy of Eastman Kodak Company.

ing photography, as it was accessible to anyone who had $1 to spend on the camera and 15 cents for the film. Early Eastman advertisements promised that anyone could use the camera, the message on which Kodak built its trusted brand. The Brownie was an incredible marketing tool, aimed specifically at children. Eastman had realized, even before hiring Jones, that his primary ad target would be the family. An 1888 ad featured a father on one knee snapping a picture of his little daughter, emphasizing the emotive nature and charm of picture-taking rather than the camera itself, a theme that Kodak continues to use in its advertising.

The Brownie packaging was decorated with imaginary sprites called brownies, the characters of Canadian illustrator Palmer Cox, and the company organized Brownie camera clubs and sponsored photography competitions for adolescent Brownie users. The camera's ad icon, the Brownie Boy, a cute, good-natured child who loved photography, began appearing in print ads shortly after the camera was launched. Eastman sensed early on that the lifeblood of his company would be film and that

The introduction of the inexpensive Brownie camera brought photography to the masses. The Brownie Boy icon was used in Kodak's ads to position the camera as the choice for children.
Courtesy of Eastman Kodak Company.

object like a tree or a house. The Kodak Girl was introduced to the United States in the late 1880s as a young, wholesome-looking lady, usually in a striped dress and holding a camera. It did not take long for her, like the camera brand she represented, to become part of American popular culture and, later, that of Britain, where she was introduced in 1901. Slogans accompanying the Kodak Girl included "Springtime is Kodak time"; "Don't forget your Kodak"; and "Save your happy memories with a Kodak." When the Kodak name became so well known that it was being used as the common noun for a camera in general, Jones and Eastman came up with a new line: "If it isn't an Eastman, it isn't a Kodak."

By the end of the 19th century, Kodak was one of the biggest advertisers in the country, with ads targeting families of the expanding middle class. In 1900 the Kodak "Brownie" camera was born, a small box camera that eliminated the need for dark-room developing and furthered Eastman's dream of democratiz-

Kodak's long-term success depended on bringing children into the franchise so they would grow up with Kodak, always needing and wanting more cameras and more film. The first batch of 5,000 Brownies sold out almost immediately, and when the second model of the Brownie came to market the next year, almost 250,000 of the original had been sold.

Kodak cameras became increasingly popular during World War I, when Kodak's advertisements focused on the importance of using snapshots to remind soldiers of home. The emotional value of photos to soldiers was so enduring that virtually the same ad—an image of a GI looking at a packet of pictures—was used again during World War II.

Between the wars, the Roaring Twenties brought motion pictures to the masses, and the movies began to capture the world's visual imagination. Because Eastman's progressive thinking assured that his company would be on the cusp of all new developments in imaging, in 1923 Kodak made amateur motion pictures a reality with the introduction of a 16-mm motion-picture camera. In 1929 the company launched its first motion-picture film designed especially for making movies with sound.

The 1920s also saw Kodak's first outdoor advertising, with thousands of small signs erected on the shoulders of U.S. highways. The signs announced upcoming photo opportunities to drivers with messages such as "Picture ahead! Kodak as you go." During the 1920s, the Kodak Girl matured into color posters that were stylish and chic, reflecting that the ad icon's clothing and personality had changed with the times.

With the onset of the 1930s, as photography was celebrating its 100th anniversary, the medium came of age and really began to flourish. In 1931 Eastman Kodak's $100,000 international amateur photography competition drew 3 million entries, and the average, untrained "snapshooter" became the target of much of the company's advertising. One ad slogan of the time read, "Snapshots you'll want tomorrow, you must make today." Everyday people looking at everyday pictures became a popular theme, one that Kodak still relied on in the 21st century with its "Everyday moments" umbrella campaign.

During World War II, civilian use of photographic equipment—like all consumer goods—was strictly rationed; by the war's end, the demand was so high that consumers had to wait for production to catch up. By the late 1940s, Kodak's marketing strategy was multilayered, separated into eight distinct product groups targeting various audiences, from the casual snapshooter (Brownie, Tourist) to the more serious 35-mm amateur (Kodak 35, Rentina).

As the century reached its halfway mark, Kodak entered the world of large-scale advertising. On 15 May 1950, it unveiled the first in its long-running series of Kodak Colorama displays—18 feet high and 60 feet wide—overlooking the main terminal of New York's Grand Central Station. An attraction viewed by close to 650,000 commuters and tourists every day, the display ran until 1989.

In the early 1950s, Kodak embarked on two major campaigns—consumer and trade—to promote picture taking, an ongoing marketing strategy. Consumer ads read, "Big weekend

All out-doors invites your Kodak

Autographic Kodaks $6.50 up

Eastman Kodak Company, Rochester, N. Y., *The Kodak City*

With the rapid spread of automobiles in the 1920s, Kodak advertising focused on the great outdoors, featuring a stylish makeover of the Kodak Girl.
Courtesy of Eastman Kodak Company.

coming up—time to take those snapshots you'll treasure all your life." Consumer work was done by JWT, while Charles L. Rumrill & Company handled professional photographic supplies.

Television Advertising

In addition to its large-scale presence in Grand Central Station, Kodak also entered the world of the small screen as TV came on the scene. Its first entry into the new medium was a short-lived series called *Norby*, which ran from January to April of 1955 and had the distinction of being the first network show to be filmed in color. In 1956 Kodak tried again, this time as sponsor of a long-established program, *The Adventures of Ozzie and Harriet*. Both were handled by JWT, which also made Kodak a participating sponsor of *The Ed Sullivan Show* in 1957. Sales of Kodak film were boosted by its move into TV. The TV spots did not differ greatly from Kodak's traditional print ads that celebrated the occasions of family photography, reminding consumers that all they needed was film, a camera, and "a little thoughtfulness" to make beautiful memories. In the late 1950s, Kodak began a Christmas campaign with the tag line "Open me first," which the company used well into the next decade for its holiday advertising. By 1958 Kodak ranked as nineteenth among the leading advertisers in the world, with a $30 million ad budget.

In 1962 Kodak for the first time recorded U.S. sales exceeding $1 billion and worldwide employment surpassing 75,000. Kodak's own milestone was followed by an American one: John Glenn became the first American to orbit the Earth—and Kodak film traveled with him to document his adventure.

Instamatic Camera

The following year, Kodak launched its first Instamatic camera, which used easy-to-load film cartridges. The launch was supported by a $3.5 million spring ad campaign in magazines and on TV. That same year, Kodak's ad department numbered 450, one of the largest in American industry and larger than most ad agencies at the time. Two years later, following the success of the Instamatic, Kodak launched a line of Instamatic movie cameras and projectors.

The 1970s marked the beginning of the decline of the professional friendship of Kodak and the Polaroid Corporation, which had been working together since the 1950s for complementary products. Polaroid needed color negative materials on a large scale, which Kodak mass produced, and Kodak needed Polaroid's business to keep its plants running full time. But the pending expiration of some of Polaroid's patents on instant film and an agreement signed in 1969 permitting Kodak to make and sell Polaroid-like color film in 1976 posed threats to their partnership.

In the meantime, Kodak introduced a new logo, a two-part red and yellow square with the word Kodak that began appearing in ads in 1972. In May 1974, Kodak commissioned Oscar recipient Marvin Hamlish to compose a ragtime musical theme for a TV spot from JWT, called "Highwire," which showed how easy it was to use the pocket-sized Instamatic in unusual settings, such as the circus. Advertising in the 1970s was devoted primarily to the Instamatic and to film, with TV ads carrying the tag line, "Kodak film. For the times of your life."

At the end of 1974, Kodak announced that for the first time in many years it did not plan to increase its advertising budget for the following year, given that sales were down for most of 1974 and earnings trailed 1973 performance. A year later Kodak told analysts that the format and design of its camera to compete with Polaroid's instant format was ready and that a target launch date was set. Thus, 1976 was the year of the showdown. After months of hinting and promising to enter the instant camera market, Kodak unveiled its new line in April 1976, posing a direct challenge to Polaroid, which had pioneered the market segment 30 years before. Ironically, the inventor of Polaroid's instant photography method, Edwin Land, first offered to sell his idea to Kodak in the 1940s, but Kodak's success at the time led Eastman to think he did not need an outsider's input and he rebuffed Land.

I had a great game, Mom. I went 3 for 4, threw out a runner at home plate and I think the shortstop likes me.

Kodak film. For the times of your life.

Kodak's most memorable campaign of the 1970s used the enduring "For the times of your life" slogan, as seen in this ad from 1975. *Courtesy of Eastman Kodak Company.*

In 1976, when the rivals went head to head, Kodak's $5 billion in sales dwarfed Polaroid's $812 million. Kodak began advertising its instant camera during the Olympic Games with ads announcing, "It's here! The Kodak Instant," and offering a three-year warranty. Later that year, Polaroid decided to face off with Kodak in court, filing suit against Kodak, charging ten patent infringements, which Kodak denied. Polaroid was offered an interim injunction in the United Kingdom, where Kodak was prohibited from manufacturing or selling its instant cameras until patent litigation was resolved. Despite Polaroid's claim that it had not increased its ad efforts in an attempt to compete with Kodak, it broke a $16 million campaign to promote its newest camera.

The following year, Kodak doubled its ad spending for its instant cameras to $12 million, deepening its battle with Polaroid by introducing "The Handle," an instant camera selling for $39.95 to compete with Polaroid's low-priced offering at $59. The ad theme was "Grab onto the Handle."

The ongoing battle between Kodak and Polaroid led to the decrease in value of both companies' stock, and the 1980s, the decade that began with Kodak's 100th anniversary, were tough on the company. Market competition from Japan was increasing; costs were high; Kodak had too many employees to support. Since mass layoffs were not part of the company's heritage, it offered an optional early-retirement package that was accepted by 5,000 staffers. Kodak began the decade with ads highlighting middle-American life: the theme was "Kodak: America's storyteller." By the end of the decade, it had moved to a "True colors" theme for Olympic and general advertising.

Kodak finally lost its drawn-out court battle with Polaroid over patent infringements and was forced to remove all its instant camera and film products from the market in 1986. Two years later, after nearly continuous positive support from the investment community and the media, Wall Street took notice that Kodak had not met its profit goals. The last year of the decade was the worst in Kodak's history, after three quarters of lower-than-expected earnings and criticism from the local Rochester media regarding the company's hiring freezes and cutbacks.

The early 1990s did not look much better for Kodak, which was suffering from a series of missteps from the two previous decades. These included its struggles with Polaroid; its decision to spend time and money developing digital photographic equipment before the market warranted it; and its entry into the pharmaceutical industry, which tripled its long-term debt. Diversion into nonfilm areas meant that Kodak's core film business lagged, as competition from Japan heated up.

A New Focus

After firing Chief Executive Officer (CEO) Kay Whitmore, a long-time Kodak engineer, the company in 1993 realized it needed a new manager—a marketer—to bring it back to life. In October of that year, Kodak announced that it had hired former Motorola CEO George Fisher, the first Kodak outsider to lead the company. Fisher took the reins of an organization plagued by more than a decade of declining market share and weak financial performance, and he came on board mediating expectations by predicting that 1994 would be the tough beginning to a slow turnaround. But by May 1994, Fisher changed his tune and started taking radical steps to bring the company back. He decided to sell off Kodak's health businesses to focus on its film and electronic imaging units and pay off its $6.9 billion in long-term debt.

In 1995 Kodak cut $50 million from the cost of its film and paper production and reduced production time for key processes. By 1996 Kodak was back on track. Its stock price hit a record high of $80 per share, double what it was when Fisher joined the company at the end of 1993. It was outperforming the Standard and Poor's 500 by 20 percent, a welcome change from three years earlier, when it was trailing the index by 50 percent.

Ad account consolidation also helped Kodak cut costs. By 1996 the company's agency roster—once occupied by 77 shops—was cut to four, with JWT and Ogilvy & Mather handling consumer products and Uniworld and Saatchi & Saatchi handling ethnic marketing and professional imaging, respectively. The consolidation began earlier that decade, when in 1992 Kodak set out on a global brand-building effort and made agency realignments resulting in a single shop in each country. It shifted camera advertising in the United States from Young & Rubicam, Inc. (Y&R), to JWT, leaving JWT as its domestic agency and Y&R to handle most international work. Ogilvy & Mather Worldwide, Kodak's primary agency as of 2000, came on the scene in 1994 to handle the company's digital and applied imaging business two months after the unit was launched. By September of the following year, Ogilvy won Kodak's $40 million to $50 million corporate branding account. Its goal was to focus on how people could make greater and more creative use of their pictures, a theme that fit with the strategy Kodak began in the early 1990s that hinged on usage groups—often defined by age groups—rather than product-driven marketing. In February 1996 Kodak dropped Y&R from its roster, leaving JWT and Ogilvy with the spoils. The streamlining left Kodak with $100 million for media spending for 1996, up from $80 million the previous year.

The company's chief marketing officer, Carl Gustin, appointed in August 1995, worked with the agencies to push Kodak's new theme line—"Take pictures. Further"—which was coined by Ogilvy. The tag line was first launched in 1996 when Kodak introduced the world to the Advanced Photo System (APS), a new photographic format developed in conjunction with Canon, Inc., Fuji Photo Film, Minolta Corporation, and Nikon, Inc. Ogilvy, the engineer of the campaign that would take Kodak into the next century, became the lead agency for Kodak's entire consumer imaging business in June 1997, when Kodak finally bid farewell to JWT after 66 years.

Ogilvy began to initiate Kodak's relationship with a new target, Generation X, via a wacky global ad campaign featuring Gen-Xers and UFOs to show how Kodak's diverse line of products from cameras to film to digital could be used by the demographic. Fisher pioneered this strategy, hoping that appealing to a new audience would help Kodak recover from its losses earlier in the decade. These losses were exacerbated by trade wars with Fuji that had become a major point of friction between the United States and Japan. In 1995 Kodak filed a petition with the U.S. government asking for an investigation of anticompetitive trade practices in the Japanese market, including price-fixing to prevent key distributors and retailers from selling U.S.-made photographic products. After a year of investigation, a U.S. trade representative confirmed the existence of trade barriers and called on Japan to discuss Kodak's concerns under the supervision of the World Trade Organization.

By mid-1996, after shedding 11,000 workers and $7.5 billion in debt, Kodak looked attractive to Wall Street for the first time in years. Daniel Carp, a 25-year Kodak veteran, was appointed to the new post of president and chief operating officer at the end of the year, and at the beginning of 1997 Fisher extended his five-year contract two additional years, until the close of 2000.

But perhaps Fisher acted too soon, because by the end of 1997 he was forced to lay off close to 11,000 more employees owing to increasing losses in sales and market share amidst the heightened film price war with Fuji. The layoffs helped the beleaguered Kodak reduce costs by $500 million and position itself in 1998 to focus on aggressive marketing of its U.S. film business as well as its APS brand, Advantix, and the growth of its digital services.

TIME AND TIME AGAIN, THE WORLD'S GREAT PICTURES
ARE TRUSTED TO ONE BRAND OF FILM. KODAK.

Photographed on Ektachrome film.

Photographed on Kodacolor Gold film.

WHY TRUST YOUR MEMORIES TO ANYTHING LESS?

© Eastman Kodak Company, 1989

TRUE COLORS.™

The "True Colors" campaign characterized Kodak film as the choice for preserving historic events and childhood memories alike.
Courtesy of Eastman Kodak Company.

By 1998 the company was melding Fisher's two key premises—digital imaging and increased picture-taking—into one by encouraging people to take more pictures by giving them different ways to use them. It introduced products such as Picture CD, allowing people to store film-based pictures on a compact disc (CD) to print at in-store PictureMaker kiosks or e-mail via Kodak's partnership with America Online, called "You've Got Pictures." The company had also discovered a way to counter Fuji's constant cost-cutting in the low-end 100-speed film market by developing a multilayered strategy that allowed it to command a premium for higher-end 400- and 800-speed film while still enjoying healthy profits in the APS arena, where a price war did not exist.

In June 1999, Fisher announced he would leave his post before his contract expired, leaving his second-in-command, Carp, to be CEO at the onset of 2000. Under Carp's watch, Kodak continued the "Take pictures. Further" umbrella theme by maintaining the focus on usage groups and whole product lines rather than specific offerings. At the start of the new millennium, Kodak embarked on a five-year, $75 million youth marketing push via Saatchi & Saatchi Kid Connection, with its Max Flash one-time-use camera as the cornerstone product. The aim was to make everyday picture-taking an intrinsic part of teen socialization, in keeping with Fisher's idea that encouraging picture-taking is a sure-fire marketing strategy for the photographic giant. Also in 2000, Kodak cast a wide net to market its digital suite of products and services to the masses, showing consumers how digital could be integrated with traditional film.

As Kodak entered the 21st century, the influence of Fisher—the only non-Kodak man to ever run the company—was clear. The number-one camera company, with 1999 sales exceeding $14 billion (and $441 million in ad spending, according to *Advertising Age*) continued to develop new digital products and services while at the same time remaining true to the core camera and film business that won it its lead position in the industry.

CARA BEARDI

Further Reading

Brayer, Elizabeth, *George Eastman: A Biography*, Baltimore, Maryland: Johns Hopkins University Press, 1996

Collins, Douglas, *The Story of Kodak*, New York: Abrams, 1990

Eastman Kodak Company, *The Business of Filmmaking*, Rochester, New York: Eastman Kodak, 1978

Frangos, Stephen J., and Steven Bennet, "Turnaround at Kodak Park," *The Business Quarterly* 58, no. 3 (1994)

Gill, Arthur, and James Fenton, *You Press the Button, We Do the Rest*, Bath, Avon: RPS Historical Group, 1980

Lubove, Seth, "Eastman Kodak: Does It Finally Have Its Act Together?" *Forbes* 26 (November 1990)

Swasy, Alicia, *Changing Focus: Kodak and the Battle to Save a Great American Company*, New York: Times Business, 1997

Uterrback, J.M., "Developing Technologies: The Eastman Kodak Story," *The McKinsey Quarterly* 1 (1995)

West, Nancy Martha, *Kodak and the Lens of Nostalgia*, Charlottesville: University Press of Virginia, 2000

E-Commerce

Dubbed the most important new advertising medium since television, the World Wide Web surpassed all expectations with its monumental growth and economic impact in the late 1990s. In a startling turnaround, however, this meteoric growth was quickly quashed in 2000 and 2001, resulting in numerous layoffs and the closing of hundreds of e-commerce and content sites—the "dot-bomb," as the collapse was dubbed.

Keys to Success

The rapid initial success the Web as a commercial medium can be attributed to three factors. First, content and commerce are more closely integrated on the Web than in other forms of advertising; users can view almost any product and be a "click" away from buying it. The proximity of content and commerce explains why Web content sites such as the *New York Times* on the Web <http://www.nytimes.com/> and CNN.com <http://www.cnn.com/> have added commercial links, while commerce sites such as those of

Coca-Cola Company <http://www.cocacola.com/> and Nike <http://www.nike.com/> have added editorial content. The Web is a crucial part of most marketing plans and advertising strategies for every "e-tailer" from Amazon.com to ZanyBrainy.com. Technologies such as interactive banner advertising, cable access, personalization engines, Java, push, and intranets and extranets have entirely rewritten the rules for on-line marketing.

Second, the advent of portable computers and screens in the 1990s made the reading of on-line content more convenient than it had been previously. As new Web start-ups compete for audiences in the 21st century, the shift of ad revenue from traditional print media to digital-media companies such as America Online (with 33 million members worldwide) will likely accelerate. Newspapers, which earn 40 percent of their revenue from classified ads, are likely to suffer as a result.

Third, most Web content is free, and global Internet advertising companies such as DoubleClick support this free content by means of a variety of strategies, ranging from direct e-mail marketing to personalized promotions. Jupiter Media Metrix measures Internet and digital-media audience usage with targeted Web-traffic measurements to gauge advertising effectiveness.

Advent of the "Dot-com"

Internet first became a household word in the mid-1990s. Speaking at the April 2000 conference of the American Society of Newspaper Editors, the oldest and largest U.S. newspaper editors' group, Steve Case, chairman and chief executive officer (CEO) of America Online, one of the world's largest interactive media companies, said:

> Ten years ago, the Internet was the exclusive province of researchers. Just five years ago, the World Wide Web barely existed, there was no talk about a "new economy," and, hard though it may be to believe, "e" was just the fifth letter in the alphabet. Today, more than 200 million people are on-line worldwide. . . . There are around 800 million Web pages, covering everything from world markets to world wrestling. And "e" has become the prefix for a massive social and economic transformation.

As Case observed, the "e" (for electronic) concept has become commonplace; in addition to e-tail, among the many new coinages that incorporate it are e-business and e-commerce. While these terms are often used interchangeably, e-commerce covers the broad range of buying and selling of goods and services on the Internet, especially the World Wide Web.

The vast access to information on the Internet spawned myriad advertising and marketing strategies. As new Web sites proliferated, so-called "dot-com marketers" faced the formidable challenge of cutting through the clutter. Beginning in the 1990s the term *dot-com* (also, *dot.com*, *dotcom*, and *dot com*) came to be widely used to refer to Web-based companies, Web spin-offs, and Internet start-ups, as well as to any Web site intended for business use. The term *dot-com* came to be shorthand for any kind of commercial Web site. (The term derives from the ".com" suffix that forms the last part of the Web address for most U.S. Internet-based commercial entities.)

Every new medium is launched via older, established media. Thus, even dot-com companies began by relying on traditional media to reach the mass market. While the average U.S. advertiser spent 29.4 percent of its national TV budget on cable in 1999, the average dot-com company spent 40.2 percent of its comparable budget on cable. The 2000 Super Bowl was nicknamed the "dot-com bowl" because of the high number of Web-based companies—17—each of which paid an average of $2.2 million for a 30-second ad to reach the estimated 160 million-plus viewers. The list of advertisers included AutoTrader.com, Britannica.com, Computer.com, E*Trade Securities, Hotjobs.com, MicroStrategy, Monster.com, and Pets.com. Fourteen of the 17 did not advertise during the previous year's Super Bowl. With so many debuting e-companies seeking to advertise in 2000, the cost of advertising was up 38 percent from the $1.6 million average of the previous year

and was predicted to continue to increase. Predicting the future, however, can be risky, and following the crash of e-commerce in 2000 and 2001, the 2002 Super Bowl saw average prices for a 30-second spot drop to $1.9 million.

Super Bowl exposure is frequently cited as the pinnacle of brand building—Apple Computer chose the 1984 telecast to launch the Macintosh—but this enormous audience is not always as receptive as advertisers had hoped. The clutter created by the proliferation of dot-com advertising—combined with their near-universal reliance on offbeat humor in commercials—has left many consumers bewildered if not annoyed.

The job-search site Monster.com took a huge risk during the 1999 Super Bowl and scored. It spent the majority of its ad budget on its phenomenally successful debut spot "I Want to Be a Yesman;" traffic on the site went up 117 percent after the ad, and the levels remained high for many months.

A naked man answering the door for a pizza delivery (Beyond.com), a young executive dropping his cell phone in a urinal (AltaVista.com), and a gerbil shot from a cannon into a brick wall (Outpost.com)—were just a few of the outrageous, horrifying, hilarious, or just plain obnoxious images used in 1999 by dot-com companies flooding the airwaves with "edgy" advertising. Despite the dominance of e-commerce spots in the 2000 Super Bowl, many critics felt that the ads were not at the same level as those from years past. As *Advertising Age* put it, "Most e-sites left little behind but gaping holes and fuzzy memories of something-or-other.com that promises to provide who-knows-what." In 2000 and 2001 the percentage of Super Bowl spots purchased by dot-com marketers declined.

Driven by the desire to go public, dot-com advertisers were more interested in getting noticed immediately and bringing traffic to their sites than in building a brand. In the attention-deficit-afflicted Internet world, there was barely time to develop a product, let alone to craft a well-thought-out strategy and creative campaign. Thus, the "Dot-Com Bowl" in 2000 proved to be a bust for some advertisers. For instance, an E*Trade ad featured two elderly gentlemen and a dancing chimp in the company's T-shirt, followed by an on-screen message, "Well, we have just wasted two million bucks. What are you doing with your money?" Several ad critics remarked that E*Trade did not say anything about why trading on-line was better than conventional trading or why it was better to trade with E*Trade than with other on-line companies. Likewise, an ad message for the on-line, direct marketing company Lifeminders.com stated, "This is the worst commercial on the Super Bowl." An ad cited as obscure and befuddling was WebMD.com's "Time wasted in healthcare" spot, in which sports legend Muhammad Ali was featured shadow boxing with the camera. The ad suggested that Ali's profound medical problems could be addressed reasonably on a Web site. Critics pointed out that there was a different voice and a different attitude in the company's representation of itself on TV and its appearance on the Web. Some dot-coms, however, may have been less concerned with generating interest among consumers than with attracting the attention of investors. The purpose of these ads may simply have been publicity—a way to get through the clutter and to be written and talked about, albeit an expensive way.

Some dot-com ads succeeded in emerging from the clutter. The first broadcast campaign of the on-line magazine Salon.com, created by Odiorne, Wilde, Narraway & Partners, San Francisco, California, was designed to reflect the diverse cast of characters who assemble on the Salon.com site. Its television spot, which featured a series of digitally contrived interactions among famous people—for example, former U.S. Attorney General Janet Reno dancing with Microsoft co-founder Bill Gates, was a metaphorical representation of *Salon* magazine's "virtual dinner party" theme.

During the 1999 and 2000 holiday seasons Amazon.com, via FCB Worldwide, San Francisco, hilariously evoked the circa-1961 days of Lawrence Welk and Mitch Miller with a sweater-clad men's chorus singing chirpy songs of Christmas cheer about the wonders of holiday shopping on-line. The TV spots for Amazon.com's on-line-shopping emporium included brand-benefiting lyrics such as: "Amazon's got a lot of books and DVDs, / like Harvard's got a lot of Ph.D.'s. / Toys and electronics and tools, / like Chinese poker has a lot of rules. / Amazon.com's got a lot."

Some Web advertisers presented TV spots that even traditional marketers could admire. Working with agency Fallon-McElligott, Minneapolis, Minnesota, Drugstore.com came up with a campaign that simultaneously informed and entertained. In one of these spots, set to a *Mission: Impossible*–like sound track, a woman relaxed in her bath as several people in jumpsuits stealthily replenished her cache of diapers, soap, aspirin—even the bubble bath resting on the edge the tub. A voice-over delivered the message: "You have better things to do than go to the drugstore. Let the drugstore come to you."

The advertising allocation for an average dot-com business was $8.2 million in 1999, of which the largest proportion—$3 million—was for on-line ads, followed by $1.9 million for television ads, according to Forrester Research. Of the remainder, $1 million was allocated for radio, $830,000 for newspapers, $570,000 for magazines, $475,000 for direct mail, $334,000 for outdoor advertising, and $160,000 for other media.

Between 1998 and 2000 it became nearly impossible to watch prime-time television or thumb through a major magazine and not see a dot-com ad. Internet ad expenditures for television (including network, spot, syndication, and cable) in the first half of 1999 exceeded $398 million, compared to $323 million in 1998 and $173 million in 1997. By the end of 1999 total revenue for the U.S. television industry from on-line and Internet services was estimated at $1 billion, according to the Television Bureau of Advertising, the local television stations' association for advertising issues.

Gaining credibility and establishing trust are central to on-line business strategies. To this end, in the late 1990s many dot-com companies were investing roughly 70 percent of their ad budgets in traditional media or off-line advertising, recognizing that these media were more effective than on-line advertising for the purposes of branding and name recognition. For example, when Priceline.com was launched in 1998, only 41 percent of U.S. households had Internet access, and the company realized it would be advertising largely to people who were not yet able to use its service. Priceline built its brand through radio and print ads, with campaigns created in-house. By late 1999 Priceline had started advertising on-line in affiliate deals, which pay Web masters a commission for sales they refer. (Affiliate marketing deals unite e-commerce sites with smaller affiliate sites, which earn money for referring customers. Affiliate deals achieve more immediate return on investment by paying for performance only. Advertising costs for this "refer-the-sale-and-get-paid" business model are significantly lower. Such relationships, which seek to drive traffic as well as sales, are available for books, credit cards, loans, and other products or services.)

A 1998 Forrester study of consumer confidence in advertising found that consumers considered on-line ads to be the least trustworthy of all forms of advertising (with direct mail the next most suspect). From the outset, therefore, any new company using the Internet as an ad medium faced the serious challenge of establishing its credibility—a task made all the more difficult after the collapse of the Internet economy.

In the early days the dot-com business model, to some extent, demanded hype. The idea was to get "eyeballs"—that is, to call attention to the Web site—in a hurry. In the late 1990s companies embarking on Internet advertising felt that they needed to move quickly to claim the top spots in their markets. Ad budgets were not a problem, as dot-coms had no shortage of venture-capital cash and investor funds. All this changed in 2000 when dot-coms began to be held to a standard that required them to show some profitability. Thus, the earlier business model has proven less popular with the market since 2000.

Role of the Agency

For all the new money the dot-com companies brought to the ad market in the late 1990s, a number of advertising agencies did not find this new kind of client easy to work with. As many of the young dot-com entrepreneurs came to traditional ad agencies seeking help in building their brands, it became clear that there was a considerable contrast in culture between the new world of the start-up Internet companies and the old world of the agencies. Over the decades ad agencies evolved practices and protocols that placed high value on long-term agency-client relationships, a sense of partnership, and structured methods of evaluating and reviewing ad strategies. These practices grew out of doing business for many years with established marketers that were risk averse and preferred methodical decision making.

The typical dot-com company, on the other hand, was often driven by a spirit of pioneering innovation, and its management was more likely to be averse to precedents and restrictions than to risk. This attitude produced an increasing number of agency-client clashes over business styles. Dot-com managers were often willing to invest long hours and give up holidays to pursue dreams of becoming rich. But most agency executives were salaried and accustomed to normal work hours. The dot-com entrepreneur was likely to be absorbed in the technology and content of his product. The agency executive often found a client with little or no understanding of traditional advertising tools. The dot-com owner grew restless, while the agency executive grew frustrated. Often the fundamental differences in business style came down to something as trivial as dress codes. The account executive long accustomed to coat-and-tie formality was sometimes distrusted by an e-client who dressed as if he or she were still in college.

As a consequence, the number of top agencies resigning the business of dot-com clients was unusually high. PlanetRx.com was an on-line drug retailer, whose agency, Goodby, Silverstein & Partners, resigned the account after a few months in 1999. The marketer had demanded an immediate campaign but could not make basic decisions on goals. When it brought in another agency to undertake a separate project, Goodby resigned. Drugstore.com had brief relationships with LeftField Advertising, San Francisco, California, and McCann-Erickson before moving to Fallon McElligott. But the company's admitted lack of commitment to any consistent approach made it a difficult client to serve, according to the *Wall Street Journal*.

Black Rocket, a small San Francisco agency, dropped Buy.com after several months, reportedly because it could not get approval on a creative direction. Another agency, Citron Haligman Bedecarre, dropped a $20-million start-up company because its CEO and marketing vice president could not agree. Publicis & Hal Riney resigned an Internet start-up in December 1999 because "the company's objectives were a moving target." These were among the growing pains of an industry with great financial resources at its disposal but few historic patterns to govern its relationships with long-established ad agencies. On the other hand, many agency people were excited by the prospects of being in the vanguard of a dot-com start-up company and left agency positions to do so. By the end of 2000, however, significant numbers were finding the instability of the e-business atmosphere chaotic and trying to return to the relatively stable atmosphere of their old agencies, many unsuccessfully as the "dot-bomb" fallout left many agencies retrenching rather than hiring.

Strategies

Advertising and marketing strategies for e-commerce can be divided into eight areas:

1. Designing and writing advertisements for "virtual storefronts," such as Lands' End's Web site <http://www.landsend.com/>, with on-line catalogs, sometimes gathered into a "virtual mall," such as ZDNet's Computershopper.com.
2. Gathering and using demographic data obtained from Web contacts or from such services as Jupiter Media Metrix and ACNielsen's NetRatings <http://www.netratings.com/ >.
3. Using on-line information services such as the electronic data interchange (EDI) for the business-to-business exchange of data, as documented by the EDI InfoNet <http://www.wpc-edi.com/>. The EDI is a set of standards for controlling the transfer of business documents, such as purchase orders and invoices, between computers. The goals of the EDI are to eliminate paperwork and to shorten response time. For it to be effective, users must agree on standards for the formatting and exchange of information.
4. Attracting public attention to a product or business with e-mail, faxes, and on-line media to reach prospects and communicate with established customers, as documented in Internet.com's Electronic Commerce Guide <http://ecommerce.internet.com/>.
5. Promoting business-to-business buying and selling, as outlined by the Interactive Advertising Bureau <http://www.iab.net/>. Such business-to-business trade may involve updating search-engine registries and specialized directories, participating in Usenet newsgroups, compiling information about customers, and using other technological means to market on-line, while incorporating traditional marketing methods.
6. Ensuring the security of business transactions, as documented by the United States Commerce Department's Computer Security Resource Clearinghouse <http://csrc.ncsl.nist.gov/>.
7. Building relationships with valued customers, providing quality customer service and support, building brand loyalty, and offering free information and services to attract and keep new customers.
8. Customizing advertising content according to the audience. Since Web sites cross national boundaries, global consumer companies such as Levi Strauss & Company <http://www.us.levi.com/> and Yahoo! <http://www.yahoo.com/> feature Internet advertising content that is attuned to verbal nuances and cultural differences or that may be offered in different languages to accommodate people from different groups and countries.

"Clicks and Mortar"

Taking a cue from e-commerce "purebreds" such as Amazon.com, most brick-and-mortar companies quickly adopted the strategy of "clicks and mortar"—the common-sense melding of everything that is fast, seamless, and slick in e-commerce with traditional services and distribution. The bookseller Barnes and Noble, for example, did not condemn its real-world stores to the wrecking ball when it launched Barnesandnoble.com. However, dot-coms and traditional retail stores did not always mix well. Dot-com spin-offs usually were either built separately from or operated outside corporate bureaucracies; they tended to have a more hip image and funding from venture-capital dollars. There were exceptions: financial services firm Charles Schwab & Company merged its independent e.Schwab division into the parent company because its subscribers also wanted access to Schwab's high level of conventional advice and service. Other companies such as Wal-Mart Stores, Inc.; Home Depot, Inc.; Staples., Inc.; and OfficeDepot, Inc., tried to integrate their on-line operations to form clicks-and-mortar alliances. Many on-line subsidiaries of retail and catalog companies such as Circuit City stores, Inc.; OfficeMax, Inc.; and Gap, Inc., attempted to integrate their operations into their parent companies.

Powerful technology-based marketing, aggressive advertising, and a wide consumer base created e-commerce successes such as eBay <http://www.ebay.com/> and Amazon.com <http://www.amazon.com/>. In spite of, in some cases, astronomical valuations on the stock market—Amazon.com's worth was estimated at more than that of the combined industries of traditional book retailing and publishing—many had yet to make a profit by the end of the 20th century, and it was unclear when they would. The largest Barnes & Noble bookstore in the United States still carried only 200,000 titles in the late 1990s. Amazon.com offered 4.5 million volumes and was "located" on some 25 million computer screens.

In their efforts to harness the full power of the Internet for promotional, advertising, and selling endeavors, marketers and advertisers adopted technological innovations that replaced mundane tasks once routinely handled by a labor-intensive sales staff, thereby streamlining business operations. Most on-line ordering systems such as that at Dell Computer Corporation's Web site <http://www.dell.com/> boasted electronic inventory, on-line pricing, custom quoting, and on-line ordering and order tracking.

DEBASHIS ("DEB") AIKAT

See also History: 1990s; Internet/World Wide Web; *and color plate in this volume*

Further Reading
Barrett, Neil, *Advertising on the Internet: How to Get Your Message Across on the World Wide Web,* London: Kogan Page, 1997; 2nd edition, 1999
Forbes, Thom, *Advertising,* Gloucester, Massachusetts: Rockport, 2000
Janal, Daniel S., *Online Marketing Handbook: How to Promote, Advertise, and Sell Your Products and Services on the Internet,* New York: Wiley, 1998
Melin, Mark, *Computer In$elligence: Transform Your Bottom Line with Interactive Marketing Magic,* Worcester, Massachusetts: Chandler House Press, 2000
Schumann, David W., and Esther Thorson, *Advertising and the World Wide Web,* Mahwah, New Jersey: Erlbaum, 1999
Sterne, Jim, *World Wide Web Marketing: Integrating the Web into Your Marketing Strategy,* New York: Wiley, 1999
Zeff, Robbin Lee, and Brad Aronson, *Advertising on the Internet,* New York: Wiley, 1997; 2nd edition, 1999

Education

A vast growth in the advertising industry preceded the introduction of advertising as a discipline in colleges. Before the Industrial Revolution, advertisements were usually simple, designed to appeal the illiterate majority—for example, a sign with a picture of a shoe posted outside a cobbler's shop. One did not need an education to create such advertisements, and very little schooling was available to most people.

During the industrial boom of the 19th century, new technologies increased the production of commodities, improved transportation, and created new media. Together, these developments led to the rise of mass consumption and facilitated the emergence of advertising as a stimulus of demand. Catalogs and flyers produced by manufacturers were among the earliest forms of modern advertising, but historians conventionally date the origins of advertising as a profession to 1841, when Volney Palmer, the first "advertising agent" in the United States, began selling newspaper space to the promoters of goods and services. Once advertising was established in the business world, the academic world began to recognize a need for trained advertising workers, and advertising education as we know it today began.

Programs and Degrees

Marketing, journalism, and advertising education at four-year degree-granting U.S. colleges and universities developed sporadically between the end of the 19th century and World War II, after which an explosive growth in the discipline occurred. In 1893, a half century after Palmer began selling ad space, advertising was the subject of a college course for the first time in a class taught by Joseph French Johnson at the Wharton School of Business, University of Pennsylvania, in Philadelphia. Although historians are not certain when the first marketing course was offered, there is evidence of marketing courses at the Wharton School as early as 1881.

The growth of advertising education in journalism programs began at about the same time; advertising education was part of the curriculum from the outset at the world's first school of journalism at the University of Missouri, which was founded in 1908 (although journalism courses were first offered at the university as early as 1878 and advertising was taught in 1898). The University of Missouri also claims to have offered the first graduate course in advertising in 1921. Growth in the graduate-level discipline was strong over the next several decades—6 institutions offered graduate courses during the 1930s; in the 1940s the number had risen to 16; in the 1950s there were 27; and 35 institutions taught graduate-level advertising classes in 1964.

Five institutions were known to offer advertising courses as part of either a business or a journalism curriculum in 1909, with the number rising to 11 by 1919. A 1955 study by Harold Hardy reported that 197 institutions taught advertising in the 1930s; 318 schools taught advertising in 1946; and 482 in 1950. Part of

In addition to college and university programs in advertising and marketing, professional schools such as Atlanta, Georgia-based Creative Circus offer certificates in creative aspects of the industry such as design and art direction.
Courtesy of Creative Circus; Phil Gable, Copywriter; Marcia Mayoral, Designer.

the difficulty in tracing this history is that advertising has been taught as a part of many diverse disciplines: in addition to its place in journalism and business programs, advertising has been included in courses in marketing, economics, psychology, English, and philosophy.

College students in the United States could not major in advertising prior to 1909, but by 1919 a total of six programs for advertising majors existed. An organized degree-granting program in advertising started at the University of Missouri around 1913 (another source claims that an advertising sequence was founded at Missouri in 1908), and New York University in New York City established an advertising major in 1915. Again, there was strong growth over time: in the 1930s there were 19 major programs; in the 1940s there were 43; in the 1950s there were 59; and in 1964 there were 63.

The University of Missouri granted the first degree in advertising in 1915. Six more institutions would grant degrees during the 1920s. In the 1930s, 13 institutions were granting advertising degrees, and the growing trend was established: 30 institutions granted degrees in the 1940s, 50 in the 1950s, and 54 institutions were granting degrees by 1964. At the end of the 1990s, only one doctoral program in advertising was in existence, at the University of Texas at Austin. Doctorates in mass communication, a discipline that includes advertising courses, are prevalent at a number of schools, and 31 such doctorates were awarded in 2000.

From fledgling programs came the first college graduates trained in the practice of advertising. Data on the number of college degrees granted prior to 1950 are very sketchy. Undergraduate degrees awarded from 1958 to 1960 totaled 1,492; from 1961 through 1964, 3,464 degrees were awarded. During the 1998–99 academic year 4,933 degrees were awarded, with another 1,816 degrees reported from joint advertising/public relations (ad/pr) programs. There were 106 master's degrees in advertising awarded from 1958 to 1960, and from 1961 through 1964 the number of master's grew to 130. No doctorate degrees are reported in this time period. In the 1998–99 academic year, 499 master's degrees were awarded by advertising programs and an additional 164 were granted by ad/pr programs. Two doctorates were awarded in 1981 (one each from the University of Illinois and the University of Tennessee). Figures from 1998–99 show that 23 individuals earned Ph.D. degrees from advertising and advertising/public relations programs. (See Appendix for list of U.S. programs in advertising.)

Noteworthy Educators

The first known individual to hold a full-time position as an advertising faculty member was Joseph E. Chasnoff in 1911, at the University of Missouri. He was succeeded a year later by John B. Powell, who would later found the first advertising student fraternity, Alpha Delta Sigma. By 1919 five institutions had full-time faculty teaching advertising. Five more institutions added advertising faculty in the 1930s; 19 more institutions hired faculty in the discipline in the 1940s; in the next decade 14 more schools added advertising faculty; and by 1964 there were 60 U.S. institutions with full-time advertising faculty.

Student Organizations

Student organizations are often a natural offshoot of campus programs, and advertising education was typical in this regard. Alpha Delta Sigma began in 1913 as a national professional advertising fraternity for men, with local chapters at the Universities of Missouri, Kentucky, and Illinois. Fifty undergraduate and 11 professional chapters had been established by 1964. Gamma Alpha Chi was founded in 1920 at the University of Missouri as a female counterpart to Alpha Delta Sigma. By 1964, 37 chapters had been founded, of which 22 were active.

In 1972 the two organizations merged into a single group, nationally headquartered at Texas Tech University. One year later they were incorporated into the American Advertising Federation

(AAF). Today there are some 120 college chapters in the AAF program. The name Alpha Delta Sigma was retained by the AAF and is used today to refer to the national honor society for advertising students.

Development since World War II

The conclusion of World War II brought about massive changes in U.S. society. Factories shifted from the manufacture of war materiel to the production of consumer goods; mass media burgeoned; and the introduction of television revolutionized mass communications. Each of these developments helped foster a demand for individuals trained in advertising to create messages and sell media space and time, and U.S. colleges and universities responded—by 1950, 30 advertising degree programs were in place in the United States, playing a prominent role in the college curriculum.

In 1959, however, studies by the Ford and Carnegie foundations led to the decline in the position of advertising in the academic structure, particularly in schools of business. Both studies recommended that the number of hands-on courses in advertising be reduced and that colleges place an increased emphasis on management and theory. The effects of these studies were evident as 13 schools of business discontinued advertising programs in the 1960s, although nine of the universities whose business schools dropped advertising continued to support advertising programs in their journalism departments.

In 1965 Billy I. Ross published his dissertation as *Advertising Education* (in conjunction with the American Academy of Advertising [AAA] and the American Association of Advertising Agencies, which is perhaps better known as the "Four A's"). That same year, he and Donald G. Hileman (dean of the College of Communication, University of Tennessee) began to issue annual updates on Ross's initial research entitled *Where Shall I Go to College to Study Advertising?* After Hileman's death in 1984, Ross continued to publish the volume annually, joined in 1991 by his associate at Texas Tech University Keith F. Johnson. In 1992 Ross also published a 25-year update *The Status of Advertising Education.*

In 1995 Ross and Johnson added separate data on joint advertising/public relations programs and on programs in public relations alone to their annual report, and the volume's name was accordingly changed to *Where Shall I Go to Study Advertising and Public Relations?* All advertising programs at degree-granting schools of journalism, mass communications, or business are included in the research. Aggregate results are published in various media and on a Web site (*http://www.mcom.ttu.edu/wsig/*). Data from 1960 to 2000 show a greater than sevenfold growth in the annual number of degrees granted and the level of enrollment, as well as a phenomenal growth in the number of faculty, from 35 to 554. (In addition, 366 faculty members currently teach part-time in advertising or advertising/public relations programs.)

Organizations for Advertising Educators

The National Association of Teachers of Advertising was founded in 1915; in 1924 the word *marketing* was added to the organiza-

tion's title, to become the National Association of Teachers of Advertising and Marketing. In 1933 the word *advertising* was dropped from the organization's name, and in 1937 it was renamed the American Marketing Association.

The AAA, the premier organization for advertising educators, began as the brainchild of Harry Hepner at Syracuse University in Syracuse, New York, in 1957, as the Advertising Federation of America (AFA). At a 1958 Dallas, Texas, meeting of the AFA, a formal structure for the organization was devised. Today the AAA has more than 600 members worldwide, including teachers of advertising and marketing as well as industry researchers.

In 1966 the Association for Education in Journalism and Mass Communication (AEJMC) established an advertising division. It currently has more than 250 members, most of whom are teachers of advertising and public relations in schools of mass communication around the world.

Advertising Education Publications

Three publications have assisted advertising education over the years. Since 1963 the *Journal of Advertising* has served as the academic journal of the AAA, which also publishes proceedings of its annual conference. The AEJMC publishes *Journalism/Mass Communications Educator,* which is specifically targeted to teachers at mass communications schools, and in 1996 the advertising division of the AEJMC began issuing the *Journal of Advertising Education,* which features articles written specifically for college advertising teachers.

Future Directions

Just as college educators have always adjusted their course criteria to reflect innovations in the advertising industry, today's advertising faculty are revising the curriculum to reflect the most recent changes in the communications industry, such as the increasing cultural and economic significance of the Internet relative to more traditional forms of print and broadcast media. Today's students are taught to use and create Web sites, to conduct research based on electronic data, and to approach advertising, promotion, and public relations from the perspective of the "global village." Furthermore, integrated marketing communications, or IMC, is an emerging discipline being pursued at many schools, most notably at the University of Colorado, Boulder, and Northwestern University, Evanston, Illinois. This field teaches students how to combine all producer-based communications into a single-message-sourced campaign.

Another recent development in advertising education is the growth of joint advertising/public relations programs, with some universities merging two independent course sequences into one (currently 44 U.S. programs offer this joint degree). Although a certain economy of scale may help motivate such mergers, this trend also reflects the fact that the communications industry of the future will likely eradicate the line of distinction between the professional roles of the advertising executive and the public relations specialist.

BILLY I. ROSS

Further Reading

Bovee, Courtland L., and William F. Arens, *Contemporary Advertising*, Homewood, Illinois: Irwin, 1982

Richards, Jef I., and Elizabeth Gigi Taylor, "Rankings of Advertising Programs by Advertising Educators," *Journal of Advertising Education* 1, no. 1 (1996)

Ross, Billy I., *Advertising Education: Programs in Four-Year American Colleges and Universities*, Lubbock: Texas Technological College, 1965

Ross, Billy I., *The Status of Advertising Education*, Baton Rouge, Louisiana: Advertising Education, 1991

Ross, Billy I., and Keith F. Johnson, *Where Shall I Go to Study Advertising and Public Relations?* Lubbock, Texas: Advertising Education Publications, 2001

A. Eicoff & Company

Founded by Alvin Eicoff in 1965; purchased by Ogilvy & Mather in 1982; continues to operate under its original name as a unit of WPP Group's OgilvyOne.

Major Clients

Guarantee Trust (Student Life Insurance)
Jelmar (Tarn-X)
Reed Union (Nu Vinyl)
Schwinn (Bowflex)
Time-Life Books (Mysteries of the Unknown)
M.B. Walton, Inc. (Roll-O-Matic)

After a succession of partnerships that dissolved amicably as the partners went their separate ways, Alvin Eicoff struck out on his own, launching A. Eicoff & Company in 1965. It soon became recognized as one of the most successful television direct-response advertising agencies, first in Chicago, Illinois, and then throughout the United States. Eicoff credited much of the agency's early success to lessons he learned from his mentor, Lee Ratner (the promoter of the insecticide d-Con and Lehigh Acres, Florida), a trailblazer in broadcast direct advertising. The Eicoff agency had a reputation as a maverick in the ad industry. Although its ads were sometimes criticized for being tacky or cheap, few criticized the agency's results. By 1973 it was billing $30 million.

Eicoff's vision was deceptively simple: create direct-response commercials to generate profitable sales. Some advertising agencies were concerned with the artistry of creative advertising for its own sake, others desired a Clio or Echo Award to gain industry recognition, and still others wanted to build a client's image. A. Eicoff & Company, however, focused on generating sales. Eicoff's oft-repeated slogan was "immediate measurable results."

To achieve such results, the Eicoff agency developed a number of novel practices and major innovations in direct-response television advertising. At the time of their implementation most of these new ideas and methods were regarded as misguided at best; however, many later achieved widespread acceptance and became standard industry practices. Among others, Eicoff introduced the carnival-style pitchman on TV, produced a consumer-oriented direct-response sales presentation, formulated the magic-number concept, instituted the key outlet marketing concept, created a sales resistance theory along with a corollary isolation factor, and compiled a product market index.

In the early days of television advertising, during the late 1940s and 1950s, Eicoff formulated the idea of using a pitchman to sell ads on television upon seeing a promoter sell an "amazing sex pill" to a live audience in Peoria, Illinois. The hackneyed phrase "amazing sex pill" gave him the inspiration—if the tactic worked in Peoria, it could work on TV. The passage from traveling medicine show and carnival barker to television commercials was a natural transition. Eicoff employed a variety of pitchmen to sell a number of products, including knife sharpeners, weed killers, fishing kits, "magic" towels, food slicers, chrome cleaners, cooking pots, fly killers, and bug sprays. The commercial lasted the length of the pitch, with added time for a tag. For example, if the pitch took 12 minutes, then the commercial was 15 minutes with a 3-minute tag. If the pitch took 26 minutes, then it was a 30-minute commercial with a 4-minute tag. The TV pitchman started dying out in the early 1960s, when the Federal Communications Commission mandated a two-minute maximum commercial break. Eicoff, among others, later resurrected the pitchman in the time-unconstrained infomercials of the late 1980s and 1990s.

The Eicoff agency developed a consumer-oriented sales presentation that outlined the stages through which a commercial had to move the consumer to achieve a direct response. These stages were summarized by the acronym TPS: "tease 'em, please 'em, and seize 'em." The idea was to tease the TV audience by showing a problem that generated a high level of concern; please the viewers by solving the problem with a unique product that consumers could not find elsewhere; and seize them with a sales offer that was too good to refuse and compelled the customer to buy on the spot. Eicoff's commercials for M.B. Walton, Inc.'s Roll-O-Matic mop exemplified the TPS approach. The commercial started the tease by showing the problem: a housewife laboring to mop a kitchen floor. The voice-over lamented, "One of the most tiring backbreaking household chores is scrubbing and waxing floors . . . the constant bending, stooping, and straining to wring out your mop." The Roll-O-Matic offered a solution that pleased: "The no-stoop, no bend, self-wringing mop." Once the pain and strain of mopping was eliminated, the finale was an offer too good to pass up: "Buy it for only $9.95, try it for 30 days, stock is limited so call today, satisfaction guaranteed or your money back."

The key outlet marketing concept, another tactic pioneered by Eicoff, offered a parallel advertising-distribution method of selling. The advertised product was sold to a selected supermarket or drugstore chain, such as Atlantic and Pacific Tea Company, Woolworth Corporation, or Walgreen Company, where the point-of-purchase display emphasized in big bold letters: "As Advertised on TV." Each television market, based on the area of dominant influence, or ADI, was treated as a profit center. Sales were tracked and ad budgets adjusted based on market-by-market profitability, which followed the Eicoff company line of immediate measurable results. Using the key outlet marketing concept, Eicoff created direct ads for successfully selling such products as housewares, lawn and garden products, small appliances, sewing devices, vitamins, and cosmetics. The concept is represented in the successful selling of BBI's Handi-Screen, a round mesh screen with a handle designed to cover a frying pan and prevent grease from splattering on the stovetop and the cook; the product was priced at $2.98. Eicoff produced the commercial for $7,000, distributed Handi-Screens at drugstore chains in more than 70 markets, and sold upwards of 4 million units in the first year (1963) alone.

The magic-number concept, another Eicoff innovation, referred to the maximum advertising expenditure allowable per sale of a product to generate a given level of profit. The theory was that if advertising expenses approximated the predetermined number, everything worked "like magic." Grant Company's Hair Wiz, for example, a product that cut hair to "save a trip to the barber" was priced at $2.98 and sold in key market outlets in 1966. The retailer received a 30 percent trade margin, leaving about $2.10. Then the costs, totaling $1, were deducted: production, 35 cents per unit; overhead and administration expense, 15 cents; miscellaneous costs, 10 cents; and targeted profit, 40 cents. Once the dollar's worth of costs were subtracted from $2.10, a magic number of $1.10 remained, which was the amount allowable for advertising to generate the desired profit per unit of 40 cents. If 1,000 units were sold in each of 50 markets a week, total profits would exceed $1 million a year

Eicoff's sales-resistance theory was based on research showing that there were times of the day and days of the week when consumers were more resistant to buying in response to advertising. Contrary to accepted direct television advertising practices, the Eicoff agency found that the more popular the show, the greater the sales resistance to the commercial—viewers were alert and did not want to be interrupted with a commercial break in the middle of their favorite TV shows. Eicoff was convinced that sales resistance would be highest during prime time and lowest during late night. Moreover, since people were most mentally alert during the middle of the workweek, sales resistance would be highest during this time. Alternatively, because people were either gearing up for work or winding down from it, sales resistance would taper off toward the weekend. Thus, direct-marketing commercials aired late at night and near the weekend would encounter the least sales resistance because viewers were the most relaxed and had the fewest distractions. Not only did Eicoff's sales-resistance theory identify the most effective commercial time, it provided another important advantage: late night was also the least expensive time to buy commercial spots.

Eicoff also developed a corollary to the sales resistance theory, which the agency termed the "isolation factor." Simply put, isolating an advertisement served to avoid the clutter created by several competitors sharing the two-minute commercial break. The agency thought this approach would also avoid confusing or irritating the viewer with multiple sales messages; it therefore positioned its ads as "the only salesman in the viewer's living room" during a commercial break.

Based on company research Eicoff compiled a product marketing index, or PMI. The PMI provided an index number that compared TV markets based on the number of units of product sold by a given number of advertising dollars. The PMI considered such factors as number of TV stations, advertising rates, product prices, a variety of demographic indices, and seasonal or geographic influences to provide rating of markets. The idea was that a given amount of advertising would sell 20 more units of product in a market having an index number of 120, with a base of 100, but 10 fewer units in a 90-indexed market. Using the PMI, the value of various TV markets was rated not merely on viewer exposure or recall, which were the standard measures of advertising effectiveness, but on actual consumer sales.

With a stream of innovative methods, A. Eicoff & Company evolved into one of the premier direct-response television advertising agencies in the United States. Alvin Eicoff gave up managing daily operations as president to become chairman in 1981, then chairman emeritus the following year. In 1997, in recognition of his many contributions to the industry, he was elected to the Direct Marketing Hall of Fame. Ron Bliwas, who joined the agency as vice president of new business in 1970, was promoted to senior vice president in 1976 and then to president and chief executive officer of the agency in 1981, a position he held at the turn of the century. The agency was purchased by Ogilvy & Mather in 1982 but continued to operate under its original name. At the close of the 20th century, under the umbrella of the WPP Group, it was one of Ogilvy's most profitable divisions.

ERIC H. SHAW

Further Reading

Bliwas, Ron, "A Direct Response Shop's Challenge: Can Your Agency Do This?" *Adweek* (8 November 1993)
Eicoff, Alvin, *Or Your Money Back: For the Business Executive, Student, or Man on the Street: A Practical Way to Turn a Minimum Investment into a Fortune Using Broadcast Advertising*, New York: Crown, 1982

Eicoff, Alvin, *Direct Marketing through Broadcast Media: TV, Radio, Cable, Infomercials, Home Shopping, and More,* Lincolnwood, Illinois: NTC Business Books, 1995

Garfield, Bob, "It's Amazing!!! So Call Now!!!" *Advertising Age* (9 November 1992)

Glick, Susan R., "Nothing Else but Television," *Screen Magazine* (11 December 1989)

Hume, Scott, "Eicoff Savors Economic Downturn," *Advertising Age* (8 October 1990)

E.I. Du Pont de Nemours & Company. *See under* Du Pont

Electronics. *See* Consumer Electronics

Employment of Minorities and Women. *See* Minorities: Employment in the Advertising Industry; Women: Careers in Advertising

---

Endorsement

A commercial endorsement is a personal recommendation for a product or service from a known person encoded into a message directed at a target audience. An endorser's role is substantially different from that of a presenter, someone who merely disseminates product information. Typically, an endorser presents the product or service in a positive light to a broad audience. The endorsement message usually places the object or service within the context of the endorser's personal experience and conveys the recommendation in a natural and interesting manner.

There are at least six types of endorsers: celebrity, expert, lay, chief executive officer (CEO), fictitious, and third-party. Celebrity endorsers, by definition, are individuals known to a large number of people because of the publicity surrounding their lives. They help increase product awareness and acceptance, especially when their personal characteristics and achievements are related to those of the product being endorsed. Examples include Michael Jordan for Nike, Whitney Houston for AT&T Corporation, Tiger Woods for American Express Company, and Bill Cosby for Philip Morris Companies' Jell-O. Expert endorsers are persons perceived to have substantial knowledge or expertise

relevant for evaluating the product. Examples include the former U.S. Surgeon General C. Everett Koop for dental care and the mutual fund manager Peter Lynch for stock investments. Lay endorsers are ordinary people who are not widely recognized but who usually resemble members of the target audience (e.g., a housewife in Maine chosen to endorse Tide Liquid Detergent in a national TV advertising campaign). In such instances endorsers are carefully chosen so that the target audience can identify with them. In addition, the spontaneity that accompanies unrehearsed testimonials from lay endorsers (e.g., when testimonials are recorded with hidden cameras) enhances the sincerity and believability of the messages being communicated. CEO endorsers (e.g., Lee Iacocca for Chrysler or Victor Kiam for Remington shavers) provide a personal statement about their companies' products. Fictitious endorsers may be cartoon characters (e.g., Mickey Mouse or the Energizer Bunny) or actors playing fictitious characters (e.g., Joe Isuzu) that aim to enhance the image and credibility of products. Finally, third-party endorsers are individuals or organizations that stake their credibility on recommendations for one product over others using devices such as the seal of approval awarded by *Good Housekeeping*.

Theoretical Basis

As explained by Gerard Tellis in his book *Advertising and Sales Promotion Strategy* (1997), the theoretical rationales that explain how endorsements work rest on three models: source credibility, source attractiveness, and meaning transfer.

A key tenet of the source credibility model is that, as the credibility of a message increases, the more likely the message is to persuade consumers. For endorsement messages, of course, the source is the endorser. Credibility, in turn, rests on two characteristics of the endorser: expertise and trustworthiness. That is, the credibility of a message increases as (a) the expertise of the endorser increases and (b) the trustworthiness of the endorser increases.

The source attractiveness model, as its name suggests, posits that the persuasiveness of an endorsement message depends on the charisma of the endorser. This, in turn, rests on three characteristics: familiarity, likeability, and the similarity of the endorser to the perspective of the audience. Finally, the meaning transfer model has substantially influenced current thought about endorsements. According to Grant McCracken, a researcher who has studied the process, the meaning transfer model suggests that the rich, powerful, and culturally distinctive meanings associated with a celebrity can be transferred to a product through the endorsement process. From the consumer's perspective, consumption of the product entails the further transfer of these meanings from the brand to the consumer. Thus, McCracken's model traces the sequential transfer of meanings to (a) the celebrity within the cultural context, (b) the product within the endorsement context, and (c) the consumer within the consumption context.

One implication that emerges from the meaning transfer model is that each celebrity embodies a complex mix of meanings. Identifying key meanings that are particularly desirable for a given brand, profiling and choosing a celebrity who possesses these meanings, and, finally, using creativity and skill to transfer them successfully to a brand is a tremendous challenge.

According to McCracken, it is useful to analyze celebrity endorsements by placing the unique, detailed, and powerful meanings packaged into a celebrity within a cultural context. These meanings can encompass specific demographic variables such as class, status, gender, and age. Thus, McCracken characterizes Peter Jennings and John Forsythe as "patrician" men and Catherine Deneuve and Audrey Hepburn as "regal" women. On the one hand, Pierce Brosnan and Diane Sawyer represent the distinction of new wealth, while Larry Hagman and Joan Collins exemplify the brazen and grasping versions of the same category. Tim Matheson and Shelley Long are exemplars of the upper-middle class, John Ritter and Christie Brinkley the middle class, and Patrick Swayze and Suzanne Somers the lower-middle class. In a similar vein, certain celebrities elegantly capture highly gender-specific cultural meanings. According to McCracken, maleness is personified at the extremes by Sylvester Stallone and Dick Cavett, with men such as Arnold Schwarzenegger, Brian Bozworth, Fred Dryer, Tony Danza, Stacey Keach, Paul Newman, Patrick Duffy, Timothy Hutton, Bob Newhart, Tony Randall, and Jeremy Brett somewhere in

"Famous Men of the Day" was one of Barbasol's best-known campaigns. In this 1929 ad baseball great Babe Ruth endorses the shaving cream. *Courtesy of Pfizer, Inc.*

between. Similarly, Loni Anderson and Sigourney Weaver represent extremes of femininity, with Cheryl Ladd, Victoria Principal, Cheryl Tiegs, Pam Dawber, Kate Jackson, and Jane Seymour between them. With respect to age, the extremes range from the militantly youthful (Pee Wee Herman) to the prematurely ancient (Danny DeVito) and from callow youth (Judge Reinhold) to age-authenticated wisdom (E.G. Marshall).

Beyond demographics, celebrities effectively portray subtle nuances in personality and distinctive lifestyles. In a 1998 study Sheila O'Mahony and Tony Meenaghan found that their subjects regarded Sean Connery as "suave, well-groomed and handsome." McCracken's examples of personalities include Ed Asner (the curmudgeon), John Larroquette (the rake), John Cleese (the irritable incompetent), Bronson Pinchot (the bewildered alien), Woody Harrelson (the good-hearted dimwit), Tracey Ulmann (the irrepressibly impudent), Ed McMahon (the indiscriminately jolly), David Letterman (the irascible), and Gary Collins (the blandly agreeable). Other celebrities are associated with distinctive lifestyles: Ken Olin of *thirtysomething* (the quintessential yuppie), Pam Dawber (the stereotypical young professional woman), Bill

Cosby (the perfect dad), Delta Burke of *Designing Women* (the perfect princess), and David Brinkley (the man of wisdom and experience).

McCracken believes that celebrities deliver unique and culturally derived meanings in a manner that noncelebrity endorsers cannot convey. For example, no ordinary person could have marshaled the forbidding severity that John Houseman brought to the Smith Barney tag line created by Ogilvy & Mather, "We make money the old-fashioned way. We earn it." A distinguished writer and producer since the 1930s, Houseman had been introduced to the public as an actor only shortly before he made the ad, when he played the role of a tyrannical but brilliant and incorruptible law professor in the 1973 film *The Paper Chase*. Through his performance in this single role, he came to personify a man with integrity and an intelligence of overwhelming power and authority, precisely the qualities Smith Barney and Ogilvy & Mather needed to empower and sustain their slogan. The commercials may have featured Houseman, but he was such a compelling actor that audiences saw only Professor Kingsfield of the movie. McCracken noted that every famous person has "particular configurations of meanings that can not be found elsewhere." Thus, when Leo McKern succeeded Houseman in the Smith Barney campaign, it was not surprising that he carried different meanings and was less credible than his predecessor.

Brief History: From Lindbergh to Jordan

The scale of the endorsement business has grown impressively over the years. Jules Alberti, president of Endorsements, Inc., has provided an early assessment of the growth in the field. Alberti estimated that for the period from 1945 to 1956, some 8,000 endorsers were used in all U.S. advertising media, pitching approximately 4,500 products; the bulk of the endorsements were for products such as apparel, household appliances, cosmetics, beverages, foods, tobacco, jewelry, and automobiles. The enterprise involved some 1,400 advertising agencies and represented well over $700 million in billings. Alberti further estimated that the endorsers received only 1 percent of the billings during this period. By contrast, according to Jeff Jensen, writing in *Advertising Age* in 1994, the earnings from endorsement contracts for a single superstar—Michael Jordan—exceeded $34 million in 1993 alone.

During its long history, advertising has seen some unlikely and strange endorsements. For example, a well-known advertisement for Zenith hearing aids featured a full-page testimonial from Eleanor Roosevelt, Charles Edison (formerly secretary of the Navy and governor of New Jersey), and the writer Rupert Hughes. The copy was brief and to the point: "These three great Americans can afford any type of hearing aid at any price. They wear the $75 Zenith hearing aid." When Charles Lindbergh took Hershey candy bars with him on his historic solo flight from New York City to Paris, France, in May 1927, Hershey rushed to the newspapers with a drawing that depicted the gallant flier at the controls of the *Spirit of St. Louis*. A novel feature of the ad was that, with Lindbergh's permission, Hershey bars were portrayed as the wings of his famous airplane. This same type of association was reprised a generation later when U.S. astronauts took a powdered orange drink called Tang into space.

Much to their chagrin, even some U.S. presidents have been linked, either directly or indirectly, with product endorsements. For example, the White House has discouraged the sale of a Christmas whiskey decanter bearing the names of several U.S. presidents. Although the advertiser claimed that "there was no intention to convey the impression that the President endorsed the product," the White House counsel cited the standing policy of opposing the sale of anything perceived to have received a president's endorsement. Another case involved Sergeant Marty Snyder, who served as Dwight D. Eisenhower's mess sergeant in World War II. When Snyder tried to market a beef stew with a label that read, "as I prepared and served to General Dwight D. Eisenhower," he encountered problems with what was seen as an implied endorsement by the White House. Moreover, the Securities and Exchange Commission discovered that potential investors in Snyder's enterprise were told that President Eisenhower had an interest in the company when he did not. It was for this reason that a temporary restraining order on the sale of the firm's stock was issued. On the other hand, the Parker Pen Company had no problems using ads that featured a news photo of then General Eisenhower, taken immediately after the German surrender, in which he was holding one of its pens.

Rules and Regulations

Broadcast sponsorship rules require transparency about the persuasive intent behind endorsements, especially when the person is paid for the endorsement. The rules are based on the principle that audiences are entitled to know when they are being persuaded and by whom. Beginning with the Radio Act of 1927 and continuing with Section 317 of the Communications Act of 1934, the broadcast sponsorship rules have required that all contents (including endorsements) broadcast for a "valuable consideration" must be announced as having been paid for, with the name of the payer given. The rationale is simple. Serious conflicts of interest can remain hidden if such information is not available to the recipients of a message. For example, a "frequent prescriber" marketing plan once proposed by Wyeth-Ayerst Laboratories offered doctors 1,000 points on American Airlines' frequent-flier program for each patient who was prescribed Inderal LA, a hypertension drug produced by the company. In another example, as part of a so-called study, the drug firm Roche paid doctors $1,200 if they prescribed a new antibiotic for 20 hospital patients. Because they did not reveal their personal gains to patients, these physicians were, in effect, "masked" expert endorsers for the drugs in question; moreover, key details (i.e., information about the existence, nature, and beneficiaries of the endorsement plans) were unknown to the patients, who thus may have viewed a doctor's endorsement in a more objective light than it deserved.

In a similar vein, "masked" celebrity endorsers can undermine the spirit of broadcast sponsorship rules if they deliberately conceal the fact that they have been paid to endorse a product. The motivation for not revealing such information is, of course, that audiences generally perceive a spokesperson who is paid to say favorable things about a product as being less than objective. A good example of a "masked" celebrity was baseball star Mickey Mantle, who once touted Voltaren, a Ciba-Geigy Corporation arthritis drug, as a miracle product on NBC's *Today* show. The incident prompted NBC's science reporter to point out later that Mantle's enthusiasm for Voltaren was understandable since he was a paid spokesperson for the company. Ciba-Geigy also employed baseball player Whitey Ford as a Voltaren endorser on a Miami, Florida, radio talk show and arranged for appearances by actress Shirley Jones to recommend its estrogen-replacement therapy Estraderm at women's seminars on menopause. The common denominator in these examples is that the endorsers' statements were carefully placed in editorial contexts in which audiences were unlikely to suspect that Ciba-Geigy had paid for them. Faced with a criminal investigation into such practices, Ciba-Geigy agreed to revamp its marketing strategies to prevent abuses in the promotion of prescription drugs.

Effectiveness

There is a considerable body of research on the most effective use of endorsements. In a 1994 study Carolyn Tripp, Thomas Jensen, and Les Carlson suggested that as the number of products endorsed by a given celebrity increases, the celebrity's likeability suffers. Research on sports celebrities has concluded that: (a) they are more effective at endorsing sports-related products than other products and (b) a long-term relationship between a sports celebrity and a product is more effective than a limited endorsement engagement. In separate studies James Martin, David Shani, and Dennis Sandler have concluded that sports celebrities who appear in a broadcast event as well as in the commercials that accompany the broadcast are likely to overshadow the endorsed product.

Researchers have also explored ways of estimating the long-term payoff of an endorser to his or her sponsor by using Q-ratings, Video Storyboard tests, and other customized approaches. Q-ratings, for example, involve the evaluation of celebrities by representative panels of respondents. The ratings represent the percentage of respondents who are familiar with a celebrity and who evaluate the person as "one of my favorites." Video Storyboard tests represent an annual national survey that queries respondents about the effectiveness and credibility of famous spokespersons in actual advertisements. From an advertiser's perspective, it is especially useful to sort such evaluations by respondents' demographic characteristics so as to obtain information about a specific celebrity's appeal to different groups in the general population. Another research approach compares respondents' perceptions about mock advertising campaigns involving different celebrities.

Researchers have even investigated the impact on stock prices of a company's announcement that it plans to hire a celebrity

A 1945 campaign for Lux showcased Hollywood actresses—in this example, Lana Turner—endorsing the beauty soap. *Courtesy of Unilever.*

endorser. A study by Lynette Mathur, Ike Mathur, and Nanda Rangan, for example, indicated that the mere anticipation surrounding Michael Jordan's return to the NBA in 1995, along with the related increase in visibility for him, triggered an average increase of almost 2 percent in the market-adjusted values of companies that had signed him as an endorser (General Mills, Inc.; McDonald's Corporation; Nike; Quaker Oats Company; and Sara Lee Company). This translated into more than $1 billion in stock market value.

With regard to endorsements as a seal of approval, Richard Beltramini and Edwin Stafford have found that consumers neither fully comprehend the meaning embodied in a seal of approval nor believe that the claims in an ad are enhanced by its presence. Nevertheless, there are many instances of third-party endorsers eager to offer recommendations for specific products, whether motivated by publicity or economic benefit. In January 1990 for example, the American Heart Association (AHA) launched a food certification program called "HeartGuide" that sought to educate consumers about saturated fat, sodium, and cholesterol in foods. All foods that satisfied the AHA guidelines were granted the HeartGuide seal of approval, which could be displayed on packaging and used in advertising. The U.S. Food and Drug Administration (FDA), however, forced the AHA to discontinue the use of the HeartGuide seal on the grounds that it misled consumers. Similarly, the FDA targeted another third-party endorsement seal, one offered by the American College of Nutrition (ACN) to Bestfoods's Mazola and Procter & Gamble Company's (P&G) Puritan oils. According to the ACN, companies that contributed $50,000 to its education fund become eligible for the seal. Other examples of third-party endorsements include that given to P&G's Citrus Hill Plus Calcium orange juice by the American Medical Women's Association and the American Cancer Society's endorsement of Florida orange juice. In addition, the AHA and the American Diabetes Association have worked with the Campbell Soup Company to develop a line of frozen mail-order meals (called Intelligent Quisine) that are specifically designed to combat high blood pressure, high cholesterol, and diabetes.

The American Medical Association (AMA) and the American Association of Retired Persons (AARP) reversed their decisions to provide endorsements for commercial products and services in return for pay. In 1997 the AMA endorsed several Sunbeam Corporation products (blood pressure monitors, heating pads, thermometers, humidifiers, and vaporizers) in return for potentially millions of dollars in royalties. Following a week of intense public criticism and allegations of conflicts of interest, the AMA dropped its plan to endorse Sunbeam's products. Similarly, the AARP backed down from its plan to endorse specific health maintenance organizations (HMOs) for Medicare participants. The decision came after the Health Care Financing Administration (HCFA) and several HMOs had expressed concern about the plan. The original AARP plan would have required HMOs to pay AARP a royalty of $20 per month for each member enrolled in the program.

Problems and Pitfalls

Companies can face numerous problems and pitfalls when they choose to use celebrities, experts, or third parties to endorse their products. One problem that has occurred fairly often is that endorsement contracts with a sports team or organization may conflict with the endorsement deals of individual players. At the 1992 Summer Olympics in Barcelona, Spain, for example, several members of the U.S. Olympic team found themselves on a collision course with the U.S. Olympic Committee (USOC). Michael Jordan, an endorser for Nike products, refused a request from the USOC that he wear Reebok gear at the medals ceremony. (Reebok had paid the USOC roughly $4 million for the right to have U.S. athletes wear its products at the awards ceremonies.) Several members of the U.S. World Cup team filed suit against the U.S. Soccer Federation and World Cup USA in 1994, arguing that the governing bodies had required team members to wear Adidas shoes. Some of the athletes had endorsement contracts with Puma shoes and potentially faced the loss of endorsement revenues if they wore Adidas.

Companies that hire celebrity endorsers can face other types of problems. In general, celebrities are vulnerable to the human frail-ties and unexpected setbacks that occur to everyone. Because celebrities are public figures who attract constant media scrutiny, however, the things that happen to them are blown out of proportion. In turn, the interests of the company that has hired celebrity endorsers can suffer by association. Even if a campaign involving a celebrity endorser is meticulously designed to benefit the product, the risk of negative fallout cannot be excluded.

Grace Kelly, for example, was once the featured endorser in advertisements for Lux Soap, whose message attributed her delicate complexion to the fact that she always used the brand. When a reporter for the *Chicago Sun-Times* asked Kelly if the ad's claims about her complexion were true, she replied, "Soap of any kind, Lux or otherwise, never touches my face." Several decades ago, the General Cigar Company conducted an advertising campaign featuring well-known couples in which the husband smoked Cigarillos, the company's famous brand. The ads depicted the wife as declaring, "I love a man who smokes a Cigarillo." Unfortunately for General Cigar, Lex Barker and Arlene Dahl, who participated in the campaign, announced their intention to divorce shortly after the commercial aired. James Garner, who was a spokesperson in a national advertising campaign for the Beef Industry Council, subsequently underwent bypass surgery, a development that was widely reported in the media. Cybill Shepard endorsed the same advertiser but later claimed in an interview that she did not eat meat. Canadian sprinter Ben Johnson's world record performance in 1987 attracted endorsement contracts from several companies, including Toshiba Canada, Mazda Canada, Japan's Kyodo Oil Company, and Diadora, an Italian sportswear marketer. The bulk of the contracts, estimated to be worth between $10 million and $15 million, were canceled, however, after Johnson tested positive for anabolic steroids during the 1988 Summer Olympics in Seoul, Korea. During 1989 Pepsi Cola aired an advertisement titled "Make a Wish" that featured pop singer Madonna. Shortly afterward, Madonna released a video that featured the controversial song "Like a Prayer," which reflected the theme of the advertisement. The ad outraged spokesmen for several Christian denominations, who demanded that Pepsi immediately end both the campaign and its association with Madonna.

Sometimes the embarrassment for advertisers becomes more personal. For seven years tennis star Billie Jean King had promoted Theragran M for E.R. Squibb & Sons. In February 1981 the account moved from Grey Advertising to Jordan, Case & McGrath, which decided to drop King. A new campaign was created and scheduled to make its debut on May 4. A week before, however, a story broke in the national media saying that King had had a sexual relationship with a former female assistant, a story King reluctantly confirmed. Although planned for months, King's sudden disappearance as the Theragran spokesperson just days later gave the impression that the advertiser and agency were reacting out of panic and perhaps intolerance. Squibb's explanation later made it clear that this was not the case, but King had difficultly thereafter finding work as an endorser for a major advertiser.

At a 1991 news conference, basketball player Earvin "Magic" Johnson announced that he was leaving the Los Angeles Lakers because he was HIV positive. At the time Johnson had endorsed several brands (Nestlé, Converse, Nintendo, Pepsi's Slice, and Kentucky Fried Chicken). In 1993 entertainer Michael Jackson was confronted with allegations of child molestation while he was on a world concert tour sponsored by Pepsi. Jackson canceled the tour and sought treatment for what was reported to be an addiction to prescription painkillers. Advertisers' interest in endorsement deals with skater Tonya Harding disappeared following her implication in a brutal attack on her rival, Nancy Kerrigan, carried out by people associated with Harding. Actor Bruce Willis's endorsements for Seagram's wine coolers ended after it was reported that he had stopped drinking alcoholic beverages. Athlete O.J. Simpson's legal battles following allegations that he had murdered his wife and one of her friends appear to have ended his career as a product endorser.

Advertisers can respond to such challenges in a proactive way, that is, by carefully checking the backgrounds of prospective endorsers. Nike, for example, evaluates potential endorsers in terms of talent, character, and style and takes a long-term perspective. As Tellis has noted, "In talent, Nike looks for players who are at the top of their category to reinforce the image of Nike as a superior performance brand. In character, Nike looks for athletes who are committed to the sport, have a sense of humor, and have an attitude that will be popular with the public. In style, Nike looks for athletes who are distinctive, draw attention to the sport, and make a statement."

Advertisers may have to react to such problems after they arise by ending endorsement campaigns in order to prevent further damage to their brands. For example, Pepsi ended its sponsorship of Jackson's world tour and stopped using him as an endorser of its products. Such action is made easier by including a so-called morals clause in the contract with the endorser that allows the advertiser to terminate the arrangement with a partial fee or no fee at all if the endorser's actions threaten the image of the brand.

SIVA K. BALASUBRAMANIAN

See also color plate in this volume

Further Reading

Agrawal, Jagdish, and Wagner A. Kamakura, "The Economic Worth of Celebrity Endorsers: An Event Study Analysis," *Journal of Marketing* 59, no. 3 (July 1995)

Balasubramanian, Siva, "Beyond Advertising and Publicity: Hybrid Messages and Public Policy Issues," *Journal of Advertising* 23, no. 4 (December 1994)

Beltramini, Richard F., and Edwin R. Stafford, "Comprehension and Perceived Believability of Seals of Approval Information in Advertising," *Journal of Advertising* 22, no. 3 (September 1993)

Freeman, William, *The Big Name,* New York: Printers' Ink Books, 1957

Frieden, Jon, "Advertising Spokesperson Effects: An Examination of Endorser Type and Gender on Two Audiences," *Journal of Advertising Research* 24, no. 5 (1984)

Jensen, Jeff, "Jordan Still King of Ad Presenter Game," *Advertising Age* (3 April 1994)

Martin, James, "Is the Athlete's Sport Important When Picking an Athlete to Endorse a Nonsport Product?" *Journal of Consumer Marketing* 13, no. 6 (1996)

Mathur, Lynette, Ike Mathur, and Nanda Rangan, "The Wealth Effects Associated with a Celebrity Endorser: The Michael Jordan Phenomenon," *Journal of Advertising Research* 37, no. 3 (May/June 1997)

McCracken, Grant, "Who Is the Celebrity Endorser? Cultural Foundations of the Endorsement Process," *Journal of Consumer Research* 16 (December 1989)

O'Mahony, Sheila, and Tony Meenaghan, "The Impact of Celebrity Endorsements on Consumers," *Irish Marketing Review* 10, no. 2 (1997–98)

Shani, David, and Dennis Sandler, "Celebrity Alone Isn't a Sure Hit," *Marketing News* (5 August 1991)

Tellis, Gerard, *Advertising and Sales Promotion Strategy,* Reading, Massachusetts: Addison-Wesley, 1997

Tripp, Carolyn, and Thomas Jensen, "The Effects of Multiple Product Endorsements by Celebrities on Consumers' Attitudes and Intentions," *Journal of Consumer Research* 20 (March 1994)

Environmental Movement

The beginning of the modern environmental movement can be traced to 1962 and Rachel Carson's book *Silent Spring,* which first raised widespread public awareness of the impact of human activities on the environment. The movement gained momentum in the United States and Western Europe in the 1970s with the establishment of Earth Day and of the Green Movement in Germany. While the 1970s was the decade of growing environmental awareness, the 1980s was the decade of environmental dangers and disasters, with the disclosure of hazards such as acid rain, global warming, and ozone depletion and incidents such as the Exxon *Valdez* oil spill, the release of toxic gases by a Union Carbide plant in Bhopal, India, and the nuclear accident at Chernobyl, in the former Soviet Union. In the United States, environmental concern was the fastest-growing national issue of the 1990s. By 2000 and the 30th anniversary of Earth Day, public opinion polls demonstrated ever-increasing consumer concern for the environment.

As support for environmentalism spread, U.S. and West European consumers expressed increasing concern about the environmental impact of their purchases and a willingness to pay the price for environmentally responsible products. In turn, consumer boycotts based on ecological concerns had an economic impact. In the United States, for example, fast-food establishments were boycotted because of their use of styrene packaging materials, and in Western Europe, boycotts targeted aerosols containing chlorofluorocarbons and bleached paper products. In Germany, the Green Party became more prominent and environmental legislation was passed that was widely recognized as the strictest in the world.

Advent of "Green Advertising"

As environmentalism became a core value for consumers—and consequently an economic and political force—advertisers responded by focusing on environmental issues. "Green advertising"—promotional messages appealing to environmentally aware consumers—first appeared in the 1970s and grew rapidly. In the United States the number of new products making environmental claims jumped from 0.5 percent in 1985 to 13 percent in 1993. In Canada, the figure rose from 2 percent in 1986 to almost 34 percent in 1991. In the United States alone, consumers spend about $110 billion annually on products from companies they believe to be socially and environmentally progressive.

In areas of the world where consumer environmental consciousness has remained relatively low, green advertising did not take hold until the 1990s. In Japan, the advent of green advertising can be traced to 1990 and consumer complaints about the environmental practices of Mitsubishi. In response, the company sponsored a "green" concert marking what would have been John Lennon's 50th birthday. Japan's other multinational corporations, such as NEC (formerly Nippon Electric Corporation) and the automobile and beer industries, were quick to follow suit, but by the late 1990s only 1 percent of all Japanese regional print advertising was classified as green. The percentage was slightly higher in Hong Kong, where the first green advertising was produced for television for the government's environmental division. The percentage of green advertising is expected to rise quickly in Asia, however, as the growing consumer movement demands corporate responsibility toward the environment.

Although nature imagery—trees, flowers, birds—has been used to sell products since the late 1800s, green advertising as it is known today—emphasizing corporate responsibility for environment-friendly policies—first appeared in the 1970s. Many of these early advertisements incorporated images and figures calculated to make an emotional appeal to consumers. One of the best known ads from this period is the 1971 public service announcement for Keep America Beautiful, featuring Iron Eyes Cody, an American Indian, on horseback, a tear rolling down his cheek as he surveys scenes of environmental degradation.

A surprising ally in the fight to save the environment— an oil company.

On February 10th Sun Company, (you know us as Sunoco) officially endorsed the CERES Principles as a general code of environmental conduct for business.

These principles, (formerly the Valdez Principles) were proposed by the CERES Organization – an independent group of environmentalists and social investors.

At the same time, CERES recognized Sun's principles of health, environment and safety as being consistent with the goals of their own principles.

As a result of this mutual recognition, Sun agrees to complete CERES' annual report which provides an extensive account of our environmental performance. We welcome this new commitment, because at Sun Company we strongly support the concept of increased public disclosure for environmental performance for all corporations.

The Sun Principles
Goals for the Prudent Operation of Our Business Dealing with:

Emission Reduction, with Special Emphasis on Toxic Substances

Increased Conservation of Water and Efficient Use of All Non-renewable Resources

Reduction and Disposal of Wastes

Increased Energy Conservation

Risk Reduction by Working Safely, Emergency Preparedness and Product Safety

Being Responsible in Handling any Health, Environmental or Safety Problems

Keeping the Public Informed and Increasing External Reporting

Maintaining Management's Commitment to Achieving these Principles

What we have done is not some superficial public relations ploy. By publicly endorsing the CERES Principles we realize we are going to attract more scrutiny than praise. But we welcome that. The reason is simple.

We run a business, and this is a business decision. We believe that the future belongs to those companies that see environmental protection as a valued condition for economic growth.

In the long run, our success as a corporation depends on our living up to these principles.

Sunoco is the first FORTUNE 500® company to endorse the CERES Principles. While we are proud of that distinction, we're especially proud that the first company to do so is an oil company.

We normally end our advertising with the words that Sunoco is "On the Driver's Side." But, when it concerns progress toward environmental protection, we're all on the same side: Drivers and pedestrians. Environmentalists and corporations.

SUN   **SUNOCO**   **On the driver's side.**

© 1993 Sun Company, Inc.

A 1993 Sunoco ad emphasizes the company's commitment to environmental responsibility.
Used by permission of Sunoco, Inc.

In the 1980s green advertising began to target the young, well-educated, activist-oriented, and increasingly upscale baby boomers who constituted much of the environmentally aware public. Taking the form of cause-related or social-venture marketing, green advertising used advertising and public relations in concert to link corporate identity with social causes—in this case the environment—to create a green company image that advertising dollars alone could not buy. Anita Roddick, founder of Body Shop International, was awarded the Order of the British Empire for her well-publicized efforts to manufacture environmentally sound personal-care products that involved no animal testing. Signs promoting environmental causes were featured in store displays, on shopping bags, and even on delivery trucks. Also around this time, Chevron Corporation began its "People Do" campaign, which has been running in print and broadcast formats for more than 20 years, using case studies to demonstrate Chevron's commitment to environmental projects. H. J. Heinz Corporation, responding to a consumer boycott of tuna, worked with the Earth Island Institute to introduce "dolphin-safe" tuna (i.e., tuna caught in nets that did not harm dolphins); its video news release of the announcement became one of the most widely aired such public relations efforts of its time. Other corporations advertised newly formed partnerships with environmental organizations, such as McDonald's with the Environmental Defense Fund, Anheuser-Busch and General Motors with the Nature Conservancy, and IBM with the World Wildlife Fund and the German Game Preservation Society.

Ups and Downs of Green Appeal

Early results confirmed the success of environmental image marketing. Evaluation of the "People Do" campaign a few years after its inception demonstrated a 22 percent increase in likely purchase behavior among the target audience. Heinz's share of the canned tuna market rose to a record-high 40 percent following the introduction of dolphin-safe tuna. Studies showed that green advertising appealed even to those consumers who were not themselves particularly active in environmental causes, that consumer recall was fairly high for environmental claims in advertising, and that green advertising claims were particularly effective with women with children and with younger consumers, groups that marketers were eager to reach.

Green advertising peaked in 1990 with advertising tie-ins to the 20th anniversary of Earth Day by many major corporations, including IBM, General Motors, and Coors. MCI and Sprint both pledged a percentage of profits to environmental groups. According to figures compiled by the J. Walter Thompson Company (JWT), the number of green print and television advertisements jumped from 41 in 1989 to 212 in 1990. The 1992 Earth Summit in Rio de Janeiro, Brazil, occasioned another green advertising peak, such as the 34-magazine, eight-language "advertorial" on "Meeting the Challenge of Sustainable Development." Small agencies such as MediaNatura emerged, specializing in green advertising, and major agencies such as Saatchi & Saatchi Advertising and JWT formed specialized green teams.

By the mid 1990s, however, green marketing started to slump. In the United States the percentage of new products introduced with green claims dropped from the 1993 high of 13 percent to less than 11 percent in 1994. Two factors contributed to the drop: consumer backlash and increasing government regulation. Polls demonstrated that the vast majority of consumers were skeptical of environmental claims in advertising; advertisements by major corporations were considered to be the least credible source of environmental information. Green consumers were also those

An ad for the Honda Insight, the first gasoline-electric hybrid car introduced in the United States, addressed concerns about conservation and air quality.

most likely to inherently distrust big business, and these consumers believed that environmental claims were too hard to test or prove, were deceptively vague, or omitted factual information that was not supportive of environmental claims. In the first five weeks of 1990, the Advertising Standards Authority received more complaints about deceptive green advertising than in all of 1989.

Articles appeared in the popular press accusing companies and organizations of "greenwashing" (the environmental equivalent of whitewashing) or producing "ecopornography." It was charged, for instance, that the products of the Body Shop were not as environmentally sound as had been advertised. Critics noted that the environmental actions outlined by Chevron in its "People Do" campaign were simply technological fixes required by government regulation, such as compliance with the Endangered Species Act, and not independent, company-initiated actions to reduce energy consumption and pollution. Observers pointed out that while generously sponsoring the Audubon Society, General Electric was also first on the list of companies creating highly polluted Superfund sites. In Great Britain, Friends of the Earth began bestowing its "green-con awards" on groups such as British Nuclear Fuels for its "Just how green are you about nuclear power?" campaign and on Higgs Furs, for its claims of "environmentally friendly" furs.

In response to consumer and media backlash and studies demonstrating that consumers wanted clarity and specificity in environmental advertising, many companies stopped using image advertising and turned to more factual advertising about the environmental advantages of their products. In the early 1990s a new kind of green advertisement—featuring rational appeals, environmental facts, and channels for consumer information, such as toll-free numbers—began to predominate. Procter & Gamble advertised its refillable Enviro-pak containers and bottles made with less plastic; McDonald's used advertising to educate the public about ways in which polystyrene was being recycled; and Wal-Mart built a prototype environmental demonstration store featuring environmentally friendly products and a comprehensive onsite recycling program.

Setting Standards

With these new environmental claims on the part of advertisers, public opinion swung in favor of government regulation of those claims. Although the U.S. Federal Trade Commission had investigated environmental claims cases as early as the 1970s—most notably that of Standard Oil of California, which claimed that an additive in Chevron gasoline would produce "pollution-free" automobile exhaust—court cases involving environmental ads did not become common until 1990. In that year, attorneys general from seven states charged Mobil with misleading advertising for claiming its Hefty brand trash bags were biodegradable when in fact conditions in most landfills would not allow the bags to biodegrade. Advertising for American Enviro Products' Bunnies diapers suffered a similar fate. Procter & Gamble was charged with misleading advertising for saying that the packaging for many of

its products was recyclable when in fact few recycling facilities existed at the time that could handle the material.

Some U.S. states, California and New York among them, passed their own laws governing green claims. In the absence of clear federal regulatory guidelines, however, many advertisers were unsure of the regulations surrounding green marketing. In 1990 confusion over the legal status of green claims prompted the ten members of the Attorneys General Task Force on Environmental Marketing, chaired by Minnesota Attorney General Hubert Humphrey III, to issue the Green Report, followed by the Green Report II in 1991. The reports made four recommendations for responsible environmental advertising:

- environmental claims should be specific, not vague
- they should reflect current waste management options
- they should be substantive
- they should be supported by scientific evidence

The National Association of Attorneys General adopted a resolution calling for national environmental marketing standards, and in February 1991, they, along with a broad coalition of consumer, business, and environmental groups and industry associations, including the American Association of Advertising Agencies, petitioned the Federal Trade Commission (FTC) for guidelines. In response, the FTC held public hearings on the issue in July 1991.

One year later the FTC, in cooperation with the Environmental Protection Agency and the U.S. Office of Consumer Affairs, issued "Guides for the Use of Environmental Marketing Claims." These guidelines, which do not have the force of law, set down six general principles: (1) all qualifications and disclosures must be clear and prominent; (2) claims must distinguish between environmental benefits due to the product and those due to the packaging; (3) claims cannot overstate environmental benefits or attributes; (4) comparative claims must give enough information that the basis for comparison is clear; (5) claims must be specific, not vague; and (6) terms used in claims must conform to standard definitions (definitional criteria were set for ten terms: *degradable, biodegradable, photodegradable, compostable, recyclable, recycled content, source reduction, refillable, ozone safe,* and *ozone friendly*).

State laws have continued to proliferate, however, with 18 states having or considering environmental marketing legislation as of 1999. The California law, which regulated the use of a number of terms, was considered the most restrictive and was challenged in court by the Association of National Advertisers. In 1992 the majority of the statute was upheld by the U.S. District Court, although one definition, that for *recyclable,* was ruled unconstitutionally vague. A two-to-one Ninth U.S. Court of Appeals decision upheld that of the lower court, based on the contention that the state has a substantial interest in protecting its citizens from "ecological puffery."

Cases against advertisers have proliferated as well, the majority being brought in reference to claims of ozone friendliness and degradability. Claims for aerosols (particularly personal care items) and plastics (particularly trash bags) have been the most heavily scrutinized, although disposable diapers, coffee filters, and disposable food-service items have each been targeted more than once. Within this uncertain legal atmosphere, many companies have severely restricted their environmental marketing activities. Kraft, General Foods, Heinz, and Andrew Jergens pulled claims of recyclability from their labels. Procter & Gamble struck the phrase "recyclable where facilities exist" from its packaging and, along with the Coca-Cola Company, eliminated its environmental marketing position.

Other countries around the world also developed voluntary guidelines in the late 1980s and early 1990s, such as those for the Incorporated Society of British Advertisers, the Australian Trade Practices Commission, and the French Environmental Advertising Code. While the United States has tried to approach regulation of environmental marketing claims on a voluntary standards basis, however, with states enacting laws on a piecemeal basis, other countries have a history of centrally imposed and enforced government regulation. Almost all European countries have green legislation, much of which concerns the use of eco-labeling programs. Germany—which has strict environmental laws and often serves as an environmental marketing test ground for multinationals such as Procter & Gamble—was the first to have an eco-labeling program. The Blue Angel program was established in 1977 by Germany's environment ministry to denote products certified by a nine-member independent jury to be more environmentally friendly than competing products. About 4,000 products in 70 product categories from approximately 1,000 companies carry the Blue Angel label. Certification allows use of the label in logos and advertising for a period of three years, at which time the product must be recertified according to updated standards. Companies are eager to pay for certification because the Blue Angel certification often guarantees a product will achieve market share leadership as consumers demonstrate purchase preference for these products.

Similar eco-labeling programs exist in more than 22 countries, including Canada, which began the Environmental Choice program in 1988; the Scandinavian countries, which adopted the Nordic Swan symbol; and Japan, where the Ecomark appeared in 1988. Standards have been particular to each country, however, and other countries have charged those with eco-label programs of "ecoprotectionism," that is protecting sales of domestic goods through the use of the labeling schemes. Some standardization took place with the establishment of the European Union daisy label in 1992.

In the United States, the Green Seal program was started in 1990 as a private effort by the Alliance for Social Responsibility to set environmental standards for 45 product categories. Like the Blue Angel program, certification allows use of the label for logos and in advertising for a three-year period, but high testing costs and lack of publicity have limited its use. As of 1994, nine companies, including GE Lighting, had received Green Seal certification but none had used it in advertising. A public service announcement promoting the eco-label was sent to 50 consumer and environmental magazines but received little to no placement. Scientific Certification Systems started an alternate system, an Environmental Report Card, much like nutrition labels on food products. Scientific Certification Systems has certified about 500 claims for 150 companies, including Apple Computer, Clorox, and Glidden, but its certification too failed to catch on with consumers. The European experience has shown that eco-labels can be a potent tool for advertisers if consumers demand environmentally sound products, but without government sponsorship such programs lack widespread consumer awareness and credibility.

Effect of Globalization

With increasing globalization and a lack of international eco-labeling standards, some critics have pronounced the death of green advertising. But many industry analysts contend that environmental marketing has now entered its third phase of development, in which only those companies truly committed to sound environmental practice remain to engage in green advertising. As an example, these analysts point to Church & Dwight, maker of Arm & Hammer baking soda products. Since its establishment in 1888, Church & Dwight has been conservation oriented, packing all boxes of Arm & Hammer baking soda produced from 1888 to 1966 with a conservation-themed card and using recycled paperboard since 1907 for its trademark yellow packaging. The company's Environmental Improvement Process has attracted industry attention. The program sets both internal life-cycle process goals based on independent environmental audits and external education goals, such as the Partners in Environmental Education Program. As part of this program, Church & Dwight provides technical support for authors of environmental books and newsletters; sponsors green radio and TV broadcasts; produces and distributes a Community Action Handbook and school curriculum; provides funds for the President's Environmental Youth Awards and environmental groups; and produces in-store consumer education displays called Enviro-centers. In turn, it has captured increased market share in many categories, and sales have increased in the past 20 years from $16 million to more than $500 million.

This new type of campaign moves away from corporate image advertising toward integrated campaigns stressing the environmental benefits achieved throughout a product's life cycle and not just a single aspect of the product or its packaging. For a company to successfully create an environmentally responsible image, management must support sound environmental practice—including external "environmental audits," special annual reports, eco-labeling, partnerships with environmental groups, and communication with stakeholders. The result is effective, credible green advertising that satisfies both the company and its consumers that a real environmental contribution is being made.

PATRICIA A. CURTIN

Further Reading

Coddington, Walter, *Environmental Marketing: Positive Strategies for Reaching the Green Consumer,* New York: McGraw-Hill, 1993

Ottman, Jacquelyn A., *Green Marketing,* Lincolnwood, Illinois: NTC Business Books, 1993; 2nd edition, 1998

Peattie, Ken, *Environmental Marketing Management: Meeting the Green Challenge,* London: Pitman, 1995

Polonsky, Michael J., and Alma T. Mintu-Wimsatt, editors,

Environmental Marketing: Strategies, Practice, Theory, and Research, New York: Haworth, 1995; London: Haworth, 1997

Wasik, John F., *Green Marketing and Management: A Global Perspective,* Cambridge, Massachusetts: Blackwell Business, 1996

Ericsson (China) Company, Ltd.

Principal Agency
Publicis & AD-Link International Advertising Company

The telecommunications giant Ericsson has been doing business in China since 1892, but its wholly owned holding company in the country—Ericsson (China) Company, Ltd.—was founded only in 1994. With its head office located in Beijing, the national capital, Ericsson China was created to extend Ericsson's control over staff issues in its joint ventures and other investment and management concerns. Today, Ericsson China oversees 22 local representative offices and eight joint ventures.

By the time Ericsson China was founded, Ericsson was already a well-known company and brand in China. But because the company had several joint ventures and local offices operating relatively independently, its image was fragmented. Ericsson China's main task was to mold a unified image that would enable Ericsson to compete more effectively in the country's telecommunications market.

Ericsson's business in China can be divided into three segments: consumer products, mobile communication systems, and information communication systems. Among these segments, consumer products (mainly cellular mobile phones and accessories) have received the most attention in the company's advertising efforts. In the 1990s cellular phone technology was relatively new in China, and most Chinese regarded cell phones as symbols of luxury and success. Correspondingly, marketers of mobile phones in China primarily targeted young and middle-aged business or professional people with relatively high incomes.

Ericsson's two strongest competitors in this market are Motorola and Nokia. Together, the three companies control more than 85 percent of China's cellular phone market. Numerous local companies also produce cell phones, but these companies are too small to compete either technologically or financially with the three major players, even though the Chinese government has tried to support the local mobile phone makers by imposing quotas on foreign companies.

Among the three giants, Motorola was at one time the absolute market leader, claiming a 70 percent–90 percent market share. Competition from Nokia and Ericsson, however, and

Motorola's own delay in introducing a global system for mobile communications (GSM) technology significantly endangered its position. By the late 1990s Motorola accounted for only 30.3 percent of the GSM market, while Ericsson and Nokia had caught up, with 29 percent and 27.3 percent market shares, respectively.

The three companies have employed very different approaches in their advertising. Ericsson's advertising in China is well known for its use of celebrities, especially movie stars, most of whom come from Hong Kong and Taiwan, which are still the main sources of popular movies in China. Celebrity commercials with well-designed stories and expert production have made Ericsson's advertisements enjoyable to watch and easy to remember.

A series of ads that ran in 1998–99 presented four love stories, called (in chronological order) "Task," "Decision," "Art," and "Love Lock," each starring different celebrities. Ericsson invested a considerable amount of money in the casts and production budgets. The "Task" commercial, for example, was shot on location in Los Angeles, California; the production involved several helicopters, machines that made artificial rain, and dozens of limousines. In a developing country such as China, this kind of lavish production is still quite rare and would undoubtedly impress consumers. The commercial was the most expensive cellular phone advertisement of 1998.

Another notable characteristic of Ericsson's advertising and general communication strategy is the emphasis on sports. The competitive energy associated with sports is often seen as emblematic of the spirit of China's young people, many of whom have rising incomes; sports-related promotions thus provide an opportunity for Ericsson to communicate with this lucrative segment of the market. One 1998 ad depicted two Ericsson 768 cellular phones, one wearing a yellow sweatshirt, the other dressed in blue, playing soccer. The choice of colors turned out to be prophetic; the finalists in the 1998 World Cup match were Brazil (yellow) and France (blue). Although some people in China have criticized Ericsson China's advertising for its portrayal of a luxurious lifestyle that is not yet compatible with the country's economic condition, the success of the company in the Chinese market to some degree belies this view.

YUPING LIU

Further Reading

"Centralized Control," *Business China* (6 February 1995)

Huang, Ning, and Chih-Ho Yu, "China—Ericsson's GSM Business Grows Rapidly," *Newsbytes News Network* (29 March 1996)

"Mobile Phones: Fast Movers," *Business China* (17 May 1993)

Stone, Rod, "Mobile Phone Giants Weigh Response to Chinese Quotas," *Dow Jones International News* (10 November 1999)

Ericsson, Inc.

Principal Agencies

Young & Rubicam, Inc.

Publicis

Lars Magnus Ericsson founded a telegraph equipment repair shop in 1876, establishing a company that more than a century later would become one of the world's largest telecommunications equipment suppliers. Even before the turn of the 20th century, the Stockholm, Sweden-based Ericsson had grown beyond its domestic borders and entered countries such as China, Russia, and Mexico.

In the 1950s the company became involved in the very early stages of the mobile communications industry, launching its first mobile phone, which weighed 40 kilograms. In 1965 Ericsson introduced an automatic mobile-phone system, and the company continued making innovations throughout the 1970s, developing a nine-kilogram mobile phone in 1974. When international commercial systems were being launched in the early 1980s, Ericsson won contracts throughout the world. By the 1990s Ericsson was a world leader in the global telecommunications equipment arena with a prominent presence in the fast-growing mobile communications industry.

Well into the 1990s Ericsson's advertising strategy was localized and focused on business clients. In 1993 the company launched an image and product campaign for its hardware and services businesses that included 14 European countries. The campaign included print ads from Ted Bates Advertising of Copenhagen, Denmark, which ran first in Germany, France, and the United Kingdom. By the middle of the decade, Ericsson was the world's largest supplier of mobile phone systems and the third-largest marketer of handsets.

In 1996 Ericsson focused its advertising efforts by consolidating its $40 million worldwide mobile phone account at Young & Rubicam, Inc. (Y&R), as it began an effort to shift its focus from business clients to consumers. In one of its first efforts to reach a consumer audience, Ericsson became the "name sponsor" of the Ericsson Stadium, home to the National Football League's Carolina Panthers in Charlotte, North Carolina. Ericsson's sponsorship of sports events also included NASCAR racing cars and golf tournaments.

In September 1996 Ericsson launched a second round of consumer-awareness campaigns for its cellular phones in an effort, in part, to make its brand a household name. The ads, created by Y&R affiliate Creswell, Munsell, Fultz & Zirbel of Cedar Rapids, Iowa, depicted people who needed phones in unusual situations. That year the company also created a Web site designed to communicate with customers and began putting its Web site address in advertising and marketing materials.

Ericsson was also making inroads into Latin America in 1996, using television to deliver a barrage of short messages and sponsor identifications to an upscale audience. The television blitz was reinforced with outdoor billboards in high-traffic urban markets throughout Latin America.

Ericsson closed 1996 by awarding CIA Medianetwork Europe its $25 million corporate and business-to-business account for continental Europe. The account had previously been split between Carat and Zenith Media. In 1997 Ericsson increased its ad spending. During the first 10 months of the year, the company spent $24.8 million on advertising, compared with $16.7 million during the first 10 months of 1996. Ericsson continued its effort to reach a consumer audience, with an estimated $40 million, six-week campaign coinciding with the launch of its GF788 digital mobile phone, which at the time was the smallest the company had ever produced. The ads, developed by Hall & Cederquist Y&R, Stockholm, and Dentsu Y&R, Singapore, aimed to illustrate the phone's small size by juxtaposing it with everyday objects. Television spots depicted landmarks such as the Eiffel Tower in miniature; outdoor ads also were used in some markets. The tag line accompanying the ads was, "So small, it will change your perspective." In some eastern European countries the phone was marketed as an alternative to fixed line phones. The campaign helped the GF788 become Ericsson's best-selling mobile phone. In another TV spot (unrelated to the GF788), aired on ABC's *Monday Night Football,* fans were shown using the glow from their Ericsson mobile phones to illuminate the stadium after a blackout.

Also in 1997 Ericsson sponsored the first World Championships of Beach Volleyball Tournament in California. The company's marketing efforts during the tournament included an extensive on-site and TV presence and sponsorship of a local volleyball clinics in the Los Angeles area. In addition, the company sponsored a consumer sweepstakes in Los Angeles, which awarded event tickets to 25 winners and gave one winner the chance to win $1 million by serving a volleyball at a target. Another significant marketing effort in 1997 was Ericsson's product placement in the James Bond motion picture *Tomorrow Never Dies*. The company supported the product placement with in-store promotions at retailers.

In October 1997 Ericsson received one of 14 European Advertising Achievement Awards, given for effective pan-European advertising. Ericsson won the award, presented by *Advertising Age International* and the European Association of Advertising Agencies, for its efforts to focus its brand more sharply and to make its high-tech brand more consumer friendly, particularly its efforts to promote its GF788 phone. The company also ranked number seven on *Advertising Age International*'s list of the top ten print advertisers in Asia. The company spent $1.93 million in advertising in Asia between January and June 1997.

By 1998, as Ericsson faced increasing competition from rivals Nokia and Motorola, consumer products accounted for approximately 80 percent of all of its external advertising. The company's primary focus during the year was its first global brand-image campaign. The "Make yourself heard" campaign from Y&R focused on people rather than specific products. The campaign was designed to be "borderless" and have a long lifespan. Ericsson's local and regional businesses had the option of choosing from different combinations of photos and ad copy to create the most appropriate message for their particular culture and audience. Until the "Make yourself heard" campaign, Ericsson's advertising efforts had primarily been product-specific campaigns.

In November 1998 Ericsson broke into *Advertising Age International*'s list of the top 100 global marketers, at number 68. In addition, Ericsson was listed as the biggest advertiser in a separate ranking of ad spending in international print media.

Ericsson continued its efforts to target business customers. In April 1999 Ericsson Digital Wireless Office Services began a print and Web campaign for MobileAdvantage, a wireless communications network that eliminated the need for mobile workers to maintain a wired phone and phone number at the office. Anderson & Lembke, New York City, created the ads.

In May of that year Ericsson featured its smallest Go-Everywhere phone in the first of a series of ads from Y&R. An actual-size photo of the Ericsson 788 phone appeared on a spread with the headline, "You are everywhere." In Africa the company received an industry award for best advertising and marketing campaign.

The year turned out to be a tumultuous one for Ericsson, though; the company faced management churn, corporate restructuring, and a volatile telecommunications market. After taking an early lead in the mobile communications market, Ericsson struggled to increase the pace of product introductions. In addition, the company was losing market share in the global wireless handset market.

Ericsson made several moves in the latter half of 1999 to combat its difficulties and signal a commitment to marketing. During the summer the company appointed Torbjorn Nilsson to the post of senior vice president of marketing and strategic business development. In October Ericsson named Publicis as lead agency to handle its global account for infrastructure. Publicis was called on to raise awareness of Ericsson's network operator services and enterprise business solutions. The company continued to work with local agencies on ongoing projects, but new projects were started with Publicis; Y&R kept Ericsson's consumer projects.

At the end of the year Ericsson Mobile Phones began planning a global brand campaign with Publicis and appointed Paula Callenbach director of brand marketing to lead the company's global brand mission in North America. The company also appointed CIA Medianetwork International, London, to develop its media communication strategy worldwide and to handle all the company's business-to-business marketing activities.

In 2000 Ericsson's marketing goals included clarifying its brand message, speeding product introductions, and reaching a younger audience. After being absent from TV advertising for 15 months, the company launched a costly campaign (estimated at $16 million–$20 million) aimed at promoting two new products: an Internet phone, the R280LX, and its T28 world phone. The campaign, created by Y&R, broke in May during CBS's prime-time programming with two spots that touted the handsets' capabilities. Designed to challenge Nokia and Motorola in the important North American market, the campaign was to include magazine and newspaper efforts beginning during the summer. Ericsson also was an initial advertiser on CBS's popular *Survivor* television show.

In an effort to reach a younger audience, Ericsson targeted 16-to-22-year-olds with a voice-activated phone and for the second year in a row sponsored the MTV Europe Music Awards. The company launched a limited edition of its A2618 mobile phone in conjunction with the sponsorship. Ericsson also offered consumers the opportunity to vote for award nominees via their mobile phones.

In Australia Ericsson began a brand advertising campaign with *Sunday* magazine. The "Signature Series" campaign was designed to communicate the scope of Ericsson's 2000 product portfolio in a consistent, cohesive manner.

In October 2000 Ericsson launched a high-profile mobile Internet campaign in the United Kingdom as part of a campaign developed by Publicis. The campaign was designed to present Ericsson's vision for the mobile Internet and demonstrate how it will affect everyday lives. The $60 million campaign used TV, billboards, business press, trade magazines, and the Internet in 15 markets on five continents. Although primarily aimed at network operators and service providers, the campaign also was designed to promote understanding of the mobile Internet among the general public.

During 2000 Ericsson became the title sponsor of the Ericsson Open, the fifth-largest tennis tournament in the world. Ericsson's sponsorship of the event included a campaign to build awareness of the tournament's new name and TV time on Fox and ESPN. Ericsson signed a five-year sponsorship deal for the tournament, which had previously been known as the Lipton Open.

Like other wireless companies, in 2000 Ericsson initiated efforts to become an advertising medium itself. In February the company launched a wireless version of its Internet Advertiser software used by ISPs to offer ad-supported Internet access. Using the software, ISPs are able to push targeted ads to wireless devices. Ericsson also bought a 29 percent stake in Mediatude, a company specializing in targeted mobile marketing services, in August 2000. Mediatude's platform enables companies to send promotional messages to selected mobile phones. Independent research released in October 2000 suggested that not only are consumers receptive to advertising messages delivered to their mobile phones, but also that they remember the brand messages and respond to them. Ericsson and Mediatude sent more than 100,000 messages to 5,000 users in a six-week consumer trial. At the end of 2000 Ericsson put its $100 million global consumer products account, which had been handled for four years by Y&R, up for review. The company announced in February 2001 that the account would go to U.K.-based advertising agency Bartle Bogle Hegarty.

KRISTEN BECKMAN

Further Reading
Cleland, Kim, "Ericsson Aims for Consumers with Cell Phone Ads," *Advertising Age* (19 September 1996)
Elkin, Tobi, "Ericsson Regroups for Global Push," *Advertising Age* (29 November 1999)
Elkin, Tobi, "Ericsson Renews Consumer Ad Focus," *Advertising Age* (13 December 1999)
Elkin, Tobi, "Ericsson Taps Callenbach to Fortify Brand's Image: Aussie Native to Build Share in N. America for Wireless Phone Company," *Advertising Age* (31 January 2000)
Elkin, Tobi, "Ericsson Ads Push Advanced Phones: Marketer Earmarks $20 Mil for Its Wireless Handsets," *Advertising Age* (29 May 2000)
Jensen, Jeff, "Telco Ericsson Calls on James Bond, Volleyball: Linkups Made to New Movie, World Tourney," *Advertising Age* (23 June 1997)
Jensen, Jeff, "Ericsson Takes Its Football Tie-in to New Level with Ad: Presence on 'MNF' Follows Link to New Bond Film," *Advertising Age* (22 September 1997)

Erwin, Wasey & Company

Founded by Louis R. Wasey, 1914; became a major U.S. agency and was among the first to develop an important network of international offices, 1930s; bought by David B. Williams Company, 1955; merged with Ruthrauff & Ryan to form Erwin, Wasey, Ruthrauff & Ryan, 1957; became part of Interpublic, Inc., 1963; Erwin, Wasey name retired, 1979.

Major Clients

Barbasol Company
Carnation Company
Minnesota Valley Canning Company
R.B. Selmer, Inc. (Kreml hair tonic)
R.J. Reynolds Tobacco Company (Camel cigarettes)

During its peak years in the 1940s and 1950s, Erwin, Wasey & Company (EW) ranked among the 20 largest advertising agencies in the United States and was among the earlier agencies to begin to build a network outside the country. By the middle 1930s, the agency operated offices in London, England; Paris, France; Stockholm, Sweden; the Hague, The Netherlands; Helsinki, Finland; and Oslo, Norway.

Born in Detroit, Michigan, in 1884, Louis R. Wasey entered advertising immediately after dropping out of college. He came to Chicago, Illinois, in 1904 and took a job at Lord & Thomas (L&T) less than a year after the retirement of Daniel Lord, just as

the agency was rapidly coming under the control of Albert Lasker. Wasey remained at L&T for a decade. He reached the rank of vice president, making $15,000 a year, owing in large part to his new business skills as a salesman. His success convinced him that he could lead his own agency, and in September 1914, a month after the start of World War I, he and Will Jefferson, an older vice president at L&T, opened a shop in Chicago as Wasey & Jefferson & Company. But Jefferson was not Wasey's first choice for a partner. Charles R. Erwin was.

The retirement of Lord in 1903 had been followed in 1906 by the sudden death of the other founder, Ambrose Thomas. When Thomas died, the agency was acquired by the young Lasker and Erwin, who was by then a senior L&T officer nearing retirement age. In 1912 Erwin sold his interest to Lasker and planned to retire on 1 February 1915. Wasey had approached him with his partnership proposal earlier, but Erwin was financially secure and had no incentive to continue working. Shortly before Erwin's retirement, Wasey contacted Erwin's wife and told her he thought her husband, who was 60 at the time, would die if he did not continue working. Presumably this strategy caused Erwin to change his mind, and in February 1915 the new agency became Erwin, Wasey & Jefferson. Within a year Jefferson retired, and the name changed once again, this time to Erwin, Wasey & Company.

Even before he left L&T, Wasey decided it was good business to invest in the companies he served. He became a stockholder in several of the companies that left L&T to become his first clients,

Erwin Wasey & Company created the phrase "contented cows" for
Carnation in the 1930s.

including the Olive Tablet Company and the Musterole Company,
both of which he had brought to L&T originally. The largest client to come out of L&T was Goodyear Tire & Rubber Company,
which was having disagreements over the agency's hard-sell creative approach.

Wasey felt it was good business to display a certain level of
prosperity, even if the prosperity was only anticipated. He bought
a reconditioned Packard and hired a chauffeur to drive him to his
appointments. He was always on the lookout for promising
investments. In the early days when his agency was still growing,
an inventor brought him a pharmaceutical on which he had just
received a patent. It was a blend of milk of magnesia and mineral
oil to aid digestion. Wasey financed and marketed the product for
several years before selling it to Sterling Products Company,
which continued advertising it for many years as Haley's M.O.,
though the Wasey agency never handled the account.

An even more famous brand the agency did handle for many
years was Barbasol, which was actually established by Wasey in
the 1920s. Using radio, EW devised one of the most enduring
early commercial jingles, which was sung for many years by
Harry Frankel under the name "Singin' Sam, the Barbasol man."
By the end of the decade, Barbasol was the country's number one
shaving cream. For years the lyrics were second nature to any
radio listener:

Barbasol, Barbasol,
No brush, no lather, no rub in,
Wet your razor, then begin.
Barbasol, Barbasol,
Soothing, smoothing, cooling Barbasol.

Years later in 1961 the jingle was revived with new lyrics. But
Wasey and his nephew, George Wasey, had sold their interests in
Barbasol in December 1956, and the account was moved to the
George Walsh Company in June 1958.

Wasey also thought it was good business to look for smart
people. Soon after opening his office in the Chicago Union Carbide Building, he hired a young writer named Arthur Kudner to
head his copy department. Kudner would go on to make an
imprint on EW. In the early 1930s he worked on the account of
the F.W. Young Company, which manufactured a foot liniment

called Absorbine Jr. It was Kudner who invented and named the
main affliction against which the brand was positioned—"athlete's foot." He became a partner and later president of EW before
breaking out to establish his own agency in 1935. (Kudner died in
1944.) Another future star Wasey would later hire, this time out
of a small Indianapolis, Indiana, agency, was Leo Burnett, who
joined the Chicago copy department in 1930. Burnett would also
open an agency of his own in 1935.

By 1920, EW was billing about $4 million a year. World War I
was over, and Wasey was eager to launch an office in London to
service American clients doing business overseas. Erwin was still
with the agency and was more cautious about expansion. Only
when Wasey suggested that his son-in-law head the office did
Erwin agree. Four years later in 1924, EW opened its first office in
New York City, which was becoming the country's major advertising hub. Wasey moved east to build the staff, and by the mid-
1920s the New York City office had become EW's flagship unit.
Kudner soon came east himself when he was offered the presidency, and Wasey moved up to chairman.

The agency became a strong advocate of product sampling,
starting with Barbasol shaving cream, which was then packaged
in tubes that could be easily made in small, sample-size portions.
Five hundred thousand samples were handed out to men in subway and elevated stations in New York City alone, a technique
that, in combination with the network radio 15-minute *Singin'
Sam* program, built the brand overnight. The agency also put Barbasol on the air, sponsoring news commentators Gabriel Heater
and Edwin C. Hill, who, it was assumed, could reach adult men.
The agency's most extensive exploitation of radio came after it
won the Carnation Company account in 1922. It became an early
sponsor of Arthur Godfrey between 1933 and 1945, before his
network fame when he was broadcasting locally on WJSV in
Washington, D.C. More famous was the 20-year radio run of the
Carnation Contented Hour starting in 1931. The format, which
took its title from the brand's longtime ad campaign that claimed
Carnation milk came from "contented cows," showcased classical
and later popular music. There were missed opportunities as well.
According to Leo Burnett, when he worked in the Chicago office a
young ventriloquist from Northwestern University came into the
agency's office to audition for possible radio work. But Wasey was
unable to imagine how a ventriloquist could have any appeal to
radio listeners, so EW passed up its chance to discover Edgar Bergen and Charlie McCarthy.

Another early radio effort, *The Camel Quarter Hour*, was
undertaken in 1931 with singer Morton Downey during a brief
period between 1931 and 1932, when the agency had the R.J. Reynolds Tobacco Company (RJR) account. The Camel brand, once
the industry leader, was in decline relative to its competition, Lucky
Strike, and RJR was prepared to go all out to restore its leadership
position. In 1931 the agency billed $10 million on Camel alone,
much of it thrown into the introduction of the first cellophane outer
wrap. By the time RJR shifted the business to the William Esty
Company in November 1932, the advertiser was spending nearly
$16 million, according to Howard Williams, who joined EW that
year and ended up owning it by 1955. The loss of the account, he

said, forced the agency to lay off 100 people. It taught him not to let the company become dependent on any single piece of business.

Accounts seemed to move in and out of EW with casual ease. General Foods, whose main agency was Young & Rubicam, Inc., reportedly had business at EW, as did Hudson automobiles and Philco Radio, all for relatively brief periods. When Burnett left to form his agency in 1935, he took with him Realsilk Hosiery Mills, Inc., Hoover, and the Minnesota Valley Canning Company, which marketed Niblets corn and Green Giant peas. Although there was no generally agreed upon ranking of ad agencies in the early 1930s, *Advertising Age* columnist William Tyler suggested in 1949 that "Erwin, Wasey was then the world's largest agency," a somewhat exaggerated claim considering the absence of the huge radio billings that the J. Walter Thompson Company (JWT) and Batten Barton Durstine & Osborn (BBDO) wielded. Tyler added that EW was about to undergo "perhaps the most precipitous decline in agency history."

If there was a decline, the agency still remained in the upper tier of leading shops. By the 1940s, it represented a large number of mid-size companies. Agency growth had largely depended upon client growth, led by Carnation and R.B. Selmer's Kreml hair tonic, which EW introduced in 1929. It was not the diversity of the agency's accounts much as the diversity of its locations that made EW unusual for its size. During the 1920s and 1930s, EW had built a considerable European network. And even during World War II, when its offices in Paris, the Hague, Helsinki, and Oslo were under Nazi occupation, $3 million of the agency's total billings of $17 million were from overseas.

Ten years later, EW's 1954 billings had more than doubled, to nearly $37 million. Growth was healthy, but not enough to keep pace with its competitors. In the same period, industry leader JWT's growth had nearly tripled; Y&R had more than tripled; and BBDO and McCann-Erickson had posted nearly five-fold growth rates. By 1955, however, EW's rank among the *Advertising Age* top 60 had fallen to 22nd.

In December of that year Howard Williams joined with his son David to buy Erwin, Wasey & Company, by then billing $35.7 million. Both men had deep roots in advertising and at EW. Howard Williams was a cousin of William Benton, founder of Benton & Bowles. He had been at EW since 1933 and its president since 1946. His son David had come to the agency in 1945 after graduating from Harvard University and serving in the army. Together, they formed the David B. Williams Company, a holding company for the purpose of buying EW. Louis Wasey, 71, was eager to retire, and so was his nephew, George Wasey, an executive vice president. But the Erwin, Wasey name would remain—despite "some moss on it"—according to the senior Williams.

Exactly why the Williamses bought the agency became clear 20 months later. On 2 September 1957 the Williams Company announced the purchase of Ruthrauff & Ryan, Inc. (R&R), originally formed in 1912 and once the sixth-largest agency in the United States, and its intention to merge it into Erwin, Wasey, Ruthrauff & Ryan, Inc. (EWR&R), effective October 1. The combined agencies billed $73 million, $19 million of which came from the EW overseas interests and another $14 million of which

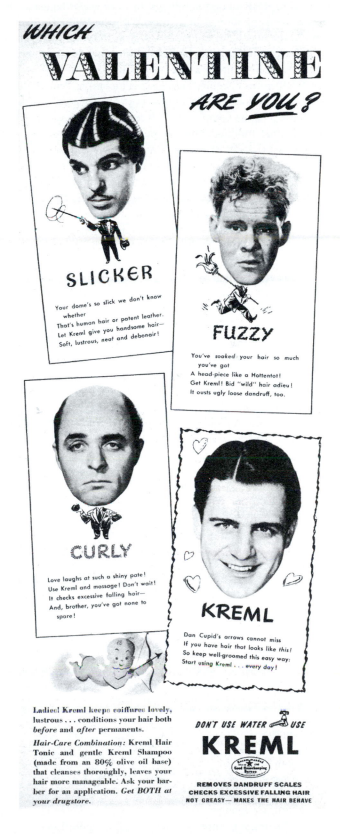

In this 1942 ad for Kreml hair tonic from Erwin, Wasey & Company, three unfortunate men—dubbed "Slicker," "Fuzzy," and "Curly"—illustrate the pitfalls of not using the hair-grooming product.

amounted to R&R's London billings. In 1957 it was hailed as the largest advertising merger in history. With the Williams team in control of the new plans board, it was clear that the R&R side of the company would likely be phased out and the new agency would attempt to institutionalize the EW legacy.

EWR&R in turn acquired a midsize Pittsburgh, Pennsylvania, agency, W.S. Walker Advertising, in 1959. But generally growth was modest. Then in October 1963 Interpublic, Inc., a marketing/communication holding company put together in January 1961 by McCann-Erickson President Marion Harper, Jr., announced the purchase of the Williams Company and its major asset EWR&R. Once again the trade press announced "the biggest deal in the history of the agency business" as Interpublic moved closer to becoming the first advertising organization to hit the half-billion point. EWR&R thus became a sister agency to Jack Tinker & Partners, McCann-Marschalk, and several smaller units under the Interpublic umbrella. It was a move that Louis Wasey did not live to see, however; he died at 77 on 29 August 1961. Under Interpublic, EWR&R continued to operate as before, although with declining volume and with its headquarters moved to Los Angeles, California. In August 1964, just before the presidential election, the Republican National Committee unexpectedly moved its advertising from the Leo Burnett Company to EWR&R in an attempt to save the election prospects of Barry Goldwater. Although EWR&R picked up the business just before the period of greatest media spending, it made no memorable creative contributions. The famous Goldwater campaign theme, "In your heart you know he's right," was the work of Burnett.

Shortly after the election, Ruthrauff & Ryan was dropped from the agency name, and the shop continued as Erwin, Wasey, Inc. The remainder of the 1960s saw steady losses, and after 1970 the agency no longer functioned as an independent entity. The parent company shifted all EW overseas units into Interpublic's international division to create a new company, Wasey, Pritchard Wood & Quadrant, Ltd. In October 1970 the New York EW office, whose billings were down to about $5 million, was combined into the McCann-Erickson flagship operation, where it functioned as McCann's medical division. EW offices in Pittsburgh; Houston, Texas; and San Juan, Puerto Rico, were closed. Finally, in 1979 the name Erwin, Wasey, which in the days before agency rankings were tabulated may or may not have briefly been the "world's largest agency," was permanently retired from the Interpublic roster.

JOHN MCDONOUGH

Further Reading

"EWR&R Buy Makes Interpublic First Agency to Near Half-Billion Mark," *Advertising Age* (14 October 1963)

"EWR&R Is Beset by Post-Merger Problems," *Advertising Age* (16 December 1957)

"H.D., D.B. Williams Are New Owners of Erwin, Wasey," *Advertising Age* (2 January 1956)

"Lou Wasey, One of the Last of the Agency Pioneers, Looks Back on 50 Years of Busy Selling," *Advertising Age* (9 January 1956)

William Esty & Company, Inc.

Founded as William Esty & Company, April 1932; purchased by Ted Bates Worldwide, Inc., and renamed William Esty Company, Inc., 1982; became part of Saatchi & Saatchi when it bought Bates, 1986; ceased to function as an independent agency when merged with Campbell-Mithun Advertising, another Bates property, to become Campbell-Mithun-Esty, 1988.

Major Clients
Ben Gay
Chesebrough-Pond's, Inc.
Colgate-Palmolive-Peet
Dristan
Nissan Motor Company
Noxzema Chemical Company (later Noxell Corporation)
R.J. Reynolds Tobacco Company
Sun Oil

The William Esty name survives as part of Campbell-Mithun-Esty, which was created in 1988 when parent companies Ted Bates and Saatchi & Saatchi merged the William Esty Company with Minneapolis, Minnesota–based Campbell-Mithun. The Esty agency, which was once among the largest in the United States, has not functioned as an independent company since then.

Founder William Esty was born in Urbana, Illinois, in 1894 and graduated from Amherst College in 1915. After graduation he worked briefly for Motion Picture News in Chicago, Illinois, before serving in the army during World War I. He returned to publishing after the war at Butterick Publishing Company and then moved to advertising, first with J.H. Cross in Philadelphia, Pennsylvania, and then with the Gorman Company in New York City. In 1925 he joined the J. Walter Thompson Company (JWT), where he began to build an important reputation for himself running the Lever Bros. account. His connections in the movie business led him to seek celebrity endorsements for Lever's Lux Soap brand, a campaign that would bring JWT to produce the *Lux Radio Theater* for the company in 1934 and make the name Lux synonymous with Hollywood.

By that time, however, Esty had left JWT. In February 1932 he took a long-term lease on an expensive office at 6 East 48th Street, New York City, formerly occupied by Benton and Bowles. With no clients or sources of income, the agency opened as William Esty & Company on 1 April 1932. "All Esty Needs is Advertisers," was the headline in an *Advertising Age* story from 30 July 1932. "Mr. Esty plans to attract accounts," the story said, and media representatives "think he will succeed and they are cultivating the new agency assiduously."

In November of that year Esty sought and won the advertising for Camel cigarettes and Prince Albert tobacco, both products of the R.J. Reynolds Tobacco Company (RJR). It was the beginning of a 33-year relationship with "Old Joe," the Barnum & Bailey camel that served as the model for the original Camel package design. The relationship would expand to include Winston in 1954 and Salem in 1956, as well as Cavalier, Doral, and other brands. It was Esty that created the "T-zone" campaign, referring to the sensitive mucous membranes of the nose and throat. In the late 1940s the agency surveyed doctors and announced in its ads that "More doctors smoke Camels than any other cigarette." The ad copy went on to claim, "Not one single case of throat irritation. Let the 30-day test prove it in your T-zone." After the Federal Trade Commission curbed health claims by cigarette makers in the 1950s, Esty fell back on quality and taste claims. For many years Camel trailed Lucky Strike in sales, but by 1950 the brand achieved a secure leadership position that it would hold for a decade. Among the most memorable of the Esty Camel campaigns was, "I'd walk a mile for a Camel," which was actually inherited by Esty, having first appeared in January 1925 on an outdoor board produced by the Reddington Company. Although N.W. Ayer was Reynolds's agency at the time, there is no reliable information as to who might have authored the line.

The Esty agency made RJR a power in radio with the *Camel Caravan,* a music series with Glen Gray (1933–36), Benny Goodman (1936–39), Bob Crosby (1939–40), and Xavier Cugat (1941–42). The series switched to comedy in 1942 with the team of Abbott and Costello, then Jimmy Durante and Gary Moore. Other Camel-sponsored programs Esty produced included *Blondie* (1939–44), the *Bob Hawk Show* (also known as *Thanks to the Yanks,* 1942–53), and *My Friend Irma* (1952–53). The agency also brought the brand into television with *Man Against Crime,* a live detective series with Ralph Bellamy, and most famously, the first evening network news program, the *Camel News Caravan* with John Cameron Swayze (1948–56) on the NBC network. In 1952 Esty experimented with film production of a detective program called *The Hunter* with Barry Nelson, which ran as a summer series for Cavalier cigarettes, another RJR brand.

Esty became a Colgate-Palmolive-Peet agency in 1944 when it created campaigns for Super Suds and Vel. The business

William Esty & Company had a long, albeit intermittent, association with Colgate-Palmolive-Peet. An ad for Colgate's Fab from the 1960s marked a renewal of the relationship between Esty and the marketer.

broadened the agency client base. Yet by 1945, although it had become the 21st-largest agency in the United States, it was dependent on RJR for about half of its $14 million in billings. In any case, as postwar ad spending rose across the board, William Esty increased its share and grew quickly. By 1947, the year of its 15th anniversary, it broke into the elite top ten in agency ranking, according to *Advertising Age* figures, with billings of $27 million. This amounted to a growth rate of 50 percent in two years, due largely to expansion of the Vel brand into related soap product categories. No major agency came close, although it was the only year Esty would rank among the top ten. That same year William Esty became chairman of the board and James Houlahan was elevated to president, a position he held until 1960. In January 1954 Esty died at his home in New Canaan, Connecticut, at age 59.

The William Esty Company became a dominant agency in the early days of television with its Reynolds and Colgate business. Super Suds was lost in 1952, but the agency won its first General Mills business the next year with the cereal Sugar Jets, followed in 1954 by O-Cell-O sponges. Two years later General Mills ended its relationship with Esty, but the agency profited when Reynolds entered the filter-tip cigarette market with Winston. Then in 1955 Colgate announced it would move the Fab account to Ted Bates & Company, Inc. Esty told Colgate that if the agency could not

The slogan, "Nobody demands more from a Datsun than Datsun," seen in this 1978 ad, helped Esty win the Nissan Motor Company account. *Copyright, Nissan (1978). Datsun is a registered trademark of Nissan.*

continue on Fab, it would prefer to resign all its Colgate business. The calculated risk backfired, and Esty lost other key brands such as Vel and Rapid Shave, along with about $15 million in billings. The agency's relationship with Colgate resumed in January 1964, however, when the agency won back Fab. Cashmere Bouquet, Halo, and Ultra Brite toothpaste followed over the next two years.

Despite the ups and downs, the growth of the agency was slow but steady through the decade. By 1960 Esty was billing a healthy $80 million from only nine clients. With a staff of 451 people, it had probably the lowest ratio of employees to billings of any major agency. It broke the $100 million barrier in 1963. The agency seemed so content with itself that in 1960 the new president, John Peace, told *Advertising Age* that Esty did not want to grow beyond $100 million.

Nestlé, which had come to Esty in June 1959 with Nescafé coffee and then other brands, departed in 1962. The agency picked up Dristan cold tablets from Whitehall Laboratories, a unit of American Home Products, but the decade would soon present Esty with some serious reversals. In 1965 it lost one of its oldest

clients, Thomas Leeming & Company, marketer of Ben-Gay, which had come to Esty in 1933. Earlier, Leeming had been purchased by Pfizer, which also moved Barbasol and Pacquin hand cream out of Esty. Another major loss was $10 million in billings from the P. Ballantine & Sons Brewery, which had been with the agency since 1955.

But the setback with the most emotional repercussions came in June 1966 when Reynolds reassigned Camel and the brand's filters, or about a sixth of Esty's $65 million in Reynolds billings, to Dancer, Fitzgerald, Sample. The stated reason was that the Camel filters business represented a conflict with Winston filters. Then in 1974 Winston, which had been launched by Esty in 1954 with the slogan "Winston tastes good like a cigarette should," followed, also moving to Dancer, Fitzgerald, Sample. To soften the blow, Reynolds moved Camel back to Esty, which still handled its Doral and Salem brands. But Salem went to Batten Barton Durstine & Osborn in 1976, soon after it ended its 28-year relationship with the American Tobacco Company.

Despite the disruptions in the association with Reynolds, the 1970s were a good decade for Esty. Spending by Warner-Lambert grew from $3 million to $25 million in three years, and spending by Nabisco and American Home Products each grew six-fold over spending in the early 1960s. Then, in June 1977, the agency was the victor in an intense competition for the Nissan Motor Company's Datsun account, worth $45 million. The winning theme was, "Nobody demands more from Datsun than Datsun."

Esty remained a major agency as it moved into the 1980s, passing the half-billion-dollar mark in billings while serving a small number of select clients. On 10 February 1982, the normally low-profile company made important news when it announced it would be acquired by Bates in the biggest advertising merger to date. Bates, which ranked second behind Young & Rubicam in worldwide billings, was by far the larger partner in the merger, with nearly $2.4 billion in gross volume compared with $550 million for Esty, but Esty continued with its name and management intact.

By the middle of the decade, however, another decline became evident. While other agencies were growing, Esty watched both its billings and income shrink in 1984 and 1985 with the loss of Winston, Chesebrough-Pond's, and the American Home Products brands Riopan and Riopan Plus. In May 1984 the agency's 40-year on-and-off relationship with Colgate ended when the Fab and Ultra Brite accounts were pulled. The reason given by the advertiser was that Esty operated exclusively in the United States and had been unable to grow on a global basis in accordance with Colgate's needs.

In May 1986 Bates, then billing $3.1 billion, agreed to a merger with Saatchi & Saatchi, creating the largest advertising company in the world and eclipsing the formation of Omnicom a week earlier. The merger brought Esty into the Saatchi family of companies by way of Bates. Again, Esty continued with its identity intact. Within a year, however, the bottom fell out for the company. In June 1986 it lost its last RJR tobacco business when Salem moved to Foote, Cone & Belding, thus ending a 74-year partnership. In March 1987 Joseph O'Donnell became president and chief executive officer. Then in April and May, Esty was hit with two devastating losses in quick succession—MasterCard and Nissan. The damage amounted to $190 million, or about 35 percent of the agency's billings.

With no immediate prospects for replacing such a considerable loss, Esty was in a vulnerable position. The parent company, Bates, looking for ways to salvage its assets, announced on 5 July 1988 that it would merge Esty with Minneapolis-based Campbell-Mithun, an agency with extensive General Mills billings. The new agency, called Campbell-Mithun-Esty, had combined billings of $800 million and was the 16th-largest U.S. agency at the time of the merger in 1989.

JOHN MCDONOUGH

Further Reading

"Bates and Esty to Merge," *Wall Street Journal* (10 February 1982)

"Esty Losing Camel Account after 33 Years," *Advertising Age* (27 June 1966)

"Esty to Merge with CM," *Wall Street Journal* (5 July 1988)

"$11,700,000 Camel Account Shifts to D-F-S from Esty," *Advertising Age* (15 August 1966)

"We Don't Want More Than $100,000,000 in Billing," *Advertising Age* (1 February 1960)

"Why Esty Got Datsun: Personalities Mesh," *Advertising Age* (20 June 1977)

"Winston Goes to D-F-S; Esty Given Camel Line," *Advertising Age* (26 August 1974)

Ethics

Almost any discussion of ethics in advertising must begin with a consideration of truth in advertising. Truth is what makes advertising credible and effective. When advertising is found to be untruthful, when claims are exaggerated or demonstrations rigged, public mistrust of all advertising increases.

In his 1994 study of decision making in advertising, Joel Davis of San Diego State University in California concluded that, for most advertising professionals, "legal considerations are not tempered by ethical considerations" when evaluating advertising. And while Davis concedes that ruling out legal liability is a reasonable first step, he is troubled that too often legal considerations are not tempered by ethical considerations. Too many professionals, he suggests, are inclined to assume if an ad is legal, it is acceptable; if advertising professionals are guided only by the letter of the law, the elimination of deceptive advertising seems a remote ideal.

For some in advertising, ethics is indeed strictly a matter of law—or more precisely, what the law will allow an advertiser to say or show about a product or service. For them, what the law allows is, therefore, truthful enough. For others, ethics is covered in industry codes such as those created by the American Association of Advertising Agencies (AAAA, or the "Four A's").

The limitation of both views is that the laws regulating advertising were written in response to specific egregious practices, and the industry codes are most often read—and perhaps best understood—by those who write them. Even though the codes deal with truthfulness and the responsibilities of advertising professionals, they are often ignored, remembered only after an ethical error has been made. How often does one hear of the Four A's codes playing a role in day-to-day creative approvals meetings or on the set of a commercial production?

Doing Ethics

In *Media Ethics: Issues and Cases*, Philip Patterson and Lee Wilkins assert that ethical thinking begins when elements in a moral system are in conflict and that ethics is an active, ongoing process rather than a code or set of rules. Many who teach ethics in schools of journalism refer to "doing ethics," the intention being to emphasize that ethics is a process rather than a set of written guidelines or encoded prohibitions.

Ethics is a process of moral reasoning and of making rational choices between what is morally justifiable and what is not. Rational is a key word because ethicists have believed since the time of the ancient Greek philosophers that people should be able to give rational explanations in support of their decisions. In terms of ethics *rational* means a decision based on more than gut feeling or the mood of the moment. "Doing ethics" means distinguishing among choices, all of which may be morally justifiable, but some more justifiable than others.

Take for example the well-known case in which marbles were put into a bowl of Campbell's vegetable soup to make the vegetables more clearly visible in a photograph. Was the decision to alter the appearance of the soup justifiable on the grounds that failing to do so would result in a less appetizing image of the product? Did the agency decision makers owe more to their client than to the consumer? Who was deceived about the true nature of the soup? Who benefited from the tampering with the soup? Who was harmed? These are the kinds of questions that typically characterize an ethical dilemma. As Patterson and Wilkins note, ethics is not so much about right versus wrong as it is about conflicting values and choices.

An ethical dilemma facing an advertising professional may require a rational choice between serving the legitimate interests of the clients and the legitimate interests of the agency. Or it may require the individual to weigh the legitimate appeal to a target audience against his or her obligations to the public at large. And the dilemmas facing the decisionmakers at agencies and client companies are compounded by the press of deadlines, the heat of competition, and the complexities of technology. Yet, time, deadlines, and competitive pressure are insufficient excuses when the ad or commercial is denounced as untruthful or unethical. What may be required is an ethical process that works even when there is little time to decide and great pressure upon the decisionmaker.

Ethical Foundations

The foundations for a belief in the importance of ethical decision making can be seen in the work of the major philosophers who shaped Western thinking about business, society, and human nature. Immanuel Kant, German philosopher and author of *Groundwork of the Metaphysics of Morals* (1785) and *Critique of Practical Reason* (1788), gave intellectual substance to the golden rule with his "categorical imperative," which implies that what is right for one is right for all. (In this sense, categorical means unconditional, without exception). Kant held that an act should be viewed as if it would become a universal law. He said the test of genuine moral obligation is that it can be universalized. Right is right and must always be done, even under the most extreme circumstances.

If Kant had been present on the set of that infamous Campbell's photo shoot, he might have asked those placing the marbles in the bottom of the soup bowl if they believed all food shots should be "propped," and if such propping should, in fact, become a universal practice accepted by all advertising agencies and food photographers.

In ancient Greece, Aristotle's "Golden Mean" defined moral virtue as the appropriate location between two extremes, the one involving excess and the other deficiency. According to this view, courage is a mean between cowardice and rashness; generosity is a mean between stinginess and wastefulness; righteous indignation, between envy and spite. A modern example of Aristotle's thinking might be the Federal Trade Commission's decision to ban cigarette advertising from broadcast media and place the surgeon general's warning labels on the packages—yet to continue to permit outdoor and print advertising of cigarettes.

The principle of utility—"Seek the greatest happiness for the greatest number"—originated with Jeremy Bentham in the 18th century and John Stuart Mill in the 19th century. Utilitarianism teaches that we are to determine what is right or wrong by considering what will yield the best consequences for the welfare of human beings. The morally right alternative produces the greatest balance of good over evil. What matters is the amount of good promoted versus the amount of evil restrained. Bentham and Mill considered happiness the sole end of human action; preventing pain and promoting pleasure were the only desirable ends. One can easily imagine utilitarianism as a defense for any number of advertising decisions if Mill's philosophy did not insist that no one person's happiness is any more valuable than that of another.

In the 1980s the philosophy of "communitarianism" came into some popularity with modern ethical thinkers. Communitarianism seeks to provide ethical guidance when confronting issues that affect the whole of society. Social justice is the predominant moral value, but it allows such virtues as altruism and benevolence to have equal footing with the more traditional virtues of truth and loyalty. Communitarianism goes beyond the utilitarian's "greatest good for the greatest number" to seek the best solutions for all of society and for the total environment.

The ethics of the Internet typify a kind of communitarianism by emphasizing equal access, sharing, cooperation, decentralization of control, and universal participation. In advertising, a believer in communitarianism might want to know what effect a particular campaign would have on the whole society and culture as well as on the targeted audience. For example, how might the sexual provocativeness and ambiguity of an ad by designer Calvin Klein featuring scantily clad teens affect the whole society, not just the intended purchasers?

Modern philosophers such as John Rawls and Sissela Bok, and ethicists in academia such as the University of Illinois's Cliff Christians and Kim Rotzell, the State University of New York's Vincent Ruggiero, and the University of Montana's Deni Elliot, are just a few who have contributed much to the academic study of media ethics. They have written books and articles of interest to advertising practitioners who seek to understand the philosophical roots of ethics and the systems one can apply today.

Ethical Systems

Ethical systems require us to think through the facts and consider competing values and principles. For decisions to be considered "ethical" there should be evidence of this kind of reasoning process leading to a defensible decision. So, for example, an approach to ethical consideration of an advertising campaign might include a process that asked such questions as:

- Does the objective of the advertising serve the best interests of the client without violating fair practices in business?
- Has the advertiser considered the impact of its message on those outside the target audience as well as those within?
- When designing research, is the advertiser seeking truthful answers or using research to ratify someone's cherished biases?
- Does the creative execution offend or humiliate members of racial or religious groups or persons with disabilities or of different sexual orientations?
- Does the advertiser accept responsibility for the relationships it establishes with consumers who trust it?

A system of ethical decision making would require advertising practitioners to consider the obligations they have to themselves, their clients, their agency, their company, their colleagues, and their society. And it could help them anticipate the consequences of their decisions more accurately.

When people see ethics not so much as a series of rules differentiating right from wrong, but as an intellectual process, then "doing ethics" means thinking about what we do. It can be a useful way to balance competing rights and even to help choose between unavoidable wrongs.

Questionable Choices

Criticism of ethics in advertising is most heavily focused on political advertising. One frequently cited example is the 1964 "Daisy" commercial run by President Lyndon B. Johnson's campaign. The ad featured the image of a mushroom cloud rising behind a little girl picking daisies. Its goal was to raise doubts about Republican candidate Barry Goldwater's fitness for office in a nuclear age, but it certainly exemplifies the observation that one man's truth may be another's distortion. A similar and more recent example was the 1988 "Willie Horton" spot created by aides to the Republican presidential nominee George H. Bush to help him defeat Massachusetts governor and Democratic candidate Michael Dukakis. At the time, Dukakis was ahead in the polls. The Horton spot was designed to remind viewers of an ex-convict who had raped a woman while he was on furlough from a Massachusetts prison. After the commercial aired, the poll numbers changed dramatically in Bush's favor, and the commercial was seen as a key factor in Dukakis's defeat.

The advertising industry has not ignored the ethical problems posed by political commercials. In 1984 the Four A's presented a code of ethics for political advertising to the U.S. Senate. The code called for advertising agencies that had not signed or did not observe the Code of Fair Campaign Practices to be excluded from representing candidates. It urged ad agencies not to knowingly misrepresent the views or stated records of any candidates or prepare any material that unfairly or prejudicially exploited the race, creed, or national origins of any candidate.

In spite of the fact that the Four A's convened panels to review complaints and that four ads were actually pulled during the 1984 campaign, not all the advertisers complied, and the process was discontinued. Throughout the past two decades, industry leaders such as John O'Toole, Alex Kroll, and Paul Alvarez have argued for codes of ethics for political advertising. And the media have instituted "ad watch" practices in the hope of identifying and perhaps diminishing the number of questionably ethical ads and commercials.

Yet ethical questions and concerns about political advertising remain, perhaps because the most salient part of the 1984 code proposal was the recommendation that "the agency should stand as an independent judge of fair campaign practices, rather than automatically yielding to the wishes of the candidate or his authorized representative." For many advertising professionals, this part of the code places the agency at loggerheads with the interests of its client, the agency's ability to make a profit, and the agency's concept of service. In effect, it creates an immediate ethical dilemma. And yet, this recommendation also comes closest to reflecting the views of modern ethicists as exactly the kind of analytical process ethical practitioners of advertising must engage in—even if they find the prospect uncomfortable and at odds with their own financial interests.

While political advertising may seem to commit the most highly visible sins, it is not alone in drawing the fire of advertising industry critics and the media. The advertising of toys and sugary foods to children was a major focus of debate between toy and cereal companies, children's advocacy groups, and the attorneys at the Federal Trade Commission during the 1970s. In 1990 Volvo Cars of North America released a TV commercial and a print ad that featured a rigged demonstration showing a "monster" truck crushing all the cars in a line except the Volvo. The commercial was designed to show the safety of the Volvo relative to its competition. In November 1990 the Texas attorney general brought suit against Volvo calling the ad a "hoax and a sham" because the Volvo vehicle shown had been reinforced with steel roof supports, while the competitors' cars had been weakened. An editorial in *Advertising Age* expressed surprise that anyone in the national ad business would deliberately rig a demonstration and suggested that the scandal might lead consumers to conclude that no ad claims could be trusted.

The portrayal of minority groups in ads is a long-running issue of contention. African-Americans have complained about the use of racial stereotypes in advertising since the days of Aunt Jemima. Some Hispanics were insulted when a telephone company ran a commercial showing a man being reminded to call his elderly mother. According to Hispanic marketers, the reminder was offensive because calling one's mother is a natural habit in this culture and no reminder is necessary.

In the 1990s criticism focused on the advertising of prescription drugs directly to consumers via television commercials and print ads. Typically, these ads urged consumers to ask their physicians for the latest drug for allergy symptoms, depression, and impotence.

Advertising exerts many significant and positive impacts on consumers. It discourages illegal drug use and drunk driving and encourages safe driving, protection of the environment, physical fitness, healthy diets, and a host of other positive social behaviors. For the most part, even its critics agree that advertising provides detailed information about products and services that are useful to consumers as well as images that charm and delight its audiences. Yet its critics thrive on the occasional—but almost always notorious—example of ethical lapse.

"The consumer is not a moron. She is your wife," said the pioneering ad executive David Ogilvy. Ultimately, learning to incorporate ethical processes into the everyday life of advertising professionals can be seen as the way to give the industry a reputation for a more empathetic and compassionate view of others, as well as to promote more truthful advertising and more rational and principled action.

BOURNE MORRIS

Further Reading

Bok, Sissela, *Lying: Moral Choice in Public and Private Life,* New York: Pantheon, 1978; London: Quartet, 1980

Buck, Rinker, "Three Cheers for Alex Kroll," *Adweek's Marketing Week* 33 (17 February 1992)

Christians, Clifford G., Mark Fackler, and Kim B. Rotzoll, *Media Ethics: Cases and Moral Reasoning,* New York: Longman, 1983; 5th edition, 1998

Davis, Joel J., "Ethics in Advertising Decisionmaking: Implications for Reducing the Incidence of Deceptive Advertising," *Journal of Consumer Affairs* 28, no. 2 (Winter 1994)

Fox, Stephen, *The Mirror Makers: A History of American Advertising and Its Creators,* New York: Morrow, 1984

Patterson, Philip, and Lee Wilkins, *Media Ethics: Issues and Cases,* Dubuque, Iowa: Brown, 1991; 3rd edition, Boston: McGraw-Hill, 1998

Rawls, John, *A Theory of Justice,* Cambridge, Massachusetts: Harvard University Press, 1971; Oxford: Clarendon, 1972

Ruggiero, Vincent Ryan, *The Moral Imperative,* Port Washington, New York: Alfred, 1973; as *Thinking Critically about Ethical Issues,* Mountain View, California: Mayfield, 1997

Stolz, Craig, "Watchdogs on Duty: Industry Groups, the Media, and Ethics Scholars of Every Ilk Plan to Keep a Sharp Eye on Political Advertising This Year," *Adweek* (Eastern edition) (3 February 1992)

Eurocom

Eurocom was formed in 1974 when Jacques Douce, head of Havas, then France's largest advertising agency, restructured his firm, making it a holding company with several agencies within its fold. It expanded overseas in the 1980s and in 1991 merged with France's third largest ad agency, Roux, Séguéla, Cayzac & Godard (RSCG), to form Euro RSCG.

Eurocom's history stretches back to 1835 with the founding by Charles-Louis Havas of France's first press agency, Agence Havas. Havas dominated the French press for over a century, supplying news stories by wire and brokering much of France's advertising space. During the 1920s it turned to advertising as well, forming an internal agency. By the eve of World War II, Havas was by far France's largest advertising agency with billings some ten times those of its closest competitor.

The French government nationalized Agence Havas in 1945, splitting off the press agency to form Agence France Press (AFP). Agence Havas (of which the government owned a majority stake) was left with interests in the sale of press space, tourism, and, under Havas Conseil, advertising. Havas Conseil was France's largest advertising agency (briefly surpassed by Publicis in the 1960s and 1970s) through most of the postwar period.

Douce came to Havas at the age of 19, immediately after the war, working at one of the agency's regional offices. A bout with tuberculosis had prevented Douce from finishing high school, but he compensated for his lack of formal education with dynamism and drive. By 1959 he was head of Havas Conseil and was responsible for much of Havas's success, bringing in clients such as Evian, L'Oréal, Simca, and General Foods.

By 1974 Douce began to fear that Havas Conseil had become too large and too impersonal for many of its clients. His plan was to fragment the agency into smaller component pieces: Havas-Conseil, Univas, Ecom, Performance-Conseil, Faits et Communi-

cations, and Polaris. (It would also have a minority interest in Bélier.) These smaller agencies, he felt, would be more responsive and personal. The newly baptized Eurocom would function as the holding company. Douce also hoped that restructuring would allay clients' conflict-of-interest fears by offering them a choice of several agencies. Douce's gamble worked; sales figures increased ten-fold, and the agencies' market share doubled over the next seven years.

Further changes occurred in the 1980s as Eurocom sought to expand globally under the leadership of Bernard Brochand. Realizing the strength and size of U.S. advertising agencies, Brochand felt Eurocom had to expand to survive. After years of negotiations, Eurocom merged its subsidiary, Havas-Conseil, with Young & Rubicam's subsidiary, Marsteller, to form Havas Conseil Marsteller (HCM) in 1985. HCM invited the Japanese advertising agency Denstu to join the partnership in 1987, forming Havas Dentsu Marsteller (HDM). Eurocom thus established its first significant presence in the United States and Asia and entered the ranks of the world's top 15 advertising agencies. Moreover, in 1986 Brochand had succeeded in increasing Eurocom's minority stake in the large agency Bélier to 95 percent. With the Bélier addition (and the acquisition of such clients as L'Oréal and Evian), Eurocom rocketed past Publicis to become France's—and Europe's—largest agency.

Alain de Pouzilhac, who succeeded Brochand in 1988, continued his predecessor's expansionism. In 1989, along with Carat Espace, the French-based media space broker, Eurocom bought a controlling interest in the British agency Wight Collins Rutherford Scott (WCRS), which had 38 offices around the world. With WCRS came its U.S. network under the leadership of Jerry Della Femina and his company Della Femina Ball: the new agency would be called EWDB. This alliance saw the quick unraveling of

Eurocom's partnership with HDM (Eurocom bought its way out of the partnership in late 1990) as Eurocom now had agencies competing with its Asian-American allies.

An unexpected buying opportunity arose for Eurocom in 1991. As a result of unsuccessful attempts to expand, RSCG was in debt for more than $200 million. RSCG had been the foremost creative agency of France for 20 years, masterminding the successful 1981 presidential campaign of François Mitterrand. RSCG had not only built France's third-largest agency, but it also had offices in the United States, most notably RSCG-Tatham with its $100 million Procter & Gamble Company account. Eurocom had extra cash as a result of selling two distribution and packaging subsidiaries, and with the French Socialist government acting as matchmaker (to prevent an outsider firm from buying RSCG), the two shops united, forming Euro RSCG. Twice as large as its rival Publicis, by the turn of the century Euro RSCG had become one of the world's top six agencies.

CLARK HULTQUIST

Further Reading

Boutelier, Denis, and Dilip Subramanian, *Le grand bluff: Pouvoir et argent dans la publicité*, Paris: Denoël, 1990
Goldman, Debra, "The French Connection," *Adweek* (Eastern edition) (16 December 1991)
Martin, Marc, *Trois siècles de publicité en France*, Paris: Éditions Odile Jacob, 1992
Rosenbaum, Andrew, "Havas to Know No Boundaries," *Advertising Age* (25 June 1990)

Europe, Eastern

The designation "Eastern Europe" gained currency during the more than four decades when Europe was divided into east and west by a political and military Iron Curtain. The region, extending from the Baltic Sea to the Balkan Peninsula, has long been a volatile area: it was the place where both world wars began, and after World War II, it became the primary battlefield in the Cold War. Probably no region of the world experienced as much change in the decade following the fall of the Berlin Wall. Although many of the Eastern European countries have much in common and, to varying degrees, share similar political and legal bureaucracies, since the fall of communism some have been much more effective than others in developing their economic systems.

Before the 1990s Eastern Europe existed in the limbo of a command economy, which precluded any role for advertising as a market tool. A visit to an East Berlin or Prague "supermarket" between 1950 and 1990 would have startled a Western shopper. One would have seen no color on the shelves because there were no brands, and there were no brands because there were only product categories, without the element of competition among providers fighting for a share of the market. In the West an extensive stratification had developed within categories. Milk, for example, was sold in a wide choice of sizes and flavors and with varying fat content. Even in the best food stores in East Berlin, however, milk was sold as a commodity, unrefrigerated and in unmarked plastic bags. Canned goods, toilet paper, dry goods, soft drinks, and other staples were all unbranded generic products.

Today more than 120 million people live in the countries of Eastern Europe, the most populous nation being Poland (38.5 million) and the least populous, Slovenia (1.9 million). The Czech Republic, Hungary, Poland, and Slovenia have largely homogenous populations, while many other countries and regions have large minority groups (Albanians in Serbia and Macedonia; Greeks in Albania; Hungarians in Romania; and Turks in Bulgaria). Several major languages are spoken, the most prominent being Slavic, including Bulgarian, Czech, Macedonian, Polish, Serbo-Croatian, Slovak, and Slovene, all of which are closely related in grammatical structure and vocabulary. Other languages include Albanian, Hungarian, and Romanian. In addition, German is widely understood by older people, while many young people speak at least some English. The word for "advertising" is *oglasavanje* in Slovenia, *promidzba* in Croatia, and *oglasuvanje* in Macedonia. In Albania it is *rekllame* and in Bulgaria *reklamirane*, both variations of the word *reklama*, derived from the Latin *reclamare* (to yell out loud).

The State of the Media

According to Ogilvy & Mather, the top media market in Eastern Europe in 1995 was Poland ($545 million in advertising expenditures), followed by Hungary ($338 million) and the Czech Republic ($326 million). By contrast, advertising expenditures in Romania totaled $85 million, while those in Slovakia and Bulgaria totaled $55 million each. Due largely to political changes and privatization, the space given to advertising in the media burgeoned in the 1990s. With the communist system having almost entirely disappeared, numerous transborder television and FM radio stations, as well as newspapers and magazines, competed to capture largely new audiences.

Early in the decade many old media outlets disappeared. Others managed to evolve and adapt, however, and some new outlets emerged. Slovenia, for example, acquired three new national television stations, three new national daily newspapers, and dozens of local radio stations, while in Bulgaria at least 23 newspapers (most now out of print) were established. Across Eastern Europe the print media's share of total advertising expenditures dropped from more than 80 percent to around 50 percent (a level roughly comparable to that in developed countries), while television's share grew from 10 percent to almost 50 percent. In absolute terms, however, the press increased its income from advertising, a result of the overall increase in use of the media. In terms of growth in advertising per capita, Hungary was the top performer in the five-year period from 1992 to 1997, with an increase from $23 to $54, a change of 134.8 percent.

In 1997 the leading Eastern European countries with percentages of households having television were Poland and Slovakia (100 percent), Bulgaria (96 percent), Hungary and Slovenia (95 percent), the Czech Republic (93 percent), Croatia (90 percent), and Romania (86 percent). The percentages of households with VCRs ranged from 53 percent in Poland to 26 percent in Romania. In terms of access to cable and satellite television, the leading countries were Slovakia (73 percent), Hungary (58 percent), Romania (53 percent), Slovenia (49 percent), Poland (48 percent), Bulgaria and Croatia (34 percent), and the Czech Republic (32 percent). In eight Eastern European nations government-run television had lost more than 10 percent of the market share by 1997, although public stations managed to hold onto their market position and tended to remain market leaders. Hungary was one of few countries showing an increase in viewing time per person, from 228 minutes per week in 1996 to 235 minutes in 1997. During the same period viewing time in Poland dropped from 256 to 213 minutes; the Czech Republic posted a decline from 200 minutes to 130.

The first regional home shopping network in Eastern Europe was launched in 1997 via satellite with news and product messages customized for different markets and broadcast in local languages. Home shopping programming was available in several countries, including Albania, the Czech Republic, Hungary, and Romania.

Telecommunications grew quickly in the 1990s, but as competition increased, industry leaders struggled to develop effective marketing strategies. Poland's market was dominated by Telekomunikacja Polska, featuring direct mail to subscribers and public relations campaigns targeting the telecommunications ministry for purposes of encouraging fair competition. The privatized MATAV continued to dominate in Hungary, but efforts to establish brand identity were limited to a new logo on pay phones. In the Czech Republic, SPT Telecom held most of the business but faced image problems as a result of weak public confidence.

The number of Internet service providers continued to grow, as did the number of cybercafés offering Internet service to the public. As a consequence, increasing numbers of consumers and firms were participating in the global on-line marketplace. The rapid adoption of the Internet as a commercial medium prompted firms to experiment with innovative ways of marketing to consumers. In Slovenia a 1997 survey conducted by the Faculty of Social Science at the University of Ljubljana found that 11 percent of the population had Internet access and that most respondents recognized graphic banner ads for products or services and knew that they could reach an advertiser's Web page by clicking on the ban-

ner. The researchers also found that 30 percent of Slovenian companies had Internet access and that more than half of survey participants said that they liked Internet ads that led them to interesting sites.

Top Advertisers

Major Western companies such as Procter & Gamble (P&G), Henkel, and Unilever began saturating the packaged-goods market in nations such as Poland, the Czech Republic, and Hungary in the mid-1990s as these countries continued their shift toward market-driven economies and as the consumer population continued to stratify into different levels of affluence. The same kinds of changes took place in the former East Germany. As early as 1991 scanners were being installed in East Berlin food and department stores, and Marlboro cigarette ads appeared in train stations. In Dresden a mobile Burger King stand was set up in the center of the city.

Agency experts in the region acknowledged that Western companies faced a serious dilemma in attempting to take maximum advantage of new opportunities while at the same time working to reduce the possibility of consumer backlash against the flood of Western goods. Market research indicated that some Eastern European consumers regarded many Western products as too expensive and consequently out of their reach. This fact partly explained why marketers looked for a range of pricing opportunities to address those portions of society that resented the "invasion" of Western companies.

The top advertisers in Eastern Europe were an interesting mix of multinational companies and homegrown industries. In 1998 *Advertising Age International* listed the top marketers for 7 of the 12 nations based upon U.S. dollar equivalent spending in television, radio, and print. P&G was first in Poland, Hungary, the Czech Republic, Slovenia, and Romania, while Unilever was first in Slovakia and second in Poland, Hungary, the Czech Republic, and Romania.

In Poland the top ten advertisers spent a total of almost $180 million in 1998; all were multinationals, including Mars, Inc.; Henkel; Daewoo Group; PepsiCo; and Colgate-Palmolive Company. P&G and Unilever spent more than $36 million and $34 million, respectively, while others ranged from $10 million to $20 million. In Hungary the top ten advertisers spent almost $100 million, with familiar names such as Philip Morris Companies, Nestlé, and Coco-Cola Company among the leaders. The total for P&G was more than $23 million, while Unilever and Henkel spent more than $18 million and $13 million, respectively. One Hungarian advertiser, Postabank Takarekpenztar, made the number ten spot.

The top advertisers in the Czech Republic spent more than $86 million and included Cokoladovny (also known as Nestlé Cokoladovny, a seasonal confectionery products company), Eurotel (a wireless telecommunications leader), Telecom (also known as Cesky Telecom, considered the leading telecommunications company in the country), and Radio Frekvence (also known as Country Radio, headquartered in Prague). P&G and Unilever spent more than $16 million and $15 million, respectively. In neighboring Slovakia the top ten, which included Globtel and Wm. Wrigley Jr. Company, spent more than $42 million. Unilever and P&G spent more than $7 million each.

In Slovenia the list was dominated by native firms, including Sportna Loterija (a company that organizes various games of chance, including instant games, TV bingo, and sports betting), Loterija Slovenije (the national lottery), Kolinska (a leading producer within the nation's food processing industry), Revoz (Slovenia's only car manufacturer), and Stimorol (chewing gums). P&G spent more than $5 million, while four other companies spent more than $2 million. The top ten spent a total of more than $23 million.

The Balkan neighbors Romania and Bulgaria differed. In Romania the top ten advertisers spent a total of more than $40 million, while in Bulgaria the figure was only about $5 million. Romania was dominated by multinationals such as Coca-Cola and RJR Nabisco, although Mobifon and Mobil Romania also made the list. The totals for P&G and Unilever were more than $7 million and $6 million, respectively. In Bulgaria the list included Philip Morris, B.A.T. (British American Tobacco) Industries, and Coca-Cola but also Bulbank, Bulgarian-Russian Investments, Zagorka Brewery (also known by the name Zagorka Pivovaren Zavod), Balkan Airlines, Interbrew, and Sofia Frans Auto. The leader, Bulbank, spent less than $1 million.

According to industry estimates, tobacco consumption soared in Eastern Europe through 1996, and cigarette marketers capitalized on national pride by developing local brands. Tobacco companies faced challenges, however, as there was a strong black market and a lack of developed distribution channels and clear rules concerning taxes and marketing. In addition, restrictions on cigarette advertising varied widely among the nations. The estimated growth in retail sales from 1995 to 2000 was 17 percent in Romania, 16 percent in Hungary, 14 percent in the Czech Republic, 12 percent in Poland, 4 percent in Slovakia, and 2 percent in Bulgaria.

Leading Agencies

A 1998 *Advertising Age* report on agencies identified the top firms in several Eastern European nations based upon gross income in U.S. dollar equivalents. In Poland DMB&B led with more than $11 million, while ITI McCann-Erickson/Poland reached almost $10 million. J. Walter Thompson (JWT) Parintex and Saatchi & Saatchi exceeded $7 million each. Six other agencies exceeded $5 million, including (in order from highest to lowest dollar figure) Ammirati Puris Lintas Warszawa, Corporate Profiles DDB, Leo Burnett Warsaw, Grey, BBDO Warsaw, and Young & Rubicam Poland. Six more agencies had a gross income that topped $1 million. In Hungary, McCann-Erickson Budapest led with more than $5 million, while four agencies—Lowe GGK Budapest, Young & Rubicam Hungary, Ogilvy & Mather, and Ammirati Puris Lintas Hungary—exceeded $4 million. Other firms exceeding $2 million included, in descending order, Bates Saatchi & Saatchi, DDB/Hungary, BBDO Budapest, Grey, and Leo Burnett Budapest.

The Golden Drum festival honors the best advertising in Central and Eastern Europe.
Courtesy of Golden Drum. Design: Zare Kerin, Kompas Design, Slovenia.

In the Czech Republic, Dorland and Mark/BBDO led with more than $7 million and $6 million, respectively. Other agencies with more than $3 million included, in order of size, Young & Rubicam Czech Republic, McCann-Erickson Prague, Euro RSCG, Leo Burnett, Grey, Ogilvy & Mather, and Ammirati Puris Lintas Czech Republic. In Slovakia, Soria & Grey led with more than $5 million, while Mark/BBDO Bratislava had more than $3 million. Wiktor/Leo Burnett and Creo/Young & Rubicam exceeded $1 million each, with two other agencies—Ogilvy & Mather and Lowe GGK Bratislava—over $500,000.

Different agencies dominated in the former Yugoslavia. In Slovenia, Studio Marketing (JWT) led with a gross income of almost $5 million, while Futura (DDB) had almost $2 million. Agencies with more than $500,000 included Publicis Virgo, S Team Bates Saatchi & Saatchi, Pristop (Grey), and Lowe Avanta Ljubljana. In neighboring Croatia, however, McCann-Erickson Croatia and BBDO Zagreb led with more than $1.1 million and $1 million, respectively. Other agencies with more than $300,000 included Digitel (Ammirati), S Team Bates Saatchi & Saatchi, and Publicis.

In Serbia, Idol & Friends (Ammirati) and S Team Bates Saatchi & Saatchi led with almost $3 million and just over $1 million, respectively. I&F Group/McCann exceeded $500,000.

Neighboring Romania and Bulgaria also had different leaders. In Romania, B.V. McCann-Erickson and Bates Centrade Saatchi & Saatchi led with almost $3 million and just over $2 million, respectively. Other agencies with a gross income exceeding $1 million included, in descending order, Graffiti/BBDO, Ammirati Puris Lintas, Ogilvy & Mather, OFC International/DMB&B, and Focus Advertising (Publicis). In Bulgaria, Ogilvy & Mather led with $900,000. Others with more than $100,000 included P.B.I./McCann-Erickson Sofia, S Team Bates Saatchi & Saatchi, Lowe GGK Sofia, Leo Burnett, Adia (Young & Rubicam), and Grey.

In Macedonia, S Team Bates Saatchi & Saatchi led with more than $300,000; Idea Plus DDB Skopje was the only other agency to exceed $100,000. In Albania the sole listing was for Grey Tirana, with a gross income in 1997 of only $34,000. No listings were available for Bosnia-Herzegovina.

At a Creative Crossroads

Western observers have described Eastern Europe at the end of the 1990s as struggling to find its "creative resonance." The industry is said to be at a creative crossroads. The best work from the region reaches an international standard of quality, although some suffers from an apparent lack of understanding of what constitutes effective advertising. At the annual Golden Drum Advertising Festival of the New Europe, which draws the top creative work from throughout Eastern Europe and former Soviet-bloc countries, simple, strong conceptual ideas and top-notch executions have marked the winners. The stylistic influence of advertising in neighboring regions is evident.

Because the industry is so new in Eastern Europe, festival jurors have cautiously avoided criticizing the region's creative sensibility. At the same time they have acknowledged that production quality is becoming so uniformly slick that ads are at risk of losing their national flavor. A "New Europe" is emerging, seemingly less focused on what dreams lie ahead than on the oddly cherished nightmare left behind. Jurors have also charged that Eastern European copywriters, art directors, and other creative personnel stop short of offering memorable, original, absorbing ideas, revealing a lack of discipline.

During the earlier transitional period, multinational clients had simply adapted or translated Western ads for Eastern European audiences. Experts are divided over whether a regional flavor or tone of voice will develop, with some claiming that life in the Baltics is as different from that in the Balkans as life in, say, Britain is from that in Italy—that the sole commonality of Eastern Europeans is the experience of having lived under communism. Others disagree, however, arguing that regional styles will eventually emerge as marketers and agencies replace expatriates with local talent, a process that was already happening at the beginning of the 21st century, and as commercials begin to include strong references to the local culture.

Several individuals have provided exemplary leadership in advancing the advertising industry in their respective Eastern European countries. They include Sandor Farkas, secretary-general of the Association of Advertising Agencies, in Hungary; Kehrt Reyner, publisher of *Media Polska* and *Marketing Polska* magazines, in Poland; Jure Apih, founder and president of the Golden Drum International Advertising Festival of the New Europe, in Slovenia; Josip Sudar, author of pioneering books on advertising in Croatia and former head of advertising in key Croatian marketing firms; Marta Tungli, secretary-general of the Hungarian Advertising Association; Ladislav Kopecky, president of the Association of Advertising Agencies, in the Czech Republic; Dragan Sakan, founder, chairman, and creative director of S Team Bates Saatchi & Saatchi, Belgrade, in Serbia; Michal Pacina, creative director of Mark/BBDO, Prague, in the Czech Republic; Csaba Foldvari, creative director of Young & Rubicam/Budapest, in Hungary; Kot Przybora, creative director of Grey Warszawa, in Poland; Jiri Mikes, vice president of the Association of Advertising Agencies, in the Czech Republic; Janez Damjan, president of the Slovenian Marketing Association; and Milcho Manchevski, author, art director, screenwriter, and scriptwriter for the acclaimed film *Before the Rain*, in Macedonia.

MICHAEL H. MCBRIDE

Further Reading

Damjan, Janez, editor, *Proceedings of the Seminar on Marketing Communications at the 3rd International Advertising Festival of the New Europe*, Portoroz, Slovenia: Slovenian Advertising Association, 1996

Damjan, Janez, editor, *Proceedings of the Seminar on Marketing Communications at the 4th International Advertising Festival of the New Europe*, Portoroz, Slovenia: Slovenian Advertising Association, 1997

Giges, Nancy S., editor, *Open Communications in the 21st Century*, London: Atalink, 1998

Ivanov, Dimitri, "Image-Conscious Eastern Europe," *New Moment* 1 (1998)

Mooij, Marieke de, *Advertising Worldwide: Concepts, Theories, and Practice of International, Multinational, and Global Advertising*, New York: Prentice Hall, 1991; 2nd edition, New York and London: Prentice Hall, 1994

Mueller, Barbara, *International Advertising: Communicating across Cultures*, Belmont, California: Wadsworth, 1996

Nowak, Jan, editor, *Marketing in Central and Eastern Europe*, New York: International Business Press, 1996

O'Neil, Patrick H., editor, *Post-Communism and the Media in Eastern Europe*, London: Cass, 1996; Portland, Oregon: Cass, 1997

Tilles, Daniel, "New Europe, New Outlook," *Adweek* (Eastern Edition) (8 December 1997)

Euro RSCG

Created by merger of Eurocom and Roux Séguéla Cayzac Godard, 1991; acquired majority stake in Dahlin Smith White, 1996; acquired Jordan McGrath Case & Partners, 1999.

Major Clients
France Telecom
Intel Corporation
Iomega Corporation
MCI (later Worldcom)
Procter & Gamble Company
Volvo

Euro RSCG was formed in 1991 when Eurocom acquired Roux Séguéla Cayzac Godard (RSCG). At that time, the combination produced Europe's largest and the world's sixth-largest advertising agency. Euro RSCG globalized its advertising business, targeting the U.S. market rather than that of France alone. By 1997 the company had moved its headquarters from Paris, France, to New York City, a shift that symbolized the agency's new worldwide focus.

The history of Euro RSCG began with the two separate agencies: Eurocom and RSCG. Eurocom, a subsidiary of the French media giant Havas, was formed in 1974 as a holding company with several smaller agencies. During the 1970s and 1980s, Eurocom was a rival in France and Europe to Publicis, Europe's top agency. Eurocom sought to expand outside of Europe through a joint venture with Young & Rubicam of the United States and Dentsu of Japan in 1987, which formed Havas Dentsu Marsteller (HDM). However, HDM did not bring Eurocom the global billings it desired. Furthermore, in 1990 Eurocom lost two valuable accounts: SNCF, the French national railroad, and the insurer UAP, and as a result of these losses some concluded that Eurocom's advertising had become stodgy. To stave off further losses and to gain a better foothold in the United States, Eurocom acquired RSCG.

RSCG had been considered France's most dynamic and creative agency since the early 1970s. During the 1980s RSCG underwent considerable expansions, which were funded mostly by loans. Expansion did not pan out as expected, however: by 1990 RSCG had $220 million of debt and few prospects for new funding; in 1991 it lost $60 million and was on the verge of bankruptcy. With a push from the French government (which did not want to see RSCG bought out by a foreign—i.e., U.S.—company), Eurocom arranged to merge with the troubled agency in 1991. Seeking to jumpstart its U.S. operations, Eurocom was particularly anxious to maintain the most desirable division of RSCG abroad, RSCG Tatham in Chicago, Illinois, which annually billed $100 million from Procter & Gamble Company (P&G). In late 1991 the deal was signed. The new firm was formidable: first in France, first in Europe, and sixth in the world in terms of billings. The chairman of the new agency, Alain de Pouzilhac, said, "We

are creating a great new European name to fight the U.S. and Japanese mastodons. We will fight like lions."

The formation of Euro RSCG brought immediate problems, particularly among its U.S. subsidiary agencies. Eurocom's relations with Jerry Della Femina, operator of one of those agencies, Della Femina McNamee, had never been good and worsened after the merger. As the parties fought, clients left, forcing Euro RSCG to buy out Della Femina in 1992. After Della Femina left, Euro RSCG reorganized its U.S. operations into seven agencies, the two most important being Euro RSCG Tatham in Chicago and Messner Vetere Berger McNamee Schmetterer/Euro RSCG in New York City.

After the merger Euro RSCG had to fight to retain the lucrative P&G account. Before acquiring RSCG, one of Eurocom's clients had been Henkel of Germany, whose interests, as a maker of home products, conflicted with those of P&G. Further problems arose for Euro RSCG when Charlotte Beers, the head of Tatham who had dealt with P&G for several years, left for Ogilvy & Mather. Euro RSCG responded by sending its international head, Jean-Michel Goudard, to P&G in Cincinnati, Ohio, to retain that crucial business. Euro RSCG ultimately sacrificed its Henkel account but realized the benefits of P&G's global reach.

Euro RSCG also had to settle potential client conflicts in Europe. Therefore, the agency reorganized itself into five separate agencies, each with 70 to 90 account managers and creative managers. These agencies retained their individual names and identities while operating under the Euro RSCG nameplate: for example, Scher, Lenoir & Lafarge became Euro RSCG Scher, Lenoir & Lafarge, and Henocq, Benitah & Julien became Euro RSCG Henocq, Benitah & Julien. According to Jacques Séguéla, president of Euro RSCG France, the new federal structure ensured that client conflicts would not arise. This European reorganization took two years but was accomplished with a minimum of layoffs and loss of clients. As a result, Euro RSCG became an advertising giant with 2,500 employees and nearly $500 million in annual billings, making the French agency twice as large as its European rival Publicis.

Even as the reorganization allowed Euro RSCG to achieve dominance in France, the alliance enabled the company to expand its focus on business outside of France during the 1990s; in time, a majority of its clients would be multinational firms based in other countries. The company's decision to focus more on foreign operations was partially precipitated by three French laws passed in the 1990s. The Evin Law (Loi Evin; 1991) forbade most tobacco and alcohol advertising in France; the Sapin Law (Loi Sapin; 1992) regulated media brokers and removed the standard agency 15 percent commission; and the Toubon Law (Loi Toubon; 1994) required that all advertising for French markets be created in French. These new regulations, along with the French recession of the early 1990s, led all French agencies to see their profits dip significantly, making the relatively unregulated U.S. market all the more attractive.

A 1996 poster from Euro RSCG used humor to sell Evian mineral water to riders of public transport in Britain.

To build its presence in the U.S. market, Euro RSCG bought two U.S. agencies in the late 1990s: Dahlin Smith White (DSW) in 1996 and Jordan McGrath Case & Partners in 1999. At the time of the acquisition, DSW was a ten-year-old firm with billings of $128 million. Furthermore, among DSW's clients were the U.S. computer chip maker Intel Corporation and the Zip-drive firm Iomega Corporation. Euro RSCG had handled Intel in Asia for the previous four years, and by acquiring Intel's estimated $100 million U.S. account, Euro RSCG established a worldwide relationship with Intel worth $150 million annually. Iomega brought Euro RSCG $35 million in billings, further giving the agency a reputation as a leading technology shop.

In addition to the obvious financial gains, the relationship with Intel benefited Euro RSCG in other ways. Before giving the agency its account, Intel insisted that Euro RSCG improve technologically. Prior to 1996 Euro RSCG had more than 100 offices worldwide, but it did not have a companywide e-mail system. Intel hoped that establishing such a worldwide computer network would produce more effective advertising by increasing connections among executives at both firms. The jointly created computer system gave users at Euro RSCG and Intel the ability to observe the progress of campaigns from start to finish and the opportunity to send instant feedback. Euro RSCG's first big U.S. campaign for Intel launched the Pentium III Chip at the 1999

Super Bowl. It was expected that Intel billings would reach $100 million worldwide.

This technology initiative from Intel encouraged Euro RSCG to expand its work in on-line advertising. In 1998 the firm reorganized its 22 interactive agencies in 12 countries into one network. At $43 million, the interactive workload remained a relatively small part of Euro RSCG's billings, but the agency's on-line clients were among its most important, including Intel, MCI (later Worldcom), and America Online, and collaboration among various Euro RSCG offices worldwide increased.

In 1999 Euro RSCG moved to become a bigger player in the United States in pharmaceutical and healthcare advertising by acquiring Jordan McGrath Case & Partners. The acquisition brought around $600 million in billings from SmithKline Beecham, Novartis, and Pharmacia & Upjohn to Euro RSCG. Moreover, Euro RSCG positioned itself to strengthen its ties to P&G; Jordan McGrath handled Bounty, Zest, Safeguard, and Era in the United States for the consumer products giant.

Internationalization of Euro RSCG was aided by changes in the company's management during the 1990s. De Pouzilhac, who created Euro RSCG before becoming chief executive officer (CEO) of Havas Advertising in 1996, believed that having Americans among the leaders of Euro RSCG would increase the company's credibility with multinational advertisers based in the United States. In 1995 Euro RSCG named Steve Dworin, an American, vice-chairman, and in 1997 the firm named another American, Robert Schmetterer, CEO, replacing the Frenchman Alain Cayzac. Schmetterer had a long association with Euro RSCG's parent company, Havas, having worked as CEO of Havas Dentsu Marsteller (HDM) in the late 1980s. He also served as a partner in the successful New York agency Messner Vetere Berger

Carey Schmetterer during the 1990s. De Pouzilhac believed that the new CEO was the best person to blend the four U.S. agencies into a single Euro RSCG brand. Further signifying Euro RSCG's commitment to U.S. expansion was the announcement accompanying Schmetterer's appointment that the new corporate headquarters would be in New York City instead of Paris.

In early 1998 the French utility and communications giant Compagnie Générale des Eaux purchased Havas for nearly $4 billion and formed a new firm, Vivendi Universal. By 2001 Vivendi had gradually reduced its ownership of Havas, however, and many observers expected that the remaining share would soon be sold.

CLARK HULTQUIST

See also Pouzilhac, Alain de

Further Reading

"Advertising: Eurover There," *The Economist* 324, no. 7766 (4 July 1992)
Crumley, Bruce, "Euro RSCG's New French Face," *Advertising Age* (26 April 1993)
"DSW Joins Euro RSCG Network, Gains Intel Account," *Brandweek* (25 March 1996)
Goldman, Debra, "The French Connection," *Adweek* (Eastern edition) (16 December 1991)
Johnson, Bradley, "Euro RSCG Takes High-Tech Leap, with Intel's Push," *Advertising Age* (16 June 1997)
Tilles, Daniel, "Paris on the Hudson," *Adweek* (Eastern edition) (31 March 1997)
Warner, Bernhard, "Euro RSCG Worldwide Commits to Online Future," *Brandweek* (28 September 1998)

Euro RSCG Tatham. *See* Tatham-Laird, Inc.

Events

As traditional media such as television and magazines proliferate and target ever-narrower groups, their audiences become smaller and more fragmented. To capture broader segments of the public, advertisers and agencies have turned increasingly to event advertising and marketing. Event advertising, also called event marketing or event sponsorship, is participation by an advertiser or marketer in events—including sports events, concerts, and cultural activities—with the goal of promoting the brand or com-

pany name to the consumer and other interested parties, such as company employees, stockholders, or local municipal officials.

Between 1989 and 1997 annual event advertising expenditures in the United States grew from $2.1 billion to $8 billion. The origins of the practice can be traced to the early days of advertising. The first broadcasts in radio and television were "sponsored" by companies that provided funding to get the programs on air. In exchange, the company's name was mentioned

A poster for the 1999 Festival de Fès, a presentation of sacred music from around the world, featured the corporate logos of the event's major sponsors.

during the broadcast. Today, companies pay a set amount of money to have their names or those of their brands incorporated into an event title or used as the designated title. Examples include the Virginia Slims Tennis Tournament and the FedEx Orange Bowl. Event advertising is similar to other forms of advertising in that it has a commercial objective: increasing brand or corporate name awareness. But a company that embarks on this type of activity may have other objectives, such as improving good will or enhancing its image.

Event advertising is used to reach a wide audience. Often the sponsor's name appears in all the media in which the event is being publicized. The company's name is seen by those who attend the actual event, as well as those who watch it on television. Indeed, those secondary audiences may be more important than the primary ones. Companies that advertise at the Super Bowl may be seen by the 100,000 or so present in the football stadium, but their names will be seen by millions more watching the game at home. The value of such large viewing audiences is reflected in the skyrocketing price for this annual event. Companies now pay $1.9 million for 30 seconds of exposure in the Super

Bowl, making it the most costly event on television. Similar prices are recorded occasionally for sponsorship of other unique television events, such as the final episode of the popular TV show *Seinfeld* in May 1998. In each case, advertisers are attracted by both the large audiences and the greater than average amount of media coverage such programs attract. Indeed, the Super Bowl now represents an occasion for many advertisers to launch new campaigns; for some, it may be their sole television exposure for the year.

Sports account for about two-thirds of expenditures in event advertising. One of the biggest sporting events is the Olympic Games. Here, companies now sponsor everything from an event to a team to the broadcast rights in a particular country. In 1996 companies paid up to $40 million to display in their ads the five interlinked Olympic rings that designate an "official" sponsor of the event. The reason they will pay so much is that the games are watched by an estimated 3.5 billion people worldwide, making it one of the biggest opportunities for reaching a global audience.

One of the problems for event advertisers is the practice used by nonsponsoring companies known as "ambush marketing." Here, a company crafts its message in such a way that people believe it is an official event advertiser even when it is not; ambush marketers buy their time at discounted rates or on several local markets so that in those markets they look like official sponsors. Both American Express and Nike have successfully employed this tactic against official Olympic advertisers Visa and Reebok.

Event advertising also provides important public relations opportunities. The company sponsoring an event may wish to impress stockholders, community leaders, or employees. Tobacco giant Philip Morris Companies is the largest sponsor of dance performances in the United States, along with many other arts events, a fact that it hopes will help soften antagonism to it as the seller of a highly controversial product. Yet event advertisers also may be subject to criticism. Nonprofit institutions may be accused of "selling out" if they accept funding from corporations that can then have undue influence on them. Both Philip Morris and Anheuser-Busch, the top two U.S. event advertisers, are accused of using such TV promotions to reach young people—even though they are not legally allowed to do so through traditional media advertising.

A newer form of event sponsorship is known as cause marketing. Here, a company links its name or its brands to specific causes. Examples include Intercontinental Hotels sponsorship of the United Nations Children's Fund (UNICEF) or Toys "R" Us giving money to support the Juvenile Diabetes Foundation. In many cases, the link is made for strategic as well as altruistic reasons. By associating their name with a good cause, the companies hope to improve their image among customers and build up their brand name.

Another late 1990s innovation is sponsorship of a building. In most cases, this is a sports arena renamed for the sponsoring company. Pepsi-Cola Company paid $50 million over a 20-year period to rename the arena in Denver, Colorado, the Pepsi Center; the former Candlestick Park in San Francisco, California, has been renamed 3Com Park; the Chicago (Illinois) Bulls play in the United Center, named after the hometown airline. This type of sponsorship offers advertisers a continuous and long-term presence, regardless of the event taking place.

Determining the impact of the sponsorship is a problem for event advertisers. Whereas TV audiences are measured via electronic meters and magazine audiences through syndicated studies, the impact of an event is harder to gauge. The effectiveness also depends on the original objectives. It may be brand awareness, which can be measured through before-and-after event surveys, or it could be improved goodwill, which might be seen subsequently through more positive press coverage. Ultimately, the goals of event advertising should be the same as for other forms of advertising: to increase sales and enhance the company's image. Some research companies offer sponsorship measurement and evaluation services. Joyce Julius & Associates, for example, can provide event advertisers with a complete event "audit" that includes measurement of attendance, media coverage, and media audiences, among other elements.

Despite the lack of syndicated or reliable measurement and the increasing costs, advertisers are turning more to this type of promotional activity. Event advertisers realize that one of the old-est definitions of advertising, "keeping one's name before the public," can readily be achieved through this type of marketing communication.

HELEN KATZ

See also color plate in this volume

Further Reading

Cornwell, T. Bettina, and Isabelle Maignan, "An International Review of Sponsorship Research," *Journal of Advertising* 27, no. 1 (Spring 1998)

Gardner, Meryl P., and Philip Shuman, "Sponsorship: An Important Component of the Promotions Mix," *Journal of Advertising* 16, no. 1 (1987)

IEG Sponsorship Report (1992–)

McDonald, Colin, "Sponsorship and the Image of the Sponsor," *European Journal of Marketing* 25, no. 11 (1991)

Meenaghan, John A., "Commercial Sponsorship," *European Journal of Marketing* 17, no. 7 (1983)

Sandler, Dennis M., and David Shani, "Olympic Sponsorship vs. 'Ambush' Marketing: Who Gets the Gold?" *Journal of Advertising Research* 29, no. 4 (August/September 1989)

Executional Variable

In paging through a magazine, one quickly notices that the advertisements differ greatly from one another in style and format. Ad messages vary because each advertiser faces unique conditions and must therefore find special ways to create the desired impact on their target audiences. The tools that advertisers and advertising agencies use to create unique messages are called executional variables.

Advertisers seek variation in their advertisements for a number of reasons. Different appeals and formats are often needed to influence different target audiences—adults as opposed to children, for example, or women rather than men. A change may also be sought when an advertiser's current campaign is wearing out and a fresh approach is needed. Advertisers frequently change their message with shifts in business or social environments, such as when buyers demand new attributes or the regulations governing an industry change. In a related vein, advertisers may vary their advertisements to take advantage of the various qualities of the media they use, such as a technical magazine versus a men's sports publication. Advertisers also select executional variables to outwit competitors, win customers, and expand markets. Even when competitors convey a similar selling proposition, they execute advertisements differently. Vigilant advertisers constantly seek ways to change and improve the effectiveness of their ads by tailoring executional variables to the vision they hold for their campaigns.

Executional variables, which comprise all the tools advertisers use to create a unique persuasive message, are divided into two major categories: executional elements (i.e., executional stimuli) and executional formats. Executional elements are all the tractable elements (e.g., signs, symbols, and cues) advertisers have at their disposal to convey various meanings and register different impressions. Executional formats dictate how a message is presented to its audience.

Executional Formats

More than 25 executional formats are found in advertising. A few clearly differ; others are quite similar, differing from their counterparts in subtle ways. Moreover, hybrid formats are often encountered, as advertisers may use more than one format in a single ad to accomplish their objectives.

An appropriate executional format is selected after advertisers and their agencies assess the situation, set the goals and objectives for the campaign, settle on a creative concept, and specify message strategy. In that way, the campaign concept and advertising strategy are executed within the selected executional format or plan.

One of the more commonly used executional formats is known as "announcer using narrative." In this format, an announcer's voice states the message through voice-over or, with others, through dialogue. Ford Motor Company, for example, used an unidentified announcer to explain a rebate on its Grand Marquis.

The demonstration is another popular format that can be executed in a variety of approaches. The main idea is to support a direct, benefit-based claim regarding a brand difference or superiority. Typically, a real or imagined scenario is used to make a direct benefit-based brand claim, highlight how benefits are meaningful and enjoyed to the fullest, support the promise, and convey instructions or show how the product is used or works. Advertisers, in using demonstrations, make them relevant to actual usage and select cues that involve the audience in the message; care must be taken, however, not to exaggerate a claim beyond credibility.

There are several variations on the demonstration format. The "torture test" demonstrates the brand undergoing a grueling examination that tests its very fabric, reliability, precision, performance, and suitability under specific conditions. Sears, Roebuck & Company used this format for several decades to demonstrate its Die Hard battery under torturous winter conditions and succeeded in bolstering its customer-based brand equity and establishing brand identity. The Banjo Minnow's infomercials used another variation, the "in-use demonstration," employing underwater shots of bass hitting the lure. Aspirin brands have locked horns for years, each employing its own "comparative demonstration" of superiority. In demonstrating the effectiveness of Bayer Aspirin, for example, its ads have claimed that doctors recommend Bayer more than any other brand of aspirin.

Another variation, "before-after tests," remain a mainstay of contemporary advertising. Procter & Gamble Company (P&G) infused a fear of negative social consequences into before-after demonstrations showing users of its Head & Shoulders dandruff shampoo. PepsiCo used a "whimsical" format in comparing the lifestyles of two chimps. One chimp, raised drinking rival soft drink Coca-Cola and then released into the wild, was shown doing fine, enjoying the forest and a friendship with Tarzan; the chimp raised drinking Pepsi was depicted as doing far better, wearing a smile, sporting a smoking jacket, and living in a tree house with Jane. Whimsical demonstrations of a brand's effects are humorous exaggerations intentionally developed, often as hyperbole, for comic effect. Because they do not convey strict literal superiority, they typically do not violate U.S. advertising law governing product comparisons.

The benefits of a brand can also be conveyed by such executional formats as "close-ups," "comparative advertising," "case histories," "customer interviews," "testimonials," "news announcements," and "problem and solution." "Close-ups" focus on a particular object or deterministic attribute of interest to buyers, leaving out other salient attributes of the product. Deterministic attributes provide benefits most important to buyers, and a top score for a deterministic attribute is often a sufficient trigger toward the selection of one brand. Many consumers who purchased a Volvo automobile said they did so because its safety features were deterministic.

Source of the Message

"Testimonials" emphasize support for a claim through advice from the spokesperson, who acts as the source of the message. Spokespersons commonly include authority figures, celebrities, or animated characters. Selection of a spokesperson is critical. Advertisers want the audience to equate the qualities of the spokesperson, or source, with specific qualities and benefits surrounding their brand or company. However, the celebrity should not overwhelm the advertisement or the brand name and message may be ignored. A "case history" is a kind of testimonial that supports an advertiser's appeal by injecting an expert, novice, celebrity, or charismatic or unusual character into a sketch that shows that character using the advertiser's brand to solve problems.

"Customer interviews or endorsements" replace special characters with real customers who serve as spokespersons, making the advertisement relevant to the audience. They reflect the particular needs of the audience, increasing the audience's perception of advertiser empathy. Savin Corporation's "We're going to win you over" campaign used endorsements from a number of national associations—such as the National Association of Legal Secretaries and the Association of Information Technology Professionals—to promote its copier machines. The endorsements were credible because legal secretaries are inundated with requests for copies of important documents that they then provide to consumers, which made them well suited to judge firsthand the functionality and reliability of copy machines.

The "news announcement" announces a dramatic technical breakthrough, an unusual promotional, a special price deal, or some other major development or improvement in the product or service that the advertiser believes will yield a substantial increase in customer value and satisfaction. The "problem-solution" format presents a direct portrayal of how one brand solves a particular problem. The service or product becomes the solution. The problem of having to scrub and polish hardwood flooring rigorously is solved in advertisements touting the ease of cleaning and polishing with Just Squirt & Mop, a flanker brand to Colgate-Palmolive Company's Murphy's Oil Soap.

The "comparative advertising" format directly or indirectly contrasts an advertiser's brand with competitive brands. Contrasts are based on such factors as features, benefits, design form, standards, and specifications. Ingredients and composition, the lack of an undesirable quality, functionality of the product and its packaging, product/service augmentation strategies, and preferences also form bases of comparison. Advertisers use either objective or subjective measures to determine brand judgment. Objective judgments are based on physical qualities or direct measurements, such as braking power, gas mileage, or the number of cup holders that characterize automobiles. R.J. Reynolds Tobacco Company used an indirect comparison based on physical measurement in contrasting the percentage of additives found in Winston cigarettes to the average amount of additives found in the top ten U.S. nonmenthol brands. Conversely, judgments can be based on subjective elements such as personal likes, dislikes, and prefer-

In this 1985 magazine ad, Michelin's emphasis on quality and dependability evoked feelings of security.
Courtesy of Michelin North America, Inc.

ences. For example, taste tests are based on personal preferences expressed by a group of participants.

Comparative formats in advertising are illegal in some countries, but in the United States comparative advertising is encouraged under the "consumer's right to know" philosophy in consumer rights legislation. Advertisers that use the comparative format, however, must conform to numerous regulatory guidelines. Comparisons must be made along at least one significant quality or attribute. In the advertisements, competitors must be fairly named, shown, and treated. Product tampering is illegal, and participants in research must have experience in the product category. If the comparison is based on preference, participants actually have to try or experience the brands. Intensive distribution, for example, cannot equate to buyer preference. Triple association tests have replaced paired comparisons as the generally accepted methodology for conducting preference tests. Here, participants are given three unlabeled items to test. Two items are the same brand, while the third is a different brand. For a marketer to claim superiority in its advertising, a significantly larger number of participants must discriminate among the three items, identifying the two like items and differentiating them from the other one, while indicating a preference for one brand over the other. If participants cannot tell the difference between brands or have no clear-cut preference, a marketer may instead use the "aspiration or parity" format.

"Aspiration or parity" is a special case of comparative advertising in which establishing brand or company superiority is not the goal. Instead, aspiration places the advertiser's brand next to a leading, high-quality, and often more expensive brand to create a perception of similarity. Aspiration attempts to wash the image and qualities of the leading brand onto the follower. Parity implies that there is no significant difference between two or more competing brands. For example, a print advertisement for Suave Daily Clarifying Shampoo for women challenged readers to judge the difference in looks between the hair of two models. Suave shampoo was used by one model while the other model shampooed with an unnamed, expensive brand. Clearly, there was no visible difference. The argument urged women both to "look and shop smart" by saving money on Suave.

"Slice of Life"

The "slice of life," or vignette, is another popular format. It is a short sketch, usually a story about the lifestyles of product users, that typically shows brand users enjoying life as they delight in the brand. In the slice-of-life format employed by White Chantilly perfume, the scene revolved around a handsome, obviously unattached man attending a meeting of a young conservative club. Sitting alone in the crowd, he looked like he would enjoy meeting someone. The message advised women that using White Chantilly perfume would "help him find you." Sometimes a satiric image of the nonuser is introduced, showing him or her to be suffering some sort of negative consequences. FedEx Corporation contrasted a sharply dressed, attractive junior executive who sent his company's package via Federal Express with another employee,

portrayed as an untidy, slovenly bungler, who chose another delivery service. Frequently, the format is built from a series of fast-paced images comprised of different scenes and people.

In contrast, the "brand image montage" format goes further than slice-of-life ads to link attitude to brand image. It focuses on life with or without the brand. The California Milk Board's "Got milk" campaign, for example, demonstrated the hardship to a family that comes when it runs out of milk. This format is suited to conveying benefits, feelings, or both. When feelings are emphasized, the challenge is to select executional elements that convey the depth of a specific feeling. The television format typically superimposes display type, music, and voice-over on the visual elements.

Another common format is the "fear appeal." It conveys the negative consequences besetting individuals who do not adhere to the message. Physical consequences threaten deterioration of a person's body caused by factors such as cancer or tooth decay, while social consequences invoke fear of social punishment. Cascade, an automatic dishwasher detergent, was promoted by its marketer, P&G, through the explicit and implicit consequences of social disapproval in its long-running "spots on the glasses" campaign. Fear appeals present an anxiety-evoking situation to shake the audience out of its complacency, and the brand or company is presented as a solution to the problem.

Another format based on emotion is "humor." One theory posits that humor is a pleasant feeling that places people in a desirable mood. Unwilling to forgo the pleasantness and lose the humorous mood, the audience accepts or yields to the message rather than arguing against it. Similarly, the distraction principle suggests that humor distracts those who receive the message from their initial position on a brand. They let down their guard, forget their initial attitude, and accept the message because they like the humor. While humorous formats are intrusive and capture attention, they tend to wear out quickly. In addition, care must be taken in designing a humorous format because humor is a matter of personal preference. The California Milk Board discovered that southern California's Hispanic mothers were not influenced by its "Got milk" campaign because they did not see humor in the commercial about a family that ran out of milk. To them the campaign's humorous take on milk deprivation was more than irrelevant, it was offensive. They believed a good mother cared about her family's well being and would not run out of milk. Once that reaction was discovered, the board changed its format to one that promoted ethnic recipes using milk, which proved more effective in influencing the Hispanic population (the "Got milk" copy was retained, however). Another disadvantage of humor is that it may distract the audience from the brand name and its selling proposition. While the readers or viewers may enjoy the humor, they may fail to learn about the brand's qualities.

The "mood/imagery" format associates a brand with a pleasant feeling or mood enjoyed by the audience. Ideas involving romance, thrill-seeking, love, and nostalgia are often used in this format. A campaign for Bacardi USA's Di Saronno Amaretto associated the product with romantic Italian moods in suggesting situations in which it could be used. The "song and dance

In this Goodyear ad from the 1920s, the longevity of the product was the focus.
Courtesy of The Goodyear Tire & Rubber Company.

spectacular" captures attention through its entertaining format, using festivity and gaiety to capture attention and possibly generate liking for the advertisement and brand.

A campaign for Taster's Choice instant coffee became a blockbuster when Nestlé USA, the brand's marketer, chose a provocative serial format for its advertising. Over time, the campaign linked the coffee to an evolving romantic relationship between a couple, moving the love story from their chance meeting in an apartment building in the United States all the way to Paris, France.

Signs, Symbols, and Cues

In addition to executional formats, managers vary the signs, symbols, and cues used to convey a message and reach their campaign objectives. Signs, symbols, and cues represent the second classification of executional variables, executional elements or stimuli. Advertisers carefully select and shape the executional elements needed to convey a precise meaning while eliminating elements that do not contribute. To stress the handling and safety of its Aquatred tire, Goodyear Tire & Rubber Company referred to it as "rain gear" while demonstrating a how it enables a van to take a sharp curve in a rain drenched road.

The most common classes of executional elements are the "basic appeal," the "source of the message," and the "slogan" or "positioning statement." Theme, tone of voice, seals and guarantees, and color also fall into this category.

A "basic appeal" builds interest in the advertiser's offering. There are at least six basic appeals, each with a unique selling proposition. "Direct, benefit-based brand claims" stress rational reasons for purchasing that derive directly from the brand's attributes. They target the cognitive, or logical thinking, dimension of attitude in claiming superiority or parity. For example, Frito-Lay, Inc., touted Tostitos Salsa and Baked Tostitos tortilla chips as having, respectively, zero grams of fat and one gram of fat per serving. In advertising its gymnasium flooring, Sport Coat stressed such benefit-based appeals as a 10-year limited warranty, indoor/outdoor applications, one-day installation, and low maintenance costs. Advertisers use direct, benefit-based claims when the audience is found to have the motivation, ability, and opportunity to process that type of information. Benefit-based claims are most effective when the audience recognizes a significant consumption problem, senses risk in making a poor choice, undertakes extended problem solving, seeks information, carefully judges competing brands, and is highly involved in the purchasing process. Rejuvenated brands often use direct, benefit-based brand claims to promote the benefits of their new features.

"Feelings-based appeals" are used when advertisers perceive that the audience cannot understand or is unwilling to process direct, benefit-based brand claims. Feelings-based claims rely on subtle emotion, pleasant feelings, warmth, and special moods to persuade the audience. Eastman Kodak Company's "Show your true colors" campaign associated warmth with its Kodacolor Gold 100 film through a series of photographs that evoked pleasant, warm feelings. Lane Furniture Company used nostalgia to influence its audience with its advertisement depicting a woman using a Lane cedar chest to safeguard cherished mementos of her mother.

Appeals that "prescribe social norms" cast people in certain roles, dramatize how others evaluate role performance, and link brands to the attainment of social rewards or the avoidance of social punishments. The rationale underlying the appeal is derived from social psychology. Psychologists believe that people periodically self-monitor themselves to assess how they are viewed by others and their likelihood of receiving social rewards or avoiding punishments. People evaluate the nature of the perceptions held by others and identify ways to change, improve, or reinforce social evaluations. Advertisers, recognizing that self-monitoring, social rewards, and social punishments strongly influence purchasing behavior, use basic appeals to link brands to the social rewards enjoyed by people occupying a certain role. An advertisement for Kudos, a healthy snack food from M&M/Mars, shows a schoolboy facing a sizable math problem on an ominous looking chalkboard. The copy argues that people who occupy a parental role ought to help their children do well in school by providing a Kudos bar as a snack.

Another basic appeal attempts to establish an image or personality for the brand. Brand image appeals use human qualities, capabilities, and personality traits as metaphors to characterize the brand. Maytag Corporation uses its friendly repairman to convey dependability and reliability for its line of household appliances. "Appeals that precipitate action" entice people to take some sort of action, such as attend a seminar or event, call a company, visit a Web site, or make a purchase. Often a sales promotion, consumer price deal, or other incentive is provided to persuade the audience to act immediately. Haggar Clothing Company offered two tickets to Super Bowl XXIX to entice consumers to visit participating retailers and attend its "Wrinkle-Free Days" event. Advertisers frequently combine basic appeals in using a "hybrid appeal." P&G combined a feelings- and direct benefit-based appeal to promote Pampers disposable diapers. The ad featured an illustration that projected a mother's love for her newborn, and the copy claimed that "81 percent of all hospitals choose Pampers to keep their babies dry."

Advertisers, in creating a specific message, also employ such executional elements as theme, tone and diction, and pace and tempo. Advertisers vary the pace or tempo of advertisements to create a specific impression. Pace, or speed, is the overall velocity or rate of movement depicted in the advertisement. Tempo concerns the integration of speed throughout the ad or among its components. A campaign for Benson & Hedges cigarettes conveyed relaxation through its slow-paced advertisements. In the ads, two Benson & Hedges cigarettes were shown in scenes of enjoyable relaxation—reclining quietly on an easy chair, on a pool float, in a hammock. Conversely, a print ad for Gatorade Thirst Quencher relied on fast-paced movement. It featured a blurry photograph of red-uniformed football players, evoking the tension and speed of the closing seconds of a hard-fought game.

To create and reinforce a specific impression, advertisers select a theme, repeating one or more executional elements for the duration of the advertising campaign. A theme provides continuity and increases recognition. Repetition of the theme links each advertisement in the campaign, increasing the audience's ability to associate one advertisement with others. Moreover, repetition increases the audience's recall of the message. Among the executional elements most commonly used to carry the theme are such variables as trade characters and spokespeople, slogans, jingles, and colors.

The Source of the Message

Another executional element, the source of the message is the prime element of an ad. The source, the person or object whose message is directed to the audience, is a powerful executional stimulus. An effective source performs a variety of key functions, such as drawing attention to the advertisement, providing trust and credibility, conveying brand knowledge, and associating feelings or personality with a brand. Among the most common sources are celebrities, experts, satisfied users, cartoon and trade characters, professional models, unseen announcers, employees or managers, and the brand or company itself. When direct, benefit-based brand claims are conveyed, credibility is the key trait advertisers seek in a source. Source credibility consists of expertise (knowledge, experience, professional judgment, and intelligence) and objectivity (honesty and integrity). Conversely, source attractiveness is the key for feelings-based appeals. Source attractiveness is measured by assessing the degree of similarity, familiarity, and liking associated with a source. "Similarity" concerns the degree to which the source and the audience share the same ideologies, attitudes, and behaviors; the greater the similarity, the more likely it is that advice from the source will be accepted. "Familiarity" describes the nature of past associations that a receiver holds for the source. "Liking" concerns the degree to which the receiver likes the source, based on such feelings as enjoyment, appreciation, admiration, regard, esteem, and physical attractiveness.

Slogans and Jingles

A third executional element, slogans (e.g., positioning statements, tag lines) and jingles, also can convey the theme. A slogan is a catchy promotional phrase that conveys in a short, compelling, and memorable way the brand's key selling proposition. Examples of slogans are BMW's "The ultimate driving machine" and Sears's "The softer side of Sears." Slogans are a continuity device found in each advertisement in a campaign. Jingles combine lyrics and music in a short, catchy song that conveys a central message. An effective jingle causes people to sing along, involving them more deeply in the ad. For example Mattress Giant's lyrics state, "For that ohh-ahh feeling. . . . Only at Mattress Giant."

Color and white space are executional elements believed to help create an impression desired by advertisers, although research findings on the effects of colors are somewhat mixed. Black, gold, and silver appear to convey strength and quality; red seems to convey passion, love, or friction; and green and blue appear to convey coolness and tranquility. Recognizing a growing concern over increases in the incidences of skin cancer, tanning lotions switched background colors to greens and blues from the yellows and oranges that characterized such advertisements up until the latter part of the 1980s. Yellow and orange tones reminded people of the danger of skin cancer attributed to exposure to intense sun.

Tone of voice is varied by advertisers to establish a certain relationship between the audience and the brand. Hennessy cognac, for example, projected a romantic tone in its advertisements.

When an advertiser wants the audience to perceive the source to be more knowledgeable or different, its ads assume a more serious tone of voice.

Seals, warranties, and guarantees are other forms of executional elements. In attempting to reduce buyers' level of perceived risk, advertisers sometimes use a seal of approval or a guarantee/warranty. For example, ads for General Motors Corporation's GM Goodwrench Service Plus convey a lifetime guarantee on automobile parts and labor.

Once selected and designed, executional elements must be carefully used to convey a dominant selling idea, produce a particular impression, and project unity. Unity implies that all the executional elements found in an advertisement appear to belong together.

In summary, executional elements and executional formats comprise the executional variables advertisers select, shape, and use to create precise impressions. Executional variables are integral components of creative advertising strategies. They must be selected and implemented with great care if advertisers are to accomplish their goals and objectives.

ALLEN E. SMITH

See also Comparative Advertising; Demonstration; Endorsement; Hard-Sell/Soft-Sell Advertising; Humor; Music and Jingles; Slogan; Spokes-Character

Further Reading

Alden, Dana L., Wayne D. Hoyer, and Chol Lee, "Identifying Global and Culture-Specific Dimensions of Humor in Advertising: A Multinational Analysis," *Journal of Marketing* 57, no. 2 (1993)

Dunn, Samuel Watson, *Advertising: Its Role in Modern Marketing,* New York: Holt Rinehart and Winston, 1961; 8th edition, by Dean M. Krugman et al., Fort Worth, Texas: Dryden Press, 1994

Felton, George, *Advertising: Concept and Copy,* Englewood Cliffs, New Jersey: Prentice- Hall, 1994

Kanso, Ali, "International Advertising Strategies: Global Commitment to Local Vision," *Journal of Advertising Research* 32, no. 1 (1992)

Kleppner, Otto, *Advertising Procedure,* New York: Prentice-Hall, 1925; 14th edition, as *Kleppner's Advertising Procedure,* by J. Thomas Russell and W. Ronald Lane, Upper Saddle River, New Jersey: Prentice-Hall, 1999

Lamb, Charles W., Jr., Joseph F. Hair, Jr., and Carl McDaniel, *Principles of Marketing,* Cincinnati, Ohio: South-Western, 1992; 5th edition, as *Marketing,* Cincinnati, Ohio: South-Western, 2000

MacInnis, Deborah J., and Bernard J. Jaworski, "Information Processing from Advertisements: Toward an Integrative Framework," *Journal of Marketing* 53, no. 3 (1989)

Mick, David G., "Consumer Research and Semiotics: Exploring the Morphology of Signs, Symbols, and Significance," *Journal of Consumer Research* 13, no. 3 (1986)

Myers, John C., and David A. Aaker, *Advertising Management,* Englewood Cliffs, New Jersey: Prentice-Hall, 1975; 5th edition, by Myers, Aaker, and Rajeev Batra, Upper Saddle River, New Jersey: Prentice-Hall, and London: Prentice-Hall International, 1996

O'Guinn, Thomas C., Chris T. Allen, and Richard J. Semenik, *Advertising,* Cincinnati, Ohio: South-Western College, 1998; 2nd edition, 2000

Parente, Donald, *Advertising Campaign Strategy: A Guide to Communication Plans,* Fort Worth, Texas: Dryden, 1996

Percy, Larry, and John R. Rossiter, "Advertising Stimulus Effects: A Review," *Journal of Current Issues and Research in Advertising* 14, no. 1 (1992)

Petty, Richard E., John T. Cacioppo, and David Schumann, "Central and Peripheral Routes to Advertising Effectiveness: The Moderating Role of Involvement," *Journal of Consumer Research* 10, no. 3 (1983)

Solomon, Michael R., and Elnora W. Stuart, *Marketing: Real People, Real Choices,* Upper Saddle River, New Jersey, and London: Prentice-Hall, 1997; 2nd edition, Upper Saddle River, New Jersey: Prentice-Hall, 2000

Wells, William, John Burnett, and Sandra Moriarty, *Advertising: Principles and Practice,* Englewood Cliffs, New Jersey: Prentice Hall, and London: Prentice-Hall International, 1989; 5th edition, Upper Saddle River, New Jersey: Prentice-Hall, 1999